PETE!

Always nice seeing you
at ☺ lux ;)

Well, here it is, my
MONSTER Book.
(I'm working on part II now —
thats why I always have
the binders with me.

"They've been calling me a
"conspiracy theorist" around
here for years.
Fuck Them!

I hope you find some thing of
interest in this mess.
Your friend,

ABERRATION in the HEARTLAND of the REAL

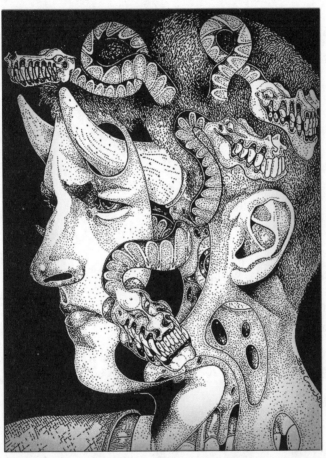

The Secret Lives of Timothy McVeigh

WENDY S. PAINTING, PhD

Aberration in the Heartland of the Real: The Secret Lives of Tim McVeigh
Copyright © 2016 Wendy S. Painting, PhD. All Rights Reserved

Cover Drawing: ©2012, 2016 Bobby Joe Crouch

Published by:
Trine Day LLC
PO Box 577
Walterville, OR 97489
1-800-556-2012
www.TrineDay.com
publisher@TrineDay.net

Library of Congress Control Number: 2016934512

Painting, Wendy S.
—1st ed.
p. cm.
Includes references and index.
Epud (ISBN-13) 978-1-63424-004-8
Mobi (ISBN-13) 978-1-63424-005-5
Print (ISBN-13) 978-1-63424-003-1
1. McVeigh, Timothy -- Political and social views. 2. Oklahoma City Federal
Building Bombing, Oklahoma City, Okla., 1995. 3. Bombing investigation --
Oklahoma -- Oklahoma City. 4. Brainwashing -- United States. 5. United States
-- Politics and government -- 20th century. I. Painting, Wendy. II. Title

First Edition
10 9 8 7 6 5 4

Printed in the USA
Distribution to the Trade by:
Independent Publishers Group (IPG)
814 North Franklin Street
Chicago, Illinois 60610
312.337.0747
www.ipgbook.com

Haven't We Done This Before?

The path of least resistance is the path of the loser.

– H. G. Wells

Now hollow fires burn out to black,
And lights are fluttering low:
Square your shoulders, lift your pack
And leave your friends and go.
O never fear, lads, naught's to dread,
Look not left nor right:
In all the endless road you tread
There's nothing but the night.

– Alfred Edward Housman

The killing was an experiment. It is just as easy to justify such a death as it is to justify an entomologist killing a beetle on a pin.

– Nathan Leopold

What is it about the petty pace of our tawdry travails that produces such horrendous abominations as the April 19, 1995 Oklahoma City Bombing? Was it simply the savage act of an unhinged honky; a disillusioned dissolute demanding attention rising out of our societal muddle, or could the action, possibly, have been some sort of underhanded government connivance? These memes and others are intricately examined in Wendy Painting's work, *Aberration in the Heartland of the Real: The Secret Lives of Tim McVeigh*.

How the tale of Timothy James McVeigh, the *face* of home-grown terrorism, plays-out depends on perspective and information. Many titillating breadcrumbs, even those strewn by McVeigh himself, have been officially devoured by the inane claims that no one else was involved. Leaving us, the long-suffering populace, in the dark with a story full of holes, and saddled with onerous new laws that have ballooned our federal government's abilities of surveillance, control and contempt.

Aberration in the Heartland of the Real gives us a deep soul-searching look at the many different, conflicting narratives that have surrounded

McVeigh and the Oklahoma City Bombing tragedy. Ms. Painting's writing draws us into the tenor of the times so activities are set within their social, cultural and historical context. Thus giving us a platform for elucidating her very interesting and intriguing analyses of the different narratives put forth during the course of public disclosures of the event and trials, plus from the continued fascinations, investigations and trepidations that have swirled around the case.

Many folks, it appears, could care less about these events from over twenty years ago, and wonder why some still do, still read books, watch documentaries – search for understanding among the tea leaves of the past. "Isn't Tim McVeigh dead?" they say. "Didn't he ask for, and receive the death penalty for his horrendous crime, I mean after all he's a baby killer, blew up the Murrah building with its day-care center. Why should we care? He's dead and gone ... good riddance!"

Well, the Antiterrorism and Effective Death Penalty Act of 1996 has had a tremendous impact on the law of *habeas corpus* in the United States, degrading our Republic, and created entirely new statutory law that limits our freedoms and liberties. And though Timothy McVeigh may have been executed, the cultural memes are still mongering fear, as "Lone Wolf" has become a trigger, sending us all scurrying into the state-security-blanket mentality.

I do not know about you, but myself personally, I am sick and tired of this whole shim-sham-shimmy charade, and am hopeful that continuing education and honest discussion will help us on our journey out of this stilted existence. There are reasons why "they" burn books, and those are similar to why TrineDay publishes. A book is such a quiet little thing, it just sits there, until someone picks it up. That's when the fireworks can start...

Aberration in the Heartland of the Real allows us to examine the many faces, and the facts behind them, which have engendered the McVeigh mythos. This book looks at the strange "tree," Timothy James McVeigh, Ms. Painting's next work, *Redacted!,* will examine the "forest," the Oklahoma City Bombing, in never-before documented detail or depth. Drawing upon thousand of hours of research and thousand of "suppressed" documents, *Redacted* will finish, what *Aberration* has begun.

I can barely wait. I love a good book.

Onwards to the Utmost of Futures

Peace,
Kris Millegan
Publisher
TrineDay
March 19, 2016

To my mother, Florence B. Humphrey, whose stories I cherish, for always sticking by me, and to Israel Painting and Seven Hassall, for their love, loyalty and for always finding a way to make me laugh when I needed to most.

Acknowledgments

I did not begin this project with the intent of writing a book, only with a personal curiosity about the historical facts and socio-cultural and political contexts and implications of the 1995 Oklahoma City bombing case. What you are about to read began as a 10-page undergraduate research paper written over 10 years ago; a paper that, over the years, developed into several longer essays and eventually, into a doctoral dissertation. At several points in this journey, I could have moved on and called it a day but everything I learned in the process demanded otherwise. That said, this book is not complete nor is it definitive. Early on, in my naiveté, I thought I could solve the case but I couldn't. However, to the dismay of some, and the dogged efforts of others, startling and game changing information about the 1995 Oklahoma City bombing continues to surface. There is much left to do. Nevertheless, I could not have undertaken this endeavor without the participation, encouragement, and assistance of many people who believed in me and/or in the importance of the topic, or both.

I would like to thank Trine Day, and particularly Kris Milligan and Kelly Ray for believing in this project, for taking this monster off my hands, and for their editorial integrity and consideration. Thank you also to those who selflessly shared their stories and insights with me over the years, some of whom risked much to do so and all of whom asked nothing in return. Some individuals who contributed much to my efforts and understanding asked to remain anonymous but their influence is felt throughout this book. Thanks to those who, throughout my long pursuit of information, offered their homes, friendship, guidance, encouragement, material and moral support, feedback and research and editorial assistance. Special thanks to anyone who ever let me drag them along on my investigatory road trips, for bearing witness to the strange and uncanny synchronicities that came to define my pursuit. To my road companions who calmly read the maps, while I was lost on the backroads, tearing out my hair, you'll be happy to know I finally broke down and bought a GPS. Thanks to those who told me to calm down or breathe during my many meltdowns. Sorry I was grumpy and weird. Thanks to those who, no matter how peculiar it seemed, never questioned my dedication or determination or told me my efforts were pointless, or that I was wasting my time, even if it appeared that way. To those who did, thanks for your feedback. Thanks to those who made me laugh, inspired me and those who helped fill my Castle Perilous with light. I couldn't have gotten out without you. For those who have passed away during this process – see you on the other side.

Epic thanks to Brian Barrett, Jeanne Bishop, Richard Booth, Larry Dangus, Esq., Kelli Grace, Thomas Johnson, Hank Meyer, Saby Reyes-Kulkarni, Adrien C. Tucker, Holland Vandennieuwenhof and Meg Walters for significant moral, editorial, and investigatory support, generous material support, and/ or all of the above. In addition, I'd like to thank (in alphabetical order) Andrea Augustine, Casey and Johnny Winston Bangerter, Michael Beaudrie, Mary Ellen Belding, Jack Blood, Brave New Books, Boulder Coffee Company, Don Browning, Russell Britain, Eve Butler, Roger Charles, Alex Constantine, Jannie Coverdale, Randy Coyne, Jason Crane, Terri Creech, Mary De Rieux, Harlan Dietrich, Rolinda Duby, Thomas Enders, Chase Everett, Phillip Ferrara, Jens Fiederer, Matthew Fletcher, Leland Freeman, Mike Frisch, Steve Gentile, Tony Gerardi, Mike Hackett, Allie Hartley, Luke A. Hartlieb, Hoppy Heidelberg, Juan Hernandez, Bruce Jackson, Stephen Jones, Ken Karnage, Charles Key, John F. King, Cynthia Knope, Mary Kohler, Wendy LaBarge, Peter K. Langan, David Langley, Catina Lawson-Wiebe, Betty and V.Z. Lawton, Carl Lebron, Jen Leist, Thomas L'Esperance, Michael Aaron Lloyd, Jenny Locicero, LUX Lounge, Randolph MacKenzie, Phil Maples, Bryan Margetts, Dan Mauck, Leticia A. Martinez, Donna McClure, Liz and John McDermott, Stacy McFacey, Lance and Johanna Meecham, Ruth Meyerowitz, Brett Munson, Brandon Murphy, Mike Nations, Rob Nigh, Paranoia Magazine, Ron Patton, "Pearl", Popeye, Kate Procious, Sage Rakestraw, Jen Rampe, Priya Reddy aka Warcry, Robb Revere, Richard Reyna, Rochester Research Associates, Jessica Stroud Sapia, Geever Schwab, Chanda Seymour, Cheri Seymour, Brian Shelton, Watermelon Slim, Elizabeth 'Betsy' Smith, Tom and Sarah Stephens, Jesse C. Trentadue, Christopher Tritico, Tristan Martin Tomaselli, Dayna Twilligear, John B. Wells, Chopstix Waits, Lyjha Wilton, Ron Woods, Louise Wu, Bethany York, Tanya Zani, and those who shall not be named here.

Thanks to the University of Buffalo's Mark Diamond Research Fund for financial assistance during one stage of this project and to the University of Texas, Dolph Briscoe Center For American History and St. Bonaventure University, Friedsam Memorial Library Archives for helping to make history accessible.

Table of contents

CONTENTS

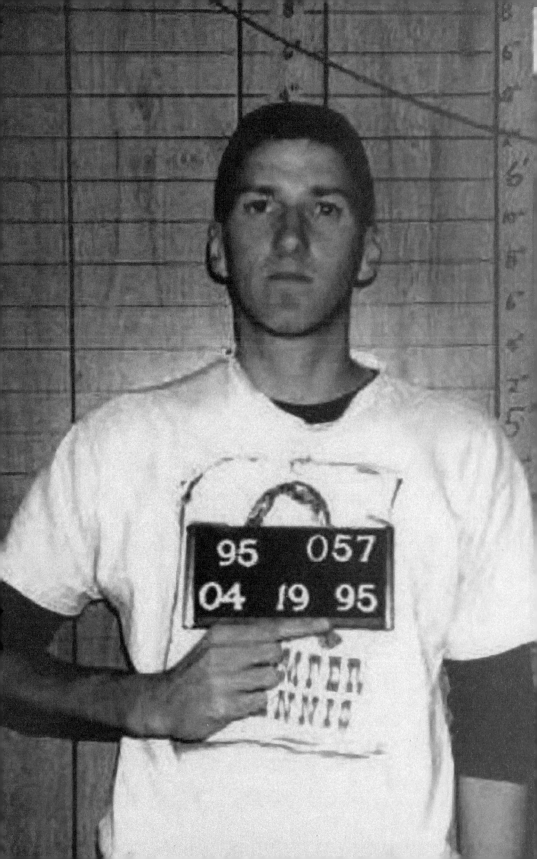

Preface

Sometimes he looked around him, horrified by the weight of it all, the career of paper. He sits in the data spew of hundreds of lives. There's no end in sight.... Let's call a meeting to analyze the blur. Let's devote our lives to understanding this moment, separating the elements of each crowded second. We will build theories that gleam like jade idols, intriguing systems of assumption.... We will follow the bullet trajectories backwards to the lives that occupy the shadows, actual men.... There is much here [in the] aberration in the heartland of the real.

–Don DeLillo, *Libra*, 1988

On April 19, 1995, at 9:02 AM, a truck bomb exploded in front of the Murrah federal building in downtown Oklahoma City, killing one hundred and sixty-eight people, including nineteen children. Two days later, authorities named twenty-seven year old Timothy McVeigh as the prime suspect in "the most deadly attack on American soil." Thereafter, his visage, quickly dubbed "The Face Of Terror," inundated the media, thus becoming seared into the archives of public memory.

In the immediate hours, weeks and months after the explosion, a number of rapidly formed and highly conflicting narratives about both the bombing and bomber appeared and spread. The stories developed over time and continue to circulate today. Their construction involves a complex and dynamic process of collaboration and competition between multiple individuals and institutions with various motives, agendas and intents (stated or implied), all of whom assert different facts based on different evaluative criteria. Authors of the stories include journalists, victims and survivors, eyewitnesses, the FBI, federal prosecutors, politicians, experts, analysts, pundits, defense attorneys and notably, McVeigh himself. Within each narrative, the material facts and chronology of events as well as the roles and identities of the villains differ, as do the acts attributed to them and their purported motives.

Today, Timothy McVeigh, an "American Terrorist," "All American Monster," and, for a time, "The Most Hated Man in America," continues to personify a wide range of prototypical Cold War and Post-Cold War identities: a Self-Styled Rambo; Survivalist; Militia Type; Gun Nut; Lone Nut; Disgruntled Soldier; Rogue Avenger; Boy Next Door Gone Bad and Quintessential Conspiracy Theorist turned Rabid Homegrown Lone Wolf Domestic Terrorist. In McVeigh's "Face of Terror" is also reflected "The Ghost of Lee

Harvey Oswald" and like Oswald, John Wilkes Booth, Sirhan Sirhan and a number of other American "Lone Gunmen," before and after McVeigh, all of whom inspired multiple competing, highly conflicting and continually evolving narratives and debates about just how *alone* these lone wolves really were.[1]

Many of the narratives that appeared after McVeigh's arrest claim to tell the *real* and sometimes, suppressed story of the 1995 Oklahoma City bombing. All of these stories were and continue to be told publicly by diverse groups and subcultures within multiple genres (fictional, historical, biographical, academic, and journalistic) and are transmitted through many media (printed, digital, televised and cinematic). Various readers and commentators have labeled these narratives, alternately, as fantastical fictional or accurate historical accounts, the stuff of conspiracy theories, cautionary tales or dangerous ideological expressions of belief (or radically cynical disbelief). McVeigh remains central within all such stories, yet appears very different depending on the version told. He may appear as one of several unnamed accomplices; a witting or unwitting "patsy" steeped in a world of shadows, spies, cross-dressing Neo-Nazis and doppelganger decoys; a modern day Manchurian Candidate, victim of nightmarish schemes and inhumane experiments hatched by faceless conspirators, or some combination thereof. Recurring elements in the plots of these stories include black helicopters, mysterious clandestine "black operators," mad scientists, brainwashing, implanted tracking and mind-control biotechnologies, faked executions and, from time to time, UFOs.

Although easily dismissed as fantastical paranoid tales, the mere existence of these narratives raises questions about and poses radical disruptions to historical and current medical, psychological, bioethical and terrorism discourses. These stories act as causes and solutions to physical and psychological terror; many products of a *covert sphere*, knowledge of which may help to distinguish between the signified and the signifier (symbols of representation and that which is represented), fact and fantasy, reality and illusion. The acceptance of one version over another depends upon pre-existing beliefs about what is logical, plausible, implausible, palatable, or simply unimaginable.

This work differs from previous treatments for a number of reasons. To begin with, it identifies and compares commonly told stories about McVeigh and the bombing, stories that more often than not rely upon recycled sources and focus exclusively on the bombing while providing only a cursory glance at McVeigh himself. This book tests all existing stories against a wealth of newly introduced biographical information gained through personal interviews and archival collections, rendering the majority of previous depictions overly simplistic, deterministic, and factually dubious or devoid of context. When these stories are compared and new information introduced, a very different picture of Generation X's own American Terrorist is revealed.

Secondly, this book differs from its predecessors by demonstrating how Timothy McVeigh himself told not only the most commonly known and officially sanctioned version (the Lone Wolf story) but, before and after his arrest, privately told versions of *all* the competing stories that would come to circulate.

Finally, the Oklahoma City bombing is continuously invoked to understand other violent acts and McVeigh as a primary figure to compare the lives, motives and actions of those who commit them, a circumstance necessitating a more complete understanding of both McVeigh and the bombing, a gap I hope this book helps to fill.

METHOD AND APPROACH

After surveying the majority of publicly available literature about the bombing and McVeigh, I began locating, interviewing and corresponding with the victims' family members, survivors, witnesses, attorneys, private investigators, journalists, McVeigh's coworkers, friends, neighbors and underworld associates including bank robbers, neo-Nazis, militia leaders and many others. I found these individuals in, among other places, Texas, Oklahoma, Arkansas, Kansas, Arizona, Nevada, Utah and New York. Simultaneously, I sought out and obtained hard to find documents relating to the case, many that are publicly introduced within this book for the first time. Newly introduced oral and archival sources include, but are not limited to, materials found within the Stephen Jones Collection located at the University of Texas, Austin and the American Terrorist Collection, located at St. Bonaventure University.

After Timothy McVeigh's sentencing in 1997, and at McVeigh's request, his lead attorney, Stephen Jones, was removed from his team of lawyers. In 1998, Jones published his account of the case, *Others Unknown*, and donated the mountains of material generated by the defense team to the Dolph Briscoe Center for American History at the University of Texas, Austin. The Jones Collection includes but is not limited to: internal defense team memorandum; meeting notes; investigatory reports; interviews with McVeigh's friends, family co-workers and outsiders; personal letters written by and to McVeigh; reports filed by defense team mental health and other experts; courtroom exhibits; audio tapes and transcripts of conversations with McVeigh, witnesses, journalists and others; FBI investigatory documents (called 302s and inserts); investigatory documents from other law enforcement and intelligence agencies; defense-generated legal briefs, filings and correspondences; newspaper clippings; and McVeigh's military and medical records. To date, I am the only researcher to have gone through the entire publicly available portion of the collection – an endeavor that took four years.

In addition, during the summer of 2012, I reviewed and transcribed the entire American Terrorist Collection located at Saint Bonaventure University, consisting of hundreds of letters written by McVeigh to his biographers after his conviction until the time of his execution as well as transcripts of hundreds of hours of their interviews with them. The American Terrorist collection picks up where the Jones Collection leaves off. The archival and oral sources introduced in this book contribute a wealth of contextual detail and information that aids in a closer comparative analysis of existing texts. The data presented operates on a number of levels relevant to several socio-cultural and political arenas and aggressively intercedes in debates about the factual details of McVeigh's life and the bombing.

Some of the documents found in the Jones Collection, including FBI investigatory documents and McVeigh's medical records, have also been obtained through my own FOIA requests. Additionally, other individuals, including Salt Lake City attorney Jesse Trentadue and Peter Langan, have generously provided duplicate versions of documents found in the Jones Collection as well as other investigatory documents not found there.

I use these sources to show how Timothy McVeigh authored *all* the competing stories about himself, not only those of the "Lone Wolf" variety. From these as well as publicly available sources, I constructed a multi-sourced timeline of McVeigh's life and critical moments leading up to the bombing. The use of this timeline helped me to identify when sources contradicted each other.

While certain details are repeated throughout this book, each time they appear within a new context and in relation to previously unknown details, in a way that, with each progressive telling, requires a new interpretation of those details and the alternate conflicting narratives discussed. Each story variation examined (as told by McVeigh and others) holds strikingly different implications about the nature of authority, reality, truth, control of the narrative, and the potential consequences of labeling certain ideas and identities as threatening, harmful, dangerous and even unthinkable. Compared against each other and to newer information introduced in this book, these stories illustrate the shifting nature of history itself and the ways that the Oklahoma City bombing acts as an example of how institutional secrecy can subjugate and silence information and knowledge and relegate it to the outskirts of officially sanctioned regimes of truth.

Timeline Of Events

May 24, 1988: Timothy James McVeigh, age 20, joins United States Army and is sent to Fort Benning, Georgia for boot camp where he meets other members of his experimental COHORT Unit, 33-year-old Terry Lynn Nichols and 20-year-old Michael Joseph Fortier.

Oct. 1, 1990: Timothy McVeigh cleared for Special Forces training.

Jan. 16, 1991 to March 29, 1991: Timothy McVeigh deployed overseas for Operation Desert Shield and Desert Storm.

April 3 to 7, 1991: Timothy McVeigh attends Fort Bragg, North Carolina for Special Forces Selection and Assessment Course (Class 5-91), undergoes psychological evaluations on April 5, and voluntarily withdraws on April 7, thereafter returning to Fort Riley, Kansas.

December 11, 1991: McVeigh ends active duty service with U.S. Army, is transferred to the New York Army National Guard, where he is obliged to serve until April 11, 1995, and returns home to New York where he works as a security guard.

June 1, 1992: McVeigh is granted an early discharge from NYANG service and is transferred to U.S. Army Reserve Control Group with service obligation end date of March 11, 1996, during which time he can be subjected to annual screening and training and active duty recall.

August 21-31, 1992: 14-year-old Sammy Weaver is shot and killed by U.S. Marshalls, and his mother, Vikki Weaver, is shot and killed by an FBI sniper during a 10-day standoff at Ruby Ridge, Idaho during which Deputy Marshal Michael Degan is shot and killed.

October 1992: McVeigh moves out of his father's house in Pendleton, New York and into an apartment in Lockport, New York. During this time, he is seen regularly at the Buffalo, Veterans Administration Hospital.

January 26, 1993: McVeigh quits his job at Burke Security and sets off on the road, traveling the gun show circuit.

February 28, 1993: About 80 BATF agents attempt to execute a search and arrest warrant against David Koresh and members of the Branch Davidian church for possession of illegal weapons on their property, Mt. Carmel, located near Waco, Texas. A firefight erupts during which 4 BATF agents are killed and 16 are wounded. Subsequently, the FBI took control of the scene, a military buildup on the property begins and military actions against the Davidians commence during a 51-day standoff between the Davidians and federal agents.

March 1993: McVeigh travels to Mt. Carmel near Waco, Texas to join crowds of supporters gathered outside the Davidian property.

April 19, 1993: The FBI and U.S. Army attack Mt. Carmel and a fire engulfs the Davidian church/residence killing 74 men, women and children.

September 13, 1994: According to Grand Jury indictment against Terry Nichols, Timothy McVeigh, and Others Unknown, the conspiracy to bomb the Murrah Federal Building in Oklahoma City begins. On the same day, the Federal Assault Weapons ban is signed into law.

November 1994: The home of Roger Edwin Moore aka Bob Miller aka Bob Anderson, an Arkansas gun dealer and associate of Timothy McVeigh, is robbed.

February 1995:

> A scheduled ATF raid of Elohim City, a white separatist community on the Arkansas-Oklahoma border is called off after a meeting between the ATF, FBI, and U.S. Attorney's Office.

> The Omnibus Counterterrorism Act of 1995 is introduced into the Senate by Sen. Joe Biden on behalf of the Clinton Administration.

April 5, 1995: A phone card in the name of 'Daryl Bridges' is used to call Elohim City.

April 15, 1995: "Robert Kling" reserves a Ryder truck from Elliot's Body Shop in Junction City, Kansas.

April 17, 1995: Robert Kling picks up Ryder truck from Elliot's Body Shop.

April 19, 1995:

> **9:02 AM**: A bomb explodes in front of the Alfred P. Murrah Federal building in Oklahoma City, killing 167 people.

> **10:20 AM**: Timothy McVeigh is pulled over and arrested while driving north on I-35, about 80 miles from Oklahoma City. He is taken to the county jail in Perry, Oklahoma.

> **9 PM**: Richard Wayne Snell, an associate of residents at Elohim City who had previously plotted to bomb the Murrah building in OKC, is executed in the state of Arkansas.

April 20, 1995: Based on witnesses in Oklahoma City and Kansas, authorities release sketches of suspects of two white males, John Doe No. 1 and John Doe No. 2.

April 21, 1995: Terry Nichols turns himself in to authorities in Herington, Kansas. Timothy McVeigh is taken into federal custody and transferred to Tinker Air Force Base near Oklahoma City where he is arraigned and then transferred to El Reno Federal Prison in Oklahoma.

June 14, 1995: The search for 'John Doe #2' is called off.

August 11, 1995: A federal grand jury indicts Timothy McVeigh and Terry Nichols for murder and conspiracy to bomb the Murrah federal building in a plot that involved McVeigh, Nichols, and Others Unknown. As part of a plea bargain, Michael Fortier agrees to testify against McVeigh and Nichols in exchange for immunity for his wife, Lori, and a reduced sentence for himself.

November 1995: Survivors, victims' family members and citizens led by OK State Representative Charles Key petition to form a State Grand Jury investigation to uncover new information about the bombing plot and, if possible, identify other conspirators.

December 1, 1995: The Tenth Circuit Court of Appeals replaces Oklahoma District Judge Wayne Alley with Denver District Judge Richard Matsch and the trials are moved to Denver, Colorado.

January 27, 1996: Four FBI workers who evaluated evidence in the Oklahoma City bombing case are transferred out of the crime lab after a federal report criticizes lab procedures

March 1996: Terry Nichols and Timothy McVeigh are transferred to the Englewood Federal Correctional Facility near Denver, Colorado.

April 24, 1996: The Antiterrorism and Effective Death Penalty Act of 1996 (AEDPA) is signed into law by Congress and President Bill Clinton.

March 31, 1997 – June 13, 1997: The trial of Timothy McVeigh results in his conviction of 11 counts of murder, 1 count of conspiracy, and 1 count of using a weapon of mass destruction. He is sentenced to death.

May 27, 1997: Michael Fortier is sentenced to 12 years in prison and fined $200,000 for failing to warn authorities about bombing plans.

June 30, 1997: Oklahoma Supreme Court unanimously rules in favor of the formation of the Grand Jury to investigate the Oklahoma City bombing.

September 29, 1997 – June 4, 1998: The trial of Terry Nichols results in his conviction for eight counts of involuntary manslaughter and one count of conspiracy.

July 13, 1999: Timothy McVeigh is transferred to a federal penitentiary in Terry Haute, Indiana.

June 11, 2001: Timothy McVeigh is executed.

May 2004 –August 2004: Terry Nichols is convicted of 161 counts of first-degree murder in state court in Oklahoma City and, after the jury deadlocks, receives 161 consecutive life sentences without the possibility of parole.

January 20, 2006: Michael Fortier is released from prison after serving 10 ½ years of his 12 year sentence.

December 2006: California Representative Dana Rohrabacher completes a two-year investigation to determine if others besides Nichols and McVeigh were involved in the Oklahoma City bombing plot.

April 30, 2015: Federal Judge Clark Waddoups files an order appointing Magistrate Judge Dustin B. Pead as Special Master to determine if the FBI tampered with a witness who was going to testify about participation in an undercover FBI operation called PATCON. In November 2015, Judge Waddoups issues an order barring participants in the Special Master's investigation from discussing the process or the particulars of their participation.

TIME

THE FACE OF TERROR

Accused bomber
Timothy McVeigh

Prologue

Constructing The Face Of Terror – A Historical Overview

THE USUAL SUSPECTS

Within an hour of the explosion, news crews from every major outlet descended on downtown Oklahoma City. An immediate and constant deluge of around-the-clock, live reports and repetitive airing of graphically gruesome images of the bombing's devastation and carnage came to signify "the worst and most deadly attack of terrorism on American soil," forever embedding both the bombing and its representation into public memory. The bombing, quickly characterized as "an attack on America's Heartland" necessitated the creation of a nationally shared narrative to explain both the event itself and the threat it represented. Initial details used to create the earliest of these stories came from mass reporting of sensationalized or sometimes wholly erroneous speculation, rumor and commentary given by counterterrorism and security experts and pundits, as well as contradictory statements issued by government and law enforcement officials. The coverage ultimately triggered, not a unified narrative, but several divergent ones.

Immediately after the blast, President Bill Clinton assured the country, "Let there be no room for doubt: we will find the people who did this. When we do, justice will be swift, certain and severe ... these people are killers and must be treated as killers."[1] Within hours, eyewitnesses in Oklahoma City gave statements to authorities. Some said they observed two and sometimes three males with "swarthy," dark complexions sitting in a brown Chevrolet pickup truck near the Murrah building just prior to the explosion, who then quickly left the scene afterward. The witnesses described the men as appearing, alternately, Middle Eastern, Arab, Hispanic or Native American. Some said they saw a white male in the driver's seat of a yellow Ryder moving truck, and a person sitting in the passenger seat parked directly in front of the Murrah who, moments before the blast, exited the vehicle and walked off in a separate direction from the driver of the Ryder who, alone or in some versions with others, sped away in a yellow four-door car.

Government spokespeople, counter-terrorism and security experts and pundits elaborated on and attempted to make sense of the information for the public, and many formulated theories about Arab jihadist perpetrators. In the days to follow, the FBI detained, questioned and released several men of Arab descent. Throughout the country, Middle Easterners became the target of harassment, hate crimes and virulent rhetorical attacks in the media. On the afternoon of April 19, the OKC Police Department (OKCPD) issued an all-points bulletin for two suspects in a brown truck. Although the OKCPD retracted the APB a few days later, it quickly became the source of ongoing confusion and speculation.

Don Browning, a retired OKCPD Canine unit officer and a first responder, recalled his experience of the confusing and rapidly shifting details surrounding the APB:

> By the evening of April 19, I started to get really concerned. The OKCPD was repeatedly broadcasting an All-Points-Bulletin to the five state area that there were three vehicles … a brown pickup truck, a blue Chevy Cavalier and another car, maybe an Oldsmobile or Buick. They were trying to keep state and region-wide law enforcement aware of the suspects and the vehicles. That evening, as we were working in the building or waiting outside of it to work again, they were still putting out a description of Persian males. They kept telling us they still had those vehicles under surveillance and said that one had headed south towards Dallas and the other two, in different directions. They had every law enforcement officer in the surrounding area and states looking for the three vehicles and they let us continue to believe that.… The guys with FBI raid jackets had become the kingpins on the scene. Everyone was begging them for information. The next afternoon I approached one of the "Agents In Charge" and I just happened to ask him, "Hey, what's the deal with the cars?" And the FBI man says, "What cars?" And I said, "Uh … the pickup and the two cars" and he says "disinformation." I said, "What?!" and he said it again "disinformation." "What are you talking about?" I asked. He says, "We can't tell the media everything we know about this." I said "Okay. Well, but you're telling law enforcement." He said it again, "disinformation" and then just walked away. Now they deny broadcasting those descriptions but I do have a copy of the teletype that was issued. Years later, I asked various other law enforcement officers about it and they also remembered the APB's being issued.[2]

The evening of April 19, during ABC's show *Nightline*, Ted Koppel cited the *Washington Post*, who cited "a source close to the investigation," who cited an anonymous source within the FBI who had reported that at least eight groups, seven of them Middle Eastern, had claimed responsibility for the bombing. Koppel opined, "If those who committed today's atrocity are, as some officials are inclined to believe, part of a fundamentalist Islamic terrorist group, then they see themselves as part of an army, sowing panic in the belly of the Great Satan.... From their point of view, today's bombing must seem a huge success." Oklahoma State Rep. and former Chairman of the House Intelligence Committee Dave McCurdy announced on CBS News that there was "very clear evidence of the involvement of fundamentalist Islamic terrorist groups." ATF director John Magaw informed CNN: "any time you have this kind of damage, this kind of explosion, you have to look [for Middle East terrorists] first." New York's *Newsday* writer Jeff Kamen, referring to the *swarthy suspects*, expressed his desire to "shoot them now, before they get us."[3]

For some, the threat of murderous Middle Easterners seemed a likely one given recent terrorist attacks such as the 1993 bombing of the World Trade Center in Manhattan. In fact, the OKC bombing followed a series of ongoing attacks against U.S. targets within the Middle East in the 1980s and early 1990s that positioned the subject of "terrorism" and "terrorists" as a central focal point within public discourse despite the vague definitions of these terms. On trial, the very same day that the Oklahoma City bombing occurred, was Ramsi Yousef, "mastermind" of the 1993 WTC plot (also involving a Ryder truck bomb). This, along with the previous attacks influenced the immediate public acceptance of the initial "Middle Eastern" OKC bombing story.

The public more readily believes explanations of terrorist incidents when they conform to existing cultural myths; and so, on April 19, 1995, the prevailing American Terrorist Myth cast barbaric Middle Easterners as the mostly likely culprit. The stereotypical Arab Terrorist featured on nightly news reports paralleled blockbuster Hollywood movies that depicted Arab Jihadists from any number of foreign countries. Films such as *The Delta Force* (1986), *Terror Squad* (1987) and *Navy Seals* (1990) helped institutionalize racially charged images of "swarthy," "dirty," "slimy," "despicable" and "demonic" Middle Eastern fanatics. These popular culture villains sported unkempt beards and headdresses and wielded bombs and guns for vague political motives explained simply in terms of their unprovoked irrational hatred of Americans. The plausibility of the theatrics seen or the degree to which they accurately reflected real world events were of little concern to eager viewers of the new terrorist action movie genre. Rather, commanding their attention were the violent aesthetics of the films; the glorious explosion and the myriad ways of depicting death and destruction; all providing a window to observe and, by proxy, engage in what film studies scholar, Stephen Prince, termed "The Theater of Mass Destruction."[4]

Thus, for the American public, the initial "Middle Eastern Terrorist" scenario of the OKC bombing was a familiar one that fit into prevailing cultural myths about terrorism and terrorists. As newer information emerged in the days following the bombing, the "Who Done It?" narrative underwent radical revisions and newer templates of terrorism appeared, all of which coalesced fact, fiction, rumor and myth with different demonized "Outsider" villains.

THE UNUSUAL SUSPECTS

As media outlets told the story of Middle Eastern terrorists, a second narrative was simultaneously forming. This emergent story was one also based on observations of OKC witnesses who began talking, first among themselves and soon to the media, about the existence of known bomb threats to the Murrah up to two weeks before April 19, one of which had resulted in the evacuation of the building on April 18. The OKC Fire Department's Chief claimed that his office had received a call from the FBI weeks prior to the bombing alerting them to a possible threat and, based on this call, there had been a state of heightened security, not just at the Murrah but covering the entire federal complex in downtown OKC on the morning of the 19th. In addition, a number of people said that in the early hours of April 19, they observed members of the OKC Sherriff and ATF bomb squad trucks and a canine search unit near the Murrah. These reports led to the construction of a story about the government's foreknowledge of the attack.

OKCPD Sgt. Don Browning recounted the strange occurrence he witnessed when he arrived at work early on the morning of April 19, before the explosion. Browning said,

> The OKCPD horse patrol was gearing up that morning; all loaded and dressed up. We were told they were being sent out for crowd control. They were en-route to downtown when the bomb went off. Why? Why crowd control? There was nothing going on in downtown. The arts fest had not started. They only ever got called out for an event. They don't just do willy nilly crowd control. There was nothing to indicate that the horse patrol was needed. There was something not quite kosher with all this. Later I was told by a secretary in the ATF office that the building had been searched for bombs late the night before, on the 18th.[5]

The FBI then introduced new plot elements and characters into the mix. The majority of accounts attribute the first concrete developments in the case to a VIN number found on the rear axle of a Ryder truck that fell from the sky after the explosion and landed in the wreckage at the blast site. By the following afternoon, Thursday, April 20, the FBI traced it to Elliot's Body Shop, a Ryder rental agency in Junction City, Kansas. There they learned that days before, on Saturday, April 15, a man using the name "Robert Kling" had made a phone reservation for the Ryder rental truck on Monday, April 17. Indeed, Kling arrived on the 17th as promised. The false ID he presented to the Elliot's employees listed Kling's birthday as April 19,

1963, and coincidently, the time-stamp on the rental agreement read 4:19 PM. The owner of the shop, Eldon Elliot, and the three other employees present at the time "Kling" picked up the Ryder, all said he came in with another man who silently stood in the back of the store and smoked cigarettes as Kling conducted the transaction.

FBI field agents began canvasing the Junction City area for leads and released two sketches based on the descriptions of the two newest suspects, both of whom came to be known respectively as "John Doe #1" (JD1) and "John Doe # 2." (JD2).

The sketch of JD1 (Kling), depicted a white male, about 5'10" in height, weighing about 180 pounds with a medium build, buzz cut, angular face with a "rough complexion," "acne" and what appeared to be a "deformed chin." JD2 was a dark-skinned man with dark hair, dark "intense" eyes, square jaw, full lips, muscular neck, in his late 20's or early 30's, approximately 5'10" in height, weighing 180 pounds with a serpent-like tattoo on his left bicep. The FBI offered a $2 million dollar reward for information leading to their arrest. The sketches matched similar reports from eyewitnesses in and around downtown OKC.

Immediately following the release of the sketches, the FBI received a slew of phone calls from people around the country who claimed to know the identities of these men. Among them was Carl Lebron, a security guard at Calspan, a defense contractor located in Buffalo, New York. On April 21, Lebron told the FBI that JD1 looked eerily similar to a former co-worker of his named Timothy McVeigh, a racist anti-Sem-

2 Men Sought In Connection With The Oklahoma City Bombing

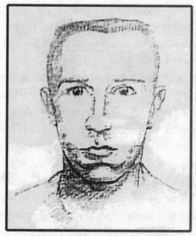

Described as being between 5-9 and 5-10.
Weighing between 175 and 180 lbs.
Visible tattoo below the sleeve of a tee-shirt.

Described as being between 5-10 and 5-11
Weighing between 180 and 185 lbs.

Information or sightings should be reported to 1-800-905-1514

13

ite who was extremely vocal about his anti-government beliefs. In fact, he continued, McVeigh's rhetoric had been so startlingly hate-filled that Lebron once secretly recorded one of their conversations, a tape of which he turned over to the FBI after the bombing. In addition, Lebron gave the FBI the name of another Calspan guard whom Lebron said he believed was John Doe 2.

Meanwhile, on Friday, April 21, as Lebron made his phone call to the Buffalo FBI office, the FBI's canvasing in Junction City, Kansas, where "Kling" rented his Ryder, led them to the Dreamland Motel. The owner of the Dreamland, Lea McGown, instantly recognized the sketch of JD1 as a recent guest who had arrived in a yellow Mercury Marquis on Friday, April 14, registered under the name "Timothy McVeigh" and, on his registration form, noted an Arizona license plate whose number was illegible as well as a Decker, Michigan home address. McVeigh had checked out early on the morning of Tuesday, April 18. McGown, her adult son and several Dreamland guests told agents that the previous Sunday, which happened to be Easter, McVeigh parked an older model, faded-yellow Ryder truck there but, by the evening of Monday, April 17, had replaced it with a newer, freshly painted model. They further recounted to the FBI agents that, during his time at Dreamland, McVeigh had received visitors in his motel room. Several guests recalled having to ask McVeigh to move the earlier, faded Ryder on more than one occasion, as it was blocking other parking spaces.

McGown had placed McVeigh in Room 25, which shared a wall with her office. Upon their arrival, she told agents she was certain that on April 16 (Easter Sunday), she had clearly heard at least one male voice and possibly two, speaking to McVeigh in his room. At least six others, all Dreamland guests and employees, also reported seeing a man with McVeigh. They described this other man as shorter than McVeigh, standing about 5'7 and weighing about 190 pounds with a muscular build, "olive" or "dark" complexion, a dragon tattoo and having dark, slicked back hair. Various Dreamland witnesses said they saw this man sitting behind the wheel of the newer Ryder, sometimes with McVeigh sitting in the passenger seat, including on the afternoon of April 17.

The Dreamland accounts were supported by Jeff Davis, a delivery person for Hunan's Chinese Restaurant, who said that at about 5:00 PM on Saturday, April 15, a caller identifying himself as "Bob Kling" had placed an order for delivery to the Dreamland, Room 25. Davis insisted that, if he had to say which JD sketch the man who answered the door and paid for the order resembled, it would be JD2, but stressed that, in actuality, the man he encountered resembled neither sketch nor the man later identified as "Timothy McVeigh."[6]

ALL AMERICAN DEMON: THE DEVIL YOU KNOW

Soon after the Elliot's, Dreamland and Lebron leads, the FBI learned that on April 19, a little over an hour after the explosion in OKC, and about an hour northwest of OKC, Oklahoma State Trooper Charlie Hangar observed a yellow, 1977 Mercury Marquis with a missing rear license plate heading away from OKC. The driver promptly pulled over to the side of the road after Hangar signaled him to do so and identified himself to Hanger as "Timothy McVeigh." Although unable to produce a bill of sale or proof of insurance for the car he was driving, McVeigh *did* disclose to Hangar that he was carrying a concealed and loaded .45 caliber Glock semi-automatic pistol, which, while registered legally in the state of New York, was nonetheless illegal in Oklahoma. Hangar placed twenty-seven year old McVeigh under arrest for the traffic violations and possession of an illegal gun and booked him in the nearby jail, located in the town of Perry, where he was to await arraignment.

Hangar described his initial impressions of McVeigh as a "clean cut," "well groomed" and "polite" young man.[7] Local officials, employees at the jail and inmates there described McVeigh's demeanor during his time in Perry as seemingly unconcerned and said he showed no reaction to the live, emotionally-charged coverage of the bombing continuously playing in the background during his booking. During his stay at the Perry jail, as he waited to appear before the arraigning judge, McVeigh made several phone calls, unsuccessfully attempting to locate and secure a bail bondsman. Based on the Lebron and Dreamland leads, the FBI tracked McVeigh to the Perry Jail on April 21, only minutes before his scheduled arraignment and release, and contacted the Perry District Attorney, requesting he stall McVeigh's arraignment.

An hour after the FBI called the DA, as agents made their way to Perry, a large crowd of ambitious news crews and civilian gawkers gathered outside the small jail/courthouse. Images of a shackled McVeigh in an orange jumpsuit, escorted by Federal agents from the front of the Perry jailhouse to a nearby black helicopter quickly inundated the airwaves. From Perry, McVeigh was taken to nearby Tinker Air Force Base for further questioning.

Upon first seeing McVeigh, the sizeable crowd that had gathered outside the Perry jail began shouting taunts at him, calling him a "creep," "murderer" and "baby killer." McVeigh, reporters said, seemed "eerily composed [and] unrepentant" and his countenance, similar to a mask whose powers of concealment seemed also to reveal his "ruthlessness and hatred." His lack of visible reaction and "thousand-yard stare" seemed to provoke and escalate the reactions of the crowd towards him. One report observed that McVeigh seemed to provide "an obliging demon" towards whom the mounting public fear and anger could be directed. What the crowd in Perry and national news viewers found most disturbing about this demon was his "gaze" and the "look in his eyes."[8] Thus, Americans (and the world) first became acquainted with Timothy James McVeigh.

The media made immediate and ongoing comparisons between McVeigh and Lee Harvey Oswald. After being appointed to act as McVeigh's lead defense attorney in early May 1995, Stephen Jones also publicly compared McVeigh's "Perry Perp Walk" to that of Oswald's. Jones commented that the repeated airing of these images had created a sense of national "déjà vous" and said "those old enough to remember 'saw' in [McVeigh] the ghost of Lee Harvey Oswald."[9] Jones later pointed out that it would have been much easier (and safer) to whisk McVeigh quickly and quietly out of the back of the Perry courthouse and accused the FBI of tipping off reporters to the scheduled perp walk during which they paraded McVeigh in front of the cameras, thereby *scripting* and orchestrating a major media event.

McVeigh's race (white), nationality (American), background (highly decorated Gulf War veteran), and clean-cut appearance starkly contrasted with the initial images of villainous Middle Easterners – a contrast accentuated even further upon the arrests of forty-year-old Terry Nichols and twenty-six year old Michael Fortier shortly thereafter. McVeigh had listed Terry Nichols of Decker, Michigan as his next of kin during his initial booking in Perry on April 19. On April 21, after hearing his name on the radio in connection with McVeigh and the bombing, Nichols promptly turned himself in to local authorities in Decker, Michigan and, at first, denied any involvement in the bombing or knowledge of McVeigh's involvement but soon after admitted to limited knowledge of McVeigh's plot. The FBI quickly identified Michael Fortier as a known acquaintance of McVeigh's at whose residence in Kingman, Arizona, McVeigh occasionally resided. Fortier, upon first being questioned by the FBI, denied any involvement and, as no material evidence existed otherwise, he was released. Within weeks though, Fortier, under round-the-clock surveillance, (by both the media and FBI), changed his story and, like Nichols, admitted that he and wife Lori had limited prior knowledge of McVeigh's plot.

The three men, all white, U.S. citizens, had met while serving in the U.S. Army. Their collective profile starkly conflicted with the existing terrorist template. This was no gang of ragtag, swarthy, wild-eyed Muslim fanatics, but patriotic white Americans and military veterans, to boot. Media attention now turned towards the suspects' purported right-wing anti-government political views, their belief in "conspiracy theories," and the larger subcultural milieu they inhabited. This semi-subterranean social realm, broadly referred to as the "Patriot Movement," consisted of loosely-affiliated, but often ideologically similar, groups and individuals who included, among others, Second Amendment advocates, paramilitary citizen militias, white supremacist separatists, pro-lifers, tax protestors, survivalists, and proponents of a range of conspiracy theories.

News articles described how McVeigh, Nichols and Fortier were part of a new generation that espoused an updated variant of much older anti-Semitic beliefs about collusion between elements within the U.S. government and the world's elite (the Illuminati) in a secret plot to establish a world government (the New World Order) and total surveillance society. The "black helicopter crowd" believed U.N. troops would soon round up, disarm, and imprison U.S. citizens within concentration camps (often to be run by FEMA). Fancying themselves modern American Revolutionaries, some were gearing up for war with the government. The events at Ruby Ridge, Idaho, in 1992 and Waco, Texas, in 1993, as well as the passage of the Brady Bill, catalyzed both the mobilization and alliance of these disparate groups and individuals.

Prior to the bombing, the emergent "movement" was virtually invisible to the public at large. Very soon after though, an increasing number of pundits, officials and "experts" linked the paranoid world views of this relatively homogenous mass of militant right-wing extremists to the willingness to commit violent criminal activity and warned that, while on the fringe, they represented a threatening and growing culture of conspiracy in the mainstream. News outlets now began to report on the strange opinions expressed by the racists, militias and "kooks" around McVeigh, some of whom knew him. Their statements to the media echoed long-established conspiracy-theory plots and introduced the beginnings of what became an entire subgroup of alternate narratives in which the bomber wittingly or otherwise becomes an Oswaldian figure. Notorious Neo-Nazi spokesperson, Aryan Nations founder Richard Butler told reporters that they suspected McVeigh was a "patsy," perhaps even a CIA agent, thereby iterating an early version of Guilty Agent stories about the bombing suspect.

On Sunday, April 23, a friend of McVeigh's in Michigan told reporters that McVeigh believed the government had implanted a tracking chip in his "rear end [so] the all-seeing eye of the government could keep an eye on him and know where he was."[10] The same day, April 23, the FBI received a call from Linda Thompson, an Indianapolis attorney, militia spokesperson and producer of an underground documentary, *Waco: The Big Lie*, which advanced a theory that the government had deliberately set the fire that killed the Branch Davidians. Thompson told agents that a certain "Dr. Jolly West," a CIA operative who conducted mind control experiments had implanted microchips in McVeigh and other U.S. soldiers. Thompson also relayed these claims to the *Indianapolis Star* who quoted her in their April 24th report. The public voicing of such sentiments introduced not only a new character (West) into the mix but also stands as the first publicly told Experimental Wolf stories about McVeigh.

While acts of politically motivated violence committed on American soil by U.S. citizens were by no means a new phenomenon, an emergent category of "homegrown domestic terrorism" increasingly occupied a central place in terrorism discourse, and the arrest of Timothy McVeigh brought forth the rhetorical coupling of conspiracy theorists (and others) with a newly emergent terrorist threat. In response, all manner of claim-makers garnered support for a range of new policies and practices meant to combat the existence and spread of threatening ideologies and subcultures.

On Monday, April 24, 1995, President Clinton assured the public that he would expand the powers and budgets granted to counter-terrorism and intelligence agencies to give law enforcement more effective means of investigating extremist groups in order to root out and eradicate whatever larger threat the bombing might indicate. Prior to the bombing, Congress refused to pass a controversial anti-terrorism bill proposed by the Clinton administration, but on April 25, the first draft of it passed in the Senate and a year later, passed in its final form with overwhelming bipartisan support.[11] The newer version of the previously proposed legislation greatly increased the powers and budgets allotted to counter-terrorism, intelligence, and law enforcement agencies with the stated goal of more effectively investigating, monitoring, and eradicating extremist groups through the FBI's and other law enforcement agencies' use of undercover surveillance and sting operations. Further, the new legislation retroactively allowed prosecutors to seek the death penalty for any suspect convicted of participation in the OKC bombing.

On April 23, the FBI announced they were still searching for anywhere from four to six other unidentified conspirators. During a press conference the next day, President Clinton promised that although the number of individuals involved in the bombing of the Murrah was unknown as yet, "no stone would be left unturned." All leads would be followed and all perpetrators found and convicted; justice would be "certain, swift, and severe" and prosecutors would seek the death penalty for those found guilty.[12] At the same press conference, Janet Reno reminded viewers that although authorities had McVeigh and Nichols in custody, the case remained open and stressed that JD2 remained at large and was considered armed and dangerous.

Although the official number of suspected participants in the bombing continued to change, on May 1, the cover of *Time* featured a photo of McVeigh, declaring his face, "The Face of Terror." On April 25, however, another Face Of Terror emerged when the FBI released a *second* sketch of the stocky, dark skinned JD2, this time with a baseball cap on. The second sketch was based on numerous eyewitnesses in Oklahoma, Kansas and Arizona who claimed to have seen McVeigh with others in the weeks, days, hours, and minutes before the explosion as well as immediately afterwards. On May 8, *Time* quoted unnamed federal investigators who said that McVeigh and the John Doe were in no way lone bombers but rather, more than likely cogs in a much larger network of extremists who had assisted in the bombing conspiracy through financing or tactical support. Then, on May 10, the *Los Angeles Times* quoted unnamed "investigators and authorities" who relayed a working theory that "John Doe 2 could be two people" who had accompanied McVeigh to OKC the morning of the bombing in order to act as "decoys" in the hope of confusing eyewitnesses and therefore authorities later (a version of the Pack Of Wolves story). The search for the John Does became "the most intensive manhunt in American history" (at the time) with the FBI conducting over 25,000 interviews and running down 43,000 leads in an attempt to find them. In the process, the FBI arrested, cleared and released several individuals, one of them live on television.

Meanwhile, as the FBI sought to determine if McVeigh had acted as a leader or follower, a "mastermind" or just one of many "foot soldiers" in a much "larger ring" of conspirators and likeminded terrorists, media outlets speculated about McVeigh's motives. Depending on the report, McVeigh's downward spiral and violent aspirations began when he "washed out" of his Special Forces try-out; became disillusioned about the role that the U.S. (and himself) had played in the Gulf War; developed "Gulf War Syndrome"; or after he became enraged by the militaristic and warlike tactics used against the Branch Davidian's at Waco, Texas and what he perceived as a general loss of civil liberties. Thus, McVeigh assumed the cloak of Disgruntled Soldier Avenger.[13]

On April 21, McVeigh was taken from Perry to nearby Tinker Air Force Base for further questioning and arraignment and, once there, was charged as the primary and, thus far, only suspect in the bombing. He was appointed two public defenders, John Coyle and Susan Otto, to whom, unknown to the public (but documented within the Jones Collection), McVeigh made a very strange confession. He told Coyle and Otto that, while in the National Guard (which he had joined after leaving active duty Army service), he had been recruited to work undercover as part of a domestic security operation. McVeigh said his mission was to infiltrate and report on Neo-Nazi's and other domestic terrorism threats. McVeigh then said that after having discovered the bombing plot, he reported it to his handlers but was instructed to continue in his role, remain embedded within the conspiracy and even go so far as to participate in the bombing; but ensure that only a couple of windows were blown out of the Murrah building. McVeigh expressed his shock that the Ryder could have caused as much damage as it did and wondered out loud if someone may have switched the truck at the last minute without his knowledge. While, within the weeks and months to come, his story would undergo radical transformation, McVeigh's initial confession to Otto and Coyle stands as, while not the first, the earliest known *post arrest* Guilty Agent story that McVeigh would tell.

From Tinker, McVeigh was taken to nearby El Reno State Prison where he remained until shortly before his trial began. Within days of his confession to them, Otto and Coyle recused themselves from the case, citing conflicts of interest. They were replaced on May 8, 1995, when Stephen Jones, a charismatic small town lawyer from Enid, Oklahoma, was appointed to defend McVeigh. According to Jones, when discussing the transfer of the case Otto cryptically warned Jones that "when you know everything I know, and you will soon enough, you will never think of the United States of America in the same way."[14]

Jones now represented the man touted in the headlines as "the most hated man in America." While *all* suspects faced the possibility of receiving a death sentence if convicted, Federal Prosecutor Joseph Hartzler announced his intent to send McVeigh specifically, "straight to hell." Facing a formidable task, Jones amassed a sizeable defense team that ultimately came to consist of fourteen attorneys, five paralegals, scores of researchers and private investigators and consultants whose fields of expertise included mental health, media analysis, forensics, explosives, terrorism, intelligence, and social-political movements.

During his first meeting with Jones, McVeigh "calmly," "proudly" and "dispassionately" confessed that, although he had not meant to kill children, he had bombed the Alfred P. Murrah federal building and had gotten caught on purpose, hoping to use his trial to demonstrate that the government's actions at Waco, Texas, on April 19, 1993, had been abusive and illegal.[15] In what the Jones Team referred to as McVeigh's "necessity defense," McVeigh believed the federal government's actions at Waco posed a threat to himself and the citizenry, as well as the constitutional foundations of the United States. Therefore, McVeigh, believing he must intervene, conceived of, planned and executed the bombing alone, as an act of self-defense in the face of an encroaching threat to his life and the lives of others.

When Jones asked about JD2, McVeigh denied that any such person existed and, ironically, accused those who insisted otherwise of being conspiracy theorists. He further informed his attorneys that he intended to "embarrass the government" during his trial and hoped that "after all the evidence is heard, the case remains a mystery" as, McVeigh explained, it had historical value and certain details about it must remain secret.[16] He also made it clear though that for the purposes of his criminal trial and historical legacy, he wanted to take full responsibility for the bombing and demanded his legal team not direct culpability towards any other individual, including (but not limited to) Nichols and Fortier (the earliest version of the Lone Wolf story).

Despite McVeigh's stated objections, during his first week as McVeigh's attorney, Jones sought a meeting with Attorney General Janet Reno with the intent of brokering a deal with federal prosecutors. He proposed that in exchange for sparing McVeigh the death penalty, Jones would offer up the identity of John Doe 2. According to Jones, although McVeigh initially agreed with this strategy, he quickly changed his mind and withdrew his permission.[17]

Jones immediately concluded that, regardless of whether or not McVeigh had acted alone, in order to mitigate the effect of McVeigh's demonization in the media, he would need to be defended, not only in a court of law, but also in the court of public opinion. To this end, Jones conceived of a public relations strategy and, in the ensuing months, formed several *quid pro quo* relationships with journalists from media outlets with whom he could exchange investigative information. At one of many subsequent press conferences, Jones announced the defense teams' intent to present McVeigh "as we believe he really is" and expose the truth about the bombing.[18]

Jones' public relations strategy backfired (or *appeared* to backfire) early on, when, on May 17, 1995, the *New York Times* published an article containing a number of highly damaging statements attributed to McVeigh, said to have been made privately to his attorney before being leaked to the press. Included was McVeigh's confession of guilt and denial that any other conspirators existed. In addition, the article discussed telephone records from McVeigh's calling card, purchased under the name "Daryl Bridges," suggesting that McVeigh had maintained connections to a number of White Power Movement organizations throughout the country, or had at least attempted to contact them using the card immediately prior to the bombing. The article also reported that McVeigh told his attorneys where authorities might find his fingerprints as well as left-over bomb-making materials and other incriminating evidence.[19]

Nobody agreed on the origins of the leaked information or the paths it had followed before finding its way into the headlines. The Jones Team and the prosecution publicly pointed fingers at each other. Jones maintained that the leaks were a result of government sabotage and, in July 1995, filed motions with the court expressing concern that prison officials and federal authorities were eavesdropping on McVeigh's meetings with attorneys and intercepting their phone calls. McVeigh, outraged, placed the blame squarely on Jones, an accusation that a number of Jones Team staffers came to agree with.

In response to the leak, McVeigh wrote the first of many scathing letters to his attorneys, complaining to them that Jones was too focused on the media and that "only days" after his assumedly confidential confession to Jones, "almost my exact words hit the front page of the *New York*

Times." McVeigh also verbalized this to a number of people on his defense team. When he learned of his client's accusations about him, Jones wrote to McVeigh and explained that the defense team's relationship with the media was an unfortunate necessity and the journalists with whom they cultivated relationships could function as extra investigators for the team. The confession article in the *Times* foreshadowed many similar leaks over the next two years, which led to a sustained attorney-client struggle, mainly between Jones and McVeigh, about, among other things, *who* would tell the story of the bombing, how it would be told and who would script and control McVeigh's public image.

While Jones publicly claimed otherwise, in his letter to McVeigh, Jones reminded his client that he (McVeigh) had given Jones permission to speak to the *New York Times.* Jones then noted McVeigh's stubborn desire to take full credit for the bombing and opined that the only reason McVeigh had given Jones permission to speak to the media was to send a "signal" to other unidentified conspirators that he was willing to accept full blame for the act of terror.

In his book, *Others Unknown: Timothy McVeigh and the Oklahoma City Bombing Conspiracy*, written after the conclusion of McVeigh's trial, Stephen Jones expressed his opinion that, from the moment they first met, McVeigh intended to take full credit for the bombing and "craved recognition, publicity, acknowledgment and he wouldn't-couldn't-let it go." Jones said that McVeigh continually asked if he could "go public and proclaim his responsibility" but to do so would be to assure McVeigh received a guilty verdict and death sentence. On the other hand, Jones said he recognized that if McVeigh was not permitted to make such a statement publicly, the other unidentified bombing conspirators (whom Jones firmly believed existed) would fear McVeigh's possible disclosure of their identities and therefore would orchestrate a "Jack Ruby incident" and attempt to assassinate McVeigh. If they believed he planned to take the fall for the bombing, they might let their guards down. Therefore, Jones said, "It was incumbent on me to find a way to protect Tim and at the same time assuage his cravings for fame." Thus, Jones said he suggested to McVeigh that they "leak" a confession to the press and McVeigh "seized on" the idea and insisted that Jones proceed. Therefore, Jones made a deal with McVeigh, agreeing to orchestrate a confession leak in exchange for McVeigh's promise not to speak to the media on his own accord. "From then on," wrote Jones, McVeigh "was effectively muzzled."[20]

McVeigh however, recalled the incident very differently in a letter to his biographers written four years later. McVeigh explained to them that, after the *New York Times* article was published, other members of his legal team learned that Jones himself had leaked the information and when Jones realized they knew, he sought McVeigh's retroactive permission to speak with the media: "Jones gave them to 'em – my own attorney! Then, 2 -3 days after [the] release, he asked me (coerced me) [into] signing a 'permission slip' attributing [my consent for the leaks]." While he considered firing Jones at this time, the thought of bringing a new attorney up to speed on his case seemed too daunting and so he "relented" and signed the consent form Jones had drafted.[21]

Indeed, in his 2012 book, former Jones Team investigator Roger Charles noted that McVeigh's authorization granting Jones permission to speak to the *Times* was signed and dated on May 18, the day *after* the story ran. Further, according to Charles, other attorneys on the team witnessed Jones bragging about having obtained McVeigh's signature even though, at the time, McVeigh had no interest in making a public confession. Charles said that despite Jones' claims that he leaked the confession to protect McVeigh and prevent him from making a lengthier, more damaging confession on television, "It was never clear how this protection was achieved by a front page confession in the country's most authoritative newspaper."[22]

McVeigh told his biographers that his misgivings about the trustworthiness of certain members of his defense team began early on and had led him to outline his security concerns to them and, on numerous occasions, warn about the dangers of diffusing confidential information too widely. McVeigh said his fears were continuously met with "a 'yea, yea, kid – you're going to teach me, your elder, something?!?!' attitude." It was at this point, McVeigh told his biographers, that he came to the realization that his "entire defense and defense team was one big 'clusterfuck'.…Quote me on that one." Yet, by the time his lawyers took him seriously, it was too late.

The *New York Times* confession was closely followed by a steady stream of similar headlines such as "McVeigh says he was bomber," "McVeigh admits role," and "McVeigh admits Oklahoma City bomb massacre." Like the *New York Times* piece, these reports publicized inflammatory and incriminating details known only to defense team members while attributing them to anonymous sources. The damning leaks of confidential attorney-client case material and its appearance in press reports continued to plague the Jones Team throughout the pre-trial phase and became, not only a recurring and defining issue for the defense team, but reflected the larger ongoing struggles over secrecy, disclosure and control of information that proved endemic to the case. According to Jones Team attorney Randy Coyne, the leaks eventually demoralized other members of the team and caused irreparable damage to the relationship between the defense team and McVeigh.[23]

While initially the relationship between Nichols' and McVeigh's defense teams were cooperative, the leaks also contributed to the disintegration of any working relationship between them. Former defense attorney for Nichols, Ron Woods, recalled a frustrating incident that began with a gesture of professional courtesy when Woods provided discovery material to Jones consisting of statements Nichols had made to the FBI. "I told [Jones] not to give [the material] to anybody," said a still frustrated Woods. However, "The very next day, [Nichols'] statements appeared in the *Los Angeles Times* and so we decided not to share information with Jones because he appeared to be talking to the media incessantly."[24]

At the time though, no matter who had leaked or who knew about it, Jones very publicly (and falsely) denied the veracity of the confession articles and doggedly pressed on with his plan to humanize his client, in doing so becoming a co-author of McVeigh's public persona. Weeks after the initial *New York Times* confession article appeared, Jones released portions of McVeigh's military records and photos of a smiling and laughing McVeigh meeting with his attorneys. Additionally, Jones made McVeigh available to several reporters and photographers for the purposes of conducting off-the-record interviews under the condition that they not photograph his client in handcuffs or ask specific questions about the bombing itself.

Among the reporters chosen to interview McVeigh and help mitigate his demonization was *Newsweek* writer David Hackworth, who conducted the first on-the-record prison interview with McVeigh in June 1995. Jones described his client as "the boy next door, the boy wonder" and told Hackworth, "He's innocent." McVeigh spoke to Hackworth about his small town childhood in rural upstate New York, his combat in the Persian Gulf, denied ever having been a militia member, expressed that he was horrified upon learning of the deaths of children in the Murrah building and stated his intent to plead not guilty.

Hackworth's article offered a very different impression of McVeigh from the seemingly cold, heartless man who had walked out of the Perry Courthouse. Hackworth wrote that, although media reports commonly depicted McVeigh as a "brooding, gun obsessed drifter," in reality, the public knew "virtually nothing" about America's newest terrorist. A fellow veteran, Hackworth observed that during their conversation, McVeigh was "in high combat form, *fully aware that his performance* in the interview was almost a matter of life and death. If he'd been in combat, he'd have [earned] a medal for his coolness under fire." In fact, wrote Hackworth, McVeigh is "a more subtle and intriguing figure…at once more clever and ingenious than his tabloid personality … savvy, world weary and very media wise. He was no militaristic automaton," "didn't seem like a baby killer" and resembled "a typical GenXer [more] than a deranged loner, much less a terrorist."

McVeigh appeared good-humored, self-aware and seemingly "normal," although this was "the image [McVeigh] wants to project" and the possibility always remained, warned Hackworth, that Timothy McVeigh "might also be the most devious con man to ever come down the pike.… At times McVeigh came across as the boy next door. But you might never want to let him into your house."

To his biographers later, McVeigh described the *Newsweek* article as accurate, but said that his "skin crawled" during the interview because he could not fully explain himself. "When [Hackworth asked] 'are you guilty?' and I have to say 'we're pleading not-guilty', [I wanted] to say 'well, I'm not guilty in a moral sense I don't think, but I've committed a crime. You can't say that.'" The Hackworth interview, he continued, had been *his* idea, but all subsequent ones had been Jones' "fucked up" idea that he nevertheless consented to for various reasons. For instance, said McVeigh, he granted CNN's Susan Candiotti an interview because he "had the hots" for her:

> I'd smile at [Candiotti] and other newswomen who came in who were hot [...] Jones wanted to make points with the media so they would help him with his investigation. He kept trying to coach me to meet with certain people. I didn't like the media but I did see one benefit, and I joked about it. I openly said, "Jones, you bring in good looking chicks, I'll meet with them." For me, it was something to jerk off to that night, for him, it was a connection with the media, for him to become a powerful person. [I met with Diane Sawyer and Barbara Walters off the record]. I was looking for a blowjob in some of these visits. One time this girl came in with one of the investigators. I think she left the seat wet she was so horny. [A high profile and popularity turns some people on.] I took a sip of her pop, passed it back to her; she said "I'm keeping this can." I felt like saying, "crawl under the table, take care of me honey."

McVeigh also left a favorable impression on other reporters who interviewed or met with him informally and who, like Hackworth, found him to be friendly, boyish and charming. Even the many reporters who never met him in person seemed to agree, including Buffalo area journalist Brandon Stickney who described him as "surprisingly normal," "a seemingly ordinary boy, someone who could be found in almost any average neighborhood in America," just a good old "all-American man."[25]

McVeigh's natural charm impressed members of his legal team as well. Stuart Wright, sociologist and consultant to the Jones defense team, described McVeigh as soft spoken, introspective, curious, friendly; possessing "a boyish quality that defied the stereotypical image of an embittered radical ... he didn't strike me as a 'terrorist.'" Likewise, Jones Team attorney Randy Coyne's first impressions were, "tall, young, serious, disciplined, articulate, and passionate."[26]

Nevertheless, mental health experts hired by the Jones Team who met with and evaluated McVeigh throughout the pretrial phase did not always buy McVeigh's *nice guy* act. For example, on August 31, 1995, clinical psychologist, neuropsychologist, psychotherapist and hypnotist, H.

Anthony Semone, Ph.D., detailed some of his clinical impressions in a memo written to Jones Team attorney Dick Burr. "It is just too easy to 'get to know Tim,'" Semone wrote. "I don't believe the apparent openness with which he greeted me, and I distrust his demonstration of warmth toward you." Semone concluded, "I think Tim is as shrewd and clever as they come…"

A review of Hackworth's *Newsweek* piece entitled "Interview with a Monster" asserted that the article provided "a closer look at McVeigh, aka American Evil Incarnate." The review argued that while Hackworth's article and the accompanying photo spread wrongfully humanized McVeigh, it also helped the public see past the now generically familiar "psychological and political caricature" of him that had been exhaustively recycled in the mass media.[27] Thus, while admitting that McVeigh's persona was rhetorically constructed and mediated and required critical deconstruction, efforts to do so were, paradoxically, seen as taboo and ethically wrong. Still, largely through the Jones PR campaign, McVeigh, the newest all-American media demon, emerged also as an all-American media darling. *Time* magazine, which had deemed McVeigh "The Face of Terror," went on to name him as a runner-up for their 1995 Man of the Year award, a distinction he lost to Newt Gingrich and shared with other runner-ups Bill Gates, Johnny Cochran, and O.J. Simpson.

During Jones' many media appearances, he repeatedly insisted that since McVeigh had been the first arrested, he became, at first, a "demon," and after, a vehicle of "catharsis" for the American public in the aftermath of the bombing. In one pre-trial court filing on October 4, 1996, Jones argued that the defense team's relationship with the press was required to negate "a year and a half of people who have constantly gone on national television and talked about killing [him], clawing out his eyes, [said] he's a monster… introvert… lunatic… right wing nut… [and] racist."[28]

Initially, other members of the defense team saw the wisdom in Jones' PR plan. Jones Team attorney Randy Coyne explained that Jones' courting of the media made sense during the early pre-trial preparation stage. His regular press conferences might help negate the many "prejudicial stories that described [McVeigh] as a right wing extremist, anti-government zealot, militia sympathizer, survivalist, and anarchist [and the] descriptions and depictions of [him] as cold, emotionless, and steely eyed." The majority of media reports "stressed the importance of guilty verdicts and hinted darkly that death would be the only suitable punishment … seriously undercut the presumption of innocence and completely compromised the possibility that McVeigh might be fairly tried either in Oklahoma or by Oklahoma jurors." Jones, said Coyne, believed that the reporters he courted "[would] be hitting the pavement and looking for the story just like investigators that are hired by the defense team and the legion of FBI agents and other investigators that worked on behalf of the federal government" and their doing so could help develop information for the Jones Team.

Still, according to Coyne, for members of the Jones Team and their client, McVeigh, Jones PR plan became an obstacle in preparing and providing an adequate defense case.

> By the time of the trial, the media became, at first, a distraction and then, ultimately, a very fickle ally if one viewed them as being an ally. At first, I don't think Tim minded so much, but then concluded, like a lot of other people did, that it wasn't in his best interest to play Tom Thumb to Stephen Jones' PT Barnum. [While] at first Jones thought the media could operate as independent investigators or the defense […] the problems came later in regards to the disclosure of defense documents and the lack of security on the defense team as far as protecting the client's confidences. There was certainly frustration with the defense team's relationship with the media.[29]

Thus began what would prove to be a highly complicated, controversial love-hate relationship between the media, McVeigh, his defense team, the victims, the FBI and prosecution, plus, positioned in the middle of the fray: the public.

Originally, Nichols and McVeigh were going to stand trial together as co-defendants on the conspiracy charges, but defense attorneys for both parties formally requested a severance fearing that, if tried together, prejudicial statements made by one could be used against the other. Both defense teams also asked the court to change the trial locations from Lawton, Oklahoma, a small town about an hour from Oklahoma City, to another state. Attorneys for Nichols, who had kept a low profile since his arrest and refused contact with the media, feared the ongoing demonization would make it impossible for him to obtain a fair trial. Public opinion polls in Oklahoma showed that the majority believed both Nichols and McVeigh were guilty and deserved the death penalty.

During the February 1996 severance and change of venue hearings, presiding Judge Richard P. Matsch noted the intensity and repetition of victim-oriented news in Oklahoma. He explained that, while reports in Oklahoma tended to humanize the victims, more often than not, they also demonized the defendants. The majority of these, observed Matsch, focused on McVeigh specifically and included the statements of victims that emphasized McVeigh's evil inhumanity. They complained that McVeigh smiled too much in court and expressed their wish that he would show remorse. Terry Nichols and Michael Fortier had not attracted the same level of public fascination as McVeigh and bore the brunt of far less media scrutiny. The shy, quiet, mousy Nichols consistently "presented himself as a man, not a monster." Bombing victims said Nichols seemed like a "nicer person," less threatening, more like a "real estate salesman" than a terrorist. Based on considerations of the victims' understandably vitriolic responses to McVeigh, Matsch granted both the severance and venue change, and relocated the trials of both to Denver, Colorado.[30]

McVeigh appeared to cling to a strange belief that if only he could explain his motivations, the victims would understand and accept him and his actions. Yet his attempts to address their feelings were often clumsy and were viewed by the victims as intentionally insulting and dismissive. At times he referred to them as the "woe is me crowd" but explained that by this he meant only those victims who seemed to display an insatiable need to seek the spotlight and were hell bent on attacking him as a person. Despite his ill-conceived efforts to get them to understand him, the highly public contention between McVeigh and the bombing victims, along with his many callous remarks towards or about them, became an integral element in the saga of his evolving public persona.

Jones' strategic relationship with the press and provocative court filings and arguments, ostensibly meant to humanize McVeigh and counter the overwhelmingly negative pre-trial publicity, only provoked further outrage among victims. Eventually, Jones' continued courting of the media culminated in a prosecutors' request that Matsch impose a limited gag order barring *all* attorneys from discussing case-related information with the press. Jones and several major media outlets made formal appeals and arguments against the request. Matsch scheduled hearings to resolve the issue and, in the interim, in what prosecutors described as "a public relations blitz," Jones held a series of press conferences wherein he continued to assert that the medias' factually inaccurate, demonizing and dehumanizing coverage, especially the widely circulated Perry perp walk footage, had prematurely (and erroneously) depicted McVeigh as guilty, scared off potential defense witnesses and, ultimately, "chiseled into the consciousness of the nation," a portrait of McVeigh as "an anti-government killer, a 'marginalized' figure, an '*aberration*', a 'person who lived alone and embittered,' and as a 'loser' whose own inadequacies produced the tragedy." Then, in a court filing during this time, Jones asserted that the most vocal bombing victims and survivors had no interest in "the facts-they don't want to be bothered with the facts. They have already formed their opinion."[31] Appalled, prosecutors implored Matsch to order a total gag order and Matsch consented, provoking criticism from First Amendment advocates and media outlets.

The gag order was met with secret relief by a number of the defense team, who themselves had become weary of Jones' antics by this time.

Coyne recalled that from the outset of his involvement with the case "I felt strongly that disproportionate time and energy were spent on ancillary media matters." Coyne said he was "frequently pulled away from [important defense related] tasks to research and brief the First Amendment and media law issues in order to preserve Jones' right to swamp the airwaves with daily public appearances and sound bites." At the time, Coyne felt that the attention given to McVeigh's 'media' defense should have subsided after Matsch issued the change of venue and severance rulings in their favor, but by then, Coyne reflected, Jones had become addicted to the attention lavished on him by the press, comparing Jones' "personal quest to saturate the media" to a "heroin junkie in the throes of withdrawal ... trying to score another fix."[32]

After Matsch issued the total gag order, a series of angry letters flew back and forth between McVeigh and Jones. McVeigh said he agreed with Matsch's decision and accused Jones of caring more about becoming a celebrity than defending him. Jones, in turn, admonished McVeigh for his ongoing "temper tantrums" and accused McVeigh of intentionally sabotaging the efforts of his own legal team by stonewalling their investigations into other conspirators so that he could use the trial to air his theories about what happened at Waco, Texas. While Jones had earlier agreed to incorporate the issue into McVeigh's defense strategy, he was not above extortion when it suited him. On November 25, 1996, Jones warned McVeigh that if he did not begin to cooperate he could "kiss the Waco aspect goodbye" and informed other members of the defense team that the time had come to be "stern" with McVeigh and suggested placing "an embargo" on attorneys' visits with him.

The following day, in retaliation, McVeigh took matters into his own hands and began making contact with reporters without Jones' knowledge or consent. He wrote a letter to the *Oklahoma Gazette* but (as he would many times), failed miserably to endear himself to the paper's local readers, or soften his negative image. McVeigh accused the FBI of using the media to control information about the bombing and of demonizing him by spreading propaganda, the same tactic they used against the Branch Davidians at Waco. The FBI, he said, had prevented the public from seeing images of "the charred remains of children's bodies" at Waco and therefore nobody cared "when these families died a slow, torturous death as they were gassed and burned alive at the hands of the FBI [or] when boastful FBI agents posed for the camera as people's lives were consumed in flames." McVeigh said "the truth" about his own case and the events at Waco "lies deeper," but in order to get it to the public, he argued, people needed to "question and analyze what they hear, and ponder the intentions of those spreading the propaganda." After the *Gazette* published the letter, the FBI came to the offices of the paper and confiscated it.[33]

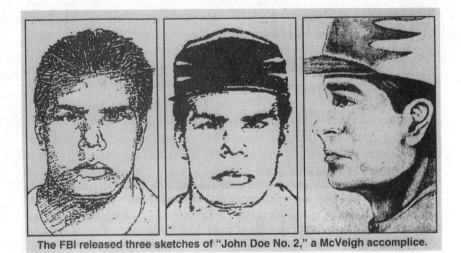

The FBI released three sketches of "John Doe No. 2," a McVeigh accomplice.

THE LEGEND OF JOHN DOE 2

For McVeigh, the only acceptable public legacy was one wherein he was a hero who, perceiving grave threats to the citizenry of the United States, had alone conceived of the plot to bomb the Murrah building and of his own volition, with only minor help from Nichols and Fortier in the preparation stages, carried out his plan alone the morning of April 19. Yet, as McVeigh became America's face of Lone Wolf terrorism, details in the Pack Of Wolves story were quickly amassing.

Early on, various members of the Jones Team and Jones, most of all, had begun to doubt McVeigh's Lone Wolf version of events. Their doubts grew with the continual emergence of evidence which strongly suggested the involvement of others in the plot, and as they increasingly perceived stark inconsistencies in McVeigh's story that often conflicted with known physical evidence and countless eyewitness statements.

An ongoing flurry of news articles (based on leaked defense team information), reported that McVeigh had links to a number of well-known Neo-Nazi and White Power Movement organizations and spokespeople and that these associations went much deeper than had been publicly discussed (or leaked) by the prosecution, FBI and defense teams. The most notable of these concerned his links to Elohim City, a white separatist community on the Oklahoma-Arkansas border known as a "safe haven" for fugitives within the White Power Movement. Shortly before the bombing, McVeigh received two speeding tickets within miles of Elohim City, and nearby motel registration records and statements made by residents there strongly suggested that McVeigh had not only called Elohim City but had visited on more than one occasion.

Oddly, in 1983, individuals associated with Elohim City had hatched their own plot to blow up the Murrah building using a car or truck bomb and the group, residing in a different racialist survivalist community, had been raided and arrested for other crimes on April 19, 1985. On the morning of April 19, 1995, the state of Arkansas executed Richard Wayne Snell, a main participant in the failed 1983 plot. On the morning of April 19, 1995, Snell's final words, addressed to Arkansas Gov. Jim Tucker, were, "Governor Tucker, look over your shoulder. Justice is coming. I wouldn't trade places with you or any of your cronies. Hail the victory. I am at peace." In the years leading up to it, Snell's impending execution attracted protests nationally from adherents to the farthest reaches of the extreme paramilitary right wing. In the two years leading to the bombing, McVeigh attended over eighty gun shows in forty states. In October 1993, only weeks after registering at a motel and receiving a speeding ticket near Elohim City, McVeigh had written his sister a letter informing her that he was traveling the country on the gun show circuit and establishing "*a network of friends.*" Information such as this certainly suggests that McVeigh had been involved in a much broader plot.[34]

Internal Jones Team memoranda noted the fact that McVeigh could not reasonably account for all of the eyewitnesses who said they saw him with others in the days leading up to April 19, 1995, as well as those who saw him with anywhere from one to four other individuals in OKC on the morning of the bombing. In fact, every person who had observed McVeigh in OKC on the morning of the bombing said he had been accompanied by other individuals and at least one of the individuals described matched initial descriptions of John Doe 2 (seen with McVeigh in OKC). Such reports (and the many supporting video surveillance tapes that also turned up missing after the FBI took possession of them) presented grave problems for a legal defense team, whose client refused to acknowledge that any of these reports could be accurate.[35]

More troubling for his defense team was that, while on *most* occasions McVeigh denied that other conspirators existed, at other times, during private conversations, he alluded to and sometimes even admitted that other individuals had participated in the bombing and occasionally offered tantalizing tidbits of information to this effect, which, when asked about later, he would deny. Much to McVeigh's consternation, the Jones Team continued to implore him to tell them the truth and numerous investigators were hired and tasked with getting to the bottom of the matter.

Over time, Jones Team investigator Richard Reyna developed a particularly close relationship with McVeigh, and in doing so, uncovered significant information about the bombing plot that for various reasons would never come to light. In one internal memo, Reyna informed Jones that based on his investigation and McVeigh's many proven connections to the far right, "It is very likely that Mr. McVeigh could have been tricked or entrapped by members of the 'movement' to carry out a specific deed which in the end, leaves Mr. McVeigh with the appearance of total responsibility." Years later, Reyna recalled the occasional tantalizing tidbits he shared, under the condition that the legal team not point fingers at anybody else, and the implications of his conversations with McVeigh:

> I spent a lot of time with [McVeigh] and he told me a lot of things that I'll take to my grave. He gave me diagrams of where to go and what to see. My job was to find out who he had been dealing with – and that's where I went. Wherever it took me. There were people that should have been brought in that weren't ... and those are things that McVeigh and I had talked about ... he was never alone, and he was always with several people. All the people that saw him the morning of the bombing definitely identified him, but they identified four to five people with him. He couldn't have organized a two car funeral alone. They were painting him to be a general of some sort, but you only had to sit down with him to know he was a frightened kid. McVeigh was just looking for a home, trying all these different organizations. It can be compared to a war, which is the mentality that the different organizations had. You have soldiers and you have generals and leaders and so forth. And the soldiers follow the directions and orders. And that's what McVeigh was doing.[36]

Once, McVeigh told Jones that if no one else was arrested for the bombing "the revolution can continue." On another occasion, he said that after Waco and the assault weapons ban, "we decided to turn the tide," "go on the offensive" and "[make] them know what it feels like to be the hunted," although he refused to specify who *we* consisted of. During yet another meeting, McVeigh, alluding to these mysterious conspirators, said he had given them his word and that "information was valuable." He then acknowledged having omitted significant information to his defense and said he had "built one lie on top of another." After expressing his regret for doing so, he promised to offer his full cooperation and disclose everything but warned that if any of the information was used against anybody else, including Fortier and Nichols, he would not cooperate in the future. McVeigh's newfound spirit of cooperation proved short-lived however. At various times during conversations with certain members of his defense, when pressed about the issue of the John Doe 2's, McVeigh said he hoped to embarrass the government during his trial by exposing the weakness of their investigation of the bombing as well as his seemingly contradictory wish that "after all the evidence is heard, the case remains a mystery," as his trial had historical value and therefore, certain details about it must remain secret.

Meanwhile, the FBI's statements about the John Doe 2's fluctuated as wildly as McVeigh's, until eventually they both removed the mysterious conspirators from the equation completely. According to FBI officials' statements to the media, by mid-June 1995, the number of unidentified conspirators had grown to anywhere from six to eight individuals. Within a month though, the FBI's assertions of a larger plot, or at least their public statements about it, began to change dramatically. On any given day FBI investigators and spokespeople alternately acknowledged and denied the existence of John Doe #2 (and 3 and 4), sometimes on the same day.[37] And then, suddenly, the FBI began promulgating an entirely new theory: that McVeigh's mysterious companions, formerly the subjects of 'the most intensive manhunt in American history' might never have existed at all, but had been the product of well-meaning but mistaken (or delusional) eyewitnesses. By July 1995, the FBI called off the search for the John Doe people altogether. This turnaround fed into growing allegations that, in the Department of Justice's (DOJ) rush to obtain convictions and death sentences for McVeigh and Nichols, the FBI's investigation of additional perpetrators had fallen by the wayside.

Beyond McVeigh's occasional confidential allusions and cryptic hints, the Jones Team found it all the more strange that for someone who claimed to hate the federal government, his version of events shifted in accordance with the latest theories aired publicly by the FBI and prosecutors, a circumstance Stephen Jones described as "Kafkaesque." Jones wrote that McVeigh's version of events and the government's "went hand in hand" and because McVeigh had regular access to media and news reports, it became easy for him to "[adjust] his story from time to time to incorporate the governments findings" and "shore up" loose ends when he became aware of them, a practice Jones said McVeigh "finely honed" over the years.[38]

For example, to his legal team, McVeigh initially denied seeing anyone else at Elliot's when he came to pick up the Ryder truck. Shortly after the FBI dismissed the sightings, however, Jones asked McVeigh to explain the statements of Elliot's employees who insisted two men came in together to rent the Ryder on April 17 and McVeigh suddenly remembered that indeed, another man whom he did not know had come in after him at Elliot's, stood next to him, smoked a cigarette and even spoke with him briefly. McVeigh: always making friends.

In August 1995, a Grand Jury met at Tinker Air Force Base to hear the government's evidence against McVeigh and Nichols. Media outlets reported that during the supposedly secret (but inevitably leaked) proceedings. McVeigh's younger sister, Jennifer, gave testimony to the Grand Jury that alluded to the involvement of a Pack of Wolves. She said that beginning in December 1993, in a series of conversations and letters, her brother confided to her that he had participated in bank robberies with others who, like him, were "at war with the system ... we have to fund our war with sometimes covert means." He compared their actions to those of "Robin Hood." He boasted to her about how he instructed the unnamed bank robbers and "showed them how to do it" and had even asked her to launder money, telling her it was proceeds from the bank robberies.

At least one Grand Juror, Hoppy Heidelberg, found the proceedings so disturbing that he defied his oath of secrecy and spoke publicly about it, thereby making public some of the information presented. Heidelberg came to feel, during the hearings, that prosecutors had prevented jurors from hearing crucial evidence and stymied their inquiries and attempts to subpoena it. None of the witnesses who saw the John Does were called to testify and despite the Grand Jury's requests, jurors were not permitted to view the surveillance tapes from in and around the Murrah building that captured the critical moments before the blast. Heidelberg further claimed the FBI had harassed and intimidated several witnesses and pressured them to change their story, an allegation supported by statements of the witnesses themselves as well as the subject of complaints filed by the defense teams.[39]

On August 11, 1995, the federal Grand Jury returned an indictment that read: "Beginning on or about September 13, 1994, and continuing thereafter until on or about April 19, 1995 [McVeigh and Nichols] did knowingly, intentionally, willfully and maliciously conspire, combine and agree together *with others unknown* to use a weapon of mass destruction." The indictment listed twenty-seven overt acts that created "a narrative of the plot" and concluded that McVeigh "attempted to recruit others to as-sist in the act of violence," a reference to McVeigh's many pre-bombing phone calls and suspicious associations. If they existed at all, the iden-tities of the "others unknown" mentioned in the indictment remained a mystery although the phrase itself suggested the possibility of additional arrests. During a press conference explaining the indictments, Janet Reno made the contradictory statement that while the investigation was ongo-ing "most of [the JD2] leads have been pursued and exhausted."

Still, while the FBI and prosecutions concern about John Doe 2 fad-ed rapidly after the Grand Jury indictments, headlines stressed the case was "A Puzzle Unfinished" and "Far From Closed." Jones later wrote that McVeigh and lead prosecutor Joseph Hartzler (who earlier threat-ened to send McVeigh "straight to hell") "had one thing in common to which they held with an unshakeable tenacity – both publicly professed that Tim McVeigh was primarily responsible for the bombing. Either way, both were wrong. And either way, both knew they were wrong." During a press conference the day after the indictment was issued, Jones opined that, "Before this investigation is over with, the government will have Tim McVeigh standing next to Lee Harvey Oswald."[40]

Meanwhile, members of the press as well as the Jones Team engaged in a monumental struggle with the government concerning their withholding of substantial information about the case from defense attorneys, an effort that closely paralleled McVeigh's own obfuscations and Heidelberg's account of government stonewalling during the Grand Jury.

Very soon after the bombing, the media's attempts to obtain information about it were somewhat stymied by the court's decision to seal hundreds of case-related documents filed by both the prosecution and defense. Major media outlets filed complaints formally objecting to the ruling and argued that by doing so, the court violated procedural sealing protocols, the First Amendment and the public's right to information about criminal trials. Prosecutors maintained that the material fell under the 1980 Classified Information Procedures Act (CIPA) and, therefore, were outside the scope of public disclosure. Despite its close relationships with the press, the Jones Team objected to unsealing the documents. Referring to the sealed material and other limits places on the public's access to information about the case, *USA Today* remarked that while the bombing "was the most public of crimes ... the man accused of committing it is getting the most secret of trials," despite the advantage this afforded to the government, "who can't always be trusted to do what's right."[41]

While the Jones Team agreed the documents should be sealed, the government's secrecy became a major and ongoing point of contention between them and the prosecution and the subject of many Jones Team court filings. The Due Process Clause of the Fourteenth Amendment to the United States Constitution dictates that prosecutors provide defense attorneys with material in the government's possession considered exculpatory to a defendant in a criminal trial per *Brady v. Maryland* (1963). Included in this is information and evidence that could influence possible conviction for a crime or sentencing (level of culpability) such as physical evidence and witness statements that contradict prosecutors' charges, which would impeach a prosecution witness or reflect their status as a paid informant.

Six months after the bombing, on November 6, 1995, the Jones team submitted its first request for such material to the D.A.'s office, noting that the government had not yet provided them with any exculpatory evidence gathered during the FBI's investigation. Only after Judge Matsch ordered them to begin handing over discovery materials to the defense in a timelier manner did prosecutors begin incremental and partial production of the materials. Jones quickly realized that significant reports were missing, including those pertaining to critical eyewitnesses such as the Elliots and Dreamland witnesses. According to Roger Charles, the government's "delays and omissions were always most pronounced on the issue of possible conspirators." Rob Nigh said, "It didn't matter how specific we were, the government's response was that everything had been provided." The back and forth between the prosecution and defense continued until the time of McVeigh's trial and after it's conclusion.[42]

Perhaps the most notable instance of withheld material concerned the surveillance footage from the cameras positioned around the Murrah building that the FBI had confiscated immediately after the blast. At the very least the footage had the potential of clearing up some of the lingering questions about who was with McVeigh the morning of the bombing. However, despite the legal efforts of the Jones Team, survivors and victims of the bombing, investigators for a later County Grand Jury and the media, the content of the tapes remained a secret, at least officially. In late October, the Associated Press reported that, according to federal law enforcement officials, while the footage showed "a glimpse of a shadowy figure in the passenger seat [of the Ryder]" because the quality of the image was poor, investigators were unable to determine the identity of the passenger. Referring to John Doe 2, one article opined, "It's like he walked into the wall and vanished."[43]

Nevertheless, Judge Matsch ruled that an order forcing the government to produce the missing surveillance tapes would not only interfere with the operations of law enforcement agencies, but that public release of the tapes could hamper the ongoing criminal proceedings. Only after the criminal trial of McVeigh had concluded did a Secret Service memo written immediately after the bombing come to the surface. The memo stated "security video tapes from the area [around the Murrah] show the truck detonation three minutes and six seconds after the *suspects* exited the truck." While the FBI and federal prosecutors continued to deny the existence of any such footage, a memo, later permitted into entry as evidence during Terry Nichols' 2004 state trial, was described by Nichols' defense team as "direct evidence of the involvement of others in the bombing conspiracy."[44]

For many, including the Jones Team and Stephen Jones particularly, that other yet unidentified suspects existed was the only way to make sense, not just of the eyewitness's accounts, but also the many unexplained calls McVeigh had made to suspicious groups and people prior to the bombing and critical gaps of unexplained time in his (and the FBI's) timeline of the plot. McVeigh's own obfuscations and changing stories seemed nonsensical no matter how he spun it on any given day. Among his shifting stories: his prior involvement in other crimes; the nature and extent of his relationship to the White Power Movement generally and the residents of Elohim City and their associates, specifically; the actual number and identities of his accomplices; the aliases and disguises he used; the extent to which he conducted surveillance of the Murrah before April 19 and his ignorance of the daycare center; the exact geographic locations and movements of McVeigh and the Ryder from the time the bomb was allegedly being built in Kansas until the moment it exploded; and, amazingly, even the clothes he wore the day of the bombing.[45]

Thus, in order to make sense of all the conflicting information, the Jones Team catalogued and constructed a chronology of McVeigh's contradictory statements, a document that eventually came to total over 500 pages. For Jones, McVeigh's statements, when read together and closely scrutinized, inadvertently confirmed the existence of JD2. Jones explained to me that, "McVeigh simply realized that he'd told me too much. He hadn't given me a name, but he'd told me too much..." One internal defense memo entitled "Is He Lying or Isn't He: SECRET" discussed their efforts, reminded those on the legal team that McVeigh had occasionally admitted to being deceptive with them, outlined his contradictory statements and concluded that McVeigh's Lone Bomber story was "riddled with inconsistencies ... the larger part of McVeigh's adult life is predicated upon lies, deceptions, cons [and] theft ... Every person has the capacity for self-deception but Tim's is seemingly infinite..."[46]

Jones said that, after realizing the extent of his obfuscations, "I then went to McVeigh and asked him how he wanted to be remembered. 'As a mastermind? A terrorist? Who's going to challenge you? Certainly not the government or the people you're protecting.' The only people challenging McVeigh, were his own lawyers." A number of angry letters about the issue flew back and forth between McVeigh and Jones but the team's pleas that he tell them the truth only resulted in increasingly hostile reactions by McVeigh.

Finally, McVeigh consented to Jones' request that he submit to a polygraph test to resolve the John Doe issue, but the results of the test suggested that, while he was honest in his claims of having participated, McVeigh was being dishonest in his insistence that no additional accomplices were involved beyond the limited participation and foreknowledge of Fortier and Nichols. Tim Domgard, who issued the test, said he had "absolutely no doubt" that McVeigh was concealing the identity of another person "involved in their situation" and predicted that McVeigh would "take the name with him to his grave."[47]

When Jones confronted him about the results, McVeigh became enraged. In a series of angry handwritten letters to his defense team, McVeigh wrote that the only way he could continue to cooperate with them was if they accepted his Lone Wolf claims and, referring to all other theories of the case, instructed them to just "drop it." The ongoing concerns about his truthfulness led to the complete deterioration of the already strained relationship between McVeigh and Jones and he informed members of his defense team that since he and Jones had reached an impasse and his efforts to resolve this had been unsuccessful (as had his occasional threats of violence), he was "going to have to resort to 'guerilla warfare' with

[Jones]" and threatened to plead guilty if the defense team did not stop their investigation.

Beliefs that others had participated still did not explain the minute details of the crime and the team considered several possibilities of what could have happened, (all of which became variants of the story types discussed in this book). Jones Team attorney Bob Wyatt outlined a handful of these possibilities: McVeigh acted alone; with others; had been contracted by a group of "right wing fanatics" or recruited by foreigners: "the government or friends of the government recruited a guy [who] thinks [the bombing was] a payback for Waco when in fact, the real objective was to overshadow and justify the actions taken by the government at Waco and discredit the Waco group and their supporters as just a bunch of nuts. In other words, the 'Manchurian Candidate' scenario." McVeigh bristled especially at the allegations that someone had used him as an Experimental Wolf and told Jones, "I haven't been brainwashed ... I did this for the movement."

Referring to a meeting between defense team members, Jones Team attorney Dick Burr wrote in another internal memo:

> The significance of the evidence that Tim did not act alone and the possibility that he may not have been the "general" – and the relationship of these facts to Tim's compulsion to convince us that he acted alone (with only fading support from Fortier and Nichols) – informed much of our subsequent discussion. [The following should aid in the contours of the defense] Tim was not acting alone at the Murrah Building ... he may not have been the primary actor...Indeed, he may not have had a primary role at all. His role may have been far less important than he has led us to believe. He may have driven the truck; he may not have. He may have been only the getaway car or decoy driver. He may in fact have been the fall guy who, though involved enough in the conspiracy and the bombing itself to be convicted, may have far less culpability than the government's theory (as well as his own story) now assigns him ... [as] credible evidence [to this end] mounts that other, as yet undisclosed people were involved, there is a risk that Tim will decompensate. If he is no longer perceived credibly as the primary actor, the view of himself as competent and valuable may fade. His fear of this happening may account for the passionate pleas he has made to all of us every now and then to 'just [or finally] believe me.'"

Eventually, mental health experts hired by the Jones Team to evaluate and treat McVeigh concluded that he was "not likely the person who came up with the idea for the bombing, but that he could very well have been the person who took responsibility for carrying it out. His strength is in carrying out orders…" However, given McVeigh's agitation about both ongoing mental health evaluations and findings as well as the defense team's investigatory attempts, they recommended the Jones Team "consider not pushing Tim any further about whether he is lying to us."[48] Jones, however, chose not to heed their advice and doggedly continued his investigation and McVeigh began referring to him as "Sherlock Jones."

It was Jones' opinion that "a defensible argument" could be constructed to show that "the government withheld evidence about the bombing from the defense, the courts, and the American people; evidence which suggests not that McVeigh was innocent, but that he was involved in a larger conspiracy." Nevertheless, even among those on the Jones Team who suspected McVeigh was shielding the identity of others, not all agreed with Jones' planned strategy of proving a larger conspiracy at the upcoming trial. Some found information about Others Unknown inconsequential and perhaps even detrimental to a defense case, including attorney Christopher Tritico, who later stated that, "Quite frankly, my view of the Others, the other conspirators, was that proving he had someone else helping him only gets him and someone else executed. It doesn't win the case…. In order to win the case, [we needed to] forget about this other guy … even if he existed. The fact that Tim didn't answer some of the questions Stephen wanted him to answer … those were questions that I would never have asked him in the first place."[49]

THE OKLAHOMA DISSIDENTS: "DANCING WITH THE DEVIL"

Acts of terrorism are complex and multi-layered, and those who survive them have equally complex reactions. Although not often acknowledged, those who survive the trauma of terroristic violence must also contend with state, legal and media institutions whose policies sometimes lead to further traumatization. In order to regain equilibrium and make sense of nonsensical events, victims take the available fragments of information about the event and use them to construct a "survivor's narrative." Victims undergo additional, compounded traumatization when critical information remains unknown, a situation that prevents them from constructing a believable narrative about their pain. The most salient need for information was experienced by the bombing's survivors and victims' family members, many of whom later recounted their early and ongoing reliance on the media to provide it.

Coinciding with Jones' struggle with the FBI and prosecutors over the discovery material and reflective of the larger struggle for information about the case and the control of this information, was the parallel struggle of a group of survivors and victim family members whom

Ambrose Evans-Pritchard dubbed the "Oklahoma City Dissidents." Since the bombing, the Dissidents had become increasingly alarmed about what they perceived to be the FBI's incremental abandonment of its search for other conspirators and the DOJ's lack of concern over prosecuting them. They became increasingly vocal in the media about their lingering questions. The Dissidents wondered, *"Was there a wider conspiracy? Did anyone who could have warned victims – even Federal law enforcement officials – know of the bomb plot beforehand? Was a government informer involved?"*[50]

In November 1995, led by Oklahoma State Rep. Charles Key, the Dissidents petitioned to form and empanel a State Grand Jury investigation to uncover new information about the bombing plot and, if possible, identify other conspirators.[51] While the Dissidents were eventually successful in empaneling the jury, they faced significant and heavy-handed institutional resistance in doing so.

Prosecutors and officials publicly accused the Dissidents of engaging in paranoid delusions and "pandering to the worst kind of paranoid conspiracy theories." News reports and editorials repeatedly echoed such sentiments, quoting experts, officials and watchdog groups who compared the suspicions and speculations of the Dissidents and others about the bombing case to Holocaust denial and claimed that such expressions were indicative of the same delusional and dangerous extremism that had created the ideological atmosphere for the bombing in the first place. Thus, the Dissidents were equated, symbolically, with Timothy McVeigh himself. In an ironic twist, foreshadowing many more to come, those most deeply impacted by the bombing, an act committed by a 'crazed conspiracy theorist,' were now themselves labeled as conspiracy theorists.[52]

Nevertheless, the Dissidents gained popular support and were featured in an ABC News segment of *20/20* that highlighted some of the known and missing evidence that fueled the growing speculations, rumors and theories. In two opinion polls at this time, 80-90% of Oklahomans favored the formation of a Grand Jury. 13,500 Oklahoma City residents signed the petition – 5,000 more than required by state law.

After a lengthy and bitter public campaign and appeals process, the Oklahoma Supreme Court unanimously ruled in favor of the formation of the Grand Jury. However, while Key would head the investigation, to the dismay of the Dissidents, Oklahoma District Attorney Robert Macy, lead prosecutor in both McVeigh's and Nichols' trials and the most aggressive opponent of the Grand Jury's formation, was appointed to oversee the Grand Jury hearings and determine what information could be presented. Nevertheless, Key established the OKC Bombing Investigation Committee (OKCBIC), made up of volunteers and a professional research staff who would conduct their own investigation and gather evidence.

Kathy Wilburn-Sanders, whose two grandsons had died in the bombing, became one of the most outspoken Dissidents. She wrote that the group's need for answers was so overwhelming they were "willing to dance with the Devil to get the truth." For the Dissidents, the Devil resided in the details. Evans-Pritchard wrote, "Documents have a habit of leaking when friendships are formed across a broad front," and therefore, in order to solve the mystery, the Dissidents formed an "unholy alliance" with a number of individuals and groups. The alliance, which traded information like baseball cards, included the Jones Team, victims' families, sympathetic investigative journalists, fringe conspiracy theorists and the mainstream media – all of whom were pursuing similar lines of inquiry about the facts surrounding the bombing.[53]

The unlikely hodgepodge of allied "truth seekers" painstakingly retraced the steps McVeigh had allegedly taken on his road to right-wing extremism. Along the way, they encountered the vast network of parties with whom McVeigh had crossed paths and possibly conspired. Like the research communities that sprang up after the JFK assassination, the OKCBIC tapped an enormous but obscure knowledge base and gathered, compiled and categorized a wealth of previously unknown information pertaining to the bombing plot.[54]

The information uncovered additional wrinkles of complexity in an already complex situation that, although often raising more questions than it answered, proved irrefutably damning to the government's story. The combined investigatory efforts led to revelations about its *prior knowledge* of the bombing and shed light on the possible identities of several other conspirators. Among the most publicized of these revelations were those concerning McVeigh's relationship to the cast of characters residing in or frequently visiting Elohim City, including Andreas Strassmeir ("Andy The German") – a German national living in the U.S. on a expired visa and head of paramilitary training at Elohim City.

Elohim City had only one telephone that was shared by the entire community. Residents there remembered that on April 5, 1995, two weeks before the bombing, McVeigh called looking for Strassmeir. McVeigh, Strassmeir, the FBI and prosecutors maintained that the two met once at a Tulsa gun show, two years earlier, in April 1993, at which point Strassmeir invited McVeigh, who introduced himself as "Tim Tuttle," to the community. Then, on April 17, 1995 and again on April 18, McVeigh called CAUSE, the racist legal organization that represented Strassmeir.[55]

Although an FBI memo dated April 20, 1995, the day after the bombing, stated "it is suspected that members of Elohim City are involved [in the bombing] either directly or indirectly through conspiracy," no real investigation into these links was conducted and Strassmeir was questioned only by telephone and only after he had been allowed to leave the country and return to Germany. Nevertheless, suspicions about him persisted. According to Roger Charles, a number of strange details and circumstances surrounding his life, "strongly suggests that Strassmeir was not the radical rightwinger he appeared to be, and might even have been a government agent of some sort, spying on extremists in the United States." Over the years, Strassmeir spoke to a handful of journalists. In 1997, while denying his involvement in the bombing, he told Evans-Pritchard that the bombing was a sting operation permeated by undercover agents and informants that "acquired a momentum of its own." Strassmeir elaborated:

> The [ATF, FBI and] different agencies weren't cooperating. In fact, they were working against each other. You even had a situation where one branch of the FBI was investigating and not sharing with another branch...The ATF had something going on with McVeigh. They were watching him-of course they were...McVeigh knew he was delivering a bomb, but he had no idea what was in that truck. He just wanted to shake things up a little; you know, make a gesture...the bomb was never meant to explode. They were going to arrest McVeigh at the site with the bomb in hand, but he didn't come at the right time...maybe he changed the time, you never know with people who are so unreliable. I have heard that they [were expecting the bomb to go off] in the middle of the night, between two and three in the morning. The truck had a transmitter, so they could track it with a radio receiving device. I don't know how they could have lost contact. I think there was misinformation that the operation had been canceled.

When asked if he thought the agents and informants would reveal themselves, Strassmeir responded:

> How can he? What happens if it was a sting operation from the very beginning? What happens if it comes out that the plant was a provocateur? What if he talked and manipulated the others into it? What then? The country couldn't handle it. The relatives of the victims are going to go crazy, and he's going to be responsible for the murder of 168 people? Of course, the informant can't come forward. He's scared shitless right now.[56]

The Dissident truth seekers also discovered connections between McVeigh and a group of Elohim City associates who called themselves "The Aryan Republican Army" (ARA) and dubbed by the press "The Midwest Bank Robbers." Considered "one of the most criminally competent paramilitary gangs in American history," between 1993 and 1995, the ARA, robbed 22 banks, netting over $250,000 in proceeds. The ultimate goal of the ARA's bank robberies was to fund and incite a race war, spark a revolution, and establish an all-white 'homeland.' When the ARA was apprehended, a mountain of bomb-making materials were found in their safe house. McVeigh denied any association but his movements throughout the country in the years leading to the bombing often closely overlapped those of the ARA; and in the years leading up to the bombing, he'd written his sister letters telling her he was involved with a group of bank robbers. Although a few of the bank robbers would allude to ARA participation in the bombing plot and there was physical and circumstancial evidence linking certain members of the ARA with the bombing, the FBI improperly destroyed some of it, failed to look closely at the bank robbers' alibis on April 19, 1995 and ultimately shut down their investigation into the connections.[57]

Wilburn Sanders wrote that, as the Dissidents' investigation advanced, "It was becoming clear that there was much we didn't know, and the people who were supposed to be on our side might be harboring some unthinkable secrets."[58] Still, the incestuous sharing of information between the Grand Jury investigators, Jones Team, Dissidents and investigative journalists continued to yield results. Perhaps the most startling were revelations about Carol Howe, a paid informant for the ATF and the FBI, who from June 1994 until March 1995 had infiltrated EC, the ARA and other groups in an ATF investigation deemed "SIGNIFICANT/SENSITIVE," meaning it had potential national security implications. Howe, who became deeply embedded within the community of extremists, filed over 70 reports with her ATF handlers and, on *numerous* occasions, warned them about an impending attack on April 19, the anniversary of the fire at Waco, and named Andreas Strassmeir and some of the ARA bank robbers (among others) as conspirators.[59]

In one report (submitted prior to the OKC bombing) Howe specifically named the Murrah Federal Building as one of three possible targets for a bombing being considered by the conspirators and reported she had, on three occasions, accompanied them to scout out the Murrah. She passed all of the seventeen polygraph tests the ATF had given her to substantiate her information. Immediately after the bombing, Howe reported to the ATF and FBI that she had seen McVeigh at Elohim City on more than one occasion in the year prior to the bombing. Corroborating her claims were a number of other undercover informants placed within EC by federal agencies and watchdog groups, including the Southern Poverty Law Center (SPLC), who independently said they saw McVeigh there on over a dozen occasions. In fact, the Dissidents' unholy alliance led to revelations about the prevalence of federal informants embedded within or very near to the bombing plot, of whom Howe was only one. Evans-Pritchard wrote, "The intrigue had become so twisted with undercover informants from different agencies tripping over each other – that it is almost impossible to disentangle." Thus emerged the story of the Closely Watched Wolves.[60]

In 1996, based on information developed by the Committee and its allies, 475 survivors and victims' family members began filing what would amount to several civil wrongful death lawsuits, as well as other legal actions initiated against government agencies including the ATF and FBI. The Plaintiffs charged that those named in the suits had failed to act on the warnings of informants and argued that the bombing had occurred amidst a sting operation and thus, the government agencies involved were partially culpable for the deaths that occurred (a mainstay within all later Closely Watched Wolves stories). The courts dismissed the lawsuits.

The Jones Team and Key investigators spoke with numerous individuals who said the FBI interviewed them regarding McVeigh, his associates and possible co-conspirators but that reports documenting these interviews had not been among the discovery information furnished by the FBI. Further, a growing number of people with crucial information about the bombing plot said that the FBI expressly instructed them not to speak to the defense team, harassed them and ordered them to destroy any notes they had taken about what they knew or witnessed. Still others reported that they had been harassed and ridiculed or subjected to other FBI methods meant to prevent them from coming forward with information. Many were scared for their jobs and reputations. Charles Key recounted:

> I did get some personal threats but I don't feel comfortable talking about that. I think the real threats were from people like the Attorney General who had the power to try and stop people from doing what they have a right to do, to investigate. That's a real threat. There were many efforts behind the scene to try and smear us in some way; an effort to do anything possible to stop and discredit us. The Assistant Attorney General was trying to control the Grand Jury. Robert Macy, who was tasked with presenting evidence, was trying to fight us every step of the way. We knew the deck was stacked against us. One of the most frustrating things was the issue of prior knowledge. It was clear that there was prior knowledge. Someone knew something was in the works, and when we asked questions about this, we attacked. We had information from a Senate Staffer. I interviewed him, and he claimed that the Justice Department was involved in a sting operation. It was never meant to get out of hand or develop to the point it did. The Sting went down the wrong path. They covered it up, he said, because the operation went bad. One of the most frustrating things was we were accused of saying the government blew the building up,

which I did not say, and I do not believe that. There is a difference between a sting operation that has gone wrong and thinking the government 'did it.' *The question is, how much prior knowledge did they have?*[61]

Roger Charles later wrote that the prosecution was worried by the large number of witnesses who recalled seeing McVeigh with others and so, with the help of "a handful of trusted FBI agents, [they] set about making the problems go away. They interviewed and re-interviewed witnesses, looking for weaknesses in their stories or ways to get them to change their minds." Included were lead FBI agents Scott Mendeloff and Jon Hersley's "extensive efforts" to "neutralize" Elliot's employees, "convince [them] that John Doe 2 was a phantom" and thereby, prevent the spectral conspirator from appearing at the trials. In fact, "Hersley was the prosecution's go-to person to resolve many of the holes in the case." Lead prosecutor Larry Mackey later acknowledged that Hersley regularly "hammered" witnesses who might aid the defense team's cases. Further, another lead FBI agent in the case, Danny Defenbaugh, disclosed that in his opinion, Hersley commonly distorted evidence, lied about his investigation (or lack thereof) and often acted outside of his authority. "We had to watch over Jon. He'd go around trying to stop viable investigations, especially if they involved other people in the conspiracy. Every time we caught him, I had to bring him in the woodshed to paddle him. Then he'd go right back at it."[62]

What's more, it appeared that the FBI was making other evidence disappear. For instance, in November 1995, the Jones Team requested transcripts of all OKCPD and OKCFD dispatch tapes of transmissions in the two weeks prior to the bombing and the day of April 19. Rather than honoring this request, later discovery material would show that the FBI had "accidently destroyed" these dispatch tapes. This was not the only instance of such shenanigans.[63]

Thus, nearly a year after they had submitted their first request, Jones informed Matsch that the government had not complied with Matsch's earlier order to turn over discovery material and that the defense team "continue[d] to learn of efforts by the Government to conceal and destroy exculpatory evidence and to obstruct the defense investigation of the facts of the case." He compared the case and the struggle to obtain the information to "Alice In Wonderland" where nothing is at it seems and nobody means exactly what they say. Jones submitted a 400-page list of still-missing information (including that uncovered by the Dissidents and Key investigators as well as still-classified reports), saying that the list "represent[ed] only the tip of the iceberg," and accurately foretold that unless the situation was rectified, much "exculpatory evidence will never be known to the defense."[64]

Prosecutors insisted that they had already turned over all the materials, had even exceeded their discovery obligations and accused the defense of going on a "fishing expedition." Much to McVeigh's displeasure, an undeterred Jones filed a motion with the Tenth Circuit Court of Appeals, arguing that there was a "high probability" that Strassmeir and other individuals at Elohim City were part of the bombing conspiracy but that the government had "engag[ed] in a willful and knowing cover-up of information supplied by its informant [Carol Howe]."[65]

Ultimately though, Matsch denied Jones' pleas to compel the prosecution to comply with discovery rules and Matsch's earlier order that they do so, ruling that Howe's testimony was "irrelevant" and that even if the defense had all of the government's information relating to the Elohim City, other suspected conspirators and everything else it sought, he would deem it inadmissible at the trial. Only after the criminal trial concluded did the Jones Team learn the extent to which the FBI failed to turn over discoverable exculpatory materials. Further revelations of withheld information continue to this day (as explained in the final chapter).[66]

THE GOOD SHIP MCVEIGH

If Jones' or McVeigh's media strategies had in any way softened the public perception of McVeigh, such progress was lost when, on March 1, 1997, just weeks before his trial began, the *Dallas Morning News* ran yet another front page "leaked confession" story which was then picked up by several other major media outlets whose front page exclusives included yet more leaked material.[67]

McVeigh blamed Jones for the breach and Jones, after alternately blaming various members of the defense team, settled on publicly pointing a finger at Richard Reyna, the defense investigator closest to McVeigh. Reyna, in turn, denied the accusation and went on to publicly blame Jones for the leaks. No matter who had 'leaked' this time, other members of the Jones Team felt that the *Dallas Morning News* article was simply the unavoidable culmination of Jones' unwise relationship with the media that had plagued their efforts since the get-go.[68]

Legal experts opined that the continuous Jones Team leaks had "done more damage to McVeigh than the government's" ... own case against him. Jones Team attorney Coyne later wrote that after the article, "Our Hindenburg of hope had vaporized" and Jones' media campaign "imploded with a vengeance... In my view, the Good Ship McVeigh had run ashore on the shoals of its captain's ego." Jones had been "hoisted by his own petard." The conflict that ensued, said Coyne, made "the shootout at the O.K. Corral [look like] a simple misunderstanding." "When McVeigh found out about the *Morning News* leak, he had "nothing short of a total conniption fit." Defense attorney Tritico said, "The media leaks sent Tim over the top, and quite frankly, I don't blame him. It was devastating to the defense right before the trial."[69]

McVeigh then attempted to have Jones removed from the case based on such mismanagement, but was unsuccessful, due largely to Jones' own thwarting of McVeigh's efforts.[70] When he failed to get Jones fired, McVeigh threatened to plead guilty. In response to the threat, Jones wrote McVeigh a letter reminding him that many members of the defense team felt that McVeigh's version of the story, while possible, was neither probable nor likely and warned that if McVeigh attempted to plead guilty, Jones would inform Judge Matsch that McVeigh was simply attempting to "take the fall" for other conspirators. In another letter, referring to McVeigh's many references to his personal 'Code of Honor', Jones chided McVeigh, "If by Code of Honor you mean we are to protect other murdering bastards, that is not something that we have any obligation to do…Certainly no one is protecting you. *You have been thrown to the wolves*":

> [In order for you to play a useful role in your own defense, you need to] eliminate the fiction that you are some self-contained individual fully capable of controlling your own destiny and actions. […] It has come time at last to grow up and recognize fully what is at stake here. We are trying to save your ass. [Your version of events] places 99% of the responsibility for the bombing of the A.P Murrah Building upon yourself. You claim to have conceived the project, organized it, financed it, thought it through and then carried it out. In your discussions with us, 'nothing' is left to chance and everything was perfectly executed, including having been [intentionally] apprehended afterwards. [The details you offer to support this story] simply appear to be irreconcilable with the facts [and] simply cannot be reconciled with the known physical evidence and eyewitnesses unless we are willing to believe that not just simply one or two, but dozens of individuals are honestly mistaken. […] What you are doing is protecting fellow conspirators…you simply have not told us the truth…I think it is entirely possible, perhaps even probable that much of what you have told us is, in fact, the truth, but the part that is not the truth may be the most critical part, i.e., the role of others . [It is the responsibility of attorneys] to investigate not only the facts, but to investigate beyond what the client has said or represented [and] nothing you can say or do can distract us from that duty… You can write to whomever you wish complaining about me, though it clearly is ill-advised.

Jones warned that if he did not give up his fictions, McVeigh would eventually break down, physically, emotionally and mentally and concluded the letter by outlining his predictions about the future of McVeigh's trial and legacy, which, Jones said, were likely no matter what McVeigh or his legal team did or did not do:

> The reality is, of course, that the odds are you will be found, condemned, not only by the verdict of the jury, but by the verdict of the American people, history, your family, and that you will be executed and put to death, not with honor, but because you will be perceived as a mass murderer, a man who committed a crime greater than Lee Harvey Oswald, John Wilkes Booth, or Ted Bundy. Not only will you die, but many of the principles you believe in will, at least temporarily, be rejected by the American people and you will be seen as a fanatical, mal-adjusted misfit who brought untold suffering to thousands of innocent people in your misguided attempt to right an imaginary wrong by resorting to revolutionary terror. You will be equated in the public's mind not with Patrick Henry, but with Adolph Hitler.[71]

THE TRIAL AND TRIBULATIONS OF TIM McVEIGH

In her 2012 book, *Killing McVeigh*, Jodi Maderia illustrates how McVeigh's trial was a site of narrative construction and negotiation for victims, survivors, the state and the larger public, which, at its conclusion would offer a solidified, officially sanctioned and publicly accepted collective version of history. Similar to the contention between McVeigh and Jones as well as that between Jones, the Dissidents and the government, the trial of Timothy McVeigh represented a struggle of who, exactly, could recount the past. Like the Key Grand Jury, McVeigh's trial was an institutional ceremony to resolve lingering ambiguity and contested truths about the bombing, not the least of which concerned John Doe 2.

By the time jury selection began for the trial of the *United States vs. Timothy McVeigh* on March 31, 1997, the government had eliminated John Doe 2 (and 3 and 4 and 5, etc.,) as a factor in the case, dismissing him/them as a product of witnesses' confusion and "unconscious transference." The week before, the *Washington Post* observed that, in a case where "each hard fact is surrounded by theory, speculation, or spin," the "shadowy" John Doe 2 would, like Bigfoot or the Loch Ness Monster, "remain eternally at large, the one who got away, the mystery man at the center of countless conspiracy theories. It's possible he never lived. It's likely that he'll never die." He had "become a legend" delegated to "the realm of myth, where truth is not only impossible to ascertain, it's almost irrelevant." Still, despite the assurances of prosecutors that the FBI had followed every possible lead in an intensive effort to identify and bring to justice everyone involved, for many, including the Dissidents and a significant portion of the American public, doubts persisted. A 1997 *Time*/CNN poll found 77% of Americans believed the FBI had not yet identified or captured all bombing conspirators and a Gallup poll reported similar results; as well as another belief held by "a considerable percentage of Americans [that] the federal government itself was involved in the bombing."

Some chalked up the persistent belief in John Doe 2 to an inability for people to accept that one man (McVeigh), with a little, but not much, help from his friends (Nichols and Fortier), could commit such an atrocity. Others blamed increasing public cynicism and distrust in the government that had become common after the JFK assassination, Vietnam, Watergate and Iran-Contra. Public confidence in the criminal justice system and law enforcement agencies, generally, and the FBI, especially, had sharply declined in the wake of Ruby Ridge, Waco, the first World Trade Center bombing, OKC and Atlanta Olympic bombings and a recent FBI Crime Lab scandal.[71]

At stake in the trial of Timothy McVeigh, was the public's trust and confidence in long-standing government institutions and McVeigh's guilty verdict could potentially act as a powerful remedy for the crisis of legitimacy caused by the FBI's ongoing "foul-ups, mishaps, and cover-ups." Oklahoma Governor Frank Keating, a former FBI agent and staunch opponent of both the Key Grand Jury and theories about John Doe 2, confidently told reporters, "We believe the system should and will work, and those responsible for this horrific act will never walk the face of this Earth again." For him, the willingness of Americans to believe that "our free institutions can commonly be corrupted to dark and evil purposes," was a result of "watching too many Oliver Stone movies. What we see on the movie screens these days demonizes government agencies and public officials. Free institutions cannot survive this kind of cynicism." In fact, Keating continued, the bombing itself was a result of just such paranoia.

Guilty verdicts in criminal trials help exorcise social demons and retroactively or pre-emptively legitimize institutional responses to it. The bombing had unleashed an abundance of previously dormant or clandestine threats including racists, militia, gun-nuts and conspiracy theorists who posed a danger to peace-loving Americans and who had quickly come to represent an emergent 'homegrown domestic terrorist' specter. Since the time of his arrest, media coverage had linked McVeigh to militias, conspiracy theorists and a number of others, said to be allied within a "loose network of autonomous anti-government groups" who inhabited the "semi-underground" world of gun shows and "remote compounds." These apocalyptic millennialists reportedly ranted and raved about black helicopters, government concentration camps for the politically incorrect, implantable microchips, the New World Order, "spaceships" and, sometimes, the "Zionist-controlled media." Many feared the viral spread of their dangerous ideas. Experts warned journalists that "America's extremists," defined as "militia members [and] conspiracy theorists of all stripes" would be watching the trial closely for details that supported their crazy theories, "anti-government or otherwise"; information that would then "absolutely flood that subculture" and potentially spark another McVeigh. On the other hand, if McVeigh was found guilty, the government could "send a clear message to racists, terrorists, militia members and other anti-government zealots" that their beliefs had no place in society and demonstrate to the rest of the world that acts of terrorism on American soil would not be tolerated.[72]

Opening arguments commenced on April 24. It was the most-covered criminal trial in the twentieth century and an absolute circus. For nine weeks, more than 2,000 media representatives from every major outlet swarmed Denver and swamped the airwaves with round-the-clock daily coverage, in-studio recaps of the previous two years, on-location commentary, up-to-the-minute updates, legal analysis, and speculations about the outcome. In an attempt to avoid the frenzied circus atmosphere that had plagued the O.J. Simpson trial, Judge Matsch banned cameras from filming inside the courtroom and relegated journalists to an area outside the courthouse known as "the bullpen." Still, each day, the courtroom quickly filled beyond its maximum capacity. Security measures in and around the courtroom were intense.

During the trial, federal prosecutors told the Lone Wolf story (with a little help from his friend Nichols). They emphasized McVeigh's anti-government views and asserted that, while Nichols had offered minimal assistance by gathering materials and building the bomb, McVeigh alone conceived of, planned, and carried out the bombing by driving (alone) to OKC and detonating the truck bomb. According to prosecutors, while it was true that both Nichols and Fortier had agreed to help McVeigh, they did so only because he had intimidated and threatened them until both, to differing extents, backed out, leaving McVeigh to execute the final stages of his plan by himself. Prosecutors attributed McVeigh's motive to bomb the Murrah to his "hatred of the government" and "rage" about the 80 Branch Davidians killed at Waco. Jones Team attorney Randy Coyne observed, as many others would, the efficiency and brevity of the prosecution's case: "The government kept their case simple, lean, and mean. They got in and got out and didn't seem to prove everything and didn't present a complete story. They certainly weren't interested in cluttering it up with alternate theories and Tim was not interested in sharing responsibility if that might mean reducing his culpability."[73]

Jones touched upon aspects of McVeigh's desired 'necessity defense' which revolved around the argument that the actions at Waco had required him to bomb the Murrah but mainly attempted to 'poke holes' in the prosecution's case and alluded that McVeigh had simply been a "designated patsy" within a larger conspiracy. Judge Matsch, however, ruled that much of the eyewitness testimony and physical evidence (or lack thereof) that Jones wanted to use, was inadmissible, thereby severely hampering his ability to raise questions in the mind of jurors about the Others Unknown.[74]

Among the absent witnesses whose testimony was ruled inadmissible were those who saw McVeigh at Elliot's, Dreamland, Geary Lake (where the bomb was allegedly built) and Oklahoma City – all of whom saw him with other individuals, collectively referred to as John Doe 2. Prosecutors dismissed as 'confused,' the statements of the many Dreamland witnesses who saw not only another unidentified man with McVeigh, but also another Ryder truck *prior* to the Elliot's rental. Despite numerous eyewitness statements and other evidence to the contrary, Prosecutors emphasized that only one truck was used in the bombing plot and told jurors that there was "no indication that McVeigh rented a second truck." Jones was unable to introduce evidence showing otherwise. McVeigh, of course, could not have been more pleased by Judge Matsch's rulings and told his attorneys so, chiding that for the past 18 months they had ignored his requests that they stop pursuing Others Unknown and John Does.[75] He did not take the stand in his own defense.

While their testimony was ruled inadmissible, Jones was able to *discuss* the testimony given to the FBI by several eyewitnesses who had reported seeing McVeigh and another person in the days leading up to the bombing and with him in the Ryder the morning of April 19. When taken together, he argued, they "provide a picture dramatically different than the one that the Government will present." Jones remarked that it defied logic to think that McVeigh, whom the government said had carefully plotted his act of terror for two years, would register at the Dreamland Motel under his own name but use an alias to rent the Ryder from Elliot's, only miles away. He then called attention to the fact that several people had access to McVeigh's phone card, and therefore, it was impossible to prove who, exactly, made many of the incriminating calls, such as those placed to Elliot's when the Ryder was reserved.

Although there were up to twenty-five surveillance cameras positioned in and around the Murrah Building on April 19, the FBI never produced them during discovery nor did they enter them as evidence at the criminal trials. The whereabouts of footage from all of the twenty-five known surveillance cameras remained unknown and Matsch did not compel the FBI to produce them. Amazingly, as none of the witnesses who saw McVeigh in the days leading up to the bombing and on the morning of April 19 testified (assumedly because they all saw him with other people) and since the surveillance tapes from the Murrah never surfaced, and while nobody argued otherwise, prosecutors never even established McVeigh's presence in OKC on the morning of the 19th.[76]

Roger Charles opined that, "Despite the FBI's protestations about leaving no stone unturned," by June 1995, only weeks into the investigation, the government had settled on the case they planned to present which, for him, "was as notable for what it left out as it was for the oddly truncated version it presented as the whole story." Jones remarked that "The factual part of the government's case was pared down to a minimum, and it went fast, like a film that's been edited to a jump cut pace – presumably so that no one would notice [its] gaps and the inconsistencies. [...] It was daring, it was high risk. Who would ever have guessed that a case, already highly circumstantial, in which the federal government was asking for the death penalty, would leave the jury without a single witness to Tim McVeigh's whereabouts [from April 17 to April 19]?"[77]

Physical evidence introduced during the trial was scarce and dubious. Criminologist and former Jones Team consultant Mark Hamm observed that the government's Lone Wolf theory failed to "explain how the bomb was built, transported to Oklahoma City and discharged." A DOJ Inspector General's (IG) inspection and Audit Report issued months earlier had strongly criticized the FBI's Crime Laboratory for mishandling evidence in several high profile cases, including (but not limited to) the 1993 World Trade Center bombing, an assassination attempt on George H.W. Bush that same year, the 1995 investigation of 'Unabomber' Ted Kaczynski, and the Oklahoma City bombing. The IG initiated its investigation after the Supervisory Special Agent in the FBI Crime Lab, Frederick Whitehurst, PhD (considered the FBI's most highly qualified bomb residue and explosives expert) went public with allegations about corrupt crime lab practices. The IG final report concluded, among other things, that the OKC bombing investigation was one of the most serious cases of evidence tampering that the IG had ever encountered and that the FBI crime lab had "repeatedly reached conclusions that incriminated the defendants without scientific basis."[78]

The FBI lab reports for the OKC bombing case had failed to document an evidentiary chain of custody and thus, reviewers could not determine the work performed or the reliability of the results in the reports in the case. Ron Woods, former defense attorney for Terry Nichols later told me, "There was evidence that there was someone else in the Dreamland Motel with McVeigh when he ordered Chinese Food delivery. The government never went in and fingerprinted or dusted for the fingerprints of anybody!" Jones Team attorney Christopher Tritico, who was specifically tasked with gathering and analyzing all material during the trial preparation and court arguments concerning the forensic aspects of the case, also discussed the Crime Lab scandal with me:

> What we learned about the Crime Lab [through the IG report] was that it was poorly managed. The FBI had an incentive system for the scientists there. If they testified in a case that resulted in a conviction, they got bonuses, which in our view, was highly unethical. They had no scientific protocols to speak of. It was just pathetic. This was supposed to be the world's premier lab! They wanted convictions and the FBI Crime Lab was suffering from this prosecutorial mentality. *The Judge would not allow any of this into evidence.* At Elliot's Body Shop where the Ryder had been rented, the FBI had gone in and took the counter. They just unbolted it from the ground and took the whole counter and took it back to the FBI crime lab to fingerprint it and they didn't find any prints on it. Another thing that surprised me was the acting head of the lab at the time, Stephen Burmiester, made a decision to mix the Oklahoma City evidence with that of the Unabomber case on a plane heading to Washington. They mixed the evidence in the same plane, and I made [FBI Agent] Burmiester admit that on the stand!"[79]

While Matsch did allow Whitehurst to testify about the Crime Lab failures in a *limited* capacity during McVeigh's criminal trial, the majority of his complaints about the lab, as well as large portions of the IG's Final Report which called into question the prosecution's theories about the chemical composition of the bomb, would be barred from entry as evidence.

FBI agent Jon Hersley testified about traces of a detonation chemical, called PDTN, found on McVeigh's clothing at the time of his arrest. Whitehurst, however, who conducted tests on McVeigh's clothes, said he did not find PDTN residue on either McVeigh's clothes or in his car, the same conclusion reached by the IG report. Prosecutors relied on receipts for the purchase of ammonium nitrate, said to be the main ingredient in the bomb, which had been found in Terry Nichols' possession, to establish a physical connection between McVeigh and the bomb. The only evidence that suggested the bomb contained ammonium nitrate were residual crystals discovered a month after the explosion. Whitehurst, in turn, argued that the heavy rain in the preceding month would have washed the crystals away. Jones argued that, "If Tim McVeigh built the bomb," the FBI would have found proof of this in his fingernails, nostrils, hair, clothes, car, shoes, socks but "they didn't." In fact, beyond its ingredients, prosecutors did not bring up the *actual* building of the bomb at Geary Lake and jurors never learned about many other forensic anomalies or inexplicable contradictions including the fact that the storage lockers the government claimed McVeigh stored bomb components in, bore no trace of explosive chemicals. Jones, describing the trial, wrote that the FBI "had to stretch the evidence to prove that McVeigh was John Doe 1" and ultimately, they could not prove McVeigh had ever even entered Elliot's Ryder rental shop at all.[80]

The three most damning witnesses called by the prosecution were McVeigh's sister and confidant, Jennifer McVeigh, and his friends Michael and Lori Fortier. After being placed under extreme duress by the FBI and the urging of McVeigh himself, Jennifer reluctantly agreed to testify against her brother and in what Stuart Wright called "the cruelest of ironies" offered what he felt was perhaps the most damning" of all those who took the stand. Her testimony, as well the many letters he wrote her in the years leading to the bombing, established his obsession with *The Turner Diaries*, his predilection towards right-wing ideologies and evolving hatred for the government.[81] It did not connect him in any material or significant way to the bombing itself.

Although at first, Michael Fortier denied any knowledge of or involvement with the plot to bomb the Murrah, he eventually confessed to having had prior knowledge about McVeigh's plans but, not taking him seriously, had failed to warn authorities. In exchange for immunity for Lori, a reduced sentence for himself and the placement of both in the witness protection program after Fortier served the sentence, the Fortier's agreed to testify against both McVeigh and Terry Nichols.

During her testimony, Lori recalled that, months before the bombing, McVeigh had come to their house and used fifteen soup cans to demonstrate to her how he planned to construct the bomb. She also said that she had helped McVeigh hide blasting caps used to construct the bomb by placing them in a box and wrapping the box in Christmas paper. As soon as she heard about the bombing on television, said Lori, she immediately knew Tim had done it. McVeigh said that other attorneys on his legal team had prepared a list of 118 cross-examination questions for the Fortier's but instead of asking them, Jones asked irrelevant questions like why she had so many soup cans and rambled on aimlessly about inconsequential topics. Still, Jones got Lori to admit that she had lied to FBI agents (as well as to her parents and friends) about her knowledge of the bombing plot until the government offered her husband an immunity deal.

Michael Fortier told jurors that, after the events at Waco in 1993, McVeigh had become very disturbed, angry, defensive and paranoid. Then, in 1994, McVeigh wrote Fortier, informing him that he (with Nichols' assistance) was planning on taking "some kind of positive offensive action" intended to avenge Waco. After this point, he had begun to confide various details about his preparations to Fortier who then agreed to help. He admitted that he had accompanied McVeigh to a rented storage space where McVeigh had stashed stolen bomb-making materials and, on one occasion, to Oklahoma City to case the Murrah building.[82]

Under cross-examination, Fortier (like Lori) admitted to having made a number of contradictory and insensitive statements to friends, family members and the FBI in the first few days after the bombing. For instance, in addition to insisting that he had nothing to do with the murders in OKC, Fortier had told friends and family, "[If they call me as a witness] I'd sit there and pick my nose and flick it at the camera." In one phone conversation (which was being monitored by the FBI) he said, "I've been thinking of trying to do those talk show circuits for a long time, coming up with some asinine story and getting my friends to go in with it." He could, he said, fabricate a story "worthy of the Enquirer" and make "a cool mil" by selling the book or movie rights to it. Lori and Michael Fortier, said Jones, were like "Tarzan and Jane.... They swing from tree to tree tying the government's case together."[83]

On May 28, 1997, the evening before closing arguments began, Jones wrote to McVeigh and told him that he was honored to have been a part of the case and that, no matter what the verdict turned out to be, he wanted him to know that every individual on the defense team had been committed to providing him the best defense possible. He then attempted to comfort his client by telling him that, through his legal team, McVeigh had achieved at least some of his original objectives for the trial: "I think the message that you would want out is out, the government is in a state of confusion and embarrassment."

The next day, the jury began deliberation. McVeigh said that, throughout the entire trial, he had known his death sentence was inevitable and therefore, "didn't waste energy on nail biting over the verdict or sentence." The other members of his legal team agreed. Christopher Tritico said, "There was no illusion that we were going to win in this case because the evidence against McVeigh, while it was circumstantial, was strong." Roger Charles said that the arguments Jones had presented during the trial, "all but conceded that his client would be found guilty."[84]

On June 2, 1997, after almost 24 hours of deliberation, the Jury found twenty-nine year old Timothy McVeigh guilty of all 11 counts against him, recommended prosecutors seek his execution and the sentencing phase of his trial began. McVeigh's parents took the stand asking the court to spare their son from execution. His mother's statements brought what appeared to reporters to be a tear to her son's eyes. "He is not a monster...," she stated, choking back her own sobs, "Yes, I am pleading for my sons' life. He is a human being." His father, always the quiet type, chose instead to play for jurors home videos showing McVeigh as a young, normal, All-American kid.[85] McVeigh said he did not want his parents to have to beg for his life as the jury had already made up its mind and attempts to change them at this point in the game were farcical.

On June 13, 1997, prior to receiving his sentence, McVeigh, for the first time throughout the proceedings, took the opportunity to speak in court on his own behalf, to quote the dissenting opinion of Judge Brandeis in a 1928 illegal wiretapping court case: "Our Government is the potent, the omnipresent teacher. For good or for ill, it teaches the whole people by its example." Then the jury sentenced Timothy McVeigh to death by lethal injection.[86]

Despite the overwhelming relief of many, not everybody felt the trial had provided any real resolution. Georgetown University law Professor Paul Rothstein remarked that Judge Matsch "held the reins so tightly, that maybe there will be some doubts throughout history as to whether there were stones left unturned." During a press conference on June 16, Stephen Jones told reporters, "There is also a considerable body of evidence that indicates that he is not guilty. Now, the jury didn't find him not guilty, but the jury didn't hear the entire evidence." McVeigh, he continued, was not evil and if the public knew the "full story" as he did, they would agree. When asked to explain, Jones said he could not talk about what he knew, mainly because McVeigh "wouldn't want me to" but then remarked that evidence existed which suggested the government had prior knowledge of the bombing.[87]

On June 30, 1997, Stephen Jones wrote a letter to Mickey Frazer, McVeigh's mother. "I just wanted to tell you how sad I am for your family and for Tim that we did not have a better result," and expressed that, "Tim was tried and convicted in the court of public opinion even before I was appointed to defend him. He has so many good qualities, and that is why I have been careful to say in all of my interviews that he is not evil or demonic, that he has many fine and noble qualities, not the least of which is empathy for the innocent." Jones' kind words and assurances failed to quell the hate McVeigh had developed for him. After his sentencing, McVeigh, successfully this time, filed a motion with the court to have Jones removed as his lead attorney. Several other members of the Jones Team continued to represent him throughout his appeals until his execution in June 2001.

The federal trial of Terry Nichols began shortly after McVeigh's concluded. Prosecutors argued that Nichols had helped McVeigh compile components and that the two had then built the bomb together. Nobody, however, including the FBI, suspected Nichols of being JD2, nor did anybody assert that he had been in OKC the morning of the bombing. Curiously, Judge Matsch allowed Nichols' defense team to introduce *some* of the evidence about the John Does not allowed at McVeigh's trial and testimony such as Carol Howe's, which was barred during McVeigh's trial. Attorney Ron Woods explained how Nichols' attorneys were not hampered by the same evidentiary restrictions and exclusion rulings as McVeigh's and this allowed them to present a great deal of information that Jones had hoped but was not allowed to present. At the very least, Woods said, this information sowed the seeds of reasonable doubt about the government's narrative in the mind of jurors.

> The Jury in Nichols case certainly had doubts. It was always our position that there was someone else with McVeigh and we spent a lot of time presenting evidence that there was someone else with McVeigh that was not Nichols, but we never could find out who that was. The evidence from the witnesses indicated there was someone else with McVeigh when he came to rent the Ryder truck. There were witnesses who saw the Ryder being driven in the streets of Oklahoma City with two people in it. There were also several reports of a third person...The government had developed this information but didn't want to present it because it was inconsistent with their theory.[88]

Before dismissing the jury in Nichols' 1997 presentencing hearing, U.S. District Judge Richard P. Matsch, who had also presided over McVeigh's trial, stated for the record that "not all of the questions have been answered" and implored the FBI to continue their investigation into other unidentified conspirators. The jury deadlocked, so Nichols was not eligible for a sentence of death.[89] Ultimately, they found him guilty on eight counts of involuntary manslaughter and conspiracy to use a weapon of mass destruction, and he received a sentence of 161 years in prison without the possibility of parole.

On May 27, 1998, Michael Fortier accepted a reduced sentence of twelve years in prison and a fine of $75,000. After his release from prison in January 2006, he and his family were placed in the Witness Protection Program and given new identities.

In 1999, after the Supreme Court rejected his appeal for a new trial, McVeigh chose to end his appeals, removed Jones as his attorney, and requested the earliest date for his execution, which was then set for May 16, 2001. However, on May 1, 2001, after the FBI disclosed that it had withheld thousands of discovery documents from McVeigh's defense team during the 1997 trial, Attorney General John Ashcroft ordered a thirty-day postponement of the execution to allow attorneys to review the documents. This, however, was not enough time for his attorneys to adequately view the materials and they had reason to believe that the documents represented only a small portion of what had been withheld during discovery. Nevertheless, Ashcroft insisted that none of the 'newly found' documents created any doubt about McVeigh's guilt and the execution would proceed. Randy Coyne said, "We were buried in FBI investigative reports known as 302's. We were given the haystacks and so set about looking for the needle. Apparently, as was revealed later, not everything that should have been turned over to us by the government, was."[90] Christopher Tritico recalled:

After the trial, I was off the case but when the evidence came out that the government had not given us all of our evidence I was re-appointed with several other members of the original defense team and was his lawyer again until the execution. When we found out about all of this evidence Tim said 'let's find out what it is at least' and authorized us to do what we had to try and stop the execution and see the evidence and of course, we were denied at every step. The documents we did get gave us leads we wanted to investigate. Can I say these leads would have radically changed the outcome of the trial? No. I can't say that but those leads led us to discover that there was another hundred boxes of evidence that we never did get to see. Now, in that 100 boxes, is there something that would have changed the outcome? Who knows? And now nobody ever will.[91]

The title of a May 12, 2001 *New York Post* article, "Dead Man Laughing: Tim The Terrorist Sneers At Victims," quoted one man whose 27 year-old daughter had died in the bombing and who, when asked his feelings about McVeigh's impending execution said, "He is enjoying this [attention] because we have created a monster." The article concluded by stating that while new evidence was coming to light in the final hours before the execution "America's most home-grown monster is laughing, when people are still crying.... Dead man laughing."[92] Still, headlines like that of CBS News, which claimed evidence the "FBI Withheld On Purpose Suggests Prosecutors Contradicted Information FBI Had On Hand" kept public doubt about the case alive.

According to public opinion polls, by June 2001, nearly two-thirds of Americans thought other individuals beyond McVeigh and Nichols had been involved in the plot. Two survivors of the bombing unsuccessfully petitioned the court to delay the execution for the sake of obtaining and preserving evidence of the crime. One of them, V.Z Lawton, said, "I lost 58 friends in the building that day and the bombers also attempted to murder me. I believe that is reason enough for me to pursue everyone who was involved in the bombing. I want justice but there can be no justice without the truth."[93] While some hoped that if McVeigh was kept alive, he might someday tell the truth about the facts surrounding the bombing, the majority of those victimized believed that, even if there was more to the story, McVeigh would never talk. In any event, Timothy McVeigh seemed to have nothing more to say. Having considered the possibility of filing another appeal, he instructed his attorneys to drop any appeals and resigned himself to death.

The Bureau of Prisons (BOP) allowed the execution to be broadcast via closed circuit television to victims' family members. 14,000 press credentials were issued, and on the morning of June 11, 2001, scores of reporters from media outlets and cable networks were gathered outside the Terre Haute prison. At 7:14 AM, after receiving a series of lethal injections, thirty -three year old Timothy James McVeigh was pronounced dead, becoming the first federally executed prisoner since 1963. As his final statement, he offered the words of William Ernest Henley from his 1875 poem *Invictus*:

> *Out of the night that covers me,*
> *Black as the pit from pole to pole,*
> *I thank whatever gods may be*
> *For my unconquerable soul.*
> *In the fell clutch of circumstance*
> *I have not winced nor cried aloud.*
> *Under the bludgeonings of chance*
> *My head is bloody, but unbowed.*
> *Beyond this place of wrath and tears*
> *Looms but the Horror of the shade,*
> *And yet the menace of the years*
> *Finds and shall find me unafraid.*
> *It matters not how strait the gate,*
> *How charged with punishment the scroll,*
> *I am the master of my fate:*
> *I am the captain of my soul.*

Timothy McVeigh and his grandfather Ed.

Narrative Types &
Recurring Depictions

By the time of his indictment on April 27, 1995, Timothy McVeigh had already been depicted as a demon; a lone wolf or one of a pack; a CIA agent; an FBI informant; patsy; government guinea pig, disgruntled soldier; fallen war hero; loser; loner; gun nut and conspiracy theorist. In the chapters that follow, I examine the origins all of these stories, compare several existing works about him to each other and introduce new, never before published information – thereby offering a "hidden biography" of Timothy McVeigh. In many ways, this book is a story about stories, the people who tell stories, the stories they tell and the reasons they tell them. Before telling McVeigh's "back story" I want to briefly outline five commonly told narrative variations: The Lone Wolf, The Pack of Wolves, The Closely-Watched Wolves, The Guilty Agent and The Experimental Wolf.

THE LONE WOLF

The Lone Wolf narrative is the least complex and most widely known account of the Oklahoma City bombing and the one officially endorsed by the U.S. government. In this story, McVeigh, *alone*, motivated by his anger over the Federal government's actions at Waco, conceived of and executed the bombing plot. While his former Army buddy, Terry Nichols, provided minimal assistance by helping McVeigh gather components for the bomb and assisting to build it, he did so under duress, fearing for the life of his family whom McVeigh threatened. Then McVeigh alone drove to Oklahoma City on the morning of April 19, 1995, to detonate it.[1]

In Lone Wolf stories, all details of the plot and the identities, motives, movements and actions of perpetrators are known. Additional, unapprehended accomplices and co-conspirators do not exist and no stone has been left unturned, no mystery remains and narrative closure is achieved. As with all the other narrative types, the Lone Wolf story originated with multiple individuals and institutions and appeared prior to McVeigh's and Nichols' trials or convictions within news reports, biographical works and in McVeigh's own letters and conversations with his defense team and reporters. Today, the Lone Wolf story is not only inscribed upon geographical locations (memorials) but also permanently embedded in consciousness and the collective national memory.

While many of the "McVeigh as Lone Wolf" accounts have been published, the most enduring and well-known of them and the one that continues to inform expert, academic and popular understandings of both the bombing and the man executed for it, is the one McVeigh himself narrated to Dan Herbeck and Lou Michel for their 2001 *authorized* biography, *American Terrorist: Timothy McVeigh and the Oklahoma City Bombing*. According to the authors, despite the ongoing appearance of his leaked 'confessions' in news reports, McVeigh's public silence about his exact role in the bombing left room for the proliferation of "conspiracy theories," but unlike Lee Harvey Oswald, there was still a chance to let McVeigh tell his story. The authors wrote that by letting him do so, they hoped to circumvent the "specter" of unresolved issues that surrounded the JFK assassination. With the publication of *American Terrorist*, readers are told, McVeigh irrefutably "becomes the confessed bomber of the Murrah Building in OKC."

McVeigh's motives for cooperating with the authors are more than a bit ironic. While readers learn of his lifelong fascination with conspiracy theories, McVeigh hoped to refute the conspiracy theories surrounding the bombing (and himself), especially those propagated by his former attorney Stephen Jones. Therefore, McVeigh (and the authors) spent a considerable amount of time addressing competing accounts and theories and denying McVeigh's documented connections to other violent extremists, the existence of JD2 (or 3 or 4) or any other related "big conspiracy." According to Herbeck and Michel, McVeigh told them his story with such frank "intensity and candor," held nothing back and provided "a depth of detail" that "jibed with witness testimony" and "perfectly fit with [the official accounts offered by] the FBI, investigators and prosecutors…" they had no reason to question his honesty and whole-heartedly believed the story he orated. Aggressively asserting the role of Lone Wolf Mastermind Bomber to his official biographers, McVeigh claimed to have carefully planned his actions down to the tiniest minutiae, including the John Wilkes Booth t-shirt he wore the morning of the bombing. He said he hoped the bombing would act as a "shot heard around the world," which would inspire and catalyze other revolutionary acts.[2]

FBI Special Agents Jon Hersley and Larry Tongate, two lead investigators in the case, felt compelled, in their 2004 book *Simple Truths: The Real Story of the Oklahoma City Bombing Investigation*, to correct "various inaccurate and irresponsible theories that this notorious event spawned" and "tell the real story" of the Oklahoma bombing. Restating their intentions throughout the book, the authors offer "a much-needed factual history of the case" and *Simple Truths* purports to offer a "contribution to accuracy in history." Tongate and Hersley summarize and advance the FBI's conclusion and the case prosecutors presented at the criminal trials of McVeigh and Nichols and assert that, having turned over every stone and followed every lead, "all other theories proved implausible [and] no credible evidence existed that anyone other than McVeigh and Nichols were involved." After all, they emphasize, McVeigh himself admitted such. In his introduction to the book, retired FBI agent and Governor of Oklahoma at the time of the bombing, Frank Keating, described the bombing as an act of "monstrous evil" but assured readers that *Simple Truths* "is the closed book on the case. Two evil men did this and two evil men paid." *Simple Truths* is illustrative of the way in which the government's Lone Wolf story is oddly similar to McVeigh's own.[3]

THE PACK OF WOLVES; AND THOSE CLOSELY WATCHED

In cases of high profile American assassinations, where one Lone Gunman appears, alternate accounts inevitably emerge asserting the involvement of multiple shooters and competing claims about their identities. Multiple gunmen rumored to have been involved in the assassination of John F. Kennedy include, but are not limited to, the CIA, KGB, Secret Service, Mossad, mafia, Anti-Castro Cubans, a plethora of intelligence operatives including Howard Hunt, David Ferrie, the three tramps, man with the umbrella, black dog man and Lee Harvey Oswald. Likewise, in some stories about the Oklahoma City bombing, where Lone Wolf bomber

McVeigh appears, others follow closely behind who populate a second, more thematically complex genre of narratives collectively referred to as The Pack of Wolves. Unlike the uniformity of Lone Wolf narratives, Pack stories have distinct variations, The Pack and The Pack Closely Watched.

Within all Pack stories and their sub variants, McVeigh is no longer the mastermind or primary villain in the bombing plot, never acts entirely alone, and is always one of several additional unidentified and/or unapprehended conspirators who helped conceive of, plan, fund and execute the bombing. Therefore, McVeigh's culpability is mitigated and his role usurped by Others Unknown. The Others are composed of several individuals who, over time, have become a single composite character widely known as John Doe #2. Within the various descriptions of the Pack, identities of the Others Unknown differ and may include a range of candidates: Islamic Jihadists, the Irish Republican Army (IRA), Columbian Drug Lords, but most often Neo-Nazi bank robbers and/or others within the White Power Movement. While the identities and roles of the Others remain the subject of inquiry and speculation, their involvement and sometimes even their existence are officially denied. Unlike the Lone Wolf template, that bases its claims to truth on *known* information and achieves total narrative closure, the defining quality of Pack stories (and all other variants) is the *unknown*; and thus, an inability to achieve resolution.

Pack accounts explain how, while over 226 people reported seeing one or more John Does with McVeigh in the months before the bombing, everyone who saw him in OKC the morning of the explosion saw him with these Others. Pack stories also explain how the participation of these Others was obscured from history by the disguises and decoy vehicles they used, generating a myriad of contradictory eyewitness descriptions of them. This confusion led to several permutations of a single conspiracy theory, all involving the officially denied Others.

Recurring themes and elements in stories about the Pack of Watched Wolves include covert surveillance practices conducted mostly by the FBI and ATF and the ongoing presence of undercover federal informants, agents, provocateurs and spies who, throughout the plot, pose as true pack wolves, all the while passing information to their government handlers. In these stories, McVeigh becomes part of a 'Sting Operation Gone Horribly Awry.'

In their failure to prevent the bombing, the government assumes a degree of culpability ranging from failure to act on intelligence, sometimes vague, sometimes detailed, and warnings of the impending bombing as well as accusations that they orchestrated it. All Pack stories allege that various government agencies have engaged in a cover-up by intentionally distorting and withholding facts about the bombing from the public.

Like all other variants, Pack stories appeared publicly immediately after McVeigh's arrest and proliferated during the years leading to McVeigh's 2001 execution, often via works of investigative journalism and news reports that connected him to various players in the White Power Movement and American paramilitary underground.[4]

While all Lone Wolf accounts have remained uniform and consistent, after McVeigh's execution, Pack stories have become increasingly complex due in part to the continuing emergence of case-related information resulting from ongoing formal and informal investigative, legal, and academic efforts.

THE GUILTY AGENT

In the fourth variation, McVeigh is depicted, not as a Lone Wolf, or even one within a Pack of Wolves, but as a Guilty Agent; a *witting* undercover operative for shadowy defense agencies in a nationwide sting operation which, for one reason or another, resulted in the bombing.

Guilty Agent stories appeared frequently in works of the conspiracy theory genre prior to the criminal trials of McVeigh and Nichols. For example, Jon Rappaport's 1995 book, *Oklahoma City Bombing: The Suppressed Truth*, argues that the bombing plot was unquestionably a conspiracy that subsequently led to a "cover-up" afterwards. While Rappaport acknowledged that, at the time of his writing, many of the details of this conspiracy and cover-up remained unknown, he nonetheless asserted that both were part of a larger effort by the federal government to run damage control in the aftermath of the Waco debacle, demonize the Patriot Movement and pass anti-terrorism legislation which would expand the budgets and powers of various government agencies, thereby allowing them to further suppress the Movement.

Rather than espousing a unified theory about the exact workings and details involved in the bombing plot, Rappaport presented several scenarios other than the then-dominant Lone Wolf story. Rappaport asserted that, if any of the alternate scenarios outlined proved true, it was likely that McVeigh had not been fully aware of all the details of the plot he was involved in but was more likely an "amateur" participant within "the visible part of a [larger] sophisticated operation," a "delivery man," "blamable man," "fall guy," "throw away," and "dupe."[5]

After McVeigh's arrest, so-called conspiracy theorists were linked to terrorism. This new batch of 'potential terrorists' and their supporters co-opted the discourse of counter-terrorism pundits by claiming that the bombing itself was the result of a conspiracy, and while the exact nature of this conspiracy was not yet known, they believed that covert state actors played a part in the carnage. In the years after McVeigh's trial and execution, Guilty Agent depictions of McVeigh have continued to proliferate online and in self-published books.[6] In this book, I discuss new information which has surfaced since 2001 and introduce new evidence to show how Guilty Agent theories are originally rooted in stories told by McVeigh himself, both prior to and after the bombing and how stories such as these may be more plausible than previously imagined.

THE EXPERIMENTAL WOLF

Finally, Experimental Wolf narratives break with many previous understandings of the bombing story and the life of Timothy McVeigh and, often, disrupt linearity and agency normally ascribed to him. In them, McVeigh, the ultimate conspiracy theorist, is rendered the victim of a conspiracy; a dupe, a Guilty Agent lacking real Agency, a traumatized automaton suffering from "Agency Panic" (the sense of being shaped or controlled by powerful external forces) and sometimes Generation X's own Manchurian Candidate.[7] Within many of these theories, either during or after his time in the Army, McVeigh was a test subject for classified experimental or refined procedures until after his arrest. McVeigh is thus depicted as a human guinea pig who, unbeknownst even to himself, (depending on the version articulated) is influenced, tracked or controlled by a number of mysterious technologies, drugs and methods, manipulated by mad scientists operating out of black-budgeted staging grounds in a number of geographical locations. Recurring themes and elements may include high level, officially sanctioned architects of death, brainwashed automatons, and, from time to time, UFO's.

A close reading of previous Experimental texts reveals a wide range of emergent literary and cultural themes found in works of science fiction, but that originate from or reflect actual historical and current circumstances, events and practices. We will outline and compare various interpretations of all Experimental stories about McVeigh or others and explore related themes and texts and the many variations of Experimental narratives, including those about Post Traumatic Stress Disorder, Gulf War Syndrome and, the most common of these, Brainwashing/Mind Control.

We will closely examine stories told by and about McVeigh, and/or fictional ones similar to those that appeared and circulated immediately after his arrest. For instance, within days, countless news articles reported that McVeigh told a number of people he believed the Army embedded a computer chip in his buttocks. Very quickly, the reports noted, the 'black helicopter crowd' suggested that he was the victim of mind control experiments. Many variations of 'Experimental' stories appeared online and in book length works prior to McVeigh's execution. More recently, they have appeared in fictional works like Tracy Letts' 2006 play *BUG* and its 2007 film adaptation of the same name as well as a January 2010 episode of *Conspiracy Theory with Jesse Ventura* entitled "Manchurian Candidate." Though no proponent of the Experimental variation has yet tested these consequently unsubstantiated claims against oral and archival records, in this book, I do so, in the process revealing a number of obscure and startling contextual and biographical details about McVeigh.

In constructing this Experimental history, I employ both fictional and nonfictional texts including those about McVeigh and update readers on recent controversial and provocative bioethical issues surrounding, among other practices, the use of *non-lethal* interrogation, surveillance and "soldier enhancement" methods. Like all others discussed thus far, McVeigh first articulated various contradictory versions of these stories privately prior to the bombing, and many appeared publicly within days of his arrest. While acknowledging the existence of Others Unknown and multiple John Does, Experimental stories emphasize McVeigh's powerlessness over his own actions, making his final statement "I am the master of my fate, the captain of my soul," rather ironic.

Perhaps one valuable contribution made by this writing is the demonstration of an underlying medical and psychological narrative that, while largely unknown, underpins a number of fictional and non-fictional representations of McVeigh. This hidden narrative sheds light on, or helps clarify, unknown or unresolved biographical elements of McVeigh's life, controversies surrounding the Gulf War and contributes to a number of larger ongoing discussions and debates surrounding current U.S. government, military and medical policies and practices. We will also explore a nearly hidden history of McVeigh's participation and experiences in the Gulf War.

All Experimental stories or variations thereof are important, no matter their truth, or the actual secrets they reveal, as within all subcategories, inscribed within McVeigh's very body (symbolically or actually) are the effects of militarism and warfare. Mind Control, or 'Experimental' stories help us to understand possible motives left unexplored about McVeigh's motivation to participate in the bombing plot, whether as a Lone Wolf, a part of a Pack or a Guilty Agent.

Chapter One

On Becoming John Rambo:
An Overview of American Madness

"Rampage" – (verb): a course of violent, riotous, or reckless action or behavior; (noun): violent behavior that is reckless, uncontrolled, or destructive.

The amok man is patently out of his mind, an automaton oblivious to his surroundings and unreachable by appeals or threats. But his rampage is preceded by lengthy brooding over failure and is carefully planned as a means of deliverance from an unbearable situation.

–Steven Pinker, *How the Mind Works*, 1997

His was an impenetrable darkness. I look at him as you peer down at a man who is lying at the bottom of a precipice where the sun never shines.

–Charles Marlow, protagonist in Joseph Conrad's *Heart of Darkness*, 1899

This is the way the world ends. Not with a bang but a whimper.

–T.S. Elliot, "The Hollow Man," 1925

THE MANY MCVEIGH'S YESTERDAY & TODAY...

Much has been written[1] about Lee Harvey Oswald who, according to the well-known narrative, on November 22, 1963, at the age of twenty-four, fired three shots from the sixth story of the Texas School Book Depository in Dallas, wounding Texas Governor John Connolly and killing President John F. Kennedy, after which he escaped the scene, via city bus, taxi and on foot, headed to a movie theatre, and shot and killed Dallas Police officer J.D. Tippet along the way. After a booth attendant called the police to report that a man had entered the theatre without buying a ticket, the police arrived and arrested Oswald. Depending on the account, Oswald either willingly submitted to police or put up a struggle and had to be subdued. Either way, he was charged with the murders of Kennedy and Tippet, but adamantly denied involvement

---

1. In the section, 'The Many McVeigh's,' I attempt only to present the stories of modern so-called Lone Gun Men as told by news articles and the patterns in these stories that emerge within media depictions

in either of the deaths. During a transfer from the Dallas police headquarters to a county jail, he proclaimed to journalists and television crews, "I didn't shoot anybody! [...] I'm just a patsy!" Two days later, Oswald himself was shot and killed on live television by nightclub owner Jack Ruby. This much we think we know.

Oswald's brief life was marked by complexity and contradiction. His father died before he was born, leaving his mother to raise him and his siblings. His mother moved often (from Louisiana to Texas to New York) and by the time he graduated high school Oswald had attended 12 different schools. Although he read voraciously and had a high IQ, he had great difficulty writing and spelling. Those who knew him at a young age described him as introverted, moody and argumentative. When he was arrested for repeated truancy in the 7th grade, the juvenile psychiatrist who evaluated him reported that Oswald was absorbed within a "vivid fantasy life, turning around the topics of omnipotence and power, through which [he] tries to compensate for his present shortcomings and frustrations." By fifteen years old, he was a self-proclaimed Socialist and Marxist. The next year he joined the Civil Air Patrol in New Orleans.

At seventeen, Oswald quit school and joined the U.S. Marine Corps because, according to his older brother, he hoped "to get out and under ... the yoke of oppression [of our] mother." While in the Marines, he was trained as a radar operator, obtained a security clearance, qualified as a sharpshooter and took (but did poorly on) a Russian language exam. Although one of his commanding officers described him as a "very competent" crew chief and "brighter than most people," Oswald expressed pro-Soviet sentiments and on a number of occasions was court-martialed, once for accidentally shooting himself in the elbow with a handgun he was not authorized to possess and another time for fighting with a sergeant. His various court-martials led to imprisonment and demotion.

At the age of twenty, Oswald defected to the Soviet Union where he lived for three years and met and married his wife Marina before returning to the U.S., claiming he became disillusioned with life in the USSR. In March 1963, Oswald allegedly purchased a rifle and revolver through the mail, using the alias "A. Hidell" and purportedly used the rifle in an attempt to shoot U.S. Major General Edwin Walker, a rabid right-wing anti-communist segregationist. The next month, he moved to New Orleans where he began propagating Pro-Castro literature but, paradoxically, associated with a number of notable right-wing individuals who had very rabid and vocal anti-communist and anti-Castro political beliefs. These individuals included, among others, former FBI agent Guy Bannister, CIA asset David Ferrie and local businessman Clay Shaw.

In New Orleans, Oswald briefly worked at a coffee company until July 1963, when he was fired for reading rifle and hunting magazines while on the job and for loitering in general. That September, he is reported to have visited the Cuban Embassy in Mexico seeking a visa that would allow entry into Cuba where he planned to stay before traveling on to the Soviet Union. Facing a delay in processing the visa, Oswald headed to Dallas where he rented a room under the name "O.H. Lee," had some contact with FBI agents, and got a job at the Texas School Book Depository.

Despite numerous official and citizen investigations and the many theories surrounding it, the JFK assassination and Oswald's subsequent murder ushered in, not only an era of televised death spectacles via politically motivated assassinations and random public shootings (with no apparent political motivation) committed by "lone nuts" but also the age of rapidly proliferating conspiracy theories, the formation of "conspiracy cultures," and a deep cynicism and distrust in the *official* stories about any one of these incidents and the creation of alternate counter-narratives.[1]

Within a few years of Oswald's appearance on the public stage, a number of other equally frustrated and listless lone nuts emerged. These included twenty-five year old Charles Whitman who, in August 1966, killed his wife and mother in their home and then commenced a sniping spree from a tower at the University of Texas, killing sixteen people and wounding thirty-two others before being shot and killed by an Austin police officer. Whitman, like Oswald, reportedly grew up in a physically and psychologically abusive home and went on to join the U.S. Marine Corps. [2] Two years later, in April 1968, James Earl Ray allegedly assassinated Rev. Dr. Martin Luther King, Jr. and a little over two months after that, in June 1968, twenty-four year old Sirhan Sirhan purportedly killed Presidential nominee, Robert F. Kennedy.

Arthur Bremer

Included among this growing family of Lone Nuts was twenty-two year old Arthur Bremer whose attempt to assassinate Democratic presidential candidate George Wallace with a .38 revolver during a campaign rally, left Wallace paralyzed from the waist down and critically wounded three others. Members of the crowd tackled Bremer and he was arrested.

Bremer grew up in an abusive and highly dysfunctional home. He later explained that as a child, "I would escape my ugly reality by pretending that I was living with a television family, and there was no yelling at home or no one to hit me." Although Bremer was gifted with a high IQ, he consistently received low grades, had trouble making friends and found school to be a lonely and torturous experience filled with bullies who scorned and ridiculed him. After graduating high school, he enrolled in college, where he was remembered as a "strange, aloof and argumentative" fellow who "rarely talked to anybody." Bremmer dropped out after one semester and got a job as a busboy, but after customers complained about his bizarre mannerisms, including talking to himself out loud, he was demoted. When he demanded his demotion be reversed, an evaluator reported that Bremer, although a "conscientious" worker, "border(ed) on the paranoid." He quit his job and for the next few years worked as an elementary school janitor during which time he became increasingly suicidal. In October 1971, Bremer was arrested for carrying a concealed weapon and was pronounced mentally ill by a court-appointed psychiatrist. Soon after, Bremer purchased a .38 revolver.[3]

On March 2, 1972, Bremer wrote in his diary, "It is my personal plan to assassinate by pistol either Richard Nixon or George Wallace," and that his purpose was "to do SOMETHING BOLD AND DRAMATIC, FORCEFUL & DYNAMIC, A STATEMENT of my manhood for the world to see." He then began to stalk Wallace, following him throughout the country. More attracted to the idea of killing Nixon, on April 11 of that year, Bremer traveled to Ottawa, Canada where Nixon was making a public appearance but decided against killing him due to the high level of security there.

After returning to his home state of Wisconsin, Bremer took two books about Sirhan Sirhan out of the library and wrote in his diary, "I am as important as the start of WWI. I just need the little opening and a second of time." He then turned his full attention to Wallace, although somewhat less enthusiastically, as Wallace was not as well-known as Nixon and his death "won't get more than three minutes on the network T.V. news." Still, on May 9, Bremer visited Wallace's local campaign headquarters and continued to follow him and attend his rallies. The day he set out for Laurel, Maryland, where Wallace was to appear next, Bremer wrote, "My cry upon firing will be 'A penny for your thoughts.' Copyright 1972. All rights reserved. Arthur H. Bremer." On May 15, 1972, Bremer, wearing dark glasses, red, white and blue clothing and a "Wallace in 72" campaign button, attended a campaign rally for Wallace. As many in the crowd jeered Wallace and even threw tomatoes at him, Bremer feigned support for him by loudly cheering and applauding. Due to the crowd's harsh reception of him, the candidate did not interact with the crowd after his speech and Bremer found no opportunity to enact his plan, but succeeded later that day at another rally just a few miles away.

When police searched his apartment they found shell boxes, a Confederate flag, pornography, Black Panther literature, newspaper clippings, Wallace campaign buttons, a book entitled *101 Things To Do In Jail* and a number of diary entries including ones that read "My country tis of thee land of sweet bigotry," "Cheer up Oswald," and "White collar, conservative, middle class, Republican, conservative robot."

In his car, which investigators described as a "hotel on wheels," were pillows, blankets, a tape recorder, a radio with police band, binoculars, a .9mm automatic pistol and the 1972 edition of *Writer's Yearbook.*

During his trial, his defense attorneys argued that Bremer was schizophrenic, legally insane and had "no emotional capacity to understand anything;" but prosecutors argued otherwise and said that, while perhaps the man was disturbed, he knew what he was doing when he attempted to kill Wallace and had done so to get attention, even calculating his arrest and subsequent media coverage of his trial. After a jury found him guilty, at the conclusion of his sentencing hearing, Bremer was given the opportunity to speak and said, "[The Prosecutor] said that he would like society to be protected from someone like me. Looking back on my life, I would have liked it if society had protected me from myself. That's all I have to say at this time."

He was sentenced to serve sixty-three years in prison but the sentence was appealed and reduced to fifty-three years. In 2007, after serving 35 years, at the age of fifty-seven, Bremer was released from prison and placed on probation until 2025.[4]

Ted Kaczynski

In their 1977 book, *Snapping: America's Epidemic of Sudden Personality Change*, Flo Conway and Jim Siegelman proclaimed that a rapidly growing "epidemic of sudden personality change" existed in America, a cultural phenomenon they dubbed "snapping," wherein *normal* individuals undergo startling personal transformations that sometimes lead them to engage in acts of random violence. To help understand the emergent phenomenon, the authors introduced their theory of "communication disorders" and a particular subset of these that they termed "Information Diseases" (IDs). They described ID's as "alterations in a person's information-processing capacities" that, unlike momentary, episodic and individualized snapping, results in a prolonged and "marked [change] of awareness, diminished conscious control [and] persisting impairments [of a person's] everyday powers of thinking, feeling, perception, memory, imagination and conscious choice."

Writing long before the emergence of the World Wide Web, the authors attributed America's ID epidemic to the unique stresses of modern life, especially information overload, as well as other isolated or ongoing traumatic experiences that, in combination, "lead to the physical breakdown of a person's entire ability to make sense of his experience," making them more suggestible to outside influences and rendering them "prone to uncontrollable urges and sudden outbursts of violence."

One such trauma, called 'Information Stress,' resulted from "obsessive absorption" with computers, television or other modern-day hobbies, noting that recent generations "have been molded, not by rich real-life experiences [but] information imparted electronically via television, film, computers and other advances in communication technologies" that convey "narrow, shallow and violent" images and messages, lead to crises of identity (at best) and actual violence (at worst) and render people mere "holograms of the society they inhabit." While the most common IDs led to "ongoing altered states of awareness," when in a "more advanced" and extreme stage, 'the delusional stage,' an individual's ability to distinguish reality, fantasy and illusion is impaired, causing them to suffer "vivid delusions" and confusion about whether they are actually awake or dreaming.[5]

In 1978, the year following the publication of *Snapping*, Theodore "Ted" Kaczynski began targeting individuals in some way connected to modern technology through planting or mailing home-made bombs that, from 1978 until 1995, killed three people and injured twenty-three others. His bombing campaign ceased when he was apprehended in April 1996, after his brother tipped off the FBI to Kaczynski's whereabouts in Lincoln, Montana, where he lived a hermetic life in a cabin without electricity or running water. After pleading guilty, he was sentenced to life without the possibility of parole.

As a child, Kaczynski was often sick and frequently hospitalized for various ailments including recurring hives. He feared other children and refused to interact with them, leading his mother to seek help for what she believed to be autism. He was, however, highly intelligent, and completed high school by the age of fifteen. At sixteen, he began attending undergraduate classes at Harvard University. While there, he, along with several other undergraduate students, became a subject for psychological tests conducted by a former interrogator for the WWII intelligence agency, the Office of Strategic Services (OSS) – Henry Murray. The tests, which lasted several months, sought to measure reactions to extreme stress and distress. Students wrote essays about themselves, were taken into a room and placed in a seat facing bright lights and a two-way mirror, hooked up to electrodes and then berated, belittled and subjected to brutal verbal attacks directed at their egos and beliefs. The experience and their reactions to it were filmed, and then played back to them repeatedly throughout the course of the study. Kaczynski's brother said that, prior to his participation in the test, his brother had been emotionally stable.

In 1962, at the age of twenty, Kaczynski graduated from Harvard and enrolled in a doctoral program at the University of Michigan, where he earned a PhD in mathematics. While there, he taught courses and published a number of papers. In 1967, he graduated and was recognized by the school for writing the best dissertation in his field that year. That same year, he began teaching geometry and calculus courses at the University of California, Berkeley. Students complained about his teaching style, told administrators that he was very nervous in a teaching environment and said he sometimes stuttered and mumbled during lectures. Two years later, he resigned from his teaching position and moved to his cabin in Montana where, in 1978 he began his bombing campaign.

In 1995, he sent a number of letters to his victims and packages to media outlets. The packages contained his 35,000-word manifesto entitled *Industrial Society and Its Future*, commonly referred to as the "Unabomber Manifesto." He demanded that outlets publish the manifesto and promised to cease the bombings if they did. Eventually, in September 1995, after he threatened to kill more people because outlets had delayed publishing his writings, the *New York Times* and *Washington Post* complied with his demands. The writing advocated world revolution against modern society and its "industrial-technological system" which he said (among other things) had destroyed human autonomy, degraded their relationship to nature and caused them to "behave in ways that are increasingly remote from the natural pattern of human behavior." This system, unless it was destroyed, would evolve until human freedom was destroyed altogether. He railed against the system for causing individuals to become overly socialized and expressed his belief that modern psychological problems were the result of individuals having to live in physical and social environments and behave in conforming ways that are radically different from those in which humans had originally evolved to exist.

Further, according to Kaczynski, the system had developed various methods of controlling individual and group responses to their unnatural and extremely stressful environments:

> Imagine a society that subjects people to conditions that make them terribly unhappy, then gives them the drugs to take away their unhappiness. Science fiction? It is already happening to some extent in our own society. It is well known that the rate of clinical depression had been greatly increasing in recent decades. We believe that this is due to disruption of the power process [...] The entertainment industry serves as an important psychological tool of the system, possibly even when it is dishing out large amounts of sex and violence. Entertainment provides modern man with an essential means of escape. While absorbed in television, videos, etc., he can forget stress, anxiety, frustration, dissatisfaction...

When he read the manifesto in the newspaper, his brother recognized Kaczynski's writing style and alerted the FBI, who then arrested him. The first psychiatrist appointed by the court diagnosed him with paranoid schizophrenia but nevertheless found him fit to stand trial. Experts who evaluated him later came to disagree with the diagnosis. While his attorneys wanted to plead insanity in order to avoid a death sentence, he adamantly insisted he was not insane and so, in order to avoid the publicity of a trial, Kaczynski agreed to plead guilty in exchange for life in prison.[6] While incarcerated at a Federal Supermax prison in Florence, Colorado, Kaczynski met, corresponded with and became friends with Timothy McVeigh. In a number of letters to his biographers, McVeigh referred to Kaczynski as his "kindred spirit."

MARK DAVID CHAPMAN

On December 8, 1980, twenty five year old Mark David Chapman shot and killed musician and cultural icon John Lennon in the lobby of his New York City apartment building, after which he calmly remained on the scene reading J.D. Salinger's 1951 novel *The Catcher in the Rye*. When the police arrived shortly afterwards, Chapman took off his coat to show the police he had no hidden weapons, told them he had acted alone and that the novel was his "statement" and explained to them, "I'm sure the big part of me is Holden Caulfield, who is the main person in the book. The small part of me is the Devil." Soon after, he claimed he could not remember aiming his gun at Lennon, but only recalled pulling the trigger.

In the years after his arrest and conviction, Chapman disclosed that, as a child, he feared his father, who was unloving towards him and physically abusive towards his mother. To cope, Chapman retreated into a fantasy life where he became king of a colony of "little people" who lived in his bedroom walls. In high school, Chapman, who was bullied for his poor athletic ability, began using drugs, skipping classes and running away from home. When he was twenty, Chapman enrolled in college and began working for the YMCA and World Vision, counseling young Vietnamese refugees in Arkansas and Beirut, Lebanon. Despite his seeming successes, when he and his girlfriend began having problems that led to their eventual break-up, Chapman became suicidal, dropped out of college and moved to Hawaii. At the age of twenty-two, after an unsuccessful attempt to end his own life with carbon monoxide, he was admitted to a hospital for psychiatric treatment where he was diagnosed with clinical depression. At age twenty-three, inspired by the book *Around The World In Eighty Days*, Chapman toured the world for six weeks.[7]

Upon returning to Hawaii, Chapman married his travel agent. He said that, about year later, on the heels of some frustrating life events, he resumed his relationship with his childhood imaginary friends (the Little People), developed an obsession with John Lennon, and his fixation with *The Catcher in the Rye* became a full-fledged obsession.

The year before he killed Lennon, Chapman wrote a letter to a friend in which he told her "I'm going nuts," signing the letter "The Catcher in the Rye." Although previously a fan of Lennon and later claiming he had no particular feelings about Lennon one way or the other, those who knew him said Chapman (an aspiring musician himself) became angered when Lennon publicly rejected the existence of God and declared that The Beatles were "more popular than Jesus." Chapman railed against Lennon for espousing a message of "peace and love" and rejection of capitalistic trappings, while accumulating great wealth – traits antithetical to *Catcher in the Rye* protagonist Holden Caulfield's ideal of "anti-phoniness." Chapman, attempting to defuse the perception that he shot Lennon simply to get attention, explained, "I understood that it [was] necessary for a man to die. A phony man had to die. But what a beautiful foundation was laid by his death. I became that book." A couple of months before the shooting, Chapman informed his wife that he planned to kill Lennon but, perhaps not taking him seriously, she failed to notify authorities. On October 23, Chapman quit his job as security guard and on his last day, signed out as "John Lennon." Days later, he bought a .38 caliber pistol.

Prior to leaving his New York hotel room early on the morning of December 8, Chapman carefully placed various personal items around his room for police to find later, including cryptic writings and a copy of *The Catcher in the Rye*, in which he had written, "This is my statement." Chapman arrived at Lennon's residence early that morning and waited there the entire day. He observed Lennon leaving the building around 5:00 PM but only asked him to autograph an album cover. When Lennon returned around 10:49 PM, Chapman fired five shots at Lennon, hitting him four times. Lennon was pronounced dead about fifteen minutes later.

A psychiatrist retained by the defense team diagnosed Chapman with schizophrenia and said that the voices of the "little people" in his head had ordered him to kill Lennon. After this initial evaluation, the defense and prosecution called in additional mental experts to evaluate him who found him to be (among other things) delusional, suffering from "grandiose visions of himself," and possibly psychotic, but still sane and competent to stand trial. Chapman's defense attorneys still planned to argue an insanity defense.

However, shortly before the trial Chapman informed his legal team and the court that he wished to change his plea to guilty as this was the will of God and denied having ever heard voices. In 1981, the presiding judge accepted his guilty plea and sentenced Chapman to twenty years to life and psychiatric treatment. Since then, Chapman, who remains married to his first wife, has been denied parole eight times and will be eligible for parole hearings again in 2016.[8]

JOHN HINCKLEY, JR.

On March 30, 1981, John Hinckley, Jr. shot at President Ronald Reagan with a .22 revolver as Reagan exited the Washington D.C. Hilton Hotel where he had just finished a speaking engagement. Although Hinckley failed to kill Reagan, he did manage to wound him along with three others including two Secret Service agents and White House Press Secretary James Brady. Hinckley was quickly apprehended. When he was searched, police found a copy of *The Catcher in the Rye*.

Hinckley grew up in a wealthy family with elite political connections, including the Bush family. He played on a number of school sports teams, was a talented pianist, popular with his classmates and, twice during high school, voted class president. Despite his popularity, Hinckley became withdrawn and isolated. After graduating high school, he attended a college in Texas on-and-off until 1980. During this time, in 1975, he relocated to Los Angeles to pursue his dream of becoming a songwriter, but was unsuccessful. In the many letters written to his family while there, Hinckley complained of his professional and economic frustrations and told them about his girlfriend "Lynn," who, in reality, did not exist. The following year, 1976, he returned to live at the home of his parents, at which time he began taking psychiatric medications (anti-depressants and tranquilizers), purchasing and familiarizing himself with firearms and grew obsessed with the 1976 movie *Taxi Driver*, its fictional protagonist Travis Bickle (played by Robert De Niro) and the film's lead actress, Jodi Foster. In the movie, loosely based on the exploits of Arthur Bremer, Bickle, a disaffected Vietnam veteran, plans to assassinate presidential candidate Senator Charles Palatine, but after being observed by the Secret Service at a campaign rally, abandons his plan. He then develops a protective relationship and obsession with a child prostitute played by Foster's character. He successfully encourages her to turn her life around.

After becoming obsessed with the movie, Hinckley began stalking Foster, sending her letters, phoning her and attending a class at Yale University where Foster was enrolled. He devised and then abandoned several schemes to write himself into history and thereby impress her (including highjacking an airplane and committing suicide in front of her). Hinckley then began collecting literature about extremist groups and American assassins including Lee Harvey Oswald, purchased a .22 pistol and "Devastator" exploding bullets. He then set his sights on President Ronald Reagan. In his efforts to impress Foster, Hinckley considered assassinating Senator Edward Kennedy and stalked him for a brief time but eventually settled on assassinating President Jimmy Carter, thereafter following him throughout several states until being arrested on a firearms charge. He then returned home and sought psychiatric treatment.

Various psychiatric evaluations diagnosed Hinckley with schizophrenia, dysthymia (a type of prolonged depression), as well as narcissistic, schizoid, borderline and passive-aggressive personality disorders. In 1982, Hinckley successfully pled not guilty by reason of insanity and was remanded to St. Elizabeth's Hospital in Washington, D.C. Hinckley had a significant effect on the role of mental health in criminal prosecutions. After his trial, a number of states modified their laws regarding the insanity defense, some completely abolishing it. Hinckley, perhaps more than any other lone nut before him, sparked gun-control debates that eventually led to the passage of the Brady Bill, gun-control legislation named after Jim Brady, the Press Secretary whom he had wounded. In 1987, Hinckley was granted the privilege of regular overnight stays with his parents and in January 2015, told reporters that he hoped to be deemed eligible for release soon and described his recent efforts to get a job at Starbucks.[9]

A number of conspiracy theories or alternate narratives have been constructed to explain the actions of this progression of assassins, just as they were about McVeigh, as well as other 'lone nuts' who followed him. Many times, these alternate narratives involved claims that the particular shooter under discussion had been set up by the CIA, FBI or both, and sometimes that they were hypnotized/brainwashed/programmed assassins of the Manchurian Candidate variety.

In April 1995, Lone Wolf Timothy McVeigh joined a long line of disaffected, listless and fantasy-prone American males who commit highly public violent crimes. Media outlets and commentators frequently made comparisons between McVeigh and nearly all of the previous Lone Gunmen, although none so much as Lee Harvey Oswald, with whom he appeared to have the most in common. His defense attorney Stephen Jones described McVeigh as a demonized symbol of American Terror and on several occasions likened him to Oswald. For instance, in 1997, *The Toronto Star* deemed both Oswald and McVeigh "blank slate[s] on which the nightmare side of American life can be projected ... spiritual brothers [and] true representatives of a type that emerges every now and then to act out a recurring American nightmare." The article pointed out the many similarities shared by Oswald and McVeigh. Both came from broken homes, were bullied as children, loved guns, joined the military and subsequently left under "a cloud of unknowns." Both grew frustrated by their many life failures, by their mid-twenties had achieved infamy by committing highly public murders and, ultimately, died in a storm of publicity nearly as intense as that surrounding the acts they committed. The article closed with the warning that acts like Oswald and McVeigh's "will happen again [in America], surely ... on some day when its inhabitants are not expecting bloodshed."[10]

In the second edition of their book, released in 1995, Conway and Siegelman discussed "the rise in reported incidents of people snapping suddenly and violently [and] sensational crimes, mass slayings and quieter instances of people snapping in everyday life situations." Average, everyday people were being "pushed to the breaking point and beyond" and becoming "anxious ... confused ... overwhelmed ... overloaded ... vulnerable to manipulation and ultimately less capable of thinking and acting as fully human beings." They attributed this situation to "traumatic social, political and technological transitions in cultures besieged by fanatical mindsets and apocalyptic messages," "masses of information, mountains of technology and an explosion of new experiences, increased pressures on minds and bodies, new strains of illnesses, spreading social turmoil, and the breakdown of basic human bonds and supporting social structures."

In this second edition, Conway and Siegelman included chapters about the events at Waco and the OKC bombing, using the actions of Timothy McVeigh as the latest example of prolonged snapping. To them, both Waco and the OKC bombing indicated a much larger group of "vulnerable minds [that] have increasing difficulty distinguishing literal messages from metaphors." They noted an increased suggestibility found in children who 'space out' while consuming television or film media and pointed out that, by the time they reach adolescence, the average American has spent tens of thousands of hours in front of television sets, has watched as many murders and "engineered acts of violence" and has been exposed to hundreds of thousands of commercials filled with "arbitrary symbols of coded commands and meaning." (Although not noted by the authors, McVeigh had watched the fire that killed the Davidians at Waco live on television while the Davidians themselves likely only watched live TV on any regular basis in the hours leading up to their deaths). The authors concluded that "the profusion of engineered images, experiences and environments" had not only undermined traditional institutions" (ex., nuclear family, education, work, government, religion) but "made information stress a fact of life" and ominously (but accurately) warned readers that "the phenomenon [of increased snapping] seems to be accelerating as a tumultuous millennium approaches."[11]

In the years following the 1995 Oklahoma City bombing (and the second edition of *Snapping*), a slew of highly dramatic and public mass shootings and other spectacles of terror and death occurred, several during the writing of this book. Unlike many of the previous acts of often random and always highly public violence, these newer and increasingly frequent spectacles seemed to have less defined, or sometimes no clear political motivation other than the frustrations of the violent actors.

Stories told about these newer Lone Gunmen inevitably reflected recurring elements found in those told about other legendary infamous American assassins and gunmen in history. All the Lone Nuts are predictably and, without fail, compared to Timothy McVeigh, himself an archetype; and his name is shorthand for young, angry and violent dealers of unexpected mass death. The modern day Oswalds, Hinkleys, Whitmans and Chapmans are likewise regularly depicted as alienated, disaffected, bullied, anti-social loners; young men lost in a violent fantasy world inspired by and drawing upon recurring images, archetypes and 'cultural scripts' in popular media. Their construction and enactment of these scripts has been attributed to a number of actual or perceived intolerable life circumstances and dysfunctions (psychological, familial, social, cultural and political) shared by the loners.

COLUMBINE

Eric Harris and Dylan Klebold, both seventeen years old, are credited with ushering in the "Age of the Mass Shooter" and the "American School Shooting Epidemic" on the morning of April 20, 1999 (Hitler's birthday), when they arrived at their high school in Columbine, Colorado, bearing an array of illegally purchased guns and explosives. During their subsequent shooting spree, they killed thirteen and wounded thirty-one others before killing themselves. Fellow students later described Harris and Klebold as "outcasts" who obsessively surfed the Internet, played video games and had, in the year leading to the shooting, adopted a paramilitary fashion style. Others noted that the shooters held extremist anarchistic and unabashedly racist political views, and had an interest in the "Doomsday" prophecies of Nostradamus.

Nothing indicated that either had an abusive or in any way troubled home life and no "comfortable or familiar psychological explanation based in individual trauma [could] explain" their act. Rather, they were reportedly inspired by Oklahoma bomber Timothy McVeigh; all three the victims of "vivid millennial dreams." While not the first school shooting or random public one, the distinctive style in which they carried out their horrific fantasy, at the time the deadliest school shooting in American history, changed discourses about violence and the ensuing media spectacle they starred in gained them celebrity, inspiring "copycat" shooters.[12]

LUKE HELDER

In 2002, twenty-one year old Luke Helder injured six people with eighteen pipe bombs filled with BBs and nails and left in mailboxes rigged to detonate upon opening. Along with the bombs were notes detailing Helder's anti-government beliefs and warnings that "mailboxes are exploding." Helder had placed the bombs in locations over a distance of 3,200 miles including Iowa, Illinois, Nebraska, Colorado and Texas. He had chosen his targets so that the bombs would create a smiley face across the United States map (an idea he borrowed from the 1999 film *Fight Club*).

Helder, a seemingly average kid by most accounts, was in a three-piece grunge rock band called Apathy whose only CD was titled *Sacks of People*. His professors at the University of Minnesota, which he attended at the time, described him as a good, quiet and polite student. Just prior to the bombings, Helder sent a six-page letter to his school newspaper explaining how each person has the ability to create their own reality and that "once you begin to realize the potential you have as a consciousness/soul/spirit, you will begin to harness the abilities you have to produce realities." He described the bombs as "attention getters" and explained, "I'm taking very drastic measures in an attempt to provide this information to you... I will die/change in the end for this, but that's ok, hahaha paradise awaits! I'm dismissing a few individuals from reality, to change all of you for the better.... I'm doing this because I care ... In the end you will know I was telling you the truth anyway." Helder later said that both the bombings and the manifesto were intended to gather media attention so that he could inform the public about government control and promote marijuana legalization and astral projection. Helder was found incompetent to stand trial in 2004 and remanded to the Federal Medical Center in Rochester, Minnesota, where he remains.[13]

SEUNG-HUI CHO

At 6:47 AM, on April 16, 2007, after a 5-year respite from the massive carnage caused by these snappers, twenty-three year old college senior Seung-Hui Cho, armed with .22 caliber and 9mm semi-automatic handguns entered a dormitory on the Virginia Polytechnic Institute and State University (Virginia Tech) campus and shot and killed two students. He then went to his own room, changed his clothes, deleted his emails and removed the hard drive from his computer. About two hours later, Cho went to a post office near the campus and, using the name 'A. Ishmael' for the return address, mailed some of his writings and a video tape to NBC News. He then walked back to campus and, carrying a backpack containing chains, locks, a hammer, nineteen 10 and 15 round magazines, 400 rounds of ammunition and his guns, entered a building full of Engineering classrooms and lecture halls, chained the front door shut and placed a note on it warning that if the door was opened, a bomb would go off. Cho proceeded to the second floor, looked inside several classrooms, entered one and opened fire. He eventually murdered thirty students and professors and wounded seventeen more before fatally shooting himself in the head. When the body was examined, the words 'Ismael Ax' were found scrawled on his arm.

Cho, a remarkably shy and quiet individual, suffered from selective mutism, severe depression and anxiety. He had been subjected to merciless bullying prior to and during his time as a student at Virginia Tech. In 2005, he was accused of stalking two female students and his English teacher complained about his bizarre classroom behaviors and disturbing writings. After an investigation, he was declared mentally ill and ordered to get treatment if he wanted to continue to attend school.

In a suicide note left in his dorm room prior to the shooting, Cho railed against "rich kids," "debauchery" and "deceitful charlatans." The package sent to NBC contained pictures of Cho holding his guns, his 1,800-word "manifesto," and 27 videos of himself in which he aimed his guns at the camera, ranted about the rich, compared himself to Jesus and extolled other "martyrs like Eric [Klebold] and Dylan [Harris]." In one, Cho stated, "You had a hundred billion chances and ways to have avoided today but you decided to spill my blood. You forced me into a corner and gave me only one option. The decision was yours. Now you have blood on your hands that will never wash off. You just loved to crucify me. You loved inducing cancer in my head, terror in my heart and ripping my soul all this time." In another he said, "I didn't have to do this. I could have left. I could have fled. But no, I will no longer run. It's not for me. For my children, for my brothers and sisters that you fuck, I did it for them."

The Virginia Tech Review Panel concluded that Cho was unable to handle the stress and fright he felt about the many responsibilities he would face after graduating and thus, created and became immersed within a fantasy in which "he would be remembered as the savior of the oppressed, the downtrodden, the poor and the rejected [...] His thought processes were so distorted that he began arguing to himself that his evil plan was actually doing good. His destructive fantasy was now becoming an obsession."[14]

In the aftermath of the "Virginia Tech massacre," as it came to be known, a number of troubling questions were raised. Proper emergency response measures were re-evaluated, as were privacy laws that prevented school officials from learning of Cho's previous mental health issues. The year after the shooting, gun control legislation was signed into law that mandated improvements to federal databases used to determine eligibility for gun purchases.

Major Nidal Malik Hassan

Ongoing debates on whether mass shootings constitute acts of terrorism, legally or in practice, became more salient when, on November 9, 2009, thirty-nine year old Major Nidal Malik Hassan, an Islamic U.S. Army psychiatrist, arrived at work armed with a semi-automatic pistol fitted with two laser sights, a .357 revolver and over 3000 rounds of ammunition. Hassan sat at a cafeteria table briefly, suddenly got up from his seat, yelled "Allahu Akbar!" and then began shooting at uniformed personnel. A civilian police officer shot him, leaving Hassan permanently paralyzed from the waist down, but not before Hassan had killed thirteen people and wounded more than thirty others.

Upon graduating high school, Hassan joined the Army and attended college while serving as an enlisted soldier. He earned a bachelor's degree in biochemistry from Virginia Tech and a medical degree from the Uniformed Services University of the Health Sciences in 2003. While an intern and resident at Walter Reed Medical Center from 2003 until 2009, he completed a Masters in Public Health and a two-year fellowship in Disaster and Preventative Psychiatry at the school's Center For Traumatic Stress. Hassan received poor evaluations from his superiors and was reprimanded for substandard work. Students and faculty there found him to be "socially isolated," "deeply troubled," "disconnected," "aloof," "paranoid," "belligerent," and "schizoid." On a number of occasions, his colleagues reported his strange behaviors to superiors and in 2008, the staff and board of directors called a meeting to discuss the reports.

In the summer of 2009, Hassan began working at the Soldier Readiness Processing Center at Ft. Hood, treating soldiers immediately before and after deployment. His colleagues there described him as "anti-American" and, at one point, the FBI had even conducted an investigation into Hassan's online correspondence with known Islamic radicals. One family member said Hassan became noticeably more agitated after his parents' deaths in 1998 and 2001. Another told of Hassan's complaints of being harassed and discriminated against at work because he was a practicing Muslim and had expressed his desire to leave the military. And yet another said that Hassan became appalled and turned against the U.S. after hearing stories from patients who had recently returned from Iraq and Afghanistan. About a month before the shootings, Hassan was notified that he would be deployed to Afghanistan, and he began to give away his belongings. He began visiting a gun range where he became proficient at hitting silhouette targets from up to 100 yards away.

An Army sanity board found Hassan sane and fit to stand trial. While the Department of Defense classified the incident as 'Workplace Violence,' a Senate report described the Fort Hood shootings as "the worst terrorist attack on U.S. soil since September 11, 2001." Media outlets noted that Hassan represented the most recent example of Lone Wolf Terrorists self-radicalized by the Internet.[15] Hassan was found guilty and sentenced to death.

JARED LEE LOUGHNER

On January 8, 2011, twenty-four year-old *loner* Jared Lee Loughner appeared at a crowded supermarket parking lot in Tucson, Arizona, where Democratic Congresswoman Gabrielle Giffords was holding a "meet-n-greet" for her constituents. Loughner opened fire on the crowd gathered there, killing six and wounding thirteen others, including Giffords, who barely survived. Upon his arrest, Loughner, who appeared calm, said he pled the Fifth and stated, "I just want you to know that I'm the only person that knew about this." When the FBI searched his house, they found bomb-making components locked away in a safe.

A friend of Loughner's said he had a troubled home life and was constantly the brunt of his father's criticisms and anger about "minor things." Others who knew him said that, growing up, Loughner had been a "talented musician" but was "shy" and had "low self-esteem." Still others described him as generally a "happy, friendly, well-liked," "sweet [and] caring" kid. A number of people noted that in the years leading to the shooting, his personality changed drastically and "he just wasn't the same." Loughner became increasingly "withdrawn," "detached," "weird," noticeably "disturbed," "someone you couldn't figure out," an "oddball and "social outcast" whose internal world had clearly gone "awry."

After dropping out of high school in 2006, Loughner began working at Quizno's restaurant and volunteering at a local animal shelter, but was dismissed from both because of a seeming inability to "understand or comprehend" instructions. He was arrested in 2006 for underage drinking and in 2007 for possessing marijuana and related paraphernalia. According to a close friend, when Loughner gave up drinking and smoking pot in late 2008, "his theories got worse … he was just off the wall." He stopped hanging out with friends and devoted most of his time to sleeping in order to "lucid dream," a topic he had become increasingly obsessed with. He faithfully kept a dream diary and developed a fascination with "semantics and how the world is really nothing – illusion," and told his friend that he'd come to the conclusion that words had no meaning. Loughner attended a Gifffords campaign question and answer event, where he asked, "If words could not be understood, then what does government mean," a question answered only by the silence of the room. Loughner felt that Giffords skirted his question and, in the years to come, occasionally expressed his dislike for her and his opinion that she was a "phony."

In 2008, Loughner called the police to report that somebody was impersonating him online, including having set up a fake MySpace account in his name with an accompanying picture of him. That same year, he attempted to join the Army but was rejected and deemed "unqualified." One friend, who had not seen Loughner since high school, said that when they met again in 2010, his old friend had become "anti-government" and seemed "radically different [than before and asked] random, weird questions that didn't go together…"

In February 2010, Loughner enrolled in community college where he often confused his teachers and classmates with meandering mumblings and random rants during class about the end of the world, government conspiracies, the monetary system, terrorism and faked space flights. Eventually, in September 2010, after becoming the subject of at least 51 campus public safety reports detailing his strange and erratic behaviors, he was suspended from attending classes pending the results of a mental health evaluation. As he refused to do so, he did not return to school. Rather, he developed a sudden but strong interest in firearms which he then started to purchase (including those he used in the shooting) and created and posted a number of disturbing You Tube videos including one that claimed college was unconstitutional and "one of the biggest scams in America."

School suspension did not dampen his interests and, in a video he made just weeks before the shooting, Loughner told his viewers, "My favorite activity is conscience dreaming; the greatest inspiration for my political business information. Some of you don't dream – sadly.... My ambition – is for informing literate dreamers about a new currency; in a few days, you know I'm conscience dreaming! Thank you!" In another, Loughner accused the government of brainwashing the populace through grammar, religion and false currency and asked (as he had years earlier), "*What is government if words have no meaning?*" In yet another internet post, Loughner announced, "there are important figures in my dreams.... Hitler, Hilary [sic.] Clinton and Giffords to name a few" and described himself as "a sleepwalker – who turns off the alarm clock."

Nor did his suspension from school temper his growing political obsessions. Besides his occasional rants about Giffords, he would also become enraged by images of "George W. Bush or [when] discussing what he considered to be the nefarious designs of government." He believed in conspiracy theories about the illegitimacy of the U.S. dollar, the 9/11 attacks, the existence of a New World Order and the impending 2012 apocalypse. Among the pictures he posted to his MySpace profile was a handgun placed upon a document titled "United States History."

At 4:12 AM on the morning of the shooting, Loughner's MySpace post stated "Goodbye friends. Please don't be mad at me. The literacy rate is below 5%. I haven't talked to one person who is literate. I want to make it out alive. The longest war in the history of the United States. Goodbye. I'm saddened with the current currency and job employment. I had a bully at school. Thank you. P.S. – Plead the Fifth!"

Loughner's arrest photo was quite disturbing; described by the *Washington Post* as "smirking and creepy, with hollow eyes ablaze." When asked about his possible motives, a close friend said to, "promote chaos," and compared Loughner's mindset to that of the Batman's nemesis, the Joker, who "fucks things up to fuck shit up, there's no rhyme or reason, he wants to watch the world burn. He probably wanted to take everyone out of their monotonous lives ... to take people out of these norms that he thought society had trapped us in."

Following his arrest, court-appointed mental health professionals diagnosed Loughner with paranoid schizophrenia and declared him incompetent to stand trial. He spent several months at a federal prison medical facility where he was forcibly administered a cocktail of psychotropic drugs, regained his sanity, and in August 2012, pled guilty to all charges against him, thereby avoided the death penalty. Loughner was given seven life sentences without parole plus 140 years and is incarcerated at the U.S. Medical Center for Federal Prisoners in Springfield, Missouri.[16]

Oscar Ramiro Ortega-Hernandez

On November 11, 2011, twenty-three year old Oscar Ramiro Ortega-Hernandez drove two thousand miles from Idaho Falls, Idaho to Washington, D.C., and fired at least eight rounds from an AK-47 style semi-automatic assault rifle at the White House. He quickly drove away but crashed (ironically) in front of the United States Institute of Peace, after which he fled on foot until, five days later, authorities located and apprehended him in Indiana, Pennsylvania. He did not resist arrest.

According to friends, he had railed against the wars in Iraq and Afghanistan and talked about Global Positioning Systems chips injected into people by the Federal government and their use of fluoride and aspartame to control Americans. On a number of occasions, he had told friends that he was "on a mission from God" to kill President Barack Obama, whom he called "the anti-Christ" and "the devil." In March 2011, he purchased more than 1,200 rounds of ammunition, the firearm used in the shooting, and a scope kit. For the next six months, he practiced shooting in desolate areas near his home. That October he made two videos that he posted on YouTube. In them, he described himself as a "cold-hearted warrior of God," praised Osama bin Laden for standing up to the United States, called for revolution against the federal government and announced, "It's time for Armageddon!" During his trial, he pled not guilty and claimed that someone had stolen his car, that he did not shoot at the White House, and that his statements to that effect after his arrest were coerced by the Secret Service. Ortega-Hernandez was found guilty, sentenced to twenty-five years in prison for terrorism and related weapons offenses and ordered to pay $94,000 in restitution.[17]

James Holmes

On July 20, 2012, twenty-four year old James Holmes, with newly-dyed bright neon orange hair, wearing earphones blasting techno music, dressed in full SWAT riot gear, a gas mask and wielding a virtual arsenal of guns, entered a sold-out midnight premier showing of the newest Batman movie *The Dark Knight Rises* in Aurora, Colorado. Just as the film's opening sequence of violence began, Holmes set off gas or smoke canisters and then opened fire on unsuspecting audience members, killing twelve and wounding seventy others. Upon his apprehension outside the theatre, he did not attempt to resist arrest. Rather, he identified himself to authorities as Batman's longstanding nemesis "The Joker" and told police that he had placed booby traps around his apartment. As promised, investigators found his apartment loaded with a complex network of explosive booby trap devices (including home-made napalm) which, despite their sophistication, failed to go off. They also found Batman paraphernalia and other "evidence of his apparent obsession with the comic book hero."

In elementary school, Holmes, who grew up in an upper-middle-class suburban home, was "nice," well behaved, polite, easy to get along with, popular, and "extremely intelligent." He always helped to take care of his younger sister and (like McVeigh) entertained other kids in the neighborhood by building an amusing but not too scary haunted house during the Halloween season. Holmes himself later said he became obsessed with killing when he was just 10 years old, an obsession, he said, which became more realistic for him over time. By high school, he had become, according to classmates and his former coach, a sullen, increasingly withdrawn, "creepy," "quiet loner," "a kind of a shadow figure ... part of us but not part of us ... hard to get to know [and] pretty invisible." During his senior year of high school in 2006, Holmes was an intern at the Salk Institute for Biological Studies where his supervisor described him as socially awkward, uncommunicative and stubborn. He was diagnosed with depression and once became so frustrated that he pulled out his hair; so much that he was left with a bald spot on the back of his head.

After graduating high school, Holmes attended the University of California at Riverside where, in 2010, he studied neuroscience and graduated in the top 1% of his class. Letters of recommendation by his teachers described him as "a very effective group leader" and a person who "takes an active role in his education, and brings a great amount of intellectual and emotional maturity into the classroom." In 2011, he was accepted into a highly competitive neuroscience PhD program at the University Of Colorado Anschutz Medical School and received a $21,600 grant from the National Institutes of Health and a $5,000 stipend from the University of Colorado, Denver. Holmes, it turned out, had a longstanding interest in "fantasy versus reality." In a home video made during this time, he explained to his peers at a science camp that he was working on the concept of "temporal illusion [which is] an illusion that allows you to change the past" and spoke of carrying on his mentor's interest in "subjective experience [or] what takes place inside the mind as opposed to the external world." The next year, however, his academic performance began to suffer. In the spring of 2012 he received poor grades on his comprehensive exams and, after failing a critical oral exam in early June, chose to withdraw from the PhD program.

Afterwards, he broke up with the only girlfriend he'd ever had, warning her to stay away from him "because I am bad news bears" and confiding that he thought he might be suffering from 'dysphoric mania,' a type of bipolar disorder, whose episodes, one psychiatrist said, include "[getting] this idea of doing something and even if your mind [tells you not to], your body moves you forward." His now ex-girlfriend urged him to seek counseling. He'd already tried that. In the months leading to Holmes' rampage, he sought help for his deteriorating mental health on several occasions from at least three campus mental health professionals. After he confessed to one of them that he wanted to kill people, the campus police were called but they declined to hospitalize him.

In the weeks before and after withdrawing from his PhD program, Holmes legally purchased two Glock 22 pistols, a Remington 870 Express Tactical shotgun, a M&P Smith & Wesson semi-automatic rifle, 6350 rounds of various kinds of ammunition and a Blackhawk Urban Assault Vest. Less than a month before the killings, Holmes filled out an application to join a local gun club. The owner of the club said that when he attempted to call Holmes back, he heard a "bizarre ... freaky... guttural ... incoherent and rambling" voice mail, "like [he] was trying to be as weird as possible." Holmes was not admitted to the gun club.

Weeks before the shooting, Holmes took a series of "menacing" selfies with his orange hair and wearing black contact lenses. The day before his rampage, he mailed his campus counselor a notebook in which he had repeatedly scrawled the question "Why?" The notebook detailed his internal debate about the best method of murdering a large amount of people and outlined the pros and cons involved in various methods under consideration including old-fashioned serial killing, biological weapons, and bombs. He then debated the best location for such an act and while he considered an airport, ultimately decided that beyond the "substantial" security at an airport, they had "too much of a terrorist history [and] terrorism isn't the message." In fact, he wrote, "the message is there is no message. Most fools will misinterpret correlation for causation, namely, relationship and work failures as causes. Both were expediting catalysts, not the reason. Causation being my state of mind for the past 15 years." That settled, he chose his target, concluding, "Finally, the last escape, mass murder at the theatre."

Although after his arrest, commentators remarked that Holmes was undoubtedly delusional, his bizarre behavior during court appearances led some to question whether he was really crazy or just acting a part in order to evade execution. Holmes first pled not guilty but after federal prosecutors announced their intention to seek the death penalty, he changed his plea to "not guilty by reason of insanity" and was ordered to undergo psychiatric evaluations. To the evaluating psychiatrist he explained that at the time of his arrest, he was under the belief that he'd only killed 3 people and wounded 20 and described his victims as simply "numbers ... a conglomerate mass ... not real people ... just kind of amorphous people...," whom he could barely see through his gas mask. Except for one man whom Holmes said remained in the front row of the theatre smiling at him right up until the end when he decided to stop shooting and calmly headed to his car. He would never forget *that* guy.

When asked why he committed such an atrocity, Holmes explained that, "If you take away a life, it adds to your own value ... anything they would have done or, like, pursued, gets canceled out and given to me," a concept he said he'd drawn from economic theory. In the end, he continued, it was either kill them or kill himself. Killing them jolted him out of his depression. Still, he added, he believed the feds had been following him in the weeks leading to the shooting and had hoped the FBI would arrest him and lock him away before he could carry out his meticulously calculated attack.

He was diagnosed with schizophrenia, delusional psychosis as well as schizoaffective, borderline, narcissistic, anxious, avoidant, and obsessive-compulsive personality disorders but, despite this, and despite his smearing feces on the walls of his prison cell, was found 'legally sane' and sentenced to 12 life sentences plus 3,318 years. During his trial, Holmes, on a cocktail of anti-psychotic medication, remained emotionless and declined to speak in his own defense.[18]

WADE MICHAEL PAGE

Unfortunately, Holmes was only one in what would be a long series of deranged acts committed by fantasy-prone Lone Gunmen that year and the two years following. On August 5, 2012, forty-one year old Wade Michael Page entered into a Sikh temple in Wisconsin, shot and killed six individuals and wounded four others before killing himself. Page, a former Army Psychological Operations specialist until 1998, had a history of bad conduct while in the Army and was very vocal about his white supremacist beliefs. The Southern Poverty Law Center had been monitoring Page's racist online ramblings for twelve years prior to the shootings.[19]

ADAM LANZA

Just a few months later, on December 14, 2012, twenty-year old Adam Lanza shot his mother with her .22 caliber rifle while she lay in bed, took her car, drove to nearby Sandy Hook Elementary School, fired 154 shots with a semiautomatic rifle, killed six adults and twenty children and then killed himself. All of the firearms used in the massacre were legal and registered to his mother.

Classmates described the "pale, tall, scrawny" and autistic Lanza as "a wicked smart kid" who "excelled in everything" and graduated three years earlier than the rest of his class but also a "kind of weird," "socially awkward," "shy and quiet," "remote," "recluse" and nearly "unknowable" individual who had a "turbulent childhood." His parents' separation, they said, had "hit the [Lanza] children hard," and that Adam, in particular, seemed "really depressed" and even "devastated" by it. Taunted by bullies at school and in the neighborhood, Lanza spent a lot of time alone in his mother's basement playing modern warfare video games including, among others, *Call of Duty*. Even as a small child, one relative remembered, Lanza dreamed of joining the U.S. Marine Corps. He had a keen interest in "aliens" and sometimes talked about "blowing things up." A search of the Lanza home revealed that he "lived amid a stockpile of disparate weaponry and macabre keepsakes" including a military-style uniform and newspaper clippings of other mass shooters in his attempt to "Outkill [the] Norway Nut Job." Like them, Lanza, "obscure in life [became] infamous in death."[20]

Aaron Alexis

The following year, on September 16, 2013, thirty-four year old African-American and former Naval Reservist, Aaron Alexis, arrived at a Washington D. C. Navy Yard, where he worked as a contractor servicing the Navy's Internet system in the Navy Sea Systems Command building. First using an 870 Remington sawed-off shotgun and then a Beretta handgun taken from a security guard whom he shot, Alexis opened fire, methodically killing fourteen people and wounding four others. When officers arrived, a firefight ensued during which Alexis himself was killed. Alexis is an exception to the fact that mass shooters have overwhelmingly been young white males, though discontented Muslims in the military are seemingly a growing threat.

Although described as a "polite" kid and "typical teenager," throughout his adult life Alexis displayed disturbing, "bizarre" and "alarming" behaviors. In 2004, at the age of twenty-five, Alexis had walked out of his grandmother's house and, later claiming to be frustrated over the parking situation there, shot three rounds from a .45 caliber pistol at the car of a nearby construction worker. He later explained to police that he had PTSD and had blacked out and only later remembered shooting at the car. His troubles, he told them, began when he participated in rescue and recovery operations in Manhattan on September 11, 2001.

In 2007, Alexis joined the Naval Reserves where he fixed electrical systems on airplanes. Despite being awarded a National Defense Service

Medal and a Global War on Terror Medal, while in the Reserves, he displayed a "pattern of misbehavior" and was cited for misconduct at least eight times before receiving an honorable discharge in 2011. Such misbehavior carried into his personal life as well, and once, in 2010, he fired a handgun into his ceiling, the bullet penetrating his upstairs neighbors' floor. He told police he accidently fired while cleaning his gun.

After his discharge from the service, Alexis retained his secret level security clearance, which allowed him to do sensitive military work for The Experts, a contracting company that serviced the Navy's Internet system. His job kept him on the road and living in hotels and, in the seven months prior to his final shooting, Alexis worked at seven different military bases in a number of states. Friends said that during the summer of 2012, Alexis became increasingly depressed, withdrawn and suffered from insomnia and compared him to "Dr. Jekyll and Mr. Hyde." After one bout of prolonged insomnia that kept him awake for three days, he sought treatment at two different VA hospitals.

In August 2012, the Newport, Rhode Island police department issued a report sent to a local Naval Base where Alexis had been cleared to work, warning that he suffered from hallucinations and was hearing voices. His employers took no action, but after making inquiries and finding him to be "unstable" they planned to recall him. Alexis held an increasingly obsessive belief he was being "targeted," controlled or influenced by Extremely Low Frequency (ELF) electro-magnetic waves. About a month and a half before the Naval Yard shooting and weeks before the police issued their warning, Alexis called 911 and reported that he was hearing voices of three individuals emanating from the "walls, floors and ceiling" of his Rhode Island hotel room. He told the dispatcher that the voices, which were keeping him awake, belonged to individuals who were following him and were being deployed from "some sort of microwave machine." Alexis said he was afraid the people were going to hurt him. In a letter found on his laptop after the shooting, Alexis wrote, "Ultra-low frequency attack is what I've been subject to for the last three months and to be perfectly honest that is what has driven me to this." On the Remington he used during the attack, Alexis had carved the words "My ELF Weapon," "End to the torment!" "Not what ya'll say" and "Better off this way!" While often used in sub-tonal submarine communications, various news outlets pointed out that among "conspiracy theorists" ELF denotes a technology deployed by the government to harass, monitor and manipulate individuals, a growing number of whom believe, like Alexis, that they are "Targeted Individuals," (or TI's).[21]

PAUL ANTHONY CIANCIA
On the morning of November 1, 2013, twenty-three year old Paul Anthony Ciancia, armed with a Smith & Wesson .223-caliber assault rifle

and carrying hundreds of rounds of ammunition, arrived at the Los Angeles International airport and entered a terminal, where he had apparently stashed a rifle and three clips. Then, in an "eerie" and "methodological" manner, he began shooting Transportation Security Administration (TSA) agents, killing one and wounding at least seven other individuals (both civilian and TSA). Soon after the rampage began, two LAX airport neutralized Ciancia by shooting him four times, including in the face. Ciancia, who "stared into space" during his arrest, was sedated upon his detainment and, for days, remained unresponsive. Towards the end of that month, Ciancia was released from the hospital and taken to a treatment facility to complete his recovery. In March 2014, he was transferred to a Federal detention facility to await his trial and in January 2015, prosecutors announced that they would seek the death penalty against him.

According to law enforcement officials, the duffle bag Ciancia carried with him during his killing spree contained "anti-government literature outlining conspiracy theories" and a one-page manifesto that exclaimed, "F U Janet Napolitano," (former Chief of Homeland Security) whom he described in it as a "bull dyke." In his writing, Ciancia detailed his "disappointment in the government," railed against the TSA's intrusive airport security searches and other government violations of privacy, and spoke of a "fiat currency," the illegitimacy of the Federal Reserve and the abuses of the "NWO"; a term countless media outlets explained referred to the New World Order – "a conspiracy theory that foresees a totalitarian one-world government" run by "secret elites" bent on sabotaging American freedoms. Ciancia expressed that, while he had "made the decision to try and kill ... TSA and pigs" in order to "instill fear in their traitorous minds" and didn't care if they were "black, white, yellow, brown, I don't discriminate," he had no interest in hurting "innocent people." Witnesses to the shooting noted that he seemed to target only TSA agents.

A local police officer in the blue-collar New Jersey town where Ciancia grew up who knew his family told reporters that Ciancia came from "a very good family. Whatever happened, it had nothing to do with his upbringing." Those who knew Ciancia remembered him as a shy, quiet and awkward teenager who played French horn, dressed all in black, seemed to have a speech impediment and was bullied in high school. One classmate said of Ciancia, "He kept to himself and ate lunch alone a lot ... I really don't remember any one person who was close to him....In four years, I never heard a word out of his mouth.... He was quiet and people would take advantage of that." Many others stated that Ciancia had never shown signs of anger or acted out violently and had no previous mental health issues although, they added, something seemed to have come over him in the years after graduating high school, perhaps set off by the death of his mother in 2009. Days before the shooting, Ciancia's brother received a text from him stating he was "thinking of taking his life" and so informed their father who, the morning of the shooting, unable to locate or contact his son, called the Los Angeles police and requested they check on him. But, by then, it was too late.[22]

JUSTIN BOURQUE

Between 2000 and 2008, an average of five mass shootings per year occurred in the United States. Those numbers spiked after 2008, with fifteen mass shootings in 2013. Mass shootings continued at an increased frequency throughout 2014.[23] The carnage caused by the lone nuts has not been exclusive to the U.S. On June 4, 2014, twenty-four year old Moncton, New Brunswick resident Justin Bourque, clad in camouflage fatigues, a matching bandana, and an ammunition belt and toting a knife, a pump-action shotgun, a semi-automatic rifle and a crossbow, calmly and purposefully walked down the residential streets of Ryder Park, where he lived at trailer #13. Bourque, said witness, looked "like a man on a mission." Said another, "He just had this blank state on his face, just a dead look in his eyes. He was calm as could be. He was just walking at a steady pace. It wasn't fast. It wasn't slow. He did not waver, not even to avoid a pothole." Within minutes, the police received a barrage of calls from concerned neighbors.

The responding officers arrived and proceeded on foot towards Bourque who laid in wait in a nearby wooded area. Upon spotting them, he opened fire, killing three police officers and wounding two others, all the while occasionally yelling out warnings to civilians to stay out of the way. A manhunt ensued, during which time over 300 police searched for Bourque in nearby wooded areas using dogs, armored vehicles and thermal imaging-equipped helicopters. Residents were asked to stay inside and lock their doors and schools, businesses and public transportation shut down. Thirty hours later, a SWAT team found Bourque in a nearby yard and apprehended him. He surrendered without incident, telling officers, "I'm done."

Bourque grew up in a close-knit Roman Catholic family with his six siblings who, along with himself, were all home-schooled. Countless friends and neighbors described the Bourque family as a loving and supportive one. Bourque himself later said that his home life was defined by religious fanaticism and he was taught to believe he was a soldier for Jesus. He recalled that, as a child, he wanted everybody to like him and looked up to the popular videogame character Mega Man X, a member of a robot military task force who must prevent his villain counterpart from wiping out all of humanity. He built model tanks and played with "little green army men" with his friends who recalled that Bourque wanted to join the armed forces, that or become an archeologist who hunted dinosaur bones.

In his late teens and early twenties he developed a love of music, played guitar, wore heavy-metal T-shirts and played *Call of Duty* for hours on end with his friends who also described him as "a great guy, very chilled, down to earth," a "big comedian." He was always doing impressions of popular culture icons like Beavis and Butthead; perhaps "quirky" but always a good and loyal friend. He was an avid hunter and, like McVeigh, had a life-long interest in firearms, collected them (legally) and was known to be very contentious about gun safety. His profile pictures on social media sites depicted him in camouflage and posing with his guns, sometimes alone and sometimes with friends. He tried to join the military at sixteen and eighteen but, lacking a high school diploma, was rejected on both occasions. He graduated high school at nineteen, but by that time was too busy drinking and smoking pot to try again.

A few years prior to the shooting, Bourque got a job at Walmart. Co-workers there said he "seemed friendly enough," but was "a little bit of an outcast" and "always seemed to have a problem with authority. Issues with parents, bosses, police [and] seemed to have a hate on for everything." He once casually discussed how, someday, he would "go out with a bang and take people with him." When a group of co-workers invited him on a camping trip, he "brought his rifle with him, without ammunition, which he held on to the whole night while drinking ... we didn't invite him the next time." Eventually he was fired from Walmart for "attitude related issues, being defiant, not doing what he was supposed to be doing ..."

According to *Maclean's*, Bourque's "downward spiral" and "disturbing descent" had begun in 2012 after his father kicked him out of the house for bringing home guns after he was told not to. After this, he became preoccupied with "faraway wars," gun ownership rights, a "looming apocalypse" and the desire to "live off the grid." Still, friends said that up until a few months before the rampage Bourque seemed like the guy he had always been, maybe a little weird but definitely unthreatening. In the months leading to the shootings though, Bourque had quit his job at a grocery store and reportedly became obsessed with "conspiracy theories." He regularly posted musings on his Facebook account in which he expressed his frustrations with the government, police, the public's preoccupation with irrelevancy such as the Academy Awards, his support of militias and the right to bear arms and belief that if war were to break out in Canada, the country would be too soft to defend themselves. "So you're okay with the government having the weaponry to annihilate all life on earth but you're upset I have a rifle that holds 30 rounds," one of his posts asked. Said another, "Obey the state, it's the law. Using the phrase 'it's the law' to validate government is a fallacy. As if a codex of pompous and incomprehensible legalese magically validates coercion, theft, intimidation and violence."

In late February 2014, he wrote, "We live under their reign, under crownless kings. Unless the people take notice, fight and destroy the 1% the battle for the future is lost, because the new age of tyrants is already upon us." In March 2014, "the third world war could be right around the corner, wishful thinking isn't gonna stop this one. This will not be like Iraq, NATO is vastly outnumbered by Russia and her allies." A few weeks later, "Canada is one of the world's most likely targets Russia would invade at the start of a war due to pushover resistance." In early April, "Ask yourself, would you fight for the future of your children or grandchildren, or your family and friends, sons and daughters? The answer is: no you're too stupid to know what to fight for, cause we're already losing the silent war you don't wanna believe is happening."

His father said that he and Bourque's mother worried about their son's financial problems and started noticing a marked change in his behavior and attitude. "It started to happen slowly and gradually … his worries and anxieties. His restlessness. His concerns over injustice and wars and stuff like that going on. [He was] over concerned. I wouldn't say paranoid, but very worried.… He was going down, down, down low and there was just nothing we could do to reach him." Concerned, they contacted a family friend and retired police officer; they were told there was nothing that could be done.

The situation suddenly appeared more alarming when in May 2014, Bourque became enraged after a pair of RCMP officers, who had shot and killed Montcon resident Dan Leveque the previous July, were cleared of wrongdoing. One friend recalled Bourque's reaction upon hearing the news. "His exact words were: 'This is absolutely bullshit that the cops can get away with this." Two days before going amok, he told his father he'd had enough of authorities and their oppressive actions. When his father told him that people who think that way end up in jail, Bourque warned that if they ever tried to stop him, he'd be armed, would defend himself and would never submit.

Before he set out on his cop-killing spree, Bourque posted lyrics by Megadeth (an American thrash metal band) on Facebook, placed the key to his gun cabinet on his front steps and his wallet on a table near his front door. His trailer was decorated with heavy-metal posters, a large confederate flag and army-themed action figures. He had a 20-gauge shotgun hung above his bed, a U.S. Army *Improvised Munitions Handbook* and an automatic rifle manual pinned to his wall as well as a pro-assault weapons poster upon which he'd written "I am not a fish, I am a man" and a propane tank with a bullet hole on his kitchen table.

During the manhunt, police posted pictures of Bourque on Twitter, and his friends began to spread news of and speculate about his snapping on Facebook. One wrote, "Fuck he lost it." Another, ""U were a friend man." Some of his friends immediately made connections between Bourque's actions and the lack of accountability for Leveque's death. One wrote that his "most respectable friend [believed it was] necessary to take justice into his own hands and set things right for the family and loved ones of the dead boy." "He's doing this for all of us…. He's righting all the wrongs" said another, to which Leveque's mom responded by writing, "it's cruel to say but I'm going to agree with you."

Upon arrest, Bourque explained to police that his actions were meant to start a rebellion against an oppressive government, commented that he "felt really accomplished" and while he knew how sick that must sound to them, and knew his victims probably had wives and kids, "every soldier has a wife and kids … it's all about whose side you chose." The "soldiers" he killed defended corrupt institutions and protected the rich from the poor and he chided one of his victims for not being a "very combat savvy guy." A court-ordered psychiatric evaluation found that Bourque had felt depressed, was romantically frustrated, "disillusioned and confused from sleep deprivation" at the time of the shooting, having just worked 15 hours on 2 hours sleep, and was "probably also withdrawing from marijuana," something he used regularly, according to the evaluator, in order to help him cope with his disdain for authority figures. Bourque said that, like so many shooters before him, he did not think he would survive his own rampage. Despite his lack of sleep and "reefer madness," Bourque had not been clinically depressed or psychotic at the time of the shooting. He was found sane, pled guilty to all charges and, on October 31, 2014, was sentenced to life without the possibility of parole for 75 years; the harshest sentence issued in Canada since 1962.[24]

The incidents outlined above provoked debates about what, exactly, could have caused these individuals to commit such extraordinary violence, not so much the reasons they themselves offered (when they did) but the real *root* of the problem. Their atrocious acts also catalyzed or reinvigorated public discourse about possible responses, and preventative and punitive measures. To read the commentary, such acts seemed easily preventable if only we could fill in the gaps of a simple formula: Identify the cause by understanding the shooter and implement the proper legislative and social regulations. The initial profile narratives constructed about all of the Lone Gunmen framed the discussions, debates and corresponding proposed solutions that followed.

The frequently suggested causes vary as much as the proposed solutions: The shooters were poorly raised. Spoiled. Abused. Suffered from a lack of attention. Craved attention. Received too much attention. Had defective genes. Defective brains. Were mentally ill without adequate access to voluntary (or involuntary) treatment and services. Were bullied. Socially alienated. Played too many video games. Watched too much television. Grew up in a sick and morally deteriorating society. Were confused and disheartened by pervasive consumerism, unable to live up to ideals largely defined by popular culture and mass media. Were able to purchase firearms (especially semi-automatic weapons) too easily. Held dangerous and hateful ideologies. Believed in conspiracy theories. Were pretty sure the end was nigh. The actions of these deranged loners, psychopathic bullies, victims, dupes and masterminds, we are told, demand, alternately or in combination, stricter gun control legislation, mental health screening and treatment and a host of other measures.[25]

The author of an April 2013 Vice.com article entitled "Conspiracy Theorists Are Dangerous Enemies To Have," said the fact that a quarter of the population believes in conspiracy theories (however undefined) was "infuriating enough to drive rationalists up a tower with a rifle and start shooting"; a nod to Texas tower shooter Charles Whitman. Among the worst and most ironic of these conspiracy theories, other commentators observed, were ones that purport the mass shootings themselves were staged theatrical events.[26]

Different but related are the concerns expressed by some, concerning certain shooters' apocalyptic beliefs about the imminent, cataclysmic end of the world as we know it and their "stockpiling" of weapons; an analysis all the more alarming given a resurgence and growth of the 'survivalist movement' in recent years (now called the "prepper movement"), a social milieu popularly typified by Ted Kaczynski and Tim McVeigh. Evidence of this renewed ideological threat included speculation about the influence that Nancy Lanza, Adam's secretive, high-strung, paranoid, gun toting, survivalist mother, possibly had on her son given her own stockpiling of food and guns based on her reportedly apocalyptic beliefs.[27]

The burgeoning multi-disciplinary academic field of terrorism studies understands terroristic events and actors through multiple social scientific lenses. Timothy McVeigh's face adorns the cover of one "terrorism studies" textbook series entitled *The Psychology of Terrorism* which attempts to understand and therefore prevent terrorism by determining (among other things) the unique psychological traits of terrorists and terrorist subcultures and includes a number of essays that use McVeigh as a case study. One of these, an essay examining the relationship between family dysfunction and acts of terrorism or mass violence, invokes McVeigh as a springboard to discuss psychological fragmentation of traumatized children, and subsequent cycles of trauma the traumatized perpetrators enact upon their victims. Essayist Timothy Gallimore attributes McVeigh's love of guns, racial ideologies and acts of terror to his having been targeted by bullies, his parents' divorce and his military experiences.[28]

More than one essay in the *Psychology of Terrorism* series concerns how and why "end of the world" mentalities are formed. One of these explains that "apocalyptic fantasies" have two key components: "first, the idea that the world will be destroyed, and second, that a remnant of humanity will be rescued from the catastrophe" but only by suffering through a myriad of "trials and tribulations." Old realities now effectively destroyed, the survivor (sometimes a previously practicing survivalist) is then able to help fashion a new post-apocalyptic world. Certainly an attractive circumstance, especially for people who feel they have no control over the fashioning of their current realities, often because of recent destabilizing personal events. While the author concedes that such 'end times' imaginings are a universal phenomenon often accompanied by violent fantasies that in reality help negotiate other underlying psychological conflicts, he expresses concern about the frequency at which "these fantasies lead to violent actions." Another essay says apocalyptic beliefs "derive from excruciating rage and humiliation." Rather than consciously attribute the source of their turmoil to its origin (often parental), it is attributed to an outside evil that, having now been identified as the cause of one's suffering, becomes "amplified to cosmic proportions." Every so often, the essay warns, a terroristic individual, in an act of misguided expression, attempts to exact vengeance upon the real source of suffering by attacking the symbolic stand-in.[29]

A very different approach is taken by Richard G. Mitchell Jr., who opposes linking terrorists with survivalists. In his 2001 book, *Dancing At Armageddon: Survivalism and Chaos in Modern Times,* Mitchell argues that in constructing "'what if' scenarios," so called survivalists are engaging in optimistic fantasy about the types of "creative transcendence [that] calamitous change" might bring; an act he views as rational in the face of an irrational world, proactive rather than reactive, "a novel exploration" of possibility rather than "a retreat from or renouncement of social life," and an examination and "reinterpretation of the cultural assumptions and intrinsic practices that undergird the institutional order." Still, critics of the book argue that Mitchell, in his rush to defend survivalists, ignores their tendency to act violently, often citing McVeigh and Kaczynski as examples.[30]

Somewhat similar to the previously discussed concept of snapping, and shedding additional light upon newer Lone Gunmen, are cultural theories about postmodern hyper-reality; a condition that results from an increasingly virtual "lived" experience in which "every means of consumption is a simulated setting, or has simulated elements, or simulated people, or simulated products. Even those things that still seem real have an increasing number of unreal elements. As a result, it is no longer clear what is real and what is unreal," what is truth, fiction, news and entertainment.[31]

In 2007, immediately after the Virginia Tech shootings, twenty-one year old Ryan Lambourn made headlines and attracted international criticism for his creation of V-Tech Rampage, an online first-person shooter video game based on Cho's massacre, wherein handgun-wielding players control a character who roams a campus and participates in "three levels of stealth and murder" making sure no witnesses are left alive. After the understandable outcry instigated by his game Lambourn, who said he designed the game for "laughs," refused to remove it from the Internet, arguing that it provides an insight into Cho's mindset. In 2013, Lambourn found himself the topic of discussion once again, this time for his newest video game, a first person simulation of Adam Lanza's Sandy Hook elementary school shootings.[32]

The advent of the postmodern era has radically disrupted the notion of identity. In a world rampant with "self-referential illusions and post-modern self-parodies," multiple, simultaneous realities and corresponding selves exist and are greatly informed, even created, by popular media. In 2012, a *Boston Globe* opinion piece expounded on the Batman Shooting, by observing how "it is possible for any of us, of any age or gender, to avoid reality all day in America by keeping our eyes fixed on our screens." While our HD flatscreen smart TV's offer untold numbers of fantasy self-images and masks from which to choose, sometimes, "when we're sold a fantasy that is so well made, that seems to tap so deeply into our very real sense of imminent catastrophe, and that seems so self-aware about the fantasy itself, certain people respond to it as if it's the Truth."[33]

In this way, singular acts of violence themselves constitute re-enactments of holographic wholesale violence as depicted in movies, video games, television, etc., that transform notions of reality into "a terrible nightmare of violence, chaos and cataclysm." Similarly, according to anthropologists Joseba Zulaika and William Douglass, highly public acts of violence "provide [an additional] arena for a chamber of horrors in which imagined events are as possible as factual ones, and the latter are frequently perceived, in their senseless atrocity, as a kind of fictional reality." In fact, the ability for terrorizing events to impact larger social landscapes and collective imaginations depend upon "their being played out on the hyperreal screens of electronic mass media," which themselves provide the models or scripts and inspiration for these acts to begin with.[34]

Oswald read about Huey Long's assassin. Sirhan read about Oswald. Bremer read about Sirhan and wrote about Oswald. Hinkley read about various American assassins including Oswald and was deeply inspired by *Taxi Driver*, a movie based on Bremer. When he drove to OKC the morning of the bombing, McVeigh wore a t-shirt with "Sic Semper Tyrannus" or "Thus Ever To Tyrants" printed on it, the words John Wilkes Booth yelled right after he shot Abraham Lincoln. McVeigh inspired the acts of other disaffected, frustrated, anti-social, loner killers who mentioned McVeigh specifically in their writings. They include Columbine shooters Klebold and Harris, Virginia Tech shooter Cho and Norway shooter Anders Breivik. Lanza kept a sizeable collection of newspaper clippings about previous Lone Gunmen including Breivik and even created a scorecard for each detailing their kill rates. And so it goes. The stories about recent Lone Gunmen (illustrated in the above compilation of media reports) echo those told about Timothy McVeigh, who himself both enacted and expanded upon certain cultural scripts and models.

The linking of McVeigh (with often only scant explanation) to those violent actors who came after him illustrates how the name "McVeigh" itself became and continues to act as cultural shorthand for a number of messy and complex issues for which simple explanations may not exist.[35] In his 2008 book, *Guys and Guns,* about school shooters, Douglas Kellner explained that "cultural studies read texts in their socio-historical contexts [and] situate[s], interpret[s], and trace[s] the effects of certain texts, artifacts and events [and] contextualizes its object in its historical matrix."[36]

Understanding McVeigh

As the FBI and American public sought to understand who, exactly, Timothy McVeigh was, so too did his defense team. When Jones Team mental health expert Lee Norton asked McVeigh about his childhood in June 1995, he told her he simply could not remember much of it, and years later made the same claim to his biographers. Perhaps more understandably, it sometimes seemed as if McVeigh had lost large portions of his memory, especially about the two years leading to the bombing.

Norton, along with defense team investigators, conducted numerous interviews with McVeigh's family and friends, and in the process, uncovered a number of biographical details about their client which he'd rather they not have. Norton observed that the details McVeigh disclosed about his early life seemed idealized and often contradicted numerous accounts of those who knew him. The mental health experts retained by the Jones Team described McVeigh's childhood and family life as lonely, devoid of empathy or affection and, according to one, Dr. Anthony Semone, a perfect environment for the formation of a future terrorist.

Tim became "deeply disturbed" and "displeased" after learning of the mental health experts' findings and opinions about his family and childhood, particularly those of Dr. Norton, whose reports, according to Dr. Semone, brought to light a number of other "family skeletons." His reaction, Semone opined, indicated a "clear affirmation of the presence of a whole lot of material in Tim's life, including the bombing, about which Tim would rather we stay ignorant. Why? The old commentary about the 'Emperor's clothes' seems particularly relevant here." Norton and Semone concluded that, in order to mask inconvenient truths about himself and his family, Tim McVeigh had engaged in a "contextually embedded delusional process" and further, displayed symptoms of an "externalized psychosis." On the other hand, sometimes there were reasons to wonder if some of the strange things he said might have at least some basis in reality. For some members of the Jones Team, a major question concerning the stories McVeigh told was whether he really believed them or not, and bizarre as they seemed, might they actually, even in part, be true? If he believed them and they were *not* true, the team would need to sort delusion from fact; but if any of his stories were true, or based in truth, they were in wholly unfamiliar territory.[37]

During the first year after his arrest, the team spent considerable time attempting to decipher the roots of McVeigh's particular mental and emotional malfunctions. Ultimately though, they found no neurological impairments or any diagnosis that could be used in a mental health defense or that served as justification for his participation in the bombing and Jones Team psychiatrist John R. Smith found McVeigh competent to stand trial.

Still, when taken together, the clinical diagnosis they assigned and profiles they constructed depict him as a narcissistic, fragmented, paranoid, delusional, suggestible, possibly amnesiac man suffering from Post-Traumatic Stress Disorder (PTSD) as well as the more controversial diagnosis, Dissociative Identity Disorder (DID). A review of the professional literature reveals all of these descriptions to be interrelated.

Narcissism refers to, among other traits, a pathological preoccupation with the survival of the self; the presentation of a cold, detached, unemotional self; a fragmented self and an inability to maintain personal coherence; a sense of omnipotence, delusions of grandeur and fantasies of self-importance. Related to narcissism's 'pathological preoccupation' with the self's survival are the survival functions of PTSD and one of its most extreme manifestations, dissociation. Plagued by intrusive thoughts, panic attacks, flashbacks, insomnia, paranoia, obsessiveness, depression and hyper-arousal, the actions and general mannerisms of individuals living with chronic PTSD often seem disorganized and bizarre to others. The experience of the trauma, isolated or ongoing, results in a radical disruption of associative pathways (formation of meaning), linear time and a shattering of the self, sense of a coherent self and continuity of self. Trauma "destroys identity, shatters the construction of self, and robs the individual of the basic human need for safety. [It] tears a part of a complex system [and] fragments the personality" leaving in its wake a "fragmented self."[38]

Dissociative Identity Disorders (DID's), as defined by the DSM-IV (2000) are extreme, severe and long-lasting manifestations of PTSD. While all people experience some dissociation in non-life threatening circumstances (eg., driving or daydreaming), DID's are more severe and long lasting-expressions of dissociated states which manifest at times of acute stress. What makes them pathological or maladaptive is, in part, the episodic amnesia often accompanying them. DID is conceived of as a set of dissociative symptoms and tendencies thought to be a coping mechanism instigated by intense traumatic experiences, often during childhood. Such experiences include extreme, repetitive physical, sexual, and/or emotional abuse, and intense coercive persuasion wherein the victim dissociates himself from a situation or experience that is too violent, traumatic, or painful to assimilate with his conscious self. Essentially, DID is a fundamental disruption of consciousness, memory, identity, or perception of environment that produces a lack of connection in a person's thoughts, memories, feelings, actions, or sense of identity. An integrative deficit wreaks havoc with an individual's ability to maintain a sense of self over time, claim ownership of personal historical events, and the ability to differentiate between the real and unreal. [39]

It was the prevailing opinion of the mental health team that Timothy McVeigh suffered from a "dissociative disorder" (among other disorders) and possessed "dissociative abilities" resulting from trauma and possible sexual abuse, which were then further exacerbated during his time in the military. McVeigh adamantly denied that he was traumatized (by anything, ever) and wanted nothing to do with a mental health defense, while Jones dismissed the results of their head-shrinking as gobbledegook.

Eventually, McVeigh's mental health became an issue between Jones Team attorney Dick Burr and Stephen Jones. Jones wrote a memo informing Burr that they had "fundamental differences" in relation to "the mental health issue." At stake was the issue of McVeigh's personal agency. Jones wrote:

> [Your career has been] devoted either philosophically or politically towards a view that people who commit violent crimes may be the victims of emotional disturbances or racism or poverty or abuse or lack of nurturing or any other behavioral aspects, which as viewed by conservatives, chiefly result in an argument to avoid responsibility for acts. [...] Tim rejects the idea that anything he may have done is the result of anything other than his own deliberate plan and desire ... and I happen to agree with him ... he does not wish to be painted as a John Hinckley, and he doesn't want us to spend

time trying to investigate chapters in his life. Tim's story is one that is undoubtedly repeated millions of time a year. His act, which he views as one in a series of revolutionary acts against the government, would then be belittled simply to the act of somebody who's "crazy'"… Tim's act is no more "crazy" than John Brown's raid on Harpers Ferry … [or] … the Haymarket Anarchist.… The bottom line is this is a plea [by Tim] for us to quit invading his privacy [or that] of his family.

In Jones' view, the reasons McVeigh developed dissociative tendencies were irrelevant, as evidenced in another letter in which Jones informed Burr that "[T]here is no conceivable set of circumstances in which we would want to explain *WHY*" Tim manifested symptoms consistent with DID. Efforts to "try and uncover the best kept family secret … when the secrets seem to be as well guarded as they are, surrounded by extraordinary defenses, will be painstaking and painful and will create the risk that Tim will shut if off anyways."

Burr responded by writing to Jones that, while he acknowledged and agreed with the decision not to put on an 'abuse excuse' case, he still felt that "evidence of Tim's dysfunctional [and] abusive family" might allow jurors to understand him, and perhaps sympathize with him, but that "If we are not interested for purposes of defense in <u>why</u> Tim developed dissociative abilities (disorder)," then it did not matter what they learned about the McVeigh family. Like Burr some of the other mental health experts, attorneys and team members believed these "skeletons" were vital to understanding Tim, but they too eventually dropped the issue based on the direct order of Stephen Jones and Tim's continual requests. Thus, no more time was spent trying to determine the traumas that had separated McVeigh from himself.

Jones ordered the defense team to cease their efforts and spend no more time "interviewing people who talk about his mother's alcoholism or sexual adventures or his father's remoteness" as such lines of inquiry could not "save Tim's life," but would only intensify the ever-widening divide and sour relationships between Tim and his defense team. Jones instructed that, if during an interview with Tim or others, unsolicited information about the McVeigh family secrets was disclosed to any member of the team, they were not to mention it explicitly in their reports, but only to refer to it by *"cryptic reference."* Further, the memo's in the Jones collection, while rich in their current form, were sanitized in anticipation of future reciprocal discovery. The most sensitive documents were kept separate from the rest and, therefore, the extent of the actual findings of the psychologists and psychiatrists were never made known to the public.

THE MCVEIGHS NEXT DOOR

Tim McVeigh's great grandfather Edward McVeigh, Sr. left Ireland in 1866 and settled in Lockport, New York, a small town about thirty miles from the city of Buffalo, Niagara Falls and the Canadian border. After graduating high school, his son, Ed Jr., obtained a well-paying job at General Motors' Harrison Radiator factory, a reliably lifelong occupation for males in the region. His son William "Bill" McVeigh was born in 1940 and, after graduating from DeSales Catholic High School, also began working at Harrison Radiator. Bill joined a local Catholic bowling league where he met and later became engaged to Mildred "Mickey" Hill. Mickey, born in 1945 in Ransomville, New York, also graduated from DeSales and when she met Bill, had dreams of becoming an airline flight attendant.

Soon after they met, Bill was drafted into the U.S. Army and, during the two years he was away, Mickey attended Hartford Airline Personnel School. Bill received an honorable discharge in 1965, just prior to his units' deployment to Vietnam and returned home, resumed his job at Harrison, and married Mickey. The newlyweds moved to nearby Pendleton, New York, a small rural community about twenty miles from Buffalo, whose population consisted of mostly white, working-class Catholic families.

Mickey and Bill had three children, Patty in 1966, Timothy on April 23, 1968 and Jennifer in 1974. All of the McVeigh children were born at Lockport Memorial Hospital, attended Lockport's Starpoint school system and received religious instruction at nearby Good Shepherd Church. The McVeigh's lived in a series of houses in Pendleton, each more spacious than the last. On the surface, the family seemed to be living the American Dream.

Nearly all of the family, friends, and neighbors who knew him described young "Timmy" as a charming, intelligent, innovative, entrepreneurial, quick-witted, cleverly mischievous boy who shared his mother's sense of humor. His innovative and entrepreneurial ideas often earned him money. In addition to be being the most popular 'neighborhood babysitter,' every Halloween, Tim set up Haunted Houses for the younger children who lived nearby and a casino where, for a small admission fee, they could play roulette. Even as a young child, one of his most notable traits was his sense of responsibility. Tim was an avid collector of comic books and referred to the collection as his "college fund."

Liz and John McDermott lived next door to the McVeigh's from the time Tim was eight years old. They described him as sensitive, aware of the needs of others, attuned to suffering and highly empathetic to people and animals. Liz McDermott remembered, "When we moved in our house there was a huge toy tank and Tim would come over and look at it often. My husband lost his job and so when Mickey invited us to go to the medieval banquet in Niagara Falls, we couldn't afford it. Tim said 'why don't we have a garage sale?' I hated garage sales. I don't go to them and I certainly didn't want to run one but Tim took it over and ran the garage sale for us and we made more than enough to go to the banquet and more than enough to give him the tank."[40]

Despite their seemingly idyllic, upwardly mobile, middle class, suburban life and the outward normalcy of the well-behaved and friendly McVeigh children, a number of troubling issues brewed under the surface of the family veneer.

Neighbors, friends and family members told the Jones Team about Mickey's overwhelming fears and belief that she was in danger. Mickey, they said, often felt persecuted by an unknown threat and tended to avoid deaths like the plague, refusing to attend even the funerals of family members. A number of people stated that, over the years, they observed paranoia "both in Tim and in members of his family." In one report, Dr. Semone described the work of Dr. Norton and elaborated upon the extent of Mickey's paranoia and the effects he felt this had on Tim's psyche. Semone wrote that Norton had "uncovered data in her extraordinary investigative efforts of episodes during Tim's very early life, five to six years of age, when his mother would induct him into what may or may not have been paranoid delusional schemes having to do with her being spied upon." Another family friend said Mickey had "always demonstrated some unusual characteristics," notably her paranoia and "would sit in the living room with the lights out, convinced that people were in the neighborhood. She was always looking out the window, always watching the window. She would do this with Tim. Sometimes Tim would call and tell us that there was someone in the neighborhood casing our houses, and we should be aware of it. It seemed 'off' to us."[41]

Whether her fears were real or not, Semone continued, her expression of them would relate "to the degree to which a child experiences his world as a deeply frightening experience. [Along with] a younger sister for whom Tim reports having also felt responsible as to her welfare, the child [in such circumstances] grows to feel a singular burden for the protection of the vulnerable ones in the family. God made big men and Colt made the .45." Tim later acknowledged that his mother had always been paranoid and recalled, "I was at her house, opening a can of tuna fish, [and] she worried about the magnetic code." But he insisted that her fears had no effect on him. Jones Team attorney, Christopher Tritico, said that Mickey McVeigh "had a mental illness long long before [the case began]. When you met her you could tell she was mentally ill."[42]

Although McVeigh later claimed to more than one person that he could not remember much of his childhood, occasionally he attempted to help fill in the gaps. Over time and in his own fragmented, inconsistent and non-chronological way, he began to paint a troubling picture of his younger years first to the Jones Team and, later, to his biographers. To his attorneys he revealed that both his mother and father had a history of mental illness and that Bill was on some type of mood medication, a disclosure that caused Dr. Halleck to opine that there was "more to Bill than we have picked up so far." To his biographers, Tim wrote that since the bombing his mother kept saying "strange things" were happening to her, but it was hard to tell if what she was saying was real, as she had always been paranoid.

Upon first meeting him, Norton reported that Tim was "cooperative" during their interview but also "guarded [and] highly defended" and displayed pronounced obsessive compulsive" features including "rigid" speech patterns and that he seemed "uncomfortable with spontaneous," unscripted conversation, especially when it involved talking about emotions. Norton, along with all of the other Jones Team mental health experts agreed and found Tim's detached demeanor, emotionless affect and difficulty displaying empathy to be traits "indicative of the emotional sterility characteristic of [the McVeigh] family." This, they said, was observable in Jennifer and, while Mickey "didn't know how" to show emotion, the lack of it was a primary character trait of their father, who also seemed "unable" to show his feelings. One family member remarked that Tim "kept his emotions inside him the way Bill did." Halleck wrote that once, during an interview with ABC News shortly after his son's arrest, Bill was visibly detached, "so distant that he was not even there."

According to Norton, Bill seemed to have "very limited insight into his own personal psychology and emotions or those of his children" but rather, was a 'hear no evil–see no evil' kind of guy who had put a lot of energy into not noticing what is going on with his kids, especially when they are hurting/confused/bewildered." It was clear that, like Tim, Bill felt safest and most comfortable staying within the realm of facts and while pleasant and friendly, had great difficulty talking about his feelings. They concluded that, while Bill was physically present in his children's lives, his very passivity rendered him "virtually absent."

Tim said that, while usually quiet, perhaps to a fault, his publicly non-confrontational father was a perfectionist who, privately, had a short and intense temper. Bill, he said, was "highly nervous, very excitable, and screwed up" and seemed to be "always complaining" about one thing or another. To his biographers, he vividly described a number of incidents of Bill's rage and, once, after recalling that he regularly went on fishing trips with his maternal grandfather as a child added, "If my dad had been there to fish with me … I just wish he was. He was working 12-15 hour days." What he remembered most about his father, he said, was that he was "great with kids … but for me, I didn't see any of the nurturing skills

... I don't remember any of the nurturing. What I remember was that he was never there for anything but to yell at me. He was the disciplinarian. I don't hate him at all. He was operating on three or four hours of sleep a night, working double shifts, playing softball... sleep deprivation will severely aggravate people."

Neighbors also acknowledged to the Jones Team that Bill could be overly critical with his son. One remarked, "Tim rarely got attention for anything good; he only heard about his mistakes" and became a perfectionist himself. A family member remarked that Tim "kept his emotions inside him the way Bill did" and a family friend and neighbor also noted the similarities between Tim and his father saying, "I think Tim is his own worst enemy. He was very rigid. He was overly responsible and conscientious. Sometimes he was hard on others. He had lofty goals for himself and he had the same expectations for others. When they didn't live up to Tim he could get his back up. He had no use for a job done half-way." Mickey said, "Bill lost his temper a lot and yelled but never hit anybody" and the children, fearing his anger, always came to her when they misbehaved and asked her to intercede on their behalf. Tim said that when his father lost his temper, he usually dealt with it by retreating to his bedroom and learned to prevent Bill's tendency to "overreact" by avoiding certain topics of discussion.

To his biographers, Tim recounted how he felt pressured by his father to be athletic. "My dad, he's a jock," he explained. "I always felt like a failure to my dad. I wasn't a jock figure. Dad always had in mind a boy should be an athletic giant. I was thin, gangly, not really coordinated. I didn't even know how to put on a jockstrap." In order to make Bill happy, Tim joined Little League but said his memories of being on the team were painful because, "Whenever my dad would go out to play sports with me ... he would recognize my non-coordination. I was an outcast. He played fast pitch softball [and] wanted to warm up his arm with his son. Truth is, all it did for me back then was show him I was uncoordinated.... I couldn't really catch the ball ... afraid of the ball ... I didn't want to be out there, didn't even want to be on the team. My dad approached [the coach] after I was picked, and said to him, 'Tim isn't that great, did you pick him because you are my friend?'... That hurt, they didn't know I was listening...."

Like many children, Tim was sometimes picked on, at first for being too short and then for being too tall, thin and uncoordinated. A number of humiliating incidents at the hands of meaner children may have led him to develop his "seething hatred of bullies – of any person, institution, or even nation that seemed to be picking on the weak."[43]

Speaking of the 1999 Columbine Shooters, Harris and Klebold, he said, "Jocks were bullying those kids in Columbine. These jocks are taught on the field of competition to dominate others. I know these kids that were involved in the shooting, they had a point that somebody should address. There needs to be something instilled in these jocks that you don't need to dominate these kids when they're walking down the hall between English and Social Studies class.... Most bullies in schools are jocks." Although unarticulated, by equating "jocks" with his father he equated his father with bullying; a correlation that suggested his bombing of the "bullies" in the Murrah was a symbolic strike at his father.

According to Tim, while Bill never learned to deal with his anger properly, the main thing he learned from his father was, ironically, the value of controlling his own. "[I] learned a deeper lesson by experiencing my dad's short temper (surprised, huh?) [...] I would never 'fly off the handle' without thinking thru my reaction and subsequent action. I would go thru life not <u>yelling</u> every time the situation was adverse, and I would not make a habit of raising my voice when not necessary to get results."

While family, friends and neighbors said Bill "worshiped Mickey," they added that there had always been clearly notable differences between them that became a growing source of contention. While she tried to "settle down" after marrying Bill, the extroverted and outwardly emotional Mickey was "always on the go," had a short attention span and constantly craved attention, excitement and social interaction. She had a yearning for travel and adventure. Domesticity seemed to both bore and suffocate her and she was ambivalent about motherhood. Bill, on the other hand, was practical, reserved, "painfully shy" and "a homebody." While Bill preferred a quiet night at home on his off time, the tall, thin, "strikingly sexy," and "well endowed" Mickey liked to go out dancing and drinking with her friends and turned heads every time she entered a room. Mickey, said one family friend, "needed more stimulation than Bill could provide."

When Tim was eight, Mickey took a job as a travel agent and was away from home for increasing amounts of time. When she did have time off from work, she liked to hang out at the local bowling alley and even worked there for a while. Sometimes she would stay out all night, and when she was home, it was begrudgingly. Friends, family and neighbors said that, because Bill worked the graveyard shift at Harrison and as Mickey's excursions and drinking intensified, there was a notable lack of supervision in the McVeigh home.

A number of others drew a more damning portrait of Mickey. According to one family member, she "wasn't much of a house wife [and] their home was always messy." Another said, "We called Mickey 'the Queen.' She never cleaned or made her kids pick up their toys. She would come home at night and just sit there, or get ready to go out bowling or socializing. We used to joke that the only time she ever cleaned her house was when they were moving. Bill would have dinner waiting when Mickey got home from work." Others described her as materialistic and greedy, "Mickey was the kind of person who always wanted more. She was never satisfied with any of their houses. ... Bill paid for everything in cash. He never even had a car payment or a credit card. He was a hard worker and frugal."

Mickey, they said, encouraged unhealthy coping skills in her children. One close relative recalled that once, having made an unexpected visit to the McVeigh home, they found the 15-year-old Patty making Whiskey Sours in the blender. Mickey, herself a heavy drinker, explained that she had suggested this, since Patty had just broken up with a boyfriend and it would make her feel better. Although Bill was aware of such occurrences and "probably didn't approve," he did nothing to prevent it and never said anything about it.

To Norton, Tim described his mother as a "freewheeling ... free spirit" who liked to hang out at bars and socialize and while she sometimes drank at home, he never saw her "staggering drunk." Yes, she took a job when he was eight, he said, but added that most of the time she was home and always made his lunch to bring to school. During their earliest conversations just weeks after his arrest, Tim claimed that while his parents "had strife all throughout their married life," they never fought in front of the children until her drinking and absences increased the tension between them. Sometimes at night while he was trying to sleep, Tim said, his parents would argue. Often, his parents' fights were about Mickey's continual demands for more sex. He later told his biographers that, sometimes, as he lay in bed at nights, through the walls he could hear his parents having sex, but mostly just heard them argue with an intensity that frightened him.

While he was still young, continued Tim, Mickey began going out drinking at night and it did not take long before his father suspected she was "sleeping around." At some point, Tim came to believe that his father's own friends became sexually involved with his mother. Family, friends and neighbors also shared rumors with the Jones Team about Mickey bringing men to the house while Bill was working. Further, based on their investigation and interviews, the team's mental health experts also suggested the possibility that Mickey, when drunk, encouraged her children to engage in inappropriate "sexual situations."[44] If such rumors were true, Tim would be in a double bind; a classic Freudian Oedipal dilemma, having usurped his father in actuality or by being made into a silent witness and therefore unwitting co-conspirator in his mother's infidelity. Further, true or not, given such unsubstantiated rumors, Tim's "disturbance" at the Jones Team's early findings became more understandable.

Over time, the stark, irreconcilable differences between Bill and Mickey became apparent not only to the McVeigh children but to their friends and family, and seemingly everyone else who knew them knew that Mickey had a *reputation* in the small town of Lockport. She was, they said, a "magnet for men," notably married men. She was "emotionally needy," "selfish," "immature," "self-absorbed," a "slut" with a "propensity for drama" and someone who desperately sought out the company and affection of men, a situation that caused many wives to become jealous of her. Jennifer said Mickey was obsessed with staying young and would become "depressed and frantic" without constant male companionship or attention. Everyone, it seemed, knew or suspected that she was cheating on Bill, and according to one family member, Bill "knew, but he buried his head in the sand." In this story, for various reasons, people end up buried in the sand.

Tim's cousin remembered that Tim "had a short fuse" in general and "wouldn't tolerate his parents' arguments for very long before he would be yelling at them to stop." On the day of Tim's execution, Jones Team expert Dr. John Smith told reporters that Mickey and Bill's arguments frightened Tim so terribly that he "took refuge in a fantasy world where he, as hero, would vanquish the bullies." A number of people described the negative effect his parents' fighting and general home environment had on Tim and how, because of it, even as a young child, he sought refuge and spent most of his time at the homes of neighbors, sometimes eating dinner and spending the night for days at a time. When his biographers asked if he loved his parents, Tim responded, "I struggle with the question ... I have very few memories of my childhood, of interaction with my parents. I can't blame them for anything that's happened to me. I was often by myself or with neighbors. Most of my memories focus on that."[45]

A neighbor who acted as one of Tim's many surrogate mother-figures told the Jones Team that, from the time he was very young, she suspected something disturbing had happened to him in the McVeigh home which had left him very troubled. Even as a child, Tim exhibited behaviors that indicated he had suffered a traumatic experience. His body image was poor and he often wore baggy clothes "to cover the shape of his body... I have always sensed that Tim had a deep hurt he could never talk about and I always felt that it could have something to do with his mother." While she could never prove Tim had been sexually abused, the thought crossed her mind. All she knew for sure was that "something [had] hurt him deeply." This was not the first allusion to possible sexual abuse.[46]

Tim found his most cherished respite at the home of his grandfather, Ed, who instructed him in a variety of domestic tasks and taught him to properly handle and shoot firearms. Speaking of his grandfather, Tim said, "I used to nap on his couch when [I] woke we'd fold blankets together, him holding the end as I picked up corners. Eventually [he] taught me how to fold a blanket by myself [...] I loved going to his house." To his grandson, Ed's knack for technology and mechanics made him seem like "MacGyver." "Occasionally," said Tim "the MacGyver influence comes out in me." As he reflected on his grandfather, Tim said the "memories flood back [and] it is easy to recognize the value of an adult guiding presence in a household." His grandfather, he said, was a "rugged individualist" and the only person he could truly claim to love.[47]

In 1978, when Tim was nine years old, unable to reconcile her domestic role and unhappy with her marriage, Mickey moved out. The McVeigh children had a choice of who they wanted to live with and, while his sisters chose to stay with their mother, Tim chose to stay with Bill. Countless friends, family and neighbors said that, after she left, they noticed a marked change in Tim. They said he became increasingly alienated, distant, disconnected and guarded. One close family friend said he became noticeably "insecure ... unable to find his niche ... almost starved for affection ... having an impenetrable shell around him which hardly anybody could break through. [After his parents broke up,] I hardly ever saw him express emotion." His best friend Steve said that Tim was clearly hurt and bitter; he knew of his mother's affairs by now and blamed her for his parents' break-up. Mickey, elaborated Steve, "told [Tim] she was going away with 'one of his uncles' and when she came back she said she was leaving. Tim told me his mother told him she didn't care about him ... It was a particularly difficult time for Tim ... he was lonely and wanted a family atmosphere."

Jennifer said her brother resented Mickey's decision to leave and, after she did, "kind of divorced himself from Mom." Next door neighbor and close family friend, Mrs. McDermott, said that even before she left Bill, Tim expressed anger towards Mickey. Other neighbors remembered him complaining that she dressed like a teenager, went away on long trips and even confided his fears that she was cheating and sometimes called her a "slut" and "pig,"; slurs, one neighbor recalled, he was scolded for on more than one occasion.

Whether he expressed such derogatory sentiments as a child, numerous individuals reported that he did so as an adult. One former Army friend recalled how Tim would call his mother a "no good whore, a slut ... never had anything good to say about his mom." Another remarked that Tim "kind of held a grudge against his mom ... it obviously still upset him. He generally referred to her as a bitch. He was not happy with her at all. He ... had no love for her I ever saw displayed."[48] Andrea Augustine, a co-worker Tim developed a close friendship with after he left the Army, described their conversations. "[Tim] told me his mother was a whore and a bitch. That's how he referred to her. He said when she was with the family she would come in drunk at all hours of the night and that she and his father would argue. He said she abandoned them when he was a lot younger – younger than a teenager – and that she left without warning. They just came home and found her gone."

Tim denied to his defense team that he ever said anything of the sort. In fact, he remembered occasionally talking to Augustine about their families but claimed he could not remember making these types of statements about his mother or even *thinking* them. While admitting Augustine had no reason to lie, he could not "think of any reason why" he would have said such things to her. Still, after his arrest, his Army friends told reporters about conversations they had with him that sounded similar, if not identical, to those Augustine described. McVeigh maintained to the Jones Team that these types of reports, which continually found their way into the media, were "a real mystery" to him. At first, he made similar denials to his biographers, but later reluctantly acknowledged he may have made such statements. "I understand human sexuality," he explained to them, "I personally believe nobody was made for one partner. I think marriage is a good social institution, for populating the earth, preventing the spread of social diseases. Aside from that, I don't see it as natural. Why would I be mad about my mom for sleeping around?" He admitted that, "My mother was devastated by all the allegations [and] accusation that I called her a bitch [and] slut… [It was] not true. She visited me in the courthouse, she walked up to me, [and] the marshals were standing right there. The first thing she said was 'did you call me a bitch and a slut?' I probably did call her that, but who knows what problems I was having that day, what kind of mood I was in. [If] I was talking to Andrea, I was probably trying to get in her pants…"

In an attempt to save her marriage, Mickey episodically returned home to Bill and Tim until finally, in 1984, the year Tim began high school, she moved to Florida and took his sisters with her, while he chose to remain with his father. Publicly as well as privately to his defense team, Tim denied that his parents' deteriorating marriage had any impact on him, much less traumatized him or that it had in any way influenced decisions he made as an adult; and allegations otherwise greatly angered him. Still, the majority of accounts (including those of the Jones Team) say that Mickey's decision to leave the family left "deep psychological wounds [and] permanent emotional scars." Tim, they believed, felt abandoned and, given the smallness of the town and the way rumors circulated, stigmatized, ashamed and embarrassed.[49]

The Education of Tim McVeigh

Beyond those real or imagined threats his mother perceived, his father's anger, his parents dissolving marriage or other turbulence that existed within the McVeigh home, a number of external threats also plagued the world of young Tim McVeigh, which he responded to by taking an interest in survivalism. He told his biographers that, in order to understand this interest, "you'd have to live during my era and live my life":

> [I] grew up during the Cold War era. People had built bomb shelters in their backyards.... The McDermott's had basement walls 8 feet thick. [It was] a fallout shelter in their basement. They told me the guy who built the house was worried about radiation from bomb fallout. My uncle's former house had its own gas tank and underground pump. [During] the gas crisis of 1974, I remember a neighbor coming in the middle of the night, siphoning gas from my dad's car and other neighbor's cars.... Gas was gold, and it was being stolen from our driveway. That instilled a feeling of righteousness in me, a feeling that you should be able to defend your property. I wanted to sit outside and guard our property.... You couldn't just shoot him because you're not in fear for your life, [and you] start thinking that the laws aren't in line with what I would call natural law.

This, he said, along with "duck and cover" drills at school caused him to adopt what he referred to as his survivalist "nuclear alert mentality" and fostered an appreciation for Cold War architecture.[50] In this, Timothy McVeigh was not unique.

The early 1980s witnessed a resurgence of early 1950s Cold War era back yard bunker builders, ever vigilant for threats of impending nuclear disaster, who had evolved from the mid-1970s gas 'hoarders' into a growing survivalist movement. While nuclear war remained on the list of fears, everyone had their own individualized, yet distinctly American apocalypse scenarios: economic collapse, communist invasion, urban riots, environmental pollution, natural disaster, technological breakdowns, and oil and fuel shortages. Some people hid away gold and silver and began growing their own food supply. Thousands of optimistic others, despite accusations of harboring fatalistic doomsday mentalities, were willing to shell out money to ensure their survival, leading to a financial "doom boom" in every major city. Entrepreneurs sold easily assembled bunkers and fallout shelters, radiation suits, prepackaged food, 2,000-gallon water and fuel tanks, metal grain containers and medical supplies as well as ammunition and guns including high-powered semiautomatic military assault weapons.[51]

With the shit clearly about to hit the fan, some headed for the hills. Religious and secular survivalist communities, sometimes referred to as "armed cults," began to appear throughout the United States and could be found among a broad political spectrum that included the right, left and apolitical, as well as Christians, Jews, New-Agers and White Supremacists. Some communities offered training courses where, for a modest fee, the forewarned could learn how to fight, shoot, and survive all manner of impending apocalypse. In 1983, the *Washington Post* reported on the building of underground condominiums in Utah and one group in the Midwest who were building "anti-gravity space ships that will leave the earth at the appointed time and orbit until the clouds of destruction have passed."[52]

According to Tim, his preoccupation with preparedness and self-sufficiency began in earnest during the worst snowstorm to hit upstate western New York in twenty years, known as the "Blizzard of 1977." Pendleton received the brunt of the fifteen-foot snowfall, and Niagara County was declared a disaster area. Telephone and power lines stopped working. The school, town and surrounding areas shut down for weeks. Thousands of people were left stranded and several died. The region's tumultuous weather compounded the turmoil within the McVeigh home. Earlier on the evening the blizzard began, Mickey left and drove to a hotel a couple of miles from their home to meet up with co-workers for drinks where she became stranded, unable to return for two days. According to some, this was the first time Tim McVeigh saliently felt abandoned by his mother and then, only months after the blizzard, she moved out and left the state.

The magnitude of the cataclysmic blizzard, coupled with his mother's absence, made a distinct impression on the nine-year-old, who, along with a growing group of Americans, began stockpiling food, water and canned supplies in the basement and convinced his father to buy a generator in case such a situation arose again. Although acutely sensitive to the many possible threats around him, popular culture provided potential models for overcoming them, one of the earliest to capture his attention being *Little House on the Prairie*, which illustrated the value of perseverance in the face of bad odds.

To his biographers, Tim explained, "I watched *Little House On The Prairie*. [I]Loved the show, loved people surviving in the Wild West.... On the show, they survived blizzards in their little cabin. [...] In the Blizzard of '77, we faced the real threat of having no food in the house, because we couldn't get anywhere. [You need to] keep in mind a 'fundamental' – it will be important later: 'survivalists' are, by their nature, <u>defensive</u> in posture ... so in a real sense, a survivalist 'goal' is an incremental effort at attaining personal freedom thru separation and independence from 'the system.' It's a yearning to live the Ingalls's on <u>Little House</u>.... A wholesome and pure life, I see nothing wrong with that [sic]."

He found ways to cope with the many looming threats and disasters he faced, both at home and in the outside world. Those who knew the McVeighs recalled that, after Mickey left Bill the first time, Tim became increasingly distant and disconnected. According to his cousin, he was "always very meticulous with his hobbies," and began to concentrate more on them. He absorbed himself in comic books, particularly Marvel's X-Men series about a gang of teenage "mutants" whose evolved genetics imbue them with superpowers. Under the guidance of their mentor, Professor X, the misfits learn to use their extraordinary powers for good, often using them to thwart the plans of evil mutants and thereby avert worldwide disaster.

Tim found another way to help him feel secure in a shifting and scary world when, at the age of seven, his grandfather Ed taught him how to shoot. According to his classmates, once, in elementary school, Tim brought his BB guns to school to demonstrate to the other children how to properly hold and load the gun and to show them how quickly he could shoot and reload. Towards the end of eighth grade, during the time he called his "bully period," his interest in shooting blossomed into a defining and lifelong interest when, on his thirteenth birthday, his grandfather gave him his very own .22 caliber hunting rifle. Despite his lack of interest in hunting animals, he enjoyed perfecting his marksmanship on inanimate targets and seemed to have a natural talent for it. On a middle school career day survey, Tim listed his future occupation as "gun shop owner."

Always a television junkie, Tim McVeigh absorbed popular culture and became a close and lifelong observer of the world as seen on TV news and depicted in blockbuster movies. The two mediums increasingly merged into a new genre of popular journalism, now termed "Infotainment." The intriguing casts of characters and dramatic plotlines featured in news stories assured continued viewer consumption and absorption that tended to blur reality, fact and fantasy, creating a "hyper-real" aesthetic for receptive consumers.

In the two years after he began high school in 1982, the U.S. announced its possession of the first cruise missiles. Civilians could now purchase home computers, including the first Apple Macintosh. Global Positioning System (GPS) technology became available. A partial core meltdown occurred at Chenobyl, a nuclear power plant in Russia, followed by a much larger catastrophic disaster there a few years later. The local consequences of an accident at one Argentinean power plant declared a level 4 on the Internal Nuclear Event Scale and technical failures at a nuclear power plant in Germany resulted in the release of Iodine-131. A nuclear world war was narrowly averted when, a Soviet military officer identified a missile-attack warning as a false alarm, although a few months later a NATO exercise was misinterpreted as a live nuclear first strike. In 1984, the tongue-in-cheek remarks of President Ronald Reagan were overheard during a sound check. "My fellow Americans," declared Reagan, "I'm pleased to tell you today that I've signed legislation that will outlaw Russia forever. We begin bombing in five minutes."[53] In the final days of the Cold War, as the threat of nuclear disaster loomed, the disarmament movement grew.

Nearly all biographical accounts mention Tim's love of the 1983 science fiction-suspense movie, *WarGames*. The hero of the movie, David Lightman, is a highly intelligent but unmotivated high school student who uses his knack for computers to hack into his school's computer system and change his grades. Lightman accidently discovers an automated NORAD supercomputer running constant military simulations and threat/risk assessments. The system's artificial intelligence [AI] has become confused between simulated and actual threats, however, and after falsely detecting the deployment of Soviet submarines (in response to Lightman's hack), the AI declares DEFCON 1 – the highest state of military alert. In order to avert World War III and impending global nuclear disaster, Lightman must engage the system in a game of wits until it becomes cognizant of the probability of mutually assured destruction and ceases its planned nuclear attack on the Soviets.

In his 1998 unauthorized biography, *One of Ours*, Richard Serrano wrote, "Tim was easily impressed. Certain movies took hold of him and he would act out their story lines and imagine himself in the center of the plots."

Tim identified with Lightman. He said that, even before the release of the movie, while still in junior high, he had begun exploring the emergent world of home computers. By ninth grade, he had taught himself programming languages, and over the next few years, his extraordinary talents became apparent as he designed sophisticated programs that allowed him to communicate via modem with other home computers. One high school teacher and family friend recounted Tim's self-taught computer acumen and "bright mind." The school was using a Commodore Pet, and Tim, on his own, created an "advanced" and "enormously long program" to locate area modems. After having constructed an early bulletin board, he chose "The Wanderer" as his online identity, a handle that became his first, but by no means last, alias. Known in his high school as a hacker, at the time an emerging subcultural identity for nerdy teenagers around the country, his favorite activities, as listed in one yearbook, were "talking pseudo-code and computers."[54]

His close friend Steve said, when they started high school (the same year Mickey left the state of New York), Tim became much more intense, obsessive even, in his interests and hobbies. Steve described how Tim's interests continually "mutated from one form to another" but "whatever he did, he did it to the hilt.... [H]e would say he had busted into other people's computers and would get convinced he was going to get caught. He'd tell me 'the feds have my house tapped; it's just a matter of time before they bust me.' But he didn't quit."

Tim described his interest in computers and hacking to his biographers: "I was on the Internet before it became popular. I kept inputting different phone numbers.... I hacked into banks, government agencies [...] I hacked into more shit on computers than I'd ever admit to. I had a Commodore 64 computer at home. [Dave Darlak and myself] hack[ed] into peoples computers from school [...]I learned how to charge phone calls to other peoples' phones [...] One day we were hacking around and a message came up 'you are all on the system illegally, and we'll turn off your phones.' [The] next day, I was scared to even take out the garbage. I thought the cops would come [...] I got into White Sands Missile Range computer system [...] White Sands was government computer, but I didn't get past their password. [...] I loved the movie *WarGames*, [Lightman] found the grid computer, and I was trying to get into that, too. I saw that movie and wrote my own program. I was inspired by that movie."

America's future Face of Terror, also came of age during the advent of mass-mediated "Terrorism Spectacles." These began in earnest in late 1979 during the Iran hostage crisis, at which time Americans learned that the United States does not negotiate with terrorists. During the subsequent Reagan and Thatcher administrations, these spectacles became firmly rooted in the minds of Americans as airplane hijackings and crashes, assassinations and bombings became recurring features in the news and popular culture. Media coverage of terroristic events became more frequent, repetitive and dramatic in content.

Throughout the 1980's, already vague common usages and official and legal definitions of terrorism, of which there were hundreds, broadened. Incrementally, understandings of what constituted *terrorism* and who was a *terrorist*, became more inclusive and came to encompass a much more expansive range of groups and acts including terroristic hoaxes and threats. Thus, the number of reported incidents of terrorism increased as did rapidly growing state and privatized counterterrorism budgets. So too did terrorism become the subject of seemingly disproportionate media coverage. The majority of mainstream prime-time mass media reports about terrorism were not only occurring more frequently, they were increasingly sensationalized in nature. Secretary of State Alexander Haig declared that the deadliest threat faced by Americans was terrorism.[55]

Television viewers learned of ongoing conflicts escalated between democratized Western nations (i.e., U.S. and Israel) and a range of independently organized and politically motivated groups and individuals in the Middle East and elsewhere. In 1983 and 1984 alone, the IRA and Sinn Fein fought with the U.K. In the largest prison break in British history, thirty-eight members of the Irish Republican Army escaped, followed shortly by an IRA car-bombing in London that killed six and injured ninety. Two train bombings in France also thought to be the work of the

IRA, killed five and injured many others, and a bombing attempt on the lives of the British Cabinet and Prime Minister Margaret Thatcher killed five, though it left Thatcher unharmed. 6,800 gold bars worth about $26 million were stolen from a vault in Heathrow Airport in London during the Brink's-MAT robbery, only a small portion of which were recovered.

U.S. troops invaded Grenada where, during a military coup, the Prime Minister and forty followers were assassinated. A Soviet jet shot down Korean Airlines flight 007 killing all 269 people on board, including a U.S. Congressman. Filipino opposition leader Benigno Aquino, Jr., was assassinated. Several people died in the attempted highjacking of Aeroflot flight 6833 in Soviet Georgia. Two members of the Indian Prime Minister's security detail were assassinated.

A bomb placed in the baggage compartment of Gulf Air flight 771 exploded, and the plane crashed in the United Arab Emirates, killing 117 people. Palestinian gunmen hijacked and took hostage passengers on an Israeli bus. Hezbollah took over a Kuwait Airlines flight, killing four passengers onboard. Their car bombs hit the U.S. Embassy in Beirut, killing 63, as well as the U.S. Marine Corps barracks, killing 241 service members. The Marines exited Beirut, but a CIA station chief, kidnapped by Islamic Jihadists, died in captivity. A Lieutenant in the U.S. Navy on a reconnaissance mission was shot down over Lebanon and held captive by Syrians. The United Nations condemned Iraq for their use of chemical weapons against Iran, and U.S. President Reagan called for an international ban on chemical weapons.

Meanwhile, hurricanes, famines and industrial disasters claimed millions of lives around the world. Hurricane Alicia hit Texas leaving twenty-two people dead and flash floods in Oklahoma claimed several lives, as did a tornado in Wisconsin. El Niño caused severe weather throughout the world. A famine in Ethiopia left over a million people dead. The worst industrial disaster in history left more than 8,000 dead and half a million injured after methyl isocyanine leaked from a Union Carbide pesticide plant in India.

During this time, "Night Stalker" Richard Ramirez murdered his first known victim. Accusations of ritual Satanic abuse of children by teachers at a preschool in a California suburb caused a national scandal and nearby a 41-year-old man randomly killed 21 people at a McDonald's restaurant. In Los Angles, a smokeable form of cocaine, known as Crack, began receiving increased media attention and its use was being called an epidemic.

It is not surprising then, that, given all these natural and manmade threats throughout the world, teenage Timothy McVeigh, already concerned with preparedness in the face of disaster, grew increasingly fascinated with Reagan-era Cold War apocalyptic and post-apocalyptic World

War III survival scenarios, as seen within popular movies of the era. He later described how he grew up gravitating towards films with plots that featured tornados, volcanoes, floods, plagues, nuclear and man-made disasters and scenarios where protagonists, oftentimes alone, must survive in harsh brave new worlds. His favorites included *Road Warrior* (1982), ABC's *The Day After (1983)*, and *Mad Max: Beyond Thunderdome* (1985), which came out the same year Tim bought his first car.

Often mentioned as influential on him was *Red Dawn*, released in 1984, a year in which fears of a looming Armageddon coincided with (or were the result of) patriotic sentiment. In this film, communist Cuban and Soviet troops invade the U.S. The invaders disarm the citizenry after obtaining lists of gun owners, arresting, imprisoning and executing some. A group of high school students calling themselves "The Wolverines," led by Jed (Patrick Swayze), form a successful guerilla resistance and are memorialized as heroes. The plots of *WarGames* and *Red Dawn*, observed Stickney, feature high school students embroiled within government conspiracies that are resolved through the protagonists' heroic actions.[56]

The film's phrases and visual images within the film appealed to the gun-toting high school boy Tim. One scene that stood out for him featured the NRA's slogan *"I'll give you my gun when you take it from my cold, dead hands"* on a bumper sticker of a pickup truck immediately before its driver is killed by the Communist villains, who indeed remove his gun from his (still warm) dead hands. One of the highest grossing movies of 1984, *Red Dawn* met with much criticism for its glorification of guns, violence and mindless patriotism, its promotion of uncritical hatred towards communist and socialist countries and its acclaimed reception by right wing extremist and second amendment advocate audiences.[57]

Mitchell's re-envisioning of survivalism proves relevant to McVeigh's early perceptions of the world, his responses to them and his related narrations. "Survivalists," wrote Mitchell, "relish inventing new narratives, new primal means and fundamental meanings by which the world may be known. [...] To find places of consequence survivalists fashion discourses of pending need, speculative circumstances of crisis and concern wherein major social institutions face imminent serious erosion or total dissolution and in which survivalists themselves play central roles in reprioritized revisioning, recover and renewal. Survivalist discourse tailors widespread rancor and disorder to fit schemes for maximizing personal competence, actualization and relevance."[58]

Serrano pessimistically observed however that, "The young McVeigh was thinking even then in the simplest of terms, how best to face an unfair world." Had his father paid better attention to his son, "he would have noticed the trademarks of many who end up on the fringes of American society – those who believe in government conspiracies and demon threats, and who trust no one in authority," reliant only on themselves. "As a teenager, [he had] embraced fantasy rather than accept the reality of the breakup of his parents' marriage. Sometimes he could not move beyond his mother's exit from his young life [and so] to shore up his defenses, he built a fortress in his secret basement world." While other teenagers worried about what brand of clothing they wore, Tim spent his money on 55-gallon barrels that he filled with water and stored in his father's basement. When asked what else Tim kept down there, Bill said, "whatever he thought he needed [including gun powder]. If everything went haywire, he'd have it there. You know, he was into survival."[59]

When asked about this, McVeigh conceded that, perhaps he did have "millenialist thinking" and recalled that when he first watched *Red Dawn*, it fit perfectly with what he already sensed about the world, he just never quite "pinned down how the end would come." All he knew was, when it did, he "didn't want to have to depend on anyone to survive. If you depend on somebody else, you are at their mercy." Mrs. Hodge (Steve's mother) noted, "[t]his was at the time he was trying to survive without his mom and without his dad." Steve remembered Tim's "preoccupation" and said, even as a teenager, he "had an arsenal which included tents, guns, k-rations and tear gas. He had many kinds of ammunition, including steel-case metal-piercing bullets."

Timothy McVeigh was not alone in his interests. The wider culture of survivalists had steadily grown since Tim's early brush with the apocalyptic blizzard of '77. A reportedly large percentage of Americans shared Tim's concerns about future nuclear winters, evidenced by increasing subscription rates to magazines like *Survive* and bestselling books like *Nuclear War Survival Skills*. Books such as *Life After Doomsday: A Survivalists Guide to Nuclear War and Other Major Disasters* (1980) and *How To Survive A Nuclear Disaster* (1982) continued to appear on shelves. Such books offered grim statistics about the likelihood of surviving a major catastrophe (manmade or natural) and informed readers about how to improve their chances of doing so.[60]

By January 1984, headlines announced, "They're Ready: The Nuclear Family, Preparing to Survive Doomsday and Beyond." Reports described this new "survivalist culture" as a family affair; parents educated their children on the value of survival, and movies like *Red Dawn*, *WarGames* and the TV film *The Day After* made apocalyptic anxieties fun for the whole family. Perhaps exacerbating threats of looming doom were government agencies like the Federal Emergency Management Agency (FEMA), who announced the creation of nationwide evacuation and relocation plans, or statements like those of President Ronald Reagan who earlier that month, in a discussion about Soviet-U.S. relations declared that, "reducing the risk of war – and especially nuclear war – is priority number one. A nuclear conflict could well be mankind's last."[61]

Mitchell explored the ways in which survivalists articulate the stories they tell to themselves and others:

> Among themselves, survivalists more often narrate than debate the cause of the coming cataclysm. Assorted calamity stories may co-exist without discord, to be retold and tailored as individuals see fit. Constructing a cataclysmic tale personalized to ones circum-stances is a survivalist prerogative and pastime. Once constructed, these tales accrue respect from survivalist others *as stories*. Quality is judged ... on the bases of artful drama, clever plot twists, and especially refinements in technical details, not on the basis of cor-respondence to the empirical. Stories need to be believable, not provable; evoke imagination, not reveal first principles or primal truths. Survivalist scenarios are akin to contemporary legends told in future tense ... accounts of happenings in which the narrator has not yet been directly involved, presented as propositions for belief, events that could occur, told as if their probability is high. ... Problems ahead must be defined as both urgently compelling and manageable in scope, neither trivial improbabilities nor certain de-struction. This is challenging, creative work.[62]

Mitchell's "survivalists narrative," provides a framework through which to read many of the threats McVeigh perceived, beyond simply re-ducing them to paranoia. McVeigh explained:

> [You need to] keep in mind a 'fundamental' – it will be import-ant later: 'survivalists' are, by their nature, <u>defensive</u> in posture... so in a real sense, a survivalist 'goal' is an incremental effort at attaining personal freedom thru separation and independence from 'the system. It's a yearning to live like the Ingalls on *Little House*. [...]Why do I have to apologize for making sure I can take care of myself, wanting to make sure I can live without someone else's help? That is, the governments help. What would these people do if there was a terrorist attack and NYC water supply was spiked? They'd probably sue if they died! It's sort of a hobby. No weirder than collecting stamps of memorizing the batting average of some retired baseball player [...]A lot of the time, I don't have pity for these people who get wiped out be-cause they didn't prepare themselves.[...] The power plant in Niagara Falls would be a secondary or tertiary bombing target because the winds are westerly. [...] Being a survivalist is about being prepared if the infrastructure is not there. [...]I have a real problem with people who demonize 'survivalists' by calling them 'hoarders,' or say they are 'hoarding' supplies. <u>By defini-</u>

tion, 'hoarding' can only take place in times of <u>shortage</u>! When food and other supplies are plentiful in our free market, it is <u>not</u> 'hoarding' to squirrel these things away!

Interestingly, the one work of popular culture he absorbed that seemed to provide a sense of comfort or optimism, or that in any way mitigated his anxieties about the encroaching disasters and cataclysms he perceived, was the *Star Trek* television series. For young Tim McVeigh and throughout his life, *Star Trek* held the answers to a number of ills and taught him how to ask questions about the world around him and think for himself. While many have commented on McVeigh's consumption of popular media, he obsessively talked about *Star Trek,* in particular, as a way to illustrate any number of issues, including those pertaining to the bombing and its victims. His attorneys remarked, "[t]he primary extent hero/role models he speaks of are Captain Kirk, Mr. Spock, and Captain Picard, all characters on *Star Trek.*"

He continued to speak and write about *Star Trek* until his execution and many letters to his biographers contain pages of his sometimes bizarre musings about the show. In fact, Tim McVeigh compared nearly everything, including himself, to characters or circumstances in the show and, undoubtedly, emulated them.

"All in all, whether it's the characters or the system of government, Star Trek: NG is an <u>in-depth</u> utopian model for the future – something for mankind to strive toward. (Especially in this, the bloodiest century since mankind first walked upright – a light of hope in these dark ages.). […] [H]ow I relate to certain key characters: <u>Picard</u>: -[the] most respected man in Star Fleet (see my [military] buddies comments [about me]). [Picard] knows all the systems, multiply proficient, highly skilled diplomat (I wish – a standard goal to aim for), <u>yet lonely man</u>. Keeps emotions in check; no quality I dislike or don't understand. <u>Worf</u> – the consummate warrior. (I do consider myself a 'warrior') (Again, see [my] *Newsweek* interview) <u>Data</u>-Android (so no emotion), logic rules ([Data is] the 'Spock equivalent -accesses stored memory on command (i.e., highly retentive) <u>La Forge</u>-Chief Engineer. Just look at the pride he takes in knowing his shit-engineering section is 'his' and he takes pride in knowing it like the back of his hand. Highly proficient in his field. I absolutely relate to the pride and care he takes in the upkeep of his systems […]I Like Picard better than Captain Kirk. Confronted with a situation, Kirk would kill people with phaser guns. Picard would say, 'Let's see what we can do to straighten this out.'"

Among other things, Timothy McVeigh was a *bona fide* nerd.

THE LOST GENERATION

Tim McVeigh began high school in 1982. Based on his high IQ scores, he attended advanced placement (AP) classes. Throughout high school, he maintained near-perfect attendance, received excellent grades and stayed out of trouble. He never caused problems; he "went to church and didn't swear, smoke, drink, use drugs, or fight." He never belonged to any specific group and seemed to get along with everyone. His classmates remembered that Tim appeared to possess an innate intelligence. He could just show up to class and ace every exam placed in front of him, without having studied.[63] He continued to collect rare coins and comic books, did not like math class but liked earth science and had a crush on a girl in his biology class whom he thought was both "pretty" and "intellectual." In his freshman year, he joined the football team, then the track team in his sophomore year. In his junior year, he was elected to student council and, with money he had squirrelled away, purchased his first car. In his senior year, he began working at a nearby Burger King and upon graduation, his classmates voted him "Most Talkative" (because he never talked or because of his ability to talk to anybody, depending on who you ask).

Steve Hodge and his mother said Tim was an "extremely conscientious" teenager, always prepared, and "the type of person who always kept big ropes in the car so that he could help people in trouble. I remember he always wanted to help people. He would get real excited if he heard about someone who needed something. He'd come over and say, 'Come on, we've got a mission!'" Likewise, his teachers remembered him as a "quiet, well-liked, conscientious," cooperative and helpful people pleaser. One classmate said he was "always trying to please other people by doing extra – extra help, [being] extra funny.... He went out of his way to make people laugh and to like him ... he was always on the outside trying to fit in."[64]

Others, including one classmate, offered a more contradictory and divided picture. Tim, he said, was "outgoing and active" but also an "unconnected loner [on] the fringes" of teenage social life.[65] Similarly, a family friend told the Jones Team that "[Tim] was always on the outside looking in wanting a place to fit in... He never quite made what he wanted to make or achieved what he wanted to achieve.... It seemed like no matter what he did he didn't quite make it. Not as a son to his mother or father or in any of the groups the other kids were involved in."

His classmates never knew him to date girls; nor did they recall his attending the senior prom. One remembered that Tim "rarely, if ever, dated" and thought the problem was that he "set his sights too high" and tried to ask out girls that were out of his league.[66] According to Tim, his parents never mentioned, much less discussed, sex with him. And whatever he knew about the subject, he learned on his own. He himself claimed that he lost his virginity in his junior year to an older, married woman he worked with at Burger King who liked his "stamina" and the fact that he was a "young buck." The affair lasted about three weeks and then fizzled out.

Soon after, he began dating another co-worker around his own age named Sarah (name changed) who said Tim was "loud and goofy" and tended to drive frighteningly fast. To her, he seemed "lost," almost as if he was raising himself, and he had an obvious resentment of his mother.[67] They dated for about six months but he broke up with her soon after he graduated high school, telling her he was not ready for a serious relationship. Tim elegantly explained to his biographers that it was with Sarah that he began to explore his sexuality, "I was interested in another girl. Sarah was a little plump, she was interested, I was horny. [...] I got Sarah on the pill, I was an honorable kid, took her to Planned Parenthood clinic in Lockport. I took her to [her] senior prom. She was my coming of age girl."

Sarah was the only girlfriend Tim McVeigh ever had. His only other known sexual partners were, like his mother, married women, often the wives of close friends including those of future co-conspirators, Terry Nichols and Michael Fortier. After his arrest, allegations that he was still a virgin or disinterested in either sex in general or woman specifically, particularly offended him. "Asexual? No way. I had no long-term love relationship, never met a woman I loved. That doesn't mean I didn't have sexual relationships. I'm very discreet. I don't need to brag about the woman I fucked. We kept it quiet [...] I never obsessed on one girl, if [a girl I asked out] said 'no' [I said] 'no problem.'"

Meanwhile, after moving to Florida with her two daughters, Mickey began drinking more heavily and her behavior became more erratic. She seemed to "see herself more as a friend than a mother" and occasionally brought her daughters to the bar and encouraged them to drink with her. Late one night, Jennifer received a call from someone at a local bar who said her mother was plastered and needed to be picked up right away. When Jennifer arrived she found Mickey, who was drunk and stoned, and had accidently locked herself in the bathroom, bumped her head, and could not remember how to get out.

Jennifer became increasingly "wild" and depressed under Mickey's roof and began drinking regularly and using drugs herself. Mickey seemed unable to settle on one location. Jennifer said that in the year after she moved to Florida, she lived in four different places and attended three high schools. Her grades began to drop significantly and, unhappy with her life in Florida, returned to the Buffalo area to live with her father. The hard working but detached Bill also seemed unable to provide the type of structure she needed. Jennifer said she would "go to bed every night with a bottle of Jack Daniels" and drink until she passed out. Her father never said anything to her about it.

As countless books about survivalism popped up in the 1980's, writers in other genres capitalized on the trend by selling books such as *How to Survive Your Marriage* and *How to Survive Your Job* as well as an increasing number of children's books about kids abandoned by their parents because of various natural or manmade disasters. The trend coincided with increased divorces rates, single-parent families and a growing number of working mothers. During this time, divorce rates slowly increased from about 12% in 1982 and 1983 to 13.4 % in 1985. No longer the exception to the rule, by the mid 1980's 'latch key kids' were becoming the norm. In 1985, 60% of mothers in Canada worked outside the home. Related books appeared including, *The Handbook for Latchkey Children and Their Parents: A Complete Guide for Latchkey Kids and Their Working Parents.*[68]

While he denied it had any negative effect on him, Tim often brought up the lack of supervision in the McVeigh home, "When I got home [from school] my mother wasn't there. These days," he said "kids get home, there is no parental influence in the household. Parents are working." Much of this he blamed on the "woman's movement" which he felt had removed mothers' presence from home life. Tim felt the previous Baby Boomer generation had full parental influence, while his, Generation X, had "some sense" of it and the next, Generation Y, would have almost none. Sometimes, in letters to his biographers, he advised them to spend time with their children as they were "in that age where they really need you."

The effects of this trend on children became a subject of debate and study. Generation X, the first to live fully within the themes of postmodernism, inhabited an unpredictable, "rapidly mutating" and "crisis ridden" world and faced an extremely uncertain future in which "previous boundaries" dissolved. Beyond the breakdown of traditional nuclear family norms, the Baby Boomers left their progeny to contend with a sense of political cynicism, new technologies, "information and media overload," identity crises, high unemployment rates, a "complex and fragile global economy [and] frightening era of war and terrorism" and domestic militarism. Many speculated that the growing numbers of 'Generation X'ers' fending for themselves were more likely to have behavioral issues, low self-esteem, depression; to abuse drugs, smoke, drink, become promiscuous, cynical and reject authority.

Studies and news reports dubbed the "latch key kids" of Tim's generation, the "lost generation" and described them as "rootless, disillusioned and apathetic ... indifferent, cheaply employed [and] frustrated people." These "slackers" were not particularly lazy, just "cynical and skeptical." Unlike their Baby Boomer parents who still tended to remain at the same job for most of their adult lives, Tim's generation tended to be more nomadic and "while not loyal to geography or employment [were] loyal to their friends ... disliked being labeled or categorized, less shallow, less materialistic than parents [and] eschewed the American Dream." On the other hand, they had enjoyed "the possibilities of technologies, identities and entrepreneurial adventures unimagined by previous generations," and thought to be more independent, self-reliant, confident, socially and technologically savvy, perhaps even, "the most technologically sophisticated" and possessing the widest repertoire of media literacy. By the late 1990's, banks and homebuilders speculated that, as they grew into adulthood, what Generation X wanted more than anything else was a sense of community, stability and permanence, both domestically and in employment.[69]

On Becoming John Rambo

By the early 1980's, the economy of western New York, in recession for decades, had reached an all-time low. Within the city of Buffalo and its outlying areas, flour and steel mills and auto factories closed, leaving thousands without jobs: part of a larger pattern of deindustrialization nationwide. Unemployment rates reached record heights as wages, property values and the area's population declined drastically. The cityscape of Buffalo was quickly decaying into a "landscape of despair." The streets appeared deserted, buildings were abandoned and houses boarded up. Buffalo's civic spirit seemed decimated by the economic blight and its populace suffered from a shared "inferiority complex."[70]

Harrison Motors, which employed both Ed and Bill McVeigh, itself subject to cutbacks and layoffs, was no longer a reliable option for recent graduates like Tim. Increasing numbers of area high school students dropped out or, if they did graduate, chose not to pursue higher education, as college did not guarantee employment. Having earned a small state scholarship, Tim enrolled in computer programming classes at nearby Bryant & Stratton Business College. He received a 99% on the school's math aptitude test, the highest in the school's history, and failed to achieve a perfect score by only fractions. Within a few short months, however, he began to feel unchallenged, grew bored and quit. He later explained, "I knew as much as most of the teachers. I wanted to learn the 'why' of things, not just the 'what.'"

The majority of biographical accounts emphasize that Tim's love of and later obsession with guns originated from the intense bond he shared with his grandfather; but those who knew the McVeigh family noted that he also shared his interest in weapons with his mother.[71] When Tim was eighteen, Mickey returned briefly to the Buffalo area, applied for a pistol permit and convinced Tim to do so as well. In April 1987, on his nineteenth birthday, he applied for and received a New York State concealed firearms permit. For both Mickey and Tim, guns may have been a symbolic cure for the ill-defined, elusive yet impending threats felt by both and, for him, a form of preventive self-defense.

Having decided that guns were a better investment than comic books, Tim sold his sizeable collection that, as a boy, he had considered his college fund. He got a job working at the Johnson Country Store, a gun shop in his hometown of Lockport and along with his friend Dave Darlak purchased ten acres of land in Olean, New York, where Tim sometimes spent days camping and firing his guns on the shooting range the two had built. In the fall of 1987, having given up on the idea of college, he got a second job as an armored truck driver at Burke Armored Security in Buffalo. Tim bragged that his co-workers there nicknamed him "The Kid" because, "I could outshoot virtually everybody."

His fascination with firearms emerged within the broader context of an American gun culture and the growing survivalist movement. All presidential candidates during the 1988 elections were members of the National Rifle Association (NRA), and there were firearms in nearly half of all American homes, with a reported 60 million handguns and 10,000 machine guns in circulation. Throughout the country, a growing number of ordinary citizens purchased 9 mm pistols, .22 automatics, .45's, 12 gauge shot guns, Uzi's, MP-5's, 9 mm submachine guns, untold rounds of ammunition, armor piercing shells, and shot at old TVs, computers, and paper targets depicting Commies and the Ayatollah Khomeini. These weekend warriors, the *Washington Post* noted in 1985, had joined "paramilitary groups, terrorists, survivalists and neo-Nazis."[72] By his late twenties, Tim McVeigh would be associated with and come to represent all of these *types* of people.

Coinciding withing the widespread American bunker mentality at this time were wildly popular television shows like *Magnum PI* (1980–1988), *The A-Team* (1983–1986), *Airwolf* (1984–1986) and *MacGyver* (1985–1992), that featured heroic narratives about the exploits of often resentful, disgruntled, renegade Vietnam veterans.[73] Perhaps important to the construction of stories McVeigh would later tell, the "A-Team" consisted of four former members of an Army Special Forces "crack commando" unit who had fought together in Vietnam. After a superior officer framed them for a bank robbery in Saigon as part of a political ploy, they were convicted and "sent to prison by a military court for a crime they didn't commit." After escaping from a "maximum security stockade," the A-Team found refuge in the "Los Angeles Underground." Now forced to live on the run, hunted by military police and intelligence officers, they survive as soldiers of fortune. Despite being "wanted by the government," each week the A-Team, out of the kindness of their heart, came to the rescue of innocent and wronged citizens who sought out their help.

Hollywood joined in, generating millions of dollars in ticket sales and merchandise for films such as *The Deer Hunter* (1978), *Apocalypse Now* (1979), *Platoon* (1986), and *Full Metal Jacket* (1987). While traditional war films told stories of soldiers banding together to defeat common enemies, post-Vietnam blockbuster films centered on recurring themes of missing POW's abandoned by their government, traumatized and "deranged" combat vets plagued by debilitating flashbacks: "My Lai's killer zombies come home, dripping blood and lunacy...a metaphor for madness itself." These films aimed to resolve lingering conflicts surrounding the country's recent humiliating and shameful war by telling fictionalized versions of historically uncomfortable tales, thereby conquering the collective nightmare of the Vietnam War through the construction of shared national fantasies and newer mythologies about it. The hyper-masculine, hyper-violent war-hero action films of the 1980's depicted "macho protagonists [who face] herculean obstacles and challenges" but who nevertheless display military heroism, selflessness, camaraderie and principled dedication to a cause larger than themselves "as the highest form of life." In this newer generation of war film, the hero, "willing to use any means at his disposal" positions himself at the forefront of chaotic violence and for the most part, prevails in the end.[74]

The most notable of these films was the *Rambo* series: *First Blood* and its sequels in 1985 and 1988. In them, the protagonist, John Rambo, emerges as a symbol of restored masculinity, betrayal and revenge in the aftermath of Vietnam. While criticized for its revisionist, cliché, and jingoistic depictions of an "ultra – macho, all-American vengeance wreaker," a nationwide Rambo *fever* emerged nonetheless, as evidenced by millions in box office sales. Tim, too, had caught Rambo fever, and the affliction would soon consume him.[75]

It was at this time that Tim, an avid reader, first encountered and began to devour a new type of literature, highly influenced by post-Vietnam cultural imaginings. Hoping to develop his marksmanship further, he began frequenting local gun clubs and area shooting ranges where, according to Stickney, "members subscribed to literature whose content ranges from information on various weapons to right wing paranoia pamphlets that claim the federal government's main goal in the future is to disarm America." He gravitated towards publications such as *Soldier of Fortune* magazine (*SOF*) that describes itself as pro-second amendment, U.S. military, strong U.S. defense, police and veterans, ardent supporters of "the basic freedom of mankind" and against "tyranny of all kinds." *SOF*, criticized for its unabashed "anti-leftist" leanings, backing of Nicaraguan "Contra" rebels and recruitment of American mercenaries to train them, had attracted a growing number of readers, many of whom, while too young to have fought in Vietnam, grew up viewing images of it in popular media. The magazine appealed also to the increasing numbers of survivalists who, like Tim, hoped to learn the "tricks of staying alive after the collapse of civilization."[76]

SOF and other, similar publications soon became a permanent staple of his literary diet. And then one day, in the back of *SOF*, Timothy McVeigh found an advertisement for the 1978 book *The Turner Diaries*, written under the pseudonym Andrew McDonald by former physics professor William Pierce, founder of the National Alliance – one of the most notorious and highly organized racist organizations in the country. Set in the not-too-distant future, the book contains the fictitious diary entries of Earl Turner, who believes that increased multi-culturalism and restrictive gun ownership legislation (The Cohen Act) poses a threat to the white race whom the Jews (and their minions, the blacks) hope to enslave and annihilate in order to establish a "Zionist Occupational Government" (ZOG). Turner organizes underground cells to wage war on "The System" by committing acts of terror including assassinations and bombings in order to destroy the repressive government, eradicate the non-white population and establish a utopian white homeland in the northwest United States. Turner and his gang of white freedom fighters achieve success after using a truck bomb to destroy a supercomputer, housed in an FBI building, which tracks and databases all U.S. citizens, especially those who, like Turner, opposed ZOG.

For groups like Pierce's National Alliance, the concept of ZOG or the formation of an "all-white homeland" was a central ideological tenet of the larger, growing White Power Movement (WPM), who praised *The Turner Diaries* for its prophetic wisdom and sought (with surprising success) to spread its message to impressionable, disaffected American youth. During the late 1980's, WPM spokespeople began to attract the attention of mainstream media, thereby further garnering alienated followers. As the WPM grew in numbers, so too did the frequency of hate crimes and WPM-participant arrests. Considered a "bible" by various white supremacy groups, *The Turner Diaries* also gained a larger audience within broader right-wing paramilitary circles. While disparate, their ranks included second-amendment advocates, survivalists, common law and sovereign citizens groups, constitutionalists, and disgruntled farmers, all of whom gravitated to the book's unabashed pro-gun message and anti-government themes.[77]

Widely referred to later as "the blue print" for the Oklahoma City bombing, by all accounts, Timothy McVeigh became obsessed with *The Turner Diaries* and its influence upon the formation of his political and racial ideologies is undeniable. *The Turner Diaries*, he said, not only helped him understand his co-workers' racism but "expose[d] me to racism I wasn't familiar with … it's very anti-black," although later he realized "everyone is an individual." He said that, prior to working at Burke, "I didn't have a racist bone in my body" and was oriented more towards "the survivalist crowd – put away your food supplies for a year, get ready for whatever disaster would be coming along, nuclear, natural. [Burke] was the first time I ever was exposed to racist comments. [From them] I learned the vernacular of racism, I picked up on it."[78] Publications like *Soldier of Fortune* and *The Turner Diaries* bolstered his already existing survivalist leanings. They exposed him to, and familiarized him with, previously unknown subcultural realms and ideas, provided new models for him to draw from in the shaping of his identity and, ultimately, played a pivotal role in the narrative constructions of the OKC bombing (and other acts of violence by the extreme Right). In a sense, McVeigh made real the deeds of the fictional Earl Turner.

Meanwhile, Burke quickly promoted the responsible and trustworthy nineteen-year-old Tim McVeigh, assigning him to high profile sites, including the Buffalo Federal Reserve Bank, despite his occasional juvenile antics and increasingly odd behavior. Tim had "started out as a good employee [but] he began having problems." His co-workers at Burke "saw a Timothy McVeigh most high school students never knew– a man influenced by war and weapon literature, angry over his home life and living in a survivalist fantasy world." [79]

According to his supervisor, Tim was a good, reliable employee who always did his job. Tim, he recalled, had a fascination with armored cars, described himself to others as a "survivalist" and told of his hopes to build his own underground bunker someday. His co-workers remembered his interest in guns, his impressive collection of firearms (he always carried one or two on him), and that he was one of the best marksmen on the shooting range – a true *crack shot*. Sometimes, they said, he tried to be funny and, once, showed up to work dressed like Rambo, decked out in camouflage and ammunition belts crisscrossed over his chest looking like he was ready for World War III. Despite his earlier praise, upon further reflection, his supervisor recalled that two of the other men assigned to ride with Tim complained that, occasionally, he put on earplugs and turned the radio up to its highest volume. In fact, he added, Tim once threatened to blow up the house of neighborhood children who had thrown snowballs at his truck.

Co-workers said that at some point he began to act increasingly high-strung, hyperactive, jumpy, erratic, intense and began carrying more guns with him to work than he could ever possibly need. His temper had grown shorter and, some days, he became angry at the drop of a hat only to, just as quickly, calm down again. Other days he was silent and acted like an introverted, preoccupied loner. According to McVeigh though, if he had acted oddly it was due to overwhelming amounts of stress, partly from working two jobs. This left him worn down and sleep-deprived, a state known to induce erratic and paranoid behavior. He would use this excuse to explain similar observations made by others, later.[80]

It was during this time, McVeigh reflected, that he grew disenchanted by the mundane and developed an overwhelming personal desire for a larger purpose in life; a warrior's "Code of Honor" as depicted in films like *Rambo*. He sought structure, purpose, camaraderie ... and guns. Later, he could, and did, cite long passages from *The Turner Diaries* from memory and evoked a particular favorite one to illustrate his growing sense of oppression: "*The chains that bind us are formed slowly, one link at a time, so we never notice the additional weight of one additional link, but eventually, it forms a chain.*" [Italics added]. McVeigh said, "I loved that [passage], it was right on. Most Americans could give a shit, as long as they have a six-pack of beer and their TV is working."

On May 12, 1988, shortly after his twentieth birthday, Timothy McVeigh, alone, drove to the Federal Building in Buffalo, New York, walked into the Army recruiter's office and informed the recruiter of his desire to become an Airborne Ranger, Green Beret or member of the Special Forces. The man assured him he could pursue this vision once he completed basic training; and so he enlisted in the U.S. Army, took his general aptitude test that same day and his physical a few days later. According to his enlistment documents, he was 6' 1" and 150 pounds, with blond hair, blue eyes and 20/20 vision. He was in good health, having no prior medical or dental issues, no allergies, and no prescribed medications.

Childhood friend Sam Dangler (name changed) said that, growing up, Tim had been a "very pro-government type of individual," was a fan of Ronald Reagan and at eighteen registered with the Republican Party, so his decision to join the military made sense. According to Steve Hodge though, it was not patriotism that propelled him, but his interest in survivalism. Tim believed the Army could provide the best weapons and survival training.

His legal team believed he joined the Army seeking *truth* and to fill a "central core of meaning" absent within him. Brandon Stickney thought his decision was influenced by the works of fiction he devoured that depicted the heroics of war, and led him to believe his future lay in commanding men in distant lands he'd only ever read about. Or perhaps, Stickney continued, Tim thought he would become a member of "the elite forces, that special breed of man set apart from the rest, a man who is authorized for secret missions."[81] Even Tim later acknowledged that he based his decision to join the Army, in part, on his desire to buttress his survival skills and viewed it as equivalent to spending four years in college, but also on the powerful influence of his favorite movies, notably *Rambo: First Blood* and *Missing in Action.*

Whatever his reasons for joining, while he claimed to be so at the time of his death, upon enlisting, Timothy James McVeigh was no longer fully the Captain of his Soul, nor Master of his Fate. Rather, he became the property of the United States Army, and the chains that would bind him proved strong ones indeed. Timothy McVeigh had just joined an experiment in progress, one from which, psychologically, there would never be an exit strategy.

Chapter Two

THE FOLLOWING RECORDS DO NOT EXIST

PART ONE
Avalanche Of Decay
(1988-1990)

BASIC TRAINING (MAY 1988)

While at the Buffalo Army recruitment center, McVeigh scored among the top ten percentile on the General Technical test. On May 30, 1988, only days after enlisting, Timothy McVeigh began Basic Combat Training at Fort Benning, Georgia, the self-proclaimed "incubator for the world's finest combat soldiers" and home to the U.S. Army School of the Americas. A recruitment *error* however, landed him in the experimental Cohesion Operational Readiness Training (COHORT) unit. The COHORT program kept soldiers together from Basic Training throughout their entire three-year enlistment cycle, with the goal of unit cohesion, *esprit de corps,* advanced group training and commitment to the unit's mission. While military theorists proposed the idea that COHORT Units would lessen "soldier turbulence" as well "high levels of psychological breakdown in battle," previous attempts to form such units had led to higher rates of AWOL's and suicides. Assumedly, in an attempt to work out these kinks, the U.S. Army formed the COHORT unit in which Tim McVeigh now found himself. To his great dismay and despite assurances to him by his recruiter, the COHORT structure prevented recruits from volunteering for Special Forces, Ranger School, or even Airborne School, for at least three years. "If the recruiter had told Tim the truth about the program he was headed for," Brandon Stickney wrote, "McVeigh probably wouldn't have enlisted." This was only one of such errors and misrepresentations the Buffalo Army recruiter made in McVeigh's case.[1]

Mark Hamm, criminologist at Indiana State University and former consultant for the Jones Team, wrote that the Army's COHORT experiment provided the "mechanism" and "most important source of indirect support for the terrorism that would later occur in Oklahoma." In fact, he said, the conspiracy to bomb the Murrah building could not have gotten off to a better start had it been orchestrated by the "best and brightest at the Pentagon." In Hamm's opinion, "there would have been no conspiracy" without the COHORT program, for it was in Basic Training that Timothy McVeigh met Terry Nichols and Michael Fortier, who would become Tim's closest friends and, later, his co-conspirators.[2] All three had enlisted on the same day in different states: McVeigh in New York, Nichols in Michigan, Fortier in Arizona; they were assigned to the COHORT Unit and placed together in a six-man squad.

Thirty-three year old organic farmer and family man, Terry Nichols, had been hit hard by the Midwest farm crisis of the 1980s and faced the impending loss of his family farm. He joined the Army at the suggestion of his soon to be ex-wife. His fellow soldiers described Nichols, the oldest man in the unit and chosen squad leader, as an introverted family man, "spastic" and "nerdy." He quickly picked up the nicknames "Pops" and "Old Man" from the younger grunts who later (if they remembered him at all) described him as "helpful," "friendly" and "outgoing."[3] One soldier said that while the mechanically inclined Nichols "often acted dumb, in reality he was very intelligent and was always reading a book or fixing something." He recalled that after one commanding officer found Nichols to be "extremely bright," he was assigned to headquarters. Another said Nichols was "a very, very nervous person and appeared that he was the type who would never want to get into trouble.... Nichols always wanted to tell on somebody if they did something wrong."

Fortier, very different from the old-fashioned Nichols, and an unlikely companion for the serious clean-cut McVeigh, was a twenty-year-old, former long-haired, flannel-wearing, grungy, pot-smoking, methamphetamine-user, described by fellow soldiers as "blunt" and outspoken in speech who, while humorous, had a "bad attitude."

However mismatched, all three shared an interest in guns, adamantly opposed gun control legislation, had an attraction to the growing survivalist movement and espoused anti-government values. Others, like Brandon Stickney, later wrote that from the very beginning of their acquaintance, Nichols and McVeigh had something else in common: overt racism.

THE SURVIVALIST'S HARD-ON (MAY-AUGUST '88)

In boot camp, and throughout his time in the Army, Tim McVeigh wrote home regularly to his friend Steve and sister Jennifer, first about the rigors of boot camp, the developing feelings of camaraderie between himself and his fellow COHORTs and then, with an increasing frequency, about ongoing world events and politics. One letter detailed the typically horrible experience he had when exposed to CS Gas during training, an experience that would haunt him later during the Waco siege and contribute to the deep sympathy he would feel for the victims.

Years after his arrest, McVeigh wrote to his biographers, "In basic training, when I was being conditioned and brainwashed, I recognized it. I knew it was happening to me, but I went along with it. In basic, when our platoon stood at attention, we had to snap to attention and say, 'blood makes the grass grow. KILL, KILL, KILL" Every time we came to attention, which must have been 20 times per day, we had to chant that. I had to prevent myself from smirking. I knew a lot of these guys around me weren't smart enough to pick up on it."

Among the characteristically recurring themes to appear in his letters home was survival in the face of possible future disasters, his descriptions sometimes reaching apocalyptic homoerotic heights. Demonstrative of his lifelong interest in mysterious topics like the lost continent of Atlantis and the Bermuda Triangle was one early letter in which he discussed his belief that the predictions of Nostradamus alluded to Iran. When asked by his attorneys what he meant by this, he told them that, at the time, he believed Iran would surely be "the beast that starts the war."

Throughout the previous eight years, the U.S. had publicly backed Iraq during the Iran-Iraq War. At the time McVeigh entered boot camp and, in the months prior to his enlistment, the U.S. launched naval strikes against Iranian oil operations. Secretly, however, the U.S. had been dealing weapons to Iran and supporting Saudi Arabia, the professed enemy of both. Indictments issued against Lt. Col. Oliver North and Vice Admiral John Poindexter for their roles in what came to be known as the Iran-Contra scandal did not prevent former CIA Director and Vice President George H.W. Bush from winning the Republican presidential nomination, despite Bush's own role in the debacle. Meanwhile, turmoil, natural and manmade, intended and accidental, foreign and domestic, dominated the headlines. Around the world airplanes crashed, bombs exploded, and politicians were assassinated. The U.K. fought the IRA; the Palestinians fought the Israelis; the Soviets began economic restructuring (perestroika). Soon after, the Geneva Accords convened. And while maintaining the highest defense budget on the planet Earth, the U.S. economy was crashing.

While impending cataclysms were nothing new to McVeigh, he was amazed at his new environment, having never before left his native region of upstate New York. A letter he wrote to Steve described his enjoyment of various training activities and late night/early morning guard duty:

> I looked into the sky. I thought I was looking at thin clouds, but...
> holy shit!!! The sky was so clear; I could actually see the Milky Way!!

I could see every damn star in the universe.... I could have sat in awe all night.... [The drought] here gives this hardcore survivalist a hard-on! I only wish I was home in the middle of a possible catastrophe! The funny thing (and terrible thing) is the Army doesn't give a shit about water conservation yet civilians are put on water restrictions. That's the gov't for you! [During bivouac training a hurricane hit near Ft. Benning and] the Medivac flew 4 people out. I had a hard-on, it was great. Mine was one of the few tents left standing at the end ... I dug a drainage ditch on the outside better than the goddamn Romans!! A tree blew over...the sand was blowing like snow in a white out. What a first time experience!!...Storms here hit hard and fast ... some of the best electrical storms I've seen.

From this point on, the content of McVeigh's letters home consistently included detailed descriptions of various weapons he was mastering or the newest guns and ammo he had purchased or acquired (at times through theft of Army property). Sometimes he sent ammunition back home for his "nest egg," claiming it had gone unused during training anyway. He told Steve that "while everybody else is getting laid," his plans for the Fourth of July that year consisted of searching pawnshops for ammunition and fireworks.

In regard to Timothy McVeigh's life in the army prior to the Gulf War, four major themes consistently emerge within existing biographical accounts: his love of guns, interest in survivalism, an inclination towards racist literature, and his outstanding performance as an infantry soldier. Archival sources reveal the existence of another pattern in his letters, however– a continued tendency to link sex with weapons, violence and possible catastrophe, a quality which, while not a conventional "Army Value," was one perhaps possessed by only the best soldiers in the U.S. Army.

His only real complaints during boot camp, it seems, were commonly shared ones: its exhausting physical demands and the traditional divide between officers and enlisted men. To Steve, he wrote, "an NCO [non-commissioned officer] is a real man, fuck those brain-dead officers. Chain of Command is so fucked up, we get the order (finally) at 5:00 PM to un-blouse our boots and take our BDU's off after the heat is gone. I just hit brain-death, that's all." Despite his "brain-death," Timothy McVeigh and the U.S. Army seemed to be well suited to each other and upon completion of Basic Training, he scored perfectly on all his tests and qualified as an Expert Sharpshooter.

AVALANCHE OF DECAY

Mark Hamm later noted that the Pentagon sealed Nichols' and McVeigh's military records, therefore making the available portion of military service and medical records a valuable addition to the Jones Collection. Within the archival collection primarily, and supported by oral and other types of documentary evidence, a mysterious narrative emerges, which tells a different story about Timothy McVeigh; a story that runs parallel to, but whose details remain strikingly absent from those told previously.

Timothy McVeigh joined the Army, in part, to hone his survival skills in the event of future disaster or cataclysm. Meanwhile, beginning in boot camp, a more elusive physiological deterioration began to occur. Briefly outlined here is a portion of this covert narrative that took place from May to October of 1988.

On May 25th and 27th, days after arriving at Ft. Benning, McVeigh received a battery of standard (and not so standard) vaccines and immunization shots for tetanus, measles, mumps, rubella, smallpox, polio, flu and two other shots meant to prevent acute respiratory disease called Adenovirus Type 4 and Type 7.[4] A week later, on the evening of June 6, 1988, at 9:40 PM, McVeigh made the first of what would be many non-routine visits seeking medical attention. The attending doctor noted that McVeigh received a "superficial abrasion" after he tripped over the man in front of him while running in formation and, since then, continued to feel dizzy. The doctor assigned him to light duty for the remainder of the day.

About a month later on July 10, he wrote a letter to his mother and sister telling them that he had recently been feeling sick, was running a fever and, because of this, expected to receive a chest x-ray. In a separate letter written two days later on July 12, he claimed to have come down with walking pneumonia, but said the doctor, at McVeigh's request, did not prescribe medication to him as, he explained in the letter, he did not want to establish a "medical profile." If he did indeed visit a doctor for a fever, an x-ray, or pneumonia, these visits remained undocumented in his medical records – a circumstance of vital importance later. Interestingly, he wrote home noting his objections to establishing a medical profile at the exact period when his lengthy and inexplicable profile, while incomplete, begins. The July 12 letter marks the first of a very few frank admissions Timothy McVeigh would make about his health or its official documentation.

His third and final *documented* medical interaction while in boot camp occurred on the morning of July 26, 1988, when he sought attention for muscle pain in his right leg that, the doctor noted, McVeigh said had been bothering him since the previous week. On August 4, 1988, he wrote to Steve telling him he had just gotten through the "middle of three bad weeks" although no medical visits are listed for the month of August.

After completing Basic Training, Private McVeigh arrived at Fort Riley, Kansas. Shortly afterwards, on September 9, 1988, though never mentioning his head and leg injuries, he wrote to Steve:

> Yesterday we got more shots. This time I was politely introduced to yellow fever, typhoid, and "Plague I" (whichever plague this one is, I'm not sure but "Plague II" didn't hurt as much in Basic!) They told us some side effects would be flu-like symptoms. One hour later, we had a ceremony to welcome the new company in. The asshole CO made a dickhead 1 ½-hour long faggot speech – it was just like the movies ... people just crumbling all around me, falling down and passing out. I almost went myself; and just as everything was going black and my knees buckled, the CO finished and turned the company over to the 1st Sgt., who immediately gave us "Rest," which is a command to talk or move as long as you don't move your right foot. I went right to my knee.

His medical records contain no entries until September 12, however. On this day his first *documented* yellow fever, typhoid, and 'Plague Shot I' vaccinations are listed, and a month later, his October 7 'Plague II' shot. No signed consent forms are included in his immunization records; and redactions that obscure the identities of doctors who administered the shots as well as any identifying information (rank, etc.) about them, are found throughout the records; the first redaction being the name of the doctor who oversaw McVeigh's yellow fever vaccination.

The earliest non-routine medical visit noted in the records after McVeigh's completion of Basic Training occurred on October 4, 1988, at 6:23 AM, when he arrived at the medical barracks complaining of chronic back pain that, he said, began three weeks prior (shortly after his second round of immunizations). The doctor noted that Pvt. McVeigh "used to lift a lot of bags at home" and oddly, although he had not been home in over five months, the pain was such that McVeigh requested an x-ray, the results of which were "normal." Two days later, on October 6, 1988, he once more saw the doctor for chronic back pain, and on October 8, one day after being given a Plague II shot, his gums began to bleed, for which he would for the first time (but certainly not last) see the Army dentist.

That November he wrote to Steve and said that, although he had come to the decision to eventually move back home to his father's house and "enclose the house in evergreens," he did not think this would *"stem the avalanche of decay"* he perceived as imminent. The phrase "avalanche of decay" came from one of his favorite films, *Mad Max II: Road Warrior* (1981), about survival in a dystopian society after nuclear war has destroyed most of the planet. His remaining letters for the duration of his military service make no further mention of shots, aches and pain, dental issues, or any of the many other symptoms (some quite bizarre), for which he would receive medical attention in the years to come.

From just May 1988 until that December, excluding visits for the immunizations, McVeigh saw the dentist three times and made four additional non-routine visits to the doctor. In just a few weeks, military doctors examined Timothy McVeigh on more occasions than civilian doctors had throughout his entire high school career and, upon his leaving the Army two years later, more times than in his entire life prior to joining the Army. McVeigh's medical records and letters reveal an unknown soldier, who, in two years active duty in the United States military received medical attention on more than seventy-five occasions, as reflected in his *available* records. Was it possible that Timothy McVeigh's avalanche of decay alluded to something more than his adolescent apocalyptic survival fantasies?

PRIVATE MCFLY

After completing Basic Training in August 1988, Pvt. McVeigh, along with the rest of his COHORT unit, including Fortier and Nichols, arrived at Fort Riley, Kansas. McVeigh and Fortier were assigned to the famous First Infantry Division (The Big Red One), Dagger Brigade, 16th Mechanized Infantry Regiment, 2nd Battalion, Charlie Company, (1st) Headquarters Platoon and remained in the same Squad while Nichols was reassigned to Bravo Company and became his Unit Commander's driver.[5]

Many of the COHORTs assigned to Dagger Brigade with McVeigh recalled the frequency of problems in Charlie Company, including excessive drug use, domestic abuse and general insubordination. McVeigh, however, was different. One soldier described the men of Charlie Company as "rude, crude, and socially unacceptable.... Warped ... there was all sorts of strange characters in that company, it was really wild." To an outsider, they seemed like "a bunch of assholes."

In contrast, those who served alongside him described Tim McVeigh as "one of the most normal guys in the whole company.." He did not smoke, drink, or use drugs. He was polite, well mannered, clean-cut, quiet, and sometimes shy; "a good guy," "down to earth," "ordinary" and "straight": "as nice a guy as you could meet." With few exceptions, he got along with everybody, "never pissed anybody off" and "tried to stay out of trouble." More than one soldier mentioned that McVeigh was one of only a few in the company that they would invite over to their house. Although no one ever knew him to date, according to a higher-ranking soldier, "Tim was the kind of guy that a girl's parents would want her to bring home – very straight and conservative. However, he wasn't the kind of guy that girls would want to date ... not wild enough."

Charlie Company COHORT Ray Barnes (name changed) shared a room with McVeigh for nearly three years prior to the Gulf War (Operations Desert Shield and Desert Storm). Barnes said, "Our Company had a lot of problems. I mean, half the time we couldn't even get floor wax. We had to buy our own. Our Company ... it wasn't the greatest but we had some good guys and in my opinion, McVeigh was right up there."[6] The descriptions offered by his fellow soldiers of his performance are, perhaps, the only consistent aspect of McVeigh's documented life not contradicted by other accounts and sources.

In the 1962 film *The Manchurian Candidate*, when asked to describe brainwashed war hero Raymond Shaw, the soldiers he served with always, automatically and unanimously, responded by reciting the words, "Raymond Shaw is the kindest, bravest, warmest, most wonderful human being I've ever known in my life." Reminiscent of this are the descriptions of McVeigh by his fellow COHORTs, over 33 of whom responded in a remarkably unanimous manner. McVeigh was smart, hardworking, and above all else, an outstanding soldier, one of the best they ever encountered. He was: a "good soldier," "great soldier," "fantastic soldier," "excellent soldier," "top soldier," "total soldier," "dynamite soldier," and "model soldier ... before things fell apart," "very military," "gung-ho," "a very squared away soldier ... out of all the soldiers in the 1st Platoon Tim was by far the most squared away." He seemed to love the Army, "always walked a very good line," took orders well, was responsible, "always cooperative" and "willing to do whatever was necessary." Not only did he follow orders, he strove to be the best at anything in which he involved himself. One fellow soldier said McVeigh "was kind of like a robot ... everything McVeigh did was for a purpose." "McVeigh," said another, "played the military 24 hours a day, seven days a week."[7] Ray Barnes said:

> *He wouldn't sleep.* He was a consummate soldier. I mean, if you gave him a cinder block and *a tooth brush* and said "make it shine" he'd follow orders to the T. If a superior officer came up and gave him an order, McVeigh'd do everything possible to carry out that order. He was a smart, detail minded person, the type that dotted I's and crossed T's. He was nice and polite, not a trouble maker or a bully. He wasn't cruel. ... Hell! I seen him pick up stray animals and help them. He wasn't a whiner, didn't complain. He was a private person and didn't open up to just anybody. He wasn't nosey, wasn't a snoop. They tried to portray him as this expert cold-hearted killer, but the truth was that girls scared the crap out of him. I think a third grader could have punked him out. I mean ... he was nerdy!

While his COHORTs seemed to think highly of him, it was also evident that Tim McVeigh just did not quite fit in. He seemed "better educated," more "serious," "kind of a loner," and "kind of nerdy, not what you'd picture as a typical infantry soldier." He maintained a large library in the small barracks and read constantly, earning him the nickname "McFly" after the geeky character from *Back To The Future*. To them it seemed he could memorize a weapons or procedure manual just by picking it up and recite the Standard Operating Procedures and regulations verbatim. Concerning all matters of military practice and protocol, he "always knew the text book answers."

Unable to pursue his ambition of joining the Special Forces for two more years (until the COHORT unit's enlistment cycle ended), he nonetheless continuously prepared to do so, his sights focused squarely on this goal. He trained, physically and mentally. Though gawky, awkward, and nerdy, he was in "excellent shape," quickly becoming known as a "PT Stud." He had the makings of a career soldier, and they all thought McVeigh would be a "lifer ... he just didn't have much of a life." On the weekends, "McFly" sometimes stayed in the barracks watching movies, but mostly spent his time maintaining his weapons, shining his boots, pressing his uniforms and studying technical and field manuals, applying this knowledge to a training program of his own design in addition to his assigned training.

Ray Barnes said, "We had a crew we called the Brew Crew. We'd all go out drinking. [McVeigh] wasn't really a person that got out and did the bar scene though. He was intelligent and read a lot. Before the Gulf, he knew that he wanted to be in the Special Forces. While everybody else was going out to the bars, running around, McVeigh was putting on a rucksack, road marching, running, swimming, lifting weights, trying to build up his body mass." Likewise, Gordon Blackcloud (name changed) said, "McVeigh was a little strong headed about what he wanted, but he was a good soldier. Before we even went to the Gulf he was already carrying backpacks and getting ready... he wanted to join the Special Forces even back then. Personally, as a friend, we could talk and BS around. He could be funny at times, and we went a lot of places together. I never seen him with any girl [laughing] and he didn't like going to the bars. He'd rather just ride around and drive and stuff like that."[8]

As he had when a child, McVeigh found ways to capitalize on his environment, and the worldly habits of those around him provided him opportunities to do so. He became his unit's "designated driver," charging small amounts of gas money. As he saved all his money and "always had a lot of cash," he thus became the "company loan shark" as well. Although the media made a lot of noise after his arrest regarding his personal business ventures while in the Army, most of his Battle Buddies said this was overblown. According to one, "sometimes we'd pay him for his trouble, but it wasn't like he was demanding payment." Rather than depicting him as greedy or predatory, his fellow soldiers said he was dependable and someone they knew they could count on. To them, he was a good friend, who many times used his own holiday leave to drive his fellow soldiers home to visit their families during the holidays, sometimes trekking across the country to do so. According to one COHORT, "Tim looked out well for the guys in the 1st Platoon. He'd taxi them around, making a lot of money in the process, but also making sure that they got back to base and were there for the next duty call. He was charging much less than a taxi and those guys could depend on him. Many times, he dragged those guys out of bars and made sure they got back to base. Tim was the kind who would look out for his fellow troops." Ray Barnes said:

> We were roommates for a good three years. Did I consider McVeigh a friend? Most definitely! Out of anybody in the Company that I could trust to do their job as a soldier, McVeigh'd have been on the top of my list. If you told him a secret and asked him not to tell anybody, he wouldn't. He could keep a secret. Did I trust him? Yes. Did I like him? Yes. 'Veigh was a good friend and I'd help him out in anything. He was there for me when I needed it. We were tight. That's what you want in a COHORT Unit. We stayed together from boot camp until your enlistment is over. You're one, day in and day out. Brothers. He was a good guy and I could trust McVeigh with my life. If he said "Hey! I got your back," he kept his word. That was McVeigh.

Although a barracks resident, McVeigh spent a good amount of time off post and so other soldiers would sometimes invite him over to have dinner with their wives and children. More than one reported that he had been good with their children and another fondly recalled that McVeigh had helped him pick out an engagement ring. Likely unknown to them however, were the letters he wrote to his sister in which he claimed to be sleeping with more than one of his COHORTs wives.

GUNS, POLITICS & MCVEIGH'S EVER-IMPENDING DOOM

Timothy McVeigh absolutely loved guns and the U.S. Army's arsenal of death allowed him to nurture this love. Here he found the time, encouragement, resources, training, incentive system and overall environment conducive to developing his already existing interests and hobbies. During his first year, he received Infantry training and was assigned a SAW (Squad Automatic Weapon) Gunner. McVeigh's self-discipline paid off and he quickly rose in rank, receiving a promotion to E-3, and Unit Weapons Specialist in January 1989. In his second year, he trained in heavier, mechanized infantry tactics at Ft. Irwin, California. While there, he received an Army Achievement Medal. In a letter written to Steve from Ft. Irwin, he gleefully bragged, "I must know how to operate and maintain every weapon in U.S. and Soviet arsenal."

Fellow soldiers described McVeigh in the same manner as others did before and after his enlistment. He was, they said, a "weapons freak," more interested in target shooting than drinking or picking up women and was ready to go out shooting with anyone, anywhere, any time. He was an excellent shot, one of the best in his company, a natural who "didn't have to work as hard at learning things like others … he could put a weapon together blindfolded." One COHORT said McVeigh loved guns like other men love football. He always owned several weapons that he procured from local gun shops, gun shows and, sometimes, even appropriated them from Uncle Sam's own stockpiles. Armed to the teeth, he had guns of all shapes and sizes stashed everywhere – off base in storage sheds, the homes of friends, the trunk of his car, and, (also against regulations) at various locations on post. Gordon Blackcloud: "For the most part, he was just like anybody else. The only thing I seen that was a little different was that he'd take stuff and put in his trunk of his car or his foot locker. He carried MRE's, guns and had canisters of CS gas in his trunk too. It wasn't too hard to get all the stuff off the base. As far as I know, he was gonna take 'em home and store 'em. Nobody was gonna tell on him."

A number of others said that McVeigh's interest in guns was a normal hobby for infantrymen and it was common for men living in the barracks to keep extra guns off base (although probably not stolen ones). Still, in letters he wrote during this time he repetitively expressed both his disagreement with and non-adherence to existing firearm regulations. In one, he wrote about mailing stolen ammunition and in another that, because he was under twenty-one, he could not buy a Glock 19 in Kansas and so had gotten a friend to buy it for him with, he said, "No waiting period or anything, right over the counter."[9]

His hobbies seemed to have driven his political ideology, more than the other way around. A constant topic of his conversations and letters was the growing debate surrounding the Second Amendment. John W. Hinckley's failed attempt to assassinate President Ronald Reagan in 1981 left three wounded and White House Press Secretary Jim Brady permanently paralyzed by a bullet in the head. Consequently, Brady's wife, Sarah, catalyzed an aggressive firearms control campaign that continues to this day. Hinckley had used a .22 caliber pistol, bought in a Dallas pawnshop and Sarah Brady argued that, had a criminal and mental health background check been conducted on Hinckley, his troubled past would have been detected and the shooting possibly prevented. She lobbied for the passage of The Brady Handgun Prevention Act, introduced during the 1987 Congressional session, calling for nationwide, mandatory seven-day waiting periods on all handgun sales, as well as criminal and mental health background checks. The bill quickly became a major legislative priority. Reagan supported the legislation, calling it crucial to the prevention of violent crimes plaguing the nation. The National Rifle Association (NRA) led an equally aggressive campaign to prevent the legislation's passage, a campaign McVeigh kept a close eye on.[10]

A number of McVeigh's letters focused on the growing controversy surrounding the Brady Bill and those "liberal mother fuckers" trying to pass gun control legislation generally. One, written to his sister just prior to the 1988 presidential elections, is the first of many to follow in which McVeigh outlines key tenets of his developing politics beyond the issue of gun control. While conceding to his sister that Republican candidate George H. W. Bush was an "idiot," he told her he still preferred Bush over Democratic candidate Michael Dukakis. "New York is turning liberal," he explained, "The problem with liberals is they're anti-freedom, big brother types ... the question is, how much is it the right of the government to take by force, which is what the IRS does? With state and federal taxes, the government takes more than 50% of what you earn. This makes you a slave, with the government saying 'thanks for growing the corn, I'll take it.' The government takes our guns, because the government cannot trust us. [Liberals] believe they can violate the constitution if it protects people from themselves."[11]

McVeigh continued to immerse himself in magazines like *Soldier of Fortune*, *Guns and Ammo* and *American Survival*. One COHORT said, "The material that Tim read was pretty neat stuff for a soldier. If anything happened, he wanted to be prepared for it." Another said he "seemed to believe that we were going to eventually have a war in this country." To them, the intensity of his love for guns and his self-identification as a survivalist was almost comical. They sometimes joked that McVeigh was a perfect caricature of the survivalists found in popular movies like *Tremors* and *Mad Max*, and McVeigh, for his part, intended to survive the post-apocalyptic world depicted in such movies. The threat as McVeigh perceived it at this time, however, was not a domestic one, but foreign. While not expressing outward hostility towards the U.S. government generally, he "frequently talked about Communism and how he was going to be ready to defend himself if this country were ever attacked."

No one remembered him speaking of or advocating plans to sabotage the government. Gordon Blackcloud said McVeigh "didn't advocate violence against the government. It just wasn't him." COHORT Howard Thompson recalled his keen and "humanitarian" awareness of global and domestic political issues and said once, after reading *Schindler's List*, McVeigh had lectured Thompson about the human capacity for cruelty. "[Tim] seemed to care about the whole world as opposed to just his country or himself," remembered Thompson, "[he] would see news of warring countries and comment that he wished the world could get together and get rid of the oppressors."

Leaving aside conflicts between Iran, Iraq and Saudi Arabia, and the imminent Gulf War, there was a lot happening at this time that undoubtedly reinforced McVeigh's militant dreams. Since he had joined the Army, fires, droughts, earthquakes, geomagnetic storms, tornados, hurricanes, typhoons, and cyclones wrought destruction throughout the world. Trains, planes, hot air balloons, and cruise ships crashed. Ferries caught fire, submarines sank, and battleships exploded. An asteroid named Asclepius was rapidly approaching the Earth.

Assassinations (successful and not), military coup d'états, protests, insurrections, and revolutions worldwide were signaling an end to the Cold War, with a united global economy emerging in its place. The most public faces of this "New World Order" were George H.W. Bush and Mikhail Gorbachev, who signed a treaty ending the production of chemical weapons and calling for the destruction of vast stockpiles of armaments in both countries. The treaty, however, was effectively broken soon after the first McDonald's fast food chain opened in Moscow.

The B-2 Stealth Bomber appeared in the skies. The first webpages and browser software ushered in the era of the World Wide Web and users of this technology contended with the release of the first Internet worm. Billions in federal aid to mega-corporate conglomerates could not prevent the continuous market crashes and industrial bankruptcies, mainly of automobile manufacturers and passenger airlines. Syringes feared to be infected with AIDS, among other medical waste, washed up on the beaches of New York and New Jersey, and the Exxon Valdez spilled over eleven million gallons of oil in Alaskan waters.

As traditional race and gender roles rapidly shifted, racially motivated crime became common, sparking heated national debates and giving rise to hate-crime legislation. In Montreal, an "anti-feminist" gunman shot and killed fourteen young women. In Beverly Hills, California, Lyle and Erik Menendez shot and killed their parents and a lone gunman in Stockton, California, killed five children and wounded thirty additional individuals before turning the gun on himself. Los Angeles implemented a ban on the sale and possession of semiautomatic firearms, George H.W. Bush banned the importation of assault weapons and U.S. Serial killer Ted Bundy met his death in an electric chair in Florida.

MY EYES HAVE BEEN OPENED

In April 1989, McVeigh and his Charlie Company COHORTs left for Heidelberg, West Germany, for orientation with the Bundeswehr (the West German Army) at their acclaimed urban warfare training camp, where they were instructed in *motivational techniques* and went on border patrol missions. His stellar performance there led McVeigh to earn the

German equivalent of an Expert Infantry badge. McVeigh later told his biographers that, while at the German installation "they learned to fight their way through houses and barns, ducking into alleys and climbing up chimneys ... to 'clear' a house by tossing in a grenade and then spraying the place with automatic weapon fire."[12]

Before giving his biographers the above account, McVeigh had told his attorneys an even stranger story about his trip to Germany. McVeigh had told them that one afternoon when he and three other men in his unit went off post, a German male approached them. His series of odd statements led McVeigh to believe the man was a German intelligence agent attempting to "blackmail" them. This story raised questions for the Jones Team and prompted them to make an official inquiry into the purpose and specific details of his assignment there. However, military records about the trip were among the portions missing from those they were able to obtain.

According to rather sensational news reports issued during this time, spies were all over the place. Media outlets reported that tens of thousands of East German and Soviet secret police and clandestine operatives or "sleeper" agents, intent on conducting assassinations, sabotage and preventing NATO-initiated disarmament efforts, had penetrated West Germany and were impersonating Bundeswehr troops. Officials alleged that the highest concentration of these shadowy East German spies was located in the region surrounding the East and West German borders. In truth, a number of joint NATO and U.S. intelligence and counter-intelligence operations were being conducted there in conjunction with the Bundeswehr's elite counter-terrorism units, GSG9 and KSK.

While the story McVeigh told the Jones team is unverifiable, the tale nonetheless stands as the first, but by no means last, instance of mysterious German men, spooks, spies, agents and/or intelligence assets appearing throughout the various narratives McVeigh would tell about the years leading up to the 1995 Oklahoma City bombing, or those told by others about the bombing itself. After his arrest, McVeigh's relationship with German national Andreas Strassmeir, a former Bundeswehr Officer, GSG9 agent and, while in the U.S., resident of the "white separatist" community Elohim City, became the subject of numerous public and private, journalistic and governmental investigations. McVeigh, it turned out, knew Strassmeir and had even called Elohim City looking for him a few days prior to the bombing. Adding to existing speculation about the extent of their relationship was an ongoing joint U.S.-German undercover intelligence-gathering operation tasked with disrupting international recruitment efforts and the flow of Neo-Nazi literature in organized hate groups. These things, in addition to other anomalies surrounding "Andy The German" (as he was called), led to theories that

Strassmeir had come to the U.S. as an undercover operative and possessed foreknowledge of or played an active role in the plot to bomb the Murrah building.[13]

Regardless of what really happened in Germany or who he actually met, McVeigh later said that the trip fundamentally altered his worldview; in part because he observed the West German army's relationship to German civilians, and the role it played in domestic operations, both distinctly different from the way things were done in the U.S. (or so he thought).[14]

> The Army helped me [to]define myself … the first two years were some of the best years of my life…. Worldviews can be altered by contact with foreign peoples, cultures, etc., in their own land … my trip to Germany had the same effect on my outlook … I became close to Fortier when we made that trip to Germany where, as a squad, we became tighter than we'd ever been…. I excelled over there and bonded with those guys. At the time, Germany had the most elaborate MOUNT Site in the world Military Operation in an Urban Terrain (*sic*). In other words, its houses and barns and you have to run through and … climb chimneys, sweep rooms, [by] kick[ing] the floor open, throw[ing] a grenade in and spray[ing] it with a machine gun…. One thing I learned in the Army was what "true freedom" was b/c in the Army, it had been taken away. Let me expand. In the military, you meet people from all over the U.S. and you even travel to foreign countries. [During my] "tour" of Germany, its museums, towns and cities, and "The Wall" – I began to gain a fundamental understanding of freedom, liberty, and free will. […] I was beginning to "see" the difference between man's law vs. God's law (aka "natural law") I also started my path towards understating that "freedom" is relative – and if you have nothing to compare to – you are relatively content. […]I learned that things I had always been taught were 'the law' were actually not, in some places.

He also explained that, while in Germany, he'd had discussions with soldiers from other states in the U.S. and that these discussions contributed to his evolving worldview as well. What stuck with him during these conversations were variances between state laws including sales and property taxes, minimum wage requirements, mandatory auto insurance and inspection, vehicle license plates, interstate tolls, speed limits, gambling prohibition, the age of consent, alcohol, fireworks and firearm regulations as well as the prices of gas. Through this observation, he continued, "the intentions of the founding fathers" and "the principle of states' rights vs. an (intended) weak central government" became clearer. Based on this change in his understanding he came to feel that greater personal freedom could be found in states with fewer Federal controls, where people could decide "how best to run affairs in their own back yard!"[15]

Indeed, the change within him at that time is reflected in the letters he wrote to his sister and Steve immediately after leaving Germany and returning to Ft. Riley; the contents of which were markedly more dramatic, strange and political than previous letters. In them, themes of social alienation, racism, sex, power and politics intertwine, revealing the depths and shifting contours of McVeigh's real and imagined internal and external worlds. A letter to Steve written shortly after his return from Germany begins with McVeigh's observation that they were growing apart as friends in part because"my eyes have been opened to the real world," whereas Steve, said McVeigh, remained physically and mentally stuck in the small town where they grew up.

> *In one year, the influence of the Army and the people around me have changed/are changing me in many ways.* The good part is that I am aware enough to notice these changes within myself; the bad part is the changes ... *I'm hesitant to wonder what 2 more years [in the Army] will do to me.* To sum up the changes in my attitude, I can only conclude that (and I say this with fair amounts of self-shame) that I led a VERY sheltered life in NY ... *I have seen things that I could never believe existed....* I am beginning to see a much larger portion of the 'whole picture' as seen, firsthand – Gang warfare, 5 deaths (4 stabbings, 1 shooting), how widespread drug use really is (people you would <u>NEVER</u> suspect ... the insignificance of "law enforcement," and many more startling things.... *To survive in the system to which I have now been exposed, I've had to change, to adapt; and I will never be the same.* I do things now out of necessity which I would have never <u>dreamt</u> of doing back home. Would you ever consider doing (besides in Road Horror Fantasy); regularly running from the police instead of pulling over; no – I cannot go on, this is turning into an admission of self-guilt ... *these things I say again, are no longer criminal; they are necessary to survive in the environment I live in....* I still feel self-shame in telling you of *the corrupt world I have slipped into,* but maybe somehow you will understand instead of condemning me. *I will never be able to live the same way again.* To hit it direct – your mom thought I was a bad influence before, she hasn't even dreamed (emphases added, underlined in original).

Like the earlier story about a German spy, the true nature of the events mentioned in this letter, if they occurred at all, remains unknown. When asked about it by the defense team, McVeigh explained that although he could not recall writing this particular letter, it nonetheless illustrated how, after his tour in Germany, his outlook had in fact changed, insofar as his distrust of law enforcement grew, and he realized that notions of *right* and *wrong* delineated by U.S. laws were "fluid, not solid."[16]

Throughout the months following his return from Germany, increasingly explicit and (until this time) uncharacteristically open ruminations about race and sex came to define McVeigh's letters. Perhaps betraying an increasingly destabilized mental state were the letters' rapid shifts and transitions in subject matter, all of which seemed removed from any coherent context. A letter dated July 4, 1989, began with McVeigh informing Steve that a Nuclear, Biological, Chemical [NBC] Environment is "a contaminated area" and his disclosure that he now slept in his locker because he suspected his roommate (Ray Barnes) had broken into the house of a female coworker and "sodomized her dog." Without offering any further explanation, context or intelligible transition, he strays from reflections of chemical warfare, homosexuality, and bestiality to racial and political topics portending his later characteristically obsessive expressions of domestic discontent.

> I'm not saying everything in the world is evil, but that <u>there is evil</u>. I used to call black people "black," because I only saw one side of the story. Now you can guess what I call them. People form opinions from the environment they live in. The problem comes along when these people begin to try and force their opinions on everyone, when these opinions are based upon only their own opinions. Take a liberal living in Amherst ... she has never seen drugs, but forms an opinion on them based on <u>propaganda generated by the mass media</u> ... she is condemning something she knows nothing about. Now substitute the word "drugs." Try guns, race, abortion, etc. This is where the <u>U.S.</u> is <u>all fucked up</u>. People having laws passed about things which they have no firsthand experience and knowledge of (underlined in original).

In letters written to Jennifer in particular, allusions to race and sex became more frequent and inappropriate. In one he admonished her that the name of her new boyfriend, "Maurice, sounds like a <u>BLACK</u> name!?! Don't even tell me that!" He then informed her that he had been sleeping with the wife of one of his co-workers, but that they agreed to be more discreet as her husband was growing suspicious: "If I dump her, I have another married chic that's been flirting with me, but I know her husband too well; she's gorgeous, but it's dangerous." One wonders if these co-workers are the same soldiers who said Tim McVeigh was such a stand-up guy, one of the few they'd invite to their houses or to family events. In any case, he concluded by suggesting that Jennifer send pictures of her and her friends as guys on post "pay good money for pictures of 15-18 year old girls!!!"[17]

While the details of McVeigh's sexuality are perhaps noteworthy, his developing racist ideology remains a debated element in later investigations and accounts about the bombing plot, and the motives attributed to those involved. In contrast to the consensus about his love of guns and his politics, popular, academic, and journalistic works vary in their conclusions about the extent of McVeigh's racism. Within weeks of his arrest, a number of news articles reported that he had been a member of the KKK and, while in the Army, had expressed prejudice towards lower-ranking black soldiers. Other reports noted that while he had never held formal membership in any racist organization, WPM literature such as *The Turner Diaries* deeply influenced him.

McVeigh's racism is fundamental to the accounts of criminologist Mark Hamm, who alleged that McVeigh acted within a larger network of organized racists in the commission of the bombing. In fact, for Hamm, McVeigh's racial views are central to the bombing story and McVeigh's developing politics. Hamm and others, including Federal prosecutors at McVeigh's criminal trial, contend that *The Turner Diaries* was, in fact, "the blueprint" for terrorist acts in general and the Oklahoma bombing specifically. Such assertions were often followed by suggestions that legislation should be passed to stem the tide of books like *The Turner Diaries* as well as the distribution of similar WPM propaganda. This is ironic in that, according to some, such efforts themselves led to a slippery slope that actually helped cause the bombing conspiracy itself.

On the other hand, some commentators argued that it was the book's focus on diminishing gun rights and it's general message of "fighting the system," not its racial and anti-Semitic content, that fascinated McVeigh. Even notable liberal intellectual writers like Gore Vidal dismissed rumors about McVeigh's racism simply as further unfounded attempts by the media and government to demonize him and confuse issues. Based on his personal research and correspondence with McVeigh, Vidal wrote, "McVeigh has no hang-ups about blacks, Jews, and all the other enemies of various 'Aryan' white nations" but rather, had been attracted to books like *The Turner Diaries* because of its pro-gun message and imagined war against the 'System.' To support his point, Vidal quotes Dr. John Smith, who said that McVeigh "made [it] very clear [that] he was not a racist [and] did not hate homosexuals."[18] Based on what McVeigh told them, his biographers supported this view and, throughout their book *American Terrorist*, de-emphasized their subject's racism as well as his connections to various WPM groups and individuals.

However, not debated was McVeigh's obsession with *The Turner Diaries*. In one letter to Steve, McVeigh described *The Turner Diaries* as "the most banned book in America." For him, "the ultimate treasure hunt" involved finding copies of it as well as other, equally obscure, subversive and controversial literature. Numerous letters written to his sister and Steve mention *The Turner Diaries* and sometimes his request that they mail him additional copies. Many soldiers recalled McVeigh's preoccupation with

The Turner Diaries, and said he carried it with him at all times and gave out copies to anyone who promised to read it. Not lost on McVeigh though, were the implications and possible consequences of distributing the book on base. After giving one fellow infantryman a copy, McVeigh explicitly warned him not to let others see it, because of its subversive and racial nature.

Ft. Riley itself had a long and troubling history of racism and, at the time McVeigh was stationed there, racial graffiti sullied many public spaces and different races self-segregated from others. Later, at the time of the bombing, a series of investigations were conducted concerning the rampant racism and neo-Nazi activity occurring there.[19] Several COHORTs, including Ray Barnes, recalled this environment and discussed the conflicts that seemed to continuously arise between solders of different races:

> There were racial problems in the unit though. I remember one black guy who was put on a medical profile after hurting his knee, but to him, he thought the Army was against him because he was black. He started complaining [and asking] "how come all the white guys get promoted and you're giving all the black guys crap detail?" Well, he ended up holding the CQ and CQ runner at gunpoint with a .357 for a couple of hours. When they finally got it away from him, it wasn't long before they just sent him home.... There was another guy that got bumped for promotion. We had a certain amount of people to go before an E5 board, and it just so happened that they picked all white guys. A black guy threw a fit and started complaining, "You're only promoting white guys!" Well, dude, everybody promoted has the time in service. They've earned their slot. So they bumped somebody and put the black guy in even though the guy they bumped had more time in service. And then, when the time came, the black guy didn't even have his stuff ready and said to another guy "let me use your stuff!" and the other guy was like "if he wants to be promoted so bad he can do like I did. Stay up late. Polish his brass. Get his ducks in a row."
>   I know they tried to portray [McVeigh] as a racist. I didn't see that. I know that after he was promoted, he roomed with a black guy that he didn't get along with. They got into it a lot. The other guy was all into religion and McVeigh, who was a self-proclaimed atheist, would bring up different subjects, and they'd argue back and forth, but it was never like it got to the point of one of them saying *"well, I'm gonna whup your ass."* McVeigh never said anything like *"you fucking nigger."* They were just going back and forth on their views. They got in a lot of arguments. I know McVeigh read *The Turner Diaries.* I read *The Turner Diaries.* It was written in the 1970s, and a lot of that stuff it predicted was coming into play. It talks about The Cohen Act, which was very close to the actual Brady Bill. It talked about a National I.D. ... that's happening

now. In some ways the book was very prophetic. The media and the FBI used the book to portray McVeigh as being a racist, but I never knew him to put on a white sheet and burn a cross. He wasn't stupid. He was very smart. He wasn't the dumb red neck they tried to portray him as. A racist red neck!! He wasn't that!

Other COHORTs gave contradictory and sometimes ambiguous accounts. One African-American COHORT reported that while he had experienced racism in the Army personally, it hadn't been from Tim McVeigh, who he said, "liked or disliked people for who they were and what type of attitude they had as opposed to what race they were." Another African-American COHORT said, "Tim didn't think that if you were white, you were necessarily right, or if you were black, that you were necessarily wrong ... I wouldn't say that Tim necessarily liked blacks, either [but] he was not the type to avoid or leave a gathering that blacks were attending. There was some segregation in the unit ... blacks would hang out with blacks and whites with whites."

Gordon Blackcloud (Native American) said McVeigh "may have been a little prejudiced" but treated soldiers of other races with respect. He would only "use the 'N' word if he was in a group of others that were using the term." One African-American soldier told a story about an incident. They were in a car and McVeigh was driving. Another car, whose driver was black, cut him off and McVeigh immediately became enraged and yelled, "that nigger cut me off!" He disregarded the remark though, explaining that he hadn't taken it personally because he knew that Tim always seemed to have a bit of a "short fuse ... it was always easy to get him riled up ... he could just get agitated pretty quickly and would get really irritated about little things like that. He never really caused any trouble though; just blew off steam."

Caucasian COHORT John Kelso said, "I always thought he was pretty racist. I wouldn't say he was open about it, but I don't know how many times I heard him say 'them frickin' niggers!'" Another described him as "the most racist bastard I ever knew," was "constantly expressing his emotions and stating that he hated niggers and Jews" and was particularly harsh with the black soldiers under him. Yet another said McVeigh "did not like blacks" and would call black children "niglets" and referred to Jews as "money hungry." In general however, the consensus among his fellow soldiers was that, while McVeigh certainly had racist tendencies and made racist statements, he "was too professional to risk his rank" and act on them. None knew of McVeigh having any formal interactions with or membership in any organized racist groups while in the Army (that came later, after his discharge).

When asked by his attorneys about this dramatic shift after returning from Germany, without commenting on the heightened sexual content in his letters, McVeigh explained that although he had *observed* black people while driving an armored car around Buffalo, it was not until he joined the Army that he had any direct contact with them. When he did, the differences in their "lifestyle" startled him. He liked rock and roll, they liked rap. To him, "the loud rough music, the low riders together with bass music, the loudness in the barracks and everywhere else, the staying up and keeping others up all night, the playing of dominoes loud all night ... seemed like a form of psychological warfare, in which black soldiers were purposefully bothering other people."

To both his attorneys and biographers, he said that, while working at Burke prior to enlisting, he might have adopted the racial attitudes of his co-workers but after joining the Army and meeting people of various races from all different regions, he realized that "everyone is an individual." He had gotten used to the clash of racial cultures, he assured them, and eventually it did not bother him anymore. While he admitted to having sometimes used racial slurs, he insisted he did so jokingly. Over time, he learned to refer to certain blacks who acted like "punks" as "niggers"; those who were "cool," were simply "black guys." McVeigh adamantly denied that he was ever a *bona fide* racist.

When asked by his legal team about allegations that he had assigned lesser duties to minorities, he responded that these were "totally false" – the results of others' "professional jealousy." Of all the people in the company, he explained, forty were black. Of these, he had a problem with only two individuals. Some of his platoon sergeants were black. He got along with them, and sometimes even gave them rides in his car. He emphasized that he had never been reprimanded or received any disciplinary action because of this alleged racism.

While the extent to which McVeigh's racist views may have taken root and manifested themselves during his time in the Army is debatable, that he held them was unquestionably evidenced during one of his early conversations with his attorneys in August 1995, during which he corrected them, saying he was not a white "supremacist," but a white "separatist." The distinction, as he explained later, is that while he did not believe non-whites are inferior, he merely wished to live in a racially exclusive and separate culture from them. He then exhibited his limited range of history despite his voracious reading habits, when he added as an afterthought, "It is true, however, that nothing of great value has ever been accomplished or contributed by a black person."[20]

Despite his claims of having shed his racist views over time, or his occasional attempts to distinguish himself from white supremacists, during the two years prior to the bombing, McVeigh actively sought out William Pierce, author of *The Turner Diaries* and figurehead of one of the best-known WPM groups, The National Alliance.

THE FAST TRACK

Neither racism nor eccentricity prevented McVeigh from a remarkably rapid climb up the Army's enlisted ranks. After returning from Germany in the Spring of 1989, he became turret gunner on the new Bradley Fighting Vehicles, a position for which he received the "Top Gun" acknowledgment. In March 1990, nearly two years after enlisting, the twenty-two-year-old McVeigh had earned the rank of Specialist E4. One Staff Sergeant described him as "one of the finest soldiers" he ever came across in his career; his "conduct and demeanor" the "standard to which the Army wanted others to aspire." Another commanding officer (CO) said Specialist McVeigh was "the best person available to represent the Army, a good role model" and therefore selected him to be Charlie Company's Reenlistment Non Commissioned Officer (NCO), tasked with the job of encouraging others to re-enlist. When Congressmen or other dignitaries visited, Command called upon McVeigh's squad, as he always made a good impression, sometimes spending his own money to maintain the weapons and gear on the division's display vehicle.

Sgt. Albert Warnement said Spc. McVeigh was on the "fast track," one of the first promotable E-4's in his Battalion, and selected to serve as an NCO in the Special Forces, pending promotion. His superiors expected that within 80 days of making E-4, he would attend the Army's Leadership Development Course (AKA "NCO School") and, upon completion, would receive promotion to E-5 (Sergeant). Eligibility to attend the Leadership Development Course for promotion to E-5 requires sponsorship by someone who is already an NCO. William Dilley explained that he gladly sponsored Spc. McVeigh as he always went "above and beyond the call of duty." Dilley described McVeigh as a model soldier, "sharp" and "good at working with others." Dilley continued, saying McVeigh was humble and shied away from competing or accepting awards for his exemplary conduct. 1st Sgt. Harris, in charge of all enlisted soldiers in Charlie Company, explained how remarkable it was that McVeigh could make rank in such short a time, especially from within a COHORT unit:

> A COHORT Unit has a large number of similarly experienced men competing for a small number of positions ... Tim was one of very few that were able to make rank in that situation ... I couldn't ask anything more from an NCO than McVeigh ... [he was] one of the three best soldiers in the company, sharp and highly disciplined.... Tim had some troops under him that he really shouldn't have because of their worthlessness.... [He] would look out for their welfare and was [so] conscientious that his soldiers were squared away that it was taking up all his personal time. I told him once to get out of the barracks, do something entertaining.... Tim was a soldier right up to the last day, maintaining 98% and above always.[21]

Despite the Army's enthusiasm for McVeigh, he was exhibiting ambivalence about climbing through the ranks and began privately questioning whether he still wished to be a career soldier. In a letter written to Steve during this time, he asked for his old friend's advice, telling him "I've been doing some hard thinking (again!) and I'm tossing around the idea of reenlisting.... I have a secure position, and am experienced at my job. Why start over again someplace else? I can 'retire' in 12 more years (at 50%) and only be 35. I really don't have to worry about the 'Cuts' the Army is making, I'm not on any bad lists." A few weeks later, though, he wrote Steve again, "I won't get any deeper into the reenlistment thing, because I know my attitude changes all the time. I will, either way, wait until the end to decide, to weigh all possible options and experiences."

Some of his ambivalence may have had to do with the fact that, while the majority of his NCOs lavished praise upon him, he had occasional clashes with a couple of them. He said he had a mutual hatred for a Sgt. Vitalis, whom McVeigh claimed took drugs with Michael Fortier. Later, when asked about a rumor that he had wet the bed so he could receive a discharge from the Army, McVeigh said this was not true and explained that a certain Sgt. Reese did not like him and once, when spots had been found on his mattress during an inspection, Reese tried to get him to pay for it out of his own pocket – something McVeigh "fought and fought." Another time, he said, Reese found a six-pack of Pepsi in his drawer, against barracks regulations. Reese "embarrassed" him by making the entire Company stand at attention until McVeigh gave the Pepsi to the guy at the CQ desk.

Another possible reason for his ambivalence was that when Charlie Company received the Army's new Bradley tanks in June 1989, it "really fucked up" their morale, organization, and cohesion. The tanks tore the unit apart and caused "brother to brother conflicts over 'mounted' versus 'dismounted' personnel." The Bradleys, he later reflected, "Were no good for any of us in the respect to physical conditioning." He believed they would quickly become obsolete and their placement with his company "filled a niche that didn't exist."

Finally, his ambivalence about the Army may have stemmed from the reactions of some of his COHORTs to his quick promotions. They called him a "brown-noser" and accused him of playing politics with the officers. His rapid climb up the ranks, explained one, had put McVeigh "in an awkward position ... where he had to give orders to guys he had been with since basic training ... sometimes people would grumble about that."

Despite his private doubts, occasional clashes with authority and the grumblings of other COHORTs, the majority of those interviewed remembered that he "took care of his soldiers," seemed to care deeply for those he was in charge of, and was supportive and helpful towards them.

Lou Johnson said that, while in the Army, Timothy McVeigh was his personal mentor:

> If I had an attitude about something Tim would say "look you have this or that flaw in your character and you need to work on it." He was there for you if you needed him ... Tim was also very fair minded and wouldn't take sides with someone because they were a better friend of his...[he was] fair ... a good judge of character : Tim was the one who thought things through and would not act impulsively. If you tell people the price is right they will jump on it, Tim would want to know why. He was not one for quick fixes or doing something just to get by. Tim was also very quiet but would actually get his point across ... never the type to start yelling or getting loud to make a point

Regardless of any discontent he may have had, McVeigh later described his first two years in the Army as "some of the best years of my life." His frustrations with the unit and desire to belong to a more "tight knit, efficient environment" revitalized his aspirations of joining the Special Forces and so, throughout the Summer of 1990, having weighed the options before him, he continued to train for this. No matter what they thought of him, there was no doubt among the other COHORTs that when the time came, McVeigh would pass the grueling try-out course. His squad leader and friend, Curtis Chandler, said that McVeigh "generally knew what he wanted to do and would make that happen, being very disciplined in that regard...I don't believe I ever saw Tim fail at anything in the military." According to Steve Hodge, Tim said he wanted to join the Special Forces "because of the close camaraderie and the elite status" and explained to him that if accepted "he would be guaranteed a mission within a year." McVeigh told his attorneys:

> I was introduced to Special Forces through a squad leader, Sgt. Chandler. We went to a briefing they had on post, the guy would come once every few months and try to recruit, and I was interested. They also recruited Delta Force. I was reasonable enough to realize that I could not meet the expectations they laid out for Delta Force, but I knew I could meet the expectations they laid out for Special Forces. They laid out exactly what you would have to do and I knew my test scores, my physical test scores, my road march, times, et cetera, fell within those parameters. We took our preliminary PT test which would be, I guess, your physical training test for them, which included something that is not done normally and that would be to swim – it was a hundred meters I think and in full BDU's, which is your full battle dress uniform. I passed all that so I was accepted to the class and given special orders to attend.

He then wrote his sister about his recent promotion, told her that the Army had big plans for him and said in June he was going to be attending "Super School" at Fort Benning for two weeks, which was a "huge privilege. They only send one person every 3 years, and it is a kick-ass course. It's hard as hell. ... We'll see come June, knowing the way things work around here." He continued, telling her that when he got out of the Army, he planned to put in an application at the Niagara County Sherriff's Department, one more of his many contradictory positions, given his new-found criticism of laws and law enforcement.

His scheduled "Super School" session was delayed until later that fall but he continued to train for it with characteristic single-minded determination throughout the remainder of the year. Allen Smith, the only other person in the company to train for Special Forces with McVeigh, observed that the other COHORTs treated the two of them differently because of their goal of joining the Special Forces. The other soldiers, said Smith, were not so dedicated to Army life, and thought it odd that they were. To others, McVeigh's dedication to advancement made sense as, said Chandler, he "was far above the everyday run-of-the-mill Army."

When McVeigh took the physical examination required to qualify for the Special Forces on August 22, 1990, he received a chest x-ray and routine blood tests, including one for HIV, the results of which were negative. When asked about his health, McVeigh reported that it was "very good" and said he was not taking any medications. When asked if he had ever had a number of specific symptoms, he responded in the negative. These symptoms included, "swollen and painful joints, frequent or severe headaches, dizziness or fainting spells, chronic or frequent colds, severe tooth or gum trouble, head injuries, skin diseases, pain or pressure in the chest, indigestion, stomach, liver or intestinal trouble, adverse reactions to serum, drugs, or medications, broken bones, tumors, growths, cysts, back pain, [or] foot trouble." Dr. Bloomquist, the examining physician, noted that a clinical evaluation for potential physical abnormalities had been deemed non-applicable, the only "additional dental defects and diseases" being his "missing teeth" which were nonetheless "acceptable." Dr. Bloomquist, in fact, signed the majority of the Special Forces physical examination forms.

The next day, on August 23, 1990, McVeigh began the month-long Primary Leadership Development Course (PLDC) at Ft. Benning. His evaluator there noted on his forms that Spc. McVeigh demonstrated "academic potential for selection to higher level school/training" and throughout the course, "displayed all the skills, knowledge, and attributes of an excellent leader throughout the Program of Instruction."[22] On September 18, 1990, McVeigh graduated from PLDC and re-enlisted the same day. On October 4, 1990, he was found to be "Qualified for Special

Forces Qualification Course" and on December 27, 1990, granted Secret Clearance.

A recurring anomaly, however, appears when one compares certain portions of McVeigh's medical records to other ones. Notably absent from his Special Forces Qualification papers, or the many letters he continued to write home, are any mention of his previous or ongoing extensive doctor and dentist visits that, when combined with the changes he experienced after returning from Germany, detail his continuing personal "avalanche of decay" and appear as evidence of his earlier warning to Steve that he would "never be the same again."

Prior to January 1989, McVeigh received five shots and immunizations, including a Plague II and Plague III shot, both of which, while later proving problematic for the Department of Defense and many veterans, may be explained as routine. Throughout 1989, four medical screenings are listed, also ostensibly routine. Not routine by any measure, however, are his twenty-six dentist visits from January 1989 until December 1990, one of which occurred on September 6, 1990, when he was in Ft. Benning attending the PLDC. McVeigh, who had never had any known dental issues prior to enlisting in the Army had, by this time, begun to lose the majority of his teeth, the records reflecting that out of thirty-two teeth, twenty-three of them had begun to decay.

Also overlooked during the Special Forces physical were seven non-routine medical visits from January 1989 until December 1990. On October 12, 1989 at 6:20 AM, McVeigh sought medical attention and complained of "skin tags," a recurring issue in the subsequent years. On November 6, 1989, he sought medical attention for a painful infection on his left foot's big toe, which, wrote the attending doctor, was "slightly swollen and red" and oozed a "clear, brownish fluid." Doctors removed the infected toenail three days later. In December 1989, he received emergency medical attention for his nose after it was broken by an African-American bouncer at a local bar when he went there to pick up drunk members of his unit and a bar fight broke out. Like his toe the month before, in a visit soon after breaking it, the doctor observed fluid leaking from McVeigh's nose, ordered x-rays and diagnosed an additional allergenic infection that, due to the fracture in his nose, had caused a cyst to form within it. A report from another "acute medical care" visit in 1990 erroneously listed McVeigh's name as "Timothy McKersh." At 6:10 AM, 'McKersh' appeared in the medical barracks complaining of "Burn Blisters." The report contains no other information.

From April 5 to May 27, 1990, McVeigh sought medical attention two more times for additional symptoms that would recur over the next couple of years: diarrhea, vomiting, abnormal bowel sounds, tenderness and cramps in his abdomen and dizziness. During his visit on May 27, the doctor diagnosed him with dehydration and gastroenteritis. The recommended over-the-counter medications relieved neither the vomiting nor diarrhea. Thus, in between his digestive dilemmas he received two additional HIV tests, in addition and *prior* to, the one given during the Special Forces qualification exam.[23] It is strange therefore that the second of these had been requested on May 27 by one Dr. Bloomquist, who about three months later performed McVeigh's Special Forces physical and found him to be qualified. Finally, at 6:25 AM on November 13, 1990, McVeigh visited the medical barracks one last time, this time complaining of pain in his shoulder that, according to the notations on the forms, he claimed to have sprained earlier by jumping off a tank. The shoulder, McVeigh explained, now had a "tick" in it.

Oddly, McVeigh failed to mention the incident in his letter to Steve written November 13, 1990, the same day he sought medical attention for his shoulder. Instead, he announced that he received his orders to attend the Special Forces try-out at Ft. Benning, which he expected to complete sometime between November 27 and December 20, after which he would return home on leave just in time for him "to see the Bills beat Miami" on their way to the Super Bowl. This was not to be, however, as the Post Commander canceled his leave, and his unit received orders to deploy to the Persian Gulf the following month and – as everybody knows, the Bills lost that year.

PART TWO:
The Big Lead-Up

"Public opinion wins war."

– Gen. Dwight Eisenhower

"Sometimes the effect of an error can be larger than the error itself.... We shouldn't unearth the past except when new events remind us that old mistakes were not just a matter of coincidence."

– Saddam Hussein to April Glaspie (U.S. Ambassador to Baghdad), speaking about Irangate, 7/25/90.

In 1960, Saudi Arabia, Kuwait, the United Arab Emirates, Iran and Iraq, the Gulf countries that collectively controlled roughly three-fourths of the world's oil reserves, founded the Organization of Petroleum Exporting Countries (OPEC) to mitigate the influence of Western multinational corporations' manipulation and control of global oil prices. OPEC nations sought to stabilize oil prices, and strengthen and assert member countries' independence, and control of their own natural resources and economy. After OPEC nationalized their natural resources and placed an embargo on sales to the U.S. in the 1970s, the availability and cost of oil skyrocketed worldwide.

In October 1977, Iranian demonstrations began against the Shah (installed in a coup d'etat by the U.K. and the USA in 1953) and continued until he was forced to flee to America in 1979, where he was treated for cancer. Iranians demanded the Shah be return to face trial and execution, to no avail. In April 1979, Iranians voted to become an Islamic Republic and that December, the Ayatollah Khomeini, who had led the Iranian Revolution, became "Supreme Leader." During the Iranian Revolution, existing tensions concerning long-standing border disputes between Iran and Iraq increased and Iraq, along with other neighboring countries including Kuwait and Saudi Arabia, feared Iran's revolutionary climate might spread and incite similar dissent within their own territories.

Iran, which shared a border not only with Iraq but also with the Soviet Union, held high strategic value in the eyes of U.S. Cold Warriors. U.S. fears of Soviet encroachment into Afghanistan and the Persian Gulf, as well as anxieties over the supply and price of oil, which had risen during the Iranian Revolution, heightened after the Ayatollah Khomeini deposed the Shah who had maintained a U.S.-approved status quo in the region, albeit a shaky one. In November 1979, Iranian revolutionaries took fifty-five American diplomats hostage at the American embassy in Tehran, accusing them of being "a nest of spies," where they were held for 444 days. The crisis ended with the signing of the Algiers Accords in January 1981, only minutes after the swearing-in of Ronald Reagan as U.S. President. Although no diplomatic relations had existed between the two nations previously, when Iraqi President Saddam Hussein agreed to help the U.S. counter the Iranian revolutionaries, a working relationship was formed. In exchange for Saddam's assistance in the matter, the U.S. provided Iraq with military intelligence, technology and weapons.

The Reagan administration viewed Iraq as a potential key to maintaining stability (or hegemony) in the Gulf region. Iran's potential destabilization of U.S.-friendly nations such as Kuwait, Saudi Arabia and other Gulf States, would undoubtedly threaten vital U.S. oil supplies and push prices even higher. Thus, when Saddam invaded Iran in September 1980, commencing the eight-year, Iran-Iraq War, he had the support of neighboring countries and the incoming Reagan administration.

In the ensuing years, a number of factors threatened to dampen the budding romance between Iraq and the U.S. The United Nations (UN) repeatedly condemned Hussein's regime for human rights violations and other violations of the Geneva Protocol, including the use of chemical weapons. The UN eventually imposed an embargo prohibiting arms sales to Iraq. A standing executive order and The Arms Export Control Act (1976) prevented the U.S. from selling arms to both Iran and Iraq outright, as did the latter's inclusion on the State Department's 1979 list of nations known to aid and support terrorist organizations. Such considerations prevented the U.S. from *overtly* providing Iraq with material and economic support. Still, the war was good for business and led to a substantial increase in the production of oil and a decrease in price as both adversaries began to produce and sell more oil to help finance their respective war efforts. In 1982, despite Iraq's known ties to international terrorist organizations, its lengthy record of human rights abuses and the very vocal objections of Congress, the State Department removed Iraq from the list.

In November 1983, President Reagan signed Presidential Directive 114. While the majority of the directive remains classified, it is known that part of it promised that the U.S. would do whatever was necessary to prevent Iraq from losing the war, including the continuation of intelligence and material support. Although Iraq's use of chemical weapons on a nearly daily basis was known to U.S. officials, a meeting between Hussein and Reagan's emissary Donald Rumsfeld in December 1983 strengthened the working relationship between the nations.

In 1984, the U.S. initiated "Operation Staunch," ostensibly to prevent the sale of weapons to Iran. That same year, the U.S. lifted its ban on arms sales to Iraq. Afterwards, and throughout the following eight years, the Reagan and Bush administrations provided the Iraqis with over $5 billion dollars of aid, secured vast amounts of loans for them and sold them an extraordinary arsenal of conventional weapons and weapons systems, including easily weaponized *dual use* chemicals. An international weapons dealing free-for-all ensued. In violation of the UN embargo and despite their knowledge of Iraq's use of mustard gas and other chemical weapons against the Kurds and Iranian civilians and military, nations around the globe scrambled to sell arms to Iraq, often through clandestine deals with other governments and using multi-national cutout companies and other *covert* channels. Iraq soon earned the dubious distinction of number one purchaser of weapons worldwide. In the opinion of one U.S. defense analyst, "When it comes to Iraq, everybody's hands were dirty."

Iraq's "doomsday" arsenal, the majority of which had originated in aid or sales from the U.S. and its allies, came to include chemical and biological weapons. According to various reports, Iraq's stockpile of refurbished military hardware included tanks, armored personnel carriers, antitank and long-range missiles, rocket launchers, bombers, cluster bombs, MiG warplanes, Mirage jet fighters, rifles and ammunition. Stockpiled Iraqi weapons of mass destruction included mustard and cyanide gas, nerve gas, nerve gas antidotes, anthrax, West Nile fever germs, botulism, salmonella, E-Coli and other bio-horrors similar to tuberculosis, pneumonia and bubonic plague.[24]

The honeymoon between Iraq and the U.S. began to wane in 1986, during the Iran-Contra Scandal, when it was learned that, throughout the previous two years, in exchange for hostages held by Iran, the U.S. supplied them with weapons to use against Saddam. Burgeoning tensions between Iraq and the U.S. became all the more apparent when, in May 1987, Iraq bombed a U.S. Naval ship in the Persian Gulf that had been mistaken for an Iranian commercial vessel, leaving 37 American crew members dead and dozens injured. While the White House officially chalked it up to an unfortunate accident, Reagan publicly blamed Iraq and warned them that the U.S. would retaliate if the attacks continued.

Further straining the relationship, in March 1988, the international community condemned Iraq for its scorched earth strategy and use of chemical weapons to kill thousands of dissident Kurds in Northern Iraq. While U.S. officials paid lip service to the accusations leveled against Iraq, U.S. policy makers viewed the alliance as vitally important to long-term political and economic objectives and therefore continued to supply Iraq with intelligence, financial and logistical support.[25]

In May 1988, Iraq recaptured the territory around its port city of Basra. That August, the U.N. brokered a cease-fire between Iran and Iraq, ending the war. The alliance between the U.S. and Iraq then began eroding rapidly, as Iraq was now a nation with a massive and still growing arsenal, enormous potential wealth, enormous debt and a seemingly paranoid leader whose first name means "the one who confronts."

The relationship between Iraq and Kuwait became terminally hostile when, after the war ended, Kuwait sold its oil for prices lower than OPEC standards and increased its production at rates exceeding OPEC regulations, drilling in disputed border territory with Iraq. To Saddam, the U.S.'s alignment with the United Arab Emirates (UAE) and Kuwait constituted acts of theft, aggression and economic warfare that, he said, violated and deprived Iraqis of their basic human rights and standard of living. UN sanctions had effectively deprived Iraq of 70% of their food supply and, in turn, the Iraqi government imposed food rationing upon its civilian population. The offenses of the U.S. were all the more egregious, Saddam protested, because for the past eight years Iraqis had shed "rivers of blood" to secure the stability of the Gulf region and protect the interests of the U.S. and its allied Arab nations. Saddam began to envision and speak of a grand global conspiracy orchestrated by Israel and their "imperialistic Zionist minions," the U.S. and Britain.[26]

While the U.S. and Iraq remained superficially cordial, the U.S. had long been aware that the relationship was fragile and prepared for the possibility of a future conflict with Iraq by establishing military bases and critical infrastructure throughout the Middle East. In 1988, the Center for Strategic and International Studies began a two-year study to determine the outcome of engaging in a war with Iraq. The following year, Secretary of Defense Dick Cheney revised the contingency plans of the United States Central Command (CENTCOM) for the "Defense of the Arabian Peninsula," expanding the plans beyond the scope of countering a Soviet invasion in the region to include the potential of an Iraqi assault on Kuwait and Saudi Arabia. In January 1990, CENTCOM, under the direction of General Norman Schwarzkopf, began running computer-simulated war games to this effect, and soon after increased its military presence in the Gulf region.

On July 21, 1990, Saddam positioned troops on the border of Iraq and Kuwait. While the Bush administration's repeated proclamations, echoed by the American media, declared the number of troops amassed on the border to be 100,000 (a number that quickly grew to a reported 200,000 and then to 400,000), the more accurate estimate of 20,000 surfaced later. It was at this time, after Saddam's "buildup" began, that the White House and Pentagon began a sustained propaganda campaign meant to justify and gain popular support for the U.S.'s intended military intervention there. Over the previous two years, the American media had increased the frequency and sensationalism of coverage with a decisively anti-Iraq flavor. A major recurring theme seen regularly on American television was Saddam's impressively horrific arsenal of conventional and chemical weapons and claims about his willingness to use them, although the U.S.'s previous and continued sale of conventional and unconventional weapons to Iraq (until as late as March 1992) remained virtually unmentioned.

During a meeting between Saddam Hussein and the U.S. Ambassador to Baghdad on July 25, 1990, Saddam expressed his belief that the motives underlying U.S. hostilities towards Iraq stemmed from its desire "to secure the flow of oil [through] flexing muscles and pressure." If the U.S. insisted on doing so, Saddam warned, Iraq would respond in kind. Saddam said that although the U.S. military undoubtedly had the ability to inflict significant damage to Iraq, "everyone can cause harm according to their ability and their size." Saddam continued, saying that if the U.S. continued to send aircraft and missiles, they risked pushing Iraqis past the point where they would "cease to care and death will be the choice for us. Then we would not care if you fired 100 missiles for each missile we fired. Because our life would have no value." While he could not deploy the entire Iraqi army to the U.S., Saddam warned, "Individual Arabs may reach you." He then announced his intent to restore "one by one" the rights of Iraqis that the U.S. had sold out in exchange for trade agreements with Kuwait, the UAE and the their 'Zionist' ally Israel.[27]

Saddam demanded that Kuwait turn over part of their oil fields that he said encroached into Iraqi territory, immediate payment of $2.4 billion in reparations, the cancelation of Iraq's debt to Kuwait, and their promise not to exceed OPEC regulations in the future. Meanwhile, American officials warned the press that Iraq's 'supergun', "the most sophisticated artillery weapon in the world" could be "modified to lob chemical shells on US troops in the Gulf."[28]

On August 2, Saddam moved a reported 100,000 poorly equipped Iraqi troops across the border into Kuwait, whose armed forces totaled a mere 16,000. The invasion drew international condemnation, and the United Nations Security Council (UNSC) immediately voted sanctions against Iraq and demanded they withdraw. The State Department reinstated Iraq as a sponsor of terrorism and a National Security Directive issued at this time included a list of U.S. motivations for an expected confrontation with Iraq, the first being "access to oil." Bush prohibited all U.S. sales to Iraq and froze all U.S.-held Iraqi assets. Subsequently, the profits of non-OPEC oil companies soared.[29]

OPERATION DESERT SHIELD

Operation Desert Shield began on August 7, 1990, when, without Congressional authorization, the Department of Defense dispatched an additional 40,000 troops to Saudi Arabia, along with 100,000 body bags. Americans heard conflicting predictions about expected casualty rates. On one hand, some military officials said that, within hours of the conflict's start, allied field hospitals might receive thousands of casualties and, in the event of a full-scale war, expected up to 10,000 dead U.S. soldiers and 45,000 wounded. Estimated Iraqi casualties were three times higher. On the other hand, some insisted the conflict would not be "another Vietnam" but rather a 'clean' war with minimal casualties and that new smart weapons could avoid collateral damage through surgical strikes. Still, it remained unknown if, and to what extent, Saddam might use chemical weapons against U.S. allied forces, a threat dangled numerous times by the White House and Pentagon. Some media outlets attempted to reassure Americans by reporting that U.S. troops were adequately equipped with protective gear and medical antidotes and that the desert winds would very likely disperse any nerve agents used.[30]

In a nationally televised speech on September 11, 1990, President George H.W. Bush threatened that if Iraq did not withdraw its troops from Kuwait, the U.S. would forcefully remove them. Among the former CIA Director's stated objectives for U.S. military intervention in the conflict, was the creation of a U.S.-led New World Order. In October, Congress heard heart-wrenching and graphic testimony about the extent of Iraq's atrocities and crimes against humanity, including the now infamous (and since revealed as completely fabricated) baby incubator story. Soon thereafter, Bush declared Saddam Hussein "worse than Hitler." During a press conference held near Walt Disney World, Bush, whose comparison of Saddam to Hitler had drawn widespread criticism, attempted to clarify, explaining that while the Holocaust was "outrageous," so was Saddam's brutalization of Kuwaiti children. He then awkwardly began to list the ways in which Hitler was kinder and gentler than Saddam.[31]

Included among the U.S.'s anti-Iraq propaganda effort was the carefully calculated demonization of Iraqis and the newly reincarnated Adolf Hitler Hussein, the "madman, lunatic, monster, barbarian" and "brutal dictator" who followed only the "laws of the jungle." Framed as an epic battle between good and evil, the U.S. regularly employed xenophobic, racist and sexualized rhetoric about Iraq's *rape* and *penetration* of Kuwait. Popular culture followed suit and sales of anti-Iraq and Saddam t-shirts, video games, songs and other merchandise became a popular fad, as did America's new yellow ribbon fetish.[32]

For Pentagon officials it was important to win the "hearts and minds" of the American people and prevent unmanaged media coverage of public dissent from spreading and morphing into Vietnam Syndrome. The term, while originally referring to PTSD, had also come to denote a general reluctance among U.S. citizens to enter another prolonged war. The realities of the Vietnam War as seen on American television and in the ghostly shells of men who did come back alive, had demoralized and repulsed them and contributed to the formation of a loud, active, and ultimately revolutionary shift in the social fabric of the country. In August 1990, Bush stated, "Whatever else we do, we aren't going to do it the Vietnam way."[33]

Rather, the media coverage of this conflict appeared more like an exciting action-adventure movie. Around-the-clock coverage during the lead-up to the U.S. and allied air assault often featured war journalists holding microphones and cameras and wearing gasmasks while perched in tank turrets charging through the Saudi desert on high-speed joy rides with no enemy in sight. After thirteen U.S. Air Force crew members died in an accidental jet crash, the White House implemented a policy of strict control and censorship of the press, citing reasons of national and battlefield operational security (OPSEC).

The new media policy banned coverage of U.S. troops arriving in the Gulf region and the return of dead bodies to the States. Further, the Department of Defense implemented its *embedded* journalist and press pool protocols requiring journalists to obtain Pentagon approval before entering the war theatre and, once there, to be assigned to military 'minders' who would escort them at all times. Those who attempted to break away risked detainment and arrest. Having little access to the battlefield, the majority of coverage and information about the war relied on the DOD's daily press briefings. All written and filmed media reports were subjected to 'security review' and, if found in violation of OPSEC, censored.

From November 8 to 10, Bush announced he was doubling the number of U.S. troops in Saudi Arabia. Among the deployed were covert U.S. Special Forces units and their British counterparts. On November 29, the UN Security Council issued a deadline of January 15, 1991, for Iraq's withdrawal from Kuwait, authorizing military intervention in the event that he failed to do so. By this time, the Pentagon claimed that a quarter-million Iraqi soldiers had massed near the border. As the deadline approached, President Bush informed Americans along with the rest of the world via television that, "We will not fail!" The deadline passed, and Iraq did not withdraw from Kuwait.[34]

JUST WATCH CNN

In November 1990, only days away from his long awaited Special Forces try-out, the primary reason for his reenlistment, McVeigh's unit, along with the rest of Ft. Riley's 1st Mechanized Infantry Division, learned of their impending deployment to the Persian Gulf. McVeigh wrote to Steve, telling him that he did not know the details about where, exactly, in the Gulf he would be or what he would be doing there. All he knew was that he would be in the desert for a while. "You probably know as much as us," he admitted, instructing him to "just watch CNN. They told us today that if any of us were an 'only child,' we wouldn't be deployed (to carry on the family name)." Several COHORTs later recalled how commanders told them that, if a ground war were to start, the majority of them, up to 75% even, could die, and described the fear they experienced upon learning this. "If there isn't a war," he wrote, "we stay for one year. If there is, I'll probably be back a lot sooner in a box... [Tell your mom to] send goodies, a year in the desert is a long time!" He continued, writing that, on the bright side, he had recently received a promotion to Corporal and expected to receive his Sergeant stripes shortly. As far as his upcoming Special Forces try-out, McVeigh later told his attorneys that when he learned of his deployment to Iraq, "[I thought] that was alright. I didn't know what would happen with the Special Forces training. I figured I could just reapply when I got back."

Friend and commanding officer, Sgt. Weathers, said that McVeigh disagreed with the decision to go to war, believing it to be just a political scheme. McVeigh, said Weathers, "did not think the United States had any business or interest in Kuwait but ... he knew it was his duty to go where he was told, and he went."[35] McVeigh himself later explained that he was aware of the wartime propaganda put forth by the U.S. at the time, "I remember Bush refusing the Kuwaiti offer to pay each soldier $5,000 – he said we weren't 'mercenaries' ... I remember [Bush's] multiple trips/junkets to Kuwait himself to receive gifts, etc." He expanded on this in a letter to his biographers, explaining how, throughout "the Big Lead Up," a lot of rhetoric was flying around including claims that all Iraqis and Saddam were evil. To him, the formulaic nature and logical progression of these amounted to "Kill Saddam = Kill Iraqis = kill the evil/destroy the evil."[36]

Granted a brief leave prior to his deployment to the Middle East, McVeigh returned home to western New York. Like the other men in his unit, he was afraid and expressed this to the loved ones he visited with there, including the neighbors at whose homes he had taken shelter as a child. Mrs. Dangler (name changed) said, "He told us he knew he was going to come home in a body bag. He was sure he was going to die. [I] wondered if there was part of him that may have wanted it to happen." Mrs. McDermott said it was the first time she saw him with tears in his eyes. While most of Charlie Company had already arrived in Saudi Arabia, when his leave was over, McVeigh returned to Fort Riley where he and thirty-seven others in his Platoon remained awaiting deployment orders. In a letter written to Steve on January 6, 1991, he announced his flight to the Gulf would be leaving that night and a month would pass before he wrote his next letter.

During a press conference in early November 1990, Defense Secretary Dick Cheney discussed the build-up and deployment of further troops to the Gulf and specifically mentioned Ft. Riley's famous 1st Mechanized Infantry Division, who were to join other armored units normally stationed in Germany. At some point after he arrived in the Gulf, McVeigh, along with other Bradley operators and teams from Charlie Company and the Marines' 1st and 2nd Divisions, became a crucial component of "VII Corp," a forward armored assault force described as "the largest armored corp ever assembled." After an extensive U.S. and allied air assault, VII Corp would spearhead the ground war, conducting initial breaching operations into Iraqi-held territory. McVeigh, specifically, became part of VII Corps' main effort, Task Force 3/37 or 'Task Force Iron,' Alpha Company, Third Platoon.[37]

THE GULF WAR SPECTACLE

"The first casualty when war comes is truth"
> – U.S. Senator Hiram Johnson, 1917

"If there is a war and if Bush has his way with the media coverage, the haunting and unforgettable face of battle will be masked for an American public"
> –Patrick Sloyan, *Washington Post*, January 13, 1991

'Thou shalt not be afraid for the terror by night; Nor for the arrow that flieth by day; Nor for the pestilence that walketh in darkness; Nor for the destruction that wasteth at noonday' – Psalm 91, reportedly read to by U.S. troops in January 1991, as Iraqi Scud Missiles targeted Saudi Arabia
> – New York Times, February 4, 1991.

Desert Shield turned into a perfect shit storm when, on the evening of January 17, 1991, U.S. and allied forces began a massive aerial assault upon Baghdad and surrounding areas. Suddenly, flashy new U.S. weapons with catchy names including the Tomahawk, Maverick and Hellfire missiles, F-16 Falcons, F-117 Stealth bombers and Cobra and Apache helicopters, disrupted the darkness of the Iraqi night. Its silence "exploded into mind numbing noise, [cars] shook with reverberation ... the ground was quaking as each new missile struck the city. The structure of [buildings] swayed and shivered." The spectacular allied air strikes were relentless, ceaselessly dropping an estimated 88,500 tons of explosives over the next forty-two days in what one journalist described as the "greatest bombardment in human history" and "heaviest bombardment any city on earth had undergone since the destruction of Hiroshima and Nagasaki."[38]

In violation of international law, the carpet-bombings employed fuel-air explosives and napalm and burned through nearly 12 million gallons of fuel per day. Military spokespeople appeared on media outlets explaining that the air assault was necessary to "shape the battlefield" by destroying Saddam's stockpiles of weapons. Primary targets of the attack included the Iraqi air and naval forces, SCUD missile launchers, weapons research facilities, chemical weapons factories, ammunition depots, oil pumping stations and supply lines in Baghdad and elsewhere as well as Saddam's command and communication facilities and aircraft and personal bunkers. Among the other ostensible military objectives was the destruction of civilian and military infrastructure throughout Iraq and Kuwait, inciting fear and horror and effecting submissiveness within Iraqi command.

While the ground war had not yet started, it must have seemed so to untold numbers of Iraqi soldiers who immediately began retreating on foot and in mobile convoys, many deserting their posts to join over a million Iraqi civilians also attempting to flee targeted areas. As they did so, U.S. pilots rained bombs upon thousands along the highways leading out of Baghdad that quickly filled with bumper-to-bumper traffic. Television viewers at home enjoyed the Pentagon's carefully selected footage of ballistic missiles lighting up the skies of Iraq. The *Guardian* described the coverage as a "hypnotic spectacle" of "moving graphics [and] death dealing explosives" akin to "a desensitizing, addictive arcade game."[39] While the Pentagon denied that the U.S. and its allies targeted Iraqi civilians, many died during the air assault. Conspicuously absent from the hypnotic spectacle of U.S. television coverage was any mention of these Iraqi civilian casualties, or the damage to critical civilian infrastructure, including the bombed-out, obliterated homes, mosques and even a baby formula plant, not to mention the shallow and expeditiously dug graves. Fleeing Iraqis and Jordanians told reporters about buses filled with civilians who were strafed by airborne munitions, describing countless burned vehicles and casualties that lined the highways and towns over seventy-five miles east of the border, deep within Iraq.

Saddam responded to the air assault by declaring, "The great showdown has begun! The mother of all battles is underway!" He further declared that Iraq would crush "the evil and satanic intentions of the White House." In the days to follow, and throughout the duration of the conflict, Iraq reportedly launched a number of SCUD missiles into Saudi Arabia and Israel. The U.S. claimed to have neutralized many of these by firing the newly repurposed Patriot Missile, the newest anti-missile missile. Later, numerous reports called into question the Pentagon's reported accuracy rates for the Patriot and Tomahawk missiles.[40]

On January 19, 1991, in the conflict's first (publicly known) commando operation, U.S. troops raided offshore oil platforms near Kuwait, capturing twelve Iraqis. Iraq threatened to transport their own prisoners (should they take any) to strategic locations to serve as human shields. American media reported that the invading Iraqis had purposely blown up a number of Kuwaiti oil fields, wells, storage tanks holding jet fuel and kerosene, installations and pipelines and, in an act that constituted a war crime, threatened to blow up more as part of a scorched earth campaign against Kuwait. On January 23, an estimated 400 million gallons of crude oil spilled into the Persian Gulf – the biggest oil spill in history at that time. Iraq claimed the spill resulted from U.S./allied bombings. Whatever the origin of the spill, winds carried the fumes in all directions and, within weeks, southerly winds pushed much of the oil into the Gulf away from the Saudi coastline, leaving behind birds and other wildlife covered with deadly goo. Neither the raids nor the oil spills affected oil prices, which, while fluctuating, had begun to drop as the value of the growing military-industrial market stocks rose.

On January 26, Colin Powell, Chairman of the Joint Chiefs of Staff, authorized U.S. military commanders in the Gulf to use nonlethal riot control gasses against Iraqi troops and POWs. Powell described the chemical compounds as "basically tear gas" and assured the media that their use certainly did not constitute chemical warfare. The nonlethal gasses, delivered by hand grenades, mortar shells and aerial bombs, he said, would be useful in urban combat such as house-to-house situations as they could effectively "immobilize" individuals, especially escaping or rioting POWs, but was less than explicit about the exact chemical agents the DOD intended (or did not intend) to use. Critics argued that the use of these gasses violated Geneva Convention rules as well as other restrictions against the use of chemical weapons.[41]

Also on January 26, as U.S. submarines began launching missiles from the Persian Gulf and Red Sea, 75,000 individuals, part of a growing, but largely unreported, anti-war movement, arrived in D.C. to march at the capital. Opposing them were 3,500 pro-war demonstrators. Meanwhile, that same day, anti-war demonstrators blocked the Golden Gate Bridge in San Francisco. The following day McVeigh's hometown team, the Buffalo Bills, lost to the New York Giants in the Super Bowl.[42]

BAD COMPANY BEHIND ENEMY LINES, SITTING DUCKS, SACRIFICIAL LAMBS & RANDOM DEATH FROM ABOVE

The ongoing allied air assault cleared the path for the impending ground war and, by February 4, 1991, "the last stage of the biggest, fastest deployment" and "largest logistical move in military history" began. More than 500,000 U.S. troops had arrived in the Gulf by this time, part of a growing number poised on the Iraq-Kuwait border. In Gen. Norman Schwarzkopf's war plan, praised by tacticians and military theorists, the VII Corp's First Armored Division was to lead the Hail Mary or Left Hook, northeast through the Iraqi deserts seeking out and destroying, specifically, "the four best paid, equipped and trained Iraqi divisions," part of the infamous Iraqi Republican Guard. Essential to Gen. Schwarzkopf's 'Hail Mary' operation was the new Bradley Fighting Vehicle (BFV), boldly touted as one of the most extensively tested and safest vehicles at the Army's disposal and essential to combat power on the ground.[43]

The Bradley had the capacity to house one infantry squad consisting of a vehicle commander, driver, gunner, and up to seven additional dismount soldiers. The Multiple Launch Rocket System (MLRS) could fire projectiles that, arriving at their intended targets, exploded in midair sending a spray of smaller *bomblets* designed to pierce the outside of armored vehicles or, if they hit the ground, exploded into shrapnel whose radius of destruction spanned the size of an American football field. Bradley manufacturers also claimed the vehicles had the capacity to drive over obstacles 3-feet high, trenches up to 8-feet deep, climb at angles of 60 degrees and were designed with amphibious underwater capabilities.

Both the military and the Bradley manufacturer claimed that it had four major advantages: mesh coats of low explosive reactive armor consisting of aluminum and depleted uranium (which added up to five tons in weight); lightweight and rapid acceleration capability; thermal optic night-sighting systems and newly designed and more accurate aiming systems. Gunners had an array of weapons at their disposal: mounted on top of the Bradley was a 25-mm. cannon, M-60 machine gun and an antitank (TOW) missile system. Thus, McVeigh now found himself in the role of Bradley gunner in one of the war's foremost advanced units tasked with breaching the front lines and trail-blazing for the 64-ton Abrams tanks following close behind. As the Bradley driver plowed through the sand, McVeigh, aided by thermal sights, would look for, and, if found, blow up land mines, incoming missiles, enemy troops, and their vehicles. Painted on the side of McVeigh's Bradley tank was the name he had given it, "Bad Company."

On February 6, 1991, about a month after he arrived in Saudi Arabia, McVeigh wrote to Steve, telling him about his recent promotion to E5 (Sergeant) and the duties this entailed, "I key the entire task force!" he explained, "Of course the glory has a price – look where I am." He apologized to Steve, writing that although he had a lot he wanted to get off his mind, he could not seem to concentrate. His thoughts, he said, "centered on one thing," the combat they had 'rehearsed' during the previous four days. "I shouldn't say what I'm about to," McVeigh disclosed, "[but] we're gonna burst through so fuckin' quick, the Iraqis will think it's a bad dream and when they blink to wake up, they'll be dead. Other people will brag about being part of the initial attack, but you can't get more 'spearhead' than my vehicle ... for now, here's all I can say (so someone knows that if I die it wasn't in the rear echelon) ... 'Shot Down in a Daze of Glory' ... I'll make it though, I have my own fire plan." Three days later, he wrote his sister telling her they had been very busy "practicing for the attack" and said he was not nervous because "If it's my time, it's my time." Still, when he wrote her again two days later, he hinted at his denied anxiety by signing the letter "love, Tim;" a closing unseen among his countless other letters written both before and after the Gulf War.

Cheerleaders for the Bradley sometimes boldly claimed that the ground war depended upon its performance but, despite his training, McVeigh had reason to be anxious. The Bradley was also among the most criticized vehicles in U.S. military history. At the time of the Gulf War, the Bradley remained untested in realistically simulated or actual combat situations. Its known failures and defects included susceptibility to catastrophic chemical fires when hit by anti-armor weapons (the armor shattered, burned and exploded); pyrotechnic prowess (the fuel tanks and ammunition exploded easily when hit); amphibious capabilities (they tended to sink); agility (they sometimes jammed or abruptly slowed to half speed); mobility (they often became stuck or dug in); and durability (the door of one fell off after it was rear-ended, leaving those inside to drive over the door repeatedly in an attempt to re-flatten it).[44]

Beginning around February 1, 1991, and continuing until after McVeigh penned his first letters from the Gulf, media outlets reported that the Army was conducting inspections of 300 to 500 of the 2,000 Bradley vehicles in the Gulf. As it turned out, many of the models positioned on the front lines had a possible transmission defect that could reduce the 6,000-pound armored personnel carrier's speed from 40 mph to 10 or cause it to jam completely, essentially rendering those inside "sitting ducks" in combat situations. Plus, the massive size of the Bradley made it more visible, thus a prime target for improvised explosive devices (IED's), enemy gun-fire and anti-tank missiles. In addition to this snafu, news outlets also continued to report Army field officers' ongoing investigations concerning the disappearance of more than fifty Bradley vehicles from a base in east Saudi Arabia, the location of the 1st Armored. When contacted by reporters, some officers claimed "terrorists" stole them. Others said American troops stole them to obtain parts for their own fleet of Bradley vehicles, in desperate need of repair.[45]

The commander of one Bradley company poised along the Saudi border told reporters that theirs' was "a destruction mission" expected to result in both extraordinary violence and extensive American causalities.[46] McVeigh later said they were the Army's "sacrificial lambs" meant to draw enemy fire. One sergeant described what many men in McVeigh's unit recalled, namely commanding officers' warnings that many of them, the majority even, would not survive the ground war's initial assault:

> McVeigh got the Bronze Star because when we started the battle, his track was the third one to cross through.... We weren't really the advanced forces; we were the guinea pigs they used. They sent us out to test the artillery on the other side ... that along with everything else....we were the breach element ... the Chaplain came up to us and said "well, out of the whole unit, 90% of yous ain't supposed to be here today talking to me." That's a great thing to hear from your Chaplain. They told us we were supposed to be dead.

The Bradley Units were not the only sitting ducks and sacrificial lambs. On February 9, 1991, Mikhail Gorbachev expressed that coalition actions in the Gulf exceeded the U.N. mandate and attempted to mediate by holding discussions with Saddam Hussein in Baghdad. On February 11, President Bush benevolently announced that neither he nor other co-alition leaders were eager to initiate a ground war. Two days later, in the early hours of February 13, U.S. Stealth fighters dropped a 2,000-pound 'penetration bomb' on a public shelter in al-Amiriyah, killing anywhere from 300 to 1,500 Iraqi civilians, mostly women and children. Journal-ist John Simpson described the gruesome carnage rescue workers found there, including "bodies fused together so that they formed entire blocks of flesh, a layer of melted human fat an inch deep lying on the surface of the water pumped in by the firemen." Pentagon spokespeople eventually admitted they had mistakenly identified it as an underground Iraqi mili-tary command center. Nevertheless, the Pentagon continued to dismiss subsequent Iraqi claims of allied attacks on civilians as propaganda.[47]

On February 14, McVeigh wrote Steve and told him he was mov-ing out in three hours to "secure Iraqi territory." From February 15 until February 20, Coalition forces conducted decoy attacks in hopes of lead-ing Iraqi commanders to think the main allied attack would occur along the Southern border of Kuwait. Although, officially, Coalition ground troops did not breach Iraqi-held territory until February 23, 1991, Gen. Schwarzkopf acknowledged later that Green Beret Special Forces units were already behind enemy lines in Iraq. Nearby, three miles outside the border of Iraq acting in a supporting role, was McVeigh's platoon along with others in Task Force Iron. On February 15, psychological warfare units from the VII Corp blasted recordings of vehicles moving, while the Task Force, including the 1st Infantry, part of the ruse, moved north and initiated a premature but pivotal attack.[48]

During the yet unknown decoy attacks, McVeigh wrote Steve and de-scribed engaging in "aggressive patrols in enemy territory as part of an "indirect fire mission." During one mission, he wrote, he was sitting in his Bradley when, through his thermals, he observed an abandoned Chevy truck near an oil pumping station and noticed the engine still appeared to be hot. Suddenly, just as he saw Iraqis exiting the truck, the tank right next to his "dispatched" the Chevy (and assumedly its former occupants), and then called in an airstrike. No one could possibly have survived, he opined, and added that his platoon received orders not to speak of the incident. Hours later, during a press briefing that he described to Steve as "hilarious," Army spokespeople denied making any incursions into Iraq or firing shots at installations there. Later though, McVeigh said he had been quite dismayed after the press conference because he "hated to hear the Army lie, to soldiers or the public."[49]

Perhaps another reason for the fear evident in McVeigh's letters was the increasing number of reported friendly-fire incidents appearing in the news reports. Although U.S. casualties during Operation Desert Storm were minuscule in comparison to previous wars, a large number of them resulted from friendly fire and anomalous accidents, information about which, complained journalists, was being withheld by the Pentagon. One such incident occurred on February 16, when a U.S. Apache helicopter fired two Hellfire anti-tank missiles and incinerated a Bradley, killing two and wounding six of the U.S. soldiers inside it. As nearby troops began evacuating their own tanks and running for cover, the Apache continued a barrage of machine gun fire, as the Apache pilot announced on the radio (heard by all) "this Bud's for you," killing an additional six.[50]

According to Stickney, McVeigh was horrified after hearing this on the radio as his unit had been within three miles of the incident, but he told his biographers that he only learned the true account of the incident months later. At the time, he said, they were informed that the Bradley had been the target of an unexpected attack by "Iraqi hit men," and said, in that moment he thought, "There's another reason to hate the Iraqi ragheads."[51] Still, in a letter to Steve on February 18, two days after the incident, he declared that if Steve could see the Multiple Launch Rocket System (MLRS) "his dick would get hard," and went on to discuss a "friendly fire kill." He acknowledged to his attorneys that within the first few hours of the ground war his platoon did receive "friendly" artillery fire that left him feeling extremely helpless, describing it as "random death from above."

On February 17, 1991, President Bush announced that Iraq's invasion of Kuwait would end "very, very soon." Reportedly, the air war alone had resulted in approximately 100,000 Iraqi deaths. On February 22, as thousands of tanks and a quarter-million U.S. troops sat poised on the Saudi-Iraq border, Bradley vehicles and Abrams tanks stretched for miles as Apache helicopters from the 101st Airborne flew overhead, shaking the earth and turning night into day in what was the largest helicopter invasion in history. The Apaches continually bombarded the Iraqi army, scattering them, as coalition ground troops pursued them, thinning out and annihilating Iraqi divisions in a desert orgy of violence. On Friday, February 21, 1991, Bush publicly warned that Iraq had one week to vacate Kuwait and, the next day, Iraqis reportedly set fire to an additional 950 Kuwaiti oil wells.[52]

THE GROUND WAR

On the evening of Saturday, February 23, 1991, networks interrupted regular television broadcasts to announce breaking news – the

Persian Gulf ground war (Operation Desert Storm) had officially begun. George Bush declared, "The liberation of Kuwait has entered the final phase," and Defense Secretary Dick Cheney issued a 'brown out,' suspending media briefings for nearly 24 hours, citing the need to maintain operational security. For media consumers, the motives of the war were already clear; evil Iraqis were rounding up, torturing and executing Kuwaitis. The next day, on Sunday, February 24, in what was called "the most sweeping armored attack since World War II" over 200,000 allied troops, including 150,000 U.S. soldiers, entered Iraq and Iraqi-occupied Kuwait. Schwarzkopf promised that the Iraqi army would be pursued vigorously: "We're going to go around, over, through, on top, underneath and any other way ... we're going to pursue them in any way it takes to get them out of Kuwait."[53]

Schwarzkopf's "Operation Desert Sabre" called for a Hail Mary flank strategy that hinged upon the VII Corps' main effort, Task Force Iron, a crucial component of which was the 1st Mechanized Infantry Division. The objective: to cross into Kuwait, head northeast towards Kuwait City and flank and cut off retreating Iraqi units along the way, clearing a passage through the desert for spearheading Marines approaching from the south. The Iraqi frontline, Saddam's line in the sand or "line of death," was said to be fortified with "deep minefields and oil filled trenches [intended to] burst into a deadly inferno." According to one commanding general of the Task Force, the strategy was to "maintain a rapid tempo ... thus not giving Iraqis time to react until it was too late and they were either dead or captured." Heavy aerial bombardment and the earlier interventions of Marines, paratrooper, psychological warfare and Special Forces units had helped to soften the border and flush out Iraqi troops who, once the ground war started, began retreating south, only to be met with tanks and Bradley vehicles. According to one fighter-bomber squadron commander, the ensuing massive Iraqi retreat was inevitable as their only other option was to attempt to hold their position and "get killed in their holes." Despite these best-laid plans, military planners anticipated high casualty rates in the breaching operation and predicted the decommissioning of the most forward-moving units for several days after the initial battle.[54]

In June 1995, weeks after his arrest, McVeigh gave the Jones Team his first (and perhaps only) hour-by-hour detailed account of his experiences during the Gulf War. His recollections of events that occurred from February 23 to February 26 tend to blend as if, for him, it had been one long, strange and terrifying day whose exact details are hard to know. He described the Gulf War to his father and sister as "one long [somewhat boring] drive in the desert." He claimed to his biographers that, even as they approached the Iraqi frontline, as he felt the ground trembling underneath him, he was still able to sleep, and, referring to the Ryder truck bomb used in Oklahoma, remarked that after this, "sleeping on the back of a 7,000 pound bomb is no big deal." Prior to making these claims though, he described to his attorney how, on the eve of the ground assault, while they were still about ten miles outside the Iraqi border, he had experienced "terror" for the first time in his life. He awoke at 2:30 AM the next morning to find "the desert shaking and rockets going off." His entire body began to shake from anxiety, and he confessed to more than one person that he did not think they would survive.[55]

In the first unofficial biography of Tim McVeigh, *All American Monster* Brandon Stickney wrote that, as McVeigh waited for the action to begin "he thought about his role until it scared him. McVeigh was in charge of a group that might not make it out alive." An article in the *New York Times* quoted a soldier with McVeigh who said, "The night before the war kicked off [McVeigh] was saying how he was scared because we were going to be part of the first wave. He was scared we weren't going to come out of it. Maybe we would get shot, blown up ... he was just concerned. I was feeling the same way, but most people didn't express it." *Playboy* also quoted this same soldier as saying, "We were in the desert, sleeping on the sand and he really thought we were going to die. He was worried that we would be killed by our own helicopters or *tanks*."[56] Other soldiers with him confirmed this, saying that McVeigh was afraid but added that, what he feared most was not enemy fire, but friendly fire from above or even being buried alive by U.S. tanks.

Making matters worse, his commanding officer, Lt. Jesus Angel Rodriguez, by all accounts terrified himself, made the decision to transfer McVeigh into his Bradley, thereby separating him from the crew he had trained with for three years. The stated primary objective for forming the COHORT units was the prevention of "psychological breakdown in battle" by building cohesion and trust among fellow soldiers. For McVeigh, who thrived on his training and regimentation, Lt. Rodriguez's decision must have seemed unthinkable and could not have calmed his already fraying nerves. Mark Hamm wrote about the wild drives through the desert with McVeigh at the turret and Roger Barnett at the wheel, but Barnett himself (and several other sources) described a very different scenario: "We were the Top Gunning team. I was the top driver, McVeigh was the top gunner, and Sgt. Albert Warnement, he was the top Bradley Commander. When we got to Saudi Arabia we were on the same track, and then our Lieutenant, he took McVeigh over to his track ... but our Lieutenant – he wasn't worth a crap."[57]

Indeed, a number of incidents involving Lt. Rodriguez compounded the fears and confusion of many others in the unit. The evening before the ground war, as they headed "balls to the wall" towards Safwan, McVeigh tried to catch some sleep in the moving Bradley and, like the previous evening, found this difficult to do. He woke suddenly, only to find Rodriguez, who was supposed to be acting as lookout, asleep. At that exact moment McVeigh spotted a land mine directly in front of them which they were about to hit. He yelled at the driver, who swerved out of the way, waking Lt. Rodriguez up.

They did appear accident prone. During one particularly chaotic moment, Sgt. 1st Class Dutton stepped on a land mine. Sgt. Robinson remembered, "We were sittin' up at night, and they told Dutton to go out and check the bunkers just to make sure there was no Iraqis and destroy any equipment that was in there. Well, he blew himself up in the process with his own weapon." Lt. Rodriguez testified later that McVeigh saved Robinson from bleeding to death by disobeying Rodriquez's order to pull out the shrapnel. McVeigh, who had specialized medic training, feared the screaming Robinson was bleeding too profusely, and instead, bandaged the wound and calmed him down.

The Jones Team later noted recurring themes throughout the stories McVeigh and other soldiers told them about their experiences in the Gulf. Several had described "a deep lack of confidence in their commanders and comrades" which they attributed to inexperience, poor training and leadership, and a general sense of being "ill equipped and ill prepared for what they were facing." Many also recalled, however, that during this frightful experience, McVeigh's presence helped calm them. Bad Company's driver said Sgt. McVeigh was "the one you wanted in the fox hole with you." Allen Smith, also in McVeigh's Bradley said he "never felt safe when Tim left the vehicle," sometimes fearing his comrades might intentionally or accidently shoot at him and that, out of the entire company, he trusted McVeigh alone.[58]

McVeigh said he was "under a tremendous amount of pressure" and felt responsible for the men in his Bradley as well as those in the tanks directly behind him. People were "going nuts." During one SCUD-attack alert a man in the back of McVeigh's Bradley, sitting directly above the ammunition storage and unable to see outside began crying, "freaked out and refused to take his gas mask off." At some point, a soldier pulled out a gun and demanded that unless he could talk to a Major, he would kill himself. The Major, in fear for his life, refused to talk to the soldier, so Sgt. McVeigh requested permission to stay and talk him down. A request the Major denied.

The High-Tech Turkey Shoot

In the weeks prior to the start of the ground war, reports about Iraqi and coalition POWs regularly appeared in the news. In the final weeks of January 1991, U.S. military police had begun building facilities to house up to 20,000 Iraqi POWs and defectors. Meanwhile, coalition spokespeople accused Iraq of violating the Geneva Protocols in their treatment of allied POWs. A number of international protocols existed establishing standards for the humane treatment of enemy and civilian POWs, not the least of which was the 1949 Geneva Convention. These protocols prohibited the torture, use of chemical weapons and the killing of both enemy and civilians prisoners as well as exposing them to live fire in combat zones.[59]

McVeigh admitted that he was terrified even before leaving the neutral zone and crossing into Iraq and had decided that if he was going to die, he would kill as many Iraqis as he could. In a letter written to Steve dated February 23, 1991, day one of the ground war, he complained that Geneva Convention rules regulating the treatment of POWs would end up getting everybody killed. Therefore, he wrote, "I've made up my mind – no prisoners.... It may be on my conscience for years; and I may be accused of killing defenseless people, but when push comes to shove and my life (along with the lives of everyone in my vehicle) is on the line, you gotta do what you gotta do."[60]

On February 24, while still in the neutral zone between Iraq and Saudi Arabia, Task Force Iron finally met with the Iraqi army. Rules of engagement dictated enemy troops be given the chance to surrender rather than be killed. Although the news "brown out" complicated attempts to construct an accurate picture of the early hours of the ground war, news outlets nonetheless described "disheveled and disarmed Iraqi prisoners shambling single file across the desert [with] smoky oil fires smudging the skies of eastern Kuwait."[61] Indeed, the Iraqis encountered by allied forces were not wild-eyed "rag-headed" terrorists, torturers, and murderers. Rather, many had open sores, appeared covered in lice and were starving, demoralized, poorly trained, inadequately armed, or completely unarmed and in the process of deserting or surrendering. According to reports, very often, the elite Iraqi Republican Guard units stood behind Iraqi soldiers confined to holes and trenches in order to prevent them from deserting. The commander of one U.S. field hospital said the Iraqi POWs were terrified of airplanes, sometimes curling up into fetal positions upon hearing them, while others suffered from acute shell shock or combat stress. Some news outlets reported that Iraqi soldiers were extremely happy upon their capture. Many commanders felt overwhelmed by their inability to care for the thousands of Iraqi POWs and feared their presence would disrupt or impede the advance.

According to McVeigh, it was on the first day of the ground war, heading north towards Safwan, that he first encountered surrendering Iraqis in a trench. After he fired at the trench, what seemed like "thousands" of Iraqis emerged waving white surrender flags. The voluntary POWs caused an extraordinary amount of tension as U.S. troops "didn't know what to do with them" and there were an insufficient number of interpreters to make sense of it all. On this occasion, he said, feeling overwhelmed, U.S. soldiers ordered the Iraqis to the rear and told them "keep walking you stupid fucking Iraqis...we don't have time to deal with hostages right now."[62]

McVeigh told the Jones Team that, when he first witnessed the surrendering Iraqis "looking up at the huge guns pointed at them," he began to realize the gap between what the Army had taught him about war and the reality of war, as well as the people who fight them. For the first time he felt sympathy for those he was supposed to kill. The Iraqis were not "evil," as the media and military told him – they were pathetic, scared, hungry, and confused. His encounters with them were so visceral he "could literally smell from a mile away 'our guys' who had patted down the surrendering Iraqis." After the initial aerial assaults, the conflict had "basically [become] a war with civilians with guns. As soon as the Americans came upon [the Iraqis], they surrendered." The narratives of other men with him in the Gulf echo McVeigh's who said the Army had not properly trained them to "face the enemy" they found in Iraq.

One COHORT, Royal Witcher, said that of all his experiences in the Gulf, the hardest to deal with were the surrendering Iraqis. Ray Barnes described the scene:

> That first day when it went from Desert Shield to Desert Storm, as we were making our way to and across the border ... all the sudden there was an Exodus – it was just like 5,000 people. They were walking to surrender.... They were giving up. I don't think any of them had a gun with them ... well, yes, some of them had guns but then they didn't have ammo, or they just had blanks. They were so hungry and dehydrated. They were offering stacks of money to the officers for a bottle of water. Offering bricks of hash for water because there it's legal to smoke hash. Can't drink whiskey, but can smoke hash.[63]

After comparing all the stories told to them by McVeigh's fellow soldiers, the Jones Team found that their interactions with Iraqis, particularly those killed later, had left a profound mark on all those interviewed. One memo observed, "They did not encounter 'the enemy' which they expected – [an enemy] they could keep at arm's length – but rather saw the humanity and frailty of the people they were required to kill." In June 1995, weeks after his arrest, McVeigh told members of his legal team that this newfound feeling of sympathy for the Iraqis, "made what happened later a lot worse." What happened later depends upon whom you ask, when you ask and, sometimes, why you ask it. After the Oklahoma bombing, news reports described McVeigh firing upon and killing Iraqi soldiers that had been attempting to surrender; an act said to foreshadow and illustrate his later ability to kill without remorse.

McVeigh described to his attorneys how, as they breached the Iraqi front lines, four Bradleys, including his own, lined up in front of an entrenched Iraqi machine gun bunker. He then fired at the trench from 1,600 meters away and, with one shot, hit his target and observed a "red cloud" emanate from it. After he fired several more rounds, "everyone in the trenches surrendered" but, just at that moment, he observed to his right members of Bravo Company, shooting at the surrendering Iraqis and, at that point, tried to get Lt. Rodriguez to radio over and tell them to stop. He said that only later did he learn that he killed two Iraqi soldiers with the one 1,600 meter shot.

He described the incident a bit differently to his biographers a few years later. He said that as they approached a "dug-in enemy machine gun nest" still over a mile away, Lt. Rodriguez ordered him to fire. He instantly saw "a flash of light," assumed it was enemy fire and, with the Bradley still moving, began to adjust his sights. As he did so, "an Iraqi soldier popped his head up for a split second," McVeigh fired at him and "the man's upper body exploded ... his head just disappeared ... like in a red mist." The shot, he said, also killed another Iraqi soldier standing nearby. Lt. Rodriguez ordered him to keep firing but McVeigh hesitated because he noticed that the rest of the dug-in Iraqis had begun to surrender, but since Lt. Rodriguez started screaming at him, he just "fired off a few more rounds, far off into the desert" to appease him. For this he earned an Army Commendation Medal and on the accompanying certificate, his commanding officer, Lt. Col. Moreno, noted that McVeigh had inspired others in his company by "destroying an enemy machine-gun encampment," killing two Iraqi soldiers and forcing thirty others to surrender.[64]

The incident is one of the few where the accounts of the COHORT unit differ. Corroborating this story were the accounts of William Dilley and his Commanding Officer First Sgt. Harris:

> **Dilley:** Tim shot an Iraqi soldier that he saw. We gave them so much time to give up and then we couldn't wait, so we had to clear the trenches so we'd go down and put rounds in them. We couldn't leave them and couldn't go by them, so we cleared the trenches. Tim saw one of the guys he shot and the Lieutenant saw it, too. I know he did because he said [Tim] had a confirmed kill. They saw the guy stand up, and Tim hit him, literally, which was a pretty decent shot, you know? That was the [only] reason [Tim] talked about it [later]. He was just there to do his job [and] was serious about the Army.

> **Harris:** Tim did well in the Gulf. We all did [laughing]. We went into the battle expecting significant American losses, up to 70%, going up against the 4th largest army in the world, and so there was a good deal of fear and anxiety when we first crossed the Iraqi

lines, but there was little resistance. A few would pop up from their trenches and fire at us, and some of those Iraqis got killed as a result. It really couldn't be helped.

However, according to others, it was McVeigh, not Bravo Company, who had continued to fire at the unarmed POW's. One man told the FBI that McVeigh had "bragged on numerous occasions about an Iraqi soldier he killed while in Desert Storm [telling] the story [of] how he'd 'killed a fucking rag head.'" Lester Robinson also described an Iraqi man with an AK-47 who seemed to appear out of nowhere and started firing at them. Since Lt. Rodriguez was "unavailable" at the time, McVeigh, feeling the AK-wielding Iraqi posed a threat, "took the initiative" and, naturally, shot him, accidently killing an unarmed man holding a white surrender flag standing close by. James Spencer concurred that McVeigh made the shot, but said the continued fire afterwards came from a different gunner on the tank Spencer himself was in but did so only after their commander (not Rodriguez) directly ordered them to open fire on surrendering Iraqis. The commander who issued the order, Spencer added apologetically, felt bad about it later. Ray Barnes offered his recollections:

> A lot of things that people said about him, like him supposedly snipering somebody with a 25 MAC at a thousand yards ... I never heard him talk about that.... But did he do it? No.... After the bombing the FBI came and hauled me in and questioned me and the CID come and paid me a visit and picked me up. Hauled me in. They were supposedly investigating possible war crimes with that 1000 yard head shot. According to the Geneva Convention that's overkill. That's one of my main gripes ... what we're dealing with now with the terrorists. It's a reason a lot of our boys are dying, because we're playing by the rules and the other team isn't.[65]

Garrett Bessler, positioned in the tank directly next to McVeigh at the time, said he heard about the allegations but insisted they were "absolutely false," emphasizing, "Tim wasn't the type to be trying to get that first kill no matter what the cost." He did recall a related incident at an unknown time that caused McVeigh to lose his temper. Bessler said that, once, Alpha and Bravo Co. Bradleys were firing at a particular target for over two hours before it dawned on them that they had sufficiently destroyed it. As soon as they stopped, "groups of Iraqis holding their rifles upside down with sheets tied to them," appeared, but Bravo "opened fire on the Iraqis, some of them went down, then others stood back up and the Bradleys opened fire again." Bessler was not sure how many they killed or even which specific Bradley vehicles fired but said that later, Army officials conducted an investigation into the incident and Bravo's role in it.

After returning from the Gulf, Bessler recounted the incident in sworn testimony and even confronted Lt. Rodriguez, who denied that he saw it, a claim Bessler thought "impossible." Nevertheless, Bessler believed the people responsible for the deaths had been "busted" and discharged from the Army. While speculative, I offer the possibility that perhaps *among* the reasons the soldiers' records later went missing were incidents such as this.

McVeigh's friend and fellow COHORT, Gordon Blackcloud, recalled the chaotic killing during their combat:

> I was a Bradley driver for the first half of the war and then a gunner. Everybody more or less fired on everybody. We took a lot of prisoners. I know we killed some of them [Iraqis]. Everybody had to ... everybody had to. My Platoon Sergeant got hit, and then I got hit in the back and then the back of the head. Another guy blew off his foot by stepping on a mine. After I got hit, we ran over there to our Platoon Sergeant and wrapped him up because we were also combat medics. My whole back was bleeding and everything, but I didn't let them take me off until we got done with our Platoon Sergeant.[66]

In unpublished letters and conversations with his biographers, McVeigh elaborated about the time "I shot that guy in the Gulf," describing it as a pivotal and meaningful experience:

> This is the point when I felt empathy for the enemy. I [understood] that these were just people too ... I'm not a coward. Anybody who knows me knows that ... I learned in the Gulf and through the news that people are the same; it doesn't matter why you kill a person, you're still killing humans. How did I feel about killing those soldiers? At the time it was instinctive, no feelings. You turn off your feelings until after you have time to deal with them. It's like a computer. You put them in memory and access them later. There was a lot of activity immediately after that. A lot of things were happening.... In the end, I can accept the fact that I did kill those Iraqis, and I think that in my heart maybe it would have been wrong, but that's life in the 20th century. Humans kill humans ... I don't kill for pleasure, and I don't kill for personal gain.

General Schwarzkopf heralded the initial assault as a "dramatic success." Coalition troops encountered minimal resistance as they entered Iraq and Iraqi-occupied Kuwait, capturing thousands of POWs along the way. Although the U.S. refused to release casualty information, seven U.S. Marines died as they passed through the Saudi village of Khafji. Still, said Schwarzkopf, this was a "remarkably light" number of casualties, and he was "delighted with the progress." Defense Secretary Dick Cheney told television viewers, "we have no interest in occupying Iraq, but ... there won't be any sanctuary inside Iraq for those forces who've been involved in occupying Kuwait."[67]

News reports later detailed how the majority of Iraqis simply did not want to fight and were killed as they vacated the vehicles and trenches they inhabited, waving white flags. John Simpson wrote that the battles of the Gulf War were not like those of World War II, but instead "merely the slaughter of tens of thousands of Third World soldiers armed only with weapons incapable of penetrating American armor. Almost every Iraqi soldier would have willingly given himself up if he had been given the chance. Even the punishment squads which were based behind the Iraqi lines to shoot deserters had little interest in obeying their orders. Many of them planned to desert themselves." The unnecessary slaughter of thousands of Iraqis came to be called by those who had been there, including McVeigh, "a high tech turkey shoot."[68] McVeigh also said that what came later was much worse, but did not elaborate.

THE BULLDOZER ASSAULT

I wish to use the words of Justice Brandeis dissenting in Olmstead to speak for me. He wrote, "Our government is the potent, the omnipresent teacher. For good or ill, it teaches the whole people by its example."

–Timothy James McVeigh at his sentencing hearing, August 4, 1997.

On February 25, 1991, fifteen hours ahead of schedule, McVeigh's division had crossed into Southern Iraq and completed what General Schwarzkopf called a "classic breaching" that would be "studied for years." McVeigh's Bradley was in the lead, moving parallel to Iraqi trenches along the Iraq-Saudi border until they shifted northward and continued for three hundred miles. For over 100 hours, the Big Red One engaged the Iraqi army in an "awesome display of death that would have shaken the most steadfast soldier," and took thousands of prisoners in the process.[69]

During the initial entry into Iraq, McVeigh's Bradley stopped briefly. The radio operator, having seen what appeared to be a large number of troops approaching, attempted to make contact with them in order to determine if they were *friendlies*. Just at that moment, the radio malfunctioned, and although the sights were not properly set on the Bradley's 25 mm, Lt. Rodriguez ordered them to drive out and investigate. Upon doing so, British troops who were cleaning out mines informed them that they had just driven into a minefield. McVeigh said that Lt. Rodriguez "almost plowed [the Brits] over." Although they didn't, the incident fore-shadowed what was to happen soon after.

In his strikingly insensitive 1994 account of the Gulf War entitled *Iron Soldiers: How America's 1ˢᵗ Armored Division Crushed Iraq's Elite Republican Guard*, military historian Tom Carhart provided a highly sanitized "feel good" version of Desert Storm; one that, it is safe to assume, passed Pentagon and military muster. Among the many stories Carhart recounted was one relayed to him by a female MP from the 3/37 Armored (McVeigh's battalion). The MP was tasked with minding the "few hundred" Iraqi POW's the 3/37ᵗʰ had thus far captured. She said that, while she minded the POW's, an Army engineering vehicle had "scooped out" a trench about twelve feet wide and six deep with wire around it. As she tried to "herd" the POWs into the trench she observed that "many of the prisoners were literally in tears, grown men groveling on their knees with uplifted hands, pleading [for] their lives." She then "realized, with a little shock, [that] they believed the Americans were about to bury them, as Iraqi leaders [had] prophesied." Because there were no translators available to the MP, she gathered up candy (which they had in abundance) and MREs, and saw to it that each POW had handfuls of the food. After they received their candy, the POW's became confusedly silent, asking themselves "Why would the Yankee Devil feed us candy if he was going to bury us?" until eventually they realized they were in no danger and "all [of the] Iraq[is'] fears vanished."[70]

From February 24 to 25, a nightmarish scene occurred that Ramsey Clark described as "the most horrifying story of all."[71] This story exposed a war very different from Carhart's or the one Americans saw on the nightly news. It was first reported on September 12, 1991, and was picked up by several news outlets whose shocking headlines declared that "U.S. Army Buried Iraqi Soldiers Alive in Gulf War."

The incident, or series of incidents, occurred near the Saudi-Iraqi border as the First Mechanized Infantry Division, in their breaching effort, tore through over seventy miles of barbed wire, minefields, bunkers and trenches about three-feet wide and six-feet deep, defended by, according to division estimates, eight thousand Iraqi soldiers. After Howitzers and rocket launchers "rained hell" upon Iraqis in their trenches, the heavily armored Abrams and Bradley vehicles broke through, "and the real slaughter began." During what came to be known as the Bulldozer Assault, Abrams tanks, outfitted with plows and scrapers, broached the trenches, shoveling mounds of sand into them, burying alive the Iraqis inside. Vulcan armored carriers and Bradley vehicles drove alongside the trenches, firing upon those attempting to surrender and others who continued to return fire with small arms. The Armored Combat Earthmovers (ACEs) cleaned up the horrifying scene afterwards by burying the scattered arms and legs still in view, so that none of the journalists arriving thirty-six hours later could report carnage.[72]

The record shows that as early as June 5, 1995 (weeks after McVeigh's arrest) the Jones Team was aware of the Bulldozer Assault and had noted their need to determine whether any member of his platoon "actually ran over Iraqi trenches (burying soldiers in them)" or if they had seen evidence of this as they approached the trenches. If any of his fellow soldiers spoke to the defense team about it, no such documentation was located in the Jones Collection. However, upon closer inspection it becomes clear that McVeigh's company, his Bradley among them, spearheaded the breaching operation and led the Bulldozer Assault.

In the few reports about it, news outlets quoted at least two individuals whom McVeigh knew. In September 1991, one of them, Col. Anthony Moreno, who commanded the First Mechanized lead brigade against the most heavily defended trenches during the assault, described it, telling reporters "what you saw was a bunch of buried trenches with people's arms and legs sticking out of them. For all I know, we could have killed thousands … as (Iraqi) soldiers saw what we were doing and how effective (ly) we were doing it, they began jumping out of their holes and surrendering. Our firepower kept the Iraqis down in their trenches. They were incapable of firing back."[73]

No existing biography of McVeigh explores the horror of the Bulldozer Assault in any depth, or even mentions it as such. In his book, Stickney simply wrote, "A lot of shooting by the Americans was directed at the enemy's dug-in trenches." Hamm acknowledged that McVeigh's "platoon was assigned to 'roll up' the trenches and nearby artillery bunkers supporting them. This involved rolling over them in Bradleys, tanks, trucks, and giant earthmovers, suffocating to death hundreds of Iraqi troops in the trenches. This tactic not only effectively killed the enemy, but the huge pile of corpses provided a sturdy foundation for a smooth crossing point for the invading forces." Herbeck and Michel did not directly address the Bulldozer Assault, the bodies buried alive or McVeigh's role in it. Rather, they allude to it obliquely by observing that the motto of the VII Corp was "If it's in front of us, it dies" and because of the sounds made by the tanks rolling over Iraqis, U.S. soldiers began to refer to the dead they'd created as "crunchies."[74]

The handful of existing news reports about the incident provide further details. Participants later said that they had carefully planned and rehearsed the Bulldozer Assault weeks before it commenced, a claim confirmed by satellite photographs. One Captain described the psychological trauma he later suffered because of his role in the slaughter. The Iraqis, he said, had been throwing down their weapons and were begging the U.S. troops to take them prisoner. "I wish we could have," he reflected, "[but] after [taking] so many thousands of prisoners, the order came down that it was endangering our men to capture anymore ... so we called in the bulldozers.... I had to give the order, order men who drove the earthmovers to just cover up the trenches... I buried hundreds of men alive... if I'd disobeyed orders I should have been shot for insubordination on the battle field ... that's war."[75]

Others also provided vivid descriptions: Cpt. Bernie Williams said, "There were times when we knew they were in a bunker and we gave them a chance to give up ... I'd tell my guns to fire off to the side and give them a chance. I would say about 60 percent of the guys gave up.... And there were some who decided to gut it out. A lot of guys were buried in bunkers, I'm sure. We just drove over them or backed into them to make the walls collapse... once we went through there, other than the ones who surrendered, there wasn't anybody left." Sgt. Joe Queen, who received a Bronze Star for his role in the attack said, "[We were] traveling at [five to seven] miles an hour just moving along the trench ... you don't see him [the Iraqis]. You're up there in the half hatch and you know what you got to do. You did it as much as you could close your eyes and do it ... I don't think they had any idea because the look on their faces as we came through the berm was just a look of shock.... I feel sorry for them that stayed in the trenches, but they did what they did for their country, just like we would ... the military furnished us with this piece of equipment, and that's what it's designed to do." An unnamed Iraqi soldier who survived the attack said, "Some of the soldiers were walking towards the [U.S.] troops holding their arms up to surrender, and the tanks moved in and killed them. They dug a hole in the ground, and then they buried the soldiers and leveled it. I really don't know how to describe ... it was horrible to witness ... I saw one soldier and his body was just torn apart by a bulldozer. The upper part was on one side and the lower on the other side."[76]

Many journalists said they had been tightly controlled and intentionally kept back from the bulldozed areas. One report observed, "It was a battlefield without the stench of urine, feces, blood and bits of flesh. The dead had eluded eyewitnesses, cameras and video footage." A war correspondent for the *Guardian* said that when he arrived at the scene, there were no bodies anywhere. When he asked a public affairs officer from the 1st where the bodies had gone, the official replied, "what bodies?" Simpson wrote, "There was an intensive effort to make sure that the scale of Iraqi losses was hidden from the world." When the Pentagon finally allowed journalists on the site, there were, "no bodies, no barbed wire, not even the trenches. It was too ugly for the public to be told about, and for that reason, it had all been thoroughly tidied away."[77]

Although the House and Senate Armed Services Committees claimed the Pentagon withheld details about the Bulldozer Assault in their final report on the Gulf War, it was justified as a legitimate *tactical maneuver* in a number of ways by those who planned and led it. In Dick Cheney's 2002 report to Congress that attempted to justify the assault, he wrote "Because of [the] uncertainties and the need to minimize loss of U.S. lives, military necessity required that the assault ... be conducted with maximum speed and violence." Other military planners claimed that, if an opportunity for the Iraqis to surrender had been announced over loudspeakers, U.S. soldiers would have had to exit their armored vehicles and engage the Iraqis in hand-to-hand combat or could even have become the targets of a chemical attack. Others said that while they had given the Iraqis a chance to surrender, the Iraqis declined the offer. When asked to estimate the total number buried, DoD spokesperson Pete Williams denied the Army had intended to bury anyone alive, but then continued, remarking that: "War is hell, I would certainly say many were buried ... I don't mean to be flippant, but there's no nice way to kill somebody in a war. There is no provision in the Geneva Convention that would prohibit this operation. The Iraqi soldiers that were killed in this process were those who chose to stay in their trenches or behind obstacles and fight during the breaching operation."[78]

The motto of Ft. Riley's First Mechanized Infantry Division (The Big Red One) claims "No mission too difficult, no sacrifice too great, duty first." Shortly after the Bulldozer incident, Maj. Gen. Thomas Rhames, the commander of the entire 1st division, declared to journalists, "I didn't come over here to fight fair." Rather, he came to "fight ... win, and save American lives," a goal Rhames achieved by burying what he claimed were 400 Iraqis during the front line breach. When reporters questioned Army officials about the incident during a press conference at Ft. Riley (where McVeigh was stationed before and after the Gulf War), officials there said that the bulldozing method had saved American lives as the Iraqi barrier posed the biggest threat to U.S. troops. Rhames said, "All I can tell you is that there were little hands and arms sticking up out of the dirt. They chose not to surrender. They chose to fight. So we buried them." Lt. Col. Stephen Hawkins, who helped plan the assault, said the point was to "terrorize" the Iraqis into surrendering, and thought it had worked: "it caused an instant hands-up in many places," remarked Hawkins.[79]

When asked if this was the Standard Operating Procedure for the U.S. Army, Col. Moreno said, "This was not doctrine. My concept is to defeat the enemy with your power and equipment. We're going to bludgeon them with every piece of equipment we've got. I'm not going to sacrifice the lives of my soldiers – that's not cost effective." Col. Lon Maggart, an officer from Ft. Riley whom McVeigh knew, said, "I know burying people like that sounds pretty nasty, but it would be even nastier if we had to put our troops in trenches and clean them out with bayonets."[80] In fact,

Moreno and Maggart, both of whom McVeigh knew, were among the first to talk to reporters about the attack. Both said that they intentionally used the 'bulldozer tactic' to minimize American casualties, although, in reality, those inside the tanks and Bradleys were likely in no danger from the small arms fire coming from the trenches. The entire ordeal, at least for their brigades, lasted about seventeen minutes. The Army later condemned and punished Moreno (who nominated McVeigh for several awards and decorations for his performance during combat in the Gulf) for providing this information to reporters.

No one can really say exactly how many Iraqi soldiers were buried alive or how many had attempted to surrender before meeting their deaths. *Newsday* and the *Guardian* cited military officials who claimed 2,000 Iraqis actually surrendered. Other sources put the number at between 11,000 and 20,000. An Iraqi soldier said he thought Americans had buried perhaps 300 of his comrades while Iraqi military spokespeople claimed the number was between one and two thousand. Some US infantry personnel told reporters they had no idea how many people they buried under the sand. Rhames said 400. Dick Cheney withheld details about it to a Congressional report on the war but did state that the Army buried 457 Iraqis in the sand. Maggart estimated that his brigade buried 650. A military source quoted in the *Jerusalem Post* said 6,000. Schwarzkopf's staff gave estimates of between 50,000 and 75,000 for the total number killed in the trenches. It was hard to obtain an accurate body count given the literal 'cover-up' that, according to the Pentagon, claimed no American casualties.[81]

While Geneva Convention protocols dictate that surrendering enemy troops be taken prisoner and not killed, the numbers of surrendering Iraqis would have been much higher had they not been summarily executed when attempting to do so. Many received medals for participating in the gory scene.

The aerial assaults that had occurred since January 16 at the barrier where the bulldozer attack took place were equally horrifying. One report, on January 25, said that much of the Iraqi artillery were destroyed by aerial "napalm and fuel air" bombings, which consisted of over 11,000 pounds of high explosives dropped thirty minutes before the Bulldozer assault began. Still, they claimed, U.S. soldiers continued to face a formidable foe and therefore had to "ignite oil in some defensive trenches," among other methods. According to a FOIA request, the U.S. Marines confirmed they had dropped 489 napalm bombs on "those poor fuckers in the trenches." The aerial and ground images of the aftermath in Basra, one military historian wrote, "ranks up there with the young Vietnamese girl running naked from a napalm attack or the Zapruder film." This was the first, but by no means the last time, that McVeigh found himself at the center of a contentious moment in U.S. history.[82]

THE PATH TO HELL IS PAVED (BASRA HIGHWAY)

... the word of God much bandied by George Bush whose word illuminated
midnight sky and confused the Baghdad cock who was betrayed by bombs
into believing day was dawning and crowed his heart out at the deadly raid
and didn't live to greet the proper morning. Now with noonday headlights
in Kuwait and the burial of the blackened in Baghdad let them remember,
all who celebrate, that their good news is someone else's bad or the light will
never dawn on poor Mankind.

– Tony Harrison, *A Cold Coming: Gulf War Poems* 1991

The Turkey Shoot was not yet over. McVeigh said that, after destroying the Iraqi bunkers and trenches, his division received orders to head north as quickly as possible to an airfield in the city of Safwan, Iraq. Thus, throughout February 25 and 26, 1991, the third and fourth days of the ground war, they pushed forward "balls to the wall ... day and night" towards Safwan. As they did, they encountered a massive sandstorm, a "world-class, biblical thunderstorm" and crossed paths with the Iraqi Republican Guard whom they engaged in two 'famed' battles. Commentators described the second, the Battle of Norfolk, which occurred in the Saudi village of Khafji, as "the most costly – and thus the most important – battle of the war." McVeigh's division suffered the most extensive casualties with forty wounded and seven dead. At first, Pentagon officials told reporters as well as the families of the dead that enemy fire had killed them, but month's later officials admitted that *all* the U.S. deaths resulted from friendly fire, mainly from American 'Silver Bullets'– sabot rounds coated in depleted uranium.[83]

After Norfolk, McVeigh's company continued towards Safwan traveling on Highway 8, a road that eventually connected with Highway 80 (or Basra Highway), a six-lane highway that connected Kuwait City to deep inside of Iraq, it's "Center of Gravity." By this time, the Iraqi army was in full retreat with untold thousands of Iraqi soldiers and civilians, in tanks, cars, school buses, ambulances and on foot, heading north on Basra Highway and nearby Highway 8. Throughout February 26 and 27, the retreating Iraqis on both roads met with "wave after wave" of extensive aerial bombardment consisting of laser guided missiles, mortars, cluster bombs and machine-gun fire from Apache and Cobra helicopters, Warthog and Thunderbolt fighter jets and other U.S. aircraft equipped with infrared optics. A U.S. pilot described the scene as "the biggest Fourth of July show you've ever seen." Another said, "I just didn't envision going up there and shooting the hell out of everything in the dark and have them not know what the hell hit them. A truck blows up to the right, the ground blows up to the left. They had no idea where we were or what was hitting them ... it looked like somebody had opened the sheep pen."[84]

U.S. ground troops aggressively pursued and killed those who managed to avoid the air assault. Footage recorded from an Apache helicopter revealed "terrified Iraqi infantrymen shot to pieces ... some were blown to bits, [and others] fled their bunkers under a firestorm." An Iraqi survivor of the attack said, "There were hundreds of cars destroyed, soldiers screaming ... it was a nightmare as bombs fell, lighting charred cars, bodies on the side of the road and soldiers sprawled on the ground, hit by cluster bombs as they tried escaping from their vehicles. I saw hundreds of soldiers like this." Reporters on the ground described seeing over sixty miles of burning oil wells, debris, and burning wreckage from thousands of abandoned and bombed military and civilian vehicles as well as the gruesome sights of wild dogs feasting on mutilated Iraqi corpses that numbered from the hundreds to thousands. One described, "[s]cores of soldiers ... in and around the vehicles, mangled and bloated in the drifting desert sands, [the vehicles] strafed, smashed, and burned beyond belief." Robert Fisk said he "lost count of the Iraqi corpses crammed into the smoldering wreckage or clumped face down in the sand."[85]

Although the official body count ranged from 200-300 to several thousand, nobody could be sure how many Iraqis died on Basra Highway and on nearby Highway 8. While some reporters observed the bodies, the majority of corpses on Basra Highway simply disappeared. Coalition troops buried, dug up, reburied and set ablaze those corpses not eaten by dogs. The *Boston Globe* reported, "Mile after wreckage-jammed mile of highway appeared as if frozen in mid-battle ... and all along the way, allied soldiers worked, burying hundreds of dead in shallow graves." An aerial photo revealed "Iraqis being dumped in a group grave by means of a front-loader – a scoop fixed to a truck." The aerial footage released by the Pentagon, however, showed "shreds of Iraq vehicles and equipment – and no bodies. It was if the desert were a sandbox and all the children had run away, leaving their toys behind."[86]

Gen. Schwarzkopf said he ordered the attack for two reasons. First, he wanted to destroy Iraqi equipment and, second, the retreating Iraqis were "a bunch of rapists, murderers, and thugs who had raped and pillaged downtown Kuwait City" and were now trying to escape. The slaughter on and around Basra Highway was so utterly incomprehensible that, to this day, it is called 'The Highway of Death.' Even war hawks described the ensuing "mother of all defeats" as one of "the grizzliest scenes of the war."[87] The world learned about the massacre through the reports of journalists who arrived shortly after, and some credited their graphic descriptions with catalyzing George Bush's February 28, 1991 cease-fire declaration.

The declared objective of the Coalition's military intervention had been to force the Iraqi army out of Kuwait, which ultimately was exactly what occurred.

Hamm wrote that it was on the Highway of Death where "McVeigh witnessed one of the greatest massacres of modern warfare: the slaughter of thousands of retreating Iraqi soldiers and civilians on the Basra Road" and quoted his CO, Cpt. Terry Guild, who said they "wandered for miles through hundreds of blackened bodies." His official biography dedicates less than one paragraph to details of the gruesome sights they witnessed on their trek to Safwan.

> [McVeigh] saw unspeakable carnage, hideously charred bodies, some of them with their heads or limbs blown off. Some [were] bloated to the size of cows as they rotted in the sun ... horribly wounded enemy soldiers, some of them without arms or legs, trying to crawl along the sand ... [and] stray dogs chewing on severed body part.... At one point, members of McVeigh's unit were told to help bury the Iraqi dead in the sand. Later, without explanation, they were told to stop the burials and leave the bodies out where they could be seen.[88]

At his criminal trial, Lt. Rodriguez testified that McVeigh had taken pictures of the dead Iraqis. McVeigh denied this, claiming it was the driver of his Bradley, not him, who had done that. Neither his biographers nor the Jones Team would see any of the rolls of pictures he took during the Gulf War, as the FBI confiscated them after the Oklahoma bombing.[89] In the story of the OKC bombing and Tim McVeigh, bodies (or evidence of them) continue to disappear.

After the harrowing two-and-a-half days of battle, orders changed, telling them to continue along Highway 8 and stop to secure El Bosna, a small town near the Iraq-Kuwait border before heading to the Safwan Airfield where the official Iraqi surrender, cease-fire negotiations and formal peace talks were scheduled to begin. Along the way, McVeigh and his friends observed similar horrors. On March 2, days after the cease-fire agreement and one day before the peace talks were to begin, artillery units from the 24th Division repeated the earlier Basra Highway attack, this time concentrating solely on the smaller Highway 8. Abrams and Bradleys fired upon and killed retreating Iraqi soldiers and civilians, including children. Gen. Barry McCaffery, who commanded the attack called it "one of the most astounding scenes of destruction I have ever participated in ... we destroyed all of them ... once we had them bottled up ... there was no way out."[90]

On March 3, 1991, Schwarzkopf arrived at Safwan and met with Iraqi generals who agreed to the terms of withdrawal. Lowry described it as a day to remember and "one that would be burned in our memory [and] history books for decades to come." McVeigh's company performed security detail during the treaty signing ceremony. One soldier captured video footage of Schwarzkopf walking down the line shaking hands with members of the security detail, including McVeigh, who was "beaming with pride." In 2011, Ray Barnes said "their little peace treaty," despite the theatrics, was, for the most part, "a big dog and pony show" on "some little dinky runway out in the middle of nowhere." President Bush announced the liberation of Kuwait and the end of the war. Officials declared Operation Desert Storm an overwhelming success.[91]

Throughout the war, Pentagon spokespeople claimed they could not release even estimated numbers of American casualties as it could affect the safety and readiness of U.S. troops. During the daily morning Pentagon Press briefings, the more than five hundred on-location journalists covering the war expressed their displeasure with this and complained about the inaccurate or wholly falsified information they continuously received, most notably about the dead. The official numbers the Pentagon would eventually release varied. In August 1991, they claimed the number of U.S. soldiers killed in action was 148, including 35 from friendly fire, and 467 more wounded, 72 from friendly fire.

As for the number of Iraqi soldiers killed, well, nobody really knew and military officials claimed that they just had not been keeping track, a lack of concern some linked to the negative effect official body counts had on public opinion during the Vietnam War. When asked about the number of dead Iraqi soldiers in March 1991, an unnamed Defense Intelligence Agency official remarked, "The guys in the field just weren't counting. They still aren't. They just poured them into common graves and covered them." A senior allied officer in Riyadh offered what he called a "ball park figure" of 100,000. In September 1991, the Pentagon claimed it was impossible to determine the total number of Iraqi soldiers who had died during the war. In a report to Congress that same month, Dick Cheney said that only 457 Iraqi bodies had been found on the battlefield but made no mention of the Bulldozer Assault. "We have no way of knowing precisely how many casualties occurred ... and we may never know," Cheney concluded. Although for years, Gen. Schwarzkopf refused to give even an estimated count other than "a very large number," in 2000, he said the number of Iraqi soldiers killed was "tens of thousands." Independent estimates range from 10,000 to about 35,000 with about another 75,000 wounded. Estimated numbers of collateral damage or Iraqi civilian deaths based on Iraqi census reports and U.N. and other allied totals range from 3,664 to 103,500 during the war and 205,500 more in the post-war period as a result of war-related damage to critical infrastructure. The U.S. claimed the number of surrendered or captured Iraqi POWs to be 110,000.[92] Ultimately, the soldiers who fought with McVeigh during the Gulf War could not agree how many POWs their company had taken; some claimed they had taken a considerable number while others said none.

At the beginning of the conflict, President Bush had reminded Americans that, as a Navy pilot during World War II, he had personally "seen the hideous face of war." For U.S. civilians, soldiers and the rest of the world, the carnage in and around Basra Highway became emblematic of this ghastly face and a symbol whose impact would resonate for years to come. In Richard Lowry's uncritical and embarrassingly glowing military history of the U.S.'s first war with Iraq, he describes how, during his flight to the Safwan peace talks, Schwarzkopf observed the "pitch black smoke" that filled the Kuwaiti air, the burning oil well fires and the Highway of Death below.[93] An early article about the incident warned that in the coming years it would be important to monitor the psychological state of U.S. troops who had been present, predicting they too would become psychological casualties of the atrocity.

Since 1991, mass graves filled with suffocated Iraqis have continued to appear. In 2003, the Saudi military began digging up and moving the graveyard of wreckage that still inhabited Bara Highway and surrounding areas in preparation for the U.S.'s second war with Iraq; a mess so extensive that the clean-up was expected to take a division of 17,000 soldiers over a month to complete. In 2011, U.S. soldiers ordered to "clean up hundreds of scorched corpses and carbonized bodies [on Basra Highway]" continued to have flashbacks of what they saw there as they loaded the bodies into bags, and dumped them in mass graves. In 2011, one soldier on the 'clean-up crew' described frequently waking up from nightmares about dead women and children melted together.[94]

Hamm described the end of the Gulf War as "the high point in McVeigh's life" but also the beginning of his "downward spiral." The grim and grisly impact McVeigh's travels on the long road to Safwan had on his frame of mind should not be underestimated.[95]

A SICK, DOG EAT DOG WORLD

On March 8, 1991, McVeigh and his COHORTs arrived at a "small farming community" off Basra Highway, where they remained for the next ten days. McVeigh said the majority of Iraqi civilians, mostly women and children, were "hungry as hell" and continuously begged them for food. Sometimes he and the others shared their MREs, despite Lt. Rodriguez's contrary order because "of what happened in Vietnam, when the children would carry bombs." McVeigh even wrote home expressing his displeasure with the orders not to feed the "starving Iraqi children." The actions of his fellow soldiers towards the Iraqis upset McVeigh as well. He spoke later about some of them who "watch[ed] the women going to the bathroom at night with thermals (infrared sights)" as they passed civilian houses, an observation that led him to understand "how technologically advanced" Americans were and recalled how he felt "offended by how much we intruded into their lives."

Once, Ray Barnes found a chest of tools and was in the process of taking them when a group of Iraqi civilians ran up screaming and accusing Barnes of stealing their tools. Another time, when they arrived in the town, the COs ordered McVeigh and some others to raid an abandoned motor pool, where they procured an Iraqi tank and dragged it away as a souvenir.

On March 17, 1991, McVeigh wrote to his sister, telling her they were pulling back from the demilitarized zone and that the war had been a success for the United States, but added, "It's a sick, dog eat dog world out there." That same day, Lt. Rodriguez returned to the States due to a death in his family, and McVeigh became the platoon commander, in charge of about thirty-six men. That evening, McVeigh and two other soldiers he'd grown close to thumbed their noses at Rodriguez by placing cases of MREs and cans of fruit cocktail on the road for the hungry Iraqis.

On March 24, 1991, a commanding officer pulled Sgt. McVeigh, now twenty-two years old, from routine duty and informed him that he had thirty minutes to pack his bags and prepare to leave. McVeigh and CO-HORT Mitch Whitmire had received their long-awaited orders to head back to Ft. Riley, gather their gear and then report to Ft. Bragg, North Carolina by April 5 for the twenty-one day Special Forces Selection and Assessment Course. Gordon Blackcloud said McVeigh "was excited and happy. He always thought he was ready [and] was ready in the Gulf when they transferred him." COHORT Maurice Ray said that when McVeigh left the Gulf everyone thought he would make it. This had always been his goal and he had, in the years they'd known him, trained very hard for this chance. While McVeigh also claimed later that he had been happy to receive the orders, other soldiers said he felt conflicted about it. Ray Barnes said, "Before he left the Gulf he was nervous because he wasn't able to train. I know people that's gone into Ranger school at 180 pounds, come out 150, 145 pounds." In a letter he penned during his flight home to Steve on March 26, 1991, McVeigh admitted that he was concerned because "class starts April 1 [and] I'm not in shape" and predicted, "*My list of headaches to come is about a mile long.*"[96]

While many people spoke of dramatic changes they observed after McVeigh's return from the Gulf War, a handful said they saw the subtle beginnings of this process before he left. They emphasized that his experiences there had made an immediate, marked, observable impression on him. Maurice Ray explained that many soldiers, including McVeigh, were very disappointed when the war ended and felt they should have "been allowed to go into Baghdad and finish what was begun," a sentiment McVeigh expressed to his cousin who had also fought in the Gulf War.

According to Sgt. Guest and fellow COHORT Garrett Bessler, McVeigh's change in attitude became apparent after witnessing the deaths of surrendering Iraqis, which, they said, he found terribly disturbing. McVeigh, said Guest, had been visibly "shaken up by the death and destruction" and started to feel disappointed about "the views of the military [and] the unit [in particular]." Bessler said McVeigh was "upset that they came all the way over and risked their lives for people to shoot at nothing." Many soldiers became disillusioned by the amount of "unnecessary firing" at Iraqis in the Gulf and, Bessler admitted, "I thought I was losing my mind over there." Curtis Chandler explained how, "It was just very frustrating to have fought a war over oil; then to be pulled off and never complete the mission ... all of us kind of wondered whether it was our war to fight and why we were fighting it. We all knew that nobody cared about Kuwait; all we cared about was that damn oil. It was kind of a common consensus among us that we were fighting a war over oil. Plus ... of all the prisoners we took, I'll tell you right now, aint a one of them wanted to fight. Not one. They were without question just stuck out in the middle of nowhere with nothing."

McVeigh later explained that he had previously believed they entered the war to protect the country, the U.S. constitution and innocent people and only at the end did he "wake up" and realize that the war "was all economics" and that he and his COHORTs had been "sent over there to protect big oil companies." He recalled their superiors' warnings of a horrible and evil enemy, but he now began to understand that the Iraqi soldiers he saw (and killed) on the frontlines were just as human as the Americans.

In an internal memorandum, the Jones Team noted that when McVeigh spoke to them about the war (as well as the victims of Waco), he often welled up with emotion and, while his expressions were unquestionably genuine and real, the sympathy he displayed seemed irreconcilable with the "striking insensitivity" he showed towards the victims of the Oklahoma bombing. It was almost as if he had an "insensitivity switch" that "turn[ed] off his feelings" and, while his ability to do this had "allowed him to get through the Gulf War," they believed it had also allowed him to "do what he did in Oklahoma City without thinking about the human beings he was about to kill." The Jones Team soon learned the full extent and capabilities of McVeigh's 'switch.'

In 1997, Mark Hamm noted an over-representation of combat veterans among the prison population and, drawing from a number of studies, discussed possible underlying psychological factors that led McVeigh to bomb the Murrah. Among them was the Army's training, fine-tuned over the years to remove soldiers' aversion to murdering other humans through highly calculated conditioning, which leads to a reflexive willingness to obey any orders, including killing. Once conditioned, soldiers retain the learned aggression and desire to kill, sometimes enacting this in the civilian world.[97]

Indeed, Lee Harvey Oswald, Texas Bell Tower sniper Charles Whitman, D.C. Beltway sniper John Allen Muhammad, Fort Hood shooter Major Nidal Malik Hassan, Naval Yard shooter Alex Alexis, serial killers Jeffery Dahmer and "Son of Sam" David Berkowitz, and of course Timothy McVeigh, all had one thing in common: U.S. military training awakened their lust to kill and refined their ability to do it. A June 9, 2001 article in the *Ottawa Citizen* warned of the inevitability of other McVeighs "strolling the streets of Canada" with undiagnosed or untreated Post Traumatic Stress Disorder (PTSD) rendering them "ticking time bomb[s] waiting to explode." The article urged Gulf War and other combat veterans to seek treatment for PTSD symptoms, which included hyper-awareness, sleep disorders, social isolation, panic attacks, anger management issues, depression and suicidal thoughts.[98]

In his 1995 book, *On Killing: The Psychological Cost of Learning to Kill in War and Society*, Lt. Col. Dave Grossman, former army Ranger, paratrooper and instructor of psychology at West Point and Military Science at Arkansas State University, wrote that soldiers experience typical "killing response stages" during and after combat. The first, fear and concern, occurs prior to engagement with the enemy. In the second, soldiers rely upon their previous military training and desensitization to killing and during the actual fighting, act reflexively and mindlessly. Immediately after, the heightened awareness and adrenaline produced during combat causes an "exhilaration stage" which, for some, becomes addictive. According to Grossman, more often than not, soldiers come to experience remorse for their acts, eventually rationalizing and accepting them, but that the period between their exhilaration and remorse is the most powerful and overwhelming time for them.[99]

Nearly twenty years after the end of the Gulf War, Ray Barnes described exactly the type of combat exhilaration Grossman wrote about:

> I'm not gonna' lie to you – I was scared over there, but at the same time I felt exhilarated. I mean, especially when you went out – you just didn't know if that was your last time. In a strange way – I'm a fear junkie. I like it. I felt alive. Your endorphins get goin' and I remember seeing this, laying on my cot reading a book and I look up and there's a glowing ball ... a shooting star ... about that time another little ball slams into it. BOOM. And you can hear the shrap-

nel. They shot a SCUD down. Then I remember we were securing the forward position for the battalion and sitting out there and all the sudden the sand just erupts. Our own people lobbing mortars at us. Actually, when I was over there I wasn't worried about the enemy … I was worried about our guys killing us … we had chopper pilots melt down a 113 Scout Vehicle because it was out there in the horizon. It was all melted down.[100]

Following closely on the heels of the thrilling heights McVeigh experienced was a looming boredom. As he sat in the small Iraqi farming community coming down from his battle high, he admitted to Steve in a letter that he was "itching to torch something." The Army appreciated such itches and rewarded McVeigh for "taking out the Iraqis." Included among these were the Good Conduct Medal, Army Commendation Medal for "valorous achievement," Southeast Service Medal with two Bronze Stars for "meritorious achievement," a Combat Infantry Badge for "proficiency in the performance of duties under hazardous combat operations," National Defense Service Medal, and the Kuwait Liberation Medal."[101]

McVeigh's fellow soldier and friend, Ted Thorne, reflected on this and told the Jones Team, "We were supposed to be tough guys, you know? They taught us how to be killers and then they send us back home to the real world. We are supposed to be normal people again, but it just don't quite work like that. An infantry unit is trained as killers; that's what an infantry person is. You can't just take a normal person and put them in there. It wouldn't work out." Another COHORT later relayed his opinion that the post OKC bombing media reports depicting McVeigh as a psychopathic killer were inaccurate:

The things we had to deal with, having to kill somebody, that was part of our job and we did it and it didn't make a difference how old or how young or how big or what color, it didn't matter. That went with the job, and Tim was responsible when it came to doing a job. He'd do it regardless of who or what, that's what we were trained to do and that's what he did. He was one of the few people in the unit I trusted to have my back. The other guys, it didn't really hit them that if you go to war, you're going to have to kill somebody. That's what you're for and most of the people couldn't comprehend that. Some people didn't take the job seriously, but Tim and I did. Tim and a lot of others became very disillusioned because of the stupidity displayed that got a lot of people killed. I remember being told by a Full Bird Colonial in basic training that if you had to kill a kid, kill them. The press is making him out to be a psychotic, crazy, maniac that likes to kill people and he's not like that. He's a soldier. He did what he was trained to do and he did what he was told to do. Killing comes with our job.

A COLD COMING

And I looked, and behold a pale horse: and his name that sat on him was Death, and Hell followed with him. And power was given unto them over the fourth part of the earth, to kill with sword, and with hunger, and with death, and with the beasts of the earth ... and there was a great earthquake; and the sun became black as sackcloth of hair, and the whole moon became as blood.

– Revelation 6:8,12

Archival, oral and journalistic records reveal the presence of other terrifying specters, seen and unseen, looming over McVeigh and his COHORTs during their harrowing trek through the desert that, thus far, have remained unexplored in previous biographical and explanatory accounts of the Oklahoma City bombing.

Even as it was being waged, scientists described the Gulf War as "an unprecedented atmospheric disaster ... an enormous unplanned experiment in the atmosphere" and warned that the chemicals released during it would threaten all living things in the region for decades to come. Some of the oil-well fires that burned throughout Iraq and Kuwait consumed nearly 3 million barrels, or 250 million gallons of oil a day, a tenth of that used worldwide daily and scientists predicted that the fires, numbering in the thousands, would burn for years, although most were extinguished within six months after the war's end. Iraq claimed the fires resulted from Allied attacks, while Allied forces said the Iraqi army had set the fires. No matter who lit them, by March 2, 1991, thick clouds of flammable, poisonous, neurotoxic, carcinogenic and sulfurous smoke, fumes and gasses had risen over 12,000 feet and spread in every direction, reportedly covering half of Kuwait. The sun was continuously blacked out, sand dunes turned black and black rain fell over the region in a radius up to 800 miles. Soot from the fires covered uniforms, hair and food. In April 1991, the U.S. Army environmental hygiene agency conducted a risk assessment of the smoke and similar related studies continued throughout the next few years.[102]

McVeigh's fellow soldiers recalled seeing the fires and described the last days of their "drive through the desert" to the Jones Team. Sgt. Bill Guest remembered seeing entire oil fields burning and said, "The sky was black. It was grey the entire time we were there. At night when you'd go to the telephone you couldn't see the stars. At the time, it wasn't hard to breathe because all the fumes seemed to be going up high, but then later we really got hit with it when it started to rain, and it all came down." McVeigh said that he personally counted fifty oil fires and was able to take pictures of some of them and recalled how as they traveled along Basra and Highway 8, the carbon from the fires blackened the sky and a "coating of black soot covered the sand for acres. Soldiers stepping over it left white footprints."[103]

In addition to the oil fires, the Allies' use of depleted uranium (DU) on tank armor and artillery shells and their bombing of Iraqi weapons facilities had released even more poisonous chemicals into the atmosphere. McVeigh's division was among the thousands of U.S. troops exposed to DU, whose effects, after one hour of exposure, scientists equated to fifty chest x-rays. A British Atomic Energy Authority report leaked to the *Independent* in November 1991, said that when coalition troops exited the Gulf, they left enough DU behind to cause at least 500,000 cancer-related deaths, the exact tonnage of DU the U.S. left behind. Of course, this in no way reflected the adverse effects that the chemical nightmare would have upon the Iraqi population.

Towards the conclusion of the war, U.S. military officials had advised soldiers and media outlets about the strong possibility that Iraq might deploy chemical weapons, but later denied that either they or Iraq had used them, although studies conducted by other countries after the war, as well as statements given by soldiers there, supported allegations that *somebody* had. In late February 1991, General Schwarzkopf publicly denied that Iraq was using chemical weapons and national security advisor Robert Gates warned that Iraqi commanders who did so would face a war crimes tribunal. Still, even after the war was over, allegations and rumors that chemical weapons had been used continued to surface.[104]

In 1993, the concerns of veterans groups, researchers and government officials prompted a Pentagon study, overseen by former Deputy Defense Secretary and current CIA Director John Duetch, tasked with inquiring into the possibility that U.S. soldiers had been exposed to chemical weapons in the Gulf. The study's 1994 report concluded that no evidence existed of Iraqi use of chemical or biological weapons or "any exposure of U.S. service members to chemical or biological warfare agents in Kuwait or Saudi Arabia." The results were suspect, given that the head of the study, Nobel laureate Joshua Lederberg, had also been on the board of directors of American Type Culture Collection, a nonprofit company that made over 70 government-approved shipments of anthrax and other deadly pathogens to Iraq between 1985 and 1989.[105]

A similar investigation by a House Oversight Committee in 1996 led to revelations that for several days, U.S. soldiers, in an attempt to destroy them, blew up munitions held in a storage bunker called "Bunker 73" in Khamisiya, 25 miles from the city of Basra. The munitions, mostly rockets, contained the nerve agent Sarin, mustard gas and other possible biological agents. In doing so, they released a cloud of (among other things) seven tons of Sarin into the air that, when carried by the winds, exposed untold numbers of people. Not knowing the bunkers contained rockets filled with sarin, they did not wear protective gear and when chemical alarms went off alerting them to the danger, officers told troops they were faulty and ordered them to disconnect the alarms.

While the number of Iraqis exposed to and affected by the Sarin release remains unknown, over the years the official number of U.S. soldiers exposed continued to grow. At first, the DOD insisted *no* troops were exposed. In September 1996, the Pentagon issued a statement that 5,000 U.S. soldiers were exposed. By October 1996, after the Pentagon set up an information hotline, the number grew to 15,000. A retired Army general, whose troops had been camped within 15 miles of Bunker 73, put the number at 24,000 and expressed concern, as his soldiers had not worn gas masks. *Newsday* estimated the number at 29,000. As of 2013, the Pentagon's estimate of how many U.S. soldiers could have been exposed to the toxins released at Khamisiya alone, reached 100,000.[106]

Years later, the Defense Department revealed that the Pentagon's Nuclear Biological and Chemical Warfare logs, which tracked the chemical alarms, had mysteriously gone missing; a circumstance one military officer compared to "the 18-minute gap on the Nixon Watergate tapes."[107] The missing records pertained, specifically, to entries from March 3 – 12, 1991: the period during which McVeigh and company trekked through the desert with the spoils of war darkening their path. One COHORT said, "They [sent] me out in the middle of this wide ocean of desert and there's about fifty dead sheep around me with no blood in sight on 'em. That's a good indication that some chemical agents [were] used." Similarly, COHORT Sam Stansky (name changed), recalled:

> They still say to this day that there were no chemicals released, but I think there was. For one, they used to go down and check the bunkers, clear out the bunkers, and there was call come over the radio that said "no one go in the bunkers anymore, because a soldier went down in and rubbed up against the wall, and got a nerve agent on him," and so they had stopped that and just started blowing the bunkers up. There's a lot of things about the war that haven't been told and the government don't want told. One night when I was on guard duty in Desert Storm, a guy was standing next to me, and this is gonna sound funny to you, but all of a sudden I saw a bright green glow that just floated through the air, and it was all over the place. And I asked the guy next to me if he saw it, too, and he said he did. That's stuff that's not being told.

In 1995, COHORT Sgt. Guest opined that he could not "legitimately say [if] we were or weren't exposed to nerve gas because of [U.S.] bombings [of Iraqi munitions]," and mused that they had only recently begun to learn about the toxicity of the air that swept over them during their trek through the desert.[108] *Somebody* knew though. A recently declassified memo dated March 23, 1991, sent from the Army Central Command Nuclear, Biological and Chemical (ARCENT NBC) staff to XVIII Airborne Corps states "ARCENT has positive confirmation (by urinalysis) of cml (chemical) agent blister casualty in VII corps." The memo went on to instruct that if asked by the press, spokespeople were to report that no chemical casualties had occurred. As of 2015, the estimated number of all U.S. soldiers exposed to nerve gas and other chemical agents totaled over 200,000.[109]

Later attempts to determine the realities and truths of the Gulf War were further complicated because, immediately after Iraq invaded Kuwait, the Defense Department sought and obtained approval by the Food and Drug Administration (FDA) to administer a cocktail of experimental drugs to troops without their informed consent, claiming that to obtain such consent was simply unfeasible. The *known* experimental drugs administered included pretreatments and vaccines meant to counter the effects of chemical and biological weapons. At the time, the FDA had previously barred the use of two of them, botulinum toxoid and Pyridostigmine Bromide (BP), on civilian populations and botulinum, specifically, *remains* unapproved by the FDA for civilian use because of its adverse side effects. Further, the doses administered to soldiers during the Gulf War were estimated based on previous tests on (actual) guinea pigs and the effects of the *combined* use of all the drugs had not been tested.

For several days prior to the start of the ground war and throughout its duration, commanders ordered soldiers to take anti-nerve gas and anti-anthrax agents as well as BP pills, the latter meant to enhance the effectiveness of the former. If they refused, they were threatened with court martials. Worse still, not only had informed consent requirements been bypassed but the military kept no records of those who received widely distributed anthrax vaccines, BP pills or botulism shots or the dosages administered.

One Army reservist recalled that, upon receiving word of his impending deployment to Iraq in January 1991, he and his battalion were given vaccinations over the course of three days until, on the last day, medics informed them they had received the entire required pre-deployment vaccination regimen. According to him, "[The] series [of vaccinations] was designed to be given over an eight month period and we received it in three days. Upon conclusion of the vaccination process, we were told to turn in our personal shot records. You are required to keep those on your person at all times. We protested but still had to turn them in." A few years later, when he went to check his records, they had been destroyed.[110]

At least one U.S. Army doctor was court martialed after refusing to dispense the daily dose of BP pills, whose effects on humans were unknown. Cpt. Yolanda Huet-Vaughn, a former U.S. Army doctor, applied for Conscientious Objector status during Operation Desert Storm in December 1990, citing as her reasons the "Nuremburg principles" and the experimental vaccines that her superiors forced her to administer. After the denial of her request for CO status, Heut-Vaughn deserted, an offense leading to her conviction and a two-and-a-half year prison sentence. Another recalled how it was common knowledge that the BPs were untested. "We knew it, and they [the army] knew it. Basically, the drugs came down through army channels as a prophylactic remedy for nerve gas. The orders were, just give 'em. You didn't have any choice. Their reasoning was, we're in a war, and we have to do unusual things." One soldier said, "I took the tablets, and I had a shot. They told us the tablets could possibly make us sterile; they said they didn't know, but you had to take them anyway. Some guys refused, but they made them." Yet another said, "We popped the [BP] pills like aspirin."[111]

During the Gulf War, McVeigh was assigned to the 24th Division, Mechanized, one of two divisions deployed to the Gulf earlier than others, a division journalist Gary Matsumoto said, were likely candidates for the first round of experimental vaccines. Indeed, like the other soldiers, many of McVeigh's COHORTs also reported receiving experimental and untested drugs, including anthrax vaccines and anti-anthrax agents as well as dousing themselves with insect repellents with *known* detrimental side effects. A large number recalled commanders' orders not to speak about the classified shots they received.

Tony Sikes (name changed) said, "We were forced to take pills. We had to take them on direct order, and most of the guys didn't want to. We found out the pills were experimental and no one was given a choice, so we were all guinea pigs for the government. Until 1993, I was led to believe that the shots and pills were classified and not to be talked about." Charlie Barton (name changed) said, "I took the anti-nerve agent pills. I don't know if Tim did or not. I was about 20 miles from where Tim was when the first SCUDS came in, and they told us to take them. I was eating them like candy. I took them about once every four to six hours."

McVeigh's COHORTs also recalled warnings of what would happen to them if they refused. Ray Barnes said, "We had to take the anti-Botulism Toxin. Everybody had to take that. This is how they put it: 'You volunteer to take it, and take it ... or don't take it and you'll get an Article 15 and you'll be tried because you're disobeying an order in a time of war.'"[112] Sam Stansky elaborated:

> We were required to take shots for anthrax in case of a chemical attack. They brought around a consent/non-consent form for the

anthrax shots, and there was a soldier or two in our company that said "no. I'm not consenting to this shot," and they called up to battalion, and the battalion commander sent down word his response which was – "I don't give a damn, they're taking the shot anyhow," and we were made to take the shot. … Right on the box it said "for test purposes only, not for human use!." … They were just forced to take the shot whether they wanted to or not. We also took anti-nerve agent pills.

Shortly after the Gulf War ended, veteran advocacy groups became concerned about the growing number of returning troops suffering from a constellation of debilitating physical symptoms, which, despite their unknown etymology, was collectively termed Gulf War Syndrome (GWS). In late 1991, the Department of Veterans Affairs obtained Congressional approval to create a Gulf War Registry for veterans in order to track their movements in the Gulf, the extent of their exposure to toxic fumes from the oil well fires and their current health status. Officials urged Gulf War veterans to report to their nearest VA for a medical screening to determine their exposure to a growing list of toxins beyond petroleum poisoning, including parasitic infection, depleted uranium, and chemical weapons such as sarin nerve gas; all later acknowledged as possible culprits in the GWS epidemic. In June 1993, officials in the Clinton administration publicly acknowledged that the depleted uranium (DU) used on U.S. tanks and artillery shells may have contributed to the growing number of Gulf War veterans displaying symptoms related to GWS. The commander of Walter Reed Medical Center agreed and, during a Congressional Hearing that year, added oil well fires to the list of suspected causes.[113]

However, despite the ostensible efforts to understand GWS and help the soldiers suffering from it, many times, soldiers who later reviewed their military medical records (often in an attempt to understand their debilitating and relentless symptoms) found that several of the vaccines and medicines they were administered prior to and during the Gulf War were not noted in them. Other times their records contained outright falsifications. And some were told their records had been destroyed because there had not been enough space to ship them back to the U.S.

The Jones Team found it odd that, given the barrage of shots and pills described by McVeigh himself as well as his fellow soldiers, upon their inspections of the available portions of his military medical records, there was no appearance of the shots and pills. Also absent from McVeigh's records are consent forms for any of the extensive medical treatments he received, including his military immunization records. In fact, the only entry in the available portion of McVeigh's military records for the entire duration of his Gulf War service appears on February 17, 1991, when he received the experimental 'botulinum toxoid' inoculation shot (the day before the ground war started and the same day that President Bush promised that Iraq's invasion of Kuwait would end very shortly).

When asked about the lone botulism shot entry, McVeigh said he believed it was, "some kind of test vaccine" and that he and the others "were used as guinea pigs." Although at the time, he had asked around about what, exactly, the shots were, nobody would speak with him about it. Only later did he learn that one of the shots given to he and his unit was an anti-anthrax inoculation although the names and chemical compositions of the other "shots" they were given, remained unknown to him. McVeigh further explained that upon arriving in the Gulf, they were ordered to take two kinds of pills, but after taking the first dose, he refused to take any more. He identified one of them as a "nerve agent pill" but was unable to identify the other.

He also described widespread use of the insecticide called DEET, one of the sixty-seven insecticides and insect repellents used in the Gulf War now linked to GWS. McVeigh said he never actually used the DEET because there were no insects, but did find it to be a "good fire starter." Among the other Gulf War exposures McVeigh described to his attorneys was radioactive armor-piercing ammunition coated with depleted uranium and he even had a picture of himself holding the weapon whose ammo he thought was radioactive: a 25 millimeter APDST (armor piercing discarding sabot tracer).

Having explained these exposures, McVeigh then helped his defense attorneys identify other strikingly absent portions of his records including, among others, the entire Gulf War period and his later Special Forces try-out. The Jones Team informed the court about the withholding of this (and other) critical information about their client and obtained permission from the court to hire two experts to review the records they *did* possess and to obtain those they did not. However, neither expert was able to do so.[114]

According to FBI records in the Jones Collection, as early as July 1995, an Inspector General from the New York State Military Affairs Office with the rank of major provided the FBI and the Army's Criminal Intelligence Division (CID) in Fort Sill, Oklahoma with some of the records. When he did so, the Major advised the FBI that the "documents can only be used for Government purpose and are covered by the Privacy Act." On March 12, 1996, the Jones Team's military records expert visited Ft. Riley, but upon his return notified the team that he "was not able to look at division files for the Desert Storm period as these records had been sent to the Office of the Joint Chiefs of Staff in Washington, DC – at their request!" Two days later, when the legal team contacted Captain Rodriguez (formerly Lt.) to discuss "certain aspects of Tim's records," he declined, explaining that two FBI agents instructed him not to discuss his knowledge of McVeigh or the contents of the records with anyone – especially the defense team.

The Jones Team soon realized Fortier's military records were incomplete as well, and that immediately after the arrest of McVeigh, Nichols and Fortier, the Pentagon had sealed the records of all three. In March 1997, the Jones Team noted that not only did they have "incomplete military records" for McVeigh, but also for Fortier and Nichols and that further, within the records they *did* have, there were "no medical or promotion records in Fortier's file and no promotion orders in Tim's file."[115]

From October 1996 until the time of McVeigh's trial in May 1997, internal defense memos reflect the Jones Team's frustration with their efforts to locate and obtain the records and, ultimately, their failure to do so. Almost as if McVeigh had known the records would be important later, he had, on at least three occasions prior to the bombing, requested a complete set from the Army including his medical records, had sent them home to his father for "safe keeping" and instructed him to put them in a secure location. However, after his sons arrest, when the FBI appeared at Bill McVeigh's door, he willingly relinquished the records to the FBI. Indeed, the military records taken from Bill McVeigh's house appear within the U.S. Attorney's receipt for materials from the FBI. However, the Jones Team realized that included among those items missing from the FBI's own search warrant inventory of what they took from the McVeigh home were McVeigh's *pre*-Gulf War military records (which included the many doctor visits), a record of the commendations from Desert Storm and another "packet of military records" undescribed. Hence, the exact nature of the shots and pills administered, the location where he received them or the doctors and medical staff present was, and remains, unknown.

The Jones Team's search for McVeigh's records coincided with national headlines that detailed the increasing number of Gulf War veterans who had developed the unexplainable Gulf War Syndrome, an illness defined by multiple, highly individualized symptoms. Unknown and unreported in the media after his arrest, was that McVeigh and many men in his unit were suffering from these symptoms. Like him, their records had been confiscated, misplaced, or destroyed.[116]

Soon after McVeigh's arrest, the FBI confiscated COHORT Ray Barnes' army photos and his service-related records, and, in 2010, Barnes emphasized that, despite promises to return them, the FBI had yet to do so. Further, in September 1995, the FBI attempted to obtain Barnes' extensive post-Gulf medical records, and ultimately issued a Grand Jury subpoena for them. Barnes was not alone. The FBI confiscated and misplaced or destroyed vital military records, photos and other service-related mementos of several men in the COHORT unit. Woody Davis (name changed) recalled, "Somehow the FBI got my name immediately [after the bombing] and came and took all the stuff, all the Army stuff, all my papers." Similarly, a frustrated Gordon Blackcloud said, "after the bombing the FBI came and took my picture ID, social security card, medical records.... I don't know why they took those. They never sent them back."[117]

McVeigh's hidden medical narrative continued after his return from the Gulf War and discharge from the military. So too did the attempt by many Gulf War veterans to obtain answers and treatment for their strange illness, though the very existence of GWS continued to be dismissed by many as psychosomatic hysteria and "conspiracy theory." The National Defense Authorization Act for the 1997 fiscal year (finalized in September 1996), includes regulatory protocols for "medical research involving human subjects," budgetary allotments totaling $10 million dollars for "independent research regarding Gulf War Syndrome" and a clause regarding a "Comptroller General Review of health care activities of Department of Defense relating to Gulf War Illness." The clause dictates (among other things) that the Comptroller General would "analyze the effectiveness of the [DOD's] medical research and clinical care programs," "analyze the scope and effectiveness" of DOD policies with respect to the "use of investigational new drugs" used during the Gulf War; "the current use of investigational new drugs to treat" Gulf War Syndrome; and "analyze the administration of medical records by the military departments in order to asses the extent to which such records *accurately* reflect the pre-deployment medical assessments, immunization records, informed consent releases, complaints during routine sick call, emergency room visits, visits with unit medics during deployment, and other relevant medical information relating to [Gulf War veterans]" (italics added).[118]

A 1998 report by the Senate Veterans Affairs Committee described the story of soldiers' toxic exposures, which included the preventive measures administered to counter them, as "one of ... inaccurate records ... and claims of Pentagon cover-up after the fact. *It illustrates issues common to many other events during the Gulf War.*"[119]

In 2008, the DOD recognized GWS as a legitimate service-related illness although, by that time, other related concerns had arisen. That same year, the *Guardian* reported that the dangers faced by soldiers in Iraq currently extend far beyond enemy fire or PTSD. The article described the region as "among the most polluted on the planet – so toxic that merely to live, eat and sleep (never mind to fight) in these zones is to risk death." Finally, in the early 2000s newly returning soldiers began to report symptoms similar to their Gulf War I predecessors, the combination of which was dubbed "The New Gulf War Illness" and "The New Agent Orange." In 2012, after years of similar requests, denials and appeals and strong opposition from the DOD, VA and Halliburton, the DOD agreed to create a registry to track soldiers exposed to harmful chemicals in Iraq and Afghanistan. In June 2014, the VA launched the "Airborne Hazards and Open Burn Pit Registry." As it turns out, thousands of soldiers returning from Gulf War II had likely been exposed to chemicals linked to the development of respiratory illnesses, cancers and neurological problems.

Medical studies have recently begun to link increasing incidences of Iraqi cancers, birth defects, infant mortality and multi-symptom toxic exposures to the same neurotoxins that affected veterans of Gulf War I.[120]

THE INVISIBLE GULF WAR SPECTACLE

In the many narratives told by McVeigh about events throughout his life, corpses appear, disappear, and reappear; a pattern best illustrated, and perhaps rooted, in his experiences during the Gulf War; a war whose carefully constructed spectacular prime-time entertainment value qualified it as the first hyper-real postmodern info-war. The mass mediated murderous extravaganza masked its managers' surreal and brutal genocidal, ecocidal and homicidal New World visions. It is difficult, if not impossible, to know exactly what occurred during the war, including who fired at whom, when and under whose orders Iraqis were buried with bulldozers, and how many met their deaths in this manner. Further, the unspeakable actions taken by McVeigh and his COHORTs on the Highway of Death or the details of the nightmarish visions they observed are unknowable as are the impact these had on them. Finally, among those things impossible to determine about the Gulf War is who, exactly, received the ostensibly preventive experimental shots and pills, who administered them, and when.

The opaque nature of the 1st Gulf War should not lessen perception of its relevancy or relationship to McVeigh's role in the bombing of the Murrah Federal Building on April 19, 1995. Surely, the traces of the Gulf War and the ghosts accompanying and perhaps driving him the morning he parked the deadly Ryder truck next to the building and walked away, heedless of the collateral damage, should not be ignored.

During his 1997 sentencing hearing, when asked if he had anything to say for himself, McVeigh, in yet one more act of appropriation, quoted a statement made by Supreme Court Justice Louis D. Brandeis, explaining his dissenting vote in a 1928 case that normalized the use of wiretaps in criminal investigations. "Our government," he said, "is the potent, the omnipresent teacher. For good or ill, it teaches the whole people by its example" and then McVeigh added, "That's all I have." While he prepared for his execution, McVeigh explained to his biographers that the Gulf War had left him feeling as if he had become just like the bullies he despised growing up. Worse, he had done so on behalf of his country, whose actions he came to see as the epitome of hypocrisy.[121]

In 1998, McVeigh wrote a piece entitled "Essay on Hypocrisy," that he sent to media outlets. He described it as admittedly "provocative," and said that it had only created further public outrage towards him. In it, he compared the Oklahoma City bombing to the U.S.'s actions in Iraq. The U.S., he said, "set the standard when it comes to the stockpiling and use of weapons of mass destruction." He noted that U.S. officials had explained the presence of any daycare located inside Iraqi government buildings as an Iraqi "shield." How was it then, McVeigh asked, that the one in the Murrah, a government "command and control center," was any different? In fact, he continued, the U.S. acknowledged it knew about children "in or near" Iraqi government buildings but bombed them nonetheless, dismissing any nonmilitary deaths as collateral damage. He pointed out that, although after the bombing the public lamented over the casualties and the media ceaselessly replayed images of dead children, both had failed to afford the Iraqi civilians who died during the Gulf War the same attention and respect. "Whether you wish to admit it or not, when you approve, morally, of the bombing of foreign targets by the U.S. military, you are approving of acts morally equivalent to the bombing in Oklahoma City.... Who are the true barbarians?"[122]

In a letter written to Gore Vidal in April 2001, months before his execution, McVeigh explained further:

> Borrowing a page from U.S. foreign policy, I decided to send a message to a government that was becoming increasingly hostile ... Bombing the Murrah was morally and strategically equivalent to the U.S. hitting a government building in Serbia, Iraq, or other nations. Based on observations of the policies of my own government, I viewed this action as an acceptable option. From this perspective, what occurred in Oklahoma City was no different than what Americans rain on the heads of others all the time, and, subsequently, my mindset was and is one of clinical detachment. [The bombing] was not personal no more than when Air Force, Army, Navy or Marine personnel bomb or launch cruise missiles against (foreign) government installations and their personnel."[123]

PART THREE:
The Ill Political Anti-McVeigh
(Post Gulf War, U.S. Army, Ft. Riley)

INTRODUCTION

Sometime after March 26, 1991, Special Forces hopefuls Timothy McVeigh and Mitch Whitmire left the deserts of Kuwait and Iraq and returned to Ft. Riley. On April 3, 1991, both arrived at Ft. Bragg to begin the twenty-one day Special Forces Assessment and Selection (SFAS) course. In all later accounts written about McVeigh or the Oklahoma bombing, the Special Forces try-out is a pivotal moment; a crossroads after which his later act of domestic terrorism became a foregone conclusion for reasons that vary depending upon the particular narrative being told. From this point forward, the story of Timothy McVeigh branches off on a number of different, highly conflicting trajectories, determined by one's conclusion about what happened at the try-out and McVeigh's reaction to it.

THE SPECIAL FORCES WASHOUT

The most commonly told and widely accepted version of McVeigh's Special Forces try-out appeared in early news reports, unauthorized biographies and was told in the courtroom by prosecutors at McVeigh's criminal trial. It is best encapsulated in McVeigh's 2001 authorized biography, *American Terrorist*. In this story, only hours after arriving at Ft. Bragg, both McVeigh and Whitmire very quickly realized how out of shape they had become while in the Gulf and the negative impact this was having on their performance there. In addition, as the story goes, on the very first day, McVeigh, who was breaking in a new pair of combat boots, developed a blister on his foot during a rucksack march. The blister plagued him so terribly that he privately concluded he could not realistically complete the course. Later that afternoon, he and Whitmire discussed their situation and both decided to voluntarily withdraw from the course, agreeing between themselves to try again later after getting back in shape. Thereafter both returned to Ft. Riley.[124]

When the rest of Charlie Company returned from the Gulf, they were surprised, even "shocked," at finding McVeigh at the base and not secreted away on a covert Special Forces mission, a goal he had obsessively prepared for throughout the time they knew him. The majority of interviews conducted by the defense team or FBI reflect that McVeigh had told most people at Ft. Riley the same story he later told the authors of *American Terrorist*. He "wasn't prepared," "wasn't ready," "not at his physical peak" and the course was just "too physically demanding." Indeed, several soldiers emphasized that many of those returning from the Gulf were out of shape and had lost weight, up to thirty or forty pounds, as much weight as was commonly lost during the SFAS itself, and added that, according to McVeigh, the CO instructed him to go back to Ft. Riley, rest and return later.

On its face, the story appears plausible. In his book, Lt. Col. Grossman described the physical effects of combat on soldiers. According to Grossman, the continued production of adrenaline and arousal of fight or flight responses during combat, the aggregate loss of sleep, lack of food and weathering of the elements induce an intense and prolonged state of fatigue that begins as soon as the action stops. Grossman observed that the physiological effects of combat are very similar to the level of physical exhaustion experienced during the eight-week SFAS course, which is designed intentionally to over-tax both the body and mind of recruits. SFAS hopefuls undergo a series of physical challenges including: obstacle courses, fifty-meter swims wearing full battle-dress uniforms, marches of more than 150 miles while carrying rifles and fifty-pound ruck sacks and regular intervals of sleep and food deprivation for up to five days at a time. The rate of attrition is high and over half of those who attempt the SFAS do not complete the course. Although those attending the SFAS course have been selected to do so based, among other things, on their exemplary physical condition, at the conclusion of the course, many are in a state of total starvation, enhanced exhaustion and near madness, some even experience repeated realistic hallucinations and most have shed over twenty pounds.

In 1998, Richard Serrano wrote that McVeigh felt he should have been given more time to recuperate from the war before being sent to the try-out and blamed the Army for his failure to pass "the one test that really mattered." In fact, the majority of accounts (early and recent) contend that McVeigh's failure to make the Army's elite "A-Team" sent him "into a psychic tailspin," rendered his life a "living nightmare" and initiated his "descent into hell" within the depths of which he transformed from "the boy next door" into the demonic face of American terror.[125]

Initial media reports that appeared immediately after the bombing quoted (and re-quoted) a number of COHORTs who said that after returning from Ft. Bragg, McVeigh was angry, upset and just not the same person they knew before. Interviews conducted by the Jones Team and FBI reflected the same. One soldier, with whom McVeigh briefly lived, told the Jones Team that, "his whole life shattered [after] he 'washed out' [of the Special Forces] and had to come back and face us." It was at this time that McVeigh became noticeably "disillusioned ... it just got ugly ... he crumbled ... just fell apart." Others said McVeigh was embarrassed, "angry," "very upset," "very disappointed," "let down," and "pissed off," although to what extent varied depending on who was speaking.[126]

During his interview with David Hackworth, published in the July 1995 edition of *Newsweek*, McVeigh denied that his failure to complete the SFAS course had any such profound effect on him and said it "wasn't the straw that broke anything." Other writers, while still keeping with Lone Wolf stories about the bombing, have rejected the "blister theory" and attribute different causes for his SFAS failure and the subsequent change in personality, including Hackworth, who thought McVeigh may have been suffering from "a post-war hangover." Hackworth opined that McVeigh, mentally and physically depressed, simply gave up, like many combat veterans who "stumble home" without a sense of danger or purpose and "lose themselves forever."[127]

Still, other versions of what occurred at the SFAS exist. On the first day of the SFAS, newly arriving recruits are administered a battery of psychological evaluations, including the Sacks Sentence Completion Test (SSCT) and the Minnesota Multiphasic Personality Inventory (MMPI). The SFAS psychological testing was an ordeal specifically "structured to put the maximum psychological pressure on those being tested." Passing the evaluation (and the SFAS itself) required that recruits demonstrate adaptability, ambition, cooperation, dependability, stamina, ingenuity, and tact "under constant physical and mental stress"[128] The military also uses tests like the MMPI and SSCT to construct nuanced predictive psychological profiles meant to determine placement suitability, especially those of a high-risk nature.

As early as May 1995, news outlets, citing unnamed military officials, reported that McVeigh had failed the psychological evaluation portion of the SFAS, and that once designated mentally unfit would have been unable to try out again. A number of soldiers gave statements to the press that supported such allegations. Stickney wrote that, in 1995, he spoke with a confidential source who confirmed that McVeigh was found not suitable for the Special Forces because "the answers [he] gave on the psychological tests were apparently a bit off center. Not the answers of a man capable of long-term assignments with the exclusive and tight Special Forces." In other words, McVeigh did not fit the psychological profile. Jones told reporters that such claims were impossible because, as McVeigh left the SFAS two days after it began, the battery of psychological tests he took had been filed away and remained unevaluated until after his arrest. For his part, McVeigh vehemently denied allegations that he failed the SFAS psychological evaluations, and his biographers wrote that in 2000, an unnamed "Army official" confirmed McVeigh's denials.[129]

Despite the insistence of McVeigh and others to the contrary and the denials and counterarguments Jones floated to the press, the defense team nonetheless sought, unsuccessfully, to clarify the allegations. During their August 1995 interview with a soldier with whom McVeigh briefly lived after the Gulf War, he conceded that while McVeigh had not been in top physical shape during the SFAS, a number of the other COHORTs believed he "washed out on the paperwork … fruit loop!"

Rather than resolving the issue, the more the Jones Team learned about the Special Forces try-out, the more questions they had. FBI records obtained by the Jones Team revealed that, rather than withdrawing on April 5 (two days after the course began), he remained there for five days, from April 3 until April 7, 1991. Initially, when the FBI questioned SFAS Commander Capt. Galland about the try-out, he said he could not recall McVeigh but upon viewing the Army's own records presented by the FBI, he remembered that, in fact, he had personally supervised McVeigh as he filled out and signed the entrance forms on April 3 and the SFAS Voluntary Withdrawal Statement on April 7. The form requires soldiers to explain their decision and on his McVeigh wrote that he was "not physically ready, 4 mile rucksack march should not have hurt as much as it did." Capt. Galland, who also personally approved the request, wrote on the form that McVeigh "is not physically ready. Maybe having a change of heart also." Galland told agents that the four-mile march was one of the course's earlier and easier activities, "especially for someone in the physical condition that McVeigh displayed during his Army Physical Fitness Test," and said he told McVeigh to return in six months and try again.[130]

Further, included among the partial records the Jones Team eventually obtained were the results of McVeigh's psychological exams, which he took on April 5, 1991, two days into the try-out and the day he reportedly withdrew. The military records specialist retained by the defense team noted that the results of the SSCT were "of particular note" but did not elaborate. He also remarked that he (for unstated reasons) was "unable to evaluate" the results of McVeigh's Army "MMPI Profile Report." But Jones Team mental health expert Dr. Tony Semone did and, in his subsequent memo, cryptically described the results as "revealing and consistent with what we are learning about Tim." The subsequent confusion about how long he had attended the SFAS, what occurred there and the reasons he left caused his attorneys to ask in an internal memo distributed to the entire legal team, "did he drop out of SF after 4-5 days, or did he flunk the psych exam?"

Their understanding of McVeigh's psychological state became even more muddled given the combined diagnosis of the Jones Team mental health experts and revelations about various incidents after he left the military. Included were recurring visits and telephone calls he made to various VA facilities in the years leading to the bombing and claims about having been implanted with a microchip while in the Army. While the issue remained unresolved, they opined that no matter what had happened at the SFAS, his experience there had left McVeigh humiliated. Similarly, according to Stickney, the SFAS failure had devastated McVeigh as now, he "would never have a chance to tell his friends and family" about long-anticipated secret missions he would go on and simply could not understand how he, the Army's model soldier, had become "an outcast, unfit to perform with the best."[131] Perhaps this explains why, both prior to and after the bombing, McVeigh told a number of conflicting stories other than the blister story about what occurred at Ft. Bragg and what caused him to leave.

When he arrived back at Ft. Riley, McVeigh told one soldier that the SFAS had been "cancelled." He once told his mother and later, on one occasion, his attorneys, that he became disillusioned during the SFAS when he learned the Special Forces were "college book" oriented rather than field oriented. To others, however, he painted another, much stranger portrait of events, the details of which vary slightly depending on who he told it to and when. These stories form the basis for many of the early and still circulating alternate narrative variations, most notably those of the Guilty Agent and Experimental variety although, as seen in the Jones Collection, McVeigh articulated variations of this story to others earlier. A letter written to his sister Jennifer in October 1993 best encapsulates the story he would tell in its most enduring form.

McVeigh told her that his disillusionment "all revolves around my arrival at Ft. Bragg." The 400 new recruits had all taken a number of "intelligence, psychological, adeptness and a whole battery of other tests." Although not specifying exactly when, he said that, one day, SFAS officers called ten E-5 Sergeants with Secret Clearances, including himself, out of formation, separated them from the others and made them "feel special" by telling them that they had been "handpicked" based on their test results, "intelligence [and] physical makeup." After receiving a classified "intelligence briefing," they were asked to "volunteer" for a special covert assignment in which they would act as "military consultants" to domestic and international civilian police and intelligence agencies. Although the exact nature and extent of the assignment remained undisclosed until they accepted the mission, it could involve a number of unsavory tasks including drug smuggling and assassinations.

In subsequent letters he informed his sister that, while at first he played along and returned to Buffalo where his 'handler' made occasional contact with him, as time went by, the more he learned about his secret mission, the more distraught he became until, eventually, he became suicidal and, in a near nervous breakdown, confided the entire ordeal to his grandfather. Soon after, he decided to "hit the road," go on the run, and "keep my path cool, in case someone is looking to shut up someone who knows too much." He acknowledged that, because of the drastic change in his personality after leaving the Army, the entire family now believed he was mentally disturbed, but assured her this was an act, all "part of the game." He asked her to keep what he disclosed to herself and warned that if she betrayed his confidence, his life could be in danger. He apologized if what he told her had "fuck[ed] [her] up" but said that he "had an urgent need for someone in the family to understand me" and "needed someone to know, in case I'm found floating in a river."

In this story, arguably among the stranger ones to circulate, McVeigh does not leave the Special Forces try-out because he is unfit, either physically or mentally, but rather, based on his superior mental and physical qualities, becomes part of a covert group acting independently from the Army or other government oversight. Out of principle and personal conviction though, he goes rogue and is forced to go into hiding and live on the run because of the secret knowledge he learned. Whether told in deception or delusion, or true, partially true, or wholly fabricated, McVeigh's stories sound similar to the popular 1980s television series, *The A-Team*, the "crack commando unit" framed for a bank robbery and who, having escaped, must live "underground" on the run and hunted by the Army. His defense team was unable to make heads or tails of such claims but did not think they had been written disingenuously and Jones Team attorney Rob Nigh, referring to the letters noted, "If Tim is lying, he's one good liar."

McVeigh later explained to his biographers that he fabricated the entire story based on news reports about just such scenarios and had done so in order to introduce his sister to his "mind set at the time" and illustrate his distrust of the government. He emphasized, however, that the story in the letter was completely plausible and within the realm of possibilities, as these things go. Herbeck and Michel wrote that because nineteen-year-old Jennifer was "impressionable," she believed her brother's "fairy tale ... was certain something terrible had happened in the military" and "figured someone in the military had deceived her brother, and when he learned the truth it had changed him forever." His biographers conclude this discussion by opining that McVeigh's rambling letter to his sister "conjure[d] up a fantastic scenario to justify his outrage" and "disappointment."[132] Indicative of other Lone Wolf (and most Pack) accounts, the authors say nothing more about the strange letter, which, in their book, exists as the only acknowledgment of any alternate account offered by McVeigh about the SFAS.

Over the years, various writers have likewise briefly touched on and then summarily dismissed the claims McVeigh made in the letter as expressions of his fantastical imagination and further evidence of his deceptiveness and manipulations. Like the "psych test" story however, other published works, in combination with oral and archival documentation, offer the possibility of a number of conflicting but parallel readings of McVeigh's Special Forces stint and subsequent downward spiral.

Even if McVeigh made up the story, his mother and sister seemed to believe it, as evidenced by FBI recordings of their conversations obtained through bugs hidden in a motel room furnished by the FBI "for their protection" shortly after McVeigh's arrest, as well as telephone wiretaps of the McVeigh family's incoming and outgoing phone calls. In one such conversation that occurred just days after his arrest, Jennifer spoke with her mother about how heavily the entire Special Forces ordeal had weighed on her brother, so much so that it led him to consider suicide but ultimately, he had simply refused to carry out his orders, thereby making himself a target. Mickey's responses to Jennifer during the conversation indicated that she had heard parts of this story from her son previously. Jennifer then went on to express her growing frustration with the FBI because, she explained, the agents continued to deny that her brother had actually been accepted into the Special Forces, fortuitously adding that, although she provided the FBI with records that proved it, she feared they had destroyed them.

Finally, McVeigh told another particularly intriguing version of this story during his first meeting with John Coyle and Susan Otto, the public defenders originally appointed to represent him. To them he said, "He had been operating within the confines of the United States government when he did what he did ... [having been] recruited by the government while serving a 4-5 month period in the National Guard ... [his] duties were to search for neo-Nazi's and other problem troops within the National Guard." The operation had gone well, and eventually his handlers instructed him to participate in the brewing plot to bomb the Murrah but to make sure the bomb only blew out a few windows of the building. He now suspected someone had switched either the truck or the explosives in it without his knowledge. Otto and Coyle, both of whom had offices in Oklahoma City, subsequently recused themselves from the case citing conflicts of interest.[133] When the Jones Team asked McVeigh about what he had told Otto and Coyle, McVeigh became very angry and began "yelling, [and] cursing," exclaiming that Coyle had no business discussing their private conversations with anyone, and that while some parts of this story were true, some were not.

For the remainder of his life, McVeigh continued to both affirm and deny to the Jones Team and others, the covert operation story, telling it a bit differently each time. While on Death Row in Terre Haute, Indiana, McVeigh met David Paul Hammer, another prisoner awaiting execution. In 2004, after McVeigh's execution, Hammer published his first book, *Secrets Worth Dying For: Timothy James McVeigh and the Oklahoma City Bombing*, based on alleged conversations between the two, followed by an updated version, *Deadly Secrets*, in 2010. According to Hammer, McVeigh told him a remarkable story:

While at the SFAS, McVeigh encountered a high-ranking official whom he referred to only as "The Major," a man he said had befriended him during the Gulf War. The Major, who McVeigh said was dressed in civilian clothing and had an unkempt appearance in general, pulled him aside and told him he was currently working for the Department of Defense on ultra-secret, need-to-know "Black Ops," whose agenda was "primarily domestic intelligence gathering and internal threat evaluations with an emphasis on direct counter action operations." The Major then described a right-wing militancy spreading rapidly throughout the United States that threatened to rip the country apart. He offered McVeigh a position in a secret unit, adding that he would be working alone for the most part but could recruit people of his own choosing as needed. When he accepted, the Major instructed McVeigh to "washout of the Special Forces ... tone down his 'hot shot' performance in the Army," and quit the Army altogether by the end of the year. In the meantime, in order to infiltrate the far right-wing paramilitary underground, McVeigh was to become familiar with the rhetoric and literature of the "extreme right ... create a plausible aura of a disgruntled soldier [and] await further instructions."

McVeigh obeyed the orders and began immersing himself in right-wing literature, something that came easy to him because, Hammer said, of "the beliefs and knowledge that already existed inside him." Eventually the Major instructed McVeigh to participate in the bombing. Hammer said, true or not, McVeigh believed the story and, in the final days of his life, became preoccupied by the idea that, somehow, through one ruse or another, the Major would prevent his execution at the last minute, perhaps by faking it, and he would be given reconstructive surgery, sent away and rewarded for his service.[134]

For obvious reasons, it is easy to dismiss this as a fantastical tale woven by Hammer, a desperate death row inmate. In fact, prior to his execution, McVeigh expressed his dislike of Hammer and warned more than one person that, after his death, Hammer would publish a book, which, McVeigh said, would be full of lies. Still, while Hammer's account must be read with a healthy dose of skepticism, it relayed details of conversations and claims McVeigh made in private, some prior to the bombing, that were not known publicly and therefore could not have been known by Hammer unless McVeigh told him. For instance, although attributing the SFAS withdrawal to McVeigh's blister, Randy Coyne, who continued as one of McVeigh's lawyers until his execution, relayed a story McVeigh sometimes told, which Coyne referred to as "The Bourne Scenario," alluding to the recent popular movie series about Jason Bourne, a rogue former CIA agent, released only *after* McVeigh's execution. [The books came earlier] Coyne explained that, until his dying day, McVeigh entertained the idea that rather than being executed, his former handlers might intervene, whisk him away and reward him for completing his mission and keeping his mouth shut.[135]

In 2007, Terry Nichols signed an affidavit stating that, prior to the bombing, McVeigh confided that a high-ranking FBI agent had recruited him to participate in undercover operations and at some point had instructed McVeigh to participate in the bombing. Nichols said McVeigh became visibly enraged during their conversation and ranted about how his "handler" changed the original target of the planned bombing, directing him to bomb the Murrah instead. While the court sealed Nichols' 2007 affidavit and supporting documents, in them he disclosed the identities of other alleged government informants and conspirators within the bombing plot and wrote that they were being protected by [the FBI/government] "in a cover-up to escape its responsibility for the loss of life in Oklahoma."[136]

With the exception of the letters to his sister, which became known to the public early on, and without knowing how often McVeigh told such stories, who he told them to or that he told them at all, various commentators have advanced several possible scenarios. In his 1998 book purporting various conspiracy theories or alternate narratives about McVeigh and the bombing, David Hoffman considered some possible explanations for the appearance of what he calls the "two McVeighs." Hoffman suggests that perhaps "someone working for the government" had duped McVeigh into believing a false cover story that "he was on an important top secret mission [and his] indifference to his arrest may simply have been indicative of his understanding that he was working for a government agency." Thus, McVeigh was telling his sister the truth about his induction into a covert operation and had been "sheep-dipped" and ordered to play the part of "a disgruntled ex-military man." McVeigh then carried out the bombing as part of this mission or, alternately, became disenchanted, refused and was therefore targeted for termination by setting him up as a "fall guy," which, Hoffman adds, is standard protocol for those who try to break from the shadowy world of deep intelligence.[137]

A NOBLE LIE: COMING HOME

After McVeigh's brief and mysterious SFAS try-out at Ft. Bragg, he returned home to the Buffalo area several times on leave. Friends and family members immediately noticed changes in his personality and, as reflected in the Jones Team's interviews with them, attributed it to his experiences in the Gulf War, rather than the failed Special Forces try-out. It seemed he had a vision of himself irreconcilable with what he saw and did in the Gulf, and was now cognizant of things his friends and family back home could never understand. Even his *official* biographers Herbeck and Michel, came to feel that "much more than his failure to make Special Forces, his experience [in the war] had soured him on the military. The more he thought about it, the worse he felt about the killing he had done for the American government," and stressed that the real reason for his disillusionment was "the lies he heard in the Persian Gulf."[138]

When he saw Steve Hodge after returning from the Gulf War, McVeigh emphasized that he had not done anything heroic during the war and called the medals and commendations he earned "overblown." To Steve, Tim seemed greatly troubled by what occurred during the war and described it as "a waste of life due to the inability of the Iraqis to fight." When he did have to fight, McVeigh said, the fighting had been "terrible." He told Steve about the friendly fire, the people he killed and the murder of surrendering Iraqis who, McVeigh said, would pop down in their trenches, wait for the firing to stop, pop back up and continue their attempts to surrender. It "seemed like a cycle" to Tim and Steve could tell it "bothered him a lot. I think seeing people suffer hurt him" and he had "had his fill of fighting." Although he had "always wanted to help people, to play the hero," Steve reflected that when the war ended, Tim turned his attention to "pointing out the injustices in the world."

His maternal cousin and godmother told the Jones Team that McVeigh appeared "bitter" and "disappointed ... I think he tried to be a good soldier – he wanted to be Number One – but [his] experiences [during the war] had a negative effect on him." His aunt said she could tell immediately that it had been "an overwhelming experience for him." To her he confided, "I had never known death before. I saw bodies lying around. After a while it began to get easier; it didn't hurt as much." Jennifer noticed that her brother was more restless, nervous and appeared "confused." His mother also observed a change in him. He told her about having to kill Iraqis and how bad he felt about it. She later said, "He did what he had to do, but it hurt him."

Former neighbors Dan and Linda Dangler (names changed) recalled he was "somber" as he recounted to them witnessing death and shooting people. They noted that when he did talk about it, he seemed odd, "straight faced – he didn't have much emotion, as if it was hard for him to remember." Mrs. McDermott, his former neighbor, could tell the war "deeply affected him," especially the starving Iraqi children. Similarly, she observed a "stark difference" in the way he spoke of his general experiences in the Gulf as opposed to those involving combat and recounted one conversation they had over dinner:

> [Tim] talked about the war as if he was numb. There was no emotion in his voice as he described an incident where their jeep had gotten stuck in the sand and some Iraqis came out and got them out and then surrendered to them. He talked as if he was pulled away from it all, as if he was there but not here. That's the way he was when he talked about anything to do with fighting or the Iraqis, but when he talked about things that had happened in the barracks, he was his usual self – the old Tim we knew. It was eerie.

According to Lt. Col. Grossman, the intensity, trauma and guilt soldiers suffer post-combat "inevitably result in a web of forgetfulness, deception and lies." This traumatic personal matrix reflects cultural and institutional practices of forgetting inconvenient truths and is exacerbated by the eventual understanding that history is written by victors. This combined with the soldiers' simultaneous yet "unconscious cover-up" of the reality of their own combat actions, results in a larger socio-cultural "conspiracy of silence" about the realities of war. Particularly difficult is the impact of realizing ones participation in unjust killing and wartime atrocities, an epiphany that wreaks havoc on a soldier's indoctrinated belief that, while violent, the actions taken on the battlefield are nonetheless noble. This is especially so for witnesses or participants in the killing of surrendering or captured enemy troops or civilians, who develop a deep, lingering and unresolvable need to justify such actions. Although Grossman wrote very shortly after the conclusion of the Gulf War, he failed to mention incidents like the Bulldozer Assault or the mass killing on Basra Highway, but he might as well have been writing specifically about them as well as McVeigh's own responses to them when, while discussing wartime atrocities, Grossman remarked:

> Killing comes with a price, and societies must learn that their soldiers will have to spend the rest of their lives living with that they have done.... Mass murder and execution can be sources of mass empowerment.... Each soldier who actively or passively participated in [mass executions] is faced with a stark choice...the soldier can resist the incredibly powerful array of forces that call for him to kill [or] can bow before the social and psychological forces that demand that he kill, and in doing so he will be strangely empowered.... He must believe that not only is this atrocity right, but it

is proof that he is morally, socially, and culturally superior to those whom he has killed. It is the ultimate act of denial of their humanity ... his mental health is totally invested in believing that what he has done is good and right ... the worst part is that when you institute and execute a policy of atrocity, you and your society must live with what you have done.[139]

THE ILL POLITICAL ANTI-MCVEIGH

By the time McVeigh returned to Ft. Riley in May 1991, the majority of his original COHORTs and Gulf War buddies had fulfilled their enlistment obligations and left the Army. Perhaps not knowing what else to do, McVeigh reenlisted on May 21, 1991, and served one final year before also deciding to leave active duty service.

Throughout the summer of 1991, he lived off base in an apartment with two other soldiers, Sgt. Richard Cerney and Corp. John Kelso, who said they quickly became offended at the way he spoke ill of his mother and were frightened by his erratic driving habits. Kelso remarked to the Jones Team that, to him, it seemed McVeigh had no respect for laws and described his memories of this time:

> [McVeigh was] a nice guy [but] had different views than most people [and] didn't act normal like [Cerney and I] did. He was real serious [and] read a lot. [He was] a loner [who just wanted] to be by himself. He'd rather sit in his room and read books than do what we were doing. Sometimes he'd hang out with Fortier. Me and Cerney were different than [him]. We drank and chased women, and he was a really private kind of person. [We] stayed up all night [and] went to work [but McVeigh] was totally opposite. Hell! He never had a girlfriend in his life that I knew of. Never used drugs ... just Mr. Clean. I would see him drink some, but it was a minor amount. He drank more after the Gulf. He had a lot of guns, and I found it unusual. I'm a hunter and I hunt a lot and I've got guns for every type of hunting: ducks, deer, geese, but he wasn't a hunter at all and still had a ton of guns. His were more for self-protection. He was a shooter. He shot a lot with anybody, anybody that wanted to go out, he always went. There was a big change in him when we got back from the Gulf. When he didn't get into Special Forces, his whole dream shattered. He had to come back and face us. No one was really harassing him about it, but he knew that we knew. I think he thought we saw him as a failure. He had no other thing on his mind before except the Special Forces and military and after that, he just crumbled. It was a 100% change.

Cerney, who had been in the Gulf with McVeigh during the war, often in the Bradley next to his, was less kind in his assessment. For one thing, Cerney explained, McVeigh was "the most racist bastard [I] ever knew." During the war, he had personally witnessed McVeigh shooting at surrendering Iraqis and, even at that time, thought that shooting people "didn't bother him in any way." In fact, he continued, Cerney said he personally believed that, if it came down to it, McVeigh would not hesitate to shoot them too, adding that McVeigh "is a cold blooded bastard [who] believes that life is very cheap." Both Cerney and Kelso said that, after the war, McVeigh had a bad attitude, kept guns around him at all times and seemed paranoid. They even sometimes joked that one day they would see McVeigh's face on a wanted poster, a foresight shared by many others prior to his arrest.

Reflective of Cerney and Kelso's impressions were six letters McVeigh wrote to Steve while living with them. In one dated July 10, 1991, he promised to show Steve his pictures from the war next time he came home but then went on to admonish Steve for not sending information he requested, specifically the contact information for Handgun Control, Inc., a gun-control advocacy group formed by Sarah Brady to have the Brady Bill legislation passed. To Steve he wrote, "I asked you about an address for Sarah Brady or HCI (so I can mail bomb her)."

McVeigh, who had never lived in a civilian space with anyone but his family, began to feel his roommates were too nosey and decided to leave. His friend, Sgt. Royal Witcher, lived off base in the nearby town of Herington, Kansas and since the two had always gotten along, in September 1991, when McVeigh asked if he could move in, Witcher agreed. Witcher recalled his increasingly odd personal life and described in detail how McVeigh kept almost no furniture in his room, hung a poncho instead of a curtain on the windows and, like a child, had Garfield the Cat blankets and sheets. McVeigh, said Witcher, was extremely shy and unable to "express himself" to women and so, never had a date.[140] According to Mark Hamm, Witcher now lived with the spokesperson for paranoia itself.

During this time, just as before the war, McVeigh continued to excel as a soldier at Ft. Riley, at least in the eyes of his superiors. At the end of September, he received his second Army Commendation medal, scored perfect in a competition, earned the distinction of Top Bradley Gunner and, once again, became the evaluator for the new Bradley training course. For McVeigh though, things were different and he no longer derived pleasure from such accolades. Other soldiers noticed an "unspoken change…a definite difference in Tim's attitude…he didn't seem to care anymore and was pretty disillusioned with the military. He wasn't as motivated and didn't have the drive that he always had." He was "hyper," "nervous," "bitter," "angry," "reclusive," and "isolated." He occasionally expressed "remorse" about the people he killed in Iraq and his political rhetoric become notably more dramatic and aggressive. They were unsure, however, if these changes were a reaction to the war or to his failure at the SFAS course.

To fellow soldier Sheffield Anderson, McVeigh spoke of returning home to upstate New York, building a bunker on his land and loading it with food, weapons and ammunition so that he could "be ready if the apocalypse hit." Steve Hodge told the Jones Team that McVeigh's characteristic "obsessiveness" towards his interests had always "mutated from one form to another," but after the war, his two most persistent ones, guns and survivalism, merged with his increasing critiques of the U.S. government's corruption. According to another soldier, McVeigh became "real bitter about everything. He read lots of books about the JFK assassination" and believed it was a conspiracy. He also began delving into and heatedly discussing books about the U.S. government's "private armies" and railed continuously about how the CIA, FBI and big business were getting out of control. About this period, Stickney wrote that McVeigh "was scared and mad, and getting madder." So much so that some of the other soldiers, who previously had at least some respect for him, began calling him "Anti-McVeigh," because he seemed to be anti-everything.

Another soldier said, McVeigh was always "strange," but rapidly became stranger. He related an incident that occurred one night while they were out driving around, during which McVeigh suddenly parked on the side of the road, "pulled out his pistol and just started rapid firing into the open field. [McVeigh] said he hadn't done that in while, and so he just felt like he had to do that ... I thought he probably went off the deep end." His new roommate Witcher, with whom McVeigh got along well, said the strangest thing he noticed was that McVeigh kept weapons "all over" the house: in the bathroom, "behind the towels," the kitchen cupboards, under the couch in the living room, in the ledge over the stairs and his car, both in the glove box and trunk. Other guns, Witcher continued, he stashed at friends' houses, but McVeigh's personal armory soon grew so large that he had to rent a storage locker in nearby Junction City. "I don't know if he was paranoid or what, or maybe he had some friends that were after him. I don't know."

McVeigh began spending more time with Terry Nichols, who lived nearby, and frequently made trips to Michigan to hang out with Terry's brother, James. McVeigh, Witcher continued, became "ill political"; amidst his obsessive consumption of news, McVeigh found at least one thing to take issue with every day. Another COHORT said he noticed that once McVeigh began spending more time with the civilian population around the base, with whom he shared similar interests and sometimes went out shooting, he became "a little more closed mouth."[141]

Some commentators suspect that McVeigh might have first become acquainted with members of the rapidly growing Patriot and Militia movements during this time. In 1990, Larry Pratt, the "father of the modern militia movement" and Executive Director of Gun Owners of America, an anti-gun-control legislation organization, published his manifesto that called for the formation of "armed civilian militias" and "civil defense units" and warned of the federal government's plan to disarm Americans. Reflective of a growing trend throughout the country, citizens' militias, paramilitary and anti-government groups had begun to appear around the Ft. Riley area and in Michigan where McVeigh spent an increasing amount of time. Economic and social disenfranchisement rooted, in part, from the 1980s farm crisis; gun control legislation; increased militarization of police; NAFTA and the military's involvement in United Nations peace-keeping operations were all indicative of Bush's New World Order, which provoked fears that the U.S. Constitution was rapidly eroding and the country was losing its sovereignty.

Oppositional right-wing groups within the increasingly popular umbrella of the Patriot Movement responded by stepping up their recruitment and propaganda efforts, targeting, among others, active-duty military personnel who were attracted to their patriotic, anti-communist, Constitutional rhetoric, combined with their professed willingness to take up arms against a corrupt government. The presence of militia, Patriot, anti-government, and paramilitary groups was strongest in states with higher numbers of gun owners and Vietnam and Gulf War combat veterans, including the Ft. Riley area, where recruitment efforts directed at soldiers were becoming more noticeable. McVeigh claimed he was never a card-carrying member of any group, but clearly, their pro-gun message and paranoid outlook appealed to him. Despite such claims, McVeigh, at different times in his life was, in fact, a card-carrying member of the KKK, the NRA, the Republican Party and of course the U.S. Army.

The atmosphere at Ft. Riley following the period immediately after the Gulf War was markedly desperate. Soldier morale was low and many considered their posting at Fort Riley as a "career ender" due, in part, to increased budget cuts and downsizing. Suicides and murder rates at the base continued to increase. Many shared the growing feeling that the government had left them by the wayside. Army intelligence officials noted that the growing number of disgruntled soldiers at Ft. Riley offered extremist ideologues a chance to expand their ranks. The "Commander" of the Kansas Citizen Militia agreed, admitting his group specifically recruited military personnel, explaining "these young men go into the military for all the right reasons, to protect the country, but they are watching themselves being turned into policemen for the wealthy interests of the few. They know it. We know it. That's why they are coming to us."[142]

In the updated 1995 edition of their book, *Snapping*, Conway and Siegelman described various ways in which political indoctrination acts as an "information disease" and argued that when a person who, for whatever reason, including trauma, has become physically and mentally wrecked, they consume information less critically and are more open to manipulation by others. They then offer McVeigh and his developing anti-government ideologies as an example of how information diseases lead to snapping. According to them, many of the patriot and militia cells used "cult-like methods" including "covert recruitment and induction, intimate group dynamics [and] ritualized indoctrination" as well as "more serious communication pathologies" that they say played a factor in the Oklahoma City bombing. The "[extremist] movements' distorted beliefs, ideas and potentially lethal information" inundated talk and short-wave radio and computer networks, appealing to the disenfranchised, like McVeigh and Nichols, who wanted to reduce the complexities of modern society and "the new global communication culture," that ultimately "give rise to new forms of mental illness and mass insanity."[143]

In 1999, cultural commentator Peter Knight also observed the rapid spread of "alternative information" during this period, largely through underground presses, talk radio, cable television shows, fax networks, home publishing and the emerging internet. Knight, however, felt that the general distrust of the government expressed and proliferated among ultra-conservatives did "not necessarily indicate the recrudescence of a paranoia 'virus' whose victims unthinkingly fall prey" to the types of insanity discussed by Conway and Siegelman. Rather, it indicated a massive shift of these beliefs from the fringes to the mainstream across both the right and left-wing spectrums that had resulted from decades of revelations about government corruption, cover-ups and conspiracies as well as the "profound economic and social restructuring" resulting from the rise of global "free-market" capitalism. In fact, Knight continued, a crisis of legitimacy permeated throughout the U.S. and "seemingly right-wing scare mongering rants about Bush's supposed plan for a new world order [were] perhaps not so far from what we might normally think of as leftist commentary." Given that, "sorting out the left from the right – and plausible from implausible – becomes virtually impossible." For Knight, Timothy McVeigh suffered from just this type of legitimacy crisis but ultimately represented one that existed "beyond the confines of the hardcore militia."[144]

In addition to the growing presence of the Patriot Movement, racial tensions that had long existed at Ft. Riley were reaching a boiling point and organized racism within the military was gaining the attention of watchdog groups and law enforcement officials. White Power organizations were engaged in their own recruitment of military personnel. McVeigh's rhetoric and behavior reflected all of this. Ivory Trone, an African-American soldier, was just out of boot camp when McVeigh became his squad leader. To the Jones Team, he described the men McVeigh hung out with as "the red neck posse" and on a number of occasions heard them use "racial affronts to blacks and other nonwhite races." He and McVeigh had a falling out when McVeigh issued an order and Trone talked back. McVeigh took him outside and "chewed him out ... threatening his career in the U.S. Army. He didn't like people questioning his authority." Trone said that was the point when he realized "McVeigh was very biased and prejudiced ... [and] judged him [Trone] on the color of his skin and not on his merit as a soldier."

McVeigh did not like most of the new soldiers arriving at Ft. Riley and told his biographers that during his final months in the Army, his overt racism resurfaced, attributing this to the disrespectful attitudes of "new black kids" coming into his unit. "You don't like your squad leader because he makes you get up at 5:00 AM. It's a basic human trait in the Army; these guys turned it into a racial thing. They didn't understand they were privates." Hence, when he noticed black soldiers wearing Black Power t-shirts around base he ordered one that said 'White Power' from the back of a survivalist magazine. To order the shirt he had to send a $20 membership fee to the North Carolina Ku Klux Klan. He did not feel the shirt was offensive since "black guys were wearing Black Power t-shirts on the base [and] they weren't supposed to ... I wanted to see what would happen ... I wanted to make a point.... Back in the Sixties people would bring Communist manifestos onto campus. Does that mean they're a Communist because they got that book and read it?"

In his exhaustive book on the history of the international White Power Movement, *The Beast Awakens*, Martin E. Lee, wrote that the majority of right-wing paramilitary groups had intimate personal and ideological connections to white supremacist groups. Lee explained in great depth how the WPM had embarked upon a systematic attempt to tone down their racial rhetoric and gain more mainstream credibility in order to attract unsuspecting, susceptible and disgruntled individuals drawn to the ideas and concepts of the militias. "Although hard core racialists – that is to say, *those who consciously embrace racism as an ideology* – remained a numerical minority, they were the motor that propelled and guided the militia movement since its inception." Indeed, McVeigh claimed his curiosity about the "patriot community and basic fundamental rights" led him to books like *The Turner Diaries*, which, in turn, led him to explore organizations like the National Alliance and the KKK. However, the real "test" of his racism, he said, was his eventual determination, based on his "moral values," that WPM literature and propaganda "manipulated young people" by falsely equating "racism with patriotism." Therefore, he explained, after becoming "very unhappy with the Klan," he let his membership expire and later traded the t-shirt for ammunition and smoke grenades.[145]

Still, McVeigh resumed his peculiar habit of reading, rereading and handing out copies of *The Turner Diaries* and had one on hand at all times, like a Baptist with his Bible. Later, both he and Stephen Jones rejected an insanity defense because, as Jones stated, his client did not "wish to be depicted as another John Hinckley." Yet McVeigh's obsession with *The Turner Diaries* (and other popular culture works) certainly evoked Hinckley as well as other bibliophile Lone Wolf assassins like Mark David Chapman, both of whom had a similar obsession with *The Catcher in the Rye*. Interestingly, Hinckley had provoked the Brady gun control legislation that, ironically, helped provoke the Oklahoma City bombing, which then prompted further debates about people like McVeigh.

McVeigh wrote to his attorneys, "I think that [*The*] *Turner Diaries* (at least the first 100 pages) should be required reading for everyone on the defense team because the truth is, it IS a blueprint. (It wasn't my specific blueprint, but it provides a good tactical and philosophical 'outline,' minus the racial thing." He downplayed his racism a couple of years later, telling his biographers that he identified not with Turner's racism but with the book's underlying message about gun rights and individual freedom. *The Turner Diaries*, he insisted, was not so much the blueprint for the bombing, but rather provided an inspirational model of resistance to gun control legislation.

Despite his disenchantment, accusations of his racism, his increasingly apparent bad attitude and strange politics, his superiors still considered him an excellent soldier; but no amount of commendations, accolades, medals or promotions could mitigate "the lies he heard in the Persian Gulf" or the abortive Special Forces experience. "The more he thought about it," wrote Herbeck and Michel, "the worse he felt about the killing he had done for the American government [and] he no longer wanted to work for the government he was beginning to hate." Thus, in late 1991, when his Battalion Commander asked McVeigh to be his personal driver, he declined and with his "eyes welling up with tears," announced he was leaving the Army.[146]

McVeigh said later that, while this position would have been less demanding, it entailed more paper work than he was willing to deal with and would have required him to rub noses with officers, whom he considered the Army's politicians. Instead, on December 31, 1991, he submitted his letter of resignation to his CO. His decision surprised his COHORTs, many of whom thought that, of all people, McVeigh would be a career soldier regardless of the new military cutbacks. Further, nobody expected he would pass up the chance to attend the SFAS again, only months away. Now, nobody was quite sure what he would do or where he would go.

A primary reason for the creation and circulation of conflicting stories about Timothy McVeigh was the little known fact that McVeigh himself authored or told them first and, like the SFAS failure, he gave different explanations to different people about his decision to leave the Army. Gordon Blackcloud recalled that, "He wasn't the cheerful guy he was before. You know? But he didn't really say too much or focus on what he was planning on doing." 1st Sgt. Bob Harris tried to talk him out of it, but his mind was set. Hartley had the impression he was going home to attend college, but McVeigh told Dan Stroud he planned to go home and become a law enforcement officer.[147]

Royal Witcher also saw him just before he left. McVeigh told Witcher and another soldier, Maurice Ray, "he was going to disappear for quite a while and wouldn't even be able to tell his parents where he would be or what he would be doing." And that, indeed, is exactly what he went on to do. Witcher recalled that both he and Ray "thought it was kinda funny and strange, at the same time… [we thought] it was just [Tim] being strange … he was always a little [strange] … but we couldn't figure out what he had gotten himself into that he couldn't tell his parents about." Allen Smith recalled, "He changed over time after he got back from the war; his temper had gotten worse." McVeigh told Smith he'd had enough of the "political B.S." that goes along with the Army, had lost interest and "just wanted to turn his back. He was so fed up he just got out…. Tim really hated it along toward the end." And another said, "The day he got out of the Army he spent his last night at my house. I don't think he was bitter as much as he just didn't know what he was going to do. I know he told me he was lost."

Stress Level 3000%

If McVeigh dropped out of his Special Forces try-out because he was in bad physical shape, as he claimed, he appeared to recover quickly. According to one of the soldiers who had joined Charlie Company immediately after the Gulf War, "Sgt. McVeigh was very gung-ho … [he] was a good runner, maintained his physical fitness, found pleasure in pushing himself physically … [he] enjoyed pushing others," especially in the 60-pound ruck-sack marches (which had supposedly given him so much trouble at Ft. Bragg). "When most started to get tired," he continued, "McVeigh found pleasure in pushing himself and others." Yet there was something else going on, something unexplored in all published accounts that may provide clues and context about his decision to leave the Army. Absent in the many letters McVeigh wrote Steve, as well as in the transcripts of FBI and defense team interviews with other soldiers, is any mention of his continued medical visits. From the time he returned from the Gulf in April until leaving the Army in December, he continued his secret life as a professional patient. Inexplicably, while large portions of

McVeigh's military medical records are found in the Jones Collection, no memoranda or correspondence were located in the collection indicating that anybody on the Jones Team noticed or discussed the frequency of his medical visits while in the Army.

It is no wonder that Cerney and Kelso found McVeigh a bit cranky, as during the summer of 1991, while living with them, McVeigh visited the dentist several times. On June 20, 1991, two of his teeth were decaying and causing him pain. On July 1, 12, 15, and 29, he returned for medical attention on at least seven different teeth. Doctors noted he had small protruding pieces of bone sticking out in his mouth, which was was infected, and the "bone chips" caused him continuous pain. In the midst of this, on July 17, he saw a doctor for the removal of moles that had recently appeared on his chin and near his ear. At the end of the summer, on August 26, 1991, at 1 PM, just prior to moving out of the apartment he shared with Cerney and Kelso, McVeigh visited the doctor, saying he was nauseated, unable to hold fluids and could not stop vomiting. He did not have a fever.[148]

In September 1991, the month he moved in with Royal Witcher, McVeigh received another typhoid vaccination. An almost unreadable document stamped "Emergency Treatment Center, Ft. Riley" shows that, sometime in October 1991, the 23-year-old combat veteran received a "medical injection" of an unknown variety after seeking medical care for unknown reasons. On October 14, he complained of pain in his right shoulder, but the radiologist, after examining results of the x-rays he ordered, found "no significant abnormalities." Meanwhile, McVeigh attended Ft. Irwin's National Training Center located in the Mojave Desert of San Bernardino County, California, and arrived back at Ft. Riley on October 20. Two days later, on October 22, at 6 AM, doctors at Ft. Riley saw him for a previously diagnosed "ulcer," as well as a "cold," that had persisted since the week before.

On October 28, 1991, he wrote to Steve "at 1630 (hrs) formation, they told us that we would be on alert as of 0430 tomorrow morning. Our bags will be packed onto a semi … we're on alert to guard a nuclear site in Utah against terrorist attacks. Great, another opportunity for my balls to fall off !!!" He had "a stress level of 3000%." He closed by saying, "I have to quit now, I have a pounding headache!" He did not mention the recent visits to the doctor.

An NCO Evaluation Report, detailing his performance from February until November 1991, recommended his promotion to a higher pay grade. A little over a week later, at 6 AM on November 7, 1991, he sought medical attention saying that for the previous four weeks his left big toe had been "deteriorating." It was "scaling," "fissuring between toes," "red," and "itching." He told the doctor that the "skin scales, then grows back, then holes appear." At 5:30 AM on November 13, he again went to the medical unit, this time complaining about facial moles located above the chin, but below the bottom lip and on the right side of his face near his ear, that interfered with shaving and requested they be removed. On a separate form entitled "Request For Civilian Medical Care" the doctor described the "skin tags" and noted two "new" moles – the first "5 mm flesh colored" and the second "2mm raised flesh colored." The previous July, and in the civilian medical referral, the doctor wrote the moles were new; but in a November 13 report, they had been there his entire "lifetime."

McVeigh arrived at the dentist again on November 20, 1991, and because of his bleeding gums, doctors ordered an x-ray. By this time, he had received so many x-rays, that fears of his testicles falling off appear reasonable. By the time he left Fort Riley, only five of his teeth remained untouched. The November 20 visit was the last *dental* visit to appear on his military records but, as will be seen, certainly not his last visit. After leaving the Army, McVeigh continued to visit private dentists throughout the country, including just days before the bombing. Often these visits occurred in mysterious circumstances. In a "Radiological Request Report" dated December 5, 1991, the attending doctor noted McVeigh's upper gastrointestinal difficulties that included his retention of gaseous secretions and the possibility of duodenitis, an inflammation of the intestine commonly caused by viral infection, bacteria, and often resulting in an ulcer.

James Rockwell, the supply sergeant for Charlie Company, said that one day McVeigh entered the Ft. Riley supply room and confided his belief that he had a "computer chip in his backside." Rockwell was not sure what McVeigh meant by this and asked him to explain. McVeigh responded that the military had "done things" to him and said, "I think they've brainwashed me or injected me with something." At the very least, Rockwell opined, McVeigh felt the Army had manipulated him into killing innocent Iraqis.[149]

On December 10, McVeigh "put in to get out" of the Army and received an honorable discharge effective December 31, 1991. The reason noted for his separation: "the early transition program... for the convenience of the government." As part of his early discharge he enlisted, or accepted a "voluntary assignment," in the New York State Army National Guard based in Tonawanda, New York, to begin immediately upon leaving Ft. Riley. The same day, December 10, he wrote Steve, "Yeah, I'll be home for Christmas, but in a way you never imagined! That's right, roll out the red carpet, hold all calls; because The Kid is comin' home! (Know of any job openings for a washed-up war hero?) See ya by the 20th; I'll need help unloading the U-Haul." The next day on December 11, 1991, he was administered anesthesia for the removal of the pesky moles, which did (or did not) recently appear. The doctor appears to have taken no tissue specimens to the lab for further testing.

Like so many aspects of his life, details about his health are conflicting and contradictory. McVeigh told his attorneys that he once had a negative incident with a Captain during a drill when the Captain "chewed him out" for visiting the medic for an ingrown toenail. Woody Davis said McVeigh had sinus problems before he left Ft. Riley. Gordon Blackcloud explained the standard protocol for obtaining medical attention: "If you wanted to see the doctor, you had to go through the chain of command. You had to see the medic first." After I told him about McVeigh's records and asked him what he thought, he said that if he was as sick as the records reflected, someone would have noticed, and the other soldiers would have given him a hard time. "We spent the whole time together as one unit, from basic to the whole deal," Blackcloud elaborated. "I don't know how he was before he came in, but he seemed to be in good health. As many times as he went to the doctor, that's what I'm sitting here trying to figure out as well, too. It seemed like he would have gotten in trouble for it being too excessive." The loquacious Ray Barnes provided the following explanation:

> He didn't have any health problems that I knew of. I think he had trouble in his feet one time, but that was when he was doing a lot of road marching and getting ready for Special Forces. When you start marching a lot of miles, you gotta take care of your feet, if they break down. I heard he hurt his leg in trying out, and that's about the only big major health thing that I can recall. He washed out of the Special Forces because he hurt his knee during the try-out. I recall him going to the dentist a few times, but it never interfered with his training. He wasn't being pulled out regularly. He may have gotten some teeth fixed, but to be honest, I didn't pay no attention to it. He didn't miss training or regular duty. If you got a tooth ache you can go to the dentist. I don't ever remember him complaining of a tooth ache. I know he had his wisdom teeth done because when an Army dentist pulls your teeth, you couldn't help but not miss it, cuz you look like a chipmunk. I don't recall him having moles. I'm looking at this picture [from boot camp] and I don't really notice any moles. I mean, if they were there they weren't red or anything.... But you gotta understand, McVeigh was a private person. If he didn't want you to know ... he didn't open up to just everybody. If he wanted you to know, he'd tell you. He wasn't a whiner and very few people he'd open up to. He never really complained. Like roommates, he didn't nosey into my business and I didn't nosey into his. We kind of just respected each other that way. If he wanted me to know, he told me. If he didn't, I didn't need to know, and I respected that.[150]

The FBI had interviewed all soldiers known to have contact with McVeigh and even harassed many of them, but Lou Johnson, who was also very sick by this time, commented on the FBI's lack of questioning during their interview. To him it seemed the FBI "didn't want to know the truth." A number of them reported the FBI and CID gave express instructions not to talk about McVeigh, not to attempt to contact him further, and not to discuss the case. None of the hundreds of FBI interviews refers to health problems. Nonetheless, after his return to upstate New York, the psychological, medical, and ideological odyssey of Timothy McVeigh continued.

Chapter Three

AMERINOID

PART ONE
Return To Buffalo
(12/91-1/93)

INTRODUCTION

The 1990s was widely dubbed "the conspiracy decade" due to what some perceived as a growing culture of paranoia, whose expressions continued to find their way into the broader public at an alarmingly increasing frequency. No longer on the pathological fringes, conspiracies had become a staple topic within the mainstream. Elected officials and pundits implied and proclaimed the existence of vast, far-reaching, right and left-wing conspiracies while the American populace simultaneously displayed a bipartisan fusion paranoia wherein the cynical, conspiratorial thinking of the rightist Patriot and Militia crowd coincided with surprisingly similar suspicious ruminations on the left.[1]

Growing numbers of Americans gravitated towards conspiracy theories as a way to make sense of actual or suspected parallel, but unseen, realities and realms populated by shadowy government and institutional forces. According to commentator Peter Knight, writing in 1999, the language of conspiracy that dominated the decade and its related "canon" of conspiracy theories (common subjects of popular entertainment and historical revisionism) involved any number of federal agencies' plots and cover-ups but of all the conspiracy theories that circulated, those about the 1960s "'Lone nut' assassinations were the cornerstone of skepticism toward government." According to public opinion polls, in 1964, 87% of Americans accepted the Warren Commission's official account of the JFK assassination. In 1993, 77-80% believed some type of government conspiracy was involved in the assassination of JFK, and in 1995, 90% rejected the notion that Oswald acted alone.[2]

Even the government was skeptical of the government. In 1992, President Clinton requested that Webster Hubbell, possible Justice Department appointee, find the answers to two pressing questions: "Who killed

JFK?" and "Are there UFO's?"[3] That same year, in order to help counter conspiracy theories about the JFK assassination, former president Gerald Ford, the only surviving member of the Warren Commission, requested that the CIA and House Select Committee on Assassinations publicly disclose all their files related to the murder which still remained classified.

Perhaps best illustrative of the permeation of conspiracy theories within popular culture was Oliver Stone's 1991 film *JFK*, which, as cultural theorist Jack Bratich pointed out, "kicked off a conspiracy panic."[4] FOX network's television series *X-Files* (1993-2002) also reflected, shaped and defined the decade's preoccupation with conspiracy theories. The show featured a pair of FBI agents tasked with investigating "fringe" and often paranormal-type cases, who find themselves surrounded by all manner of government conspiracies. Unshakable in their belief that "the truth is out there," they continue their quest despite numerous dangers posed to their lives by the conspirators, who include old white men in smoke-filled back rooms, where (as everybody knows) conspiracies are hatched. *JFK* and the *X-Files* raised questions about their relation to or reflection of actual and possible events, plausible or probable theories about them and the increasingly blurred lines between fact, fiction and metaphor.

Not surprisingly, the sponge-like McVeigh was an ardent *X-Files* fan, and after learning of the prosecution's request to disqualify *X-Files* fans from the pool of potential jurors, he requested that his attorneys specifically include them on the jury and insisted that the defense jury-screening questionnaire include the question of whether or not potential jurors were fans of the *X-Files*. To illustrate his reasons, he had attorney Randy Coyne, who had never seen the show, record an episode and view it with him. McVeigh told Coyne the show was about "covert meetings in the night, secret goings-on" and focused on a "ghost government." In a memo written to the other members of the defense team shortly after, Coyne said, "It is clear to me that the government will desperately try to keep all *X-Files* fans off Tim's jury." Coyne then attempted to explain the show to the rest of the team, telling them it was about two FBI agents who "find that the darker forces of evil are actually clandestine government officials and agencies." Coyne added that as they watched the episode, McVeigh insisted on replaying one particular scene wherein Agent Scully chooses not to kill the person believed to have murdered her sister, and declares, "The truth is, no court, no punishment is ever enough."

The turn of the millennium witnessed a spate of analysis by academic pundits of conspiracy theories. Some went so far as to claim that their proliferation had, by the 1990s, reached dangerous epidemic proportions and had "injected toxins into the public discourse" resulting in a full-blown paranoid virus whose symptoms among the body politic included heightened public fear and widespread cynicism.[5] Since then, a growing number have sought to move beyond the paranoid style thesis and, in doing so, have advanced more sympathetic takes on conspiracy theories, the people who propagate them and the "cultures of conspiracy" they comprise.

In 2009, historian Kathryn Olmstead built on the work of 1990s-era academic theorists of conspiracy theorists by examining why, exactly, such a large number of Americans believed their own government would engage in conspiracies against them and the relationship this belief had to actual conspiracies. She found that, despite their "seeming outlandishness" the wide array of conspiracy theories all had "at least one thing in common: when they charge that the government has plotted, lied, and covered up, they're often right." She concluded that, between conspiracies and official government stories, citizens should be more skeptical of the latter, "because the most dangerous conspiracies and conspiracy theories flow from the center of American government, not from the margins of society." Thus, for Olmstead, this represented "the struggle over the power to control the public's perception of an event" and posed a direct challenge to the government's authority to create an official version of an event and subsequently maintain it as the truth.[6]

While Olmstead interrogated the historicity and social function of conspiracy theories, in 2008 academic and cultural theorist Jack Bratich explored the ways they challenged existing constraints placed upon the very *possibility* of belief itself. He posited that a conspiracy theory provides a way to discuss a number of issues including race relations, "globalization, bio warfare and biomedicine." Even if they didn't get all the facts right, conspiracy theories posed a threat to the limits of acceptable belief and discourse by calling attention to the broader historical and socio-cultural contexts surrounding them. The very label "conspiracy theory" functioned not only as a description of a certain kind of narrative but also as a label deployed to disqualify certain topics from legitimate public discussion. The rash of criticism which followed the release of Stone's *JFK* revealed that its subject and its claims stood in direct opposition to existing, yet often unperceived "regimes of truth."

For these reasons he conceived of conspiracy theory as a struggle over meaning and suggested studying the specific narrative components of any given conspiracy theory as well as "where and when [it] appears, who speaks it, what else it is linked to, and what it opposes."[7] Following is an attempt to answer this call and show how, even prior to the bombing, McVeigh was caught in the midst of, and actively engaged in, a number of already existing "perception and meaning wars," many of which were amplified afterwards.

THE TRUTH IS OUT THERE

Immediately after his arrest, countless news reports linked McVeigh to certain conspiracy theories and the often right-leaning groups who propagated them. The tinfoil hat wearing, pathological political paranoiac offenders typified by McVeigh, reportedly saw black helicopters everywhere they looked, fearing U.N. troops would soon round up U.S. citizens and relocate them in concentration camps as part of the ever-dreaded New World Order. Nearly overnight, the bombing transformed conspiracy theorists into possible terrorists and, eventually, the U.S. State Department concluded that these "subcultures of conspiracy and misinformation" *caused* terrorism.[8]

This new batch of "folk devils" invigorated the paranoids' counterparts, the debunkers, who, in 1996, said conspiracy theories had spun out of control and had "leaked into the real world and created havoc." Built from "bad information" clogging the roads of the emergent digital highway, they acted as "thought contagions" that spread "information diseases." Works like *JFK* and the *X-Files* that "expose millions to their counter-narratives" now became a source of transmission for this disease. McVeigh and his ilk possessed a form of "dangerous knowledge" said to be infecting the mainstream on both the political left and right and a conspiratorial ideology that many now claimed led its adherents to commit hate crimes.[9]

Conspiracy theories about McVeigh and the bombing co-opted counter-terrorism discourses with their implied or stated claims about a government conspiracy that had actually allowed the bombing to occur, orchestrated it, and, in either scenario, now actively sought to cover up this fact. Ironically, and to McVeigh's frequently expressed dismay, conspiracy theories about the bombing incorporated him and his act into the very type of fantastical musings he enjoyed previously, but in a manner that sometimes deprived him of his intended legacy as a Lone Wolf bomber.

While, at least for a time, the Pack of Wolves narratives had not yet been labeled as conspiracy theory, the Watched Wolves and Guilty Agent narratives that appeared soon after the bombing were quickly dismissed as such. In the latter, McVeigh is depicted, not as a Lone Wolf, or even one within a Pack of Wolves, but as a Guilty Agent; a *witting* undercover operative for shadowy defense agencies in a nationwide sting operation that resulted in the bombing. The rapid spawning of these stories was reported less than a week after the bombing in the *Wall Street Journal* and the *Las Vegas Review-Journal,* among other major media outlets and, within months, were canonized in book form by author Jon Rappaport. Rappaport argued that the bombing and the cover-up of the bombing plot were part of a larger effort by a disgraced federal government to make themselves look like heroes, demonize the Patriot Movement and pass anti-terrorism legislation which would expand the budgets and powers of various government agencies; thereby allowing them to further suppress the Movement. While conceding that he didn't have all the facts just yet, Rappaport thought it likely that McVeigh himself, although he participated willingly, had not been fully aware of all the details of the plot and was only the visible face of a much larger government-sanctioned operation.

Writing in a similar vein, Garvin Phillips offered additional possible motives for the government's intentional failure to prevent the bombing (they let it happen) or direct participation in the bombing (they made it happen) including the destruction of embarrassing records stored in the Murrah building such as those relating to Gulf War Syndrome or Waco. Phillips suggested that McVeigh was tricked by his government handlers into believing he was doing something good for his country by helping to foil a terrorist plot: the Guilty Agent story McVeigh himself first told.

Like the Pack, Watched and Guilty Agent narratives, Experimental stories first appeared publicly within hours of McVeigh's arrest. Countless news reports detailed how, over the previous years, he had told a number of friends that the Army embedded a microchip in his buttock. For instance, on April 23, 1995, several news outlets quoted Michigan farmer, Phillip Morawski, who told reporters of McVeigh's claim that the government "planted one of those chips that they have for identifying cattle, sheep or goats so the all-seeing eye of the government could keep an eye on him and know where he was." Morawski recalled McVeigh telling him that the chip sometimes caused a "real sharp pain in his rear."[10]

The same day, the FBI received a phone call from Linda Thompson, an Indianapolis attorney, militia spokesperson and producer of the popular underground conspiracy documentary *Waco: The Big Lie*, one of McVeigh's favorites. According to the FBI report, Thompson "advised that the psychiatrist brought in to examine Timothy McVeigh, Louis Jolyon West, is actually a CIA operative who was responsible for implanting micro-chips in Army personnel in an experiment called 'MKUltra.'" She said West did just this to McVeigh during an "outpatient" procedure that "took 20 minutes." She then urged the FBI to prevent West from removing the chip so the FBI could determine what the CIA had done to McVeigh. The FBI report noted that Thompson's allegations had been "subsequently printed" in the following day's newspaper, *The Indianapolis Star*.

The majority of media reports and commentary about McVeigh's preaching of conspiracy theories highlighted the peculiar subculture that those like him and Thompson inhabited, posited the dangers posed by their beliefs and dismissed the theories and claims as outlandish. Undeterred, conspiracy genre writers continued to examine and expound upon this topic, however speculatively. Some Experimental Wolf accounts depict Calspan, a defense establishment research facility where McVeigh briefly worked after leaving the Army, as instrumental in the bombing story. In such stories, Calspan becomes a staging ground for darker and more sinister tales wherein McVeigh acts as an unwitting puppet controlled by mysterious and faceless handlers, (often Jolly West), sanctioned and funded by government black budgets. In addition, while so-called credible mainstream commentators briefly note McVeigh's assignment at Calspan, they view it as inconsequential to both the bombing and the ideology he harbored.

In 1996, the prominent conspiracy genre writer Jim Keith opined, "there is a possibility McVeigh was purposely washed out of his Special Forces training ... recruited into a secret specialized unit, then sent to Calspan for indoctrination, training, or as [McVeigh] believed," to have his tracking-control device implanted in his body. Keith took his cue from an earlier essay by Alex Constantine entitled "Timothy McVeigh's Rise From 'Robotic' Solider to Mad Bomber" that speculates about McVeigh's possible experiences as a security guard at the Buffalo-based defense contractor. Constantine, like Keith, found it both conceivable and "technically feasible that McVeigh was implanted with a telemetry chip ... drawn into an experimental black project" at Calspan and, in combination with more traditional behavioral modification techniques, was remotely controlled and transformed into a robotic super soldier. In this story and stories like it, Calspan, with a little rumored help from the notorious West, fanned McVeigh's rage.[11]

Referring to McVeigh's "leaked" confession just prior to his trial, Cold Warrior USMC (Ret.) "Mustang" Major Dick Culver, in his 1997 essay "The Saga of Lee Harvey," wrote, "Quite frankly, I wouldn't believe McVeigh if he confessed that his real name was Timothy McVeigh! Here's a gent held away from prying eyes for almost two years and available for the gentle 'ministrations' of a group of 'brainwashing' experts that make the Chinese Communists look like kindergarten kids!" Culver said McVeigh probably believed he was, in fact, a lone wolf bomber, so much so that Culver was willing to bet money that, if given a lie detector test to this effect, McVeigh would pass. (He didn't). "By now," Culver reasoned, "[McVeigh] could be programmed to say AND believe that black is white! Confessions are strange things indeed." Major Culver knows this because, as an intelligence officer in Vietnam, and therefore an *insider*, he had access to several North Vietnamese prisoners of war who, "within the space of approximately two hours ... confessed to the assassination of Abraham Lincoln ... if you ask the right questions and offer the proper alternative incentives, virtually anyone can be made to say anything... and believe it!" Writing shortly before McVeigh's trial began, Culver outlined various potential outcomes. One was that either through another programmed killer or his own self-destruction, McVeigh, like Oswald, would be "silenced" before his day in court. He accurately predicted the actual outcome, writing, "The ideal solution from a conspiracy stand point," would be McVeigh's conviction, speedy execution and, *voila*, "case closed!"[12]

In his 2004 update, Culver pointed out that McVeigh effectively silenced himself when he dropped his appeals and requested his execution to move forward. In both his original 1997 and later updated Experimental ruminations, Culver described Dr. Jolly West, who, he reminded readers, also happened to be Jack Ruby's former psychiatrist, was a "proponent" of mind control "biochips," and therefore, McVeigh's most likely mind-controller. In Culver's theory, McVeigh's handlers recruited him to be the "straw man" and "patsy" for the bombing based on his history of following orders and because they knew he would not ask too many questions about his mission. In keeping with the Experimental Wolf formula, Culver highlights the history of the CIA's MKUltra program to justify his allegations about Dr. West. Although Culver notes that West denied rumors that he had examined McVeigh at Tinker AFB immediately after his arraignment, Culver dismisses the denial as just another part of the cover-up. According to Culver, McVeigh was probably guilty of, at the least, driving the Ryder truck. But behind the scenes and throughout "the entire operation," he had been under the influence of brainwashing by puppeteers working at the behest of still other, invisible conspirators, whose motives included the demonization and targeting of militias and the passage of counter-terrorism legislation.

Over time, as Experimental stories gained momentum, their growing number of details became even more bizarre and tangled. Blogger Sherman H. Skolnick's June 2001 envisioning of the bombing scenario involves a pack of Watched Wolves wherein Experimental Wolf McVeigh is under surveillance by the CIA and FBI and brainwashed by unknown individuals. Similar to David Hoffman's writings, Skolnick reconciled countless sightings of McVeigh in different locations at the same time by suggesting that, like Oswald, the real McVeigh was brainwashed, while imposter McVeighs roamed the country making their presence known as part of a "staged espionage event" that intentionally or not and for any number of reasons spun out of control. In Skolnick's estimation, McVeigh's handlers include Iraqi military officers apparently evidenced by George Bush's former business relationship with Saddam Hussein and Cheney's and Hillary Clinton's connections to a French company that sold chemicals to Iraq.

Among McVeigh's conspirators are some of the "more than four-thousand" Iraqi defectors relocated in the U.S. after the Gulf War, some in Oklahoma City. In a sense, Skolnick *redeems* McVeigh's earlier killings in the Gulf War by resurrecting and vindicating the dead Iraqis and rendering them co-conspirators in a plot against the U.S. government. Skolnick concluded his account by describing the elaborate staging and spectacle of McVeigh's execution and asking whether or not "the REAL" McVeigh was ever even put to death at all.[13] As it turns out, although unknown to Skolnick, both the FBI and McVeigh's defense attorneys had conducted their own investigations into possible McVeigh doppelgangers, and occasionally, McVeigh himself wondered about them.

According to Kathryn Olmstead, with the passage of the 1966 Freedom of Information Act, average Americans gained the power to access information and, with it, to construct their own alternative narratives about national events. While the Jones Team's quest for McVeigh's records or the anomalous (but overlooked) information in the portions obtained were unknown to Devvy Kidd, she was so convinced that McVeigh "wasn't himself," "had a look-alike, [and] a biochip in his rear end, courtesy of the U.S. Army," that, in 2002, she filed a FOIA request for his military records. She sought his separation from the Army, deployment, and medical records that detailed "the insertion of a micro-chip, a bio-chip or any other object foreign to the human body," the surgical or other methods used to implant this device and those "that document any visits, phone calls or correspondence [with] Dr. Louis Jolyon (Jolly) West." A series of refusals, denials and contradictory responses by the Army followed, along with her further appeals. . Although likely unknown to her, the records Kidd sought concerned a topic the Jones Team was also conducting active research into.[14]

The possibility that McVeigh, like Elvis, was still alive gained traction, even though conspiracy theory writers did not know that McVeigh himself entertained the possibility that his execution might be faked. In September 2001, *Weekly World News* published their second "exclusive" exposé about this, entitled "Timothy McVeigh Is Alive." Within days of the bombing, the report said, the 'real' McVeigh received silicone injections to change his facial features, had his fingerprints altered and was then whisked away to a "secure location – believed to be the super secretive U.S. Air Force Base north of Las Vegas known as 'Area 51'" where he assumed a new identity.[15] Oddly, just prior to McVeigh's originally scheduled execution date of May 15, 2001, the DOJ announced the existence of documents prosecutors failed to turn over during discovery and issued a new date of June 11, 2001 for the execution. Perhaps not knowing about the delay, the tabloid *Weekly World News* published an image of an ostensibly dead "McVeigh" on his morgue slab – while he was still alive.

Experimental Wolf speculations about McVeigh in the conspiracy genre apparently inspired Tracy Letts' play *BUG* (1996), and its 2006 movie adaptation. Over time, *BUG's* protagonist Peter explains to his friend Agnes that, after World War II, the CIA brought Nazi scientists into the States to "work with the American military at Calspan," where they eventually developed the "Intelligence Manned Interface biochip... a subcutaneous transponder, a computer chip imprinted with living brain cells." This chip, when implanted in human bodies, tracks and controls individuals through electronically emitted signals but the design was flawed, unable to "get to everybody... they need a chip that will self-perpetuate, that will spread like a virus... a living breathing parasite..." The mad scientists responsible for this project "needed lab rats and they found us...

me in the Gulf and another soldier working at Calspan at the time, Tim McVeigh." An anguished Peter goes on to tell Agnes how military doctors shipped them off to Groom Lake (Area 51) where scientists inserted tracking chips under their skin and used them to conduct mind control experiments, "They *turned us into fucking zombies, remote controlled assassins...*" Although Peter thwarted their efforts by finding his chip and cutting it out, they found him and sent him back to the lab for a new experiment involving the more advanced "IMI biochip" to track him.[16]

Until this writing, there has been no examination, comparison and contextual analysis of the thematic elements found in Guilty Agent and Experimental Wolf narratives about McVeigh and no substantial factual analysis of those that include claims about Calspan or Dr. West (or his fictional counterparts). While Experimental Wolf narratives tend to rely solely on speculation and the majority seem to make outlandish leaps of logic, a close examination of counter-narratives about the Oklahoma bombing and Timothy McVeigh reveals sound reasons, or at least identifiable ones, for their existence... even if they are not true. Such stories, no matter how seemingly fantastical, provide a window through which to explore ongoing collective tensions, fears and aspirations and the limits of their articulation. On a practical level, however, purportedly true accounts, as well as fictional works, echo the very claims made by McVeigh himself, publicly and privately, prior to and after his arrest.

PART TWO
Washed Up War Hero Rent-A-Cop

INTRODUCTION

In January 1992, Timothy McVeigh returned to his hometown of Pendleton, New York, feeling, according to Stickney, like "a failure" who had been used as a "pawn" in George Bush's "bullshit Gulf War." In Hamm's evaluation, the period following his return home marked "the next crucial stage of post-traumatic stress disorder: the atrophy of his mind and body." For Herbeck and Michel, this began "the most disappointing time of his life." Over the next thirteen months, it would "drive him into a deep depression." For Timothy McVeigh, "The American Dream" was dead, buried in the sands of the Persian Gulf.[17]

When he decided to leave the Army, McVeigh incorrectly assumed his military training and status of 'war hero' would expand his opportunities for well-paying, secure employment in the civilian world. Like many returning Gulf War veterans, he faced record-low national employment rates and hiring freezes. Reflective of the country's overall lackluster economy, the Buffalo-Niagara region was experiencing high unemployment rates (6.9% in November 1991) and declining property values. Further, analysts anticipated the loss of 1.3 million defense industry jobs nationwide, a circumstance that led to calls for the grafting of defense jobs onto a new civilian economy. Only by the grace of his current Department of Defense security clearance status and New York state concealed pistol permit did McVeigh obtain a job, picking up where he had left off, working for $5 an hour as an armed security guard; this time for Burns International Security.

He also joined the New York State National Guard (NYNG). Stickney attributed this to boredom – McVeigh simply had too much idle time. In keeping with his usual inconsistencies, McVeigh told multiple stories about signing up for the NYNG, his job duties there, the conditions and the reasons he left. To Otto and Coyle, his original public defenders, as well as allegedly to Hammer, McVeigh claimed that when he was recruited into an undercover mission during the SFAS at Ft. Bragg, he received orders to report to the NYNG. He told the Jones Team that he joined to keep his rank of sergeant and his retirement benefits. To his biographers, he said the primary reason was to supplement his low-paying job at Burns.

His security guard job at Burns initially entailed a stint as a night watchman at the Buffalo Zoo and the occasional security and crowd-control detail at the Niagara Falls Convention Center for events like World Wrestling Federation matches and monster-truck rallies. However, only weeks after he began the job at Burns, his employers noticed signs of stress and anxiety, and sometimes McVeigh confused appropriate civilian versus military protocols when interacting with the public. His favorite assignment for Burns was the Buffalo Zoo; but, after receiving a series of prank phone calls and tracing them to a former disgruntled employee, McVeigh called the man's home and told his mother that if the calls didn't stop, he would burn down their house.

His Burns supervisor, Lynda Haner-Mele, told the *New York Times* that, finding McVeigh to be "a little too intense for the public," she pulled him from public events in Erie and Niagara County. While a good employee, always prompt and neatly dressed, he had some quirks: "he just couldn't deal with people.... He wasn't a person I could trust to put in a high pressure area.... If someone didn't cooperate with him, he would start yelling at them, become verbally aggressive. He could be set off easily." She described him as "a loner, a follower, not a leader ... if you said, 'Tim, watch this door. Don't let anybody through,'" he did well, but he could not seem to handle situations where he had to "react in a split second." This became apparent to her during one Convention Center event when, while checking the identification of a fifteen-year-old girl, he blew up. "Timmy snapped," said Haner-Mele, "He was very upset. It was like it was night or day.... I worried about him getting out of control." After this incident, she only posted him to low stress, low profile environments, such as guarding the back door at crowded events.[18] McVeigh, however, told his biographers that the crowd made him nervous, so he *requested* assignments with limited public interaction.

Still, her observations were consistent with those of McVeigh's friends, family, COHORTs and his legal team; all of whom noticed a unique character trait. His successes and ability to lead seemed to depend upon his having practiced, rehearsed, memorized and perfected with precision tasks required of him, but when unexpectedly asked to articulate what he knew or act spontaneously he had great difficulty, became impatient and got upset if things did not go by the book. Tim McVeigh's real strength, they said, was in following orders; not necessarily giving or getting others to follow them, a trait that comes to bear on the bombing, his particular role in it and later construction of non-Lone Wolf theories and narratives about it.

THE POLITICAL STRESSORS OF TIM MCVEIGH

Haner-Mele seemed to care for and worry about her new employee, whom she called "Timmy." She described him as paradoxically "boyish yet fiery ... he seemed more like a child to me than an adult man." She said, "He seemed almost lost, like he hadn't really grown up yet.... He didn't really carry himself like he came out of the military.... He didn't stand tall with his shoulders back. He kind of slumped. He was a very, very thin man – almost anorexic. He was the thinnest person I've ever seen." Often, she continued, he seemed socially withdrawn, sometimes cold or expressionless. He never discussed his love or home life and just "wasn't an open type of person, generally."[19]

He told the Jones Team he found his home life "stressful" during this time. For one thing, his sister returned to live with their father shortly before he did and had commandeered his bedroom, relegating him to the couch at night. His consequent inability to get adequate sleep left him agitated and "chronically overtired." Further, he said, his father complained too much, his sister partied too much, and the phone was ringing off the hook. "I got a job at Burns Security, but the stress of working in the city and the political stresses started eating at me slowly. The traffic was stressful, and so was working with idiots. The boss was an asshole, and the pay was low."

When asked to elaborate on the exact nature of his political stresses, he responded, "It's tough to offer examples of political stress at this point because it would take ten pages to explain, but they came from my heightened sense of awareness of what the news was really saying. The news would come on, and I would watch it. I was reading the papers more in depth than I used to, even." Bill McVeigh corroborated this when he recalled the alarm he felt upon seeing his son's recurring "outbursts," yelling and throwing things at the television.

In late 1991 and early 1992, there was a lot in the news. Robert Gates became the director of the CIA. Lebanon released the last of U.S. hostages held there. A U.S. District Court cleared Col. Oliver North of all charges against him relating to the Iran-Contra debacle. Iraq rejected a U.N. Security Council resolution demanding they allow U.N. weapons inspectors and other personnel unconditional access to their weapons facilities and prevented weapons inspectors from taking possession of documents relating to their nuclear weapons program, resulting in a four-day stand-off. The International Atomic Energy Agency ordered Iraq to destroy all facilities manufacturing nuclear weapons and the last oil fire in Kuwait was extinguished much sooner than originally anticipated, through the amazing work of Red Adair and company.

The Cold War officially ended when the Soviet Union dissolved, its president, Mikhail Gorbachev, resigned and Boris Yeltsin replaced him. The majority of Soviet republics seceded. China ratified the Nuclear Non-Proliferation Treaty. World leaders met to discuss the formation of the post-Cold War New World Order. The UN Security Council passed a resolution to deploy peace-keeping troops to Yugoslavia. The U.S. Coast Guard began deporting thousands of Haitian refugees seeking political asylum. David Duke, a former KKK Grand Wizard, unsuccessfully ran for Governor of Louisiana. Arkansas Governor Bill Clinton announced his intention to run for President in the upcoming elections. Magic Johnson, point guard for the LA Lakers, announced he had contracted HIV and Freddie Mercury, lead singer for Queen, died of AIDS-related pneumonia. President George Bush vomited on the Prime Minster of Japan on live TV.

Stickney noted that, even after returning home, McVeigh, always a prolific writer, "authored possibly hundreds and hundreds of letters to friends, agencies, publications, and, of course, relatives."[20] He could talk to Steve in person any time he wanted but continued to write him letters and, ostensibly to save on the price of stamps, personally dropped them in his mailbox. His letters became more political and Steve noticed his friend's opinions had become startlingly more "vehement," although he knew of no local persons or groups who shared McVeigh's strange politics. The letters he wrote to Steve at this time demonstrate the extent to which his obsession with *The Turner Diaries* had grown. For example, only weeks after returning, McVeigh wrote:

> Read this book [*The Turner Diaries*] when you have time to <u>sit down and think</u>. When I read it, I would have to stop at the end of every paragraph and examine the deeper meaning of what I had just read.

The book, without a doubt, has racial overtones, but please read it anyway, just to view the literal genius of it. You can tell it was written as propaganda, but if you can recognize this, it should not be a threat. There are MANY other ideas besides the racism that are expressed [in the book] that really are eye openers.... I know you are set on your racial views and am not giving you this book to convert you. I do, however, want you to understand that "other side" and view the pure literal genius of this piece. Again, this is accomplished by not just simply reading this, but in analyzing every sentence you've read. Think "what made the author write that paragraph," or "what deeper meaning is he trying to convey," or "how by wording it like that, is he trying to subliminally influence someone's thinking." If you look at it like that, it is a masterpiece. Again, it is a very high profile book, every pro and in between person in America knows something about it. Let me know what you think, I'm sure you will.

When Steve responded by voicing his negative reaction to the book, Tim went ballistic and in his next letter, dated February 24, 1992, he said that Steve's poor opinion of the book had caused him to lose sleep and even threatened to end their lifelong friendship. Tim accused Steve of "[turning] into the typical Amherst persona ... [who] view[s] the world with rose colored glasses ... make[s] a decent living ... ha[s] a home to go home to, a nice car to drive ... cable TV, your $900 a year health club, your warm living room and secure job, so everything is fine." Meanwhile, for Timothy McVeigh, nothing was fine.

He began writing a series of letters to local newspapers and politicians that Stickney described as a "furious jumble over numerous unrelated social and political problems."[21] Stickney's employer, the *Lockport Union-Sun & Journal,* published two of them. In the first, on February 11, 1992, McVeigh outlined his complaints about the world to which he had returned. These included rising crime rates, overcrowded prisons, increasing racism and taxes, all of which, he said, had reached "cataclysmic levels with no end in sight." To McVeigh, nobody was seeing the big picture. Curiously employing a language of illness, he explained that laws passed by career politicians only "dilute a problem for a while, until the problem comes roaring back in a worsened form (much like a strain of bacteria will alter itself to defeat a known medication)." To stem the ongoing avalanche of decay he, rather surprisingly, suggested combining ideologies and adapting the "communist idea of state sponsored health care" and closed the letter by asking, "Is civil war imminent? Do we have to shed blood to reform the current system? I hope it doesn't come to that, but it might."

In the second letter, published on March 10, 1992, he wrote that, traditionally, hunting animals for food was a means of survival. Hunters killed animals quickly with a "clean, merciful shot" and then the animal "dies in his own environment, quick and unexpected." Currently, however, people thoughtlessly purchased cellophane-wrapped meat at the grocery store, never questioning the process of how it got there in the first place. The breeding conditions of these animals, especially cattle, were cruel, and deprived animals of their innate dignity. He ended the letter by asking, "Would you rather die while living happily, or die while leading a miserable life? You tell me which is more humane." It was during this time, late winter of 1992, that McVeigh, never a hunter, drove out to a field near Attica Prison, and, in an act he said surprised even himself and left him unsettled for days, pointed his gun at a woodchuck and, like the Iraqis in their trenches, aimed at its head and killed it.

The majority of accounts written about McVeigh cite such letters as proof of his increasingly hostile and radical political leanings. For instance, Hamm said they "offer a glimpse into the right wing milieu as it existed prior to Ruby Ridge and Waco" and, not knowing the extent of McVeigh's medical odyssey, keenly observed that they also illustrated "the disintegration of [his] mind and body ... [and his] obsession with the atrophy of his body, as a correlate of the modern body politic [and] McVeigh's own private hell."[22]

THE BREAKDOWN

Simply put, Timothy McVeigh snapped. To Herbeck and Michel, he relayed the following story: One cold and snowy afternoon about three months after his return to New York, he went to his grandfather Ed McVeigh's house. Upon greeting him at the door, Ed was startled to find his grandson standing there with no shoes, socks, or shirt, dressed only in sweatpants and in an apparent "state of panic and despair." Tim refused to tell his grandfather the nature of his problem, saying only that he thought he was having a nervous breakdown and asked if he could take a nap. As he lay alone, "he was overcome by dark thoughts. He considered killing himself" but soon fell into a "deep sleep." Upon waking, he left his grandfather's house and the two never spoke of the incident again, though Tim said he would forever regret not knowing how to explain his anxieties to his grandfather.[23]

Unknown to his biographers, in bits and pieces during the two years prior to the bombing, he had told a variation of this story to his sister Jennifer who, shortly after her brother's arrest, related it to the FBI and the Jones Team. According to Jennifer, Tim told her that his classified domestic intelligence mission disturbed him greatly, "totally crashed his feelings" about the government, "shattered his dreams," left him "completely disillusioned" and sent him into "intense turmoil." His experience at the SFAS and subsequent contact with his "handlers" was "a major turning point" in his life.

After leaving the Army, he attempted to move on and put the past behind him by ignoring and trying to forget about his secret assignment but one day, a mysterious man unexpectedly arrived at the doorstep of his fathers house, reminded him of his obligations and warned that, if he failed to comply with his orders, he would face criminal charges. Her brother now believed he was being "tracked down" by the military and feared for not only his own life but the safety of his family. The burden of what he knew "continued to weigh on him" and became too great to bear alone. He "just couldn't keep it bottled up inside," "keep up the pretense that all was right with the world" ... "[live] a normal life knowing what he now knew," or arrive at a solution for his dilemma and considered suicide. Finally, in a panic, he drove to their grandfather's house, explained the situation, swore him to secrecy and cried for hours.

Jennifer said that after his breakdown, her brother was noticeably more anxious, restless, scared and acted confused. She described his fear as noticeable, "real"... "enduring," and one he would continue to express to her and others over the following three years. His claimed belief of being tracked by the Army is absent from or under-emphasized and under-examined in all previously published accounts and remains an issue which, whether real or not, appears to play a very important part in the secret life of Timothy McVeigh.

As noted previously, in his account of his alleged conversations with McVeigh, death-row inmate David Paul Hammer wrote that, while at the Special Forces try-out McVeigh was recruited by the "Major" to work on Department of Defense Black Ops projects, so secret even the Secretary of Defense was unaware that the unit even existed. Although, in Hammer's version (or the one McVeigh told him), he hadn't completely rejected the mission and was still "on board":

> [McVeigh] was to familiarize himself with the rhetoric of the extreme right ideology, and to create a plausible aura of a disgruntled soldier. He was to await further instructions. As with all other assignments, McVeigh immersed himself completely.... In December of 1991, McVeigh left the army as an active duty soldier. He returned to his Dad's home in upstate New York where he took on the role of just being a civilian; no one ever knowing of his sleeper agent status. Tim was anxious to hear from the Major and to proceed with whatever specific assignment that may lie ahead of him.[24]

A LITTLE R&R

Shortly after the incident at his grandfather's, McVeigh was promoted to a desk job as scheduling supervisor at the Burns Security HQ office. Here, he met receptionist and personnel manager Andrea Augustine, with whom he developed his only enduring and close, yet platonic, relationship with a female other than his sister. Augustine found him to be a thoughtful, nice person she could rely on and confide in, and soon their friendship extended beyond work hours. Augustine described her impressions:

> He did really well as a security guard, so they brought him in the office to do scheduling. We worked a lot in the office together. At first, he was very quiet, socially awkward, and kind of shy, but the more I started working with him the more I saw he was a nice guy. I liked his personality. He was fun. I liked working with him ... we were always talking and joking. He was joking around all the time. He was very outgoing and funny but you wouldn't know that if you first met him but after talking to him he'd come out of his shell and let loose. I never visited him at his home, but he came to mine a few times. We talked on the phone every day after work for hours though. We were good friends.

While he never went into details about it, Augustine said her new friend told her that he had killed people during the war, fondly recalled how he kept her up to date on current news events and even mentioned the letters he wrote to the local papers. Augustine, who had no political inclinations, said his occasional rants about the second amendment and other issues were of no concern, but she did note that he was "strong willed" about them. "If he believes in something," she said, "that's it. You will not change his mind." She remembered that Tim, unable to engage her in his political discussions, persistently attempted to draw his male co-workers into them, often brought related literature to work and occasionally handed out news articles. "Sometimes the guys just didn't want to get caught up talking about his political stuff. They didn't care. They would listen to him and debate, but Tim didn't care. He wanted to keep going, and they were like 'SHUT UP!'"

Still, according to her, most of their coworkers considered McVeigh a good employee who always did as instructed.[25] As scheduler at the Burns office, he managed 400 security guards in the Buffalo area, but it was only a matter of months before even the office position became a source of overwhelming anxiety for him. Thus, although technically a demotion, he requested a transfer back to guard duty and, specifically, that he be assigned to Calspan, a local defense contractor whose main facility is located across from the Buffalo International Airport.

McVeigh confirmed this to his attorneys and further explained that he got along poorly with his "tyrannical" boss at the office and since the Calspan site required a security clearance that he held, requested the transfer. Rather than having him quit altogether, he said, his higher-ups at Burns agreed to "push me out to Calspan" for some "R&R," although it was not much of a demotion, he said, because while at Calspan, despite his "doing practically nothing there," he received full benefits and was secretly paid $2 more than his supervisors. The money, he said, had not been included in his regular paycheck, and instead, he picked it up at the Burns office so the other guards would not find out.

NORTHSTAR & PATCON

Carl Le Bron, another guard posted at Calspan who became acquainted with McVeigh described his first impressions:

> I was working as a guard at Calspan a few months before McVeigh was transferred there. Calspan does security work for the government and to get posted there you have to have a background check and a security clearance, so it's hard to find people for that post. It's not a high level clearance, but a lower level one that simply allows you to walk through the buildings. McVeigh had a military background and a security clearance. When I met [him] he was a very friendly outgoing person; very straight laced, clean cut, a military type. He had a military bearing. When you met him you'd think "this guy's gonna be a cop" or something. He looked like he was fresh out of the service; in good shape.... He was really thin though. I knew from conversations we had that he was a veteran from the original Iraq conflict, but I didn't know he was in the local National Guard. Sometimes the other guys who'd been in the military would talk to him about military stuff, and they'd bring in their medals and show each other.

Lebron then described, or tried to describe, the type of work conducted at the facility he and McVeigh guarded:

> Calspan had a couple different buildings around. It's a national company, and they have office and research centers in other parts of the country, too. Mostly associated with ... well, I won't say. They have other places they do work at, too. You can find some stuff in the *Buffalo News*. If you want to ask them (Calspan) you should, but I don't want say much. I can only really talk freely about what's already been reported in the public media but I can't really go any farther than that. Anything questionable, I have to stop, I can't talk about it. I don't want to get in trouble with the Government. They do work on airplanes for the U.S. and foreign governments, NASA, as well as computer programing, car testing as far as car crashes and baby seat safety and basic stuff like that. I can tell you about the flight hangar because the public can see it.[26]

Herbeck and Michel wrote that "from the moment he set foot on the [Calspan] property, [McVeigh] was intrigued":

At every opportunity, McVeigh asked Calspan workers about their work. And when a directive came down instructing the night watchmen to steer clear of certain portions of the plant, McVeigh took it as a personal invitation to poke around. Unable to contain his curiosity, he prowled the wind and shock tunnels at night, looking in on the latest research.... In one of the Calspan buildings, McVeigh discovered that the federal government was renting out space for a secretive law enforcement project called Operation North Star. The project was housed in an ultra-secure area, with entry by special code. McVeigh had caught a glimpse of some paperwork that led him to believe that the U.S. military, Federal Marshals, and Drug Enforcement Administration agents were occupying the space.... One night, he noticed an oddly written memo on a desk. It read like an old-fashioned telegram, with the word 'STOP' following each sentence of the message. It mentioned the possibility of a two man submarine penetrating the rivers in the United States, but failed to say why. McVeigh wondered whether the government suspected drug dealers of using such subs in sophisticated smuggling operations. His guesses weren't far off: years later, the government would confirm that it had operated a secret drug interdiction program from office space at Calspan.[27]

Lebron said that, even after quitting the job and leaving upstate New York, McVeigh's interest in Calspan continued:

After McVeigh left Buffalo, he wrote me letters. In one, he said, that while he was working at Calspan as a guard, he found a document in an office of one floor of the building that was rented out to a government agency. He claimed the document stated that mini submarines were bringing drugs into the country and that, quote, "dredging operations on the Mississippi River were to support the access of submarines into the United States of America." To me, it seemed more like fantasy than fact. He invited me to share anything I may come across related to this with him, which I didn't do. I did mention it to the FBI after his arrest, though He would ask about what was going on at Calspan, and I gave general responses and spoke in generalities. I suggested to him that if he really had any evidence of something he should come forth with it.[28]

While it is unknown what McVeigh may have stumbled across in his rounds at the Calspan facility, it was here that, whether real, solely in McVeigh's imagination or some combination thereof, the Guilty Agent story he told over the subsequent years grew and where the roots of many later Experimental Wolf narratives told about him can be found. Hammer wrote that while McVeigh was still at the Special Forces/Black Op recruitment at Ft. Bragg, The Major "explained that the agenda for this se-cret unit was primarily domestic intelligence gathering and internal threat evaluations with an emphasis on direct counter-action operations." In this story, McVeigh was then instructed to quit the Army, return to Buffalo, bone up on his right-wing rhetoric and await further instruction.[29] Inter-estingly, while not publicly known until many years later, during the time McVeigh worked at Calspan it was indeed the staging ground for an un-dercover operation that involved his other employer, the National Guard; thus rendering some of the alternative stories told by McVeigh and later others, if not probable, at least more plausible and less irrational.

The 1878 Posse Comitatus Act prohibited the U.S. military from en-forcing civil law on U.S. soil without express authority from the President or Congress and/or as needed to quell "lawlessness, insurrection and re-bellion," restore government order, prevent loss of life and wanton destruc-tion of property, and protect federal property and governmental operations. Statutory amendments followed. This simply meant that, except under those circumstances, the military could not detain or arrest civilians.

Unfortunately, Posse Comitatus has been popularly misunderstood as prohibiting the military from *any* role in civilian law enforcement un-der *all* circumstances while, in truth, Posse Comitatus never applied to the use of the National Guard (which is conceived as a State military rath-er than a Federal one). Indeed, throughout U.S. history, in so-called times of national emergency, both the National Guard and active-duty troops have been called on to assist in civilian policing actions and have conduct-ed domestic intelligence and counterintelligence operations.

Throughout the 1980s, by the directives of Presidents Reagan and Bush and under the auspices of assisting the War on Drugs, incremental exceptions (or clarifications) were made to Posse Comitatus that allowed the military to assist in civilian policing by providing equipment, person-nel, facilities and sharing intelligence with local, state and federal law en-forcement agencies. Reagan-Bush era policies advanced the Low Intensity Conflict resolution model, the goal of which was the resolution of foreign and domestic conflicts by controlling targeted civilian populations by way of an integrated military and civilian police force whose roles and meth-ods would be interchangeable (i.e. police become more militarized and the military engages in civilian policing and domestic social-control functions). The Low Intensity Conflict goal was further outlined and advanced in the 1989 Defense Authorization Act (DAA), which defined the post-Cold War role of the military as one increasingly blended with civilian policing, jus-tified by claims that the transport of illegal drugs over the border posed a "direct threat to the sovereignty and security of the country."[30]

While the National Guard traditionally did not have as many restric-tions as other branches of the military when it came to civilian policing, there were some, but in 1987, the National Defense Appropriations Act directed the National Guard to provide "full cooperation" with civilian law enforcement agencies conducting counter-drug operations. By 1989, some National Guard units were participating in searches and arrests (activities previously denied them). By 1992, such practices were commonplace.[31]

Also throughout the mid-to-late 1980s and early 1990s, significant and increasing numbers of American police departments received training from Special Operations military units and were closely involved with the Navy Seals and Army Rangers. In 1989, under the authorization of the DAA, Secretary of Defense Dick Cheney initiated Operation Alliance, a Department of Defense-led effort based in Texas that, in coordination with federal, state, and local agencies, ostensibly attempted to facilitate a rapid response to the threat of illegal drugs, firearms and other contraband from crossing the U.S.-Mexican border. Operation Alliance was an "unprecedented program of police-military-security forces" using Advanced Operations on Urbanized Terrain (MOUNT), the very tactic the Army had trained McVeigh in during his trip to Germany and employing the same methods he complained about after returning.[32]

In 1989, an Alliance spinoff was initiated, codenamed 'NORTH-STAR,' which focused on the U.S.-Canadian border. While Herbeck and Michel make only brief mention of this operation and its staging at the Buffalo Calspan facility, they offer no further details, assumedly viewing it as irrelevant. According to a report issued by the National Center For State and Local Law Enforcement Training, NORTHSTAR's specific purpose was to "expand and enhance multi-agency operations and avoid unwarranted duplication and accidental interference between independent operations." Like Alliance, NORTHSTAR utilized the equipment, personnel and intelligence of, and coordinated with, several federal agencies, including the DOD, FBI, DEA, Border Patrol, Customs, U.S. Coast Guard, and New York National Guard.[33] While NORTHSTAR began as part of the counter-offensive in the War On Drugs, it came to take on national security and counter-terrorism functions as well.

The primary group responsible for conducting Alliance/NORTH-STAR operations was Joint Task Force 6 (JTF-6). JTF-6 operatives received training at the U.S. Army Special Operations Command at Fort Bragg, NC., and were subsequently deployed in the domestic field. Of the over 4,000 soldiers involved in JTF-6 in 1992, only a small portion were active-duty, including at least 50 members of the Special Forces, while the majority were culled from National Guard units. In fact, one of the main administrative functions of JTF-6 was the coordination of National Guard units. Among their duties, operatives provided intelligence analysis, armed reconnaissance, weapons, communications and training to civilian law enforcement agencies and participated in real-world tactical exercises.

Further, they provided equipment, transportation, reconnaissance and imagery and collected other types of intelligence data "pertaining to individuals, businesses, and organized crime groups which are known to be, or suspected of, engaging in criminal activity," data that was to be developed and analyzed, stored in DOD collection centers and distributed only to military units. Beyond their supporting role, JTF-6 active and reserve-duty soldiers were *lent* to civilian agencies for direct actions – long and short-term assignments to conduct surveillance and counterintelligence activities within elaborate nationwide sting operations. The role of the National Guard in the new 'total integration' policy was significant and Guard troops could perform arrests and needed no warrant to search private property, including homes and automobiles.[34]

In order to fight the War on Drugs, the Clinton administration continued to erode existing Posse Comitatus restrictions. The "war model" or "military model" of crime control led not only to an increased militarization of civilian police, now greatly assisted by the military and operating with a "war mentality," but also further use of the military in civilian law enforcement, intelligence and counter-intelligence operations. Justifications in the name of the drug war were somewhat nullified in the minds of some however, because of previous and more recent revelations of the CIA's and military's role in drug-smuggling operations.

As McVeigh guarded NORTHSTAR's regional headquarters at Calspan, his other employer at the time, the National Guard, was coordinating with another multi-agency task force as well, this one headed by the FBI, called PATCON (short for Patriot Conspiracy). While McVeigh was seemingly aware that NORTHSTAR existed (although not necessarily under that name), PATCON's existence was unknown to the public until 2007, when it was revealed through a Freedom Of Information Act request (although many details surrounding it remain hidden).

The forerunner of PATCON began during the mid-to-late 1980s when local, state, and federal law enforcement agencies became aware of and began investigations into the radical right-wing and White Power Movement (WPM) individuals, groups and organizations. While less sophisticated racists engaged in brutal hate crimes against minorities, a faction of more calculating adherents, who considered themselves part of an underground war against "the system," stayed out of sight and employed a variety of guerrilla tactics including bank robberies, counterfeit operations, weapons-trafficking, and small-scale bombings (the most notorious of these being The Order). One of the largest organized white supremacist groups in existence at this time was the Aryan Nations (AN). Individuals associated with the Idaho-based AN as well as AN leadership were directly linked to a number of violent criminal plots. Eventually, undercover FBI and ATF agents and the paid and unpaid informants they recruited penetrated most, if not all, known AN chapters; but while these efforts resulted in some arrests and convictions during the late 1980s, the plots continued.

By 1990, undercover federal informants and agents positioned within targeted groups began warning about the ongoing development of violent criminal conspiracies now involving not only the WPM but also their allies in the burgeoning Patriot Movement. Among the activities planned or executed were the theft and black market sale of automatic weapons, LAW rockets, night vision goggles, grenades, and other equipment from National Guard armories and other military bases. The FBI continued to gather information about these schemes and, in March 1991, FBI Assistant Director Larry Potts authorized PATCON, a national multi-agency domestic anti-terrorism initiative meant to disrupt these plots and bring criminal charges against the conspirators.

In January 1992, a PATCON informant revealed to the FBI the ambitious plans of one of the targeted groups, the Texas Reserve Militia (TRM), to ambush a National Guard convoy during an annual training exercise. The TRM, believing that the Guard conducted these simulations with unloaded weapons, planned to interrupt the annual exercise and steal the weapons. The FBI passed this information to the Guard and directed its field offices to maintain coordination with the DOD. An FBI teletype dated February 4, 1992, written by AD Potts to the commanding general of the Army's Criminal Investigative Division, alerted him to the existence of a number of items stolen from military bases that had been found in locations throughout the country, including gas masks and "other assorted items" such as bombs and a number of bomb-making components.[35] After this, the stated justifications and objectives of PATCON shifted and its allotted budget, manpower, reach and authorized tactics, expanded.

DREAMING IN THE APPALACHIANS

While the extent to which McVeigh had direct or indirect knowledge of ongoing domestic security operations involving his two employers is unknown, within six months he would find himself in the middle of PATCON's investigatory hub. Before this though, shortly after his assignment to Calspan, McVeigh made a series of curious decisions. Herbeck and Michel observed that in late May of 1992,

> McVeigh ended the one relationship in his life that had given him glory and satisfaction. He resigned from the Army reserve unit in Tonawanda, three months ahead of its deactivation date. He cited "employment conflict" as his reason for leaving. In addition to his office job as a scheduler at Burns, he often worked long hours of overtime as a guard. Something had to give, and cutting his connection to the United States government seemed like a good place to start.

Stickney, in his account, noted that, "Tim would spend five months and a day in the guard's employ. The Guard may be the only place in his whole life where Tim didn't leave much of an impression. Just about everywhere else he would travel in his entire twenty-seven years, there are people who remember him in some odd way – something he said or did. For some reason, the guard is the only place where, with a few notable exceptions, he would be remembered pretty much by name, a uniform tag, and time of employment only."[36]

While several men stationed at the same armory could not remember him at all, he left a faint trace of an impression on a few of them. A clerk at the NYNG armory reported to the FBI that he first met McVeigh during a two-day weekend drill and that McVeigh ended up working in the same office, also as a clerk. A NYNG sergeant in charge of the Combat Supply Company told the FBI he had limited contact with McVeigh but remembered he was part of a 23-man anti-tank missile platoon. NYNG Staff Sgt. Thomas Kazmerczak told the *Buffalo News* that McVeigh "was always good and punctual" and was the "leader of an anti-tank missile squad" while there. Captain Daniel Crowe told the FBI McVeigh "had an attendance problem" and although he had a two-year commitment to the Guard, because of an excess of sergeants there and based on his combat record, he had received an honorable discharge after six months.[37]

Characteristically, the reasons McVeigh gave his friends and family for leaving the Guard also varied. To his aunt he said the unit had been disbanded and he was being transferred to a "mechanized reserve unit" operating out of nearby Genesee Valley. One secretary at Calspan and her husband both told the FBI that they had "heard" McVeigh had been kicked out of the Guard. To friend and co-worker, Andrea Augustine, he said he left because his NYNG commitment "conflicted with his heavy work load at Burns."

Given the existence of PATCON and NORTHSTAR at this time, their objectives and relation to the National Guard, McVeigh's statements to his sister and his first attorneys are curiously noteworthy. As outlined previously, McVeigh told Jennifer that during the SFAS at Ft. Bragg he was informed that his covert assignment entailed acting as a "military consultant working hand in hand with civilian police agencies" in the U.S. Further, within days of his arrest he told public defenders Otto and Coyle he was "recruited by the government while serving a four to five month period in the National Guard" and tasked with "Neo-Nazis and other problem troops."

In December 1995, when a Jones Team investigator asked McVeigh how long he had been in the National Guard, his job description and the reasons he left, McVeigh became "clearly annoyed." McVeigh said he "could not recall his exact job description" but did remember that the unit eventually disbanded; a strange response given his detailed memories of his military career prior to joining the Guard. When he demanded to know *why* the investigator was so interested in his NYNG stint, the investigator told him that Otto and Coyle had informed the Jones Team about his earlier claims. McVeigh's severe reaction was noted in an internal defense memo: "Mr. McVeigh immediately became angry and yelled out several curse words directed at [his first attorney]. I immediately asked Mr. McVeigh if there was any truth to [those statements] and Mr. McVeigh replied that parts of it were true and other parts were untrue." Although McVeigh "soon settled down," when the investigator tried to discuss the matter again, he said that it was all "pure bullshit" and then "waved his hands in a gesture to let me know that he no longer wanted to talk about [the subject]."

Although he had earlier told the Jones Team that his job at Calspan was easy and demanded "practically nothing" from him, during a separate interview in September 1995 he said his NYNG obligations were too much for him, "I quickly found out I couldn't handle even one weekend a month. It was all fucked up." In yet another conversation, he told them a very different and somewhat strange story about his decision to leave the Guard. During the spring of 1992, he said, he began to feel "very frustrated," and, to channel his anxieties, joined a volleyball league but quit after he "almost beat up a line judge." He then joined a floor hockey league but quit because he was "out of shape." On one of his days off work, he drove to the Appalachian Mountains and when he got there, lay on the ground "fell asleep and had very intense dreams for about 30 minutes." Upon waking, he decided to quit the NYNG.

To the Jones Team, this was yet another example of the numerous, ever-changing and inconsistent stories McVeigh told about his life prior to the bombing. Still, members of the Jones Team wondered if there was any truth to the story he told his sister and public defenders, so they increased their efforts at obtaining complete military records. In the process, they learned of McVeigh's own efforts to do so earlier. In early April 1992, McVeigh requested a complete set of his military records including, among other things, a list of service related medals, awards, commendations, and his medical files. Then, on May 1, 1992, he wrote the letter to the NYNG requesting an early discharge, citing as his reason a "recent promotion at my full-time place of employment" that conflicted with his NYNG obligations. Attached to McVeigh's letter was one written on his behalf the same day by his supervisor at Burns:

> To Whom It May Concern: This communication is being sent to confirm that Timothy J. McVeigh (an employee of Burns International Security) has recently been promoted to a supervisory position. This position requires that he be on call after normal business hours, Monday through Friday, as well as all day and night on weekends. Should he receive a call, the supervisor must be available to head immediately into work (such calls are unfortunately, all too common in the security industry). The on call supervisor must han-

dle any problems dealing with sick or absent security officers, as well as problems with our respective clients. Supervisor McVeigh's Army National Guard "drills" interfere greatly with his ability to perform this specific job. As we understand that "Sergeant" McVeigh has requested to be released from his commitment with the NYARNG, we can only hope that you will grant him this reprieve.

Capt. Crowe personally reviewed and approved the requests and on May 1, 1992, wrote, "I interviewed SGT McVeigh, and in doing so, I realized that his civilian promotion to a supervisory position has caused him to work evenings and weekends. Although SGT McVeigh is requesting an early discharge, he hoped that he will be able to return and complete his military career. I understand and grant his request and hope you will do the same." On June 1, 1992, the NYNG granted his request, deactivated him and reassigned him to the Army Reserve Reinforcement Unit. His obligation to the Reserves would end on March 11, 1996, during which time he could be subjected to annual screenings and training and active duty recall at any time. The same day his transfer out of the NYNG was approved, McVeigh received notification that the DOD was in receipt of his records request, but it is unknown what, if any, portions he received.

Immediately after his NYNG discharge McVeigh sought employment and took entrance exams with the very agencies whose policies he railed against; agencies connected to both PATCON and NORTHSTAR operations. The first was with the Niagara Falls based Border Patrol, yet after passing the screening test, they informed him that no positions were available. Weeks after his arrest, the FBI attempted to locate and interview certain "close associates" of McVeigh's working in the Buffalo area Border Patrol. Next, McVeigh took the exam required for employment with the United States Marshalls Service, receiving one of the highest recorded scores. He did not get the job, however, and later blamed it on reverse discrimination due to affirmative action.[38]

AMERINOID

Steve Hodge said that after returning home, McVeigh's personality quirks became increasingly drastic to the point that he felt he no longer recognized his childhood friend. His rhetoric had now moved beyond talk of the right to bear arms and, during their infrequent conversations, McVeigh inevitably began railing about secret conspiracies involving "factions of the government who wanted to gain world domination" as well as the government's plans to set up "concentration camps" for U.S. citizens.

McVeigh's ideas did not originate in a vacuum. Rumors among militia and patriot circles about secret concentration camps had circulated for years. Ironically, despite McVeigh's anxieties about these hypothetical camps, he seemed to feel no compunction about sharing his growing library of racist, hate-mongering literature with co-workers. Lebron recalled how their conversations quickly turned from innocuous talk of UFOs and other "fun" conspiracy theories (highlighted later within this chapter) to much more serious and troubling topics. McVeigh, he said, was consumed by "reactionary 'no government' ideal[s]" and began bringing in, not just news clippings of political scandals but KKK newspapers or other magazines like *The White Patriot* that "had pictures of guys in sheets":

> He brought *The White Patriot* one day and was showing it around while the guard shack was full of people. After the bombing, another one of the guards gave it to the FBI. One time there was an article in the *Spotlight* denying the Holocaust, and we talked about that, so, I guess I'd say there was a slight disconnect from historical reality. McVeigh definitely had a more aggressive stance on racial issues. I felt like he was sharing the *Spotlight* and that type of literature because he was looking to recruit people either into an organization or into his ultimate goal, which, as you know, became apparent later.[39]

Bill McVeigh recalled that during this time his son was rarely home, but when he was, "all he would do is watch the news shows and talk about the government." McVeigh explained to his attorneys that among his complaints at this time were ongoing U.S. foreign actions he viewed as attempts to bully other countries into compliance and the government's attempts to control U.S. citizens, mainly through incrementally restrictive gun laws. Further, he was becoming even angrier about the growing militarization of domestic police forces and their increasing co-operation with U.S. troops. He was joined in this last complaint by a disparate coalition of activists and civil libertarians on the right and left.

Although the issue attracted much controversy, advocates argued it was necessary to help combat organized crime, stop domestic terrorism threats and aid in hostage situations. This came to a head in Ruby Ridge, Idaho, on August 21, 1992, after a joint ATF-FBI action adopting military tactics and, with the help of JTF-6, utilizing military equipment and personnel, turned deadly and drew attention to the very thing McVeigh was fretting over.

In 1987, a highly-paid undercover ATF confidential informant, whose real name was Kenneth Faderly but who called himself "Gus Magisano," began frequenting Aryan Nations (AN) headquarters in Coeur D'Alene, Idaho. While his main targets were high ranking AN members and associates, including AN founder Richard Butler, Gus would need to *turn* rank and file AN attendees in order to get dirt on his real targets. In an effort to appear as *the real deal*, Gus made numerous pronouncements about his intent to engage in criminal activities to further the AN cause.

One of the people he met was Randy Weaver who, while not a card-carrying member of AN, held similar views, lived off the grid in nearby Ruby Ridge, Idaho with his wife and four children, and occasionally visited there. For two years, from 1987 until late 1989, Gus incessantly attempted to persuade Weaver to sell him illegal weapons. Weaver continued to rebuff Gus but eventually, suffering financial difficulties, finally agreed to sell him two sawed-off shotguns for $300. This gave the ATF leverage against Weaver and they approached him with a deal: they would not file criminal charges against him if he agreed to became an informant and spy on Aryan Nations.

Much to their surprise, Weaver refused and the ATF filed criminal charges against him in June 1990, falsely describing Weaver as a bank robber and convict in their report. In December 1990, a federal grand jury indicted Weaver, for the possession (not sale) of illegal weapons, after which he was arrested, given a summons to appear in court and released. The date listed on the summons, however, was March 20, 1991 instead of the *actual* court date, February 19. When Weaver failed to show up for the February 19 court date (understandably, as he thought it was scheduled for March), a warrant was issued for his arrest. Weaver refused to turn himself in to authorities and instead, now a federal fugitive, chose to remain on his remote property with his family. For the next 16 months, his cabin was placed under intensive surveillance by federal authorities.

Enter twenty-one year old Johnny Bangerter, leader of the Army of Israel, a group of racist skinheads in Las Vegas and Utah and ranking member of and national spokesperson for the Aryan Nations.[i] Bangerter was related to Randy Weaver through marriage and best friends with Weaver's nephew. They had met several times at the Aryan Nations headquarters in Idaho where Bangerter acted as head of security for their meetings and 'festivals'. Bangerter himself had been unsuccessfully targeted in a number of undercover operations and was present when Weaver met Gus. Bangerter, who in later years disavowed and publicly renounced his racial ideologies, recalled the atmosphere at Aryan Nations events prior to Weaver's arrest:

> It was well known that at any Aryan Nation event, in a crowd of 300 people, there'd be at least 30 undercover federal agents in attendance to monitor us, and another third of the crowd were informants. Another handful were sent by watchdog groups such as the SPLC to infiltrate us. It was rampant, just like cops at a Grateful Dead show trying to sell people LSD. It was just a big mess. We were young kids, fresh at Aryan Nations. We were instructed by the head of security there, not to engage in crimes or even talk

---

i Bangerter, whom the *Salt Lake Tribune* described as "one of the most prominent skinheads in the country," was known for his provocative statements to the media. He made regular television appearances on daytime talk shows, including *Geraldo* and *The Montel Williams Show* on behalf of the AN and was the subject of countless news articles.

about illegal actions ... to document everything you did. That way, if somebody does try to frame you or implicate you in a crime, you have your story straight and will be protected by your alibi. Ironically, it turned out later that the head of security at Aryan Nations himself, the guy who taught us this stuff, had himself been an informant.

In time, I rose through the ranks at Aryan Nations and became one of the of the primary people responsible for implementing security measures there and I took this job to heart. We weren't so much trying to prevent the anti-Klan protestors from getting in the compound or the SPLC's subversions and attempts to get information. My instructions, directly handed down from Richard Butler, were to monitor events at Aryan Nations, spot, weed out and warn other attendees about suspected or confirmed federal agents, informants and provocateurs and prevent them from getting caught up in the sting operations the ATF and FBI were conducting.

We quickly came to learn, first hand, the tactics used in a sting operation. It was always the same thing. They would come up to you and say "Nigger this" or "Jew that," talk about automatic weapons and suggest you join them in criminal actions, sometimes *violent* criminal actions like leveling a courthouse or killing a federal judge. We knew those kinds of conversations were entrapment and conspiracy. And we would tell people, "if someone comes up to you and starts talking like that, PLEASE don't engage them in conversation." If they brought up automatic weapons or if they wanted us to mess around with explosives or commit any crimes that would result in a prison sentence, they were probably federal agents, informants or operatives of some sort and working against us. It was a dead giveaway. That's just not how we talked. That's how they *thought* we talked. That's how they wanted us to talk. And that's how Gus talked and I just knew in my gut he was ATF when I met him and he just kept saying things that, in my mind, confirmed my suspicions. I tried to warn Randy about Gus but he wouldn't listen. He didn't want to believe me.[40]

On August 5, 1992, the FBI approved the continuation and expansion of it's PATCON program. On August 21, 1992, the U.S. Marshals surveilling Weaver's property threw rocks at his cabin in an attempt to determine how the Weaver's dogs would respond. When the dogs began barking, Randy's 14-year-old son Sammy and Kevin Harris, a family friend, came outside to see why. The Marshalls, from a hidden position in the surrounding woods, then shot and killed Sammy's dog, prompting Sammy to fire a warning shot, after which he began running back towards the cabin. As he did, one of the Marshals shot him in the back, killing him instantly. Harris and the Marshals then engaged in a firefight, during which U.S. Marshal William Degan was killed.

At the start of the 12-day standoff that ensued, the Marshals were joined by hundreds of local police, agents from the ATF, FBI, US Marshals, US Border Patrol and troops from the FBI's Hostage Rescue Team and the National Guard until, eventually, 400 armed federal agents surrounded the Weaver cabin, occupied now by three surviving children (10 months to 14 years old), Weaver and Harris, and Randy's wife Vicki. In what already seemed like overkill, JTF-6 was called in to provide agents with supplies and conduct reconnaissance flights over the property using military helicopters.

In the meantime, hundreds of protestors from both the left and right of the political spectrum arrived at Ruby Ridge, getting as close to the scene as they could. Among them were undercover PATCON operatives as well as some of the most well-known Patriot and White Power movement activists, including Johnny Bangerter who recounted:

> In the summer of 1992, while Randy Weaver and his family were under siege by the federal government, I went up to Ruby Ridge. I saw what happened there first hand; many things that never even get talked about; that never got reported in the media. It is still difficult for me to think and talk about the things I saw and experienced there. The first thing I noticed when I got there was the massive military presence and hundreds of federal agents.
>
> At some point, ATF agents had thrown gunny sacks filled with phosphorous in the creek so that, if someone tried to cross over it, it would light up and alert the agents. A man, one of the protestors who'd come there to support Weaver, took his dog to the creek so it could drink some water. The ATF pointed their guns at him and ordered him to get back. The man explained that he was just trying to give his dog some water, and they started laughing and said, 'Oh. Okay. Go ahead then.' So the dog drank from the creek and the ATF agents burst out laughing even harder. We couldn't figure out what they were laughing about. I was watching the entire thing. That entire night the dog threw up blood and by the next morning, the dog was dead. Well, as strange as it sounds, the day after they put the phosphorous in the creek, everything in the creek was dead. You would never have known how many fish were in that creek until you saw them all floating up at the top, every one of them dead. They were washing up to the shore for a mile downstream. There were farm animals that drank from that water as well and they died too.
>
> Randy Weaver's nephew, John Reynolds, who was also my brother in law, was there with us. We had just found out that Sammy Weaver was dead. There was a news crew filming and we started talking to the agents standing around nearby. A ten-year-old boy was standing not too far from us and I asked the agents how they could kill a kid, how they could do something like that, and in response, an ATF agent with a beard and a cowboy hat, lowered

his rifle and aimed it at the boy as if to say 'Like this. That's how.' I couldn't believe it. For the first time I realized there are people that could perform a My Lai Massacre without thinking and then say they were just following orders. Well, I saw it firsthand at Ruby Ridge. Before that, I did not know the kind of evil that people are capable of ... but there, at Ruby Ridge, I saw it face to face. What I met up there, what I saw in the faces of those federal agents, was evil and it only got worse.

Bangerter told reporters that the federal officers present at Ruby Ridge as well as the federal government would be held responsible for allowing Sammy Weaver to be mercilessly killed "in cold blood" and warned that there would soon be a "second revolution in America....and it could be bloody."[41]

Unknown to the Weavers or their supporters outside, at some point after Sammy was killed, FBI Director Larry Potts changed the standard rules of engagement protocols for the snipers positioned around the Weaver property, who under normal circumstances could only fire if fired upon. The new rules of engagement amounted to a military assault style "shoot on sight" plan. So, when Randy, along with his oldest daughter Sara and Kevin Harris, attempted to collect Sammy's body, FBI sniper Lon Horiuchi shot Randy and then fired at Randy's wife Vicki, who was standing at the door of the cabin holding their 10-month-old daughter, Elishiba. Vicki was hit in the head and died instantly. Weaver, his three daughters and Harris remained in the house with her body for nine days and accepted the inevitability that like their mother and Sammy, they too would soon die at the hands of federal agents. Says Bangerter:

> We had just learned they'd killed Vicki and my friends Dave, Joe and I were standing around the creek when about ten ATF agents came down and stood about 20 feet away from us on the opposite side of the creek. They were so close we could have spit on them. We started yelling at them, calling them pussies and demanding they put their guns down and come fight us man to man. And then 3 or 4 more agents came down to join them. I will always remember them. There was one with a beard. One had a moustache. One had a weird hat on. They had antennas on their shoulders and ATF jackets. They were holding what looked to be submachine guns. Dave kept yelling at them to put down their guns and they did. First, the blond guy with the beard started putting his gun down and then the others put their guns down as if they were going to come fight us. So we took off our shirts and started crossing the creek to fight them. Well, as soon as we got to the middle of the creek, they picked their guns back up and pointed them at us.
>
> We started yelling "You fucking cowards! Shoot us punks!" But, at the same time, we started backing up because we knew.

We thought we were going to get shot to death right there in the middle of the river. These were real guns and there was a dead kid, and his dead mother up on that mountain and we were actually dealing with these people. We knew they were murderers and they wouldn't hesitate to kill us too. I could feel it happening. I could feel the bullets going through my chest and I could feel my heart bleeding. I knew I was dead. I remember kissing my children goodbye in my head. And we backed up. I had to change my tactics. That was real blood spilled up there. Those were real people. I had to go into some weird mode after that. I was basically begging and pleading with them. But they had no compassion. None.

Patriot Movement leader Bo Gritz and a female assistant were given permission to go up to the cabin to help clean Vicki's blood off the floor and convince Randy to surrender. While they were there, Randy and his daughter Sarah hid a three-page letter in a tampon and gave it to them. Bangerter said,

> The letter was very detailed. It said something like, 'first they shot the dog. Then they shot Sam. Then they shot Vickie.' They just laid out, in great detail, everything that had occurred. Things we didn't know about yet, things that are still not widely known. It was horrifying. Afterwards, we were convinced that Randy and everybody up at the cabin with him would be murdered.

Gritz, convinced of the same, asked Bangerter to write a letter to Randy Weaver and plead with him to surrender. Bangerter agreed and in his letter urged Randy to come down from the cabin with his daughters so they could tell the world what had happened to them. He assured Randy that the battle would be fought in court. Weaver listened and, along with his daughters and Kevin Harris, surrendered, bringing the standoff to an end.

What happened at Ruby Ridge only confirmed growing suspicions of many on both the left and right, that the U.S. was becoming a police state. Among the radical right, for both the racially minded White Power Movement and the non-racially minded Patriot Movement, it was seen as proof that the government was waging war on its own citizens using so called 'low intensity conflict' tactics. After Ruby Ridge, alliances between these formerly disparate elements of the extreme right were further solidified as the common enemy of both, the federal government, had shown the lengths it would go to suppress dissent. The collective mood of Patriots and racialists, which had been approaching a boiling point, was now fully ignited and their rhetoric of revolution escalated. In October 1992, a mock trial was held at a Patriot meeting in Estes Park, Colorado where FBI sniper Lon Horiuchi was indicted and a death warrant issued for him.

Many commentators cite the Estes Park meeting as the birth of the 'militia movement.'

Likewise, federal operations targeting far right radicals also intensified immediately after Ruby Ridge. Hundreds of recently released (but highly redacted) FBI PATCON reports warn of the possibility that the deaths at Ruby Ridge would be violently avenged and emphasize the urgent need to expand both the budget and the scope of the domestic counter-terrorism program to determine the validity of the threat, but also to prevent further working alliances from forming among different radical right-wing groups. And indeed, PATCON's budget skyrocketed, and the scope of its mission expanded greatly, both geographically and tactically.[42] PATCON assets and operatives received specific instructions to beef up their operations. Undercover agents and informants posing as ideologically committed revolutionaries within Neo-Nazi, Patriot and now militia groups expanded their infiltration and sting efforts, sometimes contriving bizarre plots to do so.

Bangerter described how his life changed after Ruby Ridge as the mood and actions of those within his movement escalated, along with the almost absurd methods used to neutralize post -Ruby Ridge radicalism:

> What happened at Ruby Ridge consumed my life so much. It was all I thought about. I would wake up in the middle of the night thinking about it how I wanted to take on the government and get revenge. I would have a couple of beers, call the office of Utah Senator Orin Hatch and shoot my mouth off about what I was going to do. I did and said such stupid stuff that I ended up making myself a perfect target for a set-up. In the end, they were like "this guy is easy. Let's try to get him to bite." I became so paranoid and brushed up against so many sting operations. I just wanted it to go away ... it was like a scene out of the most horrible nightmare you can imagine. One agent tried to get my brother and I to get on a plane under fictitious names and fly to San Diego, drive and pick up 500 M1 Grand Rifles to take them to the mine in Las Vegas, where 300 Las Vegas skinheads (who were supposed to rally there) would then use the guns to take the city of Vegas hostage and demand the release of The Order from prison. These were the kind of stings that were proposed.
>
> The [WP] movement was so heavily infiltrated with phony's, wannabe's, and federal agents, as well as from people that, from what I came to know, wouldn't have a problem killing a little kid. There really were the Buford Furrow types who were willing to go down and shoot up a school of Jewish children.

It is possible that Timothy McVeigh, who monitored the news carefully for developments in the ongoing Ruby Ridge debacle and its murderous conclusion first heard of Johnny Bangerter around this time. No matter when or how McVeigh heard of him, he would not forget about the loquacious skinhead with the fiery rhetoric. By most accounts, including his own, Ruby Ridge reinforced and fed McVeigh's existing fears, anxieties and suspicions, leading to a distinct intensification of his ideological expressions. His already alarming rhetoric became even more aggressive. If he had attempted to hide his racism and anti-Semitism in the Army, his efforts at concealment ended after Ruby Ridge, one more incident indicative of the "growing pattern of government tyranny" seemingly prophesied in *The Turner Diaries*. Stuart Wright wrote that the events at Ruby Ridge and later, Waco, as well as ongoing military-style raids against gun owners and the passage of federal gun restrictions became, for McVeigh, "part of a single conspiracy leading to inevitable outcome."[43]

Bill McVeigh began to believe that his son held "radical beliefs," and, given his mounting resistance to authority and seeming inability to "take orders," feared Timmy would eventually run into "big trouble." Throughout the summer of 1992, he began to isolate himself, took up gambling and moved from his father's house to an apartment in Buffalo. He later explained his move to his attorneys by saying that he was still unable to get any sleep at his father's house. The phone rang constantly with calls for his sister, from bookies, and from his employers at Burns. Thus, McVeigh chose not to have a phone installed in his new place, much to the consternation of his father, who now had to field callers attempting to locate his son. The Burns office gave him a pager to carry. According to Bill McVeigh, his son moved out of the house in an attempt to "sequester himself" from the IRS, to whom he refused to pay taxes, and from the Army, who called the house frequently. Apparently, McVeigh had received an overpayment notification from the Army informing him that Uncle Sam wanted his money back, but McVeigh refused to comply with these demands. The phone calls, said Bill, caused his son to become "irate."

The letters McVeigh continued to drop in Steve's mailbox illustrate the thoughts that consumed him during the Weaver standoff and after its deadly conclusion. Among McVeigh's cornucopia of complaints: Buffalo's new mandatory recycling policy was enforceable by imprisonment, work-place sexual harassment policies that made it impossible for him to talk to women, his view that Rush Limbaugh was simply too liberal and his discovery that shortwave radio shows were being "jammed by a government that does not like its message." In one letter, he demanded that Steve stop calling his father's house looking for him and then went on to discuss "Jews" and "Faggots," announce his disbelief in "the Holocaust" and berate his old friend for his liberal political views. He urged Steve to read *1984* and warned of an impending "Brave New World" wherein "Big Brother" would force the races to mix and imprison those who held "subversive" ideologies:

You don't realize it, but you've been brainwashed to lock out all facts as soon as you hear the word "Jew." Let's talk about the "Holocaust" – 6 million Jews are <u>insisted</u> to have been executed. Ok, yes, Jews were executed-just like the current ethnic cleansing in Yugoslavia but (and you're thinking <u>programmed to think</u> – "he's an anti-Semite, I will not listen any more....") But reason it out – <u>6 million</u>? What is the current population of NYC? Do you see what I'm getting out? Where the hell could <u>6 million</u> Jews "appear" from, to be executed? Has there ever been a name by name accounting?!? Oh no, to demand that would be racist! I call it researching history, to confirm its authenticity. But, you instantly believe it ... you are a liberal socialist, and you must understand that is why we will never see eye-to-eye. Our basic, fundamental principles are like yin and yang. Childhood friends, yes – but as adults we've established our own worldly views; and that's natural. (Although I consider your actual views as unnatural) I love, and hold precious personal freedom while you embrace more government control on our lives.... Read again <u>1984</u> and <u>Brave New World</u>, and think about it ... investigate or question <u>any</u> part of history, but as soon as you investigate the 'Holocaust', you must be a racist. By this method [of implying guilt] they succeed in covering up a fabricated 'tale of history' as truth.... Am I anti-Catholic if I wish to launch a search for Noah's Ark? No ... I'm trying to express my ideas, but I can't seem to word it right. People are, <u>even</u> today, put in jail for expressing opposing historical views of the 'Holocaust' yes, in jail – political prisoners...

A secretary at Calspan later told the FBI that McVeigh was a strange individual with "radical political views." She always had a feeling that he would wind up in trouble and said she had even expressed her worries to other employees at the Calspan facility. His workplace banter, when it bordered on the advocacy of illegal and violent actions, had perked the ears of other co-workers including Carl Lebron. In early September 1992, weeks after the Weaver deaths, McVeigh put in his two weeks' notice and announced his plans to leave New York State by the end of the year. Lebron then made the fortuitous decision to surreptitiously record their bizarre conversations. Describing his reasons for doing so, Lebron said:

After Ruby Ridge, he began talking about how easy it would be *to steal stuff from military bases*. I didn't think he'd end up like Randy Weaver though, you know-sitting on a mountain with the government coming after him. I didn't really think he'd act aggressively. Once I made fun of an article about a guy who was living in a bunker in his basement and he got all angry because I couldn't understand it, and he couldn't articulate why he had views to support that person.

When McVeigh started talking about the Holocaust issue and

even more so, *when he talked about the military base issue and how easy it could be to steal stuff from them,* I thought I might get him on tape saying that. I didn't feel any immediate danger from him; it's just that the things he was saying were just worrisome. I took it upon myself to record him, solely on my initiative based on the conversations we were having. I never went to anyone at Burns. No one from Calspan ever approached me and said 'What's going on with Tim?' or anything like that. No one else had any concern. He was a veteran. He had medals. I didn't even talk about it with anyone.

I made the tape within the last two weeks he worked there, right at the end of his time at Calspan. I guess I was hoping that if I got him on tape saying something I could do something with it; give it to Calspan or preferably the government and say "Is there something wrong here?" I was concerned about what he was saying ... but looking at him and accusing a veteran who's been showing off his medals, you can't just claim "Hey! This guy's a goof ball!" We were at the main gate across from the airport in the guard shack when I recorded him. I was wearing a jacket and had the recorder in my jacket. I just talked a little to see if he would say anything. He made one comment about the black guy we worked with, but other than that, nothing really substantial. I only made one tape and there was nothing useful on it except one moderate racial comment.[44]

Lebron may have underestimated the importance of the tape. The resumé of a former New Jersey police officer says he initiated and maintained his office's liaison with NORTHSTAR, which he explained was "a DOD program that enabled the transfer of surplus military equipment to law enforcement agencies. Through this program, I obtained numerous items, at no cost, for official use by the office such as Kevlar helmets and office equipment."[45] It is somewhat humorous that McVeigh, known to 'commandeer' military equipment at Ft. Riley while in the Army, now talked openly and in great detail about the exact types of actions being targeted by PATCON, and sanctioned under NORTHSTAR, that prompted Carl Lebron to secretly record their conversations at Calspan.

The Lebron recording took place on September 15, 1992, in the Calspan guard shack. The strange out-of-context shifts in McVeigh's topics are similar to those in his letters. Included were his increasingly vehement anti-Semitic rants, musings on the illegitimacy of the Federal Reserve System and advice to Lebron that he should withdraw all his money from the bank and convert it to gold so that "when the monetary system collapses" he might survive. During the conversation, unaware of the fact that he was being recorded by Lebron, McVeigh, seemingly out of nowhere, suddenly warned Lebron that at some point in the future people would come asking about him, perhaps, he said, even people from the Calspan offices and that these people would speak with all of his coworkers. McVeigh then told Lebron he would soon be leaving for Michigan, where he had a "mail drop" he checked every so often, because "that's the only way they can trace me.... I've dropped out of the system." McVeigh did not explain why Calspan or anyone else other than his family would care if he vanished.

Shortly after Lebron made the recording, McVeigh left New York. The reasons he gave for his decision varied, depending on who he gave them to and when. When he put in his two-week notice he told Andrea Augustine he was leaving to take a job as a toll collector somewhere down south. He even talked extensively about the details of the entrance exam required for the position and therefore, she said, she had no reason to question what he told her. He told his father he was moving to Michigan to live with Terry Nichols. McVeigh told the Jones Team that, at the time, debt collectors were harassing him and he was frustrated in general. He was searching for something but said he did not know what, was "definitely depressed" and decided to try his luck selling guns and military surplus items on the gun show circuit. His final letter to Steve before setting off articulated his preoccupations:

> As of January 29 [1993] I am leaving New York, to an undisclosed destination; therefore I believe this will be our last communication.... Remember – I am out there, and America will remain free. The Constitutional Laws will return! If I am "locked up," you can bet I will be labeled as either a "schizophrenic" or "white-racist." But what is it really? Just a radical political view that people/society is not ready to accept. A radical thinker is viewed as having an "illness" because he does not/ will not conform to the norm of society. Read this excerpt from an article on schizophrenia and mental illness: "Followers of Freud said the illness was caused by bad mothering; Dr. Ronald Laing called them a sane response to an insane world; novelist Ken Kesey described the hospitalized mentality as being politically oppressed, Dr. Thomas Szasz claimed that the illnesses did not really exist at all." For is it a defined "illness" to disagree with a majority view? Apparently, just as many people have been "hospitalized" for just that reason. Big Brother will do more than just jam [ham radios], he will lock you up, isolate your views – keep the sheep in the dark through oppression (underlines in original).

Since joining the Army, he had slowly but steadily become mentally unhinged and after leaving Buffalo in late 1992, became unhinged geographically as well. From the moment he left, until the day of the bombing, he constantly crisscrossed the country stopping in most, if not all states. His father said that after he left New York, "he didn't hear much from his son" and Jennifer said, "Half the time we didn't even know where Tim was."

In the simplest reading, McVeigh bugged out and decided to discover what else life had to offer. Stickney wrote that when he decided to leave

Buffalo, McVeigh "may well have made the worst decision in his entire life. He would re-enter the Circus of Losers – the hate filled group of people in Michigan, Kansas, and in Arizona who would aid in his progressive mental disintegration." By the time he left "for the Land of Fools," McVeigh's "Amerinoid status was set in stone."[46] Here, McVeigh's conspiracy to bomb the Murrah building, while perhaps not fully formed, was emerging and, nurtured on the ideological and material sustenance acquired throughout his travels, continued to grow. Certainly, this is a plausible scenario.

A much more complex reading is possible however when other, lesser-known information is brought into play and compared against unsubstantiated claims. According to David Paul Hammer, writing in 2004:

> By the summer days of August [1992], Tim was well on his way to becoming one of the anti-government zealots he was supposed to be preparing to impersonate, or so it seemed. Depending upon which version one believes, he was for real or he was acting. [To me,] he wavered in his position when recounting his reaction to the August 21st, 1992, raid by federal agents on the Ruby Ridge, Idaho cabin of Randy Weaver ... [He did say that] it was during the siege at Ruby Ridge that [he] received the call he had been waiting for. The Major, in a brief exchange, directed him to a meeting at Niagara Falls, New York set for the following day. The meeting was short and to the point. According to the Major, the Ruby Ridge fiasco was a real "cluster fuck" for federal law enforcement, and that the militia movement would use the deaths of a woman and child as a rallying call to all like-minded Americans. Tim was told to heed that call. He was given a secure telephone number where messages could be left for the Major. Tim's mission was simple – he was to become a spy. In the words of the Major, "the survivalist and militia malcontents can destroy this country. It is up to you to prevent that from happening." Over the next few months, Tim continued with his indoctrination into a right wing anti-government agenda. He cultivated sources by mail and telephone. He used his material on family, co-workers and all who would listen. No one was more concerned over these changes in Tim than his Dad. In mid-January 1993, McVeigh received a telephone call at his Dad's house. The Major informed him to wrap up his affairs and prepare for "months in the field." He was provided with an address in New Jersey where he needed to be by a certain date.[47]

Unknown to Hammer, according to Jones Team and FBI documents, McVeigh left a trail to this effect in addition to his "disaffected loner" persona. In a rather cryptic letter to a former COHORT and roommate, he wrote that while he was still working at Burns he would be leaving Buffalo soon and would be "gone for a while" as he was "going to be doing some missions." He told a Calspan secretary that he was going to work for the Pentagon. He told Lebron he'd gotten a promotion and was going to work with "military vehicles" down south but was "cagey about where exactly he was going." Andrea Augustine said that when he told her he was leaving, she begged him to stay but he "kept saying, 'You don't understand, I really have to go.' He just kept saying it."[48] McVeigh then proceeded to travel the gun show circuit, which allowed him to make connections with some of the most well known people (and many not so well known) within the White Power, Patriot and Militia movements. In Hammer's version, the Major had explained to him from the outset that:

> [S]hould Tim agree to "sign on," he would be required to sign a confidentiality agreement never to disclose any information about the unit or its work. His assignment would call for him to act separate from any other agents of the unit, relying on recruits or players of his choosing when needed. Funding and support for operations would be provided through sources unconnected to the U.S. Government in any way. Tim would be an agent acting alone, utilizing his own resourcefulness. ... As with all other assignments, McVeigh immersed himself completely. This task was made easier because of beliefs and knowledge that already existed within him.[49]

McVeigh's contradictory claims before and after the bombing could still easily and logically be passed off as manifestations of his pathological dishonesty and maybe combat-related mental illness. Except that, when coupled with decades-old archived information and recent revelations about PATCON, certain narratives that are deemed by some to be deluded conspiracy theory or fabrications, provoke closer consideration.

According to the newly released FBI documents and a 2011 article in *Newsweek*, in the aftermath of Ruby Ridge, PATCON assets and operatives were given license to engage in provocateur activities and instructed to make known their "willing[ness] to commit violence," and "advocate [the] violent overthrow of the U.S. government." Informants found steady employment for years, traveling the country attending KKK and Aryan Nation meetings, gun shows and paramilitary training compounds, selling illegal weapons and "sitting in church pews with would-be abortion clinic bombers." One recently released PATCON document discusses why a certain undercover FBI agent was particularly suited for the job. He had been in the military and had seen combat (in Vietnam), he was around the same age as the people he was assigned to target, and had "studied the white supremacy movement through the reading of numerous books and articles in the public domain..."[50]

Similar to the violent right-wing rhetoric and dissent it ostensibly sought to quell, PATCON spiraled out of control. In attempts to prove they were not "Feds," PATCON agents and informants set about successfully arranging the theft (often from military bases), sale, and purchase of related contraband, mostly weapons but sometimes explosives. More than a few suggested blowing up federal buildings and one PATCON operative tried to get his targets to blow up a nuclear power plant. Like in the FBI's COINTELPRO days, operatives started their own organizations and sometimes engaged in unjustified criminal acts. Although initiated and expanded upon as a means of gathering evidence that could be used to bring about criminal charges, PATCON rapidly shifted, first into a blanket intelligence-gathering operation and then a counter-intelligence operation using increasingly questionable means and methods. Despite the massive effort and cost of the program, PATCON did not result in any criminal charges against its targets. The program did manage to forge a more symbiotic relationship between the targets and those who targeted them and in doing so, arguably only exacerbated the problem it intended to neutralize.

Immediately after leaving Buffalo and up until the morning of April 19, 1995, Timothy McVeigh made connections with a number of individuals either targeted or operating under PATCON, or both. More than one federal informant has come forward to say that his handlers knew about McVeigh's (and friends') terroristic escapades prior to the bombing. Certainly, in a way that can only be described as uncanny, his geographic meanderings line up, from Texas to Tennessee to Utah to New Jersey to Arizona and so on; as do his actions and the specific relationships he sought. The question is begged: Was McVeigh the Forrest Gump of right-wing domestic terrorism, always in the right place at the right time, or was he working for somebody? If he wasn't, he probably should have been.

PART THREE
An Incommunicable Thing

WHO HAS KNOWN GREAT HEIGHTS

Who has known heights and depths shall not again know peace – not as the calm heart knows low lived walls; a garden close. And though he tread the humble ways of men, he shall not speak the common tongue again. Who has known heights shall bear forever more, an incommunicable thing that hurts his heart, as if a wing beat at the portal, challenging; And yes-lured by the gleam his vision wore – Who once has trodden stars seeks peace no more.

– Mary Brent Whiteside, "Who Has Known Heights,"[ii] 1936.

_____

ii. A poem Timothy McVeigh asked his attorneys to provide him a photocopy of and one he shared

Within weeks after his arrest, Timothy McVeigh, much like the fictional Rambo, came to epitomize the "image of a disillusioned and embittered soldier." Given their high rates of unemployment, divorce, homelessness, alcohol abuse and seeming propensity to commit random, senseless violence, the "emerging profile of Gulf War veterans" was a dismal one.[51] Soon after the bombing, questions arose about whether McVeigh's military training or Post Traumatic Stress Disorder (PTSD) had contributed to his act of violence and if those same factors contributed to violent acts committed by other Gulf War Veterans, an increasingly reported phenomenon. While the post-war image of the combat veteran gone berserk was a familiar one, much to the displeasure of some Gulf War vets, McVeigh quickly became a powerful and often-invoked symbol for other real-life Rambo's.

Trauma theorists posit that the experience of trauma, isolated or ongoing, results in a radical disruption of associative pathways, linear time, and the ability to form meaning about an event. Trauma "destroys identity," shatters the sense of a coherent self and continuity of one's self and "fragments the personality."[52] Those suffering from PTSD are plagued by intrusive thoughts, panic attacks, flashbacks, insomnia, paranoia, obsessiveness, depression and hyper-arousal. Their actions and general mannerisms may seem disorganized and bizarre to others.

Only days after the bombing, Dan Herbeck noted that "[m]any people who know McVeigh have said he returned from Desert Storm as a changed, more aggressive man."[53] To both his defense team and biographers, McVeigh acknowledged that, after leaving the Army, he began to experience a number of symptoms often linked to PTSD including confusion, depression, despair, restlessness, anxiety, irritability, insomnia and periods of mania. His military experiences, he said, left him unable to relate to others and, because of this, he felt the need to isolate himself from friends and family. Both publicly and privately, he admitted that his "disenchantment" became so great that he considered suicide.

McVeigh occasionally spoke to his defense team about various traumas he endured, including his military training, Special Forces try-out and, in particular, the killing he saw and participated in during the Gulf War. To attorney Dick Burr he explained that, "I was a pawn [for] the government" and after returning from the Gulf, "I was different from most other people, because I had killed someone. Once you cross the line [of taking a life], you can't go back … it is hard to live in society anymore." Based on what he and others told them, the Jones Team mental health experts agreed that McVeigh suffered from acute PTSD, which, they suspected, had began much earlier in his life, reached an irreversible climax after the war and came to a final breaking point after the death of his grandfather.

---

with his official biographer years later, telling them it aptly described his dilemma.

He admitted to them that he had sought help at the Buffalo VA and, after leaving the region, at VAs in other states as well but they refused to treat him anonymously, so he gave up. He explained that, "I [didn't] want to be known as someone with a mental illness" and feared a PTSD diagnosis would affect future employment opportunities. Further, he believed treatment was a "cop out," the very label PTSD, "an excuse" and thought he should be able to deal with his turmoil himself.

Mark Hamm wrote that, while still in Buffalo, McVeigh became engulfed by a persistent and "stone cold" obsession with killing, death, and "vast and gigantic conspiracy theories born of apocalyptic thinking." The "atrophy" and "disintegration of [his] mind and body" quickly became apparent to those who knew him. After mapping McVeigh's peculiar political and ideological journey, Hamm briefly speculated about links between McVeigh's disintegrating mental health and the act of terrorism he engaged in and suggested that both had, in part, resulted from a "delayed reaction to war." He compared McVeigh to World War II veterans who, through repetitive military training, had been carefully "conditioned to follow orders and trained in the art of killing" but after returning to the civilian world, retained their carefully crafted "need to kill" and engaged in acts of violence and aggression.[54]

Indeed, McVeigh described numerous instances after the war when his "combat sense[s]" had "kicked in," including throughout the planning of the bombing, the day of the bombing and during the 'Perry Perp Walk.' Based on recent studies at the time of his writing, Hamm raised the possibility that neurological changes in the hippocampus region of the brain caused by exposure to traumatic and uncontrollable events, in combination with his military training, may "begin to explain what happened to Timothy McVeigh."[55]

Though there is no evidence to show that he was aware of it, the experiences of McVeigh's fellow COHORTs paralleled his own. A number of those who shared their stories with Jones Team investigators remarked that the Gulf War was the beginning of their own troubles and revealed that they too continued to suffer from a host of symptoms commonly associated with PTSD, which began upon their return from the Gulf. The specific symptoms they named included mood swings, increased anger, memory loss, nightmares, insomnia, flashbacks, nervousness, anxiety, reclusiveness, night sweats, startle responses, and shakiness.

Their stories, remarkably similar to each other, shed light not only on McVeigh's experiences but also those of many other combat veterans both before and after Operation Desert Storm. Since the Global War on Terror began, PTSD diagnosis in U.S. soldiers, sometimes deployed to current theatres of war up to six times, have reached epidemic levels, as have corresponding suicide rates; 22 per day according to some estimates.

As soldiers of the wars in Afghanistan and Iraq continue to "come home to roost," so to speak, PTSD, its relationship to military service and anti-social and violent acts committed by combat veterans remain highly relevant. A number of recent reports and studies detail developments in new PTSD treatments and add to growing debates over soldiers' violence, their frustrated attempts to seek treatment for psychological turmoil related to their combat, along with newer, controversial methods used to reverse their pain. Further, based on the military's use of operant conditioning, hyper-realistic training and desensitization to create a killer reflex, unique sentencing guidelines for capital cases involving combat veterans have been proposed and, in the case of nonviolent crimes, enacted.

McVeigh's Mysterious Foot Flu

Shortly after the Gulf War ended, news outlets began reporting on the rapidly increasing number of Gulf War veterans who said they were experiencing a physical illness often described as a persistent flu; dubbed "Gulf War Syndrome" [GWS]. Some claimed this flu had begun while they were still in the Gulf. The most commonly cited symptoms included: chronic joint, muscle and other pain, headaches, extreme fatigue, diarrhea and other digestive maladies, ulcers, sore gums, brittle teeth, loss of teeth, sinus infections, respiratory difficulties, nosebleeds, hair loss, recurring rashes, cancerous growths (including warts and other skin disorders), insomnia, confusion, depression, mood swings, dizziness, persistent nightmares, memory loss, blackouts as well as higher rates of miscarriages and birth defects. While the cause of the epidemic (whose actual existence was disputed) remained unknown, a number of suspects emerged. Included were chemical and biological warfare vaccines and treatments, actual exposure to nerve agents, anti-nerve agents (not just their inoculants), mustard gas or the use (by Americans or Iraqis) of other forms of unconventional chemical warfare, SCUD missiles, infectious diseases common to the Gulf region, oil well fires, burning landfills, depleted uranium (used in tanks and ammunition), pesticides, diesel fuel and the paint used on the Bradley tanks.

Veterans' advocacy groups, fearing "another Agent Orange situation," pressed the government to conduct further investigations into the illness and its causes.[56] In August 1992, the Department of Veteran Affairs (VA) announced the creation of a Gulf War Registry that would collect data about the health of Gulf War vets and track future changes in it. That same month, the VA in Buffalo, New York began their Gulf War Registry.

As noted, many, if not the majority of accounts, attribute McVeigh's failure to become a member of the Army's elite Special Forces, in part, to a blister on his foot. The available portion of his military medical records (not mentioned in *any* previous writings) reflect that, in November 1991, the month before he left the Army, he sought medical attention for, among several other issues, a "deteriorating" big toe. While not claiming that McVeigh *received* treatment for PTSD at the Buffalo VA (only that he looked into it), Herbeck and Michel wrote that, after leaving the Army and returning home, McVeigh visited there for a foot ailment and, over the course of two months, beginning around December 1991, continued to receive weekly treatments for his podiatric ills. His experiences there were positive and rewarding.

Herbeck and Michel wrote:

> Oddly enough, McVeigh did have one experience during this time that helped him see that not everything about the American government was bad. When a *persistent and painful wart* kept returning to his toe, he called the Veterans Affairs Medical Center in Buffalo and found out that *he qualified for free treatment because he was a veteran earning less than twelve thousand dollars annually.* Lacking health insurance, he decided to take advantage of the government benefit. He had already spent eighty dollars of his own money on a Lockport physician, but the laser treatment he received had failed to remove *the growth, which had first appeared during the Gulf War.* Each week, while an acidic cream was applied to his wart, he schmoozed the VA doctor, 'You get back from people what you feed them' McVeigh would say. *After two months of treatment, the wart vanished.* The hospital's medical staff also *checked him for the mysterious malady known as Gulf War syndrome.* But McVeigh exhibited *no signs of fatigue, headaches, memory loss, or other symptoms* associated with the illness; he was issued a clean bill of health (Italics added).[57]

Here, Timothy James McVeigh, while depressed and not the physical specimen the Special Forces sought was, nevertheless, a perfectly healthy young man. For Herbeck and Michel (whose writing the majority of secondary and most widely known historical accounts are based on), this is the end of McVeigh's medical narrative. His motive for bombing the Murrah was rooted in political and ideological disease alone. He did not suffer from the constellation of mysterious symptoms reported by a growing number of returning vets. They based their opinion upon what McVeigh told them during their discussions and correspondence with him in 1999 and 2000. However, in what appears somewhat of a contradictory slip-up on McVeigh's part and one overlooked by his biographers, in a letter he wrote them contained in the American Terrorist Collection, he said, "When I read of government deception, lies, corruption– it's cumulative. (I'm highly retentive!) I remember Laos, Cambodia. I recall Iran Contra and CIA drug running. I remember (and experienced) the Desert Storm

Syndrome denials and the bureaucratic bullshit denials, etc., etc., etc., ad infinitum (Is that what they say?)"

Characteristically, however, several conflicting versions about McVeigh's visits to the Buffalo VA exist. One of the earliest, written by Dan Herbeck, appeared in a *Buffalo News* article only a week after his arrest. In it, Herbeck cited an anonymous government source who said McVeigh, claiming he earned below poverty level wages, participated in a free screening exam at the Buffalo VA to determine if he had "Persian Gulf Syndrome." The Director for the Buffalo VA's Persian Gulf clinic, Dr. Robert Talluto, said that while he could not discuss the results of the exam, the FBI was currently reviewing McVeigh's medical records.[58]

Only days later, another, slightly different version of the 'Buffalo VA' story appeared in *USA Today*. In this one, McVeigh, on one occasion, sought treatment for a skin rash and, while there, requested and was denied compensation for service-related Gulf War Syndrome. Brandon Stickney, citing an unnamed source, repeated this story in his 1996 book and added that the visit occurred in the spring of 1992. He opined that when McVeigh returned home, although "undetected at the time, [he] may have been suffering from Persian Gulf War Syndrome" which, by the time he left town, "probably had quite a hold on [him]." Thus, while not elaborating on this, Stickney hints that GWS might have played a factor in his motive to bomb the Murrah.[59]

A third version appeared during a conversation with his defense team (prior to his discussions with his biographers), at which time McVeigh said that, while at the VA for a "wart," he took the GWS evaluation test and checked "yes" to all possible GWS related exposures and symptoms listed on the accompanying form. In fact, McVeigh said he mentioned his sickness to relentless debt collectors in order to get them off his back and, in the summer of 1992, shortly before leaving Buffalo, told them that he had no money and had been "feeling sick since Desert Storm." He further claimed that because he had a credit card issued by the Department of Defense, they stopped bothering him.

When the defense team asked McVeigh about "Dr. Talluto," the VA doctor mentioned in the news reports, McVeigh told them he was a "Jewish podiatrist" that he saw for about two months and got along well with him. The fact, he said, that he got along with Talluto so well, was proof of his (McVeigh's) "non-supremacist character." Upon further investigation, however, the defense team noted that Talluto was not a doctor, "only a counselor" and "denied ever knowing McVeigh." In fact, Talluto's secretary told them that another "counselor" saw McVeigh at the Buffalo VA but refused to give them the name of the doctor.

Although not mentioned in the subsequent article, in his correspondence with *Playboy* journalist Jonathan Franklin, six months after his arrest, McVeigh said he discussed GWS with the staff at the Buffalo VA but that, at some point, he went there to retrieve his medical and service records, only to learn they had been lost. Archival records in the Jones Collection reveal that a couple of months after his breakdown at his grandfather's house, and days after he resigned from the NYNG, McVeigh personally requested these records on at least three occasions. The first known request occurred on April 6, 1992, followed the next day, April 7, 1992, by a request for financial compensation "for removal of planter warts," which, not being deemed service-related, was denied. The second occurred on May 7, 1992 and the third on May 22, 1992. Although admittedly speculative, I posit that perhaps McVeigh sought the extensive medical profile that, while still in boot camp, he had told his sister he did not want to establish.

Beyond Stickney's brief mention that McVeigh was physically ill upon his return from the Army, no other works (biographical, journalistic or scholarly) have discussed this, and Stickney does not provide details about the nature of his symptoms. Furthermore, the available archival and oral records certainly suggest that he had been physically ill, during and after his time in the Army, as well as after his arrest.

Interestingly, unknown not only to his biographers but also to seemingly all others who have written about him, during his three years in the Army, McVeigh exhibited and sought medical attention on more than seventy-five occasions for a number of symptoms commonly associated with GWS. These included muscle and joint pain, bleeding gums, rapid tooth decay in almost all teeth, unexplained vomiting and diarrhea, strange moles, skin growths, blurred vision, fatigue, anxiety, ulcers and recurring skin scales and skin tags. While many of his COHORT group could not remember or did not discuss him having any physical ailments, a close friend of his with whom he had served in the Gulf said that after the war McVeigh began to have "unknown health problems," including stomach ulcers, a claim confirmed by his available medical records; although, in them, the ulcers appear *prior* to the war.

Bill McVeigh said when his son came home, beyond being more irritable, unreliable, distant, and unpredictable, he "seemed to have a number of health problems after his return from the military ... he took a lot of Pepto Bismol for his stomach and had problems with his feet. He went to the VA hospital a lot." According to his aunt, "he had terrible, terrible, headaches and constant stomach problems when he returned. It got so bad, I told him to go to the VA hospital and talk to them about it. I thought he needed help."

Steve's mother said, "Something happened in the year after he returned from the Gulf," he was more agitated, did not appear to be getting enough sleep, complained of various physical ailments and "popped Tums all the time." His co-workers at Burns, including his supervisor, noted his increasing anxiety, erratic behaviors, insomnia, and extreme weight loss. Andrea Augustine said she knew of no health problems he may have had, but was aware of his growing stress. Carl Lebron said McVeigh seemed healthy to him, "other than mental issues."[60]

Others made similar observations after he left the Buffalo region. James Nichols had a lot to say about McVeigh's health and remembered that McVeigh first mentioned he was sick during a visit in June 1992 (shortly after he requested his records), and on a number of occasions in the years leading to the bombing, McVeigh continued to bring up various ailments he suffered from. James said McVeigh often complained of "severe fatigue, muscular aches, his joints ached, his teeth hurt, [and] his gums hurt. He had no energy and was always tired." In fact, James said, McVeigh often wondered whether a "secret shot" he received in the Army, or Gulf War Syndrome, might account for his symptoms and, on more than one occasion, visited the VA in Saginaw, Michigan to determine the causes and alleviate the symptoms. In late 1993, he saw a dentist there. Another man in Michigan who knew McVeigh for a number of years said that he'd always suspected McVeigh had been "messed up" by exposure to chemicals during the Gulf War and acted stranger than usual when he returned.[61]

When McVeigh returned to Buffalo for his grandfather's funeral in November 1994, he made a six-hour phone call to an Indiana chapter of the American Legion, a veteran's advocacy organization that, among other things, lobbies in support of veteran benefits and issues involving the VA hospital system. In January 1995, McVeigh (or someone using his calling card), placed phone calls from the Bay Regional Medical Center in Bay City, Michigan. In early February 1995, he wrote his sister and told her he was having "funny health problems" and suspected his exposure to radioactive ammunition was to blame. He then continued, telling her "medical programs are one of the most effective means of control available to a government. The control of medicine and drugs is mandatory" and enclosed several articles about vaccines along with the letter. On three consecutive days at the end of that month, in late February 1995, McVeigh called the Prescott, Arizona Veterans Medical Center from his motel room in nearby Kingman.[62] He visited a civilian dentist in Kingman on April 4, 1995, just weeks before the bombing and paid in cash. He told the dentist he planned to apply for a job and felt the cavity on his front tooth was unsightly. He refused to let the dentist take an x-ray though, claiming he could not afford it.[63]

According to the records in the Jones Collection, at the time of McVeigh's arrest, Trooper Charlie Hangar found a pack of Rolaids among his possessions. A couple of years later, however, he told his biographers that Hangar found "Motrin in a little Tylenol container." When Hangar asked him what the prescription was, McVeigh told him "it was from the Army hospital two years ago [1993] but you can get the same thing over the counter. It's just Ibuprofen, 2400 mg's."

Jones Team mental health expert, Dr. John Smith, first met with McVeigh at El Reno Prison on June 6, 1995, weeks after his arrest. On June 18, 1995, Smith made the first of several recommendations to the court that resulted in somewhat less restrictive confinement conditions. Despite this, throughout his pretrial imprisonment, McVeigh experienced increasingly severe physical and psychological problems commonly associated with confinement and constant surveillance, which he had also displayed earlier and that had begun while in the Army. For example, nearly a year later, Smith observed some of the symptoms noted in McVeigh's military medical records:

> [I observed] striking differences in Mr. McVeigh, both physically and psychologically, his physical condition has significantly deteriorated [...] He is obviously deteriorating physically. During the interview, he had a spontaneous nosebleed, and [said] that for the last several weeks at least, he has been having episodic spontaneous nose bleeds of an undetermined cause [and he is] clearly not digesting or integrating his food. [...] His hands are red and scaly, a new development as far as his skin condition is concerned.

Perhaps related to his previous extensive medical and dental history, McVeigh, soon after his arrest, displayed a consistent aversion to prison doctors and dentists, which he claimed later to his biographers was based on privacy concerns but which, in conversations with his defense team, he attributed to a number of additional issues. In October 1995, he saw a doctor for a recurring skin rash on his forehead and then, just days later, informed Dick Burr that he did not want to see any more doctors; the first of several such requests. Once, when he came down with a cold, McVeigh refused the flu shot offered to him and explained by simply stating, "No needles." In one conversation with his attorneys, he expressed concern that the prison staff was putting "depressants" in his food.

During one of several visits to a prison dentist, this one in December 1995, when asked if had ever had any cavities, he claimed he had only ever had one in his entire life but had it fixed in early 1995. He then expressed concern that the dentist would inject him with "sodium pentothal." In fact, the following month, when the prison dentist refused to see him, claiming he was having problems with his machinery, he told Randy Coyne that he suspected the dentist was deceiving him. He then stressed that he was in need of immediate attention and feared that, if the dentist did not see him soon, he would "lose teeth from the decay as a result." The month after this, on two separate occasions, he told Coyne and defense attorney Rob Nigh that he thought the dentist might have placed a listening device in his tooth, but both times retracted his statement soon after making it, claiming he had been joking. His regular visits to the dentist continued along with his profound distrust of them.

According to David Paul Hammer, who knew nothing of McVeigh's health records, while on death row McVeigh continued to seek out medical treatment but simultaneously expressed his deep distrust of doctors and the possibility that the public would learn of his health problems. He wrote that McVeigh "would get sick and describe his symptoms to those close to him in order for them to inform the physician's assistant and send the prescriptions to him. About the only illness he would admit to was acid reflux, only because it was so well documented, and he was so incredibly miserable, without his antacids he couldn't tolerate it."

When viewed chronologically, rather than in disparate chunks of disconnected factoids, the information presented above gives a number of McVeigh's letters and statements a deeper level of meaning than ascribed to them previously. For instance, prior to the bombing, a number of McVeigh's letters alluded to medical issues or employed medical metaphors and a language of illness, often to make political points. In his December 1991 and February 1992 editorials, written months before he first requested his records and sought compensation for GWS, he compared politicians to strains of bacteria that, when treated by medication, are diluted only to re-emerge "in a worsened form" and later, suggested adopting the "communist idea of state sponsored health care."

In her 2009 anthropological ethnographic study of GWS, Susie Kilshaw examined the conflicting narratives told about the phenomenon, including those put forth by governments, media, the medical establishment and particularly Gulf War vets themselves. She argued that such an approach provided a great deal of "insight into the cultural, social and psychological dimensions of the construction of illness [as well as] the ways this has influenced sufferers' understandings." Kilshaw's analysis of GWS ultimately concerned a larger biomedical dichotomy that depicts illnesses as either physical or psychological rather than "a combination and intertwining of natural, biological, social, cultural and psychological factors." Of note was her observation that the 'idioms of distress' and other culturally bound communicative expressions sick soldiers use to talk about their dilemma hints at "collective social angst." Their "shared bodily language" allowed them to articulate their pain to others but also acted as "a form of commentary" about a number of social, cultural and political circumstances.[64]

The stories presented here, told by McVeigh, his COHORTs, media and government, not only support and add to Kilshaw's work but also open space to re-contextualize understandings of McVeigh and the Oklahoma City bombing case.

Gulf Lore Syndrome

With the exception of Lou Johnson, who said McVeigh had some "funny health problems" after returning from the Gulf, when questioned by the FBI and the Jones Team, McVeigh's COHORTs never mentioned the recurring ailments, corresponding doctors, and dentist visits noted in his military records. Similarly, there is no evidence that McVeigh knew of their ongoing issues and if they ever discussed it with him, he seems not to have mentioned it to his attorneys, journalists who interviewed him or biographers. However, like McVeigh, they too seemed to suffer, not only from psychological ailments after the war but persistent physical ones as well, the details of which a good number of them did disclose to the Jones Team. Many had developed strange symptoms linked to Gulf War Syndrome, sometimes very similar to McVeigh's own. Their stories follow a similar pattern of other Gulf War veterans throughout the country.[iii]

Lou Johnson said that ever since he "got back from the desert" he had been having problems including recurring rashes and an abscessed rectal canal. At the time he spoke with the Jones Team, he was undergoing "Saudi Syndrome Evaluation" and waiting on the results. James Lane and Sam Stansky also developed rashes and skin bumps "similar to poison ivy." Lane said he had "bad sleep problems," had lost over twenty pounds since the war and could not gain it back no matter what he did. Gordon Blackcloud had recurring muscle spasms, memory loss, degenerating eyesight and his teeth were falling out. His first child miscarried, and his second died at birth with a throat "pushed all the way to the side." Stansky's child was also born with severe birth defects and respiratory problems.

Many of the COHORTs began to suspect that, not only did the government know what had caused their deteriorating health and were actively covering up and falsely denying this knowledge to avoid having to deal with it but, worse, some began to wonder if they had been used as guinea pigs, 'pawns' in a massive government medical experiment.

Lou Johnson stated that, despite the government's continued denial that either the U.S. or Iraq had used chemical warfare agents, he knew they had been exposed and thought his post-war physical problems were a side effect of this. Bob Host suspected insecticides, the fumes from oil well fires or even nerve gas but said the government would not confirm their exposure or provide further information about the possibility. He

---

iii. Author's Disclaimer: While I changed some of the names of McVeigh's COHORTs in previous chapters of this book, I have changed all of the soldiers who disclosed their medical symptoms and conditions to the Jones Team, even if they are referred to by their real names in previous sections, as none of their disclosures have appeared in published reports. I have chosen to protect all of their identities in this section as some of the soldiers were seeking compensation for their Gulf War related illnesses at the time they spoke with the Jones Team and, like Gulf War veterans throughout the country, many met with serious resistance from the Veterans Administration. Transcripts of all of these conversations are on file with the author as are those I spoke with myself.

explained, "They [the government] are afraid of Gulf War Syndrome. If you're talking Gulf War Syndrome, you're gonna get a lot of closed mouths because it's not just ten men, you're talking about thousands right now."

Tony Sikes said, "I wondered if some of the problems were caused by the pills we were forced to take.... We found out the pills were experimental, and no one was given a choice, so we were all guinea pigs for the government. Until 1993, I was led to believe that the shots and pills were classified and not to be talked about." Blackcloud said he definitely believed that exposure to something during the Gulf War had made him sick. He wondered, like many of the others, if it was the experimental vaccines and drugs, "some of the stuff that blew up [that] came down wind" during the war, his combat experience, or a combination of all of these factors. James Lane said he was "concerned about the anti-nerve agent pills we were ordered to take." Likewise, Sam Stansky named anthrax shots and nerve agent pills and remarked, "I believe there was stuff used that the public is not being told about, and the government is not releasing the information. I think it's because they don't want to spend the money. I think maybe it was the pills or the shots or the chemicals that were released over there, although they still say to this day that there were no chemicals released, but I think there was.... That's stuff that's not being told..."

For some Gulf War veterans, the story of GWS was "a story of conspiracy, of secret chemicals and dangerous medicines." Not everyone agreed though. Ongoing medical investigations had yet to identify a cluster of symptoms unique to GWS and not potentially related to other diagnoses. Further, as no causal chain, much less a singular cause for GWS had emerged, many scientists and commentators concluded that no physical syndrome existed at all. The lack of coherent medical explanation or identifiable organic epidemiology led dominant medical, government and media establishments to dismiss GWS, often pejoratively, as a somatic psychologically bound syndrome. It was "all in their heads."[65]

In September 1992, an editorial in the *Boston Globe* headlined, "Operation Desert Whine" emphasized, as many experts and commentators would over the years, that GWS was hatched from the minds of malingering soldiers. The physical symptoms reported by Gulf War veterans were either wholly fabricated or expressions of their psychological pathologies, manifestations of soldiers' anxieties more akin to PTSD than Vietnam-era Agent Orange complications. Some likened GWS to an "information disease" that spread, not through known medical means, but as a viral meme on the internet rumor mill and exposure to other soldiers' accounts as reported by the media.[66] The black and white "mind over matter" debate about GWS was a heated one. For skeptics and deniers, media reports that lent validity to soldiers' claims of failing health or did not attempt to debunk these claims and cut them off at the pass, were to blame. Thus, GWS became just another conspiracy theory in a decade ripe with them.

Reflecting the rhetorical style that often accompanied dismissals of GWS as a real phenomenon was a March 1997 *Reason* magazine article entitled "Gulf Lore Syndrome," that invited readers to step into "a world [where] science is replaced by rumor." In this world, veterans, "convinced they are the victims of a conspiracy deeper and broader than anything on "The X-Files," claimed to have "skin blistering semen and glowing vomit." The article compared the commonly reported GWS symptoms to "Elvis sightings" and warned that soldiers who believed they had GWS would remain trapped in a world, "terrorized by rumors about their health" until they saw reality for what it was and stopped insisting they were sick.[67] While perhaps overstating the point, the author of the article expressed one side of the growing and highly polarizing atmosphere surrounding discussions about GWS during this time and throughout the next decade.

The struggle over definitions and meanings was one waged upon academic grounds as well as medical, political and journalistic ones. Illustrating this was Elaine Showalter's 1997 *Hystories: Hysterical Epidemics and Modern Culture*, published by Columbia University Press. In it, Showalter went so far as to compare GWS to other conspiracy theories such as alien abductions and satanic cults which, while pervasive, remained beyond the boundaries of rational discourse (or at least as she defined it). Stories about GWS represented a "plague of paranoia."[68] Showalter emphasized how viral rumors like those surrounding GWS and the above mentioned conspiracy theories only serve to demonize, scapegoat and erroneously ascribe particular guilty agents as the causal force behind political and psychological events and circumstances.

On the other hand, a growing number of academics' theorizing about the meaning and implications of American conspiracy culture cited the preponderance of post-Watergate revelations about actual government conspiracies, cover-ups and abuses to questions whether any specific conspiracy theory was metaphorically rooted in, if not directly linked to actual ones, including GWS. Among them was Peter Knight, who in 1999 wrote:

> It would come as no surprise, to learn that the military is refusing to investigate properly – if not actually covering up the truth about the appalling catalogue of illnesses associated with the war in the Persian Gulf, illnesses quite conceivably caused by either careless or deliberate exposure of soldiers to unknown risk, be it pesticides, cocktails of anti-nerve gas drugs, or (in one conspiracy theory) uranium-enriched missile casings.[69]

Despite the supportive approach taken by more sympathetic commentators like Knight, more often than not, Gulf War veterans seeking information about and help for their symptoms were dismissed and told they were psychosomatic in nature, evidence of their malingering, or that they'd succumbed to ill-informed hysterical conspiracy theories. Thus, some chose not to address or seek medical attention for their symptoms at all. Certainly many of McVeigh's COHORTs had become frustrated with the VA in their attempts.

At the time of his interview with the Jones Team in 1995, Stansky said that he actually reenlisted in order to get medical care for his child (born with birth defects) and had sought treatment for his own failing health. He had participated in a "Desert Storm Syndrome physical" but in 1993, VA doctors told him that PTSD was responsible for his symptoms and referred him to the mental health division. James Lane said he had gone to the doctor at least five times in order to determine the cause of his symptoms but said rather than answers, all the doctors gave him was Prednisone, which helped but did not stop his rashes from coming back. Lane said when he asked his doctors if something during the war might have caused his rashes and sleep problems, they said they did not have the answers to that question and as his inquiries to the VA only resulted in him getting "the run-around," he eventually gave up trying to obtain answers altogether. Blackcloud said he, too, brought up his symptoms to the VA but had not heard back from them "in a long time" and after 1995, "didn't even mess with the VA anymore."

For a layperson, not to mention a sick soldier, determining the truth was nearly impossible. For every scientific study arguing that no evidence of an actual physical illness existed, an equal number of simultaneously conducted studies with contradictory results argued the opposite. A number of studies continued to show that Gulf War vets displayed higher rates of physical illnesses when compared to the general civilian population and argued that detractors denied this reality simply because it did not fit into known medical models.

It is often said that conspiracy theories tend to equate the absence of evidence to proof of a conspiracy. Certainly, the fact that pertinent government records detailing occurrences and circumstances related to possible causes of GWS (e.g., chemical warfare logs and military medical records) continued to go missing, failed to inspire confidence in official denials about the reality of GWS. Later revelations only served to bolster conspiracy theories about GWS and intensify the already contentious debate. Throughout the 1990s and 2000s, from various congressional investigations, scientific studies and government admissions, a number of commonly suspected causes of GWS became more credible. Among those suspected causes that were initially dismissed but incrementally became more plausible were a number of chemical warfare agents such as sarin gas, depleted uranium, oil well fires as well as various ingredients in the experimental vaccines and pills administered to soldiers (some of which are discussed in previous chapters of this book).

The U.S. government seemed to recognize potential harmful exposures only after they became undeniable, often through investigative journalism. Official acknowledgement followed in June 1993 when officials in the Clinton administration and Walter Reed Medical Center publicly announced that the DU used on U.S. tanks and artillery shells may have contributed to GWS. Among the thousands of U.S. troops exposed to DU was McVeigh's division.

In July 2000, Lou Johnson, the only COHORT to acknowledge McVeigh's deteriorating health, wrote to McVeigh, at that time on death row awaiting execution. In his letter, Johnson discussed his ongoing struggles with the Veterans Administration and said he planned to go to law school because, "I'm sick of seeing vets get fucked by the VA and the government. If not law, then teaching. Maybe I can change some of these college kid's idiot thinking." He said after seven years of fighting with "the bastards at the VA" who continuously "fucked up" his records, the Board of Veterans Appeals finally determined that his problems were service-related.

As the Rambo character reflected angst resulting from, among other things, the Vietnam-related Agent Orange scandal, fictional works of popular culture came to articulate shared environmental and political concerns raised by the mysterious and controversial GWS. Tracy Letts' fictional play, *BUG*, first performed in 1996, published in 2006, and adapted to film in 2007, depicts a Gulf War veteran named Peter who confides to another character that, during the war, Army "doctors came in and really worked us over with shots and pills, ostensibly for inoculation but ... there was something else going on too. A lot of the guys got sick, vomiting, and diarrhea, migraines, blackouts. One guy had an epileptic seizure." Peter also began to "feel funny" and the Army shipped him back to a military hospital in the United States where he meets Timothy McVeigh. Over the next four years, Peter says, he and McVeigh were human guinea pigs, experimental test subjects for Army doctors who injected them with, among other things, various vaccines and inoculations that had devastating side effects. Peter tells bits and pieces of his story throughout the course of the unfolding plot thereby building tension about whether or not many of the strange claims he makes (which he himself undoubtedly believes) are delusional or in some way based in reality.

A disturbing picture reflective of the story told by Peter in BUG emerges when one reviews (in chronological sequence) the intricate details within the available portions of McVeigh's military medical records, as well as other archival defense documents and oral testimony pertaining to his COHORTs, and juxtaposes these against the public history of GWS.

Only after McVeigh's execution when, in 2008, the number of Gulf War veterans reportedly suffering from ailments linked to GWS reached over 700,000, did the Department Of Defense recognize it as a legitimate service-related illness and, while money continued to be allotted for studies of its causes and treatments, to this day, no consensus exists. In 2010, the VA announced it was reviewing the 300,000 compensation claims filed by Gulf War vets, acknowledging that some of them had been wrongfully denied. More recently, a November 2012 study published in the *Archives of Neurology* found that one in four suffered from GWS symptoms attributed to nervous system damage resulting from exposure to neurotoxins including the nerve agent sarin and widely distributed anti-nerve agent pills. Similar studies have argued that exposure to pesticides, in combination with exposure to these other neurotoxins, cause Parkinson's disease. The 2012 study divided GWS symptoms into three categories: cognitive and depressive; confusion and memory loss, described as similar to Alzheimer's disease; and severe chronic body pain, all of which McVeigh and his COHORTs reported nearly twenty years earlier.

MCVEIGH'S VIRAL CONSPIRACY THEORY SYNDROME

Two weeks after the Oklahoma City bombing, the FBI conducted an interview with Peter Salino (name changed), a Buffalo resident suffering from HIV who volunteered at a local nonprofit AIDS Awareness outreach program. Salino said he first met Timothy McVeigh in 1992 when his supervisor at the program directed him to contact "Tim," a man who had called the outreach office claiming to be a student at Buffalo State University who was interested in volunteer work. Throughout the following year, he and Tim met regularly. During one discussion, Tim said he had a great interest in helping AIDS patients and was thinking about starting his own outreach initiative, but needed access to a computer to do so.

Salino described Tim as a strange and contradictory person who was vague about where he lived and said that on at least three occasions he had dropped Tim off at the Buffalo VA medical center. Tim told Salino that he was undergoing treatment there for manic depression and paranoid schizophrenia and said he sometimes blacked out and while he could perform tasks in this state, later had no memory of what he did. He explained that the blackouts usually lasted for two to three days, but that one had lasted nearly two months. On one occasion, Tim told Salino that he used to be in the Army but that the experience had been a negative one and, several times, remarked that he had a past life he had not told Salino about; but advised Salino to be careful of him because of this. Salino told the FBI that sometimes Tim would "flip out," suddenly become angry and yell incoherently about the federal government. One of Tim's main gripes, he told Salino, was Social Security's rejection of his application for medical benefits.[70]

While Salino's story is quite strange, the statements of others lend support to it and (true or not) it touches upon another, larger discursive pattern that, I believe, correlates to the specter of Gulf War Syndrome that seemed to haunt McVeigh and his COHORTs. When the Jones Team interviewed Steve Hodge's mother, she said that after McVeigh returned home from the Army he developed a strange obsession with the AIDS virus. In a letter McVeigh wrote to Steve after leaving the Buffalo area in late 1992, he included clippings of news articles about a recent CIA drug running scandal and wrote, "The U.S. government waged biological warfare against its citizens as a means of population control." Steve said that in previous conversations McVeigh "insisted" that the government "engineered the AIDS virus and introduced it into the public," first in Africa through a smallpox vaccine, and fluoride in the water supply was also poisoning people.

Perhaps McVeigh became fascinated with HIV and AIDS after reading the news. After all, as he later explained, during this time he began to pay attention to what the news was really saying. The state of New York had the highest rate of AIDS diagnoses in the country, and although some Buffalo area patients described the refusal of some doctors and dentists to treat them, local hospitals were conducting experimental trials in an attempt to find a treatment. Interestingly, local news reports said that, among the symptoms displayed by those infected with the immune-weakening virus, was an infection of the gums that often led to the removal of the majority, or all, of a patients teeth. In June 1992, local AIDS hotlines received 6,400 callers requesting information about the virus and 1,000 seeking AIDS tests. In August of 1992, the Centers for Disease Control urged public health clinics to test all patients for HIV.[71]

In an unrelated initiative that same month, the Buffalo VA established their Gulf War Registry. Earlier, in March 1991, doctors from Walter Reed Army Medical Center warned that Middle East infectious diseases could manifest several years after their contraction and banned Gulf War veterans from donating blood after 27 of them contracted a parasitic disease. By November 1994, newspapers warned of a newer threat faced by U.S. troops described as "more insidious than Iraqi tanks or Haitian machetes." While it is unknown how great the Haitian machete threat of 1994 was exactly, the report described diseases such as AIDS, malaria and hepatitis as the new Iraqi tanks. Some reports suggested that, despite their immunizations for things like hepatitis B and rabies, the fear of chemical warfare and AIDS alone was enough to cause soldiers to develop symptoms linked to GWS.[72]

In fact, given his voracious consumption of news, McVeigh likely came across at least a few of the many reports that established links between GWS and immune system reactions or failures and to AIDS/HIV in particular. Kilshaw noted that both media reports and the vets she spoke to make explicit links between HIV and AIDS and GWS. On a number of occasions, McVeigh's Army doctors ordered AIDS tests for him, and while a routine practice, his continued, but secret, medical visits led to at least one of them. Later, quite a few studies found that many of the symptoms commonly linked to GWS were analogues to various acute chronic illnesses, persistent viral infections and auto-immune deficiencies including HIV, AIDS, herpes, hepatitis and papilloma, the latter commonly causing persistent blister-like warts on a number of areas including the feet. More than a few studies reported that patients treated for GWS responded positively when treated in the same manner as those treated for auto-immune deficiencies, including repeated rounds of strong antibiotics. Rather than being an illness rooted in a patient's mind, these studies further emphasize that anxiety itself weakens the immune system and exacerbates these types of chronic illness.

In 1999, the Association of American Physicians and Surgeons linked several chronic illnesses, including GWS and AIDS/HIV, to mycoplasmal infections resulting from micro-organisms that display characteristics of both viruses and bacteria and reported positive results from treating them with antibiotics, vitamin support and immune enhancers. A scientist whose research was described as something that might be seen on *The X-Files*, had been commissioned by the VA to study the role of mycoplasma in GWS, believed that, as it appeared in the blood of Gulf War vets, it seemed "genetically engineered" and resembled "a gene from HIV." The scientist's claim is similar to a vet featured in a magazine article that claimed one of the preventative injections administered to some soldiers included an untested component chemical resembling "HIV genes" that creates "the [immune-weakening] condition that allows for the development of AIDS."[73]

Eventually, after years of previous denials, the Pentagon incrementally acknowledged that the experimental anthrax vaccine given to U.S. soldiers during the Gulf War contained the adjuvant squalene. It turned out that, not only had "officials repeatedly lied about the relationship of squalene," throughout the 1990s, the U.S. military conducted experimental tests of vaccines for, among other things, AIDS/HIV, malaria, and herpes using civilians and soldiers while the Pentagon, in other countries, including Thailand, conducted experimental trials of HIV vaccinations not authorized in the U.S.[74]

In fact, by February 1996, GWS had come to act as a "powerful metaphor for disease" for a generation of Americans who suspected that GWS itself had been "created by the hubris of modern science ... one of our terrible Frankenstein monsters." Conspiracy theories about the government's responsibility for the creation of GWS were similar to those about AIDS. McVeigh's belief that the U.S. government created and released AIDS into the population was one shared with a large number of Americans, particularly African-Americans. Cultural commentator Jodi Dean wrote that the growing popularity of the AIDS conspiracy coincided with speculations during this same period that the CIA introduced crack cocaine into the black community. Both conspiracy theories, said Dean, had roots in the Tuskegee syphilis experiments, other "unethical medical practices" and genocidal practices historically and systematically employed by the U.S. government to oppress black Americans.[75]

In 2005, journalist Margaret Cook reported on a study conducted by the University of Oregon, which found that over half of the African-American population believed that HIV was man-made and had been intentionally spread within their community by the government as a form of genocide. According to this lore, HIV was created in chimpanzees by the CIA in the 1950s and first introduced to the public via polio vaccines and later, within the gay population, through experimental Hepatitis vaccines. Others simply believed that, one way or another, their community functioned as government "guinea pigs."[76]

The continued belief in conspiracy theories of this type is founded upon actual experiments on humans involving radioactive isotopes, viruses, psychoactive drugs, cancer cells, mustard gas, fluoride, various vaccines, as well as chemical and biological weapons that continued well into the 1990s. The unwitting test subjects included, among others: soldiers, prisoners, veterans, cancer patients, and children. Cook, for one, did not discount out of hand such seemingly paranoid scenarios as ridiculous or implausible and, like Dean, opined that suspicions and conspiracy theories about government science experiments were not as outlandish or unfounded as they may first appear when the practices of the U.S. after Nuremburg are considered. Cook warned that, even if the government did not create AIDS, its previous abusive research practices posed a danger nonetheless, as victimized individuals and populations may be suspicious of and reject (for good reason) harmless protective measures such as vaccines, when offered.

Further, throughout the 1990s, the government made a number of admissions about just such experiments that had occurred decades previous. A presidential advisory panel established in 1994 resulted in the declassification of documents pertaining to the use of civilians and soldier guinea pigs. The panel found that while "the great majority" of these had been "conducted to advance biomedical science," the intent of many was to advance national defense interests. The Committee issued an official apology and paid settlements to many of the victims, an act of public apology and "performance of public contrition" that cultural theorist Bridget Brown noted had become "commonplace" and "almost comical" by the 1990s. Brown observed that, while "the historical apology has become part of a collective, national narrative of retrieved memories … official apologies for historical abuses lead not to public healing, but to confusion over to what extent abuses of power are pathologies" and "result in a deep intractable cynicism and suspicion of powers that be."[77]

Cultural theorist Jack Z. Bratich cited the "AIDS conspiracy theory" as one shared by both the left and right. He wrote that, while they may have had good reasons for their beliefs (many noted by Bratich), detractors tended to psychologize the issue, deeming the belief evidence of "race paranoia," an irrational belief in a very real genocidal structure. Bratich concludes that the more pertinent question is not whether the U.S. government created and intentionally spread AIDS but rather, why even the suggestion of this unthinkable scenario provoked debunkers' virulent responses. AIDS, for conspiracy theorists, acts as "a sign to be decoded, demystified and uncovered, revealing a truth of social and historical relations underneath it (i.e., genocide, New World Order, population control)."[78]

Kilshaw wrote that soldiers' discussions about GWS were "a form of commentary" that used a "shared bodily language" to express "collective social angst" and "distress" within a "world of shared social meaning" that existed on "the fault lines of culture."[79] The "narratives of suspicion" offered by McVeigh and his COHORT, like those of thousands of other Gulf War veterans, are closely related to, and founded in, the same circumstances that have led many in the African-American community to believe that the government not only created AIDS but also administered it to the citizenry. After all, many realized only later that the entire Gulf War itself had been a massive theatrical experiment in technology and genocidal greed. It is possible that, even if under an erroneous belief that the Army had administered vaccines or inoculants that led to his physical ailment, the fact that McVeigh embraced this belief speaks to additional motivations for his participation in the bombing plot that have hitherto remained unexplored.

Finally, the movie *BUG* illustrates how works of fiction in popular culture voice shared concerns about biomedicine and its relationship to bio-warfare. In *BUG*, as Peter slowly reveals details of his story, the audience learns that eventually he escaped the military hospital where he and McVeigh had been kept as experimental test subjects, but since then, a plague of "bugs'"continued to burrow under his skin. He explains that the U.S. Army first sprayed the bugs over Baghdad during the Gulf War and later tested them on him and McVeigh. The bugs bite him, feed off his blood and leave marks all over his body. Peter convinces his friend Agnes that the bugs (and bug bites) are real and warns her, "I don't know that I'm not carrying some contagion. That's how they start, typhoid, Legionaries' disease, some government screw up, AIDS..."

One scientist contracted by the VA to study links between mycoplasmal infections and GWS described the former as a "stealth-like" germ that "burrow[s] deep in the cells."[80] In addition to "Haitian machetes," AIDS, malaria and hepatitis, another insidious threat that reportedly plagued troops deployed to the Gulf region included leishmianis, a disease caused by snails that burrow under human skin and travel to the intestines. One informant in Kilshaw's study described vaccines as a prevention solution that "goes in your blood stream" to help the immune system by creating a "barrier" for "the germ" or "the bug."[81] In BUG, Peter covers the walls of a motel room as well as everything in the room with tinfoil in order to prevent his 'bugs' from emitting signals that would alert his handlers to his whereabouts. Kilshaw also wrote about one of her informants, a Gulf War veteran who covered his walls with tinfoil to prevent infections that might weaken his immune system. Furthermore, Peter's story in BUG and some of McVeigh's documented symptoms resemble those associated with Morgellons disease, which causes red spots to cover the body that eventually begin to ooze pus and blood. The cause of Morgellons, a disease many HIV/AIDS patients contract, is strands of bacterial fibers that, like Peter's bugs, burrow under the skin. "It's not just contact," said one scientist studying Morgellons, "it's something injecting itself beneath the skin."[82] Like GWS, skeptics of Morgellons claim the only thing those diagnosed with it share is delusional parasitosis, the belief that bugs are crawling all over one's body.

While Letts certainly did not review McVeigh's military records, and McVeigh never claimed he had literal bugs, the story offered by Peter is similar to those told by McVeigh about himself, those who knew him and, later, within subcultural realms. Like McVeigh, BUG employs the language of suspicion and conspiracy to evoke collective (but vague) memories of a number of disturbing episodes in recent American history. Although Peter claims his handlers tried to set him up as John Doe 2, he escaped. Insofar as he expresses beliefs and fears about these episodes similar to McVeigh and as relayed by Salino, Steve Hodge, his mother and others, Peter represents McVeigh, but also "McVeigh" types, past and current.

PART FOUR
HOWLING AT THE MOON

Behind the hieroglyphic streets there would either be a transcendent meaning, or only the earth.... Another mode of meaning behind the obvious, or none. Either Oedipa in the orbiting of a true paranoia, or a real Tristero. For there either was some Tristero beyond the appearance of the legacy of America, or there was just America and if there was just America then it seemed the only wa[y] she could continue, and manage to be at all relevant to it, was as an alien, unfurrowed, assumed full circle into some paranoia.

– Thomas Pynchon, *The Crying of Lot 49*, 1966.

History as we know it is a lie...

–*Dark Skies*, 1996.

CLOSE ENCOUNTERS OF THE BUFFALO KIND

I get these messages from other planets. I'm apparently some kind of agent from another planet, but I haven't got my orders clearly decoded yet.

– William S. Burroughs to Jack Kerouac, 1957.

Since the end of World War II, works of popular science fiction have nurtured American imaginations with stories of flying saucers, UFOs, space travel, aliens and mad scientists. Baby boomers and beyond grew up on tales of Nevada's mysterious Area 51, unexplained crashes of strange aircraft in the deserts of Roswell, New Mexico, advanced technologies (alien or otherwise) and living monstrosities created by science gone haywire. These imaginings caught on and science fiction soon blurred with the parameters of possible reality. By 1990, three out of five Americans believed in UFOs, half the population believed they had personally encountered a UFO, between 27% and 50% thought the U.S. government was covering up knowledge about the existence of aliens and one in fifty believed that, at one time or another, they themselves had been abducted by aliens.[83]

Not since the 1950s had Americans displayed such a fascination with UFOs and, since that time, it had become a polarizing topic. On one side were the skeptical *debunkers* and on the other, *true believers*, some of whom claimed to have personally observed UFOs or encountered non-human beings from outer space who, occasionally, took the opportunity to kidnap them. In the middle was a confused but entertained public. Maybe aliens crashed in Roswell, New Mexico, in 1947; maybe they didn't. Maybe the Air Force recovered non-human vehicles containing living or dead space travelers and stored them at secret underground hangars, or maybe not. Maybe the government was testing futuristic aerial vehicles over "Area 51" in Nevada (a location whose operational existence remained, at the time, denied), but then again ... maybe they weren't. And what about those relentless Men In Black? Who were they, anyways?

Depending on who you asked, UFO sightings could be attributable to naturally occurring phenomena such as "glowing globes of electricity" that tended to appear just prior to earthquakes. Others said that the perplexed sky watchers had observed actual but human-engineered aerial hardware including weather balloons, satellites or classified experimental military aircraft testing new non-lethal sound and electric weapons as well as stealth and, perhaps, highly classified anti-gravity capabilities. The skeptics agreed that the great majority, if not all sightings, originated from the human imagination alone. If not fabrications, hoaxes or practical jokes then perhaps the sightings were caused by sleep paralysis or vision-producing hypnogogic sleep conditions. For others, the sightings evidenced mass hysteria caused by apocalyptic anxieties as the dreaded "Y2K" rapidly approached; psychic disturbances coinciding with political and economic upheavals as theorized by Carl Jung in 1958. The most ardent skeptics warned that those engaged in the obsessive quest for answers about UFOs were similar to a dangerous cult that threatened the sanity of growing numbers of people and that the coddling of the phenomena within American popular culture and by the entertainment industry only compounded matters.

According to another emergent and newly articulated theory, individuals' memories of UFOs and abductions were, in fact, false memories *implanted* through hypnosis by well-meaning but over eager therapists with highly suggestible clients. Many UFO skeptics supported this theory and it even found support among some conspiracy theorists, who added their own twist: those fortunate enough to undergo such an experience had, unfortunately, been the subjects of unwitting mind control experiments performed on hapless and unsuspecting individuals by factions of a secret government that inserted false memories of UFOs to cover other unthinkable ones. Worse, the government had engaged in a massive misinformation and disinformation campaign to spread UFO mania to shield their activities.

Thus, the fracturing debate divided even the conspiracy theorists who, among themselves, disagreed about the meaning of the recent oddly populated skies. Some held an unshakable belief in extra-terrestrial interstellar spacecraft. For them, a number of possible reasons existed for the recent rash of UFOs traveling to earth from the farthest reaches of outer space: the exploitation of earth's resources along with the domination and enslavement of humankind; a malevolent or benevolent but rigorous study of humans whose methodology consisted of abducting and performing bizarre medical procedures, often involving the implantation of tracking devices in human bodies, thereby allowing the curious alien scientists to monitor their subjects; delivering warnings about humankind's imminent destruction of the planet and themselves along with it; and/or to help usher in a peaceful and long awaited New World Order. Still, if you replaced "Aliens" with "Shadow Government," similarities between the basic narrative formulae of both versions became apparent. Either way, the government was covering up something – their own evil plots or the existence of extraterrestrial life.

Luckily for upstate western New Yorkers and their Canadian neighbors, in September 1992, the Buffalo News published a list of "Encounter Clues" to help readers determine whether or not they had made contact with aliens or UFOs and, a month later, a *Calgary Herald* article entitled "The Skies Are Full of UFO's" added to the list. Indicators included: observations of strange lights in the sky followed by amnesia or 'missing time,' unexplained bodily scarring, nosebleeds and pregnancies, as well as recurring and vivid dreams of flying saucers or medical examinations; an overwhelming fear of the dark or being outside alone, feelings of being watched and sensing sentient, yet unseen, presences. If this sounded familiar to anyone, groups of believers, skeptics, and the "expert" guest speakers hosted by both, met regularly in the Buffalo/Niagara/Ontario region.[84]

A good thing too, as newspapers told of a growing number of local UFO sightings, abductions and individuals experiencing periods of missing time. Of course, there was nothing new about this. Western New York had been plagued by UFO's for decades – like that time when a Buffalo area teenager was busy milking his cows in his barn when he heard an unexplained noise outside just as the airwaves of the radio he was listening to filled with unintelligible static and his milking machinery stalled. When he went outside to see what was going on he saw a "silver-colored football-shaped object with sharply defined edges hovering just above tree top level." The craft made "beeping" sounds, emitted "red vapor," and then suddenly, made a loud booming sound, sharply ascended, turning the clouds green in the process and disappeared. Four other people reported similar sightings within the next 40 minutes. Although they searched the area, neither the New York State Police or the Air Force found anything to indicate the cause of the disturbance, except for a "purple-colored, oily substance" found on a nearby sod sample. Similar sightings in the area continued, usually involving aircraft displaying formations of unusual lights, maintaining fixed positions and that, on at least one occasion, emitted soft purring like sounds "like a bagful of kittens."[85]

Reflecting national patterns, the phenomena continued regionally and shared or group UFO sightings seemed to increase in the early 1990s as seen in a number of *Buffalo News* articles and elsewhere. In February 1994, the good people of Ellicottville, an outlying suburb of Buffalo, reported sightings of a "flying humanoid-like man with [a] rocket pack" who made no noise but was accompanied by "Huey-type helicopters" that flew (just as silently) alongside him. Scores of witnesses simultaneously called the local paper to report unexplained flying black objects of differing shapes and sizes with red lights hovering over fields, illuminating the skies. After his "Close Encounter of the Ellicott Kind," one concerned citizen snapped a photo. Although, as these things tend to go, the origins of the beams of light captured in it were indeterminable. That same month, handfuls of people near Syracuse saw a craft with two rows of bright lights fly over a cornfield and suddenly plummet to the ground, but when Fort Drum dispatched two helicopters equipped with night vision devices to investigate, they found no trace of the spaceship. [86]

The growing number of sightings in the region during the early to mid-1990s and the public's growing attention to them provoked the ire of the proudly rational minded, who chalked them up to boredom as, "now that the Loch Ness Monster has been revealed as a hoax, and the Kennedy assassination has been discussed to exhaustion, UFOs remain the last outpost of cosmic intrigue." For the undecided, the question remained, "if extraterrestrials have found Earth, what will happen to our culture, religion, science and politics, and how will we react to these presumably superior beings?" The real issue for believers, however, was not *if* they existed, but as expressed in the topics of a seminar held at the local Ramada Inn, the more pressing issue was, "The World Wide UFO Cover-UP" and the need to uncover "UFOs: The History and Evidence!"[87]

More neutral commentators like Jodi Dean, writing in the late 1990s, felt the prevalence of such beliefs provided "an especially revealing window [to examine] current American paranoia and distrust" and thought stories about UFOs and space exploration allowed for an interrogation of "the link between American technology and American identity."[88] Concerns about UFO's and their alien occupants were reflected in fictional works as well, in which the villains not only acted as symbolic stand-ins for Cold-War Communist Others but also mirrored the actual activities and aspirations of the U.S. defense industry.

BUFFALO'S AREA 51

Far to the east, down in the pink sky, something has just sparked, very brightly. A new star, nothing less noticeable … it's a vapor trail. Already a finger's width higher now. But not from an airplane. Airplanes are not launched

*vertically. This is the new, and still Most Secret, German rocket bomb....
Already the rocket, gone pure ballistic, has risen higher. But invisible now....
The missile, sixty miles high, must be coming up on the peak of its trajectory
by now ... beginning its fall ... now ... He won't hear the thing come in. It
travels faster than the speed of sound. The first news you get of it is the blast."*

–Thomas Pynchon, *Gravity's Rainbow*, 1973

In 1992, McVeigh was transferred upon his request from his desk job in the Burns office to an armed night watchman position at Calspan, a local aerospace research and development center. There he met Carl Lebron, another guard with whom he discussed all manner of strange topics. Lebron said he and McVeigh shared a mutual interest in "conspiracy theories ... UFOs, strip clubs and the usual political type stuff" and while he found McVeigh's conspiracy theories "more radical" than the ones he was willing to consider, McVeigh was still "into UFOs" and both men occasionally brought in "UFO magazines" to discuss.[89] In fact, upon his transfer to Calspan, McVeigh hit the conspiracy theory jackpot. As fate would have it, McVeigh and Lebron guarded a facility whose yearly multi-million dollar defense contracts helped generate the very flying saucer lore they discussed there. The fascinating history of Calspan takes place in the context of Cold-War era fears and hopes that, today, have evolved into the realization of technologies and practices previously considered science-fiction fantasy.

In 1934, the Buffalo based Curtiss-Wright Aircraft Corporation established the Flight Research Laboratory across from the Buffalo airport and built a revolutionary wind tunnel to study high-velocity flight. The wind tunnel ensured Curtiss-Wright's place as the largest airplane manufacturer and second largest corporation in the U.S. during World War II. Towards the end of World War II, after a scandal regarding Curtiss-Wright's involvement in a conspiracy to sell defective airplane parts to the U.S. military, they donated the facility, valued at $2.5 million, to Cornell University, who renamed it 'CAL' (Cornell Aeronautical Laboratory). This was the first, but by no means last time, that the CAL lab turned into a political and scientific hot potato. Operating under the auspices of its newly formed Graduate School of Aerospace Engineering, CAL conducted advanced aviation and technological research and development with the goals of maintaining U.S. air superiority and achieving innovations in commercial flight as well as non-aviation related advances in diverse fields including robotics and transportation.

The period immediately following World War II was one of controversy for the aerospace research industry, especially as it concerned the fate of hundreds of Nazi scientists in a U.S. venture code-named "Project Paperclip." While now a matter of public record, Paperclip remained secret for decades. As World War II ended, the U.S. and Soviets scrambled to gather the expertise of Nazi scientists, whose developments during the war included prototypes for supersonic rockets, guided missiles, atomic and chemical weapons, aerial vehicles, stealth technologies and aviation medicine. Under the authorization of President Truman, Project Paperclip secretly transferred more than 700 German scientists and their research projects to the U.S., where they began new lives under assumed names and busied themselves with work meant to ensure U.S. superiority in the upcoming Cold War Space Race. Nazis with new identities entered the top echelons of the American aerospace industry including the USAF and all other branches of the military, NASA and major private aerospace companies including Northrop Aviation, Lockheed, Martin-Marietta and North American Aviation.

The Paperclipped Nazi scientists developed some of the U.S.'s most spectacular technologies, including stealth bombers, guided cruise missiles and hypersonic aircraft. One of them, Werner von Braun, designed the V-2 Missile, grandfather to today's cruise missiles. Their ranks included a number of *bona fide* SS war criminals who, in the course of their coveted research, sanctioned, authorized or were directly responsible for thousands of deaths. Another was "the father of space medicine" and former Luftwaffe colonel, Hubertus Strughold, whose love of science led him to place prisoners at Dachau and Auschwitz in low-pressure chambers to determine human resiliency to high-altitude and high-speed flight, resulting in many gruesome deaths. Some of his other experiments, also performed on concentration camp inmates, entailed his placing them in freezing water for long periods of time and performing invasive surgical procedures without anesthetic. As the pioneer of aeromedical research, Strughold studied the effects of oxygen deprivation using epileptic children. Although the staff of the Nuremburg Trials and U.S. Army Intelligence documents listed him as a war criminal, Strughold apparently redeemed himself when he designed NASA's on-board life support systems and for the remainder of his life, continued to hold a number of esteemed positions in the U.S. defense establishment, where he went about developing methods to allow humans to travel safely into outer space.[90]

Paperclip provides the context for the U.S.'s illustrious aerospace and space exploration history and for what Jack Beilman, former researcher at Calspan, described as the mostly secret history of Calspan's immense contributions to aeronautics development; a significant amount of which was conducted at the lab McVeigh and Lebron guarded. Paperclip has also inspired numerous works of fiction including the classic Thomas Pynchon novel, *Gravity's Rainbow*. *BUG* alludes to Paperclip when Peter says after the Gulf War he was taken to Groom Lake (Area 51) and became the experimental subject for a military doctor named Dr. Sweet. Such experiments began, explained Peter, when "the CIA had smuggled Nazi scientists into the States to work with the American military at Calspan" where they developed tracking devices – brain implants.

Paperclip is also a staple subject within the conspiracy theory genre. No self-respecting conspiracy writer would neglect to mention it, and many argue that any major aerospace company after WWII would have on-staff at least one of its own Paperclip Nazis. Paperclip, however, is one of the subjects where the boundary separating the conspiracy genre and "credible" mainstream journalism becomes porous. In his book (not classified as within the conspiracy theory genre), *The Hunt For Zero Point: Inside the Classified World of Antigravity*, Nick Cook, a writer for *Jane's Defense Weekly* traced the Paperclip paper trail to startling conclusions about some of the U.S.'s technological plunder of Germany after WWII. Apparently, within underground German factories, Nazi rocket scientists, using slave labor, had been experimenting with anti-gravity aircraft and, according to Cook, had made some advances in the field of what, at the time, was called "Electrogravitics." The relocated Nazi rocket scientists continued developing their gravity-defying classified work upon their arrival in the U.S., during the 1950s until at least the mid-1970s, financed by 'deep black' budgets. When it came to anti-gravity research, Cook wrote, "Everybody has a finger in the pie." "Everybody" included Buffalo-based aerospace companies Bell and Curtiss-Wright and Avro, a Canadian company, all associated with CAL. For Cook, the testing of anti-gravity and other experimental technologies and aircraft accounted for a number of UFO sightings after World War II, including many over the skies of the U.S.-Canadian border.[91]

After World War II and the Soviets' launching of Sputnik, America "reached for the stars," and the CAL became an epicenter for leading airplane design and manufacturing, pioneering developments that played a major role in helping the U.S. catch up in the Space Race. According to the American Institute of Aeronautics and Astronautics, "Nearly every military aircraft and space vehicle developed in the United States from the end of World War II until the present day has been tested at the facility, now known as Calspan."[92] In early 1992, Calspan was, among other things, continuing the work begun during the Paperclip era by further developing hypersonic flight speed capabilities. Perhaps, as they sat around the Calspan guard shack, Lebron and McVeigh discussed the lab's "X-Planes" or other experimental aircraft that often enough had been humorously mistaken for UFOs of non-terrestrial origin and resulted in a perplexed public. Operations at Calspan undoubtedly influenced UFO lore.

Shortly before McVeigh left his job at the end of 1992, Calspan (at the time a subsidiary of Arvin Industries International) merged with another company, headed by former astronaut Joseph Allen, to form 'Space Industries International, Inc.,' and combined their aeronautic and industrial space research operations to make headway in the growing commercial space sector including the design, testing and eventual manufacture of "private spacecraft." Analysts at the time estimated that by the year 2000, the commercialization of space would generate billions of dollars in revenue.[93] Indeed, conspiracy writers like Jim Keith, likely read by the two CAL guards, surmised that the U.S. government/corporate ruling elite, with the help of their Nazi allies, had foreknowledge of some impending world disaster and, accordingly, planned to leave Space Station Earth and resettle on colonized planets. Once there, batches of enslaved and zombified humans could perform the more mundane workings of such an ambitious project.

Such evil machinations of the murderous-minded elite made sense to McVeigh, who saw in his favorite television show a similar but more utopian vision, outlined in a letter to his biographers:

> Star Trek holds the key! [...] The social structure of the society, the political beliefs of "The Federation" ... including 'The Prime Directive' [...] To Sum [sic]: Humanity should come together (voluntarily, not by bombs or sanctions, each nation as they're ready) for the common goal of colonization of other planets.[...] The most important reason? Right now we have "all of our eggs in one basket" – any global catastrophe ("extinction event" – there was an asteroid scare just last week) would wipe out not only our species, but all we've worked for, all of our knowledge, experience, and progress (however it may seem we degenerate, we have still advanced as a whole)[...] Preservation of the species... of knowledge. A cure to the number one reason for conflict: territorial disputes. Everyone can have their own world (by everyone I mean every nation state, every political belief system, every religious faction, etc.,).Of course, you'd have to establish ethical guidelines for "dominating" other pre-existing life. [This would be a] remedy for population-expansion problems (too many people competing for limited space, resources, I believe, is the root of most of our problems today: conflict, environment degradation, species extinction, etc.,). [We should] focus for our post-Cold War energies (rather than them manifesting in violence).[94]

Among the technological loot seized from the Nazis after WWII was the drone. While other countries including the U.S. had tinkered with the idea of unmanned aircraft previously, they hadn't gotten as far as the Nazi's. Air Force Intelligence documents related to Paperclip operations describe, in Cook's words, Nazi development and late-stage testing of "Vesco's Fireball drone: a pilotless, remote controlled aircraft that disrupted the energies and electronic systems of Allied bombers"

Before, during and after McVeigh guarded its secrets, Calspan, aided by multi-million dollar contracts from the DOD and all branches of the military made significant contributions to the further development and testing of remotely controlled aircraft capable of unusual and risky maneuvers human pilots could not perform, and the training and interface systems necessary for those who would "pilot" them. Perhaps coincidently, an unrelated article in the *Buffalo News* written by a Calspan engineer noted that most UFO sightings involved "lights and apparently solid objects that execute incredible maneuvers such as high-speed, right-angle turns; sudden starts and stops; 'falling leaf' descent, and silent hovering followed by rapid acceleration capabilities far beyond any known aircraft on Earth."[95]

In the early 1990s, major aerospace companies, suffering the decline of ballistic missile projects and other defense contract staples, turned to drone development and production to offset the losses. Enthusiasts emphasized their successful use on the front lines of the Gulf War, their precision, and ability to carry television cameras, sensors and jamming equipment that, they promised, would reduce casualties and fatalities in future wars. Even at this time, analysts and proponents projected their commercial use in domestic law enforcement surveillance, drug enforcement and customs operations by 2003. In the meantime, though, U.S. drones proved themselves useful in foreign peace-keeping operations and in the late 1990s when drones were now equipped not just with cameras but with laser targeting systems. While it sounded like something out of a science fiction movie, the hope, or at least the justification often offered, was to create an "empty battlefield" and as the necessary satellite, computing, and artificial intelligence capabilities improved, the vision became all the more realistic.[96] Still, outside of industry observers, drones didn't command wide-scale public attention.

And then 9/11 happened. After that, drones such as the Global Hawk and Predator carrying Hellfire missiles swarmed the skies of Afghanistan and then Iraq, theatres of war that Peter Pace, vice chairman of the Joint Chiefs said "provides a tremendous laboratory" to test the Pentagon's new toys. Someday, there could even be "whole squadrons of pilotless attack planes," and would make up 90% of all combat aircraft by 2025, media outlets gleefully announced in November 2001.[97] The CIA (at the time the main overseers and users of drones) pressed for increased use of attack drones, implying that if they'd had them sooner they could have killed Osama Bin Laden, thereby preventing 9/11. As the months went on, drones were increasingly credited with victories in the Global War on Terror. Admittedly, drones crashed more often than war wagers would have liked ... but this was a work in progress.

The real winners in all of this though, were not the American people per se, but the entire aerospace industry. After 9/11, Defense Secretary Donald Rumsfeld, long criticized for his efforts to "transform" the military by endowing it with the ability to project American power anywhere at any time at a moment's notice (or pre-emptively sooner), was now heralded as a prophet. In Rumsfeld's vision, once America's international technological killing capability was secure, military priority could be shifted towards "homeland defense" because, as he explained, "new threats have arrived, quite literally, at our doorstep."[98] Although Calspan had remained quietly in the background working towards such Rumsfeldian visions previously, the post 9/11 world presented the very backdrop needed for them to shine once more. And shine they did.

Among their other contributions, in 2004, Calspan began testing the Autonomous Aerial Refueling (AAR) system for unmanned aerial vehicles over Lake Ontario. The AAR, hailed as "a game changer" in 2012, significantly increased the range and endurance of aircraft carrier-based drones from which other drones are deployed. The test flights, said Calspan President Louis Knotts, were not only an important contribution to the military's operations in Iraq and Afghanistan, as the drone performed invaluable surveillance and combat functions as "eye[s] in the sky," but also made an important contribution to the local economy.[99] They soon expanded their local operations across from the Buffalo airport and built new facilities in the economically blighted chemical wasteland of nearby Niagara Falls, which had become the smelly armpit of western New York since its glory days of yore.

In 2005, Sea Technology reported on the ongoing development of lighter-than-air High Altitude Airships (HAA), resembling giant zeppelins, powered conventionally or by fuel and solar-cell technology, that could remain in the air for over six months at a time. The Calspan University of Buffalo Research Center was among those helping to ensure their imminent use in military, commercial and Homeland Security operations. In 2007, a *Guardian* headline alarmingly asked if "the U.S. [is] launching a blimp to spy on its population" and warned that those paranoid of persistent surveillance and eyes in the sky "tracking their every move" had until 2009 "to dig a bunker and [a] set of underground tunnels." Readers were informed that it would only take eleven HAA's to "watch every square meter of the whole country." By 2014, analysts seduced by dirigible dreams said that, while still in their infancy, expensive, clumsy and prone to randomly fall out of the sky, the stratospheric sky monstrosities would have the ability to "peer into distant galaxies" in the not so distant future. Local test flights over civilian airspace, intended to work out the kinks in the new, space-aged, experimental HAA aircraft, continue at the time of this writing.[100]

On September 11, 2013, Calspan successfully tested a simulation of the Unmanned Carrier Launched Airborne Surveillance and Strike (UNCLASS) control software that they had designed. In April 2014, the Navy announced that they would begin building UNCLASS systems, described as "squadrons of robotic top guns" weighing up to 80,000 pounds each that, when launched from the AAR's, would have the capacity to drop 500 pound bombs and could carry up to 3,000 pounds of other "payload."[101] And so on.

Of course, not everybody was enthusiastic about ongoing drone development and use. In August 2012, it was announced that as part of the FAA Modernization and Reform Act (2012), western New York (already the site of one of the 64 drone bases in the U.S.) was in the running to become one of six regions designated to conduct further drone research and testing to begin no later than September 2015. Protestors throughout the country, suspicious of secretive defense projects, unauthorized surveillances, (poorly and well executed) targeted attacks abroad, and for some the fear of a robot takeover (think Skynet), held signs saying "Make jobs, not drones," while drone proponents argued this is exactly what the booming commercial and defense drone industry would do.

From 2002 to the present, U.S. drones have rained hell on the declared war zones of Iraq and Afghanistan as well as covertly in undeclared war zones, including Pakistan, Yemen and Somalia, killing thousands. Among the dead are civilians, nearly half of them, children – all written off as "collateral damage." A June 2013 opinion piece about "collateral damage" caused by America's "Drone Wars" noted that many "decry the very notion that Obama is anything close to the warmongering Bush" but since his presidency began, he has sanctioned "seven times more covert drone strikes than his predecessor, George W. Bush" a number that continues to rise.

According to some estimates, in 2013 alone, drones had killed more than 2,500 people, more than 300 of whom were civilians, while 70-plus were children. And those are just the ones we know about. Accurate body counts are difficult in such awkward situations, however, even with advancements in battlefield technologies, ostensibly developed for accuracy's sake. Governments of countries victimized by drones say that the body count is higher. In 2013, Pakistan claimed that since they began their reign of aerial terror over a decade ago, U.S. drones have killed over 3,000 Pakistani civilians, including children and some infants, making the collateral damage toll much higher than the militant or combatant causality rate. Further, the drones have laid waste to the region's wildlife, civilian property and livestock. In June of the same year, Pakistan submitted a resolution to the National Assembly denouncing "the never-ending US drone attacks" and demanded the U.S. government stop the slaughter, which, they pointed out, violates the country's sovereignty as well as a number of UN Human Rights resolutions and charters as well as international treaties and Geneva Convention provisions.[102]

By 2015, covert drone strikes in regions outside of the U.S.'s declared war zones, authorized by the Obama administration and carried out by the CIA and the Pentagon's Special Forces outfit, Joint Special Operations Command, had reportedly killed six times as many people and twice as many civilians as those authorized under the Bush administration. In April of that year, the ACLU announced that while it is known that U.S. drones have killed thousands, "no one outside the government has a clear idea of who's being killed, or why" – as the government does not release information about the targets of individual drone strikes or the numbers of civilian deaths caused by them. Even the laws governing the use of drone strikes remain hidden from the public and, until recently, the CIA, citing National Security, refused to acknowledge that a drone program even existed.[103]

Who needs good old-fashioned assassins when you've got flying robots to do your wet work? Some argue that drones are a much more humane method of dealing with insurgents than say, GITMO or other black sites of extraordinary rendition. Said Lt. Gen. Michael Flynn, former head of the Defense Intelligence Agency, "We don't capture people anymore." As it turns out though, the secret killings of specific targets in the U.S.'s drone assassination program was highly ineffective. So-called terrorists and militants who became targets for this method of death were tracked with meta-data from computers, phones and cell Simcards that then determined the location for the strike. Lo and behold, there are some issues of accuracy with this method. As one whistleblower who leaked documents about the drone assassination program pointed out in October 2015, "The entire time you thought you were going after this really hot target, you wind up realizing it was his mother's phone the whole time."

In fact, the number of misattributed people targeted for death is stunning, despite President Obama's (joking?) promise that drones would only be used to murder "terrorists who pose a continuing and imminent threat to the American people [and when there is] near-certainty that no civilians will be killed or injured." Of the 200 known to have been killed in drone strikes between January 2012 to February 2013, 35 were actually targets. Everybody else, including children, just happened to be in the wrong place at the wrong time. No matter; unidentified corpses are classified as enemies, and the Pentagon plans to increase the use of drone flights.[104]

Since 2011, the United States Air Force, using exciting massive multi-player video game-like simulators, has trained more drone pilots than fighter and bomber pilots combined. In response, groups like Veterans For Peace have produced flashy ad campaign videos, calling attention to the U.S.'s murder by drone addiction and the ways that those "smart warriors" who remotely control them, are kept detached from the destructive and lethal consequences of their actions. Pointing out the high rates of PTSD in those who kill from afar, activist groups' Please Don't Fly campaign urges service members to refuse to press the "kill button." A growing number of military drone pilots have indeed left the service or sought transfer, including Brandon Bryant, who told *Democracy Now* that he chose to quit the Air Force after developing doubts about the precision of drones he controlled as well as suspicions that the majority of his 1,626 confirmed kills, had probably not been terrorists after all.[105] Despite the dissenting voices of Negative Nelly's like Bryant and company, environmentally conscious war mongers can take solace in the next planned addition to the U.S. unmanned arsenal, high-flying solar-powered drones.

Today, law enforcement agencies, including local and state police, the FBI, Homeland Security, Border Patrol and the Department of Defense, increasingly use drones for domestic reconnaissance and surveillance. While these Brave New Drones openly spy on and police Americans, thus far U.S. citizens have not been subjected to the types of aerial attacks suffered by those in Afghanistan, Pakistan, Syria, Somalia and elsewhere. But, as they say, what's good for the goose.... When the FAA authorized the commercial use of drones in domestic airspace in 2012, it estimated that nearly 30,000 drones would populate U.S. skies by 2020, conjuring thoughts of all-seeing private security firms and unmanned mercenary drone armies.

Collective anxieties about drones find avenues of expression in popular culture, whose works may prove not only entertaining but frighteningly prophetic. Drones act as cultural icons, fetishes and memes appearing in fictional books, television, film, video games, art, music and fashion. There are even Lego drones. Drones blur our understanding of reality and science-fiction fantasy. The very thought of a drone (a term denoting anything from a toy helicopter to a foam plane to a Global Hawk to a Predator) is vague and dreamlike. During an episode of one popular TV comedy a lead character jokingly remarked that drones are not "real" but rather (like conspiracy theories), "a collection of thoughts, feelings, isolated facts and nebulous paranoias." Fictional drones not only deal death but also face a number of challenges posed by terrorists' attempts to disable them and rogue supercomputer controllers who seek to wield them for malevolent intents. Drones show up in popular love songs throughout the world with lady-killer lyrics that swoon "my gaze is as deadly as a drone attack" and "drones in the morning, drones in the night, I'm trying to find a pretty drone to take home tonight."

The drones' appearance in popular realms not only reflect wider cultural realities and fears and facilitate conversations about these realities and fears but also provide arenas of resistance to them. A New York street artist arrested and charged with 56 counts of criminal forgery said that, when he depicted drones with the iPod logo, he was trying to "start a conversation" about unmanned aircraft.[106] Fashion developers make hoodies with anti-thermal-imaging capabilities. Meanwhile, some people are just happy that Amazon drones will now deliver books to your doorstep, saving the U.S. Postal Service a lot of unnecessary work.

You too can have a personal drone controllable from laptop or smartphone and if you can't afford to buy one ($449 on Amazon.com), the do-it-yourself drone community is growing. Each month over 1,000 new personal drones take flight. In fact, civilian-owned drones outnumber those operated by the U.S. military. But if you don't have time to sit around playing with your drone all day, bestow upon it a brain in the form of an embeddable micro-processor computer chip. Let it do what so many seem incapable of doing. Let drones think for themselves. Perhaps this will cut back on reported 'wandering drones' like the Navy craft that stumbled into D.C. airspace or fiascos such as the Mexican army drone that crashed in an El Paso backyard in December of 2010; or the $4 million dollar MQ-9 Reaper drone (one of a fleet that regularly flies over upstate Western New York) that, in November 2013, after being dispatched from Fort Drum during a training mission, crashed into Lake Ontario and remained missing.[107]

Pesky privately owned drones dropping illegal drugs in prison yards and getting in the way of important business at airports and disaster sites are cited for the commercial development of drone-killing counter measures, such as the "death ray" laser gun that can knock a drone out by turning it off in midair from a mile away. Just such a death ray might have come in handy when Buffalo's drone chickens came home to roost in late 2014. Twice that year, drones appeared over runways at the Buffalo International Airport, but nobody could determine who owned the "seagull-sized intruders" or why they had been deployed. They joined the FAA's list of "unwanted drone sightings"; a list I imagine does not include military, defense and law enforcement drones seen by increasingly aware sky watchers.

THE TWILIGHT ZONE

> *Beware when fighting a dragon that you do not become one.*
>
> –Chinese Proverb

> *There is a fifth dimension beyond that which is known to man. It is a dimension as vast as space and as timeless as infinity. It is the middle ground be-*

tween light and shadow, between science and superstition, and it lies between the pit of man's fears and the summit of his knowledge. This is the dimension of imagination. It is an area which we call the Twilight Zone.

–Rod Sterling, *The Twilight Zone*, Season 1, 1959

I'm not at liberty to reveal the nature of my work. This secrecy pains me from time to time. Any bureaucracy that functions in secret inevitably lends itself to corruption. But these rules I have pledged to uphold. I believe a pledge is sacred.... Well, I may reveal this much: among my many tasks is the maintenance of deep space monitors aimed at galaxies beyond our own. We routinely receive various communications, space garbage, to decode and examine."

– Major Briggs, *Twin Peaks*, Season 2, 1990

Brandon Stickney wrote that, by the time Timothy McVeigh left Buffalo, New York and headed for the "Land of Fools," his "Amerinoid status" was already "set in stone" but quickly became exacerbated by the social world in which he immersed himself, populated by people who only contributed to "his progressive mental disintegration." Included among the "government conspiracies" with which McVeigh soon became intimately familiar were ones about "alien spaceships" in the deserts of America.[108] Stickney may have been more right that he knew, or than anyone has previously noted.

In 1993, the *Buffalo News* reported on a growing trend of people with moonbeams in their eyes making pilgrimages to the deserts of Nevada in an effort to breach the secrets of "Area 51," also known as "Groom Lake" and "Dreamland." Although at first military officials remained silent, refusing to acknowledge that the site existed at all, eventually they said Dreamland was simply a testing site for classified experimental aircraft and electronic jamming equipment and a staging ground for war games. Others, however, insisted that the truth was much stranger and the government was covering up its knowledge of beings from other worlds. For them, Area 51 was a place where aliens and humankind co-operated in the building of flying saucers, hid technologies that could end war and hunger, hoarded limitless supplies of energy and performed "grotesque genetic experiments" against the will of abductees.[109] As there had yet to appear a smoking ray-gun that could settle the debate, it fell to UFO buffs to determine fact from homegrown American mythology. On the face of things, it would seem that, after leaving Buffalo, McVeigh too heeded this call and set off on his own pilgrimage to Area 51.

As he awaited trial, McVeigh continued to read the news obsessively. In July 1996, he came across the headline: "Poll Spots Belief In UFO's." The report said nearly 50% of Americans believed the government was hiding proof of UFOs, 20% believed they had alien origins and 12% claimed to have seen a UFO. He drew a line to these statistics on a clipping of the article and wrote to his attorneys, "These are the type of people we do want on a jury." If the prosecutors did not want X-Files fans, maybe they would not think to ask potential jurors if they believed in UFOs.[110]

In October 1995, McVeigh explained to his defense team that Area 51 was also sometimes called "Dreamland" and was operated by the Department of Defense and the Wackenhut Security company. The installation was very secure and there were signs at the entrance that said "Deadly Force Authorized." McVeigh advised that more nuclear testing was conducted near this location than all of the nuclear testing conducted by Russia. Towards the end of his life, McVeigh outlined his conclusions about the goings-on at the real Area 51, but might as well have been speaking of Calspan. Area 51 is a super-secret military installation whose existence, still denied by the government, is so classified it cannot be found on maps. Their mission, he said, was to "test all the ultra-modern government experimental programs out there." He explained,

> I believe that while there are such things [as UFOs], it is impractical [to think] that they are aliens. I'm sure there are these super-secret government experimental vehicles. For many reasons, for physical reasons, I do not believe aliens can travel at this point. So the answer to UFOs is that nobody can deny the government continually has secret programs that they call "black budget programs" and "black projects" and that's what I'm sure most of these sightings are.

In 2007, Calspan, now with facilities around the country, established its newest prestigious research facility located at, of all places, Roswell, New Mexico. *Popular Science* dubbed the Roswell "Calspan Bicycle Works" site, "the New Area 51."[111] Before continuing with the history of Calspan, I will briefly outline McVeigh's trip to the actual Area 51 after he left Buffalo, the possible relationship this trip might have to the bombing plot, and explore the intersection of fact, folklore, rumor and disinformation in this and related stories.

In some of the more entertaining Experimental Wolf legends, McVeigh, or one of his doubles, appeared in Area 51 prior to the bombing where he underwent various procedures including the injection of bio-tracking chips and brainwashing. In other variations, McVeigh appeared at Area 51 after his arrest, and while there, was transformed into an entirely new person. Although it has escaped the notice of other commentators, who generally claim to focus on "facts" rather than rumors, it is in and around Area 51 that all diverging narratives (Lone, Pack, Watched, Guilty Agent, Experimental) intersect and where truth once again blurs with fiction, especially the confabulations floated by McVeigh. Despite fantastical, science fictional cultural musings about aliens and UFOs hidden away at Area 51, McVeigh's later conflicting stories about his own trip there may not only have direct relevance to the commission of the bombing, but also reveal a hidden history whose rhizomic tentacles touch upon a number of issues that converge in the contradictory tales he told.

After leaving his hometown, McVeigh traveled the country on the gun show circuit. He told his biographers that, during a commute from Fortier's in Arizona to the Nichols brothers in Michigan, he paid a visit to the famed Area 51. His official biographers relayed McVeigh's colorful description of this particular adventure:

> [McVeigh] thought nothing of taking a detour five hundred miles to visit the site that interested him. And his first stop was a at a place that had taken on legendary status in more than one fringe community in American culture – the mysterious Area 51 military installation in Roswell, New Mexico. McVeigh had heard the many rumors about the site – that the military tested exotic aircraft, possibly even UFO's, at the remote outpost; that a UFO had once crashed at the site, and alien life forms had been found on the inside, but the incident had been kept secret. But it was more than just curiosity that drove McVeigh there. He was ready to stir up a little trouble too. McVeigh was outraged by reports that the federal government had posted threatening signs at the site, warning that the use of deadly force had been authorized against people who crossed a certain boundary into the installation. McVeigh wanted to test that one. He wanted to test his right as an American to walk on the public land – and he wanted to carry a gun there. McVeigh was eager to stand up to the rent-a – cops he had heard patrolled Area 51; as a former rent-a-cop himself, he knew that they possessed no greater right to make an arrest than the average citizen.... Armed with his Ruger Mini 30, semiautomatic rifle, he was prepared to confront anyone who tried to stop him...

Having arrived at Area 51, the camera-wielding McVeigh passed a "deadly force" sign and, to his dismay, another that warned against taking photographs. He kept driving, and after observing, not Men In Black, but two white security guards in a white, unmarked jeep, McVeigh leapt into a nearby gully and "ducked for cover" where he waited "motionless and undetected, following his military instincts" while the confused guards looked into his empty car. As he did so, it occurred to McVeigh that the guards were "sitting ducks" and, had he wanted to, he could have shot them. In that moment, however, it dawned on him that they were not his true enemies, and so, mercifully, restrained himself. That evening, under the cover of darkness, he hiked up a mountain with the objective of taking pictures of the legendary, super-secret installation. About halfway up, he saw a Black Hawk helicopter pass over him that then hovered about thirty yards directly in front of him. McVeigh thought about shooting the helicopter too, but "wasn't in combat mode, not yet" and so instead, he just waved to it. The helicopter, apparently unconcerned with his presence, flew away. McVeigh continued with his photo shoot. The next morning as he was leaving he noted a white van following him off the property. Rather than shooting these rent-a-cops, McVeigh gave them "a friendly 'Hi!'" after which, "the spooked guards drove off."[112]

In this account, McVeigh's visit to Area 51, while interesting and colorful, is not really convincing and reads more like a spy novel but, predictably, he and others told different versions of the story.

Michael Fortier claimed that McVeigh made more than one trip to Area 51. Fortier told the FBI that in February 1995, while on their way back to Kingman from gun shows in Nevada and Utah, he and McVeigh made two trips to Area 51, the first in the middle of the night, and the second during the day. Fortier said, on the second trip they "saw an older man with a young boy going to Area 51" and later, McVeigh sent him pictures he'd taken of one of his solo excursions there.

A different and perhaps more important story about McVeigh's trips to Area 51 was the one given to the FBI on April 28, 1995, by Kevin Nicholas, a friend of McVeigh's in Michigan. Nicholas described McVeigh as "a wanderer" who would get a job out west in Arizona and Nevada for six months or so, quit, return to Michigan, and then leave again. This pattern continued from 1993 to 1995, during which McVeigh found time to attend major gun shows throughout the country, selling guns under one of many aliases he used, "Tim Tuttle" being the only one Nicholas could remember. While on the road, McVeigh sometimes called Nicholas and, while a guest at Nicholas' house, made several long distance calls but "would never use a cordless telephone" believing "the frequency can be intercepted." Nicholas advised the FBI that, if they wanted to find John Doe #2, they should look near the Nevada-Arizona border as McVeigh had told him that he and others, whose identities Nicholas did not know, had a "stockpile of guns, ammunition, and survival supplies stashed in the desert near 'Area 51.'"[113]

Nicholas said that during one of his visits to Michigan, McVeigh took out a letter from a man who wanted to arrange a meeting with him near Area 51 for a "gun deal." McVeigh suspected the man was either FBI or ATF and so did not respond to the letter directly, but went to the "predetermined place stated in the letter and through binoculars, watched to see who arrived; however, no one came." After telling this story, McVeigh burned the letter in front of Nicholas. McVeigh added that, since he had been in the area anyway, he took the opportunity to visit Area 51, a place he described to Nicholas as "a secret military installation where crashed Unidentified Flying Objects and alien beings were kept for study by the military." When McVeigh returned to Michigan in December 1994, he even showed Nicholas about two-dozen pictures and one VHS tape he had taken there.

The month before, in November 1994, in Needles, California, a town that sits directly nestled on the borders of Nevada, Arizona and California, a local water authority official found a note nailed to a utility pole addressed to "S.C." It read, in part, "A man with nothing left to lose is a very dangerous man and his energy/anger can be focused toward a common/righteous goal ... I'm not looking for talkers, I'm looking for fighters." The letter, written in McVeigh's handwriting was signed "Tim T."[114] The intended recipient of the letter, the man McVeigh said he was supposed to meet near Area 51, turned out to be a highly skilled chemist and federal fugitive named Stephen Garrett Colbern.

Colbern, the son of a U.S. Army Reserve Colonel and Department of Corrections dentist, was remembered by his former classmates and high school physics teacher in Oxnard, California as a highly intelligent, nerdy loner who, even as a teenager, was obsessed with guns, snakes, chemistry and bomb making. One high school friend recounted how Colbern, whom he said had a hard time controlling his temper during their Dungeons and Dragons games, would often practice building and detonating ammonium nitrate bombs in the desert. After graduating high school in 1978, Colbern attended UCLA where he studied chemistry. Dan Mauck (name changed) told the FBI that he met Colbern in 1984, when they were both graduate students. Although they became friends, Mauck began to suspect Colbern was stealing chemicals from the lab, including ammonium nitrate and told his supervisor and other professors about it. They did nothing and even warned him to "leave it alone." Mauck said Colbern was "very anti-Semitic" and believed Jews ran the world as part of a U.N. conspiracy. A man he worked with later said, "He was a Nazi." Colbern's uncle told the FBI that his nephew was a paranoid schizophrenic who was capable of participating in a bombing and, in fact, he had always worried that someday his nephew would end up being a "mad bomber."[115]

Colbern used a number of aliases including Bill Carson and "John Conner," the latter referring to the protagonist of the 1984 movie *The Terminator*, who leads a fight against Skynet, an AI supercomputer bent on taking over the world with its cyborg minions, the Terminators. Colbern/Conner had close connections with various remnants of the Arizona Patriots (as did Michael Fortier), a group of tax protestors who had attracted notoriety in the mid 1980s after several members were arrested for criminal activities committed in the hopes of sparking a white supremacist revolution and overthrowing the government

By 1995, a number of individuals connected to the Arizona Patriots could be found lingering in and around the Kingman, Arizona area. More than a few people reported that Colbern made frequent trips to the desert for target practice and stored "survival materials" in caves stretching from Arizona to California. It seemed he had a lot in common with McVeigh, who also frequently made excursions into the isolated areas surrounding Kingman, sometimes for days at a time, loaded with backpacks and weapons and, according to several people, stashed guns, ammo and other items of note in remote desert locations; including near Area 51.

Throughout 1993 and 1994, Colbern divided his time by working at Cedars-Sinai hospital in Beverly Hills where he conducted DNA research and holing himself up in a trailer in Bullhead City, Arizona where, according to his neighbors, he walked around in camouflage fatigues, lived in squalor, had animals including snakes he raised crawling all over the trailer and at one point, had about 50 animals scattered around it's small yard.

In July 1994, Colbern was pulled over about half an hour from Los Angeles. After acting belligerently towards the police, his car was searched and (according to court records) they found an assault weapon, additional loaded firearms, a silencer, metal knuckles, a device to convert semi-automatic weapons into fully automatic ones, gun enthusiast magazines, a video camera and a VHS tape that showed a .50 caliber Browning machine gun lying on what turned out to be his living room floor with Colbern narrating assembly instructions. They also found a bill from a private storage unit facility in Bullhead City, Arizona issued the previous month (June 1994), the same month that McVeigh lived in Golden Valley, just minutes from Bullhead City. After his July 1994 arrest, Colbern was arraigned, released on bail and given a summons to appear in court that October. When Colbern failed to show up for his court date, a warrant was issued for his arrest and he became the subject of an ATF investigation. The following month (November 1994), around the time McVeigh made his visit to Area 51, Colbern mailed his employers at the DNA lab a resignation letter and another to his girlfriend, telling her he wanted to avenge Waco.

McVeigh and Colbern had a few other things in common. On April 14, 1995, four days before the Oklahoma City bombing, a US Marshall arrived in Kingman looking for the fugitive Colbern and questioned the manager of the post office where Colbern (as well as McVeigh and a couple other notables) rented boxes. In this and subsequent interviews, she described Colbern as someone who came in occasionally during March and April 1995, to pick up mail for a man who turned out to be Timothy McVeigh. In fact, it turned out that the only two people authorized to pick up McVeigh's mail were Michael Fortier and Steven Colbern.[116] After the bombing on April 19, the manhunt for Colbern, which had been ongoing at the time of the bombing, intensified.

When the FBI arrived to search his trailer in Bullhead City, Colbern was not there, but agents found bags of ammonium nitrate inside a truck parked in the back yard. It took about a week for the FBI to locate Colbern in Oatman, about twenty minutes from Kingman and forty from Bullhead City. Colbern was working as a dishwasher at a local restaurant but, according to his boss, about three weeks before the bombing he had taken off, saying he had to attend to his mother who'd had a stroke. Colbern did not come back to work until the weekend after the bombing. Authorities learned that he resided in a trailer with at least two other men who, along with Colbern, operated a crystal meth lab in a small shed on the lot.[117]

When he was finally arrested in early May 1995, the 35 year-old Colbern told authorities that he did not know McVeigh but soon after, realizing his alibi the day of the bombing was dubious at best and now facing additional criminal charges, Colbern asked for a deal and signed a proffer letter issued by U.S. Attorneys. He then proceeded to tell the FBI agents his story. Colbern said that after his arrest the previous July, he had become increasingly concerned about the "New World Order threat" which, he explained, was a plot involving the U.S., U.N. and "foreign banking interests" to confiscate Americans' guns and implant "computer chip(s) in the hand or forehead of all American citizens," in order to control them. Based on his political concerns, Colbern decided that, rather than show up to his court date, he would go on the run and seek out others who shared his views and from then on, used only pay phones.

First, he said, he contacted the Militia of Montana, whose organizer John Trochman later turned out to be an FBI informant. They put him in touch with a group connected to a number of white supremacist organizations including the Aryan Nations (a group populated, at this time, by untold numbers of ATF and FBI informants and agents). Aryan Nations put him in touch with a group in the Ozarks (most likely Elohim City, whose leader was an FBI informant, as were several people living in the small community). Through them, he learned of Arkansas gun dealer Roger Moore and his girlfriend Karen Anderson, who ran a mail-order gun and ammunition business and had many associates in the movement. Unknown to his customers and friends, Moore, who himself used a number of aliases, was a highly protected federal asset/informant whose connections with shadowy covert government operators, mercenaries and international arms dealers, could be traced at least as the Vietnam era but most notably during the Iran-Contra era. When Colbern contacted Moore (whom he knew as 'Bob Anderson'), Moore suggested he contact a man named Tim Tuttle, who Moore described as the "leader of hard core guys in Kingman" and "a former member of the Special Forces" who had been "over trained." Tuttle, said Moore, was "very restless," "traveled frequently" and regularly camped in the Hualapai Mountains. Moore gave Colbern a P.O. Box address in Kingman where he could write to Tuttle.

Colbern told the FBI that he only attempted to contact Tuttle once, by sending a letter to the Kingman address Moore had provided, but, despite his desire to thwart implantable chips and the New World Order, when Moore informed Colbern that Tuttle had left a note on the utility pole in Needles, he (Colbern) got paranoid, and thus never went to pick it up and abandoned the idea of joining any group. Rather, he had holed up in a mining shaft until about January 1995, when he rejoined society and moved to Oatman. Colbern insisted that he never met with Tim McVeigh in person and had nothing to do with the bombing. And that would be the end of the story, as told by Stephen Garrett Colbern to the FBI.

When the FBI approached Moore and Anderson in late May 1995, Moore denied knowing Colbern but a few days later recalled that, actually, Colbern had been a fairly regular customer of his for the last couple of years and, come to think of it, he and Karen spoke on the phone with Colbern on a fairly regular basis. They had first become acquainted in the fall of 1992 (nearly two years earlier than in Colbern's account) when he and Anderson began shipping ammunition to him in Arizona, including .50 caliber ammunition. Moore said Colbern never mentioned he was a fugitive but did seem paranoid about black helicopters that he thought were used by law enforcement agencies. Colbern had told him about a run-in he'd had with police during which they'd found a video tape connecting him to paramilitary activities. He also told Moore about the caches of weapons he had stored in more than one desert cave.

At first, Moore denied that he'd given Colbern contact information for anybody, but later remembered that, oh yeah, he *had* given him an address for McVeigh/Tuttle. Although Colbern had told the FBI that he sometimes wrote letters to Anderson and Moore, Moore did not produce the letters and neglected to mention this when he spoke with the FBI (or the FBI did not note it in their report). Moore maintained that he had only ever spoken with Colbern on the phone and had never met him in person. Oddly, though, the resignation letter Colbern sent to his employers at Cedar Sinai was postmarked from a town in Arkansas only miles from the home of Roger Moore and not too far from Elohim City.

Maybe they were being honest. Maybe Moore never met Colbern in person as he claimed and maybe Colbern never met with a man named "Tuttle," but according to others, he did meet a man named McVeigh. Both of the men who shared the Oatman meth lab trailer with Colbern told the FBI that Colbern frequently discussed making ammonium nitrate bombs and one of them said he was nearly positive McVeigh had visited the trailer … recently, in fact. Michael Fortier, who had been resolute about his intent not to cooperate with the FBI's investigation and who was under 24-hour surveillance, immediately upon learning of Colbern's arrest in May 1995, went to the FBI agents sitting in a car outside his house and offered to cooperate. Fortier, it turned out, used to buy crystal meth from the trailer inhabited by chemistry guru Colbern. Jim Rosencrans, who grew up with Fortier in Kingman and who also knew McVeigh, years later said McVeigh distributed weapons for Moore along the west coast, which Moore fraudulently claimed had been stolen in a home invasion. When asked about Colbern, Rosencrans acknowledged having known him, expressed extreme anger towards him, but refused to elaborate.

In the early and mid-1990s, the area surrounding Kingman was swarming with paramilitary groups with whom Fortier had become acquainted and, while it was something federal prosecutors chose not to bring up during his trial, during his time in the Wild West, McVeigh formed relationships with a number of high profile Neo-Nazis, other white supremacists and former or aspiring terrorists. When questioned by the FBI, a number of people said they recognized McVeigh and had seen him before, but that they knew him by other names including Tim Tuttle and Sergeant Mac. McVeigh admitted to his attorneys that he had used these and other aliases as well as disguises during his travels and interactions with his many "underground right wing connections" who, unlike movement spokespeople, avoided the limelight so they could engage in their activities unimpeded.

Among the organized groups he associated himself with were the Aryan Nations and National Alliance, whose founder wrote *The Turner Diaries*. McVeigh attended at least one Bullhead City National Alliance chapter meeting and in the days before the bombing, placed at least ten calls to their regional headquarters (located near Kingman). McVeigh explained that he was looking for an "Army" to disseminate literature and progress his rebellion further and although he never found it, he came close with the Bullhead National Alliance. His occasional allusions about a much larger group continued to waver though.

Some have argued that Colbern was one of the John Does ultimately forgotten about by the FBI. The Jones Team described Colbern as a "hot suspect of the FBI, at least for a while." Mark Hamm, in his seminal Pack of Wolves book, suggests that Colbern acted in conjunction with McVeigh, Nichols and Fortier as part of one of four independently operating cells whose job was to gather explosives. Roger Charles noted that Colbern had both the "qualifications" and "ideological inclinations" to fill the position and observed that the FBI "appeared indifferent" to the mountain of incriminating evidence against Colbern and was "oddly quick in dismissing [him] as a suspect." In fact, the FBI never questioned Colbern about his shared mailbox with McVeigh and, in a logic that defies logic, determined he was too weird to have been involved in the bombing plot. Terry Nichols' attorneys complained that the FBI "even knew what Colbern smelled like," yet failed to turn over any of the evidence they gathered about him to either defense team. The failure of the prosecutors to turn over discovery material about a number of individuals was a recurring one and, according to Roger Charles, "The delays and omissions were always most pronounced on the issue of possible conspirators." Colbern served a little less than four years for his 1994 charge and received little mention at the trials of either Nichols or McVeigh.[118]

What does this mean in relation to Area 51, UFOs, and Timothy McVeigh? While McVeigh's trip to Area 51 was likely a cover for activities related to the bombing plot, the story does not end there. However, a digression is in order, for reasons which will soon become clear.

In the summer of 1997, the *Guardian* published a series of articles about the continuing mass pilgrimages of curious and markedly paranoid Americans to Area 51 who, by then, constituted the most prominent counterculture in America. While still poking fun at those who believed Area 51 was a place where "captured spaceships and aliens are kept and dissected," the *Guardian* acknowledged that the CIA's recent admission that many UFO sightings were in fact, experimental aircraft, did nothing to reduce the suspicions of some who continued to wonder what had been omitted from the admission and what else was being covered up?

By now, the subjects of UFOs, aliens, and the growing phenomenon of alien abductions were a "catalyst for splintered fragments of belief"; a topical hub that posed a great threat, ideas that acted as magnets for "militia types" who warned of space invasions staged by the Illuminati to usher in the long-planned-for world government. In fact, according to the *Guardian*, all of this "gobbledygook" was "the launch pad for the 1995 Oklahoma City bombing." The fear was that UFO mania, formerly the domain of those on the fringe who chose to exist within an isolated "alternative twilight zone," was now shifting into the "middle-American mainstream."[119] The perception that UFO/alien mania was America's newest favorite but dangerous pastime only grew after the 1997 mass suicide of 39 members of the Heaven's Gate cult in San Diego, in their attempt to catch a ride on the Hale-Bopp comet, which, they thought, would deliver them to their alien makers. In reality of course, the belief in aliens and UFOs caused far less deaths than say, car accidents or airplane crashes.

Beyond the commentary offered by popular media to make sense of UFO cults and self-proclaimed alien abductees, academics in various disciplines offered frameworks within which they could be understood. The aim of folklorists, cultural theorists and social scientists is not to determine the factual truth of reported encounters, but the reason so many people tell these stories, the often-allegorical meaning of the stories themselves and the thinking of those who tell them. For them, the interstellar craze is best understood by identifying recurring elements in the stories of those who claim to have had personal encounters with space neighbors.[120]

Thomas E. Bullard, writing about UFO abduction reports in 1989, identified narrative similarities in sighting and abduction accounts and traditional folk stories about other "visitors" such as devils, angels, demons, fairies and human excursions into mythological underworlds. For him, this indicated that abductee and citizen research groups initially became attracted to the UFO abduction scenario, because it offered a language with which to express a deeply human yearning for a larger, unseen reality. Kimberly Ball is one of a number of commentators who assert that UFOs and alien abduction stories indicate "millennial anxieties over an anticipated hyper-technological future" so seemingly futuristic it appears "alien." The stories told help augment the lack of a framework with which to conceive of, let alone discuss, rapid technological advancements that will inevitably transform society and humanity itself.[121]

Christopher Roth, in his 2005 essay "Ufology as Anthropology: Race, Extraterrestrials and the Occult" adeptly demonstrates the shared intellectual roots, belief structures and discursive practices between Ufology and science, anthropology, religion, and mysticism generally. For him, the crossovers are most salient in relation to the issue of race. "Put simply," wrote Roth, "ufology is in one sense all about race, and it has more to do with terrestrial racial schemes as social and cultural constructs than most UFO believers are aware." Ross argues that UFO discourse is nearly inseparable from existing but "older anthropological discourses that had legitimized a hierarchical racial and class order." The aliens resemble anthropologists, zoologists or entomologists, who abduct, examine, tag and release hapless human specimens back into their "natural habitat." The question that preoccupies ufology, he says, is the role that humans will play in what appears to be "the unfolding of an interplanetary, interracial drama."[122]

In his detailed tracing of pivotal moments in the evolution of UFO lore, Roth identifies 18th century notions of polygenism: "the doctrine or belief that existing human races have evolved from two or more distinct ancestral types," and the attribution of physical variations among humans to "biologically distinct races, some superior to others." These so-called scientific truths in turn influenced the mystical philosophies of Helena Petrova Blavatsky and the Theosophical Society in the late 1800s. Theosophy envisions the history of humanity as a highly ordered classification of seven "Root Races," one for each continent, that represent, or are responsible for, successive stages of human development. The first of these originated from the moon and initially appeared on earth in their ethereal form. Another, the Lemurians, were the first to take physical "humanoid" form including distinctions of gender and inhabited South Asia and consisted of, among others, black Africans. Much like the biblical Nephilim however, the Lemurians fell from grace after mating with animals, thereby spawning a "lower" race of unintelligent mongrels. The sheer biologically-based stupidity of the mongrels left them reliant upon the mercy of the superior Venetians who helped them build their own cultures and civilizations, including ancient Egypt. Unfortunately for the Venetians, the continent they inhabited, Atlantis, sank into the ocean; a tragedy that allowed a fifth race, the Aryans, to usurp their supremacy. By the Victorian age, the descendants of the Aryans, the Anglo-Saxons, had taken their rightful but temporary place in the order of things. Theosophy's sixth and seventh root races are said to be slowly but surely emerging, sometimes with the assistance of divine intervention (genetic manipulation) and their eventual appearance on earth in large numbers will coincide with all manner of apocalyptic occurrences, including sinking continents and climate change.[123]

The attempts of the "alien" invaders (as imagined by mostly white people) to manipulate and sway human genetics thereby creating new races, their meddling attempts to fix *bad* DNA and their obsessive efforts to preserve the human race, but especially their own "race" sound eerily similar to projects advanced by eugenicists and advocated by historical as well as modern Nazi's and white racialists. Certainly, such conceptions appealed to Hitler and the mystically-minded SS, who themselves, through their Vril and Thule Societies, sought contact with extraterrestrial beings and called forth and even built (or attempted to build) their own spaceships. Several influential 1950s-era Ufologists were either the direct disciples of Blavatsky or had been greatly influenced by her doctrines. Included were prominent faces of the U.S.'s pro-Hitler/Nazi party such as William Dudley Pelley, founder of the Silver Shirt organization. Roth finds it "significant that the 1950s contactee movement was founded by [a] white supremacist theosophist in the aftermath of the Second World War," and goes on to highlight how previous and current typologies of aliens (Greys, Martians, Nordics, etc.,) parallel past and current conceptions of race, immigration and colonialism.[124]

In his book, *Black Sun: Aryan Cults, Esoteric Nazism And The Politics Of Identity*, Nicholas Goodrick-Clarke, outlines the complex (and close) relationship between organized white racialists' relationships to aliens and UFO lore. While it had been intertwined previously, during the 1950s, legends began to emerge about the Third Reich's' continued existence in underground advanced technology complexes in the Arctic, South America and Antarctica, which for some explained many UFO sightings. Someday, "against a scenario of increasing racial chaos and economic catastrophe, thousands of Nazi UFOs [would] one day fly forth to restore German world power in an apocalyptic act of deliverance."[125] By the late 1970s, Neo-Nazi writers developed this concept further and, mixing it with Nordic mythology, advanced the idea that intergalactic aliens who had some shared heritage with Aryans had helped the inner-earth dwelling Nazi's to build their own UFO's in an ongoing Aryan/interdimensional alliance. By the 1980s and early 1990s, such stories were firmly established in certain neo-Nazi groups, who themselves continued to expand on them, adding some peculiar details along the way. By the mid 1990s, many of these ideas became entrenched within larger UFO lore.

While Roth recognized that many, even the majority, of UFO/Abductee buffs eschew the assertion that not far beneath the surface of UFO/Alien stories exists a virulent yet veiled anti-Semitism and racism, it is clear that some folks gravitate towards the aliens' clear eugenicist agenda. Among the theories about the intent of the visitors' ceaseless invasions, abductions and genetic mutilations is an eventual "Noah's Ark" scenario wherein humans/hybrids will be chosen to act as new Adams and Eves in a celestial multi-dimensional Eden ... but only after massive global cataclysm. However, by the time this new Utopia can be established, humans will appear very different from what you and I know today, largely through the aliens' foresight and thoughtful bio-technological intervention. In the meantime, hybrid children of abductees or those who self-identify as "dual humans" (hybrids) represent one manner by which "an American WASP can be ethnic."[126] While perhaps hybrid is "the new black" for some, other interstellar enthusiasts might argue that a more advanced society would embrace the Alien Cyborging of America, as this would distill humanity into its purest racial form (the de-browning of America).

Among Theosophy's direct but "more militant and UFO-oriented" descendants is a group called the Church Universal and Triumphant (CUT). Roth says that CUT's thinly veiled anti-Semitic doctrine purports the existence of an ungodly "counterfeit race" of "human automatons" (the Jews) that walk the earth but, because of their wickedness, are destined for destruction.[127] In the 1980s, the congregation built underground bunkers at their compound near Yellowstone National Park where they stockpiled food, weapons and even a rumored armored personnel carrier, as dictated by the counsel of the church's invisible celestial hierarchy; the Ascended Masters, who spoke through CUTs leader, Elizabeth Clare Prophet. CUT ran afoul of federal authorities on more than one occasion, most often in regard to their weapons stockpiles, use of false names to purchase weapons and recurring lapses of memory concerning IRS tax deadlines. In light of the church's history, McVeigh's trip to CUT's Montana headquarters in 1994 (around the time he made his visit to Area 51) is noteworthy. The polygenetic foundations of theosophy are mimicked by those of Christian Identity, a religion adhered to by certain sects of white separatists and supremacists, most notably Aryan Nations but also Elohim City, a community whose residents, as noted earlier, McVeigh would be linked to, having made an appearance there himself a time or two.

Although Roth does not discuss their particular racially charged interdimensional theology, numerous others have, including Goodrick-Clarke. The theology of Christian Identity, a religion practiced by some of the most violent subsets of white separatists and supremacists, hinges on ideas about racial purity, survival, and an ongoing interdimensional race war. As the story goes, the biblical Eve generated two bloodlines, one with her human, Aryan husband Adam and the other with the "serpent" Satan who appeared to her in humanoid form. Adam's descendants constitute the only real, legitimate humans, while the bastard offspring of Satan and Eve, although they walk the earth in human form, are actually demonic imposters on a timeless mission to enslave and ultimately destroy Adam's Aryan descendants (the real humans). Today, the lying spawns of Satan himself deceptively call themselves Jews in an attempt to trick everybody and usurp the real chosen people of God – the Aryans.

In this cosmology, other races are genetically degraded sub-human "mud people," the offspring of pre-Adamic creatures whose "extraterrestrial origins" resulted from the ranks of Lucifer's rebellious angels that had fallen to earth "from elsewhere in the galaxy."[128] When the Luciferian rebellion failed, God imprisoned the mud people on the earth in the form of animals. When God created the Garden of Eden for Adam and Eve, he populated it with these sub-human animals and gave Aryan Adam complete dominion over them (kind of like the Theosophical Lemurians). Their descendants consist of all other non-white races (mainly blacks) who, at some point in time, aligned themselves with the fake shapeshifting Jews, and ever since that time, have manipulated and engaged in a program whose ultimate goal is the destruction of the Aryan bloodline. This axis of interdimensional evil will do just about anything to make sure they succeed; including enacting integration policies in public schools, promoting homosexuality and spreading AIDS.

Locked in a cosmic battle with human-appearing imposters, Aryans must remain constantly vigilant to the (literally) devilish schemes of the Jews. Aryan victory is only achievable through the eugenic purification of the race (at this point nearly destroyed through race mixing) and the reclaiming of earth, their God given birthright. Before that can even happen, the struggle will turn apocalyptically violent. While Christian Identity does not have a set belief about aliens per se, their cosmology closely parallels that of other mystical white racist sects and either way, nobody is debating that when it comes to those wily fake Jews, the fate of the planet is at stake. The more important question is not *if* aliens exist but *if they do,* which side are they on?

While the links between Nazi beliefs and those about aliens and UFO's are important to understand, what the majority of mainstream commentary and theorizing surrounding the UFO and contactee movements fail to take into account (including those commentators not focused on racial ideologies) is that the world of UFO mania is, and has always been, highly infiltrated. A sizable amount of information propagated by the UFO movement was intentionally planted there by the U.S. intelligence community. A handful of writers however, most notably Jodi Dean, Greg Bishop, and investigative journalist Mark Pilkington, have presented credible and well-documented histories of the U.S. government's attempts to contain, exert control over and shape the public's never-ending fascination, inquiries and speculations about UFOs.

In the mid to late 1940s, Americans began seeing strange lights and aircraft in the sky; sightings the military feared could indicate a foreign intrusion into American airspace perhaps by advanced Soviet aircraft originating from captured Nazi technologies. It is not surprising then, that from this time forward (if not earlier), UFO's became a subject of some interest to the U.S. intelligence community. In 1947, the U.S. Air Force initiated Project Sign with the objective of studying the UFO phenomenon and determining what threat, if any, the sightings represented. In the final analysis, Sign concluded that although UFOs did not pose a threat to national security, UFO investigations should remain under the control of the military ... just in case. The sightings continued however and strange legends, including those about downed extraterrestrial aircraft and their space invader pilots, spread rapidly throughout popular culture.

In an attempt to mitigate the rumors, Project Sign became Project Grudge in late 1948 but, unlike its predecessor, Grudge began with the official position that UFOs did not exist and attributed the sightings to mass hallucinations. Grudge recognized that, even if UFOs were not real, the Soviets could exploit the American public's increasing preoccupation with them and weaken citizens' faith in their government as, for citizens, government denials coupled with continuing sightings a dishonest government makes. Further, and perhaps worse, if the American people insisted on believing that they saw strange things in the sky, their inquiries might uncover the very real and ongoing testing and development of U.S. advanced military aircraft, and sooner or later the Soviets would find out about it and improve on it. Jodie Dean explained:

To decrease the likelihood of mass manipulation, Project Grudge waged a propaganda campaign to alleviate public fears of UFOs while downplaying sighting reports in general. A primary element of this campaign involved stripping away the credibility of those who thought they saw something strange in the sky. Properly trained observers (scientists and military experts) would then provide "true" explanations [...] Witnesses were dismissed as drunk, hysterical, crazy, or deeply twisted and dishonest. [Yet] the official ridicule had a reverse effect: suspicions that there was really something to hide [managed to] shift the problem of credibility from UFO witnesses to the U.S. government and military. [...] The flying saucer community undercut military assurances of security [...] Few other positions in Cold War society provided so consistent and potentially fundamental a challenge to military competence and integrity [...] [and] military and scientific hegemony. [...] Military legitimacy rested on a disavowal of the unknown ... it was outside the parameters of truth, dangerously threatening to a security ever dependent on a stable, predictable, containable, real. In the face of the possibility of aliens, the military looked weak, unable to provide the safety it promised. In the face of charges of conspiracy, the government looked corrupt, indistinguishable from its own representation of the community enemy.

As part of this discrediting, government officials utilized friendly journalists and media outlets to debunk and make light of UFO reports. Pilkington noted that the decision to intervene in the UFO debate and discredit (sometimes maliciously) those who claimed to see strange, unexplainable aircraft in the sky, stands as an example of one of many early acts of Cold War "ontological aggression" leveled by the U.S. government against its own citizens and foreign populations alike. These perception management efforts began (for our purposes) in earnest in 1951 when President Harry S. Truman created the Psychological Strategy Board (PSB), whose purpose was to intervene in American popular culture and religious and intellectual domains in order to promote "the American way of life" and neutralize "doctrines hostile to foreign objectives." Rendering those who claimed to have seen UFO's foolish was just a part of this larger objective.

Despite the efforts to malign UFO buffs, the larger public wasn't buying the 'mass hallucination' explanation. Too many people had already seen too much and the number of sightings only continued to increase. In response, citizen UFO research groups formed, whose purpose was simply to solve the mystery but which inadvertently, by their very existence, posed challenges to the very "limits to and criteria for government secrecy." Included among these groups was NICAP (National Investigative Committee on Aerial Phenomena), APRO (Aerial Phenomena Research Organization) and later, MUFON (Mutual UFO Network). As these and other UFO research groups as well as related subcultures that sprung up during the Cold War's 'culture of containment' engaged in a dogged quest for information, they asked questions that posed a direct challenge to the institutional secrecy of the military-industrial space complex.

By the time the PSB was created in 1951, reports of UFO sightings had not only increased but had become more dramatic. Thus, in early 1952, CIA Director Walter B. Smith wrote to PSB Director Raymond Allen that he was "transmitting to the National Security Council a proposal in which it is concluded that the problems associated with unidentified flying objects appear to have implications for psychological warfare as well as for intelligence operations. I suggest that we discuss [at a] board meeting the possible offensive of and defense of utilization of these phenomena for psychological warfare purposes."[132]

In March 1952, the Air Force's Project Grudge became Project Blue Book and the military made the unauthorized release of information about UFO sightings a criminal act. The following year, 1953, the CIA established a separate investigative panel to look into UFO sightings and analyze data gathered by Blue Book and its predecessors. Chairing the CIA initiated panel was a physicist from Cal Tech and director of the Pentagon's Weapons Systems Evaluations Group named Dr. Howard P. Robertson, who also happened to be one of the U.S. scientists tasked with scooping up Nazis and their research at the close of World War II. From the outset, Robertson instructed his staff that the job of the panel was to convince the public that UFO sightings stemmed from naturally occurring phenomena and not defense research or aliens from outer space. After meeting for twelve days, the Robertson panel concluded that the growing number of UFO sightings were "clogging ... channels of communication by irrelevant reports" and that the best possible course of action was to reduce "mass hysteria" by intensifying ongoing UFO debunking initiatives.[133]

The panel's findings, outlined in the *Report of Meetings of the Office of Scientific Intelligence Scientific Advisory Panel on Unidentified Flying Objects, 1953*, explained that the "'debunking' aim would result in reduction of public interest in 'flying saucers' which today evoke a strong psychological reaction ... this education could be accomplished by mass media, television, motion pictures and popular articles." (Even Walt Disney would end up getting in on the perception management act.) They further recommended (and this is important) surveillance and close monitoring of citizen UFO research organizations "because of their potentially great influence on mass thinking if widespread sightings should occur. The apparent irresponsibility and the possible use of such groups for subversive purposes should be kept in mind." The sightings, they feared, would lead to a "morbid national psychology in which skillful hostile propaganda could include hysterical behavior and harmful distrust of duly constituted authority."[134]

The PSB's interest in UFO's (or American's fascination with them) and new objective of finding ways to exploit the situation for psychological warfare purposes was the context in which the CIA-initiated Robertson panel was formed. The actual outcome of the panel went beyond simply intervening in popular culture and perception and placing American citizen-formed research groups under surveillance. Rather, it resulted in the escalation of the government's "ontological aggression" through, as Pilkington explains, a sophisticated program to muddy the waters by "creating noise, a surplus of information and bogus documentation-data-chaff known in the business as disinformation – [a] favorite technique of the intelligence and counterintelligence agencies."[135]

And that's about the time that things really got weird.

As passive intelligence gathering and perception management efforts had failed to demystify UFO's, the CIA and military intelligence agencies adopted a more aggressive approach; one that not only made UFO believers seem crazy but actually, at times, drove them insane. These operations were intended, not to squelch the propagation of UFO/ alien legends (this had proved impossible) but to induce and perpetuate them thereby rendering those who claimed to have seen anything out of the ordinary in the skies or even those who just sought to understand the phenomena, appear as outlandish as possible.

This took place concurrently and in association with the CIA's MKUltra project, which explored the possibilities of brainwashing, often by using unsuspecting civilians (foreign and domestic) as unwitting experimental test subjects. Their hearts, minds and bodies became the testing grounds for various hallucinogens and other chemicals as scientists attempted to erase memories and create new ones. In fact, the government's post-Robertson panel's UFO perception management initiative could be described as a blend between the FBI's COINTELPRO program, the CIA's MKUltra program (and similar ones before and after) and military psychological operations (PSYOPS). An example of the latter occurred during the Vietnam War when the existing myths and superstitions of the local insurgent populations were exploited for the purposes of causing fear, confusion and demoralization. To remove this context when studying the UFO/abductee movements is a grave mistake and crucial oversight made by even the most unbiased cultural commentators, social scientists, anthropologists, psychologists and journalists who have attempted to understand the movements and the people involved in them.

While all of the methods employed had been used against the UFO buffs earlier, after the Robertson Panel, the interventions were conducted in a more organized, systematic, sustained and intensified manner.

To begin with, UFO sightings (and on occasion alien encounters) were staged in the U.S. and elsewhere, after which witness' reports about what they saw and their subsequent activities could be studied, both psychologically (how did they react at the time of the sighting and afterwards) and sociologically (whom did they tell and how did the information travel).

Secondly, the Air Force, CIA, NSA and other agencies continued to spy on the UFO community by embedding operatives within citizen UFO research groups but rather than simply gathering information, the operatives acted as disinformation specialists, real life Men In Black, or "Mirage Men" who targeted select individuals, often those who had already gained some clout and respect among their peers. The Mirage Men would approach the targeted individual, either directly or through an intermediary, and offer to provide the Truth about what the government was hiding, sometimes in exchange for information about the latest rumors, trends and goings on in the UFO community. Having secured the target's willing or unknowing compliance, the operatives would provide them with faked government documents about human/alien treaties, super-secret underground military bases that doubled as alien strongholds and faked footage of alien autopsies. Some Mirage Men, having gained clout and influence within the subculture (sometimes even as *spokespeople* of citizen groups), would then proceed to make the most outrageous claims that, while persuading some already True Believers who then propagated and added to these stories, only tended to make UFO discourse appear ludicrous to the larger populace.

Finally, fictional movies and purportedly nonfictional documentaries about aliens and UFOs were funded with the effect of, not only controlling popular conceptions of UFO's, but linking even the most run-of-the-mill UFO sightings to delusional beliefs in aliens. The benefit of all of this was not to dissuade the belief in aliens and UFO's as it had once been, but to nurture and exploit these beliefs, thereby shielding or drawing attention away from the research, development, testing and real world use of actual classified next generation aircraft and technologies and weapons (including, among others, biological, radiological and electronic ones).

Once the disinformation program was underway, the number of UFO sightings grew and the details reported by the witnesses became more bizarre and baffling. While not quite knowing what, exactly, was going on, the UFO buffs sensed that something was off. The wool was being pulled over their eyes, but how?! The government had something to do with it, they knew something, but what?! Eventually, the nation's largest citizen UFO research groups began to cry COVER-UP! And not just to each other. Letters were written to government agencies and politicians, demanding an answer. In order to help put them at ease, and restore faith in government, Congressional hearings were held to look into the accusations, first in 1960 and again in 1966. Predictably, the hearings gave the intelligence services a clean bill of health (the government had done what it could to understand the UFO phenomena and rightfully concluded it was imaginary). This caused the ranks of the increasingly suspicious citizen UFO research groups to swell further, and membership reached record numbers, a growth that only presented another opportunity for the shadowy perception managers.

After the hearings concluded, the Air Force, backed by other government agencies, contracted with the University of Colorado to established a body that, while posing as an independent investigatory committee tasked with further study of UFOs, was, rather, a working group meant to depict those who reported seeing UFO's and those who dared question the government's honesty in the matter as mentally unstable and devised further methods of actually making them so.[136] Actual but human covert research and development of advanced technologies (like those over Area 51) and other unsavory projects would draw less attention and criticism from more credible people if shielded by a cacophonous circus of stories about alien invasions, such as those that culminated in the great "abduction panic of the 1980s and 1990s" during which great masses of people came to believe that they had been kidnapped and victimized by otherworldly intruders.[137] Meanwhile, the secrets these operations meant to contain were constantly under the threat of leaking. Like the time some guys, and the widows of other guys who actually had worked at Area 51, sued the Pentagon alleging that the chemicals they worked with there had caused them to develop cancer.

Perhaps best illustrative of the disinformation process at play and the long lasting effects it can have, is the classic case of Paul Bennewitz, a patriotic and brilliantly skilled but overly trusting and highly imaginative engineer, physicist and defense contractor. In 1979, Bennewitz began picking up strange radio transmissions and seeing unexplainable lights in the sky near his home located across from Kirtland Air Force base in New Mexico. Fearing this might be some sort of threat to national security, perhaps from another planet, Bennewitz contacted the base security services. They sent out an intelligence officer named Richard Doty who befriended Bennewitz, thus beginning what Pilkington describes as "one of the strangest espionage campaigns of the post-war era."[138] Then the NSA got in on the act.

Rather than just tell Bennewitz that he was seeing tests of their own classified aircraft and ask him to remain silent about his observations, Doty and his higher-ups intentionally amplified his interstellar suspicions. Over the next few years, Bennewitz was put under constant and obvious surveillance and courted by Mirage Men like Doty who "passed him fake government documents, gave him a computer that appeared to be receiving transmissions from malevolent ETs and created a fake UFO base" for him to find.[139] Bennewitz, emboldened by his government 'friends' was encouraged to believe and came to believe, that he had stumbled on to the ET secret ... and he was scared. The aliens were not our friends. They were invaders engaged in a horrible plot against humanity and would stop at nothing, even abducting and torturing children.

These Men In Black recruited some of the most well respected UFO researchers to help trick Bennewitz, ironically lured by promises that if they spied on the UFO movement and passed bogus but official looking information to Bennewitz (and others), they themselves would receive the *actual* proof about government's classified knowledge of alien life. But Bennewitz didn't know this and immersed himself in the subculture with only the best of intentions. He was, he thought, going to help them understand the truth and to this end, he shared his unknowingly bogus information ... and as it at least superficially *appeared* to have official bona fides, it spread like wildfire. The lies fed to Bennewitz spawned "a rich pseudo-history of human-alien interaction that stretched back at least two thousand years" and led to much of the UFO/ alien mythology that appeared in its wake.[140] Bennewitz himself, however, having been the constant target of aggressive psychological warfare for years, became increasingly paranoid and delusional, scattered and afraid until eventually, in 1988, his family had him committed to a mental institution.

Today, the Bennewitz affair acts as a cautionary tale among the UFO/ contactee subcultures although not a very effective one as, despite that the deceptive government origins of his information were revealed to the community, many elements of the alien narrative that had been spun from it were accepted as truth. Sincere curiosity coupled with bad information generated a mythology that was built upon by using more bad information and became entrenched in the imaginations of a mostly honest and well-meaning populace, some of whom developed an unshakable fanatical faith in the Bennewitz lies, even when those lies were exposed as such. Bennewitz himself refused to believe what had happened when Doty and others explained it to them. The lies were everything he knew to be true.

Occasionally, professional government sanctioned disinformers became whistleblowers and revealed the role they played in disrupting and discrediting UFO groups and their friends in the growing contactee movement. Implicated in the deception were the CIA, Air Force, Navy, NSA and Defense Intelligence Agency, to name a few.

For some, especially after the Bennewitz affair, the sanctioned interventions, past and present, were obvious given the prevalence of individuals with military intelligence and CIA backgrounds who showed up out of nowhere and, offering what they said was forbidden information fruit, quickly became highly regarded members and spokespeople within UFO /contactee research organizations (including APRO, NICAP and MU-FON). While government employment does not preclude interest in the phenomena under study, the Johnny-come-lately interlopers attracted the suspicion of some of their more paranoid and critical minded peers who perceived they were using their positions to spin elaborate yarns (disguised as disclosures), yarns that stretched the tolerance of even the most imaginative science fictions writers and led to deep and lasting schisms among sky watchers.[141]

"Small ripples of irrationality can make big waves" and the types of irrationality seeded by military and civilian intelligence agencies followed a repeated pattern lasting decades.[142] Within days of his arrest, news reports noted the influence that the lunatic rantings of Milton William Cooper had over the thinking of Timothy McVeigh and when his attorneys asked him what public figures might help them understand his way of thinking, William Cooper was one of the people he said they might want to talk with. They did.

Cooper, "a kook's kook" if there ever was one, had first appeared on the UFO scene in 1988, just as Bennewitz was getting locked up in the booby hatch.[143] Cooper really made a name for himself the next year though, when he spoke (at the behest of admitted and known Mirage Men) at a MUFON conference in Las Vegas. There he delivered what was perhaps the most intriguing and bizarre tale they ever heard (which is saying a lot). He claimed that after reporting a UFO sighting to his commanders while serving in the Air Force during Vietnam, he was recruited into a secret military intelligence unit tasked with recovering crashed flying saucers and, at some point, was transferred into Naval Intelligence. In the course of his duties, he was exposed to highly classified information and now, out of the kindness of his heart, wanted to share this with the world even though his former employers kept trying to prevent him from doing so.

Cooper laid out the information he 'uncovered' in his rambling, internally contradictory and often-incoherent book *Behold A Pale Horse*, published in 1991. Within the book, his subsequent writings and short wave radio program, Cooper outlined a highly complex "unified conspiracy theory" that assimilated elements of all manner of already circulating counter narratives and even introduced a few of his own.[144] A large portion of Cooper's mythology, at least the part of it that concerns aliens and UFO's, is directly traceable to, if not wholly grafted from, the fabricated disinformation fed to Paul Bennewitz, and through him, the larger UFO/contactee community. The story he told would develop and change afterward, and together, in my paraphasing, went something like this:

Chlorophyll based aliens landed in Roswell, New Mexico in 1949, after which President Truman created the NSA to communicate with them. The CIA was created for the same purpose. For the next few years, many alien piloted UFO's crashed on earth and inside of them were found the bodies of countless dead aliens and more than a few living ones. In 1954, the U.S. government, and specifically President Eisenhower (who was determined to "wrestle and beat the alien problem"), cut a deal with the extraterrestrials, via their ambassador "His Omnipotent Highness Krill" who explained that he and the other aliens of his planet were facing extinction. The terms of the treatise continued to be negotiated over time, with a little give here from the U.S. and a lot of take there from Krill and his people. Ultimately, the U.S. gave the aliens free reign to experiment on humans as, in order to save themselves, they needed to tinker around with human genetics and extract glands, enzymes and blood plasma. In return, the aliens provided the U.S. government with advanced technology and as an added bonus, in what became an interplanetary exchange program, the aliens sent some of their scientists to come stay in a network of underground bunkers specifically built with the aliens needs in mind. One of the bases was Area 51, where (in 1991) at least 600 aliens lived. Krill put the government in touch with other races of space people including the Etherians, with whom more deals were cut.

People in the government who didn't care for this type of thing were abducted, driven to nervous breakdowns, or murdered. John F. Kennedy, who knew that the aliens already had a base on the moon and was about to blow the lid off the alien/government alliance cover-up, was assassinated by his driver who shot him in the head with "a gas pressure device developed by aliens from the Trilateral Commission" or alternately, in a later version, a deadly shellfish toxin. This can all clearly be seen in the Zapruder film by the way. Kennedy wasn't even supposed to know about the aliens but someone in the inner circle of knowers, who called themselves Majesty 12, had loose lips and therefore Kennedy had to die. MJ 12 didn't like Kennedy anyways, which is obvious when you look at who some of its members were: Allen Dulles, John Foster Dulles, J. Edgar Hoover and George H.W. Bush, to name just a few. The Secret Government created UFO research organizations, especially MUFON, in order to spread disinformation and cover their tracks.

Sometimes the humans and aliens didn't get along and engaged in various skirmishes. Like that time during the Vietnam War, when the aliens abducted entire villages and more than a few U.S. soldiers, whom they then mutilated before dropping them back to earth. These kind of hijinks were meant as a warning to the humans that they better get with the alien program...or else. Plus, an ice age was coming and the humans knew that when that happened, they would need the aliens' help. So they decided to work together and formed a plan.

By the year 1998 (or alternately, 2000), Lucifer would return to earth, by way of a satanic ritual involving the pyramid of Giza and George H.W. Bush. Once the satanic forces were let loose upon the earth, the ruling elite (consisting now of both humans and aliens) would usher in the new millennium by revealing the truth about the alien/human alliance and in the ensuing panic, would declare martial law, imprison people (especially Americans and gun owners) in concentration camps, thereby allowing them to usher in a socialist New World Order.

In anticipation of this, the conspirators sometimes attempted to destabilize things a little by hypnotically inducing people to commit mass murder and other devilish acts. Given that homosexuals, blacks and Hispanics would most likely be the ones to screw up the plan, and to help insure the compliance of the soon to be enslaved sheeple, the aliens and government conspired to do a host of horrible things, including introducing and spreading AIDS and Prozac, and abducting people and implanting tracking and mind control devices into them. After the New World Order was established and everything was under control, the cure for AIDS would be revealed and any of the survivors who had gotten it, would be okay; a pretty nice gesture on the part of the overlords if you think about it.

There was a chance that this could all be prevented, but that would require the sheeple to rise up and fight aliens, humans and hybrids alike in a war of apocalyptic proportions. "I present to you that the peaceful citizens of this nation are fully justified in taking whatever steps may be necessary, including violence, to identify, counter-attack and destroy the enemy ... you must be prepared to fight, and if necessary to die to preserve your God given right to freedom" advised Cooper.[145]

There's more to it than that, but you get the picture.

Behold A Pale Horse caused an immediate sensation within the UFO subculture and Cooper became a popular speaker on the UFO conference circuit. Backing him was former CIA pilot, international arms merchant, and Iran-Contra player with deep intelligence ties turned Mirage Man, John Lear, and Bill Moore, an admitted disinformer and major player in the Bennewitz affair. Both Lear and Moore fed Cooper information originating from the Bennewitz operation; Cooper then embellished and added to this information.

Cooper drew the ire of a sizeable portion of earnest UFO researchers immediately upon his emergence in the scene. Given his relationship with people like John Lear, the contradictory, divisive and outrageous stories Cooper propagated, his complete lack of documentation and the obviously fabricated documentation he did produce, Cooper had a difficult time making friends in the UFO community. Many of his peers made no secret of their opinion that he was a drunk lying fascist, and Cooper, in turn, continued to accuse his peers of being part of the big conspiracy. Sometimes, when they questioned him or called him out, Cooper threatened to beat them up or kill them. Those who didn't think Cooper was intentionally lying tended to attribute his nonsense to the fact that he was just dumb and gullible.

Still, Cooper's book amalgamated nearly the entire history of UFO alien narratives (as well as most popular science fiction movies and books) that had been circulating in other fringe subcultures for quite some time. Everyone could find at least a few things they recognized in the book and it circulated rapidly. Even Louis Farrakhan was a fan.

In *The United States Of Paranoia*, Jesse Walker remarks on how more so than any other era, during the 1990s the subcultural legends of "militiamen, hippies, black nationalists, ufologists ... activists opposed to drug war abuses ... sovereign citizens ... [and] white separatists" overlapped and blended.[146] Indeed, *Behold A Pale Horse* lifted from Patriot, Militia, and white supremacist rhetoric and after the book came out, Cooper made the rounds in those circles as well. After the UFO crowd began to scorn and debunk him, he focused more on the villainies of the federal government and deemphasized the interstellar aspects of his master narrative until, eventually, Cooper suggested that he may have made some inaccurate conclusions and the entire alien alliance thing had probably been a lie planted by satanic elements of the U.S. government who would, in the not too distant future, stage a false flag hostile alien takeover ... and usher in the New World Order.

Cooper went on to form his own freedom fighters called the Arizona Militia, described in one report as "a far right wing movement preparing to repel alien invaders."[147] He actively encouraged stocking up on as much food and assault rifles as possible, telling his fans that this could only improve the odds of survival once the hostile alien/government takeover began (or in his post-alien days, just the government). Cooper, having now married UFO's and aliens to militias within the popular consciousness, also set about marrying all of them to the White Power Movement, whose events he also began attending.[148]

It wasn't just the heavy hitters in the UFO crowd that shunned and reviled Cooper, so too did run-of-the-mill conspiracy theory notables and those in the Patriot movement; many of whom denounced Cooper as nothing more than a "fraud, a liar and a charlatan."[149] It didn't help that he accused them too of being CIA agents, Illuminati dupes, and disinformation plants. Pretty much everybody knew that Cooper had stolen the ideas and research of others, in some cases blatantly plagiarized them and had lied about his military background (a particularly gruesome offense among the Patriots). As it turned out, Cooper's official military records reflected he had only been a low-level clerk although, of course, if he was even kind of who he said he was, it would not be documented in his official records.

After the Oklahoma City bombing, news reports linked Cooper's tirades to McVeigh's mindset and warned of the millennial cult typified by both that had snatched so many minds as of late. The reports neglected to mention the disdain that most of those within the Patriot movement felt and had loudly expressed towards Cooper (that part of the story was only reported later, in articles about Cooper's 2001 death). Cooper, said the 1995 reports, was actually the militia crowds' ideal presidential candidate, and a guru to tyranny haters everywhere; his book, "the manifesto of the militia movement."[150] This, of course, really pissed off the Patriots, who had just suffered the most crippling blow to any shred of respectability among the mainstream they had enjoyed.

The Oklahoma City bombing caused Cooper a lot of grief but he kept trucking, and continued to spread the word. Some people listened, sometimes important or influential people. In early summer of 2000, the South African Minister of Health distributed photocopied pages of *Behold A Pale Horse* to members of the senior officials of the Health Committee, in support of her suspicion that something other than or in addition to HIV might cause AIDS and that AIDS itself might be the result of an international conspiracy intended to reduce the African population.

Since 1998, Cooper had been a federal fugitive wanted for tax evasion. His life came to a spectacular end in November 2001, after a firefight broke out between him and local Apache County Sheriffs, one of whom Cooper shot in the head. The Sheriff's were attempting to arrest him on a warrant resulting from an aggravated assault with a deadly weapon charge which had resulted from an earlier altercation with the local Sherriffs that resulted from an even earlier altercation with his neighbors. Cooper had never been easy to get along with.

Although previously viewed as a "freak show, an assemblage of maniacs best ignored," once McVeigh was arrested for the bombing, said one report, the "whole movement stands accused." After all, McVeigh was a fan of Cooper's radio show, and Cooper was, according to the Clinton administration "America's most dangerous host," and everybody now knew that even if Patriot movement spokespeople didn't publicly promote the views of people like Cooper, they shared them and so did gun owners and people who questioned the government's versions of any number of events for that matter.[151] If you didn't toe the line of the status quo, you were as crazy as Cooper or Timothy McVeigh who himself represented exactly what even the most normal Americans could become if dangerous kooks like William Cooper continued to spread their hate filled horse manure.

Along with several other recognizable names in the UFO and Patriot crowds who pegged Cooper for a Mirage Man, was Jim Keith, a kind of jack-of-all-trades conspiracy guy. To Keith, Cooper was just another in a long line of official disinformers who had injected epistemological toxins into subversive but legitimate subcultural discourses and *Behold A Pale Horse*, more than likely was:

> [C]reated as "grey" disinformation, calculated to confuse and de-fuse the issues of elitist control, mind control, genocide, and secret space programs, by revealing yet concealing the these truths.[...] It would not be the first instance of the government (in either it's overt or cover manifestations) using disinformation vectors to con-fuse, pacify, or stampede the populace in directions of its choosing. [...] There is much evidence to suggest that the UFO field itself [is] largely a blind, made of fun house mirrors generated to twist facts, to conceal and not reveal them.... The success [of a disinfor-mation campaign] is that it must contain some elements of truth in order to be credible. Once the information is believed, the work of the counterintelligence specialist is complete.... What better way to generate confusion about testing of advanced post Stealth tech-nology.... When evaluating suspected disinformation, we can pro-ceed on the basis that the content of a cover up or disinformation story can possibly offer an idea of what is being hidden, since [...] to create an effective, self-perpetuating ruse, there must be a mix of truth and falsehood. This practice confuses and discredits past and future reports that are factual, linking them in the public mind with whatever incredible elements the disinformers may have in-jected.... The purpose would be to discredit these subjects and shunt debate into enclaves of UFO True Believers, who could be counted on to hallucinate, embroider and heavily merchandise the information, thus continuing the work of the disinformers.[...] The success [of disinformation campaigns] is dependent upon dropping information upon a target or 'mark' in such a way that the person will accept it as truth and will repeat, and even defend it.[152]

Despite that a lot of the interstellar themed information was obvious-ly taken from the bad information fed to Paul Bennewitz, main stream news reports that ridiculed Cooper, and by extension a wide range of fringe movements and their participants, liked to point out that a lot of Cooper's *information* originated with "things the UFOlogists made up as jokes." While that had happened on occasion, Cooper had also worked closely with known disinforming Mirage Men like John Lear and, out of stupidity or nefarious intent, incorporated and popularized a lot of intentionally planted disinformation. When people like Lear or Cooper were asked about their position on actual abusive government practices against Americans and others, they consistently took the position that these were a 'smokescreen' for the larger human/alien drama and were of no consequence in the face of the extraterrestrial threat. So, the disinfo campaign was going swimmingly even if Cooper wasn't a witting part of it (which seems unlikely).

Cooper's death helped to "write the final scene of a paranoid drama authored by Cooper himself" – said one report, indicative of so many others that overlook the actual role of the government in creating and spreading alien/UFO related theories. But then again, to acknowledge this would feed into the very paranoia such cultural crusaders were trying to combat.[153] Plus, if the government helped create and spread the kinds of astounding nonsense floated by Cooper, and if Cooper had helped corrupt the mind of McVeigh, then the government kind of helped make McVeigh, and that's the kind of thing that Cooper would say, so best not to bring it up.

But that's not all. Jim Keith also observed how certain recurring circulating elements of stories propagated by right wing organizations like the John Birch Society, mystical minded neo-Nazi groups, the unabashedly racist *Spotlight* newspaper, and run of the mill non-racist conspiracy theory subcultures subtly melded with those advanced by UFO groups thereby effectively aligning all of these subcultures. With the merger of their diverse ideas into fantastical narratives like Cooper's, disinformation campaigns and counterintelligence operations targeting a number of subcultures whom the government found problematic, could kill multiple birds with one stone. If it's not broke, don't fix it and if government disinformation interventions worked so well before, why would such interventions cease? Surely not because a bureaucracy somehow grew a conscience. As Pilkington demonstrated, the UFO disinformation game is ongoing.[154] Which brings me to my point.

The admittedly abbreviated yet sordid history of UFO sightings/ alien abductions and the government's surveillance and disruption of people and citizen groups who looked into these things, casts the lineup of speakers for MUFONs 2010 national symposium in Irvine, California, in an interesting light.

Big names appearing there included retired Air Force Intelligence officer George Filer and Stanton T. Friedman, the latter described by the *Huffington Post* as "a former nuclear physicist ... the original civilian investigator of the Roswell UFO incident and one of the most outspoken scientists who believes there is overwhelming evidence that alien space crafts are visiting earth." Jodi Dean described Friedman as "a nuclear physicist who earns his living lecturing on UFOs [and] argues that government confirmation of contact with aliens and their superior technology will shatter earthly economic and political structures" and, because of this, the government is actively covering up this information. Friedman and Filer are also alleged disinformation agents. Joining them at the conference was former John Doe #2 candidate, Steven Colbern, who had disappeared from the public's view after the conclusion of McVeigh's trial, only to rise again as a MUFON spokesperson. The title of the paper Colbern delivered at the event: "Analysis Report on Metal Samples from the 1947 UFO Crash on the Plains of San Augustine, New Mexico."[155]

Soon after, Colbern appeared as a guest on the radio show *Coast-to-Coast AM*, a long-standing favorite among conspiracy theorists everywhere. Colbern's area of expertise was not spacecraft wreckage but "Alien Implants." His biography on the show's website describes Colbern as a "Chemist/Material Scientist" and "Nano-technologies specialist" with 20 years of experience. His most recent project did not involve gathering bomb components and hob-knobbing with America's most notorious neo-Nazis, but analyzing samples of "alleged alien implants" on behalf of a Dr. Roger Leir, a highly recognizable name within the UFO/ contactee community. Leir claimed to have removed the implants from patients of his who claimed to be alien abductees.

After intensive study, Colbern found that the implants were "foreign to the host body" yet "do not produce immune response(s)" but did emit radio signals prior to their removal. This was possible because, Colbern explained, the implants were "sophisticated nano-technological devices with carbon nanotube electronics built right in," at least 100 times more advanced than current human technological capability. Colbern said he did not know who put the implants in the non-consenting human bodies, but speculated they were "part of a sophisticated electronics/communication system meant to generate certain scalar frequencies – possibly used to transmit sensory and physiological information – what the subject is seeing and hearing." In fact, of the 17 implants Leir and Colbern had allegedly found thus far, only one was identifiable as having earthly origins while the others might be "extremely advanced electronic communication devices which are relating information to someone, somewhere," most likely an alien civilization attempting to manipulate the DNA of humankind.[156]

After his 2010 appearance on *Coast To Coast*, Steven Colbern garnered quite a following, not so much with UFO buffs but among alien abductee circles and made regular appearances on the UFO/abductee circuit. For a modest fee, Colbern uses his sophisticated scientific equipment (a metal detector) to scan for hidden implants and attempts to determine if a person is, in actuality, a hybrid infused with alien DNA. Through the "data set" garnered by those he scanned, Colbern discovered other telltale signs of alien abduction which included alien hair samples as well as traces of invisible dyes detectible only through ultra violet lighting and "impossible to wash off," which when detected on the human body indicate that an individual had been recently snatched and was now being monitored. "It would be nice for people to take this seriously," Colbern pleaded during his appearance on *The Voice of Russia* radio show in December 2013, "because it's one of the biggest stories of the 21st century that we're not alone in the universe and we're being visited."[157]

These days, when Stephen Colbern is not removing and analyzing alien implants, he spends his time arguing on internet forums about the existence of UFO's and aliens, the former he claims to have seen "several times." Colbern is very open about expressing his frustration with the "pathological disbelief" and "magical thinking" of those who do not believe in UFOs. In one online debate that apparently went on for longer than he was comfortable with, Colbern accused his opponent of engaging in "some type of agenda-driven propaganda campaign," a somewhat ironic and even humorous accusation, all things considered. The twenty years that have passed since the Oklahoma City bombing do not appear to have tempered Colbern's more earthly political and racial concerns as seen in a rant he orated on an underground webcast in July 2015. During the two-hour broadcast, in between outbursts about those government scumbags intent on enslaving humanity and his ex-wife and her family who were communist plants, Colbern stated he was not concerned with race per se but clashes of culture and the Arab "rag heads" bent on destroying the American way of life.[158]

For some, the history of UFO lore, UFO lore itself, U.S. Paperclip Nazis, the U.S. intelligence network and the American extreme right wing have always been and continue to be, intertwined. Regarding the crossover among those in the UFO community and the racist right, Alex Constantine wrote, "The surface of the underground movement swarms with seemingly delusional quasi-mystical savants. [While] [b]eneath [is] a hidden world of terror – with origins in the waste of war-struck Europe and the beating hearts of some of Nazi Germany's most ruthless military scientists. From these cold chambers exploded many of the mysteries that have since riddled the postwar world." Similarly, for Jodi Dean, the public's ongoing fascination with Area 51 (and I would add, legends about underground Nazis) represented "the hidden, secret, and denied costs of the Cold War." The scientific and technological advances of the American flight development and space program are inseparable from Project Paperclip, which remains "an element of history that continues to elude narrative, a history of black budgets, experiments on civilian populations and a community of secrets."[159]

In his private letters and conversations, McVeigh told stories linking, however loosely, Steve Colbern to Area 51, UFOs and black operations. Colbern, once so deeply worried about the Jews, the New World Order and implantable microchips, doesn't seem to have much to say publicly about the first two and makes a living by (literally) digging out the third. In an online memorial for recently deceased UFOlogist and contactee luminary, Bud Hopkins, Colbern thanked Hopkins for revealing "that aliens are contacting people in their bedrooms in the dead of night – or even while driving their vehicles – manipulating their minds, and memories, and even conducting medical and breeding experiments, in a large scale program of activity that may be influencing the future of the human race; possibly even altering our genetic makeup."[160]

Nearly twenty years earlier, when the authorities caught up with him in May 1995, Colbern was cooking meth in a trailer on the outskirts of Kingman, Arizona which was, in Mark Hamm's description, "overrun with rattlesnakes ... inside [were] reams of hate literature, along with stolen medical supplies, more than a dozen assault rifles, bomb-building manuals, a cache of Chinese-made AK-47 bullets, and explosives."[161] Were the medical supplies used to remove microchips? The rifles to stave off the alien threat? I jest.

Colbern's real beliefs about aliens and UFOs both prior to the Oklahoma City bombing and currently are unknown. Perhaps he has yet to make a final determination about whether or not UFOs and Aliens are actually illusions created by "global elites" as a pretext for establishing the ever-looming New World Order and his implant related activities offer a way to turn a quick buck in the meantime. Perhaps he is a true believer holding out hope that the alien overlords will offer their assistance in reversing the genetic impurity of the white race. Given his apparent technical expertise, perhaps he will be there to assist when the time comes for governments and aliens to embed all living people with tracking chips. Maybe that was his purpose deep down in those desert mineshafts. Maybe he was looking for clues of his alien ancestors, of likeminded Nazis from the days of yore, or a hybrid combination of both and, thinking they might be living in the furthest reaches of Earth's hollow core, went as deep underground as he could manage. Maybe he believes the stories he tells the abductees that come to him seeking his assurance and advice. Maybe he doesn't. Maybe convincing people that they are in fact chipped victims of the skypeople has a much darker purpose. Perhaps the types of claims made by Leir (now deceased) and Colbern are nothing more than intentional disinformation, lies meant to mask the use of existing or impending technologies of control, although on whose behalf, I am unaware.[162]

No matter what you make of it all, Colbern and the spoken and unspoken details of McVeigh's 'Area 51' stories illustrate how even the most fantastical legends have roots in and shed light on actual events, not only in McVeigh's life but in America's less apparent history, as does so much else in the back story of the Oklahoma City bombing.

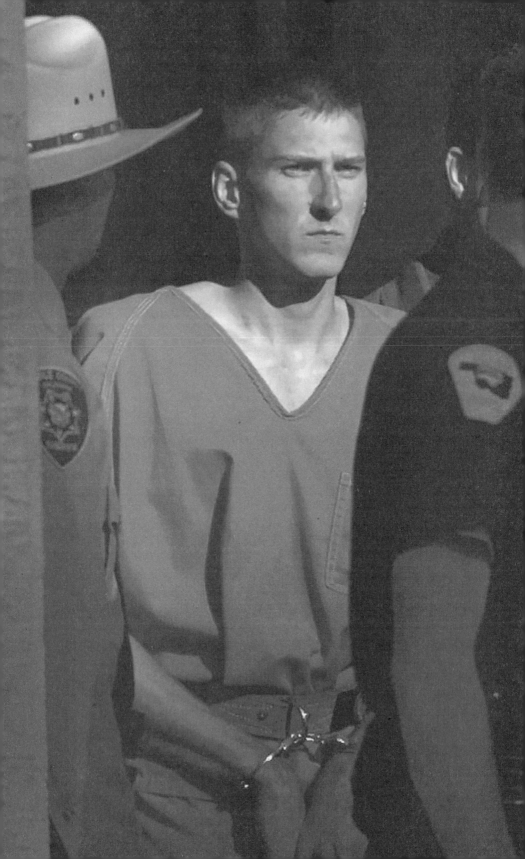

Chapter Four:

Mcveigh's Imperceptibly Binding Chains

PART ONE
The Tale of the Dastardly Doppelgangers and the Manchurian Terrorist

> *If the world is where we hide from ourselves, what do we do when the world is no longer accessible? We invent a false name, invent a destiny, purchase a firearm through the mail.*
>
> – CIA agent and black operator, Wit Everett, from Don DeLillo's, *Libra*, 1988

> *The Apparatus is precisely what we can't see or name. We can't measure it, gentlemen, or take its photograph. It is the mystery we can't get hold of, the plot we can't uncover. This doesn't mean there are no plotters.*
>
> –paranoid radio talk show host, 'Weird Beard', DeLillo, *Libra*, 1988

What follows is an amalgamation of conflicting narratives whose internal contradictions, points of intersection and digression, once identified, confound any particular version, reveal critical gaps in and between them, clear a path for new interpretive possibilities, and demonstrate the historical quandary left in McVeigh's wake.[1]

---

1. Authors note: In the following chapter, I highlight many (but not all) key elements found within each of the distinct narratives told about McVeigh, his movements in the two years leading up to the bombing of the Alfred P. Murrah federal building on April 19, 1995 and the commission of the bombing itself. These conflicting narratives are referred to as Lone, Pack, Watched, Guilty, and Experimental, respectively. When possible, I add newly discovered information. While much of the information presented in Chapter Four, Part One is documented (through investigatory and eyewitness reports and the accounts of involved parties), I have also included apocryphal elements

On the other hand, while not attempting to argue any one particular theory of the case, by pitting all the narratives about McVeigh and the bombing against each other and highlighting certain aspects of each, I *do* hope to undermine *any* version that insultingly argues that the reality of either can be understood by a few Simple Truths.

LEAVING BUFFALO: LATE 1992-EARLY 1993

While in the Army, Timothy McVeigh, the model soldier, visited military doctors and dentists at a startling rate. Shortly before he quit the Army, he confided to his supply sergeant, James Rockwell, his belief that he had a "computer chip in his backside," that the military had "done things" to him he was unhappy about and added, "I think they've brainwashed me or injected me with something."[1] Upon returning home, he made regular visits to the Buffalo VA, where, according to statements made to the FBI, military doctors treated him for paranoid schizophrenia, a condition that caused him to black out for long periods of time and left him with a secret life he could not remember. At this time, he expressed his growing concern about the availability of health care, medical abuse conspiracies and the privacy of his personal medical records, the totality of which remains undetermined.

In his final letter to Steve Hodge before quitting his job and setting off on the road in late 1992, McVeigh said he was "leaving for an undisclosed location" and that this might be their last communication for some time. He told Steve to read *1984* and *Brave New World,* warning that "Big Brother" is capable of more than just "jamming ham radio frequencies, they will lock you up." He lamented about the long line of dissidents before him that had been diagnosed as "mentally ill" and even involuntarily "hospitalized" for failing to "fit in with the norm." Someday, McVeigh said, he too might be "locked up" and labeled "schizophrenic" or a "white racist." He explained that schizophrenia and other mental illnesses are only social constructs, "sane responses to an insane world," and he was simply a "radical political thinker [and] extremist in every sense of the word."

He then issued similar warnings to others, including his former Calspan co-worker Carl Lebron, to whom he claimed someday people would come looking for him (McVeigh), perhaps even people from Calspan. Lebron said McVeigh was "cagey about where he was going," but did mention he had taken a "civilian job painting military vehicles." He told a handful of other individuals that he was leaving town to work in an

---

found within all versions, although I have attempted to make it clear and obvious when doing so. Admittedly, I focus more on those narratives that have received less 'mainstream' attention but whose existence demands further research as these stories tend to be the most readily dismissed and least scrutinized. I do this, not in an attempt to *solve* the mysteries that still surround the bombing, to prove any one version or theory or to build a coherent air-tight historical master narrative, but to illustrate the frustrating complexity faced by those who have attempted to do any of these things.

unspecified but military related capacity. His attorneys noted the need to make a list of all the people he had said this to. Unknown to them, during this same time McVeigh told Terry Nichols that while in the Army, he had been recruited to carry out undercover missions.

According to David Paul Hammer, McVeigh said that in late 1992, while still in Buffalo, he received a call from his handler, the "Major," who told McVeigh to get his affairs in order and be ready to enter the field for several months. McVeigh was then drilled extensively for days about his knowledge of "well known and obscure figures" in the extreme right-wing anti-government movement, their rhetoric, and his ability to use it convincingly. After proving his skills, McVeigh was instructed to travel the gun show circuit and "immerse, inform on, and assess the actions of those in the right wing, anti-government movement." While he would have only minimal contact with his handlers during this time, McVeigh was to report his progress by leaving voice-mails at a secured telephone number given to him by the Major.[2]

McVeigh's old Army buddy, Terry Nichols, would ultimately be tried in a federal and state court for his participation in the bombing. After the conclusion of his state trial, when he could no longer be tried again, Nichols, who had never spoke publicly about his knowledge of the bombing, began to tell his story. He said that during a visit with McVeigh in December 1992, McVeigh told him that, while in the Army, "he had been recruited to carry out undercover missions. [He] did not say who recruited him, or specify the nature of his mission. McVeigh did say, however, that he was to begin making contacts with a 'network' of people after the first of the year and that he was to take no action in furtherance of this mission until called upon [and] would soon be making his first contact "down south.'"[3]

Although the existence of the FBI's PATCON operation remained unknown for another 15 years (until 2007), in August 1992, on the heels of Ruby Ridge, the focus of PATCON's ostensive fact-finding mission was reauthorized and expanded. Rather than seeking incriminating information about any one particular individual for the purposes of criminal prosecution, operatives were now to gather "information concerning a nationwide 'Alliance' of white supremacist groups being formed to fight the U.S. government."[4]

Whether internal or external, actual or imaginary, his decision to leave was based on overwhelming and powerful forces, so much so that it almost seemed he had no choice in the matter. His friend and former co-worker at Burns, Andrea Augustine, said the last time she saw him, she could tell he wanted to stay and he almost did, "but then he kept saying 'You don't understand, I really have to go.' He just kept saying it."[5]

From the time he left New York in January 1993 until the summer of 1993, McVeigh's activities are difficult to trace due to a lack of documentation in some instances and an overwhelming but conflicting amount in others. Stickney described this period as "the lost days." While largely untraceable,

"McVeigh's life turned into what could only be called a lost crusade … but it was during this odyssey of uncertainty that he became seriously involved in a dangerous world." Whether of his own volition or under instructions, McVeigh now began his long, arduous descent into the "paramilitary underworld" of conspiracy theorists, anti-Semites, racists, militias, tax protestors, Second Amendment advocates and others who mobilized in the shadow of the looming Brady Bill. At this point, wrote Stickney, McVeigh believed "Big Brother was now watching *him*. The Government had become the enemy and was now keeping tabs on him [and he] believed a black car was following him when he went out driving." McVeigh began leading a "double life" and took measures to insure that it "remained well hidden."[6] He stayed on the move, traveling the country, rented a number of mailboxes in various states under a number of assumed names, took to using several aliases and began to use a calling card in the name of "Daryl Bridges" to communicate. Later, Michael Fortier's mother, Irene, would tell CNN that Timothy McVeigh had lived two lives and the truth was going to come out.

Various people later reported that from this time until the day of the bombing they had known the man they saw in the televised perp walk, not as Timothy McVeigh, but as (alternately) Chuck, Daryl Bridges, Steve Murphy, Robert Kling (born April 19, 1972), Mike Havens, Mike Foley, Sergeant Mac, Shawn Rivers, Joe Rivers, David Gilmore, Richard Mentan, Tim Tuttle, Tom Tuttle, Terry Tuttle, Jerry Tuttle, Tom Snead, Tim Sneed, Tim McEegie, Tim McNay, Tim McVey, Tim Johnson and Timmy, among other names. He kept multiple driver's licenses and alternate license plates. Phone records indicate that, during this time, somebody used his Daryl Bridges' calling card to place 685 calls to individuals and businesses throughout the country.

Shortly after leaving western New York, McVeigh sent his sister an article about fifty-one-year-old retired Sgt. Maj. Lawrence Freedman, a former Green Beret, who had died in Somalia the previous December, reportedly from an exploding anti-tank mine. Local obituaries did not print notices of his death and the only thing the Pentagon had to say was that Freedman, "a civilian employee of the U.S. government," died in Somalia during a classified mission. Brig. Gen. Richard Potter Jr., an old friend of Freedman's and deputy commander of the Army Special Operations Command, told reporters, "The record will not reflect the many operations he participated in."

Freedman's father said, "He was a secret to all of us." Soon, those who knew Freedman began to understand "the bigger picture" about the secret life of the man they thought they knew. Freedman "died as he had lived: fast, hard and discreetly." It turned out that Freedman was a "consummate soldier," Special Forces medic in Vietnam and survivor of a failed Delta Force rescue mission during the 1979-80 Iran Hostage Crisis, where eight of his fellow elite super-soldiers died. He had also been among the first to train the Delta Force Anti-Terrorist unit at the JFK Special Warfare Center in Fort Bragg. As an expert sniper, Freedman instructed the Secret Service on presidential convoy procedures. After retiring in 1990, he began two years of "special assignments," sometimes disappearing for weeks at a time "into the military underworld of the Delta Force" which included covert assignments in North and Central America, the Middle East, Bosnia and Africa. The Pentagon refused to answer the elder Freedman's questions about the circumstances surrounding the death of his son.[7] Freedman, McVeigh told his sister, was the first known casualty of US covert operations in Somalia.

Throughout the next two years, McVeigh sent his sister news clippings about a number of political corruption scandals, many involving clandestine operations similar to those he said he learned about during the Special Forces tryout; one about the arrest of two brothers who attempted to transport 66 pounds of cocaine on an Air Force plane. Others pertained to CIA smuggling of heroin into the U.S. and the explosion of Pan Am Flight 103 over Lockerbie, Scotland.

McVeigh then made his way to a number of locations of interest including the headquarters of the Militia of Montana, where he was introduced to other visitors, including Aryan Nations members, as a "mercenary" named 'Sergeant Mac.' He also began making phone calls to WPM groups including a Pennsylvania chapter of the National Alliance.[8]

Early on his travels, in January 1993, while at a gun show in Ft. Lauderdale, Florida, he met Roger Moore, a gun dealer who divided his time between Arkansas and southern Florida. McVeigh was selling 'White Power' t-shirts and copies of *The Turner Diaries*, and the two struck up a conversation. No stranger to the extreme right, Moore claimed to have been involved with training anti-Castro Cubans. By the 1970's and 1980's, he was a self-made millionaire mainly, he said, by building speedboats for government agencies including the CIA and other elite clientele. Moore ran with the 'Iran/Contra' crowd (think Ollie North), had numerous international arms dealing associates and was in tight with Civilian Military Assistance, a group of CIA-backed mercenaries who, during the late 1980's were involved in the U.S.'s clandestine activities in Nicaragua and later, at the exact time McVeigh met Moore, were a key group in the FBI's PATCON operation (although whether as targets, assets or both is unclear). Like McVeigh, Moore employed numerous aliases but most people knew him as Bob Miller or Bob Anderson. Moore was a familiar face on the gun show circuit where he promoted his homemade porn distribution enterprise and mail order firearms business.

In the preceding years, Moore himself had been the subject of state and federal investigations on more than one occasion. From 1989 until March 1993, the Arkansas and Oregon State Police, as well as the ATF, FBI and Department of Defense, would investigate Moore for various infractions including plans to mail hundreds of pounds of C4 explosives through the mail; sale of government property stolen from military installations (including ammunition); intent to sell explosives and bootlegged porn (origins of which are unknown); and the sale of ammunition, grenades, and flares, that he, again, shipped through the mail. Each time an investigation into Moore's activities was begun, it was just as quickly ended, mainly through the request or inaction of the FBI.[9] After the bombing, Moore claimed he was a government informant, although by the looks of it, he was much more than that. According to Terry Nichols, Moore, one of the first contacts in McVeigh's "network of friends," helped instruct McVeigh on the ins and outs of the gun show circuit, where he would spin the web of contacts needed to carry out the bombing. Either way, Moore and McVeigh became fast friends. They met up again a couple weeks later, and Moore invited McVeigh to stop by his Arkansas ranch some time.

There were already rumors circulating among the Patriot crowd that the federal government was taking extra-legal measures to disarm American citizens and after April 19, 1993, the rumors would become self-evident fact. This began when, in June 1992, the ATF initiated an investigation of a religious sect in Waco, Texas, the Branch Davidians, who lived communally on a plot of land called Mt. Carmel. The leader of the sect, David Koresh, often bought semi-automatic weapons at wholesale prices and then sold them for a profit; questions arose about the legality of these sales. Although they could have asked to inspect his stock of guns, in the words of a later Congressional investigation report, before pursuing traditional avenues of investigation, the ATF instead decided to "pursue a military-style raid" (or "dynamic entry") on Mt. Carmel.

A federal magistrate denied the ATF's first request for a warrant on the grounds of insufficient evidence. Three weeks later, the ATF tried again, this time filing affidavits in support of their request, which included a copious amount of "misleading and factually inaccurate statements, substantial irrelevant and confusing information, and failed to properly qualify witnesses' testimony." In the affidavit seeking a warrant and throughout the events that followed, the ATF and later, FBI, would characterize the Davidians within their internal reports and to the media as "a dangerous extremist organization" and "cult."

Once the warrant to search the Davidian complex was obtained, the ATF concocted a story about a meth lab operating out of Mt. Carmel; a fabrication that, under Operation Alliance, allowed Joint Task Force 6 to provide military assistance for the planned raid. Thus began what the Department of the Treasury would describe as the "largest enforcement effort ever mounted by ATF and one of the largest in the history of law enforcement."[10] Throughout January and February 1993, the National

Guard flew military surveillance aircraft over Mt. Carmel while the Special Forces trained ATF agents in urban combat (MOUNT) techniques. This of course caught the attention of the media and word of the goings-on at Waco spread rapidly through Patriot circles.

When the ATF finally attempted to serve their search warrant on February 28, 1993, they did so by way of 80 federal agents decked out in full combat gear: camouflage fatigues, Kevlar helmets, flak jackets and wielding submachine guns, semi-automatic and sniper rifles and grenades. All of this while military Blackhawk helicopters flew overhead. A firefight broke out between the Davidians and ATF agents, leaving six congregants and four ATF agents dead. The FBI's Hostage Rescue Team then arrived, beginning a 50-day standoff and a stunning display of federal power that included Abrams tanks as well as, much to McVeigh's dismay, Bradley Fighting Vehicles, Combat Engineering Vehicles (Earth Movers) and more than 800 federal and state agents, and additional military personnel.

During this time, media broadcasts continuously spread ill-informed (and often totally erroneous) dehumanizing characterizations of the Davidian "cult" who had been "brainwashed" by their leader David Koresh who they said was sexually abusing the sect's children, despite the fact that an earlier investigation found these allegations baseless. Much of the rhetoric and false information cited by the media originated with spokespeople from the Cult Awareness Network (CAN), a group that had formed in 1971 (under a different name) as a support group for parents whose children had run off to join non-traditional religious groups. It quickly transformed into a lobbying group and public awareness organization whose primary mission was to combat "mind control" and "brainwashing" used by unconventional new religious movements deemed "cults." Unfortunately, the term was a dubious and vaguely defined one. When deposed in one of many lawsuits concerning CAN's violation of human and civil rights, CAN Executive Director Cynthia Kisser offered this definition: "a cult is an organization – an organization can be large or small; size is not the determinant- that has expressive devotion to a leader, principle or idea."[11]

To counter the so-called brainwashing and break the hypnotic trance cult members were under, CAN (and other cult-busting groups) employed controversial methods including kidnapping individuals and subjecting them to involuntary 'deprogramming,' a process that utilized the exact methods they accused the brainwashers of using, and sometimes were much worse. In their efforts to un-brainwash alleged victims, CAN de-programmers had been known to beat, drug and sexually assault non-compliant individuals they'd 'rescued' (kidnapped). And some of them made a lot of money doing this.

The ATF's original affidavit to obtain the search warrant contained hyperbole very similar to that used by CAN 'experts' and a number of unfounded accusations and inaccurate claims within it had originated from one of CAN's most notorious de-programmers (who had deprogrammed a former Davidian). Ranking CAN members acted as consultants to the ATF and FBI during the siege (although to what extent is debated) and CAN spokespeople appeared regularly in the media, spreading what would only later be revealed as false but titillating stories about the depravity of the Davidians and publicly urging the FBI to use lethal force against them. In response to growing public outcry and criticism about the massive military buildup in Waco, Attorney General Janet Reno and President Bill Clinton capitalized on the moral panic generated by CAN and repeated the unfounded claims and outright lies to the American people. In doing so, they further demonized the Davidians and largely neutralized criticism about all manner of illegalities that had already, and were about to, occur in Waco. Janet Reno in particular had a history of invoking the safety of children to authorize overreaching operations.

Things were not looking good for the Davidians and religious freedom organizations and Civil Libertarians on the right *and* left began expressing their objections to and horror with the methods being used at Waco. Although the FBI made sure the media could not get within miles of Mt. Carmel, countless protestors, spectators and media crews began arriving and got as close as they could. While individuals and groups from all political spectrums rallied on behalf of the Davidians, the national media focused on the most extreme, and therefore entertaining, voices, notably that of Indianapolis attorney and self-proclaimed "Acting Adjunct General of the Unorganized Militia of the United States" Linda Thompson. Thompson proclaimed to as many media outlets as she could that the events at Waco were evidence of the government's declaration of war on non-traditional religions and put out a rallying cry for Patriots to join her at Waco and "assemble with long arms, vehicles (including tracked and armored), aircraft, and any available gear..."[12]

For many, statements such as this only served to reinforce negative stereotypes and escalate the tension brewing at Waco. Some, however, chose to answer the calls to action put out by Thompson and others, including McVeigh, who arrived at Waco ten days into the standoff. He spent his time there observing, talking to people and selling 2nd Amendment bumper stickers. He told a student journalist who interviewed and photographed him, that people should pay closer attention to the government and "heed any warning signs" that it might be overstepping its legitimate role.[13]

McVeigh left Waco while the siege was still ongoing and headed to Terry Nichols' house in Michigan, planning to return in a few days with Nichols. On April 19, 1993, hours before they were about to begin their drive to Texas, McVeigh watched live television coverage of a fire that broke out inside the Davidian church, which, when all was said and done, consumed the lives of seventy-six men, women and children. In that moment, McVeigh unalterably snapped; his already existing frustrations and outrage now wholly consumed him as he saw the ATF and FBI's use of heavy-handed, lethal tactics, while the media justified this by spinning the Davidians into demons.

Any number of things about the events at Waco deeply disturbed McVeigh. To begin with, many of the same ATF and FBI agents who had been involved in the Ruby Ridge fiasco less than a year before were also involved at Waco. Although many debated the sequence of events that led to the deaths, nobody debated that for 181 days, authorities subjected the sect to a number of psychological warfare tactics in what they called a "stress escalation program." This included blasting sounds of dying rabbits, Nancy Sinatra's song These Boots Were Made For Walkin' and flooded those inside with bright lights for days on end. Worse still, Bradley vehicles relentlessly circled the compound and eventually charged the building, ramming holes in it and inserting pyrotechnic tear gas rounds or 'CS gas', an act that some said caused the fire that burned and asphyxiated those inside. Perhaps worst of all, during the six-hour fire the Bradley vehicles (equipped with plows) demolished the walls of the building and trapped most of the still-alive Davidians inside.[14]

As the listless drifter watched the fiery conclusion live on TV, his calling became clear. His attorneys later noted that, while cold and callous towards his own victims, every time he spoke of the deaths of the Davidians, his eyes welled up with tears. Most accounts and theories cite Waco as the primary motive for the bombing in Oklahoma, noting its occurrence on the second anniversary of that tragedy.

Linda Thompson, who helped rally the Patriots to Waco, was known for making outrageous statements. Although her documentary, Waco: The Big Lie, about the government conspiracy to kill the Davidians was well received among the movement (until more credible ones came out), even her most militant gun-toting comrades viewed her with suspicion – as a possible agent provocateur, government agent or simply insane. She frequently said things that, at best, could discredit all of them or worse, could only result in further state repression for everyone; like the time she tried to rally Patriots to come, heavily armed, to Washington D.C., storm the Capital building, place officials under citizen's arrest and try them for treason. Their skepticism was just fine with Thompson because Thompson, like William Cooper, viewed many of her camouflage colleagues with as much suspicion as they viewed her and like Cooper, made no secret about it but, rather, took any chance presented to accuse one or another of her peers of being CIA, FBI or ATF agents. Thompson, in fact, was a regular guest on Cooper's show. After Waco, Thompson became (at least for the mainstream press) the "Joan of Arc of the Militia Patriot movement."[15]

On April 23, 1995, just days after the bombing, Thompson called the FBI and expressed her belief (often-repeated later) that one of the objectives of the bombing was to destroy ATF records relating to the Waco operation. She then told agents about various people she believed were spying on her or trying to discredit her. The FBI report documenting the call noted that the agent Thompson spoke to instructed her to call back when she had facts, not theories, to support her allegations. She then called back a couple of hours later to report that Dr. Louis Jolyon "Jolly" West, "the psychiatrist brought in to examine" Timothy McVeigh after his arrest, was "actually a CIA operative responsible for implanting micro-chips in Army personnel in an experiment called MKUltra" and had done this to McVeigh during a twenty-minute outpatient procedure. Thompson then warned the agent she was speaking with that "the FBI must stop West from taking the chip out of McVeigh so that the FBI can probe what the CIA did."

Two days after her call to the FBI, Thompson posted an announcement to a Patriot Network computer bulletin board. She began by declaring, "The FBI just threatened me" and went on to outline an incoherent theory of the bombing (and its cover-up) involving Japan, the White House, and the FBI. She said that when she called the FBI to report her information she was told that if she didn't stop her investigations McVeigh's actions would be blamed on her and she would find herself becoming a co-defendant. About a week after that, she showed up at the Marion County Indiana prosecutors office, armed, seeking to file battery and stalking charges against a local journalist. When told that she did not have enough evidence to do so, Thompson began "yelling and screaming" about a number of things. The CIA was trying to murder her, she said, because she knew too much about their weapons sales to Third World countries and those in the government responsible for the Oklahoma bombing were trying to kill her by shooting beams from radio frequency weapons into her head, and that they'd already killed six of her friends this way. She was arrested.[16]

Archived computer bulletin board discussions posted immediately after the bombing illustrate that at least some of those on the fringe she supposedly represented viewed her OKC related antics as intentionally misleading distractions with proto-fascist undertones much like those of William Cooper. "Thompson and Bill Cooper are two peas in the same pod," said one commentator. Still, while Cooper was depicted as McVeigh's ideological father, Thompson was his "guiding light," his paramilitary mother figure. Thomson herself bragged to the *National Enquirer* about how "The FBI told me that Timothy McVeigh reveres me."[17]

McVeigh appeared to play down his reverence for Thompson though, describing her to his attorneys as a "flake." He *had* called her once, a few months after the fire at Waco, he added, but she accused him of being in the CIA and refused to speak with him. Whatever he felt about her personally, by all accounts McVeigh had passed out Thompson's Waco documentary with as much vigor as he did *The Turner Diaries*. So much so that the film was mentioned at his trial to illustrate how the "conspiratorial worldview" led to just the type of mindset that resulted in the bombing. Unfortunately, the media's eagerness to quote Thompson's reliably bizarre statements had the effect of equating any later questioning of the government's investigation and final narrative of the bombing (or the actions at Waco) to the kind of lunacy floated by Thompson.

Perhaps frustrated that the FBI wasn't taking her information seriously, Thompson called the Jones Team in June 1995 and during a long, rambling monologue, complained about other Patriot figures who were secret Israeli Mossad and NSA agents; corrected the misperception that McVeigh's "chip" was in his rear end (it was, she said, actually in his nose or behind his ear); and warned them that Jolly West, the "CIA contract psychiatrist ... involved in Nazi experiments," had been visiting McVeigh, perhaps without their or even his knowledge of it. She actually had more information than this, she told them, and wished she could offer it to them but her phones were bugged and she'd probably be killed if she shared what she'd uncovered. However, she recommended they speak with William Cooper who could relay at least *some* of this information and gave them his phone number.

McVeigh became part of the very "Conspiracy Theory" lore said to have infected him. A portion of this lore involved the machinations of Dr. Jolly West who, in certain circles, including Thompson's, was thought of as a "demon-in-the-flesh," a "true deceiver" that employed his "fork tongue and crocodile tears" to falsely label law abiding but politically dissenting individuals as dangerous criminals and the groups they associated with as "cults." West was rumored to have been present during the Waco siege itself. While the rumor remains unsubstantiated, it seemed plausible to conspiracy writers who pointed out that the good doctor was, after all, "the preeminent don of [the] CIA's psychological warfare program" and had designed the very types of tactics used against the Davidians to try and draw them out (or make them go crazy).[18]

Indeed, PSYOPS *were* a forte of West's, as were a number of other topics relevant to those conducting the Waco operation. West had established his expertise on the topics of cults as early as 1978 and in the years to follow, never shied away from an opportunity to call attention to the multiple thousands of cults operating throughout the U.S., into whose foul clutches millions of young people had been lured. At a 1983 CAN conference, West, a highly valued member of the organization, advanced the idea of developing a "medical model" (a "device" or "technique") through which the "cancer" of "fake religions" could be destroyed, although how West became the decider of *real* and *fake* I am unaware. By

1993, West had been on a "43-year mission to rid the world of cults" and appeared frequently in the media to offer his learned opinions about the events at Waco. He warned that "like a social bacteria," cults would "infect" the masses and openly lamented that Americans' unhealthy obsession with freedom of speech and religion had hampered the ability of law enforcement agencies to eradicate the disease.[19]

But as numerous academics would later conclude, it was the type of rhetoric used by West and his cult-busting CAN colleagues that aided the FBI and ATF's dehumanizing disinformation campaign against the Davidians and reinforced the unfortunate perception that the events at Waco had been necessary and the deaths there inevitable. So when conspiracy theorists alleged that Dr. West helped design the psychological torture used against the Davidians, they had some basis for suspecting this, and when they described the federal government's actions as political and religious suppression, they weren't alone, however much the words and actions of people like Linda Thompson made it appear so.

In 1995, Conway and Siegelman (often mentioned along with West in a number of post-Waco articles) issued the revised, 2nd edition of their book, *Snapping*. This edition focused mainly on new religious movements, or, as they referred to them, "cults" and borrowed heavily from and cited Dr. West in their interpretation of the events at Waco, which they said represented a clear case of groupthink, religious brainwashing and "collective snapping." While they were referring to the Davidians, perhaps they could have applied this to the federal authorities as well. Instead of a more probing analysis, they repeated many of the unsubstantiated or wholly fabricated claims made about the Davidians by the media and government, to argue that the dangerous "driving forces" of groups like the Davidians were located within "the information dimension … the domain of beliefs, emotions, ideologies and other messages passing among people." Through "pathologies of communications," the Davidian's had spread very powerful and deadly "information diseases" to many, including Timothy McVeigh, and in doing so, had helped instigate widespread "collective snapping."[20]

As nobody likes a snapper and certainly, nobody enjoyed the fruits of collective snapping, in the aftermath of Waco, ATF Director John Magaw announced that federal agencies would be keeping close watch on groups suspected to be cults. If any of these groups had been on edge before, this could not have helped lessen their anxieties. For a number of people, both on the left and the right, the events at Waco represented, not a growing threat of brainwashing cults, but the willingness of federal authorities to use whatever means necessary to quell dissent and assert their authority, even if it meant murdering American citizens to prove a point. As with Ruby Ridge, the government's actions at Waco proved more paranoid than the paranoid people they killed. Rather than quell so-called anti-government dissent, the deaths at Waco only further mobilized and united the conglomerate of diverse groups that made up the Patriot Movement.

According to Hammer (known himself to have snapped a time or two), McVeigh told him that, as he watched the fire that extinguished the lives of the Davidians on television, he spotted the Major in the background. McVeigh, said Hammer, was sincerely upset about what had happened there and although unsure of why the Major was there, his presence caused McVeigh to reassess his secret mission. He now began to question how the information he provided about so many groups and individuals (including those he had met at Waco), would be used and wondered what threat they really presented. McVeigh's role in the Major's operation would soon shift from passive intelligence gathering to something else entirely. In the aftermath of Waco, McVeigh was instructed to cull from his widening circle of radical associates in the right-wing underground, a team of men who would be willing to take military-type action, "when the time was right." And while unaware of what this future action might consist of, he did as he was told.[21]

No matter the origin or truth of Hammer's account, there is no doubt that McVeigh now intensified his networking efforts and his rapidly growing cadré of new friends has been well documented by a number of writers including Hamm, Wright, Pritchard, Charles and others.[22] Over the next two years, he attended over 80 gun shows in 40 different states. Whatever kind of wolf he was, Lone, Pack, Watched, Guilty Agent or Experimental, McVeigh succeeded in establishing connections with the farthest reaches of the extreme right, including some of the most recognizable faces in the movement; but also many who tended to avoid publicity rather than court it. In all narrative variations, it is at this point that McVeigh could no longer stave off the powerful and mysterious forces that compelled him to enact his violent imaginings. But for some, the question remains: Who helped him?

AFTER WACO: SPRING AND SUMMER 1993

In late April 1993, while at a gun show in Tulsa, Oklahoma, McVeigh met some of the residents of Elohim City and after making some small talk, one of them, a German named Andy Strassmeir, invited him to come out for a visit. During this gun show, McVeigh helped man Roger Moore's booth and hung out with Moore's mistress, Karen Anderson. When the gun show ended, he took Moore up on his invitation to visit the Arkansas ranch, conveniently located a couple of hours from Elohim City. McVeigh stayed with Moore and Anderson for two days. Moore told the FBI that he quickly grew agitated with McVeigh, who was a bad guest "took over the house" and ate too much of their food. McVeigh, said Moore, was "antsy," too consumed with anything he happened to be reading about at any given moment. He was "hyper" about black helicopters and *The Turn-*

er Diaries, and kept pestering Moore to read the book.[23] Karen Anderson found him to be helpful though and he spent a good portion of his time helping her put together "M-60" kits, which only further agitated Moore. After he overheard Moore and Anderson argue about him, McVeigh left.

The next month, McVeigh made his way to Kingman, Arizona, and maintained a residence there until the end of that summer. He first stayed at the home of Michael Fortier and in June rented a trailer in the Canyon West Trailer Park. He briefly worked at a security company who assigned him to guard a chemical plant. It is at this time, while in Kingman, that McVeigh began experimenting with methamphetamines and using the alias "Tim Tuttle." He opened a P.O. Box at the Mail Room; a box that, according to the manager there, was also later checked by the militant Jew-hating, snake raising, methamphetamine chemist turned alien implant expert, Steven Colbern.

Not content with simply maintaining communication with old friends, McVeigh busied himself by making new ones. While in Kingman, McVeigh made countless phone calls to militia and WPM activists around the country, including Linda Thompson, who accused him of being a CIA plant but, more significantly, to individuals associated with the local chapter of the National Alliance. McVeigh called Moore immediately before or after placing many of these calls. Although it is unknown what they discussed, both McVeigh and Nichols made claims (independent of each other) that it was at this time that Moore began providing explosives to McVeigh.

On several occasions, he visited a local shooting range with Michael Fortier, signing himself in as Tim Tuttle and Fortier as "Mike James" each time. When the FBI showed the sign-in sheet to Fortier later, he was perplexed. Fortier, a frequent visitor to the range, said in all the times he had been there, he had never signed in, never knew of anyone else signing in and further, had never used the name Mike James in his life (although he would be provided a new identity later, as part of the witness protection program). Similar to Sirhan Sirhan, whose day-long rapid-fire target practice using hollow point bullets at a gun range attracted the attention of others, more than one individual remembered McVeigh's erratic behavior at the gun club, where he wildly fired hundreds of rounds at random targets with a disturbing vigor. Said one shooter, "Quite frankly, it scared the hell out of me. He pretty much went crazy, emptying on anything – trees, rocks, anything there. He just went ballistic."[24]

McVeigh used Kingman as a jumping-off point for his gun show activities and other travels, which became more frequent and extensive throughout the latter part of summer and until the early fall of 1993. Increasingly preoccupied by what had happened at Waco, he wrote Steve Hodge a letter venting about the ATF's murder of the Davidians and announcing that, "the time for playing games is over." He was reportedly spotted at a number of racist enclaves. Although he denied it, one FBI informant claimed that McVeigh attended a KKK rally in Tennessee during which he hung out with various members of Aryan Nations (a group which was, at the time, a major focus of PATCON operations).

McVeigh also visited a number of military installations in an attempt to determine how easy it would be to steal weapons and explosives from these locations. This was the very thing that, not so long before, state and federal law enforcement agencies investigated Moore for, the exact thing McVeigh spoke about to Carl Lebron before setting out on his journey, and the very crime for which PATCON was ostensibly initiated. Interestingly, Roger Moore also spent a portion of that summer visiting military bases in an attempt to, according to *American Terrorist*, search for evidence about the New World Order's buildup of U.N. troops and equipment at these locations, a rather flimsy reason, all things considered.

McVeigh now added a new item to his gun show inventory: fuse lit flare launchers that could be converted into "rocket launchers." Moore had designed the launchers and McVeigh gave customers who bought them Moore's contact information so that they could purchase replacements flares of which McVeigh said Moore had "thousands ... just tons of them." In August, the racist *Spotlight* newspaper carried an advertisement placed by Tim Tuttle who was selling what has been described as "a military-style antitank launcher replica" "a surplus rocket launcher" or just a "rocket launcher."[25] When an Arizona public safety officer showed up at a Phoenix gun show to investigate the rocket launcher Tuttle had advertised, he encountered a man who identified himself as Tim McVeigh who was selling flare launchers and a bunch of anti-ATF and FBI propaganda. After a brief conversation, the officer concluded McVeigh was not Tuttle. This was a strange determination given that when the officer asked what the flare launcher could be used for, McVeigh responded that they could be used to shoot down ATF helicopters and demonstrated to him how to convert them into incendiary flamethrowers. McVeigh's response alarmed the officer enough to report the incident to the ATF and FBI.

FALL 1993

Plots carry their own logic. There is a tendency in plots to move toward death.
   – CIA agent and black operator, Win Everett, DeLillo, *Libra*, 1988

In September 1993, McVeigh attended the annual Soldier of Fortune convention in Las Vegas, where he met up with and manned a table for Roger Moore, a regular attendee of the event. The four-day convention is a "paramilitary theme park" widely attended by civilians but also a hot destination for ex- and current military including 'Special Forces' types as well as police officers, and security professionals.[26] Attendees can take part in a variety of combat training seminars (knife fighting, hand to hand combat, etc.); compete in shooting contests; listen in on lectures about a number of paramilitary and law enforcement related topics; join a civilian militia; recruit members into their own militia or just peruse the hundreds of merchant tables hawking guns and survival gear. The convention was also noted as a place where attendees can connect with recruiters looking to enlist mercenaries for missions to third world countries (such as those conducted by Roger Moore's friends in the Civilian Military Assistance), or even with representatives from domestic law enforcement agencies openly seeking to recruit undercover informants.

While neglecting to mention that he provided explosives to McVeigh, Roger Moore did tell the FBI that he and McVeigh got into an argument at the convention. McVeigh heard one of Moore's customers use the word "Patriot" and when the man walked away from Moore's table, McVeigh eagerly ran after him and began talking to him about Waco. Moore said he was concerned because he had noticed that the man was wearing some sort of law enforcement badge under his coat and feared McVeigh would cause trouble for Moore by making a spectacle of himself. To top it off, after talking to the badged man, McVeigh came back to the table, announced he was going for a lunch break and then vanished for two hours. When he did return, Moore laid into McVeigh for his long absence, and they argued loudly until convention organizers came over to reprimand them, after which Moore told McVeigh he was no longer welcome there. That's the version of the story as told by both Moore and McVeigh.

In another version, McVeigh met up with the Major at the SOF convention and they discussed the information McVeigh had provided thus far. The Major assured McVeigh that he had only been at Waco as an observer and had no active part in what happened there. McVeigh knew he was lying when, later in the discussion, the Major instructed him to take his team of men, which he should have assembled by now, and prepare to carry out a domestic bombing. The intent of the bombing, which would be blamed on the patriot, militia and survivalist movements, was to take the wind out of their anti-government sails. The Major then gave him a large infusion of cash.

While the true nature of what happened at the convention may never be known, what *is* known is that a few weeks later McVeigh began compiling bomb-making materials and continued to do so for the next year. After leaving Las Vegas, McVeigh continued on his travels, making sure to write to Steve Hodge regularly and rant to him about the tyranny of the federal government, and especially about what had happened at Waco. In one letter, he accused Steve of suffering from a "learning disability" that prevented him from understanding the concept of Liberty and the impending enslavement of mankind. McVeigh, said Hammer, claimed that he was intentionally leaving behind an incriminating paper trail and had been ordered to do so. When Hammer asked why, McVeigh explained, "It had to be known that I hated the government. Even my own family had to believe my cover otherwise I could have ended up dead before the mission was completed."[27]

In a later iteration of Hammer's Guilty Agent story (not included in the first), McVeigh said that as he roamed the country after the SOF convention, he stopped at Executive Security International School (ESI) headquartered in Grand Junction, Colorado, a training facility that some of his former Gulf War colleagues were now associated with. ESI's promotional material describes it as a "private school [that] provides training in executive protection, investigation and intelligence operations, including anti-terrorism." Part of the privatized counter-terrorism and security industry, with many locations throughout Colorado, in 1990 *Management Review* described ESI as "the Harvard of bodyguard schools." For the most part, ESI instructors are ex-members of Special Forces, as well as former and current FBI, CIA, DEA, Secret Service, and local law enforcement agents; but other instructors have included editors of *Soldier Of Fortune Magazine*. One ESI instructor described it as a school for "professional paranoids" but then added, "The line between paranoia and awareness is very fine."[28]

While it is unknown if McVeigh actually had any type of association with ESI, he could have. According to FBI investigatory reports as well as internal defense team records, very shortly after leaving Buffalo, McVeigh did travel to Boulder, Colorado and set up a mailbox to which, for a time, he had his mail forwarded from boxes he'd opened in other states. This puzzled his attorneys, who wondered in an internal memo why he had been in Colorado for any length of time that would warrant his opening a mailbox there.[29] Interestingly, ESI is mentioned in James Gibson's book, *Warrior Dreams: Violence And Manhood In Post-Vietnam America,* as one of a growing number of security training (mercenary) schools that were popping up in the late 1980's and early 1990's that actively recruited at the annual Soldier Of Fortune conventions.

In the fall of 1993, McVeigh made his way to the home of Terry Nichols in Michigan, where he stayed until January, during which time he used Michigan rather than Kingman as the jumping-off point for his continued travels. He also began having an affair with Terry's wife Marife while Terry was at work.

Terry's brother, James, described how during this time, McVeigh talked about the possibility that a "secret shot" he was administered in the Army had caused him to develop Gulf War Syndrome. McVeigh, he said, had gone so far as to visit the VA hospital in Saginaw because "his bones ached, his teeth hurt, his gums hurt, he had no energy and was always tired." MCVeigh also voiced his suspicion that a 'tracking chip' might have been injected in him but when James suggested he go to the hospital to find out, McVeigh declined, saying it was unlikely they would tell him the truth even if they did find one. James then suggested he see a private doctor and even made an appointment with one on his behalf, but McVeigh "backed off" and failed to show up. James said he did not dismiss the idea out of hand because he and Terry had used tracking chips in their turkeys for years. James added, as an aside, and likely unaware of the Guilty Agent stories he was telling some people, that McVeigh had probably been under surveillance for the last couple of years and, most likely, his watchers opened a file on him when he went to Waco.

Other individuals, including a man in Michigan and one in Kansas, independently spoke to reporters about similar conversations they'd had with McVeigh. One of them, Phil Morawski, said McVeigh told him the government "planted one of those chips that they have for identifying cattle, sheep or goats, so the all-seeing eye of the government could keep an eye on him and know where he was." The chip, McVeigh complained, sometimes caused a "real sharp pain in his rear."[30]

Moore told the FBI that he ran into McVeigh again at a gun show in Knob Creek, Kentucky during the first week of October but that McVeigh mainly spoke with Karen Anderson. On October 11, 1993, McVeigh received a traffic ticket for passing on a double yellow line, about four miles from Elohim City. In the Pack of Wolves, Watched Wolves and Guilty Agent stories, McVeigh visited Elohim City and thus began the plot to bomb the Murrah federal building. For many, including Mark Hamm, the conspiracy involved McVeigh and a number of people associated with the White Power Movement (WPM). McVeigh's Pack Of Wolves would consist of, among others, Steven Colbern, Michael Fortier and (to a lesser extent) Terry Nichols, but also a number of full time and on-again-off-again residents of Elohim City such as Andreas Strassmeir and most notably, a group of racist bank robbers who called themselves the Aryan Republican Army (ARA).

While the rudimentary details of the plot would have been discussed at the October 1993 "planning session," it was further developed during subsequent meetings. They would act within small isolated cells, each with a different purpose (funding, gathering material, bomb making, delivery, etc.,). Throughout the lead-up to the bombing, the conspirators used fake identification and referred to each other only by aliases. As they gathered the necessary materials and bomb making components, false paper trails were laid in order to confuse investigators later. Certain conspirators even acted as decoys or 'doubles' for others (including McVeigh). On the day of the bombing the conspirators employed disguises and decoy Ryder trucks; thereby confusing eyewitnesses.

Funding for the bombing would come, in part, from bank robberies, some of which McVeigh would participate in. Hamm overlaid McVeigh's movements throughout the country from this time forward with those of the ARA bank robbers and found that their locations often coincided. Sounding much like a conspiracy theorist himself, Hamm said, "so many random coincidences have to be statistically impossible. There must have been some larger card at play." A review of Hamm's 2002 book noted that, through a process "akin to placing layers of the same film animation frame on top of each other –a remarkable series of concurrent and complimentary events that fit so snugly together it became hard, if not impossible to regard them as simple coincidence."[31]

To his attorneys and biographers, McVeigh denied having ever been to Elohim City. At the time he received the October 1993 speeding ticket, he said, he and Terry Nichols were simply on their way to a gun show in Indiana. In the months to come though, he bragged to his sister about his involvement with a group of bank robbers and, at one point even asked her to launder money, telling her it was proceeds from a bank robbery. In one letter, he claimed to be generating funds for the revolution through robbing banks. He had friends who, like him, were "At war with the system." Bank robbers weren't criminals, he explained. The banks and the Federal Reserve were the real criminals who controlled people through worthless paper. Bank robbers were more like "Robin Hood, and our gov't the evil king."

After his arrest, he told his attorneys that he and Terry Nichols had thrown around the idea of robbing banks and even "cased" one bank in an attempt to ascertain the schedule for armored car deliveries, as this was the only time the bank vaults would be opened. In the end though, they never got around to actually robbing banks. In a taped three-day long conversation with his biographers towards the end of his life, he gave contradictory responses when asked about his involvement with bank robberies. In one candid moment very early on in the interview session, he responded by saying that, "Yes," there had been *a* bank robbery but quickly instructed them to "Leave it at that." Tim refused to offer more information except to say that everything had been planned down to the most minute detail. The things that could not be planned, "that's part of the fun." Much later in the three-day interview, when asked again about the bank robberies, he said there weren't any.

Still, an FBI report from May 1995 details their investigation of a California bank robber, whose modus operandi was very similar to that "believed to have been used by subject McVeigh and his associates." At least one of the ARA bank robbers has publicly stated that he had "no doubt whatsoever" that members of the gang were involved in the bombing.[32] For some reason though, the FBI destroyed surveillance tapes that captured the ARA bank robberies at a time when legal proceedings and criminal trials related to the robberies were ongoing. The FBI and prosecutors chose not to make a big deal about the bank robbery connection, perhaps because, as was later learned, there was more than one federal informant embedded within the gang.

On October 20, 1993, eight days after receiving the ticket near Elohim City, McVeigh sent his sister a Guilty Agent-themed letter, which, while filled with hyperbolic political rants, also encapsulated a story that he would tell in private later and others would expand on publicly after his arrest. In it, he said he desperately needed someone to understand him and she was probably the only person who could "comprehend/accept" what he was about to say. Part of the reason he seemed so secretive was because if he was honest about what he was doing and why "they'd think I was wacko ... no one, I mean <u>NO ONE</u> has heard this before [because] I realize, in the normal world, [what I have to say] sound[s] <u>VERY</u> unbelievable and crazy."

He then laid out the story of how during the Special Forces tryout he was recruited into an undercover unit "to do some work for the government on the domestic, as well as international, front." The unit would be acting as military "consultants" working "hand-in-hand with civilian police agencies" to "quiet" anyone deemed a "security risk." They would fund their "many covert operations" through illegal actions including drug running. His quitting the Army and his claims of becoming "disillusioned" by the Special Forces were only a cover story. While living at home and working at Burns he found it increasingly difficult to keep his secret and "pretend that I didn't know what I knew." Eventually, unable to "live with this information bottled up inside of me," and his feelings vacillating between "rage," "acceptance" and "denial," he considered committing suicide (leading to the incident at their grandfather's house). Because of the nature of what he now knew "my life may well have been/may be at risk" if he exposed it (which is why he was telling *only* her). The newspaper clippings he sent her shortly after leaving Buffalo about Lawrence Freedman, the special ops operator killed in Somalia, had been a "clue." He begged her not to tell anybody because if she did, it would "very honestly, seriously endanger <u>my</u> life." He lamented that, "my whole family thinks I'm *mentally deficient* – which is part of the game ... (It's like a great weight has been lifted off my shoulders, to finally tell <u>someone</u>) ... I needed someone to know, in case I'm found floating in a river." Later, his attorneys, referring to this particular letter, opined, "If this is a lie, Tim is one good liar."

In a letter that followed soon after, he told her he had "documentation" to support his claims and had additional things he wanted to tell her but would rather do it in person. In fact, he wrote, "I spend most of my time gathering and amassing 'evidence.' Maybe someday I'll have a chance to show some/all of it to you. Maybe it would be a mistake to show you all that now, anyway... I don't want to fuck up your future." He then informed her that he was on the run, "trying to keep my path 'cool'" as, since he already knew too much, someone might come looking for him and try to shut him up. He was establishing a *"network of friends,"* and now had "ears all over the country" so that if someone did come looking for him, he would hear about it through his grapevine and disappear into the "underground." He closed the letter by saying that just writing the letter had brought back a lot of memories for him, "it doesn't even seem like it could happen to me, that I've been everywhere I've been, done everything I've done, seen and heard everything I have. I know it must be ten times harder for you to grasp."

Jennifer later told the FBI that for a number of reasons, she believed what he was telling her and his mother said he'd told her a similar story. It is unclear *what* he was telling her, though. Was he amassing evidence *against* his network of friends or of the government's corruption? Did he "know too much" about the undercover mission and had now abandoned it or too much about the evils of the government, or both or something else entirely? When he said he was expected to fund covert operations through illegal activities, did he really mean fund the bombing through bank robberies? Most have read these letters as fairy tales spun by McVeigh, perhaps in an attempt to impress his little sister. True, partly true or totally fabricated, it is at this juncture that the Guilty Agent story breaks off into a divergent strand, one in which McVeigh rejects his role and like The A-Team, is hunted by the government and forced to stay on the run.

On November 22, 1993, while staying at the home of Terry and Marife Nichols, Timothy McVeigh found their infant son, Jason, dead, having apparently accidently suffocated in a plastic bag. He tried to revive the boy and, at the same time, calm Marife, but to no avail. McVeigh said that while all of this was happening he snapped into "combat mode." After failing to resuscitate Jason, he called the police and in the meantime, placed his lifeless body on (he later realized) the very same spot where he had stood months earlier watching the fires at Waco kill the children inside. When the police arrived, he identified himself as Tim Tuttle but later said this was accidental, a force of habit. Gwen Strider, the aunt of McVeigh's friend Kevin Nicholas, who became a sort of motherly figure for McVeigh in Michigan, recalled that Jason's death "ripped Tim completely apart," his inability to save Jason devastated him. He had "loved the baby ... eaten with him ... played with him, taken care of him" and for a week after the incident, had "not been himself." Like many people who knew him throughout his life, Gwen said that McVeigh was great with children and children, including her own, loved him. After the bombing, rumors of foul play arose (McVeigh killed him to keep Terry Nichols in check; James Nichols and McVeigh killed him because the child was racially mixed). As McVeigh recounted the incident in great detail to his biographers years later, he sometimes slipped into the present tense.[33]

The month after Jason's death, McVeigh visited a dentist in Marlette, Michigan, about an hour from Nichols' farm. Soon after, he used the alias Tim Tuttle when he purchased nitro-methane, sold as model airplane fuel, at a hobby shop in Marlette.

WINTER TO SUMMER 1994

In January 1994, McVeigh called Roger Moore's ranch in Arkansas to announce that he was passing through town and was hoping to stop by and stay the night. Moore was in Florida at the time but his girlfriend, Karen Anderson, was there and told him that would be fine. Anderson told the FBI that she let McVeigh sleep in her bedroom, and she slept in a different bedroom. Given McVeigh's history of sleeping with his friends' girlfriends and wives, questions later arose about the actual sleeping arrangements. The red-headed Anderson was a firecracker; just the kind of incendiary men who frequented gun shows might like. McVeigh told Hammer that Anderson had a reputation for sleeping with the young men she met on the gun show circuit, entrapping them in her senior-citizen sex web by showing them the bootlegged porn she and Moore secretly sold. In Hammer's account, Anderson tried to hire McVeigh and his bank robber friends to kill Moore.

McVeigh, as always, claimed he was just passing through Arkansas on the way to a gun show; nothing unseemly had happened between them, sexual or otherwise. Moore, however, grew jealous of the attention she lavished on him, a circumstance that put further strain on their friendship. Mark Hamm suggests that Anderson facilitated communication between McVeigh and other participants of the bombing, pointing out that she knew Elohim City resident Andy Strassmeir and ARA bank robber Richard Guthrie. Anderson herself testified in court that, during this visit, she urged McVeigh to contact Steven Colbern, who in Hamm's estimation "played a crucial role in the Oklahoma bombing conspiracy." [34]

Either way, Anderson's assertion that McVeigh called the house shortly before he arrived was curious because that call, along with other calls Moore and Anderson claimed McVeigh made to their house, was not found on the Daryl Bridges calling card records. This was significant because part of the FBI and prosecutors justification for dismissing the possibility of additional conspirators was their logically unsound belief that, in Roger Charles' words, "the Daryl Bridges phone records could track anything and everything related to the plot." [35] If the calling card records didn't show a call, then McVeigh must not have made it. That the records shed light on the plot is not in question, but the records themselves, which nearly defined the structure of the government's case against McVeigh, did not reveal *who* made the calls nor did they preclude the use of alternate methods of communication.

In February 1994, McVeigh once more established himself in Kingman and, except for countless road trips to locations throughout the country, remained there until that summer. In a letter to his sister during this time, he wrote that "seeing as it's been more than two years since I got out [of the Army], things may well be okay now" but told her that if anyone "unusual" came looking for him, she should contact him at Fortier's trailer in Kingman. One is left to wonder *what* would be "okay now" and *why* would it matter when he got out of the Army? *Who* was going to come looking for him? Why did he keep warning people about this possibility? Was he delusional? Paranoid? If he was being honest in the letter, then he *had* abandoned his undercover mission and went rogue (making him an ex-Guilty Agent in a Pack of Watched Wolves). If that was the case, it seems unlikely that his handlers would have forgiven him for this, even if it had been two years. If McVeigh was indeed a Guilty Agent and had carried out orders up until the day of the bombing, as he would claim to others (including his first attorneys), then this letter was a cover story. He realized he had already told his sister too much and had to somehow fix the damage by telling her he quit his secret mission – only to (as Hammer claims) continue with it.

McVeigh told his biographers that, knowing he was about to "go afoul of the law in a big way," he told her these things as a way of trying to preemptively mitigate her inevitable disappointment in him.[36] The problem with this is that he'd been telling variations of the Guilty Agent story, letting details of it slip out here and there, and warning about the people who'd come looking for him before he had ever left the Buffalo area, somehow pre-emptively covering his tracks before he even knew why he would need to.

During his stay in Kingman throughout early to mid-1994, McVeigh briefly worked at another security company, then with Fortier at a local True Value hardware store and continued to ply his wares at gun shows. During this time, he became friends with Walter "Mac" McCarty, a Korean War USMC veteran who earned his living by giving shooting lessons and was known for organizing local gun control protests. McCarty told the *Sunday Times of London* that McVeigh (whom he knew as Tuttle) seemed like two distinctly different people. "In public, he was quiet and polite and he had this big, easy smile" but other times, especially when talking about politics, he snapped and "got real mean and savage. He was one highly-strung young man. I don't think I ever saw anyone with such hatred in him. He was bitter about just about everything....I tell you he was running right on the edge." He had even watched his young friend cry while they watched a video about Waco. He described McVeigh as impressionable and opined that frustrated men like McVeigh make "great brainwashing material."[37]

In early 1994, McVeigh rented a house in the outlying town of Golden Valley, located just yards from a former member of the Arizona Patriots and current ranking member of the local National Alliance who said McVeigh attended two of their meetings that he knew of. In one strange and unsubstantiated variation of the Experimental Wolf story, while at a Disabled Veterans group in Kingman, McVeigh met Mike Gadbaw, an older Vietnam veteran whom he let stay at his Golden Valley house. Gadbaw, who remained in the house for several years after McVeigh's execution, said that the local VA had used both he and McVeigh as guinea pigs.[38] McVeigh never mentioned anyone named Gadbaw and Fortier testified that McVeigh lived alone in the Golden Valley house.[39]

McVeigh's mother, Mickey, believed that the FBI and others began watching her and her family at this time, in anticipation of the bombing. James Rosencrans said it was during this time that it became obvious to more than one person in the Kingman area including McVeigh himself that McVeigh was being watched. On more than one occasion, McVeigh had pointed out surveillance vehicles he said were following him. By association, McVeigh's friends and associates (including Rosencrans and Fortier) had also been under surveillance. Were the Watchers related to the people McVeigh said might come looking for him?

Maybe Gadbaw was confused about who he lived with. After all, a number of alternate or "double" McVeighs emerged in the Kingman area during his extended stays there and this would happen in many other locations at an increasing frequency in the months to come. Bob Ragin, the man who owned the trailer park where McVeigh lived the summer before told the *New York Times* that McVeigh was "an ideal tenant." However, in an earlier *Times* article on April 23, 1995, Ragin was quoted as saying that his former tenant McVeigh acted like an "arrogant loner," always wore Army fatigues, played loud music, threw beer cans, had a barking dog and a pregnant girlfriend. [40] Although most quickly dismissed this as a case of mistaken identity and chalked it up to Ragin's confusion, FBI and defense team reports confuse the issue.

Ragin wasn't the only one who made such claims. A man who worked with McVeigh at State Security Service in the summer of 1993 during the time he lived in Ragin's trailer, told the FBI that McVeigh was fired after about two months and added, as an aside, that McVeigh had been involved with an underage girl. About a year later, in the summer of 1994, McVeigh briefly had another job in Kingman guarding a warehouse distribution center. His supervisor there told the FBI that although McVeigh quit the job on good terms, he thought McVeigh was a "creep" and while he worked there a rumor was floating around that McVeigh hung out with an underage girl who was between six and eight months pregnant. A co-worker at the Kingman hardware store he worked at told the FBI that McVeigh sometimes attended community bingo games in Golden Valley, and on more than one occasion showed up to bingo night accompanied by another man and a "very pregnant female" who seemed to be in some sort of relationship with McVeigh. They made the other players nervous because McVeigh and the other man openly wore their handguns into the bingo hall.

A bewildered defense team noted the number of such reports in the Kingman area and mentioned another FBI report they had come across detailing a 16-year-old pregnant girl who lived across the street from Fortier and had been seeing (and smoking meth with) McVeigh. The defense wondered whether McVeigh was the father of any of these babies. In a private discussion between his sister and mother after the bombing, Mickey asked Jennifer about the rumors of Tim having had a pregnant girlfriend. Jennifer, not knowing the FBI was bugging the room, responded that she didn't believe it because, as far as she knew, there never was a girlfriend. Interestingly, the 1994 sightings coincided with one of McVeigh's visits to Las Vegas, during which he applied for a job at Loomis Armored Car Company. On the application, McVeigh disclosed his debts but said they were the fault of a girlfriend who ran up his credit cards. He took the required psychological examination but did not get the job.

Adding to the confusion are ATF and FBI reports detailing their numerous conversations with Richard Rogers, who lived in the Kingman area. Rogers claimed he met McVeigh after picking him up hitchhiking about thirty miles outside of Kingman and, over a period of about a year and a half, had several sexual encounters with him. While the veracity of this story is unknown, it is interesting that both the FBI and ATF conducted several interviews with Rogers. His lurid stories were humorously fascinating though, so one can see why. David Paul Hammer, unaware of these reports, claimed McVeigh sometimes expressed attraction to males and had "sexual identity problems."[41] Given all the confusion over which McVeigh was which, even among people he saw on a daily basis, it would seem he had a number of identity problems beyond those of a sexual nature.

Pregnant girlfriend, gay lover or no, or maybe because of them, McVeigh quit his job and left the Kingman area and continued his "extraordinary itinerant lifestyle [and] barely stopped moving, frantically crisscrossing the country in his car [and] paid for everything in cash." His friends, family and former co-workers had no idea where he was and could only get in touch with him through his Kingman mailbox (the one Steven Colbern was about to start using with McVeigh's authorization).[42]

Two letters McVeigh wrote his sister during this period displayed a return address in Kingman, Arizona, but the postmarks revealed he had mailed them from Los Angeles and Las Vegas. Nichols lived in Vegas at the time and implant aficionado Colbern worked in Los Angeles until his arrest that summer, after which he became a fugitive and lived in mineshafts not too far from Kingman. It was, in fact, during this same period that Moore told Colbern about Tuttle, the former Special Forces guy he knew who had been over-trained and now led a bunch of mean motherfuckers out in the desert with whom Colbern would *almost* cross paths near Area 51. At the time of Colbern's July 1994 arrest, police found a receipt for a storage-shed rental in Bullhead City (at a time when McVeigh lived only minutes away). Maybe Colbern crossed paths with one of the other McVeigh/Tuttle characters running around the desert. And maybe there was something in the water because McVeigh himself soon began renting storage spaces in various locations including one in Golden Valley where he kept ammonium nitrate; one of a few incriminating storage sheds he said had not been discovered. Mark Hamm, among others, argued that Colbern, (who Hamm said made the meth Fortier, McVeigh and friends smoked), "was the mastermind behind the actual construction of the bomb"; that he was assisted by another man who lived with him in the meth lab trailer and that there was "likely ... another unidentified man involved in this cell, a phantom bomb builder."[43]

Hammer wrote that during one of McVeigh's trips to Las Vegas, the Major introduced him to a man he referred to only as "Poindexter" but who the Major said would help with the construction of the bomb. Poindexter came to an unfortunate end the night before the bombing though, having been murdered and thrown in the back of the Ryder truck (more on that later). Unknown to Hammer, Jim Rosencrans told the FBI that in the summer of 1994, he saw McVeigh spending time with a clean-cut man with glasses, 35-40 years old, whose name he said he didn't know and who he never saw before, or after that brief time, but who he described as a "geek" and a "Poindexter." As Rosencrans knew Colbern, he and Poindexter were not the same person, although Poindexter *could* have been Nichols or possibly Hamm's phantom bomb maker.

In fact, from here on out, McVeigh, if he wasn't being confused with other people who happened to have the same name, job, friends and interests, he was being seen with other people who nobody could quite identify later (collectively called the John Does).

In August 1994, McVeigh attended a motorcycle rally in Sturgis, South Dakota where he wore what prosecutors later called a disguise, which consisted of – a bandana; arguably the least effective disguise ever conceived of. McVeigh must not have thought so, though, because he continued to wear his biker disguise, including at a racing track in Texas where he purchased ammonium nitrate.

Interestingly, around this time, PATCON operative Bob Matthews was instructed by his FBI handlers to attend a paramilitary training camp in San Saba, Texas. Highly redacted FBI PATCON reports from 1991 described the camp as a 160-acre ranch run by the Texas Light Militia (TLM), a group known to be stockpiling weapons and explosives, specifically stolen military grade C4. The FBI had several high-level undercover informants and agents in TLM, who reported on the groups plans to train people "in the use of weapons and explosives for the purpose of using force against the U.S. government at a future time."[44] TLM was closely aligned with other problematic organizations including Aryan Nations, the KKK, and Civilian Material Assistance (the latter closely associated with Roger Moore), and members of those groups attended TLM's monthly training sessions.

When Matthews attended the TLM training camp in 1994, he saw Timothy McVeigh and Elohim City resident and illegal alien Andy Strassmeir (associated with the TLM since he arrived in the U.S.). During this session, attendees received instruction on how to convert Marine Corps-issued flare guns into grenade launchers. Immediately after the bombing, Matthews contacted his handler Don Jarrett to tell him he recognized McVeigh as the man he saw at the camp with Andy the German. Jarrett, however, informed Matthews that this was old news; that McVeigh had associated with other similar groups and that undercover FBI assets (other than Matthews) had been monitoring McVeigh in the run-up to the bombing. While he wasn't interested in McVeigh's appearance at the Texas camp, Jarrett did ask Matthews if he had ever seen McVeigh in Arizona (as Matthews had infiltrated groups there as well). Matthews had not. The FBI's harassment of Matthews and their attempt to prevent him from testifying about this and other incidents is currently the subject of a Federal Court-appointed investigation into the FBI's overall effort to silence key witnesses and withhold information about the bombing.

Information provided by Joe Hurley, an informant working for, first the Secret Service, and then the FBI, ATF and Missouri State Highway Patrol, led to the arrest of Wyatt Duane Waggoner in September 1994. Waggoner, ultimately convicted on six explosives and weapons violations, had planned to blow up a courthouse using an ANFO truck bomb and a rocket launcher and had been involved in bank robberies in order to fund his plan. After the OKC bombing, Hurley (like Matthews and others) said he met McVeigh at a paramilitary training camp attended by radical right wing mercenaries willing to carry out acts of terror, for the right price.

SEPTEMBER 1994

According to the federal indictment issued him, the conspiracy to bomb the Murrah building began on September 13, 1994 and involved McVeigh, Nichols and the mysterious Others Unknown. Interestingly, McVeigh registered at the El Siesta Motel located just minutes from the remote Elohim City on this same day.

Roger Moore said that although he and McVeigh continued to communicate after the robbery, the last time they saw each other in person was the previous spring when McVeigh stopped by his Arkansas ranch. McVeigh, he said, had become noticeably more paranoid. He slept by the windows so he'd know if anybody was approaching the house and kept handguns under his pillow. He kept rapid-firing his automatic pistol in the driveway and harping on Waco.

McVeigh left a couple of days later, although Moore wasn't sure why, as there had been no altercation between them. That's what Moore told the FBI. McVeigh said he stopped by in an attempt to "patch things up" with Moore, but left after only one day because Moore suddenly accused him of stealing his flare launcher design. McVeigh said he sold about ten of the "rocket launchers" based on Moore's design but thought it would be okay since by doing so he was helping Moore sell the replacement flares. Neither would admit to seeing the other at any point after that although through slips of the tongue, McVeigh's defense team (and later others) learned that they had.

During a conversation, defense investigator Richard Reyna informed McVeigh that Moore would likely testify against him in court. McVeigh said he didn't think that would happen because Moore would never dare. When Reyna told McVeigh to "wake up and smell the coffee," McVeigh became visibly angry. If Moore ever decided to testify against him, said McVeigh, "there was enough evidence available to sink Roger Moore." He then explained to Reyna that on several occasions, including in August and September 1994, Moore sold him "Kinestiks" (one of the components used in the truck bomb). In fact, said McVeigh, Moore sold Kinestiks and many other things he wasn't supposed to, but not to "just anybody." If the FBI had ever bothered to search Moore's house, they would have found not only "more weapons than were found at the Davidian Compound..." but cases of explosives as well. In a conversation with his biographers after his conviction, McVeigh said that while he was unsure of how much he should talk about Moore, there was a lot more to Moore than people knew. He explained to them that if Moore's house had ever been searched, Moore would have been arrested on the spot because he sold an aluminum powder used to boost ammonium nitrate; and the chemical traces of it would have been "all over his fucking house," which would have matched those found on McVeigh after his arrest. Not only that, McVeigh continued, Moore provided him with blasting caps and cannon fuse (also components of the OKC bomb) but again, it had never become an issue in the investigation or in his criminal trial.[45]

Years later, in 2005, Nichols told the FBI where they could find a box of explosives that he had hidden prior to the bombing. He said that the box would have a shipping label in the name of 'Robert Miller' (Moore's alias) and Moore's fingerprints would be all over the box.[46] Sure enough, the FBI found the box of explosives right where Nichols said it would be but, for some reason, they didn't attempt to match the fingerprints found on the box for another three years, by which time the results were found to be inconclusive.

Even if McVeigh and Nichols were just attempting to shift blame from themselves to Moore, their statements would fail to explain other episodes in Moore's life. In 1989, a confidential informant told the ATF that 'Robert Miller' in Arkansas offered to mail him 100 pounds of C4 explosives. The telephone number and address provided by the informant traced back to Roger Moore and Karen Anderson. While "Robert Miller" was a known alias of Moore, when the ATF contacted the Arkansas State Police Intelligence Unit and gave them this information, they were told that it was just a case of "mistaken identity" and the ATF's investigation of Moore was quickly dropped. Other, subsequent investigations involving weapons and explosives and Roger Moore were also dropped.[47]

Moore must have forgotten about the explosives he gave and sold McVeigh as well as a number of other things in his life because he told the FBI that he *never* sold anything that would have brought the attention of the ATF and had even stopped selling guns because of "difficulties raised by the Brady Bill." Another thing Roger Moore forgot was that he and McVeigh were both at the 1994 Soldier Of Fortune convention that ran from September 15 to 18 and, according to DOJ gun show records provided by the DOJ to the Jones Team, McVeigh was working a table registered under Moore's name.[48] Also in attendance were a number of White Power spokespeople whom McVeigh attempted to call in the days leading up to the bombing, including Kirk Lyons and Dave Holloway, both closely associated with Elohim City and suspected German operative Andy Strassmeir, both spokespeople for CAUSE (whose offices, like Elohim City, McVeigh would call in the days before the bombing).

Also in attendance at the 1994 SOF convention was Utah skinhead leader Johnny Bangerter. While standing around a row of tables packed with militia and White Power keepsakes, Bangerter had the unfortunate privilege of meeting an ATF informant from Las Vegas named John Brinar, who was congregated near Moore's table. Bangerter recalled that Moore (using his alias Bob Miller) "wanted to give us, not *sell* us, but *give* us a safety flare converted into a shoulder-fired missile launcher. If you just glanced at it, it kind of looked like a toy but it was supposed to be able to divert heat seeking missiles and thwart infra-red searches. We accepted the launcher and, at the same time, Brinar tried to give us another type of fake rocket launcher, which was supposed to launch grenades. They were very cheap looking and you could tell those were bullshit, so I declined that offer."[49]

Not long after, Brinar started showing up at Bangerter's house trying to get him to take part in a number of plots, including trafficking illegal firearms and stolen military hardware (specifically night vision goggles and C4 explosives), killing federal judges and a bombing plot using... you might have guessed ... an ANFO-loaded Ryder truck (all defining features of the PATCON operations). Bangerter, who, during his time in Aryan Nations, had learned the ropes of a set-up and the signs of a sting, was suspicious of Brinar and rebuffed his efforts (written about extensively in my next book, *Redacted*). Brinar was persistent, though, and kept trying until, one day, he suddenly disappeared.

Imagine Bangerter's surprise (or lack thereof) when Brinar appeared in a series of news articles for his involvement in an ATF sting operation run out of a Las Vegas gun shop. Brinar had gotten caught up in a sting operation very similar to the one Roger Moore was involved with in the late 1980's. It was also similar to and running concurrent with a PATCON operation that involved a gun store in Phoenix named (no joke), "Lone Wolf Guns," which sold automatic weapons to right-wing extremists and outlaw biker gangs. More recently, the curiously named gun shop was implicated in the "Fast and Furious" scandal. Years after he disappeared, Brinar would write Bangerter and ask his forgiveness, admitting that he himself had been busted on a weapons charge and subsequently induced to entrap other people in exchange for leniency. During late 1994 and early 1995 though, Brinar was still busy trying to entrap Johnny Bangerter.

OCTOBER-NOVEMBER 1994

On November 1, 1994, McVeigh asked Terry Nichols to rob Roger Moore, saying that, as Moore and Nichols didn't know each other, Moore wouldn't suspect Nichols. He assured Nichols that it would be easy, and Moore would give him "absolutely no trouble at all."[50] Nichols could keep most of the cash and the only thing McVeigh wanted were the guns. Nichols said, when he declined the proposal, McVeigh threatened his family and thus he eventually relented. Now that it was agreed, McVeigh told him exactly when and what to do. Nichols was to rob Moore on November 5, a day Karen Anderson would be out of town and Moore would be alone, although how McVeigh knew this is unclear. McVeigh further instructed Nichols not to take anything that belonged to Karen Anderson. He gave very detailed instructions as to where everything Nichols should take would be found. Included were a number of unregistered guns with no serial numbers. McVeigh told Fortier that the objective of robbing Moore was to obtain a list of names he kept of people in the "movement" because Moore had threatened that if he ever ran afoul of the law and needed a get out of jail free card, he would hand over the names to the Feds.

Meanwhile, on November 4, 1994, Stephen Colbern mailed a resignation letter to his employers at the California DNA lab from Texarkana, Arkansas (about two hours from Moore's place). Karen Anderson, who left for Louisiana that same morning, told the FBI that at some point during the drive she mailed a letter for Colbern, who told Anderson that the letter was for his girlfriend and he didn't want her to know where he was. Colbern's relationship to what happened next, if any, is unknown.

The next day, on November 5, Roger Moore walked out of his house and was robbed blind, at least according to Moore. Everything after that is a bit blurry or rather, Moore's account of what happened tended to change quite a bit, depending on who he was talking to and when. When all was said and done the robber had taken between $9,000 and $24,000 in cash, precious metals and stones, keys to safety deposit boxes at banks in Arkansas and Florida, between 66 and 77 guns valued at about $66,000 and other stuff, none of which belonged to Karen Anderson. When the robber left, Moore went to the house of his next-door neighbors, Verta and Walt Powell, who, along with their son Lance, immediately thought Moore sounded disingenuous and suspected he was lying about *something*. They became even more doubtful of his story when, later that afternoon, they learned that Moore had not even called the police to report the robbery because, as Moore explained to them, it had been an attempt by the government to keep him "in check."[51] They eventually convinced a begrudging Moore to call the police.

Unfortunately, Moore could not produce serial numbers for the stolen weapons. As a responsible law abiding unlicensed gun dealer, he certainly kept a list, he said, but it had been hidden in a secret compartment in his van that only he and Anderson knew about. When the van was recovered just miles away, wouldn't you know it? – The robbers found the compartment and took the list, but, for some odd reason, had left the $600 in cash that was also stashed there. When the responding Sheriff asked him who he thought might have done this, Moore named a few people he suspected, including McVeigh. He also accused the Sheriff's office of conspiring with McVeigh to rob him. (McVeigh of course had a solid alibi, having been at a gun show in Ohio). The neighbors told the Sheriff (outside of Moore's earshot) that they thought Moore was making the entire thing up. When the Sheriff left, Moore complained to his neighbors that an investigation of the robbery would "blow his cover." Whatever he meant by that, Moore continued to make claims about his cover being blown to a number of people throughout the next two years. The FBI became concerned later that McVeigh's and Nichols' defense teams would speak with the neighbors about the robbery.[52]

Nobody except the FBI believed Moore's robbery story, including the insurance adjusters. They had a number of reasons for doubting him, beyond the lack of serial numbers for the guns, the large amount of cash and other valuables he said had been taken and the fact that critical details just didn't make sense or that he kept changing those details. One adjuster said that Moore's story sounded like a "rehearsed script." Moore told at least three people who worked for his insurance company that the federal government was involved in the robbery.[53] It was only natural that some doubts would arise.

Nichols later said that Moore *was* compliant, just like McVeigh predicted he would be; so much so that during the robbery, Nichols wondered if Moore had been in on the plan all along. The cash was not hidden where McVeigh said it would be. It was lying out on Moore's desk! As Nichols was leaving, Moore even told him about a remote location where he should drop off Moore's van (that Nichols was stealing). Maybe that was just the kind of nice guy Moore was.

The night of the robbery, McVeigh called Fortier and, using Moore's alias, told him "Terry did Bob."[54] He warned Fortier that Moore would send private investigators to look for him. When McVeigh saw his sister a couple weeks later, he told her he was upset because somebody was supposed to be murdered, but wasn't. Although she didn't know the details, his sister believed him.

It is well documented that items belonging to Roger Moore, including his bank box keys and fake ID in the name of his alias 'Bob Miller', ended up in a storage shed in Las Vegas that Terry Nichols rented and an ARA storage shed in Ohio. The guns themselves, at least some of them, were given away, sold and planted on people up and down the west coast in Arizona, Nevada, Utah, and California (and likely a number of other locations as well). As it turned out, a lot of Moore's guns weren't registered at all; according to Moore this was because he feared that if he declared them all, the boyfriend of some insurance agent might hear about it and try to rob him. It is not difficult to imagine that the real list of "stolen" property is longer than the one Moore gave the police or his insurance company. Certainly, if he had fake IDs or illegal explosives lying around, he would not have told investigators about it. One also wonders what happened to the underground pornography peddled by Moore and Anderson.

Over the years, different theories about the motives and identities of Moore's robbers have been suggested. FBI and prosecutors argued that the sole purpose of the robbery was to fund the bombing. The indictment against Nichols and McVeigh said that they "caused the robbery of Roger Moore," though not that they actually committed it, and some have questioned whether Nichols even robbed Moore at all. Others have suggested that members of the ARA, with or without Nichols' assistance, robbed Moore; that Moore was supposed to be killed after the robbery (as directed by Karen Anderson, McVeigh or both); that the robbery was an insurance scam orchestrated by Moore himself; and/or that the robbery never happened at all but was Moore's way to get guns and other materials into the hands of McVeigh and others, without getting his own hands dirty. In 2005, Nichols himself explained that a couple of months after the robbery, McVeigh finally admitted that it had been staged with Moore's cooperation and the purpose was to shield Moore from being implicated, directly or indirectly, in the bombing.[55]

According to an ATF informant who had infiltrated Elohim City, it was in November 1994, that she along with two other frequent faces there, Andreas Strassmeir and Dennis Mahon made their first of a few trips to Oklahoma City to scout the Murrah building and determine its desirability as a possible bombing target.

In the year leading up to the bombing, and increasingly in the six months before, scores of people reported that they had seen McVeigh with unidentified individuals. One of them was Bill Maloney, a realtor in Carthage, Missouri, who called the FBI and told them an intriguing story. Maloney said that on November 2, 1994, (three days before the Moore robbery and the day after Nichols says McVeigh bullied him into robbing Moore), three men came into his office. One of them, "Tim," had called the previous month and made an appointment to come discuss a plot of land Maloney was brokering. Tim arrived when he said he would, along with two other men who identified themselves as "Nichols" and "Jacks." Maloney, who had received naval intelligence training in memory recall, said that as he spoke with Tim he noticed a discolored upper right eyetooth and realized it was a filling. Maloney described all three of the men as having a confident military bearing, although the man who called himself Jacks seemed to be in charge of the group. During the course of their conversation, the men said things that caused Maloney to become suspicious, so much so that he asked one of them, Jacks, to look over a map which Maloney placed in a safe after they left. Maloney later gave the map that had the fingerprints of the mysterious Jacks to the FBI. Maloney wasn't delusional; other employees in the office confirmed that the men had indeed come in; and one of them remembered that they had been driving a car with Arizona license plates. When the FBI took McVeigh's handwriting sample later, agents observed his teeth and saw the same discoloration on the same tooth, exactly as Maloney reported.

According to an FBI report dated December 11, 1995, about eight months after Maloney reported the incident, "Dr. Michael G. Gelles, Psy. [Psychologist], Naval Criminal Investigative Service (NCIS) ... traveled [with an FBI agent] to [Maloney Real Estate] for the purpose of interviewing witness [Natalie Yards] under hypnosis." Yards, a receptionist at Maloney Real Estate, had been in the office the day Tim and friends had shown up. The FBI report details how Gelles interviewed Yards and placed her under a "hypnotic trance" that lasted over an hour. While under Gelles' hypnosis, Young provided "new information" including "the color, make, model and year of the vehicle as well as a partial [Arizona] license plate number [for the car driven by] the trio" that visited the office. This rather amazing report raises a couple of questions, one of which is, how many other eyewitnesses were hypnotized during the bombing investigation and if the hypnosis was able to produce "new information" relevant to the FBI's investigation, why weren't more of them hypnotized?

Gelles' background in counter-intelligence work (explored in more detail later) makes this story all the more interesting.[56] But there's more to the Maloney story. About a week after McVeigh arrived in Kingman in February 1994, so did two "drifters," sixty-year-old Robert Jacks and his companion, thirty-five-year old Gary Land. Land and Jacks, using a California driver's license, promptly rented a mailbox at the same small Kingman Post Office as McVeigh, which they closed that August, the same week McVeigh left town. They probably didn't miss McVeigh much though, because from November of that year until April 1995, Lands and

Jacks rented three different rooms at or near motels McVeigh often stayed at on dates that coincided with his presence.[57]

If that wasn't enough of a coincidence, early on April 19, 1995, the morning of the Oklahoma City bombing, Land and Jacks registered at a motel in Vinita, Oklahoma, two hours Northeast of Oklahoma City and two hours North of Elohim City, where McVeigh allegedly planned to seek refuge after the bombing. That evening, about ten hours after McVeigh's arrest in Perry, Lands and Jacks checked out of the Vinita motel and for reasons unexplained, rented a motel room in Perry, stayed there for only a few hours, checked out and checked back into their Vinita motel. Maybe the bed was uncomfortable.

On May 1, the FBI put out an all-points bulletin for Gary Allen Land and Robert Jacks, and the next day, at 5:30 AM, a heavily armed FBI tactical squad arrested Jacks and Land at another motel in Carthage, Missouri, an hour from Maloney's office. An FBI spokesperson told reporters that the "trail of Mr. Land and Mr. Jacks proved the strongest lead yet in the search for a second suspect and for a wider circle of conspirators they believe to have been responsible for the explosion [...] Several officials said that they strongly suspect Mr. Land is John Doe No. 2." Witnesses in Kansas and Oklahoma came forward stating they had seen McVeigh with them, but both Land and Jacks denied knowing McVeigh or having ever seen him. On May 3, 18 hours after their arrest, Lands and Jacks reportedly passed a polygraph examination and the FBI released them. FBI spokespeople then claimed that the two mens' uncanny parallel movements to McVeigh's were an unfortunate coincidence.[58]

When reporters finally caught up to them, Land was driving a 1981 Thunderbird with Arizona plates, the same car that Yards remembered seeing at Maloney's office while under hypnosis (although this connection was unknown to reporters). While not widely reported, years before Terry Nichols had owned property in Cassville, Missouri next door to another property owned by a man named Robert Jacks. Maloney, however, said that the Jacks who traveled around with Land wasn't the same as the one who came into his office. If nothing else, the bombing plot and its investigation may be best described as the most massive case of coincidences and mistaken identities *ever*.

In late November 1994, Ed McVeigh, Tim's grandfather and the only person he ever publicly admitted to loving, died. By the time Bill McVeigh located his elusive son, the funeral was over, but upon receiving the news, he returned home immediately. According to a childhood friend, who saw him at this time, "[Tim] had slowly deteriorated and turned into a paranoid person. He got stranger and stranger.... He was a troubled person."[59] A friend of the McVeigh family said that his strange political rantings caused them to worry if he had joined a cult. Steve Hodge's mother thought he was "going to crack" and worried he might be suicidal. Steve shared her concerns. He noticed that McVeigh now kept a gun with him in the front seat of his car and, like his mother, thought his old friend was "ready to snap."

McVeigh told his attorneys (and biographers) about an eerie and mysterious message he found on his dead grandfather's answering machine. The message, left in a woman's voice, said, "Pick up the phone. This is Jesus Christ. You're coming to see me tomorrow." He said he could never figure out what this meant or who would have left it. Defense mental health expert Lee Norton wrote that when his grandfather died, McVeigh, already suffering from PTSD, reached a final breaking point. Combined with everything else, Ed McVeigh's death left Tim feeling like he had no control and "show[ed] him that what he once thought was real and concrete is in fact, amorphous and fleeting."

McVeigh stayed in New York for a short time in order to help settle his grandfather's estate. While there, he received calls from a credit card company hounding him about outstanding debt. He told his attorneys that when he finally spoke with a representative he explained that he was "feeling sick from Desert Storm" and because his credit card was issued by the Department of Defense, they eventually stopped bothering him. From his father's house, he placed a six-hour call to the American Legion in Indianapolis.

McVeigh went to visit another friend from high school, Laurie, who hadn't heard from him in over two years, except when he sent her newspaper clippings about various politicians he told her not to vote for. Laurie said that when she saw him, he told her that "'they' had called him and asked him to do some 'military training.'" She had no idea who he was talking about and he didn't elaborate. He did tell her that he would only be gone for a couple of weeks, a couple of months at most, and would then be returning home. She never heard from him again. He visited with Steve, this time to say goodbye. They shook hands and McVeigh said, "I hope to see you in the next life." It was the last time they saw each other.

Since leaving town nearly two years before, McVeigh had occasionally sent letters to Calspan security guard Carl Lebron discussing Waco and Calspan's relationship to an undercover operation and asked him to photocopy classified documents housed at the Calspan facility about Operation North Star, which Lebron declined to do. While in town in November 1994, he made time to visit Lebron at Calspan. Lebron asked him why he had stopped by and McVeigh replied mysteriously "targets of opportunity," but offered no further explanation. He railed at Lebron for complaining about conspiracies, but doing nothing about them; and then left. He also visited Andrea Augustine. Augustine said she had the impression he was living out of his car and asked him a number of questions about his life, but instead of answering them, "he would blow me off … give me an answer to stop asking him … would change the subject … diverted me.… At the time, I thought he was being silly." Augustine would not see him again until after his arrest for the OKC bombing. Meanwhile, shortly after he was back on the road, he wrote to her and told her to contact him if she needed someone "killed or blown up, a shoulder, refuge or fertilization from good stock." He cryptically closed the letter by reminding her that "people may change superficially but not underneath. Remember that."[60]

DECEMBER 1994 TO FEBRUARY 1995

"A few agents of the thought Police moved always among them, spreading false rumors and marking down and eliminating the few individuals who were judged capable of becoming dangerous..."

- George Orwell, *1984*

Late December to early February 1995 saw McVeigh in Ohio, Illinois, Kansas and Michigan (among other places) transporting explosives and off-loading the loot from the Moore affair to various individuals, some of whose identities remain unknown, but who some members of the Jones Team suspected were co-conspirators "higher up on the food chain" than McVeigh, and whom he was trying to protect. Interestingly, Moore and McVeigh remained in close contact after the so-called robbery. They communicated mainly by cryptic letters, the contents of which indicated, not only that they still trusted each other and were even on "remarkably good terms," but also that Moore was in some way involved with the bombing plot, whose details were now rapidly coming together.[61]

Shortly before Christmas, McVeigh made his way back to Michigan. He had been driving across the country with stolen mercury switches and explosive blasting caps in boxes made to look like Christmas presents in the trunk of his car if he got into an accident. Afterwards, although he simply told most people he had been rear-ended, he wrote a letter to Roger Moore and Karen Anderson telling them that a black sedan which he believed to be a government vehicle had tried to run him off the road and caused him to total his car. Authorities later found, yes, mercury switches, blasting caps and boxes wrapped as Christmas presents, in an ARA bank robbery gang safe house in Ohio. The FBI had them destroyed, despite that they were evidence of the bank robberies and possibly the bombing; and criminal trials in both were ongoing. Also found in the safe house was an ID in the name of Roger Moore's alias, Bob Miller, as well as surveillance footage of properties including Roger Moore's, although nothing came of this either.

In between gun shows, McVeigh spent a considerable amount of time with Gwen Strider and her family and, after some urging on her part, joined them for Christmas dinner. He gave her a t-shirt with a Waco slogan on it, a set of used tires and a waterbed. Strider and her family, including her children, enjoyed McVeigh's company and said he was always smiling. "He was like a little kid and excited to be included" in their family holiday. During their conversations, it became clear that he was "very bitten by the Waco situation" but he wasn't overly negative, just seemed to want people to understand what "really happened" there. McVeigh, she told the Jones Team, "believed" (not just "thought") that when he was receiving his immunizations during the Gulf War, he had been injected with a microchip. He also believed that babies in California (where Colbern lived) were being implanted with microchips as part of some kind of a government experiment. Although it seemed strange, it didn't seem overly outrageous as she herself had seen a news report about pets being implanted with tracking chips. She felt that he probably had a good reason for his beliefs and if what he said about his own chip wasn't true, perhaps he had somehow "brainwashed himself."

During this visit, McVeigh told Strider that he would like to live a normal life someday, to get married and have kids, but he just couldn't right now. He had too many obligations. She thought he sounded suicidal and told him this. He responded by denying he had any urge to commit suicide but added, "When I go people will know I've been here." It was obvious to her and her entire family how happy he was with them and everyone urged him to stay, but to no avail. Strider said that as they hugged goodbye, she had a gut feeling she would never see him again. And she was right.

It was during this visit, in early January 1995, that McVeigh, in a conversation with Terry Nichols, accidently let it slip during "a fit of rage" that his "high level handler" was none other than Larry Potts, lead FBI agent at Ruby Ridge and the siege at Waco, Texas. Nichols said McVeigh was extremely angry and accused Potts of "manipulating him and forcing him to 'go off script,'" which Nichols took to mean that the target of the bombing and the date it was to occur had been changed by someone other than McVeigh.[62] Nichols, who knew McVeigh was planning a bombing, had helped him gather materials for it and even helped him build a bomb (although probably not the one that was actually used), and said that McVeigh never told him his specific target. Fortier, though, did know. McVeigh had told him when they drove past it the previous month, the same month that sightings of McVeigh inside the building began.

Just before he left Michigan, McVeigh (or someone using his calling card) placed three phone calls from the Bay Regional Medical Center. Although Strider never saw him again, about a month or so after he left, McVeigh wrote her a letter and told her about a government supercomputer database that contained the names of "suspected subversives and terrorists," ranked in order of threat. He believed his name was in the database. He expected that his health would began to deteriorate within the next year or two and felt it was better to "burn out than rot away in some nursing home."

He wrote his sister a series of letters telling her about his "funny health problems," and how "medical programs are one of the most effective means of control available to a government. The control of medicine and drugs is mandatory." He enclosed several articles about vaccines. He warned her to "keep an eye out" for private investigators who, he said, were likely to be looking for him and emphasized, "They could be anybody, and they don't follow the rules. Be especially careful at bars, etc., where they will try to get you to talk." In another letter he wrote that "They" would be watching and recording her and told her not to send any mail to him because "the G-men might come get it out of my box." He signed the letter to his sister "Tim T.," the first and last time he would do so. Jim Rosencrans told the FBI that when McVeigh made his way back to Kingman that winter, he was very obviously being followed by a government-issue-surveillance van whose occupants didn't even attempt to hide what they were doing.

Throughout the months of February to April 1995, McVeigh checked in and out of motels in Kingman, where guests and managers remembered he always wore camouflage and seemed to have a steady stream of visitors. The managers of the Belle Art Lodge said he checked in there using his real name on January 31, 1995 and registered to stay until February 8. A few days after checking in, five men and one woman visited him in his room and continued to show up over the course of the week. They were so loud the managers refused to let him extend his stay. Throughout that month, McVeigh, or somebody using Daryl Bridges' calling card, placed phone calls from McVeigh's Kingman motel rooms at an obsessive frequency. On February 17, 18 and 19, calls were placed from his room at the Hilltop Motel in Kingman to the Prescott, Arizona Veterans Medical Center.[63] The following month, this ceaseless barrage of phone calls continued.

He met with a mysterious man in a Kingman diner, named Ron, whose description matched that of Poindexter. When a waitress there spoke with the defense team, she expressed fear for her life, telling them that the mysterious man was "ex-military" who was now part of a seven-man "militia group formed by the US Army and trained to assassinate people in Vietnam." McVeigh acknowledged that he knew the waitress and had frequented the diner, but for the life of him, could not recall this Ron person. McVeigh appeared at a National Alliance meeting in Bullhead, Arizona (as "Chuck") and aroused the suspicions of other attendees. He showed up at another National Alliance meeting in Oklahoma City and appeared in the Murrah building. He made his way to Galveston, Texas, to purchase explosives, attended a gun show in Reno, Nevada, one in Iowa as "Joe Rivers" and in the last week of February 1995, as "Tim Tuttle" in St. George, Utah.

A man who worked with Michael Fortier told the FBI that in late fall 1994, Fortier had given him a pamphlet from an anti-government group in Utah. In late December, McVeigh told more than one person that he would be teaching a survival class in southern Utah but when the Jones Team asked him about this, he said he made the entire story up and that there never had been any class. McVeigh had given Fortier about a third of Roger Moore's guns to sell but when, in early 1995, he learned that Fortier had not yet gotten rid of them, he insisted Fortier accompany him to some west coast gun shows including one in St. George, Utah. Coincidently, Roger Moore (aka Bob Miller) had connections to a network of international arms merchants and right-wing gun dealers operating throughout the state of Utah.

Johnny Bangerter lived in LaVerkin, Utah (minutes from St. George). He and his group of Christian Identity skinheads, The Army of Israel, held regular survival-training sessions in nearby Zion National Park and sometimes hosted guest trainers from other groups including the Aryan Nations and National Alliance. During late 1994 and early 1995, ATF informant John Brinar was still trying to get Bangerter embroiled in various plots and kept dropping the name 'Bob Miller,' the man Johnny had met at the Soldier of Fortune convention.

It was precisely during this time, in December 1994 and January 1995, that Johnny Bangerter's family began receiving a series of strange phone calls from a man who called himself Chuck. Chuck mentioned the names of people in the movement in the Kingman area who Johnny and his family knew, including Dick Coffman, organizer of the Bullhead City National Alliance. The caller left several messages, saying he would be passing through St. George soon and wanted to meet up with Johnny. A family friend who had taken down one of the messages recalled that Chuck sounded upset and stressed out, as if he was under some kind of pressure. In this same period, Coffman contacted Johnny and suggested he meet with a guy named Tim and invited Johnny to attend an upcoming National Alliance meeting in Nevada. In the end though, for various reason, Johnny never made contact with either Chuck or Tim – nor did he attend the meeting. Timothy McVeigh did attend the meeting though, accompanied by two other men, one of whom turned out to be Michael Fortier; although the identity of the other, older-looking man remains unknown. Two other attendees, including Richard Coffman, confirmed their presence. Although the entire meeting was videotaped, the tape has never surfaced.

On the weekend of February 25 to 27, 1995, McVeigh, accompanied by Michael Fortier, registered at the Dixie Palm Motel in St. George, Utah. Over the course of the previous week, Johnny's mother Mary received several phone calls from a man named "Tim" who said was looking for Johnny. Like Chuck, Tim explained that they had mutual friends in Kingman and that he "had a lot of great ideas" he wanted to run past Johnny. Each time, Mary told the caller that Johnny wasn't home but the caller, undeterred, gave Mary the number of the motel he was staying at in St. George, asking that she pass it along to Johnny. She did, but Johnny, who by now was becoming annoyed with the calls and more than a bit suspicious of the caller, instructed his mother that if he called again, to tell him that he had gone out of town on a camping trip. He didn't call back. Instead, he showed up at the house that Saturday while Johnny was at work. When Mary heard the knock at the door, she peeked her head out and saw a man who introduced himself as Tim and explained that he was the one who'd been calling the house. When she explained that Johnny wasn't home, Tim asked if he could come inside and wait. Mary apologized and said she had some errands to run, so that wouldn't be possible. Johnny's sister, Brenda, who was also at home, described the unexpected visitor as arrogant, rude and pushy.[64]

The next day, Sunday, Johnny, along with several of his friends, attended the Crossroads Of The West gun show in St. George. While there, he approached the booth of a man selling stickers, t-shirts and literature. Johnny noticed that the man's baseball cap said "Is Your Church ATF Approved?" (a reference to the incident at Waco). Johnny complimented him on the hat and they shook hands. At that same moment, a man named Harry Contries, who had been walking around the show taking pictures, pointed his camera towards them, told them to "say cheese" and snapped a picture. Contries was well known in the Utah area and associated with the old-time arms dealers (a number of whom were well acquainted with Roger Moore/Bob Miller). Johnny said that, although it was not the normal practice to take pictures at the show, he didn't think much of it at the time and continued his chat with the man at the booth. Eventually though, wanting to look at the other tables, Johnny excused himself and the man handed him a business card with the words "Tim Tuttle: Weapons Parts, Kits" printed on it. Only later, did Johnny realize that the man he had spoken to was the same man he met at the gun show and Mary and Brenda realize that McVeigh was the man who had shown up at the house.[65] Although the Contries picture never surfaced and its whereabouts are unknown, it turned out that McVeigh, as Tuttle, was at the show selling Roger Moore's guns. It is unknown if Fortier, who had accompanied McVeigh to St. George, was at the gun show as well.

Given Bangerter's high visibility in the white power movement at the time, his habit of making highly inflammatory statements to the media and his association with some of the government's most wanted Nazi's, it would be easy to think that maybe he had a deeper connection to McVeigh than he was willing to admit. Almost *too* easy.

Sure enough, the story got a lot weirder almost exactly one year after McVeigh's appearance in St George, and nearly ten months after the bombing. The Jones Team had obtained a set of phone records showing that Bangerter had made a number of highly incriminating calls that directly linked him to McVeigh and the bombing. When Jones Team investigator Richard Reyna showed up at Bangerter's house and presented him with the incriminating paper trail (including the phone records), Bangerter was baffled and insisted he didn't make any of those calls and that he only met McVeigh that one time … but his name was Tuttle. Stranger still, the FBI had never questioned Bangerter as to whether or not he had ever been in contact with McVeigh. Therefore, when Reyna arrived Bangerter still had Tuttle's business card and gave it to him. Reyna, of course, did not believe Bangerter, and continued his investigation of McVeigh's west coast connections, all the while being trailed and followed by government agents.

Somewhere along the way, the phone records had been leaked to major media outlets, who began reporting on Bangerter and his good friend McVeigh and the likelihood that Bangerter would be indicted for charges relating to the plot. Bangerter's so-called allies on the fringe right followed suit, seizing and reporting on the story with more unfounded sensational detail than the mainstream media, calling him "Bombin' Johnny Bangerter" and, because the FBI had not bothered to question him, accused him of being a federal informant and the government's "pet Nazi."[66]

Eventually, Judge Matsch, at Reyna's insistence, issued a subpoena allowing Reyna to obtain a copy of Bangerter's phone records directly from the phone company and, much to Reyna's surprise, *none* of the incriminating calls were listed on them. What's more, the order of calls listed in the real phone records appeared out of order on the bogus ones. It was at this point that both Reyna and Johnny Bangerter realized that someone had gone out of their way to fabricate the records and pass them off to the Jones Team and the media. Bangerter recalled:

> When Reyna realized the incriminating calls were not in the real phone records, he was scared. I was scared. All of the sudden it was like Godzilla's coming. And that was the feeling we all got. That Godzilla was coming. Reyna said this was some high level stuff, a matter of national security and if it got out, we would all be in danger and could even end up dead. I will never forget his face. He wasn't acting. He couldn't disguise it or fake it … he couldn't even think. It was like "Hey Reyna! You forgot your underwear." He was so freaked out, he was blank. Enough to where, if I ever live to 85, however long I live, when I'm lying on my death bed, when my life is flashing in front of me, his face when he found out will be there. Within 24 hours of obtaining the real records that showed I was innocent, Reyna called my house and told me to hurry up and turn on CNN. I did and there was Janet Reno and FBI Director Louie Freeh stepping onto a podium. Reno announced that all further indictments in the bombing were being dropped, that there would be no further indictments and no additional suspects would

be pursued. It was the shortest press conference I ever saw. Reyna came right over to our house. He was in utter disbelief. He knew what he thought had happened, and that was that the other indictments were dropped because at least some of them were based on fabricated evidence and the truth of it was bound to come out and if that happened, there'd be an uproar.

Eventually the truth about the records did get out when Kevin Flynn wrote about it in the *Rocky Mountain News*. Flynn really did his homework and when he fully realized what had happened, he was shocked. Even though there was no uproar, it was very brazen for a reporter in the mainstream press to even suggest a conspiracy related to the bombing much more so to expose the fact that there had been an effort to try and frame someone like me. But really, I was the easiest person in the world to frame with the kind of rhetoric I spouted all the time and the kinds of statements I made on television. Still, when I was speaking with Flynn about what had happened, it was all very fresh in my mind. I was paranoid and rightfully so. I had been through so much, so many sting operations. I knew how they worked. I don't know how far he went in his investigation but when Flynn found about the records he was very troubled. Like Reyna, he thought he was talking to a dead man. It was all very eerie.

Flynn's November 1997 article, entitled "Who Painted The Phony Trail Of Guilt," announced that skinhead leader Johnny Bangerter believed authorities were trying to frame him in the Oklahoma City bombing and, as it turned out, a trail of fabricated evidence "led to Johnny Bangerter's front door," which indicated that indeed, "someone" *had* tried to frame him. Still, the question of who and why remained. At the time, Bangerter was sure the records were just one in a long line of attempts to set him up that had begun after Ruby Ridge. Flynn quoted Reyna who said, "I don't blame (Johnny) for thinking the feds did it ... someone got his actual records.... Whoever did this did a good job. It was too authentic."[67]

In the months to come, the Jones Team learned that the government was actively conducting investigations in the St. George area, investigations they suspected related to Bangerter and his group. They couldn't be sure though, because despite Judge Matsch's orders that the Feds turn over information about their St. George probe, they *refused* to do so. In addition, they learned that the FBI had questioned Coffman about McVeigh's many phone calls but Coffman denied having ever spoken to McVeigh, saying that a man named Tuttle had left a message on the National Alliance answering machine, but they had never spoken in person. The FBI was seemingly content with this, despite the fact that Coffman misrepresented the number of calls and refused their request to take a polygraph. They never asked him about Fortier or about Bangerter's claims that Coffman had tried to connect him with "Tim."

The government had never really needed to question Bangerter about anything, because a handful of federal informants had been reporting on his activities for quite some time. Sounding very reminiscent of PAT-CON operations as well as the ATF operation involving John Brinar, is an account written by former ATF agent Jay Dobyns, in his internet blog. Dobyns explains how, during the 1990's, he and his partners were conducting undercover investigations of extremists in the Las Vegas area. This involved "buying machine guns, sawed off shotguns, homemade nitroglycerin." Eventually they moved on to more "high profile target[s]" including Patriot Movement spokesperson Bo Gritz and "befriended 'all-stars' of the movement like Johnny Bangerter." In fact, Dobyns wrote that he and his partner even "trained with Bangerter and the members of his Army of Israel." When they got close to the real "shotcallers" however, they were instructed to "disengage the target" and end their investigations, an order Dobyns says originated with the "White House or CIA."[68]

Meanwhile, the ATF had an active plan to raid Elohim City, primarily based on information provided by an informant who told about all manner of violent plots brewing there, one of which was the bombing of a federal building (the Murrah being one potential target she named). In preparation for the raid, the ATF requested the assistance of the INS, as one of the men they planned to arrest was illegal alien Andy Strassmeir. In later February 1995, Bob Ricks, chief of the Dallas FBI headquarters, called a meeting with the head of the Tulsa ATF office. During the meeting, Ricks revealed that the FBI had at least six of their own informants in the mix at Elohim City and were engaged in other related undercover operations elsewhere that an ATF raid might foil. Therefore, at the FBI's urging, the ATF called off their scheduled raid. The ATF's informant in Elohim City, wrote Evans-Pritchard "had stepped on a land mine ... she [and her handlers] had unwittingly stumbled on a much bigger sting being conducted by the FBI" which appeared to be "a counterintelligence operation approved at the highest levels in Washington," one of the reasons the FBI sought to protect Strassmeir.[69]

MARCH AND APRIL 1995

The right understanding of any matter and a misunderstanding of the same matter do not wholly exclude each other.

– Franz Kafka, *The Trial*

It was a bright cold day in April, and the clocks were striking thirteen.

– George Orwell, *1984*

About two weeks after McVeigh appeared at the St. George gun show and on Johnny Bangerter's doorstep, he showed up in the Fort Riley, Kansas, area with two and sometimes three unknown men. Scores of witnesses reported these sightings to the FBI immediately after the bombing, one of them a retired Army Lieutenant Colonel and Special Forces Advisor who had unfortunately come down with a "brain infection" and was unable to offer further information. Another man reported that on March 9, 1995, he boarded a bus in Kansas that was headed to Pueblo, Colorado. He sat down next to a fidgety passenger who called himself "Tim McNey," whom he now recognized as Timothy McVeigh. The FBI sought information about a vendor named "Tim Tuttle" and his registration at a gun show in Colorado on the dates of March 10 to 12, 1995. In Hammer's Guilty Agent story, McVeigh received final instructions in explosives at ESI in Colorado during this time and on March 17, traveled back to Las Vegas to meet with the Major who instructed McVeigh to check in on a daily basis until he completed his mission.

Since the previous September, Cary Gagan, an informant for the U.S. Marshals, who regularly traveled from Denver to Las Vegas to Kingman, Arizona, had been providing information to handlers in Denver about an ongoing plot to blow up federal buildings. The Department of Justice issued a letter of immunity for Gagan, who was instructed to maintain his contact with the conspirators and report any developments. On March 17, 1995, Gagan informed his handlers that he had met with some of the conspirators at a motel room in Las Vegas where they had reviewed drawings of the Murrah building. Based on this and other information, the U.S. Marshalls issued a general warning to their regional offices that federal courthouses and government installations may become targets of terrorist attacks.

A man using the name "Steve Murphy" but listing McVeigh's address registered as a vendor at a gun show in Prescott, Arizona to be held on March 18, but, according to the organizer, never showed up. At the end of the month, McVeigh sent his sister his military records for safekeeping and on March 31, checked into the Imperial Motel in Kingman, where he allegedly stayed until April 12. According to the Lone Wolf story, McVeigh remained in his room, alone, leaving only to get food, although guests at the motel said he had a number of visitors. His defense team noted that while the handwriting on the original registration form at the Imperial "resembled" McVeigh's, the registration extension form dated April 7, had very obviously been filled out by someone other than McVeigh. During his stay at the Imperial, McVeigh (or somebody using his calling card) placed a number of calls to Coffman's local National Alliance office; a Ryder rental shop in Lake Havasu, Arizona; to Elohim City and to the CAUSE foundation in North Carolina, an organization catering to legal defense efforts of the racist right.[70] According to Hammer, McVeigh spent this time with the mysterious bomb maker, Poindexter.

On April 6, 1995, U.S. Marshal's informant, Cary Gagan, called his Denver handlers and relayed that he had just returned from a meeting in

Kingman, Arizona where he learned that the bombing was to occur within the next two weeks.

It would seem *something* strange was going on in Kingman. A heavily redacted FBI document, written about four months after the bombing, recounts information provided by a man very familiar with the remotest parts of the outlying desert there. The man, who had been out hiking during this time, heard what he thought was a plane going down and saw a plume of smoke. Fearing somebody may have been hurt, the man went towards the plume and eventually saw two strange people in the distance with no vehicle, which he said was "highly unusual" where they were. When he got closer to them, they "disappeared" but there were tracks on the ground and they had "obviously" hidden in some nearby brush. In retrospect, the man thought maybe he had witnessed a "test run" for the OKC bombing. Not long after this occurred, he returned to the area and saw "a large group of individuals clad in white robes with colored sashes" and a large trailer. He could not understand how they got the trailer so far out into that terrain. The area, he said, was filled with "isolationists, survivalists, paramilitary groups and some religious individuals all focused on Idaho" (probably referring to Aryan Nations.) The man advised that he had lived there for a long time and was very knowledgeable about these "cult groups." He had heard, from a source he refused to name, that McVeigh had visited a couple of these desert dwelling paramilitary groups and that McVeigh had only been a "good soldier" in the plot, "not a general." He believed that "when all is said and done," this area of Arizona would yield the individuals directing McVeigh. [71]

Later, Michael Drosnin, a reporter for the *Washington Post* and the *Wall Street Journal*, contacted first the FBI and then the Jones Team. He told them that shortly before the bombing, McVeigh had met with a Cuban man at a "hideout" and "compound" in the most remote desert areas surrounding Kingman. The man, who Drosnin said, had a "military bearing," had many Arab connections and used many aliases, sometimes "Arab-sounding." He was known as an "army officer," sometimes passed himself off as a "priest" and had some kind of connection with the Branch Davidians. Drosnin's story also paralleled Cary Gagen's in some ways.

Drosnin told the FBI agents that he really hoped this information didn't "come back to haunt" the FBI but he felt it was important they check out the lead before the group disappeared. [72] Drosnin, trying to secure an interview with McVeigh, told Jones that if he could confront McVeigh with this information, McVeigh would be shocked and would immediately know who and what he was talking about. However, Drosnin advised, based on what he now knew, he did not believe McVeigh knew the man's *true* identity or who he really was and would be very interested in this information. Once he knew, McVeigh would not want to protect the man. The story told by Drosnin, who would not reveal the source of his information, was similar in some ways to those told by others, including the previously mentioned man in the desert; and Drosnin's descriptions of the strange Cuban man matched sightings of McVeigh with a darker skinned man in Kingman. When his attorneys asked McVeigh about this, rather than deny he knew anything about it or call Drosnin crazy, as he normally would have, McVeigh emphatically insisted that his defense team should not deal with Drosnin, saying that he was "bad news" and "obviously has sources and can dig out information."

On April 4, 1995, just two weeks before the bombing, McVeigh visited a dentist's office in Kingman but refused to let him take an x-ray, claiming he could not afford it. The dentist filled a cavity for McVeigh, who explained that he planned to apply for a job and the cavity (on the front tooth) was unsightly. He paid in cash. The visit perplexed his defense team. They wondered why he would have a cavity filled right before the bombing. Was the tooth causing him pain or did he want to get rid of an identifying mark? Despite the Kingman dentist record and the many Army dentist visits, after his arrest, McVeigh told a prison dentist that, in early 1995, he had one cavity filled but other than that, had no dental problems … ever … in his life.

On April 7, the flurry of telephone calls made from McVeigh's motel room stopped; and then resumed on April 11. On those dates, he appeared at the Fortier family dinner in Kingman, Arizona, but also in Colorado, Kansas, and Oklahoma. An overwhelming number of multiple McVeighs (as well as multiple Ryder trucks and John Doe 2's) appeared at critical times and locations throughout the weeks leading to the bombing and the frequency of such appearances increased as April 19 approached. Witnesses from different areas of the country and who didn't know each other, reported that the McVeigh they saw made a point of announcing his name (McVey, McNey, McVeigh) and told them to remember it because they would hear it again soon.

Sightings of McVeigh inside the Murrah building began as early as December 1994, but became more frequent in the weeks immediately prior to April 19, 1995. Numerous McVeighs, sometimes alone and sometimes with other individuals, visited the Murrah daycare center, the Veterans Administration and Social Security offices, the mail room, elevators, snack bar, vending machines, lobby, underground parking lot and the basement tunnels that run below Oklahoma City, including those directly under the Murrah. Employees described them, alternately, as good-looking, having distinct facial markings, wearing an earring, dressed neatly, dressed sloppily, holding a walkie-talkie or rummaging through the mail.

These "McVeighs" sometimes smiled, scowled or spoke. One McVeigh came into the daycare center and told the manager that he and his children had just moved to the area. Instead of questions parents normally ask, McVeigh asked about the security cameras and construction of the building. Three men came into the Veterans Administration office. One of them explained he was looking for a job and identified himself as Tim "McVey" from upstate New York, even making a point of spelling out his name (like the McNey on the bus to Colorado had). Still, McVeigh insisted to his attorneys and biographers, "I've never been in the Murrah building in my life."

Approximately two weeks before the bombing, employees at the federal courthouse in downtown Oklahoma City were advised to be extra vigilant of suspicious people who might be wandering the building and a number of employees who worked in the federal complex downtown, including at the Murrah, began hearing rumors about bomb threats. Although the FBI would deny it, Harvey Weathers, a deputy chief of the Oklahoma City Fire Department said that on Friday, April 14, 1995, his office received notice from the FBI that they were to be alert for "terrorist activity in the near future," and warned that individuals of interest may enter the city that weekend.[73]

On April 14, 1995, Timothy McVeigh checked into the Dreamland Motel in Junction City, Kansas, listing James Nichols' house in Michigan as his permanent address. Guests there recalled McVeigh, or someone who closely resembled him, but who had tattoos, glasses, an abundance of body hair and other features, depending on who was talking. The owner of the motel, her son and the guests said the man parked two different Ryder trucks there at different times, first a smaller, faded older-looking one and then a larger, newer one. On April 15, 'Robert Kling' placed a delivery order for Chinese food to McVeigh's room at the Dreamland. The delivery driver insisted that the man who answered the door in no way resembled McVeigh, Nichols or John Doe #2 sketches.

On April 17, a man with a pockmarked face rented a Ryder truck from Elliot's Body Shop, just miles away from the Dreamland. The man presented a South Dakota driver's license in the name of Bob Kling, born April 19, 1972. The time stamp on the rental receipt was 4:19 PM. Depending on who you ask, Kling either did or did not come into the store with another man, later known as John Doe #2. Roger Charles wrote, "The prosecution could never prove that McVeigh rented the Ryder truck in person, or that he – or his surrogate, had done so alone."[74] In fact, during his trial, prosecutors could not conclusively place the ambiguously elusive bomber at Elliot's at all.

At around 5 AM on April 18, 1995, McVeigh left the Dreamland Motel, driving the second of the two Ryders he had parked there during his stay. McVeigh (most times) claimed that he and Nichols built the truck bomb in Kansas that day, after which he, alone, drove the bomb-laden Ryder from Kansas to Oklahoma. At some point after crossing the state line, he pulled off the road and parked the Ryder in a small gravel lot near (but not at) a motel where he remained until early the next morning, at which point he headed to Oklahoma City to deliver death to those inside the Murrah. For the first time in a long time though, he had failed to leave even a shred of paper in the paper trail he had so carefully laid throughout the previous two years.

Witnesses saw McVeigh, a Ryder truck and two other men at a restaurant in Perry, Oklahoma, around 7:30 PM, then at a McDonald's in Oklahoma City with an unknown number of people at an unknown time. Then with one other man at a convenience store in Oklahoma City around 9:30 PM and at the same store around midnight, now accompanied by a lone "hooker" (more on that later). When his defense team asked McVeigh where the truck was during the missing time the night before the bombing, he responded by saying, "Maybe it was in a government warehouse being loaded with explosives." Among the things in his possession at the time of his arrest were handwritten directions to a storage warehouse in Oklahoma City.

In Hammer's story, McVeigh, Poindexter and ARA bank robber Richard Guthrie completed the real bomb around 9 PM on April 18 after which they dropped Guthrie and the fake truck bomb off at a motel near Oklahoma City. McVeigh and Poindexter made their way to a warehouse in Oklahoma City, where they met with The Major and Roberto, the man who had tested McVeigh on his knowledge of right-wing rhetoric nearly two years before. The Major and Roberto killed Poindexter and dumped his body in the back of the Ryder truck.

An ATF spokesperson told a group of reporters that there *had* been an ongoing sensitive sting operation (the nature of which he left undefined) and, as part of that, the Murrah building was under surveillance throughout the night of April 18, but the stake-out was discontinued at around 6:00 AM on the morning of April 19. He later retracted his statement, but that really didn't matter because, even before he made it, several eyewitnesses reported that they saw bomb disposal units near the Murrah building and federal courthouse and members of the Oklahoma City bomb squad confirmed they searched the courthouse for bombs that morning.

The surveillance teams and bomb disposal units weren't the only early birds out and about on the morning of April 19. Starting around 7 AM, multiple incarnations of McVeigh (and friends) began appearing at different locations throughout Oklahoma City, driving very different vehicles; all of them accompanied by various unidentified companions. Despite this (or perhaps because of it) no eyewitness who saw a McVeigh that morning was called to testify in court and therefore, as the security footage from all of the cameras around the Murrah had gone missing, McVeigh was never conclusively placed at the scene at all.

At 8:32 AM CST (Oklahoma time), the Department of Justice in Washington D.C. received a strange phone call from a man who refused to give his name. The caller said that the federal building in Oklahoma City had just been bombed. He knew, he said, because he was standing across the street as they spoke. A half-hour later, at 9:02 AM, the deadly explosion ripped through the Murrah building. Immediately after, many McVeigh's, accompanied by the various unidentified companions, were seen speeding off in equally various vehicles, except for one McVeigh variant, who a few people saw standing not too far from the blast sight calmly watching the commotion and horror. One peculiar McVeigh, with a pock-marked face and stained teeth, was seen standing around talking to two other people about four blocks from the Murrah. A man who walked by them said the McVeigh figure turned to his companions and coldly remarked, "Shit happens doesn't it?"

About 90 minutes after the bomb exploded in OKC and about 60 miles north of there, Timothy James McVeigh was pulled over for driving without a rear license plate. He was arrested for driving an unregistered vehicle and carrying an unregistered concealed pistol. For some reason the name on the booking card at the local jail listed him as 'Bruce James McVeigh.' About ten hours later, Lands and Jacks, the strange drifters who seemed to follow McVeigh, left their motel room near Elohim City and checked in at a motel in Perry; but left after only a couple of hours. Prior to his being named a suspect in the bombing, as McVeigh sat in the Perry jail, Roger Moore contacted at least two bail/bond companies in an attempt to arrange bail for him. Stephen Jones told terrorism expert Stephen Sloan that McVeigh's arrest in Perry had actually been "detrimental to the federal investigation [of the bombing] because there [were] indications that the FBI had a lead on Tim the day of the bombing or perhaps the next day, [had already] tracked him to Perry and they wanted to wait until Tim bonded out to follow him and see where he went." At the last minute, however, the ATF tracked McVeigh to the Perry jail, which really "screwed things up for the FBI."

Referring to his demeanor prior to the FBI's retrieval of him two days later, the county prosecutor said McVeigh had an "eerie calm ... you wouldn't look into his eyes and say 'There's evil exuding.' You just looked into his eyes and said, 'There's nothing.'" A number of outlets reported that, when the FBI finally did come to collect him, McVeigh refused to answer any questions, gave only his name, rank and serial number but (at least according to one report) did mention that he had been implanted with a "bio-chip." This article explained that those who inhabited the same world as McVeigh believed that eventually all people would be implanted with tracking microchips, and now McVeigh himself "is claiming to be one of the participants (or victims of) these fantastical control projects."[75]

Regardless of what he did or did not say to his captors, after the FBI questioned him in Perry, the U.S. Marshals transported him to Tinker Air Force Base for arraignment. As agents led him to a nearby black helicopter, McVeigh expressed concern for his safety, telling them he feared another Lee

Harvey Oswald-Jack Ruby incident and requested a bulletproof vest; a luxury the agents declined to grant him. During the televised 'Perry Perp Walk,' McVeigh's cold blue eyes stared straight ahead, with "the hundred mile stare of the lost soldier – his tall, thin frame draped in orange prison clothing."[76]

Within days, Irene Fortier (Mike's mother) told reporters McVeigh had lived a double life and the truth would eventually come out. Terry Nichols' ex-wife Lana Padilla told Diane Sawyer that the McVeigh she saw on television during the perp walk was "not the same person," there was something off, something unrecognizable about his face.[77] A handful of other people made similar statements.

Here we are presented with a problem of multiple McVeigh's; a man whose cold demeanor and accused crime transformed him into an unrecognizable monster even in the eyes of those who knew him. Then there were those pesky flesh-and-blood McVeigh's who repeatedly appeared at different locations simultaneously, so much so that the detail-minded former Jones Team investigator, Roger Charles, referred to them as McVeigh "surrogates" and "the McVeigh character." While the FBI *briefly* conducted an investigation into the use of possible McVeigh "look-alikes" in the bombing plot, they discontinued this line of inquiry as early as May 10, 1995, even as reports of this type were still forthcoming. The Jones Team also looked into this possibility and, occasionally, McVeigh himself wondered if someone had impersonated him without his knowing it (which, whether he liked it or not, would have indicated a larger conspiracy).[78]

Pack Of Wolves narratives and some of their Watched Wolves counterparts suggest that at least *some* of the doubles were McVeigh's clever masquerading co-conspirators, and given his associates' fondness for disguises, use of decoys and fake identification, this is also a reasonable proposition, up to a point. Lone Wolf stories, however, attribute *all* sightings of McVeigh duplicates and all John Doe 2's to mistaken or overly imaginative eyewitnesses. They insist McVeigh doubles, if they did exist, were simply those he created through his many aliases and (bad) disguises. And certainly, that is also true, to a point. From the outset, McVeigh constructed, enacted and left documentation of a number of shadow-selves (an issue explored in the next chapter).

All other narratives of the bombing (Guilty Agent and Experimental), purport that McVeigh, like Lee Harvey Oswald, was "an ordinary man who became caught up in a complicated web of intrigue and deception." Here, the bombing plot involves any number of individuals watched over, guided or orchestrated by institutions who possessed both the motive and resources to commit the crime, and the ability to set up patsies and scapegoats to take the fall and protect certain individuals after the fact. In a nod to such stories, a 1997 *Toronto Star* article described Oswald and McVeigh as "spiritual brothers, true representatives of a type that emerges every now and then to act out a recurring American nightmare." In fact, Oswald acts as the prototype of McVeigh "and of all the McVeigh's to come" Both men echoed earlier and influenced later depictions of "The Patsy" and the "Sympathetic Assassin."[79]

Like Oswald, McVeigh has the uncanny yet consistent ability to appear in two places at once, sometimes loudly identifying themselves by variations of his name and then making easily remembered spectacles of themselves. Like Oswald, McVeigh made connections to a number of groups and individuals whom the FBI had placed under systematic surveillance and was himself under surveillance by any number of intelligence agencies (military, ATF, FBI, private). Like Oswald, McVeigh was in constant contact not only with numerous potential *bad guys* but known intelligence assets and agents, like Roger Moore, who despite his probable involvement in the plot walked away, as he had so many times before, unscathed and, just months after the bombing, the FBI systematically dropped him from their inquiry. In addition, while Oswald can be placed near the scene of the crime, no *direct* evidence exists that he killed JFK. Similarly, no physical evidence and only dubious eyewitness evidence existed that McVeigh rented a Ryder truck and ultimately, although he was in Oklahoma City the morning of the bombing, nobody can quite say for sure where he was, when and what exactly he was doing there.

In Guilty Agent stories, McVeigh does misrepresent himself, leading a double life as an undercover operative. His racist rants, odd behavior and appearances in radical right-wing enclaves, were all part of his carefully constructed "legend" even if the legend jibed with his authentic self. But alongside of him, working concurrently, likely without his knowledge, are imposters implanted and controlled by shadowy intelligence agencies. Whether the real McVeigh went rogue, went off the reservation, or carried out his orders as directed, it matters little, as there is always another McVeigh ready to fill to his shoes. Three years before the assassination of John F. Kennedy, FBI Director J. Edgar Hoover informed the State Department there was a possibility that an "imposter" was attempting to pass himself off as Lee Harvey Oswald and thanked them in advance for any information they could provide about him.[80] The FBI of the 1990's sought to avoid these types of mysteries in McVeigh's case. But unlike Oswald, who insisted certain incriminating pictures of him were doctored and faked, once McVeigh became America's Face Of Terrorism, he sought to conform his story to the FBI's.

Finally, some have envisioned a plot wherein Experimental Wolf McVeigh had been brainwashed or medically manipulated in a manner that induced him to act as an easily tracked Guilty Agent within a Pack Of Watched Wolves, but to compliantly and even enthusiastically accept his role as Lone Wolf bomber afterwards. Such an amalgamation of narratives was told about Oswald as well and to one degree or another, was told by McVeigh about himself.[81] At times, such stories purport that unseen operators staged the execution of the *actual* McVeigh and, McVeigh, too, entertained this possibility. In a sense, the Experimental Wolf scenario, that consists of and combines all other versions, reconciles the many contradictions between all of the stories, including the multiple McVeigh's, into a grand-master narrative in which everything fits neatly – much like the Lone Wolf story, except that Experimental Wolf stories incorporate, rather than ignore and dismiss, contradictions.

Beyond the problem of multiple McVeigh's, there is the issue of the confusing array of companions who surrounded the bomber and the emergence of several coinciding possible plot trajectories, all of which somehow coalesce in Oklahoma City on the morning of April 19, 1995. In the wake of this confusing trail, the bombing plot itself seems to take on a life of its own, sweeping up into its grasp ever-widening rings of people, many people in different locations with different motives, who participate in seemingly disparate events, possibly related to its culmination. A plot that, in the words of CIA assassination mastermind Win Everett in Don DeLeillo's novel *Libra*, carried its own internal logic. Rather than a grand conspiracy, the plot consists of several small random conspiracies, and like DeLillo's *Libra*, "members of the conspiracy are simultaneously inside and outside of the plot," and "each conspirator, seeing no further than his own interests, fears or desires for revenge, moves in a private direction." The mystery of solving the crime, involves identifying "the connection between chance and design, between contingency and conspiracy."[82] In this situation, understandings of "conventional history," in this case the Lone Wolf story, or any other purportedly true version:

> ...may be only one possible system, one that has screened out most "rings" and whose "points of intersection" are strictly defined by cause and effect. However, if history is conceived instead as an open system or a conglomerate of interacting systems, the opposition between random event and cause/effect sequences would no longer obtain: certain occurrences would appear to be random only because they are located on "rings" that are not intersecting at visible points, and certain "patterns [could] emerge outside the bounds of cause and effect."[83]

Philosophical musings aside, what *is* clear, is that the story of the Oklahoma City bombing and Timothy McVeigh is one fraught with multiple irreconcilabilities: multiple unidentified conspirators; multiple people each with multiple aliases, alibis, doubles, decoys, doppelgangers, imposters, look-a-likes and impersonators; even multiple Ryder trucks. The quandary is exacerbated by the dilemma of unreliable narrators (McVeigh, Nichols, Roger Moore, the FBI, etc.,) and further compounded by the dismissal, distortion and systematic destruction of evidence, a good portion of which was credible and beyond reproach. While it seems reasonable to reject any single piece of evidence as aberrant, it is another thing altogether to reject the entire body of contradictions. Admittedly, there seems no way to present all of the information or the intricacy of evidential detail and come out with a coherent story that does not wrongly dismiss critical elements of the others. Still, it must be acknowledged that the history of the case, as most people understand it, is problematic, naïve, and the continued evocation of the bombing or McVeigh in service of various agendas is irresponsible, when it relies on the Lone Wolf or Pack of Wolves narratives, and ignores wider implications.

PART TWO:
The Experts

Most people actually use the word paranoid to denote an overly suspicious person. But the suspicious thinking of a paranoid is more than the normal mistrust and doubt implied by the word. It is suspicion in the literal meaning: to look below the surface for details.... But sometimes the imaginary enemies turned out to be real...

–*Whispers: The Voices Of Paranoia*, 1994, Ronald K. Siegel, PhD, pharmacologist, professor at UCLA Department Of Psychiatry and Behavioral Science, colleague and co-author with Dr. Jolly West.

INTRODUCTION

On April 21, 1995, a black helicopter transferred McVeigh to Tinker Air Force Base in Oklahoma City where he remained in a cell with eight-foot tall thick glass walls until his arraignment at 8:30 PM the next day. There he met with two public defenders appointed to represent him, Susan Otto and John W. Coyle III. Herbeck and Michel wrote that upon meeting Otto and Coyle, an "unashamed" McVeigh "dropped a thunderbolt" and, for thirty minutes, proceeded to confess his guilt to them, "giving them as many details as he could about his action." According to his biographers, his "secret confessions" were part of his long term "strategy [...] While refusing to plead guilty to the charges against him, he was honest – brutally so – with the lawyers and investigators who were assigned to help him." Within days though, Otto and Coyle asked the judge to remove them from the case, citing conflicts of interest. Still, they impressed McVeigh because, he said, "they never betrayed him" and "kept their knowledge to themselves."[84]

Not reported and assumedly unknown to McVeigh's biographers (who mainly relied on Tim's own account) was McVeigh's first and assumedly private Guilty Agent confession to Otto and Coyle; a strange claim that they soon relayed to his replacement attorneys. As outlined previously, McVeigh told them that he had been recruited into an undercover operation and tasked with tracking neo-Nazis. Having discovered a bombing plot, his government handlers instructed him to embed himself in it. However, the bomb was only supposed to blow out a few windows of the Murrah and because of this, he suspected that somebody switched the truck or the explosives in it without his knowledge. Later, when Jones Team investigator Richard Reyna asked McVeigh about his strange statements to Otto and Coyle, McVeigh became very angry and began "yelling, [and] cursing," and exclaimed that Coyle had no business discussing their private conversations with anyone, and told Reyna that while some parts of the story were true, some were not.

It was at Tinker AFB that McVeigh not only began to tell his Guilty Agent story to people outside of his private world, but it was also a central location in Experimental stories told by others, stories that in many ways were elaborations of the stories McVeigh told before his arrest. As fate would have it, on the same day McVeigh arrived at Tinker, the villainous Dr. Jolly West, then head of UCLA's Neuropsychiatric Institute, showed up in Oklahoma City to coordinate a psychological trauma team for survivors and first responders on behalf of the American Psychological Association (APA). The trauma team, along with several other disaster relief initiatives, used Tinker as a coordinating and staging site.[85] In Experimental Wolf stories, West's presence in OKC so soon after the bombing implied something much darker: his charitable activities there were simply a cover to manipulate the memories of critical eyewitnesses and shield his secret visits with McVeigh, whom he set about mind controlling until McVeigh, as obnoxiously as possible, confessed to being the Lone Wolf mastermind and (thanks to West) believed his own false confession wholeheartedly.

Seemingly imbued with psychic powers, on the evening of April 19, (before anybody knew exactly *what* had happened in OKC and prior to McVeigh's name being announced as a suspect), Dr. West appeared on Larry King Live to discuss the "lone nut" who had bombed the Murrah building.[86] On April 22, the day after his arraignment, McVeigh was transferred to El Reno Federal Correctional Facility, located about 25 miles from OKC. The same day, Linda Thompson called the FBI to report that Jolly West was examining McVeigh at El Reno, and while McVeigh himself seems never to have discussed West, in the years to come, unsubstantiated rumors about West's regular visits with McVeigh at El Reno proliferated.

A couple of weeks after Otto and Coyle asked to be removed from the case, they were replaced by Stephen Jones. According to Jones, before meeting McVeigh, he met with Otto and Coyle to discuss the transfer of the case, at which time Otto cryptically warned, "When you know everything I know – and you will soon enough – you will never think of the United States of America in the same way." On May 5, Jones and McVeigh met for the first time.[87] In an internal defense memo, Jones recalled that as soon as he sat down across from his new client, McVeigh, suddenly and without context declared, "I'm not brainwashed," a statement Jones found "curious" and "odd." The memo does not detail Jones's reaction or McVeigh's subsequent explanation, if any, but Jones did discuss other aspects of the meeting in his book. At some point during their ten-hour long discussion, McVeigh calmly and dispassionately confessed his guilt. When he asked McVeigh about John Doe #2, McVeigh denied any such person existed and insisted that he had acted alone. Immediately after the meeting, Jones held a press conference during which he informed reporters that he intended to bring out the truth of the bombing, which he compared to the assassinations of JFK and MLK, and during a follow-up press conference soon after, compared McVeigh to Lee Oswald.

News outlets reported that at both Tinker and El Reno, McVeigh was being kept in isolation under constant surveillance. After his transfer to El Reno on April 22, he was confined to a nine by five-foot isolation cell with guards standing outside at all times, and Federal authorities in D.C. monitoring him 24 hours a day through live-feed CCTV cameras. On May 18, 1995, McVeigh complained to one of the attorneys on his new legal team that prison guards had taken pictures of his penis and he feared these pictures and the constant video recordings would become public. He did not want people buying black market copies of the "Life and Times of Tim McVeigh in Prison." He threatened that if the prison did not remove the camera in his cell, he would go on a hunger strike and if that didn't work, he would take more active measures (although he did not specify what those might be). On May 25, 1995, Jones asked the court for permission and funds to hire experts who could evaluate McVeigh's physical and mental health to determine if he was competent to stand trial, expressing concern about the conditions of McVeigh's confinement and its impact on his mental state. Jones told the court, "I see the cameras as simply an attempt to engage in a kind of psychological warfare, and I think, ultimately, perhaps, would have an effect on [McVeigh's] mental stability, which might in turn affect the trial."[88]

After the court approved Jones' request, he set about recruiting a team of mental health experts, all with interesting areas of expertise. Among them was Dr. John R. Smith, an Oklahoma City psychiatrist and retired

Air Force Captain, who specialized in aggression, violence, hypnosis and the mental and physical effects of combat for Vietnam Veterans. Smith also acted as, among other things, consultant for the University of Oklahoma's Department of Psychiatry and Behavioral Services, the Veteran's Affairs Administration Hospital in OKC, the security services in Pakistan and, later, a contractor treating active duty members of the US military at various installations, including Guantanamo prison camp.[89]

Smith first met with McVeigh at El Reno Prison on June 6, 1995. Two days later, on June 8, the court sealed the psychological records of both McVeigh and Nichols. On June 18, Smith made recommendations resulting in somewhat less restrictive conditions and the cameras in his cell were turned off for four hours each day, although guards were posted outside his cell at those times. McVeigh continued to express concern about the prison guards' observations of him that were noted in a logbook. After one incident, during which he may or may not have been hearing voices that were or were not simply hallucinations, McVeigh said the guards might have written that he was delusional and therefore asked that his attorneys have the prison logbooks sealed. He further asked that Smith's reports be available to future mental health experts retained by the defense, explaining to attorney Rob Nigh that he wanted "them to know he is not completely crazy prior to the time they come to visit."[90]

Smith granted many media interviews about his involvement in the case and countless outlets reported that Smith spent over 20 hours with McVeigh before deeming him fit to stand trial. Smith, we are told, evaluated McVeigh with the sole objective of making such a determination and, in the end, diagnosed him with depression and PTSD. As an adult, said Smith, McVeigh dealt with his trauma the same way he did as a child. He "created [a] superhero role for himself [and] fantasized all these monsters, which he fought." Still, despite his active fantasy life, Smith said McVeigh was not delusional, competent to stand trial, and had been "fully aware" of what he was doing when he bombed the Murrah.[91] Smith's initial findings, submitted to the Jones Team on June 18 were a bit more complex than reported. Smith's diagnosis did include "long term significant depressive illnesses" and PTSD but also "paranoia … character/personality disorders; borderline personality disorder with obsessive features [and] grandiose features and perfectionist." McVeigh never mentioned this to his biographers.

McVeigh's account of the reason Jones hired Smith in the first place is also slightly different. To his biographers he said that Jones thought the details of his life and the bombing plot (as he described it) sounded so "surreal" that Jones "wanted to check if I was 'brainwashed' (his idea, not mine)" and determine "if I was delusional [or] competent to stand trial… so that's why Dr. Smith came in." McVeigh explained how they met repeatedly throughout a three-week period:

Given time to explain all, [Smith] (being from OKC and having bombing victim clients himself) and I actually formed a bond- and he told [Jones] I was fine. [...] I don't fault [Jones] for not believing me at the get go (it all sounds so surreal) [...] I was seen repeatedly by 3 defense "shrinks'"... pre-trial. I got along great with 2; the 3rd grew frustrated b/c his job was to formulate a possible 'mental defect' mitigation – and he couldn't find any basis for such. None of these three professionals, when everything was explained, found anything wrong with me.

There was nothing wrong with McVeigh – according to McVeigh. He hadn't been brainwashed and nobody put a microchip in him.[92] Smith must not have cleared up the "brainwashing" issue to Jones' satisfaction because internal defense memos reveal that even after his June 18 report, the possibility of some type of mind control remained an issue, however speculative. The defense team kept an ongoing shared *to do* list that delegated various tasks to different members. As per a discussion between Rob Nigh and McVeigh on June 28, ten days after Smith submitted his first report, the task of following up on information "concerning microchips being implanted in military personnel or others" and, a few months later, "Army enlistees subjected to brainwashing and/or electronic mind control experiments" was added to the list.

In the majority of accounts, Smith's involvement with McVeigh ended after he found him fit to stand trial that June. For instance, attorney Randall Coyne said, "the good Dr. John Smith was the mental health professional who met with and evaluated Tim. He was looking at him with a view towards competency and sanity. My sense was that Smith's interviews with McVeigh were not helpful to the defense; therefore, Smith's participation in the defense was curtailed. We didn't call him as a witness; we didn't offer a mental health defense. To my knowledge he wasn't treating Tim."[93] In reality, the extent of Smith and the other mental health experts' involvement in the case, as well as their findings, are much more telling than McVeigh let on or than some of the other attorneys on the team, even those closest to him, may have known.

According to court affidavits and internal defense memos, Smith met with McVeigh not just for three weeks as McVeigh claimed, but intermittently until at least the time of his trial. Their meetings extended beyond competency evaluations in July 1995, when attorney Rob Nigh informed the team that McVeigh "said he concurred with our decision not to have Smith continue to see him but apparently there is one issue bothering Tim that he wants to speak to Dr. Smith about." McVeigh asked that Smith come back to see him "just one more time" and Smith agreed under the condition that Jones and attorney Dick Burr understood "he did so only based on McVeigh's request." (I'm not sure *why* Smith would stress that or what the alternative implications of his visit could be).

Although Smith is the most often mentioned mental expert to have been involved with McVeigh, and despite McVeigh's claims that only two or three "shrinks" saw him, Jones briefly noted in his book that "Dr. Smith was only one of several" psychiatrists to see McVeigh. Among those who saw him on a regular basis were clinical and forensic psychiatrist, Lee Norton, Ph.D, forensic psychologist Dr. Seymour Halleck and clinical psychologist, neuro-psychologist, psychotherapist and hypnotist, H. Anthony Semone, Ph.D.[94]

Trauma specialist Lee Norton began meeting with McVeigh in June 1995, continued to see him throughout preparation for his trial and con-ducted many of the defense team interviews with McVeigh's friends, fam-ily members and co-workers. She felt that the shattering of his psyche began during childhood and continued throughout his adult life, most markedly after the Gulf War, he experienced "increasing fragmentation." McVeigh told Norton that during the Special Forces tryout "he was told what they 'really did,' which included bringing illegal substances into the country and hunting and killing potentially innocent people." According to Norton, his inability "to reconcile his 'perfect' image of the 'good' that the Army performed for the sake of the country to what he was told their actual mission may at times involve," caused him to experience a remark-able, even earth shattering, sense of "dissonance."

To the Jones Team, McVeigh sometimes expressed confusion about individuals who swore they met him and who seemed to have accurate details about where he was and when, but McVeigh said he could not re-member. Norton wrote that, in fact, there was "clear affirmation of the presence of a whole lot of material in Tim's life, including the bombing, about which Tim would rather stay ignorant" and so, he had engaged in a "contextually embedded delusional process." Further, he displayed symp-toms of an "externalized psychosis" (a paranoid delusion that is acted upon).[95] In clinical terms, a delusion is a firmly held, false belief and incor-rect inference about external reality that is considered pathological when, despite what most other people within one's culture or subculture believe and when presented with proof to the contrary, the person defends and vigorously maintains the beliefs. Unlike other delusions, contextually em-bedded delusions do not necessarily depend on whether a particular be-lief is true, false, possible, probable or plausible, but rather the process by which one arrives at the belief, the manner one communicates and enacts it and the extent to which the belief negatively impacts the believer or other people. While unstated, Norton's diagnosis seems to hint that she, for one, suspected McVeigh's Guilty Agent recruitment story was based on something that, even if it wasn't true, was grounded and supported by his larger context, and did not represent a complete break from reality.

Whatever context the delusions sprung from, in Dr. Norton's estimation, McVeigh's fictional world was much more entrenched than the simple "fantasy world" as described by Smith. The other mental health experts as well as the other attorneys on the team soon came to agree. In fact, a recurring concern underlying much of the story of McVeigh's life and the bombing itself is one of delineating delusion and determining the real versus the unreal. For the Jones Team too, a major question concerning any of the stories McVeigh told was whether he really believed them or not and if so, why? Were any of them true or simply delusional imaginings?

For instance, McVeigh initially told Otto and Coyle that the day of the bombing he had been operating "within the confines of the United States government," and that the truck might have been switched because the bomb was not supposed to have caused the horrific damage it did. To begin with, this would imply that he was not as familiar with the truck as he should have been if he'd been in it before, even slept in it, and had been the only one to drive it (as he claimed). *Maybe* he was delusional.

Interestingly however, although he had no way of knowing about the conversation between McVeigh, Otto and Coyle, a little over a week after the bombing, on April 28, 1995, Bobby Joe Farrington, a federal inmate in Texas with deep connections to the White Power Movement, contacted the FBI and told them a strange story which he would repeat with slight variations to McVeigh's defense team and then the media, a summary of which is as follows:

Farrington was introduced to a mercenary named "Sergeant Mac" but who was, in reality, Timothy McVeigh. Farrington implicated a number of people whom he said ordered, sanctioned and provided material support for the bombing. Most were connected to Aryan Nations, the National Alliance and Militia Of Montana.[96] Sergeant Mac, he said, turned out to be "a real idiot" who disobeyed orders and "blew up the wrong place." He was actually supposed to blow up the courthouse. He was also supposed to detonate the bomb at night but took it upon himself to change the timing. While later media reports detailing his claims are very different from the accounts he initially gave the FBI and Jones Team, Farrington passed a polygraph issued by the FBI. Maybe *he* was delusional.

A year after the bombing, the Jones Team had tallied up numerous credible sightings of McVeigh with other individuals during the 24 hours prior to the bombing, when he was supposed to be alone in the Ryder. These sightings, opined the defense team in one memo, supported the theory that "the Ryder trucks were switched" and McVeigh had not built the actual truck bomb, as he now insisted. A decade later Terry Nichols would describe McVeigh's angry outburst upon learning that both the target and the time of the bombing had been changed. Which of the switched bombing target and truck stories were delusional, which ones true, which intentional deceptions and which ones combinations of all three?

Another perhaps more disturbing example of the confusion that arose between what might be real and what was patently unreal, involves one of the lingering mysteries surrounding the Oklahoma City bombing: an unidentified shaved leg clad in a combat boot found in the rubble at the blast site. The official explanation of the leg kept changing. It belonged to a black woman, to a white man. It was buried with one person, dug up, examined, placed in a grave with a different individual, and dug up again before authorities admitted they simply didn't know to whom the leg belonged. Ultimately, the Medical Examiner had to concede that no person or leg was missing from the survivors and victims of the bombing. Speculation abounded that the leg belonged to John Doe #2. McVeigh displayed a fascination with the leg and often mentioned it in conversations with his attorneys, once glibly remarking that the limb would "fuel conspiracy theory for years." In late August 1995, McVeigh indicated that the leg belonged to an ex-convict from Utah. The defense wondered why he would even have this detailed information and where and how he obtained it. He brought up the leg again soon after, this time during a meeting with attorney Rob Nigh on September 10, 1995. Nigh wrote:

> The following bracketed information was provided by Tim after he wrote on a legal pad "THIS IS NOT TRUE BUT WILL TEST FOR A BUG" [Tim said that he wanted to talk about the leg that was discovered. Tim said he was embarrassed but that he picked up a prostitute in Junction City and had tried to kill her because she would be able to recognize him. He says that he stuffed her body in a barrel "ahead of time." He said "I can't figure out how the leg survived." Tim said the hooker was wearing combat boots when he picked her up. He (Tim) asked me (Nigh) to "check it out" and notes that combat boots have "heavy duty soles."]

Clearly Nigh thought McVeigh was delusional. Jones Team investigator Scott Anderson, in notes from his meeting with McVeigh the following day, reported a similar conversation:

> There were many comments made during my visit with Tim that left me very uneasy about either the mental condition of Tim or just the fact that some of things he is saying is disturbing. He mentioned off handedly about being honest with his defense team and pulled out a small sheet of paper. He mentioned that he knew that there would be a missing persons report sooner or later in Junction City and that he didn't understand how a body could get blown to pieces leaving a leg and combat boot intact. I quickly asked him what he was talking about, to which he told me that he had known about the leg from the beginning and that the left leg belonged to a

prostitute that he had picked up in Junction City before he had left. He took her down with him and I gathered from other comments he made that he had killed her, and put her in army dress. He then said that he placed her body in front of the cone of the bomb and left it to be disintegrated from the explosion. He was still holding his piece of paper, which he then slid to me across the table, which said to not believe a word he was saying, that all of it was made up, and that he was doing this to find out if the room was truly bugged. All of this was very disturbing, due to the fact that his confession stories with different twists and turns are getting more prevalent and they are useless to us, but could possibly contain some truth, but may be written off because we believe that he is delusional.

While McVeigh later claimed that the only thing he threw in the back of the Ryder was his Robert Kling ID card, the larger context of these disturbing conversations illustrate that, while *seemingly* delusional, they were also plausible. Employees at an Albertson's store in Oklahoma City reported to the FBI on April 22, 1995 that, the evening before the bombing on April 18, McVeigh, or someone who looked very like him, and a man who resembled the John Doe #2 sketch, came into the store. A couple of hours later, McVeigh came back in, this time with a prostitute. Other, less "credible" witnesses also reported this to the FBI. An FBI report dated September 19, 1995, about a week *after* McVeigh relayed his grizzly story to members of the Jones Team, details an equally bizarre story told by a man in Texas. Among his other claims, the man said that "the leg found inside of the boot in front of the federal building belonged to a black female prostitute who was sitting in the front passenger seat of the [Ryder] truck and the black female had been dead two or three days prior to the bombing."[97]

Among the possessions found on McVeigh at the time of his arrest were handwritten directions to Emerik's, a storage and warehouse space in Oklahoma City, although the FBI did not question the managers there until December 1995. The following month, on January 16, 1996, McVeigh's attorneys asked where the Ryder truck was from the day it was supposed to be in Kansas on April 18 until it arrived in Oklahoma City early on April 19. McVeigh responded, "Maybe it was in a government warehouse being loaded with explosives." According to David Paul Hammer, McVeigh claimed the leg belonged to 'Poindexter,' the man who helped build the bomb at a warehouse in OKC the evening before the bombing. No longer needed, Poindexter had been killed and his leg placed in the back of the truck.

Unknown to both McVeigh's and Nichols' defense teams, DNA tests on the leg were conducted in a private lab in 1997 but, while the Oklahoma Medical Examiner was given a copy of the results, they remain confidential. In December 2015, the FBI disclosed that they were unaware that DNA tests were conducted or the existence of a report detailing the findings, but said they would look into the matter. However, according to an FBI crime lab spokesperson, the FBI would only perform new DNA tests, using more advanced techniques, if the original FBI agents in charge of the case requested it.

For many, including Oklahoma County District Attorney Wes Lane, in charge of Terry Nichols' 2001 state trial, Stephen Jones, California Rep. Dana Rohrabacher (who conducted his own investigation) and a host of others involved in the investigations and trials, the leg indicates the long denied existence of John Doe #2. Roger Charles said that the FBI could not risk exposing known conspirators because it would, in turn, expose a complex network of government informants and undercover investigations. Former FBI agent Bob Ricks, a lead agent in the bombing case, told reporters that this was hogwash. He was "very confident" that McVeigh was alone in OKC on April 19, 1995, and dismissed rumors about unidentified conspirators as "conspiracy theories."[98] Perhaps, a knee-jerk reaction?

The truth about the leg may never be known.

THE MANY FACES OF TIM MCVEIGH

Spying is attractive to loonies.... Psychopaths, who are people who spend their lives making up stories, revel in the field

– CIA contract researcher, Harvard Psychiatrist, Dr. Harry Murray,
Explorations Of Personality, 1938

Doublethink means the power of holding two contradictory beliefs in one's mind simultaneously, and accepting both of them.

– George Orwell, *1984*

If you want to keep a secret, you must also hide it from yourself.

George Orwell, *1984*

There is also a legend of a place called the Black Lodge, the shadow-self of the White Lodge. The legend says that every spirit must pass through there on the way to perfection. There, you will meet your own shadow self. My people call it The Dweller on the Threshold.... But it is said, if you confront the Black Lodge with imperfect courage, it will utterly annihilate your soul.

– Deputy Hawk, *Twin Peaks*

McVeigh strongly resented suggestions that another person (or people) may have influenced, manipulated, directed or even controlled him.

Nevertheless, the overall opinion of the mental health experts was that it was unlikely McVeigh came up with the idea to bomb the Murrah building and may not have even played a "primary role," but was part of "a larger conspiracy" that went "much deeper" than McVeigh was willing to let on. For legal purposes it didn't really matter, because the government wanted to pin the bombing almost exclusively on him, and he insisted on taking complete responsibility for it. This wasn't surprising, in a psychological sense, as, they noted, "his strength is in carrying out orders." McVeigh appeared "psychologically incapable of revealing who [they] are and what their role was."[99]

But, *why*? Although for legal reasons it didn't matter why, in the attempt to understand him better, the mental health experts, other consultants, attorneys and investigators considered several possibilities, a few of them of the Experimental Wolf variety, dubbed "fringe leads" but based on actual but puzzling information about McVeigh and the bombing.

Among the "fringe" possibilities considered: While in the military, McVeigh was exposed to "considerable trauma – and who knows what else" that led not only to Gulf War Syndrome (a medical disorder) but had also left a "chemical imprint" on his brain resulting in uncontrollable violent impulses.

Or: Others Unknown had recruited him into an already existing plot, using any number of possible pretexts; after which they set about psychologically manipulating him, pushing him "over the edge" and setting him up as a "fall guy." Then of course, there was the "Manchurian Candidate" scenario, the fringiest of them all, but one continuously explicated or alluded to in internal memos. Despite the sometimes-vague allusions, more than one member of the Jones Team has told me that the juiciest discussions were not memorialized in the memos or were only discussed using cryptic references as per Jones' instruction. What *was* memorialized is noteworthy.

In one memo, Dr. Seymour Halleck suggested the possibility of a fringe scenario, noting that he had an "eerie feeling" that something bizarre had happened to McVeigh, although the specifics of his theory are only hinted at in references to previous conversations not found in the internal memos. Still, Halleck's "eerie feeling" is interesting for the fact that after bringing it up he went on to clearly express his opinion that beyond McVeigh's "traditional" and "contextually embedded" delusions, his "most remarkable feature" was his "suggestibility." He was, Halleck informed the attorneys, "*highly suggestible*" (italics added).

Since childhood, McVeigh had – more than most – a sponge-like ability to absorb and internalize information. Jones Team investigator Roger Charles wrote that, when McVeigh left the army, he was already in the process of "coming unstuck from mainstream society" and afterward, his very sense of self dissolved. "Politics," said Charles "was the means by which McVeigh forged a new identity." Just as he enacted various roles prior to leaving the Army (The Survivalist, The Good Soldier), McVeigh had *re-enacted* the deeds of the fictional Earl Turner, protagonist of *The Turner Diaries*. While waging an underground racist revolution, our hero constructs a truck bomb from fertilizer, and uses it to blow up a federal building in order to destroy a database and force a change in The System.[100]

Unreported were the early observations of his legal team that, "[t]he primary [...] hero/role models [Tim] speaks of are Captain Kirk, Mr. Spock, and Captain Picard, all characters on *Star Trek*," and wondered at his tendency to speak of characters in *Star Trek* as actual models of reality. Letters written to his biographers after his conviction also illustrate his sometimes bizarre, always obsessive, musings about the show that continued until the time of his execution. Prior to and after his trial McVeigh compared nearly everything, including himself, to characters or circumstances in *Star Trek* (sometimes illogically) and, over the years, undoubtedly emulated them.

McVeigh's fragmentation actually went a little deeper than subtly manifested emulations of popular culture. Indeed, the prevailing opinion of all the Jones Team mental health experts, including Smith, was that McVeigh possessed "dissociative abilities" which, having seemingly taken on a life (or lives) of their own, led them to diagnose him with a "dissociative disorder."

Dissociative Identity Disorders (DID) are defined as extreme and long lasting manifestation of traumatic stress resulting in "a disruption of and/or discontinuity in the normal integration of consciousness, memory, identity, emotion, perception, body representation, motor control, and behavior." While everybody experiences some forms of dissociation in non-life threatening circumstances (e.g. daydreaming), DIDs are more severe and long-lasting expressions of dissociated states which manifest at times of acute or prolonged stress. What makes dissociative states pathological or maladaptive is the inability to control their occurrence and the *episodic amnesia* often accompanying them. DID is a fundamental disruption of consciousness, memory, identity, or perception of environment that severs connections between a person's thoughts, memories, feelings, actions, or sense of identity; an integrative deficit that wreaks havoc with an individual's ability to maintain a sense of self over time, claim ownership of personal historical events, and to differentiate between the real and unreal. In extreme manifestations, those who suffer from DID's may "call themselves different names" and "have different personality states," who appear and "take over" the primary personality.[101] Those displaying symptoms of DID tend to be highly suggestible and *easily hypnotizable*.

The Jones Team mental health workers' clinical diagnoses, and the independent and collective profiles of McVeigh they constructed, when taken together, depict him as a narcissistic, fragmented, paranoid, delusional, psychotic, suggestible, amnesiac man suffering from PTSD and Dissociative Identity Disorder. Thus, rather than finding him normal and not delusional as he claimed, the experts found McVeigh to be perplexingly disturbed and recommended he undergo further psychological testing. Jones did not, however, intend to put on a mental health defense and informed Burr that he (for once) agreed with McVeigh who, he said, "does not wish to be painted as a John Hinckley."[102]

To be clear, the term "multiple personality disorder" is not found within the Jones documents, although such a prognosis is the most extreme manifestation of DID. Regardless, the concept of dissociation presented one way to explain, not only McVeigh's frequent memory lapses, but also the many distinct identities he enacted throughout his life and the increasing frequency of their number and appearance leading to the bombing. Many of these *personae* had specific names and functions. Some appeared only briefly, generally for a specific task; others enacted and maintained consistently over long periods. It would seem he had varying degrees of control over and memory of them, depending on the circumstances.[103] No matter how structured and embedded his compartmentalized mind, how he managed his mental modules, or why and how they even existed, it seemed that at some point Timothy McVeigh fragmented into multiple self-states. When viewed as a product of fragmented selves, the inconsistent narratives he frequently offered look somewhat more consistent. This also aligns with the strange observations made by others who knew him (or claimed to) before the bombing, and the publicly disseminated Experimental Wolf narratives that came to surround him.

Reminiscent of the account given to the FBI by a volunteer at a Buffalo area AIDS outreach program, Peter Salino (name changed), about McVeigh's strange trips to the VA hospital and blackouts during which he had no memory of his actions, an individual with Dissociative Amnesia suffers a loss of autobiographical memory for specific past experiences. Dissociative Fugue pertains to "amnesia [that] covers the whole (or, at least, a large part) of the patient's life; it is also accompanied by a loss of personal identity and, in many cases, physical relocation (hence its name)." During a flight from reality in which they seek out new environments, an individual in a state of Dissociative Fugue "may behave quite normally in the new environment, but very differently from his usual behavior. When he returns [...] he does not remember the events of the fugue." While a fugue can last for long periods or may consist of a single episode, longer fugue states may include the establishment of a new identity or identities.[104] While aliases and disguises are often employed as critical components of a successful criminal endeavor, the individual utilizing such methods is conscious and in control when they do so. DID implies that the subject is *not* in control; or may be to a weakened extent.

Literature about dissociation notes that while the real person or "host" cannot remember them, the dissociated *personae* tend to leave a trail of evidence and clues to their existence. Even with the failure of several government agencies to turn over critical discovery material about their investigations, and the manipulation and destruction of information, the Jones Team was able to chronicle many of McVeigh's movements throughout the country. The many motel records, speeding tickets, phone records, receipts, photographs, and letters support the idea that several characters with distinct claims of self-identity within McVeigh have contributed to the trail in a conspiracy of multiple selves.

More than a few of his known identities, personas, idealizations, and introjections seem scripted from the popular culture he absorbed, while the origin of others remains unknown. "Tim Tuttle" frequented gun shows, his name apparently borrowed from the main character in the film *Brazil,* Harry Tuttle: a vigilante terrorist out to fix a corrupt system. In Arizona, Montana and Idaho, a mercenary known as "Sergeant Mac" emerged. "Daryl Bridges" made numerous and incriminating phone calls to several well-known (and not so well-known) neo-Nazis. "Shawn Rivers" maintained a series of storage spaces throughout the country and filled them with stolen guns, disguises, and bomb-making materials, and "Tim Johnson" checked into a few motels. Although McVeigh said the existence and functions of "Shawn Masters" and "Terry Masters" were unknown to him, they nevertheless left trails of their existence. "Robert Kling," reminiscent perhaps of the race of warriors called Klingons in McVeigh's beloved *Star Trek,* was born April 19, 1972. Kling rented a Ryder truck and ordered Chinese food, but had it delivered to Timothy McVeigh's room at the Dreamland motel.

The McVeigh as Dissociated Bomber scenario presents further linkages and intersections between Experimental and Guilty Agent stories, and recurrent narrative elements found in both. Dr. Jolly West, ace practitioner of all things creepy, was among the experts quoted in a 1985 *Washington Post* article about "the quirks of the modern spy" and other deep-cover operators who inhabit the "shadowy world of counterintelligence." According to West, people choose to become spies, secret agents and operatives for a handful reasons: loyalty to one's country or an ideal; revenge; to damage those whose secrets they sell and betray; as well as what West called a "bag of mixed psychological motivations." His colleagues expounded on this bag, saying operatives are overly romantic thrill-seeking escapists with a need for control, a desire for power, narcissistic and conceited. They are empowered by the very secrets they harbor and their ability to conceal information, including about their own selves. A State Department consultant said that the operator "lives a life of half-secrets and half-truths. He can live life without having to confront reality."

It is these very character weaknesses that spy recruiters and handlers count on and exploit. West said recruiters and handlers are "espionage professionals" and described them as "very smart ... they know how to get their subject involved just a little bit, doing something that seems harmless" and end up seducing them into taking actions they normally would never consider. In the old "carrot and stick approach," the carrot could be any number of things the recruited spy desires (mentally or materially) while the stick, wielded on noncompliant agents, is blackmail. The handlers threaten to expose the operative for the very actions he or she was ordered to take in the first place. There is no getting out of the game, said West, "The bottom line is that you work for them forever."

West's colleagues warned of the devastating psychological effects professional imposters suffer, paranoia being one of the most frequent consequences. This could also be a reason they got into that line of work in the first place. Said Dr. Murray Miron, psychologist and FBI consultant, "there is power in information, in intelligence … the paranoiac typically lives in a fearful state of discovery" – at any moment his ineptitudes, weaknesses, dirty secrets and innermost thoughts could be exposed. A life of secrecy therefore becomes imperative and thus, the already paranoia-prone person turns his "psychological quirk" into a full-blown career. "Dealing in secrecy [becomes] an almost drug-like nurturance of paranoiac impulses:"[105] An intoxicating thrill-ride for the skillfully paranoid professional spook … until it's not.

Remember Michael Gelles, the navy counter-intelligence professional called in by the FBI to hypnotize the woman who saw Tim McVeigh with two other guys at Maloney's real estate office in Missouri? Gelles, not just a one-trick hypno-pony, also had some insight into the workings of McVeigh's real or imagined career as a government-sponsored covert warrior on a secret mission. In 2000, Gelles, Chief Psychologist for Naval Criminal Intelligence Service (NCIS) (among his other titles) made headlines for his NCIS internship program, which trained college students and agents of regional, state, federal and international law enforcement organizations, in effective undercover intelligence-gathering methods and sting operation protocols. Students of the program, explained Gelles, learn "what it's like to pretend to be somebody else."[106] Students took a battery of psychological tests to identify their unique personality traits with the intent of creating better, more convincing misrepresentations and then further developed and tested their new identities. The school was like an incubator for monster liars, and Gelles the midwife to the false personas the students birthed.

After he retired in 2006, Gelles began a new life as a private security consultant to high tech internationals where Gelles may or may not have taught "undercover techniques" and shadow self-construction to private citizens acting on behalf of government agencies without democratic oversight (somewhat like ESI, where McVeigh did or did not receive additional training for his mission). But that's just speculation.

The proper screening, recruitment and training of deep-cover operators has become a popular topic of late, mainly due to the increasing numbers of former and current undercover intelligence and police agents roaming around plighted by all manner of psychological problems caused or exacerbated by the peculiar stresses involved in undercover work. Ongoing studies seek to devise ways of preventing field operators from going off the underground reservation, so to speak.

The undercover agent's mission requires intense immersion into the world of their target, the concealment and suppression of their own identity, the creation and convincing enactment of false ones, sometimes having to stay "in character" for years at a time, especially in deep-cover operations. Thus, they must be creative and convincing liars able to maintain fictitious identities and fabricated life histories. The constant effort to detect threats to and prevent discovery of their true identity/agenda, all the while finding or creating opportunities to achieve their objectives and fulfill their mission, is a mental meat-grinder, leading to paranoia and debilitating fatigue.[107]

Acting largely autonomously and separated from friends and family, they live a lonely existence and are particularly prone to developing deep attachments to their targets. They may come to identify with targeted individuals and groups and question the utility of certain laws, the purpose and rightness of their assignment, and their own involvement in it. It then becomes justifiable to engage in criminal activity beyond what is necessary to maintain their cover or achieve their objective. Insufficient guidance, instruction and encouragement from handlers and low pay versus the risks they are expected to take, leads to further resentment, disillusionment, alienation and feelings of sympathy towards their targets. They may become indoctrinated into the very group they are investigating, especially when their mission involves prolonged exposure to "'subversive' environments" such as those encountered in investigations of suspected terrorist organizations or cells. Even when they are given leave from the operation (briefly or permanently), undercover operators have a difficult time settling back into their former identity and, for varying lengths of time, "retain the undercover lifestyle in terms of hairstyle, language, demeanor" and continue to enact the "mannerisms and idiosyncrasies" of their fake personalities.[108] Or worse.

Due to the very particular demands of undercover work, a number of problems tend to arise during and after an operation. The development of "noteworthy occupational maladjustment, psychiatric disturbances and unusual personality changes" is common, including symptoms associated with PTSD in varying degrees of severity and duration, such as extreme narcissism, confusion, psychosis, paranoia, disorientation, depersonalization, memory distortion, fleeting as well as longer lasting uncontrollable dissociative states, described as "out of context pseudo-identity reenactments" (a term coined by West). Also, "reappearance of false identity outside an operational context," and simply "loss of self." An article in the *American Criminal Law Review* succinctly observed, "Undercover officers are at serious risk of developing 'split personality' or experiencing the 'self as unreal...traits characteristic of dissociative identity disorder, in which multiple personalities recurrently take over a person's behavior.'"[109] Avoiding this type of fragmentation is a bit of a double bind for operatives, as success requires their ability to call up false identities on demand and convincingly enact them (including entire fake personal histories), or face disastrous consequences. The psychological process is very similar to uncontrolled multiple-personality manifestations seen in those suffering from severe forms of structural dissociative identity disorders.

Sometimes the undercover agent's alter ego(s) linger, appearing or reappearing at inappropriate non-work related moments, before and after the mission ends, both in social and public contexts as well as private ones. Sometimes they are not even consciously aware that the undercover identity has come to the surface and taken over. Sometimes the operator forgets who they really are (or were prior to the mission). Sometimes they forget their real name. Sometimes, like the criminals they were created to catch, spy on or entrap, they commit crimes, occasionally violent ones. In some cases, the altered state, once birthed, developed, and enacted over a sustained period is hard to bury. In a sense it has acquired its own survival imperative and other needs related to, but distinct from, that of the original operator. They are generally not the most pleasant people you'll ever meet.[110]

Several factors are said to increase the likelihood that a once intentionally assumed alter identity will surface in an uncontrolled fashion. These include the disillusionment experienced when the agent realizes that the promises and enticements used to recruit them were false, plus the lack of warning about the nastier things that tend to go along with this line of work. A number of pre-existing character traits are thought to increase the likelihood that an agent will experience dissociative symptoms during or after their mission. These include neuroticism, narcissism, poorly defined self-image and higher predispositions to experience varying degrees of normal, everyday episodic dissociative states (eg., "spacing out"). The stress of being in the field amplifies certain existing traits and quirks making for "extremely narcissistic vigilante covert operators for whom 'the thrill of deception and manipulation' ... then becomes an end in itself."[111]

For the most part, recruits undergo minimal training, although historically, certain methods involved in rigorous training programs and settings have led to unintended consequences. For instance, during try-outs, recruits may be subjected to highly stressful situations to see if they break their cover. A series of deceptions might be orchestrated, including being told they have failed and did not make the cut, for the purposes of observing their reactions. Such methods engender lingering "suspicion and distrust" about the very institution on whose behalf they work. In fact, observed one study, "agents readily admit that the most troublesome symptoms of anxiety and paranoia do not typically arise with uncertainty over the enemy [or target], but more when it is the employer's motives that are perceived to be the source of the threat."[112] By this time though, it may be too late to back out.

The techniques and intensity of mission preparation may correlate to later issues. Interestingly, while studies are ongoing, it is currently thought that symptoms are less likely to appear, or at least to appear outside of the agents' control, if they undergo hypnosis prior to enacting their deceptive selves rather than (or in addition to) the role-playing techniques traditionally used. The most psychologically vulnerable time for the spy is during the actual work itself. One study pointed out that, agents in the midst of an operation, more so than before or after, exhibited "elevated psychiatric symptoms [similar to] those of psychiatric outpatients."[113] The deeper the cover and longer the mission, the more entrenched the false persona becomes, the more likely they will suffer psychological problems, and the longer and more severe those problems will be. The more stressful, dangerous and complex the mission, the higher the stakes, the worse it becomes for the operator. Making a marijuana bust is probably not going to cause long term personality pathologies or dissociative identity disorders, but being embedded with the mafia for three years might. Agents embedded in terrorism investigations are said to have it the worst.

While some studies argue that overly strenuous and abusive selection and training contributes to blowback in the form of unhinged undercover operators, a recently published law journal article by Nicholas Wamsley urged both public and private organizations involved in covert work to implement the selection and training program used by the Special Forces called SERE (Survival, Evasion, Resistance, Escape). The thinking is that SERE's psychological evaluation process, the most demanding in existence, the high-intensity stresses induced and the physical and psychological gauntlet SERE candidates undergo, would "greatly reduce the number of unfit candidates working in undercover situations."[114] Wamsley's solution is an interesting one and based on a certain logic. But his argument for increased privatization of undercover activity and the expansion of it, into realms beyond even the minimal oversight of state-run covert operations, is as baffling as its implications are nightmarish.

After the Jones Team obtained the results of the psychological tests McVeigh took during the SFAS (Special Forces tryout), they noted that the results were consistent with what they were learning about him, although this observation is not elaborated on. In one conversation between McVeigh and Dr. Halleck, however, McVeigh expressed his frustration that there were "things out there" that his defense team was not discussing with him and offered the example of his military psychological records, which he had not even known his defense team possessed until Halleck told him about it. He then explained that the reason the SFAS psychological tests indicated he was "paranoid and angry" was because he had just gotten back from the Gulf War when he took them, and "was reeling with the anger" he had developed there.

Before and after this conversation, McVeigh claimed that while at his Special Forces tryout, after taking "intelligence, psychological, adeptness, and a whole battery of other tests," he and nine others were asked to "volunteer" to "do some work for the government." They would act as "military consultants [working] hand-in-hand with civilian police agencies" to contain and neutralize security threats and would be expected to perform illegal actions in the course of their work. While he may have easily pulled the details for this story from recent revelations about other, similiar actions, he seems to have been married to the idea that he in some way acted on behalf of the government in a private capacity. He told his attorneys that if they wanted to understand him better, they should obtain a copy of the July 1995 issue of *Soldier Of Fortune Magazine*. The titles of two featured articles in that particular issue were "Delta/Seal Combat Camp For Civilians" and "Private Spies: Hire Your Own CIA Agent." His mother and sister thought he actually had trained with the Special Forces rather than simply attending the tryout. His sister emphasized that whatever happened at the SFAS, it had fundamentally altered him.[115]

As these things go, there is ample historical precedent to show that, strange as it might have sounded, there was nothing impossible about the Guilty Agent story McVeigh told his sister.[116] Whatever their purpose and whoever signs their paychecks, all operatives working in an undercover capacity must gain the trust of their targets. They do so by "smoke and mirrors," illusions meant to manipulate impressions, contrive situations, using schemes (ruses, pretexts, scams, cons, decoys, staged introductions to "frame the context in which the agent is inserted."[117] Throughout the duration of their assignments, they must be able to convincingly (and sometimes spontaneously) create and maintain fake identities and cover stories, resist integration and, if interrogated, remain calm, and provide false information. As we have seen, sometimes they become so immersed that they trick even themselves into thinking they are the people they pretended to be or were told to become. In this light, McVeigh's actions before and after the bombing may take on new meaning, even if the undercover mission he thought he was engaged in was purely imaginary.

Some commentators combine both scenarios by suggesting that McVeigh's secret mission was both real *and* imaginary. While the Jones Team discussed it previously, David Hoffman more candidly outlined such a suggestion when he asked whether it was possible that McVeigh had been lied to: "Someone – whom McVeigh thought was working for the government, gave him a cover story – convinced him he was [on] an important top secret mission." For him, McVeigh's "seeming indifference upon his arrest" could indicate this belief. A number of his character traits, Hoffman points out, would have made him both an ideal "undercover operative and a perfect fall guy." Others have noted that, like Oswald, McVeigh left the military "under a cloud of unknowns," became politically alienated, engaged in restless nomadic wanderings, had a deep desire to be recognized by a strong father figure and a desperate need to "assert himself," to do something important, to write himself into history; all easily exploitable traits that made both men "a natural sucker" for *real* conspirators (whoever they may be).[118] Certainly, his psychological profile fit that of the typical spy as highlighted by Dr. Jolly West and friends in 1985.

McVeigh's documented dissociative disorder and other revelations only compound matters and add to an already complex array of information that must be considered when evaluating his Guilty Agent claims and, in fact, open doors for the creation of Experimental Wolf stories. Fabricated undercover identities exacerbate role confusion and can take on a life of their own, a nearly predictable occurrence when certain psychological profiles with dissociative predispositions are taken into account. What's more, hypnosis can and is used to aid in the creation and maintenance of controlled alter personalities for use in undercover work that are then further developed and structurally entrenched during real-world field deployment. The more predisposed to dissociative experiences, the more suggestible they tend to be and the easier they are to hypnotize. Conspiracy theorists have known this for a long time though. That's partly why Jolly West causes them such antagonistic fascination. The funny thing about West is that he wasn't just an expert on cults, undercover operators and spy handling but hypnosis and dissociative states as well. West wasn't interested in curing dissociative disorders though, he was specifically concerned with ways to induce dissociation and, wouldn't you know it, he was one of the primary architects of the military's SERE program (more on that shortly).[119]

A number of theorists conceive of John F. Kennedy's assassination as the first major post-modern event; an event that spawned multiple chronologies, theories and histories and a pervasive paranoia about secret government machinations in general. Central to this were questions about the true identity of the ambiguous and multiplicitous Lee Harvey Oswald, the first true post-modern subject, whose many identities could mean any number of things. McVeigh's *seeming* inability to keep his many identities straight, keep track of all of their movements and relationships, or even remember them, is another trait he shared with DeLillo's fictionalized Oswald. DeLillo's Oswald is a man plagued by a number of uncanny other Oswalds whose existence deeply disturb the "real Oswald's" concept of singular self. DeLillo explained that this depiction was inspired by an observation that the real-life Oswald seemed to be "scripted out of doctored photos, tourist cards, change of address cards, mail order forms, visa applications, altered signatures, pseudonyms. His life as we've come to know it is a construction of doubles." Like McVeigh, DeLillo's Oswald, "becomes one of those people whose fantasy life is much more important than his real life. The world of espionage, into which Oswald drifts, is a particularly dangerous one for such an individual, since it is a breeding ground for paranoia, illusion, and multiple identities."[120]

THE VERACITY OF TIM MCVEIGH

Every person has the capacity for self-deception, but Tim's is seemingly infinite.

–Internal Jones Team Defense Memo, 'Is He Lying Or Isn't He?' 1996

What science may never be able to explain is our inflapable fear of the alien among us; a fear which often drives us not to search for understanding, but to deceive, inveigle, and obfuscate. To obfuscate the truth not only from others, but from ourselves.

– Agent Dana Scully, *The X-Files*, 1999

According to Herbeck and Michel, the most cited account in discussions about McVeigh, "Jones simply did not believe McVeigh's contention that he acted alone... [and] was convinced there was a much bigger conspiracy involved [but] McVeigh never wavered from his story."[121] According to archival documents and those who knew him, McVeigh *did* waver and at various times alluded or admitted to other conspirators, only to later deny such admissions; or near admissions. Over time, in bits and pieces, McVeigh presented several possibilities about the reality of the bombing; he had acted alone; he was one in a group of conspirators whom he refused to name because, as he himself said, "I gave them my word"; or as an agent for covert powers in a vast conspiracy. Sometimes it was almost as if he wanted to tell them, but stopped just short of doing so. Rather, he hinted, alluded, suggested, smiled and arched his eyebrows in just such a way as if to suggest they were getting closer to the truth. But his hints, in combination with the inconsistent details and changing stories he offered them made it nearly impossible to know what, if anything, he said was true.[122]

The questions remained: Even if something he said was not true, did he really believe it was and, if so, why? Were they fantasies he took refuge in?

Calculated lies and "chicken feed" meant to misdirect their investigatory and legal defense efforts? Partial truths mixed with misleading deceptions? The ambiguity surrounding McVeigh's version of events and his sporadic, yet enduring, *delusions* dictated that his defense team carefully consider the possibility, plausibility, probability and rationale for any one version he offered, including the most outrageous and then weigh it against supporting or negating evidence. But, as the Jones Team engaged in an increasingly aggressive effort to determine the truth about the bombing, McVeigh resisted at every turn. Their cumulative efforts deeply disturbed him as their ongoing inquiries and investigation threatened to undermine his Lone Wolf legacy.[123]

Several internal defense memos reveal the extent to which the Jones Team went to determine his lies from his truths. One undated memo entitled, "Is He Lying Or Isn't He? – SECRET," outlines and compares conflicting statements he had made over time and essentially encapsulates the content of many others. The memo illustrates the ways in which at least some of the Jones Team were coming to view him:

> Tim is a masterful manipulator and con man. The better part of his adult life is predicated upon lies, deceptions and cons. His story is riddled with inconsistencies.... His psyche is such that he often says and advocates the opposite of what he truly believes.... Even when not completely lying, he's prone to hyperbole and exaggeration [and displays] delusions of grandeur... Tim is confident of his intelligence and his ability to lie and deceive....Tim tells us he's telling the truth, and he purports to value truth, integrity and honor ... Tim is lying to us, and he uses the same strategies of deception on us that he used on others; diversion. He takes the offensive with us, dominating conversations (and attempting to do the same strategically in terms of the case) to steer it in the direction he wants rather than risk letting us probe around in the topics we are desperate to know. When we get close to finding something out Tim gets indignant and defensive. His recent hysteria over [the] subpoenaing of the phone records is a case in point. Why would he care unless, buried within them, they are going to prove him a liar? By his own admission, Tim lied to us from the beginning, and though he says he is now coming clean, the truth is that he's just exchanged old lies for fresh ones. The larger part of his adult life is predicated upon lies, deceptions, cons, theft and adultery and yet, Tim continues to assert, with a straight face even, that truth, integrity and honor are his predominant characteristics as a man. Every person has the capacity for self-deception but Tim's is seemingly infinite...

By August 1995, Jones had reached the limit of his tolerance for McVeigh's obfuscations (even if they were symptomatic of his mental illness) and his nonsensical Lone Wolf story, and convinced him to take a polygraph test. The results of the polygraph indicated McVeigh was dishonest when he stated no other conspirators beyond Nichols and Fortier had participated in the bombing plot. Tim Domgard, who conducted the polygraph, told Jones, "there's absolutely no doubt in my mind [that McVeigh is] attempting to keep someone's identity, who is involved in this situation, from me" and predicted, "he would take the name with him to his grave."[124] After Jones confronted him with the results, McVeigh (who assumedly thought he could pass the test) became enraged and said he found the test results unacceptable. He insisted they were wrong and based on inaccurate science. In two handwritten letters about the results he wrote:

> To rest on these polygraph results is not an option, because somehow they are wrong.... I give my word on my sacred honor that I am telling the truth.... I will submit to anything to prove my word to you, for the trust of my legal team is really all that I have left.... I am absolutely, psychologically in "a tailspin" .... If I cannot gain your full trust, then I have very few (unpleasant) options left.... I will submit to further polygraph's, *SODIUM Pentothal, hypnosis, or even fucking torture* to recover the honor and integrity that I have lost today... I admit that I cannot explain the results, but I am adamant that they are flawed and wrong.... I cannot live with these results, period. [...]I am betrayed, bitter, and on the literal verge of psychosis.... I will not face anyone who thinks I am untruthful.[125]

To Halleck, McVeigh's hissy fits indicated he was concealing something and said he (McVeigh) kept bringing up the polygraph results in their discussions. In fact, said Halleck, McVeigh had become "obsessed" by the failed polygraph test. After one conversation with him, he wrote, "Tim was very bothered by the polygraph results and kept coming back to that. He said he was going to be watching each of his lawyers quite carefully to see whether any particular lawyer seems not to believe him anymore. He said that if people do not believe him, he will be very upset." And upset he got, once threatening to "hit" the next "motherfucker" who asked him about where he parked his getaway car "soooo hard that their mama's gonna get a black eye!" He told Jones that the problem, as he saw it, was that Jones kept showing up and presenting him with a "new and improved list of the most eligible co-conspirators," but the problem would naturally resolve itself once Jones ran out of "names of the living." McVeigh continued, "I'll suck it up if necessary – but just know that it makes me want to smack you."

Despite McVeigh's threats, his story about the car kept changing and the doubts of his legal team persisted all the more so after the polygraph, until finally McVeigh requested that no member of his legal team visit him unless it was crucially necessary. Of course, while not every member of the team agreed that it even mattered who else participated in the bombing, at least as far McVeigh's legal defense was concerned, Jones felt it was important and, further emboldened, continued his inquiries. Thus, the failed polygraph, along with the defense leaks, precipitated the near total collapse of McVeigh's relationship with his legal team.[126]

Frustrated with their inability to get McVeigh to "come clean" or even keep his stories straight, Jones asked the mental health experts to make recommendations about how better to induce McVeigh to give up the information he so carefully guarded. Dr. Semone wrote that McVeigh "is as shrewd and clever as they come," and suggested tapping into his "Stockholm Syndrome" (his reliance on them for everything) and using it to their advantage. Circumstances, including McVeigh's deteriorating mental health and refusal to cooperate with his defense team, became such that Dr. Semone expressed his belief that it was "absolutely clear… that the mental health issues cannot be divorced from the legal effort" and recommended that the legal team approach him as "both legal client and clinical patient."[127] In response, in October 1995, Jones wrote McVeigh:

> I think sometimes you must feel that there is no one that you can communicate with […] So here is my suggestion: You seem to have gotten along well with Dr. Smith. Why don't we rearrange the Dr. Smith appointments once a week and let him be your therapist with the understanding that anything you say to him is privileged. In other words, *we will alter his situation* so that he is not part of the psychiatric and psychological team, but is there for you and you alone. Nothing that you say to Dr. Smith will be repeated to any member of the defense team, except myself, and will only be repeated with your express authorization to Dr. Smith. … Dr. Smith is highly regarded, he is close by … and I think he would value this relationship and do you an outstanding job.

In his response letter to Jones, McVeigh told him that, in his opinion, they should just "sack all these doctors, at least in the context of seeing me." In fact, he said, he had made it known to all of them that he didn't even "completely agree with the science of psychiatry," and the only thing the doctor visits accomplished was to make him "extremely defensive," "uncomfortable" and even more stressed out. That said, McVeigh closed the letter by saying that he would consider Jones' suggestion about bringing Smith back in and asked for a week to think about it as "it's hard for me to admit that I would need to call in a 'professional.'" Smith and McVeigh would continue their visits but not for a few more months.

ORWELLIAN REVERSAL

[H]is case was unfolding itself, while up in the attics the Court officials were poring over the charge papers.… It looked like a kind of torture sanctioned

*by the Court, arising from his case and concomitant with it […] Even that
has its reason; it is often better to be in chains than to be free*

— Franz Kafka, *The Trial*, 1925

*All coercive techniques are designed to induce regression. […] The deprivation
of stimuli induces regression by depriving the subject's mind of contact with
an outer world and thus forcing it upon itself [while] the calculated provision
of stimuli … tends to make the regressed subject view the interrogator as a fa-
ther-figure [thereby] strengthening the subject's tendencies toward compliance.
[…] As regression proceeds, almost all resisters feel the growing internal stress
that results from wanting simultaneously to conceal and divulge … As the
sights and sounds of the outside world fade away, its significance for the inter-
rogate tends to do likewise. [The outside world] is replaced by the interrogation
room [and] the dynamic relationship between [interrogator and interrogat-
ed] … As the interrogation goes on, the subject tends increasingly to divulge or
withhold in accordance with the values of the interrogation world rather than
those of the outside world.[…] If resistance is encountered … non-coercive
methods of sapping opposition and strengthening the tendency to yield and
cooperate may be applied…. The use of unsuccessful techniques will of itself
increase the interrogatee's will and ability to resist. The effectiveness of most
non-coercive techniques depends upon their unsettling effect…. The aim is to
enhance this effect, to disrupt radically the familiar emotional and psychological associations of the subject. When this aim is achieved, resistance is seriously
impaired. […] The aim of the Alice in Wonderland or confusion technique is
to confound the expectations and conditioned reactions of the interrogatee…
The confusion technique is designed not only to obliterate the familiar, but to
replace it with the weird … as the process continues, day after day as necessary,
[the situation] becomes mentally intolerable [and] he is likely to make significant admissions, or even pour out his story.*

— KUBARK *Counterintelligence Interrogation Manual*, CIA, 1963

*We'd like to know a little bit about you for our files. We'd like to help you learn
to help yourself. Look around you all you see are sympathetic eyes. Stroll around
the grounds until you feel at home. […] Hide it in the hiding place where no one
ever goes. Put it in your pantry with your cupcakes. It's a little secret just the Robinson's affair. Most of all you've got to hide it from the kids. […] Laugh about
it, shout about it, when you've got to choose. Every way you look at this you lose.*

— Simon and Garfunkel, 'Mrs. Robinson', 1968

McVeigh's Special Forces assessment psychological exam revealed an
already existing tendency towards, among other things, paranoia,
a trait he shared with his mother, Mickey; who may have imparted her

own paranoid thinking to her son. After his arrest, as McVeigh's paranoia became more pronounced, so too did his mother's, who constructed her own Experimental Guilty Agent narrative about her son and, like him, began to suffer a rapid mental decline. In a series of internal memos, Dick Burr and Lee Norton described their impressions of her as well as those close to her:

In July 1995, Norton thought Mickey was "in a state of emotional crisis" (understandably), displayed "symptoms consistent with mild to moderate paranoia" and was probably suffering from "significant depression with anxious and paranoid features." When they met, Mickey was preoccupied with making sure Norton was who she said she was and even after Norton showed her multiple forms of identification, Mickey remained suspicious. She told Norton that she was under constant surveillance and people followed her wherever she went. She provided pictures of "devices on her phone wires which she believes are phone taps," about which Norton noted, "She may be correct." Mickey wondered if "Tim gave her house keys to the FBI." The bombing, Mickey told Norton, was "part of a government conspiracy in which her son was the 'Lee Harvey Oswald'" and although she knew more about the conspiracy, she couldn't talk about it as doing so could put her and her family at further risk.[128]

Jennifer told Norton that her mother was becoming "increasingly incoherent" and paranoid. Jennifer, no fan of the FBI at this point in her life, remarked that her mother was becoming obsessed with the FBI and the notion that they were following her, tapping her phones and even encouraging her to have a nervous breakdown "as part of the larger conspiracy of the case." She thought the government was controlling the information she heard on the radio and asked Jennifer to get ahold of Tim's attorneys so that they could "make the government quit controlling her radio." She believed the defense team was "in league" with the FBI and could control what they did. Jennifer said she thought her mother was taking sleeping pills given to her by "the Coast Guard doctor" (health care was available to her through the Coast Guard via her new husband). Mickey's attorney confirmed that her condition was growing worse but said he felt it best that she not seek treatment through the Coast Guard as the quality of care they provided was questionable and they could very well leak information.[129]

In October, Dick Burr and Lee Norton met with her again after which Norton noted that Mickey was experiencing "pervasive paranoia sometimes accompanied by auditory hallucinations." She told them there was an ongoing plot to make her think she was going crazy, she was being stalked, and her life was being threatened. Cars and trucks followed her and their drivers talked about her on the CB radio, except they called her "he" in order to trick her and hide what they were doing. She thought a dentist she had seen some months ago intentionally introduced an infection into her jaw. Her friends, neighbors and even her own husband were in league with the FBI's machinations against her, said Mickey. At first, she thought her husband was just helping them gather information but more recently he "introduced noxious gasses into the air conditioning vents" in an attempt to asphyxiate her. He had also tried to give her poisoned brownies. Her husband had since left her.

Sometimes, she said, her calls to innocuous places like her credit card company were rerouted to the local FBI office. She was receiving communications through the local radio station and could "hear them speaking 'between the lines' about her whereabouts." In fact, both her television stations and her radio were being controlled externally. Sometimes she would be watching the news and the announcer would say that next up was a report about the Oklahoma bombing and, all of the sudden, cartoons like Tom and Jerry would cut in and replace the news program, making it so she couldn't get information about developments in the case. If that wasn't bad enough, "they" could even watch her through her television and her efforts to thwart this by throwing a blanket over it were futile because "the signals can go through all the electrical outlets."

She could hear people at a distance, including a sniper in her father's yard, who she heard say, "I have a clear head-shot of her." Mickey attributed her newly amplified sense of hearing, which Norton said, "sound[ed] more like auditory hallucinations," to her heightened anxiety that had kicked off self-preservation abilities. She had even developed a telepathic connection to her son and knew what he was thinking about in prison. She thought it was "possible [that] Tim could have been brainwashed at some point in time [and] was absolutely certain it [was] possible [that] someone could have implanted a chip in his butt," explaining that, if they can do it to dogs just by lifting up a flap of their skin and slipping in a needle, "they can certainly do it to humans." She thought the chips were used to track people, possibly children, in order to prevent them from being kidnapped. Now more than ever, she was convinced that her son was "a patsy in all of this."[130] Her family wanted to commit her, but she said she couldn't let that happen because then the news would announce, "Mother Of Mad Bomber Cracks Up." Norton closed this particular memo by noting that while her delusional symptoms seemed to have spiraled out of control, it was possible she'd always had them, but to a much lesser extent and it was imperative they learn how this had affected McVeigh's developing world view.

Finally, in November, after another meeting, Dick Burr outlined his impressions, which were very similar in content to what he and Norton observed the prior month, including "the most striking impression [that] Mickey is extremely paranoid." She had seen at least two more dentists recently but thought they too had done something harmful to her. Sometimes her things would go missing, like her credit cards and identification, and once, all her cigarettes had been taken out of the pack in her purse and lined up, one by one, on the seat of her car. She had finally overcome her jaw infection and since then, it seemed people had backed off a bit from trying to confuse her and make her think she was crazy. She told Burr that she believed that her son would try to cover or protect other people, even if it meant taking the blame, because he always wanted so much to please everybody. The government, she said, had made her son into a "scapegoat."[131]

Mickey was clearly suffering from severe delusions that had increasingly made her life unmanageable. Still, the defense team acknowledged, *some* of them were based in reality although, wrote Burr, it appeared most of them were not. The FBI was following and spying on various members of the Jones Team, so why wouldn't they follow the McVeigh family?

Cameras hidden inside television sets were nothing new and had been used in undercover investigations for quite some time. In fact, McVeigh's Army friend, Ray Barnes, later told me that when he was scheduled to testify at McVeigh's trial, the FBI put him up in hotel and soon after, a compromising video taken from inside his hotel room had been mailed to his wife. Electronic bracelets were being used to prevent child abduction and tracking chips were being marketed for this purpose as well. Much of what Mickey thought was happening to her, wasn't, but as it turned out, the FBI *had* bugged the McVeigh family homes, phones and the motels the FBI put them up in at various times during their investigation. Transcripts of conversations recorded by the wiretaps and bugs just days after the bombing, prior to Mickey's mental decomposition, reveal that both his mother and sister believed that McVeigh had been recruited into some sort of a covert operation. Their beliefs were based not on their paranoia, but because this is exactly what he had told them years earlier and, at the time, they had no reason to question his honesty.

Like Lee Harvey Oswald's mother, Marguerite, had done, Mickey McVeigh spoke publicly about her son's innocence, claimed he worked in some sort of undercover capacity for the government and accused mysterious forces of spying on her family prior to and after they framed her son. Unlike Marguerite Oswald, Mickey McVeigh's claims and assumedly her distress, led to her involuntary confinement in a psychiatric facility in early 1997.

As early as May 1995, McVeigh told his defense team that he was suffering from Gulf War Illness and said he and his COHORTs were "used as guinea pigs" for some sort of "test vaccine." When they obtained a partial set of his military medical records (not the psychological test records), McVeigh appeared to be "sensitive" about some of the entries in it but did inform them that certain entries that should be there, including immunizations, were missing. The Jones Team conducted research into the issue of Gulf War Illness but at that time, its existence was a topic of heated debate and study.

As he had in the military and in the years and weeks before the bombing, throughout his time in prison, McVeigh continued to see doctors and dentists on a regular basis, for many of the same symptoms he had previously.[132] Once, within days of seeing a prison doctor for a recurring skin rash on his forehead in October 1995, McVeigh informed Dick Burr that he did not want to see the medical doctors anymore, the first of several such requests. In fact, throughout his time at El Reno prison, while awaiting trial, McVeigh expressed a deep distrust of and anxiety about the prison staff generally, and their medical staff specifically. He told his attorneys that the prison guards were drugging his food. Was McVeigh as bat-shit crazy as his mother seemed to be?

Earlier that summer, several news outlets reported that hypodermic syringes were among the contents of food trays delivered to McVeigh and Nichols. This led to the suspension of Chuck Mildner, the Chief of Security at the prison in charge of the guards who delivered the trays. The prison warden, R.G. Thompson, assured reporters that, despite the syringes, the inmates were not at risk and the issue was "an internal personnel matter" (whatever that means).[133] The strange thing was that Mildner was not suspended because syringes were delivered to the inmates under his watch but because, after the incident, he tightened security and put preventive measures in place to stop such things from happening.[134] Mildner's supervisors overrode and countermanded the security measures, after which additional contraband (this time unspecified) was found on their trays. After Mildner's suspension resulted in an outcry from other correctional officers, Warden Thompson clumsily explained that the only reason he suspended Mildner was that he opened his big mouth about the incident; an act Warden Thompson said he viewed as a threat to McVeigh and Nichols' privacy. (No matter that both were under constant CCTV surveillance and that attorney-client meeting rooms at the prison were bugged).

James Nichols wrote that while at El Reno Prison, both his brother Terry and McVeigh "received a hypodermic syringe and cigarette butts on their food trays, apparently from someone who was making a point that the two prisoners were not 'out of reach.'" During this same time, he continued, "Terry's fingernails began turning black – which could indicate that he was being subjected to a slow poisoning – [but] immediately after the condition and Terry's suspicions were brought to the attention of his attorneys, the condition mysteriously 'cleared up.'"[135] While the contents of the syringes are unknown, according to an internal defense memo, the day after "the flap at the prison over [the] syringes, Tim found bugs in his food [but] does not want this information released to the press." The Jones Team seems to have been unaware of the exact nature of these goings on, as they filed motions requesting that the court compel El Reno prison (and any other agency that would know) to disclose any security threats to McVeigh. The court sealed the motions.

The death of an El Reno prison guard who worked under Mildner on McVeigh's cell-block resulted in suspicion from within conspiracy theory circles that the guard had seen something he shouldn't have, perhaps even visits by the spectral Dr. Jolly West who, they speculated, was probably on one of his brainwashing excursions. It was even possible, some said, that West was there to mentally program McVeigh into killing himself so he couldn't spill the bombing beans. Rumor had it he'd been seen going in and out of the prison. Dr. West aside (for just a short time longer), the fact remains that in the two years after the bombing, there *were* suspicious deaths of people in a position to have insider knowledge about McVeigh or the bombing. Included among them was the aforementioned guard, whose mother and others that knew him told Oklahoma State Representative Charles Key that shortly before he died, he told them he feared for his life because of important information he'd learned about McVeigh.

In any event, as much as he wanted it kept under wraps, McVeigh's own fear of the prison security guards continued, and in late February, he told one defense team member that the night before, a guard had come into his cell to retrieve his dinner tray and purposely dropped it on his head while he was sleeping. When he expressed concerns about the actions of certain guards to the warden, the warden told McVeigh he was paranoid. Later, when he came down with a cold, McVeigh refused the flu shot offered to him, insisting he wanted "no needles." In another incident, when McVeigh complained of heartburn, the BOP medical technicians told him that bacteria can cause heartburn and drew his blood, and told McVeigh they were testing it for bacteria. His attorneys, much to their displeasure, discovered that "since they took the blood, they are going to 'type' it for the U.S. Marshalls for security purposes." While this un-granted access to their client understandably upset the defense team, it also couldn't have helped relieve McVeigh's anxieties about DNA databases.

After Dr. John Smith's June 1995 recommendations to the court that some of McVeigh's prison restrictions be eased, the prison agreed to turn off the surveillance cameras for at least a few hours a day but, according to Stephen Jones, the Bureau of Prisons "fudged" on their promise and the cameras kept rolling.[136] By October, due to his prison conditions, the failed polygraph and his legal team's continuous effort to get him to tell them the truth, McVeigh had plummeted into a state of deep depression and anger. By January 1996, he began to say very strange things (think hooker legs in Ryder trucks). Attorney Amber McLaughlin said that during one meeting, McVeigh "discussed the possibility that human beings have not evolved into a higher form of mankind since only 30% of the brain is used. He wondered if Egyptians might have been a higher life form who built the pyramids through the power of their minds. This could be evidence that the human brain is degenerating. I think," added McLaughlin, "Tim may be spending too much time alone, but I did not tell him this)." McVeigh suggested they watch the 1988 film *They Live*, a favorite of his about a drifter who learns that aliens masquerading as humans are controlling humankind through subliminal messages in mass media. The aliens were only detectable with special glasses.

Throughout that winter, things grew progressively worse. McVeigh complained that, despite the orders of the court, his prison conditions were actually worsening, including the ability to see natural sunlight for only an hour a week. He expressed concern that his "mind is deteriorating." He feared he was rapidly losing his memory and said that if not recorded in his attorneys' memos, his "ideas and insights may be lost forever." These insights during this time included not only his profound thoughts on aliens and Egyptians but also his allusions to the participation of others in the bombing, a broader cover-up or conspiracy, and the presence of a government informant within the plot.

The negative psychiatric effects of prolonged isolation and solitary confinement on prison inmates are well established, particularly in regards to those in the pre-trial stage. Confusion, disorientation, intense agitation, sleeplessness, the inability to concentrate, loss of memory, obsessions, preoccupations, paranoia, panic, dissociation, hallucinations, irrational aggression, and psychotic delirium, to name a few. An often-observed phenomenon is the tendency of the prisoner to believe that their confinement is an attempt to "break them down" psychologically. Furthermore, for those already unhinged, these confinement conditions cause "severe exacerbation or recurrence" of pre-existing psychiatric symptoms.[137]

On the other hand, James Nichols said that around the time of the syringe incident, McVeigh called him and complained that he was being kept in isolation and expressed his desire to act as his own attorney. After a number of strange incidents, James came to believe that Jones was intentionally keeping McVeigh in increasingly isolated circumstances against his wishes and preventing him from communicating with anyone he could trust. Finally, in January 1996, during one court hearing, McVeigh, through one of his defense investigators, slipped James and others a note that they were to destroy after reading. According to James, in the note McVeigh expressed his regret at being unable to call or write them but said his hands were tied and "the psychological profilers at Quantico" were watching him closely. The note, said James, was McVeigh's attempt to inform them "the psychologists were messing with his head [and] in fact, profiling the case inside Tim's head to fit the FBI's allegations.... He was trying to tell us what they were doing to his mind while in total isolation." Jones himself wrote that McVeigh's stories changed in accordance with the FBI's, describing it as a Kafkaesque situation.

James believed McVeigh knew more than he could ever safely say and that the powers-that-were would go to great lengths to prevent him from revealing what he knew. At the time, McVeigh "still had the wherewithal to cry for help" but "unfortunately, at the time, we didn't know how to answer that cry."[138]

Likely unknown to James Nichols were the mental health experts' observations that, despite the negative impact the constant surveillance had on McVeigh, the more intense the surveillance became, the more "mentally off balance" McVeigh became and, when this happened, the more compliant and open he tended to be. Meanwhile, McVeigh made it known that he questioned the legitimacy of the mental health profession in general and thought the "shrinks" were just trying to "dig something up." And on the latter point, he was right.

McVeigh didn't want a mental health defense and rejected that his actions were caused by anything other than his own carefully thought out decisions, a position Jones philosophically if not factually agreed with. "Our job," Jones wrote, "is not to 'cure him' or to engage in psychoanalysis…instead we should concentrate on getting Tim to tell us the complete truth." Jones agreed with a recommendation made by Dr. Smith in his initial report that mental health experts meet with McVeigh and apply psychological pressure, "test" and "push" him, until he disclosed the information Jones sought. Not everybody agreed and felt they should let him "progress naturally" rather than "break him down" as Smith advised. But Jones was the boss. While the exact process of how the testing and pushing occurred and at what point it began in earnest is unknown; that it did occur seems a reasonable supposition. In February 1996, the month after James Nichols says he received McVeigh's strange note, McVeigh refused to meet with Dr. Halleck, because, he said, Halleck was trying to cycle through his innermost thoughts and emotions at a pace he didn't like. He was probing too deeply too fast.

In early March 1996, McVeigh once more expressed that he was suffering from "extreme mental anguish" both because of his prison conditions and because of the "psychological warfare" the prison guards were waging against him. He informed his defense team that he had finally found a way to "fight back" by initiating what he called "an Orwellian reversal" that consisted of him communicating with the guards who watched him in his cell remotely via live feed CCTV cameras by holding up signs with the guard's names on them. That same month, after seeking assurance that anything he disclosed to Dr. Smith would remain private, Nigh explained that while the government had copies of Smith's letters to the Jones Team, "perhaps the public would not." Apparently satisfied with this, McVeigh then requested to see Dr. Smith again, as soon as possible. McVeigh elaborated, saying, he "could see that he was attempting to *isolate himself,* and wanted to 'nip the problem in the bud' before it got out of hand… Of course, Dr. Smith was able to see him […] and I believe that you are both familiar with what transpired after that" (italics added). While what exactly did transpire "after that" remains unknown, Smith visited him at least twice that month and continued to see him after his transfer to Englewood, Colorado, as did the other mental health experts.

In a letter written to the defense team by Dr. Smith following one of the March 1996 El Reno meetings, Smith said he had recently visited McVeigh for the first time in months and was taken aback by what he found. McVeigh's health had taken a remarkable turn for the worse since their last visit. Smith wrote:

> [I observed] striking differences in Mr. McVeigh, both physically and psychologically, his physical condition has significantly deteriorated.... [He] has always been a rather tall, thin man [and the last time I saw him] he was vigorous ... spirited [and] spontaneous [in conversation. But on this occasion] his eyes were sunken, black rimmed, and his body seemed anorexic. He is obviously deteriorating physically.... During the interview, he had a spontaneous nosebleed, and [said] that for the last several weeks at least, he has been having episodic spontaneous nose bleeds of an undetermined cause [and he is] clearly not digesting or integrating his food.... He is always light complexioned but it is striking how pale he is.... His hands are red and scaly, a new development as far as his skin condition is concerned...

Apparently McVeigh had not explained to Smith that he had sought medical attention for some of these very symptoms prior to the bombing.

Smith also noted that McVeigh had lapsed into a "deep despair and depression" to the point where he was "reluctant to say what he thought ... out of concern that [what he says] will be interpreted or seen by others as being paranoid. This has undoubtedly led him to withhold information... from his defense team." He told Smith that he had been feeling an "impulse to give up," although it was later noted that this "might be precisely what the Government is trying to accomplish." Smith said the afflictions of McVeigh's confinement were in large part to blame for his condition (no sunlight, constantly watched, not allowed to read in his cell, minimal if any sunlight and when recreation was granted, it was in a cage called "The Thunderdome").

Smith thought McVeigh had been very open and forthcoming with him in revealing his emotional state and warned that if the deterioration continued at the same rate, he would be unfit to stand trial. He recommended McVeigh have a complete physical and at the very least, be allowed sunlight, as this may help slow down or even salvage his mental and physical health. After Smith's visit in March, a physician's assistant came to check on McVeigh once a day and a physician came once a week.

McVeigh continued to request that Smith see him but also informed his defense team in writing that, "I would like a motion filed with the court requesting that any and all video monitoring and/or recording of me either at the federal courthouse or in my permanent cell once I am on trial, not be used in any evidentiary, examinatorial, or display fashion. That is, if I am to be on camera or audio monitored, it is for security only, and can't be viewed by a psychiatrist, psychologist, behavioral analyst, or by any type of senior Justice Dept. officials for the purpose of gawking or display."

Just days after Smith's memo warning the Jones Team about the deterioration of Timothy McVeigh, Burr informed Jones that McVeigh's prison conditions "promote[d] mental and physical deterioration rather than retard it" and there was no reason for him to be "guarded by three guards and filmed everywhere he goes. The [recordings] are designed to wear him down and ruin his mental and emotional health, and although denied, *probably to assist the behavioral science unit of the FBI laboratory, and ultimately the prosecution*" (Italics added).

Were the suspicions of the defense team born from the same delusional paranoia exhibited by McVeigh and his mother? Had McVeigh somehow infected them with his pathological paranoid information disease? Just as the paranoid imaginings of McVeigh and his mother had, at least, some basis in reality, so too did those of the Jones Team.

On May 3, 1995, newspapers reported that a dozen FBI profilers were scrutinizing McVeigh's entire life, from his "lust for elite military missions to Army psychological tests and medical checkups" in order to build a psychological profile that may help uncover his role in the plot (i.e, leader or follower). Former FBI profiler Robert Ressler said, "The biggest key is in his military records. They offer a wealth of information. If there is any indication of a mental disorder, I suspect it would be in the health records." Ressler brought up McVeigh's microchip belief as a sign of his paranoid delusions but did not think a paranoid psychotic could have accomplished the bombing alone and suggested a terrorist cell could have used him. FBI consultant and Northeastern University professor Allen Burgess said the profile would help interrogators. "The name of the game is to get him to the point where he is going to babble like a baby." But, since the FBI could not use Gestapo-like tactics such as beatings with a hose, "although we'd like them to," they had to rely on clues in the profile. Later that year FBI profiler all-star, John Douglas, said that people like McVeigh "are comfortable in a structured environment, they do very well. But outside of a structured environment, without that rigidity, he just can't survive. On the other hand, he's probably doing fine now in jail. I bet they would say he's a model prisoner."[139]

Once again, the writings and career of eyewitness hypnotist Michael Gelles, might have given the FBI, Jones, or whoever else, some pointers about the best way to extract coveted information from McVeigh's deteriorating mind (although Burgess seemed pretty clear on what he thought they should do). You see, Gelles wasn't just the FBI's go-to hypnotist guy he was an interrogation guru, one of only eleven members of the "Government Experts Committee on Educing Information" and trailblazer in the field of operational psychology for that matter, having formed the Naval Criminal Investigative Service's Psychological Services Unit. Operational psychology, a discipline born from the O.S.S. (precursor to the CIA) wields the "arts" of psychology and psychiatry, not for clinical therapeutic reasons, but for investigatory purposes with the ultimate goal of gaining strategic information and advantage. This involves understanding a target's capabilities, personalities and intentions and developing ways of better extracting information, ostensibly from bad guys. The specific mission of the NCIS, of which Gelles' pet unit was a part, involved "preventing terrorism, protecting secrets, and reducing crime."[140] (While whose and what types of secrets it protected is not mentioned in the literature I reviewed, perhaps "extracting and exploiting secrets" might be added to the mission list). Either way, in 2003, the unabashed Gelles, who trained interrogators and profilers at Quantico, authored a comforting article about the role of psychologists and psychiatrists asked to do things that conflict with standard ethical guidelines when acting as consultants in terrorism, espionage and intelligence cases with vital national security implications. Doctor-Patient confidentiality, wrote Gelles, does not exist in such evaluations, nor does the presumption that the professional is acting in the best interest of the subject. In fact, they may be acting in just the opposite capacity, using their expertise to cause "arrest, detention, prosecution, physical injury or even death." One instance of such largely "uncharted waters" includes circumstances where "the consultant has professional contact with the individual," but national security concerns "dictate that the true purpose of the contact be withheld from the subject of the investigation." For instance, a psychologist might attend a party and mingle with guests, including the subject, with the intent of covertly evaluating them. In any case, no informed consent is required, and a "detainee" or subject may never know the professional identity of the expert whose purpose is to gather incriminating evidence against them.[141]

Gelles described the very type of paranoid world that Timothy McVeigh had inhabited for quite some time, one in which anybody can turn out to be someone other than whom they claim to be.

PART THREE
The Guilty Agent
Or All-American Mind Control

PAGING DR. WEST

On March 9, 1996, Dr. John Smith visited with McVeigh. The next day, McVeigh asked Rob Nigh if he could "shut down" Dr. Halleck and cancel his scheduled appointment with him. He would, he said, "rather have Smith instead." On March 11, Smith wrote a letter warning Dick Burr about the startlingly rapid rate at which McVeigh was deteriorating, both mentally and physically. On March 12, Stephen Jones personally called Smith to inquire about "the literature and the effects of surveillance." Smith told Jones, "Most of the effects of surveillance have to do with brainwashing during the Korean War [and] that's where the literature got started." As a side note, but in a manner implying they had spoken of him before, Smith informed Jones that (drumroll) "[Dr.] West was interested in that at one time ... that's how he originally made his name ... and what led to him being a part of the Patty Hearst thing." Unbeknownst to conspiracy theorists everywhere, as a student at Oklahoma State University, McVeigh's regular and trusted 'therapist,' Dr. John Smith (the only "shrink" he ever liked,) studied directly under none other than Dr. Louis Jolyon West.

Maybe it was Smith's glowing recommendation of West or maybe all those rumors about West finally seeped into the minds of the defense team, but two days later, on March 14, Jones Team attorney Andrew Murphy called Dr. West at his UCLA office. Transcripts of the conversation imply that someone from the Jones Team had spoken to West about McVeigh already (most likely Jones himself). Murphy informed West that Dr. Smith had been meeting with McVeigh and West acknowledged Smith as a former student. McVeigh, said Murphy, was "suffering from what Dr. Smith defined as 'exceptional circumstances,' [under] continuous surveillance and he said you were the honcho on that area of medicine." West, never one to toot his own horn, simply replied, "I know a lot about it." Again implying that a previous conversation, perhaps via Smith or with another member of the Jones Team, had occurred along the way, Murphy continued, telling West, "I also understand that you are willing to come down and see Tim."

West said he would be willing to if the Jones Team was willing to accept his fee, which, he said, was "about double" what someone local would charge, but then again, he explained, he was "an authority" on the effects of confinement and sleep deprivation. West added:

> On the other hand, I don't think there is anybody in that part of the country who has the same kind of background that I do ... I'm 71 years old. I've been Professor of Psychiatry here at UCLA for 27 years since I left OU. During the first 20 of those years, I was chairman of the department here as I have been there, and director of the neuropsychiatric institute here and I've had a lot of positions and so on I'm pretty well known. My research experience has covered, going back to the 50's, the effects of different kinds of confinement.... There is a small [body] of medical literature about the effects of solitary confinement, but I'm the authority on the effects of people being, let's say, subjected to situations in which they had

no privacy. American captives of the Chinese Communists during the Korean War who were held that way, but there is very little literature on it as far as I know.

West then offered to send over some literature about constant surveillance and promised to send along his academic resume (CV) "to give you an idea of what you're looking at." Indeed, West kept his word and his CV is located in the Jones Collection. Despite ramped speculation, if West visited McVeigh or if the Jones Team had any further communication with him, it is unknown to me and, while I've looked (*believe me I've looked*), no documentation to this effect has yet surfaced. Every rumor traces back only to more rumors, although as mentioned, the earliest of these are tied to Linda, "The CIA Is Zapping My Brain," Thompson. And there the creepy trail ends. When asked, years later, members of the Jones Team, including Jones himself, seemed not to know the extent of either West or Smith's involvement with McVeigh, or avoided the question.[142]

In 1998, David Hoffman observed, "Recent history is replete with cases of individuals who calmly walk into a restaurant, schoolyard, or post office and inexplicably begin shooting large numbers of people as though they were in a trance." Hoffman described what, years earlier, Conway and Siegelman termed "snapping" and what, tragically, recent history has continued to witness at a seemingly exponential rate. Rather than resulting from "information diseases," though, Hoffman asks if these snappers are the subjects of "CIA 'sleeper' mind control experiments." According to Hoffman, "McVeigh was subjected to psychological torture while in prison" which, he says, got so bad that, "eventually" his attorneys "called in a psychiatrist to help treat [his] anxiety." Could it be, Hoffman wondered, that McVeigh "was an Army/CIA guinea pig involved in a classified telemetric/mind control experiment?" Given the plague of missing Gulf War vet medical records throughout the country, Hoffman thought it reasonable to assume that entries for telemetric mind control would be purged from McVeigh's. For whatever reason, the Jones Team had begun researching just such a scenario nearly a year prior to their call to West.

In any event, although Hoffman does not name or mention Smith in his account, he, like others, does posit that Dr. Jolly West "mind controlled" McVeigh during his brief stay at Tinker Air Force Base immediately following his arrest and perp walk. He noted West's presence at Tinker during McVeigh's arraignment (ostensibly heading a psychological disaster response team). West himself had disclosed this to the Jones Team, telling them that while it wouldn't affect his impartiality, they should be aware of it. When Hoffman interviewed West and asked if he treated McVeigh, West curiously responded, "No, I haven't been asked to do that. I think his lawyer wouldn't want someone he didn't trust."[143] Hoffman didn't buy it and West certainly didn't bring up his student Smith, who McVeigh trusted more than most.

Author Robert Guffey noted, "Dr. West ... acts as a kind of dowsing rod for anyone attempting to track down government mind control experiments. Wherever one finds 'Jolly', the CIA isn't too far behind."[144] How did Dr. Jolly West, just a Jewish kid from Brooklyn, become such a notorious, legendary figure? Why do many, if not all, stories about brainwashing and technologies of control roads eventually lead to and intersect with West? How did persistent rumors come to surround West, generally, and speculations about his relationship to McVeigh, specifically? Why does he continue to appear as McVeigh's CIA Mind-Controller/Microchip-Implanter? In what ways do legends about West relate to other episodes detailed in this writing? In short, when West offered to send his CV to the Jones Team, what, exactly, were they looking at?

AMERICAN MIND CONTROL 101 OR, RAMBO'S NIGHTMARE

For, after all, how do we know that two and two make four? Or that the force of gravity works? Or that the past is unchangeable? If both the past and the external world exist only in the mind, and if the mind itself is controllable – what then?

–George Orwell, *1984*

Power is in tearing human minds to pieces and putting them together again in new shapes of your own choosing.

–George Orwell, *1984.*

Hello darkness, my old friend. I've come to talk with you again because a vision softly creeping left its seeds while I was sleeping and the vision that was planted in my brain still remains within the sound of silence...

– Paul Simon, "The Sound of Silence."

During World War II, leading academic journals reported on the military's successful use of hypnosis. In his 1943 book, *Hypnosis*, head of the Psychology Department at Colgate University, Dr. George Estabrooks bragged about the military's use of hypnosis during wartime, particularly the creation of hypnotic couriers with clinically created duel personalities who could deliver messages that they would have no recollection of later. Estabrooks told of the sheep-dipping of agents who would be given a fake dishonorable discharge from the military, subjected to hypnotic programing that allowed them to convincingly infiltrate enemy groups, after which they would report to their handlers with amazing recall of the information they gleaned. After the conclusion of the war, the 1947 National Security Act and the creation of the CIA that same year established rhetorical justification, covert infrastructure, and the extra-legal means necessary to initiate a series of ambitious yet unsavory and highly secretive research projects. In short, it was at this time, in the earliest years of the Cold War, that the CIA and U.S. military began a sustained, disciplined and well-funded foray into mind control.[145]

Among the events to catalyze such research efforts was the arrest of Cardinal Jozef Mindzenty by Communists in Budapest for espionage and subversion. Mindszenty, held and interrogated for thirty-nine days, eventually confessed, despite a startling lack of evidence against him. During his three-day public 'trial' in 1949, he displayed a robotic, zombie-like demeanor and spoke in a "monotonous mechanical chant." That same year, the United States Air Force commissioned Yale psychologist Irving Jannis to study the Mindszenty case. Jannis concluded that Mindszenty's strange behavior was a result of a series of electroshock-induced convulsions combined with drugs, sleep deprivation and hypnosis, which induced a somnambulistic trance that allowed his captors to implant false memories, thereby assuring his compliance, his false confession and even his own belief in his false confession. Jannis advised that the U.S. intelligence community conduct "systematic" experiments, using the same methods, to see if they too could induce false confessions.[146] Their efforts to do so were quickly met with success.

In 1950, the CIA initiated Project BLUEBIRD, expanded and renamed ARTICHOKE in 1951, conducted in coordination with Army and Navy researchers. According to CIA documents, the objectives of the projects included identifying "offensive uses of unconventional" and "unorthodox methods," to gain "control of an individual by application of special interrogation techniques" and the ability to reverse engineer these methods to "prevent unauthorized extraction of information" in the event of capture. In addition, researchers sought to create "an exploitable alteration of personality" by developing effective and reliable ways of inducing enhanced memory capacity, implanting false memories, and assuring compliance in formerly noncompliant people generally. Methods of doing so included (but were not limited to): truth serums, other biological and chemical agents, hypnosis, induction of somnambulistic trances, post-hypnotic suggestions and controls, sensory stimulation, electroshock, psycho-surgery (partial lobotomy), "brain damage … so called 'black psychiatry,' [classical] Pavlovian conditioning, 'Brainwashing' or any other methods" possibly useful for "interrogation, subversion, or seduction" and resistance."[147] To achieve these aims, the U.S. government drew from the expertise of newly re-cruited Paperclip Nazi "mind scientists" and their handlers. Progress towards the research objectives was rapid.

Researchers had a wide variety of drugs as well as human test sub-jects at their disposal, including unwitting CIA agents and assets of questionable loyalty (i.e., suspected moles, plants and double agents). More often though, test subjects were found among unsuspecting ci-vilian "volunteers" deemed *expendable*, such as drug addicts, prisoners and patients at sanitariums and hospitals. The research projects also culled an endless supply of subjects from the military population. Sol-diers made exceptionally good candidates for experiments because they could not sue for damages resulting from harm done to them by mil-itary doctors and were the only population for whom a modicum of legally informed consent did not apply. Experiments designed to ensure strategic military and intelligence advantage resulted in a number of ad-verse effects for the unwitting lab rats including paranoia, depression, epilepsy and death. The possibility that, in some cases, certain *terminal experiments*, could lead to death, was one taken into account during the inception, planning and execution of the research.

For the already burgeoning art of American brainwashing, the Kore-an War (1950-1953) was a godsend. The Korean War provided further justification, institutionalization and acceleration of America's mind-con-trol initiatives and, shortly after entering the war, the U.S. practiced and further developed their "advanced" techniques on North Korean prison-ers of war held in Japan.[148]

One CIA project-related memo, asked if it was possible to "get control of an individual to the point where he will do our bidding against his will and even against fundamental laws of nature, such as self-preservation?" Methods considered included: "[seizing] a subject and ... by post [hyp-notic control] have him crash an airplane [or cause] a train wreck...." Per-haps the question was rhetorical, because those engaged in active research into the question during the early Cold War mind-control race certainly thought so and had made this abundantly clear. Public agencies such as the CIA/OSS, the DOD, Naval and Air Force Intelligence and their pri-vate think-tank counterparts such as RAND, continued to issue reports identifying and outlining the ability to control behaviors, regulate mem-ories, and elicit false confessions. In fact, despite conventional beliefs that a person could not be hypnotized to commit acts that went against their personal ethics, Estabrooks and other leading hypnotists claimed other-wise. In 1950, a popular magazine quoted the good Dr. Estabrooks, who claimed, "I can hypnotize a man – without his knowledge or consent – into committing treason against the United States," and warned that if he could do it, so could the Communists. In one of Estabrooks' more compassionate research proposals to his spooky backers, he expressed the opinion that any loss of life that might result from experiments in which hypnotized individuals were commanded to murder, would be justified; "...a very trifling portion of that enormous wastage in human life which is part and parcel of war."[149]

Research and development of brainwashing took on added urgency after a group of USAF pilots, held as POWs, confessed to the use of biological warfare agents (anthrax, typhus, cholera, and plague) against the North Koreans. Thousands more (apparently brainwashed) POW's had signed petitions making similar confessions and pleading with the U.S. to end the war. Once released, some of the American POW's who had "succumbed to Communism" were taken to military hospitals where Army officials said, "The best techniques of modern psychiatry would be used in their preparation for return to society." It is unknown what this "special treatment" consisted of.[150] In any event, after the POW's confession SNAFU, the CIA, military, intelligence and defense establishment sought the knowledge of leading academics to help close the "mind control gap."

Enter the ubiquitous and legendary Dr. Louis Jolyon 'Jolly' West, born in New York City in 1924, the eldest of three and only son of Russian Jewish immigrants who eventually, along with their children, settled in Wisconsin. Although the West family was poor, his mother instilled in him a "sense of power and destiny" and when World War II began, West joined the Army hoping, he said, "to show Hitler there were Jews who knew how to fight, and to kill. ... I was a bloodthirsty young fellow."[151] The Army had other plans for West though, and sent him to medical school in Minnesota, where he achieved the rank of Major and was transferred into the Air Force Medical Corps, who sent him to study psychiatry at Cornell Medical School, during which time the Korean War had begun. While there, West became quite proficient in the art of hypnosis. In 1952, he became the Chief of Psychiatry at Lackland Air Force Base in San Antonio, Texas, where his career as psychiatric pioneer began.

While at Lackland, West conducted his seminal study of American Korean War POW confessions, which led to his unified theory of behavior control, termed "Debility, Dependency, and Dread" (DDD), "the definitive study on Communist psychological tactics."[152] West argued that the POWs were not the victims of mysterious communist voodoo, but had been psychologically broken through the systematic use of fear, hunger, sleep deprivation, humiliation and spontaneous and random relief from these conditions. The resulting futility, disorientation, loss of sense of space and time, hallucinations, and psychological regression produced a weakening and collapse of the prisoners' will, dissociative and automaton-like states and, eventually, utter dependence upon and total compliance with captors. At a certain point, prisoners, no longer able to grin and bear it, switched to a mindless "autopilot" state that eventually degraded into something resembling a Zombie. Essentially, West asserted that a controller could form, break and remake an individual's sense of coherent identity by subjecting them to DDD. West's theory of DDD became instrumental to all early and subsequent government mind-control endeavors. It was used to inoculate soldiers to enemy interrogation and brainwashing and, conversely, to retrieve information stored in the deepest recesses of the mind in some and induce desired behaviors in others, even when such actions were against their conscious will.

A January 14, 1953 CIA memorandum entitled "Interrogation Techniques" explicated the valuable potential that West's work could have to ongoing efforts:

> If the services of Major Louis J. West, USAF (MC), a trained hypnotist, can be obtained, and another man well grounded in conventional psychological interrogation and polygraph techniques, and the services of Lt. Col [deleted], a well-balanced interrogation research centre [sic.] could be established in an especially selected location.[153]

Dr. West was Chief of Psychiatry at Lackland Air Force Base when, in 1953, the USAF created its prototypical offshore "prison camp" or "stress inoculation" school in Chinhae, South Korea. West's colleagues, Dr. Albert Biderman (sociologist), Dr. Robert J. Lifton (psychiatrist), Dr. Lawrence Hinkle, Jr. (neurologist, Cornell), and Dr. Harold Wolff (human ecologist, Cornell) acted as directors and instructors at the school. There, student soldiers learned to resist torture and interrogation not only through simulations involving self-inflicted pain, extreme sleep deprivation and isolation, but also through actual torture by instructors. The idea was that through forced standing for long periods, electric shock, kneeling on broomsticks, and forcefully inserting foreign objects into the bodies of students, if captured in the future, they could endure similar treatment at the hands of enemies. As the most effective ways to extract information from unwilling informants, students received instruction on how to perpetrate these abuses upon others. Similar schools were also established in the United States.

West's theory of DDD forms the theoretical and operational foundations for counter-intelligence manuals used by the CIA, Special Forces and all other military and intelligence "survival schools;" the very type of schools from which McVeigh aspired to graduate. Education programs founded upon or using DDD theories included USAF Survival School (1953), USAF Survival, Evasion, Resistance, and Escape (SERE) course (est., 1955), U.S. Army's Special Warfare School at Fort Bragg, NC

(1959), the infamous School of the Americas and the CIA's "premiere course" in survival training conducted at a remote location in Virginia known as 'The Farm.'[154]

In 1953, based on a recommendation by Dr. Wolff, head of Cornell University's Neurology Department (1932-1962) and President of the American Neurological Association (1960-1966), the CIA established Cornell's Human Ecology Fund (HEF), a front-organization used to channel money into various research projects. In the shade of the HEF, the CIA expanded their efforts and initiated Project MKUltra, an endeavor historian Alfred McCoy described as "a veritable Manhattan Project of the mind," that operated under the auspices of the CIA's notorious Technical Services Division, headed by the infamous CIA chemist, Dr. Sidney Gotlieb.[155]

The CIA's newest unconventional Cold War weapons race would utilize a revolutionary multi-disciplinary, vacuum cleaner approach and draw from and recruit all imaginable academic disciplines in both the sciences and humanities. Protection of classified research involved compartmentalization, secrecy agreements, and outright deceit. Through countless respectable private charitable organizations and publicly funded "dummy institutions" (universities, hospitals, etc.), MKUltra research was staged in a way which left the public, and many researchers directly involved in the work, unaware of the project's ultimate objectives, future uses, and source of funding. Private and public charitable organizations used to funnel money to MKUltra research included the Josiah Macy Foundation, the Ford and Rockefeller Foundations, the National Institute Of Public Health, Federal Bureau of Drug Abuse, Federal Bureau of Narcotics, Veterans Administration, Department of Health, Education and Welfare, Food and Drug Administration, and the Law Enforcement Assistance Administration, to name a few.

MKUltra, while not the only project of this type, was the main one under which all manner of outrageous behavior control research was conducted. The aims of MKUltra and related government research and development efforts, included, as summarized by Rebecca Lemov: "[C]ertain stratospheric drugs; the hypnosis of secret agents, programming them to carry out missions unaware; the possibility of mind control machines; the possibility of carrying out mass brainwashing, coercion or subtle attitude adjustment and behavioral modification; the use of electroshock, intensive drugging, and lobotomy to control or "drive" an individual; the effects of extended sensory deprivation on one's state of mind; and the possibility that any of the above might be an effective interrogation tool or a way of making someone forget having been interrogated in the first place."[156] Essentially, MKUltra, along with numerous similar projects conducted by other agencies during this time, was designed to manipulate, control and engineer the behaviors of individuals and groups by any means necessary.

U.S. intelligence agencies, notably the CIA, used fronts like HEF to provide legitimacy and funding for research using actual human subjects. There was no doubt on the part of the architects of these programs that the research would, at times, cause significant harm to subjects. Similar to their predecessor projects (both Nazi and American), the experiments used non-informed and non-consenting human subjects including house-wives, soldiers, minority populations, psychiatric patients, drug addicts, prostitutes, johns, prison inmates, and children.[157]

In his research, Wolff placed his subjects in "untenable situations" and disoriented states induced through lengthy periods of sleep deprivation, in order to break and reprogram their thoughts and behaviors. Included were 100 Chinese refugees whom Wolff hoped to turn into secret agents that would then repatriate and infiltrate their home country and, in the event of capture and interrogation, be able to withstand their captors' attempts at extracting information and brainwashing. Like West's, almost all U.S. interrogation and counter-insurgency manuals put out by the CIA and military from that time until the present include methods based on Wolff's work.

Dr. Ewen Cameron, funded by the HEF and Rockefeller Foundation, expanded upon Wolff's work in his experiments in a sanitarium at McGill University's Allan Memorial Institute in Montreal (1957-1964). His subjects consisted mostly of depressed homemakers that checked in for nerves and anxiety; for which they received large doses of LSD, Thorazine, Seconal, and high-voltage electro-shocks as Cameron sought to obliterate their memories and fully regress them into infantile states. Afterwards, Cameron placed them in sensory isolation rooms, keeping them in drug-induced comas for months at a time, all the while playing nonstop recorded messages as a way of reprogramming their underlying personality structures, in a process Cameron called "psychic driving."

The research of Dr. West and his closest colleagues was equally well-funded and unrestricted in scope or method and, as it was unknown to the public, free from scrutiny. HEF (along with the military) had in fact funded the work that led West to conceive of and expand his theory of DDD and to become a leading national expert in the use of hypnosis for clandestine purposes. West's research attracted attention and, in 1954, at the age of 29, the University of Oklahoma's School of Medicine appointed him head of their Department of Psychiatry, Neurology and Behavioral Science, where he would first meet his student and McVeigh's future trusted psychiatrist, Dr. John R. Smith.

In 1956, the Oklahoma Turnpike Authority contracted West to study whether or not light-reflectors on the highway hypnotize drivers and, in the process, he discovered the phenomenon of "highway hypnosis," which is really not hypnosis at all but a common form of dissociation.[158]

That same year, West accepted the first of many seemingly simultaneous appointments at numerous military and VA facilities and began research under two top-secret MKUltra-funded projects entitled "psychophysiological studies of hypnosis and suggestibility" and, as part of this, authored a report entitled "Studies of dissociated states" outlining his findings:

> The literature concerning clinical entities ordinarily considered to constitute the dissociative reactions is fairly well limited to case studies of patients with fugues, amnesia, somnambulisms, and multiple personalities. Unpublished studies by the writer have led him to a greatly expanded concept of dissociation. [...] There is considerable experimental evidence pointing to the significant role played by dissociative mechanisms in the production of the various phenomena of hypnosis. In fact, hypnosis may be considered a pure-culture, laboratory controlled dissociative reaction. Of the entire phenomenology of the various states described above, there is not one single manifestation which cannot be produced experimentally in the hypnotic subject. Thus, through the use of hypnosis as a laboratory device, the dissociative mechanisms can be studied with a high degree of objectivity [...] Experiments involving altered personality function as a result of environmental manipulation (chiefly sensory isolation) have yielded promising leads in terms of suggestibility and the production of trance-like sates. There is reason to believe that environmental manipulations can affect the tendencies for dissociative phenomena to occur [...] all of the above recommended experimental procedures will require special equipment, special methodologies and special skills... [a] research team is being developed at [redacted] a unique laboratory must be organized and constructed. This laboratory will include a special chamber, in which all physiologically significant aspects of the environment can be controlled. This chamber will contain, among other things, a broad-spectrum polygraph for simultaneous recordings of a variety of physiological reactions of the individual being studied. In this setting various hypnotic, pharmacologic, and sensory-environmental variables will be manipulated in a controlled fashion and quantitative continuous recordings of the reactions of the experimental subjects will be made[159]

Like CIA-funded researchers Drs. George Estabrooks and Martin Orne, West advised the CIA about the creation of multiple personalities through hypnosis, post-hypnotic suggestion and amnesia, enhanced by mind-altering drugs like LSD and other methods such as electroshock and in combination with classical operant conditioning. West's unique research interests landed him a number of prestigious appointments and professional positions and, throughout his career, he wrote prolifically about a number of MK-related topics. A good portion of West's work remains classified.[160]

West had not yet achieved infamy though, as much of his work was secret at the time (and, in fact, remains so today). Rather, he became a media go-to guy, always ready to offer his insight into all things strange and troublesome. West was the on-call media commentator during a highly publicized fund-raising stunt in 1957, in which a famous radio announcer stayed awake for seven days straight. West explained to reporters that extended lack of sleep could bring out latent psychopathic tendencies. There was a great medical interest in sleep deprivation, he said, but the research was "handicapped by the difficulty of trying to produce the disease in a laboratory for study." This was because, according to West, no doctor was willing to produce real mental illness in a person just to study it. In 1959, newspapers reported on a phenomenon called micro-sleep, or "flash blackouts," during which people appeared awake, and even walked around with open eyes, but were in effect, sleeping, as evidenced by brainwave tests. West, along with Dr. Harold L. Williams, a psychologist at Walter Reed Army Institute of Research, presented the first scientific report on micro-sleep. Newspapers reminded readers that West knew all about this stuff, having conducted extensive studies into false confessions and other kooky behaviors induced through sleep deprivation.[161]

Throughout the 1960's, as West continued to build his resumé and media profile, the CIA and military refined and exported their survival/interrogation schools, offering training programs for "friendly democratic" governments abroad. While the doctrine of psychological warfare (PSYWAR) had existed previously, in 1953 CIA Director Allen Dulles declared psychological operations (PSYOPS) as the primary weapon with which the Cold War would be fought. In 1962, Army officials announced a dire need to cull psychological expertise to fight a "new kind of war" that could exploit "national vulnerabilities" in a way that would neutralize political opponents, namely indigenous left-wing resistance movements, through understanding the way they think. This then led to the military's "unprecedented and wholly unique financial support for psychological research" as well as other social science research.[162]

The rapidly growing body of government-funded psychological and social science research, including West's DDD, moved into the application phase in the early 1960's, and from this, a newer, improved and greatly expanded form of PSYWAR emerged. While technically considered "unconventional," PSYWAR actually became more conventional than traditional military actions and central to U.S. policies regarding so-called Third World countries where, apparently hearts and minds were to be won, and if that didn't work, kidnapped, brutalized and killed with newly trained death squads. Ever-evolving psychological operations (PSYOPS) were waged against insurgents and insurgency movements within high-value Cold War theatres including South America, Asia and Indo-China; theatres that also came to serve as test sites for new methods of mind control, interrogation and torture.

Drawing heavily from West's conception of DDD and the related work of Wolff and Hinkle; and central to ongoing PSYWARs and those to come, was the CIA's infamous 1963 KUBARK Counter-intelligence Interrogation Manual. KUBARK was instrumental in conveying the most efficient means of coercion and interrogation, including sensory deprivation, isolation, "threats and fear, debility, pain, heightened suggestibility and hypnosis, narcosis," and even mock executions. According to KUBARK, successful interrogation involved the gradual "regression of the [subjects] personality," most efficiently achieved through DDD techniques and those "designed not only to obliterate the familiar, but to replace it with the weird," ultimately rendering the situation "mentally intolerable" thereby, through the systematic escalation of tactics, eroding psychological defenses and structures, inducing regression, and forcing compliance.[163] KUBARK was a required textbook for CIA agents and interrogators.

Some of the more brutal and deadly techniques developed by the CIA and military were taught to the repressive security forces of Third World countries in Latin America and Asia by U.S. "consultants" working under the CIA controlled Office Of Public Safety (OPS). Amazingly considered a form of 'foreign aid,' John F. Kennedy established the OPS in 1962 as part of a larger "counter-insurgency" effort meant to avoid the appearance of waging traditional war. In 1965, Army Intelligence initiated Project X, intended "to develop an exportable foreign intelligence package to provide counterinsurgency techniques learned in Vietnam to Latin American countries."[164]

In 1967, the CIA coordinated the diverse counter-insurgency efforts of various agencies, including those of the OPS, in what was called the Phoenix Program, described by CIA director William Colby as "an essential part of the war effort [...] designed to protect the Vietnamese from terrorism" but in actuality was "the culmination of the CIA's mind-control project." The joint counter-terror operation was headed by CIA director William Colby and executed, largely, by the Army Special Forces, who themselves relied on the guidance of theories and methods of PSYWAR and DDD as outlined in military intelligence manuals such as KUBARK. Phoenix targeted, arrested, abducted, interrogated, starved, tortured, mutilated and killed untold thousands of alleged Vietcong sympathizers. PSYWAR also involved staging False Flag operations involving "a campaign of highly publicized atrocities (blamed on leftists) progressing in stages of psychological terrorism, culminating in mass beheadings and mutilations." Phoenix also functioned as an enormous factory for human experiments of the "terminal" variety that led to death as esteemed U.S. psychologists observed and advised. In this nightmare, prisoners, whose status as civilian or combatant was unclear, were abducted and treated to a cornucopia of "unconventional methods": (electroshock, throwing people out of airplanes, "cutting off the fingers, ears, fingernails and sexual organs," and inserting dowels into the brains of certain prisoners while others were forces to watch).[165]

The most notorious OPS "public safety advisor" was FBI agent and CIA consultant Dan Mitrione. Sharing the devilish details of the CIA's newly developed dark art with nearly every U.S.-backed state in Central and South America, Mitrione taught, normalized and institutionalized their police forces' use of systematic physical and psychological torture. His school of information extraction was founded upon the theories and methods of DDD, PSYWAR and KUBARK. Mitrione instructed that effective interrogation included (but was not limited to) placing subjects within cramped temperature and sensory-input controlled boxes, electroshock, sexual humiliation, forced standing, beating, abduction and the torture of prisoners' families. He demonstrated his lessons to students using pregnant women, children and random "beggars" off the street who sometimes ended up dead.

Some of the details of the U.S.'s counterinsurgency programs came to light when Mitrione was himself abducted and murdered in Montevideo in 1970. Ostensibly, in an attempt to eliminate torture, Congress dissolved the OPS in 1975, although in name only, as similar programs under the direction of DOD and U.S. military as advised by the CIA, continued to propagate the techniques of systematic torture. The Army's Project X existed until at least 1991. In a baffling twist of language, counter-insurgency programs came to be known as counter-terror programs, but the methods remained the same. While many of the records were destroyed, several details of the Phoenix program as well as Mitrione's pedagogic work, are echoed in more recent official U.S. interrogation and survival manuals and practices, all clearly based on the foundational theories and writings of West, Wolff and other MKUltra researchers.

Meanwhile, after a 1963 internal audit report by the CIA, MKUltra was renamed MK-SEARCH, and identical research resumed. Countless state and federal law enforcement, military and intelligence agencies continued to act in conjunction with, and/or under the direction of, the CIA, both domestically and abroad. Never a slacker, West remained quite busy.

He not only continued his work on those topics but also took on other hobbies and was appointed to a number of additional prestigious positions. He also wrote extensively on, among other things, LSD; hypnosis; the ability to induce anxiety through hypnosis; hallucinations; suggestibility; sleep deprivation; dissociative reactions; brainwashing; violence (specifically racial violence and how to prevent it); scuba diving; "the marihuana problem" [sic.] ; inducing false memories; and transcendental meditation.[166]

Though West later told the Jones Team that he had a "pretty good reputation in Oklahoma," a number of Oklahomans remember him as the former head of University of Oklahoma's School of Medicine who, in 1962, accidently killed 'Tusko,' a 7000-pound Asiatic male elephant. Tusko met his demise after West injected him with a heroic yet poorly calculated dose of LSD, apparently the largest known dose of LSD administered up to that time, in an effort to reproduce symptoms of "recurring elephantine temper tantrums." One recent news report noted, "Rumors persist that West was on LSD during the experiment and follow-up autopsy." A few years later, West's unfortunate killing of Tusko was mentioned in a news report with the headline, "Elephant Never Had a Chance After LSD Shot." The report discussed theories that LSD could actually increase IQ scores, arguments for and against the therapeutic use of LSD, the testing of LSD on "20 hippies of both sexes" at Northwestern University and the "adverse" effects of tests on the hippies.[167]

West knew all about LSD and hippies. He admitted to taking LSD himself, first in 1953, at a time, he said, when doctors believed it would help shed light on the causes of insanity. He smoked pot, too. The first time in 1946, in order to understand its effects but did not smoke it again until 1966, when, West explained, "I went to Haight Ashbury. I did it to prove to youngsters living there that I wasn't a narcotics agent myself." The hippies' suspicions were understandable, given their aversion to police in general, but also due to the recent activities of Federal Bureau of Narcotics agent and CIA asset, George H. White. By day, White busted drug dealers and, by night, conducted the MK-funded Operation Midnight Climax, an effort to lure unwitting test subjects to one of three CIA safe houses in San Francisco, dose them with acid and other drugs, and monitor their behavior; especially, their sexual behavior. White retired in 1966, just as West resumed his pot smoking with the "youngsters."[168]

Besides himself and elephants, West had some other notable test subjects upon which to conduct his own LSD experiments; namely, college students and hippies, whom West studied "in their natural habitat" – apartments rented in San Francisco that, like White's 'safe houses,' functioned as labs. One CIA agent described Haight Ashbury during this time as "a human guinea pig farm." Besides just learning how LSD could be used (alone or in combination with other methods) to exploit individuals, the less-addled hippies were involved in anti-war demonstrations and other forms of radical politics. LSD, known to alter the existing belief structures and politics of those who took it, presented a possible means of neutralizing undesired political activism and affiliation. West, it seemed, picked up in 1967 right where White left off. An archive of West's work at UCLA contains some of his related unpublished papers including one entitled "Make Love Not War: Notes on the Sexual Customs of Some American Hippies." Whatever West's reasons for hanging out with the youngsters and monitoring them, he subsequently published many papers outlining his deep understanding of hippie culture. One wonders if West ever used LSD to induce 'temper tantrums' in the hippies.[169]

Perhaps in an effort to neutralize increasing public panic about the growing use of LSD, a 1966 article in a local Oklahoma newspaper, declared that, despite "vague" and "unconfirmed" rumors of the drug's popularity, there had only been two confirmed cases of LSD use in the entire state within the past year. In fact, said the article, "Doctors across the state reported the drug is not in use for treatment or research because of its unpredictable side effects." Among the state's doctors quoted in the article was West who said that, while there'd been "a great deal of talk" about the drug, there'd been little use, at least in Oklahoma, as young people there were "still concentrating on alcohol."[170] Although the accuracy of this report is doubtful at best, LSD use probably *was* less frequent in Oklahoma, as, aside from the elephant, a good portion of West's hallucinogenic adventures occurred in California.

West eventually did gain notoriety for advocating the selective prohibition and supply of pharmaceutical drugs to problematic populations as a way of exercising "political control" over those who would engage in "active, organized, vigorous political protest and dissent." Making a direct comparison to Huxley's *Brave New World*, and in a suggestion that sounded a lot like the dystopian vision painted by McVeigh to Steve and certainly could not have made his hippie friends all too happy, West wrote:

> Control can be through prohibition or supply. The total or even partial prohibition of drugs gives the government considerable leverage for other types of control. An example would be the selective application of drug laws permitting immediate search, or "no knock" entry, against selected components of the population such as members of certain minority groups or political organizations. But a government could also supply drugs to help control a population [with] the governing element employing drugs selectively to manipulate the governed in various ways.[171]

In 1964, West, then Head of Psychiatry, Neurology and Behavioral Sciences at Oklahoma University School Of Medicine, along with Dr. Chester M. Pierce, Chief of Psychiatric Services at the Oklahoma City

VA Hospital (who helped West dose Tusko), presented the findings of their study of the lives of nine "negro" protesters, who from 1958 until 1962, opposed unjust racial laws through civil disobedience. West and Pierce found that, for the most part, they went on to lead successful lives, although they tended to focus more on "the race crisis and its ramifications" than they did international, national or even local current events. They had faced many hurdles in their fight for justice however, including "saboteurs, those who consciously or unconsciously try to prolong the conflict rather than resolve it, the cynics, the publicity seekers, political misfits..." As well as the "psychiatric cases, the neurotically guilty whites seeking martyrdom in the Negro cause and neurotically guilty Negros seeking to perpetrate their own oppression of all varieties on both sides and anti-social characters seeking a setting for violence."[172]

There are conflicting stories about West's views on race. It has been reported that after the 1965 riots in Watts, West recommended that particularly bothersome African-Americans and Hispanics undergo chemical sterilization. West continued to study and make horrible recommendations about the proper way of handling rebellious individuals and groups who, according to West, included "Black Power Advocates of the Negro revolt and the psychedelic flower children whose mystical and pharmacological rejection of Western society is perhaps the most profound of all." A recent book, *The Protest Psychosis: How Schizophrenia Became A Black Disease,* details the ways in which psychiatry and psychiatric diagnosis have been used historically as a means of subjugating African-Americans. In the 1960's and 1970's particularly, mainstream psychiatry continuously argued that protest caused schizophrenic symptoms among black folk. The authors offer several examples including the work of Dr. West, whose 1964 paper in the *International Journal Of Social Psychiatry* asserted that civil rights activism led "negroes" to become delusional and even develop "dangerous, aggressive feelings." On the other hand, according to West's wife, "Jolly appointed the first blacks to the [OU] medical faculty," and they both regularly participated in Civil Rights demonstrations.[173] Further, West later involved himself in South Africa's apartheid problem, testifying on behalf of political prisoners there, although some have argued that was a cover for, of course, nefarious activities.

Either way, the topic of homegrown insurgency on the part of any race was of special interest for many researchers during this time – but particularly for West. This interest, along with his other specialized and obscure areas of expertise (hypnosis, brainwashing, dissociation, and the psychological effects of captivity), led to West's involvement in a number of high-profile criminal cases. Pioneer of, participant in, and at the center of the U.S. government's attempt to create perfect Manchurian Candidates through inducing structured dissociation, his long and prolific career helped spawn legends about not only West himself, but also a sizable body of mind control narratives of which those about McVeigh are only a small fraction. During the 1960s and 1970s, West examined and became personally familiar with America's most notorious criminal faces of his generation, including Jack Ruby, Sirhan Sirhan and Patty Hearst.

In March 1964, a jury convicted Jack Ruby of murdering Lee Harvey Oswald and sentenced him to death. Afterwards, Ruby began making public claims about a much larger conspiracy surrounding JFK's assassination. He wished to reveal details about it, he said, but fearing for his life, could not unless he was transferred to a prison location anywhere but in the state of Texas. In late April 1964, Ruby's newly appointed defense attorney, Hubert Winston Smith, argued that the pre-trial mental evaluations that found Ruby amnesiac but sane, and included a spinal tap, electroencephalographs, as well as other neurological, and physical exams, had been inadequate.

Because of this, his trial attorneys had found themselves in a situation they said was "similar to one where vital evidence is locked up in a safe and the combination lost." They had been able to argue that Ruby acted in a fugue or dissociative state, but never got much further than that. Smith said that since then, evidence had surfaced that Ruby had "either an organic amnesia … or has repressed into his unconscious memory certain details" about his killing of Oswald. Smith asked the judge to remand Ruby to a hospital where a qualified doctor such as, let's say, Dr. Jolyon West, could perform further psychological evaluations of Ruby, this time using hypnosis and truth serum. A new evaluation, if performed by West, would, Smith argued, "very likely … retrieve repressed material" that would then allow him "to provide the court and society at large with invaluable evidence." The defense was granted permission to retain West.

About a week later, according to Sheriff Bill Decker, Ruby asked a prison guard for a drink of water and, just as the guard was about to retrieve it for him, Ruby deliberately rammed his head into his cell wall. Ruby was rushed to the hospital for x-rays. but after being returned to his cell, attempted to rip his clothing into strips. West visited Ruby later that evening. At this point, Ruby's sister, Eva Grant of Dallas, requested that the judge empanel a new jury to determine whether her brother was currently insane. Just before a scheduled hearing on the issue, Dr. West told reporters that Ruby was "preoccupied with delusions of persecution of Jews" and was "obviously psychotic." Still, even after Ruby's head banging and West's opinion, the judge refused to hospitalize him.[174]

In late May 1964, Ruby's defense attorney demanded an immediate sanity hearing, to which the prosecutor replied that there was "no need whatsoever" for such a hearing because Ruby was sane. The judge said he would delay ruling on the issue until three evaluating psychiatrists submitted their reports. One of the evaluators, Dr. William Beavers, said that Ruby was suffering from "a covert delusional system" that revolved around threats to his "race" and family because of his participation in a larger conspiracy. Dr. West also reported that Ruby was delusional and now believed he was "responsible for the slaughter of millions of Jews" throughout America. The sanity hearing was again delayed, this time based on the reasoning of the prosecutor that if they all just waited until October, Ruby's condition would either have improved or deteriorated to such an extent that there would be no question about his sanity.[175]

On June 7, Supreme Court Justice Earl Warren (heading the ongoing Warren Commission) questioned Ruby in his cell. Ruby requested that Warren allow him (Ruby) to undergo sodium pentothal (truth serum) or a polygraph test. He wanted to tell them the truth of the matter, how he had been "used for a purpose," but had a psychic blocking mechanism similar to "brainwashing" that prevented him from articulating all of the details. Plus, he said, his life was in danger. His "people" were being "tortured and mutilated." In the two weeks after his chat with Warren, Ruby's condition deteriorated rapidly and he was rushed to a hospital where Dr. West met with him. West talked to Ruby for about 90 minutes after which he recommended hospitalization. Ruby, said West, was "in a paranoid state" to a degree that he could not be treated from his prison cell. If he wasn't treated, West warned, Ruby would become hopelessly insane and if that happened, he could not be executed. In 1966, in part based on West's findings that Ruby suffered from a mental illness when he shot Oswald, the Texas Court of Appeals overturned Ruby's conviction and sentencing. Shortly after his visits with West began, Ruby insisted that powerful people were trying to silence him and that they'd poisoned him. In 1967, days before his new trial date, Jack Ruby died of a strangely quick-acting cancer.[176]

During the brief conversation between Jones Team member Andrew Murphy and Dr. West, West spoke briefly about the Ruby case. He said Jack Ruby's prison conditions caused him to become "psychotic" and "deranged" and implied Ruby's case had relevancy to McVeigh's:

> I never did publish my account of the Ruby case. I've been told many times I should because I probably understand Jack Ruby better than anyone else, but I just didn't have the heart to do it at the time, and then after he died, I decided to hell with it. There is no doubt about what he did, but the question [remains as to] why and the circumstances under which he then became mentally deranged, which he wasn't before. He was not a normal person but he wasn't psychotic either, but he did become psychotic afterwards and that's another story. I can describe it if it comes to that.

Over time, the hazy facts surrounding the assassination itself, criticisms of the Warren Commission Report, the manufacturing of public perceptions of the event by various officials and agencies, the claims of Jack Ruby and the involvement of West and his colleagues generated a number of conspiracy theories and ultimately helped usher in an era of public paranoia and distrust.[177] West never did describe "it" that I know of, but certainly in the years to come legends would have West mind-controlling Ruby, as he would, supposedly, do later to McVeigh.

Similar to Timothy McVeigh, and other contemporary "lone gunmen," eyewitnesses told police that, after firing the fatal shots that killed Robert Kennedy on June 4, 1968, Sirhan Sirhan's eyes seemed "peaceful" and he appeared "purged." Upon his arrest, Sirhan made strange comments to authorities, including his remark to one LAPD officer that, "we're all puppets." Sirhan had, and continued to have, no memory of the shooting. A number of mental health experts evaluated Sirhan prior to and after his trial. The pre-trial findings, however, only confused jurors. UC Berkley psychiatrist Bernard Diamond felt that Sirhan was easily hypnotizable, highly suggestible and throughout his life, was subject to "bizarre involuntary dissociative trances." He determined that at the time of the shooting, Sirhan, was "in a twilight state"; "out of contact with reality, in a trance in which he had no voluntary control over his will, his judgment, his feeling or his actions." However, Diamond told jurors, Sirhan had programmed himself through self-hypnosis.[178] Trance or no trance, in April 1969, jurors found him guilty and sentenced him to death, later commuted to life in prison.

Psychiatrists continued to evaluate Sirhan after his conviction and made similar determinations, although not all of them agreed that he had programmed himself. Among them was Dr. Eduard Simson-Kallas, Chief Psychologist at San Quentin Prison. In Simson's opinion Sirhan had been hypnotically "prepared by someone," other than Sirhan himself. After noting his conclusions in a report, the prison warden ordered Simson to cease his visits with Sirhan, after which Simson resigned. Years later, Simson wrote that, "Whatever the truth … it still remains locked in Sirhan's other, still anonymous mind." Adding to this was Columbia University psychiatrist, Dr. Herbert Spiegel, an internationally esteemed leading authority in hypnosis. Sirhan's post-trial legal team consulted with Spiegel, sharing with him all of Sirhan's previous psychiatric reports and other information. Spiegel believed that Sirhan had been programmed by a group of people; "one senior programmer and many accessories," part of a larger project "very carefully designed by people who were expert in brainwashing victims."

After the consultations, Spiegel filed an affidavit with his attorney in the event that something was to happen to him. In the years to come, respectable psychiatrists who evaluated Sirhan echoed the sentiments of Simson and

Spiegel. A motion, filed by Sirhan's attorneys in November 2011, argued that Sirhan "was an involuntary participant in the crimes being committed because he was subjected to sophisticated hypno-programming and memory implantation techniques which rendered him unable to consciously control his thoughts and actions at the time the crimes were being committed."[179]

Throughout the years, allegations have arisen about West's involvement with Sirhan Sirhan (either before or after his arrest) and while unsubstantiated, given the period, the region, the issues at hand, and West's areas of expertise, it's certainly possible. A textbook dedicated to West recounts the story of a patient who arrived at the UCLA hospital. The first-year resident examining the patient had a difficult time diagnosing the problem, and called in the Chair of the department, Dr. West. West, who published a chapter on dissociative identity disorders in 1967 that was, we are told "years ahead of its time," took a great interest in the patient and eventually discovered they suffered from Multiple Personality Disorder (DID's most severe manifestation). The resident felt very grateful for West's help, they wrote, because "in 1971, only four faculty members at UCLA had ever seen a multiple personality patient" but luckily, "Dr. West had experience in this area."[180] Lucky indeed.

However, even if rumors that West had some type of involvement with Sirhan are untrue, the allegations are understandable given that another MK ULTRA-funded expert hypnotist who later worked directly under West at UCLA, Dr. William Kroger, bragged of having hypnotized Sirhan. One author noted that the final chapters of Kroger's 1976 book, *Hypnosis and Behavior Modification: Imaginary Conditioning*, "describe the chilling possibilities offered by combining hypnosis with electrical stimulation of the brain, brain implants, and conditioning." Similar allusions were supposedly made by another Korean War-era MK ULTRA architect in the Los Angeles area, Dr. William J. Bryan. Byran was put on probation by the California Board Of Medical Examiners in 1969, after they learned of his hypnosis and sexual abuse of a number of female patients.

Come to think of it, West was a pretty persuasive guy with the ladies himself, as noted by, among others, his son, who commented on his father's not so secret philandering. Rumors about West's own proclivity to combine hypnosis with sexual abuse linger. While I do not know the truth of this one way or the other, I once met a sociologist at an academic conference whose family had been close to the West family. She fondly remembered Dr. West, but did mention his numerous illegitimate children, the product of his flings with his secretaries and students. One wonders what (or who) in the world could have ever persuaded these women to engage in such behavior. Well, moving on.

In 1974, the Symbionese Liberation Army (SLA) kidnapped heiress Patty Hearst, kept her confined in a dark closet and subjected her to continuous verbal, physical and sexual abuse. Eventually, Hearst adopted the ideology of her captors and took the alter-identity of "Tania," who went on to participate in the SLA's criminal escapades, including a bank robbery, for which she served 22 months in prison. In her participation in the SLA crimes, Hearst adopted more than one alter-identity and donned many disguises. During her 1975 bank robbery trial, both the defense and prosecution called in several expert psychologists and psychiatrists. Testifying in Hearst's defense were preeminent MK-funded notables Robert Jay Lifton, Dr. Martin Orne and Dr. Jolly West, all three leading experts on dissociative pathologies and recurring villains in mind-control narratives. (Orne wrote the preface to Kroger's 1976 book). Like West, Lifton and Orne made extensive studies of dissociative states in returning American POW's during the Korean War.[181]

West interviewed Hearst for over 40 hours after her arrest and concluded that the SLA's use of DDD techniques (which he had developed) led Hearst to form multiple alter-egos. Her captors' treatment had created intense confusion, fear and anxiety, causing her to develop "dissociate features" including lapses of memory, dream-like states and a sense of unreality. Her desire to survive her ordeal led to the symbolic death of her former self, and the formation of a new self who could effectively deal with the demands of her captors. West compared Hearst's zombie-like demeanor to that of Cardinal Mindszenty, and said she had the "Mindszenty look," often seen on the faces of individuals subjected to mock trials. Lifton, West, and Orne all argued, in their own ways, that the trauma Hearst suffered during her captivity (like McVeigh's traumas) had produced dissociative states, comparing them to shell shock and "survivor's syndrome" experienced by concentration camp victims and POW's. Similarly, court-appointed psychiatrist Margaret Singer, a controversial close colleague of West, Orne and Lifton, described Hearst as a "zombie," as did the jurors at her trial. Historian William Graebner wrote that the defense experts offered numerous depictions of Hearst: "Patty as Korean War POW, Patty as Vietnam veteran, Patty as concentration camp survivor, Patty as a Communist victim, Patty as a zombie."[182]

What was at stake, in a philosophical sense, was an age-old issue that also applies to McVeigh: the "problem of the mutable self" and the problems of identity performance that have resulted from "modernity's disruption" of normal expectations concerning "community, tradition, and bedrock expectations about one's life and what one could expect from it." Nobody, including Patty Hearst, knew who the hell they were, or who they were supposed to be anymore. It fell to jurors and the public to decide whether Hearst had acted of her free will or if she, as a means of survival, became another person altogether and, if so, whether it had been the "other person" who committed the crimes she was accused of. Ultimately, the jurors concluded that even as "Tania," Patty Hearst had retained agency for her illegal actions and thus found her guilty, with mitigating circumstances.[183]

For some though, West's involvement with Hearst takes a more suspicious tone, given his later involvement with behavior modification experiments at Vacaville Medical Prison in California. It turns out that Hearst's abductor and the head of the SLA, Donald Defreeze, had been one of the subjects in these experiments. So for them, what was at stake was something else entirely, mainly these crazy shrinks running around with a *carte blanche* to perform bizarre experiments and trying to control everyone.

Throughout the 1960's and 70's, researchers working in defense intelligence initiatives expanded on the "national security" related work of West and friends. The DOD, Federal Bureau of Narcotics (FBN), U.S. Army, Office of Naval Intelligence and other agencies continued the search for methods and technologies of interrogation, control and coercion and, in the process, pioneered newer, more effective uses for mind-altering drugs, other chemical and biological agents, radiology, isolation, high-frequency radio waves, drug-induced comas, electro-shock, lobotomy, psychosurgeries, and brain implants. Yes, brain implants.

The surgical implanting of remote radio frequency-controlled devices in human brains had begun earlier. In 1952, while at Yale, Dr. Jose Delgado wrote his first paper on implanting electrodes into human brains and designed the "stimoceiver," a device that, when surgically embedded in the brain, received signals that could stimulate a wide range of behaviors in humans and animals and induce powerful emotions, hallucinations or physical sensations, including pain. Among Delgado's achievements was his shocking 1964 experiment involving placing a stimoceiver in the brain of a bull, controlling its aggressive rage and stopping it in mid-charge with the press of a button. Delgado also tested his brain implants on, among others, children and mental patients.[184]

Although he wasn't aware of the extent, Delgado was not alone in his efforts to control humans remotely through implanted electrodes. It was the topic of several CIA and military funded research projects. In 1960, after Saul Sell, head of the Dept. of Medical Psychology at the USAF School of Aviation Medicine (1948-1958) and soon to be founder of Christian Texas University's Institute of Behavioral Research (1962), proposed building a computer that would read and translate brainwaves, he received CIA funding to research "Techniques for Activating the Human Organism by Remote Electronic Means." CIA reports detail that remote control implants were operational in animals by 1961 and the future of their use in humans looked bright.[185]

By 1963 and continuing in the years to come, another implant enthusiast, Tulane University psychiatrist, Dr. Robert Heath, was tinkering around with the use of brain implants to (among other things) cure homosexuality and achieved at least a modicum of behavioral control in this way. Subjects of these implant experiments were not asked for, nor did they give, informed consent. They included the usual cadré of drug addicts, prisoners, sexual deviants, mental patients, orphans and minorities. Despite how crazy it may have sounded in the mid 1990's, such implants were no secret and results of some experiments were published in leading academic journals.

In fact, the emerging discipline of cybernetics (the melding of machine and man) and the creation of cyborgs (humans whose functions can be controlled through electronic or electro-mechanical means) were enthusiastically endorsed by CIA Director Richard Helms. In a 1964 memo to the Warren Commission, Helms reported that the Soviets were already well aware of the fact that cybernetics could "be used in molding of a child's character, the inculcation of knowledge and techniques, the amassing of experience, the establishment of social behavior patterns ... all functions which can be summarized as control of the growth processes of the individual."[186] In the late 1960's and early 1970's, thanks to major government funding, the development of technologies of remote control was rapid.

During the Vietnam War, a CIA neuro-surgeon under the guise of a front company called Scientific Engineering Institute, implanted electrodes in the brains of Vietcong prisoners and through this sent radio frequencies that caused defecation and vomiting in their subjects. The CIA agents then placed them in a room, gave them knives, and then set about stimulating various portions of the brain in an effort to induce them to become violent. After the experiment ended, U.S. Army Special Forces Green Berets, who provided security during the experiments, took them out back, shot them and burned their bodies. In 1970, General William Westmoreland, commander of all U.S. forces during the Vietnam War, predicted, "on the battlefield of the future, enemy forces will be located, tracked and targeted almost instantaneously through the use of data links, computer assisted intelligence evaluation, and automated fire control."[187] History has shown that all of this hard work paid off.

The year before, in a 1969 memo written to the National Security Agency (NSA), Delgado, who by this time had greatly improved upon his stimoceiver, predicted the use of implantable two-way receiving/transmitting devices in the brain to send satellite-relayed messages, what the military now calls "synthetic telepathy." In the NSA memo Delgado described these as "nearly microscopic receiver devices that collect, and transmit audio, color, video and location coordinates" relayed through satellites to command centers, which could then send encrypted messages back to the receiver "in the form of post-hypnotic suggestion." Delgado's memos were pleas for funding. He believed, as outlined in his book published the same year (1969), *Physical Control Of The Mind: Toward A Psychocivilized Society*, that the ills of mankind could be cured through the establishment of a society of technological control in which brains were manipulated from cradle to grave. No dystopia, for Delgado, such methods presented "a process of mental liberation and self-domination which is a continuation of our evolution." The "future man," he said, would be happier, smarter, and more efficient. The only question, for Delgado, was "who is going to exert the power of behavior control?"[188] Who, indeed?

Delgado's work was heavily cited in the 1970 book, *Violence and the Brain*, written by psychiatrists Vernon H. Mark (Harvard) and Frank R. Ervin (UCLA). The book, an aggressive plea for funding, succinctly outlines at least some of the already operational applications for brain implants and EEG brain mapping to predict, prevent and induce violent behaviors including murder and riots. For Mark and Ervin, violence was much more of a brain problem than a socio-cultural one. The year prior, in 1969, West left Oklahoma and headed to California to begin his new positions as the Director of UCLA's Neuropsychiatric Institute and Chair of the Department of Psychiatry and Bio-behavioral Sciences at the UCLA School of Medicine. His enthusiasm for Mark and Ervin's philosophies and methods soon landed him in hot water (more on that soon).

In late 1971, a Senate Subcommittee chaired by Sam J. Ervin, Jr. (no relation to Dr. Ervin) began an investigation into "individual rights and the federal role in behavior modification." The committee was catalyzed after realizing that several federally funded programs already under investigation pointed: "collectively to the emergence of a new technology of behavior control which posed serious questions [about the] protection of the constitutional rights of individuals."[189]

A year later, in 1972, the Hastings Center, a leading bioethics research institute, held their "Conference on Control of Human Behavior Through Drugs." The topics of discussion were ethical questions relating to "personal liberty and behavior control technology" and the challenges of both to the accepted "medical model" paradigm. The Hastings Center's report detailing the conference explained that science now possessed technological surveillance methods and means to control mood, emotion, desire and ultimately, behavior; the methods to do so becoming "increasingly effective" at an "accelerating" rate. Included were "psychological conditioning techniques, psycho-pharmaceutical discoveries and neurological methods for controlling brain functions electronically or chemically [which] singly or in combination, conditioning, drugs, and brain implantations are the most important..." It was expected that these methods would be implemented "in the very near future." Newer biotechnologies on display at the conference included "electronic chips, smaller than a little fingernail, which can be implanted under the scalp to serve as trans-mitters/receivers for electrodes buried deep in the brain." While possible, reversal of procedures such as this was admittedly difficult.[190]

The messiness of the brain implants didn't even matter that much though because, by the 1960's, viable methods of controlling humans through other means had been developed and were in an early stage of operational use. Not mentioned in the 1972 Hastings report, were other government-funded projects that much earlier had sought to and even-tually did develop psychotronic, telemetric, electromagnetic, bioelectric, and other energy-based weapons. Such methods, even in their earlier stages, could induce emotions, sounds, words, sentences, thoughts or even behaviors. Perfected in the decades to come, and dubbed "the sound of silence" by some in the intelligence community, today they are com-monly referred to as "non-lethal" weapons and can be used against groups (crowd control) and, through brain mapping, can target specific individ-uals. In 1972, the potential social control and military applications were (and remain) endless.

The Hastings Report did acknowledge that, while such technologies would help quell criminal and "socially deviant" behaviors, as definitions of crime and mental illness expanded and the technologies grew more exact and efficient, it would become "more difficult to segregate [the] po-litical or quasi-political implementations from its clearly medical ones. If uncontrollable aggression can be flawlessly controlled, for instance, and the *victim* of it made happier thereby, then its political expression can be just as cured as its personal one, however – by the same technique – and the patient will be grateful afterwards, so who's to object?" These technol-ogies, their users, uses, and regulation touched upon issues of agency, free will, individual vs. collective good, and potentially likely political abus-es when, after "some initial coercive step, consent can be flawlessly engi-neered." The questions asked by "the community of experts in psychosur-gery and electrical brain stimulation" about "control over psychosurgery and electrical stimulation of the brain," raised unprecedented social and political dilemmas and consequences and therefore demanded "a redefi-nition of human freedom and other civil rights in very intimate emotion-al, elemental, and biological terms."[191]

Another topic of discussion at the 1972 conference was the use and regulation of drugs as a method of control over both individuals and groups. Drugs, like biotechnologies, had definite, if controversial, mil-itary and political applications. Several participants supported the view that, rather than simply as agents of healing and pain management, the most effective use of such drugs were "as controlling agents when linked with other kinds of social and psychological pressures." Dr. Wayne Evans, representing the U.S. Army Research Institute, spoke of "a developing capacity to deliver drugs to large numbers of the population at a time," and specifically mentioned "anti-riot and anti-aggression gasses."[192]

Just prior to the conference, the Hastings Center had begun a project exploring possible ways to identify violent predispositions and ways of controlling violence through technology, medicine, and psychology in general. The 1972 report and a subsequent report issued a few years later, noted the valuable contributions made to their efforts by West, described as the foremost expert on the uses of exotic drugs for, among other uses, "medication," "behavior reinforcement," "self-exploration [and] counter-intelligence and social control."[193]

Throughout his career, West, patriotic guy that he was, acted as Chief Psychiatrist and Psychiatric Consultant to a number of military and Veteran Administration hospitals throughout the country, and chair of several related policy committees. West was mentioned in several news reports in 1969 and 1970, discussing the inadequacies and underfunding of the VA system and the tendency of doctors to give veterans a "Chemical Brainwash" rather than treat them. In 1969, along with a number of psychiatrists and doctors he worked with, West testified at a Senate Subcommittee about the desperate need to provide services to the growing number of men returning from Vietnam who were flooding VA hospitals. West said that there were "thousands and thousands" of shell-shocked Vietnam veterans drugged up on tranquilizers and walking around in a "chemical cocoon." Men like them, he said, could be seen at "any mental hospital … we are chemically lobotomizing thousands and thousands of patients, and we can keep it up for years … they are easy to identify because the drugs used make them move slowly and stiffly … with an invisible barrier between them and the rest of the world." VA's around the country didn't even compare to those in California, the worst of which, the Brentwood VA, he said, "lagged 20 to 25 years behind current psychiatric trends." (West didn't mention the fact that this particular VA specialized in "psycho-social medicine" and that he happened to work there).

According to West's California colleague and associate, Dr. Russell Lee, what was needed was "a major program of health facilities and services research at 10 to 20 VA hospitals that would then become centers for such research" as well as post-discharge mental hygiene programs. Dr. Stewart Wolf, a colleague and associate of West's from Oklahoma specializing in neuroscience research, also urged the government to approve further funding. A retired Colonel said that many men were coming back from the war with doubts about their reasons for being there to begin with and wondered if it had all been "a cruel hoax, an American tragedy [that left them] holding the bag." The testimony caused quite an alarm and one subsequent editorial remarked that these men had already given so much for their country, and asked if they have "to give their minds, too?"[194]

Apparently they did. The final report of Senator Ervin's Subcommittee investigation (not issued until the end of 1974), found that of all the federally funded behavioral research and modification programs, "the most notable" were those of the Veteran Administration. The report noted some serious concerns about the "extensive involvement" of the VA "in a wide variety of methods of altering the behavior of individuals" that likely violated their rights. VA patients could be (and were) subjected to all manner of techniques meant to alter behavior against their will and despite their objections. Included were experiments on soldiers such as those conducted at Edgewood Chemical Arsenal in Maryland where, from 1952 until 1974, over 7,000 soldiers were, without their consent, administered various drugs such as LSD and exposed to, among other things, radiation. For some reason West forgot to mention this in his "Chemical Cocoon" spiel.

What's more, the committee learned of "numerous psychosurgical operations" that, although performed under the guise of therapy aimed at "producing a more 'normal' human being were in reality, experimental, and no more effective than the lobotomies of the 1950's. These types of surgeries were performed to alter the thoughts, social behaviors, personality and subjective experiences" of the patient. Included was the implanting of electrodes in the brain that could act as "electric amplifiers," to remotely record electric signals and elicit specific behavioral responses. While the committee did not mention West (at least in relation to VA's), he was associated with a handful of the ones they identified as performing such operations. In their 1974 report, the committee acknowledged that it had no idea if such operations continued.[195]

The committee's report did discuss one particularly disturbing account about an otherwise normal and functioning man named "Thomas" who had been hospitalized at a civilian hospital for depression in 1965. The committee did not mention that it was an MK funded hospital, as MKUltra and similar mind control projects were not yet publicly known. Regardless, while Thomas was not psychotic and had never displayed violent tendencies, Dr.'s Vernon Mark and Frank Ervin deemed him incurable and implanted "multiple electrodes" in his brain, telling his mother that he had simply undergone a "minor surgical operation." The doctors removed the implants a year later (or so they said) and Thomas was released from the hospital. Weeks later, now exhibiting severe confusion and disorientation, he was arrested for a minor offense and sent to a VA hospital (where West happened to work). Thomas told the VA doctors that the civilian hospital he'd just been released from was "controlling him [by] microwaves [and] electrodes in his brain." He said they could control his moods and actions, and could turn him "up or down" at will. After hearing his story, the VA doctors, *assumedly* unknowing of what had actually occurred, diagnosed him as schizophrenic, delusional and paranoid and declared him totally disabled.[196] I'm not saying Dr. West tortured this man, but he would soon sing the praises of the men who did and even suggested they come work on his own implant project.

In the meantime, all hell was breaking loose. Or so it seemed. Newspapers throughout the country reported on the cataclysmic level of violence overrunning the streets of America. In fact, there appeared to be "an epidemic of mass murders in California." Experts quoted in the reports told of the current inability but dire need for psychiatry to develop accurate methods of predicting who would become violent or commit violent acts in order to prevent them. Many of the reports quoted leading government funded mind-control doctors who, in retrospect, seemed to be driving the public panic in a desperate attempt to secure more funding which, for a few reasons, was becoming more difficult to obtain.[197]

Then, wouldn't you know it, in January 1973, California Governor Ronald Reagan addressed Congress asking for $1.5 million dollars to help him wage "a new attack on crime" via the creation of the UCLA Center for the Study and Reduction of Violence that, he said, would help "rid society of this cancer of violence." Although there had been other "violence study centers" established throughout the country, the Center was to be the most advanced and far reaching of them all. The Center had been West's idea. He drafted the proposal and, as its architect, he would head and direct it. The Center was West's baby, the culmination and synthesis of his many diverse research topics thus far. Its creation had the blessing and support of a number of high-level state officials and the full support of Gov. Reagan. The overwhelming support for the project came at just the right time as, wrote one UCLA psychiatrist working under West, "federal funds for research support had dried up."[198]

Initially, news reports billed the Center as "an effort to reduce murder, rape, gang wars, assassinations and the battery and abuse of children" to which the Center's proposal (written by West) added, "suicide ... senseless maniacal killings, mass murders ... deadly mayhem on the highways [and] skyjackings." Said the state health and welfare secretary, Dr. Earl Brian, "a lot of things are being done by a lot of people in a lot of places" and the Center would help create a preventative profile of violence prone individuals. It would "bring together the best minds" with the intent of coordinating ongoing research, initiating an array of new studies, and developing practical applications to "predict, control and prevent" the eruptions of those prone to such behavior."[199]

This was important because, as West explained in the Center's proposal, a "veritable plague" of violent incidents were occurring at a higher rate than ever before, a rate that was only increasing and "the specter of unproved attack haunts city-dwellers alone outdoors after dark." To make matters worse, people weren't just hurt by unknown faceless criminal specters, husbands hurt wives, parents hurt children, children hurt other children, people hurt and killed themselves. In these desperate times, desperate measures were called for. Previous and ongoing violence studies tended only to focus on "social conditions, neighborhood problems, and penal reforms." West's Center had no concern for such issues but instead sought to get at the heart (and mind) of the matter.[200] Plans for the Center quickly moved forward.

The Center would be located mainly on the UCLA campus but also at satellite facilities including state mental hospitals. It would be financed by a combination of state and federal funds provided by agencies including the California Council of Criminal Justice, California Department of Mental Hygiene, the Department of Health, and the California Health and Welfare Agency. The bulk of the money, however, would come from the DOJ's Law Enforcement Assistance Agency (LEAA).

There were some problems though. The mind control research network, who for so long enjoyed ample freedom and funding, and of which West was an integral part, had been the subject of bad publicity as of late. While for decades, the public was unaware of horrific government-funded experiments using human guinea pigs, the recent exposure of a couple of them led to a rapid exposure of several additional ones. One such revelation concerned Vacaville Medical Facility, a prison hospital that was to be the Center's primary satellite location but where Clockwork Orange-type activities had been occurring. For years, Vacaville had been a testing ground for the Army's research into diseases endemic to Vietnam, vaccines for "the plague," the effect of pesticides and other chemicals.[201]

In addition, and what brought the facility to the attention of the public, was an ongoing brutal behavior-modification program there in which highly addictive and experimental drugs were tested on non-consenting prisoners that led to at least three deaths and, a year after the Center was proposed, the kidnapping of Patty Hearst. West had already secured the use of the prisoners as test subjects, which probably wasn't difficult, given what had already been going on there.

As additional details of West's proposed Center emerged and the good people of California learned what he was planning for them, a firestorm erupted. This concerned the specific research projects he hoped to initiate, the methods they would incorporate, the populations he hoped to cull test subjects from and the expert staff he recommended to work under him. To begin with, the Center's most intensive work was to occur at a nearby Nike Missile Base, an Army installation with a vast and complex underground network that the Army was prepared to "turn over" for the Center's use. According to West, "it is accessible, but relatively remote ...

securely fenced ... we could put it to very good use ... studies could be carried out there, in an isolated but convenient location of experimental or model programs for the alteration of undesirable behavior."[202]

The Center planned to, among other things: test drugs and hormones that could induce or inhibit violence; conduct comparative studies of violence among certain ethnic groups and determine genetic factors (important for possible eugenic "selective breeding" initiatives) and devise other methods of predicting who, in fact, would become violent later in life. This would come in handy as the Center also planned to assist law enforcement agencies develop a computer database containing profiles on "pre-delinquent children" (whatever that means) who could then be tracked throughout their lives (or worse). No parental consent required. Methods of prediction, modification, and control ("treatment") included solitary confinement, electro-shock, mind-altering drugs, chemotherapy, "programming" individuals with audio and visual stimuli and bio-feedback devices, EEG's and other "electro-physiology" technologies. Currently, wrote West, "it is possible... to arouse violent reactions by applying minute electric stimulation [to deeply buried areas in the brain.]" and "to record bioelectrical changes in the brains of freely moving subjects, through the use of remote monitoring techniques." One of the major tasks of the Center was to improve on these technologies for "large scale screening" of the broader population. This was, he explained, "essential" in order to identify the potentially violent people and those with whom "they interact" so that "corrective and preventative measures can be undertaken, for their own protection and for the safety of society."[203]

Who would be the good doctor's lucky test subjects for the Center's many ambitious projects? They would be culled from the usual mix of prisoners, patients at "mental hospitals" and other "special community facilities," sexual deviants, sex offenders, "hyperkinetic children," and unspecified members "in the community ... or wherever practical." West also made specific mention of neighborhoods with predominantly black and Hispanic populations.[204] All of this came to light in March 1973 when West's proposal was leaked and caused concern, to say the least, but what really put a cramp in his brain-child (pun intended) was the whole brain implant thing. Although he denied it later, West's proposal clearly contained his intent to implant all manner of behavior technologies into the minds of test subjects.

The resulting public outcry was intense. West had recommended some of the shadiest MKUltra luminaries in the fields of social sciences, humanities, law enforcement and education (among others) to help run the program. Even without yet knowing the extent of the CIA/military backed research that had occurred, eyebrows were archly raised. When state officials said that the "best minds" could be tapped to help with the

Center, they referred to people like UCLA Drs. Barton Ingraham and Gerald W. Smith, who wanted to put "permanent radio receiver transmitters in the brains of parolees" linked to a computer. They could be perpetually tracked and monitored and if the computer detected the "probability of misbehavior," an electrical shock would be sent straight to their brain and alert police to their whereabouts. As it stood, a number of prototype devices of this sort were already being field tested. Also included on the list was Dr. Ralph K. Schwizgebel, author of *Psychotechnology: Electronic Control Of The Mind* (1972), who "conducted substantial research into" and whose book described the present and potential use of brain implants to determine and control "the location, activities, and even thoughts" of individuals.[205]

While the list is extensive, among his A-Team, West also hoped to include Drs. Vernon Mark and Frank Ervin, authors of *Violence And The Brain*, who implanted the electrodes into the heads of non-consenting subjects including, among others, the aforementioned Thomas. Ervin, Mark, and another notorious mind scientist, Dr. William Sweet, had previously sought funds for the Center on behalf of West from a Congressional appropriations committee but, in the words of the Senate report, were denied after an investigation discovered, "the shoddy operation they were running and the scientific invalidity of the approach they were taking."

By "invalid," the subcommittee may have referred to the arguments of Drs. Sweet, Mark and Ervin that rioting minorities probably had brain damage, easily fixable through their particular "treatment." By "shoddy," they explicitly did refer to the fact that when these doctors bothered to get consent from patients, they did so during a time when their brains were being "stimulated" and/or that their treatments resulted in the death and permanent insanity of more than one patient. Even Jose Delgado (of stimoceiver fame) had called their work "sloppy."[206]

It turns out, the main funding source, LEAA, (who funded Sweet, Ervin and Mark) was even more lax with their ethical guidelines concerning the use of psychosurgery and brain implants than the VA and their involvement with the Center is what really peaked the Senate Subcommittee's interest. Their 1974 report noted no less than 537 ongoing LEAA behavior modification initiatives. Further, West's proposal contained no mention of ethical safeguards that would be established to protect the rights of test subjects. Why would it? He'd been working without such guidelines his entire career.

In April 1973, the month after the Center's unsavory details emerged, UCLA and Jolly West became the targets of protests. One news outlet sarcastically reported that those who opposed brain surgery as a way of treating violence could themselves become violent at an upcoming protest of the Center. During a press conference, two Berkley psychiatrists said the Center was "a political effort hiding behind the supposed neutrality of science." Terry Kupers, a physician and fellow in community psychiatry at the UCLA Neuropsychiatric Institute, said the Center's proposed study on child abuse and other topics could serve as a "Trojan Horse" by covering up what he felt to be "highly dangerous projects" and would undoubtedly lead to a "1984-type scenario."[207] Protest groups called the Center "racist, sexist and fascist" and a student body referendum voted to condemn the center. Three UCLA students were jailed after chaining themselves to the furniture in Dr. West's office.

After the controversy broke, the California State Senate Committee on Health and Welfare held hearings about West's intended magnum opus. One of the most vocal critics included Senator Sam Ervin, whose Subcommittee report on federally funded behavior modification programs noted the high likelihood that the Center would develop technologies and methods that would be used by "government authorities" for political purposes. The report urged UCLA to avoid becoming a place where "politicians obtain the techniques for scientific pacification of our population."[208]

Soon, esteemed professionals associated with the Center began to distance themselves from it. The LEAA withdrew its funding from the Center and announced that it would curtail all "biomedical and behavioral research immediately" until further notice. However, in reality, they dropped only 2 or 3 of the 537 ongoing ethically dubious projects under their direction. Interestingly, years later, a UCLA colleague described West in almost worshipful tones in his essay "Medal Ethics." He wrote (with not the least bit of sarcasm), "On the local scene a major factor in the shift of interest in medical ethics has been [the result of] the quiet support and encouragement that Jolly West has given in the field of human values in medicine." He then goes on to say something even more perplexing, when he recalls how, in 1973, he was approached by "a group known as the Medical Faculty Wives Club" who asked him to organize a panel about medical ethics. He naturally sought West's assistance in this matter and West "promptly advised me to have Frank Ervin" speak on the panel, as Ervin had recently been working on plans for the Center with West and "was very much versed in ethical dilemmas in the practice of medicine."[209]

The project, at least as far as public funding was concerned, was scrapped, although one of the would-be directors of the Center told reporters that private foundations had shown a great interest and predicted it would be fully funded by private organizations within two years. Although West changed the name of the Center to the "Project for Study of Life Threatening Behavior," and continued to revise his proposal, reportedly

9 times by 1978, what he stated versus what he intended became increasingly dubious. West even appointed a respected UCLA doctor to act as an ethical oversight director, but the doctor quickly resigned. Another UCLA psychiatrist, who worked closely with West, in his recounting of the subsequent controversy over the Center, remarked that of course the Center was to focus on low income and ethnic minority individuals because, after all, those populations were overrepresented in crime and prison statistics. The writer then derided those silly people who thought the Center would perform unethical experiments or feared the potential political abuses of the Center's work. What they learned, he said, was that one has to be very careful of the "disastrous effect" of publicity when it comes to proposing experimental research, "especially if the experiments involve human subjects, and particularly if they have some relevant application to political-social life."[210]

Eventually, West's long awaited project died for good, reportedly for lack of funding; hence, remarked one news article, "it appears that violence will continue to remain an enigma and the rapist a cipher." Rape might have become non-existent and Jolly West may have achieved his dreams, if it weren't for those meddling hippies, who he claimed to understand so well. West later said that the Center's demise "was the most frustrating experience of my career," a result of accusations, all of which were "utter nonsense," that had originated with "ironically, many [of the same] liberal organizations I belonged to."[211]

Revelations about the Center and other brutal government-funded experiments led to Congressional investigations and hearings in 1975 and 1976, and a few additional hearings and investigations in the years to come. During this time, the existence of MKUltra and related programs became known, but the full details remain hidden, as CIA Director Richard Helms ordered the bulk of the files destroyed. One can only imagine what they contained.[212] The official hearings surrounding harmful government experiments, as with most official hearings and investigations, were limited in the time periods they examined (always ten or more years in the past, never on present projects), as well as the full scope of the projects. They characteristically tended to avoid some of the more gruesome allegations, including the sexual abuse of children in mind-control projects.

While the torture, brainwashing and interrogation methods involved were *publicly* disavowed after the 1972 Congressional Hearings, during the Reagan Administration, such practices gained favor once more, specifically in areas such as Honduras, Nicaragua, Ecuador, Guatemala, and El Salvador. The CIA's KUBARK manual, containing "the principle coercive techniques of interrogation" gave birth to the even more horrendous

1983 *Human Resource Exploitation Manual*, used, like its predecessor, to instruct the security forces of third-world military dictatorships in the fine dark arts of enhanced interrogation. Throughout South and Central American countries, disappearing, torture and murder of dissidents became commonplace. Interestingly, West, whose methodologies were contained in both the 1963 and 1983 manuals, told reporters in 1985 that his efforts were now concentrated on setting up a center at UCLA to study victims of torture, most notably the flocks of Asian and Latin American immigrants fleeing repressive governments. "There are probably more torture victims in [Southern California] than any other place in the world, except in those countries where torture is still sanctioned, officially or unofficially," he remarked with an irony completely lost on the reporter.[213]

Today, the direct lineage of the CIA/military funded activities of West and friends during the Cold War can be seen in the practices now (in part) known to have occurred at Guantanamo Bay, Abu Ghraib and other "black" sites used for interrogation and torture in the Global War On Terror (GWOT). Detainees were (and likely still are) subjected to a wide range of psychological warfare tactics meant to extract information, sometimes at undisclosed locations in countries with little to no human rights laws. Either way, they get treated to some of the best interrogation methods that Special Forces SERE training has to offer. The first of the "high value" detainees, Abu Zabaydah, was captured in Pakistan and taken to a secret Thai prison where, according to his interrogator (a CIA contractor and SERE psychologist), he was "treated like a dog." Forced to lie naked in a box he came to call his "tiny coffin" for weeks at a time, in combination with other well documented routine interrogation horrors, he was given what one CIA officer called the "Clockwork Orange kind of approach." It worked insofar as he confessed to all manner of horrifying terrorist plots including plans to blow up "American banks, supermarkets, malls, the Statue Of Liberty, the Golden Gate Bridge, and nuclear power plants" but was unsuccessful insofar as none of the things he confessed to were true.[214] The old Mindszenty trick.

Interrogation (and just routine treatment for that matter) at Guantanamo Bay, Abu Ghraib and other detention sites includes (but is not limited to) repetitive blasting of obnoxious music and sounds, waterboarding, forced standing, sleep deprivation, beatings, sexual humiliation; the entire gamut of DDD coercion methods, really. While first reported in 2004, only recently has attention focused on other, less pleasant practices including rape of women and children (captured with their parents). Reported Seymour Hersh, "The women were passing messages saying, "Please come and kill me, because of what's happened." Basically, "what happened," happened to women who were arrested with their children, and in cases that have been recorded, said Hersh, "[t]he boys were sodomized with the cameras rolling. The worst about all of them is the soundtrack of the boys shrieking that your government has. They are in total terror it's going to come out." In 2011, the rape of men was added to the list.[215] Said Cofer Black, head of CIA counter-terrorism in 2001, "After 9/11, the gloves came off." (Were they ever really on?)

In this political environment, psychologists and psychiatrists picked up better paying gigs working as interrogators or interrogation consultants, an activity fully supported by influential professional organizations like the American Psychological Association [APA] and American Psychiatric Association; even if their methods violated the Geneva Convention. This should come as no surprise, given the sordid history of many past APA presidents' and high ranking members' involvement in MK type research and really, who better to help disorient newly captured terrorist prisoners? In fact, the APA remains the only group of professionals who have not wholly condemned the use of torture, and in fact have "stricter, more specific standards for the treatment of laboratory animals than for human subjects such as [GITMO] detainees." According to psychologist Frank Summers, this is because the APA knows better than to bite the funding hand that feeds them. Their dependency on the military and defense establishment for the funding and therefore the growth of their field leads to a "blind loyalty" and the defense and justification of abusive interrogation practices and professional penalization of those who speak out against this policy. "Indeed," wrote Michael Welch, a professor of criminology at Rutgers University, "the genealogy of modern torture reveals that its theoretical foundations strongly depend on behavioral and psychological research," of the type that the highly respected members of the American Psychological and Psychiatric Associations who oversee and administer it are well aquatinted with. Not just that, but abusive psychological and psychiatric methods that originate with and are at first contained within the military, have a way of seeping into and becoming institutionalized by the broader fields as practiced in civilian realms.[216]

Not long after the Global War on Terror began, the Defense Department called on inconvenient eyewitness hypnotist, Dr. Michael Gelles, and his military team of non-clinical psychologists (NCIS) to form a Behavioral Science Consultation Team to "establish rapport with detainees." Apparently, this was supposed to curtain potential and ongoing abuses while still extracting valuable information. Gelles trained interrogators and in some instances assisted in interrogations at GITMO and other sites where "reversed" SERE techniques were used against POWs. He would later note that, even after it became clear that abusive SERE methods were too costly in the court of public opinion, it was hard to put the brakes on. For some, it was too easy and too addicting to brutalize other people. The problem, explained Gelles, was that "once you take the dogs off the leash, you cannot put them back on."

In a 2003 essay co-authored by Gelles, he argued that it is ridiculous to expect psychologists and other mental health experts working in national security fields to follow ethical guidelines expected of others in their profession. Gelles himself has made it clear that he does not believe that psychologists participating in these scenarios should be sanctioned (by a court of law or by professional associations like the APA). Rather, he says, he believes in "the accounting of history" not "an accountability of individuals."[217]

After representing Timothy McVeigh, attorney Randy Coyne went on to represent, among others, a handful of GWOT POW's, including at least one "high value" detainee and detailed the problematic nature of representing so-called terrorists within the "Orwellian labyrinth of security rules" that renders any attempt to do so a nearly impossible "ordeal." The majority of inmates, he said, had never committed known hostile acts against the U.S., or anyone else for that matter, unless "fleeing from American forces qualifies as a 'hostile act.'"[218]

For his part, McVeigh's favorite head-shrinker and Dr. Jolly West's pupil, Dr. John Smith, having closed his private practice in Oklahoma City in 2004, took a position at Fort Bragg, where he helped soldiers returning from Iraq and Afghanistan work through some of the issues they developed there. In 2008, Smith began to appear at academic conferences and in news articles to discuss "the psychological impact of being a guard at Guantanamo Prison," which he called "an overlooked group of victims." His case study concerned a guard who developed such severe PTSD that two other psychiatrists gave up on him and referred him to Smith. Apparently, detainees brutalized the guard. Smith said the prisoners "threw feces and urine on him," mocked him and even had the audacity to try and pressure the guard into sneaking out letters to their families. This type of behavior left the guard "confused and terrified." He did, Smith acknowledged, participate in their torturous interrogations, but the sessions only resulted in the detainees' "psychotic reactions: bizarre screaming and crying," leaving the poor guard all the more stressed out and causing him to cry as well.

After treating this guard, an influx of others sought out Smith's services. Luckily for the guards, in January 2009, President Obama promised to close Gitmo and other CIA "black sites" within a year, announcing "I can say without exception or equivocation that the United States will not torture."[219] As discussed earlier, drones are more effective for dealing with known terrorists. As of May 2016, the detainees remain at Gitmo. It seems nobody really knows what to do with them. Certainly, they can't just be allowed to walk around willy-nilly, after so many years of abuse.

Speaking of violence, in the years after the Center closed, West bravely continued his strange career as a researcher, media commentator and government-appointed expert. In the 1980's, besides his never realized plans of opening a torture victim center at UCLA, West spoke at and chaired exclusive American Psychiatric Association conference sessions, where he expounded upon such topics as "Multiple Personality: Diagnosis And Treatment" and "Terrorism And Group Influence: The Psychodynamics Of Terrorism."[220] He ended up acting as the chair of the APA's Task Force On Terrorism, whatever that entails. He then set about pissing off Scientologists (with all his talk about cults) as well as self-professed victims of child sexual abuse and implanted false memories.

In 1994, West was one of a handful of experts appointed by Congress to the Institute of Medicine Committee to Review the Health Consequences of Service During Gulf War, a good fit, given the experimental nature of the war itself. The next year he got a call from the Jones Team about their dissociated patient Tim McVeigh, dejected about the conditions of his confinement and for some reason unable to remember a whole slew of important things. There was probably no better person to consult.

Maybe I've gotten West all wrong. A psychiatric textbook dedicated to his career written by close colleagues and students of his, praise him. He was "a driving force in our profession," "an implacable foe of every form of discrimination," not one to be tainted by "all the sleaze and corruption that appears to have affected the American society at many different levels," "a shining example of [the] profession," a true light in the darkness despite all those "false charges that he was an operative of the Central Intelligence Agency" (the only time the agency is listed in the book).[221]

Perhaps not surprising then were the psychiatric and psychological professional societies' glowing obituaries of Dr. West. Upon his death in 1999, they honored him for his contributions to research and clinical practice that included, among others, a better understanding of the effects of inhumane acts, social violence, sleep deprivation, mind-altering hallucinogenic drugs, hallucinations in general, hypnosis, suggestibility, pain perception and dissociative states and dreams. He was, we are told, "the outline of an American success story," who, guided by "egalitarian principles ... battled ceaselessly for individual freedom and dignity, opposing prejudice, bias, bigotry, violence, torture, and the subjugation, punishment, and mistreatment of others by governments.... He took the side of the poor, minorities, children, the disenfranchised, the mentally ill, the uneducated, and the weak." A memorial fund in his name was established, as was the "Award for Excellence in Psychiatry." (Did anybody besides the hippies even read his Center proposal!?) Newspaper articles did at least note that that he was, in fact, "an expert on cults, torture and brainwashing." Said one colleague, "above all, [Jolly was] a colorful figure, an alive person who loved being on the stage."[222]

West appears in many pivotal landmark episodes in American history, real, imagined, or just alleged. Here is West at POW brainwashing camps; at black sites conducting experiments on U.S. soldiers; handling America's most notoriously legendary assassins and patsies, terrorists and spies; with cults who "brainwash" soon to be dead congregants, including Jones Town, Waco and Heaven's Gate; fighting those who might implant false memories or alternately implanting false memories himself. Here is West hobnobbing with America's Foremost Mind-Controlled "Hypo-Programmed" Amnesiac Sex Slaves. My FOIA requests about West, meant to help clarify fact from legend, have been unsuccessful. It turns out that many government records about him were destroyed in a fire. Nothing like a good fire.

Despite all the humanitarian rhetoric of West and other officials about predicting and preventing violence and monitoring those who did or would perhaps someday act violently, West's proposed Center For The Study And Reduction Of Violence was, in actuality, in the words of one headline, a dystopic "Chamber of Horrors," and a rather racist one at that. West's Center was a nightmare of epic proportions, but there was a method to his madness. Rebecca Lemov described West's ultimate goal as "access to total knowledge: He spoke of building a massive databank of consciousness itself, which would consist of bioelectrical recordings – gathered through electromyography, electro-oculography, rheoencephlography, and CAT scans – subsequently analyzed and coded, then stored in a centralized location such as the National Institute of Mental Health or the National Medical Library. The dreams of knowledge and power that had fueled human engineering for decades were propelled forward."[223]

West tends to be remembered either as a bold yet benevolent pioneer and progressive humanitarian who sought to liberate mankind or a shadowy malevolent clandestine operator and pioneer of some of the most frightening types of invisible chains meant to control and enslave humankind. In this more disturbing depiction he becomes the "mad scientist" who implanted a "chip" into McVeigh's head or rear end, depending.

PART FOUR
Calspan: Rise of The Robots
& The Database That Could

There will come a time when it isn't "They're spying on me through my phone" anymore. Eventually, it will be, "My phone is spying on me."

– Phillip K. Dick, mid 1970's

We monitor many frequencies. We listen always. Came a voice, out of the babel of tongues, speaking to us. It played us a mighty dub.

– William Gibson, *Neuromancer*, 1984

Brainwashing became a term applied to every circumstance in which one person was influenced by others to change his behavior or thinking. And when a word comes to mean too much, it loses what value it may have had. Brainwashing isn't a term I use myself, except in order to dismiss it and then focus on what really happened.

– Dr. Louis Jolyon West, 1985

After World War II, an increasing number of fictional and nonfictional "conspiracy narratives" emerged, many of them displaying what cultural theorist Timothy Melley termed "Agency Panic," an "intense anxiety about the apparent loss of autonomy or self-control." The first of two major defining features of Agency Panic is an "uncertainty about the causes of individual actions," sometimes manifesting in suspicions that external forces are controlling, "programing," or brainwashing the will of oneself or others. The second concerns the motive and means of the external controlling forces themselves, who are often identified as "large, and often vague, organizations," on whose behalf the faceless controllers operate.[224]

The panic itself results, in part, from a sense that one is not in control and an inability to glean more specific information about the ubiquitous "Them," who do the controlling. Agency Panic is not a psychiatric diagnosis, however, but a cultural condition, an affliction of the masses born from technological and political realities or potentialities. Both admittedly fictional and purportedly nonfictional stories about mind control, display linear shifts and changes that parallel the development and use of technologies of control and attempt to give voice to difficult, perhaps even impossible to voice, cultural anxieties about real world conditions.

The most famous of these fictions is Robert Condon's 1959 novel, *The Manchurian Candidate*, which tells the story of Raymond Shaw, an American G.I. captured by Communists during the Korean War. Held as a P.O.W., Shaw is brainwashed through DDD and Pavlovian conditioning to act as a sleeper assassin, unaware of the manipulations of his controllers and the "triggers" implanted within him that can call him into action. Only at the end, do we learn that Shaw's mother, the wife of a powerful, high profile right wing politician modeled after Joseph McCarthy, essentially sanctioned Shaw's brainwash, as a means of realizing her own political aspirations.

For some, the novel represents McCarthy-era fears of Communism and the U.S. government's responses to it (cultural anxieties). But, as others have pointed out, the U.S. government's fomenting of this fear acted itself as a *strategic fiction* that, among other things, shielded their own development of advanced mind control methods and technologies and the testing and use of these on U.S. citizens. This "Cold War duplicity" had the effect of dissociating the public's knowledge of the state from its actual workings, replacing fact and history with implanted screen memories and skewed perceptions.[225] While it would be decades before the public had an inkling of the actual scope of such activities, the novel and its 1962 film adaptation of the same name, went on to inspire many other works of fiction about mind control as well as narratives about the actual brainwashing of "real" assassins, including Lee Harvey Oswald.

Len Deighton's 1962 novel *The IPCRESS File*, and its 1965 film adaptation by the same name, tells the story of a covert intelligence officer brainwashed through "Induction of Psychoneurosis by Conditioned Reflex Under Stress," a process that employs a combination of West's DDD and Ewen Cameron's more technologically inclined psychic driving techniques. The subject is made pliable through sensory and sleep deprivation, an alternate inundation of visual and electronic stimuli and through hypnosis and post hypnotic suggestion, the controller implants cues and triggers into the sleeper who can now transmit information deeply encoded within his mind.

Harry Benson, the protagonist of Michael Crichton's 1972 novel, *The Terminal Man*, is a brilliant computer programmer who is helping to develop artificial intelligence for the Department of Defense. After a car accident, Benson begins to suffer from epileptic seizures and amnesiac blackouts during which he becomes violent and is preoccupied with a persistent delusion that "machines are conspiring to take over the world."

In late 1970, Benson, was arrested after attacking a man while in the throes of a seizure and was referred to the Neuropsychiatric Research Unit of a Los Angeles University hospital. The Unit's director, Dr. Roger McPherson, had been waiting for just such a patient upon whom to test an experimental new operation, the implanting of electrodes deep in the brain controlled by an implantable computer "the size of a postage stamp" elsewhere in the body. The computer, detecting the onset of a seizure, would prevent it by stimulating portions of the brain. Due to his seizures, Benson is a walking "ticking time bomb" that the procedure could diffuse.

McPherson and his staff understand the controversial nature of the procedure though and the potential loss of funding if the operation enflames the ignorant publics' fear of brainwashing. Therefore, they must be very careful about how they sell the experimental operation to the public. McPherson explains that "there's a lot of crap theory floating around" about the social and cultural roots of violence, when in reality, "people who engage in repetitive violent acts – like certain policemen, gangsters [and] rioters" are actually afflicted with brain damage.

Ellis, a surgeon working under McPherson, echoes the director's sentiments, when he tells reporters that "a high percentage of violent people ... have brain damage," and cites Texas tower shooter Charles Whitman and Lee Harvey Oswald, as examples. This, he says, "shoots down a lot of theories about poverty and discrimination and social injustice and social disorganization ... you can't correct physical brain damage with social remedies." Benson's operation is only the first step towards the realization of McPherson's true vision, the development of computer circuitry made from living human nerve cells and ultimately, brain prostheses.

McPherson and his staff proceed with the operation, against the advice of Benson's psychiatrist (also working in the research unit), who feels that it will only exacerbate his delusions about the threat of intelligent machines. Afterward, McPherson says, "we have created a man with not one brain but two.... We have created a man who is one single, large, complex, computer terminal."[226] Eventually, Benson, tormented by the technology, attempts to destroy the state-of-the-art computer mainframe located in the basement of the hospital that controls his implanted technology, but is killed by his psychiatrist in the process.

At the start of the novel, Crichton includes a historically accurate timeline of implantable technologies as well as an accompanying bibliography in which the recent works of Jose Delgado, Frank Ervin and Vernon Mark are noted. In a postscript included in subsequent editions, Crichton explains that after the release of the book, several neurologists informed him that epilepsy and brain damage do not, in fact, cause violence, although Crichton insisted he was not so sure. Not mentioned by Critchon but noted in the 1974 Senate Subcommittee report concerning federal funding of behavior modification, was that Crichton based his "terrifying" novel on the actual work of Drs. Ervin (UCLA), Mark and William Sweet, and the character of Benson, on one of their patients. Not mentioned by either, but noted by literary critic David Seed, is the fact that Critchon, himself, an M.D., studied under Dr. Mark and Benson's character was inspired by 'Thomas,' the man driven insane by the above-mentioned doctors' operation on him. *The Terminal Man*, says Seed, follows in a long line of literature wherein the mad scientist proves unable to control their experimental subject and depicts the "male-gendered arrogance" surrounding existing "medical technology that proves to have links with military hardware."[227]

In 1978, Don DeLillo announced the advent of an "age of connections, links [and] secret relationships" which he called "the age of conspiracy." That same year, H.W. Bowart released his groundbreaking non-fiction bestseller, *Operation Mind Control*, which included a forward by Robert Condon, author of *The Manchurian Candidate*. In it, Bowart conceived of "The Cryptocracy," a large incestuous institutional network of bureaucratic government agencies and private corporations involved in mind control research and operations.

By 2000, embeddable tracking and control implants were no longer thought of as futuristic technology, people were choosing to have them placed in themselves and their children, although you were still crazy if you claimed to have one involuntarily. Developed by alliances of private and public institutions, this technology, when coupled with the internet and advances in micro-technology, offered an untold number of brave new capabilities. There was a rumor going around that the military had placed them in soldiers during the Gulf War. In the 2004 remake of *The Manchurian Candidate*, Shaw is a Gulf War veteran. His brainwashing no longer relies on DDD and hypnosis, but now involves a private defense contractor utilizing "hi-tech brain implants and subcutaneous chips [that] remote control the subject [through] invasive technology, literally drilling into the brain ... platoon members are inculcated with manufactured memories, with memory chips implanted, [and] wires and I.V. tubes..."[228]

As previously discussed, although he denied it later, at various times within a span of three years, McVeigh told a number of different people in different locations throughout the country that he'd been implanted with *something* while in the Army. The first known instance occurred in early 1992 at Fort Riley, while McVeigh was still in the Army, but shortly before deciding (or being directed to) end his active duty military career. In reference to reports about McVeigh's alleged implantable tracking chip, a July 1995 *Globe and Mail* article derided such nonsense, opining that paranoid beliefs of this type originated from the public's "fear of high-tech surveillance" and "a rumor that microchips are now being implanted in babies just after birth."[229] McVeigh had discussed the latter with a number of people including Buffalo area AIDS/HIV volunteer, Peter Salino and his Michigan friend Gwen Strider, among others.

Upon his arrest, McVeigh displayed a disturbing "eerie calm" and reportedly gave only minimal identification information (name, rank, serial number), and somewhere along the way, at least as reported by one outlet, claimed to have a "bio-chip," as part of, what the report described as a "fantastical control project."[230] Whatever the truth of such reports, soon after his arrest, the Jones Team began looking into a variety of *fringe* type subjects that they suspected in some way pertained to McVeigh. In May 1995, they began research into Gulf War Illness-related issues including experimental vaccines and immunizations. In June, they began research into "micro-chips being implanted into military personnel and others." In October, they began research into "enlistees who are subjected to brainwashing and/or electromagnetic mind control experiments." The findings of this research are unknown to me and ultimately, for their purposes, none of these topics would come to bear upon his criminal trial.

McVeigh's "extra leg," government sanctioned covert operative, lone bomber and other stories demonstrate how, having stepped into the real or imagined world of Timothy McVeigh, the Jones Team seemed to have a difficult time determining what, exactly, might be delusion, paranoia, outright deception or what, in fact, might be *the truth*, or at the very least, somewhat truthful. To help resolve this, the Jones Team mental health experts attempted to understand the inner workings of McVeigh's mind and the autobiographical details of his life, speaking to many people who knew him in their effort to do so. Meanwhile, and for quite some time, his attorneys attempted to obtain a complete set of his military records that may have helped fill in some of the gaps. When they called Ft. Riley to obtain the records, however, they learned that they had been transferred to the Office of the Joint Chiefs of Staff, who themselves requested them from the FBI.

In a conversation with Dick Burr in October 1995, when asked if he was paranoid, while not mentioning any "chip," McVeigh described himself as someone who experienced a spectrum of paranoia, that ranged from "situational awareness" to "extra cautious" to occasionally "paranoid," but, he added, this stemmed from his "knowledge of modern technology." To illustrate his point McVeigh described a then recent *New York Times* story he had read, about "police using high technology to fight crime and the privacy issues raised by videotaping public areas and using hidden microphones" at airports and malls. McVeigh then made a slippery slope argument against the practice, citing a line in *The Turner Diaries* to support his point. "Because the chains that bind us were forged imperceptibly, link by link, we submitted."

Peter, the paranoid protagonist of Tracy Letts' 1996 play, *BUG*, and its 2006 movie adaptation, that follows the play nearly exactly, is a Gulf War veteran who may or may not be AWOL. Peter tells his new friend Agnes that after military doctors implanted a crude tracking device under his skin, he escaped from the VA hospital, only to be apprehended. Afterward, the doctors replaced his primitive tracking chip with a newer model, "the Intelligence Manned Interface biochip, a subcutaneous transponder, a computer chip imprinted with living brain cells," a "bug sack" that, when placed in the teeth, is able to spawn additional "bugs." Peter was not the only lab rat used to test the biochip; they also tested it on "another soldier working at Calspan at the time, Tim McVeigh." By the time he meets Agnes, Peter is plagued by an infestation of "self-perpetuating ... rapidly multiplying, brainwashing bugs." Burrowed under his skin and teeth, the bugs emit signals back to his controllers. When Agnes suggests that Peter see a dentist, he refuses, telling her that doing so would only assist the Army doctors who are trying to recapture him. In one of *BUG*'s more disturbing scenes, Peter enters the bathroom of the dingy Oklahoma City motel room he now shares with Agnes, only to emerge covered in blood, having pulled out one of his teeth with pliers in an attempt to remove the bug sack tracking device in his tooth. Eventually Peter's viral paranoia infects Agnes too, and she becomes convinced that Peter's bugs are now crawling under her skin as well. In order to shield themselves from the bugs and prevent them from transmitting their whereabouts to the Army doctors, Agnes and Peter cover the motel room and everything in it with tinfoil.

BUG convincingly leads viewers to believe that Peter's claims are the result of drug-induced delusions and this is how the majority of critics have interpreted his actions, although questions are raised when the sound of approaching helicopters (assumedly black) surround the motel room, growing increasingly louder until finally, there is an unexpected knock at the door. At the door is Dr. Sweet, Peter's former Army psychologist from whose care he has escaped. Sweet attempts to convince Peter to return to the hospital. When Agnes protests, Dr. Sweet concedes, "I am his doctor. He is my project.... We made a mistake. I made a mistake. I didn't know what they were using it for. What they're doing. It's dangerous ... it's wrong." As the hovering helicopters grow louder, Dr. Sweet confirms that the motel room is under surveillance by a variety of covert agencies, and he tells Peter that he will be better off if he willingly surrenders to Sweet, but cannot guarantee what will happen if the other spooks catch him first. Peter, finding this option unacceptable, tells Agnes that Dr. Sweet is a robot, and proceeds to stab the doctor to death. Peter and Agnes, alone once more in their tinfoil-covered dwelling, invoke the deaths of the Branch Davidian's at Waco, Texas, when they douse the room with ammonium nitrate and perish in a fire that they themselves set.

BUG appears to be an amalgamation of purportedly nonfictional stories circulating in the realms of conspiracy theorists for quite some time, details reported after McVeigh's arrest and the incorporation of both into newer mind control narratives that appeared on the internet after. Most interestingly though, is the close parallels of details in BUG with those in a 1994 book written by Ronald K. Siegel, PhD, esteemed experimental psychology researcher at UCLA's Department of Psychiatry and Behavioral Science, who happened to be a close colleague of Dr. West. The book, Whispers: The Voices Of Paranoia, offers several case studies of Siegel's interaction with and study of paranoiacs throughout his career, at least three of which seem to have found their way into BUG.

Included is the case of Dr. Edwin Tolman, a biophysicist with a high level clearance and Director of "a supersecret research unit for an aerospace company in California," who believes he is being targeted by an advanced satellite system called POSSE (Personal Orbit Satellite for Surveillance and Enforcement). POSSE, Tolman says, uses low frequency electromagnetic energy (ELF), to track him and insert troubling visual images into his brain. The second relevant case study concerns a woman who believes that a dentist has implanted receiver/ transmitter nanotechnology into her teeth. The technology was developed by the military and, for the most part, has been kept secret while a network of dentists implant the devices into their patients to "harass and spy on them." Siegel reminds readers that the woman is not alone in her belief, but one of a number of people who have made similar claims, some of whom go to extreme lengths to remove the imagined devices themselves.[231] Finally, Siegel documents several individuals who have come to believe that bugs have infiltrated their bodies, self-mutilate in an attempt to stop the bugs, and in some cases, are able to convince people close to them that the bugs are real and have targeted them too. In one case, a man who believes his bugs originated from the machinations of secretive government agencies, kills himself in front of his family.

Throughout the book, Siegel makes reference to tricking or deceiving the individuals whose paranoia he was documenting and studying, including at times misrepresenting himself and his interest in them, at least until he can get their cooperation. This is necessary to get inside their head. In the case of the infiltrating bugs, Seigel, rightfully, attributes the bugs to the effects of powerful drugs such as cocaine and amphetamines. In the other two cases outlined above (involving tracking and control implants, and satellites), Siegel acknowledged that the technologies exist. Nevertheless, he dismisses their claims as delusional, in part, because he does not think the technologies are in an operative stage of development and, even if they were, would not be tested or used against people in such cruel ways.

While Siegel presents an elegant case for chalking up the beliefs of those he studies to paranoid delusions, he makes at least one critical omission. In his recounting the case of Dr. Tolman, the aerospace developer who claimed POSSE was projecting images into his field of vision, Siegel neglects to mention a paper he wrote in 1968 that explored, although not satellites, technologies that could accomplish this very thing. Siegel, funded in part by the Defense Research Board of Canada, designed a device called FOCUS (Flexible Optical Control Unit Stimulator) as described in his 1968 paper entitled "A Device for Chronically Controlled Visual Input," published in the *Journal Of The Experimental Analysis Of Behavior*. In it, Siegel discussed the device's ability to maintain "direct control of visual input" and bring "visual stimuli directly to the eye." The further development of this, and the inducement of specific visual images, he wrote, "is both feasible and useful."[232] Given this, Siegel's omission in his 1994 book, his peppering of sarcastic ridicule of Tolman throughout the account, and quite frankly, his connection to UCLA shortly after publishing his 1968 paper, takes on a somewhat more ominous meaning, as does the subtext of *BUG*.

Unlike Siegel, who refuses to consider larger cultural reasons why his very real research *subjects* might have developed their delusions, one reviewer of *BUG*'s 2006 cinematic adaptation did consider such factors in relation to Peter, who happens to display a long line of peculiar delusions discussed by Siegel. The reviewer felt that while Peter was manipulative and "violently unhinged," "a familiar American type, the paranoid loner with a shady past," his bugs were manifestations of a profound uncertainty about the militaristic applications of hyper-miniaturized technology, rapid advances in nanotechnology and the increasing reach of the state.[233] All such stories, fictional and purportedly true, raise questions about the relationship between technological development, behavioral conditioning, and the loss (or theft) of autonomy and control. The real and imagined history of American brainwashing and its lengthy tentacles begins to help make sense of speculation, legend, and fact embedded within stories about McVeigh, Calspan, Dr. Jolyon West, and the intersection of all three. With that in mind, let us look once more at McVeigh's alleged implanted microchip in relation to the wider socio-cultural context in which it appeared.

On December 14, 1994, 26-year-old psychology student, Ralph Tortorici, walked into a classroom at the University of Albany, and with a high-caliber rifle and hunting knife, held the class hostage. Tortorici believed he was part of a secret government experiment and was implanted with a tracking device in his penis and a computer chip in his brain that could control his thoughts and emotions. He demanded to speak to somebody about the experiment but before this could happen, students overtook him and he was arrested.

In fact, although they didn't usually take hostages or act violently, claims of this sort were becoming increasingly common. A few years later, UA shut down the "X-Files" type research of psychology professor Kathryn Kelley, PhD. Since the hostage incident, Kelley had been investigating the claims of those like Tortorici that suspected or believed they'd been involuntarily implanted with communications devices for "monitoring and control." In her related lectures and papers, Dr. Kelley noted instances of implant research funded by the NSA and DOD and the usually disenfranchised populations upon whom these devices were tested. She and her team of graduate students identified several companies who had developed "trans-tympanic transducers," instruments that function as mini-telephones, sending voice messages to the inner ear. She also spoke of RAAT's (radio wave, auditory, assaultive, transmitting implants).

"When (short-wave) operators transmit to or scan RAAT implants in victims, they can talk to the victims remotely and anonymously, and hear the victim's speech and thoughts." They could be easily implanted, leaving only minor stiches in the ear. She pointed out that, despite this, implant claims are generally interpreted as an indicator of schizophrenia. Her colleagues became concerned that she actually believed such implants would be commonplace in the future.[234]

In September 1995, the *Journal of Nervous and Mental Disease* published an article detailing the "delusions" of two individuals who complained of electronic devices implanted in the fillings of their teeth. Their respective psychiatrists, having concluded that they were mentally ill, intervened to prevent the dental extractions they sought and prescribed antipsychotic drugs instead. According to the authors of the article, the crux of the problem, what made them crazy, was that neither seemed to realize the implausibility of their claims. Various theorists have posited that "anomalous sensory experiences" and episodic illnesses provide fodder for delusions. For instance, dental pain can correlate to the belief that an outside force (government, spouse, parent, etc.,) had implanted a "chip" in one's tooth for the purposes of remotely tracking, controlling or both.

A 2002 article in *Psychiatry* added to a small list of case studies about this belief, and recommended diagnostic criteria for a 'culturally bound' delusion including "the specific delusional belief of having a microchip implanted in one's body." This article, while acknowledging that such technologies do exist, said the belief itself is nonetheless "not credible in their local cultural context" and therefore, is delusional. Larger social, cultural and political events and circumstances, including technological innovations and other scientific developments "may cause fact and fiction to become enmeshed in the delusional belief" which, when organized around a particular theme (tracking chip) is considered a "systematized delusion."[235] For instance, Jose Delgado pioneered the development of such technologies during the first half of the twentieth century and, along with his contemporaries, went on to advocate their use in a program of political control for larger society. On the other hand, poor "Thomas," who Drs. Ervin, Sweet and Mark implanted, certainly wasn't delusional when he claimed cruel doctors wrongfully placed implants in his brain.

No matter what explanation any one member of the Jones Team suspected or believed about the famed chip, the fact remains that, as an adult, beginning during the time he was in the Army, McVeigh became inexplicably familiar with the dentist's chair. His teeth continued to attract attention after his arrest and soon became the subject of shared delusions.

As previously noted, excluding his numerous Army dentist visits, McVeigh saw a dentist in Michigan in late 1993. His 'discolored eye tooth' was noted by Realtor Bob Maloney in November 1994, and he saw an Arizona dentist in April 1995, just weeks prior to the bombing. Stephen Jones said that while he was at Tinker AFB, the FBI attempted to obtain McVeigh's handwriting sample, but McVeigh refused to comply and was not compelled to, as a judge sustained the objections his attorneys raised. "I now know," said Jones, "that in reality [the FBI] really didn't care about the handwriting sample. They were hoping that McVeigh could speak because they wanted to look at his teeth."[236]

Given McVeigh's observable cavities, his unusual dental records and his earlier offer to prove his honesty by subjecting himself to truth serums or torture, his response to a prison dentist who, in December 1995, asked him if he ever had any cavities, is curious. McVeigh told the dentist that he only ever had one cavity in his entire life and had it fixed in early 1995. In a memo detailing the visit, Randall Coyne wrote, "Tim wants to be sure he is not injected with sodium pentothal" and so asked the dentist, "How do I know you won't give me sodium pentothal instead of Novocain?" [To which] the dentist sharply replied, "This ain't Nazi Germany," but Morris, the unit manager chimed in, telling McVeigh "The truth is you don't know."[237] Teeth and truth, for whatever reason, appear inexorably mixed up in this story.

Prior to his arrest, McVeigh claimed that his tracking chip was located in his buttocks, the part of his body cited in all reports that detail this belief. Not reported however, is that after his arrest, McVeigh's chip seems to have moved into his teeth. Randy Coyne noted that, after two dentist visits during the first week of February 1996, McVeigh joked to Coyne "the dentist implanted a microchip in his tooth and the government was now "listening to everything I say." He repeated this claim about a week later, as noted by Jones Team attorney Rob Nigh on February 15, 1996, who wrote, "Tim told me he recently received dental work, and is confident our conversations are being monitored via a transmitter installed in his tooth. He wanted me to make sure and indicate in the memorandum that he was kidding about the transmitter. I, on the other hand, am not so sure. I think there may in fact be a transmitter."

McVeigh became enraged when, after his conviction, he saw a 2000 article by investigative journalist and Jones Team ally J.D. Cash, who had written extensively about the bombing while moonlighting as a defense investigator. Cash wrote that the Jones Team perceived McVeigh's paranoia early on and had serious concerns about his mental health, specifically in regard to the chip. While he insisted to them he had not been "brainwashed," said Cash, McVeigh "claimed the government had been able to track him all over the country because of a homing device they had planted in his buttock while in the army [that] allowed agents to follow him with their satellites. Thus, to avoid surveillance, McVeigh said he often lived in caves, especially caves located in the deserts around Kingman, Arizona."[238]

McVeigh wrote to his biographers about the article and told them Jones was responsible for leaking the fact of their concern over his mental state, denied that he ever lived in caves, insisted he did not have an obsession with Patrick Henry, as the article claimed, only a fascination; "nothing delusional." He downplayed his earlier implant claims, attempted to assure them that he never once honestly believed he had a tracking chip. Further, he insisted he had not been brainwashed or manipulated and that any paranoia he had about prison doctors was reasonable.

> [In the Army] I had a rapport with the medical platoon. I had a friend or two in there. Through personal curiosity, buttressed by my own survivalist training, I would ask questions and was always inquisitive about medical procedures. Right before the Gulf War, we got a booster shot, right in the ass. It was to boost our immune systems, our globulins. [It was] a big shot, 5 cc's as opposed to the normal 4 cc's. There were people who couldn't sit down for the whole day. Some of them passed out later in the morning in physical training exercises. It was a big ass shot. I'll give credit where credit is due. I believe Sheffield Anderson, the guy who was always starting rumors in the company such as "Congress didn't pass the budget, we're not going to get paid this month" (he'd get people all upset). I think he was the one who started the rumor [about the] computer microchip they put in your butt. People from my generation can make that joke because we know that computer chips are used, not in troops, but in experiments with pets. ... I think one community in California wanted to put them in children. Me and Anderson, part of Generation X, we felt free to joke about it (the computer chip). One day we were sitting around James Nichols' kitchen table at this farmhouse, and I told somebody, as a joke, that I had a computer butt chip put in me, in the Gulf War. Whoever was at that table that day didn't know me well enough to know I was joking and has spread that rumor ever since my arrest. It was a joke to start with. I knew from my medical training that it wasn't true.
>
> I was the principle [in the bombing]. I used [Terry] Nichols and anybody else that was involved. There was no secret person manipulating me behind the scenes. I'm friggin' old enough to know when somebody is using me. I'm not a brainless individual. In fact, I'm very world weary, you might say. More so than what would meet the eye in my country boy appearance. The Army did that to me. My aversion to prison doctors was based on my privacy concerns. I didn't want prison officials to take a picture of my penis and write "the life and times of Tim McVeigh in prison." Hmmm ... was this delusional or realist?

There are a few issues with this. For one, his "rapport with the medical platoon" and inquisitiveness about "medical procedures" do not mention more than 75 known doctor and dentist visits while in the Army. Secondly, while he couched the chip in terms of a joke his generation would *get*, and while that is true, he made the claim to a number of other people, who then reported it either to the Jones Team and FBI, independently of each other. One of them was Gwen Strider who stressed that he didn't just "think" he had a chip, he firmly "believed it." Another was Terry Nichols' brother James, who spent a lot of time with McVeigh and knew him well, or perhaps as well as one could, also said McVeigh thought he was "chipped" and also that he considered having his chip removed but, like *BUG*'s Peter, felt that it would do more harm than good.

To my knowledge, the fictional *BUG*, although an admittedly indirect representation, is the only account, other than private ones, to locate McVeigh's chip in his mouth. Critical context surrounding this story is revealed through juxtaposing McVeigh's "real life" microchip with those depicted in other stories, fictional and non. *BUG*, a story of brainwashing, surveillance, paranoia, control, and controllers, has roots in and unknowingly borrows from actual circumstances and events pertaining to McVeigh's life. *BUG*'s depiction, in combination with previous published accounts and archival and oral sources, demonstrates the ways in which fact, fiction, and folklore blur and the difficulty of determining which is which.

In BUG's Dr. Sweet, we can see the many purported "authors" of McVeigh's hidden Experimental medical narrative. Dr. Sweet acts as a stand-in for Dr. West, who himself, within conspiracy legends, acts as a stand-in for his other, faceless, unidentified mind controller colleagues. Even his name, Dr. Sweet, is lifted from the annals of American mind control history, Dr. William Sweet being a close colleague of Drs. West, Mark and Ervin. Within seemingly paranoiac conspiratorial mind control or brainwashing narratives, the recurring appearance of relentlessly cruel controllers and technologies of social control are positioned in opposition to the last bastion of human agency, one's very body and the interior recesses of the mind. But beyond UFO's and covert hybrid private/government domestic security operations, how does Calspan fit into this strange story?

While chatter from within conspiracy theorist realms about McVeigh's connections to West and microchips began within days of the bombing, it was Alex Constantine who, in 1996, first introduced Calspan to these stories. In pondering McVeigh's reported belief of having been chipped, Constantine noted that it was at least "technically feasible [that] McVeigh was implanted with a telemetry chip [and] drawn into an experimental black project" involving the Buffalo facility McVeigh guarded. Other writers, sometimes with arguably less astute research habits, quickly honed in on this possibility and Calspan became the location where McVeigh was sent "for indoctrination [or] training" and in at least one instance (BUG), found it's way into fiction. The story continued to proliferate over the next two decades, becoming self-evident (to some) that "CIA doctors at Calspan" helped manage McVeigh and are currently colluding with NASA to scan, classify and database the brainwaves/thoughts" of just about everyone." Some people were not so convinced. The blog of one former Calspan intern, ridiculed these conspiracy theories and noted that the only "doctors" he ever encountered there "were PhD aerospace engineers," most of whom were also professors at nearby University of Buffalo.[239] So what was all the fuss about Calspan and what made a link between Calspan, Dr. West, and McVeigh's microchip seem feasible?

The roots of the legend begin in 1948, when Jolly West began his psychiatric residency at Cornell Medical Center in New York City, after which he took a position as psychiatric assistant at Cornell Medical College from 1952 until 1954, before moving on to Oklahoma City. Also at Cornell Medical College at this time were several doctors of note, including Lawrence Hinkle and Harold Wolff, both of whom were instrumental in mind control projects predating MKUltra and who established and administered the Human Ecology Fund, *one* of the major cut-outs through which CIA channeled money to MKUltra research. Cornell Aeronautical Laboratory (at the time known as CAL and later Calspan) was a satellite facility of Cornell University until the 1970's. A number of other MK funded doctors were associated with Cornell and experiments on unwitting subjects occurred there during the years CAL was under its auspices. In addition, Calspan's clients were, for the most part, the very government agencies funding MK type research. While not a direct link (between West and Calspan), the interconnection provides the basic infrastructure for the Experimental Wolf narrative and a *potential* link in funding, agenda, and possible lack of methodological restraint.[240]

Although best known for its crash test dummies, throughout its history CAL (and then Calspan) received billions of dollars of defense related subcontracts. DOD and other defense industry-related contracts made up over two-thirds of CAL's total research and development budget during the Cold War, and over half of their projects remain classified, designated 'Top Secret.' Calspan contributed to more than just early and later-stage drones to the Pentagon's Brave New unconventional arsenal. It was instrumental in developing "non-lethal" electronic weapons, microwave technologies, biotechnologies including electronic telemetric devices (i.e., implantable microchips) and other human tracking and monitoring technologies, and systems to allow for the interface between man and machine.

When Dr. Peter Venkman warned Dr. Ray Stanz not to "cross the streams" in the 1984 movie *Ghostbusters*, he wasn't talking to Calspan about aerospace medicine, psychotronics, cybernetics, and surveillance, but as it concerns the fate of humanity, he might as well have been. While Calspan's accomplishments and fields of study are legion, for the purposes of this discussion, four areas of pioneering research and development concern us which, while related, would eventually converge, culminating in many of McVeigh's dystopic anxieties about societies' imperceptibly binding chains and the bleak visions of conspiracy theorists.

From the outset, CAL was in the electronic warfare business. They employed only the cream of the mental crop including scientists involved in the Manhattan Project and one physicist who, during World War II, discovered the ability to "talk over" or "speech modulate" infrared light, thereby transmitting and directing verbal communications to precise locations. In 1958, they transmitted microwave signals "at more than triple the power thought possible" at that time, thereby increasing the effectiveness and range of radar, which led to their creation of Doppler. In 1966, CAL completed REDCAP, an electromagnetic warfare simulation system, and the preeminent electromagnetic threat detection and war-games system used by all major U.S. defense agencies. CAL maintained and improved upon REDCAP until its transfer to Edwards AFB in the late 1990's.[241]

They were also in the robot business. A 1958 news article headlined "Navy Working On Electronic Robot 'Brain'" told of a psychologist at CAL who had, on behalf of the Office Of Naval Research (ONR), thought up and then, designed and built the prototype of an "electronic robot" named "Perceptron." The robot could match some of the functions of the human brain but eventually, would be able to "perceive, recognize and identify its surroundings without any human training or control," assist with piloting tasks, translating language (written or vocal) and the "automatic unearthing of scientific and other information buried in library books." In 1960, two NASA scientists coined the term "cyborg," short for "cybernetic organism" (the blending of man and computer). One of the earliest attempts to build a cyborg occurred in 1962, when the Air Force commissioned CAL to explore and design a "powered suit of armor" to amplify natural human capabilities. By 1964, they had developed the 'Man Amplifier,' a wearable exoskeleton that "link[ed] man and machine" and could "augment and amplify [an operator's] strength and endurance and provide biofeedback to controllers in real time" thereby testing the overall "man = machine capability." The Man Amplifier promised to "make a superman out of a mere mortal."[242] These were exciting times and the DOD provided additional funds for further progress towards this aim.

Beginning, for our purposes, in 1950, the ONR, Air Force and NASA (another major CAL patron), collaborated closely with the CIA and were steeped in unethical chemical and behavioral modification research. A covert behavioral modification research contract funded a 1958 symposium on sensory deprivation at Harvard Medical School. Attending the symposium were, among others, Norbert Wiener, considered the father of cybernetics. In the coming decades, all three agencies contributed significant funding to CAL's work.[243]

In addition, CAL was big on tracking and surveillance technologies and related databases. In the late 1950's, CAL's talent for all things remote, gained them a contract to develop "advanced 'eyes'" ("combat surveillance systems" and eventually total information capabilities) for those who would fight on and command the battlefields of the future in both "large scale and limited war" scenarios. In 1967, the FBI awarded CAL a contract to develop the first automated "electro-optical" fingerprint reader, which culminated in the "FINDER" system, first presented at the Electronic Crime Countermeasures conference on April 19, 1972 (the year CAL become Calspan). In his foresighted 1978 book, *Technospies,* Ford Rowan specifically mentioned FINDER as one of the technological developments that, along with associated repositories of information gathered, threatened the privacy and civil liberties of all Americans. Nevertheless, the Buffalo based company continued to improve upon FINDER and engineer other "electronic and intelligence gathering" systems for "law enforcement agencies and other interested groups."[244]

In 1969, at the height of the Vietnam War, the public learned of CAL's ARPA and DOD funded aerial radar surveillance tests and classified "counter-insurgency" research projects in Thailand. The lab became an embarrassing liability for Cornell University, already under fire for revelations about their MK type activities, and in 1972, the University cut them loose, leaving CAL (now changed to Calspan) free to pursue all the lucrative military contracts they desired. After this, the laboratory continued to change ownership, going from the hands of one well-known private defense contractor to the next. In actuality, of the five-member Calspan Board Of Directors, two were higher-ups at Cornell University and the school kept a 68% interest in Calspan until at least 1978 when Arvin bought them out.

In 1976, Calspan attempted to sell their fingerprint search and identification computer (now called Fingermatch) to a South African mining company, to help them control black mine workers. Conflicting reports exist as to whether the State Department blocked the sale or if the futuristic system was too expensive for the mining company. Despite protests over the systems' potential for human rights abuses, they were, however, able to sell the systems to a number of cities in the United States and other countries including Kuwait. Throughout the following decades, under various owners, Calspan serviced its clients through the development, creation, and testing of both classified and publicly acknowledged strategic defense initiatives.[245]

Since its establishment in 1958, NASA was a major CAL funder. Sometimes in collaboration with various defense agencies including the Air Force, NASA funded biomedical studies pertaining to the effects of space on humans, radiobiology, weightlessness, and space medicine. NASA's radiation experiments used human subjects, included total body irradiation and, in conjunction with the DOD, the effects of radiation on the human eye. NASA had no policy about test subject's informed consent until 1972. CAL was part of NASA's broader "Aerospace Medicine and Biology" research initiative that, during the 1960's and 1970's explored, among other things: hypnotic conditioning to reduce fatigue, the effects of hypothermic stress, the effects and uses of ultra-high and ultra-low radiofrequency; x-rays, and microwave radiation on humans, brain wave monitoring, and "implantable telemetry systems for use in animal monitoring."[246]

In 1973, on behalf of the National Institute of Health, Calspan conducted research into "implant device development." In 1977, on behalf of the U.S. Department of Health, Calspan scientists investigated "materials compatible with human blood" in an effort to develop better prosthetic devices.[247] The lead scientist on that project, Dr. Robert Baier (who worked on the 1973 project), happened to hold many positions related to military, industry and university biotechnologies research, won many awards for his innovations in that area, and is widely published on the topics of dental and medical implant technology. So perhaps *he* might have been able to figure out what was going on in McVeigh's mouth and elsewhere.

A 1986 Calspan report entitled "Future Research Needs in Biomechanics" was cited in an issue of *Engineering In Medicine And Biology Magazine* (co-written by a Calspan associate). The paper discussed exciting new developments in biomedical devices and materials that held great medical potential. Soon, drugs would be remotely dispensable and prosthesis and implantable devices would degrade naturally into the body, electrical stimulations would help cure paralysis, and centralized computers would be able to track elderly people through their medical devices. Best yet "major breakthroughs" in mapping the human genome, were going to revolutionize biomechanics research in the not too distant future. [248]

The University of Buffalo Research Foundation, Calspan Research Center (CUBRC) (est., 1983), "a pioneering collaboration" of public and private interests, released a 1986 report co-authored by the School of Aerospace Medicine (SAM) at Brooks AFB, about a joint project partially funded by the Army Medical R&D Command at Ft. Detrick, MD. In this study, researchers induced sleep deprivation, heightened states of confusion, frustration, anxiety, anger, and depression in USAF pilots to determine the effects of these states on performance. Related research investigated the effects of several drugs for their sedative, amnesiac and hypnotic effects as well as their potential to enhance performance. More than one of these studies involved the effects of Pyridostigmine Bromide, a drug that has been consistently linked to Gulf War Illness. In the late 1980's and early 1990's, Calspan, funded by NASA, USAF Wright Research and Development Center, USAF SAM, Walter Reed Army Institute (among others), further explored "human performance variables." These same funders supported research, which, while not conducted by Calspan, was presented at the same conferences on topics including the psychological and physiological factors and responses contributing to "the susceptibility of Blacks and Caucasians to cold sensitivity," and the effects of various drugs on EEG readings.[249]

Meanwhile, as early as the 1950's, government funded scientists became aware that sound could be induced in both hearing and deaf persons from thousands of feet away using extremely low and high frequency electromagnetic energy (ELF, EHF) radio frequency (RF) amplifiers. These same methods could be used to induce unpleasant bodily sensations. In 1962, Cornell researcher Alan Frey was hopeful that this would eventually replace remote stimulation of the nervous system "without the damage caused by electrodes." CAL researcher Clyde E. Ingalls then expanded on Frey's work, as proposed in his 1967 paper "Sensation Of Hearing In Electromagnetic Fields." In 1974, DOD researcher J.F. Shapitz wrote about the ability of "the spoken word of the hypnotist [to] be conveyed by modulated electro-magnetic energy directly into the subconscious parts of the human brain - i.e., without employing any technical devices for receiving or transcoding the messages and without the person exposed to such influence having a chance to control the information input consciously." His belief was based on his ongoing experimentation and he purposed further experiments, the results of which remain classified. The next year, in 1975, the Director of a VA neuropsychology research laboratory in Kansas City was able to beam words into heads using "voice regulated microwaves" (or so he claimed in a report).[250]

In 1976, Calspan received a $4 million contract from the Air Force to study the best applications of "new electronic countermeasures" and, in 1978, a $4.6 million contract for "analysis of systems to help weapons penetrate enemy defense(s)." A 1980 article in *Military Review* entitled "The New Mental Battlefield: 'Beam Me Up, Spock,'" described newly developed and already operational lethal psychotronic weapons. The more conventional of these used electromagnetic energy and biofeed-back to manipulate human psychology and behavior. Electromagnetics, said the article, held the key to the creation of a "Manchurian Candidate," and the military was harnessing, mimicking and weaponizing a range of parapsychological phenomenon including telepathy and "telepathic hypnosis." The author, U.S. Army Special Forces Vietnam veteran and Director of the Non-Lethal Weapons Laboratory at Los Alamos National Laboratory, John Alexander, told of their use in "the not too distant future."[251] For whatever its worth, Alexander was implicated in the government sponsored alien disinformation campaign discussed earlier and was very encouraging of Colbern and Leir's alien implant detection and removal endeavors.

In the post-Cold War world, electromagnetic pulse generators, lasers, and microwave devices could remotely destroy car engines, telephones, radars, computers and all other modern technology the world had come to depend on. Deemed non-lethal, these still classified weapons could explode eyeballs and cook internal organs. If they had been widely available during the Gulf War, one military spokesperson said that a single pulse beam could have taken out the entire Iraqi army. Whose bright idea was this? According to military historians, John Alexander's 1980 article about the possible uses of telepathy and brain waves had captured the attention of the high brass and catalyzed research into "soft kill" technology. He has since established himself as an expert in this realm. In 1993, the *Wall Street Journal* depicted the battlefield of the future as one filled with induced sounds, and nonlethal weapons that could "dazzle [enemies] with lasers, putting them to sleep with calmative chemicals and even confusing them with holographic projections in the clouds above them – perhaps images of Muslim martyrs telling them to go home." These kinder, gentler methods could help subdue the U.S. domestic civilian and prison population as well. If it came to that. Calspan remained at the forefront of radiofrequency and electromagnetic applications and electronic warfare simulations, helping to realize this vision.[252]

In 1994, Canadian neuroscientist and head of Laurentian University's neuroscience behavioral lab, Dr. Michael Persinger, attracted attention for his creation (and display) of the 'God Helmet.' Persinger's helmet used magnetic wire coils to send electromagnetic waves into the brain's field, thereby inducing feelings of anger, fear, mystical experiences, and even alien abduction experiences. Best yet, Persinger told reporters that "autobiographical pseudo memories" (false memories) of unusual events (alien visitation, etc.,) could be created in nearly 50% of "readily hypnotizable subjects." Persinger, colleague of Dr. Jolly West and an accomplished hypnotist in his own right, would know, as the defense establishment funded the research of both and both were involved with the Pentagon's parapsychology studies, thought by many to be a cover for other, more nefarious activities relating to weaponized electromagnetics. In 1995, the DOD through the Air Force awarded a grant for phase II of research into "communicating via the microwave auditory effect."[253]

Some argue that while inducing sounds is well established, inducing understandable words or sentences is not, but that certainly didn't stop researchers from trying. From the late 1970's until currently, several patents to this effect have been filed and a growing number of academic and technical papers have outlined these 'voice to skull' technologies. Perhaps not surprisingly, the 1980's and 1990's witnessed a growing number of individuals who claimed voices or subliminal thoughts were being beamed directly into their heads or that they were being subjected to other forms of electromagnetic and RF harassment, claims considered patently delusional.

It is about this time, in the early to mid-1990's, that all of Calspan's streams thus far discussed, electromagnetic warfare, aerospace medicine, "human potential" research, cybernetics, biometric surveillance and related databases, seem to collide, with implications reaching far beyond the life and times of Timothy McVeigh.

Among the gripes McVeigh voiced to Buffalo area HIV/AID's outreach volunteer Peter Salino in 1992, was his belief that government agencies like Social Security kept too much information on US citizens and thought someone should figure out a way to destroy their files. Once, he said he wanted to set fire to the Buffalo federal building because of the large amounts of private data about people stored there. According to Salino, McVeigh railed against the Center for Missing and Exploited Children because he felt they were part of a larger effort to track all individuals. McVeigh warned Salino that by the year 2000 the government, in conjunction with the center, would collect the "handprints, footprints and DNA records" of the entire population. This, he said, was only one example of the government's invasions of privacy and its plans of "keeping track of people," which ultimately would lead to a total global DNA surveillance society in the not-too-distant future.[254] Lending some credibility to McVeigh's "paranoia" was the actual creation of massive DNA databases prior to and after his death.

In January of 1992, the DOD announced their plans to create a massive databank of genetic information, the first of its kind. The stated intent was to replace traditional dog tags with genetic ones that could help identify the remains of U.S. soldiers. The FBI had also begun pilot DNA "fingerprinting" programs. Governor Mario Cuomo was among the early enthusiasts and in May 1992, proposed that the state of New York begin gathering DNA samples from convicted murderers and sex offenders. Ethical concerns about DNA profiling and databases voiced at this time included the accuracy and confidentiality of the data and the availability of such information to employers, civilian and federal law enforcement agencies and the potential use of DNA information to predict mental and physical illness. In 1996, the state of New York's DNA databank became operational. In recent years, DNA databases have proven to be beneficial in overturning false convictions as well as locating and convicting guilty parties.

Meanwhile, the FBI and Department of Homeland security have created their own vast databases. Improving upon their FINDER system over the decades, Calspan, in conjunction with UltraScan Corp., another Buffalo-area business started by a former Calspan employee, created 'Ultra-Scan,' an "ultrasonic fingerprint imaging" system, first tested on methadone maintenance patients beginning in 2001. In March 2003, CUBRC created the Western New York Population Health Observatory whose twofold purpose included bioterrorism and health surveillance systems. Later that year, this partnership resulted in the founding of the Department of Homeland Security-funded Center for Unified Biometrics and Sensors (CUBS), an interdisciplinary initiative to design newer biometric systems that could identify people by facial features, gait and even chemical signatures. In 2006, CUBRC presented their ongoing research to the defense intelligence community at a "Sensor Fusion Conference" whose topics included current "challenges in DOD, Government Security and Intelligence and Homeland Security applications," "complete battlefield awareness," and "total data fusion" so that "warfighters" could "better locate, track and eliminate their enemies."[255]

While civil libertarians warned about the impending total surveillance society, the military said biometrics was important in the fight against "insurgents and terrorists." Biometric information, including DNA and iris scans, were regularly taken in the War on Terror from over two-million individuals including those working on military bases, detainees and "suspicious" looking Afghanis and Iraqis. In some cases, the U.S.'s genetic sweep encompassed entire villages.

In 2010, CUBRC formed a partnership with Akonni Biosystems, Inc., to better serve military and homeland security markets and the Army awarded both companies a joint, collaborative contract the following year. Based in Maryland, Akonni develops, manufactures, and sells "genetic diagnostic and disease surveillance solutions." The company regularly received grants and contracts from government agencies including, one in 2010 from the National Institute Of Health to develop a rapid molecular test for genotyping. Their corporate board includes CUBRC's Director of Biomedical Research as well as the Buffalo lab's President and CEO, who happens to be Akonni's Director. Other CUBRC members of Akonni's board have interesting military biomedical research and development backgrounds. In 2011, Akonni signed a licensing agreement with the U.S. Army Medical Research Institute allowing them to market diagnostic tests with "global bio-securities applications."[256] The next year, projections of CUBRC's revenue were more hopeful than ever after being awarded two new federal biomedical contracts worth over $100 million.

DNA appeared in the news throughout 2012 as the Senate approved Gov. Cuomo's DNA expansion bill, allowing law enforcement officials to take DNA samples for all criminal suspects, no matter the severity of the crime, while Congress allocated millions to help clear up the DNA backlog from the growing number of samples gathered. That same year, the Canadian military announced its own plans to expand biometric data collection to include scans of irises and faces at a distance and, in cooperation with the U.S., to begin using biometric systems on the border. As of 2015, many, if not most, local and state agencies share access to and information with the FBI's federal DNA database, called CODIS. Meanwhile civil liberties groups continue to warn of the sweeping dangers such databases pose and actual abuses that have occurred. Even if their warnings prove true, there is no going back as most "civilized" nations operate their own DNA databases.

Around the time McVeigh applied for a job with the Department of Transportation, shortly before leaving Buffalo but while still working at Calspan, the DOT, in conjunction with Calspan, was developing experimental "highways of the future" as part of the DOT's plans for the National Intelligent Transportation System, i.e., "smart highways." Satellites would track GPS outfitted "smart cars" and, in the event of an emergency such as a car crash, transmit location data to the local sheriffs. In 1995, privacy advocates, warned that these smart highways, eventually renamed Intelligent Vehicle Highways System (IVHS) would monitor and record citizens' movements and thereby gather private information about them beyond the scope of the DOT's needs. Despite their concerns, in 1998, the smart system was transmitting the "exact location" of at least 500 vehicles in the Buffalo area to a "government satellite" via a black box installed in the cars and Calspan planned to install 3,000 more.

That same year, the *Washington Times* ran an article by philosophy professor and journalist David Oderberg, envisioned a world in which "smart buildings" would track the movements of all individuals via technologies. All financial transactions would rely on technology and, humans, now reduced to cattle, would go about their daily business unconcerned with the Orwellian implications.[257]

Nine years earlier, at a 1989 Engineering in Medicine and Biology Society (EMBS) conference themed "AI Systems in Government Conference" researchers from CUBRC presented on their recent DARPA funded project called CUBRICON, a super intelligence man-machine interface system designed to imitate the ability of humans to accept various sensory input while simultaneously producing output. Despite the predictions about the Robot Brain of the 1950s, there were some kinks in the development of a "completely intelligent interface" including gaps of knowledge about human intelligence in general and the differences between people and their brains, although advances in brain sciences were quickly trying to fill those gaps. Calspan's CUBRICON was mentioned in a 1991 *Computer World* article about the Pentagons funding of research with "peacetime" applications. At the 1991 EMBS conference, CUBRC advanced prominent ongoing projects including one related to Biomedical Sensor Technology, funded in part by NASA.[258]

A *Washington Times* article named Dr. Carl Sanders as the inventor of the "Intelligent Manned Interface Biochip" (the name of Peter's updated chip in *BUG*). According to Sanders, satellites had the ability to track people implanted with the chip, and that this was done "with military personnel in the Iraq war." Cultural theorists Douglass Kellner and Steven Best described the 1991 Gulf War as a laboratory used for testing the battlefield applications of new technologies that blurred the boundaries previously separating humans and technology and transformed soldiers into prototypes for "cyborg soldiers" with imparted "high tech skills," through enhancement drugs and implantable "psycotechnologies." They went on to explain how recent scientific and technological developments had bridged the gap "between science fiction and science fact, between literary imagination and mind boggling techno science realities."[259] These included forms of biological control, nuerotechnologies (including biochips and brain implants to control individual thought and behavior), self-assembling nanotechnologies, artificial intelligence, pharmacogenics and cybergenomics.

Shortly after McVeigh returned home from the Army, on April 22, 1992, the *Buffalo News* reported on the rapid growth of the biotechnologies industry, one of the fastest growing industries in the country. Analysts estimated that by the year 2000, biotechnologies would generate $50 billion annually. In fact, several joint U.S. – Canadian biotechnologies ventures were underway. Biotechnologies had already led to revolutionary agriculture and food processing methods and enthusiasts prophesied that they would lead to the discovery of the cure for, among other ills, the common cold, cancer, cystic fibrosis, and AIDS. Best yet, biotechnologies were expected to create thousands of jobs for upstate Western New York.

Alex Constantine noted a handful of individuals with direct connections to Calspan, whose research had unsettling potential. Included was James Llinas, head of Calspan's Buffalo division who, in 1995, spoke at the Navy Center for Applied Research in Artificial Intelligence about his research into bioengineering and artificial intelligence systems. Another was Calspan notable, former astronaut Richard Covey, formerly joint director for electronic warfare at Eglin AFB, who engaged in, according to the AF's press release "tracking of mammals [Dolphins] with subminiature telemetry devices" with "programmable capabilities ranging from frequency, transmission mode, input scaling and signal conditioning."[260]

A March 1995 article in *Defense News* entitled "Naval Research Lab Attempts to Meld Neurons and Chips: Studies May Produce Army of 'Zombies'" announced that the battles of the future would be waged using "genetically engineered organisms, such as rodents, whose minds are controlled by computer chips engineered with living brain cells.... The research, called Hippocampal Neuron Patterning, grows live neurons on computer chips." The research and development for HNP was funded by the Office Of Naval Research, a major client for Calspan as well. Sounding much like the distant ancestor of Perceptron, the early 1950's Calspan robot (also funded by the ONR), HNP researchers were sure the new technology would produce computers that could "learn" like a real human brain. Other researchers noted that HNP could be "used to control a living species" and still others touted its medical potentials including the ability to enhance memory by popping one of the chips in the brain. Some warned of its "horrendous applications." While the article assured readers that genetically engineered soldiers would be unleashed on enemies, Lawrence Korb, a senior fellow at the Brookings Institute, said that technology like HNP, "could potentially be used on people to create zombie armies."[261]

In 1996, Tom Brown, the Mayor of St. Peters, Missouri, drew flak from his constituents when he spoke openly at a Chamber of Commerce meeting about turning their town into "an electronic village of the future." Mayor Brown thought it would be nifty if cash was eliminated, subcutaneous microchips carried one's medical history and fiber optics monitored traffic. Some townspeople were not so enthusiastic, however, calling his plan "too Frankenstein, too Revelations, too Orwellian" and expressed concern about the Mayor's "common sense." In 1999, controversial futurist and silicon chip inventor, Ray Kurzweil, predicted a merging of man and microchip and machine. By 2008, he said, many people would have computerized components embedded in their bodies and "some would have their brains scanned in order to upload their personalities into a computer. What's more, within the next 20 years, computers would "look human and claim to be human" and who have "convincing virtual bodies ... display emotion ... [and] have spiritual experiences." Even better, humans would get to have computer generated sex partners.[262]

In April 2000, the U.S. Army's 82nd Airborne Division began conducting training exercises or "war-games" at Ft. Benning that pit human soldiers against cyborgs, other human soldiers outfitted with high tech "Land Warrior" suits. The helmets of the suits were equipped with telescopic, infrared, and nighttime vision capabilities as well as computerized battlefield maps detailing their location and that of other platoon members. Remote commanders determined where to direct air strikes by utilizing information processed in the cyborg soldiers 'on board computer.' The Army expected to put 34,000 Land Warrior suits into the operational field that same year, just in time for the post 9/11 wars. Also in development in 2000, DARPA's new human armor called "Exoskeletons for Human Augmentation,' apparently a descendant of Calspan's 'Man Amplifier.' In 2000, the *South China Morning Post* reported the future possibility of embedded implants that would "translate" individuals' thoughts and upload them into a network. The article, which mentions McVeigh's chip, noted concerns voiced by cultural theorists and scientists about the ethical dilemmas of creating cyborgs.[263]

In 2002, growing numbers of people were opting to have GPS tracking chips, called 'VeriChips,' implanted in their arms that could locate and identify them and provide medical information in the event of an emergency. A 2004 article of *The Journal Of High Technology Law*, predicted that it was "only a matter of time" before subcutaneous tracking devices replaced traditional military dog tags and raised ethical and legal questions about compulsory military implants, conscientious objector status to chipping, consequences of refusal, and the removal of the chip upon discharge from the military. Military implants, noted the article, could pose threats to constitutional rights ostensibly guaranteed to both civilians and soldiers including the right against self-incrimination, or recourse to civil torts claims if the chip happens to cause harm to the soldier, let's say in an experimental test of such technologies. The author then pointed out that, "The very use of the chip [might] be considered classified" and, if that was the case, would be considered a military or state secret and therefore not discoverable in a court of law or to the public generally. When the remake of *The Manchurian Candidate* came out that same year (2004), *USA Today* quoted the film's science advisor, neurologist Jay Lombard, as saying that everything in the movie was already or would soon be "completely possible" and Standard University professor Judy Illes pointed out that "brain chip implants" were already used to treat Parkinson's and obsessive-compulsive disorder. The same article quoted a psychologist who said that while he'd met many people who claimed the CIA implanted them with a control device, he never saw proof of it in any brain scan.[264]

In 2006, the *Guardian* reported on a new dental ID chip implanted in fillings that stores personal information. The purported benefits: the ability to ID bodies in the event of terrorist attacks or natural disasters.

Those who have undergone the implant process describe it as less painful than having a cavity filled. Microsoft, among other well-known companies, currently owns patents for implantable technologies such as 'audio tooth implants' to facilitate wireless communication with cell phones and computers. While acknowledging the beneficial uses of such technologies to aid hearing and vision defects and movement disorders, news reports often mention their other, more dystopian possibilities.[265]

On October 4, 2007, the *Buffalo News* observed that the entire world enjoyed the legacy of Cold-War era Calspan research, the offspring of which included cell phones, Google Earth, Global Positioning Systems and other luxuries related to military and commercial telecommunications satellites and satellite imagery.

This type of pioneering, while perhaps making our lives more comfortable, unfortunately upset twenty-one year old Oscar Ramiro Ortega-Hernandez who, in 2011, fired shots at the White House with a semi-automatic rifle, claiming the president "intended to implant computer chips in children to track them." Those who knew Hernandez described his "bizarre behavior" before the shooting, including his warnings of a government plot to "install Global Positioning System (GPS) devices … chips inside the bodies of U.S. citizens in order to track them."[266] The topic of a cyber-security conference, held at SUNY Utica/Rome's Institute of Technology in June 2012, was the burgeoning nanotechnology industry and the applications of combining cyber and nanotechnologies. Keynote speaker Lt. Gen. Ted F. Bowld (ret.) predicted that, in the not too distant future, all individuals would have radio frequency identification chips implanted within them in order to unlock their Internet-connected devices.[267]

That probably wouldn't be necessary eventually, as researchers at the University of Buffalo were feverishly working on nanotechnologies research and had already demonstrated the ability to remotely manipulate cells, neurons "and even animal behavior" through exposing nanoparticles in cell membranes to magnetic fields directed via radiofrequencies. The researchers hoped to "unravel the signaling networks that control animal behavior." The *New Scientist* pointed out that the UB researchers were among other biologists hoping to "take charge of living cells using little more than radio waves," which if tailored to specific "genetic machinery" (DNA) in humans, could kill cancerous cells and induce antibodies and immune responses.[268]

In his 2012 book, *Mind Wars: Brain Science and the Military in the 21st Century*, leading bio-ethicist and Hastings Center fellow Jonathan Moreno described how already existing implantable brain devices will enhance soldiers' memory and abilities, and the soon to occur use of these technologies in warfare. In addition, were "noninvasive" directed electrical energies that can not only remotely control individuals but also can detect and *read* neural activity at a distance, i.e, read minds. He suggests that "just as telephones and Internet technologies have gone wireless" neural implants allow for "direct connections to the Internet" and "brain to brain interfacing." Moreno wrote of the inevitability that nanotechnologies would provide "direct links between neuronal tissues and machines."

According to Moreno, the major challenge faced by scientists currently, was the creation of systems that would enable a scenario very similar to *Star Trek*'s The Borg, "a species of beings that were once organic but have assimilated mechanical and electronic parts" and have lost their status as individual beings but rather are more akin to a "collective ... ant colony." Another not too distant "science fiction scenario" involves "an army of robots capable of movement nearly as precise as that of a human soldier, each controlled by an individual hundreds or even thousands of miles away." While some have expressed concern over such technologies, often funded by DARPA, the DOD, and other defense related agencies, Moreno depicted them in noble terms lauding their ability to "develop and implement cognitive, behavioral, and pharmacological interventions that will prevent the deleterious effects of stress on warfighters." This, he says, is the culmination of defense industry driven science developed in the atmosphere of "total war."[269]

In February 2013, the Obama administration announced plans for the 'Brain Activity Map' project intended to advance artificial intelligence, help cure various diseases and mental health issues and, ultimately, create a massive network of "national brain observatories." Although Dr. West would be happy, The Terminal Man's Benson might not be. The project, soon renamed BRAIN (Brain Research Through Advancing Innovative Nuerotechnologies), was similar to but expected to "dwarf the Human Genome Project." The vaguely defined project could take up to ten years to complete but nanotechnologist and neuroscientist advocates said new technologies would speed the brain-mapping process. Notably, they hoped to create "fleets of molecule size machines to noninvasively act as sensors to measure and store brain activity at the cellular level [...] using synthetic DNA as a storage mechanism for brain activity."[270] What the administration neglected to mention was that the project was not new or even *planned*, but rather the effort had been ongoing for quite some time and critics of BRAIN cited the secrecy surrounding DARPA's control over certain aspects of the project.

Experts said the surgically attached brain-controlled exoskeleton donned by the protagonist of the 2013 futuristic movie *Elysium*, would be a reality within a decade. This left some to fear whether or not technologies' ability to turn soldiers into stronger, better, faster, more durable, human killing machines might eliminate humans from the battlefield altogether, leaving many people without job prospects. News articles about BRAIN quoted the most recent predictions of Ray Kurzweil, which were the same as those he made back in 1996 although, this time, they didn't sound so outlandish, including those about uploading people's personalities and memories, which to some sounded too much like the 1990 movie *Total Recall*. Others worried that recent DOD advances in "erasing" and even "overwriting" traumatic memories of soldiers would remove necessary ethical considerations involved in war waging and argued that although painful, battlefield soldiers should have to remember their actions. Despite the naysayers, those diverse private and public organizations working on BRAIN promised that the project would lead not only to better medical devices, but also to improvements on existing high-end consumer products that allow users to control their favorite technologies by thought alone, including phones, video game consoles, and tablets.[271]

The protagonist of *Intelligence*, a CBS action-drama that aired for one season in 2014, works for an elite U.S. government cybersecurity agency, and has been implanted with a microchip in his brain through which he connects directly to the "global information grid" (Internet) and has access to unlimited encrypted, classified data. His enemies include brain-implanted super spies controlled by other governments. Meghan Ory, a co-star of the show, gleefully told reporters, "The thing that's really cool about the show is that it's not science that's 100 years in the future – we're maybe 10 or 20 years away from this being possible.... We're all going to have chips in our brains."[272]

Moreno's science fiction-sounding world appeared increasingly less fictional. According to NPR, in May 2014, DARPA launched a $70 million project to "help military personnel with psychiatric disorders using electronic devices implanted in the brain." Through this method, "volunteer" soldiers would be monitored and electric stimulations sent directly to the brain would help eliminate a wide range of dysfunction and get soldiers standing on their feet and ready to fight again. Brain implants would clear up depression, PTSD and just general anxiety caused by the horrors of war. In 2015, the consumer magazine *Electronics For You* announced the release of a new implant that didn't need to be surgically implanted, but could just be "injected directly into the brain using a syringe."[273] And so it goes.

So-called "conspiracy theory" writers of the 1990's relied on circumstantial details to speculate the *possibility* that McVeigh had somehow come under the influence of malevolent forces. In doing so, they linked McVeigh to Calspan to Dr. Jolly West and those within his professional sphere. These stories, at the very least, point to shared concerns about actual black budgeted abuses of the past. Given the gaps left in the known history of these events, a seeming collective amnesia about them and the overall willingness to dismiss them as aberrant unfortunate occurrences that have since been corrected rather than an institutionally endemic on-going dilemma, the stories raise questions about the potential for future abuses when it comes to medical and technological methods of control.

McVeigh's privately expressed concerns, beliefs and actual experiences, when viewed in context and hindsight reveal, if not concrete connections, then at least the traces of Calspan and West; traces relevant to a number of current debates about the relationship of psychology, psychiatry, neurology and the larger medical field to technology, terrorism, counter-terrorism, social control, bioethics, dissent, and human rights abuses. All the more so, when developed in a hyper-militarized environment.

In July 1995, the *Globe* made a mocking comparison between McVeigh's 'chipped' posterior and *Johnny Mnemonic*, the titular character in William Gibson's 1981 short story (and 1995 film adaptation of the same name), a courier of secret information for shadowy, underworld organizations through his surgically implanted memory enhancing brain devices. In 2010, a number of states in the U.S. were considering or had already passed legislation banning the involuntary implantation of microchips in humans, a practice one news article quipped appeared "so sinister and so secretive there isn't any clear indication [it's] actually occurring. Anywhere. At all." Except, of course, the article sarcastically remarked, that time the Army put one in Tim McVeigh.[274]

Still, a 2009 Hastings Center report listed behavior control among the stated ethical issues that led to the creation of the organization. Modifications of the brain for the purposes of social control and the reduction of violence and aggression, said the report, have needlessly attracted "ominous" representations that emphasize threats to the perceived free will of the individual. On the other hand, the report acknowledged the danger of the "Wizard of Oz" factor' i.e., who controls such methods and how. Despite the report's comforting inclusion of this warning, their 2010 report debated the ethics of medical professionals' participation in the development of "medicalized weapons" which, while 'non-lethal,' incapacitate individuals via nueroscientific, physiological, and pharmaceutical means such as lasers, inaudible audio and chemicals.[275]

While not mentioned in the report, the Center had backed the work of Dr. Jolly West, pioneer and outspoken proponent of the use of these methods for social control and massive databanks to profile (via brain maps) and track all *potential* thought criminals or violent offenders; a pioneering vision seen in the "brain observatories" initiated by the Obama administration. The irony and tragedy of this is that paranoiac panic about existing technologies and abusive medical aims, contributed to the type of violent behaviors that such means and methods are ostensibly meant to control. Aiding in the effort, are publicly funded private defense contractors, publicly lauded for helping to develop medical technologies while developing the weapons applications of these same technologies behind closed doors.

Leaving aside Calspan's housing of Operation Northstar, an initiative spun off of Operation Alliance and closely related to PATCON and its relation to McVeigh's real or imagined secret mission, Calspan intersects with McVeigh's fears of societies' imperceptibly binding chains and legends about Dr. Jolly West and mind control in general, in a number of important and interrelated ways. The Buffalo Calspan facility McVeigh guarded was itself brain deep in the same militaristic cybernetic "total information" (total control) Brave New waters as Drs. West, Sweet, Delgado, and friends. Stories about Calspan, like West, allow for the formation of linkages between various episodes in American history. A closer understanding of several seemingly unconnected elements that continue to appear in Experimental narratives about McVeigh and others, bring to the forefront major concerns about the current technological capabilities of the defense industry.

Fictional and nonfictional cultural texts are always already political in that they "reflect as well as produce ideology: They 'reflect, embody, reveal, mirror, symbolize' through 'reproducing (consciously or unconsciously) the myths, ideas, concepts, beliefs, images of an historical period.'" Purportedly nonfictional conspiracy narratives, the claims of self-proclaimed victims of government funded mind control, medical abuse, surveillance and psychotropic harassment, and fictional works like *BUG*, that depict the aforementioned subjects, all indicate, in the words of Jodi Dean, a shared and well-founded fear that "the U.S. government values technology more than it values the body of their citizens."[276]

The protagonist of the 1997 film, *Conspiracy Theory*, Jerry Fletcher, played by Mel Gibson, is an ultra-conspiracy theorist, obsessive-compulsive taxi driver who writes and publishes a conspiracy newspaper. Fletcher stumbles upon what he believes to be a plot by NASA to kill the president using a secret space weapon/weather modification device. Vindicating his paranoia, however, is his abduction by CIA psychiatrist Dr. Jonas who forcibly doses Fletcher with LSD, interrogates, and tortures him; an experience leaving Fletcher with a sense of *déjà vu* and a vague memory of having experienced this before. Eventually, Fletcher learns he was an experimental MKUltra test subject for Dr. Jonas who attempted to turn him into a mind-controlled assassin until John Hinckley, Jr. shot Ronald Reagan, at which point the program was shut down.

Dr. Jones, evocative of Dr. West, explains that the objective of MK ULTRA, which he described as "science, sanctioned by the government," was to "take an ordinary man and turn him into an assassin ... it involved hallucinogenic research, electroshock to induce vegetative states, terminal experiments in sensory deprivation." He continues, saying the experiments were sometimes "terminal ... resulting in [the] death" of subjects. Filled with references to numerous other American conspiracy theories, especially brainwashing, *Conspiracy Theory* details Fletcher's obsessive compulsion to acquire numerous copies of *The Catcher in the Rye* and black helicopters that hunt him down when he attempts to evade the various government surveillances imposed upon him. Upon the movie's release in 1997, McVeigh faced his death sentence, suffering from "paranoia" similar to that of the fictional Fletcher and believed, for rational or irrational reasons, fantasized or deceptively claimed that he, too, was a cog in a larger subterranean machine, about to become a subject in one final experiment.

PART FIVE
The Bourne Scenario

Everybody's first patient is a dead body.

–Louis Jolyon West, MD, quoted in *American Medical News*, January 7, 1991

For me to feel less lonely, all that remained to hope was that, on the day of my execution there should be a huge crowd of spectators, and that they should treat me with howls of execration.

– The Anti-hero, Merusault in Camus' *The Stranger*, 1942

Tune into to what I'm trying to say to you. Do you know what a Sin Eater is? Well, that's what we are. We are the Sin Eaters. It means that we take the moral excrement that we find in this equation and we bury it down deep inside of us so that the rest of our cause can stay pure. That is the job. We are morally indefensible and absolutely necessary. You understand?

– USAF Col. (Ret.) Eric Byer, Operation Outcome Damage Assessment Team, *The Bourne Legacy*, 2012

For every sufferer instinctively seeks a cause for his suffering; more exactly, an agent; still more specifically, a guilty agent who is susceptible to suffering – in short, some living thing upon which he can vent his affects: for the venting of his affects represents the greatest attempt on the part of the suffering to win relief, anesthesia.

Frederik Nietzsche, *The Genealogy of Morals*, 1877

The truth is no court, no punishment is ever enough.

– FBI Special Agent Dana Scully, *The X-Files*, 1996

In January 1996, during a conversation with Jones Team attorney Randy Coyne, Timothy McVeigh expressed his "dread" that if found guilty, he would be incarcerated at a Super-Max facility, a possibility his guards at El Reno assured him was inevitable. Coyne then relayed to the other defense team members that, "In the event Tim is sentenced to anything less than death, he suggested he would prefer a death sentence."[277] On May 2, 1997, Jones Team attorney Bob Wyatt, a partner in Jones' law firm, sent Jones his letter of resignation. In the letter, Wyatt wrote that while Wyatt was aware that McVeigh had made similar statements to others on the defense team, he wanted Jones to know that when he had met with McVeigh just a few days before, McVeigh "clearly acknowledged that others were involved and that is why there is so much factual conflict."

On June 3, 1997, a jury returned their verdict, finding McVeigh guilty of eleven counts of murder (the federal agents killed), conspiracy, and using a weapon of mass destruction in what was "the worst act of domestic terrorism in American history."[278] During his sentencing hearing, when asked if he had anything to say on his own behalf, he simply quoted the dissenting opinion of Judge Brandeis in a 1928 illegal wiretapping court case: "Our Government is the potent, the omnipresent teacher. For good or for ill, it teaches the whole people by its example." On June 13, 1997, McVeigh was sentenced to death. Roger Charles wrote that after his sentencing, all the members of the Jones defense team knew that McVeigh would take his secrets to the grave with him, including the identities of other conspirators, and he was happy to go down in history as the sole mastermind and lone executioner of the Oklahoma City bombing plot.

As he feared, McVeigh was transferred to the Super-Max prison in Colorado and began his appeals. McVeigh had Jones removed from his post-sentencing appeals team, although as per his request, other, formerly subordinate members of the Jones Team continued to represent him, including attorneys Rob Nigh, Randy Coyne, Christopher Tritico and Dick Burr. In July 1999, McVeigh was transferred to the death-row facility in Terre Haute, Indiana. In conversations with his biographers after his conviction, McVeigh reflected on his then ongoing appeals and callously stated that whether the state assisted his suicide or not, he had won. If he died, his trial had still demonstrated the corruption of the government, and if he lived, he further aggravated those who wanted him dead.

In December 2000, McVeigh decided he would go to his death willingly and as quickly as possible. He successfully engaged in a precedent-setting legal battle with the state to prevent the autopsy of his body, ordered his attorneys to drop his appeals and filed to have his execution date sped up. His requests met with little resistance and an execution date of May 16, 2001 was set. However, on May 11, 2001, the FBI suddenly announced that they'd withheld several hundred investigatory documents that should have been turned over during discovery prior to his criminal trial.

Attorney General John Ashcroft delayed the execution for one month, and as his attorneys tried to make sense of them, additional documents were released. These included reports about other possible bombing suspects. The FBI chalked up their withholding of the material to bad record keeping and praised themselves for "doing the right thing" and releasing the documents. His attorneys argued that they were not given enough time to inspect the ones they had and expressed their suspicions that there were likely additional documents where those came from, but McVeigh was not interested in pursuing the matter.

Christopher Tritico's explanation of McVeigh's stated reasons for giving up his appeals is consistent with the most widely known and commonly accepted account:

> Tim felt that if he won the appeal all he would get would be life in prison in a Supermax where he's in an 8 by 10 cell, 23 hours a day by himself. In other words, he would spend the rest of his life alone in solitude and he just said 'I don't want to live like this,' so he stopped the appeals. Then when he found out about the evidence the government had not given us, he said 'let's find out what it is at least,' and so he authorized us to do what we did to try and stop the execution to see the evidence, and of course, we were denied at every step. And then right before we went to the U.S. Supreme Court where we thought we might get a stay of execution, he ordered us to stop again. I don't think anybody wants to die but he had resigned himself to the fact that that was his fate. So when he got ready to do it, it was time. He was resolute. The last time I met with him he was sane. He was rational. He understood what he was doing. He knew why he wanted to do it. It wasn't something we felt we should argue with him about because he had a rational basis for the decisions he was making and so we didn't try to intervene.[279]

Bruce Jackson, seminal ethnographer of death row culture, noted that since the 19th century, there have been three major changes in the United States' capital punishment procedures. The first is the issue of mens rea, or the criminal intent or mind of the offender at the time of his offense, which became a factor in sanctioning and legitimizing executions. The second change involves the level of physical pain inflicted on the condemned and the time it took to induce their death, both of which were minimized over time. Finally, while criminal trials and sentencing hearings may be public affairs, criminals are no longer hung at the gallows in the public square for all to see. Rather, with the exception of select witnesses, prison officials, and the state's designated death dealers, the sanctioned killing of criminals has become a private matter. The act of putting criminals to death, wrote Bruce Jackson "is not televised" and yet "[i]nvariably, at least one of the officials interviewed informs the public how well or badly the condemned accepted the administration of death."[280]

The execution of Timothy McVeigh was both a mundane and exceptional act. In April 2001, in a precedent-setting decision, John Ashcroft granted about 145 survivors and victims' family members in Oklahoma City the privilege of watching McVeigh die live via CCTV cameras.[281] A media company unsuccessfully sought the rights to broadcast the execution live on the Internet. Soon after, a U.S. Circuit Court of Appeals overturned a federal judge's earlier order to videotape McVeigh's execution for use as evidence in a different trial. McVeigh himself said he supported both the Internet broadcasting and videotaping of his death.

Oddly, in late May 2001, about a week after McVeigh's execution was delayed due to the FBI's release of the withheld documents, the front page of the *Weekly World News* announced, "Dead McVeigh On Morgue Slab," complete with a large picture of McVeigh, eyes closed, mouth hanging open and allegedly dead. On June 6, the still very much alive McVeigh mailed the tabloid cover and the accompanying article that discussed his death in the past tense, entitled "Exclusive Photo of Timothy McVeigh Will Rock America," to his biographers. In the accompanying letter, the last one he would write to them, he said he'd also sent a copy of the tabloid to the coroners' attorney "chastising them for leaking!" Ironically, the letter, which he closed by drawing a smiley face, arrived in their Buffalo mail box on June 11, the morning of his execution.

In the final months and weeks leading up to his death, McVeigh seemed to be "acting himself." He joked around and was "calm" and "in amazingly good spirits." According to partial prison logs released through FOIA requests, with the execution just days away, he became restless. He watched television, mainly news coverage, paced in his cell and, unable to sleep, tossed and turned in his bed, all the while "smiling" to himself. In the final 10 hours of his life, he simply stared at the wall, "grimacing."[282] According to Stephen Jones, his former client knew his final moments would become a matter of public record and so thus, as he had throughout his life, projected a façade of control.

On the morning of June 11, 2001, swarms of media outlets and other spectators gathered outside the prison and provided extensive coverage of the execution, both inside and outside the prison, as well as from the site of the CCTV broadcast in Oklahoma City. T-shirts were sold with slogans like "The worst is yet to come McVeigh-Hell," "Die

Die Die," and "You are the weakest link-goodbye" above the image of two needles.

At seven o'clock that morning, prison officials drew back the curtain, allowing witnesses to see 33-year-old Timothy McVeigh, now much thinner, paler and with circles under his eyes. He was "wrapped tightly in a light grey sheet," and strapped to a gurney. The prison warden then read the execution order. An execution team in an adjacent room fed a series of three chemicals through intravenous tubes inserted into his right leg: sodium pentothal to put him to sleep, pancuronium bromide to paralyze him and stop his breathing, and potassium chloride to stop his heart.

After receiving his lethal doses, the communicative terrorist looked pointedly towards the two witness rooms and into the CCTV cameras and nodded to the unseen witnesses, acknowledging their presence in what seemed an "unafraid," "satisfied," and "twisted kind of pleasure." Many of those watching through the glass or on the remote telecast said they felt McVeigh's purposeful gaze focused on them personally. His unblinking "coal black" eyes "stared right through" witnesses and coupled with "a totally expressionless blank stare," formed a "cocky" and "proud" "look of defiance." McVeigh then "stared blankly" ahead for about five seconds, put his head back down, stared "stoically" at the ceiling, appeared to fend off sleep, swallowed, blinked, went unconscious, and grew pale. His eyes glossed over. His lips turned white. His jaw quivered, his body twitched and then, shortly before 7:14 AM, his eyes, which remained open, rolled back in his head, his face frozen as "blank" and "defiant" in death as in life.[283]

He never apologized or expressed remorse; his final statement, an appropriation of a poem, declaring to the world that he was, in the end, "master of my fate, captain of my soul." President George W. Bush agreed, telling the country that justice had been done and McVeigh had "met the fate he chose for himself six years ago."[284] He remains the only person executed for a terrorist act, although his crime is classified simply as "murder."

McVeigh had not been overly concerned about the FBI's last-minute release of withheld documents. He wanted to die and, by that point, had said all he wanted to say. After the release of Stephen Jones' book, *Others Unknown* in 1998, McVeigh began to write his *tell-all* confessional letters to Dan Herbeck and Lou Michel, his official biographers, who set about writing their book, *American Terrorist*, released just weeks before his execution. The book told the story of the Oklahoma City bombing as McVeigh wanted it told and, for the most part, was the same story told by the government to the American people. In it, McVeigh was the Lone Wolf bomber who, alone, conceived of, planned, and executed the deaths of 168 people with the objective of righting the wrongs of a tyrannical federal government. Any minimal assistance he had during the preparation stage came from Michael Fortier and Terry Nichols, whom he cajoled, tricked and, finally, threatened in order to gain their cooperation. Just like the Department of Justice claimed, says the book, no investigative stone was left unturned and no mystery remained. *American Terrorist* remains the most widely cited account, both of McVeigh's life and of the bombing.

However, behind the scenes, McVeigh was characteristically narrating and hinting at other, very different versions whose details irreconcilably conflict with his official Lone Wolf story. In one of his earliest meetings with members of the Jones Team, McVeigh expressed that while he intended to take full legal responsibility for the bombing and would therefore keep certain details of the plot a secret, even from them. He hoped that when all was said and done, the truth of the bombing would remain a mystery. His post-sentencing actions betray the fact that McVeigh had kept critical details secret and that the government would, for whatever reason, seek to do the same. His actions also indicate that, for whatever reason, McVeigh took steps to insure that, after his death, at least some of the secrets he'd so vigorously guarded would eventually surface.

One example of this was his request made shortly before his execution to Bob Popovich, a friend of his from Michigan. He asked that after his death, Popovich initiate an effort to have all sealed court documents in his case opened up, telling him that if the effort was successful, a conspiracy would be uncovered.

The messages he sent to Salt Lake City attorney Jesse Trentadue provides another example of this. In August 1995, Jesse received a call informing him that his brother Kenneth had committed suicide by hanging himself at the Federal Transfer Center in Oklahoma City, where he was being held after being picked up and imprisoned for a minor parole violation. Prison officials pressured Jesse to have the body of his brother cremated, even offering to incur the costs, contrary to standard procedure. The family declined and when Kenneth's corpse was finally returned to them, they learned why officials had made such an unusual offer. The condition of his body revealed that Kenneth had been brutally beaten and tortured. He was severely bruised from head to toe and had suffered three major blows to the head. His face and the bottoms of his feet had been lacerated (the latter a common method of torture) and his throat had been slashed.

In 2001, Timothy McVeigh contacted Jesse from death row and told him a strange story. Kenneth, McVeigh said, looked remarkably like ARA bank robber Richard Guthrie. Guthrie and Kenneth Trentadue were the same height, weight, had the same color hair and eyes, the same facial hair, and even had a nearly identical tattoo placed in the same location on their arms. Guthrie bore a remarkable resemblance to some of the John Doe 2 sketches and he was suspected of having been involved in the bombing, at least temporarily, until the issue of the John Doe 2's was dropped. The FBI, said McVeigh, under the mistaken belief that Kenneth was Guthrie, had sought to question him at the holding center. The interrogation had gotten horribly out of control and resulted in Kenneth's murder. Sure enough, after Guthrie was apprehended in connection with the bank robberies, he, like Kenneth, was found dead hanging in his cell. Only weeks before, Guthrie told a journalist that he planned to "blow the lid" off the Oklahoma City bombing investigation.[285]

At the time McVeigh relayed this, Jesse knew nothing about the bank robbers and only what he'd heard on the news about the bombing, but soon set out to learn everything he could about both. McVeigh's tip ultimately set him on an investigatory trail that led Jesse to uncover mountains of additional buried and aggressively suppressed information about both his brother's death and the bombing plot. Included among these discoveries was the existence of PATCON. (The details of the Trentadue story are explored in the postscript of this book).

Finally, according to David Paul Hammer, while McVeigh was telling his biographers the Lone Wolf story, he was simultaneously narrating his Guilty Agent story to Hammer, with the understanding that Hammer would not disclose what was said until after his official biography came out and only after he was dead.

Thus far, previously published works, oral testimony, and archival documents have demonstrated the ways in which *all* of the competing narratives about McVeigh and the bombing originated with McVeigh, who told variations of them all, prior to and after his arrest. Only afterwards were his stories expanded upon and circulated by other individuals and groups with diverse motives, including the government, the victims' family members and survivors, investigative journalists, and conspiracy theorists. With a few exceptions, in numerous instances (perhaps most instances), those telling any one of the many conflicting versions did so without knowing that they originated with McVeigh. Also demonstrated are the ways in which McVeigh's many questionable stories (from Lone Wolf to Experimental Wolf and everything in between) were rooted in works of popular culture, shared public histories, collective "subcultural knowledges" and, most notably, his actual experiences.

Among the most striking of these stories, or at least the strangest, is one about McVeigh's death, or, rather, his immortality. While speculative elements of this story were publicly told and circulated prior to his criminal trial, it was expanded upon immediately after his execution. On June 12, 2001, a story appeared on the Internet entitled "The Big Bad Wolf Is Dead! Or Is He…" For years, said the Internet post, there were rumors that McVeigh had been "trained by the U.S. military to take a fall for the unexplainable!" The trial was a show and the "execution would be faked," with McVeigh's full cooperation. He had been trained, in part of an MKUltra-like program, to withstand his prison sentence and "told he would be given millions of dollars and a new face and a new identity" and "sent to South America," if he cooperated with the public deception. In May 2001, perhaps in an attempt to repair the credibility damage done when they wrongly declared McVeigh dead weeks before his execution, *Weekly World News* announced, "Timothy McVeigh is Alive!" The CIA, said the tabloid, staged the terrorist's death, gave him reconstructive surgery, and set him loose to start his "new life underground."[286] In the months and years to come, such stories continued to proliferate.

What is not widely known is that, as with all of the other conflicting narratives about McVeigh and the bombing, McVeigh himself first voiced the essential elements of this apparently delusional story. The earliest trace of it that I have found occurred in August 1995, in a memo written by Randy Coyne. McVeigh, said Coyne, raised the "possibility of a plea bargain. He said the government could use me for a special mission. They could say they executed me. They want to punish me. They wouldn't have to worry about losing me…" While admitting the chances of this happening were remote, he insisted it was a possibility.[287] It is unknown when the possibility that he would escape death first occurred to him, but by 2001 it grew beyond speculation and developed into his occasionally stated belief.

In 2011, Randy Coyne referred to this, the last Guilty Agent story McVeigh told, as "The Bourne Scenario" – a reference to Jason Bourne, the central character of a series of spy novels written by Robert Ludlum and their film adaptations, the first of which was released in 2002.

> When the jury returned with the guilty verdict [McVeigh] seemed stoic, forlorn [but] didn't seem afraid. I think for the most part he was realistic. There were moments of, I don't how to describe it, a psychiatrist would say there were moments, from time to time, where he entertained the delusion that there might be some way he would not be executed…. There were delusions he had. He thought about the possibility of 'The Bourne Scenario' and talked about being a special assignment guy and not being executed for the bombing. He sometimes mentioned he thought maybe they would pull him out at the last minute and fake his execution, and he would be placed on special assignment and used for something. That's something he talked about. He never articulated his reasons for saying that, just said there were forces at work that might make that happen.[288]

Death row inmate David Paul Hammer (whose books Coyne was unaware of when he told me this) detailed McVeigh's legal efforts to prevent the autopsy of his body and his decision to give up his appeals. Hammer, though, ascribed a very different motive for McVeigh's decision than the one McVeigh publicly stated and that most people accept. The prevention of the autopsy was one of the final steps necessary for McVeigh to complete his mission. At least that's what Hammer says McVeigh said. According to Hammer, who was unaware of the 1995 memo or Coyne's later statements about the Bourne Scenario, McVeigh insisted his apprehension about the mutilation of his corpse was part of a "script" devised by the Major.

> McVeigh seemed to genuinely believe that the bombing had been a legitimate mission on the scale of a military objective ... he was not at all certain that he would be actually executed. One scenario envisioned by Tim had the "Major" or members of his team infiltrating the execution process and replacing the lethal drugs with alternate drugs designed to feign the appearance of death. McVeigh was adamantly opposed to having an autopsy on his remains, mainly because of this prospect. According to McVeigh the CIA and other US agencies involved in covert missions had developed drugs to create the illusion of death in the human body and disguise signs of life. Tim would be administered these drugs by his executioners, and once his body was released to his legal representative, a squad of medical personnel would revive him. He would then undergo reconstructive surgery, and be rewarded for his efforts and loyalty to those he served.[289]

> I don't know whether it was his paranoia, or something more, but as McVeigh's execution date approached, he told me he wasn't sure he was going to die. [...] This is farfetched, but it does reveal McVeigh's mindset. [...] [The morning of June 11, 2001] Timothy McVeigh walked past my cell here on death row and gave me the nod on his way to the death chamber. Sometimes I think about that moment, I still wonder if Timothy McVeigh was really executed at all.[290]

In 2010, attorney Christopher Tritico commented on Hammer's claims. Tritico, also unknowing of Coyne's earlier notations and observations, insisted McVeigh never made any such assertion, which, understandably, sounded outrageous to him.

> I don't believe for one minute that Tim made those statements. This is the first I ever heard about it. But look, knowing Tim the way I know Tim, that wouldn't have happened. I just don't believe it. Now here's the thing about the autopsy, and this is one of the things I actually respect about Tim a lot, is that he did not want to be a martyr for anybody. He wasn't looking for that out of life.

He didn't want this autopsy report to be all over the internet. His ashes were scattered by Rob Nigh, and Nigh is the only person on the face of this earth that knows where those ashes were scattered. Nobody knows where it is. Rob hasn't told me or anybody else, and that was something that Tim wanted. He didn't want this place where neo-Nazis, or whatever you want to call them, would come and pay homage to him. He just didn't want it. He didn't want this autopsy that would live on beyond him, and he didn't want a final resting place that would become a shrine to weirdos or whatever.[291]

McVeigh gave very similar reasons to his biographers about his decision to forego an autopsy and the cremation of his body. Then again, Tritico had no knowledge of McVeigh's Army medical records, the real findings of the team's mental health experts or his ongoing physical deterioration while in prison. When asked about all of these he said McVeigh "appeared healthy to me" and had no physical or mental health problems "that he knew of." In fact, in conversations with members of the legal team the phrase "that I know of" appears often, many times followed by a disclaimer about the highly compartmentalized structure of the defense team. Tritico handled aspects of the case relating to physical evidence such as fingerprints and chemical traces. The legal defense efforts of the Jones Team, he said, generated a mountainous body of documents, "probably a million documents in Tim's case," and added, "I probably read about ten thousand of them but the only person on his own defense team that read every document in the case was Tim." No one member of the Jones Team had been privy to all of the information produced.

Further, without exception, all former members of the Jones Team that I spoke with, investigators and attorneys alike, claimed that, more so than any of the others on the team, *they knew McVeigh best*, were closest to him and had gained his *real* trust, therefore they each had special insight the others did not have. No matter who was closest to McVeigh or who, if anyone, McVeigh trusted, Tritico seemed to trust McVeigh, as evidenced by his suggestion that, "If you really want to understand Tim McVeigh's psyche," read *American Terrorist*. Of course, given the leaky nature of the Jones Team, for McVeigh to admit to anyone other than a select few individuals his belief that he might get snatched up and reassigned rather than die, would undermine the intended message of the bombing and transform his political act into a random act committed by a crazed delusional lunatic.

What sense can be made of this, the last story McVeigh would tell?

An essay by Benjamin Beit-Hallahmi, published in a textbook series entitled *Psychology of Terrorism*, offers one possible interpretation. The essay concerns beliefs about immortality held by groups and individuals, specifically in the context of apocalyptic End Times scenarios. Here, after a series of cataclysmic, supernaturally driven events, select individuals and groups will experience rebirth, either metaphorically or literally, through resurrection. Reinvention of the self, says Beit-Hallahmi, is not only a fundamental element of the "American dream" but also a universally shared hope of escaping and transcending ones "destiny and identity." According to him, apocalyptical beliefs about immortality involve a type of "magic thinking" that often begins in response to dramatic personal events.[292] Certainly, McVeigh was facing a dramatic destiny he might have wanted to escape.

A related, but less religiously centered explanation is that McVeigh suffered from "Cotard delusions," a clinical term referring to an individual's belief that they are already dead, and in less frequently seen manifestations, that they are immortal. Both variations are associated with depression and psychosis caused by neurological or other physiological dysfunction or, alternately, appears as an attempt to quell overwhelming existential fears, especially those about one's own death. According to acclaimed forensic psychiatrist Dorothy Otnow Lewis, a belief in one's immortality and the denial of one's eventual death, results from the unique logic of dissociation, which itself is comparable to "the logic of dreams."[293] Individuals traumatized by witnessing the death of others or experiencing prolonged fear may display ambivalence about their lives and the lives of others, a preoccupation with or increased interest in death, unrealistic, magical understandings about it, a heightened sense of invulnerability and fantasies about having some special protection or exemption from it. McVeigh's ongoing claim that he might not die at the time of his execution is a belief seen not only among the religious but also the traumatically dissociated, both of whom sometimes believe that, even if they appear dead, they will somehow escape actual death.

On another level, the use of the name "Bourne Scenario" for McVeigh's strange beliefs, should remind us of key elements found within other stories he told about himself, some of which other people came to believe as well. Furthermore, whether factually true or not, the Bourne Scenario helps to explain why such stories exist in the first place. Jason Bourne, the fictional protagonist of three Robert Ludlum novels (1980-2001), seven novels written by others after Ludlum's death, and several film adaptations, is an alias adopted by American Foreign Service Officer David Webb, whose family is killed by the U.S.'s bombing of Cambodia during the Vietnam War. Afterwards, the CIA inducts Webb into a secret Special Forces unit called Medusa, essentially a fictionalized version of the real life Phoenix Project death squads. His assignment is to assassinate suspected Viet Cong organizers and collaborators. In the course of his mission, he assassinates a double agent named Jason Bourne. Webb eventually becomes part of a CIA black operation called Treadstone, at which point he begins to use the name Jason Bourne as his primary alias, of which he has many. In the novels, Bourne is tasked with establishing a "legend" by taking credit for acts of terrorism and assassinations in order to lure and catch a real terrorist. In the films, Bourne's assignment consists of spying on and assassinating select targets – including the leaders of other countries.

At some point, a fisherman finds Bourne, who has been shot in the back and left for dead. Bourne has total amnesia; no memory of what happened to him, his name, or his past. As the fisherman tends to Bourne's wounds, he finds a device implanted under his skin. The device contains coded clues that Bourne follows in an attempt to figure out who he is. Along the way, he finds a stash of passports and other forms of identification, all in different names but bearing his picture, including one in the name of Jason Bourne.

Over time, he learns of his previous, but unremembered, role as the first subject in Operation Treadstone's experimental "behavioral modification" assassin-training program. An encounter with the doctor who oversaw the experiments triggers Bourne's recovery of some of these memories. Throughout the series Bourne endlessly relives his previous life through painful flashbacks and must live on the run, hunted by other CIA assassins, former government programmers and handlers who relentlessly seek to kill him in order to tie up Treadstone's loose ends and keep it hidden from the public. Bourne is able to stay alive only by the killer instincts installed in him through his Treadstone training. Although Treadstone has been terminated, Bourne learns of its successor, Operation Blackbriar, a CIA assassination program that targets U.S. citizens and is run by the agencies' counterterrorism division. As Bourne sets out to expose Blackbriar, the hunt for him escalates.

The advertisement for the 2012 film *The Bourne Legacy*, reads "Welcome To The Program." Bourne does not appear in this instalment. Rather, he has become the prototype for other, better constructed and controlled professional assassins and/or patsies, created under Blackbriar's successor, a DOD covert program code-named Operation Outcome. As it turns out, many of the former Treadstone/Blackbriar operatives suffered a range of debilitating physical and psychiatric symptoms including depression, uncontrolled outbursts of anger, obsessive-compulsive tendencies, and headaches. This, in combination with the rogue actions of Bourne, "a malfunctioning $30 million weapon," led to the creation of Outcome, a program that culls its subjects from active duty Army personnel, transforming them into lone wolf super soldiers and spies through genetic modifications, and highly addicting physically and mentally-enhancing pills.[294] All Outcome operatives are implanted with tracking chips, including the protagonist Aaron Cross.

The film depicts an Operation Outcome-created brainwashed mass shooter and a host of villains including the CIA, military, pharmaceutical companies, scientists and mental health professionals with questionable ethics who act as shadowy controllers. One of them, a cruel government psychologist-programmer-interrogator, masquerades as a grief counselor in order to cover for his programming of human subjects. After the public learns of Treadstone and Outcome, the FBI and Senate hold investigations, causing the project's overseer, an Air Force Colonel, to order the elimination (death) of all Outcome test-subject/field agents through lethal injections containing a "genomic targeting" virus.[295]

A number of thematic parallels exist between the fictional Bourne stories and the purportedly nonfictional stories told by and about McVeigh, the brief exploration of which may help to shed light on (or perhaps further confuse) the reasons they appeal to groups and individuals.

Jason Bourne suffers from dissociative fugue. As noted, traumatic dissociation is an affliction generally resulting from extreme stress sometimes coupled by physical injury such as neurological damage, after which, in pronounced cases, an individual may lose their autobiographical memories and sense of identity. In a dissociative fugue state, this occurs suddenly and the dissociated person travels to other geographical regions ("fugue" meaning "flight"). Fugues can last hours, days, or months. In cases of prolonged fugues, the person relocates and lives under a different name under the belief they are that person until, suddenly, they remember who they really are, but lose all memory of the dissociated pseudo-life they've just led.[296]

The first clinically documented case was recorded in 1891 and involved a man named Reverend Ansel Bourne. Other documented dissociative fugue states have involved Vietnam veterans, described by them as "going bush." One assumed the identity of a friend recently killed in combat. Although true dissociative fugue is uncommon, amnesia and dissociation in general and fugue states specifically are a long-standing element in fiction. Hollywood's government-trained operatives and assassins frequently fall victim to the seeming occupational hazard of forgetting who they are and what they have done. In both fiction and real life, however, with dissociative fugue state amnesia, "the show-reel of personal life malfunctions," and "narrative gaps infiltrate [the] story."[297]

Ludlum's creation of Jason Bourne in 1980 followed a deluge of revelations in the mid-to-late 1970's about the U.S. government's Cold War covert actions, including sanctioned assassinations and the effort to create amnesiac assassins to carry them out. After Bourne forces the public disclosure of Treadstone, a CIA official who believed the program had been terminated laments that he'll have to face an oversight committee, and asks what he's supposed to tell them. He solves this by having the director of Treadstone killed and lying to the oversight committee, telling them the project had simply been a training program that was ultimately economically untenable and scrapped. Thereby, the full scope and activities of Treadstone remain undisclosed. Both the novels and the films highlight the futility and compromise of Congressional oversight investigations and committees, which tend to learn just enough to assure the public that the threat has been uncovered, unsavory goings-on have been documented, and the problems corrected. In this way and through this process, narrative gaps about the covert workings of the state infiltrate, and remain dissociated from American history.

Psychiatric literature outlines the case study of a Vietnam veteran who witnessed the death of his platoon leader and the killing of a Vietnamese "boy-soldier" in 1968, who began experiencing recurring dissociated fugue states. These continued intermittently for 20 years until the late 1980's, often after stressful life events. Finally, in 1991, his wife saw a television show about animals who were tracked for research purposes by matchbox-sized homing-devices. She suggested her husband also be outfitted with one, which he was and that, while not preventing future occurrences, seemed to reduce the stress his fugues caused her. The authors of the case study hoped that this "innovate application of bio-technological advances to psychiatric practices" would, with advances in telecommunications, lead to the use of "smaller, simpler and cheaper tracking devices."[298]

The Bourne of the post 9/11 era, and his successor in *The Bourne Legacy*, Aaron Cross, must contend with, avoid and even co-opt persistent global surveillance networking systems. Bourne (and Cross) traverse a "frenetic gamut of electronic spyware and computerized mapping ... magnetic remote trackers, security cam footage," CCTV cameras, GPS tracking cell phones, biometrics identifiers, drones and a host of other now mundane technologies including those implanted in the very bodies of the hunter turned hunted. Similar to McVeigh's "Orwellian reversal," viewers engage in a fantasy in which the very technologies the heroes must confront, offer the ways and means of resistance. While Jason Bourne did not appear in *The Bourne Legacy*, he is expected to in the newest Bourne film, to be released in 2016. Actor Matt Damon, who plays Bourne, explained that the new film takes place in "a post-Snowden world" and will touch on issues about "spying, civil liberties, and the nature of democracy."[298]

In *The Bourne Legacy*, Cross has it a bit worse than Bourne, who faces not only "the erosion of the private will by surveillance and brutality but of organic biogenetic tampering" and the secret interventions of neurobiology. Although he is not subjected to generic tampering, in a sense, Jason Bourne's body "is never entirely his own," and as far as his employers are concerned, is nothing more than government property, a multimillion dollar investment.[300] The fact that Bourne and Cross have been technologized through implanted tracking devices render their bodies an even costlier investment. While Bourne must decipher and follow clues left by his now dissociated body as well as the clues left within it in the form of his microchip, Cross divests himself of his chip by placing it in a wolf, thereby making the wolf a sacrificial decoy.

The Bourne stories, like McVeigh's Bourne Scenario, resist closure by including seemingly infinite layers of conspiracies and cover-ups which, when revealed, lead only to revelations about even more disturbing ones. This book's final disturbing revelation about McVeigh may well provide fuel for existing and future narrative fires about "McBourne" (or whatever Manchurian Candidate comes next) and concerns Alan Doerhoff, McVeigh's lead executioner and his specially chosen team of death dealers.

In 2007, Doerhoff, a Missouri physician, gave testimony at a closed trial concerning the illegality of an impending execution that violated the Eighth Amendment against cruel and unusual punishment. The trial revealed that, Doerhoff, who testified under the name "John Doe 1," had been the subject of over twenty malpractice suits, his right to practice medicine had been revoked at two hospitals, and he had been reprimanded by a state board for concealing this information ... all prior to his execution of Timothy McVeigh.

Doerhoff testified that, for years, he designed and carried out execution protocols for the State of Missouri without consulting anyone. During one execution, he reduced the dose of anesthetic by half because, he said, it was difficult to put the entire amount in the syringe. When Doerhoff was asked about the exact doses of lethal drugs he typically used, he responded by saying, "I am dyslexic ... so it's not unusual for me to make mistakes" and was, he added, simply "not good with numbers." When asked if he used calculations to determine lethal dosages of drugs he administered, Doerhoff exclaimed "Heavens, no!"

For the most part, Doerhoff continued, he simply made up procedures as he went along – and admittedly sometimes mixed up the name of the drugs he used to kill people. He insisted though that, despite his dyslexic disadvantage and poor math skills, he could always tell when he'd properly anesthetized an inmate by watching them through cracks in the blinds behind a glass window. Doerhoff conducted some of his Missouri executions in the dark with only a flashlight and a team that often included "nonmedical people" who had never handled a syringe in their lives.

Among those on McVeigh's execution team was a man who, although a registered nurse, had an extensive criminal record that included acts of violence and threats of violence. He had to seek permission from his probation officer to leave the state of Missouri in order to help Doerhoff kill McVeigh. Doerhoff's professional shortcomings also included poor record-keeping practices, which made investigations into his previous executions nearly impossible.

Dr. Mark Heath, a Columbia University anesthesiologist, became one of the foremost experts in lethal injection after McVeigh's 2001 execution. His interest began when he read that McVeigh's executioners used what sounded to him like a bizarre and nonsensical combination of drugs and that McVeigh's eyes leaked "tears" after receiving his doses. This indicated to Heath, not that McVeigh became sad, but that Doerhoff failed to administer the proper dose of sodium pentothal. In fact, said Dr. Heath, Dr. Doerhoff "[didn't] know what he was talking about when it comes to the use of sodium pentothal," the drug used to induce sleep and render the death painless.[301]

Although lethal injection is thought of as a more humane alternative to hangings, the electric chair or firing squads, lethal injections can actually take longer and be more painful, more brutal. This is especially so when any of the drugs that make up the lethal cocktail are miscalculated. If not properly anesthetized, the prisoner may experience feelings of suffocation and burning from the inside. Despite Doerhoff's self-assured peep through the window-blinds, the second of the three lethal injection drugs, the paralyzing agent, prevents the condemned from doing anything but lying motionless and expressionless, making Doerhoff's guesstimates about whether or not the inmate has received an adequate dose of anesthesia, astoundingly callow. Thus we are presented with yet another story; one in which, on June 11, 2001, America's least competent executioner killed America's most notorious terrorist.

Until 2007, Doerhoff enjoyed anonymity as he went about his business of ushering in state-sanctioned deaths. After the *St. Louis Post-Dispatch* revealed his name, legislators passed a bill making the identities of executioners a state secret. A number of comparisons can be made about the intents and methods of modern executions and torture. Both are acts of "total theatre" that take place on skillfully designed stages and reveal only what the dispassionate playwrights and directors wish them too, never anything more or less.[302] Sometimes interrogation and torture involve the staging of mock executions to induce fear, and sometimes executions involve torture. The identities of those who perpetrate both are state secrets.

The Cold War notion of the *sleeper agent* was fictionally and factually associated with brainwashing, hypnosis, torture, interrogation, espionage, sabotage, and assassination. Cold War sleepers unknowingly carrying out actions scripted by others; but after 9/11, the "sleeper" concept became increasingly associated with witting terrorists and an invisible but constant terrorist threat. No matter what era they appear in, at some point, all Sleepers must awake and remember who they really are. While it appeared to the public that McVeigh succumbed to death's sleep, in the Bourne Scenario, his controllers awaken him from his slumber. Like the tales of tracking chips in McVeigh's buttocks and tooth, in the years after his execution, his personal, privately told Bourne Scenario took on a narrative life of its own and, like those about Elvis, legends about McVeigh's fake death continue to circulate, each year gaining new speculative details.[303]

The lineage of fictional amnesiac assassin Jason Bourne can be traced to Raymond Shaw, protagonist of *The Manchurian Candidate*. Like Shaw, Bourne "is both the agent and the victim of a government program designed to turn him into a lethal human weapon." Unlike the 1959 version of Shaw, who is the victim of an outside enemy, Bourne's dilemma is a result of the U.S.'s own actions, policies, and agencies. He is a tool and weapon of the U.S. security state itself and the intrusive memories that plague him, but always remain just out of reach, are allegories for the details of an already always unknowable secret national history and the very "spectacle of amnesia" required to maintain national security secrets. The Bourne movies hint at such national secrets when viewers witness some of the behavioral modification techniques used to transform Bourne into an efficient killer, scenes clearly inspired by events at Abu Ghraib and Guantanamo Bay. The Bourne stories, said one cultural critic, raise, "troubling questions about the use of violence" and the ways in which "national security managers" determine that a former U.S. solider "is himself a security threat and needs to be terminated. [...] Shockingly, as it turns out, a man trained, programmed, and authorized to maim and kill, is disposable."[304]

McVeigh, like Bourne, seems to have had some serious memory malfunctions and knowingly or otherwise, enacted a number of different personalities, each with different functions. Like Bourne, he at times believed and sometimes claimed to be or have been, involved in an undercover operation of some sort. He had been (and this cannot be stressed too much), the subject of experimental vaccines and drugs before the first Gulf War and exposed to terrible chemicals in the "Turkey Shoot." He believed himself to have been the subject of experimental medical procedures including, like Bourne, implanted with a tracking chip. Further, he claimed to at least one person that he sometimes suffered from recurring blackouts that usually lasted two or three days, but in one instance, several weeks. During these episodes, he did things he could not remember later, episodes that sound a lot like dissociative fugue states.

In the Bourne Scenario, McVeigh's decision to block an autopsy of his body was his effort to help those behind the scenes stage a theatrical "smoke and mirrors" execution, as was his *alleged* autopsy. Dead men, however, tell no tales, and McVeigh was assuredly a teller of tales. Is it possible that his autopsy would have told yet another suppressed story by revealing evidence of the many physical illnesses that plagued him since joining the Army? Was McVeigh's very body the site of some other unimaginable state secret? If so, the lack of an autopsy is simply one more in a long line of cover-ups. Or may it have worked both ways? Was his execution staged, and McVeigh spirited to some remote location to be used one last time as an Experimental Wolf, only to be taken out back and shot by shady doctors after getting the most value out of their investment? The possibility is chilling to contemplate and yet, a number of details about the bombing and the subsequent obfuscation, as well as the details of McVeigh's life, call to mind the maxim: Truth is stranger than Fiction.

On June 11, 2012, I found myself sitting in the basement of a private university in the remote mountain regions of western New York. I was going through a private archival collection that contained transcripts of conversations between McVeigh and his biographers as well as the letters he wrote them during the final two years of his life. In response to a question about what he would change if he could, he wrote:

> The "culture of secrecy" in government. I would open up everything to public disclosure and scrutiny. No more "black budget" crap, no more redacting government documents [...] Government secrecy means government operates by "conspiracy" (decisions in secret). It breeds suspicions of cover-ups and actual cover-ups, and hey, let's be real – if someone / some entity feels they're doing right (morally), there's no need for secrecy [including] the CIA policy of non-disclosure of names of employees (past or current). You only keep something secret or hidden because you know it's wrong or you fear reprisal – but why fear reprisal if you're the white knight right?

On the other hand, not long after writing this, he told them that Stephen Jones still controlled his case file and he feared that after he filed his appeal, which in part would claim that Jones provided inadequate legal counsel, Jones would find a way to "overtly or covertly" release the material to the public. What Jones was holding onto, he warned them, was "the most relevant stuff." He was sure that someday a lot of it would be "leaked. [The materials in the 'case file' are] supposed to be protected. Jones thinks he can donate them.... He thinks he owns them. We're fighting him on that." McVeigh fretted that if his legal documents were released "20 years from now," it would be too late for him to defend himself from anything within them, a lot of which, he said, was inaccurate, the result of both malice and honest mistakes.

During discussions about his case file, he focused on the FBI 302's, making it seem as if this would be the source of inaccurate information. What he did not mention was that the "case file" consisted of more than 500 boxes of potentially embarrassing documents including his letters, some of his military records, statements by his family, neighbors, friends, and fellow soldiers, and many (but not all) of his attorney memoranda documenting the Jones Teams' conversations with him.[305] What he did say, his last words on the issue at least to his biographers, were that if somebody accessed this material, especially if they already had it out for him, "it could look pretty damning." Finally, he warned that the release of his case material would eclipse public interest in their book, *American Terrorist*, the authorized biography of Tim McVeigh.

That is what I read on June 11, 2012, the anniversary of McVeigh's execution. As soon as I did, the hairs on the back of my neck stood up and chills went through me. I immediately went outside to smoke a cigarette. I felt dizzy. For four years, I had spent months at a time in the very boxes he was talking about. The boxes of legal files Jones donated, that Jones told me about, that became the basis for the book you have just read. I am, to date, the *only* person to have gone through the entire publicly available portions of this case file. Timothy McVeigh emphasized to his biographers that same sentiment he expressed to his attorneys prior to his criminal trial: No matter what happened, he did not want somebody coming along writing the secret lives of Timothy McVeigh, at least in a way that expanded beyond his own dictation.

Even after years of historical and investigatory research, when it comes to the majority of McVeigh's stories, I cannot claim to know with absolute certainty where truth, deception, fantasy, and confabulation begin and end. Throughout this book, I have laid out what I know and what other people have claimed to know. I have provided information to help test competing stories, in the process telling a few new ones. Minimally, I feel I have provided context to help explain why certain people might find certain stories believable or at least possible and why seemingly fantastic stories continue to be told.[306] I have tried to corroborate claims made by others and when I could not, attempted to present information in a way that would indicate this.

People tell a lot of stories, to themselves and others. They tell stories for various reasons, depending on the story being told, the person telling the story and the intended audience of a story. Sometimes stories are true. Sometimes they are not. Some stories continue to be told and take on a life of their own. While the major elements, basic structure, and plot of a story may remain consistent, a story changes, however slightly, with each new telling. This is true even when people intend to and think they are telling true stories. The meaning depends entirely on context; and this too changes. Stories are dynamic, not static. Stories are not photographs and they are not video recordings. They are not and can never be exact representations of what occurred at any given time, even if told within minutes of an event, especially involving many people. There are always missing details. There are always gaps.

Bruce Jackson wrote that real life often doesn't make sense, meaning not everything in life can be explained sufficiently. Sometimes things just happen in a whirlwind of contingency and chance. Even so, he said, the stories people tell each other should make sense, except under certain circumstances. Jackson said he could think of five permissible situations for telling nonsensical, fractured, and contradictory stories: when told by a young child, when told by the daily press, when communicating a myth, when describing a dream, and finally, when told by delusional paranoid psychotics. Stories told by "psychotic murderers," wrote Jackson, "are clutter; they make no sense.... They can't tell a straight story." Nevertheless, their disjoined, fragmented, and contradictory stories serve a larger purpose. They help to create a clearly defined line in the shared cultural sand by delineating innocence and guilt, the right and wrong time to kill, "the boundaries of society, the corridors of power, the heart of legitimacy, the good and the evil."[307]

Underneath the surface of McVeigh's life story, as told by himself and others, is a mystifying, enigmatic, and at the same time all-too-familiar tale of dysfunction, patriotism, medical abuse, torture, interrogation, militarism, the frightening reach of technology, perceived betrayal, secrecy, misdirection, violent spectacles, and remorseless murder. The complete history of the OKC bombing and the events leading up to it will probably never be known, due to withheld, ignored, manipulated, redacted and destroyed evidence. It is, in all its details and variations, a story about expendable people, a story that just doesn't make sense. In a broader sense, stories told about McVeigh by himself and others, true, partially true, or totally fabricated, point to America's hidden history and the lengths that folks will go to conceal it. As far as his decision to have his body cremated, McVeigh told his biographers that he did not want somebody digging up his body in 100 years, "saying this is the real Tim McVeigh." While awaiting his trial, he expressed a particular fascination with one X-Files episode called "Apocrypha," that depicted doctors tending to barely alive disfigured people who eventually died, after which an official coldly instructed the doctors to get rid of the bodies – to have them destroyed.

The terrorist is an elusive, slippery figure, evoked for various reasons and intentions. On May 1, 1995, *Time* magazine declared the likeness of Timothy McVeigh as "The Face Of Terror," a title he retained in the years to come, usurped only briefly by Osama Bin Laden. Amazingly, the corpses of the two Faces of Terrorism of my generation are nonexistent.

WEEKLY WORLD
NEWS.

MORE THAN 13
EXCITING STORI
& FEATURE
INSI

DEAD McVEIGH ON MORGUE SLAB!

PHOTO THE GOVT. DOESN'T WANT YOU TO SEE!

Epilogue

Wearing The Wolf's Head

You don't fight the fight you know you can win, you fight the fight you have to fight, whether you can win or not.

— Jesse Trentadue, Feb. 2015

Caput Gerat Lupinum

— Latin for "Let Him Bear The Wolf's Head," an Old English common law writ of outlawry. Once issued, an outlawed individual was stripped of all legal protections and recourse and banished from society, after which they became, in the eyes of the law, a wolf or other wild animal, who could be legally hunted down and killed by any person who found or encountered them.

The headline of a June 19, 1995, letter to the *Chicago Tribune* asked if Timothy McVeigh was "Oswald's Ghost." If not possessed by Oswald, said the writer, the ghost of Lee Harvey Oswald could nevertheless be seen hovering around him. Either way, both men offered "the public what it wanted, a face and an explanation," a name upon which to hang "the outrage of a grieving country." While the current location of Oswald's ghost is unknown to me, I find it ironic, comically strange almost, that confusion about the finality of McVeigh's death exists not only among the most fantastical of Internet conspiracy theorists (and McVeigh himself) but also among those who propagate the official version of events, that of the Lone Wolf (including McVeigh himself). The perfect (and perhaps most extreme) example of this occurred on April 19, 2010, the fifteenth anniversary of the bombing, when MSNBC aired a two-hour special, *The McVeigh Tapes: Confessions of an American Terrorist*, narrated by Rachael Maddow. Reviews of the special announced "McVeigh is dead … and yet very much with us" and "McVeigh's victims were silenced forever, but their killer, it turns out, lives on."[1]

Although presented as a "documentary," its theatrical production places it more accurately in the category of "docufiction"; a genre wherein "documentary and fiction breed to create a better truth."[2] The show used a look-alike actor to portray McVeigh in key scenes leading up to and after the bombing, sequences made more realistic by digitally placing McVeigh's face, mapped in 3D, over the actor's and overlaying previously unheard audiotapes of prison interviews with McVeigh conducted by the authors of *American Terrorist*. Viewers hear McVeigh narrate his confession while simultaneously witnessing cartoonish versions of Nichols and McVeigh building the bomb; McVeigh, alone, pulling the Ryder up to the front of the Murrah building, igniting the detonation fuse, and calmly walking away as the ground shakes underneath him. Such scenes are interspersed with interviews of victims' family members, survivors, first responders, defense and prosecution attorneys, law enforcement officials, McVeigh's former friends, and Dr. John Smith, his now deceased prison psychiatrist.

Further heightening the emotional intensity, viewers hear McVeigh's cold and callous thoughts about survivors and victim family members. Maddow comments that, despite her opposition to capital punishment, McVeigh's "profoundly unsympathetic – even repugnant" statements caused her to rethink this position. The authors of *American Terrorist* appear and inform viewers of a recent rise in the militia and Tea Party movements, an increase in weapons purchases and stockpiling, and swelling anti-government angst in response to growing government regulations, widespread unemployment, and health care reform debates. Maddow, the Ann Coulter of the political left, concludes by saying that even though nine years have passed since his execution, "we are left worrying that Timothy McVeigh's voice from the grave echoes in a new rising tide of American anti-government extremism." Reviewers described the anniversary special as "creepy," "jarring," "scary and chilling," a "cautionary tale," a "somber warning" about "unchecked fanaticism" and the dangers posed by "fringe lunatics who cannot distinguish between fantasy and reality," a not-too-subtle reminder of the need to monitor dangerous individuals, ideologies, and groups.[3]

Despite its dehumanizing and villainous depiction of him, the *The McVeigh Tapes* nevertheless relied upon McVeigh as a primary, credible, and authoritative source of information about both himself and the bombing. The motives and veracity of McVeigh's Lone Wolf story, like those of the experts, FBI agents or the government officials featured in the show are left unchallenged and unquestioned. Through critical omissions, *The McVeigh Tapes* dismisses a wealth of conflicting evidence about the facts of the bombing plot, including those particulars that had recently surfaced. This, coupled with the emotional narratives of the bombing victims that circumvent critical audience reception, impose upon the viewer a "historical" truth, the questioning of which is equated to the very types of devilish ideology and psychological disturbance supposedly typified by McVeigh himself.

The blending of authoritative experts and officials, narrator commentary, emotionally laden testimony and the posthumous voice of McVeigh, with cartoonish video-game graphics creates the illusion of reality and transforms acts of political violence into digestible popular memes, whose worth is found in their perceived entertainment value rather than the factual or evidential integrity. In this way, *The McVeigh Tapes* is an artifact that exemplifies "Mass Mediated Spectacles of Terrorism"; terms that refer to the porousness and fluidity of boundaries between fact, fiction, news and entertainment.[4] The show not only rendered McVeigh the first terrorist to come back from the dead and scare American television viewers, but perfectly illustrates the ongoing and aggressive nature of a large body of Lone Wolf texts to present "self-evident truths" about both McVeigh and the bombing, through a self-authorizing framework and in a manner that resists alternate information and interpretations.

In February 2012, the FBI issued a warning about the resurgence of "Lone Wolf Terrorism" whose perpetrators they compared to Timothy McVeigh, the "prototypical lone wolf extremist." The recurring comparisons of newer "Lone Wolves Weaned on Hate" to McVeigh, use terminology, labels, descriptions and media framing to explain their actions, ideologies and motivations, remarkably similar and in some cases, exactly the same, as those used in initial media reports about McVeigh himself. Often detailed are perpetrators' transformations from "Boy Next Door" into "Homegrown Lone Wolves." Such texts, while keeping with the Lone Wolf script that asserts the bombing plot was a lonely one, is still able to implicate broader segments of society by equating them with McVeigh, a phenomenon *The New Yorker* referred to in January 2016 as "the McVeigh stigma." Not content to leave dead enough alone, reports of this type warn of the ubiquitous "specter of militia past," the ghostly gang who assumedly keep McVeigh company in the afterlife when not busy rising from the dead intent on infecting others with the not quite clinical affliction of "McVeigh madness."[5]

The acts, prevented acts or ascribed fantasies of "Terrorists Next Door" (including apparently undead ones), even when their ideological motivation, if any, is unclear, provoke political and cultural debates about the need for measures to prevent, detect, and punish actual or aspiring terroristic wolves like those enacted in the aftermath of the Oklahoma City bombing. These debates weigh the demands for tighter security measures in public spaces, stricter gun laws, and mental health screenings against the preservation of civil liberties, with the latter usually getting the short end of the stick. For two decades, the name Timothy McVeigh has functioned as shorthand in discussions about Lone Wolf terrorists, the threat of right-wing ideologues, mass shooters, conspiracy theorists, disgruntled veterans, and dissenters generally. Given the conflicting information that has ceaselessly surfaced since his 2001 execution, the tendency to do so is simplistic and unproductive at best, intentionally deceptive and agenda-driven at worst. Whatever the intent, when the name McVeigh is mentioned in reports, (usually as a means of demonizing other people and groups), everybody knows what is being discussed, or at least venomously thinks and asserts that they do. But they don't.

While Bourne Scenario enthusiasts claim the Lonely Wolf lived on, those who tote the official line make an even stranger claim, or when not explicated, an even stranger subtextual implication. In their minds, Lone Wolf McVeigh died but then somehow managed to return from the dead and possess untold numbers of potential terrorists who must be exorcized of his "unconquerable soul" by whatever means necessary. It seems to me, they don't *want* McVeigh to die, that his absence would rob them of a convenient spectral demon who reliably offers a means of reducing the complexities of actual threats to buzz words, pop psychology, and politically expedient narratives.

For all the talk of understanding violence and those who commit it, (talk that tends to increase budgets, pass legislation, and justify unrelated restrictive and intrusive measures but never actually dampens the initially proclaimed threat), I'm not convinced the people who (sincerely or with an agenda) tout the McVeigh as Lone Wolf or even the Pack story without the Watched Wolf caveat, or who label politically undesirables as "McVeighs," really *want* to understand much of anything. Here's why:

While the details of Lone Wolf accounts have remained consistent, after McVeigh's 2001 execution, all other narrative variations became increasingly complex due in part to the continuing emergence of case-related information resulting from ongoing formal and informal investigative, legal, and academic efforts. A 2006 Congressional Oversight investigation, more than one major network television exposé, scholarly works, lawsuits, and countless investigative journalism reports, have continued to document additional instances of informant's warnings and other intelligence failures pertaining to the OKC bombing, comparable to those that occurred prior to the events of September 11, 2001.[6]

Included are two academically published books, both written by scholars of politically contentious social movements and former Jones Team consultants. The first of these was Indiana State University criminologist Mark Hamm's *In Bad Company: America's Terrorist Underground*, published in 2001 and the second, Lamar University sociologist Stuart Wright's book *Patriots, Politics, and The Oklahoma City Bombing*, published in 2007. Both purport what Hamm coined the "Multiple John Doe #2 Theory," consisting of the usual litany of assorted bank robbers, white separatists, neo-Nazi's and gun show attendees. Both note the presence of more than a few federal agency and watchdog organization informants among the conspirators and their attempts to warn authorities about an impending attack.

In Bad Company, valuable for its sociological insight, while telling a more plausible story of the bomb plot than that of the Lone Wolf, and noting many of the related failures of intelligence surrounding the bombing, does not proffer possible reasons for the failures or explore the ways in which networks of informants contributed to the plot.[7]

Wright placed the bombing in the context of an escalating "trajectory of contention" between 'insurgents' and agents of social control. In the years leading to the bombing, both sides of the conflict (Patriot Movement versus law enforcement officials, watchdog groups, and policy makers) increasingly employed dramatic "war narratives" about the need to neutralize the looming threat represented by the other. This was aided in large part by sensationalized media reports that only confirmed and fueled their perceptions resulting in and justifying acts of violence by the "insurgents" and the increased use of militaristic tactics by law enforcement agencies (think Waco, Ruby Ridge, etc.,), budget increases and the passage of arguably unnecessary legislation.[8]

Wright noted the ways in which the sizeable body of case-related information linking McVeigh to other conspirators that surfaced since 2001 allowed for the construction of "a more complete picture," one very different from the government's "lone wolf theory" that had "steadily disintegrated with each new revelation." Included among them was a Secret Service memo uncovered by Associated Press investigative journalist John Solomon in 2004. The memo referred to security cameras around the Murrah, stating the "security video tapes from the area show the truck detonation three minutes and six seconds after the suspects [plural] exited the truck." While the FBI and federal prosecutors denied the existence of any such footage, the memo was allowed to be entered in as evidence during Nichols' 2004 state trial. This and other "newly discovered" evidence about the Others Unknown, created significant reasonable doubt among jurors and significantly undermined the story of the bombing as told by the FBI and DOJ.[9] The continual appearance of *newly discovered evidence* such as the memo within media headlines and news reports, was followed by the FBI's announcement in early 2004 that they planned to conduct a formal review of their previous investigation and initiate a new inquiry into McVeigh's connections to the right-wing underground; the results of which have yet to be revealed.

More importantly (for the purpose of this discussion), Wright's conception of a much larger bombing plot, did not just mention but *emphasized* the proliferation of undercover informants and related intelligence-gathering efforts of law enforcement agencies prior to the bombing. Ultimately, Wright concluded much more vigorously than Hamm, who didn't seem to think it all that important, that several state and federal officials from different agencies had varying degrees of foreknowledge of the impending bombing, for one reason or another neglected to act on this knowledge and thereby, failed to prevent it.[10] This was, of course, not a new or unique theory, but one whose legitimization outside of "paranoid" circles was aided, in part, by Wright's scholarly status. Wright went a few steps further than just documenting prior knowledge; he also called attention to the FBI's destruction of critical photographic and video evidence, a pattern noted but left unexplained. The deep embedding of intelligence agents and assets outlined by Wright is crucial to understanding McVeigh's role in the plot and many of the little known stories told by and about McVeigh both prior to and after the bombing, and the related manipulation and destruction of evidence afterward.

Other ongoing developments in the case occurring shortly before and at the time of Wright's writing include a History Channel special in late 2004 that detailed contradictory evidence and lingering mysteries surrounding the bombing and the 2005 publication of *After Oklahoma City*, a book by Oklahoma City dissident Kathy Wilbern-Sanders, whose two young grandsons died in the bombing. She outlined the personal impact that the bombing and its cover-up had on grieving families and their process of uncovering evidence in the early stages of the investigation.

Perhaps the most significant development at the time was a largely ignored 2006 Congressional Investigation led by Congressman Dana Rohrabacher (R-CA), that looked at lingering questions about "serious but circumstantial evidence" pertaining to the involvement of other conspirators in the bombing plot. While the investigation did not look into any question that had not already been raised previously (embedded informants, prior warnings, McVeigh's relationship to various groups and individuals, etc.,) it did so with the authority of the government. The committee's final report detailed a number of roadblocks faced by investigators including ex-FBI Special Agent and former Governor of Oklahoma Frank Keating's strange request that "the investigation be called off" shortly after it began.

Another roadblock the committee documented was the FBI's refusal to cooperate, and Department of Justice's refusal to disclose (among other things) the whereabouts of one ARA bank robber who, at best, was thought to possess critical information about the bombing and its perpetrators and, at worst, was a possible suspect himself. About these and other instances of the FBI's "needless defensive" obfuscations, the report noted, "Federal law enforcement has been accused of an institutional mind-set that congressional oversight is a nuisance to be avoided or blocked. That mind-set was painfully obvious during this subcommittee's inquiry into the Oklahoma City bombing."[11]

Former Oklahoma State Representative Charles Key, who spearheaded the empaneling of the similarly railroaded state Grand Jury that convened in 1997, recounted:

> The [Rohrabacher] investigators came to Oklahoma City and we met with them, discussing the bombing and what we thought was the most important piece of evidence they could obtain – the surveillance tapes that were in Murrah federal building and in the downtown area. I told them they should demand to the FBI that the tapes be released and reviewed. They said they did not have the ability to do that, they tried and were unsuccessful. During the criminal trials, the Justice Department had said they couldn't do this, or couldn't do [that] simply because of the ongoing trial or investigation, but the Justice Department continued to deny this material to the Congressional Investigators even after the trial had concluded. They continued to use the exact same excuses to prevent obtaining information that's been sought for such a long time.[12]

According to the 2006 Rohrabacher Committee report, in June 1995, two months into the Oklahoma City bombing investigation "The FBI, much to the frustration of some of its own investigators, discarded the possibility of the existence of John Doe Two" and despite evidence to the contrary, "authorities still contend McVeigh was alone [the morning of the bombing]." It then expressed the opinion of the committee that "The FBI was not justified in calling off any further investigation into John Doe Two" but had done so nevertheless. Further, the FBI failed to conduct an adequate investigation of the many credible links between McVeigh and others, links that may have led to the discovery of his other conspirators, and seemingly ignored crucial evidence about the origins and ultimate location of some of the explosives possessed by McVeigh and Nichols.

The report concluded by expressing the committee's belief that, "Authorities erred in allowing Timothy McVeigh to move forward the time of his execution while major questions remained about whether others were involved in the crime. [...] the McVeigh execution should have been further delayed until there was greater consensus on the subject of John Doe Two." Noting that "the average condemned inmate spends well over a decade on death row" and McVeigh spent only four years, the report opines, "Perhaps McVeigh would have continued to adamantly deny anyone else's involvement but simply keeping him alive closer to the typical death row stay would have allowed more opportunity for determining the truth."[13] A convenient circumstance for some; disconcerting for others.

In 2007, the BBC aired their own special about the bombing conspiracy noting the many questions that remained. The show featured former FBI agent Danny Coulson, involved in the initial OKC bombing investigation. Coulson said that he was told by his superiors not to investigate the links between McVeigh and Elohim City and felt that the only way to resolve the lingering mysteries in the case was to convene a federal grand jury investigation. FBI agent Jon Hersley (lead agent in charge of the OKC investigation, and author of *Simple Truths*) disagreed and said that the FBI did such a thorough investigation that they actually "over-investigated parts of the case."[14]

Despite some of their criticisms of Stephen Jones, a number of former members of the Jones Team came to similar conclusions about the case. The most recent to voice them being Jones Team investigator and award-winning journalist and producer Roger Charles in his 2012 book, *Oklahoma City: What the Investigation Missed – And Why It Still Matters*, the latest full-length investigatory text. The book, co-written by Andrew Gumbel (*Huffington Post, Guardian*), details *some* of the results of Roger Charles' 20-year research and investigation, provides a comprehensive source of well-documented information and contributes significant details about the inner workings of the FBI's investigation, or lack thereof, while managing to avoid making speculative claims. A glowing review in the *Wall Street Journal* said Charles' "extraordinarily well-researched" book demonstrates how, in their zeal to obtain convictions against McVeigh and Nichols and avoid confusing jurors, the FBI's "investigation of the bombing was badly flawed and missed, or disregarded, evidence of a larger conspiracy," thereby raising the question, "How far did the conspiracy go?"[15]

For a moment, between the publication of Wright's book in 2007 and Charles' book in 2012, it almost seemed as if the most widely popular narrative and publicly accepted history of the bombing had changed forever. In March 2011, nearly a year after the airing of MSNBC's *The McVeigh Tapes*, entertainment outlets mounted the planned filming of *O.K.C.*, to be produced by Oscar winner filmmaker Barry Levinson (*Rain Man, Good Morning Vietnam, Wag The Dog*). The upcoming movie was described as Hollywood's fictionalized, but based on true events, take on the Oklahoma City bombing conspiracy. Announcements of the upcoming production noted that the script for the "political thriller," written by Clay Wold, was based on the experiences of his brother, Chad, a Jones Team legal clerk who spent "months" of his life "attempting to investigate evidence that others were involved in the terrorist act, often at the risk of his own career and safety." *O.K.C.* is the story of the intrepid Jones Team clerk's "determination to expose the truth," an effort that ultimately led him "to a bigger conspiracy and nearly destroyed the young man." The film promised to expose "the real circumstances" surrounding the 1995 bombing.

Not everyone was happy about the type of clarifications made by Hamm, Wright, John Solomon, the Rohrabacher Committee, or Roger Charles. Nor were they enthusiastic about fictionalized depictions along these lines. An anonymous editorial expressed the hope that Levinson's movie would "stick to the facts" and be "accurate and devoid of embellishment," rather than a movie that only "muddles history" and dishonors bombing victims; a sentiment not expressed about the observably embellished and aggressively deceptive MSNBC bombing anniversary special. Similar sounding write-ups appeared, all offering an abbreviated Lone Wolf accounting of reality. The film was never made and like the John Doe 2's and Murrah surveillance tapes, it quickly disappeared down the memory hole.[16]

Memory is fleeting. Just before McVeigh's criminal trial began, a scandal erupted concerning the corrupt and compromised practices of the FBI crime lab that had manipulated its findings to bolster convictions. The scandal was quickly forgotten because, after all, this was the work of isolated people and corrective measures had been enacted. Or so the public was led to believe. History repeated itself in April 2015, when the FBI made a "startling admission" that for over 20 years its forensic experts gave flawed testimony at criminal trials, some ending in the death penalty. The mistakes, purportedly unintentional, were always in favor of the prosecution. Innocent people had been convicted; some had been put to death. The revelations were a "colossal disaster … a sinkhole … a systemic failure." Interestingly, the CNN segment that reported these revelations on April 19, 2015, transitioned into a piece about the anniversary of the Oklahoma City bombing, never once mentioning the earlier crime lab scandal or the questions that still surround the physical evidence in that case. Viewers were informed that, back in 1995, law enforcement really had to scramble to figure out what had happened but, luckily, these days, people who pose potential threats on the scale of McVeigh are under a much stronger "microscope"; an assertion that, ironically, implies that the new McVeighs will be detected and stopped before they have a chance to strike.[17]

One man who knows all about the types of treacherous institutional and public memory holes outlined above (and throughout this book) is

Salt Lake City attorney Jesse Trentadue. For 20 years and counting he has walked through fire to retrieve some of the critical information that has fallen into those holes and continues to act as a force of reckoning for memory-hole diggers, although to do so he has gone down a road even the most determined and bravest of truth seekers dare not tread. He is, as one news article noted, "no liberal crusader, nor is he an anti-government conspiracy theorist." However, as fate would have it, in his quest to learn why his brother was murdered, Jesse Trentadue uncovered (and continues to uncover) the most explosive and aggressively suppressed information withheld from the public about the bombing to date, ensuring that the questions about it remain in public view.[18]

The horrible story began when on June 10, 1995, Jesse's brother, Kenneth Michael Trentadue, a 44 year-old Vietnam veteran, was driving home to his new wife and child in San Diego, California. Kenneth was pulled over during a routine traffic stop near the California-Mexico border where he'd been working a construction job. Wanted on a parole violation that occurred six years earlier, he was taken into custody and incarcerated in a San Diego jail until August 18, when he was inexplicably transferred to a Federal Transfer Center (FTC) in Oklahoma City, to be held there temporarily until his parole violation hearing. The next day, he called his family and let them know where he was. According to his family, Kenneth wasn't upset, knowing he'd most likely be released immediately after the hearing or at worst, would serve no more than another two months. If anything, he sounded upbeat and hopeful. He was looking forward to the future. As a young man returning home from the Vietnam War, he'd gotten into his share of trouble but since 1988, had pieced his life back together. He'd recently gotten married and had just become the proud father of a baby boy. Kenneth and his family spoke briefly and he promised to call back the next day, but his call never came.[19]

Early on the morning of August 21, the acting FTC warden called the Trentadue family to inform them that Kenneth had hung himself in his cell the night before. The warden then urged them to have Kenneth cremated and made an unprecedented offer to have the prison incur the expense of the cremation. The family insisted Kenneth's body be returned to them unmolested and eventually, one week later, after several heated and bizarre phone calls, the prison complied.[20] Upon seeing his body, the family realized why prison officials, despite their protests, had been so insistent on a cremation. Kenneth's corpse was so heavily caked with makeup that, at first, the wounds underneath were barely visible. When his wife and mother cleaned off the makeup, it became evident that Kenneth had been brutally tortured and murdered. He was covered from head to toe with bruises, lacerations, and obvious fingerprint impressions. His skull was smashed in three places and, perhaps most damning, his throat was slashed.

On August 30, 1995, when services for his brother concluded, Jesse wrote a heartbreaking letter of complaint to the Bureau of Prisons and enclosed photographs of Kenneth's body. Any reasonable person could see that this was no suicide, Jesse wrote, and, after outlining various possibilities about how such injuries could have occurred, expressed his opinion that the prison was in some way responsible.[21] Two days later, the BOP issued a press release claiming that Kenneth's injuries were self-inflicted and over time concocted an amazing story about how Kenneth had tried to hang himself but fell. Since that didn't work, he attempted to slit his throat with a tube of toothpaste before making a second, and this time, successful attempt to hang himself.

What the press release failed to mention was that, over the BOP's objections, a medical examiner had performed an autopsy as required by state law. The day after Kenneth died, Kevin Rowland, Chief Investigator for the Medical Examiner's Office, filed a report with the local FBI noting his belief that Kenneth's injuries were "inconsistent with a suicide," and indicated "foul play." Fred Jordon, Oklahoma Chief Medical Examiner, listed the cause of death as "unknown" pending investigation and, despite the BOP's demands, refused to classify it as a suicide. In the days and months to follow, Rowland filed additional reports noting his suspicion that Kenneth had been tortured and murdered and the fact that prison officials refused to grant investigators access to the cell itself. Rather, they were only allowed to view the cell from outside, by peering between the bars, although by that time it didn't matter because the cell had been scrubbed clean in violation of standard procedure in inmate deaths, suspicious or otherwise.[22]

Because the Medical Examiner's Office had officially noted their concerns through the proper channels, the BOP was required by law to investigate the matter, although, anticipating a lawsuit, filed their documentation of the supposed investigation in such a way as to be shielded from public discovery through FOIA or court actions. In the following months and years, Jesse attempted to use every legal means available to discover the facts surrounding his brother's death, a task that proved exceedingly difficult due in part to the BOP's destruction of a great deal of evidence including, among other things, crime scene photos, prison logbooks and Kenneth's bloodstained clothing. And then there was the issue of the video-tapes of Kenneth's cell the morning he was found, the contents of which were erased.

Eventually, over the objections of Medical Examiner Chief Investigator Kevin Rowland, Oklahoma City District Attorney Bob Macy issued a final ruling that Kenneth had committed suicide. Macy, you will remember, was the lead prosecutor in the Oklahoma City bombing case and after unsuccessfully attempting to prevent the formation of the state Grand Jury investigation of the bombing, was appointed to oversee and control it. The significance of this to Jesse however, would not become apparent for another six years.[23]

In 1996, due to the negative attention of media outlets and support of sympathetic legislators that the case was receiving, the DOJ's Civil Rights Division assumed responsibility for the investigation and recommended evidence be presented to a federal grand jury, which would decide whether or not to issue any indictments. Meanwhile, the local FBI office set about discrediting the reputation of Fred Jordon, who had conducted Kenneth's autopsy and had refused to rule the death a suicide; even a forensic pathologist, hired by the DOJ to give a second opinion, had also reached the same conclusion as Jordon.[24]

The Grand Jury heard only evidence cherry-picked by the government and declined to issue any criminal indictments. It took two months for the DOJ to inform the family or the public of this, because, as inflammatory internal reports, emails and handwritten DOJ notes later revealed, they were busy devising a "roll-out plan," about how they would handle fallout from the lack of indictments, including the very real possibility of a Congressional or Senate investigation. "We ain't looking for press on this," said one email. DOJ officials compared the damage control effort to "coordinating the invasion of Normandy" which, they said, would necessitate a long list of "Trentadues and Trentadon'ts." Leading and controlling the effort was future Attorney General Eric Holder, who at the time was Deputy and Acting Attorney General, second only in command to Janet Reno.

Holder's plan, dubbed by him and his DOJ team, "the Trentadue Mission," apparently included sending FBI agents to harass any person with influence who might affect an outcome other than the one the DOJ desired. Oklahoma Assistant Attorney General Patrick Crawley informed a DOJ attorney that, in what he described as an "Alice through the Looking Glass" situation, the BOP and FBI had obfuscated the truth of Kenneth's death. The agencies had

> ...prevented the medical examiner from conducting a thorough and complete investigation into the death, destroyed evidence, and otherwise harassed and harangued Dr. Jordan and his staff. The absurdity of this situation is that your clients [DOJ officials] outwardly represent law enforcement or at least some arm of licit government.... It appears that your clients, and perhaps others within the Department of Justice, have been abusing the powers of their respective offices. If this is true, all Americans should be very frightened [of the DOJ].

The calculated and malicious pressure placed on Jordon finally became too much for him and, in July 1998, he complied and changed Kenneth's official cause of death to suicide, although in private he continued to maintain otherwise.[25]

In the meantime, just as the BOP had feared, the Trentadue family filed a wrongful death lawsuit through which additionally damaging information surfaced despite the government's efforts to destroy relevant evidence in the case that would reveal the identities of Kenneth's murderers, including blood samples from inside the cell that belonged to individuals other than Kenneth Trentadue. Then there were eyewitnesses, including a prison guard who told his neighbor that Kenneth was hung after he died in order to cover up the fact that he had been killed. In 1999, Alden Gillis Baker, an inmate in an adjacent cell came forward to say he witnessed the murder and was willing to testify at the civil suit. He never got the chance because, soon after Baker told his lawyer that he feared for his life, he too was found dead, hanging in his cell. Although Baker's death was ruled a suicide, he was not the last helpful witness to turn up dead.[26]

In a strange and cruel maneuver, the DOJ requested that U.S. District Judge Tim Leonard, who presided over the civil suit, legally muzzle the Trentadue family. Specifically, the DOJ requested that the judge issue an order barring the Trentadue family from discussing with the media or any branch of law enforcement (including the DOJ itself) any evidence revealed through discovery or presented at the trial that might implicate federal employees in criminal acts including perjury or obstruction of justice. In August 1998, Judge Leonard complied with the DOJ request, explaining that he did not want the suit to become "a pipeline of information to non-parties over whom the court has no supervision."[27]

While the civil suit was still being litigated and the Trentadue family gagged, the DOJ's Office Of Inspector General (OIG) conducted another brief investigation but sealed their November 1999 report. However, they did release a summary of the report relaying their finding that employees of the FBI had mishandled evidence and lied to their superiors, to the OIG, and to the courts about their actions during their initial investigation into Kenneth's death. In 2001, the Trentadue family was awarded $1.1 million for "emotional distress," not for the BOP's role in Kenneth's death, but from their deceptive and otherwise shameful conduct afterwards. Money wasn't what Jesse Trentadue was after. He simply wanted answers about his brother's death and, now, the reason the BOP, FBI, and DOJ would go to such great lengths and spend millions of dollars to prevent him or the public from obtaining these answers.[28]

It was at this time that Timothy McVeigh contacted Jesse Trentadue and told him the FBI killed his brother during an interrogation
gone awry. The FBI, advised McVeigh, had mistaken Kenneth for ARA
bank robber Richard Guthrie, whose whereabouts in August 1995 were
unknown, but whom the FBI suspected had information about, if not
direct, involvement in the Oklahoma City bombing. When he saw pictures of Guthrie, Jesse was struck by how closely he resembled Kenneth.
Even stranger, after his arrest for the bank robberies in 1996, Guthrie
(like Kenneth, and Baker before him) was found hanging in his prison
cell, after threatening to tell the media everything he knew about the
bombing, which, Guthrie indicated, was quite a bit.[29] Many speculated
that had he lived, Guthrie would have revealed McVeigh's links to specific members of the ARA bank robbery gang (including Guthrie himself), some of the residents at Elohim City, the identities of federal informants, and the participation of all three groups in the bombing plot.

Thus, Jesse set out to learn what he could about the bank robbers,
his search for justice and truth for his brother becoming forever-after inexorably intertwined with the Oklahoma City bombing conspiracy. As
Jesse himself explained, he didn't start out trying to solve the Oklahoma
City bombing but "as it happened, every lead I came across took me
back to the bombing in Oklahoma City in April of 1995, including the
message I received from Tim McVeigh shortly before he was executed."
He quickly encountered the very institutional secrecy and denials that
long plagued both his brother's and the OKC bombing case. Nevertheless, where others, including the Oklahoma Dissidents and the Jones
Team had failed to obtain information about a larger conspiracy, Jesse
succeeded; but only because, in the words of journalist Andrew Gumbel, ever since the death of his brother, Jesse Trentadue had "been all
over the federal government like a bad case of lice."[30]

Jesse Trentadue's lousy information-seeking infestation, as it concerns the
OKC bombing, began in earnest in 2005, when he began filing Freedom
Of Information Act requests to federal agencies for information about the
bank robbers, the FBI's and other federal agencies' investigation of them
and their possible links to McVeigh. For the most part, the FBI responded
by denying that any such information existed. The majority of documents
they did produce were heavily redacted and virtually unreadable. Even so,
the released documents revealed that prior to calling off their search for
additional conspirators in the bombing, the FBI had actively investigated
links between McVeigh, the ARA, Elohim City and others with possible
connection to the bombing and the existence of additional informants
embedded within the plot beyond those already known about. Significantly, the documents referenced an FBI informant from Arkansas who

had infiltrated militia and patriot groups around the country; a probable reference to Roger Moore, who provided explosives to McVeigh. Further, Jesse obtained documentation indicating links between McVeigh and bank robber Guthrie, which lent weight to the tip-off McVeigh gave Jesse in 2001.[31]

Some of the documents produced in response to Jesse's FOIA's made reference to other related documents, which should have been produced but weren't. His requests for these as well as other, more specific information were met with similar denials including one instance where the CIA acknowledged the existence of the sought information but refused to turn it over for reasons of National Security. Every time an agency (most often the FBI) failed to release the requested information or denied its existence, Jesse appealed, all the while continuing to file additional requests for other information. In doing so, he continued to uncover ever more damning information and encountered further obfuscations until, eventually, his appeals set legal precedent.

In 2006, U.S. District Judge Dale Kimball, who presided over Jesse's appeals at this time, opined that he had "unearthed significant evidence of foul play" in his brother's death, and "posed some very good questions" about the factual history of the bombing. Kimball found it "troubling" that the FBI had failed to produce "so many of the documents" referenced in the material they had turned over and further observed that the material Jesse had obtained "indicate[d] that there was an undercover operative in with McVeigh and members of various militia groups who aided and supported McVeigh. Plaintiff wonders why, given the subject matter, there are no earlier records that have been produced by the FBI."[32] When Kimball ordered the FBI to turn over all of the information Jesse sought, they responded by giving him another 150 pages of heavily redacted documents, some of which they had previously claimed did not exist. Jesse responded by arguing that this was only a fraction of what the FBI continued to withhold and Kimball once more ordered the FBI to look again. After the agency predictably returned with claims that the sought-after documents did not exist, Jesse produced heavily redacted copies of some of them, which had been anonymously leaked to him.

Until this day, a pattern has continued wherein Jesse seeks information, the FBI claims it doesn't exist, Jesse proves it does, judges ordered the FBI to search harder and the FBI comes back with even more heavily redacted pages. The majority of the information federal agencies have sought to withhold concerns informants embedded in or in close proximity to the bombing plot, the number of which continued to increase until it became undeniable that something larger than the bombing plot itself had been going on. Jesse's quest and the unthinkable information it resulted in, increasingly appeared in national news media. He had forced the discovery of information about the bombing and the machinations and troubling methodologies of the FBI.[33]

Although apparently unread by Rachel Maddow and the producers of *The McVeigh Tapes*, by 2007, major media outlets began to ask the very same questions about the bombing that so-called conspiracy theorists had been asking for years and advancing the very theory about Kenneth's death that Timothy McVeigh offered to Jesse years earlier. *Democracy Now* reported that the information Jesse "dug up suggest that the FBI knew about the plot to bomb the Alfred P. Murrah federal building" and did "little to prevent it." Trentadue was credited with revealing "a widespread informant operation" that had allowed the FBI and ATF to know "well in advance of April 1995 that there was a bombing in place and/or [in the] planning," as well as the identities of those involved, although both agencies "did nothing to stop it."[34] Amazing as such acknowledgements may seem, in 2007, Jesse was just warming up. There were still many more questions than there were answers.

With the blessing and support of the surviving Oklahoma Dissidents (bombing survivors and victim family members), Jesse next requested copies of the twenty or more missing surveillance tapes from cameras that surrounded the Murrah building on April 19, 1995, all in different locations and managed by different companies. The tapes, which captured the moments before and after the bombing, could clear up the issue of who was with McVeigh that day. The FBI insisted that they could not locate the tapes and therefore, they did not exist. But, unbeknownst to the FBI, Jesse possessed FBI documents proving otherwise, which he presented to the court.

In 2009, having denied their existence for 15 years, the FBI released video footage from four of the 22 or so cameras in and around the Murrah. Oddly though, while the cameras, operated by four different local businesses using four separate systems, contained several uninterrupted hours of footage prior to the explosion, all of them simultaneously malfunctioned at the same time; which just happened to be the moment the Ryder truck pulled up to the front of the Murrah building. The footage then resumes minutes after the blast. While some of the released footage came from a camera inside the Murrah, the FBI claimed there was no camera posted on the outside of the building and insisted there were no more tapes beyond those they suddenly *discovered* and dutifully provided.

When he appealed in 2010, Jesse submitted irrefutable evidence to the contrary, including the FBI's own reports documenting agents gathering tapes from a great many more cameras than they claimed to exist. In addition, he presented sworn affidavits and photographs proving there were cameras on the outside of the Murrah in a position to capture the Ryder and its occupants. He argued that the FBI was withholding footage from additional cameras and that the miraculously malfunctioning video the FBI *had* turned over was doctored. The judge bluntly asked the FBI where the footage from the other cameras was, to which the FBI responded that, although additional footage capturing the worst attack of terrorism on American soil had once existed, it had since been "lost." In 2011, citing the public importance of the tapes, Federal Judge Clark Waddoups ordered the FBI to conduct another search for the tapes and further, to explain why FBI officials had previously made false statements to the court about those tapes.[35]

During a trial over the matter in July 2014, OKCPD officer and first responder Don Browning testified to what he had stated in his earlier submitted sworn affidavit. Browning, in what the court found to be "the most compelling testimony" heard at the trial, said that in the immediate aftermath of the bombing, as rescue workers were trying to recover as many survivors as they could, the FBI ordered them to halt the search. When Browning protested that there was a woman trapped inside the building who was still alive, a female FBI agent told him "that there were files so critical to the government that there would be no recovery effort" until the files were retrieved. As he waited for this to happen, Browning observed a group of FBI agents place a ladder up against the Murrah that they then used to retrieve a surveillance camera on the front of the building, the bracketing, and much of the wiring – essentially anything to indicate that the camera had ever been there. The FBI denied this and called Jesse's witness a liar. Jesse, however, happened to have two photographs that had appeared in news articles shortly after the bombing. One showed a camera on the building and the other, a ladder against the building but no camera.

A colorful back-and-forth exchange ensued between Jesse, the FBI's witness and the judge. Waddoups eventually opined that the evidence and testimony presented by Jesse "supports an inference that these cameras were removed from the Murrah Building that morning [April 19, 1995] to conceal the fact that there was a security system in place that may have recorded the perpetrators," and that the FBI "failed to prove" that the camera didn't exist. The finding implies that the agency's pattern of lying to the court was an ongoing one.[36] Their continued insistence that nobody was with McVeigh and the Ryder in Oklahoma City on April 19, 1995, was becoming increasingly tenuous and raised a number of questions. Even if the many eyewitnesses were unreliable (as the government argued), how could the FBI or anybody else for that matter, know one way or another if, in fact, the tapes didn't exist or were lost? Along with the tenacity of their claims, the motives behind losing, hiding or destroying the tapes also appeared increasingly sketchy.

The reasons prompting the FBI's stubborn obfuscations became all the more suspicious when, in 2007, J.M. Berger, a writer for *Foreign Policy* and *Intelwire*, filed FOIA requests seeking information about federal surveillance of a Texas militia and the FBI responded with several redacted documents, some of which contained reference to "PATCON." Hoping to find out more, Berger and Jesse Trentadue requested more information through FOIA, the results of which (while highly redacted) revealed the FBI led a multiagency national sting/provocateur network called PATCON, that, as we now know, somehow kept crossing paths with McVeigh and correlated to information about the FBI's informant network Jesse had already discovered. The PATCON developments ultimately allowed Jesse to forge further precedent-setting investigative paths and, in the process, fill in some major gaps in the known history of the Oklahoma City bombing.

Jesse recalled how, in 2011, as he continued appeals in the surveillance tape case and pieced together the specifics of PATCON, he received a call from a man named John Matthews who told Jesse that while he (Jesse) had "all the pieces" he didn't "see the big picture."[37] Matthews told Jesse he had been a deep-cover PATCON informant and offered the name of his former handler, FBI Special Agent Don Jarrett, stationed in the Phoenix, Arizona office. Matthews, a Vietnam veteran, was dying from Agent Orange-related cancer. Jesse's story had moved him so much that he wanted to relieve himself of some PATCON secrets he harbored before he died and, in July 2011, traveled across the country to meet with Jesse.

Matthews explained that the majority of undercover PATCON informants faced criminal charges and became involved in exchange for reduction or dropping of those charges. Matthews however, said he chose to go undercover out of concern over the danger posed by extremist right-wing groups. He believed that he could serve his country by informing on them and thus went undercover for PATCON in 1992. Eventually though, after successfully infiltrating twenty-three groups, Matthews realized that although he was initially told, "the objective was to infiltrate and monitor," he came to understand that, actually, "the objective was to infiltrate and incite." Matthews outlined a number of instances in which PATCON operatives had provided the ideas, detailed instructions, and even live C4 explosives and automatic weapons to targeted individuals as a way of entrapping them into terrorist plots, so the FBI could capitalize on foiled and actualized plots.[38]

Matthews said both Ruby Ridge and Waco were PATCON operations and he believed Oklahoma City was too because, while he wasn't involved in the latter, he knew of other "PATCON guys" who had been. In fact, Matthews told Jesse that the year prior to the Oklahoma City bombing he had seen Timothy McVeigh at a militia training camp in Texas. McVeigh, whose name he didn't know at the time, was with a German man and they were instructing camp attendees in the art of converting flare guns into grenade launchers (explored previously in this book). After McVeigh was arrested, Matthews immediately recognized him and called Jarrett to tell him that this was the same man he saw at the Texas training camp. Jarrett assured Matthews that they (the FBI) already knew and told him to "forget about it."[39] Matthews said he was disturbed by this for a few reasons. For one, this indicated that the FBI probably had informants spying on each other. Secondly, if they were watching McVeigh and friends back then, they had likely continued watching them throughout the bombing plot. Matthews provided Jesse with emails between him and Jarrett as well as other proof that he was whom he claimed to be, including awards he received for his undercover service.

Much of what Matthews said fit with what Jesse already knew. The PATCON documents in his possession named the camp as an initial PATCON target and Don Jarrett, the man Matthews named as his handler, appeared on several of the FBI investigatory reports about the bombing. Jesse also knew that McVeigh and Roger Moore had been involved in the creation of rocket and grenade launchers and that such activity was of interest to PATCON. In addition, Matthews was just one of several informants and operatives who had crossed paths with McVeigh – and the German that Matthews saw with McVeigh sounded a lot like Andy Strassmeir.

Matthews told Jesse that he just wanted to tell his story before he died and inform the public about what had happened so Jesse referred him to Jon Solomon, a former writer for the Associated Press and current editor of *Newsweek*. Solomon and his team spent four months confirming everything Matthews said. Solomon excitedly told Jesse that he had confirmed everything and the eight-page story, which was supposed to run on the last Monday of November 2011, was going to be incredible: it would really blow the cover off PATCON. When the story came out however, while it featured Matthews predominantly on the cover, and confirmed many of his stories, it never once mentioned PATCON and left out a lot of other crucial details, most of which dealt with provocateur activities. The real story had been quashed by the FBI, the DOJ *and* the Obama Administration. With only a few exceptions, other major media outlets have yet to report on either the existence or implications of, in the words of an *Examiner* article, the "murderous covert program called PATCON."[40]

Putting the *Newsweek* fiasco behind him, Matthews agreed to testify at the July 2014 federal court trial, where Judge Waddoups was to make a ruling about the FBI's release (or withholding) of the April 19, 1995 OKC surveillance footage (and other issues). Jesse believed that Matthew's testimony about his role in PATCON and his having seen McVeigh at the PATCON-infiltrated militia training camp, would help provide motive for the FBI's continued denial about the bombing's relationship to a sting operation and their withholding of surveillance footage from April 19, 1995. Jesse told the judge that the reason the FBI could not find the tapes was that they would show that the person in the Ryder truck with McVeigh was one of theirs. The trial resulted in an entirely different conflict about other FBI shenanigans.

Matthews feared his testimony would draw retaliation and the judge took his concerns seriously, granting him permission to testify on CCTV from a remote facility whose location would be kept secret from the FBI. At the last minute however, Matthews went missing. Neither Jesse nor Roger Charles (who was also in close contact with Matthews) could find him. Charles finally reached Matthews, who said he wasn't going to testify because FBI agent Adam Quirk had contacted him and told him to "stand down," that it was "best for everyone" if he didn't testify, and made serious threats about what would happen if he did. Further, Quirk allegedly added, if he couldn't get out of it, Matthews had better come down with "a bad case of the I Don't Remembers." His former handler Don Jarrett allegedly repeated the warning.[41]

Jesse then explained to presiding Judge Waddoups what had happened, and why his witness backed out. The judge was concerned and ordered the FBI to investigate the allegations of witness tampering. Not surprisingly, the FBI found that there was no basis for the claims of threatening a witness, but when the judge learned that their investigation consisted of simply asking the FBI agent if he had threatened Matthews, he ordered them to conduct a more thorough investigation, a report of their findings, and set a date for evidentiary hearings in the matter. Waddoups said that Matthews' testimony about PATCON would likely influence his decisions about the surveillance tapes (the original issue). Although the evidence before him led to a "reasonable inference of wrongdoing" by the FBI, he was going to give both sides a chance to set the record straight.[42]

During the November 2014 hearing, the FBI, not in the business of setting records straight, failed to provide a report of their findings. After Waddoups expressed his displeasure, the FBI (a few days later) submitted an un-indexed *redacted* version of a report which claimed, in part, that because Matthews' former handler Don Jarrett was retired and no longer worked for the FBI, he was not required to answer any questions about his duties as an agent. Because it was a civil matter, the court could not issue a subpoena outside the state of Utah. Jesse countered the FBI's denials of the allegations with emails, letters, affidavits, and other evidence supporting his claims, including some written by Matthews himself.

An outraged Judge Waddoups observed that the FBI's redacted report failed to "dispel the court's concern" and announced that he would adjourn the proceedings while he decided whether or not to implement the judicial oversight mechanism of appointing a Special Master, who would investigate the FBI's witness tampering and insure the bureau's compliance with the court's orders. Further, Waddoups, who said he was "perplexed" by the FBI's willful disregard of his court, told the FBI to prepare arguments concerning why he shouldn't hold them in contempt of court. The FBI insisted such measures were unnecessary and that the court had no basis or jurisdiction to impose oversight over the agency. Despite the FBI's objections, Waddoups sustained the adjournment and reiterated his decision, telling both sides that the allegations were "too important of an issue to leave with ambiguities."[43]

On April 30, 2015, Judge Waddoups filed an order appointing Magistrate Judge Dustin B. Pead as Special Master in the case and, at some point afterward, placed a seal on the case and a gag order on everyone involved, assumedly until Pead concludes his investigation into the FBI's alleged witness tampering. Waddoups ordered the FBI to turn over an un-redacted version of their earlier report detailing their investigation of themselves, as well as a slew of other un-redacted materials for Pead's review. If, during his investigation, the FBI claims that certain materials are privileged and not subject to disclosure to the court or Jesse, Pead will determine whether they are or not. Further, Pead will oversee the FBI's and Jesse's cross-examination of each other and their witnesses, including Roger Charles and Agents Quirk and Jarrett, "in the interest of completing the record on this issue" and may ask the witnesses "additional questions as he believes in his discretion are appropriate to make a complete record."[44]

Pending the results of Pead's investigation, Waddoups postponed further decisions about or investigations into the FBI's compliance, or lack thereof, with Waddoups' May 2011 order to turn over the surveillance tapes and related documents. If Pead's findings are unfavorable toward the FBI, Waddoups may hold a new trial about the tapes and instruct Pead to oversee and enforce the FBI's compliance. Pead's investigation is ongoing and under seal, but as of January 2016, Special Master Pead was in the process of deposing witnesses.

In authorizing and initiating Pead's investigation, Waddoups wasn't trying to embarrass the FBI and stick it to "The Man," Waddoups *is* The

Man and was trying to insure the integrity of his court as well as the larger American justice system. For two decades, critical eyewitnesses in the bombing case have claimed that the FBI had harassed them and pressured them into changing their stories. Some of their accounts are heartbreaking. Waddoups' decision to initiate judicial investigation of the FBI's witness tampering and obstruction of justice in the Oklahoma City bombing case provides official acknowledgement of the types of abusive institutional practices that have proved, not aberrations, but defining factors in the case. Nevertheless, the FBI continues to deny they or any other government agency or official had any foreknowledge of the bombing or the existence of John Doe #2, calling claims to the contrary "ridiculous" speculative conspiracy theories.[45]

Jesse's efforts have not always met with success but the failures are noteworthy for the insight they provide. For instance, in late 2006, Jesse requested twelve CIA documents pertaining to the bombing and its subsequent investigation, suspecting that the documents implicate the involvement of German intelligence operative Andreas Strassmeir and his relationship to McVeigh. The CIA refused to turn them over, naturally claiming that to do so would jeopardize national security. In 2010, after years of appeals, a federal judge ruled that the CIA was not required to release the documents. The judge added, however, that it was "clear that the CIA and DOJ were cooperating in the prosecution of Mr. McVeigh." In response to the ruling, Jesse dismissed the national security excuse, calling it "the king's X, the ultimate protection," a fail-safe way to insure that embarrassing information remains hidden. Jesse explained to reporters that the ruling was a "good thing" because, minimally, the existence of the documents revealed either that the CIA unlawfully involved itself in domestic matters or that there was a foreign connection it was legitimately investigating.[46]

It wasn't the last time Jesse Trentadue encountered the looming and invisible specter of National Security. It happened again when he stumbled upon the existence of the FBI's "Sensitive Informant Program," a program that judges with the 10th Circuit Court of Appeals equated to FBI misconduct. The snitches in this program were not your run-of-the mill informants; these were carefully selected and placed within management and executive levels of influential major media outlets such as ABC and CBS News. The FBI program also recruited and planted informants among the staffs of federal judges, congressmen, and senators as well as in the White House and defense teams in high profile criminal cases, including Timothy McVeigh's. Jesse filed a FOIA asking for a copy of the FBI's Sensitive Informant manuals that would explain how they recruited and placed their plants. "I thought they'd come back and say,

'We would never do that because that would be illegal and unconstitutional!' Instead, they came back and said 'Yeah. We do that. We have manuals on that but you can't have them because of National Security."[47] The judge in that case wasn't buying it and demanded they return with un-redacted copies of the manuals, although this has yet to occur. Though this briefly appeared in the news, the existence, scope, and breadth of the program and its implications were largely overlooked, even among civil libertarians' highly vocal outrage over the post-9/11, post-Snowden spying scandals.

Even when failing to obtain the specific information he seeks, Jesse Trentadue still manages to contribute to the public's understanding of the inner workings and secret machinations of the FBI generally. Although one DOJ attorney mockingly testified that there was no indication that the FBI has a "nefarious, secret record-keeping system," it turned out they do. Referring to the documents suddenly discovered just prior to McVeigh's execution, a 2007 National Association Of Criminal Defense Layers (NACDL) press release asked how "the single-greatest record-keeping agency in the United States" ends up losing important information? Especially information crucial to highly public capital cases and, in any event, they are legally required to turn over in even the most mundane of cases? As it so happens, the answer to that question is that the FBI maintained (and assumedly continues to maintain) their very own memory hole where the bureau's "Real X-Files" are kept, inaccessible even to prosecutors and most FBI agents.[48]

In 2004, reporter John Solomon first learned of the system, which, at the time of the bombing, was called the "Zero Files." After Solomon's discovery (aided by FBI whistleblowers), Jesse, trying to figure out where all the FBI's information about their investigation into his brother's death had disappeared to, began to unravel its threads. The "Zero Files" are a special set of secret files kept by the FBI specifically for the purpose of obstructing justice. According to FBI agent Ricardo Ojeda, who himself was assigned to the OKC investigation, the Zero Files contained "reports [and] information the FBI would not generally want disclosed ... and which were kept separate from a specific case file." The files were "kept internally" and "typically not turned over" to either prosecution or defense attorneys during criminal trials.[49] This includes exculpatory evidence (evidence gathered during an investigation that is favorable to a defendant) that may help establish the innocence of those accused of criminal acts. The system was nothing new, even in 1995. It had originally been called the "June Files" and was created in the 1970's, renamed The Zero Files in the early 1990's and renamed again in 1996, this time becoming the "I-Drive" files. Discovery of the Zero Files led to the initiatives of other organizations, media outlets, and attorneys that further detailed the existence of such systems. Jesse's actions, specifically, revealed a separate but similar FBI file-hiding classification called the "S-Drive."

A brief *Iowa Law Review* article in 2006 described some of the troubling issues raised by the Zero Files (in 2006 the 'I-Drive'), adding that the file-hiding systems only exacerbated the already existing issue of discovery abuses. The article noted the FBI's routine failure to turn over discoverable information during criminal trials, citing the trials of Timothy McVeigh, Ted Kaczynski and the Ruby Ridge defendants as an example. These and other cases illustrated that "even when the FBI knows where evidence critical to an investigation is located, history suggests that the FBI may be reluctant to disclose it." This is part of what many law journal articles and news reports have identified as a much larger and endemic pattern of prosecutorial misconduct. While withholding exculpatory evidence from defense attorneys is "the most common form" of such misconduct and can occasionally result in overturning a conviction, there is little to no recourse for holding specific prosecutors responsible, and oversight to guard against such abuses is virtually non-existent.[50]

The existence of these and other elaborate file-hiding systems goes a long way in explaining the FBI's continued confidence in withholding information about the bombing while deceptively denying its existence. For a short time, national news outlets reported on how the FBI's "practice of hiding evidence in secret databases" was not an aberrant one, confined to a few cases. Rather, it was "routine," part of a much broader and ongoing pattern. In 2009, a media studies organization found that the FBI's rate of failing to turn over public information was five times higher than that of other major federal agencies. "If information were a river," said a 2009 Associated Press article "the FBI would be a dam," using the case of Jesse Trentadue to illustrate this.[51]

The issue comes to bear not only on the supposed right to a fair trial, but also the government's ability to cover up its own mistakes and misconduct, such as those that occurred in the death of Kenneth Trentadue and the Oklahoma City bombing. An *Oklahoma Law Review* article about precedents set by Jesse Trentadue's efforts argued for more transparency in government, noting that while "government officials can always be counted on to tout their exploits and successes," they could also be reliably counted on to hide their mistakes, abuses and deceptions. "The Trentadue case," concluded the article, "demonstrates the need to reveal government secrets [in order] to expose the possible cover up of a murder," and exemplifies how "even minor factual data could expose a conspiracy that stretches through several government agencies." PATCON, by the way, involved several government agencies, as did NORTHSTAR and Alliance. Referring specifically to PATCON, Jesse said, "Let me put it to you this way, you've got the Secret Service involved, the ATF, FBI, Department Of Defense, CIA ... really, everybody but the IRS."[52]

When Eric Holder was nominated to become Attorney General in 2008, Jesse wrote a scathing letter to Senate Judiciary Committee Chairman Patrick Leahy, informing him of the "key role" that Holder, in his capacity as Deputy Attorney General, played in the cover-up of his brother's torture and murder. This was not just his personal "shocking opinion" explained Jesse, but one supported by the DOJ's own records. He suggested the nominating committee look into this and closed by strongly advising against appointing Holder to the position. Sure enough, only a few years after Holder became Attorney General, strange connections began to surface between PATCON, its operative Matthews, his FBI handler Don Jarrett, government-sanctioned gun-running, sting operations gone awry, hundreds of violent murders, a little gun store in Arizona called Lone Wolf Trading Company, and Eric Holder. As it turned out, Holder went a long way in covering up and containing the 'Fast and Furious' scandal that broke in 2010, through his (gasp) hiding and destroying related documents from Congressional investigators and authorizing DOJ officials to hinder access to the majority of other ones. Fast And Furious, said Jesse Trentadue, "is part of the legacy of PATCON." It was by no means the last scandal whose trail led back to Holder who, ironically, spent an inordinate amount of time publicly expressing his fear of radical lone wolf terrorists, guns, and the need to combat these evils.[53]

Speaking of combatting these evils ... after the 1995 Oklahoma City bombing and until the time of McVeigh's 2001 execution, the FBI and ATF made continuous announcements about how their use of undercover agents and paid informants (whose numbers increased markedly after the bombing) had led to the uncovering and thwarting of violent plots brewed by McVeigh-like extremist conspiracy theorists. In fact, prior to April 19, 1995, the FBI was investigating 100 cases of domestic terrorism, which by 1998 had grown to over 900 and continued to grow as the millennium neared. Media outlets and government officials praised the FBI's covert interventions for preventing these disastrous plots from coming to fruition; successes that went unquestioned and seemed to negate the damage from unacknowledged or aggressively denied intelligence failures in the OKC bombing case.[54]

Only after 9/11 did it become clear to growing numbers of people that use of the phrase "terror plot" by authorities does not always "equate to a concrete level of danger," or sometimes to any danger whatsoever, other than the FBI's own undercover counter-terrorism operations and methods.[55] According to the FBI and other national security managers, their post-9/11 efforts to thwart domestic "terrorist plots" using covert methods, including electronic and physical surveillance and undercover agents and paid informants, have been wildly successful. However, around 2007 and increasing exponentially thereafter, growing number of news articles and investigative reports, watchdog organizations and legal scholars have raised seriously troubling questions about these practices.

A 2011 news report said the FBI had created a "massive network of spies to prevent another domestic attack," but then asked if they were "busting terrorism plots- or leading them?" A 2014 *Human Rights Watch* report (among others) indicated the latter. As it turns out, undercover FBI operatives regularly provided cash, explosives, guns, and other materials and supplied the terroristic ideas and plans to targeted individuals, after which FBI agents swooped in to arrest them for plotting violent conspiracies. With the goal of identifying and neutralizing potential Lone Wolves, FBI agents and informants target "tens of thousands of law-abiding people, seeking to identify those disgruntled few who might participate in a plot given the means and the opportunity. And then, in case after case, the government provides the plot, the means, and the opportunity." The next step in the process involves the arrest of the "Terrorist" (or in some cases, Pack Of Terrorists) and an FBI press conference "announcing another foiled plot."[56] Sensational headlines follow.

A 2015 *Creighton Law Review* article explained how use of the highly emotive term "terrorist plot" is very often misleading, as many times, no plot existed prior to the intervention of undercover operators, and serious questions exist about whether or not a plot ever would have existed without the intervention of the government – most often the FBI. That is not to say that no threats exist or that counter-terrorism agencies have never prevented an act of terrorism, only that the claimed number of legitimate plots have been greatly exaggerated and that, when the details of the case are examined closely, they often appear to have been hatched from the minds of government operatives themselves.[57]

As they did during COINTELPRO in the 1960's and PATCON in the 1990's, the FBI sometimes creates terrorist cells or organizations precisely to recruit and ensnare individuals, getting them to voice interest in committing violent acts, many times so grandiose that these "perpetrators" would have no inclination, technical skill or means of carrying them out. In doing so, violent ideologies and would-be insurgents' will to action is strengthened and encouraged. Moreover, the

FBI, when no better, more legitimate target presents itself, has a habit of going after "vulnerable people, including those with intellectual and mental disabilities and the indigent. The government, acting through informants, then actively develop[s] the plot, persuade[s] and sometimes pressur[es] the target to participate, and provide[s] the resources to carry it out." Another result of this is an exaggerated public perception of terroristic threats. In a vicious yet ongoing cycle, the DOJ uses the "foiled terror plot" script as a "mantra" that reinforces skewed perceptions, generates public fear, justifies continued civil rights violations and abuses and invites further dissent, which can be used to frame more so-called terrorists.[58]

The FBI's creation and subsequent thwarting of its own terrorism plots has become a common occurrence, involving not just a few instances, but "nearly all high-profile terrorism cases" since 9/11 (if not, I might add, many before that). The "fake terror plots" are so prevalent at this point, that the tactic and phenomenon is becoming its own field of academic study.[59]

A few examples of the exhaustive number of federally sponsored terrorism plots or their FBI-prepped plotters that have received widespread media attention include (but is by no means limited to): the D.C. and New York subway bombing plots, the "Christmas Tree bomber" in Portland, Oregon, "The Liberty City 7" in Miami accused of conspiring to blow up the Chicago Sears Tower, and the second "Underwear Bomber," to name a few. Not confined to Islamic Jihadists, the FBI operatives do not discriminate and have been implicated in a number of other left-wing anarchist and right-wing plots including that of the "Hutaree Militia" in Michigan. Brandon Darby, a paid FBI informant/agent provocateur who infiltrated left-leaning groups, proposed a plot to bomb a bookstore I myself frequent in Austin, Texas. Some say Darby's deceptions directly resulted in the death of a peace activist (among other things).

Protest over learning that this or that political activist has been an informer (or agent) all along or that those who share the same political beliefs as you have been targeted and entrapped, are contained within the political milieu immediately affected by these practices, to the detriment of everyone. While the left touted bookstore-bomber provocateur Brandon Darby as an example of how "the U.S. government is using informants to wage war on dissent," he became "widely respected," a "hero" even, among the right. Unfortunately, both sides are readily willing to defend those in their camp targeted by overreaching undercover activities and too readily willing to throw those in the other camp under the bus, without pausing to reflect how the same repressive measures used against one side one day, will inevitably be used against the other, the next.[60]

It seems you can't go anywhere these days without a fed trying to hand you a bomb and some blueprints. Recently, a mentally ill homeless man in my hometown of Rochester, New York, was arrested for his own "terrorist plot" after the FBI drove him to Walmart, bought him a machete and other tools of terror, and pressured him into voicing his desire to hack up people at a local bar on New Year's Eve. The arrest immediately made national news and everyone was freaking out. One local news article actually reported that the man had been arrested for "carrying out an attack," as if the Machete Massacre of 2016 had already occurred! The Mayor canceled the city's fireworks so that more police could patrol the city looking for terrorists. It took about twenty-four hours before the FBI's own role in the "totally bogus" machete plot surfaced and an additional twenty-four hours of outrage and cries of injustice, before the incident was forgotten.[61]

Even when terrorism-related charges are thrown out or reduced, sentencing delayed and convictions overturned due to investigatory misconduct, overreach and entrapment, media coverage of these developments tends to pale in comparison to the DOJ/FBI initial announcement that yet another terrorist has been stopped. Thereby nothing is done to reduce the public's unwarranted fears or lessen their ignorance. This is necessary because if government-disseminated threats about terrorism fails to result in observable and memorable spectacles or arrests, national security managers would soon lose the public's support and money, as would untold thousands of paid informants. However, if accused terrorists are arrested for plots that never would have been hatched without government intervention, it calls into question the original information leading to the surveillance agencies' self-promoting claims of having foiled a terrorist plot, and the legitimacy of the diabolical methods used to do it.

Without access to the complete records of "FBI surveillance and sting operations" (and we know how that goes), it is very difficult to know if the FBI's actions stopped anything at all. However, "because these operations are covert and because itemizing details of *failed* sting operations would raise the possibility of defamation of the suspect, there cannot be a public record of all sting operations," (italics added) especially unsuccessful ones or those that have clearly *caused* violence.[62]

The creation of terrorism is essential to waging and winning a war on terror and the FBI's role in post-9/11 terrorism "plots" was foreshadowed by and is just one more legacy of the murder of Kenneth Trentadue (and its cover-up), PATCON and the Oklahoma City bombing. The difference is that the OKC bombing plot actually came to fruition and resulted in 168 deaths. If we are to accept, as more than one federal judge seems to have, that the Oklahoma City bombing occurred in the context of and had connections to a larger sting operation, and that somehow this sting operation went awry, we must ask why and how. Personally, I wonder how, given everything we now know, it is so difficult for some to believe that a federal "counter-terrorism" sting operation could get that far out of control. A more heated and less frequently posed questions is: at what point does a plot to entrap become a sanctioned plot to kill, directly or through an intentional looking away? At what point *does* a so-called terror plot become an FBI plot? Or the plot of another national security-minded agency? Where does the boundary lie?

Even as information continues to surface that makes counter narratives about the 1995 Oklahoma City bombing all the more viable, and even as gaping questions about the plot linger, strong resistance to the evidence still exists and those who ask questions — victims, survivors, historians and journalists alike — are labeled themselves as, or equated to, conspiracy theorists at best, and at worst, to terrorists.[63]

If, for two decades and three presidential administrations, such great effort has been made to tell a patently false story about "the worst case of domestic terrorism on American soil," a story consistently told whenever it is politically expedient, we have to ask questions about the facts and circumstances of other mass spectacles of violence, however uncomfortable this feels. Not to disrespect or cause further harm to victims (as some have claimed such questioning does), but to gain insight. Only through an accurate understanding of any horrific event, is there the possibility of preventing similar ones in the future. If our understanding and knowledge of an event is inaccurate, ineffective and unnecessary measures will result. As it stands currently, the full story of the Oklahoma City bombing (and therefore its *real* implications) is, as Jesse Trentadue observed – the story of what is missing.

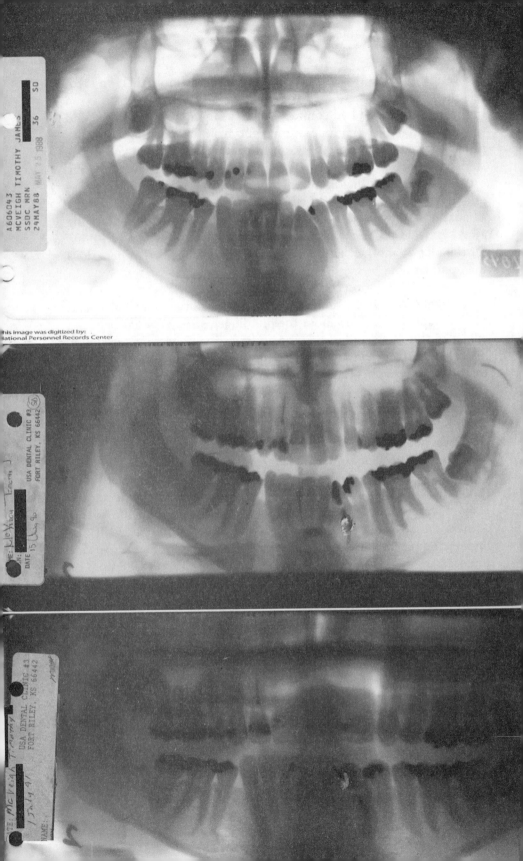

Notes

PREFACE

1. Brandon Stickney, *All American Monster: The Unauthorized Biography of Timothy McVeigh*, Prometheus Books, 1996; Jennifer Gideon "United States V. McVeigh: Defending The 'Most Hated Man In America'" *Oklahoma Law Review* (V. 51, N. 4, 1998); Dan Herbeck and Lou Michel, *American Terrorist: Timothy McVeigh and the Oklahoma City Bombing*, HarpersColins Publishers Inc., 2001; *Time Magazine* 'Face of Terror' (cover), May 1, 1995; *New York Times* "New Face of Terror Crimes: 'Lone Wolf' Weaned on Hate" Aug. 16, 1999; Jones, Stephen *Others Unknown: Timothy McVeigh and the Oklahoma City Bombing Conspiracy*. New York, Public Affairs, 1998:9.

PROLOGUE

1. Richard Serrano, *One of Ours: Timothy McVeigh and the Oklahoma City Bombing*. New York, London, W. W. Norton & Co Inc., 1998: 187.

2. Author interview of Don Browning, Dec. 23, 2009, Oklahoma City, Oklahoma.

3. FAIR (Fairness And Accuracy In Reporting) "The Oklahoma City Bombing: The Jihad That Wasn't" July 1, 1995, Jim Naureckas; Mathieu Deflem "The Globalization of Heartland Terror: International Dimensions of the Oklahoma City Bombing" paper presented at annual meeting of the Law & Society Association, Toronto, Canada. June 1995; *USA Today* "No Place Is Safe" April 20, 1995; *Nightline*, April 20, 1995, transcript 3629; *Boston Herald* "Send the Bombers to Hell" April 20, 1995; CAIR (Council on American-Islamic Relations) "Rush To Judgement: A Special Report on Anti-Muslim Stereotyping, Harassment and Hate Crimes Following the Bombing of Oklahoma City's Murrah Federal Building," April 19, 1995" 1995; *Village Voice* "We Have Met The Enemy" May 9, 1995, Richard Goldstein; *Boston Globe* "U.S. All Heart but no Spine" April 20, 1995.

4. Steven Prince. *Firestorm: American Film in the Age of Terrorism*. Columbia University Press, 2009: 17-70.

5. Author interview of Don Browning, Dec. 23, 2009, Oklahoma City, Oklahoma. V.Z. Lawton, who worked in the HUD office inside the Murrah and who survived the bombing, later testified that the day before the bombing he met four employees of the General Services Administration (GSA), an agency in charge of security for the Murrah and other federal buildings. The GSA employees told Lawton that the GSA headquarters sent them from Fort Worth to check security in the Murrah's security. (Associated Press July 16, 1997; Author interview with V. Z. Lawton Dec. 15, 2008, Oklahoma City, Oklahoma).

6. Information for 'The Unusual Suspects' derived from several sources including, but not limited to: Serrano; *Sunday Times* (London) "The Oklahoma Suspect Awaits Day of Reckoning" April 21, 1995 Tim Kelsey; *Washington Post* "In all the speculation and spin surrounding the Oklahoma City bombing John Doe 2 had become a legend—the central figure in countless conspiracy theories that attempt to explain an incomprehensible horror. Did he ever really exist?" March 23, 1997, Peter Carlson.

7. *Sunday Times*, May 21, 1995.

8. *Vancouver Sun,* (British Columbia) "The most hated man in America: Timothy McVeigh's life story is terrifying for a lot of reasons," July 15, 1995; Jody Lynne Madeira, Jody Lynee. *Killing McVeigh: The Death Penalty and the Myth of Closure.* New York University Press, 2012: 9-12.

9. Jones 1998:9.

10. *Dayton Daily News* "The Militia: 'I think (McVeigh) was a Little Off but Not Too Much" April 23, 1995.

11. The Comprehensive Terrorism Prevention Act of 1995, unsuccessfully proposed prior to the bombing, was re-introduced on April 27, 1995, and passed six weeks later on June 7. The Omnibus Counter Terrorism Act of 1995 and the Effective Death Penalty Act of 1996 (AEDPA) were among the legislative measures adopted quickly after the bombing. In February 1995, Sen. Joseph Biden introduced AEDPA, which Senate majority leader Bob Dole described as "the toughest and most effective anti-terrorist bill" to date. At the time, however, Republicans vehemently contested it citing the overly broad powers it granted to the federal government. On April 25, 1995, the Senate unanimously passed the Anti-Terrorism Resolution and Congress passed the final draft of the bill a year after the bombing in April 1996.

12. Weekly Compilation of Presidential Documents, April 24, 1995.

13. *USA Today* "FBI Agents Dissect McVeigh's Past" May 3, 1995.

14. Jones 1998: 31,359; Jones had worked as Richard Nixon's personal researcher and, interestingly, had served as general counsel for the Oklahoma ACLU at the same time, a position he stepped down from when the ACLU publicly called for Nixon's resignation. Jones had a history of representing unpopular clients such as Keith Green, arrested during an anti-war protest at the University of Oklahoma in which he had carried a Vietcong Flag and represented Abbie Hoffman when the Oklahoma State University banned him from speaking on campus.

15. *Vancouver Sun* July 15, 1995; Jones 1998: xiii, 51, 136.

16. Jones 1998: xviii.

17. Roger G. Charles., Andrew Gumbel. *Oklahoma City: What the Investigation Missed – and Why It Still Matters.* Harper Collins, 2012 (referred to throughout this book as 'Charles') : citing conversation with Jones Sept. 17, 2010.

18. *New York Times* "McVeigh Says He'll Plead Not Guilty" June 26, 1995.

19. *New York Times* "McVeigh is reported to claim responsibility for the bombing" May 17, 1995.

20. Jones 1998: 60, 61.

21. American Terrorist Collection.

22. Charles, 218-220.

23. *The Columbian* "McVeigh Says He Is Bomber" May 17, 1995; *Newsweek,* July, 3, 1995, David Hackworth ; *Seattle Times* "McVeigh Says He Was Bomber- Lawyer Doubts Purported Confession" May 17, 1995; *Las Vegas Review Journal* "Report: McVeigh admits role" May 17, 1995; *The Times* "McVeigh Admits Oklahoma City Bomb Massacre" May 18, 1995; See also: Randall Coyne, "Collateral Damage In Defense Of Timothy McVeigh" *Cooley Journal of Ethics and Responsibility* 1 (2006).

24. Author interview with Ron Woods, Houston, Texas, December 20, 2010.

25. Stickney, 16.

26. Stuart A. Wright, *Patriots, Politics, and the Oklahoma City Bombing.* Cambridge University Press, 2007: 3,4; Coyne 2006:22.

27. *Pittsburgh Post-Gazette* "Interview with a monster" June 29, 1995, Bill Steigerwald.

28. Jones 1998: 352, 357; U.S. v McVeigh and Nichols, Oct. 4, 1996.

29. Coyne 2006: 24; Author interview with Randy Coyne, Oklahoma City, Oklahoma, Jan. 5, 2011.

30. Madeira 2012: 107; *Boston Globe*, Dec. 18, 1997. Shortly after the change of venue was granted, victims' advocacy groups petitioned the court to install closed circuit television (CCTV) cameras in the Denver courtroom. When Matsch denied their petition, advocacy groups allied with prosecutors and solicited the aid of Congress, which then added an amendment to the pending Anti-Terrorism and Effective Death Penalty Act allowing victims to view the proceedings remotely though CCTV cameras. The Jones Team objected and argued the cameras would provide a daily reminder to jurors of the "large faceless [group] of grievously injured persons [who] are depending on the jury to return the only verdict (guilty) and sentence (death) this group will find acceptable" and would place "enormous psychological pressure" on jurors to please the victims. Further, the cameras might dissuade defense witnesses from speaking frankly during their testimony. Matsch eventually upheld the AEDPA amendment, finding the alternative of delaying the trials while the issue was resolved in court unacceptable. A room within the OKC FAA Center that seated 320 people was designated for survivors and victims' family members who could view the live CCTV feed after filing an application. The court approved 832 of the 1,200 applications submitted. Matsch, still concerned that the trials would devolve into an emotional fiasco, barred trial attendees from wearing religious symbols, displaying photographs of victims, crying, or displaying any emotional reactions during the proceedings and reminded victims "this is not theater, this is a trial." See: Jones 1998 :xiii; Jones and Hillerman 1998; Jones and Gideon 1998; Wright 2007:6,7; Madeira 2012: 14, 96,97, 107-114, 136, 142, 164, 167; New York Times "All-American Defendant? Lawyer Works to Soften Image of Bombing Suspect" June 2, 1996.

31. Jones 1998: 352, 357; *United States v. McVeigh and Nichols*, Pre-trial Transcript, "Hearing on Motions," 96-CR-68-M (D. Colo., October 4, 1996).; *Las Vegas Review-Journal*, Aug. 24, 1996; Madeira 115; *NewsOK* "McVeigh Seeks Approval To Do 8 Media Interviews" Aug. 21 ,1996, Nolan Clay.

32. Coyne 2006:24,25.

33. *Esquire* May 2001; American Terrorist Collection; CNN "FBI seizes angry letter written by McVeigh" April 9, 1997.

34. Authorities learned of the original 1983 plan to bomb the Murrah from James Ellison, founder of the Covenant, the Sword, and the Arm of the Lord (CSA), a white supremacist paramilitary group located nearby and closely associated with Elohim City (EC). On April 19, 1985, 200 state and federal authorities raided the CSA's compound. A standoff ensued which ended four days later when Rev. Robert Millar, Sr., the 'patriarch' of EC, negotiated a truce. EC came to act as the repository for many former CSA members after the group had disbanded. On April 19, the morning of his execution, Snell watched coverage of the bombing. His final words, addressed to Arkansas Gov. Jim Tucker, were, "Governor Tucker, look over your shoulder. Justice is coming. I wouldn't trade places with you or any of your cronies. Hail the victory. I am at peace" (Charles 15). In addition to Elohim City, McVeigh had made numerous phone calls to several other well-known White Power Movement [WPM] organizations and spokespeople, many of whom had close links to Snell and Elohim City, including various chapters of the National Alliance as well as the North Carolina headquarters for CAUSE, a kind of White racist ACLU. McVeigh was less than forthcoming about his phone calls. McVeigh claimed he made the calls seeking a place to hide after the bombing. For some, the calls implied that McVeigh had facilitated communication between terrorist cells involved in the bombing plot.

35. In the Lone Wolf version of events that would be told by the FBI and prosecutors during McVeigh's criminal trial (as well as publicly by McVeigh and then within many subsequent 'authoritative' books on the subject), McVeigh, using his real name, checked into the Dreamland Motel where he stayed, alone, from April 15 until the morning of April 19. On April 17, he (alone) picked up the Ryder truck from nearby Elliot's Body Shop and the following day, April 18, drove

it a few miles away to Geary Lake State Park. There, he and Nichols (whom he had coerced and threatened into helping) packed the Ryder with explosives. Nichols then returned home to his Kansas farm and McVeigh went back to the Dreamland, parked the Ryder in the Dreamland parking lot and slept in it. The next morning, on April 19 at about 7 AM, McVeigh (alone) drove the Ryder to OKC and after arriving there, McVeigh, alone, detonated the bomb at 9:02 AM and, once more alone, drove away from OKC.

The owner of the Dreamland Motel in Junction City, Kansas, her son, a Chinese food delivery driver and numerous guests, told the FBI that not only did they see McVeigh with other people during his stay there but that they saw him with two distinctly different Ryder trucks, an older faded one and a newer one. Likewise, all of the employees at Elliot's body shop said that another man had come into the shop with 'Kling', aka McVeigh, when he picked up the Ryder. Their descriptions of this man resulted in the first John Doe 2 sketch and matched the descriptions given by eyewitnesses in OKC. According to Elliot's employees however, the FBI repeatedly tried to browbeat them into changing their stories. In addition, a number of individuals on the route from Junction City to OKC saw McVeigh with other individuals in the early morning hours of April 19. Further, scores of witnesses had seen McVeigh with others in the days leading up to and on the day of the bombing and all of the individuals who observed McVeigh in OKC on the morning of the bombing, saw him accompanied by other individuals, at least one of whom matched initial descriptions of JD2. For example, Mike Moroz, who worked at Johnny's Tire, just blocks from the Murrah, said that at about 8 AM a Ryder truck sped erratically into the parking lot. Moroz went outside and asked how he could help. The driver got out of the truck and asked for directions to a building very near the Murrah. For the next five minutes, Moroz explained the directions but the driver, he said, seemed "confused." The man got back in the truck and sat there for another ten minutes before leaving. Moroz made fun of the man with his manager, who also witnessed the exchange. Moroz later picked McVeigh out of a lineup, and prosecutors used his positive identification of him at McVeigh's arraignment. Danny Wilkerson, who worked at a convenience store in the Regency Towers apartments across the street from the Murrah, said that at about 8:45 AM, he sold McVeigh two sodas and a pack of cigarettes while another man drove the Ryder around the block and briefly stopped to get out and use the payphone across from the store. When he left, McVeigh got back in the Ryder driven by another man. When the Jones Team and media outlets attempted to view the video tape, they learned that it had inexplicably gone missing.

Such reports (and the many video surveillance tapes that also turned up missing after the FBI took possession of them) presented grave problems for a legal defense team whose client refused to acknowledge that any of these reports could be accurate.

Eyewitness accounts of John Doe 2 have been documented extensively in previous books about the bombing. See: *London Sunday Times* April 21, 1995; David Hoffman. *The Oklahoma City Bombing and the Politics of Terror*. Feral House 1998 citing FBI FD-383 (FBI Facial Identification Fact Sheet) of Tom Kessinger April 20, 1995; Jones 1998; *Rocky Mountain News* Jan. 18, 1998; Mark Hamm. *In Bad Company: Americans Terrorist Underground*. Northeastern University Press, 2002; Wright 2007; Charles 2012; *Final Report of the Oklahoma City Bombing Committee* 2001.

36. Author interview with Richard Reyna, Texas, Jan. 5, 2011 (with Holland Vandennieuwenhof).

37. For instance, on May 21, Oklahoma FBI spokesperson Dan Vogel denied the accuracy of news reports from a few days earlier in which sources claimed that law enforcement officials had identified JD2 and eliminated him as a suspect and another report that quoted an unnamed official who said the person in the JD2 composite sketch was "an erroneous lead." Vogel asserted that the FBI was "still trying to locate and identify [JD2]" and was even "soliciting the public's cooperation" to do so. (*Las Vegas Review-Journal*, May 21, 1995).

38. Jones 1998: xviii ; Jones 1998: Xviii, 48, 49, 63 , 134. Jones collection documents are rife with internal defense team discussions about McVeigh's allusion to other unidentified conspirators.

39. Hoffman 1998: 65 citing his interview with Hoppy Heidelberg; Author interview with Hoppy

Heidelberg, Dec. 2008, Oklahoma. After Heidelberg wrote to George T. Russell, the presiding judge at the time, a letter about his dissatisfaction with the Jury, and notably the lack of 'follow through' on the John Doe 2 issue, Russell, dismissed Heidelberg from the Jury and shortly after, Heidelberg went public about the evidence presented or lack thereof.

40. Jones 1998: xiii, 117; 136; *New York Times*, Aug. 13, 1995; *USA Today*, Aug. 14, 1995.

41. The Jones Team argued against unsealing the documents but that the fact that "more than half of the documents in this case have been filed secretly, with no identification in the docket sheet as to what was being filed," defied legal norms. CBS issued a statement that "in the matter presented here, the interest asserted by [McVeigh] and the government do not override the presumption of openness that is at the foundation of our judicial system." Ultimately, Matsch decided to unseal evidence subpoenaed in the case, promised to unseal the financial records after the trial concluded but refused to provide the Jones Team with transcripts of Grand Jury testimony (Jones and Hillerman 57, 58; USA v McVeigh and Nichols, Motion to Unseal Records, et.al., 1995; *Denver Post* Jan. 29, 1996; *Denver Post* Feb. 28, 1996, *USA Today* April 24, 1997; Jones Collection).

42. Jones 1998:8; Charles 290. While the Middle Eastern theory was largely cast aside after McVeigh's arrest, for Jones and others, it remained a possibility that WPM conspirators acted in conjunction and conspiratorial collaboration with Middle Eastern terrorist cells, or as Jones wrote, "Islamic Radical Fundamentalists." One theory explored by Jones was that Terry Nichols had made frequent visits to the Philippines in the years prior to the bombing , not to obtain a mail order bride as he claimed, but to connect with other terrorist minded individuals, hone his bomb-making abilities and act as a liaison between Muslim terrorists and white nationalists. Among the materials that Jones sought but prosecutors claimed fell under CIPA exclusions were information about Middle Eastern terrorist cells.

43. *Kansas City Star* "Camera saw figure in bomb truck , Oklahoma City video is unclear, but it may show John Doe No. 2" Oct. 28, 1995; *Washington Post* "Videotape Of Bomb Truck May Show John Doe No. 2" Oct. 29, 1995. One internal defense memo written by Jones Team attorney Dick Burr, stated that he (Burr) had "[told the others members of the defense team about] the newly emerging evidence that John Doe 2 was observed getting out of the passenger side of the truck, and that a pick-up truck bearing an Arizona license plate traceable to Tim was seen in (and perhaps photographed) parking in front of the Ryder truck" (Jones Collection).

44. Wright 193; *Philadelphia Daily News* Oct. 28, 1995; Stickney 1996:258. While the FBI and federal prosecutors had for years continued to deny the existence of any such footage, the memo, which was permitted entry as evidence during Terry Nichols' 2004 state trial, was described by Nichols' defense team as "direct evidence of the involvement of others in the bombing conspiracy" (Wright 193).

45. In addition to the Murrah surveillance tapes the Jones team also sought copies of photographs taken by Sheri Moore who, arriving at the Murrah building for an appointment in the Social Security office on April 19, at 9 AM observed a brown pickup truck parked illegally in a handicapped spot very close to a Ryder truck. Annoyed, and carrying a camera, Moore took pictures of the truck. The explosion occurred after she took them as she approached the entrance. She dropped the film off to be developed, and when she went to pick it up two weeks later, FBI agents were waiting for her, intervened and took both the pictures, which never surfaced again.

46. Author interview with Stephen Jones, Dec. 27, 2007, Oklahoma City, Oklahoma.

47. Jones 1998:123.

48. As they waited to find out Matsch's ruling on whether or not to impose a total gag order, Jones held 'auditions' for who would have the privilege of interviewing McVeigh and argued at press conferences and court appearances that it was necessary to allow McVeigh to participate in televised interviews. Dick Burr disagreed and in one memo wrote. "Now that we are having more reason to believe that others were involved [in the bombing] perhaps as the principals, [and if] Tim

is overstating his role to us, why wouldn't he do so, at least by inference, in a television interview? I think the risk outweighs the possible humanizing benefit, especially if he can be humanized by others until he is ready to humanize himself and not take more credit than he is due (or than the government can establish he is due)." Jones then submitted a motion to the Bureau of Prisons requesting they intercept McVeigh's incoming and outgoing mail and route it to Jones himself in order to prevent McVeigh from making a public confession prior to trial, an act that further enraged McVeigh who, of course, greatly resented such attempts to control him.

49. Author interview of Stephen Jones, Oklahoma City, Oklahoma, Dec. 27, 2007; Author interview of Christopher Tritico, Houston, Texas, Dec. 27, 2010.

50. *New York Times*, Oklahoma Grandparents Turn Grief Into a Quest" March 5, 1996, Jo Thomas.

51. Charles Key recalled, "I got to the point where I decided there was something wrong. It seemed like a cover-up. I asked myself if I could walk away from this or not? If this was someone else's problem? I couldn't do that. I felt in my gut that someone had to do something. We all don't always do that in life but occasionally we do and this time I looked and decided to do something. Our goal was to get the Grand Jury empaneled and then present the information." One attorney representing the Dissidents in a civil lawsuit insisted there was a very distinct possibility that several individuals within the government had "possessed knowledge" about the impending bombing.

  A Noble Lie: Oklahoma City 1995 (film) Free Mind Films, 2011, Director: James Lane. Producers: Holland Vandennieuwenhof, Chris Emery, Wendy Painting. Writers: Holland Vendennieuwenhof, Wendy Painting; Author interview of Charles Key, Oklahoma City, Oklahoma, Oct. 15, 2010; *Tulsa World* "U.S. May Become Defendant in Case" May 12, 1996.

52. Associated Press, Dec. 29, 1998; *Daily Oklahoman*, Dec. 25, 1996; *Tulsa World*, May 12, 1996.

  One attorney representing the Dissidents, retorted by explaining that his clients were not comparable to those who continued to debate about "who shot Lincoln," and further, that they were not floating "Oliver Stone-type conspiracy theories." Rather, there was a very distinct possibility that several individuals within the government had "possessed knowledge" about the impending bombing.

53. Kathy Wilburn-Sanders, *After Oklahoma City: A Grieving Grandmother Uncovers Shocking Truths about the bombing… and Herself.* Master Strategies, 2005:96; Ambrose Evans-Pritchard, *The Secret Life of Bill Clinton: The Unreported Stories.* Regnery Publishing, 1997: 20 also published in *Human Events* "What Really Happened in the Oklahoma City Bombing? May Victims' Families Believe FBI Knew Bombing Was Being Planned" Oct 21, 1997.

  Rep. Key led the OKCBIC, who gathered materials, to present to the Grand Jury. The Committee was responsible for gathering case-related documents, identifying, locating, and interviewing eyewitnesses, taking their statements and obtaining sworn affidavits. Among the most outspoken of the Dissidents were Glenn Wilburn and his wife Kathy, whose two grandsons died in the explosion. In his 1998 book that deals with the bombing conspiracy, Ambrose Evans-Pritchard called the Wilburn's and their daughter Edye, "the nerve center of the Oklahoma Dissident movement." Another major force among them was J.D. Cash, a writer for the *McCurtain County Gazette*. Cash was independently investigating Timothy McVeigh's connections to Elohim City and the Aryan Republican Army, a gang of bank robbers who frequented there and their possible involvement in the plot. Cash went on to act as an investigator for both the Dissidents and the Jones Team. Cash worked closely with Richard Reyna and went on many investigative excursions with Reyna and other members of the defense. Illustrative of the close-knit nature of the investigative 'nerve center,' when Glenn Wilburn died in 1997, his pallbearers included Cash, Reyna, and OK State Rep. Charles Key. Evans-Pritchard also formed a very close relationship to the Dissidents. Today, Cash is posthumously recognized as one of the foremost investigative journalists and researchers to approach the bombing and traces of his work are found in all depictions other than Lone Wolf.

54. Although they had gathered mountains of documents and sworn statements, the Committee's limited subpoena power hampered them, and exclusionary regulations and the Open Records Act

prevented them from presenting much of the material obtained to the Grand Jury. Committee members published the *Final Report of the Oklahoma City Bombing Investigation Committee* privately in 2001. *The Final Report* includes court documents, sworn affidavits, and Grand Jury testimony of over 80 eyewitness accounts of those who saw John Doe #2 and several who observed the Bomb Squad in downtown early on the morning of the 19th. It remains the only comprehensive collection of such material published to date and exists as a kind of investigator's guide to the bombing.

55. As usual, McVeigh never mentioned the EC call to his attorneys until they learned of it. When attorney Randy Coyne asked him about it in December 1995, McVeigh said he remembered meeting Strassmeir at a Tulsa gun show where McVeigh was working a table for a friend of his (and a suspected government informant), Roger Moore. McVeigh said Strassmeir approached his table and explained that he was on a 'shopping trip' for the EC community. After chatting for some time, Strassmeir called over two other men he had come to the show with whom McVeigh described as "Okies." Strassmeir told the men, "This guy feels the way we do." McVeigh explained to Coyne that this statement meant that they were like "brothers in arms." At that point, McVeigh said, Strassmeir invited him to visit EC and produced a business card that had the "rural route where the camp was located" on it. McVeigh elaborated, telling Coyne that EC was a white separatist compound also known as "City of the Universe," and that it was "pretty fucking hard core." During his April 18 call to CAUSE (a legal organization who represented Strassmeir), McVeigh had a lengthy conversation with Dave Holloway, longtime associate and occasional Elohim City resident, as well as the partner of Kirk Lyons, the head of CAUSE. According to Holloway, McVeigh told Holloway that someone needed to 'take action' and revenge Waco.

In the Lone Wolf version of events, although McVeigh never visited the community of racist revolutionaries, he called EC either looking to recruit others into the plot or looking for a place to go after the bombing. Strassmeir was not there when he called, however, and McVeigh told the person who answered the phone to tell Strassmeir he might stop by. Many however, including members of the Jones Team, the Dissidents, and a handful of investigative reporters covering the case believed that McVeigh's association with EC went deeper than a single phone call. Evidence showed that he visited there at least twice prior to and after the conception of the conspiracy. For instance, Morris Dees, spokesperson and attorney for the Southern Poverty Law Center, told Jones Team consultant and criminologist Mark Hamm that his own sources inside EC confirm that McVeigh was there on more than a dozen occasions. Other sources inside EC admitted to Mark Hamm as well as investigative journalists J.D. Cash and William Jasper that they too saw McVeigh at EC in late 1994. According to Pack Of Wolves stories, the purpose for his presence there was to discuss forming the phantom cells who would eventually work together to bomb the Murrah.

56. Charles 99, 297, 298; Evans-Pritchard 73, 90, 9.

While the FBI initially showed interest in the mysterious German, in a letter written to Jones weeks before McVeigh's trial began, prosecutor Beth Wilkinson announced, "at no time did the FBI consider Andreas Strassmeir a subject of the Oklahoma City bombing investigation."

57. To accomplish their goal of establishing a white homeland, the ARA used a tactical phantom cell structure in the commission of their criminal activities. They always used disguises, including ex-president masks and sometimes ATF and FBI jackets. They left fake explosive devices to buy getaway time. They always used fake names, even with each other, and used them to buy cheap getaway cars, including, once, in the name of an FBI agent investigating them. The ARA operated a number of safe houses throughout the country which, when searched by authorities after their arrest, were found to contain wigs, disguises, fake IDs, phone cards and police scanners; pistols and semiautomatic weapons as well as a mountain of bomb making components. Bomb making components found in ARA safe houses included timers, switches, live grenades, pipe bombs, blasting caps wrapped in Christmas paper, the same way McVeigh disguised his own explosives. Investigators also found a driver's license for 'Bob Miller,' the alias of McVeigh's friend and suspected government informant Roger Moore.

Criminologist and Jones Team consultant Mark Hamm wrote that, while McVeigh's movements are generally well documented by the long paper trial he left, his whereabouts during the few days prior to and after the first 10 of the 22 ARA bank robberies are unknown. He argued that McVeigh participated in some of them. For instance, on December 11, 1994, McVeigh attended a gun show in Overland Park, Kansas, the location of an ARA safe house. In attendance at the gun show were four members of the ARA. Hamm wrote that the fact that they all "ended up in the same town on the same day in December 1994 ... without all this being somehow correlated, is extremely unlikely, if not statistically impossible." According to another Jones Team consultant, Stuart Wright, the likelihood that they were all there at once without making contact is improbable.

Illustrative of their close links with other White Power groups being investigated by Key and Jones' teams alike was Michael Brescia, one of the younger bank robbers and whom many suspected of being involved in the bombings. Brescia had been Strassmeir's roommate while living at EC.

Associated Press investigative journalist Jon Solomon also linked McVeigh to the ARA bank robbers. Solomon revealed that, during its investigation of an ARA bank robbery in Ohio, the FBI believed that the surveillance video inside the bank showed an image of McVeigh and sent it to the FBI crime lab, which deemed it inconclusive. Then, against standard procedure, the Bureau ordered the video destroyed despite the fact that the appeals of one bank robber as well as McVeigh were still pending. None of the known ARA members had substantiated, or even viable, alibis for the day of the bombing. Very soon after his arrest, Peter Langan illuminated authorities about some of the more obvious connections between the bombing, McVeigh and the ARA. He told agents that his compatriots had "the blood of Oklahoma City on their hands." Afterwards, federal prosecutors in the bombing case offered Langan a plea bargain for critical information he had about the bombing. However, they withdrew the offer shortly after, when it was decided not to look into the bank robbers' alibis on the day of the bombing.

Given all of this, as well as the many other compelling links between McVeigh and the ARA not mentioned here, the FBI's quick dismissal of their investigation into the ARA bank robbers' connections to the OKC bombing, seems hasty if not unfathomable. See also: Hamm 2002; Wright; Charles; Associated Press "FBI Linked McVeigh to Group After Bombing" Feb. 12, 2003, pg. 3A, John Solomon; *Philadelphia Inquirer* March 3, 1997.

58. Wilburn- Sanders 74.

59. Howe had originally been retained as an informant to spy on her ex-boyfriend, KKK and White Aryan Resistance (WAR) organizer, Dennis Mahon, who often stayed at EC and happened to be a close friend of Andreas Strassmeir. Howe addressed her reports to her handler, ATF Agent Angela Finley. Finley's first report summarizing Howe's information, dated August 30, 1994, states that "WAR has approximately 20-25 active, 50 non active and 200 underground members locally. The primary training location is called Elohim City... Mahon and his organization are preparing for a race war and war with the government in the near future and it is believed that they are rapidly stockpiling weapons." Howe, as instructed, and despite the fact that the known penalty for informants was death, strengthened her association with, and continued her infiltration of EC, eventually becoming fully integrated into the community. In Finley's report based on Howe's information, dated November 29, 1994, Finley stated that Strassmeir and his EC crew were actively discussing plans to take "direct actions and [conduct] operations [against the government] such as assassinations, bombings, and mass shootings." In early 1995, Howe told Finley that the atmosphere at EC had become increasingly paranoid.

The FBI briefly considered Mahon a potential JD2, however, as with Strassmeir, abandoned this theory. For his part, Mahon refused to testify at the Key Grand Jury proceedings and invoked his Fifth Amendment rights protecting him from self-incrimination. Prior to this, however, he bragged to Richard Reyna and J.D. Cash that he knew McVeigh under the name 'Tim Tuttle,' hosted him at EC and knew the identities of others who participated in the bombing. Mahon continued to make similar claims over the subsequent years. In June 2009, authorities arrested Mahon for his 2004 pipe bombing of Don Logan, the African American "diversity director" for the town of Scottsdale, Arizona, based on information provided by a female informant in an undercover sting operation instructed to pose as a racist white separatist. Prosecutors said that Mahon encourages acts of 'lone wolf' terrorism against minorities and the government. In May 2013, a federal judge sentenced the then sixty one year old Mahon to forty years in prison. The judge said the bombing was an "act of domestic terrorism" intended to spread hate and racism.

60. Charles 99,297,298; Evans-Pritchard 65,73, 90, 91; Associated Press Feb. 13, 2002.

In February 1995, based on Howe's information and the reports of at least two other undercover informants at EC who, like Howe, claimed Strassmeir and associates were actively plotting to bomb a federal building, the FBI sought to arrest him and issued a 'Be On The Lookout' for him. Meanwhile, the ATF planned to conduct a raid on the community and requested assistance of the INS, citing Strassmeir's status as an illegal alien. Unknown to the ATF, the FBI had been conducting its own concurrent undercover investigation into EC and so, on February 23, only days before the raid was to occur, the FBI asked the ATF to cancel their raid, ostensibly fearing the compromise of their undercover operatives there. Evans-Pritchard says the FBI prevented the planned raid on EC because Howe and Finley had "stepped on a landmine" and "unwittingly stumbled on a much bigger sting being conducted by the FBI," a counterintelligence operation approved at the highest levels in Washington. On March 3, 1995, immediately after canceling the raid, Bob Ricks, current Chief of the Dallas FBI office and former FBI's media spokesperson at Waco, called a meeting between the agencies to "discuss the investigation of Elohim City." Afterwards, the FBI insisted that the ATF deactivate Howe as an informant, although both the FBI and ATF reactivated her immediately after the bombing. Only days after calling off the raid, the ATFs investigation into WAR disintegrated, as did the plans to arrest Strassmeir. Based on his interviews with ATF and FBI agents involved in the case, Roger Charles suggested the possibility that a turf war between the two agencies caused the cancellation of the raid.

An FBI memo dated April 20, 1995, a day after the bombing, said "it is suspected that members of Elohim City are involved [in the bombing] either directly or indirectly through conspiracy." Not long after, the FBI issued another alert for Strassmeir. However, the following month, CAUSE attorney Kirk Lyons (whom McVeigh had called) helped Strassmeir leave the U.S. and return to Germany, in part by using a false name at customs. The FBI interviewed him by telephone a year after he left the US, which Strassmeir later described as "a joke, they didn't want to know anything." Also immediately after the bombing, Howe reported that she had seen McVeigh at Elohim City on more than one occasion. Howe said she first met 'Tim Tuttle' at EC around Christmas of 1994. Corroborating her claims were a number of other informants placed within EC by federal agencies and watchdog groups, including the Southern Poverty Law Center (SPLC), who independently said they saw McVeigh there on over a dozen occasions. Morris Dees, spokesperson for the Southern Poverty Law Center, corroborated Howe and told Mark Hamm that his own 'undercover' sources at EC also reported seeing McVeigh there on over a dozen occasions. Other sources inside EC admitted to Hamm as well as investigative journalists J.D. Cash and William Jasper that they too saw McVeigh at EC in late 1994. As it turned out, in December 1995, the SPLC sent a report to the FBI bombing task force describing Strassmeir as an "associate" of McVeigh's and claimed that McVeigh had made a visit to EC shortly before the bombing. During one of Richard Reyna's many trips to EC, the 'patriarch' of the community, Robert Millar, told Reyna that Strassmeir was a government agent, informant, McVeigh's accomplice or some combination thereof.

Yet, while the FBI initially showed interest in the mysterious German, in a letter written to Jones weeks before McVeigh's trial began, prosecutor Beth Wilkinson announced, "at no time did the FBI consider Andreas Strassmeir a subject of the Oklahoma City bombing investigation." Various researchers, journalists and investigators have raised a number of possibilities over the years. Evans-Pritchard is among those who felt that Strassmeir was involved in a joint U.S.-German intelligence operation whose mission was to locate the source of Neo-Nazi propaganda passed between the U.S. and Germany. Others believed he was an operative involved in covert intelligence gathering and sting operations conducted by various agencies, including the FBI, that targeted extreme right Patriot and WPM movements. The issue of McVeigh's proximity to ongoing domestic intelligence operations is explored further in later chapters throughout this book.

In fact, the Dissidents' unholy alliance led to revelations about the presence of federal informants embedded within the bombing plot in addition to Howe, including Robert Millar, the patriarch of Elohim City. According to Stephen Jones, "Robert Millar, at the same time he was the leader of Elohim City, was an FBI informant. This was during the same time that the government said the conspiracy started, September and October 1994. Also at this time, Carol Howe had given information to the ATF that Strassmeir and Mahon were planning on blowing up government buildings and engaging in mass murder. The Bureau did not tell us any of this, but if you start with April 19th and you go backwards, what Howe said before the bombing is pretty incriminating evidence that the government knew something was going on. I think that they did" (Author interview with Stephen Jones, Consultation, Dec. 27, 2007). The Elohim City revelations became a central point of contention within the Jones Team's struggle over discovery material and a key focus of the Dissidents investigation. Both sought information about key WPM figures and organizations with whom McVeigh had been in contact and about whom the FBI had gathered information during the course of its investigation both prior to and after the bombing.

61. Evans-Pritchard 18; Jones 1998:240; Author interview with Charles Key, Oklahoma City, Oklahoma, May 2, 2008; Charles Key interview, Oct. 15, 2010 in *A Noble Lie*, 2011.

Dissident Glenn Wilburn said "[some] people don't want to talk, you know. They're afraid of retribution from the federal government, they're scared for their jobs." Witnesses whose statements conflicted with that presented by federal prosecutors in the criminal trials reported attempts by Macy and Edmonson to discredit them including telling the media that Key's efforts amounted to "howling at the moon." Despite this, the Key investigation produced a wealth of new information, much of it damning to the Lone Wolf case the government was preparing to present at McVeigh's trial.

62. Charles 308-310.

Dissident Jannie Coverdale described her personal search for answers, during which she became acquainted with a number of eyewitness, including Eldon Elliot, the owner of Elliot's Ryder rental. Coverdale said that, when they met, she told Eldon that she wanted to know what happened on the day McVeigh came in to rent the truck. Elliot replied, "You mean, when Tim and his friend came in?" to which she responded, "Tim wasn't alone?" Elliot said, 'No. He wasn't alone.' He then explained to Coverdale how he had told the FBI this, but "the FBI told him he didn't see what he knows he saw… The last time I saw Eldon," Coverdale said, "he was on 20/20. He was crying on TV and kept saying 'I know what I saw.' He insisted that there was someone else with Tim" (Author interview with Jannie Coverdale, Oklahoma City, Oklahoma, May 28, 2008 and July 1, 2008).

Hersley would go on to co-author a book about the bombing, which while simplistic, misleading and at times factually inaccurate, was appropriately titled, *Simple Truths: The Real Story of the Oklahoma City Bombing*.

63. Although prosecutors continued to counter that they had fulfilled their Brady obligations, the Jones Team had, by other means, obtained an FBI log sheet detailing several reports about McVeigh's alleged involvement with the WPM. The sheet mentioned a number of specific persons the FBI deemed 'of interest,' many of whom were already a subject of both Key's and Jones' investigations. Included was Elohim City resident Andy Strassmeir. Also named on the FBI log sheet was Dennis Mahon and detailed statements made to the FBI by members of the Aryan Nations who claimed McVeigh was present at various WPM meetings and gatherings, including at EC. These statements support the contention of others who told Jones Team and Key investigators as well as the FBI that McVeigh attended National Alliance meetings in the Arizona-Nevada region.

Jones sought the log sheets in discovery and eventually, the DOJ capitulated (kind of), producing some of the FBI log sheet material. This led Jones to fire off an admonishing letter to the DOJ. Many of the documents turned over, said Jones were "very heavily redacted, far beyond what might be needed to protect the identity of the source (if such deletion was in fact justified). Not only are the names of the subjects of the interview reports redacted, but the names of the reporting agents are also deleted. The dates of key events and significant observations are excised. Entire paragraphs are blacked out." Additionally, the FBI had misspelled the names of many persons of interest, thereby making them unlikely to be locatable in computer database searches. Included were the names of Howe, Strassmeir and Millar, among others. Jones contacted Judge Matsch and insisted an evidentiary hearing was necessary to, once again, compel the government's compliance, arguing that, while the government had produced a small portion of the material requested, they nonetheless failed to turn over a "great majority" of it and Matsch did not compel them. Prosecutors continued to withhold information about not only the larger WPM, but the Howe investigation into Elohim City as well.

See: Pritchard 1997:72-76; Charles 2012: 288-294; Jones Collection.

64. The material sought by the Jones Team, included: reports of various law enforcement and intelligence agencies investigations generated prior to, after or in connection with the bombing investigation including those pertaining to: John Doe #2, including all witness statements taken by the FBI including reports, especially those dealing with "other suspects seen in [OK] in the two days prior to April 19, 1995" and sightings of JD2 at Geary Lake; "any and all audio and/or video recordings which captured the images or sounds of the Murrah building explosion"; various surveillance tapes from gas stations and restaurants that McVeigh had visited; "far right political groups"; threats made to federal buildings or heightened security orders for any federal building since 1993 generally and those concerning the Murrah specifically, knowledge of a criminal conspiracy to bomb the Murrah; immunity agreements granted to undercover informants within ongoing bombing plots since 1993 and the identities of individuals who entered into plea bargains with prosecutors; call logs and transcripts of wiretaps and video surveillance conducted on suspects in connection to the case, both prior to and after April 19, 1995; a subsequent request sought the receipt for the Chinese Food delivery signed by Robert Kling; statements given to the FBI about other bombing plots by members of the Aryan Nations and other white supremacist groups; documents about "a safe house" in the Kingman area where "the government has obtained food, water [and] weapons" and where they conducted "survivalist activity"; letters McVeigh had written to his sister which were confiscated by the FBI; McVeigh's pre-April 19 attempt to rent a Ryder truck in Minneapolis; motel records for Nichols and McVeigh; details of 'bomb sweeps' at the Murrah prior to April 19 and the whereabouts of the bomb squad on April 19; measurements of the Ryder allegedly used; and the list of people who applied for the FBI's $2 million dollar reward money for information leading to arrests.

65. Along with the old material sought earlier the new list also included: Further, the Jones Team sought "an admission or denial" by officials that McVeigh's former friend and seeming insurgent 'mentor,' Roger Moore aka Bob Millar, whom McVeigh allegedly robbed to finance the bombing was, as many suspected, for good reason, a government informant.

Only after the criminal trial concluded did the Jones Team learn the extent to which the FBI failed to turn over discoverable and sometimes exculpatory materials, including by one count, at least 43,000 'lead sheets' and 3,100 additional reports generated by interviews with witnesses. Jones later explained that while in April 1995, the government was still interested in investigating, by July 1995, prosecutors realized that all they had was circumstantial evidence against McVeigh along with a damning amount of exculpatory evidence that they knew they would be required to turn over. So, in order to give themselves "time to clean up the case" prosecutors delayed producing the discovery material and in the meantime made a big show of insisting John Doe 2 did not exist. "In order to get the death penalty, had to create the impression that just these two Army drifters, Nichols and McVeigh, had been responsible. They really couldn't expect to get the death penalty if people thought there were others involved, so they had to put on a campaign that there were no others, that we'd got them all. [...] You can construct a defensible argument that the government withheld evidence about the bombing from the defense, the courts, and the American people; evidence which suggests not that McVeigh was innocent, but that he was involved in a larger conspiracy" (Author interview of Stephen Jones, Oklahoma City, Oklahoma, Dec. 27, 2007).

The Nichols Team encountered the same type of stonewalling and engaged in a similar effort to obtain exculpatory materials. Defense investigators for both teams sought to question witnesses whose identities they discovered either through the Brady material or whose names appeared in the media but who, when contacted, refused to cooperate, claiming the FBI had specifically instructed them not to speak to either defense team or cooperate with them in any manner. Eventually, Ron Woods, lead attorney for Nichols, brokered a deal with prosecutors wherein the government would provide investigative reports in exchange for the defense team's investigative memos and while the government did not keep their end of the bargain, this is partially why the Jones Team began keeping two sets of memoranda and obscured information within the 'regular' set.

66. The Key Jury convened for 18 months. Despite revelations about government informants' warnings of an impending bombing or the testimony given by over 26 witnesses who had seen McVeigh with John Doe #2, no criminal indictments against additional conspirators would result. The Grand Jury did acknowledged, however, "[w]e cannot affirmatively state that absolutely no one else was involved in the bombing of the Alfred P. Murrah Federal building." Key responded by stating that the truth had not been told and that there was "clear and convincing evidence that there were others involved."

67. The DMN article stated that during a private conversation with his defense McVeigh had explained the chemical composition of the bomb and responding to a question about why he had chosen the early hours of April 19th, quoting the leaked memo reportedly written by a member of the defense team, said, "Mr. McVeigh looked directly into my eyes and told me, That would not have gotten the point across to the government. We needed a body count to make our point..." Worse still, during this conversation McVeigh had referred to the children killed as "collateral damage." Countless news outlets including CNN and ABC immediately picked up the DMN story, and *Playboy* and Reuters published their own equally damning stories based on a confidential chronology of McVeigh's pre-bombing activities that had been prepared by his legal team.

68. At first Jones *publicly* denied that McVeigh made the statements attributed to him in the DMN leaked confession article and those that followed. Then, over the next few weeks, Jones floated a number of shifting theories about the leaks to the media including the theory that defense team investigator Richard Reyna had leaked the material as a hoax to ease the minds of unnamed conspirators and get them to talk with Jones Team investigators. Jones then put an 'official' explanation on record with the court when, in a letter to Judge Matsch, he explained that the memo had been illegally downloaded from a defense team member's laptop that had been "hacked." The *Dallas Morning News* adamantly denied this allegation.

In one letter from Jones to Hartzler dated March 26, 1997, Jones stated that some of the discovery material provided to them by the prosecution had itself originated with the defense's own investigation and demanded the identities of the individuals leaking the material. In another incident, an investigative reporter from a local Oklahoma City news station obtained phone records relevant to the case and sold them to several media outlets including ABC News. Eventually though, it was determined by investigators and agreed upon by Judge Matsch that these phone records were complete fabrications, although the question of how and by whom remained unknown.

The exact identity of who leaked and why created enormously disruptive contention within the team. Everyone was suspect and everyone had a theory about what had happened. *In private*, Jones alternately accused several different members of leaking the information. According to Stuart Wright, "[a] cloud of suspicion enveloped us all," and Jones accused Wright and others of "secretly garnering evidence for the opposition, perhaps to sell or leak to the media ... it was a surreal episode" (Wright 7-9).

Defense investigator Richard Reyna, whom Jones eventually publicly accused of leaking the confidential material, became very close to McVeigh during the course of the investigation and was able to get McVeigh to open up with him, perhaps more so than anybody else on the Jones Team. Reyna recalled how the *Morning News* leak eventually led to his separation from McVeigh's defense team as well as the stress of the investigation itself. Reyna recounted how, when the leaks began, he confronted Jones and told him that the FBI and ATF were following him wherever he went. He warned Jones that the meetings between members of the defense team as well as with their client were being bugged. Reyna said that the "entire experience was very horrible" and that many of the members on the defense team were there for publicity, not for the good of the client. Reyna said that his final meeting with McVeigh was very distressing. McVeigh said that his discussions with other people on the defense was being leaked and so Reyna suggested that everybody on the defense team take a polygraph test and they would see who was leaking.

"My last meeting with McVeigh was bad. He said his meetings with people were being leaked out. I suggested to him 'Why don't I take a polygraph test and then let's do everybody else and see who's leaking' and that's when they began to keep me away from him. And then they tried to discredit me. ...They didn't like it because Tim was opening up with me. Jones didn't like it. It got to the point where I would say 'I need to go see Tim' and they'd say 'No. No. No. We're concerned about his state of mind. We don't want this and we don't want that.' I said 'Well, how am I supposed to function here with your guys blocking me? I got all the other investigators leaking all the information. I got the fucking FBI following me around and the white supremacists wanted to kill me. [...] At first, when Jones began to accuse me publicly of revealing information from interviews with McVeigh, I kept quiet. I knew it wasn't true. I worked for no one but Jones. Finally though, when I couldn't bear anymore of the bullshit. I came out on *Good Morning America* or one of those shows. I told Matt Lauer on camera that I'd pay for the polygraph, that I didn't release any of that information, they [Jones Team] did and I want them to say they did. Then Jones had several lawyers contact me and say 'we know you were screwed over but if you could just quit talking to the press and give Tim a break.' I was trying to help Tim though but even after I was gone, information was being leaked out. It didn't matter, whatever Tim was saying....the pipeline was just incredible." (Author consultation with Richard Reyna, Texas, Jan. 5, 2011 with Holland Vandennieuwenhof).

Either way, the *Dallas Morning News* article signaled the total collapse of McVeigh's relationship with Jones, whom he blamed for the leaks. McVeigh complained to other members of his legal team that the leaks had aided the FBI's investigation and, ultimately, the government's case against him.

69. *Tulsa World*, March 17, 1997; Coyne 2006: 2,28; Author interview with Christopher Tritico, Houston, Texas, Dec. 10, 2010.

70. Tritico said that after the DMN article, "Tim was rightfully very upset and I went and met with him and [to] came back in the fold and [he] worked with us but as soon as the trial was over, he told us he did not want to work with Stephen Jones anymore. Stephen's idea of how to try the case and Tim's idea of how to defend himself were two very different things. He felt that Stephen spent too much time talking to the media and not enough time preparing his defense, and all those things combined into his decision to fire Stephen. (Author interview with Christopher Tritico, Houston, Texas, Dec. 10, 2010). Coyne said, "[When McVeigh found out about the DMN leak, he had] nothing short of a total conniption fit. McVeigh desperately attempted to call his attorneys [...] to discuss what to do about Jones [...but...] the secretaries had received orders from Jones that McVeigh's calls were to be routed to him—and no one else. In frustration, McVeigh called the federal courthouse and asked to speak to Judge Matsch. [...] The clerk suggested that McVeigh talk to his lawyer. McVeigh pleaded with the clerk that the suggestion was the root of the problem. He didn't want to talk to his lawyer—he *needed* to talk about his lawyer. [At this point other attorneys on the team] seriously considered resigning, but we concluded that Jones would never resign, and that we could best serve McVeigh by staying on board and performing legal triage. Bent, bowed, utterly humiliated and damned near broken, we continued on, media mavens began chirping that a guilty verdict was inevitable." (Coyne 2006: 26, 28).

On March 12, 1997, McVeigh contacted the court and attempted to arrange a meeting with Matsch to discuss Jones' removal, but Jones, heading him off at the pass, thwarted all McVeigh's efforts to do so. McVeigh later recalled to his biographers how, "I tried to have [Jones] removed...I called the court clerk who told me to call my lawyer. I said 'that's the problem!'" He then approached a third-party attorney to communicate his wish to Judge Matsch. But the attorney, in turn, informed Jones of McVeigh's efforts. Finally, McVeigh wrote an affidavit outlining his complaints against Jones and gave it to a member of the staff he trusted to deliver to the judge, but Jones prevented the staff member from delivering the affidavit to the court, eventually telling McVeigh that he "did not want [my] dissatisfaction [with Jones] to become a part of the public court file." When Jones became aware of McVeigh's wish to have him removed, he met with Matsch privately in a closed 'in camera' session to discuss the *Morning News* story and other leaks. McVeigh learned of the meeting, which, to him, indicated "collusion" between Matsch and Jones. He later detailed the conversation based on transcripts of the meeting. According to McVeigh, Jones suggested to Matsch "maybe if we hurry up and go to trial, the problem will take care of itself" and Matsch agreed. After the meeting, Jones told McVeigh that Matsch denied his request to have Jones removed because, if he did, the entire defense staff would have to be replaced as well. Jones then attempted to assure McVeigh that, although the *Morning News* confession had been a "hoax," he had already fired those responsible. (American Terrorist Collection)

McVeigh's pre-trial attempt to have Jones removed became central to his post-conviction Habeas appeal, prepared with the help of several former Jones Team attorneys, including Dick Burr and Randy Coyne. Both continued to act as McVeigh's attorneys during his appeals and both believed Jones had acted fraudulently and unethically in his dealings with McVeigh.

71. Hamm 2002: 21, 24; *Washington Post* "In all the speculation and spin surrounding the Oklahoma City bombing John Doe 2 had become a legend—the central figure in countless conspiracy theories that attempt to explain an incomprehensible horror. Did he ever really exist?" March 23, 1997, Peter Carlson.

Four days after the bombing, a Gallup Poll showed that 39% of Americans felt the federal government had become too large, a sentiment that, a year later rose to 50%. During the lead up to the trial, news reports cited public opinion polls as evidence of this predilection for suspicious cynicism. 51% of Americans felt it was likely that state actors had played a direct role in JFK's assassination. 48% believed the government was lying about chemical warfare during the Persian Gulf War and 60% thought they continued to withhold information about Agent Orange during Vietnam. One third believed that TWA Flight 800 had been shot down. An even higher number believed federal agents had intentionally set fire to the Branch Davidian compound and the majority of the population thought the CIA facilitated the sales of crack cocaine to African Americans.

72. *The Columbian* May 30, 1997; *St. Louis Post-Dispatch* "Spreading cynicism fuels beliefs in conspiracies" July 4, 1997; *Star Tribune* "Oklahoma City bombing case; On trial: Militia subculture As Timothy McVeigh's trial opens today, the spotlight turns on an anti-government hate that may or may not be worth fearing" March 31, 1997; Chermak 167.

73. Herbeck and Michel 339; Opening Statements in United States vs. Timothy McVeigh found at http://law2.umkc.edu/faculty/projects/ftrials/mcveigh/prosecutionopen.html; Author interview of Randy Coyne, Oklahoma, Jan. 5, 2011.

74. Jones also attempted to establish that Terry Nichols' involvement in the plot was much deeper than the government claimed and that he had utilized foreign contacts in the Middle East, including Ramsi Yousef (WTC I) to acquire the skills needed to build the bomb, skills McVeigh did not possess.

ATF informant Carol Howe was willing to testify on behalf of the defense and her attorney provided information about her undercover role to the Jones Team, which had been withheld from them during the discovery process. Shortly before McVeigh's trial, Howe and her boyfriend were arrested for possession of explosives. She was ultimately acquitted of the charges after McVeigh's trial, as she had acquired them in her role as an undercover informant for the ATF and FBI. Nonetheless, Howe was flown to Denver in shackles and the government would not allow anyone from the Jones Team to talk with her directly. Although Howe's attorney said that she could give "compelling testimony in support of a potential conspiracy theory," Matsch barred it from entry, saying it "would confuse or mislead the jury." Jones filed a writ of mandamus claiming that the government was attempting to silence Howe. An appeals court denied the Writ and upheld Matsch's decision to disallow Howe's testimony.

75. Charles 232.

Christopher Tritico explained the defense's strategy of countering the government's case by attempting to raise doubts in the minds of jurors about the story presented by the prosecution: "[The government presented] a circumstantial case and the way we attacked it was to poke holes in what the government did present. In a circumstantial evidence case, when there is no direct evidence that the person is guilty that it is your obligation as a defense attorney, to attack, at every front, the circumstantial evidence that the government has and their burden of proof is to prove beyond a reasonable doubt. [The] job then, is to keep poking at that reasonable doubt, to put that doubt in the jury's mind" (Author interview of Christopher Tritico, Houston, Texas, Dec. 20, 2010).

76. On April 27, 1995, during McVeigh's preliminary hearing, FBI agent Jon Hersley went into great depth in his description of video footage from a surveillance camera located at the Regency Towers, located across the street from the Murrah which he said captured images of the Ryder truck and a yellow Mercury only moments before the explosion. Hersley's statement to the court under oath was quite curious as, after McVeigh's indictment, the government (and then McVeigh) would claim that McVeigh's yellow Mercury sat parked in a lot untouched for two days before the bombing and McVeigh returned to it only after the explosion. Further, despite Hersley's testimony, the whereabouts of footage from all of the twenty-five known surveillance cameras remained unknown and Matsch did not compel the FBI to produce them. Christopher Tritico later said, "There was no direct evidence that Tim McVeigh detonated the bomb that blew up the building. There was a Ryder truck that was rented but there was no photograph of Tim McVeigh sitting in front of the Murrah building" (Author interview of Christopher Tritico, Houston, Texas, Dec. 20, 2010). The full content of the surveillance tapes, which, it is assumed would show McVeigh (alone or with others) in OKC on April 19, have never been made public and, as of September 2015, attempts to obtain them from the FBI remain the subject of an ongoing lawsuits, a subject explored in detail in the conclusion of this book. See also, Trentadue vs. Federal Bureau of Investigation, United States Department of Justice Office of Information and Privacy and United States Central Intelligence Agency, April 1, 2010; Jones Collection.

77. Charles 232,234; Jones 1998: 316,317,326.

78. Indiana State University criminologist and former Jones Team consultant Stuart Wright wrote that "the [IG] report, based on an 18 month investigation, found widespread mishandling of forensic evidence, including posed or manufactured evidence, unscientific speculation favorable to the prosecution, inappropriate techniques of analysis, use of degraded or unchecked equipment, biased and false testimony, and generally, persistent violations of standard operating procedures at the crime lab, that directly impacted the Oklahoma City bombing case" (Wright 2007).

79. For eight years, Whitehurst, considered the FBI's most highly qualified bomb residue and explosives expert, had continued to tell his superiors about ongoing corruption within and mismanagement of the lab, which, he said, adversely affected the conclusions and testimony given by FBI Lab experts in over fifty-five cases, including the aforementioned. However, rather than correcting the problems, the FBI dismissed Whitehurst (described by his superiors in one performance evaluation as "the most outstanding forensic chemist in the lab's explosive trace unit") from his position, subjected him to various forms of harassment and ordered him not to speak to his former co-workers or attorneys about the allegations. When his superiors failed to take action, Whitehurst publicly exposed the crime lab and in doing so, instigated the IG to conduct an investigation. The Chief of the crime lab gave false testimony to Congress and FBI Director Louis Freeh concerning Whitehurst's allegations and the events leading to his suspension. However, in 1988, after Whitehurst sued the FBI for wrongful termination, the FBI agreed to a $1.6 million-dollar settlement as well as $258,580 for Whitehurst's legal fees.

Wright 13; Hamm 2002: 192; Charles 316; *Washington Times* "FBI Lab Woes Put 50 Cases in Jeopardy" Feb. 14, 1997; *Washington Times* "Experts Questioned FBI Lab Practices Years Before

Inspector General Report" (unknown date)- Articles found in Jones Collection; FBI *Draft Report of the Department of Justice Office of the Inspector General Report* Feb. 12, 1997; Author interview of Ron Woods, Houston, Texas, Dec. 20, 2010; Author interview of Christopher Tritico, Houston, Texas, Dec. 20, 2010 ; Jones 1998: 277-285; Evans-Pritchard 1998:7-17; Jones Collection.

80. Jones 1998: 230,231,322; Author interview of Ron Woods, Houston, Texas, Dec. 20, 2010; Author interview of Christopher Tritico, Houston, Texas, Dec. 20, 2010; See also, Charles 103-107.

Roger Charles pointed out that the handwriting on the rental contract was inconclusive and further, the FBI "could barely figure out how he arrived in time to sign the contract." Security cameras at a McDonald's in Junction City revealed McVeigh ate there prior to arriving at Elliot's and Prosecutors claimed that McVeigh walked a mile and half from the McDonald's to Elliot's. However, it rained that entire day and the Elliot's witness said 'Kling' did not appear to be wet when he arrived, indicating somebody gave him a ride. Although McVeigh claimed that, a 'kid,' whose identity he did not know, had stopped and gave him a ride, authorities never identified the person and he never came forward. Although the Fortier's testified to helping McVeigh create the 'Kling' ID used to rent the truck, it remained possible that someone else had used the ID. For the defense, this raised two possibilities of what may have transpired: John Doe 2 drove McVeigh to Elliot's or another individual who resembled McVeigh rented the truck, both viewed as plausible within all tellings of the story other than the *Lone Wolf.* If the witnesses' statements from Elliot's were correct, Charles opined, the McVeigh lookalike was very possible as employees there described JD1, the man later identified as McVeigh as "shorter, with rougher skin and an odd way of chewing tobacco" (231). McVeigh did not smoke.

81. Wright 2007: 11.

82. Prior to his testimony, Fortier had denied being aware of the daycare center located on the first floor of Murrah, which was clearly visible from the front of the building. Prosecutors never asked him about this question during the trial.

83. *McCurtain Daily Gazette* "Jury Begins Its Deliberations In McVeigh Trial," May 30 1997, J.D. Cash.

84. Author interview with Christopher Tritico, Houston, Texas, Dec. 20, 2010; Charles 323

85. *Buffalo News* "He's Not a Monster' McVeigh's Parents Beg Jurors To Spare Son From Death Sentence" June 11, 1997, Lou Michel. Pg. 1A.

86. Olmstead vs US, 277 US 438, 1928.

87. *American Bar Association Journal* (July 1997); *Denver Post* "McVeigh painted as 'patsy' Defense lawyer hints at foreign connections" June 16, 1997, Jim Kirksey.

88. Author interview with Ron Woods, Houston, Texas, Dec. 20, 2010.

89. Hamm, 2002: 24, 25.

Ron Woods said, "As we knew and as the government conceded, Nichols was home in Kansas on the morning of April 19th […] Our defense of Nichols, basically centered on this [and the third person]. […] The government did not have a whole lot of evidence on Nichols and the jury hung up for a week with ten out of twelve of them feeling he was not guilty, but two jurors said they were not leaving without convicting him of something and so they convicted him of the least culpable state of involuntary manslaughter- but in order to do this they also had to find him guilty of conspiracy to use a weapon of mass destruction. When they came back in with that verdict and the Judge said 'okay, now we're going into the penalty and sentencing stage and the conspiracy count includes the death penalty'. I watched them and they all looked at each other in shock. When we presented the evidence during the sentencing phase they went in and hung up and said 'we can't agree.' They had come to the conclusion so early on that Nichols was so minimally involved that they hung on the punishment" (Author interview with Ron Woods, Houston, Texas, Dec. 20, 2010).

90. Author interview with Randy Coyne, Oklahoma, Dec. 5, 2011.

91. Author interview with Christopher Tritico, Houston, Texas, Dec. 20, 2010.

92. *New York Post* "Dead Man Laughing: Tim the Terrorist Sneers at Victims" May 12, 2001, Steve Dunleavy.

93 . Gallup Poll "American's Less Concerned About Terrorist Attacks Five Years After Oklahoma City" April 19, 2000 (http://www.gallup.com/poll/2983/americans-less-concerned-about-terrorist-attacks-five-years-after-oklahoma-city.aspx); V.Z. Lawton "Without the Truth There Can Be No Justice" 911truth.org, April 21, 2006.

Narrative Types & Recurring Depictions

1. Canonical Lone Wolf treatments of the Oklahoma City bombing and McVeigh include *All American Monster: The Unauthorized Biography of Timothy McVeigh*, written by Brandon Stickney and published by Prometheus Books in 1996; *Apocalypse in America: Waco and Ruby Ridge Revenged*, written by Mark Hamm and published by Northeastern University Press in 1997; *American Terrorist: Timothy McVeigh and the Oklahoma City Bombing*, written by Dan Herbeck and Lou Michel and published by Regan Books, HarpersColins Publishers Inc., in 2001; *Simple Truths: The Real Story of the Oklahoma City Bombing*, written by Jon Hersley, Larry Tongate and Bob Burke and published by Oklahoma Heritage Association in 2004; and an MSNBC television Special narrated by Rachel Maddow called "The McVeigh Tapes: Confessions of an American Terrorist" that aired on April 19, 2010.

Lone Wolf Terrorism is a term used by experts, academics, watchdog organizations, and the media to denote a particular tactical strategy of political violence. Terrorism studies scholars have defined *Lone Wolf Terrorism* as "political violence perpetrated by individuals who act alone; who do not belong to an organized terrorist group or network; who act without the direct influence of a leader or hierarchy; and whose tactics and methods are conceived and directed by the individual without any direct outside command or direction." Others have conceived of the phenomena of Lone Wolf vs. Group Terrorism (Pack of Wolves) as occurring within a spectrum and argue that Lone Wolf Terrorists, in the truest sense of the term, must meet the following criteria of 'Loneness': (1) they self-radicalize (2) they have no contact with other 'militants or belligerents'(3) they conceive of their act of violence alone with no 'influence, encouragement or inspiration' from any outside party (4) they conduct all planning alone (4) they receive no direct or indirect assistance or support and (5) they execute all stages of their attack alone.

The strategies of *Lone Wolf* resistance (sometimes called Leaderless Resistance), as defined, adopted and popularized by the broader extreme-right 'underground' throughout the 1980's and early 1990's were widely credited with informing McVeigh's own actions and inspired the aspirations of subsequent Lone Wolves. See: Fred Burton., Scott Stewart, "The 'Lone Wolf' Disconnect" Stratfor Global Intelligence (website) Jan. 30, 2008; Mark Hamm, "Lone Wolf Terrorism in America: Forging a New Way of Looking at an Old Problem" Indiana State University citing Ramon Spaaij, *Understanding Lone Wolf Terrorism: Global Patterns, Motivations, and Prevention*. Springer, Heidelberg, London, New York, 2012 (and) "The Enigma of Lone Wolf Terrorism: An Assessment." *Studies in Conflict & Terrorism*, V. 33 (2010) pg. 854-870.

2. Herbeck and Michel: XIX- XXI, 224, 286, 295, 300, 317, 382. *American Terrorist* continues as the foremost book cited about McVeigh and the bombing.

Brandon Stickney's 1996 book, *All American Monster: The Unauthorized Biography of Timothy McVeigh*, was written and released prior to the start of McVeigh's trial. Stickney hailed from the same region as McVeigh and worked as a reporter for the *Lockport Union Sun & Journal*, a small local newspaper that published McVeigh's provocative 'letters to the editor' prior to the bombing. To write his book, Stickney compiled a lengthy and extensive bibliography of existing media accounts and helped to establish a narrative chronology and structural template used by many subsequent works.

Stickney's interviews exposed a handful of previously unreported and underreported biographical details that Stickney claimed McVeigh hoped would remain secret; primarily those pertaining to the inner workings and dysfunctions of the McVeigh family. Perhaps the most valuable contribution made by *All American Monster* is the inclusion of observations by McVeigh's friends and family members, who described his rapid physical and mental deterioration, increasingly volatile outbursts, strange conspiratorial claims and the listless post-combat boredom he suffered after returning from the Gulf War. Stickney determined that this post war discontent, along with his consuming outrage over the government's actions at Ruby Ridge and Waco, led him to bomb the Murrah. Stickney employed a formula commonly seen in terrorism literature in his identification and tracking of the origins and process of radicalization that lead people to commit acts of political violence. In the end, Stickney concluded that both nature and nurture were equally important to the formation of his terrorist monster and found no single trauma or cause for his violence; not his parents' divorce, failure to become an Army Ranger or the right wing milieu he inhabited. Rather, Timothy McVeigh "was a seemingly ordinary boy, someone who could be found in almost any average neighborhood in America ... [whose] life is the tale of an all-American man desperately seeking a meaning to his existence and a direction ..."

Despite the fact that neither McVeigh nor Nichols had yet to be convicted or that the FBI investigation was ongoing, Stickney unequivocally concluded that McVeigh was indeed the primary perpetrator and that no larger conspiracy existed. Many of the factual, hypothetical and speculative claims that appear within *All American Monster* would appear in subsequently published fictional, nonfictional, journalistic, popular and academic works about McVeigh and the bombing. Although arguably premature, Stickney's depiction of McVeigh is the first full-length book to position him as 'Lone Wolf' mastermind.

Professor of criminology at Indiana State University, Mark Hamm, published his first book about the bombing, *Apocalypse in Oklahoma: Waco and Ruby Ridge Revenged*, in 1997. Released prior to McVeigh's trial and conviction, *Apocalypse* was the first scholarly book-length publication to advance the Lone Wolf theory about McVeigh's role in the bombing. Hamm described the historical context of the bombing plot employing critical social and cultural theories to introduce new perspectives about McVeigh's motivations and describe the historical context of the bombing plot, contributions that have informed a number of scholarly works since.

In his own speculative yet well-documented chronology, Hamm highlighted McVeigh, Nichols, and Fortier's association with 'known faces' of the extreme right, but after introducing evidence to illustrate where others might have entered into the plot, rejected the notion that they did. Hamm acknowledged that crucial information required to make any final determination was not as yet available and therefore the case remained "unsolved" and while existing alternate narratives involving additional perpetrators within a much larger plot ranged in complexity, 'the truth' was much simpler. A more plausible explanation for the bombing, purported Hamm, was the one endorsed and publicly advanced by McVeigh himself that "McVeigh acted as a lone wolf" and dismissed all alternate theories as a result of the public's desperate need to "identify the real enemy." Hamm pointed out that, while ideological similarities existed between McVeigh and the far right, the investigation failed to turn up any material evidence of the involvement of others in the bombing and thus left politicians and the media with a choice: to depict McVeigh as "a terrorist" – and the bombing an "act of a madman" – or focus on "the institutions and individuals who had indirectly supported the plot." Ultimately, they chose the former.

Ironically, Hamm alleged that the ATF and FBI, among others, "indirectly supported" the bombers by acting with "malfeasance" in choosing to ignore critical intelligence collected about McVeigh in the years leading to the bombing, an accusation also made by others pejoratively labeled (and thus dismissed) as "conspiracy theories." Specifically, Hamm said there was evidence to show that the FBI and ATF were aware of at least some of McVeigh's suspicious activities and associations, including his links to Elohim City. In fact, Hamm wrote, the FBI, ATF or both, had probably opened a file on McVeigh but for reasons Hamm does not examine, failed to initiate a proactive investigation and, thus, discover the plot and prevent the bombing. Perhaps informing Hamm's 'intelligence failure' theory but undisclosed in *Apocalypse*, was his role as a paid expert consultant for McVeigh's defense team. Noteworthy, however, is that while he makes mention of the 'failed intelligence theory' in *Apocalypse*, he nonetheless advances a *Lone Wolf* version of events. In Hamm's 2002 book about the bombing, he expanded on the 'intelligence failure' theory and came to a very different conclusion from that argued in *Apocalypse*.

3. While allegations about the FBI's harassment of eyewitnesses and attempts to get them to change their stories were ignored, a recent book by former Jones Team investigator Roger Charles provides 'insider' knowledge about Jon Hersley's role in the harassment. Included were his "extensive efforts" to "neutralize" eyewitnesses who reported seeing others with McVeigh, "convince [them] that John Doe 2 was a phantom" and thereby, prevent the spectral conspirator from appearing at the trials. In fact, Charles wrote, "Hersley was the prosecution's go-to person to resolve many of the holes in the case." Lead prosecutor Larry Mackey later acknowledged that Hersley regularly "hammered" witnesses who might aid the defense team's cases. Further, lead FBI agent Danny Defenbaugh also disclosed that, in his opinion, *Hersley commonly distorted evidence, lied about his investigation (or lack thereof) and often acted outside of his authority*, "We had to watch over Jon. He'd go around trying to stop viable investigations, especially if they involved other people in the conspiracy. Every time we caught him, I had to bring him in the woodshed to paddle him. Then he'd go right back at it." (Charles 2012: 308-10).

4. Canonical Pack and Watched Wolves treatments of the Oklahoma City bombing and McVeigh include *The Secret Life of Bill Clinton: The Unreported Stories*, written by Ambrose Evans-Pritchard and published by Regnery Publishing in 1997; *Others Unknown: Timothy McVeigh and the Oklahoma City Bombing Conspiracy*, written by Stephen Jones and published by Public Affairs in 1998; *The Oklahoma City Bombing and the Politics of Terror*, written by David Hoffman and published by Feral House in 1998; *Final Report on the Bombing of the Alfred P. Murrah Building*, prepared by the Oklahoma City Bombing Investigation Committee and published by Hervey's Booklink in 2001; *In Bad Company: Americans Terrorist Underground*, written by Mark Hamm and published by Northeastern University Press in 2002; *Patriots, Politics, and the Oklahoma City Bombing*, written by Stuart A. Wright and published by Cambridge University Press in 2007.

(*Others Unknown*, 1998): The most comprehensive and seminal body of book length works detailing and advancing *Pack* stories are those authored by attorneys or experts who worked for McVeigh's defense team. While Mark Hamm published his *Lone Wolf* account the previous year, McVeigh's lead defense attorney Stephen Jones published his *Pack* book, *Others Unknown: Timothy McVeigh and the Oklahoma City Bombing Conspiracy*, in 1998. The cover of *Others Unknown* promises to tell "The Real Story," a common and familiar claim made by works of narrative variants. The title is taken from the criminal indictment against McVeigh and Nichols and encapsulates the plot of the book; i.e., Jones' quest to identify other conspirators, despite the prosecution's claims that the crime was "an open and shut case" or the "systematic [and] deliberate attempts [by the government] to prevent" the American people from learning the truth. The August 1995 criminal indictments asserted that Nichols and McVeigh had "conspired with Others Unknown" to bomb the Murrah. In Jones' book, readers learn that "the real story" is "complex, shadowy, and sinister."

Jones recounts, at length, the reasons for his unshakable doubts about the veracity of McVeigh's confessions and frustrations with his omissions and partial admissions while simultaneously contending with ongoing FBI and DOJ refusals to produce exculpatory discovery materials. Jones wrote that, despite his client's wishes, this "Kafkaesque" situation left him with no other option but to retain several experts and align himself with journalists, the Dissidents, and right wing/ white supremacist extremists. Although obstructed at every turn, Jones' costly, time-consuming and controversial search for the *Others Unknown* helped uncover the earliest information pertaining to the government's 'prior knowledge' (i.e. the ARA, Elohim City and other WPM actors). Ultimately, though, Jones failed to follow through on the book cover's promise to tell the "real story" by concluding that, due to both the government and McVeigh's intentional blockage and obfuscation, the case remained a mystery. Hence, Jones could not solve the case, offer a unified theory about it or explain the failures of intelligence.

Jones depicts his former client as the "ghost of Lee Harvey Oswald," a man who became entangled in a much larger conspiracy that ultimately shielded everyone except himself. Jones describes McVeigh as a narcissistic, megalomaniacal patsy who, because of his craving for publicity, desired to take full credit for the bombing, but a "designated patsy" nonetheless. Indeed, Others Unknown reads largely as a forum for Jones to defend himself against McVeigh's public accusations that Jones violated his attorney-client confidentiality, resulting in the many 'confession' leaks to the media. Jones' accusations that McVeigh craved publicity were ones McVeigh first leveled against Jones prior to his trial and subsequently in media interviews as well as to his biographers. Jones argues that McVeigh himself waived this confidentiality, and had even encouraged Jones to write the book (all publicly denied by McVeigh). According to Jones, McVeigh's unsuccessful attempt in August 1997 to have him removed as his attorney constituted a waiver of attorney client privilege. After the publication of Others Unknown, McVeigh filed a 50 page motion for a new trial, claiming that Jones provided inadequate, ineffective and unprofessional legal representation, claiming that Jones was not motivated by a desire to defend him but to gain celebrity and 'cash in' on his high-profile client.

Ironically, Jones' book catalyzed McVeigh's decision to cooperate in the writing of American Terrorist – the exemplary Lone Wolf text. American Terrorist and Others Unknown illustrate the differences in the plots of Lone vs. Pack stories as well as the complex and contradictory dynamics involved in the relationships between McVeigh, Jones, other members of the defense team, the Dissidents, mainstream and independent media, and the state (FBI, DOJ, etc.). Further, Others Unknown embodies the ongoing struggle between Jones and McVeigh over who would tell the story, how, when and to whom, resulting in internal defense team contentions as well as McVeigh's ongoing and increasingly aggressive public assertions of sole responsibility.

(The Oklahoma Dissidents & The Politics of Terror, 1998): After the trial of Tim McVeigh concluded, various authors expanded upon previous Pack texts. Included was award-winning British journalist Ambrose Evans-Pritchard's seminal 1997 book, The Secret Life of Bill Clinton, dedicated to, among others, the Dissidents and "the people of Oklahoma who deserve the truth" and "have refused to accept the half-truths" of the Department of Justice. Pritchard describes the OKC bombing as the "most tragic event" in the U.S. since the JFK assassination and one that had an immediate "catalytic effect" of garnering support for the expansion of anti-terrorist powers and budgets. Pritchard wrote that, at stake during McVeigh's trial was not only the matter of determining his guilt or innocence but justice itself. In his opinion, McVeigh's criminal trial "did not bring out the full story," and in fact, had been "skillfully managed to ensure that collateral revelations were kept to a minimum." Pritchard focused on the involvement of the ARA and Elohim City and concluded that, given the number of informants who issued warnings, the bombing was most likely "a sting operation that went disastrously wrong," followed by a DOJ and FBI cover-up so well executed Pritchard "could never have imaged the machinery of cover-up could be so oppressively efficient."

Similarly, in his encyclopedic 1998 book, The Oklahoma City Bombing and the Politics of Terror, conspiracy-genre writer David Hoffman posited two theories: Either the bombing was a sting gone wrong, or a deliberate black operation. Hoffman, like many others writers, acknowledges that the 'truth' of the bombing is unreachable given the vast amount of missing data. Still, he concludes that the event was likely a deep-cover black operation orchestrated by powerful but faceless elites and executed in the typical style of a tactical "strategy of tension." A term that most often refers to state-sponsored terrorism described as "a tactic which consists in committing bombings and attributing them to others. By the term 'tension' one refers to emotional tension that creates a sentiment of fear. By the term 'strategy' one refers to what feeds the fear of the people towards one particular group" (Daniele Gasner, Dec. 29, 2006, Voltairenet.com) Hoffman presents a number of depictions, all of which paint McVeigh as an Oswald type, even wryly describing the Ryder truck as "The Mannlicher-Carcanno Bomb."

5. Jon Rappaport. Oklahoma City Bombing: The Suppressed Truth. The Book Tree, 1995: 1,101,14,15.

6. Canonical Guilty Agent books include: Jim Keith. *OKBOMB! Conspiracy and Cover-up* Adventures Unlimited Press, Kempton, Illinois, 1996; David Paul Hammer. *Secrets Worth Dying For: Timothy James McVeigh and the Oklahoma City Bombing.* 1st Books Library, 2004: vi, 122; David Paul Hammer. *Deadly Secrets: Timothy McVeigh and the Oklahoma City Bombing.* Bloomfield, Indiana, Textstream, 2010. Canonical Guilty Agent works about McVeigh published after his 2001 execution will be explored throughout this book and at its conclusion.

On April 25, 1995, only days after McVeigh's arrest and perp walk, the front page of the *San Francisco Chronicle* announced, "Militia[s] Feed on Conspiracy Theories/Bombing Called Government Plot to Create Hysteria." The article portrayed the McVeigh variety of conspiracy theorists as tinfoil hat-wearing, pathological political paranoiacs, who saw "mysterious black helicopters" everywhere they looked. For them, the bombing was part of an attempt by the U.S. government to undermine the U.S. Constitution and implement a "New World Order." Worse, their beliefs had them actively "preparing for war with government troops and police." Several other initial news articles in major outlets contained quotes by militia spokespeople who claimed that McVeigh was probably just an Oswald-like patsy set up to vilify and demonize the growing Patriot Movement, alleging that the government itself was *knowingly responsible* for the bombing and that McVeigh had acted as their willing puppet. They included McVeigh's "fellow patriots," "members of weekend militias" and of course, "conspiracy theorists" who continued to vocalize their insistence that McVeigh was simply a convenient "stooge," masking the faces of the *real* perpetrators. John Trochman, a well-known voice within the Patriot Movement, leader of the Montana Militia and now known government informant, told reporters McVeigh was a victim of the "Oswald Syndrome; [...], "a patsy" whose sole function was to "provide deep cover for the CIA...after all," Trochman asked, "Who trained him? The military." For conspiracy theorists like Trochman, the real story was easy to suppress because "the American people have been so brainwashed they can't see the truth anymore" (*Omaha World Herald* "An Inconsequential Verdict in the Eyes of McVeigh Sympathizers, He'll Always Be Innocent, Jury Selection" March 30, 1997.)

In addition to the above-mentioned quotes, Guilty Agent stories appeared frequently in works of the conspiracy theory 'genre' prior to the criminal trials of McVeigh and Nichols. For example, Jon Rappaport's 1995 book *Oklahoma City Bombing: The Suppressed Truth*, whose cover claims to be "The Book That Shatters The Cover Up" argues that the bombing plot was unquestionably a conspiracy that subsequently led to a "cover-up". While Rappaport acknowledged that, at the time of his writing, many of the details of this conspiracy and cover-up remained unknown, he nonetheless asserted that both were part of a larger effort by the federal government to run damage control in the aftermath of the Waco debacle, demonize the Patriot Movement and pass anti-terrorism legislation which would expand the budgets and powers of various government agencies, thereby allowing them to further suppress the Movement. Rather than espousing a 'unified theory' about the exact workings and details involved in the bombing plot, Rappaport presented several alternative scenarios to the then-dominant Lone Wolf story. Rappaport asserted that, if any of these proved true, it was likely that McVeigh had not been fully aware of all the details of the plot but was more likely an "amateur" participant within "the visible part of a [larger] sophisticated operation," a "delivery man," "blamable man," "fall guy," "throw away" and "dupe. " Similarly, Jim Keith's 1996 book *OKBomb! Conspiracy and Cover-Up* listed the numerous unaccounted for sightings of John Doe 2, eleven "striking incongruities in the behavior of Timothy McVeigh" not accounted for by the official story and outlined evidence suggesting the government's prior knowledge of the bombing. While Keith did not argue in favor of any one of them, he proposed various conspiracy theories as possibilities to account for inconsistencies in the Lone Wolf story.

7. An in-depth discussion of 'Agency Panic' is found in Timothy Melley, *Empire of Conspiracy: The Culture of Paranoia in Postwar America*, Cornell University Pres, Ithaca, New York, 2000.

Chapter One: On Becoming John Rambo

1. Warren Commission Report (Ch.1, pg. 19; Ch. 3, pg. 117; Ch. 7, pg. 378), (Appendix 13, pg. 670-682,); Warren Commission Hearings (Testimony of Howard Brennan, Vol. 3, pg. 143), (Testimony of John E. Donovan, Vol. 8, pg. 290-298), (Testimony of John Edward Pic), (Interview with Mrs. John Edward Pic, Vol. 22, pg. 687), Vol. 25, pg. 123; Acron.net "Report of Renatus Hartogs, May 1, 1953" ; Anthony Summers, *Not In Your Lifetime*, Marlowe & Company, New York, New York, 1998: pg. 235; Alex Cox, *The President And The Provocateur: The Parallel Lives of JFK and Lee Harvey Oswald*, Feral House, Port Townsend, Washington, 2013.

2. In a note written the day before the Tower incident, Whitman wrote, "…I do not really understand myself these days. I am supposed to be an average reasonable and intelligent young man. However, lately, (I cannot recall when it started) I have been a victim of many unusual and irrational thoughts." He asked that his brain be studied by scientists who could figure out what was wrong with him (Time Life Books, *Mass Murderess*, Time Life Education, 1993: 5).

3. One week after the 1971 arrest, Bremer met a woman named Joan whom he began dating but she broke up with him after a number of incidents involving his inappropriate and "weird" behaviors. Bremer refused to accept the breakup, shaved his head and began stalking Joan.

4. *Pittsburg Post-Gazette,* May 17, 1972; *Eugene Register Guard*, May 16, 1972; *Life*, May 26, 1972; Time.com "Arthur Bremer's Notes from the Underground" May 29, 1972; *Milwaukee Sentinel*, May 12, 1973; Arthur Bremer, *An Assassin's Diary*, Harpers Magazine Press, 1973.

5. Flo Conway., Jim Siegelman, *Snapping: America's Epidemic of Sudden Personality Change, 2nd Edition*, Stillpoint Press, New York, NY, 1995: pgs. 147-150, 150, 156,301-312.

6. Theodore Kaczynski, *The Unabomber Manifesto: Industrial Society and Its Future and Control of Human Behavior*, 1995; *New York Times* "Excerpts From Letter by 'Terrorist Group' FC, Which Says It Sent Bombs" April 26, 1995; *Washington Post* "Paper Assails Industrial – Technological System" June 30, 1995.

7. After graduating high school, Chapman attended college and worked for World Vision, an international humanitarian aid organization, first with Vietnamese refugees housed at a resettlement camp in Arkansas and then continued his work with refugees in Lebanon. In time, Chapman became an area coordinator and key aide to the programs director, who invited Chapman to attend meetings with high-level government officials.

World Vision has been described by some as a 'CIA Front' and within more conspiratorial narratives, has been implicated in U.S. mind control experiments, the 1978 mass suicides at Jim Jones' People's Temple in Guyana, and as an unseen but important influence in the actions of Mark David Chapman and John Hinckley, Jr. , whose father was President of the organization.

During his six-week trip, Chapman traveled to a number of countries including (but not limited to) Bangkok, Beirut, Dublin, Tokyo, Seoul, Hong Kong, Singapore, Paris and London. The next year, he married and began working as a printer at the same hospital he had been an inpatient at previously but was fired after a series of altercations with the hospital staff. Chapman's hospitalization and employment at the Hawaii hospital are critical within mind control themed stories that emerged after the Lennon assassination.

8. Fenton Bresler. *Who Killed John Lennon?* St. Martin's Press, 1990; Jack Jones, *Let me Take You Down: Inside the Mind of Mark David Chapman, the Man Who Shot John Lennon*, Virgin, London, England, 2001; Peter Knight, *Conspiracy Theories in American History: An Encyclopedia, Volume 1*, ABC-CLIO Inc., Santa Barbara, California, 2003:426-428; Salvador Asturcia, *Rethinking John Lennon's Assassination- the FBI's War on Rock Stars* Ravening Wolf Publishing Company 2006; CNN "Lennon's killer denied parole again" Aug. 12, 2008; *USA Today* "John Lennon Killer Chapman Denied Parole In NY" Sept. 7, 2010, Carolyn Thompson; *Buffalo News* "Lennon's killer transferred to Wende facility" May 15, 2012, Matt Gryta; Crime Library.com "To The Brink and Back" Fred McGunagle; The *Times* (London) "Reagan gunman: I want Starbucks job" June 8, 2015; Daily Mirror "John Lennon killer denied 8th parole bid" Aug. 24, 2014.

9. After one ruling in 2009, Hinkley's privileges expanded allowing him to leave the hospital for up to ten days at a time although he was forbidden to speak with the media (whom he aggressively courted) and required to carry a GPS cell phone with him at all times, in order to track his movements.

10. *Toronto Star*, June 7, 1997.

11. Conway and Siegelman 1995: 299, 303, 308, 312.

12. Strozier, Charles B. "Youth Violence and The Apocalyptic" *The American Journal of Psychoanalysis* 62 no. 3 (2002): 285. Not discussed in this book but among the shooters to emerge prior to the Columbine incident were thirty-two year old Frederick Martin Davidson (Aug. 15, 1996) and sixteen year old Kip Kinkel (May 20, 1998).

13. United States Postal Service "2002 Annual Report of Investigations: Violent Crime" 2002; *Time* "Person of the Week: Lucas Helder" May 9, 2002; CNN "Feds: Suspect admitted pope bomb spree" May 9, 2002; *The Badger Herald* "News Analysis: Newspapers receipt of shady mail a daily occurrence"; *WQAD Report* "Experts say mailbox bomb suspect unlikely to be freed soon" April 6, 2004; Disovery.com "Why Conspiracy Theories Provoke Violence" Jan. 30, 2013; Associated Press "Luke Helder, Mailbox Bombing Suspect, To Face Mental Competence Hearing" May 13, 2013.

School shooters who emerged in the period after Luke Heller (2002) include, but are not limited to forty-two year old Peter Odighizuwa (2002) and forty-one year old Robert Flores (2002).

14. NBCNews.com "Gunman sent package to NBC News" April 19, 2007, Alex Johnson; MSNBC "Massacre at Virginia Tech" April 20, 2007, Ewen MacAskill; *The Guardian* "Families rebuke NBC for broadcast of killer's rant" Aug. 21, 2007; "Mass Shootings at Virginia Tech April 16, 2007: Report of the Virginia Tech Review Panel (Massengill Report) Aug. 2007: Appendix N, "A Theoretical Profile of Seung Hui Cho."

15. *Daily Telegraph* "Fort Hood shootings: the meaning of 'Allahu Akbar'" Nov. 6, 2009; KMBC-TV Kansas City Ch. 9 "Local Slider Describes Fort Hood Shooting" Nov. 6, 2009; New York Times "President, at Service, Hails Fort Hood's Fallen" Nov. 11, 2009; NPR "Walter Reed Officials Asked: Was Hassan Psychotic?" Nov. 11, 2009; *New York Times* "Investigators Study Tangle of Clues on Fort Hood Suspect" Nov. 14, 2009; A Special Report by Joseph I. Lieberman, Chairman Susan M. Collins, Ranking Member U.S. Senate Committee on Homeland Security and Governmental Affairs "A Ticking Time Bomb Counterterrorism Lessons From The U.S. Government's Failure To Prevent The Fort Hood Attack" Washington D.C. 20510, February 2011; *Christian Science Monitor* "Opinion: Fort Hood attack: Did Army ignore red flags out of political correctness?" Feb. 3, 2011; *USA Today* "Nidal Hasan found guilty in Fort Hood killings" Aug. 23, 2013.

16. *KGUN-TV* "9OYS Investigates: Who is Jared Loughner" Jan. 8, 2011, Tammy Vo; ABC "Jared Loughner Radically Changed Before Alleged Shooting, Friend Says" Jan. 9, 2011, Lee Ferran, Jason Ryan, Emily Friedman; *Arizona Republic* "Jared Lee Loughner, suspect in Gabrielle Giffords shooting, had college run-ins" Jan. 9, 2011, Robert Anglen; Nick Baumann; *Los Angeles Times* "Jared Lee Laughner's parents alone with their anguish, neighbor says" Jan. 10, 2011, Sam Quinones; *USA Today* "Friends, co-workers: Shooting suspect had curious, dark change" Jan. 11, 2011, Gary Strauss, Peter Eisler, Jack Gillum, William M. Welch; CBS "Sheriff Releases Loughner's Arrest Records" Jan. 12, 2011; *Los Angeles Times* "School releases You Tube post from Loughner" Jan. 15, 2011, Rong-Gong Lin II, Rick Rojas; *New York Times* "Looking Behind the Mug-Shot Grin" Jan. 15, 2011, Dan Barry; *Mother Jones* "Exclusive: Loughner Friend Explains Alleged Gunman's Grudge Against Giffords" Jan. 20, 2011; *New York Times* "Lawyers for Defendant in Gifford's Shooting Seem to Be Searching for Illness" Aug. 17, 2011, Marc Lacy; *Telegraph Herald* "Court Grapples with Medicating Loughner" Aug. 31, 2011, Paul Ellias; *Spokesman Review* "FBI Releases Loughner Files: Agency believed Giffords' shooter planned second attack" July 26, 2014.

The morning of the shooting, a police officer pulled Loughner over for running a red light. Although Loughner acted oddly (at first calm, then crying, then laughing), he was let go.

17. *Huffington Post* "Oscar Ramiro Ortega-Hernandez's Lawyers" Statements From Accused White House Shooter Were Coerced" Jan. 16, 2013; Rollcall.com "Idaho Man Who Fired at White House in 2011 Sentenced to 25 Years" March 31, 2014; Salt Lake Tribune "Suspect in White House shooting had Utah ties" Nov. 19, 2011.

18. *Time* Magazine "Who Is James Holmes, the Aurora Shooting Suspect?" July 20, 2012, Nick Carbone, Erin Skarda ;ABC News "Colorado Movie Shooting: Who is James Holmes?" July 21, 2012, Christian Ng, Olivia Katrandjian; ABC News "Colorado Shooting Suspect James Holmes Was Turned Away From Gun Range" July 22, 2012, Christian Ng, Olivia Katrandjian, Pierre Thomas, Jack Date; *Daily Beast* "James Holmes Suggested He Suffered From 'Dysphoric Mania' Weeks Before Attack" Aug. 28, 2012, Eliza Shapiro; *Denver Post* "Long Odds to clear Holmes" June 7, 2013, John Ingold; Fox News "Massacre suspect James Holmes' gun-range application drew red flag," July 22, 2012; *Christian Science Monitor*, "Colorado shooting suspect James Holmes was an 'unusually bad intern'" July 23, 2012; *New York Daily News* "Suspected Aurora shooter James Holmes brilliant? Not by a long shot, says former Salk Institute supervisor John Jacobson" July 23, 2012; 5 NBC Chicago. "Man accused in Colo. shooting was accepted to UIUC" Aug. 10, 2012; *Denver Post* "Notebook details theater attack plans" May 28, 2015; *Irish Mirror* "James Holmes trial: Batman gunman's notebook shows he planned attack after harboring obsession to kill for 10 years" May 28, 2015; *Daily News* "Murder Ink" May 29, 2015; *Daily News* "Colo. Shooter eyed capture" May 30, 2015; *Los Angeles Times* "Aurora theater massacre, as told by the gunman" June 3, 2015; *Irish Mirror* "James Holmes trial: Batman gunman smears feces on wall of his cell but is ruled sane by doctors" June 6, 2015 ; *The Columbian* "Colo. Shooter's ex urged him to see therapist" June 12, 2015 ; *Denver Post* "Final Witness planned" June 15, 2015 ; *Charleston Gazette-Mail* "Coach says shooter a 'shadow figure'" July 24, 2015 ; thespec.com "I still love him' says tearful sister of mass killer James Holmes" July 28, 2015 ; thespec.com "From happy to boy to mass killer: The story of James Holmes" July 30, 2015 ; *The Daily Gleaner* "Surprise ending in Colorado cinema shooting trial" Aug. 10, 2015; *Legal Monitor Worldwide* "Capital punishment would have been doubtful for Colorado theater shooter James Holmes" Aug. 13, 2015 ; *Irish Mirror* "James Holmes: Batman killer is 'monster' destined for 'most painful part of hell' victim's family tells court" Aug. 25, 2015 ; *Chicago Daily Herald* "Judge formally sentences James Holmes to life in prison" Aug. 27, 2015 ; *Newsday* "The trap in James Holmes' apartment" Sep. 11, 2015 ; Daily News "An Aurora Horror" Sep. 11, 2015 .
   Police reportedly later retracted their statement that Holmes identified himself as The Joker.

19. *Jewish Exponent* "Shooting Highlight 'Lone Wolf' Threats" April 17, 2014.

20. *Washington Post* "Parents' breakup devastated Lanza, ex-neighbors recall" Dec.15, 2012; *Gazette (Montreal)* "Gunman recalled as quiet, fidgety, student; With No Facebook page, Adam Lanza avoided attention and left few footprints" Dec. 15, 2012, David M. Halbfinger; *Edmonton Journal* "Killer was 'a socially awkward kid': Adam Lanza was intelligent but emotionless, ex classmates say" Dec.15, 2012, David M. Halbfinger; *Newsday* "Newtown Shooting: Unknowable to the End" Dec. 16, 2012; *New York Post* "Blood Sport Newtown Shooter Tried To Outkill Norway Nut Job" Feb.19, 2013, Andy Soltis; *New York Times* "Newtown Killer's Obsessions, in Chilling Detail" March 28, 2013, N. R. Kleinfield, Ray Rivera, Serge F. Kovaleski.
   Other, 'conspiracy theories' similar to those that exist about the nefarious uses of ELF weapons surround HAARP, short for High Frequency Active Aural Research Program, a Department of Defense initiative staged out of Alaska purportedly to study the relationship between the ionosphere and radio signals. More suspicious minded individuals, however, believe HAARP has weather modification and control capabilities as well as monitoring and remote influencing capabilities, the sort sometimes attributed to ELF weapons.

21. *Washington Post* "Weather control conspiracy theories: scientifically unjustifiable" (Commentary), Aug. 16, 2013, Dennis Merserau; *Washington Post* "DC Navy Yard rampage leaves 14 dead; alleged shooter killed, ID'd as Aaron Alexis" Sep. 16, 2013, Ashley Halsey, III, Peter Hermann, Clarence Williams; *New York Times* "Suspect in Shooting Had Interest in Thai Culture, and Prob-

lems With the Law" Sep. 17, 2013; *Washington Post* "Aaron Alexis, Navy Yard Shooting Suspect, started deteriorating last year" Sep. 17, 2013; *Washington Post* "FBI Chief: Navy Yard gunman seemed to pick targets randomly" Sep. 19, 2013, Sari Horwitz, Susan Svrluga, Paul Duggan; *Washington Post* "Warning signs unheeded" Sep. 22, 2013; *USA Today* "Navy Yard shooter feared electromagnetic control; Federal officials detail delusions, release video of Alexis stalking halls" Sep. 26, 2013, Kevin Johnson, Doug Stanglin; *New York Times* "Gunman Said Electronic Brain Attacks Drove Him to Violence, F.B.I. Says" Sep. 26, 2013, Michael S. Schmidt.

22. NBC News "Shooter opens fire at Los Angeles International Airport" Nov. 1, 2013; *Daily News* "KILL THE TSA AND PIGS' 7 people hurt, agent shot dead, Cops blast, susp in 'methodic' attack" Nov. 2, 2013; *Los Angeles Times* "Suspect in LAX attack kept to self; Former classmates described the N.J. native as shy and quiet but did not see him as a threat" Nov. 2, 2013; *New York Post* "Bloody end of lax SLAY rampage Gory scene as cops shoot psycho in face" Nov. 3, 2013; *Commercial Appeal* "Shooter viewed TSA as 'traitorous'" Nov. 3, 2013; Reuters "Accused Los Angeles airport gunman to be moved to federal detention" March 3, 2014; *Pasadena Star-News* "Federal prosecutors to seek death penalty for accused LAX shooter Paul Ciancia" Jan. 3, 2015.

23. *Newsday* "Cops' new police in mass shootings; run toward gunfire; no more waiting: to save lives, officers now pushed to enter hostile situations sooner, using special training and tactical support" June 9, 2014.

On April 2, 2014, thirty-four year old Iraq war veteran, Ivan Lopez, stationed at Ft. Hood, killed three people and wounded sixteen others at the base before killing himself. At the time of the incident, Lopez was undergoing treatment for depression, anxiety and PTSD for which he was prescribed the sleep disorder drug Ambien. He had recently asked for a transfer, telling his superiors he was being "picked on" by other soldiers (CNN.com "Official: Fort Hood gunman claimed he was picked on by follow soldiers" April 7, 2014). In May 2014, another public shooting was committed by 22 year old Elliot Rodgers, followed by another in June 2014 committed by 26 year old, Aaron Ybarra.

24. CTV News "3 RCMP officers dead, 2 wounded in Moncton shooting." June 4, 2014; *National Post* "Moncton shooting leaves city on lockdown – Justin Bourque at large" June 5, 2014; National Post "Moncton shooter waved away civilian who tried to help fallen officer, witness says" June 5, 2014; Globe and Mail "Suspect in Moncton shooting talked about going out 'with a bang'" June 5, 2014 ; National Post "Moncton shooting manhunt has quickly become one of Canada's largest police operations." June 6, 2014; BBC News "Canada shootings: Man arrested in Moncton, New Brunswick" June 6, 2014 ; Associated Press "Canadian police charge suspect over shooting deaths of three Mounties." June 6, 2014; *Globe and Mail* "Moncton suspect was in rage, then despondent before Mountie shooting" July 4, 2014 ; CTV News "Mountie killer Justin Bourque sentenced to 75 years before parole eligibility" Oct 30, 2014 ; CTV News "Justin Bourque sentencing exhibits made public" Dec. 5, 2014 ; CBC News "Justin Bourque had 'kit' ready the night of Mountie shootings" Dec. 6, 2014; CTV News "Justin Bourque was sleep deprived before Moncton shooting" Dec. 8, 2014; CBC News "Justin Bourque felt 'tired of being oppressed' report reveals" Dec. 8, 2014; CBC News "Moncton shooting: Justin Bourque armed with rifle, shotgun" June 5, 2014; CBC News "Justin Bourque: Latest revelations about man charged in Moncton shooting" Sep. 4, 2014.

25. Proposed responses and solutions included: 'Active shooter' training for educators, security guards, TSA officials, police and everyday citizens. Discarding outmoded views of civil liberties for the sake of public safety. Changing privacy laws and creating more sophisticated databases that would allow schools, employers and firearm merchants to conduct more thorough background checks. Enacting laws that would require mental health professionals to report clients who may pose such threats (however defined). Mandatory treatment and/or involuntary institutionalization for those deemed mentally ill. Prosecuting perpetrators of mass shootings as terrorists. Executing them. Closer monitoring of social media by law enforcement agencies. Refusing to broadcast too many details about the shooters and/or incidents in the mass media. Subtle manip-

ulation of social media, spamming and trolling, guided by knowledgeable experts who could halt the spread of erroneous, dangerous and contagious ideologies and beliefs (conspiracy theories).

26. Vice.com "Conspiracy Theorists Are Dangerous Enemies To Have" April 24, 2013; Disovery. com "Why Conspiracy Theories Provoke Violence" Jan. 30, 2013; *Newsweek* "The Plots to Destroy America: Conspiracy Theories Are A Clear And Present Danger" May 23, 2014.

27. *Christian Science Monitor* "'Survivalist' murder suspect goes to ground in huge earthen 'bug out' bunker' April 28, 2012, Patrick Christian Jonson; *Irish Daily Mail* "Killers Mother had stockpiled food and guns for the collapse of the world" Dec. 17, 2012, Tom Leonard;

28. Timothy Gallimore "Unresolved Trauma: Fuel for the Cycle of Violence and Terrorism" in *The Psychology of Terrorism: Clinical Aspects and Responses. V. 2*, Chris E. Stout, Ed., Westport, Connecticut, London, Praeger, 2002:143-164.

29. Benjamin Beit- Hallahmi. "Rebirth and Death: The Violent Potential of Apocalyptic Dream" pg. 163- 189 and Jerry S. Piven, "On the Psychosis (Religion) of Terrorists" pg. 119-148, both in *The Psychology of Terrorism V. 3: Theoretical Understandings and Perspectives* ed. Chris E. Stout., Westport, Connecticut, London, Praeger, 2002.

30. Mitchell 3, 8-10;*St. John's Telegram* (Newfoundland) "Just an ordinary doomsday fanatic: Author says survivalists are reacting rationally to a crazy world" March 17, 2002, Elaine Cassel.

31. Carl Boggs and Tom Pollard. *A World In Chaos: Social Crisis and the Rise of Postmodern Cinema.* Lanham, Maryland, Roman & Littlefield Publishers, Inc., 2003: 34 quoting Ritzer 1999:172-186.

32. *The Australian* "Massacre game creator defiant" May 17, 2007; *Hobart-Mercury* "University massacre game 'just for laughs'" May 17, 2007; *New York Daily News* "Sick Sandy Hook videogame lets players shoot mom, collect ammo and fire into school" Nov. 20, 2013.

33. *Boston Globe* "Fantasy, masks, and James Holmes, the 'Dark Knight Rises' killer" July 20, 2012, Ty Burr.

34. Carl Boggs and Tom Pollard.,. *A World In Chaos: Social Crisis and the Rise of Postmodern Cinema.* Lanham, Maryland, Roman & Littlefield Publishers, Inc., 2003: 53; Joseba Zulaika and William Douglass., A. *Terror And Taboo: The Follies, Fables, and Faces of Terrorism.* New York, London, Rutledge, 1996: 4, 17.

35. Gallimore; Parnas et. al. 2010; William H. Reid. "Controlling Political Terrorism: Practicality, Not Psychology" (pg. 1-8) and Ruben Ardila, "The Phycology of the Terrorist: Behavioral Perspectives" (pg. 9-15) in *The Psychology of Terrorism: Clinical Aspects and Responses, V. 1*, Chris E. Stout Ed., Praeger, Westport, Connecticut, London, 2002.

36. Douglas Kellner. *Guys and Guns Amok: Domestic Terrorism and School Shootings from the Oklahoma City Bombing to the Virginia Tech Massacre*, Boulder, London, Paradigm Publishers, 2008:11.

37. Clinically, the term 'psychosis' denotes a 'loss of contact with reality,' often accompanied by delusions, false beliefs based on incorrect inferences about external reality that are firmly held to without accurate, corresponding or sufficient evidence despite evidence to the contrary and in opposition to what the majority of people accept as true. A contextual delusion is a belief which, under closer scrutiny, seems reasonable, even rational, when supported by the contextual circumstances surrounding it. Unlike a run of the mill delusion, a contextually embedded delusion does not necessarily depend upon the *truth, falsity, possibility, probably or plausibility* of the claim or belief but rather, the process through which a person arrives at a delusional conclusion, the experience of the belief, the manner by which an individual communicates and enacts it and the extent of its negative impact upon the life of the individual and lives of those around them. In the absence of falsifying evidence to disprove a strange belief, the possibility remains that a bizarre claim might be real.

38. See: J.E. (Hans) Hovens., Boris Drozdek., "The Terror of Torture: A Continuum of Evil" (pg. 75-103) and Teri L. Elliot. "Children and Trauma: An Overview of Reactions, Mediating Factors,

and Practical Interventions That Can Be Implemented" (pg. 49-73) and Gallimore in *The Psychology of Terrorism: Clinical Aspects and Responses, V. 2*, Chris E. Stout Ed., Praeger, Westport, Connecticut, London, 2002: 144, 152; Elizabeth, F. Howell., *The Dissociative Mind* The Analytic Press, Hillsdale, NJ., London 2005: viii, 16, 17, 26, 27, 219; William Graebner. *Patty's Got A Gun: Patricia Hearst in 1970's America* University of Chicago Press, Chicago, London, 2008: 127.

39. The definition of DID is one found amongst the literature (see previous note). DID and other dissociative disorders were included and expanded upon within the DSM-V (2013). The resurgence of this diagnosis, renewed research efforts and the recent growth of literature addressing dissociation, generally, and as pathological specifically, dovetails and incorporates recent advances in neuroscience and trauma studies.

40. Author interview with Liz and John McDermott, Buffalo, NY, Oct. 6, 2010.

41. When not otherwise cited, quotes by various individuals originate with interviews conducted by the Jones Team attorney, investigators, and mental health experts or those conducted by the FBI and are found within the Jones Collection. For a list of interview dates and a general description of the person interviewed (McVeigh family friend, military interview, McVeigh extended family member, etc.,), see Jones Collection. Due to privacy concerns, the names of individuals interviewed are not included in my citations although copies of all of the interviews are on file with the author.

42. Author Interview with Christopher Tritico, Houston, Texas, Dec. 27, 2010.

43. Herbeck and Michel, 20.

44. see endnote 46.

45. Herbeck and Michel, 7.

46. Certain members of the Jones Team came to believe that Mickey might have encouraged her children to participate in "sexual situations." The allegations of Mickey's having exposed her son to inappropriate sexual situations, was based on information learned by the Jones Team after interviews with McVeigh family friends and neighbors. I think it's fair to mention that such rumors are just that, rumors, and I have no further information to corroborate them beyond their brief mention in Jones Team memos. They very well could be the result of over eager defense investigators or gossipy neighbors.

47. Jones Collection; BBC June 11, 2001; American Terrorist Collection.
    Tim said that as a child, he trashed his bedroom, threw darts at the walls, and ran string from his light switch to his bed so he could read late into the night without getting up to turn off the light. Once, he remembered, he had used a rope to try and 'grapple' out the window but became stuck half way down and ended up damaging the ledge and twisting his ankles trying to climb back up.

48. *New York Times*, Dec. 31, 1995; ABC News, April 11, 1996, both quoted by Stickney 1996: 83.

49. Stickney 82, 83.

50. Herbeck and Michel, 39.

51. *Christian Science Monitor* "How to Survive the Survivalists" Sep. 18, 1980, Melvin Maddocks; *New York Times* "In California, The 'Private Societies' Flaunt Firepower" Dec. 17, 1980, Wayne King; *New York Times* "Fearing Society's Collapse, Survivalists Cache Goods" Jan. 15, 1981, Wayne King; *Washington Post* "Survivalists; The Posse in Maryland is Ready to Ride" June 26, 1983, Mike Sager; *Globe and Mail* "Beating the Bomb" Rachael Migler, Sep. 29, 1984.

52. *Washington Post*, June 26, 1983.

53. *New York Times* "Texts of Statements By U.S. and Soviet on Jest" Aug. 16, 1984.

54. Serrano, 21; Stickney, 75; Hamm 1997: 126.
    Years later, as a result of his security clearance, McVeigh obtained a job as a guard at the Calspan

research and development facility in Buffalo, NY, where, among other things, the REDCAP program was located which, very much like the AI computer Lightman squares off with, also ran hyper-realistic simulated war games.

55. In 1978, the CIA reported 3,336 acts of terrorism, after which definitions of terrorism expanded, and in 1980, the number rose to 6,714. When CIA director William Casey expanded definitions to include actions taken by the Soviets, statistics of international terrorism incidents doubled. Although between 1980 and 1985, only seventeen deaths had been attributed to terrorist violence worldwide, *New York Times'* coverage of terrorism increased 60% and by 1986, the paper published an average of four stories per day on the topic. CBS dedicated as much coverage to the hostage crisis in Tehran as it did to the Vietnam War. The 1985 TWA hostage crisis would make up 65% percent of televised news content and 30% of major newspapers content at that time (Livingston 1-7,182; Zulaika and Douglass 8, 9, 12,13, 16-23; Chermak; Matthew Carr. *The Infernal Machine: A History of Terrorism From the Assassination of Tsar Alexander.* The New Press, 2007: 205, 206).

56. Stickney, 74.

57. The title of the movie *Red Dawn* would be used as the military's designation for the operation to capture Saddam Hussein in 2003; an operation that involved hundreds of soldiers, themselves referred to as Wolverine 1 and 2, respectively. The remake of *Red Dawn* was released in 2012. The remake contained many of the same underlying themes as the original but also some interesting differences. In the 2012 version, North Korea invades the U.S. and Daryl, a member of The Wolverines who, in the original, informs on his cohorts and alerts the Soviets to their location, in the remake, is tagged with a subcutaneous tracking transmitter (micro-chip) thereby unwittingly alerting 'the enemy' to the Wolverines hideout.

58. Mitchell 9,10.

59. Serrano, 20.

60. Bruce D. Clayton, PhD. *Life After Doomsday: A Survivalists Guide to Nuclear War and Other Major Disasters.* The Dial Press, New York, New York, 1980; Robert C. Smith. *How To Survive A Nuclear Disaster* Zebra Books, 1982.

61. *Washington Post* "Meet the Whitneys: They're Ready: The Nuclear Family, Preparing to Survive Doomsday and Beyond" January 18, 1984, Phil McCombs.

62. Mitchell, 14,15.

63. Hamm 1997: 125.

64. Jones Collection; Hamm 1997: 126; Stickney 77 citing *Buffalo News* April 23, 1995.

65. Hamm 1997: 126; Stickney 77 citing *Buffalo News* April 23, 1995.

66. Hamm 1997: 125.

67. Herbeck and Michel 2001: 34.

68. *Guardian* Dec. 20, 2012; *Globe and Mail* Sep. 2, 1985; Lynette Long, Thomas Long. *The Handbook for Latchkey Children and Their Parents: A Complete Guide for Latchkey Kids and Their Working Parents.* Arbor House Publishing Company, New York. 1983.

69. *Connecticut Post* Nov. 11, 2005; *National Mortgage News* July 5, 1999; *Ottawa Citizen* March 6, 1999; Kellner 2008:61-63.

70. On Becoming John Rambo *Washington Post* "Poised to Enter the Big Time, Buffalo Puts Up the Numbers" Sep. 6, 1989, Howard Kurtz; *Toronto Star* "Well, hello Buffalo" Sep. 24, 1989, Peter Gorrie.

71. After her son's arrest, when the FBI questioned Mickey, she could provide little details about his life after she moved to Florida. While she was unable to recall his medical history, where he

was in the years before the bombing or who his friends were, according to the FBI report at least, she did remember many of the guns her son had owned and could describe them in detail. Among them, she told the agents, were a .357 Magnum Desert Eagle, a .44 Magnum Desert Eagle, a .357 Python, and a .45 Magnum Desert Eagle.

72. *Washington Post* "Playing With Firepower! Brrp! Machine Guns Are Much in Demand- And America's Ramboing Down to the Range" Sep.26, 1985, Art Harris; *Globe and Mail* "Americans are tragically obsessed with a four letter word: guns" Feb. 13, 1988, Michele Landsberg.

73. *Sunday Times* "The Politics of Machismo/ Analysis of the Rambo movie cult" July 7, 1985, Dewey Gram.

74. *Globe and Mail*, June 10, 1995; Bogs and Pollard 54,164.

75. *Sunday Times*, July 7, 1985; *Washington Post* , Sep. 26 ,1985.

76. *New York Times* "Mercenary Magazine Widens Appeal" Sep.23, 1985, Iver Peterson; *Soldier of Fortune Magazine* "about us" (website) http://www.sofmag.com/about; Stickney 80, 81; Herbeck and Michel 49,50; Chermak, Ch. 7.

    SOF was founded in 1975, by a Vietnam veteran former Green Beret and mercenary for hire. *SOF* reports on warfare, insurgencies and terrorism worldwide. The controversial magazine, is known for its recruitment of mercenaries and 'guns for hire' advertisements. Other examples of such literature include *SCOPE*, a Second Amendment rights publication that also dealt with other 'government intrusion' issues in such articles as "The FBI Wants Ability to Wiretap 1 in 1,000 Americans."

77. The growth and ideologies of the WPM in the late 1980's and early 1990's have been written about by a number of scholars including: Mark S. Hamm. *American Skinheads. The Criminology and Control of Hate Crime.* Praeger. Westport, Connecticut. 1993; Hamm 2002; Ridgeway, James. *Blood in the Face: The Ku Klux Klan, Aryan Nations, Nazi Skinheads, and the Rise of a New White Culture.* Basic Books. 2nd Ed., 1996., New York, New York; Kaplan, Jeffery. *Radical Religion in America: Millenarian Movements from the Far; Right to the Children of Noah.* Syracuse University Press. Syracuse, New York. 1997; Dyer, Joel. *Harvest of Rage: Why Oklahoma City is Only The Beginning.* Basic Books. Boulder, Colorado 1998; Chermak; Wright.

78. In the years leading to the bombing, Tim gave away countless editions of *The Turner Diaries* and sold it at gun shows. Like Mark David Chapman's obsession with *The Catcher in the Rye*, McVeigh had the book in his possession constantly, made several calls to its author (and his followers), gave it out to everyone he could, and had cut-out and handwritten portions of it with him at the time of his arrest. Works about the bombing or McVeigh tend to ignore, downplay, or emphasize his racism as well as his alleged associations with various WPM organizations, spokespeople and adherents or their possible role in the bombing.

79. Hamm 1997:127; Stickney 81.

80. *New York Times* "John Doe No. 1- A Special Report: A Life of Solitude and Obsessions" May 4, 1995, Robert D. McFadden; Stickney, 81-85 Citing *Buffalo News* (no title) 4/23/95 & *Media Bypass* 3/96; Hamm 1997:127, 128, 253.

81. Jones Collection; Stickney, 86.

Chapter Two:

Unless otherwise stated, information and quotes in Chapter Two that pertain to McVeigh's military and medical records are found in the Jones Collection. Other information quoted but not cited is found in American Terrorist Collection and the Jones Collection, listed in an index at the end of this book. All military related and defense related documents found in the Jones Collection are on file with the author. Due to privacy concerns, the names of some individuals have been changed.

1. Herbeck and Michel, 51; Lt. Col. Kenneth C. Scull, "Cohesion: What We Learned from CO-HORT" U.S. Army War College Study Project, Unclassified, AD-A223 529, April 2, 1990; Stickney, 90, 93. Historically, a 'Cohort' was a unit within the Roman legions. The Army's COHORT experiment, modeled on Roman, British and even Nazi troop organization practices, began in 1981 in an attempt to correct Vietnam War era rapid rotation policies, said to have contributed to the low morale of soldiers during the war. Normally, soldiers were reassigned as individuals and not companies or units and during the Vietnam War, were rotated out of their units in 12-month cycles and tactical commanders in 6-month cycles. In the first COHORT experiment, an entire company (about 120 soldiers) were brought in together, trained together, assigned together to a major unit as a company and deployed together overseas. The same cohesion system was to be implemented for regiments of 3000 soldiers as well. When possible, members of a given company within the COHORT unit were to be drawn from the same geographical region. It was hoped that COHORT units would be more stable than other ones, their soldiers more loyal to their companies thereby more combat effective, and that by placing commanders in battalions and brigades for 30 months rather than the standard 18, would allow for continuity of leadership, the lack of which was also said to have contributed to unit incohesion during Vietnam. In the early 1980's COHORT companies, battalions with similar missions and weapons (ex. Mechanized infantry) would be grouped together as a regiment. In late 1982, there were 40 COHORT companies with an expected formation of 80 additional ones by 1985. By 1985, however, the Army had deemed the COHORT program too costly and cumbersome and therefore decided to greatly descale and revamp the COHORT experience to smaller groups of soldiers, which by 1987, were company sized. By 1987, critics of the COHORT companies said that it decreased, rather than increased morale, as it hampered a soldiers change of promotion and desired transfers. [See also: *New York Times* "Vietnam And The Military Mind" Jan. 10, 1982; *New York Times* "Army Is Revising Use Of Regiments" Dec. 22, 1982; *New York Times* "Army Chief Wanted G.I. Wedded To His Unit" June 23, 1983; *Washington Post* "Army Planning to Modify Unit-Assignment Program: COHORT Plan Viewed as Too Cumbersome, Costly" Nov. 8, 1986; *Washington Post* "Army Trainers Seek to Bolster Infantry's Line" Nov. 7, 1987.

2. Hamm 1997: 136, 137.

3. Herbeck and Michel 49-66; Hamm 1997: 128-139; Stickney 93.

Although some soldiers said they could not remember him spending much time with Nichols early on, Stickney says that from the beginning "McVeigh clung to Nichols." Nichols would leave the Army on a hardship discharge before the Gulf War began, citing 'family reason' as the issue necessitating this.

4. List of Immunizations given to McVeigh on May 25, 1988: Tetanus-Diphtheria Toxoids, Tuberculosis (PPD), Measles/Mumps/Rubella (MMR), Adenovirus Type 4 and 7 (fort acute respiratory disease"), Smallpox, Oral Poliovirus, and Influenza vaccines and immunizations.

5. Brigade: 3,000 to 5,000 solders; Battalion: 300 to 1,000 soldiers; Company: 62 to 190 soldiers; Platoon: 16 to 44 soldiers; Squad: 9 or 10 soldiers (on average).

6. Author interview with Ray Barnes, Arkansas, Nov. 10, 2010 (with Holland Vandennieuwenhof); Jones Collection.

7. Jones Collection; *New York Times*, May 4, 1995; *Newsweek*, July 3, 1995.

8. Author interview with Ray Barnes, Arkansas, Nov. 10, 2010 (with Holland Vandennieuwenhof); Author interview with Gordon Blackcloud, Oklahoma, Jan. 16, 2011 (with Holland Vandennieuwenhof).

9. Jones Collection; Gordon Blackcloud interview with author, Oklahoma, Jan. 16, 2011 (with Holland Vandennieuwenhof).

10. President Bill Clinton eventually signed the bill into law in 1993. McVeigh's lead attorney Ste-

phen Jones [who had also represented] Hinckley's parents, often compared McVeigh to Hinckley who in turn lends himself to comparisons with recent 'apolitical' mass shooters such as Lanza and Holmes.

11. McVeigh's mention of corn could refer to the 1980s farm crisis, which would have been a topic of discussion between McVeigh and Nichols (who lost his family farm during the crisis and was notably bitter about it). Further, it could also reflect the agricultural dilemmas faced by his neighbors in upstate New York at the time.

12. Herbeck and Michel, 63.
   During the Gulf War, McVeigh became part of 'VII Corp,' specifically the First Armored Division headquartered in Germany. Prior to the war, VII Corp conducted Bradley training at Fort Irwin's National Training Center's desert warfare course where McVeigh had also trained with his Bradley.

13. In 1991, German domestic intelligence agencies released that there were nearly 40,000 "right wing" extremists in West Germany, many of whom held "white supremacist" ideologies. Both Strassmeir and McVeigh had connections to Oklahoma KKK spokesperson, Dennis Mahon. As early as 1991, Mahon was under investigation by U.S. and German intelligence agencies for trips he made to Germany in previous years recruiting radical right wing Germans for the White Power Movement (WPM). Outlawed in Germany, a growing amount of hate literature flowed from U.S. sources and participation in extreme right wing fascist hate groups increased. Other connections between McVeigh and targets of joint German/U.S. intelligence operations, at the time of the bombing, include the National Alliance, whose organizers and chapters McVeigh made frequent contact with.

14. *Washington Post* "Germans' Kristallnacht Observance Ends in Clash of Leftists, Neo Nazi's" January 10, 1991, "FBI Targets U.S. – German Neo- Nazi Tie; Americans Who Aid Fascists to Be Probed" December 15, 1993, "Hate Groups: an International Cooperative" May 11, 1995; *Chicago Tribune* "German Leader Blames U.S. for Fascism" December 21, 1993; *Boston Globe* "US, Germany Joining Forces to Fight Hate Groups" June 24, 1994, "Germany Raids Neo-Nazi Smuggling Ring; seeks US Hate mail Author" March 24, 1995; Evans-Pritchard 1997; *BBC Monitoring International Reports* "German intelligence agency said strengthened 'far right scene'" January 7, 2012.

15. In addition to these more politically oriented shifts in perspective, McVeigh's religious views changed or 'evolved' after his return from Germany. He explained to his biographers, "When I broke free from the coercive Catholic influence and joined the Army I was able to think for myself. What it comes down to is, what feels right, what a lot of people call Natural law. There's an answer for everything in the human heart. I'm a scientific person who doesn't necessarily subscribe to religion. I believe there's a higher power, an unexplained consciousness… there's science, religion and philosophy. Science is my religion. I must admit to myself and acknowledge there must be a higher power (Big Bang theory). Even with the Big Bang theory [you] still need an explanation for the start of the universe. Most religions say you must bow down and worship their God. [In Star Trek] people are convinced that a woman with a laser beam is God. I don't recognize an all-powerful being. I recognized there are powers higher than I. I have a hard time accepting there's a higher power that cared what we do. I don't insult other peoples religions. I believe people have a right to believe what they will."

16. Jones Collection.
   McVeigh also explained to his attorneys that it was during this time that he realized women had no place in the military. During a two-week training course, he said, "they put this woman in our class… and it was just a joke. We had to post extra guards so she could go to the bathroom, she couldn't pull her weight digging, she couldn't carry the M-60 when it was her turn to be assigned to it. You started seeing the infantry was no place for a woman. And it was immediately after this course that I started paying heightened attention to the political atmosphere [and those making

claims that] women should be allowed in combat, it was their right, equal rights. I started taking exception and this might have opened my political arena also."

17. Jones Collection.

In subsequent letters to Jennifer but written in this same time period, McVeigh inquired about a different new boyfriend of hers, this one named Tom, and suggested she date his new roommate Michael Fortier instead; even sending his sister a picture of Fortier as well as his address and requesting that she write him. He closed that letter rather abruptly by announcing that Mike "just came in [the room] telling me he slashed some dude up last night..." In others, he used homophobic terms like 'faggot' which he later explained did not reflect that he was homophobic, but that such language was normal in the military and was "a way of coping with being thrown together with a bunch of other men."

18. Gore Vidal. *Perpetual War for Perpetual Peace*. New York, Thunder's Mouth Press/ Nation Books. 2002:105.

19. See: *Washington Post* "3 White Soldiers Held in Slaying of Black Couple; Ft. Bragg Suspect's Supremacist Views Were Well- Known, N.C. Officials Say" Dec. 9, 1995; *Guardian* "Murder Shocks US Army Intro Racism Inquiry: Growing Evidence of white supremacism worries the generals" Dec. 14, 1995, "The Modern US Army: Unfit for Service?" Aug.21, 2012; *Washington Times* "Purging the armed forces of racists" Dec.19, 1995; *Christian Science Monitor* "Army Brass Rattled By Ties of Soldiers To White Supremacists" Dec. 19, 1995; *Salt Lake Tribune* "Skinheads Considered Most Violent Group of Extreme Right" Jan. 21, 1996.

20. Jones Collection; American Terrorist Collection.

To his biographers McVeigh spoke of Brent Williams (name changed), a black COHORT who respected him; a respect, he said he "gained through fire and water" during their combat in the Gulf. He had heard that one African American man in his COHORT joined the Black Panthers and said if that was true he would like to "congratulate him" and wondered if he may be connected to the "Black Panthers down in Texas," a group he'd seen on television "in parade after that guy got dragged to death behind his car" (American Terrorist Collection).

21. McVeigh made E-4 on March 1, 1990 and was promoted to E-5 on February 1, 1991, shortly after deployment to Iraq.

22. The chief evaluating officer for the PLDC course that began on August 23, 1990, noted on forms that while McVeigh was not evaluated for his "written communication" skills or "research ability" McVeigh held "academic potential." Good marks academically, well delivered instructional assignments and good use of resources all point to an outstanding [NCO]. Throughout the course, he displayed an enthusiastic attitude and a willingness to help his peers whenever necessary" (Jones Collection).

23. The additional HIV testing occurred on April 25 and May 27, 1990, the latter requested by Dr. Bloomquist.

24. *New York Times* "Confrontation in the Gulf: Excerpts from Iraqi Document on Meeting With U.S. Envoy" Sep. 23, 1990.

Included among the various governments who began selling arms to Iraq, were the Soviet Union, the UK, France, China, Chile, West Germany as well as a number of multinational arms manufacturers and dealers. In 1984 alone, Iraq spent an estimated $14 billion dollars (60% of their gross national product) on these. Meanwhile the Iraqi population starved. Weapons sold to Iran eventually found their way to terrorist groups such as Hezbollah.

25. In December 1988, Iraq purchased $1.5 million worth of pesticides from Dow Chemical, despite warnings that they were highly toxic, could result in untold accidental deaths, or their weaponization.

26. In an April 1990 meeting with Senator Bob Dole, Saddam complained of continued U.S. ef-

forts to demonize him in the press and asked Dole, "has the Zionist mentality taken control of you to the point that it has deprived you of your humanity?" (Simpson 117). The grand conspiracy Saddam perceived against him and his nation, however, had not prevented the U.S. from continuing to share intelligence, their conventional and chemical weapons sales to Iraq or the exporting of these by privately owned U.S. companies.

27. *New York Times*, Sep. 23, 1990.

28. *Washington Post* "How Saddam Built His War Machine; West Provided Much of the Necessary Technology, Expertise" Sep. 17, 1990.

29. *Washington Post* "Fog Of War: The White House: National Security Directive 54" Jan. 15, 1991.
     Journalist John Simpson wrote about later revelations that the CIA had known in advance about Iraq's impending invasion and had deliberately done nothing to prevent it. See: John Simpson, *The Wars Against Saddam: Taking the Hard Road to Baghdad*. Macmillan, London, Basingstoke, Oxford, 2004.

30. *Boston Globe* "US Military Medical Crews Prepare for War's Casualties" Dec. 25, 1990, Colin Nickerson.
     In the city of Samarra (about 45 miles from Baghdad), a chemical warfare facility was reported to be operational and while, claiming to produce insecticides for civilian use, was in reality manufacturing nerve agents that could be used against the U.S.

31. *Toronto Star* "Judgment Day: Will Tuesdays Mid-Term U.S. Elections Signal the Beginnings of the End of the Bush-Reagan Presidential Dynasty" Nov. 4, 1990. Pg. H1, Linda Diebel.
     As part of this a U.S. public relations firm Hill & Knowlton concocted stories of Iraqis' atrocities including the false testimony given to Congress in October 1990 about the slaughter of Kuwaiti infants removed from incubators and left on the floor to die. It was only later, in January 1992, that the doctor who testified about the incubator abuses admitted they had been wholly untrue. Other propaganda contrived by Hill & Knowlton included stories about Iraq's chemical weapons, nuclear capabilities, ability to facilitate terror attacks around the globe and pictures of the horrors perpetrated by Iraq displayed at the United Nations, the halls of Congress and television. The media then widely circulated these stories, often quoting White House and Pentagon spokespeople whose frequent mention of them rallied Americans in support of the war.

32. Cultural critic Douglass Kellner noted, "Throughout American history, vengeance for rape—especially the rape of white women by people of color—has been used to legitimate [legitimize] political and military action against colored people" (2004:8). See: Douglas Kellner "The Persian Gulf TV War Revisited" Ch. 7 in *Reporting War: Journalism in Wartime* Stuart Allan, Barbie Zelizer, Eds., Rutledge, 2004.

33. Simpson 179.

34. *Washington Times* "War- Bush: 'We Will Not Fail'" Jan. 17, 1991, Frank J. Murray.

35. Stickney 110, 111.

36. American Terrorist Collection.
     Always an avid consumer of the news, by the time McVeigh learned about his deployment to the Gulf, he likely saw the few reports published that were critical of the war like the September 1990, *Washington Post* article entitled "How Saddam Built His War Machine: West Provided Much of the Necessary Technology, Expertise." Just prior to his execution McVeigh discussed his perception of Gulf War propaganda on *60 Minutes*. He elaborated to his biographers, comparing the type of media hype seen during 'The Big Lead-Up' to the Gulf War to that seen during the Waco siege. He outlined a number of first hand experiences with "wartime propaganda" during the Gulf War about which he said, "All of these experiences gave me a very unique and personal experience with, and perspective on, WARTIME propaganda. So, imagine my shock and disillusionment when, re-

turning home from such as war, I recognized the same propaganda being utilized against American citizens – first Ruby Ridge, but real bad at Waco. Wartime propaganda being used against Americans!" This, McVeigh said, showed him the value of propaganda as a "war tool." He then offered another equation, to explain- "David Koresh = all Davidians evil, Kill Koresh = Kill Davidians = destroy the evil" (American Terrorist Collection).

37. Richard Lowry *THE GULF WAR CHRONICLES: A Military History of the First War with Iraq*. Lincoln, NE, iUniverse, 2003: 69, 70.

The VII Corps consisted of the 1st and 2nd Marine Division and the Army's 2nd and 3rd Armored Division, 1st Calvary, 2nd Armored Calvary Regiment, and the 1st Infantry Division.

38. Simpson 199-202.

39. The *Guardian* (London) "The war through hypnotized spectacles - Lavish production, pity about the script. Hugh Hebert on the bizarre music hall of television's Gulf War coverage" Hugh Hebert, Jan. 26, 1991 (A).

40. *Washington Post* "U.S., Allies Launch Massive Air War Against Targets in Iraq and Kuwait" Jan. 17, 1991, Rick Atkinson, David S. Broder.

Throughout the Persian Gulf War, military spokespeople and pundits repeatedly claimed that U.S. Patriot Missiles were successfully repelling Iraqi SCUD warheads fired at Saudi Arabia and Israel though in later years, this claim was hotly contested. In the years to come, various critics, including DOD think tanks, Air Force spokespeople, Israeli Defense Forces, American and Israeli media, and the Congressional Research General Accounting Office claimed that they had shown anywhere from a zero to forty percent success rate. Israeli military officials claimed the Patriots had caused more damage than they prevented as, more often than not, they failed to vaporize the SCUD, instead blowing them up and scattering Patriot and SCUD debris on the ground below. Further, while the Pentagon promised that the new precision guided 'smart bombs' would reduce civilian casualties, only 9% of bombs dropped by the U.S. were 'smart.' According to the Pentagon, the accuracy rate of the remaining 'dumb bombs' was less than 25%. The success rate of the Tomahawk missiles, estimated by the Pentagon at 98% at the start of the war, dropped to less than 10% by 1999.

41. *New York Times*. "War in the Gulf: Weapons; Pentagon Said to Authorize U.S. Use of Nonlethal Gas" Jan. 26, 1991, Patrick E. Tyler.

The UN held that the use of tear gas and other nonlethal agents was prohibited by the 1925 Geneva Protocol, but during World War II, the French used riot control agents, the Germans, chlorine, while both sides used mustard gas. An executive order issued by President Gerald Ford in 1975 restricted the use of lethal and non-lethal gases, but the use of riot-control agents was reauthorized during the invasion of Panama.

42. On February 4, 1991, three thousand, five hundred people congregated around the White House to show support for the war and counter the growing numbers of anti-war protesters. According to Douglass Kellner, a critical component of the U.S. Gulf War propaganda machine involved the press pool system and the systematic exclusion of anti-war demonstrations or even dissenting opinions in news coverage. A study by media watchdog group FAIR found that only 29 of the 2,855 minutes of television coverage from August 8 to January 3, addressed opposition to U.S. military intervention in the Gulf. When the anti-war movement did receive coverage, it tended to be negative, depicted them as mobs of unruly anti-American terrorist sympathizers. Still, Kellner says that the night before the war began, 50% of Americans were opposed to it (*New York Times*. Jan. 26, 1991; *Pantagraph* Jan. 27, 1991; *New York Times* Feb. 4, 1991, A, F; *Guardian* Jan. 21, 1991; *Wall Street Journal* "Jan. 22, 1991; Simpson 212; Kellner 2004:9).

During the last weeks of January, as Iraqi troops continued their advance into Kuwait, U.S. Marines fired artillery, mortar rounds and TOW missiles at them and their bunkers. In the parlance of the day, Iraqi forces became "bogged down" on January 29, 1991, when a Kuwait radio station owned by the CIA encouraged a Shi'ite uprising in Saudi Arabia – diverting the attention, resources, and manpower of the Iraq Army to quell the uprising (*New York Times*, Feb. 4 1991; Kellner 2004:9).

43. *New York Times* "War In The Gulf: Logistics; From Bombs to Burgers, Gulf War Involves Biggest Supply Effort Ever" John Kifner, February 4, 1991 (B); Tom Carhart. *Iron Soldiers: How America's 1st Armored Division Crushed Iraq's Elite Republican Guard.* New York, Pocket Books, 1994: 5, 6.

By January 17, the number of combat ready soldiers from the Army's First Infantry Division totaled 23,000 as well as thousands of Bradley Fighting Vehicles attached to the elite VII Corp that, along with McVeigh had begun arriving in early January. In addition to operating the large fleet of front-line advance moving Bradley Vehicles, the VII Corp (McVeigh included) was responsible for operating the Multiple Launch Rocket System (MLRS).

44. During Operations Desert Shield and Storm, FMC Corp. , the manufacturer of the Bradley, was one of the largest U.S. defense contractors in the Gulf, contracted to supply defense systems and industrial chemicals to clients around the world, replace and supply damaged oil production equipment in Kuwait, petroleum equipment plants in Saudi Arabia, and oil production facilities in Iran. In 1985, after Col. James Burton, a testing supervisor in the Pentagons office of Research and Engineering filed an internal complaint, Congress leveled heavy criticism against the Bradleys, claiming the Army skewed the results of simulated combat testing of the vehicle, although the Army denied this. Col. Burton, although commended by Congress for speaking out, was subsequently transferred to Alaska, ultimately leading to his decision to retire early. In early 1989, Saudi Arabia agreed to purchase 200 Bradley's for an estimated $550 million dollars, to be received by early 1991. On February 11, 1991, *The Wall Street Journal* quoted one FMC executive as saying that while the companies' profits had taken a turn for the worse, allied bombs and Iraq's scorched earth policy promised to raise them and informed reporters of FMC's willingness to provide Kuwait with the equipment they may need if they successfully regained control of their country. In 1992, FMC began building a newer type of Bradley, designed for electronic warfare and outfitted with radio and radar transmission and interception capabilities, described as a "combined spy and traffic cop." In 1996, FMC had agreed to pay the U.S. government $13 million dollars for defrauding the government by inflating the costs of the vehicle from 1991 to 1994, allegations that started with another company whistle blower, Robert Neargarder. FMC sold its operations in 1997. In 1998, after a nearly twelve year long court battle, $125 million dollars was awarded to the U.S. Army, who still had a reported 9,000 Bradley's in use, as part of a federal jury's verdict against FMC Corporation, who had been contracted with manufacturing and supplying the Bradley's to the Army. The jury found that FMC had misled the Army about the safety of the vehicle. The suit had begun in 1986 when former FMC whistle blower Henry Boisvert, complained that the vehicles had not passed all the tests FMC claimed they had. (See: *Washington Post* "Army Says 12 Bradleys Sank" April 27, 1987, Sandy Johnson; *Wall Street Journal.* "Crisis Management: FMC Moves to Keep Clients Like the Army Supplied During War—Maker of Armored Vehicles, Oil Field Gear Also Eyes Post Conflict Contracts—Salesman Frets About Scuds" Feb. 11, 1991, Robert Johnson; *Washington Post* "Gulf War Leaves Environment Severely Wounded" March 2, 1991, Thomas W. Lippman; *San Francisco Chronicle.* "FMC Unveils New Bradley Fighting Vehicle" Jan. 23, 1992, Don Clark; *San Francisco Chronicle.* "$125 Million Verdict in Bradley Fighting Vehicle Suit" April 15, 1998, Manny Fernandez).

45. In total, an estimated 2,200 Bradley's were used during the Gulf War alongside M1 Abrams tanks, the latter consuming five or more gallons of fuel per mile.

Other vital military equipment reported missing included an AC-130 plane. The *Wall Street Journal* reported on February 11 that one commander of a Bradley Unit had called the manufacturers, desperately announcing his willingness to pay out of his own pocket for spare parts needed to fix the Bradleys in his fleet.

46. *New York Times* "War In The Gulf: The Troops; War Cries and Whistling in the Dark" Philip Shenon, Feb. 4, 1991 (B).

47. Simpson 203-205.

Reports about the numbers of casualties in the Iraqi shelter bombing varied, the lowest number, 300, is found in Herbeck and Michel 's 2001 book while a slightly higher number of 500 was reported by *USA Today*, and the highest number, 1,500, was reported by Ramsey Clark (See: Ramsey Clark. *The Fire This Time, U.S. War Crimes in the Gulf*. Emeryville, California, Thunder's Mouth Press, 1994).

48. Also on February 15, Iraq announced it would agree to withdraw from Kuwait under the condition that Israel pull out of occupied Arab regions, the Saudi's forgive past Iraqi debts and the coalition foot the bill to rebuild the severely damaged Iraqi infrastructure. Israel and the U.S., however, declined the offer.

49. Jones Collection; Herbeck and Michel 70.

50. On January 30, 1991, eleven U.S. Marines died after an American Maverick missile hit their personnel carrier. The Marines had been part of a forward reconnaissance patrol engaged in combat with Iraqi troops west of Khafji. Such events, said CENTCOM Chief of Staff, Major General Robert Johnston, were unfortunate, but normal, occurrences in war. A growing number of journalists alleged that, during the daily Pentagon press briefings (the only sanctioned source of information for them), inaccurate or wholly falsified information was being given to them. One example of this were the initial claims of military spokespeople that U.S. Marines had not played significant roles in the Khafji attacks. As journalists were not allowed there by the Pentagon, it was left to maverick reporters and photographers who had breached the Pentagons' policy and gone there independently. On February 2, another U.S. Marine was killed by bombs dropped by American planes, who had confused the U.S. convoy with an Iraqi one. On February 4, 1991, that 'mechanical failures' caused an American B-52 to crash over the Indian Ocean. One AH-1 Cobra and one UH-1 Marine Corps helicopters accidentally crashed over Saudi Arabia, killing the six passengers inside them.

On February 26, another friendly fire incident during allied bombings killed seven U.S. Army soldiers. Ultimately, during the entire ground war alone, cluster munitions and 'bomblets' dropped from U.S. Air Force planes killed at least 14 U.S. troops and wounded an additional hundred. The February 16 incident raised the number of U.S. 'friendly fire' casualties to ten out of every fourteen deaths.

51. Stickney, 112; Herbeck and Michel, 69,70.

52. *USA Today* "1991 Gulf War Chronology" Sep. 30, 1996.

53. *Washington Post* "Allies Meet Little Resistance, Capture Thousands of POWS" Feb. 25, 1991, Rick Atkinson, William Claiborne.

54. *Washington Post* Feb. 25, 1991; Carhart 1994: 202; USA Today Sep. 30, 1996.

The air assault the evening before the ground war started was much less spectacular than was originally planned as smoke from burning oil wells, now reported to cover over half of Kuwait, reduced visibility leading to the cancellation of some sorties.

55. Stickney 111, 112; American Terrorist Collection: Jones Collection.

56. Both quotes cited in Stickney 111, 112 citing *New York Times* May 4, 1995.

57. This unexpected and inexplicable transfer away from his crew likely unnerved McVeigh greatly as, according to one fellow COHORT in the Bradley crew McVeigh trained with, he was a smart and excellent soldier, but "if he was faced with something he hadn't been trained in, he wouldn't react well...he was the type that needed to have practiced or been trained in a task" (Jones Collection).

58. Jones Collection: A former attorney on the Jones Team, Randall Coyne said, "McVeigh was an exemplary soldier obviously. There were a lot of Bronze Stars handed out during the Gulf War, but not as many with a V for Valor like he had. I put a witness on during the sentencing trial who described Tim as being Iron Mike. Iron Mike is this statue they have when they go to basic train-

ing, I think, and he knew Tim to be like him, the exemplary statue of the model soldier; he's the guy you'd want with you if you were in combat. He's the guy watching your back. He's the guy who would not desert you. He's the guy who might sacrifice his life for yours. That was his impression of Tim as a soldier and a fellow military professional" (Author interview with Randall Coyne, Feb. 14, 2011, Oklahoma).

59. In December 1990, the U.S. Navy's ship Comfort had been designated specifically for Iraqis captured during the 'commando' oil platform raids. Later, Iraqi's paraded British pilots they had captured through the streets of Baghdad.

The photos of captured allied troops released by Iraq became a subject of debate within the American media. ABC chose to show the pictures but not broadcast the audio, fearing it would add to the effectiveness of Iraqi propaganda efforts. CNN, NBC and CBS aired the photos as well as audio of nine U.S. POWs denouncing the aggressive actions of America against Iraq. The allied prisoners had been placed in highly targeted areas to act as human shields, as Iraq claimed civilian facilities continued to be targeted. Article 23 of the Geneva Convention dictated, "No prisoner may at any time be sent to, or detained in areas where he may be exposed to the fire of the combat zone, nor may his presence be used to render certain points or areas immune from military operations." Iraq claimed however that as long as the U.S. continued to violate the Geneva Convention in their treatment of Iraqi and Palestinian POWs, so too would they.

60. Jones Collection: Interestingly, Dr. John R. Smith, widely cited for finding McVeigh "sane" was an expert in POW conditions and his teacher, Dr. Jolly West the leading U.S. expert on the topic, came to appear within several Experimental Wolf narratives about the bombing and McVeigh. The record shows that the Jones Team called West because McVeigh's conditions of confinement had led to his mental and physical deterioration and for this reason, among others, Dr. Smith 'treated' McVeigh regularly while he awaited trial.

61. *Washington Post,*Feb. 25, 1991.

On February 24, an estimated 8,400 U.S. soldiers and 3,000 Abrams tanks, Bradley's and other personnel carriers from the First Infantry Division came up against a reported 8,000 Iraqi soldiers on Basra Highway.

62. Jones Collection; Herbeck and Michel 72, 73.

63. Author interview with Ray Barnes, Nov. 10, 2011, Arkansas (with Holland Vandennieuwenhof).

64. Herbeck and Michel,73-75.

65. Jones Collection; Author interview with Ray Barnes, Nov. 10, 2011, Arkansas (with Holland Vandennieuwenhof).

66. Author interview with Gordon Blackcloud, Jan. 16, 2011, Oklahoma with Holland Vandennieuwenhof).

67. *Washington Post* Feb. 25, 1991.

68. Herbeck and Michel 72.

69. Andrew Leyden. *Gulf War Debriefing Book: An After Action Report*, Hellgate Press, Grants Pass, Oregon, 1997:176; Lowry 113.

70. Carhart, 208.

71. Simpson 208, 210.

72. Simpson 210.

73. *Newsday* Sep. 12, 1991.

74. Stickney, 112; Hamm 1997:147; Herbeck and Michel, 72.

75. *National Catholic Register* "The Bulldozer Assault" Dec. 8, 2002, J.P. Zmirak.

76. *Newsday* Sep. 12, 1991; *San Francisco Chronicle* "The Best Way To Kill People" Sep. 16, 1991, Editorial, Arthur Hoppe; *Guardian* "Bloodless Words Bloody War: In a *Guardian*/Channel 4 investigation across three continents, Maggie O'Kane follows the trail of lies, cover-up and carnage that were the truth behind the 'clean' was in the Gulf" Dec.16, 1995.

77. *Guardian* "The unseen Gulf War: 'What I saw was a bunch of filled – in trenches with people's arms and legs sticking out of them. For all I know, we could have killed thousands': Patrick J. Sloyan on how the mass slaughter of a group of Iraqis went unreported" Feb. 14, 2003, Patrick Sloyan; Simpson 209, 210.

78. *Pantagraph* "Iraqis Buried Alive In Army Offensive" Sep. 13, 1991; *Globe and Mail* "Iraqi troops buried alive, Pentagon admits 'No nice way to kill somebody in war,' Washington spokesman says" Sep. 13, 1991.

79. Lowry 114; *Seattle Post-Intelligencer* "U.S. Forced Buried Enemy Forces Alive During Gulf War" Sep. 13, 1991; *Globe and Mail* Sep. 13, 1991.

A U.S. Marine Corps officer involved in the VII Corps Bulldozer Assault told the Washington Post that the 'bulldozer' tactic was getting a bad reputation in the media: "As officers involved in ground combat, our primary concern is mission accomplishment. Next on our list -- and it is a very close second -- is our fervent desire to bring all of our Marines and soldiers home alive. By contrast, preserving the life of the enemy who is trying to stop us from reaching our goals by killing us is quite low on our list of priorities. If the enemy chooses to surrender, he will be treated with as much care as we can possibly give him. If he chooses instead to fight, he must be destroyed" (Sep. 21, 1991).

80. *Newsday* "Iraqis Buried Alive –U.S. Attacked With Bulldozers During Gulf War Ground Attack" Sep. 12, 1991, Patrick J. Sloyan.

Although the U.S. claimed no American casualties resulted from the Bulldozer Assault, Pentagon officials later released a belated statement saying that one U.S. soldier was killed and one wounded during the breaching maneuver.

81. *PBS Frontline* cited by *National Catholic Register* Dec. 8, 2002; *Seattle Post- Intelligencer* Sep. 13, 1991; *Las Vegas Review Journal* "U.S. foes in Gulf War buried alive" Sep. 13, 1991.

Cheney's 2002 report to Congress attempted to justify the Bulldozer Assault. In it, he wrote "Because of these uncertainties and the need to minimize loss of U.S. lives, military necessity required that the assault ... be conducted with maximum speed and violence ... There is a gap in the law of war in defining precisely when surrender takes effect or how it may be accomplished. An attempt at surrender in the midst of a hard-fought battle is neither easily communicated nor received" (*Pantagraph* Sep. 13, 1991).

A classified log created by division officers reported that 150 had been buried and 500 taken prisoner. Other estimates for the number of prisoners taken that day are as high as 2,000 and lower estimates of the numbers buried ranged from 44 to 80 to a couple of hundred to 650. Pentagon sources were quoted as saying 457 Iraqis were buried dead in 56 temporary burial sites during the war and the sites had been marked and reported to the Red Cross. Another report claimed the Iraqi government found 44 bodies. After claiming no U.S. soldiers had been killed, the Pentagon released a statement saying one U.S. soldier was killed and one wounded during the Bulldozer "maneuver."

82. *Washington Post* Feb. 25, 1991; *Guardian* Dec. 16, 1995; Lowry 220; *National Catholic Register* Dec. 8, 2002.

83. Jones Collection.

After the war's end, it would later surface that, on February 27, the deaths of the Marines and nine British soldiers, the wounding of forty more and the destruction of five Abrams and five Bradleys during 'the Battle of Norfolk', had all been the result of friendly fire. When the body of Sgt. Tony

Applegate (killed during Norfolk) returned home, despite the letter signed by Maj. Gen. Thomas Rhane (commander of the First Mech. Inf. Div.) explaining he "was killed as a result of enemy action" his widow became suspicious. Mrs. Applegate said, "The coffin didn't weigh anything. I wondered if Tony was really in there." The only portion of his body in the casket turned out to be a charred hipbone. Her husband was the gunner on a M1A1 Abrams tank that another Abrams hit with a sabot round, or 'Silver Bullet' that travels about a mile per second, its tip coated with dense depleted uranium. The sabot ignited a fire in Applegate's tank that burned for two days. Army officials thought his body had been sucked through a three-inch vacuum created by the round. 21-year-old Spec. Tony Kidd also died from an American Silver Bullet during Norfolk. Initially, military officials told the families that their loved ones had simply been 'killed in action' but when, in August 1992, the Pentagon admitted they had died from friendly fire they acknowledged they had hidden the truth "to permit exhaustive investigations" into each death. Lt. Col. John Brown, commander of the brigade who inflicted and received the highest number of friendly fire casualties during The Battle of Norfolk explained such fratricide as "the dark side of war." (*Calgary Herald,* May 23, 1992).

84. Lowry 122; *Stars and Stripes* "U.S. Troops revisit scene of deadly Gulf War barrage" Feb. 23, 2003, Joseph Giordono; *Globe and Mail* "Getting Blown to Bits in the Dark," Feb.25, 1991.

85. *Globe and Mail* Feb. 25, 1991; Guardian "Carnage on a forgotten road: A Highway that was not cleared after the ceasefire" April 11, 1991; Press Association (UK) "Kuwait's Highway of Horror" March 2, 1991 Gordon Airs; *Independent* "Horror, destruction and shame along Saddam's road to ruin" March 2, 1991, Robert Fisk; *Los Angeles Times* "On Forgotten Kuwait Road, 60 Miles of Wounds of War" March 10, 1991, Bob Drogin; *Washington Post* "In Postwar Iraq, Bridges Rebuilt but Not the Nation's Spirit" Feb. 9, 1993, Nora Boustany.

Estimated numbers of retreating Iraqi soldiers and civilians range from 10,000 to 80,000 and the number of Iraqi vehicles on Basra Highway, was estimated at approximately 2,000.

Kuwaitis living in the area said many Iraqis attempted to flee but those who escaped the aerial assault became the targets of coalition ground forces. Speaking of a quarter mile traffic jam that trapped several hundred retreating vehicles, A U.S. officer told Press Association (UK) reporter Gordon Airs, "we have taken out about 80 bodies from this tangled mess so far- but God knows how many are still in there." Airs described his impressions of the scene, writing, "The few who managed to get north of the bottle neck trap did not last long either. All along the highway lay wrecked and burned out military vehicles and civilian cars, most of which had been abandoned during the attacks. With even more bodies lying alongside the road" (Guardian, April 11, 1991).

86. *Boston Globe* March 2, 1991; *Digital Journalist,* "The Unseen Gulf War," Dec. 2002, Peter Turnley; Globe and Mail Nov. 5, 2002; Globalsecurity.org "Hammurabi Division" no date; *Stars and Stripes* Feb. 23, 2003; *Independent* March 21, 1991.

The body count ranged from 200 to 300 (the official count) to thousands. The official 200-300 body count had first appeared in the *Washington Post* and was based upon the estimates of one journalist who visited the scene shortly after. A British officer recalled his regiment "found and buried women and children" (Globalsecurity.org; *Stars and Stripes* Feb. 23, 2003).

87. *Stars and Stripes* Feb. 23, 2003; Lowry 140, 155.

88. Hamm 1997:148 ; Herbeck and Michel, 75.

89. Concerning Lt. Rodriguez' testimony that McVeigh took pictures of dead Iraqi's McVeigh said this was "Not true. (This testimony was not malicious on his part, just bad recall.) Someone on our vehicle did take such pictures (I don't wish to name him), but I felt it was just "wrong" (one of those intuitive feelings – like a desecration of the dead or something. I was even offered copies of these and declined. My Desert Storm photo album collection (confiscated by the FBI, so they knew) had no such pictures – reinforcing this fact." In another conversation with his biographers, McVeigh said that the driver of his Bradley took pictures of dead bodies and gave him a copy, "we had a rapport, and he respected my ability. After the war, he gave me a set of his pictures. When he gave me that set I went

through them that day, with him right there, in his house. I went through and said I don't want these. The only ones I kept were of the destroyed vehicles and stuff. He was in a better position than me to take pictures because I was the gunner, I never had much chance to jump out of the turret and take pictures. When you're in a defensive position, driver doesn't have anything to do, but the gunner is constantly scanning. Lt. Rodriguez also took as set of pictures and gave me a copy of his. You can identify his photos by a Teenage Mutant Ninja Turtle in the corner of the photo. [...] [there were] no dead bodies in my entire collection" (American Terrorist Collection).

90. *New Yorker* "Annals of War: Overwhelming Force – What Happened in the Final Days of the Gulf War?" May 22, 2000, pg. 48-82, Seymour Hersh.

Before heading towards the small town El Bosna, McVeigh's division had to stop at Safwan Airfield where Saddam was to sign a surrender agreement and coalition and Iraqis negotiated a cease-fire yet much to the dismay of Gen. Schwarzkopf, the VII Corp had not secured the town of Safwan. Under direct orders from Gen. Schwarzkopf, McVeigh's division continued towards Safwan. Upon arriving there, however, they learned that due to confusion resulting from, 'the fog of war,' the division tasked with ousting the Iraqis occupying the location had failed to do so. On March 1, Major General Rhame commanded Lt. Moreno to take his brigade and convince the Iraqis to leave peacefully or kill them. Moreno informed the Iraqi generals that they had one hour to vacate, threatening them with his impressive fleet of armored Bradley vehicles and Abrams tanks. After a Bradley almost ran over the car of one Iraqi General, they agreed to leave, and thus, the First Infantry Division, this time with no shots fired, helped to end the war.

91. Lowe 210, 211; Hamm 1997:149 ; Herbeck and Michel,80; Author interview with Ray Barnes, Nov. 10, 2011, Arkansas (with Holland Vandennieuwenhof).

92. *Village Voice* "The Grim Recent History of Iraq: Facts and Shivers" May 6, 2003, James Ridge-way; Department of Veterans Affairs "Gulf War Veterans Information System" May 1997; *Daily Sitka Sentinel* (Sitka, Alaska) "Iraq Military Death Toll: More Than 100,000?" March 22, 1991; *Newsday* "Iraqis Buried Alive—U.S. Attacked With Bulldozers During Gulf War Ground Attack" Sep. 12,1991

Estimates of total coalition casualties cited 379 dead and 776 wounded. A large number of civilians died due to the nonstop aerial bombardment and the massive fires that ensued, although estimated numbers vary.

93.*Washington Post* "Text of Bush's Radio Address" Jan. 6, 1991; Lowry 210, 211.

In 2003, as allied forces began clearing the Basra Highway area, many of the newly arriving U.S. soldiers did not know how the road had gotten its nickname, but hearing their CO's call it that, adopted the name themselves. One nineteen year old Howitzer gunner remarked, "They should just keep calling it the Highway of Death, because that's what this is designed to inflict" (*Stars and Stripes* Feb. 23, 2003).

94. *Las Vegas Review Journal* "Unyielding Anguish" Dec.21, 2011, Keith Rogers .

95. Hamm 1997:149.

96. Jones Collection; Author interview with Gordon Blackcloud, Jan. 16, 2011, Oklahoma (with Holland Vandennieuwenhof); Author interview with Ray Barnes, Nov. 10, 2010, Arkansas (with Holland Vandennieuwenhof).

Herbeck and Michel wrote that McVeigh, a highly respected noncommissioned officer, was happy and hopeful about his promising future. He had heroically contributed to the triumphant war effort and his dream of becoming an elite warrior in the Green Berets was now in his grasp. However, Hamm cited two other soldiers who said McVeigh had mixed feelings about leaving the Gulf and attending the Special Forces course as his four months in the desert had physically and mentally taxed him, and he worried he was not ready for the extreme rigors of the SFCQ.

97. Hamm's theories were based on studies of World War II veterans who, through repetitive military training, had been carefully "conditioned to follow orders and trained in the art of killing." Once

conditioned, they retained their "need to kill." In their blood lust they tended, after leaving the theatre of war, towards increasing acts of violence and aggression within the civilian world. Military training and conditioning, postulated Hamm, may also account for the over-representation of Vietnam and Gulf War era veterans within prison populations (See Hamm 1997: 150- 159).

98. McVeigh told his attorneys he had sought treatment for PTSD, but each time, had decided not to pursue it as, "I [didn't] want to be known as someone with a mental illness." Further, like many others he felt treatment "was just an excuse, and that I should be able to handle it myself" (Jones Collection). I explore McVeigh's attempts to get help for his post war difficulties in later chapters.

99. Lt. Col. Dave Grossman, *On Killing: The Psychological Cost of Learning to Kill in War and Society*. Boston, New York, London, Bay Back Books, 1995: 231-245.

100. Author interview with Ray Barnes, Nov. 10, 2011, Arkansas (with Holland Vandennieuwenhof).

101. Jones Collection; Herbeck and Michel, 75.

102. The media reported that the invading Iraqis had purposefully blown up a number of Kuwaiti oil fields, wells, storage tanks holding jet fuel and kerosene, installations and pipelines and, in an act that constituted a war crime, threatened to blow up more as part of a 'scorched earth' campaign against Kuwait. Iraq claimed the spill resulted from allied bombings. The region's winds carried the fumes in all directions. The ongoing oil field raids and oil spills did not affect the price of oil that, although fluctuating, had begun to drop as the value of defense related stocks climbed. Although many had been lit earlier, the greatest amount of oil well fires set occurred after February 20, 1991. Aerial photos revealed several oil well fires in Kuwait which Leyden speculated, might have been set by Iraqis hoping the smoke would shield their visibility from bombers or disrupt heat sensitive munitions or, alternately, may have been ignited by "errant American strikes that hit the facilitates by accident." U.S. commanders acknowledged setting some oil on fire in Iraqi defensive trenches.

Beyond oil well fires, the spoils of war seeped into the sea as well. In January 1991, Saddam commanded his generals to begin opening pipeline valves leading to the Kuwait Sea, dumping millions of barrels of oil into it and resulting in the largest oil spill in history. The amount of oil spilled into the Kuwait Sea, estimated at 400 million barrels, twice the size of any other oil spill in history, 25 times the size of the Exxon Valdez spill and destroyed marine life and eviscerated sea birds, coral reefs and turtles (Leyden 199: 144; *Washington Post* "Gulf War Leaves Environment Severely Wounded" March 2, 1991, Thomas W. Lippman; Jeff Wheelwright, *The Irritable Heart: The Medical Mystery of the Gulf War* W.W. Norton & Co. New York, New York 2001: 60, 63; John Simpson, *The Wars Against Saddam: Taking the Hard Road to Baghdad* Macmillan, 2004).

103. Jones Collection; Herbeck and Michel 78.

104. Eventually, in 1992, a Senate Committee investigation into the U.S.'s sales of unconventional weapons to Iraq issued a report entitled "U.S. Chemical and Biological Warfare Related Dual Use Exports to Iraq."

105. *Newsday* "Undisclosed Connection / Scientist On Gulf War Syndrome Linked To Supplier Of Iraqi Anthrax" Nov. 27, 1996, Patrick Sloyan; *Newsweek* "Head of Gulf War Illness Panel Had Ties To Chemical Supplier" Nov. 28, 1996, Patrick Sloyan.

106. The U.S. bombed a reportedly operational chemical plant in the city of Samarra (about 45 miles from Baghdad) which Iraq claimed was used to produce insecticides for civilian use, but according to U.S. military officials, was actually manufacturing nerve agents that could be used against the U.S.

107. *Austin-American Statesman* "Gap found in records on exposure to nerve gas; Gulf War documents covering explosions of Iraqi missiles are missing" Oct. 4, 1996, Patrick J. Sloyan.

108. Jones Collection.

109. *Newsweek* "U.S. Nerve Gas Hit Our Own Troops In Iraq" March 27, 2015, Barbara Koeppel.

110. *EHS Today* "Gulf War Syndrome: Things Are Not Always As They Seem" June 23, 2014.

111. *Guardian* "Gulf Syndrome Victims Point To Nerve Gas Pills" Dec. 24, 1993, Simon Tisdale.

112. Jones Collection; Author interview with Ray Barnes, Nov. 10, 2011, Arkansas (with Holland Vandennieuwenhof).

Steve Hodge, among others, told the Jones Team that McVeigh later spoke with him about the shots they received in the Gulf, shot which they were told would protect them from the effects of chemical warfare.

113. The Veterans Administration in Buffalo, New York, began their Gulf War Registry in August 1992, which by September 1992 had screened an estimated one hundred and fifty Gulf War veterans of the 1,500 in the region and by 1994, 466.

114. In July 1995, the legal team would file an 'Application for Subpoena and Supporting Brief' and made it known to the court that "*the records provided are not complete*." At this point, the Jones Team hired a military records expert to suggest several locations where these records, notably those detailing his service in the Gulf, might be located although ultimately, the experts' suggestions did not lead to the Jones Team's obtaining them. For this reason, by February 1996, the defense team successfully requested that the court allow them to replace their then current military records expert with a different one.

115. Jones Collection; Hamm 1997:140.

116. In 1997, the Senate Armed Services Committee held hearings on [the Military Personnel Review Act of 1997, which, for the Jones Team, were of special concern because of "the effect of the proposed legislation in cases where a military department has destroyed or misplaced its records" and because the legislation, if passed, would "abrogate the rights service members have enjoyed since 1870.'" Although they could not obtain the complete set of records, including medical ones, the Jones Team discovered discrepancies in information listed about McVeigh, specifically, his height and, within internal memos, discussed their need to have the *complete* records available to them in order to introduce portions into evidence during the upcoming criminal trial.

Oddly, the list of symptoms commonly associated with GWS came to include hair loss, sore gums, persistent dreams and nightmares, muscle and joint pain, bleeding gums, rapid tooth decay in almost all teeth, unexplained vomiting and diarrhea, strange moles, skin growths, blurred vision, fatigue, anxiety, ulcers and recurring skin scaled and skin tags. The available portion of medical records reflects that during his three years in the Army, McVeigh sought medical attention on *more than seventy occasions* for all of these symptoms.

The twenty-five most commonly reported symptoms of the Gulf War Syndrome are: fatigue, skin problems, rashes, memory loss, blackouts, joint pain, headaches, personality changes, diarrhea, muscle pain (weakness, spasms, tremors), pain (back, shoulder, neck, etc.), vision problems, shortness of breath, sleep disturbances, hair loss, numbness in the extremities, bleeding gums, reproductive problems, chest pain, abdominal pain, fever, nausea/vomiting, dizziness, nasal discharges, and sensory sensitivity.

117. Jones Collection; Author interview with Ray Barnes, Nov. 10, 2011, Arkansas (with Holland Vandennieuwenhof); Author interview with Gordon Blackcloud, Jan. 16, 2011 (with Holland Vandennieuwenhof).

118. Public Law 104-201-Sept. 23, 1996 "National Defense Authorization Act For Fiscal Year 1997" (10 USC 1071, Sec. 742, 743, 744).

119. Wheelwright 166.

120. *Guardian*, Nov. 11, 2008 In July 2014, *EHS Today*, an occupational safety journal, reported, "Contractors were assigned the task of properly disposing of any and all trash on military installations in Iraq, Afghanistan and other locations in the Middle East. Instead of using incinerators,

the contractors disposed of the waste through burn pits and in the process, exposed thousands of veterans to toxins that place them at serious risk of respiratory illnesses, cancers and other occupational diseases" (*EHS Today* "The Toxic Wounds of War" July 2, 2014).

121 Herbeck and Michel 351).

122. Associated Press, May 29, 1998.

123. Vidal 109,110, italics included.

124. With a few slight variations, the version of the Special Forces 'tryout' as told in *American Terrorist* (2001), was first found in *Newsweek* (July 3, 1995), the writings of Stickney (1996) and Hamm (1997) as well as countless news reports and court testimony.

125. Serrano 42; *New York Times* "John Doe No. 1- A Special Report: A Life of Solitude and Obsessions" May 4, 1995, Robert D. McFadden; *Newsweek* "The Subject Speaks Out" July 3, 1995, David Hackworth and Peter Annin; Stickney 118; Hamm 1997:150.

126. Jones Collection; Jones Team attorney Randy Coyne said that, "In one sense, the Oklahoma City bombing can be attributed to a blister" that ultimately left him deeply disenchanted and "profoundly depressed" (Author interview with Randy Coyne, Jan. 18, 2011, Oklahoma.

127. *Newsweek* July 3, 1995.

128. USAF, William Saier "An Assessment of Assessment: Is Selective Manning Right For USAF Special Operations Aircrew?" Research Report. Air War College Air University Maxwell Air Force Base, Alabama. April 1995; *Washington Post*, July 2, 1995; *New York Times*, Dec. 31, 1995.

An April 1995 research report by the Air War College at Maxwell Air Force Base details some of the desirable traits looked for in Special Forces candidates. Included among these were individuals of "above average intelligence," and who tended to be "assertive; self-sufficient; ...not extremely introverted or extroverted...not necessarily people who are emotionally stable" but who were "forthright," "hard to fool, and not dependent on others." The report discussed the use and function of psychological testing among the military's 'Special Operations' units. The administering of these tests began in World War I. The purpose of the tests was to "weed out unacceptable draftees and identify potential offenders." After World War II, the OSS (predecessor to the CIA) recognized the need to "eliminate 'bad' recruits" (spies) and so established a 'school' of psychologists and psychiatrists to develop better methods to do so. A bad recruit was, among other things, "stupid, apathetic, sullen, resentful, arrogant, or insulting." Further, undesirables were "blabs...sloths, irritants, bad actors, and free talkers." Those whom the intelligence communities valued displayed "motivation for assignment; energy and initiative; effective intelligence; emotional stability; social relations; leadership; and security" (3-10). Both tests are designed to identify an individual's attitudes towards family, sex, interpersonal relationships, self-concepts, personality structures, responses to both internal and external stimuli, emotional adjustment and maturity levels, contact with reality, the ways in which conflicts are resolved and identify possible psychological dysfunctions including hypochondria, depression, hysteria, psychosis, paranoia, obsessiveness, mania, and introversion. Included as part of the evaluation were recruits reactions to at least five days of sleep deprivation.

129. Jones Collection; Stickney 117; Herbeck and Michel 407.

Although Stickney includes this statement from his unnamed military source about McVeigh's failure of the SFAS psychological evaluation, he also rejected the claim, based on the same reasoning as Jones.

130. Jones Collection.

Included among the documents the Army provided the FBI was a SFAS Data Questionnaire, Statement of Understanding and Honor System statement all three signed by McVeigh and dated April 3. However, the FBI noted he signed his SFAS physical fitness scorecard and Voluntary Withdrawal Statement on April 7, 1991. Although it is most likely a typo, one FBI document noted that McVeigh signed the Withdrawal Statement on July 4, 1991. If McVeigh left in April 1991, he would have been eligible to try again sometime around September 1991.

131. Jones Collection; Stickney 119.

132. Herbeck and Michel 146.

133. While Jones does not discuss McVeigh's strange claims to Otto and Coyle, he did write that after he was appointed to the case, Otto cryptically warned him, "When you know everything I know, Stephen, and you will soon enough, you will never think of the United States of America in the same way [again]" (Jones 1998:31).

134. David Paul Hammer. *Secrets Worth Dying For: Timothy James McVeigh and the Oklahoma City Bombing*. 1st Books Library, 2004.: 148-150.

135. Author interview with Randy Coyne, Jan. 18, 2011, Oklahoma.

McVeigh mentioned David Paul Hammer in at least 16 letters he wrote to his biographers, in most of them expressing his distrust and dislike of Hammer (American Terrorist Collection).

136. *Nichols Affidavit* filed in U.S. District Court, Utah on Feb. 9, 2007.

Nichols, no longer able to appeal his guilty verdict or sentence, said in his affidavit that the purpose of his 2007 disclosures were intended to help the victims find closure.

137. David Hoffman. *The Oklahoma City Bombing and the Politics of Terror* Feral House Venice, California, 1998: 61,66, 361.

To explain the term 'Sheep Dipped,' Hoffman quotes former CIA-DOD liaison L. Fletcher Prouty's book, *The Secret Team*. Prouty wrote that Sheep Dipping "is an intricate Army-devised process by which a man who is in the service as a full career soldier or officer agrees to go through all the legal and official motions of resigning from the service. Then, rather than actually being released, his records are pulled from the Army personnel files and transferred to a special Army intelligence file. Substitute but nonetheless real appearing records are then processed, and the man 'leaves' the service" (61, 66,361).

138. Herbeck and Michel 92

139. Grossman 31, 36, 190-216.

140. *New York Times*, May 4, 1995.

141. Jones Collection; Hamm 1997:151; Herbeck and Michel, 87; *New York Times*, May 4, 1995 and July 5, 1995; Stickney, 120,125, 127; *London Sunday Times* "All American Monster" Sep. 3, 1995, James Dalrymple.

142. *Boston Globe* "A Kansas Base for Malcontent Army Station Is Seen as a Potential Militia Breeding Ground" April 26, 1995, Charles M. Sennott.

143. Conway & Siegelman 1995: 343, 347, 349,358.

144. Knight 1999: 26, 30, 31; Conway and Siegelman 1995: 27.

145. Martin A. Lee, *The Beast Reawakens: Fascism's Resurgence from Hitler's Spymasters to Today's Neo-Nazi Groups and Right Wing Extremists*. New York, Rutledge, 1997: 346; American Terrorist Collection

McVeigh would later change his mind concerning the KKK at this time in his life as, later, he would make contact with and request an application for another KKK chapter in Arkansas.

146. Herbeck and Michel, 90-92 .

The incident was the second known time in his adult life that Tim McVeigh cried in front of someone, the first being when he thought he was about to die just prior to leaving for the Persian Gulf. Later, several Jones Team members realized his eyes often 'welled up with tears' when he talked about Waco, but maintained his coldness when speaking of his own victims.

147. Jones Collection; Author interview with Gordon Blackcloud, Nov. 16, 2011, Oklahoma (with Holland Vandennieuwenhof).

148. Jones Collection.

The first appearance of medical attention he received since returning from the Gulf occurring on June 20, 1991, when he visited the dentist because two of his teeth were decaying and were causing him pain. Soon after on July 1st he returned on the 12th, 15th, and 29th of that month with attention being given to at least 7 different teeth. On the 15th he reported that there were small pieces of bone sticking out, he was in pain, and his mouth was infected. He complained of "bone chips" and continued pain again on the 29th of that month.

149. Charles 170.

150. Author interview with Gordon Blackcloud, Jan. 16, 2011, Oklahoma (with Holland Vanden-nieuwenhof); Author interview with Ray Barnes, Nov. 10, 2010, Arkansas (with Holland Vanden-nieuwenhof).

Chapter Three: Amerinoid

1 "Fusion Paranoia," a term coined by Michael Kelly in 1995, refers to "the convergence of politi-cal wings in the conspiracy theory milieu." Beyond the conspiratorial musings of the 'reactionary right,' the so called 'conspiracy theories' that circulated among the 'intellectual left' at this time touched upon a variety of issues including the U.S. government's involvement in domestic and foreign assassinations and coups, surveillance and infiltration of the New Left, drug and arms run-ning during an alleged War on Drugs, policies targeting minorities, the cover-up of facts surround-ing the Gulf War and Gulf War Syndrome (Jack Z. Bratich, Jack Z. *Conspiracy Panics: Political Rationality and Popular Culture.* Albany, New York, State University of New York Press, 2008:36 citing *Los Angeles Times* "America the Enemy" June 18, 1995, Nina J. Easton).

2. *Gallup New Service* "Most Americans Believe Oswald Conspired With Others to Kill JFK" April 11, 2011, Darren K. Carlson ; Peter Knight,. "'A Plague of Paranoia': Theories of Conspiracy Theo-ry Since the 1960s" (pg. 23-50) in *Fear Itself: Enemies Real & Imagined in American Culture.* Nancy Lusignan, Ed., West Lafayette, Indiana, Purdue University Press, 1999: 28, .29

Knight listed a number of subjects often appearing within the "canon" of conspiracy theory. They included the deaths of JFK, RFK, MLK, Malcolm X and Marilyn Monroe; various classi-fied government programs including MK- ULTRA, Operation Paperclip, Phoenix, Mongoose, Majestic 12, COINTELPRO; the lives of various assassins including Lee Harvey Oswald, James Earl Ray, Sirhan Sirhan, Arthur Herman Bremer, Mark David Chapman and John Hinckley, Jr.; as well as theories about soldiers Missing in Action (MIA), LSD, CIA, FBI, NSA, DIA, Octopus, Gemstone, Roswell, Area 51, Jonestown, Chappaquiddick, Waco, Oklahoma, Watergate, Iraqgate, Iran-Contra, October Surprise, Savings & Loan, BCCI, Whitewater, Lockerbie, TWA Flight 800, Ebola, AIDS, crack cocaine, military industrial complex, grassy knoll, magic bullet, lone nut."

3. Kathryn Olmstead, *Real Enemies: Conspiracy Theories and American Democracy, World War I to 9/11* Oxford University Press, Oxford, New York , 2009: 173 citing Hubbell 1997.

4. Jack Z. Bratich, *Conspiracy Panics: Political Rationality and Popular Culture*, State University of New York Press, Albany, New York, 2008: 54.

5. Olmstead, 2009: 237.

6. Olmstead, 2009: 3, 6, 239.

7. Bratich, 2008: 6,3, 19.

8. Bratich, 2008:13.

9. *Ottawa Citizen* "Conspiracy Theories Spin Out of Control on the Web" Nov. 16, 1996, Chris Cobb; *Washington Post* "Reality Check: You Can't Believe Everything You Read. But You'd Better

Believe This" December 4, 1996, Joel Achenbach; Bratich, 2008:5, 7, 99.

10. *Dayton Daily News* "The Militia: 'I think (McVeigh) was a Little Off but Not Too Much" April 23, 1995, Wes Hill.

11. Jim Keith, *OKBOMB! Conspiracy and Cover-up* Adventures Unlimited Press, Kempton, Illinois, 1996:196; Alex Constantine, *Virtual Government: CIA Mind Control Operations in America*. Los Angeles, California, Feral House, 1997:255.
   Other works discussing Calspan (in relation to mind control)or Jolly West include Jim Keith's 1998 book, *Mind Control, World Control: An Encyclopedia of Mind Control* and David Hoffman's 1998 book, *The Oklahoma City Bombing and the Politics of Terror*, both of which repeat and somewhat add to Constantine's version.

12. Dick Culver, "Introduction to The Saga of 'Lee Harvey' McVeigh" on *Culvers Shooting Page* (website) March 23, 1997, updated 2004. http://www.jouster.com/index.html.
   Culver described the several shifting explanations Stephen Jones gave the media about McVeigh's leaked confession "fishy" and asked what price Jones demanded to sell out McVeigh.

13. Sherman H. Skolnick,., "The Secrets of Timothy McVeigh" (website) June 15, 2001 Skolnick-report.com) http://www.skolnicksreport.com/tmsecrets.html.

14. Devvy Kidd, "McVeigh's Second Trial" (website) August 1, 2005 on NewsWithViews.com http://www.newswithviews.com/Devvy/kidd119.htm.
   Others, like Salt Lake City attorney Jesse Trentadue, did achieve success with FOIA, prying loose critical information about the bombing plot (and the surveillance of it) from the vaults of monolithic agencies engaging in institutional secrecy.

15. *Weekly World News* "Exclusive: Timothy McVeigh is Alive" Sep. 18, 2001, Cliff Lindecker.

16. Letts, Tracy *BUG* (play) Dramatists Play Service. Northern University Press, New York, New York, 2006, first performed September 1996; *BUG* (film), William Friedkin, dir, L.I.F.T. Production, Bug LLC, DMK Medienfonds, Lionsgate 2006.

17. Stickney 129; Hamm 1997:157; Michel and Herbeck 95.

18. *New York Times* "John Doe No. 1- A Special Report: A Life of Solitude and Obsessions" May 4, 1995, Robert D. McFadden.

19. *New York Times*, May 4, 1995.

20. Stickney 136.

21. Stickney 137.

22. Hamm 1997:157- 159.

23. Herbeck and Michel102,103.

24. Hammer 2004 140-151.

25. Author interview with Andrea Augustine, Buffalo, New York, Oct. 22, 2010.

26. Author interview with Carl Lebron, April 10, 2010, Buffalo, New York.

27. Herbeck and Michel 111,112.

28. Author interview with Carl Lebron, April 10, 2010, Buffalo, New York.

29. Hammer 2004:140-151.

30. William W. Medel., Murl D. Munger., "Strategic Planning and the Drug Threat" A Joint Study Initiative by The National Interagency Counterdrug Institute The Strategic Studies Institute U.S. Army War College and The Foreign Military Studies Office. Fort Leavenworth, Kansas, August 1997:61.

31. Bradley Balko, *Rise of the Warrior Cop: The Militarization of America's Police Forces*, Public Affairs, New York, New York, 2014:158, 180.

The NG could already search vehicles, buildings, and private homes without a warrant, but the 1989 DAA removed any existing restrictions placed on the NG's ability to conduct civilian law enforcement activities. By 1997, the National Guards domestic interdiction program was the largest in the DOD.

32. Wright 104.

33. Chief Steven T. Kernes ""Law Enforcement Resource Guide for Small Town and Rural Agencies" National Center For State and Local Law Enforcement Training, Student text 9016, 2001; 15.

Operation Alliance Command Group included representatives from the Bureau of Alcohol, Tobacco and Firearms; Drug Enforcement Administration; Federal Bureau of Investigation; Immigration and Naturalization Service/Border Patrol; Internal Revenue Service; Joint Task Force Six (DoD); U.S. Coast Guard; U.S. Customs Service; Department of Interior; U.S. Forestry Service; U.S. Marshals Service; U.S. Secret Service; and scores of state agencies.

34. Kernes 2001: 15, 16.

The 1989 DAA allotted $300 million to the DOD, $40 million of which to the NG. The 1991 DAA allotted $1.08 billion to the DOD, $160 million of which to the NG. According to Balko, by 1992, the NG assisted in "20,000 arrests, searched 120,000 automobiles, entered 1,200 private buildings without a search warrant" and entered private property without a warrant 6,500 times (Balko: 180). By 1997, the National Guard was conducting 1300 missions a day in connection with JTF-6.

35. FBI Teletype. Feb. 4, 1992. To: Major General Peter T. Berry, Commanding General, Criminal Investigative Division, United States Army, Falls Church, Virginia. From: Larry Potts, Assistant Director, Criminal Investigation Division. Sub: Information Regarding Possible Planned Attack on National Guard Convoy; FBI Teletype #0450 MRI 01669 "To: Director, Priority" Oct. 2, 1992. The February 1992 teletype included the disclaimer though that "The above information is unsubstantiated and has not been corroborated." Assorted items mentioned in the teletype that had been discovered during one PATCON investigation in Birmingham, Alabama during July and September 1991, included ammonium nitrate, fuel oil, dynamite, blasting caps, smokeless powder with homemade light bulb initiators and nails.

36. Herbeck and Michel, 108; Stickney, 136.

37. Jones Collection; *Buffalo News* "McVeigh received medical exam here following Gulf War; FBI checking suspects records at Veterans Hospital for leads." April 28, 1995, Dan Herbeck, Mike Vogel.

Cpt. Crowe, issued and signed his NYNG ID on February 4, 1992 which had an expiration date of April 11, 1995. His actual obligation to the Guard was to end on May 26, 1996. One member of the National Guard interviewed by the FBI said McVeigh told him that, during the war, after he shot at the Iraqis a large number of them surrendered and further described "tank battles" he had seen during which Iraqi tanks blew up allied ones. He also said he met McVeigh after the Gulf War during a two-day weekend drill "in a U.S. Army Reserve Unit in Tonawanda, New York." The FBI neglected to ask or note when this was. During their conversations, the man continued, McVeigh "seemed to favor the Americans' role in the Gulf War" and did not express distaste for the government. (Jones Collection).

38. According to Herbeck and Michel, McVeigh found the idea of "guarding prisoners, protecting federal judges, [and] hunting for dangerous fugitives" intriguing (Herbeck and Michel 99,100). About a year after his arrest, two (named) U.S. Marshalls made a surprise visit to McVeigh for the purposes of interviewing him, quite to the dismay of his attorneys who were neither notified nor present. In the course of the interview, he reminded the Marshalls that he had scored 101.8 on their employment test in 1992, adding that this should come as no surprise "revelation" to them because the FBI had confiscated all the related paperwork from his father's house. (Jones Collection).

39. Author interview with Carl Lebron, April 10, 2010, Buffalo, New York.

The Spotlight (1975-2001) was a weekly newspaper published by the populist, nationalist, right wing, anti-communist Liberty Lobby. The paper supported David Duke's political campaigns, alternative medicine and regularly covered 'anti-government' and 'conspiracy theory' articles. In 1992, it had 90,000 subscribers. The Anti-Defamation league had called the paper anti-Semitic. E. Howard Hunt sued the paper for defamation after they published an article claiming he was involved in the JFK assassination and famed attorney Mark Lane, defended them. In 2001, the name of the paper was changed to the *American Free Press*. The White Patriot Party, labeled as a terrorist organization by The National Consortium for the Study of Terrorism and Responses to Terrorism, is a white supremacist organization with ties to the Ku Klux Klan and Christian Identity groups. The organizations' newspaper *The White Patriot* claims to provide 'News For White People.'

40. Author interviews with Johnny Bangerter from December 2010 to February 2015 (sometimes with Holland Vandennieuwenhof).

41. Jess Walter. *Ruby Ridge: The Truth an Tragedy of the Randy Weaver Family*. HarperCollins, 2002: 222, 223.

42. According to newly released PATCON documents, after Ruby Ridge, PATCON's budget expanded by $186,746.19. PATCON operatives were instructed to rent safe houses for surveillance or other operational needs. Equipment used included CCTV, Pen register phone taps, and "Nagra body recorders." Locations of PATCON operations included, but were not limited to, Texas, Alabama, Colorado, California, Idaho, Tennessee, Utah, Ohio, Kentucky, Maryland, etc.

Johnny Bangerter would come to be involved in the OKC bombing saga in a remarkable way. His entire life story is amazing: unless I had verified it through a number of news reports, conversations with other individuals and records within the Jones Collection, I would have found it unbelievable.. In the years following the Ruby Ridge incident, a remarkably strange series of events came to entwine Bangerter with PATCON, McVeigh and the OKC bombing plot investigations (explored later in this book and in my follow-up book, REDACTED).

43. Wright 5, 15.

44. Author interview with Carl Lebron, Oct. 22, 2010, Buffalo, New York.

45. getprivateinvestigatorjobs.com "Resume of March Griswold" undated. www.getprivateinvestigatorjobs.com/resumes/Arnold-MD/Marc-Griswold-7821351.html.

46. Stickney 144, 145, 183.

47. Hammer 2004: 151,152.

48. Jones Collection; Author interview with Andrea Augustine, Buffalo, New York, Oct. 22, 2010; Author interview with Carl Lebron, April 10, 2010, Buffalo, New York.

49. Hammer 2004:140-151.

50. *Newsweek*, "My Life as a White Supremacist: An FBI mole speaks for the first time about life in the seedy world of right-wing terror." November 21, 2011, R.M. Schneiderman; FBI document "PATCON, Knoxville, 100A-KY-61785-35" May 26, 1994.

According to newly released PATCON documents, after Ruby Ridge, PATCON's budget expanded by $186,746.19. PATCON operatives were instructed to rent safe houses for surveillance or other operational needs. Equipment used included CCTV, Pen register phone taps, and "Nagra body recorders." Locations of PATCON operations included, but were not limited to, Texas, Alabama, Colorado, California, Idaho, Tennessee, Utah, Ohio, Kentucky, Maryland, etc.

51. *New York Times* "The Gulf War Veteran: Victorious in War, Not Yet at Peace" May 28, 1995, Eric Schmitt.

52. *The Psychology of Terrorism: Clinical Aspects and Responses*. V. 2, Chris E. Stout, Ed., Westport,

Connecticut, London, Praeger, (2002).

53. *Buffalo News* "McVeigh received medical exam here following Gulf War; FBI checking suspects records at Veterans Hospital for leads." April 28,1995, Dan Herbeck, Mike Vogel.

54. Hamm 1997: 156,157,150.

55. Hamm 1997: 151.
    Hamm (1997) pointed out that the hippocampus, an area of the brain that helps to control, store, and retrieve memory had effectively postponed emotional reactions to the intensities of combat of many Vietnam veterans.

56. *Washington Post* "Veterans groups call for study of possible Desert Storm illnesses" April 29, 1992.

57. Herbeck and Michel 2001:110.
    Herbeck and Michel based this passage on what McVeigh told them. He said, "In late 1992…I visited the VA hospital for treatment of a wart on my toe that developed in the Gulf. I had it removed by laser at the Lockport clinic in about December 1991 ... It came back though so I sought chemical treatment…applied repeatedly over six to eight weeks at the VA... I made weekly trips there, all prior to my Gulf War Syndrome exam… [At] the vets hospital they wanted to screen me for Gulf War Syndrome. They screened me, and I checked out healthy" (American Terrorist Collection).

58. *Buffalo News* April 28, 1995.
    McVeigh acknowledged to the Jones Team that he knew both Dr. Talluto and Dr. Finkelstein, two Buffalo area VA doctors quoted in news articles.

59. Stickney 117,135; *USA Today* "Unraveling McVeigh: Past offers a few clues into psyche" May 2, 1995, Steve Komarow; Kirk Spitzer.

60. Jones Collection; Author interview with Andrea Augustine, Buffalo, New York, Oct. 22, 2010; Author interview with Carl Lebron, April 10, 2010, Buffalo, New York; Author interview with Carl Lebron, Oct. 22, 2010, Buffalo, New York.

61. Jones Collection; *Dayton Daily News* "The Militia: 'I Think (McVeigh) Was A Little Off But Not Too Much'" April 23, 1995, Wes Hills, Pg. 1 A.

62. Jones Collection.
    Oddly, according to FBI reports, a US Naval Dentist was staying in a motel room next door to McVeigh's.

63. Hammer 2004:80.

64. Susie Kilshaw. *Impotent Warriors: Gulf War Syndrome, Vulnerability and Masculinity*. New York, Oxford, Bergham Books, 2009: 2-5.

65. Kilshaw 2.

66. *Boston Globe* "Operation Desert Whine" (editorial), Sep. 23, 1992, Alex Beam.

67. *Reason* "Gulf Lore Syndrome" March 1997, Michael Fumento.

68. Elaine Showalter. *Hystories: Hysterical Epidemics and Modern Culture*. Columbia University Press, New York, 1997:8.

69. Peter Knight, "'A Plague of Paranoia': Theories of Conspiracy Theory Since the 1960s" (pg. 23-50) in *Fear Itself: Enemies Real & Imagined in American Culture*. Nancy Lusignan, Ed., West Lafayette, Indiana, Purdue University Press, 1999: 23, 24.

70. Salino said he had not seen Tim since late 1992. Strange as it sounded, much of what was written in the FBI's report based on their conversation with Salino corresponds to other details either given by people who knew McVeigh or statements he himself made. Further, Salino's name is mentioned in his role as local AIDS educator in *Buffalo News* articles spanning from 1992 to 1997.

71. In 1992, 50% of those treated for AIDS at Erie County Medical Center were Caucasian, and 12% African American. By August of that year, of the 1 million Americans diagnosed with HIV in 1992, over 23,000 had developed AIDS.

72. *National Geographic News Services* "U.S. Military Fights Illness Overseas Haiti, Persian Gulf Are Hot Spots" Nov. 6, 1994, Suzanne Possehl .

73. *San Antonio Express News* "'Stealth' Germ Theory Invading Gulf War Illness Debate" June 7, 1998, Don Finley; Kilshaw 97.

Mycoplasmas had first been linked to infections in humans in the 1930s and 1940s and were a major cause of pneumonia and, as of 1996, had been identified in those suffering from arthritis, leukemia, urinary tract infections and AIDS.

74. *Insight on the News* "Gulf War Mystery and HIV" Nov. 3, 1997, (investigative report) Paul M. Rodriguez.

75. *Guardian* "Acts of God and Microbes and Men" Feb. 1, 1996, Natasha Walter; Jodi Dean, *Aliens in America: Conspiracy Cultures from Outerspace to Cyberspace.* Ithaca, New York, Cornell University Press, 1998:142.

76. *New Statesman* "Blame the government: Observations on HIV." By Margaret Cook" Feb. 7, 2005, Margaret Cook.

77. Advisory Committee on Human Radiation Experiments, *Final Report of the Advisory Committee on Human Radiation Experiments,* Oxford University Press, New York, 1996; Bridget Brown, *They Know Us Better Than We Know Ourselves: The History and Politics of Alien Abduction,* New York University Press, New York, 2007: 118-120.

78. Bratich 101, 120.

79. Kilshaw 5, 9, 228.

80. *San Antonio Express News,* June 7, 1998.

81. Kilshaw 96.

82. *Texas Monthly,* "Under My Skin" October 2006, Jim Atkinson.

83. In January 1994, the Congressional General Accounting Office began a study to determine if the government suppressed information regarding allegations of having removed alien corpses from a crashed flying saucer in Roswell, New Mexico in 1947. Although, the Air Force later claimed the only thing that had crashed in the desert was a weather balloon, the records of the incident were missing, which contributed to skeptics persistent inquiries and complaints about the rumored cover-up and requests for an investigation of the matter until finally, as one official said, "willing to take a stab at it" (*Buffalo News* "GAO To Probe Claims U.S. Suppressed Data On '47 Crash Of Purported UFO" Jan. 23, 1994). In September of that same year, the investigation concluded that the wreckage from the crash had still come from a weather balloon.

84. *Buffalo News* "Encounter Clues" Sep.20, 1992; *Calgary Herald* "The Skies Are Full of UFO's" Oct. 9, 1992.

Buffalo was the national headquarters for The Committee for the Scientific Investigation of Claims of the Paranormal, a national debunking organization run by former senior editor of Aviation Week and Space Technology and University of Buffalo professor Phillip Klass.

85. *Buffalo News* "Incident At Cherry Creek Still Unexplained 35 Years Later" Aug. 12, 2000, Robert A. Galganski .

86. Thecid.com "UFO Sightings 1994" http://thecid.com/ufo/uf14/uf0/140169.htm ; *Buffalo News* "A Saucer Full Of Mystery In The Hills Of Ellicottville" April 24, 1994, Donn Esmonde; *Buffalo News* "Search Resumes In Field After Report UFO Landed" April 15, 1994.

87. *Buffalo News* April 24, 1994; *Buffalo News* "Where to Find Out More About UFOs" Aug. 1, 1993;

Buffalo News "Presenting The Case For Close Encounters" March 20, 1995, Nicole Peradotto.

88. Dean 10, 11.

89. Author interview with Carl Lebron, Buffalo, New York, April 10, 2010.

90. Strughold, a Rockefeller Foundation Fellow in the 1920s, conducted aviation medicine and physiology research in the U.S. during this time. Among the positions Strughold later held in the U.S. from 1947 until 1986, was chief scientist at the US Army Air Force Aeromedical Center and the National Aeronautics and Space Administration (NASA)'s Aerospace Medical Division as well as professor of Space Medicine at the US Air Force School of Aviation Medicine. He received a number of esteemed accolades and honors, posthumously revoked after revelations that in the 1950s he placed humans in sealed 'space cabin' chambers for long periods to determine the effects. The revoked honors included an esteemed aerospace library at Brook AFB named in his honor in 1977, renamed in 1995, his placement in the International Space Hall of Fame, removed in 2006 and a Society of Air and Space Medicine award in his name in 2004.

91. Nick Cook. *The Hunt For Zero Point: Inside the Classified World of Antigravity Technology* Broadway Books, New York, 2001: 20.

Many conspiracy writers claim the entire SS intelligence network was simply grafted onto, or formed the foundation of, the U.S. Alex Constantine notes the roles of the Rockefeller and Carnegie Foundations, IG Farben and Nazi sympathizer Allen Dulles in the great American Nazi heist, opining, "Nuremburg was an inside job." Jim Keith points out the pre-existing popularity of eugenics among American elites that predated and coincided with the Nazi atrocities of World War II that continued afterward, with the help of SS expertise. The enigmatic conspiracy theorist 'Commander X' explains how, as various Nazis stood trial for experiments on humans in Nuremburg, the U.S. was conducting similar experiments on the Nazi 'show' criminals. (See also: Constantine, Alex *Virtual Government: CIA Mind Control Operations in America* Feral House, Los Angeles, California, 1997; Keith, Jim. Mind *Control and UFOs: Casebook on Alternative 3* Adventures Unlimited Press, Kempton, Illinois, 1999; Commander X., Swartz, Tim, R., *Mind Stalkers: Mind Control of the Masses* Global Communications, New Brunswick, NJ, 2012).

92. *Buffalo News* "50 Years Ago, Sputnik Changed Everything; Local Firms Played a Big Role In Ability of U.S. to Catch Up" Oct. 4, 2007, Stephen T. Watson; American Institute of Aeronautics and Astronautics "The History of Aerospace Research at Cornell Aeronautical Laboratory and Calspan 1946 to 1996" AIAA 2004-5884, Vol. 1 in " The Furnas Years – 1946 to 1954." Space 2004 Conference 28-30 September 2004 San Diego, California.

Among the projects Calspan contributed to was the testing at Bikini Atoll. Calspan's creations included the futuristic "X-Plane" series including the Bell X-1, a supersonic plane that broke the sound barrier in 1947. Other CAL aerospace innovations include the jet aircraft (based on Paperclip prototypes), the 'James Bond rocket belt' (1948), the flight simulator (1966), design and testing of NASA's first space shuttle (1967), and development of the 'Star Wars' space defense program (1986) and the first commercial helicopter. On October 4, 2007, *Buffalo News* observed that the entire world enjoyed the legacy of Cold War-era Calspan research, the offspring of which included cell phones, Google Earth, Global Positioning Systems and other luxuries related to military and commercial telecommunications satellites and satellite imagery. In 2010, the AIAA designated the CAL facility as a Historic Aerospace Site.

93. In 1991, the commercial space sector had grown 29% while, that same year, Calspan generated over $214 million in sales, their primary customer being the U.S. government including a 1991 contract with NASA worth $150 million.

94. McVeigh may well have benefited from the wisdom of physicist and nationally known UFO buff, Stanton Friedman, who, at MUFONs 2011 national symposium (the pre-eminent UFOologist convention), informed audiences that "there are loads of civilizations out there all over the place ... [the aliens] would instantly recognize that we don't qualify for membership in a galactic

federation (*Huffington Post* "Roswell UFO Controversy: Former Air Force Officer Says Gen. Ramey Lied to Cover Up Space Crash" July 22, 2011).

95. Cook 72; *Buffalo News* "An Objective Look at UFOs" Oct. 25, 1998, pg. 5H, Robert A. Galganski.

96. *St. Louis Post-Dispatch* "Unmanned Aerial Vehicles Make Sense When The Cost Is Blood And Money" Oct. 22, 2000.

97. *Atlanta Journal Constitution* "Backgrounder: Drones: Unmanned craft past test with flying colors; Pentagon surprised by success" Nov. 30, 2001.

98. *St. Louis Post- Dispatch* "Afghan War Revises Call To Change How We Build Planes, Fight Foes; Boeing Could Be Among Firms That Benefit Most" Dec. 2, 2001.

99. *Buffalo News* "Calspan Goal: Let Unmanned Aircraft Refuel In Midair; Spy planes could keep flying without landing for fuel" Nov. 4, 2007, Matt Glynn; *The Leader* (Lexington Park) "Tanking up the Drones" Jan. 24, 2012.

100. *Guardian* "Technology: Newly asked questions: Is the US launching a blimp to spy on its population?" Jan. 25, 2007; The Times Of India "Modern airships brace for space odyssey" Aug. 2014.

101. *The Leader* Jan. 24, 2012; *Ars Technica* "Top Gun, robot-style: Navy moves ahead on carrier-based drone program" April 23, 2014, Sean Gallagher.

102. *Daily Mail* "We Bought Into The Lie That Obama Would Be Different- But He's Just The Same as Bush" June 26, 2013, pg. 26; *Business Recorder* "PTI Submits Resolution in National Assembly Against Drone Attacks" June 11, 2013.
    In 2013, the New York Times reported 3,000 drone-related deaths in Yemen, Pakistan and Somalia since 2009. The Bureau of Investigative Journalism reported that collateral includes 349 deaths (49 civilians and 2 children) killed in 56 confirmed covert drone strikes in Yemen since 2002 but add that 99 unconfirmed attacks resulted in 455 additional deaths (50 civilian and 11 children). 3,567 people including 890 civilians and 197 children as well as 1,485 wounded were the collateral exacted from U.S. covert death dealing drone strikes since 2004. They further report that not so covert drone actions killed 881 Pakistani civilians, including at least 176 children since 2004. But that BIJ report was issued in January 2013 (*Bureau of Investigative Journalism* "Obama 2013 Pakistan drone strikes" Jan. 3, 2013. *Business Recorder*, June 11, 2013).

103. *Plus Media Solutions* "Washington: Many Drone Deaths, Little Information" April 28, 2015.

104. *Newsweek* "Leaked Documents Reveal New Details About the U.S.'s Lethal Drone Programs" Oct. 15, 2015, Lauren Walker; Lucy Steigerwald "Drones, Torture, and the Impatient State" Antiwar.com, Oct. 21, 2015.

105. *Kashmir Images* (India) "Drone Music" May 4, 2015.

106. The Verge.com "Romancing The Drone: How America's Flying Robots Are Invading Pop Culture" Feb. 18, 2013, Joshua Kopstien.

107. *Guardian* "Anti-Drone 'Death Ray' Can Blast Vehicles Out Of The Sky From A mile Away" Oct. 7, 2015; *Buffalo News* "Drones above airports pose threat in Buffalo, nationally; Seagull size intruders tied to 2 incidents here" Dec. 8, 2014.

108. Stickney 144, 145.

109. *Buffalo News* "UFO Fans Trek to Desert For Close Encounters; Hunt for Little Green Men is Big Business in Desolate Area of Nevada" April 25, 1993, Carol Masciola.

110. Jones Collection: Jones Team Defense News Database citing *Daily Oklahoman* "Poll Spots Belief in UFO's" July 3, 1996.

111. *Popular Mechanics* "New Area 51: Mohave's Desert Outpost Holds Space Flight's Future" Sep.

20, 2009, Joe Pappalardo.

112. Herbeck and Michel 155, 156.

113. Nicholas continued, telling agents about one of McVeigh's visits to Michigan in August 1993 during which McVeigh became terribly upset about what had happened at Waco, Texas the previous April and said he had visited the Branch Davidian property during the siege. During this visit, McVeigh gave Nicholas a copy of Linda Thompson's video about the government's involvement in a conspiracy that led to the Waco fires and their cover-up after the fact. Unknown to Nicholas, days after the Oklahoma bombing, Thompson, the film's writer and producer, told the FBI that a Dr. Jolly West had implanted a tracking chip in McVeigh.

114. Herbeck and Michel 184, 185; Charles 204.

115. Jones Collection; Charles 217; Hamm 2002: 193.

116. Colbern's activities and links to McVeigh are partially documented in Roger Charles 2012 book. In personal emails and conversations, Charles has told me that, although it is not in the book, the Marshall's learned of the McVeigh/ Colbern mailbox connection on April 14, 1995. His book wrongly states that the mailbox 'tip' was a bad lead but Charles says this is not correct and, as documented in the endnotes of the book, the mailbox connection was confirmed by a Secret Service memo dated May 5, 1995 as well a U.S. Marshall's report dated May 6, 1995.

117. One of his meth making roommates said that Colbern had been with him, in their trailer, on the morning of the bombing and had been there throughout the week before as well.

118. Jones Collection; Hamm 2001: 204; Charles 204, 217,222, 290.

119. *Guardian* "Pass Notes No. 1029- UFOs" June 3, 1997; *Guardian* "CIA Comes Clean Over UFOs That Were Spy Planes" Aug. 4, 1997, Ed Vulliamy; *Guardian* "UFORIA: American has long had its believers in visitors from space. Once dismissed as a few loonies, they are no longer alone...Ed Vulliamy on the growing tide of conviction that is sweeping the country" August 5, 1997, Ed Vulliamy.

120. Among the most commonly noted elements are the extraterrestrials: ability to exert paralyzing control over their victims through methods such as hypnosis; telepathic communication; performance of harrowing and intrusive medical examinations upon their human 'subjects' that often take place in sterile environments, on cold steel-like tables and using a host of strange tools including "eyelike scanning devices" and probes with which they extract skin, blood and other bodily fluids samples. Encounters with the off-planet or off-dimensional visitors sometimes concluded with the implanting "a tiny device into the brain" into the subject or worse, their impregnation of female victims through nonsexual means with 'hybrid' alien/ human babies only to traumatically remove them later from the host body in which they were incubated. The experiences are most often followed by full or partial amnesia ('missing time') which, once 'recovered,' help explain debilitating psychological and physical symptoms suffered by the abductee including flashbacks, anxiety, burning eyes, sunburned skin, puncture wounds and gastrointestinal upset.

121. Thomas E. Bullard, "UFO Abduction Reports: The Supernatural Kidnap Narrative Returns in Technological Guise" *The Journal of American Folklore* 102 no. 404 (1989): 147-170; Kimberly Ball "UFO- Abduction Narratives and the Technology of Tradition" *Cultural Analysis* 9 (2010): 99-128.
     For Ball, the existence of UFO and abductee stories indicate not only the apprehensions about surveillance, manipulation and control felt by the abductees but among the larger, non-abductee population who "sense that we are in a profound transition" but lack the language to articulate fears that "advancements in technology will overwhelm humanity, changing it into something unrecognizable as human, into something alien." The emergence of these stories and details added to them overtime coincide with real world technological developments, their use by governing elites and civilian accessibility to them. The same technologies that allow for the availability of personal computers, phones and medical devices such as pacemakers, neurological simulators and cochle-

ar implants and the building of massive digital databases, while aiding humanity, have abusive potential as well. Such anxiety-provoking potential is mirrored in stories about the emotionless alien abductors' ability to "locate, monitor, and/or control abductees" through strange devices and telepathy. "After all," wrote Ball, "what aliens seek during abduction is, largely, information."

122. Christopher, R. Roth, "Ufology as Anthropology: Race, Extraterrestrials, and the Occult" (pg. 38-93) in *E.T. Culture: Anthropology in Outerspaces* Debbora Battaglia Ed., Duke University Press, Durham, North Carolina, London, 2006.

123. Definition of Polygenism taken from Merriam Webster Dictionary (website), 'Polygenism'; Roth 44, 46.

Theosophy purports the first root race of Lemurians to include black Africans and Dravidians; the fourth "Atlantians," Mongols and Mesoamericans; the fifth race of Aryans include Semites, North Indian Aryans, Westerly Aryans inhabited the Gobi Desert, Tibet, South Asia and Europe including Iranians and Europeans including the Celts and Teutonic Anglo Saxons.

124. Roth 61.

Roth points out that for Latino-American immigrants, Native Americans and other minority populations, white Americans are the aliens, possibly a contributing factor in the more recent growth of abductees identifying themselves as alien human hybrids.

125. Nicholas Goodrick-Clarke, *Black Sun: Aryan Cults, Esoteric Nazism And The Politics Of Identity*, New York University Press, New York and London, 2002:160.

126. Roth 90..

127. Roth 57

128. Goodrick-Clarke 240.

129. Dean 26-42.

130. Mark Pilkington, *Mirage Men: An Adventure into Paranoia, Espionage, Psychological Warfare, and UFO's*, Skyhorse Publishing, 2010: 29; Pilkington 75 citing Frances Stonor Saunders, *Who Paid the Piper? CIA and the Cultural Cold War*, Granta, 1999..

131. Dean 39.

132. Pilkington 78 citing CIA memo ER-3-2809,10 February 1952.

133. Memorandum for the Assistant Director for Scientific Intelligence from F C Durant, 'Report of Meetings of the Office of Scientific Intelligence Scientific Advisory Panel on Unidentified Flying Objects, January 14–18, 1953, Feb. 16, 1953; CIA memorandum to Deputy Director / Intelligence from James Q Reber, 13th October 1952.

134. Memorandum for the Assistant Director for Scientific Intelligence from F C Durant, Feb. 16, 1953.

135. Pilkington 13.

136. After the 1966 hearings ended, the Air Force (under Blue Book) contracted the University of Colorado to conduct yet another UFO study. The President of the university outlined the operating philosophy of his UFO research committee informing its members: "Our study would be conducted almost exclusively by nonbelievers ... the trick would be, I think, to describe the project so that, to the public, it would appear a totally objective study but, to the scientific community, would [still appear objective]." The investigation, he continued, was to focus, "not on the physical phenomena, rather on the people who are observing [and on] the psychology and sociology of persons and groups who report seeing UFOs" (Dean 38 citing Memo. To E. James Archer and Thurston E. Manning, From: Robert J. Low, SUB: Some Thoughts on the UFO Project, Aug. 9, 1966; Dr. Edward U. Condon, Scientific Director, *Scientific Study of Unidentified Flying Objects*, University of Colorado, Contract No. 44620-67-C-0035, with United States Air Force, 1968).

137. Pilkington 99.

138. Pilkington 11.

139. Pilkington 12.

140. Pilkington 12.

141. For instance, Zechel de Rochefort, Vice President of NICAP in 1956, was a member of the CIA Psychological Warfare staff and, in 1979, retired CIA agent Allen P. Hall replaced him. Other CIA employees retained positions as NICAP Presidential Assistant and members of their various subcommittees. Other well known disinformers who were part of these counterintelligence operations included George Adamski, J. Allen Hynek, and John Lear, some of the most influential people in the UFO/ contactee subcultures.

142. Pilkington 24.

143. *Reason* "Death Wish: How rebels punch their own ticket" Dec. 7, 2001, Brian Doherty.

144. *Mail & Guardian*, "Govt Aids nut linked to Ku Klux Klan" Sep. 8, 2000.

145. *Mail & Guardian*, Sep. 8, 2000; *The Observer* "Cults 2" May 21, 1995; Donna Kossy, *Kooks A Guide to the Outer Limits Of Human Belief*, Feral House, May 1994; William Cooper, *Behold A Pale Horse*, Light Technology Publishing, Sedona, Arizona, 1991.

146. Jesse Walker, *The United States Of Paranoia: A Conspiracy Theory*, Harpercollins, 2013.

147. *Mail & Guardian*, Sep. 8, 2000.
    At some point, Cooper began calling himself the 'Director of Intelligence Service of the Second Continental Army.'

148. Cooper attended KKK events and had his nearly imaginary 'militia' train with them. Cooper said that while he wasn't member of the Klan, the organization itself was "misunderstood," and patriots should support them because they were vigilant monitors of threats posed by the U.S. government to American sovereignty and would probably be one of the only groups, along with his, to survive the coming alien/ human or just human/ human wars (*Mail & Guardian* "Govt Aids nut linked to Ku Klux Klan" Sep. 8, 2000).

149. *Mail & Guardian*, Sep. 8, 2000.

150. *Guardian* "New Trial May Solve Riddle of Oklahoma bombing" Nov. 3, 1997; *The Observer* "Cults 2" May 21, 1995; *New York* "All Conspiracy Theories Are Connected: 'It is possible that one or more conclusions may be wrong'" Nov. 18, 2013, Boris Kachka.

151. *Guardian* , Nov. 3, 1997; *The Observer*, May 21, 1995; *New York*, Nov. 18, 2013.

152. Keith 1999: 169,173, 186.

153. *Reason* "Death Wish: How rebels punch their own ticket" Dec. 7, 2001, Brian Doherty.

154. As a side note, the Lizard people also appear in the racist and violent religion of Christian Identity, as well as the teachings of UFOlogy superstar David Icke, best known for his 'reptoid hypothesis.' If you look at what Icke is saying, it also sounds (with a couple marked differences) a lot like what William Cooper said who, as mentioned, was saying what the government originally told Bennewitz types. In Icke's story, a long, long time ago, aliens from outer space called 'Anunnaki' traveled to Earth with the intent of creating a race of slaves. Once there, the aliens used their advanced biotechnological know-how, to splice their own genetic material with that of Earth's original occupants thereby creating humans. The Anunnaki didn't really have time to oversee the human slaves though, so they interbred with another extraterrestrial race called the 'Nordics' that happened to have blond hair and blue eyes. This race mixing resulted in a 'super-hybrid' race of human slave masters. The reptilian side of the family makes them emotionless, cruel, controlling, racist, fascist, and ritualistic while the Anunnaki side allows them to shape-shift (into very tall

lizards) and read minds. In Icke's world, a large percentage, perhaps the majority, of ruling elites (including both George Bush's) have Anunnaki / Aryan bloodlines. Throughout time, the lizard slave masters have exerted control over pretty much everything through secret societies such as the Illuminati as well as international banking systems (an assertion nobody with past due student loans would disagree with). Feeding off human fear and negativity, the covert snake people are responsible for the worst atrocities committed by humankind. The endgame, for the lizard people, is the establishment of the New World Order, a dystopian situation requiring....you guessed it... the implanting of microchips in all humans. In Icke's estimation, the end of this particular cosmic struggle can only come about by the evolution of human consciousness and the acceptance that underneath it all, reptilians, humans and hybrids alike are all the same, all God's creatures, each one a component of a larger cosmic consciousness.

Icke's teachings have been embraced by modern day Nazi's and new age hippies alike, although Icke himself has often been accused of pandering veiled anti-Semitism. His critics argue that he works too closely with racist militants (who invite him to speak at events or who republish his writings) and point out (among other things) that, if you replace the words 'Reptilian' or 'International Banker' with 'Jews' Icke's real feelings become clear. Others disagree, and offer more optimistic readings of Icke arguing that despite all the lizardly doom and gloom, his writings tend to advance a universal message of love and acceptance and anticipate a utopian era in which everybody can just get along.

155. *Huffington Post* "Roswell UFO Controversy: Former Air Force Officer Says Gen. Ramey Lied to Cover Up Space Crash" July 22, 2011; Steve Colbern, Steve. "Analysis Report on Metal Samples from the 1947 UFO Crash on the Plains of San Augustine, New Mexico" Oct.14, 2010.

156. *Coast to Coast AM with George Noory* (radio show) "Alien Implants" Nov. 05, 2010. http://www.coasttocoastam.com/show/2010/11/05.

157. *Voice of Russia* "Alien implants 'diamond tools would not cut it, that's unheard of' -scientist" Dec. 12, 2013.

158. "Bad UFO's" (Blog) Comments by "Colbern Steve," January 4, 17, 18, 21, 2013. http://badufos.blogspot.com/2012/12/is-interstellar-travel-preposterous.html ; "Raventstar's Witching Hour 07-18-2015 Steve Colbern Hour One" https://www.youtube.com/watch?v=0Kv4GN-jc_k and "Hour Two" https://www.youtube.com/watch?v=ExpU0NHuO2k&spfreload=10.

159. Constantine 75; Dean 119, 188.

160. "Tributes To UFO Abduction Researcher Budd Hopkins" http://www.lindacortilecase.com/tributes-to-ufo-abduction-researcher-budd-hopkins.html.

161. Hamm 2002: 194.

162. I refer you to Dr. Roger K. Leir, D.P.M., *The Aliens And The Scalpel: Scientific Proof of Extraterrestrial Implants In Humans*, Granite Publishing, LLC, Columbus, N.C., 1998. Leir mentions in his book a number of individuals with intelligence backgrounds who have been directly linked to UFO disinformation schemes. Leir notes the generous contribution made by these individuals in his attempt to locate and remove alien implants.

Chapter Four:

1. Roger G. Charles., Andrew Gumbel. *Oklahoma City: What the Investigation Missed – and Why It Still Matters*. New York, New York, Harper Collins, 2012:170.

2. David Paul Hammer, *Secrets Worth Dying For: Timothy James McVeigh and the Oklahoma City Bombing*. 1st Books Library, 2004: 151-153; David Paul Hammer, *Deadly Secrets: Timothy McVeigh and the Oklahoma City Bombing*. Bloomfield, Indiana, Textstream, 2010: 33-35.

3. Declaration of Terry Lynn Nichols, Feb. 9, 2007, entered as Document 100 in Jesse C. Trentadue vs. FBI and FBI Oklahoma City Field Office, Case No.: 2:04 CV 00772 DAK, USDC, Utah,

Central Division, Feb. 16, 2007.

4. FBI document, 100A-KX-61785-35, unknown date, unclassified on May 26, 1999, unknown author.

5. Author interview with Andrea Augustine, Buffalo, New York, Oct. 22, 2010.

6. Stickney, 150, 153, 160.

7. Jones Collection; *Buffalo News* "Covert Somali Trip Ended in Death Ex-Soldier's Life Largely A Mystery To Family, Friends" Jan. 24, 1993.
   The *Buffalo News* described the many mourners at his funeral that included "bikers, Green Berets, combat veterans, children, generals, spies and nationals from around the world including Vietnam and Panama. Some, said one report, "looked like they could rip your throat out… the kind of guys who you're afraid to look into their eyes, because you know there'd be nothing there." After his death, Freedman's family did learn about previously unknown medals he had earned including a Bronze Star for valor in Vietnam, a Purple Heart and about 20 other medals he never told them about.

8. While at the Militia of Montana headquarters, McVeigh reportedly bragged to one Aryan Nations member that he knew Thom Robb, leader of a KKK chapter in Arkansas. And indeed, McVeigh had filled out an application to become a member of this chapter a few months earlier, around the same time he began calling a Pennsylvania chapter of the National Alliance.

9. In May 1989 by the Arkansas State Police and the ATF, for offering to ship 100 pounds of C4 explosives in the mail to a confidential ATF informant. The investigation was dropped as quickly as it had begun. In June 1989, Moore had been arrested in Salt Lake City for theft of government property in a Department of Defense / FBI undercover investigation called 'Operation Punchout,' which was looking into theft of equipment from military installations. To do so, undercover agents set up a fake surplus store and when individuals came in trying hawk the equipment, they were arrested. Roger Moore was one of the first to show up, offering to provide ammunition, explosives and bootlegged porn videos that he said he got from an "underground" network. The criminal charges against Moore were dropped in 1991 at the request of the FBI who cited "lack of evidence" and no further investigation into the matter was conducted. In early March 1993, the Arkansas and Oregon State Police exchanged information with the FBI about Moore's sale of ammunition, grenades and flare launchers to a felon but once again, nothing came of it (Charles 241, 242; FBI 302. File #174A-OC-56120, Salt Lake City, Utah. March 5, 1996 with attached 'Criminal History' of Roger Moore aka Bob Moore', Aug 23, 1991; FBI 302. J File # 174A-OC- 56120, Lead Control 13857, Jan. 11 and 18, 1996).

10. U.S. District Court. 1993. Application and Affidavit for Search Warrant. WP3-15M. Western District of Texas. Filed Feb. 26, 1993; Wright pg. 152-155, 160 -165 citing U.S. Department of the Treasury, 1993, Report of the Department of Treasury on the Bureau of Alcohol, Tobacco, and Firearms Investigation of Vernon Wayne Howell, Also Known as David Koresh (pg. 134) and Investigation into the Activities of Federal Law Enforcement Agencies Toward the Branch Davidians, Thirteenth Report by the Committee on Government Reform and Oversight Prepared in Conjunction with the Committee on the Judiciary, Aug. 2, 1996 (pg. 12, 3,11); *Atlanta Journal and Constitution* "Report: Military Wary of Waco Plan" Oct. 31, 1999, Mark England.

11. *The Kokomo Tribune* (Kokomo, Indiana) "Nuts get too much notice" Aug. 7, 1995 ; Anson Shupe and Susan E. Darnell "CAN, We Hardly Knew Ye: Sex, Drugs, Deprogrammers' Kickbacks, and Corporate Crime in (old) Cult Awareness Network" A paper presented at the 2000 meeting of the Society for the Scientific Study of Religion, Oct. 21, 2000. Citing Deposition of Cynthia s. Kisser in Cynthia Kisser vs. The Chicago Crusader, Et Al., Circuit Court of Cooke County, Illinois. Sep. 30, 1994, No. 92 L 08593.
   When asked if the Democratic Party would be considered a cult, Kisser agreed it would.

12. Kenneth Stern, *A Force Upon the Plain*, Simon & Shuster, New York, 1996: 61.

That the Davidians were an interracial sect, did not stop some of the more public relations savvy white supremacists spokespeople from making their way to Waco, among them Louis Beam, master propagandist, strategist and 'ambassador at large' for the Aryan Nations.

13. Later, confusion existed among his defense team as to the number of pilgrimages McVeigh made to Waco, as well as their dates and duration of the visits. McVeigh himself acknowledged that he returned to Mt. Carmel about one year after the fire there.

14. Wright 164 citing *Report of the Deputy Attorney General on the Events at Waco, Texas, February 28 to April 19, 1993* (report), United States Department of Justice, Oct. 8, 1993 (pg. 138).

15. *Indianapolis Star* headlined "Government behind Oklahoma blast, claims militia advocate" R. Joseph Gelarden, unknown date.

16. Linda Thompson online post entitled "FBI Threat" on April 25, 1995 reprinted in UFO Updates Digest V. 1.19, The Mutual UFO Network Of Ontario, May 14, 1995 ; *Logansport Pharos Tribune* (Logansport, Indiana) "Militia Leader Claims Government Trying To Kill Her" May 14, 1995.

17. Linda Thompson online post entitled "FBI Threat" on April 25, 1995 reprinted in *UFO Updates Digest* V. 1.19, The Mutual UFO Network Of Ontario, May 14, 1995; *National Enquirer* "America's Queen Of Hate" unknown date reprinted in *UFO Updates Digest* V. 1.19, The Mutual UFO Network Of Ontario, May 14, 1995.

18. Robert Sterling "Beast of the Month: Dr. Louis Jolyon West, CIA 'Cult Expert' and Brainwasher" *The Konformist*, May 1997.

19. L.J. West, Transcription of speech delivered to the Citizens Freedom Foundation, Oct 28, 1983, pg. 1415; *Salt Lake Tribune* "Psychiatrist Brings 43 Year Crusade to Utah- Ridding World of Cults" Oct. 9, 1993, JoAnn Jacobson-Wells; *Boston Globe* "After Waco, The Focus Shift To Other Cults" April 30, 1993, Larry Tye.

Explained West: "A good approach if you were interested in curing a cancer is to find a chemical that kills the malignant cells and spares those that are healthy. What would be the effect of a device or technique which, when applied by society to any organization calling itself religious, would have no untoward effect upon bona fide religions, but would be deadly to the fakes?...Malignant cells or fake religions wouldn't survive it. Healthy cells or bona fide religions and altruistic organizations would not be harmed" (West, Oct 28, 1983).Throughout the 1980's, West was often quoted in the media in his capacity as an expert on cults and was a highly valued member of CAN, having served on the editorial board of their magazine, *Cultic Studies Journal* and a regular keynote speaker at their conferences. In 1986, West was commended by the *Toronto Star* for helping put the bacterial "cultists under a psychological microscope." When West received CAN's Leo J. Ryan award in 1989, CAN described him as "an individual who exhibits extraordinary courage, tenacity and perseverance in the battle against tyranny over the mind of man;" a highly ironic accolade. (*Toronto Star* "Aftermath of a Cult" Aug. 18, 1986, Jamie Talan; Jones Collection: Curriculum Vitae of Jolyn West, PhD: Leo J. Ryan Award, National Cult Awareness Network.

In March 1993, as McVeigh was arriving at Waco, West was named in a lawsuit filed by Scientologist students at UCLA against the school (where he taught), charging that since the 1980's, university funds had been wrongfully been diverted to finance West's "anti-religious" activities on behalf of CAN, and in doing so, had helped violate First Amendment rights. Other lawsuits noting West's relationship with CAN as well as CAN's violation of human and civil rights followed (John Van Dyke and Mario Majorski v. Regents Of The University Of California, Et., Al., CV 92-3459 JSL, USDC Central District Of California, Filed March 11, 1993). CAN was eventually bankrupted as a result of several lawsuits accusing the organization of violating civil and human rights, some noting West's relationship to the organization. In 1986, an estimated 2,500 cults existed in the country that had reportedly lured somewhere between one and three million Americans, depending on who was counting, most between eighteen and twenty-five years old, into their clutches.

The number of deaths at Waco and West's own media presence apparently decreased this number, as, in October 1993, West reduced his estimate to 2,400 active cults in the U.S (*Toronto Star* "Aug. 18, 1986; *Salt Lake Tribune* Oct. 9, 1993). According to West and his colleagues, former cult members suffered a number of symptoms including depression, loneliness, sleeplessness, anger, violent outbursts, disorientation, memory loss, hallucinations, nightmares and sexual dysfunction, all similar to what is now described as PTSD (another area of expertise for West).

20. Conway and Siegelman., 1995: 261-264.

What happened at Waco, they argued, had been part of an ongoing process they termed the "death spiral," consisting of a plague of "armed apocalyptic cults, murderous satanic sects, radical political groups and paramilitary survivalist sects [that seemed to] break out repeatedly in violent shootouts and flame-filled cataclysms." Interestingly, another millennial, apocalyptic brainwashing cult mentioned in the news articles featuring West, Conway and Siegelman was the Church Universal and Triumphant; a congregation McVeigh also visited during his travels, as noted in the previous section of this writing.

21. Hammer 2004: 156.

22. McVeigh himself added to the list of notable faces he'd met in his travels. During the July 1995 conversation in which McVeigh told his attorneys about having called Linda Thompson, he also spoke of having crossed paths with several "visible folks in the Patriot community" often mentioned in news articles as contemporaries and comrades of Thompson, including Bo Gritz, Jack McLamb, Mark Kornke, Ray Pratt, and others.

23. FBI 302 Roger Moore, Karen Anderson, May 19, 1995, SA Mark A. Jesse interview on May 11, 1995.

24. *New York Times* "Terror In Oklahoma: The Suspect; One Man's Complex Path to Extremism" April 23, 1995, Robert D. McFadden.

It does seem strange that Fortier would use a fake name in a small town he had lived in all his life and where his family was well known. McVeigh would have known this, so it seems equally odd that he would assign Fortier a fake identity. This raises the question of whether someone else besides Fortier accompanied McVeigh to the shooting range. Fortier's statements to the FBI about the log in sheets and the log in sheet are found in the Jones Collection.

25. Stickney 160; Hamm 2002: 149; Hamm 1997: 168.

26. James William Gibson, *Warrior Dreams: Violence And Manhood In Post-Vietnam America*, Hill and Wang, New York, 1994: 142-169.

27. Jones Collection; Hammer 2004: 159.

28. Hammer 2010: 39, 41; Steve Kovsky "Corporate terrorism: a new global threat." *Management Review*, Oct. 1990: *Rocky Mountain News* "Bodyguards Learn Trade In Aspen Terrorism Focuses Increased Attention On Protective Services" Oct. 15, 2001, Deborah Frazier.

ESI's founder, Bob Duggan, explained that during the 1960's, he was a Marxist Revolutionary mercenary in South America until Pol Pot's genocidal actions caused him to change his politics, at which point Duggan returned to the U.S., where he taught counterterrorism courses at, among other places, the Army Intelligence School in Arizona before going on to open his own school (a story that raises a few questions).

29. The FBI checked the phone records of a number of locations in Colorado during their investigation, although their checking of phone records throughout the country probably stands as the most thorough aspect of their investigation.

30. *Houston Chronicle* "He'd had enough of rules'; McVeigh reportedly became more extremist after Gulf War" April 23, 1995; *Dayton Daily News* "The Militia: 'I think (McVeigh) was a Little Off but Not Too Much" April 23, 1995, Wes Hills.

Terry Nichols worked for a rancher in Kansas from March to October 1994. When interviewed by the Jones Team, both he and his son recalled McVeigh's 'tracking chip' story and when I asked the son about this in May 2009, he again confirmed the story.

31. *Independent* "The Oklahoma Conspiracy: Next Week, One Man Will Be Executed For Carrying Out America's Worst Peacetime Atrocity. Timothy McVeigh Claims To Have Acted Alone. But New Evidence Reveals He Was Part of an Underground Network Of White Supremacists" May 11, 2001, Andrew Gumbel.

32. FBI 302, 174A-OC-56120-E-4206, May 4, 1995; FOX News "Did Oklahoma City Bombers Have Help?" April 17, 2005.

33. American Terrorist Collection; Strider quote: Jones Collection.

To his biographers, McVeigh recounted "[Marife] came bursting in my room, I was sleeping in the nude, I jumped up, I could tell just from a dead sleep, from living with her for so long… from the tone of her choice penetrating my ear while my mind was sleeping, I could tell it didn't matter if I jumped up naked, there was something too bad going on. So it was a time to not even worry about the modesty of the fact that this was my friends wife. ..I threw on a pair of pants on real quick. She had run to the room and taken Jason's body, put it in front of my door and to tell you the truth I'm well versed with CPR, I kneel down, I checked for a pulse on the jugular, I couldn't feel anything. I'm not feeling a pulse, I'm touching cold clammy skin. I'm starting to get a suspicion that he's been out too long. He's cold. A body maintains heat for a while and he feels like room temperature. I went to the wrist, figuring if I couldn't get it in the neck, id tried the wrist. Couldn't get it in the wrist. So I decided to check for breathing. First, I bent down by his mouth, didn't feel anything on my ear, so I pulled his shirt up and that's when I knew, I was going to watch for the rise and fall of his chest and maybe start CPR, but when I pulled it up, my knuckles touched his rib cage and breast plate an even that was cold and I noticed if his core, the core of his body is cold, he's been out for a few hours. [I called 911… and while we waited for them to arrive] my military training kicked in and I was calm… she's freaking out. She's a civilian. She never had the military experience so she doesn't have control over her emotions. So she's naturally freaking out and I'm not holding that against her by using that phrase freaking out. […] and I laid him on the same spot where I had stood for the WACO fire in fact it was right outside the kitchen. […]Marife is freaking out and screaming over the phone […]I instinctively took charge…..[…..] I tried to block out Marife, but she's screaming. She's now kneeling down and she's screaming and pulling Jason by the shoulders. […]I physically picked Marife up and carried her all the way up the steps, cradle in my arms. As I was carrying her up, and I don't know where I got the strength, I was out of shape at that point…." (American Terrorist Collection: Appendix C).

34. Hamm 2002: 166.

35. Charles 233.

36. "Every time I talked to her," said McVeigh, "I knew exactly what I was saying… I had to somehow prepare her to accept that I'm about to afoul of the law in a big way. I was trying to help her understand her brother….sometimes I [was] convey[ing] things directly. Other times, [I was] trying to convey things between the lines. This was my attempt to lessen the blow to her, when it eventually came" (American Terrorist Collection).

37. *Sunday Times* "All American Monster" September 3, 1995, James Dalrymple; Associated Press wire report, no title, Aug. 9, 1995; Charles 223.

38. Gadbaw claimed that even after McVeigh left the area six months later, he continued to stay there on occasion. Records do indicate that a man by this name lived at the same Golden Valley house McVeigh did, but at a different time.

39. Given that Kingman, Arizona is one of the creepiest places I have ever been to in my life, I would not be overly surprised if there was even a hint of truth in any of the rumors about some of

the stranger things to happen there.

40. Stickney 152; *New York Times*, April 23, 1995.

New York Times "TERROR IN OKLAHOMA: THE SUSPECT: One Man's Complex Path to Extremism" April 23, 1995.

41. Hammer 2005:167.

Rogers told the FBI that McVeigh offered him $5 to drive him back into town but as Rogers felt "a little horny" at the time, he informed his passenger that he wanted to have casual sex with him. McVeigh was agreeable to this plan, so they checked into a nearby motel (Charles 278). Perhaps because the story was just that interesting, the ATF and FBI kept coming back to take further statements from Rogers, all of which contain strange details, like the time Rogers discussed his and McVeigh's sexual relationship with Rick Corvette (whoever that is). In perhaps one of the strangest law enforcement reports ever written or at least that I've ever seen, the ATF noted that, according to Rogers, McVeigh "liked to suck nice DICK and suck nice BALLS [sic.]" (Jones Collection). Beyond the name of individuals, which are usually completely capitalized in law enforcement reports, the only other words to appear in all capital letters in this report are 'Dick and 'Balls.' I personally refer to this as 'The Dick And Balls Report.' Rogers reports are found in the Jones Collection.

42. Quote: *Independent*, May 11, 2001.

In the letters between McVeigh and Steve Hodge throughout the summer of 1994, the two old friends discussed or debated a number of conspiracy theories, with Steve always arguing against the ones McVeigh floated. "Do me a favor," Steve wrote, "perhaps in your next letter you could let me in on what you've been up to for the last year and a half. I mean I've heard loads about your views on politics but it seems to me you must have covered some ground. Where have you been and what have you done, what have you seen in the last year?" Steve expressed his relief that the two remained friends and that their friendship still meant something to 'Tim' because Steve himself would never turn his back on a friend. He continued, saying that if anyone else said the things 'Tim' did, Steve would think they were crazy, but because Steve valued Tim, he listened to his 'conspiracy theories' but did not know what to make of the information. Steve closed the letter by asking Tim not to stop writing because he, Steve, would be greatly upset if he did so (Jones Collection).

43. Hamm 2002: 195.

44. U.S. Department of Justice, Federal Bureau of Investigation, San Antonio, Texas, Sub: Texas Reserve Militia, June 24, 1991.

45. Jones Collection; American Terrorist Collection.

McVeigh told his biographers that Moore, Anderson and "another guy" used to "make their own exploding top bullets" with the powder and Moore had the chemicals "all over his fucking house" and the traces would have matched those found on him (McVeigh) after his arrest" (American Terrorist Collection).

Roger Charles provides a detailed account of Moore's links to components used to make the OKC bomb.

46. Declaration of Terry Lynn Nichols, Feb. 9, 2007, entered as Document 100 in Jesse C. Trentadue vs. FBI and FBI Oklahoma City Field Office, Case No.: 2:04 CV 00772 DAK, USDC, Utah, Central Division, Feb. 16, 2007.

47. Alliance Services Investigative Memorandum. To: Michael A. Tigar, Ronald G. Woods, From: John W. Hough, RE: The Enigma Of Roger Moore, Dec. 18, 1996 citing FBI Insert #E7052 'Birdsong' Jan. 11, 1996 and Jan. 18, 1996; and Don Birdsong Memo dated Nov. 20, 1996 (also cited by Charles, pg. 391); Alliance Services Investigative Memorandum. To: Michael E. Tigar, Ronald G. Woods, From: Roland Leeds. Re: Roger Moore. Case: Nichols. Oct. 10, 1996; FBI 302, Lead Control #13857; Jan. 11 and 18, 1996, SA Steven Crutchfield.

48. Alliance Services Investigative Memorandum. Dec. 18, 1996 citing FBI Insert #E7052 Jan. 11, 1996 and Jan. 18, 1996; and Don Birdsong Memo dated Nov. 20, 1996 (also cited by Charles, pg. 391); Alliance Services Investigative Memorandum. Oct. 10, 1996; FBI 302, #13857; Jan. 11 and 18, 1996.

On November 22, 1996, the DOJ provided the Jones Team with a list of gun shows McVeigh attended including the 1994 SOF convention where he shared a table with Roger Moore. On December 26, 1995, the FBI interviewed Dolores Grochowski, the owner of the Valley Motel in Las Vegas. She told them that Roger Moore usually stayed with them during the annual Soldier Of Fortune conventions. She said that Moore sometimes registered under his wife's name, Carol Moore. Moore had registered in his own name from September 15, 1994 until September 18, 1994, listing his home address in Hot Springs, Arkansas. Grochowski said that during the 1994 SOF convention, she received a call asking to be connected to Bob Miller in Moore's room. When her daughter asked Moore why he was getting calls under a different name, he said it was for business reasons. She did not, however, have phone records for the calls. McVeigh told his attorneys he was at the 1994 SOF convention and described it to them. He was also seen there by Johnny Bangerter.

49. Author interviews with Johnny Bangerter from December 2010 to February 2015 (sometimes with Holland Vandennieuwenhof).

50. Declaration of Terry Lynn Nichols, Feb. 9, 2007, entered as Document 100 in Jesse C. Trentadue vs. FBI and FBI Oklahoma City Field Office, Case No.: 2:04 CV 00772 DAK, USDC, Utah, Central Division, Feb. 16, 2007.

Roger Charles, along with summaries of the Moore robbery investigation prepared by Nichols defense team go out into great detail about the events surrounding the alleged robbery.

51. Charles 250,393 citing Walt, Verta and Lance Powell testimony at Nichols trial on December 3 and 4, 1997 and their interviews with Nichols' defense team on November 12 and 13, 1996.

The gist of Moore's story goes like this: As Moore stood in his driveway, he was waylaid by an armed man with a shifting description. The robber bound Moore's wrists with plastic cuffs or duct tape or both and instructed him to go back in the house, warning that another robber was waiting outside and would shoot Moore if he tried to escape. Moore never actually saw the second man. One of the robbers did or did not fire a warning shot in the air. Moore went back in the house at which point the robber began gathering everything of value, except those things that belonged to Karen Anderson.

Moore told Verta what happened and asked to use the phone as his phone lines had been cut. Moore called somebody and spoke in hushed tones. Verta had Moore stay with her and asked her husband and son to come home right away. The more Moore told them, the more suspicious the entire situation seemed to them. He seemed to be putting on an act and immediately knew the exact spot where his phones lines had been cut. The Powell's dog, who barked at everything, hadn't made a peep all morning. When they asked why he had not yet reported the robbery to the police, Moore told them that the robbery had been an attempt by the government to shut down a movement he was leading and keep him "in check" (Charles 250 citing interviews with Verta and Lance Powell on Dec. 3 and Dec. 4, 1994).

52. According to an investigative memo prepared by Nichols defense team later, the FBI was preoccupied with the thought that either of the defense teams would contact and speak with the Powell's, as demonstrated in the reports they wrote after speaking with Moore about the robbery (Alliance Services Investigative Memorandum. To: Michael E. Tigar, Ronald G. Woods, From: Roland Leeds. Re: Roger Moore. Case: Nichols. Oct. 10, 1996).

53. Alliance Services Investigative Memorandum. To: Michael A. Tigar, Ronald G. Woods, From: John W. Hough, RE: The Enigma Of Roger Moore, Dec. 18, 1996 citing Transcript of Spivey's interview of Roger Moore on 11-16-94; Priddy memo dated 11-17-96; Dies memo dated 11-18-96; Spivey memo 11-25-96; Policy # 18911153801, Claim # G7 15764, Claim Date, Nov. 5, 1994, Nov. 16, 1994.

To one adjuster Moore said that the way the robber behaved suggested Special Forces or Navy Seal type training. He told an insurance agent that he could not describe the robber because he "never saw him" and also that the robbery had been an "inside job" and the "government" had been involved. She recalled that More seemed "very knowledgeable" about the government and the FBI. He even showed her a "badge" which he told her he shouldn't even be showing her and then asked her not to tell anyone. He told a customer service representative for the insurance company that the "federal government" was involved and said he didn't want the robbery to attract any publicity.

54. Charles 251,393 citing Michael Fortier's testimony at McVeigh trial.

55. According to Nichols "McVeigh said that I was chosen to carry out the robbery so that if he was polygraphed he could truthfully testify that he did not know the robber....he and Moore came up with the plan to stage a robbery so that if any investigation of the bombing tracked back to Moore, Moore could claim he was the victim of a home robbery rather than a supplier of funds and explosives used to carry out the attack..." (Declaration of Terry Lynn Nichols, Feb. 9, 2007, Trentadue vs. FBI and FBI Oklahoma City Field Office, Feb. 16, 2007).

56. Gelles' career includes over 16 years of counterintelligence work. He was Chief Psychologist for the NCIS and Chair of the Police Psychological Services Section of the International Association of Chiefs of Police until his retirement in 2006. After retiring from public service, Gelles began a new life as a private security consultant to high tech multinationals (kind of like the work performed by ESI). Gelles is explored further later in this chapter.

57. While Lands and Jacks appeared in news reports briefly, the fact that their arrival and departure from Kingman coincide with McVeigh's was never publicly reported; although the related FBI investigatory reports are found in the Jones Collection.

58. *New York Times* "TERROR IN OKLAHOMA: The Overview; F.B.I Issues Alert For 2 More Sought In Bombing Inquiry" May 2,1995.

59. *New York Times* "John Doe No. 1- A Special Report: A Life of Solitude and Obsessions" May 4, 1995, Robert D. McFadden.

60. Herbeck and Michel 181; Author interview with Carl Lebron, April 10, 2010, Buffalo, New York; Author interview with Andrea Augustine, Buffalo, New York, Oct. 22, 2010.

61. Charles 256.

62 Declaration of Terry Lynn Nichols, Feb. 9, 2007, entered as Document 100 in Trentadue vs. FBI and FBI Oklahoma City Field Office, Feb. 16, 2007.

63. On February 19, 1995, while McVeigh was staying at the Hilltop, a Naval dentist was staying in the room next door, although he later told the FBI he did not interact with either MCV or Nichols, nor did he see them.

64. Jones Collection; Author interviews with Johnny Bangerter from December 2010 to February 2015 (sometimes with Holland Vandennieuwenhof); Author interviews with Mary Bangerter from December 2010 to January 2011 (sometimes with Holland Vandennieuwenhof).

Mary, a former police sketch artist, vividly recalled the incident: At the time, I felt bad because Tim had been trying to contact Johnny the entire week. Johnny kept putting him off though and I felt bad for him because he seemed so earnest about it. He told me he came all the way out here to meet Johnny and whatever he had to say to him seemed very important. I never forgot his face. He was kind of skinny and tall. He had a fresh, innocent looking kid face and the sun was behind him. It was shining in his hair. Only later, when I saw his face on the news, did I realize: it wasn't just by chance he stayed in St. George at the Dixie Palms Motel. It was all about getting involved with Johnny. He really did make a big effort to get a hold of him. The phone bills were in my daughter's name so how in the heck 'Tim' got our number is beyond me.

65. Author interviews with Johnny Bangerter from December 2010 to February 2015 (sometimes with Holland Vandennieuwenhof).

66. *The John Doe Times*, Vol. III, No. I, Dec. 28, 1996, Mike Vanderbough.

67 *Rocky Mountain News*, "Who Painted The Phony Trail Of Guilt? Racist Militia Leader Denies Link To The Oklahoma Bombing, Stays Ready For A Shootout" Nov. 2, 1997.

The story of Bangerter's scrape with McVeigh was the subject of several Jones Team memos as well as an article in the *Rocky Mountain News*. Johnny Bangerter (a major character in my second book, *Redacted*) has confirmed the story to me as have other individuals. Parts of the story (those dealing with the Jones Team and the fabricated records) were confirmed to me by defense investigator Richard Reyna. As found in the Jones Collection, I have a copy of both the fabricated phone records and the real ones Reyna eventually obtained that did not include the incriminating phone calls.

68 Jay Dobyns "April 19: An Untold Personal ATF Story" April 20, 2015 http://blog.jaydobyns-group.com/?p=827.

I should note that, from 2010 until summer of 2015, Johnny Bangerter had mentioned many of the same people and places noted by Dobyns, prior to my finding Dobyns blog in fall 2015.

69. Evans-Pritchard 63 citing: Criminal Alien Information, INS, Jan. 9, 1995; Trooper Safety Alert, Angela Finley, ATF; FBI Memo from FBI Dallas Office to ATF Tulsa Office, Feb. 23, 1995.

70. CAUSE was a legal foundation that catered to defense efforts for those on the extreme, racist right. The founder and staff of CAUSE were deeply connected, to Elohim City, the National Alliance and Aryan Nations and CAUSE organizers had been keynote speakers at the September 1994 Soldier Of Fortune convention, attended by both Moore and McVeigh.

71. The man continued walking around but lost his bearings. He came on an area with several hand painted signs that said "Wayne's Place" and warning to quickly get off Wayne's property. The man said he went back after the bombing but the signs disappeared.

72. Drosnin told the FBI he knew the exact location but he wanted them to accompany him there as he feared that if he confronted them alone, the people at the compound would run, or worse.

73. Evans Pritchard 15 citing Glen Wilburn interview with Harvey Weathers; OKCBI Final Report 266,267,437,438; FBI report by Oklahoma County Grand Jury Final Report, No. CJ-95-7278, June 30, 1997 citing *USA Today*, unknown title, April 20, 1995.

74. Charles 351. A significant number of McVeigh doppelgangers roaming the country had acne or pock-marked faces, as did the one who rented the Ryder at Elliot's and a few the morning of the bombing in Oklahoma City.

75. CNN "The Road to Oklahoma" November 19, 1995; *The Observer* "Cults 2" May 21, 1995. *Newsweek* "The Subject Speaks Out" July 3, 1995.

76. Stickney 178.

77. ABC News 'Prime Time Live' May 10, 1995.

78. Although reports of double McVeighs continued, the FBI, according to their reports, ended its investigation of McVeigh "look-alike" information on May 16, 1995. McVeigh, who sometimes seemed legitimately baffled by his shadow selves, felt the FBI's decision to stop looking deeper into the doppelgangers illustrated their general willingness to abandon viable avenues of investigation.

79. Hoffman 36 ; *Toronto Star* "Lee Harvey Oswald revisited Why Oklahoma City bomber Timothy McVeigh can be seen as spiritual brother to JFK assassin" June 7, 1997, Philip Marchand.

The *Toronto Star* article noted McVeigh's resemblance to Don DeLillo's 1988 depiction of the fictionalized Oswald in his book *Libra*.

80. *Minneapolis Tribune* "Efforts to open Oswald's grave blocked by my brother" Aug. 15, 1980.

Those who knew Oswald offered highly conflicting accounts of him: He could or could not drive a car; he could not shoot to save his life, he was an excellent sharpshooter; he was a communist, an anti-communist or an undercover double agent of both factions.

Those who have researched Oswald's life painstakingly detail (among other things): his movements throughout the United States and abroad, connections and associations to both extreme right and left wing revolutionaries and groups whom the FBI had placed under intense surveillance; intelligence agencies' ongoing surveillance of Oswald himself, his communications with the FBI and other intelligence agencies and assets, and the simultaneous sightings of more than one Oswald in different locations. This leads to a number of possibilities, any one of which could have culminated in the assassination of the President in a high-level conspiracy involving many players including Oswald lookalikes. Similar to those about McVeigh, among the possibilities suggested about Oswald: Oswald was inducted into a naval intelligence operation in which he adopted the role of disgruntled U.S. soldier and, under this guise, defected to the Soviet Union; upon returning to the United States, quickly set about establishing his legend as an extremist and became an FBI informant and/or was assigned by another agency (CIA, military, etc.,) to conduct 'deep cover' operations investigating national security threats which involved infiltrating both the extreme right and left.

81. In 1972, writer Walter Bowart hypothesized, as others would about McVeigh, that the many conflicting descriptions of Oswald make sense if he had externally induced multiple personalities. Noting that some 'Oswalds' reportedly could drive and, others could not, and likewise, some were expert marksman and could hardly shoot at all, Bowart wrote that Oswald "might have been an excellent shot in one zombie state and in another he might have been so blocked so that he could not even aim a rifle. In one state he might have had the ability to drive a car, while in another state he might have had a post hypnotic block so that he could not drive" (W. H. Bowart Operation Mind Control Dell Publishing Co. Inc. New York, New York 1978: 186.).

82. Michael James Rizza "The Dislocation of Agency in Don DeLillo's *Libra*" Critique: *Studies in Contemporary Fiction*, V. 49 No. 2, 2008: 174,176,179; Bill Millard "The Fable Of The Ants: Myopic Interaction In DeLillo's *Libra*" Postmodern Culture, V. 4, No. 2, 1994: part 8; John Johnston "Superlinear Fiction or Historical Diagram?: Don DeLillo's *Libra*" Modern Fiction Studies, V. 40 No. 2, 1994: 337-338.

"Plots," remarked Win Everett, "carry their own logic. There is a tendency of plots to move toward death…a narrative plot no less than a conspiracy of armed men" (Don DeLillo, *Libra*, Viking, New York, 1988: 221).

83. Johnston 337,338 quoting Gilles Deleuze, *Différence et Répétition*, P.U.F. Paris, 1968: 44.

84. Herbeck and Michel 259, 277, 278.

85. Beyond a number of news articles, West confirmed during a 1996 'consultation' conversation with Jones Team attorney Andrew Murphy that he had been present twice in Oklahoma City after the bombing as part of an initiative administering psychiatric services to survivors and first responders and training sessions to local mental health services. West added, "Now this won't affect my objectivity with respect to your client at all, but it is something that you should know."

86. Robert Guffey. *Cryptoscatology: Conspiracy Theory as Art Form*. TrineDay, Walterville, Oregon, 2012: 49 (citing *Larry King Live*, April 19, 1995).

While the reasons for West's central place in the Experimental legends will be explored in great depth shortly, the rumors themselves seem to have begun with alleged sightings of West visiting the facility, with Thompson's call to the FBI is the first instance they appear.

87. Jones 1998: 31, 359.

Jones said that on May 4 he met with Otto, Coyle and McVeigh so that Otto and Coyle could "pass the baton" to Jones and only the next day, May 5, did Jones meet with his new client (Jones

Collection).

88. Jones request to court found in Jones Collection; Stickney 233 (citing *Niagara Gazette* no date).

McVeigh told his legal team that there were three ways he could deal with the perceived abuse: "legal resistance, active resistance and passive resistance," and while he was currently taking the passive path, if something was not done soon, he would "quickly move to active resistance." The warden responded to McVeigh's hunger strike threats by telling him he had a choice; he could change his attitude and do "easy time" or continue with his complaints and do "hard time" (Jones Collection). Although the conversation is detailed in an internal defense memo, to his biographers McVeigh denied ever having gone on or threatened to go on a hunger strike.

89. While it is unknown how Jones chose to employ Smith, in 1993 Smith had testified on behalf of Ronald Veatch, a client of John Coyle, one of McVeigh's first public defenders. Veatch claimed that his millionaire father-in-law worked with Oklahoma Judge Wayne Alley in covert CIA operations and now his father-in-law, Alley, the CIA and a host of other intelligence and law enforcement agencies were tormenting him. Alley was one of the Judges in Oklahoma who told reporters that he received prior warning of threats in downtown OKC in the two weeks leading up to the bombing and had, in fact, not gone to work on April 19. Alley was the first judge assigned to hear McVeigh's case, but was later removed after defense attorneys argued that he had a conflict of interest. Perhaps unrelated, while he was still McVeigh's judge, Alley refused to compel the CIA to turn over case related files to the defense ... but then again so did the next judge who replaced him. Jones would call Smith in as an expert in other cases, after McVeigh's conviction.

90. Dr. David B. Foster, a psychiatrist Jones consulted on June 4, 1995, two days before Smith's visit. Jones and attorney Dick Burr told Foster that while McVeigh "was not brainwashed" he was nonetheless "capable of being brainwashed" (Jones Collection). Foster was soon retained by Ted Kaczynski's defense team until Kaczynski, who himself had some legitimate concerns about being brainwashed, fired Foster.

After Smith's intervention, McVeigh was permitted to send and receive mail, read newspapers, receive visitors and listen to the radio, but could not watch television. Further, the BOP agreed to shut off the surveillance cameras for four hours a day so McVeigh could read his legal mail.

91. *New Yorker* "From Oklahoma City to Oslo" July 26, 2011, Mark Singer.

92. McVeigh acknowledged to his biographers that he had told Jones he wasn't brainwashed but said he had done so sarcastically and only months later when one of the other attorneys told him that Smith was called in to determine if he had been. McVeigh also said he knew he was being brainwashed in basic training when he and his COHORTs were ordered to chant "KILL KILL KILL" but that the military hadn't brainwashed him to commit the bombing or into believing that "the ends justified the means," they only introduced him to the "cruelty of the real world" (American Terrorist Collection).

93. Author Interview with Randall Coyne, January 5, 2011, Oklahoma City, Oklahoma.

94. Jones 1998:63.

Lee Norton, Ph.D., M.S.W., L.C.S.W., was technically an investigator for the defense team and was not hired to treat McVeigh per se although she spent quite a bit of time with him. Norton began visiting McVeigh in June, just days before Smith did. In her private practice, she specialized in treating survivors of chronic childhood abuse as well as traumatic stress, dissociative disorders, military trauma and combat PTSD. She is currently the owner of the Center For Trauma Therapy located in Nashville, Tennessee and Melbourne, Florida. Anthony Semone first began visiting McVeigh in August 1995. Among his other professional activities, Semone evaluates, treats and testifies about 'post-shooting trauma' and PTSD suffered by law enforcement in the line of duty as well as a professional firearms training and education instructor. Seymour Halleck, who first began seeing McVeigh in September 1995, is considered an early pioneer of and contributor to the field of criminal forensic psychiatry. Semone and Halleck had a fair amount of previous experience with high profile cases. The defense team also consulted with a handful of other mental health experts who assumedly never visited with McVeigh. They included (but were not limited to) David B. Foster and Elizabeth Loftus.

95. Clinically, Psychosis denotes a 'loss of contact with reality,' often accompanied by frighteningly paranoid delusions and disorganized speech that jumps from topic to topic without explicating the links between them. Diagnostic features and characteristics include: (Hallucinations)- sensory perception without corresponding external stimuli; (Delusions)- beliefs strongly held to without accurate, corresponding or sufficient evidence; (Catatonia)- profoundly agitated states wherein experiences of reality are impaired or distorted that lead to immobility, freezing states, excessive, bizarre and extreme motor activity and/or expressions of preoccupation with ideas that impair experiences of reality; (Thought Disorders)- disorganized, bizarre and incomprehensible speech and writing and a loosening of semantic associations; and (Impaired Social Cognition) – hostility, suspicion, grandiosity.

96. Sergeant Mac was with a man with a heavy German accent when Farrington met him. Farrington said that among others, Richard Butler, head of the Aryan Nations, Dick Coffman, organizer for the Arizona National Alliance, and John Trochman, head of the Militia Of Montana (FBI informant and friend of Roger Moore) all sanctioned and provided material support. In 2011, I wrote to Farrington who, at the time was in prison in Texas. In response, I received an email from his attorney asking me not to contact him again.

97. The man whose story is related in the September 1995 FBI report, Wade Alan Nehman, also told the FBI about a white slavery ring he was involved with and the location of two bodies connected to the ring. He said one of the pilots for the ring was a "government snitch." Nehman was known to have and had been convicted for the murders of four people although the convictions were overturned based on procedural errors in securing his confession.

98. *Washington Times* "Oklahoma City bombing secret: DNA extracted from unknown leg" Dec. 7, 2015.

99. Based on what they knew, his legal team considered the possibility that McVeigh may not have even driven the truck to the Murrah, had driven one of the decoy trucks or maybe just the getaway car. In fact, when Jones was asked about the extra leg DNA fiasco in December 2015, he told reporters, "I don't think anyone thinks the car McVeigh was pulled over in was the actual getaway car. He parked it five blocks away and backed it in so that the rear license plate could not be seen. He then used a highlighter to write on a piece of cardboard saying, 'Not abandoned. Please do not tow. Will move by April 23 (needs battery and cable).' But he also left all this political literature in the car, the theory being that a week later the car would draw attention, and the literature would be there to explain why the federal building was bombed. In this scenario, whoever was going to give him a ride didn't show up, so he had to hoof it back to the car and then head north on the highway, where a trooper stopped him" (*Washington Times*, Dec. 7, 2015). Still, in 1995, Richard Burr expressed his opinion that while McVeigh's participation in televised interviews may cause viewers to have empathy for him, "I do not think he can resist the urge to take credit and to give himself up. Now that we are having more reason to believe that others were involved --- perhaps as the principals – I am even more concerned about this."

100. Jones Collection; Charles 170,178.

Note that, as discussed in the previous chapter, according to one man in Buffalo, AIDS outreach volunteer, Peter Salino, McVeigh suggested someone should blow up the Social Security building because of their database of personal records. McVeigh also complained to Gwen Strider about a mysterious terrorism database he believed contained his name.

The Turner Diaries, written by racist figurehead and organizer William Pierce under the pseudonym Andrew McDonald, would become not only a 'bible' for the White Power Movement but was often referred to in the media and by the FBI as 'the blue print' for the Oklahoma City bombing. Set in the not too distant future, the book contains the fictitious diary entries of Earl Turner, whose days were spent forming underground cells of fighters opposed to "The System" after increasing multi-culturalism and restrictive gun ownership legislation (The Cohen Act) threatens to permanently alter and enslave all of society. The guerrilla fighters live underground, and engage in terrorist acts such as assassinations and bombings, ultimately destroying an FBI building with a truck bomb, in order to erase the records stored in the supercomputer located there. The white American 'freedom fighters' are eventually successful in gaining control over North West United States, establishing a twisted utopian white homeland, and eradicating the nonwhite population.

101. American Psychiatric Association. *Diagnostic And Statistical Manual Of Mental Disorders*, 5th Ed. Washington, D.C. 2013; Bethany L. Brand Gregory S. Chasson "Distinguishing Simulated From Genuine Dissociative Identity Disorder on the MMPI-2" *Psychological Trauma: Theory, Research, Practice, and Policy*. V.7 No. 1, 2015: 94; See also: See: Hovens (pg. 75-103) and Elliot (pg. 49-73) and Gallimore in *The Psychology of Terrorism: Clinical Aspects and Responses*, V. 2, Chris E. Stout Ed., Praeger, Westport, Connecticut, London, 2002; Elizabeth, F. Howell., *The Dissociative Mind* The Analytic Press, Hillsdale, NJ., London 2005; William, Graebner. *Patty's Got A Gun: Patricia Hearst in 1970's America* University of Chicago Press, Chicago, London, 2008.

DID is conceived of as a set of dissociative symptoms and tendencies thought to be a coping mechanism instigated by intense traumatic experiences, often during childhood. Such experiences include extreme, repetitive physical, sexual, and/or emotional abuse, and intense coercive persuasion wherein the victim literally dissociates himself from a situation or experience that's too violent, traumatic, or painful to assimilate with his conscious self. The five major components of dissociation include disturbances in memory (including amnesia), de-realization, depersonalization, a discontinuity of personal existence, and hallucinatory phenomena.

Clinical and popular conceptions of dissociation have changed significantly over time. The 1954 edition of the Diagnostic and Statistical Manuel of Mental Disorders (DSM-I) described a cluster of deviant behaviors and role confusions termed 'hysterical neurosis' and 'conversion disorders,' respectively, both of which refer to pathological dissociation. In 1956, Louis Jolyon 'Jolly' West, M.D., a leading expert in dissociative states, wrote, "Dissociative phenomena are found in everyday life. Such manifestations include "highway hypnosis," states of "fascination" in flyers, hypnagogic and phantasy hallucinations, transient aesthesias, and many other examples. These reactions have many features in common with a variety of clinical disorders including "sleep paralysis," trance states, Gilles de la Tourette's disease, latah, "Arctic hysteria," and a number of other disturbances in addition to the well-known dissociative reactions of the text-books...." At the time of McVeigh's diagnosis (and currently), the DSM included in the definition of DID: (a) the presence of two or more distinct identities or personality states (each with its own relatively enduring pattern of perceiving, relating to, and thinking about the environment and self); (b) at least two of these identities or personality states recurrently take control of a person's behavior; (c) inability to recall important personal information that is too extensive to be explained by ordinary forgetfulness; (d) the disturbance is not due to direct physiological effects of a substance or a general medical condition. DID and other dissociative disorders were included and expanded upon within the DSM-V (2013). The resurgence of this diagnosis, renewed research efforts and the recent growth of literature addressing dissociation, generally, and as pathological specifically, dovetails and incorporates recent advances in neuroscience and trauma studies.

102. Narcissism refers to, among other traits, a pathological preoccupation with the survival of the self; the presentation of a cold, detached, unemotional self; a fragmented self and an inability to maintain personal coherence; a sense of omnipotence, delusions of grandeur and fantasies of self-importance.

On October 18, 1995, Dr. Halleck noted suspicions among the mental health experts based on interviews conducted with McVeigh family members, family friends and neighbors that McVeigh's mother had acted in inappropriate ways with her son, "probably not sexual relations but perhaps things like inviting him to see her when naked, then feigning surprise." A family would friend would later tell them that when Bill was at work, Mickey would have men over and that Tim was a witness to her actions, something that, as a young child, must have left him terribly conflicted. Dissociative Identity Disorder is most prevalent among those who have experienced sexually related trauma, especially as young children. The dissociative traits adapted to protect the mind from the horrors of the trauma tend to remain as adaptive techniques throughout life.

Jones explained to Burr how "Tim's story is one that is undoubtedly repeated millions of time a year. His act, which he views as one in a series of revolutionary acts against the government, would then be belittled simply to the act of somebody who's 'crazy'... Tim's act is no more 'crazy than John Brown's raid on Harpers Ferry [or] the Haymarket Anarchist." In Burr's response letter, he noted "if we are not interested for purposes of defense in why Tim developed dissociative abilities (disorder)," then it did not matter what they learned about the McVeigh family. Jones told Burr, "[Your career has been] devoted either philosophically or politically towards a view that people who commit violent crimes may be the victims of emotional disturbances or racism or poverty or abuse or lack of nurturing or any other behavioral aspects, which as viewed by conservatives, chiefly result in an argument to avoid responsibility for acts...Tim rejects the idea that anything he may have done is the result of anything other than his own deliberate plan and desire...and I happen to agree with him...he does not wish to painted as a John Hinckley, and he doesn't want us to spend time trying to investigate chapters in his life... The bottom line is this is a plea [by Tim] for us to quit invading his privacy [or that] of his family. Our job is not to 'cure him' or to engage in psychoanalysis...instead we should concentrate on getting Tim to tell us the complete truth."

103. When McVeigh discovered the dead body of Nichols' infant son, after unsuccessfully trying to revive the child, he called the police. Although not consciously attempting to obscure his true identity 'Tim McVeigh,' when asked his name, responded automatically and 'accidentally' by offering the name of Tim Tuttle, one of the more developed and often used alias/ identities/ personae. McVeigh said he had meant to use the Kling identity when he checked into the nearby Dreamland Motel, but inexplicably listed the name 'Tim McVeigh' on the registration form. When he ordered Chinese food delivery to his room there, he did so under the name Kling, telling his attorneys later that he was "trying to get in Kling mode" (although admittedly this did not explain why the physical descriptions of Kling consistently conflicted with McVeigh's actual physical traits). Although unnamed, at times McVeigh consciously or not undoubtedly became the living personification of Earl Turner. Finally, while perhaps a clerical error, the name Bruce James McVeigh was listed on the booking card at the time of 'Tim McVeigh's' arrest.

104. John F. Kihlstrom "Dissociative Disorders" *Annual Review of Clinical Psychology* 1:2005 (pg. 227-253; Ernest R. Hillgard, *Divided Consciousness: Multiple Controls in Human Thought and Action* (Expanded Ed.,) New York, Chicester, Brisbane, Toronto, Singapore, John Wiley and Sons, 1977: 22, 66, 80.

The DSM –V (2013) defines Dissociative Amnesia as (a) one or more episodes of inability to recall important personal information, usually of a traumatic or stressful nature but also everyday occurrences. These memory lapses are too extensive to be explained by originally forgetfulness; (b) has no other causes (substances, organic); (c) resulting in symptoms that cause clinically significant distress or impairment in social, occupational or other important areas of functioning. An individual with Dissociative Amnesia suffers a loss of autobiographical memory for specific past experiences.

105. *Washington Post* "The Psychology Of a Modern Spy" June 15, 1985, Molly Sinclair and Chris Spolar.

It turns out, as reported in the article, that paranoia, like a disease, is contagious. The paranoid spy contaminates those he encounters with his own suspicion, sometimes intentionally in order to destabilize them and make them more compliant to his will.

106. *Florida Times Union* "Undercover School" March 21, 2000.

Among his other notable positions, Gelles was Chair of the Police Psychological Services Section of the International Association of Chiefs of Police.

107. If unable to maintain their cover, and their true identities and objectives are discovered, undercover agents face physical harm and professional failure. Undercovers act largely autonomously

with occasional assistance from handlers of other assets who may make brief appearances as 'cover persons' in deceptive support roles meant to further convince targets that the operative's cover story or legend is real.

108. Michael L. Arter "Undercover And Under Stress: The Impact Of Undercover Assignments On Police Officers" Doctoral Dissertation. Indiana University of Pennsylvania. May 2005: 50, 54 Arter 50, 54 (referencing Michel Giordo "Health and legal issues in undercover narcotics investigation: Misrepresented evidence." *Behavioral Sciences & the Law*, V. 3 No. 3: 1985; G. T. Marx. *Undercover: Police surveillance in America*. Berkeley, CA, University of California Press, 1985); Nicholas Wamsley "Big Brother Gone Awry: Undercover Policing Facing Legitimacy Crisis" *American Criminal Law Review*, Winter 2015: 190 (referencing and quoting Elizabeth E. Joh "Breaking The Law To Enforce It: Undercover Police Participation In Crime" *Stanford Law Review*, 2009; Laurence Miller "Undercover Policing: A Psychological and Operational Guide" Police & Criminal Psychology, Fall 2006).

One undercover field agent said that when they were doing undercover drug investigations there were clear good guys and bad guys but once they switched to investigating "subversive activities" his previous clarity about "white hats and black hats" was replaced by "white hats and grey hats. And my hat got grey. But they were my only friends…You develop a closeness that is psychologically difficult to close off." Debates about good guys and bad guys aside, the once idealistic operator comes to inhabit "a nebulous mire where right and wrong overlap, intertwine, and imitate each other" (Wamsley 2015:191; Arter 2005:53).

109. Michel Girodo, Trevor Deck, Melanie Morrison, "Dissociative Type-Identity Disturbances In Undercover Agents: Socio-Cognitive Factors Behind False –Identity Appearances And Reenactments" *Social Behavior And Personality*. V.30 No. 7. 2002:632,640; Wamsley 190 (referencing and quoting *Huffington Post*, "NYPD Internal Affairs Office Present When Bikers Attacked SUV, Sources Say" Oct. 10, 2013; NBC, N.Y, "Undercover NYPD Arrested For Role In Assault on SUV Driver" Oct. 9, 2013; *International Business Times* "Who Is Wojciech Braszcok? Meet The Undercover Cop Who Took Part In NYC Biker Gang Assault On SUV Driver" Oct. 9, 2013).

Other commonly reported symptoms and maladaptive behaviors include, to varying degrees of severity and duration, anxiety, loneliness, depression, guilt, fatigue, poor impulse control, substance abuse, high risk behavior, interpersonal insensitivity, mistrust, uncontrolled anger and other emotional outbursts, hostility, corruption, misconduct, deception (in now 'inappropriate' situations), and phobias.

110. Originally created to convince (in some cases) bad guys that they too are bad guys, the alter egos are not always the most pleasant of people. They are deceitful and lawless.

111. Girodo, et. al., 2002:642; Wamsley 194 (referencing and quoting Miller 2006).

Undercovers agents are generally recruited at a young age and lured through a number of inducements, many of which turn out to be untrue (that is, after all, the name of the game). They then feel pressured to make a decision right away without learning about the aforementioned nastier things that go along with this type of work. With some exceptions, including military operatives, psychological testing and profiling identifying predisposition and susceptibility to any number of existing mental imbalances and profiling is minimal. Mainly they are chosen on physical traits, because of gender and race and the language they speak.

112. Michel Giordo "Undercover Agent Assessment Centers: Crafting Vice and Virtue for Imposters" *Journal of Social Behavior & Personality* V. 12 No. 5, 1997:242.

113. Giordo 1997:243.

114. Wamsley 189. While there are reasons to disagree with Wamsley's proposed solution, including issues of general concerns about further militarization of law enforcement, that it ignores the very studies it cites and may very well help to create rogue and unfit operators.

115. As noted previously, he told several people he was going to be conducting some 'missions'

prior to setting off on his real or imaginary one.

116. Many undercover operations gather evidence of past or future criminal activity; the latter, 'pre-crime' variety involves coaxing targets into revealing their willingness or predisposition to commit illegal actions. A number of government agencies employ covert methods for other purposes though. Efforts pertaining to national security, sometimes falling under the rubric of 'fusion intelligence sup-port activities,' may seek to obtain socio-cultural information on targeted groups for the purposes of strategic planning, policy formation, threat assessment and counterinsurgency operations. Sociocul-tural intelligence refers to data about "social, cultural, and human domain data" that provides under-standings of "identity-related, communal, cultural, and other factors [that] influence [the] decisions, perspectives and behaviors" of the individual and groups examined (Robert R. Tomes "Toward A Smarter Military Socio-Cultural Intelligence and National Security" Parameters V. 45 N.2, 2015:62). Examples include operations such as Alliance, Northstar and PATCON; PATCON because despite wide-ranging blanket information gathered about target populations, no criminal prosecutions re-sulted from the operation so, given its scope, duration and actual accomplishments, it is not wholly unreasonable to wonder if another, deeper, objective existed.

Private companies, sometimes acting as 'contractors,' do deploy undercover operatives, and are able to do so with far less oversight than government agencies. "In 1981, Executive Order 12333 granted U.S. intelligence agencies the right to enter into contracts with private companies for authorized intelligence purposes which need not be disclosed. This provided a basis for some of the arms smuggling operations using private airlines in the Contra war in Nicaragua" (Jeremy Kuzmarov "The Privatization of War: Private Mercenaries and the "War on Terror" in American Foreign Policy" Asia – *Pacific Journal*, Dec. 31, 2014) The Washington Post reported that in 2010, 1,931 private companies were working on intelligence, counter-terrorism, or homeland security for the U.S. government (Washington Post "A Hidden World, Growing Beyond Control" July 19, 2010). Historically, clandestine activities have sometimes involved diversion of property (theft) for funding purposes, sabotage, propaganda, blackmail and, in certain circumstances, violence.

117. Girodo 1997:248.

118. Hoffman, 1998: 36,61,62; *Toronto Star* "Lee Harvey Oswald revisited Why Oklahoma City bomber Timothy McVeigh can be seen as spiritual brother to JFK assassin" June 7, 1997, Philip Marchand.

119. Smith was not unfamiliar with Dissociative Identity Disorder, especially ones involving mil-itary personnel. Beyond having studied under Dr. Jolly West, in 1999, Stephen Jones retained Smith as an expert in defense of an Air Force sergeant accused of murdering his ex-wife's boy-friend. Smith testified that the man was dissociated and on "automatic pilot" when he committed the murder (NewsOK "$400,000 Bond Set In Enid Murder Case" Aug 28, 1999).

120. *Rolling Stone*, "American Blood: A Journey through the Labyrinth of Dallas and JFK" Dec. 3, 1983; *Toronto Star* , June 7, 1997.

121. Herbeck and Michel, 286.

122. The frequent discrepancies in McVeigh's bombing story included, but were not limited to: prior involvement in other crimes; his exact relationship with the WPM, generally, and residents of Elohim City and the Aryan Republican Army bank robbers, specifically; his actual number of accomplices, their identities; the aliases and disguises he used; the extent to which he conducted surveillance of the Murrah before the 19th of April and his ignorance of the daycare center located there; his (and the Ryder's) movements and exact locations from the time the bomb was allegedly built in Kansas until the time it was delivered to the Murrah and even the clothes he wore the day of the bombing.

Dr. Halleck said that during one recent conversation, McVeigh hinted at and seemed ready to discuss his co-conspirators but sought Halleck's assurance that he would not write a book "telling the whole world in ten years who else was involved in this thing." Halleck assured him he wouldn't but decided not to push him about the issue and McVeigh did not elaborate in this instance. During this same conversation, Halleck said he felt that somebody should confront McVeigh about what Lee Norton had learned about him through his interviews but wanted to wait a few weeks, as he had not yet gotten all the information he could from him and he would probably shut down if confronted.

123. Members of the Jones Team who suspected or believed others were involved based this belief on the existence of many eye witnesses who reported that they observed McVeigh with these Others at various times (including during the rental of the Ryder truck and the morning of the bombing); his phone calls to Elohim City (and other notable faces within the WPM) in the days and weeks leading up to it; and the analysis of several counter-terrorism experts who concluded that additional manpower had been needed to accomplish the bombing.

124. Jones 1998:125.

125. Psychosis is a medical term denotes a 'loss of contact with reality,' often accompanied by frighteningly paranoid delusions and disorganized speech that jumps from topic to topic without explicating the links between them.

126. His ongoing anger concerning the polygraph results and their continued disbelief could be seen when, after being asked by his legal team on several occasions to describe the morning of the bombing McVeigh responded by writing that "if one more motherfucker asks me where I parked my car, I'm gonna hit them sooo [sic.] hard their mama's gonna get a black eye! Instead of 'testing' me, I suggest you put this information to use...if you can't put it to use, why the fuck ask me about it 100-odd times." The problem was he kept changing the story so, despite his threats, their doubts persisted. Some members of the Jones Team found information about Others Unknown inconsequential and perhaps even detrimental to a defense case including attorney Christopher Tritico who later stated that, " Quite frankly, my view of the Others, the other conspirators, was that proving he had someone else helping him only gets him and someone else executed. It doesn't win the case... In order to win the case, [we needed to] forget about this other guy... even if he existed. The fact that Tim didn't answer some of the questions Stephen wanted him to answer... those were questions that I would never have asked him in the first place" (Author interview of Stephen Jones, Oklahoma City, Oklahoma, Dec. 27, 2007; Author interview of Christopher Tritico, Houston, Texas, Dec. 27, 2010).

127. At the same time, Halleck noted that McVeigh had become increasingly depressed and agitated about the lack of privacy his confinement afforded him.

128. Mickey told Norton that she had isolated herself from the outside world, suspicious of even her friends' motives for associating with her at a time like this. Mickey told Norton that she was suffering physical discomfort from a recent tooth extraction and was facing other stress including the fact that her husband, 15 years younger than her, had fallen out of love with her and was going to divorce her.

129. Mickey's attorney confirmed to Norton both what Norton herself had observed and what Jennifer had told her, mainly that she had become (like her son) "increasingly paranoid and fragmented." He told Norton that at first he thought her concerns might be warranted given the nature of the case but her grasp of reality seemed to be waning beyond what he could consider possible.

130. Mickey suggested to Norton and Burr that, "there were actually two forces at work, the malevolent FBI which was trying to get information and make her think she was crazy, and a benevolent, unknown group who were trying to protect [her]" (Jones Collection).

131. Burr made a point of noting that of all the people in McVeigh's life, Mickey was the most open in expressing her true thoughts and feelings, in fact she was the first to do so with any depth. Despite how frightened and painful her world was, she had tried very hard to be mentally "present" during their conversation.

132. McVeigh's visits with doctors continued after his trial until his death. David Paul Hammer, not knowing about McVeigh's previous medical history (unless McVeigh told him), wrote that while on death row, McVeigh was so self-conscious about his legacy that sometimes "he would get sick and describe his symptoms to those close to him in order for them to inform the physician's assistant and send the prescriptions [he needed] to him. About the only illness he would admit to was acid reflux and, only because it was so well documented as he was so incredibly miserable with his antacids he couldn't tolerate it" (Hammer 2004: 80).

133. *Seattle Times* "Syringes Found On Oklahoma Bomb Suspects' Food Trays"Aug. 28, 1995;
At first, Warden Thompson denied the incident ever happened but the number of other guards who said it had, made it hard to deny. Ten years later two El Reno guards were found guilty of causing the death of an inmate after they set fire to his mattress although their sentences were deferred.

134. Mildner issued an order that only one officer be allowed to handle the food trays delivered to McVeigh and Nichols and that all trays be dispersed randomly to all prisoners.

135. Jones Collection; James Nichols, *Freedom's End: Conspiracy In Oklahoma, as Told To Robert S. Papovich.* Freedoms End, Decker, Michigan. 1997: 345, 346.

136. Jones Collection; Jones 1998/2001: 140.

137. Stuart Grassian "Psychiatric Effects of Solitary Confinement" *Washington University Journal of Law & Policy*, V. 22, No. 24, 2006: 333.

138. Nichols 343-355.
In March 1996, Jones informed James and a Nichols family friend that all letters to McVeigh would go through him from now on. While James Nichols was certainly not a neutral source and there would be logical reasons why communication with him could harm McVeigh in a legal sense, it does appear that Jones exerted a great amount of control over McVeigh's communications with the outside world, especially when McVeigh tried to have Jones fired (see Introduction).

139. *USA Today,* "FBI Agents Dissect McVeigh's Past" May 3, 1995, Haya El Nasser; *USA Today,* "Inquisitors Probe For Clues in Mind of Oklahoma Blast Suspect" May 4, 1995; *New York Times* "McVeigh's Mind: A Special Report, Oklahoma Bombing Suspect, Unraveling of a Frayed Life" Dec. 31, 1995, John Kifner.
The May 1995 article noted that the FBI was in possession of the military records and then relayed rumors that he had performed less than perfectly on his Special Forces psychological testing.

140. Russell E. Palarea, Ph.D. (Psychological Services Unit, Naval Criminal Investigative Service) "Expert Opinion: Operation Psychology: An Emerging Discipline" AP-LS News, Fall 2007: 9-11; *Educing Information: Interrogation: Science and Art, Foundations for the Future.* Intelligence Science Board , Center for Strategic Intelligence Research, National Defense Intelligence College, Intelligence Science Board, NDIC Press, Washington, D.C. , December 2006.

141. Michael G. Gelles., Charles Patrick Ewing. "Ethical Concerns in Forensic Consultation Regarding National Safety and Security" *Journal of Threat Assessment* V. 2 No. 3, 2003: 96, 97.

142. Towards the end of 1996, the Jones Team renewed their attempts, begun in late 1995, to obtain from the DOJ surveillance tapes from McVeigh's arrival at Tinker Air Force base as well as details about the FEMA and OK State Dept. of Mental Health funded 'Project Heartland,' the trauma team West coordinated from Tinker. On the same day the Jones Team placed the call to West, they began a renewed search for the missing portions of McVeigh's military records. When, in 2007, I asked Jones if West had any involvement with McVeigh, Jones prevaricated, and while he clearly remembered who West was and mentioned West's involvement in the Patty Hearst case, said he had "no knowledge that [Dr.] West had any first hand involvement in the case." Then, without being asked about Tinker AFB, continued, "I now know," said Jones, "that in reality [the FBI] really didn't care about the handwriting sample. They were hoping that McVeigh could speak

because they wanted to look at his teeth" (Author interview of Stephen Jones, Oklahoma City, Oklahoma, Dec. 27, 2007). Jones did not mention that Smith was West's student or that the defense team called West at least once, inquiring about his services but at the time I was unaware of the phone calls the Jones Team made to West. In 2011, Coyne was less sure but still ambiguous. When asked about the involvement of West, if any, Coyne responded "not to my knowledge. He may have been [involved]" (Author Interview with Randall Coyne, January 5, 2011, Oklahoma City, Oklahoma). Coyne's response appears sincere in light of the fact that Coyne (and other Jones Team attorneys like Christopher Tritico) did not know Smith had continued to treat McVeigh past his evaluation.

143. Hoffman 55, 59, 60. Beyond a number of news articles, West confirmed during a 1996 'consultation' conversation with Jones Team attorney Andrew Murphy that he had been present twice in Oklahoma City after the bombing as part of an initiative administering psychiatric services to survivors and first responders and training sessions to local mental health services. West added, "Now this won't affect my objectivity with respect to your client at all, but it is something that you should know" (Jones Collection).In fact, the Jones Team requested records that would help them construct a chronology of the events of McVeigh's time at Tinker Air Force Base, although the reasons for this could have nothing to do with West.

144. Robert Guffey. *Cryptoscatology: Conspiracy Theory as Art Form.* TrineDay, Walterville, Oregon, 2012.

145. In 1948, the U.S. Navy initiated Project CHATTER, whose objective was to test an assortment of drugs to determine if any of them increase the odds of extracting information during interrogations. CHATTER ended in 1953, shortly before the Korean War ended.

146. Irving L. Jannis, "Are the Cominform Countries Using Hypnotic Techniques to Elicit Confessions in Public Trials?" Santa Monica, Rand Corporation, Air Force Project Rand Research Memorandum, RM-161, April 25, 1949: 1,3,6-7, 16-20; Alfred W. McCoy, *A Question of Torture: CIA Interrogation from the Cold War to the War on Terror*, New York: Holt, 2006: 22.

147. CIA MKUltra Document "Narrative Description of the Overt and Covert Activities of [Redacted] January 1, 1950 in CIA MKUltra Documents, disk 2, MORI ID no. 190882, National Security Archive; CIA "Report of the Ad Hoc Medical Study Group" Jan. 15, 1953; Senate, Select Committee TO Study Government Operations With Respect to Government Activities, 94th Congress, 2nd sess. *Foreign and Military intelligence, Book 1: Final Report,* Washington: Government Printing Office, 1976; CIA Memorandum For: Director Of Central Intelligence, Sub: Successful Application of Narco-Hypnotic Interrogation (Artichoke)), July 14, 1952 (as found in Box 5, CIA Behavior Control Experiments Collection, National Security Archives, Washington, D.C.)

Among the U.S officials instrumental in the Project Paperclip effort who would soon play an important role in Bluebird and other subsequent mind control studies was Boris Pash.

On June 5, 1951, defense and intelligence officials from the U.S., U.K., and Canada met in Montreal to discuss the looming threat of communist brainwashing.

148. American's use of "advanced" techniques on North Korean POW's: John Marks, *The Search For The Manchurian Candidate: The CIA and Mind Control, The Secret History of the Behavioral Sciences*, Dell Publishing, New York, 1979 (in 1988 edition: 25,232 citing numerous CIA documents released to Marks through FOIA in 1977).

Techniques used by Americans on the North Korean POW's, included (among others) traditional hypnosis, drugs and electroshock. While it is widely reported that the term 'brainwashing' resulted from North Korean methods of interrogation, the term first appeared within CIA documents as early as January 1950, prior to the war. The term 'brainwashing' is often said to have been both coined and popularized by journalist Edward Hunter when he used it in a September 1950 Miami News article, and in his 1951 book *Brainwashing in Red China*. Hunter illustrated for readers strange and seemingly magical ways in which Communists were coercing, indoctrinating, and controlling both their own citizens and potentially innocent Americans. According to historians Alfred McCoy and Timothy Melley however, Hunter was a known OSS/CIA propaganda asset and they point out the real origins of the term within CIA documents prior to the start of the Korean War or the publication of Hunt's article. Melley says "[t]he public concept of brainwashing was from the beginning a creation of the CIA" a term whose invention and dissemination into popular consciousness was intended both to "fuel public anxiety" surrounding Communism and to justify their own foray into 'mind control' (Timothy Melley "Brain Warfare: The Covert Sphere, Terrorism, and the Legacy of the Cold War" *Grey Room* 48: Fall 2011, pg. 19-40).

149. CIA "Narrative Description of the Overt and Covert Activities of [Redacted] Jan. 1, 1950; *San Francisco Gate* "How Brainwashing Came To Life And Thrived" Aug. 1, 2004;Marks 21-25, 31, 232 (in 1988 edition: 25,232 citing numerous CIA documents released through FOIA in 1977); George Estabrooks quoted in Argossy, February 1950 (as cited in several works including W. H. Boward. *Operation Mind Control*, 1978).

Estabrooks proposal concerning the possibility of inducing individuals to commit murder opined that, "Any 'accidents' that might occur during the experiments will simply be charged to profit and loss, a very trifling portion of that enormous wastage in human life which is part and parcel of war."

150. *The Brooklyn Daily Eagle* (Brooklyn, NY) "'Brain-Washing' Cure Undertaken At Valley Force" May 2, 1953.

151. *Los Angeles Times* "Louis J. and Kathryn West: Probers of the Mind, Dedicated Activists: He Is Director of the Neuropsychiatric Institute at UCLA" Oct. 27, 1985, Michael Berges.

152. Frank Summers, PhD., ABPP "Making Sense of the APA: A History of the Relationship Between Psychology and the Military" *Psychoanalytic Dialogues: The International Journal of Relational Perspectives*, 2008: 624.

153. Jim Keith, *Mind Control, World Control*, Adventures Unlimited Press, Kempton, Illinois, 1997:113 (referencing Glenn Krawczyk "Mind Control Techniques and Tactics of the New World Order" Nexus Magazine, December/ January 1993.

While I have been able to locate the original Nexus Magazine reproducing the text of the January 1953 CIA memo, I have been unable to find mention of this same memo elsewhere. However, West's resume listing various dates and locations associated with his military service as well as news articles corroborating the establishment of just such a center corroborate the substance of the memo as quoted by Keith and Krawczyk.

154. Other schools using DDD as a central tenant of their educational program included: Army and Navy training programs at Camp Mackall, NC (est., 1953) and USMC survival school located at Glenview Naval Air Station, IL (est. 1955).

In September 1955, a news article announced that the US Air Force was testing new methods that the U.S. might use someday to extract information from prisoners of war. The program was operating out of Stead Air Force Base in Nevada. The article noted that pilots were trained to withstand enemy brainwashing techniques if captured. Quoted in the article was Maj. John Oliphant, "an ex POW himself" who said that the Stead was also a center for setting practices for US enemy captives. "The U.S. military does not, of course, torture prisoners of war," reported the article, but getting all possible information from them was important. Historically, such methods have ranged from "the physically brutal to the psychologically subtle." Thus far, 20,000 combat air crewman undergoing the 17 day survival training school at Stead had been subjected to "Chinese interrogation tricks," so that they would be prepared if ever taken prisoner. The news reports opined, "presumably they are more civilized than torturers" but instead, "are believed to rely more on psychological suggestion" and "weird masks, eerie costumes and strange and fearsome rites in a darkened room sometimes can induce a flesh crawling horror of the unknown that will loosen a prisoners tongue" (Monroe Morning World (Monroe, Louisiana) "Air Force Tests New Ways To

Get Information From War Prisoners" Sep. 18, 1955). While West is not mentioned in the article, from 1956 until 1958, he was on the Advisory Council of the US Air Force Office of Scientific Research, Behavioral Sciences Division. In 1965, West emphasized to reporters that soldiers could be trained to resist brainwashing and mentioned the existence of just such a program at Stead Air Force Base in Reno, Nevada. There, said West, soldiers are subjected to indoctrination, mock interrogations, forced marches and other techniques including sleep deprivation, and minimal food. Through such methods, soldiers learn that there is a ceiling to pain, that the situation is temporary, and that there are ways they can refuse to hear or give themselves to unwanted suggestions; all of which allows them to survive such an ordeal intact for up to 6 months (The Evening Review (East Liverpool, Ohio) "Can A Brain Be Washed?" Dec. 10, 1965).

155. Alfred W. McCoy, *A Question of Torture: CIA Interrogation from the Cold War to the War on Terror*, New York: Holt, 2006: 7.

HEF was originally called the Society for the Investigation of Human Ecology but was changed to HEF in 1961.

156. Rebecca Lemov, *World As Laboratory: Experiments With Mice, Mazes, and Men*, Hill and Wang, New York, 2005: 201.

In addition, declassified MKUltra founding documents, list the objectives of conducting research into "aspects of the magicians' art useful in covert operations [including] surreptitious delivery of drug[s]," polygraphs, "toxins, drugs, and biochemical in human tissues; provision of exotic pathogens [and] effective delivery systems," sprays and aerosols and other chemical and biological warfare techniques (John Marks, *The Search For The Manchurian Candidate*, Times Books, 1979; Harvey Weinstein, *Father, Son, and CIA*, Lorimer, 1988:129, 130 (both Lemov and Weinstein citing and referring to numerous CIA documents released to Marks through FOIA in 1977). MK- DELTA was established at the same time as MKUltra and acted as the operational arm of MKUltra mainly as it pertained to "the use of biochemical in clandestine operations" (Bowart citing Allen Dulles CIA memo April 3, 1953).

157. In his proposal for a similar project also housed at Cornell, called QK- Hilltop, Wolff requested of the CIA that, "where any of the studies involve potential harm to the subject, we expect the Agency to make available suitable subjects and a proper place for the performance of necessary experiments." (CIA documents cited by several authors including Michael Otterman, *American Torture: From The Cold War To Abu Ghraib and Beyond* Melbourne University Press, London 2007:25; Wienstien 140; Marks 33). Researchers found witting subjects by offering addiction patients at the Addiction Research Center in Lexington, Kentucky, their drug of choice in exchange for participation in the studies including marijuana, cocaine, PCP, ether, mescaline, and heroin. Although the program was later scrapped, the effects endured by the soldiers at Edgewood Chemical Arsenal who were given powerful drugs and exposed to radiation, did not prevent the CIA from considering the possibility of putting LSD in a city water supply to incapacitate civilian populations.

158. *The Lawton Constitution* (Lawton, Oklahoma) "Does Turnpike Hypnotize Drivers?" April 25, 1956; *The Indian Journal* (Eufaula, Oklahoma). "New Highways Cause Hypnosis" June 11, 1959

West told the *LA Times* that when OU offered him the position he at first declined, citing his commitment to the Air Force but through the direct intervention of Oklahoma Senator Mike Monroney, arrangements were made for him to work both at OU and for the Air Force and for two years he went back and forth from Lackland AFB to OU.

159. J.L. West "Psychophysiological Studies of Hypnosis and Suggestibility" and "Studies of Dissociative States" (proposal) MK ULTRA Subproject 43 (cited in Colin A. Ross, *The C.I.A. Doctors: Human Rights Violations By American Psychiatrists*, Greenleaf Book Group Press, 2006: 107,109).

West received a $20,800 grant for this project in 1956. In the paper attached to his grant proposal, West wrote: "Dissociative phenomena are found in everyday life. Such manifestations include "highway hypnosis," states of "fascination" in flyers, hypnagogic and phantasy hallucinations, transient aesthesias, and many other examples. These reactions have many features in common with a variety of clinical disorders including "sleep paralysis," trance states, Gilles de la Tourette's disease, latah, "Arctic hysteria," and a number of other disturbances in addition to the well-known dissociative reactions of the text-books...." West continued to write on dissociation, and authored a chapter in a 1967 psychiatric textbook, entitled "Dissociative Reaction." In it, West explained that dissociation concerned "psycho biological modulation of information ---incoming, stored, and outgoing—by the brain" and explained that dissociative responses occurred within a continuum of normal to pathological.

160. During the 1950's West's publications, appointments and other professional activities included: USAF Office of Scientific Research Advisory Council for the Behavioral Sciences Division (1955-1975); Consultant in Psychiatry at the OKC VA Hospital (1956-1969), Chief of Oklahoma Medical Research Foundation in OKC (1956-1969) as well as Consultant in Psychiatry at the Air Force Hospital, at Force Base, Oklahoma (1956-1966); ASAF National Consultant in Psychiatry to the Surgeon General (1956- 1958); Board of Directors and Board of Scientific Advisors for the Institute for Research in Hypnosis, the American Medical Association's Council on Mental Health and Committee on Hypnosis (1958-1966); *The International Journal of Clinical and Experimental Hypnosis* (editor, 1958-1966).

Topics of West's writings and titles of his papers during the 1950's include: the effects of hypnotic suggestion on pain perception and galvanic skin responses (1952); measuring psychopathology using the MMPI (1953); the effect of drugs on emotions (1955); evaluations of subcoma insulin therapy (1955); alcoholism in the military (1956); and medical and psychiatric considerations in survival training (1956); "Brainwashing, Conditioning, and DDD (Debility, Dependency, and Dread)" (1957); Chinese Communist's use of forceful indoctrination methods on US Air Force prisoners held by them (1957); "An Approach to the Problem of Homosexuality in the Military Service" (1958); POW's, "psychiatric aspects of training for honorable survival as a POW" (1958), a paper published by the Air Force Personnel and Training Research Center, portions of which remained classified as of 1995; the effects of sleep deprivation (1959).

161. *The News-Palladium* (Benton Harbor, Michigan) "Eight Days Minus Sleep Is His Goal" Jan. 20, 1959; Carrol *Daily Times Herald* (Carroll, Iowa) "Nears Goal of No Sleep in 8/12 Days; Polio Stunt Turns Into a Scientific Achievement" Jan. 28, 1959 ; *The Lawton Constitution* (Lawton, Oklahoma) "Sleeplessness Dangers Cited" June 26, 1958; *The Oregon Statesman* (Salem, Oregon) "Test Hints Loss of Sleep Stirs Latent Psychopathic Tendencies" June 26, 1958; *The Lincoln Star* (Lincoln, Nebraska) "All of us are 'Micro-Sleep' Walkers in Waking Hours' June 21, 1959.

West, Chief psychiatrist at OU and psychiatric consultant to the surgeon general of the US Air Force was Chief of the 12-man team of psychiatrists, psychologists and medical doctors observing the entire contest to determine the mental and physical effects of sleep deprivation. A man only identified as "Williams" monitored an instrument-packed room from nearby Hotel Astor in order to monitor changes in the brain and central nervous system. West explained, "Every utterance, every attitude during this great stress has been noted down. There is nothing we haven't measured. We know him through and through and I'll tell you something, he's a mad man." West later told reporters that for three months after the contest, the radio announcer had "paranoiac ideas- feelings of being persecuted." Finally, West told reporters, the man sought treatment at a VA hospital.

Reports about micro-sleep note that Dr. West was the expert who conducted exhaustive studies to determine why US pilots would give false confessions about the US' use of germ warfare. After considering hypnosis, conditioned reflex, "and a number of diabolical schemes," West concluded that sleep deprivation was a major factor as it provokes delusions, hallucinations and confusions to the point where, by the time the pilots made the false confessions, they were technically temporarily insane. This was supported when the disc jockey West observed, underwent progressive disorientation. In 1959, the U.S. Junior Chamber of Commerce nominated West for the distinction of being one of the "Ten Most Outstanding Young Men In America." Whatever else he was, West was outstanding. The titles of his work stand out prominently among other researchers at this time.

162. Frank Summers, PhD., ABPP "Making Sense of the APA: A History of the Relationship Between Psychology and the Military" *Psychoanalytic Dialogues: The International Journal of Relational Perspectives*, 2008: 624 (citing E. Karcher., Army social science programs and plans. In *Symposium Proceedings. The U.S. Army's Limited War Mission and Social Science Research*, Washington, D.C., March 1962: 348) and Summers 625.

PSYWAR refers to "any action which is practiced mainly by psychological methods with the aim of evoking a planned psychological reaction in other people" (Béla Szunyogh, *Psychological warfare: an introduction to ideological propaganda and the techniques of psychological warfare*. William-Frederick Press. 1953: 13). PSYWAR is meant to influence value and belief systems, emotions, motives, reasoning and ultimately, the behaviors of individuals and groups, to destroy will and morale, and induce confession and is often employed in combination with black and false flag operations.

In 1942, the OSS, who already had their own PSYWAR division, defined PSYWAR as: "the coordination and use of all means, including moral and physical, by which the end is attained--other than those of recognized military operations, but including the psychological exploitation of the result of those recognized military actions--which tend to destroy the will of the enemy to achieve victory and to damage his political or economic capacity to do so; which tend to deprive the enemy of the support, assistance or sympathy of his allies or associates or of neutrals, or to prevent his acquisition of such support, assistance, or sympathy; or which tend to create, maintain, or increase the will to victory of our own people and allies to acquire, maintain, or to increase the support, assistance and sympathy of neutrals" (Alfred H. Paddock, Jr., *US Army Special Warfare, Its Origins, Psychological and Unconventional Warfare, 1941-1952*, Washington, DC: National Defense University Press, 1982:11). In 1952, Brigadier General Robert A. McClure, 'the founder of American PSYWAR,' established the Psychological Warfare Center at Fort Bragg, North Carolina.

163. *Newsweek* "A Tortured Past: The CIA's extensive use of enhanced interrogation techniques started long before 9/11" Dec. 26, 2014, Jeff Stein; Otterman:58; CIA, *KUBARK Counterintelligence Interrogation* (July 1963); Melley 2011: 33.

KUBARK also contained allusions to "medical, chemical or electrical methods or materials ... used to induce acquiescence" (KUBARK 1963). Historian and cultural critic Timothy Melley, explained what was meant by 'weird': "the central principle of [KUBARK] is to create radical ontological uncertainty in the subject by advancing and slowing clocks, preventing knowledge of day and night, feeding the prisoner at bizarre intervals, drugging and moving the prisoner during sleep, inquiring why he tried to hang himself (when he did not), and so on" (Melley 2011: 33). While KUBARK quoted liberally from major MK funded psychiatrists and psychologists including Hinckle, Wolff, Hebb, and Biderman, at least one newsreport claimed that KUBARK was actually the work of Dr. West and Dr. William Sargent, his British counterpart (See *Sunday Express* "British doctor who tortured his patients in NHS hospitals" Oct. 26, 2008). KUBARK made mention of ongoing MKUltra experiments (although not referred to by that name), but lamented that while some of them had applications for counterintelligence interrogations, they had not yet been tested in the field. But this was about to change.

164. McCoy 71 (citing DOD Memo, Sub: USSOUTHCOM CI Training-Supplemental Information (U) July 31, 1991 and DOD Memo, SUB: Interim Report on Improper Material in USSOUTHCOM Training Manuals, Oct. 4, 1991.

OPS provided the foreign police forces with interrogation equipment including polygraph and electroshock machines. By 1971, OSP had trained over one million police officers in 47 countries by 1971 including in South Vietnam, Brazil, Uruguay, Iran, Philippines, and the Dominican Republic.

In the years leading up to and throughout the Vietnam War, CIA and military mind control/brainwashing/interrogation research expanded beyond behavioral approaches and came to include mass persuasion and propaganda methods.

165. McCoy 64, and 67 (citing House of Representatives, 92nd Congress, 1st Sess., Subcommittee of the Committee on Government Operations, Hearings on Aug. 2, 1971, "US Assistance Programs In Vietnam" Washington, Government Printing Office, 1971:349); Alex Constantine. *Psychic Dictatorship In The U.S.A.* Feral House. Portland, Oregon. 1995:172; William Blum, *Killing Hope: U.S. Military And CIA Interventions Since World War II.* Common Courage Press. Monroe, ME. 1995:51, 52, 58 (citing *New York Times* "Dark Side Of Up: Colby of CIA- CIA of Colby" July 1, 1973; *Washington Post,* "Sterile, Depersonalized Murder" Aug. 3, 1971; *New York Times,* "Ex-Soldiers Report Vietnam Slayings," Aug. 3, 1971).

The numbers of dead are unknown; it is estimated that by 1972, the U.S. Phoenix personnel killed 20,000 while the police forces they trained, working under U.S. Phoenix operators were responsible for upwards of 108-109 deaths.

166. Beyond those already noted previously, from 1963 until 1973, when limited information about MKUltra, MK-SEARCH and some other related projects was made known to the public, West's official appointments and professional activities, included: Professor and eventually Head of the Department of Psychiatry at University of Oklahoma School of Medicine's Neurology and Behavioral Sciences in Oklahoma City (1954 to 1969), during which time he also served as Psychiatrist and Chief at University of Oklahoma Hospitals; Chief Consultant to the USAF Aero-Space Medical Center (1961-1966); North American Co- Chairman of the Section on Clinical Hypnosis (1962-1968); U.S. Veterans Administration's National Advisory Committee on Psychiatry, Neurology, and Psychology (member, 1968-1972, chairman, 1970-1972); VA's Special Medical Advisory Group; President and President and Vice President of the Pavlovian Society.

Some of the topics and titles of papers written and presented by West from 1960 until 1973, include (but are not limited to): psychophysiology of hypnosis (1960); the applicability of personality theory and drive concepts to the study of suggestibility (1962); physiological theories of hypnosis (1962); training in medical hypnosis (1962); the use of hypnosis in medical practice (1963); hypnosis and experimental psychopathology (1963); 'the problem of hypnotizability (1963); the experimental usefulness of hypnosis in psychopathology (1964); the 'dangers of hypnosis' (1965); the hypnotic induction of anxiety (1965); dissociative reactions (1967); 'Hallucinations (1962, 1965); the psychosis and psychopathology of sleep deprivation (1962, 1967); his general theory of hallucinations and dreams (1962); 'some psychiatric aspects of civil defense' (1962); brainwashing, sensory isolation, sleep (in general) (1963); elephants and psychiatry (1963); brainwashing and the American character (1964); 'exposing the myth that Korea GI's weren't tough' (1964); monkeys and brainwashing (1964); "Sexual Behavior and Military Law" (1965); 'types of inpatients' (1965); the treatment of insomnia (1966); personality changes linked to sleep deprivation (1966); the dynamics of scuba diving (1966); and 'brainwashing, conditioning, and DDD (debility, dependency, and dread)' (1966); 'transcendental meditation and other nonprofessional psychotherapies' (1967); 'biosocial adaptation and correlates of acculturation in the Tarahumara ecosystem' (1970); behavior therapy (1972).

167. *The Ottawa Journal* (Ottawa, Canada) "Elephant Never Had a Chance After LSD Shot" March 4, 1969; The Guardian "Life: Far Out: Tusko's Last Trip" Feb, 26, 2004.

According to one account, Tusko had actually died of muscle spasms and heart failure in response to the LSD West gave him rather than as a 'direct' result of the LSD itself. The poor guy just got overwhelmed with the good doctor's medicine. In another account, Tusko died after having passed out and West injected him with another drug meant to revive him. Another account, published in The Guardian in 2002, says Tusko died of asphyxiation.

168. *San Bernardino County Sun* (San Bernardino, California) "Doctor Reveals Why Youth Take Drugs" March 17, 1970;Lemov 202.

In April 1960, West was an honored guest at an Arizona Medical Association conference along with Col. George H. White (Federal Bureau of Narcotics). White was awarded the Treasury Medal for exceptional service for his wiping out narcotic rings in the Middle East and Europe as a special undercover agent. During WWII, White served in the OSS. In 1960, White was district supervisor of the State of California, Nevada and Arizona. He had been with the FBN for 25 years and was a recognized authority on narcotic law enforcement. White was known for being a cruel, ruthless person.

169. Lee and Shlain, 188, 189 (quoting and referencing Nicholas von Hoffman, *We Are The People Our Parents Warned Us Against*, Fawcett Publications, Greenwich Village, NY, 1973; Louis Jolyon West and James R. Allen "Flight From Violence: The Hippies And The Green Rebellion" *American Journal Of Psychiatry*, Sep. 3, 1968); UCLA Library Special Collections, Charles E. Young Research Library 'Louis Jolyon West papers' 2014.

Related topics and titles of papers written and presented by West from 1960 until 1973, include (but are not limited to): the use of LSD in psychotherapy (1960); psychopharmacology (1961); "Lysergic Acid Diethylamide: Its Effects on a Male Asiatic Elephant." (1962) ; hallucinogens (1967, 1972); 'the marihuana [sic] problem' and the effects of marijuana (1968); 'runaways, hippies and marijuana' (1971); 'the green rebellion' (1967); 'hippie culture' and 'the two hippie worlds – true and 'plastic' (1968); 'three rebellions: red, black and green' (1968); 'campus unrest and counter culture' (1970); 'Flight from violence: Hippies and the green rebellion' (1971); 'runaways, hippies and marijuana' (1971); psychiatrists and social problems (1971); violence (1972).

170. *The Lawton Constitution* (Lawton, Oklahoma) "Two Instances Of LSD Use Are Confirmed" Aug 17, 1966.

Another doctor quoted in the article, Dr. Vernon Sisney, a psychologist at the OKC VA hospital, said there was little evidence that LSD was being used in Oklahoma.

171. L. J. West., R. K. Siegel, *Hallucinations: Behavior, Experience, and Theory*, New York: John Wiley & Sons. 1975:288.

172. Pierce and West found that the experiences of the 9 'negro protesters' only strengthened their already existing character strengths and had given them confidence to become leaders and they went on to lead successful lives, personally and professionally. Their only related weakness appeared to be that they focused more on "the race crisis and its ramifications" than they did international, national or even local current events. By May of 1964, when West and Pierce presented their findings, "almost all" OKC restaurants, hotels and amusement parks had eliminated racial segregation and the City Council was even "considering outlawing racial discrimination in places of public accommodation" (*The Des Moines Register* (Des Moines, Iowa) "How Nations First Sit-In Affected Lives of 8 Negroes" May 10, 1964).

173. *St. Louis Dispatch* "Letters From the People: Covert Testing Endangered American Lives" (editorial) Aug. 15, 1994; *The Danville Register* (Danville, Virginia) "Campus Rebels Yearning For Omnipotence They Held In Cradle, Says Psychiatrist" Nov. 10, 1968; *The Gastonia Gazette* (Gastonia, North Carolina) "When His Majesty has become 20 years old" Nov. 11, 1968; Jonathan M. Metzl, *The Protest Psychosis: How Schizophrenia Became A Black Disease*, Beacon Press, Boston, MA, 2010:101 (discussing and quoting Louis J. West, M.D., Chester M. Pierce "Six Years Of Sit-Ins: Psychodynamic Causes And Effects" *International Journal Of Social Psychiatry*, V. 12 No. 1, 1966, pg. 73-80.

Los Angeles Times Oct. 27, 1985.

One of the 'black's West appointed to OU was Chester Pierce, with whom he dosed Tusko and wrote the aforementioned article in 1966. Related topics and titles of papers written and presented by West from 1960 until 1973, include (but are not limited to): 'principles that should underlie federal legislation for drug abuse control' (1970); alcoholism and narcotics' (1970); 'the drug abuse crisis in perspective' (1972); 'the therapy of human injustice' (1962); the act of violence (1963); racial violence (1965); 'prevention of racial violence in the urban ghetto' (1967); 'psychobiology of racial violence' (1967); psychiatry and civil rights (1968).

174. *Valley Morning Star* (Harlingen, Texas) "More Mental Testing Asked For Jack Ruby" April 23, 1964; *Greely Daly Tribune* (Greely, Texas) "Ruby Insanity Trial Now Appears Certain" April 27, 1964; *Florence Morning News* (Florence, South Carolina) "Ruby Beats Head Against Cell Wall In

Jailer's Absence" April 27, 1964.

Ruby's previous attorneys had claimed, during his trial that Ruby had suffered some sort of epilepsy that caused him to black out and kill Oswald. While the pre-trial mental evaluation indicated that Ruby was emotionally disturbed, had marked symptoms of depression, lapses of memory, but was sane, his post-trial attorney, Smith, said the medical experts who issued the pre-trial tests "were deprived of corroborative and/or clinching evidence." About a week after his attorney's request to retain Dr. West, when his jailer was momentarily absent, Ruby deliberately rammed his head into the wall, according to Sheriff Bill Decker. Decker said that Ruby had refused to go to bed and had been talking with one of the guards assigned to watch him around the clock. At about 1 am he had asked the guard for a drink of water and, just as the guard was about to leave the cell, Ruby lowered his head, took several fast steps and then rammed his head against the cell wall until the guard restrained him. Ruby did not lose consciousness during the incident. He was then rushed to a Dallas hospital under heavy guard for examination and X-rays that revealed that the only damage he suffered was a knot on his head. After he was returned to his cell, Ruby attempted to rip his clothing into strips and so, as a precautionary measure, all furniture was removed from his cell and only the mattress left. Later that evening, Dr. West visited Ruby but when asked about Ruby's condition by reporters, West declined to reveal his findings. Media accounts said that after the head banging incident, during the April 1964 hearing to determine if Ruby was to be remanded to a hospital, Ruby appeared extremely pale and obviously agitated.

175. *Tucson Daily Citizen* (Tucson, Arizona) "Give Ruby Immediate Hearing, Says Lawyer" May 21, 1964; Testimony of Dr. William Robert Beavers as given to Mr. Arlen Specter, Assistant Council of the President's Commission (Warren Commission), Dallas County Jail, Dallas, Texas, July 18, 1964.

176. *The Corpus Christi Caller –Times* (Corpus Christi, Texas) "Psychiatrist Flies To Visit Jack Ruby" June 19, 1964; *The Times Record* (Troy, New York) "Claim Ruby Incoherent" June 20, 1964; *The New-Herald* (Franklin, Pennsylvania) "Ruby's Transfer Will Be Sought" June 22, 1964; *The Brownville Herald* (Brownville, Texas) "Law Bars Ruby From Hospital" July 2, 1964; *Tucson Daily Citizen* (Tucson, Arizona) "Held Incompetent: Guardian For Ruby Sought In Application" July 17, 1964; Bowart 197-200.

After he evaluated Ruby at the Dallas hospital on June 19, 1964, West said Ruby's condition was not different from that of "thousands of mental patients found in asylums across the nation" and warned that if he was not treated in a hospital, Ruby would become hopelessly insane. The next day, his attorney told reporters that Ruby had become so incoherent that nobody could communicate with him and that he was unable to help his defense attorneys prepare their appeal of his death sentence. A few days later, his attorney added that Ruby was "not in touch with reality at all times" and was having "delusions that people are persecuting his family...the man evidently has suicidal tendencies" as he had once charged his head against his cell and another time, tried to jam his finger into a light socket. In early July 1964, Dr. West told reporters that attempts to treat Ruby's mental illness in jail had failed and that his condition was rapidly becoming incurable. Because of this, said West, Ruby would never be executed. Ruby, according to the news report, had only taken one tranquilizing pill. Later that month (July 1964), Jack Ruby's brother Sam Ruby filed an application for legal guardianship of Jack Ruby (age 54) claiming he was "of unsound mind and wholly incompetent." The application was supported by Dr. Emanuel Tanay of Detroit and Dr. West. The application went on to say that there was reason to believe that outside persons would try to exploit Ruby for their own gain. At the time, Ruby's estate consisted of one diamond ring, a wristwatch, and personal items including clothing, books and letters (held by the Dallas City Police Department) as well as "valuable interest in rights to property." The latter would include his rights to the publication of his life story.

177. FBI Director J. Edgar Hoover admitted to White House aide Walter Jenkins, "The thing I am most concerned about...is having something issued so we can convince the public that Oswald is

the real assassin." Assistant Attorney General Nicholas Katzenbach wrote to President Johnson aide Bill Moyers that (1)" The public must be satisfied Oswald was the assassin; that he did not have confederates who are still at large; and that the evidence was such that he would have been convicted at trial" and (2) "Speculation about Oswald's motivation ought to be cut off" (Ray Pratt, Projecting Paranoia: Conspiratorial Visions In American Film, University Of Kansas Press, Lawrence, Kansas, 2001: 222 citing Arthur Schlesinger Jr., *Robert Kennedy and His Times*, V.2, 1978:643).

The issue of hypnotism was recurring in the Kennedy case. David Ferrie, CIA asset and associate of Oswald's was a self-taught hypnotist. Sodium pentothal and hypnosis would be used to test the memories of at least one witness who said they saw Oswald with others, including Ferrie, at critical times prior to the assassination. One news report, noted but dismissed by the Warren Commission, concerned the statements of Bob Mulholland, who told NBC News reporters that a man named 'Fairy' had placed Oswald under hypnosis at Jack Ruby's bar, The Carousel. Mulholland later retracted his statement, saying that's just what he overheard the FBI saying.

178. *The Brownsville Herald* (Brownsville, Texas) "Defense Claiming Sirhan In Trance" Feb. 14, 1969; Shane O'Sullivan, *Who Killed Bobby? The Unsolved Murder of Robert F. Kennedy*, Union Square Press, New York/London, 2008: 39, 296 citing Bernard Diamond's testimony at Sirhan Sirhan's 1969 trial.

179. William Turner and John Christian, *The Assassination Of Robert F. Kennedy: The Conspiracy And Cover-up*, Avalon Publishing Group, Inc., New York, 1978 (paperback edition 2006): 199, 202 (quoting Affidavit by Dr. Simon –Kallas, March 9, 1973; letter from Herbert Spiegel to authors Sep. 3, 1974); O'Sullivan 393 (quoting and referring to author's interviews with Herbert Spiegel); CNN "Convicted RFK assassin Sirhan Sirhan seeks prison release" November 27, 2011, Michael Martinez.

Spiegel explained, "Highly hypnotizable persons, when under the control of unscrupulous persons, are the most vulnerable" to commit acts they never would under normal circumstances. While some think that people cannot be hypnotized to do something against their moral code, they do acknowledge that the person can be convinced that what they are told to do, is actually for the greater good; a belief incorporates the action into their moral code (O'Sullivan 208).

180. Stephen S. Marmer "Dissociation in the 1990's" pg. 238 to 246 in *The Mosaic of Contemporary Psychiatry in Perspective*, Kales, Pierce, Greenblat (editors) Springer-Verlag New York, Inc. 1992.

181. In fact, concludes the author, if we would all just follow West's lead, everybody would have a clearer understanding of dissociation and multiple personality in general. And they are probably right.

Walter Bowart pointed out that Orne, who testified that Hearst was dissociated and brainwashed, would have known very well, given his former career as Head of the Naval Research Committee on Hypnosis and his development of many related coercion methods used by the military.

182. William Graebner, *Patty's Got A Gun: Patricia Hearst In 1970's America*, University of Chicago Press, Chicago, IL, 2008: 6, 69-71 (quoting Patricia Hearst Trial Transcript).

183. Graebner 4.

While Hearst's attorneys were unsuccessful in their attempt to convince the jury she was less culpable for her crimes because of her multiplicity and identity confusion, the 1977 book, *The Many Minds of Billy Milligan*, detailed the first case where multiple personality and dissociation were successfully used as a criminal defense, in this case, for an accused serial rapist.

184. Delgado's work was funded by the Office of Naval Research from 1954 until at least 1960. The CIA took a great interest in the work of Dr. John Lilly, who by 1953 had (like Delgado) devised a way to use implantable electrodes stimulate certain portions of a monkey's brain to induce erections and ejaculation. Lilly refused to conduct classified research, and therefore fell out with the CIA in 1958.

185. According to his obituary Sell "stressed the significance of organism—environment interac-

tions in understanding and predicting behavior; he also emphasized the need to study behavior in its natural setting." His specialized areas of research included "adaptability screening of Air Force pilots," "selection and performance prediction among pilots and aviation personnel" including for NASA, "large-scale personality studies for the Office of Education" developing variables for social adjustment predictions. During his career, Sell received a number of awards including the 1955 Aerospace Medical Association's Longacre Award (*American Psychologist* "Saul B. Sells (1913-1988)" (Obituary) 43:12 Dec. 1988, pg. 1088).

By 1961, at least one CIA report told of the ability to control the movements of dogs using this method. A follow up report just months later, told of successful demonstrations using several species of animals and plans to conduct "special investigations and evaluations" to determine the application "of these techniques to man." (Marks 225,246,247 citing numerous CIA documents released to Marks through FOIA in 1977).

186. Bowart 256 Richard Helms memo to Warren Commission, 1964.

187. General William Westmoreland, July 1970 as quoted by Steven Best, PhD, Douglas Kellner, *The Postmodern Adventure: Science, Technology, and Cultural Studies at the Third Millennium*, The Guilford Press, New York, 2001:85.

188. Jose Delgado, Overview of National Security Agency Technology, 1969; Jose M.R. Delgado, *Physical Control Of The Mind: Toward A Psychocivilized Society*, Harpers, New York, 1969.

189. U.S. Senate Committee on the Judiciary Subcommittee On Constitutional Rights "Individual Rights And The Federal Role In Behavior Modification" U.S. Government Printing Office, Washington, D.C., November 1994:19.

190. Hastings Center Report. V.2. Nov 1972 "Confronting The Other" by Peter Stienfel (pg. 4-6)";Informed Consent: When Can it Be Withdrawn?" by Robert M. Veatch, and Madeline Brady., Jonas Robtscher., "Manipulating the Brain" Brian Hilton (pg. 11); Perry London, "Personal Liberty and Behavior Control Technology" The Hastings Center Report, V. 2 No. 1, Feb. 1972: pg. 4-7.

191. Hastings Center Report. Nov. 1972.

192. Hastings Center Report. Nov. 1972.

193. Hastings Center Report. V.2. Nov 1972 ; Hastings Center Report "Researching Violence: Science, Politics, & Public Controversy" V9, April 1979: pg. 1-19.

194. *Arizona Republic* (Phoenix, Arizona) "Vets 'poor' medical care blamed on Nixon scrimping" Dec. 16, 1969; Hope Star (Hope, Arkansas) "War Causalities Are Also on Mental Side" Dec. 16, 1969; *Independent* (Long Beach, California) "Education in VA Hospitals Urged to End Care Crisis" Dec. 17, 1969; The Times Standard (Eureka, California) "Chemical Brainwash" Dec. 24, 1969; *The Fresno Bee* (Fresno, CA) "Witnesses Tell of Inadequate Care For Veterans" Feb. 1, 1970; *The Fresno Bee* (Fresno, California) ""Commentary: War Still Remains 'Hell'" March 28, 1970.

In 1969, West testified that there were more than 250 patients for each psychiatrist. Sen. Alan Cranston (D-Calif) put the number higher, citing 1 psychiatrist to every 535 patients.

195. Judiciary Subcommittee On Constitutional Rights, Nov. 1994:39-41 (citing subcommittee interviews and Stephen L. Chorover, *Psychology Today*, May 1974).

196. Judiciary Subcommittee On Constitutional Rights, Nov. 1994:64, 647.

197. *The Fresno Bee* "Executions Stir Questions On Insanity Link" Nov. 10, 1973.

The epidemic, at least in California, was partially blamed on Gov. Reagan who planned to phase out state hospitals by 1982. The legislature accused him of "dumping" murderers like Charles Manson into the community. News articles reminded readers that some of the most notorious murderers' of recent time where being held at these facilities. Health And Welfare Secretary Earl Brian clamed 62 Californians were killed in mass murders since 1969, some by former mental patients, while the California State Employees Association claimed 75 and claimed all were the acts of former state hospital mental patients. Some experts said the numbers could be accounted for by random variation and that there was no correlation to former mental patients and acts of violence while other experts said violence was predictable.

198. *The Times* (San Mateo, CA) $850 Million Reagan Proposes Sate Tax Return" Jan. 11, 1973; Robert E. Litman "Suicide and Violence Reduction: Research and Publicity" pg.281 to 290 in The Mosaic of Contemporary Psychiatry in Perspective, Kales, Pierce, Greenblat (editors) Springer-Verlag New York, Inc. 1992.

199. *Valley News* (Van Nuys, CA) "From Violent Behavior Study Center At UCLA" Feb. 13, 1973; *Santa Cruz Sentinel* (Santa Cruz, CA) "Study Of Violent Behavior" Jan. 14, 1973; Judiciary Subcommittee On Constitutional Rights, Nov. 1974: 332 (referencing CSRV, Project Description, Sep. 1, 1972).

200. Judiciary Subcommittee On Constitutional Rights, Nov. 1974: 324-326 (referencing CSRV, Project Description).
According to the proposal, within the next two years in California alone, it was estimated that violent criminals would victimize one out of every hundred people.

201. *Science News* "A Clockwork Orange in a California Prison" March 11, 1972.
Some of the recent revelations about government-funded abuses included Tuskegee syphilis experiments and the sterilization of African American teenage girls. Vacaville was thrust into the public eye when a family member of an inmate who had died as a result of the experiments at San Quinton Prison, filed a wrongful death lawsuit.

202. Judiciary Subcommittee On Constitutional Rights, Nov. 1974: 36 (quoting Letter from Louis Jolyon West, M.D. to J.M. Stubblebine, PhD, California Director of Health Jan. 22, 1973).

203. Judiciary Subcommittee On Constitutional Rights, Nov. 1974: 26, 35, 37, 327, 328 (referencing and quoting CSRV, Project Description).

204. Judiciary Subcommittee On Constitutional Rights, Nov. 1974: 326 (referencing and quoting CSRV, Project Description).

205. Judiciary Subcommittee On Constitutional Rights, Nov. 1974: 356 (partially referring to Ingraham and Smith "The Use of Electronics in the Observation and Control of Human Behavior and Its Possible Use in Rehabilitation and Parole" *Issues In Criminology*, V. 7 No. 2, 1972).
Also included on West's A-Team list was William Herrmann, CIA agent and counter-insurgency expert for private CIA front companies who would soon become embroiled in the Iran Contra scandal.

206. Judiciary Subcommittee On Constitutional Rights, Nov. 1974: 352,353 (referencing and quoting CSRV, Project Description).
In May 1972, Harvard University MK notable Dr. William Sweet, appeared before an appropriations committee and testified on behalf of himself and several other leading psychiatrists and neurologists including Sweet's co-worker, Dr. Vernon Mark, and Dr. West ("of the Brain Research Institute"). Sweet explained the need for the Senate to approve $1 million in funding for research centers where brains could be scanned with EEG's to understand, predict and develop ways of preventing violence. Sweet cited the creepy brain research network's previous studies on prisoners to add legitimacy to his funding request. He noted that in a study of 24 patients, 2 had required brain implants to allow the doctors to monitor and manipulate areas of the brain associated with violence (Judiciary Subcommittee On Constitutional Rights, Nov. 1994 citing Statement of Dr. William H. Sweet, Harvard Medical School, before Senate Labor-HEWW Appropriations Hearings, May 23, 1972). Funding was denied.

207. *The San Bernardino County Sun* (San Bernardino, California) "Violence Study Fears Outlined" May 10, 1973.
During a press conference the next month (May 1973), Drs. Lee Coleman (a Berkley psychi-

atrist) and Edward Opton (a psychologist at the Wright Institute in Berkley) said that some of the medical researchers associated with the Center planned to alter behaviors through performing psychosurgery. They further said that a proposed experiment using hormones to curb aggressive behavior was tantamount to "chemical castration." Coleman and Opton represented the Committee Opposing Psychiatric Abuse of Prisoners. Even if consent was given, patients confined at the Center and prisoners with mental problems, through promises of rewards and shortened sentences, could be persuaded to consent and become the subject of experimental procedures they might not otherwise have. Another concern cited was law enforcement agencies funding of the Center which, said Coleman, would compromise the scientific objectivity of work performed there.

208. Judiciary Subcommittee On Constitutional Rights, Nov. 1974: 351-353 (referencing and quoting CSRV, Project Description).

Senator Leo Ryan was also a critic of the Center. Ryan himself was soon murdered at Jonestown just prior to the 'Kool-Aid' incident and there is good reason to believe that Jonestown itself had begun as one of California's strange behavior modification experiments. Regardless, Dr. West would be a favorite media go-to guy to help explain what happened at Jonestown and one imagines he wasn't all that heartbroken about Ryan's murder, although he certainly capitalized on it after the formation of the Cult Awareness Network.

209. *The Van Nuys News* (Van Nuys, California) "Advisory Unit Backs Plan for Violence Study Center" April 17, 1973; *Independent Press Telegram* (Long Beach, California) "The Rapist," July 14, 1974; Bernard Towers "Medical Ethics" pg. 66 to 75 in *The Mosaic of Contemporary Psychiatry in Perspective*, Kales, Pierce, Greenblat (editors) Springer-Verlag New York, Inc. 1992.

210. Robert E. Litman "Suicide and Violence Reduction: Research and Publicity" pg. 281 to 290 in *The Mosaic of Contemporary Psychiatry in Perspective*, Kales, Pierce, Greenblat (editors) Springer-Verlag New York, Inc. 1992.

211. *The Van Nuys News* April 17, 1973; *Independent Press Telegram* July 14, 1974.; *Los Angeles Times*, Oct. 27, 1985.

Even though his plans were laid out in writing, for the rest of his life West denied that his intentions for the Center were anything other than pleasant and ethical.

212. The Hastings Center terminated their 'violence' project due to persistent and heated controversy, attracted by West and the findings of several Congressional, Senate, and House investigations and hearings. Their 1979 report entitled "Research Violence: Science, Politics & Public Controversy," outlines the issues of debate, a large portion of which revolved around and included the comments of Dr. West.

213. KUBARK 1963; *Los Angeles Times*, Oct. 27, 1985.

214. Jane Mayer, *The Dark Side: The Inside Story Of How The War On Terror Turned Into A War On American Ideals*, Doubelday, New York, 2008: 139-181.

215. Salon.com "Hersh: Children sodomized at Abu Ghraib, on tape" July 15, 2004; *Guardian* "The rape of men: the darkest secret of war" July 16, 2011.

216. McCoy 183; Frank Summers, PhD., ABPP "Making Sense of the APA: A History of the Relationship Between Psychology and the Military" *Psychoanalytic Dialogues*, V. 18, 2008:633; Michael Welch "Illusions in Truth Seeking: The Perils of Interrogation and Torture in the War on Terror" *Social Justice*, V. 37 No. 2-3, 2010-2011: 131; See also Otterman.

Summers and others argue that those psychological practices originating with and at first contained within the military very often end up becoming institutionalized within the broader field of psychology. Throughout the Global War on Terrorism, psychologists have insisted on their right to participate in interrogations at illegal detention centers, despite human rights violations. Michael Welch pointed out how, under the guise of science and professionalism, the brutal realities of torture are obscured and further, the rhetoric used to justify 'enhanced' fact-finding fails to acknowledge its ineffectiveness. Despite the clear violations of the Geneva Convention and other international laws, the field of psychology has a symbiotic relationship with the military/ intelligence community, and to repay them, offer legal arguments and legitimization for the military to continue its use of torture. By 2008, within the Iraqi and Afghanistan theaters of war, rates of PTSD reached up to 40% and suicides increased exponentially. According to one report, there were 51 suicides in 2001 to 2,100 in 2007. For this reason, as seen previously hundreds of new psychologists are being employed by the VA.

217. *Vanity Fair* "Rorschach and Awe" June 30, 2007; *Guardian* "US report on 'enhanced interrogation' concludes: torture doesn't work" Dec. 9, 2014; Jeff Kaye "Ethical Interrogations or Torture with a Pretty Name? New Documents Expose Fake 'Rapport' Schemes." Shadow Proof Dec. 9, 2009 ; The Constitution Project "The Report of The Constitution Project's Task Force on Detainee Treatment" Washington, DC, 2012 (citing Task Force staff interview with Dr. Michael Gelles, March 15, 2012).

In 1999, despite his many professional accolades, Gelles became the subject of some, albeit brief, bad publicity for his role in the brutal interrogation of Naval officer Daniel M King. During Gelles' interrogation of King, suspected of espionage, Gelles pressured him into giving a false confession. After being held without charges and subjected to sleep deprivation, threats, 24-hour daily surveillance and interrogated for 12 to 19 hours a day for 29 days, King 'confessed' although he quickly recanted. After, King was imprisoned at Quantico USMC base for 500 days where he remained in a six by nine foot cell. But when Gelles became a leading member of a prominent 2005 American Psychological Association task force on torture and interrogation, he gained a reputation for his highly public criticisms of abusive military interrogation techniques.

He still managed to attract the ire of at least *some* bleeding heart liberals, this time for his assistance in conducting interrogations and training of interrogators. While some viewed him as a champion and critic of interrogation practices, a man on a self-proclaimed mission to help reform torturous techniques, others suspected he was simply a strawman, leaking limited disclosures while covering for even more nightmarish scenarios than those he revealed. Gelles' later enthusiasm for "ethical interrogation" came at the exact moment when a whole slew of embarrassing criminal charges and scandals were about to break. One close observer of the post 9/11 torture scandal, called the "rapport scheme" designed by Gelles, "torture with a pretty name." Gelles, he said, "is a major ideologue for a certain kind of abusive interrogation [that] propagates cruel, inhuman and degrading forms of interrogation, themselves banned by law and international treaty [that often amount] to the level of full torture..." (Kaye). Given what has come to light in just the past few years about the extent of torture and some of the actual nearly unthinkable methods employed, it looks like those paranoid terrorist sympathizers may have been on to something. Following Gelles's retirement in 2006, he began a new life as a private security consultant to high tech multinationals.

218. Randall T. Coyne "Reflections on Representing Guantánamo Detainees: A Law Professor's Reflections On Representing Guantanamo Detainees" *Northeastern University Law Journal*, V. 1 No. 1, 2007: 100, 103.

Among those Coyne represented was Ahmed Khalfan Ghailani, a 'high value detainee' held in solitary confinement for four years while awaiting a military tribunal. Coyne noted that of those detained at GITMO, which he called an "American gulag," 86% had been turned in by neighbors who read leaflets dropped over Afghanistan by Americans announcing they could earn "wealth and power beyond [their] dreams" in exchange for seeing something and saying something, i.e., turning over other individuals to the U.S. occupying forces. Nevertheless, the vast majority of detainees at GITMO were not al Qaeda fighters and 40% had no definitive connections to al Qaeda whatsoever.

219. John R. Smith, M.D., "Psychological Impact on Guards at Guantanamo Bay Prison Camp- A Case Study Plus Others" Proceedings of the American Academy of Forensic Sciences, Volume XIV, Feb. 2008; *Counterpunch* "Confessions Of A GITMO Guard" Feb. 26, 2008; Sun Sentinel

"Guantanamo Camp To Close" Jan. 23, 2009.

Smith said the guards often return home only to display a higher rate of mental disturbances, depression, insomnia, nightmares, flashbacks and suicide. One guard Smith treated recalled that within his first month working there four people, two guards and two inmates, committed suicide. After leaving, the guards could not escape the memories of the abuses they perpetrated and witnessed. One guard remembered an inmate literally attempting to chew his arm off after attempting to hang himself. On the other hand, Amnesty International UK confirmed the high rate of suicide among inmates and said that their conditions left them psychotic to the point that "even those eventually released from the camp will be mentally scarred for the rest of their lives" (Guardian Feb. 25, 2008). Smith had a long history of military and defense funding as well. In 1983, the American Journal of Orthospychiatry published two of Smith's articles entitled, "On Health and Disorder in Vietnam Veterans: An Invited Commentary" which examined "assumptions about combat as a tolerable stress" as well as "the stress recovery process for survivors of catastrophe." A 1986, Seattle Times article quoted Smith (and West) in their reporting of PTSD and the role of psychologists and psychiatrists in victims of terrorist attacks.

220. Program for the American Psychiatric Association 135th Annual Meeting, Toronto Canada, May 15-16, 1982.

The intersection between West's expertise (Dissociative and Multiple Personality Disorders) and the issue of terrorism is interesting to say the least and explored in the conclusion of this book. West's papers and statements about cults are found in the endnotes of this chapter in the discussion of Waco. After the 1970's, beyond West's many papers on the topic of cults, he also wrote about: "Post Traumatic Anxiety" (1984); "Effects of Isolation on the Evidence of Detainees" (1985); and "Torture and Brainwashing" (1994). From 1987 until 1988, West chaired the APA's Task Force on Terrorism and from 1985 until 1999 was Editor of the *Journal of Violence, Aggression, Terrorism*. At the dawn of the 'Age of Terrorism,' a 1986, Seattle Times article quoted West (and Smith) in their reporting of PTSD and the role of psychologists and psychiatrists in victims of terrorist attacks.

In the early 1990's, he acted as a member of the medical oversight board for the remote viewing research of Science Applications International Corp. Remote viewing and other ESP phenomena are a long standing topic of interest to MKUltra and government funded researchers as well, many of whom helped to develop some of the 'non-lethal' weapons we know and love today.

221. Anthony Kales, MD, Chester M. Pierce, MD, Milton Greenblatt, MD "Preface" (pg. v to vii), Milton Greenblatt "LJ West's Place in Social and Community Psychiatry" (pg. 3 to 13), Towers, (pg. 66 to 75), and Margaret Thaler Singer and Marsha Emmer Addis "Cults, Coercion, and Contumely" (pg. 130 to 141), in *The Mosaic of Contemporary Psychiatry in Perspective*, Kales, Pierce, Greenblat (editors) Springer-Verlag New York, Inc. 1992.

222. Archives General Psychiatry "Obituaries: Louis Jolyon Wet, MD (1924-1999)" Vol. 56, July 1999: *San Jose Mercury News* "Louis West, Expert On Brainwashing" Jan. 8, 1999; *New York Times* "Paid Notice: Deaths, Dr. Louis Jolyon West" Jan. 11, 1999; *New York Times* "Louis J. West, 74, Psychiatrist Who Studied Extremes, Dies" Jan. 9, 1999.

The *Archives General Psychiatry* obituary informs readers that: "Jolly West served his country and his profession well. He was a consultant for the US Air Force, the Veterans Administration, the US Information Agency, US National Academy of Sciences, the Peace Corps, the National Institute of Mental Health, the Department of Health and Human Services, the American Medical Association, the American Psychiatric Association, the American specialty boards, and private foundations. He served on the editorial boards of 12 publications and on many medical school committees. He also received many honors and awards, including an honorary doctorate of humane letters from Hebrew Union College, Los Angeles, Calif. During his career he gave numerous prestigious endowed lectures, both in the United States and abroad."

223. *Santa Cruz Sentinel* "A Chamber Of Horrors Prediction" May 10, 1973; Lemov 201.

224. Timothy Melley. *Empire Of Conspiracy: The Culture Of Paranoia In Postwar America*, Cornell

University Press, Ithaca, NY, 1999: 58-63.

225. Timothy Melley, *The Covert Sphere: Secrecy, Fiction, and the National Security State*, Cornell University Press, Ithaca, New York, 2012:42.

William Jennings Bryan, the California hypnotist and suspected programmer of Sirhan Sirhan acted as a technical consultant on the movie set of *The Manchurian Candidate*.

226. Michael Crichton, *The Terminal Man*, Alfred A. Knopf, New York, 1972: 17, 24, 45, 89, 100.

227. Judiciary Subcommittee On Constitutional Rights, Nov. 1974: 352; David Seed, *Brainwashing: The Fictions Of Mind Control: A Study of Novels and Films Since World War II*, Kent State University Press, Kent and London, 2004:203.

228. Melley, *Empire of Conspiracy*, 1999: 57 (quoting DeLillo "Running Dog" 1978:111); Junghyun Hwang "From the End of History to Nostalgia: The Manchurian Candidate, Then and Now" *Journal of Transnational American Studies* V. 2, No. 1, 2010: 11, 12.

In addition to the CIA, Bowart included a number of other government agencies in the Cryptocracy including the NSA, DIA, all branches of military intelligence, DOJ, Dept. Of Health, Bureau of Prisons, Bureau of Narcotics, Energy Commission, Veterans Administration, National Science Foundation, among others, as well as several airline, aerospace and oil companies.

229. *Globe and Mail* "OKLAHOMA BOMBING: Whodunit? The Jews, the UN, the Japanese or the evil Clinton? As usual, the conspiracy theorists have transformed what seems painfully obvious into a tangle of paranoia" July 8, 1995.

230. CNN "The Road to Oklahoma" Nov. 19, 1995; *The Observer* "Cults 2" May 21, 1995.

231.Ronald K. Siegel, PhD. Whispers: The Voices Of Paranoia, Crown Publications, Inc. 1994, New York, First Touchstone Edition, 1996: 58, 96. Siegel notes that among those who have claimed to have tooth implants was Dennis Sweeney, who in 1980, assassinated former Congressman Allard K. Lowenstein, believing Lowenstein was part of a CIA conspiracy that had implanted a device in his teeth that transmitted words into his brain. Sweeney had gone so far as to gouge out his dental crowns with a hacksaw blade to end.

232. Ronald K. Siegel, "A Device for Chronically Controlled Visual Input," *Journal Of The Experimental Analysis Of Behavior*, V. 11 No. 5, 1968: 559, 560.

233. Moviefanfare.com "Is Bug the Most Relevant Thriller Today?" Sep. 27, 2010, George D. Allen; Una Chaudhuri "Bug Bytes: Insects, Information, and Interspecies Theatricality" *Theatre Journal* V. 65 No. 2, Oct. 2013.

234. *Albany Times Union* "UAlbany Suspends Implants Research: Albany professor whose work is at issue focused on surgically inserted mind-control devices" Aug. 25, 1999,Andrew Brownstein Tortorici told authorities that his actions were a way to inform people about the government conspiracy that had victimized him. His attorneys said that he was clearly delusional and psychotic but he was found sane and guilty in 1996. In August 1999, he was found dead in his prison cell, his death ruled a suicide. While the University had previously approved Kelley's plan to study the ways that communication devices could be used for "monitoring and control," after a student complained that Dr. Kelley would not dismiss him from one of her lectures, the administration ordered her to cease research or lecture on the "X-Files" realms of government mind control and surveillance. Kelley, a fully tenured professor, claimed the edict was violating her academic freedom.

In 1991, MRI and CT scans identified "paramagnetic metallic foreign bodies" (implants) in the head and chest of Brian Wronge, an African American incarcerated at Elmira and Arthur Kill correctional facilities from 1979 until 1989. Upon further examination, miniature radio implants were found in his eardrums. When he sued the state of New York, claiming the prison implanted them in him as part of an experiment, the judge instructed him to find a surgeon who would remove one of the devices. He was unable to, however, as while a number of physicians confirmed the implants, all refused to remove them, some citing fear of government retaliation (*The City Sun* "Charge of Holocaust: Medical Experiment on Black Inmate" Dec. 15, 1993, Matifa Angaza; *The City Sun* "Implant Victim Refused Help by 'Humanitarian' Physicians" no date; also discussed in Gena Mason, "The Micropchipping of America: Human Rights Implications of Human Bar Codes" Selected Works of Gena V. Mason, July 2009).

235. Ariel Eytan, Christophe Liberek, Isabelle Graf, Jean Golaz, "Case Study: Electronic Chip Implant: A New Culture Bound Syndrome?" *Psychiatry* 65:1 (2002) pg. 72,73 ; L. Sher "Socio-political events and technical innovations may affect the content of delusions and the course of psychotic disorders" *Medical Hypothesis* 55:6 (2000) pg. 506-509.

A culture bound syndrome is defined as "recurrent, locality specific patterns of aberrant behavior and troubling experience that may or may not be linked to a particular diagnostic category" (Etyan, 72).

236. Author interview with Stephen Jones, Oklahoma City, Oklahoma, Dec. 28, 2007.

237. McVeigh, when asked about his experiences at Tinker, told a reporter that while there, the government did obtain his handwriting sample. So they must have just been killing two birds.

The following month, In November, Morris, the Unit Manager at El Reno, informed McVeigh that the dentist was having "problems with the machinery" and could not see him that day. When McVeigh asked if he could see him the next day, Morris said it might be a couple of weeks. He became convinced that Morris was deceiving him, as there were five dentists' chairs and lots of equipment. He expressed to Coyne his immediate need for dental work and feared if the dentist did not see him soon, he would "lose teeth from the decay as a result."

238. *McCurtain County Gazette* "McVeigh's Revolution Driven by Drugs and Paranoia" Dec. 6, 2000. JD Cash.

239. Jim Keith, Jim. *OKBOMB! Conspiracy and Cover-up* Adventures Unlimited Press, Kempton, Illinois, 1996:196; Alex Constantine, *Virtual Government: CIA Mind Control Operations in America*. Los Angeles, California, Feral House, 1997:255; Surveillanceissues.com "Did You Know" Jan. 22, 105, (http://www.surveillanceissues.com/did-you-know/); Jim Rarey "Medium Rare: The Murder Of David Kelly" From The Wilderness Publications, Oct. 29, 2003 (http://www.fromthewilderness.com/free/ww3/111203_kelly_2.html); *Quantum Moxie: Thoughts Of A Selective Subjectivist* "Priceless Conspiracy Theory" Feb. 20, 2009 (https://quantummoxie.wordpress.com/2009/02/20/priceless-conspiracy-theory/).

While Keith's book was published first, it drew from an online essay written by Constantine. Other works discussing Calspan (in relation to mind control) or Jolly West include Jim Keith's 1998 book, *Mind Control, World Control: An Encyclopedia of Mind Control* and David Hoffman's 1998 book, *The Oklahoma City Bombing and the Politics of Terror*, both of which repeat and somewhat add to Constantine's version.

The blog of an unnamed former intern at Calspan, said that employees there "had [McVeigh's] picture up on the door of the fridge so they could toss insults at him. He was apparently a freak when he was employed there...the security at the time was a joke" and the only "doctors" he saw "were PhD aerospace engineers," most of whom were also professors at nearby University of Buffalo (*Quantum Moxie*).

240. The Cornell Medical College in Ithaca, New York is a three-hour drive from Buffalo. In 1954, Cornell University Medical School Human Ecology Studies Program conducted the early experiments of the CIA's Project QKHILLTOP, the precursor to MKUltra. An abbreviated list of MKUltra funding to Cornell doctors (not including other defense related funding under other projects) includes: Dr. Harold Wolff (Cornell, MK funding in 1956 for studies of the effect of stress on the brain); unknown doctor(s), Cornell, MK funding 1955, 1956 for top secret study of defector psychology/ formation of a study group of brainwashing experts); unknown doctor(s), (Cornell, MK funding in 1958 for study of immigrant adjustment using unwitting subjects). Other MK- Ultra

funded psychiatrists associated with Cornell included Dr. Paul McHugh (Assistant Professor of Psychiatry and Neurology, Cornell, 1964 to 1968); Dr. Sidney L. Werkman, received MD from Cornell in 1952 working directly under Dr. Wolff). Also closely associated with Cornell's MK doctors since the 1950's, was Albert D. Bidderman, whose 1961 book, *The Manipulation Of Human Behavior*, includes an essay by Hinkle and sings the praises of Jolly West.

241. *Anderson Herald* (Anderson, Indiana) ·"Power Of Microwaves Transmissions Tripled" March 5, 1958.

In the mid 1940's, at a time when CAL could already telemetrically monitor manned flights as well as the first experimental drones and had helped in the development of supersonic electronically guided missiles and bombs. Their remote observations were not limited to the skies though; they were in charge of underwater monitoring for the testing of atomic bombs at Bikini Atoll. REDCAP refers to 'Real Time Electromagnetic Digitally Controlled Analyzer Processor.'

242. *Freeport Journal Standard* (Freeport, Illinois" "Navy Working On Electronic Robot 'Brain'" July 7, 1958; N. J. Mizen "Preliminary Design for the Shoulders and Arms of a Powered, Exoskeletal Structure" Cornell Aeronautical Laboratory Report, VO-1692-V-4, 1965; H. Kazerooni, Ryan Stegar, Lhua Huang "Hybrid Control of the Berkeley Lower Extremity Exoskeleton (BLE-EX)" *The International Journal of Robotics Research*, V. 25, No. 5-6, 2006 (pg. 561-573) a paper first presented at the Proceedings of the 2005 IEEE International Conference on Robotics and Automation, Barcelona, Spain, April 2005; *The Salem News* (Salem, Ohio) No Title, May 24, 1964

Perceptron was different from other, ordinary computers because it did "not have to be fed facts and figures in advance" (*Freeport Journal Standard* July 7, 1958). In 1969, CAL released their next medical development, Myron, an instrument to measure neuromuscular behaviors.

243. The ONR pioneered the field of experimental psychology, and under its Psychological Sciences program, contracted out research to 58 universities from the years 1950 to 1952 alone. As seen earlier, the Air Force outsourced much of it's behavior modification and interrogation studies (See, McCoy).

244. *The Logansport Press* (Logansport, Indiana) "Study TV To Send Back Battle Reports"· Fri, Dec 20, 1957; *The Sandusky Register* (Sandusky, Ohio) · "Study Combat Surveillance" Wed, Jan 8, 1958; Department Of Justice, Federal Bureau Of Investigation vs. Calspan Corporation, Appeal NO. 78-501, US Court of Customs and Patent Appeals, June 8, 1978.

FINDER: FINgerprint DEscription Reader. The FBI would later sue Calspan, claiming they owned exclusive rights to use the name 'FINDER.' The FBI lost. In August 1974, Martin-Marietta's Data Systems unit assumed control of operations at Calspan's computer center, proving them with data processing resource management. Calspan engineer Carmen J. Tona developed "electronic and intelligence gathering" technologies for the Erie County Sheriff's and Amherst Police Departments during the 1960's and 70's and was appointed by President Ford in 1975 to review federal and state law pertaining to electronic surveillance. While working at Calspan, Tona served on the Eerie County Sheriff's scientific staff and acted as a consultant to the Buffalo and Amherst Police. (*Buffalo News* July 31, 2001).

245. *Cornell Daily Sun* "CU Lab Sought South African Sale" Oct. 19, 1978.

Said Frank Zurn, a Cornell University representative and on Calspan's Board of Directors, "we had high hopes that we might get that business down there (in South Africa) but said the sale was probably blocked because of "the political situation in South Africa" (*Cornell Daily Sun*, Oct. 19, 1978).

Among the defense initiatives Calspan helped realize over the next four decades were radar systems, satellite and aerial data collection and other electronic intelligence gathering and monitoring systems, military aircraft, systems and weapons as well as non-conventional military hardware and applications including countermeasures to chemical and electromagnetic warfare and terrorist attacks.

246. NASA "Aerospace Medicine and Biology" Supplemental 127, April 1974.

At the time Congress issued their report, NASA had yet to produce "a complete list or accounting of NASA sponsored studies" (Interim Report of the Advisory Committee on Human Radiation Experiments, October 21, 1994). NASA first established ethical guidelines and policies relating to experiments in 1969, although informed consent polices were not in effect until 1972.

Given the titles of some of the reports CAL issued to NASA and ONR, it appears possible that they conducted some experiments on humans. Among the many other topics relating to physiological and psychological human factors explored by Calspan was "human tolerance to environmental elements," (CAL, 1960); "the effects of acceleration on visual brightness discrimination" (CAL, Inc., Physiological Psychology Branch, Office of Naval Research, Washington, D. C. ,1961); "A survey of bioastronautics, 1961-1962: resources for research and development" (CAL, 1962); "vision and unusual gravitational forces" (*Human Factors,* V. 5, June 1963, listed in "Aerospace Medicine and Biology, Cumulative Index, 1966" Scientific And Technical Information Branch NASA, Washington, DC, Jan. 1966).

247. Public Health Service, National Institute Of Health Division Of Computer Research and Technology "Report of Program Activities July 1, 1973 through June 30, 1974" referring to Individual Project Report "Implant Device Development" John W. Boretos, Robert E. Baier, et. al, .; "Investigations Of Materials Compatible With Blood" Contract Number: N01-HV-3-2953, R.E. Baier, PhD, Principal Investigator (Calspan) in U.S. Department of Health, Education and Welfare, Public Health Service, National Institutes of Health, "Devices Technology Branch Contractors Conference Proceedings, Dec. 12-14, 1977" DHEW Publication No. (NIH) 78-16011, 1977.

Baier's career included postdoctoral research at the U.S. Naval Research Lab, 1966-1968; Executive Director of the NY Center for Advanced Technology in Health-care Instruments and Devices. 1984 -1989; member of the U.S. Army Research Laboratory Biotechnology Assessment Committee, 1992; and member of the Army's Biotechnology Working Group, 2004 to present (Roswell Park Cancer Institute "Molecular and Cellular Biophysics and Biochemistry Graduate Studies Program 2011-2012"). Baier's current research involves the boundaries between living tissues and man-made devices.

248. Neuman, Brill, Gibbons, Greatbatch, Mates, Rushmer "Research Directions in Biomedical Engineering" *Engineering In Medicine And Biology Magazine,* Sep. 1989 (with a citation for "United States National Committee on Biomechanics: future Research Needs in Biomechanics" Calspan Corp. Buffalo, July, 1986).

249. *Buffalo News* "Charles E. Treanor: Calspan physicist and engineer" May 30, 2012; Ronald L. Jackson, Donald E. Roberts, Randy A. Cote, Patrick McNeal, Janet T. Fay "Psychological and Physiological Responses of Blacks and Caucasians to Hand Cooling" Army Research Institute of Environmental Medicine, Natick, MA, ADA215646, Final Report, Sep. 1985 – June 1989. June 1989.

CUBRC was established as a non-for-profit with its main offices on Genesee Street. The 1986 CAL study used twenty-one Air Force pilots as subjects Stresses included risk taking, sleep deprivation and induced heightened states of confusion, frustration, anxiety, tension, anger, depression, vigor, and fatigue. Other funding came from the Joint Working Group on Drug Dependent Degradation in Military Performance. Like McVeigh's COHORTs, the pilots in the Calspan work performance study were kept in the same pairs during the entire experiment in order "to decrease the variability in performance associated with changing crew members" (Concurrent Validation of Four Workload and Fatigue Measures," Proceedings of The Fourth International Symposium On Aviation Psychology, Sponsored by The Aviation Psychology Laboratory, The Ohio State University and The Association of Aviation Psychologists, April 27 - 30, 1987). In 1987, Calspan was a runner up for NASA's Excellence Award For Quality and Productivity.

Calspan, generally able to avoid the type of bad publicity garnered by most defense contractors received at least some of their share when, in 1993, it was learned that the Buffalo facility utilized human corpses, including those of children, as crash test dummies.

250. A. H. Frey "Human auditory system response to modulated electromagnetic energy" *Journal of Applied Physiology*, V. 17,1962: 689-692; Schapitz, J.F., "Experimental investigation of effectiveness of psycho physiological manipulation using modulated electromagnetic fields for direct information transmission into the brain (experimental proceedings)," January 1974 (quoted in: U.S Department of Health, Education, And Welfare, Public Health Service, Food and Drug Administration, "Biological Effects of Electromagnetic Waves" Selected Papers of the USNC/ URSI Annual Meeting, Boulder, Colorado, Volume I, Oct. 20-23, 1975: 31); Don R. Justesen "Microwaves and Behavior" *American Psychologist*, V. 30 No. 3, March 1975: 396.

251. *Wall Street Journal*, no title, May 24, 1976, pg. 2; *Wall Street Journal*, no title, Sep. 13, 1978, pg. 2; Lt. Col. John B. Alexander, US Army "The New Mental Battlefield: 'Beam Me Up, Spock'" *Military Review* Dec. 1980.

Parapsychological phenomenon include out of body experiences, precognition, and telekinesis, "telepathic behavior modification" wherein a person could be hypnotized from miles away using only the power of directed thought and remote transfer of bioenergy. The term 'psyhcotronic' literally means "the interaction of mind and matter" (Alexander 47-52). Psychotronics uses energy, radio wave and sound weapons "to control or alter the psyche or to attack the various sensory and data processing systems of the human organism" and "confuse or destroy the signals that keep the body in equilibrium." Beyond projecting voices and thoughts, the immediate "bio-effects" of psychotronic assaults on the bodies' electrochemical system are legion and it's long term effects remain to be seen (*Bulletin of Atomic Scientists* "All in the (Russian) mind?" V. 54 No. 4, July/ –August 1998: 11; *US News & World Report* "Wonder Weapons" July 7, 1997).

252. *Wall Street Journal* "Nonlethal Arms, New Class of Weapons Could Incapacitate Foe Yet Limit Casualties - Military Sees Role for Lasers, Electromagnetic Pulses, Other High-Tech Tricks - Sticky Roads, Stalled Tanks" Jan. 6, 1993.

Alex Constantine pointed out that at a 1994 US Army Research Lab conference, Paul Brodnicki, Director of Advanced Systems at Calspan, chaired a panel on electronic warfare simulations, which included a paper entitled "Radio-Frequency Self-Protection."

253. *Globe and Mail* "Alien Abduction: Close encounters of the neurological kind: A Sudbury Scientist Examines The Nuerophenomenological structure in the brain that may cause mystical, alien and out of the body experiences" Nov. 26, 1994, Salem Alaton; SBIR.gov "Communicating VIA the Microwave Auditory Effect" Agency Tracking Number 19903, 1995.

Persinger had long argued that mystical and religious experiences and near death and out- of -body experiences were the result of neural activity, what he calls 'nuerophenomenology.' When a senior academic from the University of West England paid a visit to his lab, she had her own "close encounter of the neurological kind" and described how, after she put on the helmet, she felt as if her body was being pulled in different directions, not in her control, felt the presence of another 'being,' and experienced sudden anger and fear (*Globe and Mail*, Nov. 26, 1994). According to researcher Colin Ross, Persinger received defense funding for experiments concerning the ability of magnetic fields to create false memories. Both Dr. Persinger and West were on the board of False Memory Syndrome Foundation, often criticized for its relationship to several high-ranking MK doctors and suspected of being a cover operation to shield actual mind control experiments by discrediting victims.

254. It is worth remembering that just as the protagonist of *The Terminal Man* (1972) attempts to destroy the computer controlling his brain implants, in McVeigh's favorite book, *The Turner Diaries* (1978), Earl Turner uses a truck bomb to blow up an FBI building in D.C. in order to destroy the massive supercomputer database stored there.

The 'Tim' that Salino knew made frequent visits to the Buffalo VA for mental health treatment and claimed to suffer from blackouts that usually lasted for two to three days but once lasted for nearly two months. During his 'missing time,' Tim said he could perform tasks but did not remember doing so later. Salino described 'Tim' as contradictory, secretive and prone to violent outbursts. In fact, Tim warned Salino to be careful of him because he had a "past life" about which he did not elaborate.

255. *Rochester Business Journal* "2001 Entrepreneur of the Year: John Schneider, Ultra-Scan Corp." June 29, 2001; *Frost & Sullivan Market* "Insight Movers & Shakers Interview with Dr. John K. Schneider, Founder, President and Chief Technology Officer, Ultra-Scan Corporation" Sep. 14, 2006; *Health & Medicine Week* "Surveillance: Population Health Observatory to conduct regional bioterrorism monitoring" March 24, 2003, pg. 50; *Buffalo News* "UB's Biometrics Research Center May Develop Security Products" Nov. 11, 2003, Fred O. Williams; *Business Wire* "Objectivity Announces Sponsorship of the 3rd Annual Sensor Fusion Conference Addressing the Defense and Intelligence Community" Nov. 15, 2006.

The UltraScan project likely began much earlier in 1994, when Calspan was announced as one of the companies in the running for a British government contract to develop "the first comprehensive national automated fingerprint recognition system," the UK's first use of a fingerprint database (*Financial Times* "Fingerprint decision near" May 12, 1994).

256. *TransWorldNews* "Akonni Biosystems, Inc.." Feb. 29, 2012; *Zoom Company Information* "Akonni Biosystems Inc." Nov. 2015; *Medical Device Daily* "Agreements/ Contracts: Kingman added into Mayo Clinic Network" Oct. 20, 2011.

In 2010, $800,000 was earmarked from New York State's budget for Akonni/CUBRC defense related projects. The 2011 U.S. Army awarded CUBRC/ Akonni a contract to develop an automatic chemical/ biological threat detection system to help "warfighters" face the challenges posed by "biological warfare and terrorism." Interestingly, a *Medical Device Daily* article noting the Akonni/ CUBRC 2011 Army contract, also listed the collaborating of the Mayo Clinic's telemedicine networking system with the Kingman Regional Medical Center in Kingman, Arizona. The next year, in 2012, CUBRC received two government contracts, one from the Biomedical Advanced Research and Development Authority for $67.2 million to develop anti-biotics for anthrax, plague and common life-threatening bacteria. One wonders if perhaps these could be targeted to specific DNA.

257. *Buffalo News* "Calspan given highway grant" Aug. 28, 1993; *USA Today* "'Smart' autos will call 911 when hit" Oct. 4, 1995; *Washington Times* "He's got it under his skin" Oct. 5 1998, David S Oderberg; *St. Louis Post-Dispatch* "Car Device Is Being Tested That Will Call 911 After A Car Crash" May 31, 1998.

In August of 1993, CALSPAN received a $3.054 million dollar federal grant to research automated highway systems to develop new technologies that, according to Congressman Jack Quinn, would be "built into [Buffalo's] highways of the future" (*Buffalo News* Aug. 28, 1993). Over the next two years, CALSPAN received $3 million more to expand its "Buffalo based experiment to make highways safer." This included 4,000 vehicles with 'black boxes' that could record when and where car accidents occurred. The technology was already in use by the U.S. military. CALSPAN's experiment was part of the Dept. of Transportation's plans for a National Intelligent Transportation System (*Buffalo News*. Oct. 6, 1995). Since this time, CALSPAN has continued its project to build 'smart highways' in Buffalo.

258. *Computerworld* "Pentagon Funds Peacetime Projects" Feb. 11, 1991; "Multi-modal output composition for human-computer dialogues" Identifier: 10.1109/AISIG.1989.47332, AI Systems in Government Conference, 1989.

EMBS begin in 1952, with the formation of Radio Engineers (IRE) Professional Group on Medical Electronics (PGME), to investigate "problems in biology and medicine which might be aided in solution by use of electronic engineering principles and devices. In 1963, after several mergers with other professional societies, the PGME became the Engineering in Medicine and Biology Society (EMBS), now the largest international organization of biomedical engineers.

259. Sanders quote cited in *Washington Times*, Oct. 5 1998; Steven Best, Douglass Kellner. *The Post Modern Adventure: Science, Technology, and Cultural Studies at the Third Millennium* The Guilford Press, New York, London, 2001: 103, 83, .86

260. Constantine 252-256.

261. *Defense News* "Naval Research Lab Attempts To Meld Neurons and Chips: Studies May Produce Army of Zombies" March 30, 1995 (quoted in part by Constantine: 252-256).

262. *St. Louis Post-Dispatch* "Mayor Touts Technology For Town; Microchips, Fiber Optics Brining Dick Tracy, Buck Rogers To Life" March 6, 1996; *Pittsburg Post-Gazette* "Life Support: Silicon Implant Inventor Forecasts A Merging Of Mind And Microchip" Feb. 9, 1999, Reed Kanaley

In 1998, the European Parliament issued a report entitled "An Appraisal Of Technologies Of Political Control." The report identified the current and near future potential abuses of recent "developments in surveillance technologies," "new prison control systems," "innovations in crowd control weapons," and new "torture and interrogation techniques and technologies" (European Parliament, Scientific and Technological Options Assessment, STOA, No. PE 166 499, Directorate General Of Research, Luxembourg, Jan. 6, 1998).

263. *Edmonton Journal* "U.S. Army Testing 'computerized' soldiers: 'Cyborgs' will take on regular troops in a fake battle this summer" April 1, 2000., Jay Brookman; *South China Morning Post*, "Building Better People With Chips And Censors" Oct. 10, 2000.

264. Marren Sanders "Chipping: Could A High Tech Dog Tag Find Future American MIAs?" *The Journal Of High Technology Law*, V. 4 No. 1, 2004; *USA Today* "Mind Control: More Than Just A Plot Point?" July 29, 2004, Dan Vergano.

The FDA, said the report, did not consider the Verchip implants to be medical devices.

265. In 2002, the dental chip sold for about $200 and the scanner to read the information in it, $1,000- $3,000. In 2010, a tooth tracker patent holding dentist, told reporters he hoped to see everyone in the United States outfitted with the 'tell all chip.' The benefit of placing the tracker in the tooth, he said, was that you do not feel it and the body cannot reject it.

In an interesting coincidence, West wrote his first and only known paper on dentistry in 1991, entitled "Dental Management of Patients with Major Depression."

266. *Washington Post*, "Exam Urged in White House Shooting" Dec. 9, 2011, Paul Duggan; CNN "White House Shooting Suspect Competent To Aid In His Defense, Attorney Says" Dec. 14, 2011.

267. In addition to SUNY, the June 2012 Cyber Information Challenges Conference was by, among others, The Cyber New York Alliance, Armed Forces Communications and Electronic Association, Erie Canal Chapter. A major reason the conference was held at SUNY was the Air Force Research Lab Rome Laboratory located 15 miles away. The Rome Lab conducts highly classified research and development including "supercomputers to help the military sift thought piles of video surveillance data gathered from drones and satellites" (*Post Standard* 6/13/12).

268. Buffalo.edu "With Magnetic Nanoparticles, Scientists Remotely Control Neurons and Animal Behavior: Research Could Lead To Remote Stimulation Of Cells To Treat Cancer Or Diabetes" New Release, July 6, 2010, Ellen Goldbaum; *New Scientist* "Tune on, Tune In, Control Life" V. 214, No. 2868, June 9, 2012, Phil Ball.

UB was very proud of the researchers, as they aimed to slash humanities and social sciences by 2020 and gear themselves towards sciences, especially molecular recognition in biological systems, bioinformatics, and integrated nanostructure systems. Thus far, the researchers at UB had only been able to cause worms with nano-sized cell receivers implanted in their heads dance, but an announcement from the school told of the potential of remotely manipulated nanoparticles to develop a cure for cancer, diabetes, and some neurological disorders through remote manipulation of cells. The dancing worms were "just the beginning," announced the *New Scientist*. Researchers elsewhere were busy "targeting other hosts and implanting receivers in ion channels, DNA strands, and anti-bodies. Even better than nano-cells though were carbon nano-tubes, that act as stronger, more reliable radio receivers, antennas, amplifiers, and tuners. Scientists had recently demonstrated the ability to lower blood sugar levels in mice through magnetic field radio frequency targeting genetically modified nano-cells implanted in the mouse's brain. Some geneticists argue that DNA transmits information through radio waves.

269. Moreno, Jonathan D., *Mind Wars: Brian Science and the Military in the 21st Century*. 2nd ed., New York, Bellvue Literary Press, 2012:56-58, 71, 72, 73.

Moreno is a Bioethicist at the University of Pennsylvania and former staff member of the Hasting Center. He has also been a senior staff member for three Presidential advisory commissions and a member of several Pentagon advisory committees.

Among those advancements he outlined, developed with funding from DARPA, the DOD and other defense agencies were: "technologies to enable remote integration and control of biological systems at the system/organ/ tissue/ cellular / molecular scales [...]advanced signal processing techniques for the decoding of neural signs in real time, specifically those associated with operationally relevant cognitive events [and] new approaches for understanding and predicting the behavior of individuals and groups. [...]biological approaches for maintaining the warfighter's performance [and] capabilities [on the battlefield]...biological approaches for minimizing the after effects of battle injuries, including nuerotrauma ... [other] bio-inspired systems...understanding the human effects of non-lethal weapons... ... interface of biology with magnetics... advanced signal processing techniques for the decoding of neural signs in real time, specifically those associated with operationally relevant cognitive events, including target detection, errors, and other decision making processes...novel interfaces and sensor designs for interacting with the central and peripheral nervous systems, with a particular emphasis on noninvasive and/or non-contact approaches...new approaches for understanding and predicting the behavior of individuals and groups...technologies to engineer field medical therapies at the point of care..." (2012:26, 27).

270. *New York Times* "Obama Seeking to Boost Study of Human Brain" Feb. 17, 2013, John Markoff; See also, David A. Tesini, *International Journal of Childhood Education* "Development of a Biometric Infant Identification Tool: A New Safeguard through Innovation" 24:2 (2009); *Guardian* "Man Or Machine? The Age Of The Robot Blurs Sci-Fi and Cutting Edge Science" April 24, 2013; *Nature* "Brain Storm" Nov. 7, 2013, Helen Shen.

By 2013, the U.S. Food and Drug Administration had approved artificial retinas that restored partial sight to the blind.

271. Private companies like Allied Minds Devices, have partnered with the Department of Defense and federally funded research institutes in the further development and commercialization of new and improved devices (implantable and remote) to monitor and influence the mind using materials more conducive to implantation in the human body and more efficient telemetric guidance systems. Meanwhile, companies like Mind Technologies, Inc. and Jedi Mind, Inc. are devising more efficient "thought controlled applications" for consumers including the 'EEG headset' that allows the user to operate computer software and technologies made by the same company (*The Hamilton Spectator*, "Cyber hybrids far fetched? Just wait." Jan. 13, 2014 ; *Daily the Pak Banker* "Mind Technologies, Inc. Applications Approved for Sale on Emotiv Site" April 4, 2011).

As of 2010, George Lucas was suing Jedi Mind, Inc., for copyright infringement. The name of the company refers to the 'mind trick' used in Lucas' *Star Wars* movies wherein a "spectrum of force powers [influence] the thoughts of sentient creatures, most commonly used to coerce into agreement by suggestion through voice manipulation, or to cause one to reveal information [allowing] the practitioners to resolve matters in a non-violent way" (*Times of Oman* "Lucas sues to stop 'Jedi Mind' wireless headset" Aug. 27, 2010).

272. *The Hamilton Spectator* (Ontario) "Cyber hybrids far fetched? Just wait." Jan. 13, 2014.

The creators of Intelligence said they were inspired by researchers at the University Of Pittsburgh School Of Medicine who implanted brain electrodes into a paralyzed woman, thereby allowing her to control an arm prosthesis through thought alone.

273. NPR.org "Military Plans To Test Brain Implants To Fight Mental Disorders" May 27, 2010; *Electronics For You* "Tech News: Technology At Your Service, Technology To Put Electronics Into The Brain" July 1, 2015.

274. *The Globe and Mail* "OKLAHOMA BOMBING Whodunit? The Jews, the UN, the Japanese or the

evil Clinton? As usual, the conspiracy theorists have transformed what seems painfully obvious into a tangle of paranoia" July 8, 1995. *The Virginian Pilot* "Hold the microchip and pass the butter" Feb. 25, 2010.

275. W. Gaylin "Behavior control: from the brain to the mind" *Hastings Center Report,* 39(3) 2009; Michael L. Gross "Medicalized Weapons & Modern War" *Hastings Center Report,* 40 (1) 2010 .

276. Ray Pratt. *Projecting Paranoia: Conspiratorial Visions in American Film* University of Kansas Press, Lawrence, Kansas, 2001: 31 (quoting Stuart Samuels 1979: 204,205); Dean 119, 188.

277. McVeigh's anxiety centered on the fact that all cells contained cameras at the high security Supermax prisons and the fact that inmates were kept in near total isolation.

278. *Washington Post* "McVeigh Guilty On All 11 Counts" June 3, 1997.

279. Author interview with Christopher Tritico, Dec. 27, 2010, Houston, Texas.

280. Bruce Jackson ,*The Story Is True: The Art and Meaning of Telling Stories* Temple University Press, Philadelphia, PA., 2007:196.

281. Ten "civilian witnesses" chosen through a lottery would be granted access to watch the execution from the prison, 10 media witnesses, and 6 of McVeigh's choosing. John Ashcroft said, "The transmission to the victims in the Oklahoma City area will begin at the same time the curtain is opened for viewing ... All witnesses will see Mr. McVeigh on the execution table and they will be able to hear any final statement Mr. McVeigh makes" (News24.com "McVeigh's execution on CCTV" April 13, 2001).

282. *New York Times* "Lawyer Says McVeigh Appears Calm and Prepared To Die: June 11, 2001, Rick Bragg; *Business Insider* "20 years after the Oklahoma City bombing, Timothy McVeigh remains the only terrorist executed by US" April 19, 2015, Ryan Gorman; CBS News "McVeigh's Last Day" Jan.. 5, 2002 (as first reported by Associated Press).

283. Jody Lynn Maderia. *Killing McVeigh: The Death Penalty and the Myth of Closure* New York University Press, 2012: 216, 223, 224-226, 231-258; MSNBC "Live: McVeigh Execution" June 11, 2001; *Baltimore Sun* "U.S. Executes McVeigh, 'unbowed' until end" June 12, 2001; *New York Times* "Lawyer Says McVeigh Appears Calm and Prepared to Die" June 11, 2001; *Evening Times* (Glasgow) "Bomber made eye contact as he died ;Relatives of victims of Oklahoma blast see murderer of 168 executed" June 11, 2001; *Birmingham Evening Mail* "Put To Death: Oklahoma Bomber McVeigh Executed By Lethal Injection" June 11, 2001.

284. *Baltimore Sun,* June 12, 2001.

285. Rep. Dana Rohrabacher, *Chairman's Report Oversight and Investigations Subcommittee of the House International Relations Committee.* Dec. 26, 2006.

While it may be tempting to chalk up the story McVeigh told Jesse Trentadue to his last ditch attempt to stick it to the man, his frequent mention of Jesse Trentadue in letters to his biographers and others in April and May 2001, indicate otherwise. McVeigh, for whatever reason, seemed preoccupied by the Trentadue case.

286. 247news.com "The big bad wolf is dead! Or is he..." June 12, 2001; *Weekly World News,* "Timothy McVeigh is Alive" Sep.18, 2001, Cliff Lindecker.

287. McVeigh may have hinted at the story in June 1997 after his conviction when, in an attempt to console his grief stricken mother, he instructed her to think of his imprisonment as if he was "away in the Army again, on assignment for the military" (Herbeck and Michel 347).

288. Author interview with Randall Coyne, Jan. 18, 2011, Oklahoma City, Oklahoma.

289. Hammer 2004:184,192.

290. Hammer 2010: 224.

291. Author interview with Christopher Tritico, Dec. 27, 2010, Houston, Texas.

The year before, in 2009, Rob Nigh, who still acted as the executor of McVeigh's estate, said very much the same thing. Nigh explained how, after the execution, he personally took possession of McVeigh's ashes and scattered them in a secret location.

292. Benjamin Beit- Hallahmi, "Rebirth and Death: The Violent Potential of Apocalyptic Dream" pg. 163-189 in *The Psychology of Terrorism V. 3: Theoretical Understandings and Perspectives* Chris E. Stout Ed., Praeger, Westport, Connecticut, London, 2002: 163,166-168, 174.

293. Dorothy Otnow Lewis, *Guilty By Reason Of Insanity: A Psychiatrist Probes The Minds Of Killers*, Fawcett, 1998:179.

In a conversation with Lee Norton, McVeigh explained that by 1994, he "felt like he had lived through the Gulf War when he should have died ... It was just a numbers deal that he didn't. He felt [this and other] factors coming together were his sign to [do the bombing] – to take on a mission that was almost certain to end in his death ... he was at the bottom anyways" (Jones Collection).

294. The Outcome enhancements include, among others, neural regeneration, and electricity, sensory function and pain suppression. An accident at Ft. Detrick in 1985 led to the unintended discovery of chemicals used to their development.

295. In one scene, a subordinate working under Outcome's USAF overseer, protests the orders to 'terminate' Outcome operatives, "Do you understand their full utility? We just set Iran's missile program back thirty-six months with one deep cover agent. The best action recon out of North Korea in the last two years came from Outcome. Do you know how long we waited to get a real long-term operative inside Pakistani ISI? You're asking me to wipe the most valuable intel gathering assets we've ever put in the field!" (*The Bourne Legacy*, 2012).

296. "Dissociative fugue (DF) is a rapid-onset, time-limited disorder of episodic memory, usually related to an emotional or a psychological trauma rather than to an organic cause. There is often a period of flight or wandering of variable duration accompanied by unawareness of any problem and loss of personal identity. In dissociative disorders the normally well integrated functions of memory, identity, perception and consciousness are separated (dissociated). When patients gain awareness, they frequently remain unaware of their condition with reference to their amnesic period and often show a generalized flat affect" (Comparelli, DeCarolis, Kotzalidis, et. al., "A Woman Lost In The Cemetery: A Case Of Time Limited Amnesia" *Neurocase* V. 16 No. 1, 2010). "Dissociative fugue is a rare disorder which has been described as sudden, unexpected, travel away from home or one's customary place of daily activities, with the inability to recall some or all of one's past" (Chintan Madhusudan Raval, Sunnetkumar Upadhyaya, Bharat Navinchandra Pancha "Dissociative fugue: Recurrent episodes in a young Adult" Industrial *Psychiatry Journal* V. 24 No. 1, 2015). Dissociative fugue states typically last up to a few months until, at some point, their former memories begin to surface, leading to much confusion on the part of the dissociated, as they fully believed they were the person they had only recently become.

297. A.D. Macleod "Posttraumatic stress disorder, dissociative fugue and a locator beacon" *Australian & New Zealand Journal of Psychiatry*, V. 33, 1999: 102-104; Sallie Baxendale "Memories Aren't Made Of This: Amnesia At The Movies" British Medical Journal, V. 329 No. 7480, December 2004: 1481.

Reverend Bourne was a long time pillar of his Rhode Island community. Throughout his life, Bourne had suffered from headaches and sometimes blackouts usually lasting no more than an hour. In 1887, he went to the bank, withdrew money, traveled to a small town in Pennsylvania, and assumed the name A. J. Brown. As Brown, he rented space where he set up a general store, and became the town's shopkeeper and a member of the community. About two months later, he awoke suddenly in the middle of the night, terrified, and unknowing of where he was or how he got there. He refused to believe so much time had passed since taking the money out of the bank, as it seemed only yesterday. His family was contacted, retrieved him and took him to William James, a psychoanalyst, who placed him under hypnosis and was able to call up the Brown personality as well as Brown's memories. James wrote that while the two personalities seemed to have no knowledge of each other, "The Brown personality seems to be nothing but a rather shrunken, dejected, and amnesic extract of Mr. Bourne himself" (Ernest R. Hilgard, *Divided Consciousness: Multiple Controls in Human Thought and Action*, Wiley, 1977: 22-24).

298. Macleod 103, 104.

299. Garrett Stewart "Surveillance Cinema" Film Quarterly V. 66 No. 2, 2012; *The Hindu* "Jason Bourne Gets His Memory Back In 'Bourne 5': Matt Damon" Sep. 28, 2015.

300. Stewart 2012; Allan Hepburn. *Intrigue : Espionage and Culture*. New Haven, CT, USA: Yale University Press, 2005: 9, 10.

301. Jeff Stryker. "Lethal Injections: Medicine and Research." *Hastings Center Report* V. 38 No. 1, 2008; *New York Times* "The Needle and the Damage Done" Feb. 11, 2007, Elizabeth Weil; *Talk Left: The Politics of Crime* (website) "Missouri Executioner Had a Criminal Past" January 21, 2008; *Talk Left: The Politics of Crime* (website) "Dyslexic Execution MD Worked for Feds, Not Just Missouri" Nov.17, 2007.
    At the time of the 2007 trial, Doerhoff had supervised 54 executions.

302. Alfred McCoy , *A Question of Torture: CIA Interrogation, from the Cold War to the War on Terror*, Henry Holt and Co., LTD., New York, New York, 2007: 10.
    The practice of torture, like that of executions, serves a number of social functions, including punishment and a terror-producing deterrent to quell unrest and uprising. The threat of torture, like the punishment of death, may catalyze confessions, even if false. It also has a distinct medical aspect, as it is (supposedly) a highly calculated, precise process requiring the psychological and ethical dissociation of the person tasked with carrying out the state's mandate. While, unlike the American Psychological Association, the American Medical Association, the American Society of Anesthesiologists, and certain state medical boards forbid physicians from participating in executions, directly or indirectly, state courts have overruled this dictate, as executions are not considered a medical procedure.

303. In 2007, a participant in an essay posted on an online discussion board insisted that the execution "was all smoke in mirrors" and McVeigh, simply "an MKUltra experiment." Greg Szymanski "Oklahoma City Bomber Still Alive And Living In South America - FBI Whistleblower John Peeler" Blog. Jan.12, 2007.

304. Timothy Melley, "Brain Warfare: The Covert Sphere, Terrorism, and the Legacy of the Cold War" *Grey Room* 48 (2011): 22,23,34,35; Klaus Dodd, "Jason Bourne: Gender, Geopolitics and Representations of National Security" *Journal of Popular Film and Television* 2010: 22.
    Melley credits the term 'public secrets' to Taussig, *Defacement: Public Secrecy and the Labor of the Negative*, Stanford University Press, 1999. Melley credits the term 'spectacle of amnesia' to Rogin "Make My Day! Spectacle as Amnesia in Imperial Politics" *Representations* 29: 1990 (99-123).
    Melley, "Brain Warfare: The Covert Sphere, Terrorism, and the Legacy of the Cold War" *Grey Room*, V. 45, Fall 2011: 34.

305. About his 'case file' still in Jones' possession, specifically the FBI investigatory reports, called 302s, McVeigh said "There are completely false accounts in there. People who made shit up because they had prejudice against me and people who had no malice but got stuff wrong. [All] of the FBI 302s [are] negative. Nothing appears in the FBI 302 if it's positive. I could have opened a thousand doors for old ladies in my lifetime, but the one time I don't it will be in the 302. The other 1000 you'd never see referenced." McVeigh warned his biographers that if the material in the 'case file' became public, it would "ruin any interest" in *American Terrorist* or at least "greatly diminish it." According to McVeigh, the only upshot was that if Jones did leak all the material, he would risk "proving the very allegations against him- namely, [that] he's scum." He concluded by telling them to cross their fingers and hope Jones didn't blow their chance to release an exclusive book and instructing them not to take less than $1 million for the movie rights to the book (American Terrorist Collection).

306. It is probably wise to keep in mind though that many of McVeigh's most bizarre claims, be

they deceptions or delusions, are found to have some basis in reality, their origins and major elements of them traceable to actual circumstances and events in his life.

307. Jackson 198,202.

Endnotes: Epilogue

1. *Chicago Tribune* "Oswald's Ghost?" (letter) June 19, 1995, Jim Langan; *Washington Post*, "'McVeigh': A Chilling Portrait Of Seething Hate" April 19, 2010, Hank Stuever; *Philadelphia Daily News* "Ellen Gray: MSNBC's 'McVeigh Tapes' just a bit creepy" April 19, 2010; MSNBC. com "15 years later, hear McVeigh's confession: New documentary marks OKC anniversary, stirs emotion before it airs" April 15, 2010.

2. Chuleenan Svetvilas "Hybrid Reality: When Documentary and Fiction Breed to Create a Better Truth" *Documentary Magazine*, June 2004.

3. MSNBC, *The McVeigh Tapes: Confessions of an American Terrorist* (television special) April 19, 2010; *Washington Post*, April 19, 2010; *Philadelphia Daily News* April 19, 2010; MSNBC.com April 15, 2010.

4. The 1995 Oklahoma City bombing continues to inspire the production of purportedly fact based narratives (generally within news, scholarly and government accounts), but also fictional works in which McVeigh often appears in his role as 'Lone Wolf Bomber' and his supposed motivations for bombing the Murrah including events like Waco are recreated. When not explicit, these fictional works contain obvious trace references of McVeigh and the bombing. Such works of fiction include, but are not limited to the films *Fight Club* (David Fincher, 1999) and *Arlington Road* (Mark Pellington, 1999); the play *Terre Haute* (Edmund White 2006); a CBS docudrama *The Good Wife* (2011); and the novels Breaking and Entering (Eileen Pollack 2012) and *The Mirage* (Matthew Ruff 2012).

5. *The New Yorker* "The Far-Right Revival: A Thirty Year War?" Jan. 12, 2016, Evan Osnos; *The Daily Astorian* "Southern Exposure: Specter of militia past clouds ranchers' legitimate concerns" Jan. 13, 2016, R.J. Marx ; *Newsweek* "How Timothy McVeigh's Ideals Entered The Mainstream" June 1, 2015, Nina Burleigh.

6. The first significant post-execution full length book was *Final Report of the Oklahoma City Bombing Investigation Committee*, published privately in late 2001 by members of the Oklahoma City Bombing Investigation Committee. As discussed in the Introduction of this book, the OKCBI Committee, made up of victim family members, survivors, and citizens of Oklahoma and led by state Rep. Charles Key, was hampered during their initial task of obtaining and presenting evidence for the state of Oklahoma Grand Jury, which convened in 1997. The *Final Report* includes court documents, sworn affidavits, and Grand Jury testimony of over 80 eyewitness accounts of those who saw John Doe #2 and several who observed the Bomb Squad in downtown early the morning of the April 19, 1995.

7. Hamm 2001: 24-26, 191

Like a number of academic works before and after, *In Bad Company* used the bombing as a case study through which to examine the contentious political subculture inhabited by McVeigh and the reasons and processes of right-wing radicalization. Hamm offered a number of social, cultural, economic, and political theories about why individuals participate in violent subcultures and organized hate groups. Hamm argued that there was no singular "cause" for the radicalization of McVeigh and others but rather, that radicalization was the result of a number of "influences" that coalesced to create a "fertile situation" from which a dangerously violent underground subculture emerged. These influences included religious beliefs, personal pathology, political ideologies, militaristic popular culture, and shifting economic, political, and cultural circumstances.

In Mark Hamm's previous book, *Apocalypse In Oklahoma: Waco and Ruby Ridge Revenged*, published in 1997 prior to the start of McVeigh's trial, Hamm advocated a Lone Wolf theory of the bombing. By the time he published *In Bad Company* in 2001, Hamm had come to strikingly different conclusions arguing for a Pack of Wolves plot. The bombing, said Hamm, was a highly sophisticated act whose execution involved equally sophisticated criminal skill sets which McVeigh alone did not possess. The ever-elusive John Does, wrote Hamm, were not "a figment of anybody's imagination" (as many Lone Wolf proponents alleged) but "several men" working within "secret paramilitary cells" who assisted McVeigh in the conception, planning, and execution of the bombing, a scenario he termed the 'Multiple John Doe #2 Theory.' Hamm's John Doe 2's consisted of the usual Pack Of Wolves suspects, including ARA bank robbery gang, residents of Elohim City and other assorted Nazi's like paramilitary nano-chip locator Stephen Colbern. Despite the ways in which Hamm stops short of addressing the 'failures of intelligence,' *In Bad Company* was the first book-length academic publication to offer a coherent and detailed alternative narrative about the bombing. While other Non-Lone Wolf books had been published previously, they did not tell a linear story, but rather offered a series of fragmented arguments against the official (Lone Wolf) story. The book did help to account, albeit circumstantially, for the many eyewitnesses' statements and reconciled gaps in the chronology offered by prosecutors. *In Bad Company* reflects the ways in which conceptualizations of the bombing and McVeigh's role in it, changed over time. In retrospect, the impact of *In Bad Company* was that it acted as a catalyst for some social scientists to exclude the OKC bombing from the rubric of Lone Wolf Terrorism and McVeigh from the category of Lone Wolf Terrorist and is often cited in academic literature about terrorism.

8. Wright 2007: 5, 22-26, 32-37, 96,97, 115, 159 166, 191, 215.

In a general sense, like Hamm before him, in *Patriots, Politics and The Oklahoma City Bombing* Wright explored contentious right-wing social movements and subcultures and the formation and enactment of McVeigh's "insurgent consciousness." More specifically, Wright focused on the ways in which the Patriot Movement was framed as a public threat, largely through the media. Agents of social control employed this framing to justify their own policies and the increased militarization of law enforcement (as seen in Ruby Ridge and Waco). This resulted in further mobilization and escalated responses, sometimes violent responses, on the part of the Patriot Movement, in what Wright called a "trajectory of contention," and says the plan to bomb the Murrah federal building was a culmination of escalated mutual threat construction by both 'sides.' Wright concludes by explaining how, given its inhumanity and horror, the bombing, rather than being the 'shot heard round the world' or signal to other revolutionaries to take action, instead marked the processes which began the Patriot movements' demobilization. Wright concluded that, after the bombing, local armed militias essentially dissipated as did the threat represented by the extreme right; a conclusion contradictory to the continued announcements by the FBI, Homeland Security, and watchdog groups like the Southern Poverty Law Center who, after the 2008 Presidential election of Barack Obama, asserted that militia, and neo-Nazi groups skyrocketed.

9. Wright 2007: xiv, 181-193 citing Associated Press, "Documents suggests McVeigh not alone at bombing scene" April 20, 2004 (An earlier version of Solomon's report appeared in the Associated Press on February 25, 2004, in an article entitled "AP finds documents showing FBI destroyed proof possibly tying robbers to Oklahoma City bombing").

On May 26, 2004, a state jury found Nichols guilty of 161 counts of 1st degree murder and he was given 161 consecutive life terms without parole. Wright and others claim that the newly 'discovered' Secret Service memo along with the introduction of other evidence, created reasonable doubt among jurors who deadlocked during the penalty stage and ultimately spared Nichols from a death sentence. Other newly introduced evidence in the 2004 trial included previously unheard testimony of several additional eyewitnesses who, within hours of the bombing, reported to the FBI they observed the Ryder with two individuals within it. In a press conference after the conclusion of the 2004 trial, the jury foreman explained to NPR, "the government dropped the ball. I think there are other people out there." In Wright's estimation, the bombing plot consisted of "as many as ten persons were involved in the assembly and delivery of the bomb," a theory that accounts for numerous conflicting eyewitness accounts. Wright also expanded Hamm's 'Multiple JD2 theory' beyond McVeigh's associates within the ARA, Elohim City and the WPM to include other associates connected to the militia and Patriot movements whom Wright specifically alleges coordinated their efforts (with McVeigh) "under the cover of the gun show circuit." Wright says the involvement of so many conspirators explains and accounts for over 226 eyewitnesses who saw McVeigh with others prior to the bombing (many of whom testified at the state grand jury proceedings).

10. Wright 2007: 180-193.

Wright also called attention to not only the FBI and ATF's failure to pass on critical information about the plot brewing at Elohim City but also to the FBI's possession and destruction of photographic and video evidence linking McVeigh to members of the ARA bank robbery gang.

11. Representative Dana Rohrabacher, "Chairman's Report Oversight and Investigations Subcommittee of the House International Relations Committee: The Oklahoma City Bombing: Was There A Foreign Connection?" 2006 ['Rohrabacher Report'].

One possible reason Congressman Rohrabacher's investigation may have been ignored by Wright and others was its initial focus on long dormant and politically volatile 'Middle Eastern connection' theories about the bombing that fall out of the scope of domestic right-wing terrorist explorations. While Rohrabacher initially set out to investigate some of the loose ends relating to possible Middle Eastern suspects, his committee ultimately also examined evidence of a larger homegrown conspiracy. The Chairman's report detailing the investigation's findings begins by stating that while McVeigh and Nichols were responsible for the bombing and that upon their convictions, "justice was served," admits that, "from the time of the bombing until today, questions persist as to whether others were involved..." These questions included, but were not limited to: Terry Nichols' activities in the Philippines and his possible connections to a number of foreign terrorists and terrorist groups; the numerous John Doe 2 sightings and their identities; McVeigh's connection to Elohim City and various associated individuals; his relationship with the ARA bank robbers, and the claims made by some of the robbers about the involvement of other ones in the bombing plot; the warnings of ATF and FBI informants about the impending bombing; and the fact that McVeigh's "own defense team had significant internal doubts about [his] candor with them" when he claimed no additional conspirators existed. The report continued, saying, "If the Oversight and Investigations Subcommittee was successful, it should have resulted in a positive affirmation of federal law enforcement's willingness to find and share vital information. Instead, Justice Department officials (and perhaps, the CIA) were less than responsive in crucial stages of this investigation, exemplifying needless defensiveness." To which I would ask if perhaps the defiant displays of defensiveness were not needless at all but based on a reason unknown to or unarticulated by the committee.

12. Oklahoma State Representative Charles Key interview with author, Oklahoma City, Oklahoma. May 24, 2008.

13. Rohrabacher Report, 2006.

14. BBC "Oklahoma Bomb: The Conspiracy Files" (television show) March 4, 2007; *BBC News* "Call to re-open Oklahoma bomb case" March 2, 2007.

15. *Wall Street Journal* "REVIEW: Spring Books: Investigating the Investigation" April 14, 2012

The *Wall Street Journal* review noted (among other things) that, "Among the glaring gaps in the investigation was the failure of the FBI to attempt to match the more than 1,000 unidentified latent fingerprints found in the investigation -- taken from McVeigh's car and motel room, as well as from the office where he had rented the truck -- to the FBI's computerized database or even to perform a comparison among them to see how many belonged to the same people. This failure proved important because, as the authors demonstrate, almost all the eyewitnesses to the crime claimed that McVeigh was not alone.[...] Certainly eyewitnesses testimony can be unreliable, but 24 mistaken witnesses –and no accurate ones? [...] There is no shortage of suspects in this bizarre universe, including gun-show scamsters, bank robbers, drug addicts, and neo-Nazis."

16. *Tulsa World* "Famous filmmaker making OKC bombing movie" March 3, 2011; *Daily Variety* "Helmer's got 'Gotti' May 3, 2011; *A.V. Club* "Barry Levinson making film about the Oklahoma City bombing" March 3, 2011, Sean O'Neal; *Tulsa World* "Hollywood should stick to facts in OKC bombing movie" (editorial) March 5, 2011; Slashfilm.com "Barry Levinson Will Direct Timothy McVeigh Bombing Movie 'O.K.C.'" March 3, 2011, Russ Fischer.

The unnamed author of one editorial wrote that, while he hoped for the best, he (or she) suspected O.K.C would "be a farce" filled with "wild theories" and "take a turn toward a conspiracy that didn't exist" (*Tulsa World*, March 5, 2011). Another write up expressed the opinion that if O.K.C. planned to assert that anyone but McVeigh, the "pure sociopath," was involved with the bombing, the movie would be "infuriating beyond belief" (Slashfilm.com, March 3, 2011). O.K.C, another write-up predicted, would probably explore any number of "oft floated theories" of the bombing relating to the identities of McVeigh's other conspirators, and no matter which one (if any) it settled on was bound to be "inflammatory" and upset Oklahomans (*A.V. Club*, March 3, 2011).

17. CNN " FBI Admits Years of Bad Testimony; Lessons Learned from Oklahoma City Bombing; One Year Later" April 19, 201.

18. *Mother Jones* "In Search of John Doe No. 2: The Story the Feds Never Told About the Oklahoma City Bombing" Aug. 3, 2007, James Ridgeway.

19. Jesse explained that Kenneth, like many Vietnam veterans, had come home with a drug habit that inevitably resulted in trouble with the law. Kenneth had been released on parole in 1988, and although he had a minor violation in 1989, nothing had ever come of it until his 1995 arrest. Since his release, Kenneth had turned his life around and stayed out of trouble. Jesse later obtained transcripts of the taped phone calls between Kenneth and his family from the OKC Transfer Center which showed that at no time, did Kenneth indicate any worry or concern about his hearing but rather, only that he was eager to return to his family.

20. Jesse said, "I found out later that an autopsy had already been done. The federal government didn't want one done but the state of Oklahoma required one for deaths of inmates. The federal government didn't want an autopsy done and went twice to the Oklahoma medical examiner's office, asking to have Kenny cremated. It took a week to get his body released and home and I kept getting the run around from the federal government and finally, I just said "Why don't you keep him?!" (*A Noble Lie: Oklahoma City 1995*, Free Mind Films, 2011) During the many phone calls trying to secure the release of Kenneth's body, the prison warden continued to make strange statements indicating they believed Kenneth was somebody else entirely. For instance, when Kenneth's mother said that Kenneth's wife would decide what was to become of Kenneth's body, the warden "went ballistic" and said Kenneth did not have a wife. When his aggrieved and perplexed mother finally said that Kenneth's brother, Jesse, would contact the prison and handle the situation, the warden once again became outraged and yelled that Kenneth didn't have any siblings. The warden continued to make these types of strange statements and further, attempted to have Kenneth cremated despite the wishes of his family (*McCurtain County Gazette* "In The Matter of Kenneth Michael Trentadue" April 7, 2004, J.D. Cash).

21. In his August 30, 1995 letter of complaint to the BOP, Jesse wrote, "This is how you returned my brother to us.... My brother had been so badly beaten that I personally saw several mourners leave the viewing to vomit in the parking lot! Anyone seeing my brother's battered body with his bruised and lacerated forehead, throat cut, and blue-black knuckles would not have concluded that his death was either easy or a 'suicide'! [...]Had my brother been less of a man, you[r] guards would have been able to kill him without inflicting so much injury to his body. Had that occurred, Kenney's family would forever have been guilt-ridden... with the pain of thinking that Kenneth took his own life and that we had somehow failed him. By making the fight he did for his life, Ken has saved us that pain and God bless him for having done so!" (Letter. From: Jesse C. Trentadue To: Marie Carter, Acting Warden, Federal Transfer Center, Oklahoma City, Oklahoma, RE: Kenneth Michael Trentadue, Aug. 30, 1995).

22. Kenneth's cell had been scrubbed cleaned the morning he was found dead. Upon receiving his body and noting its condition, the medical examiner issued orders to preserve the cell but the orders were ignored. Instead, the cell was repainted; covering up pencil scrawls on the wall that officials claimed was Kenneth's suicide note. Prison officials had taken pictures of the alleged note, which, according to a written report, said "My Minds No Longer It's Friend" and "Love Ya Familia!" and, for some reason, "Love Paul." When he was allowed to inspect the cell 6 months after Kenneth's death, Jordon conducted a luminal test and found traces of now invisible blood belonging to someone other than Kenneth, throughout the cell.

23. In October 1995, BOP attorneys issued an internal memo observing the likelihood that the Trentadue family would file suit against the BOP, hence filed all resulting documentation as 'Attorney Work Products' thereby making them undiscoverable in a court action. In 1995, the FBI ostensibly conducted it's own investigation of Kenneth's death in response to Medical Examiner Rowland's reports, but never looked in the cell or collected any evidence. Nor did they speak to the inmates who were in adjacent cells. Their investigation consisted of speaking with prison officials. In subsequent years, Jesse Trentadue did obtain some information, none of it favorable to the BOP. For instance, although a prison medic initially said he attempted to perform CPR, he later admitted he hadn't and that, in fact no effort had been made to resuscitate Kenneth Trentadue. On August 21, 1995, a prison guard passing by Kenneth's cell found his body hanging from a bedsheet noose at 3:02 AM. The guard reported the death and videographers came to document the scene; however, the content of the tapes were erased as an FBI agent was later forced to admit in a later civil suit. When the family requested the photos of Kenneth's cell (taken while he was still in it), they were told the pictures had been lost although they showed back up in the FBI's files many years later. By the time Kenneth's body was given to the medical examiner, his clothing had been destroyed.

Due to eroded public confidence in the BOP and FBI resulting from allegations about mishandled, lost, and destroyed evidence in the case, lead state prosecutor Bob Macy was asked to conduct his own independent investigation into the death. Ultimately, Macy found only favorable information about both agencies. In subsequent years, the extent of conflict of interest between Macy, his staffers and the other agencies investigations into the death became a matter of public record.

24. The Trentadue case had attracted the media attention as well as the attention of at least three state senators, one of whom personally told Janet Reno that he believed Kenneth had been murdered. Medical Examiner Fred Jordon had conducted an autopsy and detailed his findings in the days following Kenneth's death but was told by the FBI in late 1995 not to release the report until they concluded their own investigation. Therefore, the Trentadue family was unaware that an autopsy had even been performed until this time. Beyond recording his findings in official report including the autopsy report, Jordon told the U.S. Attorney's office in Oklahoma City hat Kenneth Trentadue had been "abused and tortured." In one medical examiner office memo, Jordon wrote that it was "very likely this man was killed." Jordon went so far as to place several calls to Attorney General Janet Reno about the Trentadue matter but she refused to take the calls. He finally got the attention of U.S. Attorney in Oklahoma City, Patrick Ryan, who initiated the Grand Jury investigation, largely because of Jordon and pressure from sympathetic legislators (who told Reno they would hold a Senate Judiciary Committee investigation into the matter if her office continued to do nothing).

25. Letter. From: Jesse C. Trentadue. To: Honorable Patrick Leahy, Chairman, Senate Judiciary Committee, United States Senate, RE: Mr. Eric Holder, Nominee for Attorney General (with attached internal DOJ documents), Dec. 19, 2008; *Mother Jones*, Aug. 3, 2007.

Immediately, after the formation of the Grand Jury investigation and in the years to follow, Jordon complained to a number of people that he was being pressured to rule Trentadue's injuries, self-inflicted. In July 1997, Fred Jordon told local reporters, "I think it's very likely [Kenney] was murdered. I'm not able to prove it....You see a body covered with blood, removed from the room as Mr. Trentadue was, soaked in blood, covered with bruises, and you try to gain access to the scene, and the government of the United States says no, you can't.... At that point, we have no crime scene, so there are still questions about the death of Kenneth Trentadue that will never be answered because of the actions of the U.S. government." Thus, Fred Jordon became a great liability for the DOJ as they attempted to cover up the death of Kenneth Trentadue. The pressure and threats of retribution became so great that, in August 1997, Jordon wrote the IRS and requested a protective audit, outlining his concerns about DOJ and FBI retributive actions and sought the help of elected officials. After he changed his findings, Jordon wrote a deposition in which he stated that from "the very beginning of the case" the outset, he had been harassed by the DOJ and that he still believed Kenneth had been beaten (Mother Jones Aug. 3, 2007).

According to internal FBI correspondence, the Bureau considered charging Jesse Trentadue with obstruction of justice which would "place him as a target on one of our investigations and would also prohibit [him] from testifying before the Grand Jury" (*McCurtain County Gazette*, April 7, 2004).

26. During the wrongful death suit, agents from the Oklahoma Bureau of Investigation (OKCBI) testified that the blood of someone other than Kenneth had been found in the cell and that the noose he allegedly hung himself with contained no cut marks, although prison officials had cut it down. Jesse had obtained an internal FBI memo that detailed the statements of the prison guard who claimed Kenneth had been murdered and then hung.

27. *McCurtain County Gazette*, April 7, 2004.

28. In 1999, the U.S. Inspector General found that the FBI and BOP had conducted an inadequate investigation into Kenneth's death and that several federal agents and officials had committed perjury, provided false and inaccurate statements, and mishandled evidence. Some of the FBI agents who conducted the initial investigation of Kenneth's death refused to comply with the IG's requests for documents, although they were never sanctioned for their defiance. Like the Grand Jury, they too exonerated FBI and prison officials in the death itself and failed to indict anyone for the murder.

When Jesse filed a complaint with the President's Council on Efficiency and Integrity, a White House agency, about the OIG's "shoddy" investigation, it dismissed the complaint but sent him 55 pages of evidence submitted by the OIG, all but 350 words of which were redacted.

After the Trentadue family won their civil suit, the DOJ appealed but in 2008, the ruling was upheld although the amount awarded to the Trentadue family was reduced to $900,000. Although they have yet to receive the majority of the money awarded to them, the Trentadue family continues to offer a $250,000 reward for information leading to an arrest and conviction of Kenneth's murderers.

29. Early on, in 1996, Jesse had received an anonymous call making the same claim as McVeigh made to him in 2001 that his brother fit a profile and was killed during an FBI interrogation. At that time however, the claim sounded unbelievable and Jesse wrote it off as a prank. The anonymous caller may have been an earlier message originating with McVeigh himself. While Jesse began his investigation into Kenneth's death sincerely believing the FBI would do anything in their power to help, by the time he received McVeigh's message, he had learned otherwise and was ready to pursue the lead. As Jesse quickly discovered, the resemblance between Guthrie and Kenneth Trentadue was uncanny. They were the same height (5'8'), had the same color hair and eyes, as well as the same physique and both had the same dragon tattoo on the same location on their arm, a tattoo that several of the John Doe 2 eyewitnesses also reported. The day before he died, Guthrie had arranged for an interview with a journalist whom he promised to reveal explosive information about the bombing too.

30. Scott Horton "They Are Lying To You About The Oklahoma City Bombing" (radio interview with Jesse Trentadue) Antiwar.com, March 30, 2010; Andrew Gumbel "A Coverup Under Two

Presidents: The Unsolved Mystery of the Oklahoma City Bombing" truthdig.com, Feb. 21, 2006.

31. Jesse's FOIAs led to the discovery of at least three additional federal informants placed within Elohim City and/or bank robbery gang in the years leading up to the bombing, and further information about those whose identities were already known. In addition, his FOIA results revealed that for some reason, the CIA was maintaining active satellite surveillance over both Elohim City and Oklahoma City at the time of the bombing, although the results of this surveillance remain unknown.

32. Jesse C. Trentadue vs. Federal Bureau Of Investigation [FBI] and FBI's Oklahoma City Field Office, U.S. District Court, Utah, Central Division, "Amended Memorandum Decision And Order" Case No. 2:04CV772 DAK, March 30, 2006.

Southern Poverty Law Center spokesman Morris Dees made a statement during a press conference that the SPLC had had their own informants within Elohim City prior to the bombing and that they had warned the FBI of the impending attack in Oklahoma. When he learned of Dees' statement, Jesse filed a Freedom of Information Act request seeking all information that had been given by the SPLC to the FBI as it related to the Oklahoma City bombing investigation, both prior to and after April 19, 1995, specifically in regards to Elohim City, the ARA and their links to Timothy McVeigh. The FBI's response to Jesse's FOIA denied the material existed. Jesse appealed and submitted to the court two FBI memos which had been leaked to him. The memos, written in 1996 and authored by then FBI Director Louis Freeh, describe a nationwide undercover sting operation involving acts of planned domestic terrorism. An informant within this sting, Freeh wrote, had reported that on April 16, 1995, three days before the bombing, McVeigh had called Elohim City requesting additional help in the planned attack. In 2006, after Jesse submitted the memos to the court, the FBI was ordered to search once more for the requested material. In turn, the FBI produced 58 pages of heavily redacted investigatory documents. Among them was an FBI report discussing a joint FBI/ SPLC undercover sting operation, whose scope was national, and whose targets were several patriot, militia, and/or neo-Nazi groups. The sting operation seemed to have captured McVeigh and his cohorts in its net. Jesse observed that although the documents had made reference to an ongoing and long term investigation prior to April 19, 1995, all documents produced had been written days after the bombing. Not satisfied, Jesse requested those written prior.

33. The 2006 Congressional Oversight Committee investigation noted the FBI's apparently intentional attempt to hide the truth concerning the death of Kenneth Trentadue. Also supportive of Jesse's efforts was former FBI Deputy Assistant Director Danny Coulson, who had been in charge of evidence gathered from the Murrah after the attack. In March 2007, Coulson told BBC that he was "calling for a federal grand jury investigation into the bombing, because he questions whether everyone involved was caught." Coulson says that the "FBI headquarters prematurely shut down their investigation into the alleged links" between Elohim City and the bombing (BBC News "Call to reopen Oklahoma bomb case" March 2, 2007).

In 2008, Jesse sought (with much resistance by the FBI and Bureau of Prisons) to depose Terry Nichols, former death row inmate as well as self-proclaimed confidant of Timothy McVeigh, David Paul Hammer, and convicted ARA bank robber Peter Langan. Since the time of his arrest for the bank robberies and the death of his childhood friend and partner in crime, Richard Lee Guthrie, Langan maintained that he had information about the bombing. Included was Langan's knowledge about the participation of members of the bank robbery gang, but that "the federal government has gone to extreme lengths to prevent those fragments of the truth from coming out and coming together as a coherent story" (Jesse Trentadue vs. FBI, FBI OKC Field Office, Case no: 2;04 CV 00772 DAK, April 16, 2007 "Declaration Of Peter Kevin Langan" April 9, 2007). Although the FBI and BOP sought to block Jesse's depositions, in 2008, the court ruled in Jesse's favor and allowed him to depose Nichols, Langan, and Hammer with the stipulation that the depositions not be videotaped. At this time Nichols, not able to be re-tried, offered to reveal more information about the bombing, however, shortly when Nichols wrote a letter to the DOJ to this effect, then Attorney General John Ashcroft barred him from *all* media contact.

34. *Democracy Now* "In Search of John Doe No. 2: The Story the Feds Never Told About the Oklahoma City Bombing" Aug. 3, 2007.

35. Jesse said that when they released the partial footage in 2010, the FBI didn't know he had the documents proving they collected tapes from many more cameras than the small portion they acknowledged and therefore only released footage from cameras (they thought) he was aware of. When the FBI's first witness got on the stand, he presented a document pertaining to one of the cameras and asked if they found that footage, and he said he had. Jesse did this a couple of times and then suddenly presented the FBI documents pertaining to other cameras, asking if he had turned that footage over, to which the witnesses responded he had not. He would then remind witnesses that his FOIA requested not only the footage but the documentation of who took possession of it. The witness stated that the FBI had only turned over documents pertaining to footage that had been "placed in evidence" after the bombing. Jesse asked, "So if it doesn't go into evidence, I don't get it even though you may have it?" And the witnesses said that was correct. The judge then interrupted and said the FOIA request specified footage and related documentation in the FBI's possession and had never mentioned "evidence." After reminding the witness of this, the judge asked the witness if he had heard him correctly, to which the witness, "in the government's arrogance," responded, "of course you did." Jesse said, "I knew from this, the first witness that they were in a world of shit" (Jesse Trentadue, Feb. 8, 2015).

Jesse submitted two sworn affidavits by individuals who told a very different story than that told by the FBI. OKCPD first responder Don Browning arrived at the site of the explosion only moments after it had occurred. While assisting in the location and rescue of people trapped by Browning says that he and other rescuers were ordered to cease their efforts and evacuate the building, something Browning found "strange given the carnage and need to move quickly in hopes of locating and hopefully saving more victims trapped by the blast." Security expert and subcontractor Joe Bradford Cooley swore in his affidavit that he had made several inspections of the Murrah's security system, including in the days before the bombing and that it had been functioning as it should (United States District Court for the District of Utah, Central Division. Trentadue vs. FBI, DOJ, CIA. Case No. 2:08cv788CW, "Declaration of Joe Bradford Cooley" Feb. 1, 2010 and "Declaration of Don Browning" Feb. 16, 2010).

In addition, when a trial was held on the issue in July 2014, Jesse presented other witnesses who lived in downtown Oklahoma City and who told of other surveillance cameras in and around the building. He then cross-examined lead OKC bombing investigator Jon Hersley, who during McVeigh's preliminary hearing one week after the bombing, testified about footage from a camera down the street from the Murrah that showed McVeigh driving the truck up to the Murrah on the morning of the bombing. Jesse reminded him of this earlier testimony after which Hersley responded that he had been "mistaken" (Jesse Trentadue, Feb. 8, 2015). After this, the FBI finally admitted that while at least some of the tapes had once existed, they had since been "lost." Federal Judge Clark Waddoups then ordered the FBI to respond by June 30, 2011 and give a reason why they could not conduct a further search and explain why FBI officials had previously made false and inaccurate statements to the court about the tapes. (*Mother Jones*, July 21, 2011).

36. Trentadue V. Federal Bureau Of Investigation, et. al. "Plaintiffs Proposed Finding Of Fact" U.S. Case No. 2:08-cv-0788, April 20, 2014.

37. Author interview with Jesse Trentadue, Feb. 8, 2015, Salt Lake City, Utah.

38. Jesse explained that Matthews, who had infiltrated 23 groups, told him a "horrifying story." Matthews told him that during one of their operations in the 1990's, the FBI had given a targeted group 168 pounds of C4 explosives and the blueprints for a detailed plan that involved blowing up the cooling system at Browns Ferry Nuclear Power Plant, which if it were to occur would cause a meltdown resulting in thousands of deaths. The FBI had provided the idea, the plan, and the materials. This was during the time of Waco and Ruby Ridge when PATCON operatives had "plans

cooking all over the country" and Matthews was in the thick of it. The idea was that if several of these incidents occurred in the same time frame, the FBI could "roll in and say 'We've got a rebellion going on'" (Author interview with Jesse Trentadue, Feb. 8, 2015, Salt Lake City, Utah). PATCON had gone so far as to recruit members into fake FBI militia and Patriot groups thereby propagating and spreading the very violent ideologies it was meant to combat.

39. Author interview with Jesse Trentadue, Feb. 8, 2015, Salt Lake City, Utah.

40. Examiner.com "The article Newsweek gutted—more proof of FBI corruption" Nov. 25 2011, Anthony Martin.

Matthew's, who was featured prominently on the cover of *Newsweek*, was furious. He had taken a lot of risks by coming forward and telling his story. He told Jesse that the men who ran PATCON and the people he himself had spied on were "still out there." Having omitted the reasons he told it in the first place, the story made him a target for no good reason and he regretted coming forward.

41. Author interview with Jesse Trentadue, Feb. 8, 2015, Salt Lake City, Utah; *Salt Lake Tribune* "Lawyer says FBI threatened witness in OKC bombing records trial" July 31, 2014; *Salt Lake Tribune* "FBI to probe tampering claims in OKC bombing records case" Aug. 26, 2014.

According to one news outlet, the FBI threatened Matthews that if he testified, they would take away his VA benefits thereby preventing him from receiving treatment for his Agent Orange related cancer. Jesse Trentadue believes that the FBI threatened Matthews' family.

42. Jesse Trentadue V. United States Central Intelligence Agency, et. al. U.S. District Court For The District Of Utah, Central Division, Case No. 2:08-cv-0788, April 30, 2015.

43. Trentadue V. CIA, et. al. U.S. Case No. 2:08-cv-0788, April 30, 2015; *Desert Morning News* "Judge scolds FBI in bombing video case" Nov. 14, 2014.

A Special Master acts as the 'eyes and ears' of the judge who appoints them. Special Master's may be appointed if a case (1) "involves an especially complex or technical area of the law" (2) requires heightened, time consuming discovery oversight" (3) "calls for fact intensive non-jury determinations" or (4) "entails a long post-trial or post-settlement stage…or monitoring and compelling compliance with injunctive relief." (David R. Cohen, "Litigation: The Judge, the Special Master, and You" American Bar Association, Jan./ Feb. 2015).

44. Trentadue V. CIA, et. al. U.S. Case No. 2:08-cv-0788, "Memorandum Decision And Order Appointing Special Master" April 30, 2015.

45. *Desert Morning News*, Nov. 14, 2014.

46. *Desert Morning News* "Ruling reveals CIA involvement in Oklahoma City bombing investigation" March 31, 2010.

47. Author interview with Jesse Trentadue, Feb. 8, 2015, Salt Lake City, Utah.

Prior to the FBI's acknowledgement of the program, an ABC News spokesperson told the Center For Public Integrity, a media watchdog organization, that the alleged program was of "grave concern" to the network because it could "create a perception of collusion between the government and the news organization," endanger journalists suspected of "acting as government agents," and "raise the specter of the government trying to spy on a news organization" (John Solomon, Aaron Mehta "Memo Suggests FBI Had Mole Inside ABC News In 1990's: Agents Treated Reporter Like Informant, Raising Question: Who Else?" Center For Public Integrity, April 5, 2011 updated May 19, 2014).

48. National Association Of Criminal Defense Lawyers "The FBI's I-Drives- The Real 'X-Files'" Aug. 9, 2007, Jack King, NACDL Public Affairs Director .

49. *Mother Jones* "Did the FBI Bury Oklahoma City Bombing Evidence?" July 21, 2011, James Ridgeway.

Prosecutors are required to turn over exculpatory evidence as per Brady vs. Maryland. Such information includes "deals made with state's witnesses, crime scene evidence that could be tested for DNA, information that could discredit a state's witness and portions of police reports that could be favorable to the defendant" (*Huffington Post*, Aug. 1, 2013). Through a loophole, I-Drive files are excluded from this, thereby making it a convenient way to lose inconvenient information unfavorable to a prosecutor's case.

50. Allison J. Doherty "The FBI's I-drive and the right to a fair trial" *Iowa Law Review,* V. 91 No. 1571, July 2006; *Huffington Post* "The Untouchables: America's Misbehaving Prosecutors, And The System That Protects Them" Aug. 1, 2013, Radley Balko.

51. Doherty 2006;*Desert Morning News* "Judge Wants FBI to explain possibly missing Oklahoma City bombing videotapes" May 11, 2011; *Mother Jones* "July 21, 2011; *Desert Morning News* "Records show FBI practice of hiding evidence in secret databases" May 13, 2011; Association Press "FBI finds nothing for 2 out of 3 who seek records" March 13, 2009.

52. Amanda Marie Swain "Trentadue v. Integrity Committee: An Attempt to Reign in the Expansion of the Freedom of Information Act's 5th Exemption" *Oklahoma Law Review* V. 61: 2008, pg. 371-394; Author interview with Jesse Trentadue, Feb. 8, 2015, Salt Lake City, Utah.

53. Letter. Jesse C. Trentadue to Honorable Patrick Leahey, Chairman, Senate Judiciary Committee, United States Senate, RE: Mr. Eric Holder, Nominee for Attorney General (with attached internal DOJ documents), Dec. 19, 2008; *Mother Jones*, Aug. 3, 2007; William Norman Grigg "False Flags, Biker Gangs, and the PATCON Legacy" Lewrockwell.com, May 20, 2015.

It turns out that in the course of his undercover PATCON related activities, Matthews' handler Don Jarrett instructed him to help biker gangs in Arizona modify semi-automatic weapons into automatic ones, which were then sold through an Arizona gun store called, no lie, Lone Wolf Trading Co.. The authorities had full knowledge of the gangs' involvement in international drug running and the sale of the guns. Coincidentally (maybe), this was during the same time that McVeigh himself was offloading automatic weapons supposedly stolen from federal asset and weapons trafficker, Roger Moore, all of which was supposedly investigated by the FBI and DOJ. Matthews' story about PATCON sanctioned weapons running mentions a number of locations in Arizona where McVeigh also appeared. The Lone Wolf gun store/ PATCON/ Matthews/ biker gang connections may provide insight into McVeigh's strange claims that part of his undercover mission was to involve international drug running. Matthews' gun running account was confirmed by emails between him and Don Jarrett, that became part of the Fast And Furious investigations.

The Lone Wolf gun store ended up being "ground zero" for ATF's sale of untraceable weapons to Mexican criminal cartels, more than a few of which were used in the commission of hundreds of violent murders. Revealed by a whistleblower in 2010, the ATF operation, ostensibly meant to track the guns thereby exposing and arresting traffickers, in reality accomplished exactly the opposite (*Dallas Morning News* "Was a gun lost in a failed government sting used in Garland shooting?" (editorial) Aug. 4, 2015). In 2011, Holder was investigated and in 2012, exonerated by the DOJ's Office of Inspector General; the same office that briefly investigated Kenneth Trentadue's death and then sealed the findings. In later 2013, Holder, not for the first or last time, expressed that what he was most afraid of were "individuals who get radicalized in a variety of ways," sometimes radicalizing themselves, and end up committing "lone wolf" terrorist attacks. He then deflected questions about his authorization of egregious domestic surveillance tactics and programs and said NSA whistleblower Edward Snowden should not be offered clemency, perhaps not surprising given Holder's penchant for both egregious domestic operations and secret keeping (CNN "Holder fears 'lone wolf' terrorist attack, doesn't want TSA armed" Nov. 5, 2013). As Attorney General of the DOJ, Holder would also attract attention for his broad subpoenas on the emails and phone records of the Associated Press and Fox News. President Obama's response to this was to ask Holder to investigate allegations about the misconduct of Holder himself and his subordinates, just one more instance of the government being asked to police and investigate itself.

54. In the wake of the Oklahoma City bombing, the FBI increased it's already extensive (although

as yet unknown) surveillance of so called and self-proclaimed right wing militia and patriot groups with the stated objective of detecting the next terrorist attack before it could happen. While these efforts were largely praised in the media, even at the time, defense lawyers, judges, and juries acknowledged the use of government provocateurs in these plots and number of "terrorist cabals plotting violent rebellion" supposedly uncovered, resulted in acquittals, mistrials, mixed verdicts, and reduced charges. Prior to OKC, claims about pervasive levels of infiltration were passed off as paranoia (*Toronto Star* "Poison in a nest of Vipers U.S. agents are infiltrating right-wing militias in a bid to stop terrorism. But are they pushing the groups into violence?" June 2, 1997).

55. Robert Bejesky, "Sixty Shades Of Terror Plots: Locating The Actus Reus And The Hypothetical Line For Entrapment." Creighton Law Review, V. 48, No. 393, June 2015.

56. *Mother Jones* "The Informants" July 29, 2011, Trever Aaronson; Columbia Human Rights Institute "Illusions of Justice: Human Rights Abuses in US Terrorism Prosecutions" July 2014.

57. Bejesky 447, 448.

For instance, the *Creighton Law Review* article notes that the DOJ claimed to have secured 261 "terrorism or terrorism related" convictions between September 2001 and July 2006, when in reality, there were only two cases of "attempted terrorist activity" (Bejesky 393-395).

58. Human Rights Watch, July 2014; Bejesky 393-395, 449.

59. Bejesky 399 (citing Columbia Human Rights Watch, July 2014 and Reuters "FBI entrapped suspects in almost all high-profile terrorism cases in the U.S." July 21, 2014); *Guardian* "Fake terror plots, paid informants: the tactics of FBI 'entrapment' questioned' Nov. 16, 2011, Paul Harris.

60. Thomas Hintze, "What informs an informant?" wagingnonviolence.org, Sep. 11, 2013; Fox News "From left-wing activist to conservative hero: New documentary spotlights Brandon Darby's strange trip" Sep. 11, 2013.

61. *WHAM* (Rochester, NY) "Rochester man charged with planning ISIS attack at bar on NYE" Dec. 31, 2015; Alternet.org "ISIS New Year's Eve Terror Plot Story Is Totally Bogus" Jan. 1, 2016, Adam Johnson.

While the first paragraph of the article claimed that attack had already occurred, the remainder of the article actually reported on the would-be terrorist's foiled machete machinations, although left a number of critical details out including that he was a homeless panhandler; that the plot was suggested to him a network of undercover FBI agents and informants who then took him to Walmart and bought him his machete, knife and other things he would apparently need for an attack; or that he attempted to back out of the 'plot' numerous times only to be cajoled by the undercovers. One observant commentator did note that, "As the war on terror enters its 15th year, at some point these formulaic FBI terror sting operations should be reported on with far more nuance and skepticism. Key claims by the DOJ should not be rounded up to scariest possibly framing, mitigating factors like mental illness and FBI pressure should be highlighted rather than buried in paragraph 23, and material evidence of actual terrorist involvement should be confirmed rather than smuggled in vague framing about the claims of a mentally unstable man" (Alternet. com, Jan. 1, 2016).

Bejesky points out that "select facts, contained in principal and publicly- available court records, may not always convey the extent that FBI sources and undercover agents goad or reassure suspected terrorists, but precedent continues to aggregate with successful prosecutions. If undercover FBI and informants did not encourage, support, portray interest in, and assert devotion to the cause of terrorism (or even the glory of martyrdom), the target of a sting operation might become more reluctant to participate, become suspicious, exclude associates, or lose interest" (Bejesky 442). Yet when the full record is withheld from the public and the media picks the most sensational quotes or law enforcement agencies exaggerate the nature of a case, or the media reports but does not question or investigate possible uncorroborated allegations, the full context and therefore reality of an event remain unknown to the public.

In the face of a real threat, a number of difficult but important questions are raised. "Does law enforcement arrest suspects prematurely and before it is known that an attack would have occurred, or, in the case of sting operations, does law enforcement facilitate a fake plot with a suspect who would not have actually perpetrated a real plot or does law enforcement intervention thwart a real plot that would have manifested had there been no fake plot?" (Bejesky 400).

62. Bejesky 447, 448.

63. Here are some questions about the Oklahoma City bombing plot that keep me up at night, questions I do not feel disrespect the bombing's victims: Who was involved and why? Through what chain of events did they become involved? What were each specific individual's roles and functions in the plot? What happened on April 19, 1995, the day the plot was executed? Who was with McVeigh, prior to and on the day of the bombing? Where are they now? Then there are the equally disturbing (and unanswered) questions about what happened after the bombing. Where did the surveillance footage go? Why was it 'lost' if that is, in fact, what happened. Who lost them? Why weren't they penalized for losing evidence in the most sensational act of domestic terrorism yet? If that isn't what happened, if they weren't lost, why was the public prevented from seeing them? Who made this decision? Why would McVeigh, who claimed to hate pretty much anything the government ever did, especially the actions of agencies like the FBI, publicly go along with the FBI and prosecutors story?

Select Bibliography

A Noble Lie: Oklahoma City 1995 (film) Free Mind Films, 2011, Director: James Lane. Writers: Holland Vandennieuwenhof, Wendy Painting

Associated Press "Document: Oklahoma City Bombing Was Taped" April 20, 2004

Associated Press "Attorney: Oklahoma City Bombing Tapes Appear Edited" Sep. 27, 2009

Ballard, James, David. *Terrorism, Media And Public Policy: The Oklahoma City Bombing.* Hampton Press, 2005

Berger, J.M. "PATCON Revealed: An Exclusive Look Inside The FBI's Secret War With the Militia Movement" *Intelwire.* Oct. 8, 2007

Berger, J.M. "Patriot Games: How the FBI spent a decade hunting white supremacists and missed Timothy McVeigh" *Foreign Policy.* April 18, 2012

Buffalo News "McVeigh Predicted Conspiracy Claims" Feb. 26, 2004, Dan Herbeck, Lou Michel

BUG (film), William Friedkin, dir, L.I.F.T. Production, Bug LLC, DMK Medienfonds, Lionsgate, 2006

Charles, Roger G.; Andrew Gumbel. *Oklahoma City: What the Investigation Missed – and Why It Still Matters.* Harper Collins, 2012

Chermak, Stephen. *Searching for a Demon: The Media Construction of the Militia Movement.* Northeastern University Press, 2002

Conspiracy: Oklahoma City Bombing (television) History Channel, Jan. 15, 2008

Constantine, Alex. *Virtual Government: CIA Mind Control Operations in America* Feral House, 1997

Coyne, Randall. "Collateral Damage In Defense Of Timothy McVeigh" *Cooley Journal of Ethics and Responsibility* 1 (1) 2006: 19-32

Esquire "The Prison Letters of Timothy McVeigh" 13 (5) May 2001, Phil Bacharach.

Evans-Pritchard, Ambrose. *The Secret Life of Bill Clinton: The Unreported Stories.* Regnery Publishing, 1997

FOX News "Did Oklahoma City Bombers Have Help?" April 17, 2005

Hamm, Mark. *Apocalypse in America: Waco and Ruby Ridge Revenged.* Northeastern University Press, 1997

Hamm, Mark. *In Bad Company: Americans Terrorist Underground.* Northeastern University Press, 2002

Hammer, David Paul. *Secrets Worth Dying For: Timothy James McVeigh and the Oklahoma City Bombing.* 1st Books Library, 2004

Hammer, David Paul. *Deadly Secrets: Timothy McVeigh and the Oklahoma City Bombing.* Textstream, 2010

Harvard Law Review "Blown Away? The Bill of Rights after Oklahoma City" 109 (8) June 1996: 2074-2091

Herbeck, Dan; Lou Michel. *American Terrorist: Timothy McVeigh and the Oklahoma City Bombing.* Regan Books, HarpersColins Publishers Inc., 2001

Hersley, Jon; Larry Tongate; Bob Burke. *Simple Truths: The Real Story of the Oklahoma City Bombing.* Oklahoma Heritage Association, 2004

Hoffman, David. *The Oklahoma City Bombing and the Politics of Terror.* Feral House. 1998

Independent (UK) "The Oklahoma Conspiracy: Next Week, One Man Will Be Executed For Carrying Out America's Worst Peacetime Atrocity. Timothy McVeigh Claims To Have Acted Alone. But New Evidence Reveals He Was Part of an Underground Network Of White Supremacists" May 11, 2001, Andrew Gumbel

Jones, Stephen. *Others Unknown: Timothy McVeigh and the Oklahoma City Bombing Conspiracy.* Public Affairs, 1998

Jones, Stephen; Holly Hillerman. "McVeigh, McJustice, McMedia" University of Chicago Legal Forum 53 (1998)

Jones, Stephen; Jennifer Gideon. "United States V. McVeigh: Defending The 'Most Hated Man In America" *Oklahoma Law Review* 51 (4) 1998

Keith, Jim. *OKBOMB! Conspiracy and Cover-up.* Adventures Unlimited Press. 1996

Letts, Tracy. *BUG* (Play) Dramatists Play Service. Northern University Press, 2006

Madeira, Jody Lynee. *Killing McVeigh: The Death Penalty and the Myth of Closure.* New York University Press, 2012

McVeigh, Timothy James. *"An Essay on Hypocrisy"* March 1998

Mother Jones "In Search of John Doe No. 2: The Story the Feds Never Told About the Oklahoma City Bombing" July/Aug. 2007, James Ridgeway

Mother Jones "Did the FBI Bury Oklahoma City Bombing Evidence?" July 21, 2011, James Ridgeway

Newsweek "The Subject Speaks Out" July 3, 1995, David Hackworth and Peter Annin

Newsweek "Live From Death Row" April 9, 2001, Lou Michel, Dan Herbeck

Newsweek "My Life as a White Supremacist: An FBI mole speaks for the first time about life in the seedy world of right-wing terror." Nov. 21, 2011, R.M. Schneiderman

New York Times "Terror In Oklahoma: The Suspect; One Man's Complex Path to Extremism" April 23, 1995, Robert D. McFadden

New York Times "Terror in Oklahoma: The Far Right; Bomb Echoes Extremists' Tactics" April 26, 1995, Keith Schneider

New York Times "John Doe No. 1- A Special Report: A Life of Solitude and Obsessions" May 4, 1995, Robert D. McFadden

New York Times "A Puzzle Unfinished- A Special Report: Despite Oklahoma Charges, The Case is Far From Closed" Aug. 13, 1995, John Kifner

New York Times "Oklahoma Bombing Suspect: Unraveling a Frayed Life" Dec. 31, 1995

New York Times "Oklahoma Grandparents Turn Grief Into a Quest" March 5, 1996, Jo Thomas

New York Times "New Face of Terror Crimes: 'Lone Wolf' Weaned on Hate" Aug. 16, 1999, Jo Thomas

Nichols, James. *Freedom's End: Conspiracy In Olkahoma, as Told To Robert S. Papovich.* Freedoms End, 1997

Oklahoma City Bombing Investigation Committee. *Final Report on the Bombing of the Alfred P. Murrah Building.* Hervey's Booklink., 2001

Rappaport, Jon. *Oklahoma City Bombing: The Suppressed Truth.* The Book Tree, 1995

Rohrabacher, Dana. *Chairman's Report: The Oklahoma City Bombing: Was There A Foreign Connection?* Oversight and Investigations Subcommittee of the House International Relations Committee. Dec. 26, 2006

Serrano, Richard. *One of Ours: Timothy McVeigh and the Oklahoma City Bombing.* W. W. Norton & Co Inc., 1998

Stickney, Brandon. *All American Monster: The Unauthorized Biography of Timothy McVeigh.* Prometheus Books, 1996

Sunday Times Magazine of London "All American Monster" Sept. 3, 1995, James Dalrymple

Sunday Telegraph "Informant Accuses FBI Over Oklahoma Bomb" July 20, 1997

Swain, Amanda Marie. "Trentadue v. Integrity Committee: An Attempt to Reign in the Expansion of the Freedom if Information Act's 5th Exemption" *Oklahoma Law Review* 61 (2008): 371-394

The Conspiracy Files 'Oklahoma Bomb: The Conspiracy Files' (television) BBC, Dec. 7, 2006

The McVeigh Tapes: Confessions of an American Terrorist. (television) MSNBC, April 29, 2010

Time Magazine "The Face of Terror" May 1, 1995 (Cover)

Toronto Star "Lee Harvey Oswald revisited Why Oklahoma City bomber Timothy McVeigh can be seen as spiritual brother to JFK assassin" June 7, 1997, Philip Marchand

United States District Court, District Of Utah, Central Division. "Declaration Of Terry Lynn Nichols, February 9, 2007" Jesse C. Trentadue vs. Federal Bureau Of Investigation and Federal Bureau Of Investigation's Oklahoma City Field Office. Case No. 2:04 CV 00772 DAK

United States District Court, District Of Utah, Central Division. "Plaintiff's Reply Memorandum, RE: Motion To Strike August 25, 2015 Hearing" (Aug. 26, 2014) and "Plaintiff's Reply Memorandum, RE: Motion To Strike August 25, 2015 Hearing" (Aug. 25, 2014) Jesse C. Trentadue V. United States Central Intelligence Agency, et. al. Case No. 2:08-cv-0788

Vancouver Sun (British Columbia) "The most hated man in America: Timothy McVeigh's life story is terrifying for a lot of reasons" July 15, 1995

Vidal, Gore. "The Meaning Of Timothy McVeigh" *Vanity Fair*, Nov 10, 2008

Vidal, Gore. *Perpetual War for Perpetual Peace.* Thunder's Mouth Press/ Nation Books. 2002

Washington Post "A Ordinary Boy's Extraordinary Rage: After a Long Search For Order, Timothy McVeigh Finally Found a World He Could Fit Into" July 2, 1995, Dale Russakock, Serge Kovaleski

Washington Post "In all the speculation and spin surrounding the Oklahoma City bombing John Doe 2 had become a legend—the central figure in countless conspiracy theories that attempt to explain an incomprehensible horror. Did he ever really exist?" March 23, 1997, Peter Carlson

Washington Post "An Explosion of Conspiracy Theories in the Oklahoma City Bombing" Dec. 21, 1998, William Gibson

Wilburn- Sanders, Kathy Wilburn. *After Oklahoma City: A Grieving Grandmother Uncovers Shocking Truths about the bombing... and Herself.* Master Strategies, 2005

Wright Stuart A. *Patriots, Politics, and the Oklahoma City Bombing.* Cambridge University Press, 2007

PREFACE

For sources used but not directly quoted in the Preface, see:

Ballard, James, David. *Terrorism, Media And Public Policy: The Oklahoma City Bombing.* Hampton Press, 2005

Baym, Geoffrey. "Constructing Moral Authority: We in the Discourse of Television News" *Western Journal of Communication,* 64 (1) 2000

Carr, Matthew. *The Infernal Machine: A History of Terrorism From the Assassination of Tsar Alexander II to AL-Qaeda.* The New Press, 2006

Globe and Mail. "OKLAHOMA BOMBING Whodunit? The Jews, the UN, the Japanese or the evil Clinton? As usual, the conspiracy theorists have transformed what seems painfully obvious into a tangle of paranoia" July 8, 1995.

Houston Chronicle "Death row inmate might aid Nichols" April 5, 2004, Tim Talley

Independent "The Other Hannibal Lector" Jan. 31, 2004, Andrew Gumbel

Independent "The Oklahoma Conspiracy: Next Week, One Man Will Be Executed For Carrying Out America's Worst Peacetime Atrocity. Timothy McVeigh Claims To Have Acted Alone. But New Evidence Reveals He Was Part of an Underground Network Of White Supremacists" May 11, 2001, Andrew Gumbel

Keeley, Brian L. "Of Conspiracy Theories" *Journal of Philosophy* 96 (3) 1999: 109-126

Livingston, Steven. *The Terrorism Spectacle.* Westview Press, 1994

Salt Lake Tribune "According to Oklahoma bombing conspirator, ranking officials were involved in the attack" Feb. 21, 2007, Pamela Manson

San Francisco Chronicle "Militias Feed on Conspiracy Theories/ Bombing called government plot to create hysteria" April 25, 1995

Sunday Telegraph "Informant Accuses FBI Over Oklahoma Bomb" July 20, 1997.

Takacs, Stacy. *Terrorism TV: Popular Entertainment in Post 9/11 America.* University Press of Kansas, 2012

Tulsa World "'John Doe No. 2' Claim Denied; Prosecutors Say Man Not Suspect" Jan. 8, 1997

USA Today "Unraveling McVeigh: Past offers a few clues into psyche" May 2, 1995

Washington Times "Small Town turns out to vent rage at 'creep'" April 22, 1995

CHAPTER ONE

For sources used but not directly quoted in Chapter One, see:

Clarke, James W., *Defining Danger: American Assassins and the New Domestic Terrorists*. Transaction Publishers, 2007

Livingston, Steven. *The Terrorism Spectacle*. Westview Press, 1994

Red Dawn (film) John Milius, dir. MGM/ UA Entertainment Co., 1984

Rodrigues, Adriono, et. al., "Construct Representation and Definitions in Psychopathology: The Case of Delusion" *Philosophy, Ethics and Humanities in Medicine* 5 (5) 2010: 1-6

The A-Team (television) NBC, Jan. 23, 1983 – March 8, 1987

Van Buuren, Jelle. "Performative Violence? The Multitude of Lone Wolf Terrorism" *Terrorism:*

An Electric Journal and Knowledge Base, Inter-University Center for Terrorism Studies 1 (1) 2012

War Games (film) John Badham, dir. MGM/ UA Entertainment Co. 1983

CHAPTER TWO
(PARTS ONE, TWO AND THREE)

For sources used but not directly quoted in Chapter Two (Parts One, Two and Three), see:

Aarts, Paul; Michael Renner. "Oil and the Gulf War" *Middle East Research and Information Project* 21. 171 (1991)

Armchairgeneral.com "'Greatest Tank Battles' on Military Channel – Review" Dec. 30, 2010

Army Times "Senate Okays More TAP Classes, Burn Pit Registry" Dec. 20, 2012, Rick Maze

Army Times "Senate Panel Approves Burn Pit Registry" Sept. 12, 2012, Patricia Kime

Army Times "Companies Seek to Dismiss Suit on Burn Pit Risk" Jul. 13, 2012, Patricia Kime

Associated Press "Stocks Decline, Oil Prices Higher as War Continues" Jan. 22, 1991

Associated Press "Iraq Says POW Killed; Allies Destroy Convoy" Jan. 30, 1991

Associated Press "Some Who Kill May Hark Back to Military Training" Oct. 26, 2002

Austin American Statesman "Iraqi's Expand Border Force/ 265,000 Troops Near Saudi Arabia, U.S. Estimates" Aug. 29, 1990, John M. Broder, Melisa Healy

Austin American Statesman "Flaw In Some Bradleys Gets Fast Response From Army" Feb. 3, 1991, John King

Austin American Statesman "Army: Iraqis Buried Alive / U.S. Trench-fighting Tactic Killed Thousands in Gulf War" Sept. 12, 1991, Patrick J. Sloyan

Bennis, Phyllis; Michel Moushabeck (eds). *Beyond the Storm: A Gulf Crisis Reader*. Olive Branch Pres. 1991

Best, Steven; Douglass Kellner. *The Post Modern Adventure: Science, Technology, and Cultural Studies at the Third Millennium*. The Guilford Press, 2001

Bloomberg Business Week "Toting the Casualties of War" Feb. 5, 2003

Aviation Week & Space Technology "Army Scales Back Assessments of Patriot's Success in Gulf War" 136 (15) April 13, 1992: 64, David F. Bond

Boston Globe "World Waits on Brink of War: Late Effort at Diplomacy in Gulf Fails" Jan. 16, 1991, Michael Kranish

Boston Globe "Commandos Capture Iraqis on Offshore Rig" Jan. 20, 1991, Walter V. Robinson

Business Wire "Saudi Arabia to Buy 200 Bradley Fighting Vehicles" Jan. 5, 1989, R.W. Highlander

Calgary Herald (Alberta, Canada) "Friendly Fire: U.S. Tried to Hide Darker Side of the Gulf

War" May 23, 1992, (editorial), Patrick Sloyan Clark, Ramsey. *The Fire This Time, U.S. War Crimes in the Gulf*. Thunder's Mouth Press, 1994

Conetta, Carl. *The Wages of War: Iraqi Combatant and Noncombatant Fatalities in the 2003 Conflict*. Monograph #8. Project on Defense Alternatives, Commonwealth Institute, Oct. 2003

Digital Journalist "What Bodies?" Nov. 2002, Patrick Sloyan

Florida Times-Union "Ex General Fears 24, 000 Exposed to Gas" Sept. 19, 1996

Florida Times-Union "Gulf War Warning No Shock; Fort Stewart Vets Recall Lax Moves" Sept. 21, 1996, Jewel Radford

Florida Times-Union "Gap in Gulf War Logs Fuel Conspiracy Talk" Oct. 5, 1996, Patrick Sloyan

Globe and Mail "Crisis in the Gulf: Background 'Geneva Conventions POWs' treatment under scrutiny" Jan. 22, 1991, Estanislao Oziewicz

Globe and Mail "Crisis in the Gulf: Iraqi POWs Terrified, U.S. Says" Jan. 30, 1991

Guardian "War in the Gulf: Scuds and POWs Steal the Show- Media Watch" Jan. 21, 1991

Guardian "Captured Iraqis Hungry, Says US" Jan. 26, 1991, David Fairhall

Foreign Policy Magazine "The Gulf War: How Many Iraqis Died?" March 1993: 108-124, John G. Heidenrich

Houston Chronicle "Last-ditch Pitches for Peace; But U.S. Claims Iraqis Hold Key" Jan.15, 1991, Ellen Nimmons

Jerusalem Post "Buried Alive" Sep. 15, 1991

Klotzer, Charles L. "A Lesson for Americans: Desert Storm Operation Reports Were Full of Lies and Distortions" *St. Louis Journalism Review* 32 (250) 2002: 34-35

Knight – Ridder News Service "Ground Conflict Gives Armored Vehicles Chance For Vindication" Feb.10, 1991, Nolan Walters Livingston, Steven. *The Terrorism Spectacle.* Westview Press, 1994

Los Angeles Times "Army: Iraqis Buried Alive / U.S. Trench- fighting Tactic Killed Thousands in Gulf War" Sept. 12, 1991, Patrick J. Sloyan

Las Vegas Review Journal "No Victory Parade for Mr. Bush" Jan.23, 1992, Garry Wills

Matsumoto, Gary. *Vaccine A: The Covert Government Experiment That's Killing Our Soldiers and Why GI's Are Only the First Victims,* Basic Books. New York, 2009

Mendible, Myra. "Post-Vietnam Syndrome: National Identity, War and the Politics of Humiliation" *Radical Psychology.* 7 (2008)

Mirra, Carl. "The Mutation of the Vietnam Syndrome: Underreported Resistance During The 1991 Persian Gulf War" *Peace & Change,* 36 (2011): 262- 284

New York Times "Tests of Bradley Armored Vehicle Criticized" Apr. 18, 1986, Charles Mohr

New York Times "Confrontation in the Gulf: The U.N.; France and 3 Arab States Issue an Appeal to Hussein" Jan. 15, 1991, Paul Lewis

New York Times "War In The Gulf: Iraq Shows 2 More It Calls U.S. Airmen; Sites for 20,000 Prisoners" Jan.23, 1991, Malcolm W. Browne

New York Times "War in the Gulf: Overview; U.S. Bombers Hit Iraqi's Air Bases And Supply Lines" Feb. 4, 1991, Eric Schmitt

New York Times "War in the Gulf: Iraq; Baghdad's Refugees Find No Safety From Bombs" Feb. 4, 1991

New York Times "War in the Gulf: Troop Carrier; Armored Vehicle Is Checked For Defective Transmissions" Feb. 4, 1991, Kieth Bradsher

New York Times "War in the Gulf; Censors Screen Pooled Reports" Feb. 4, 1991

New York Times "War in the Gulf; Covering the War; Press and the Military: Old Suspicions" Feb. 4, 1991, R. W. Apple, Jr.

New York Times "U.S. Army Buried Iraqi Soldiers Alive in Gulf War" Sept. 15, 1991, Eric Schmitt

Nutter, Thomas J.; Brian Y. Cooper. "Persistent Modification of Na1.9 Following Dhronic Exposure to Insecticides and Pyridostigmine Bromide." *Toxicology and Applied Pharmacology,* 277 (3) 2014: 298-309

O'Connor, Michael J. "Bearing True Faith and Allegiance-Allowing Recovery for Soldiers under Fire in Military Experiments that Violate the Nuremberg Code." *Suffolk Transnational Law Review,* 25 (2001): 649

Omaha World Herald, "Cells of Militia Grew in Kansas in Recent Years" April 26, 1995

Pantagraph "Allies Anticipate 'Huge Numbers' of POWs" Jan. 27, 1991

Picano, James, J.; Robert R. Roland. "Assessing Psychological Suitability for High-Risk Military Jobs" in *The Oxford Handbook of Military Psychology* (Janice H. Laurence and Michael D. Matthews, eds.) Oxford University Press, 2012

San Antonio Express-News "Call Gulf War What it Was – a Massacre"(Editorial) May 26, 2000, Robert Jensen

San Francisco Chronicle. "U.S. 'Bomblets' Blamed For 14 GI Deaths" Sept. 20, 1991, Patrick J. Sloyan

Seattle Post Intelligencer "Skies Over Kuwait Become UW Lab" June 24, 1991, Tom Paulson

Spectrum "Tech Researchers to Study Insecticide Exposure" Nov. 19, 1998, Stewart MacInnis

St. Louis Dispatch "Schwarzkopf's Strategy Keeps Iraqis Guessing" Feb.26, 1991, Patrick J. Sloyan

Sunday Herald "How Did Iraq Get Its Weapons? We Sold Them" Sept. 8, 1992

Telegraph Herald (Dubuque, IA) "Some Killers Utilize Military Training; McVeigh, Whitman: Experts Say Veterans Are Not More Likely to be Murderers but Are More Proficient" Oct. 26, 2002

The A-Team (television) NBC, Jan. 23, 1983 – March 8, 1987

The Nation "The Pentagon's Radioactive Bullet: An Investigative Report by Bill Mesler" Oct. 21, 1996, Bill Messler

The Times "Gulf Shell Link to Illness Admitted" June 10, 1993, Wolfgang Munchau

Time "They Didn't Have to Die" Aug. 26, 1991, B. van Voorst

Toronto Star "Its Pass the Ammo and Load the Film as Hollywood Prepared Saudi Invasion" Sept. 3, 1990

Toronto Star "Oil Fields in Kuwait Set Ablaze" Jan. 23, 1991, Bill Taylor

Toronto Star "Could Dust Be the Cause of War Vets' Ailments?" May 12, 2011

United Nations Security Council Resolution 678, Iraq / Kuwait, Published Nov. 29, 1990

USA Today "Coming Home: Trauma of War Hits Troops and Families" Mar. 13, 1991

Virginia Tech News "Study Of Insecticide Neurotoxicity Yields Clues To Onset Of Parkinson's Disease" March 24, 2003

Virginia Tech Science Blog. "Gulf War Troop Exposure to Pesticides To Be Studies By Virginia Tech Researchers. Nov. 10, 1998

Wall Street Journal. "Officer Who Ignited Army – Vehicle Flap Won't Go To Alaska – Air Force Transfer Prevented; Col. Burton Sparked Effort To Have Tests Performed" March 15, 1985, John J. Fialka

Wall Street Journal "POWs Upstage Anti-War Activities on TW" Jan.22, 1991, Dorothy Rabinowitz

Wall Street Journal "Raytheon Defends Its Patriot Missiles Performance in War" April 26, 1991

Washington Post "The War You Won't See; Why the Bush Administration Plans to Restrict Coverage of Gulf Combat" Jan. 13, 1991, Patrick J. Sloyan

Washington Post "Scientists: War Has Caused an Environmental Catastrophe" March 2, 1991

Washington Post "Air Force Hunted Motor Home in War's 'Get Saddam' Mission" June 23, 1991, Patrick J. Sloyan

Washington Post "War in the Trenches" Sept. 21, 1991

Washington Post "Gulf Veterans Still Paying the Price; Some Troops Count Jobs, Marriages, Health Among War's Casualties" Jan. 17, 1992, Sandra Evans

Washington Post "U.S. Aware of Iraqi Terrorism: Documents Undercut U.S. Prewar Stance On Baghdad's Record" June 6, 1992, Jeffery Smith

Washington Post "U.S. Had Key Role in Iraq Buildup" Dec. 30, 2002, Michael Dobbs White House National Security Directive 45, Sub: U.S. Policy In Response To The Iraqi Invasion Of Kuwait, Aug. 20, 1990

Worcester Telegram & Gazette (MA) "US To Boost Gulf Force By 150,000 Bush Hopes Saddam Comes To" Nov. 9, 1990

For more information about Gulf War Illness, see Chapter Three, Part Three: 'An Incommunicable Thing' and related citations and bibliography.

CHAPTER THREE: AMERINOID-PART ONE: RETURN TO BUFFALO DEC. 1991 TO JAN. 1993

For sources used but not directly quoted in the Chapter Three, Part One, see:

Callahan, Bob. *Who Shot JFK? A Guide To Conspiracy Theories,* Simon and Shuster, 1993

The X-Files (television) FOX Sep. 10, 1993 to May 19, 2002

Las Vegas Review Journal "Bombers had help Gritz says" April 25, 1995, Susan Greene

New Republic "The Road to Oklahoma City: Inside the world of the Waco-obsessed right" May 15, 1995, Alex Heard

Phillips. Garvin. "The Bombing of the Alfred P. Murrah Federal Building in Oklahoma City" *Rense.com,* no date

San Francisco Chronicle "Militia Feed on Conspiracy Theories/Bombing Called Government Plot to Create Hysteria" Apr. 25, 1995

The Economist "The Death Of A President" Oct. 9, 1993

Toronto Star "Righteous 'Patriots' Testing U.S. Authority Far- Right Groups Angry at 'Tyranny' of Government" Apr. 25, 1995

Wall Street Journal "Some Militiamen See A Government Plot In Oklahoma Blast --- They Think Feds Orchestrated Bombing in Their State To Discredit the Factions" Apr. 24, 1995, Robert Tomsho

Washington Post "An Explosion of Conspiracy Theories in the Oklahoma City Bombing" Dec. 21, 1998, William Gibson

CHAPTER THREE PART TWO: WASHED UP WAR HERO RENT-A-COP

For sources used but not directly quoted in the Chapter Three, Part Two, see:

Abbot, Michael H. "The Army and the Drug War: Politics or National Security?" *Parameters,* Dec. 1988: 95-112

Berger, J.M. "PATCON Revealed: An Exclusive Look Inside The FBI's Secret War With the Militia Movement" *Intelwire,* Oct. 8, 2007

Bryant, Major Leroy C., "The Posse Comitatus Act, the Military, and Drug Interdiction: Just How Far Can We Go" *The Army Lawyer,* Dec. 1990

Dobratz, Betty A.; Waldner, Lisa K. "In Search of Understanding The White Power Movement: An Introduction" *Journal of Political and Military Sociology,* 34 (1) 2006: (1-9)

Hamm, Mark. *American Skinheads: The Criminology and Control of Hate Crime.* Praeger.1993

Johnson, Sr. Major Harry E. *Against All Enemies – Using Counterdrug Operations To Train For Infantry Wartime Missions.* School of Advanced Military Studies. U.S. Army Command and General Staff College. 1991

Kent, Jonathan. "Border Bargains and the 'New' Sovereignty: Canada - U.S. Border Policies from 2001 to 2005 in Perspective" *Geopolitics,* 16 (4) 2011: 793-818

Lyons, Matthew N. "Homeland Security: Low-Intensity Conflict Targets Non-Citizens" (report) Political Research Associates. April 1, 2002

Mendel, W. W. "Countering the Drug Threat With Interagency Teamwork" pg. 206-230 in *Global Dimensions of High Intensity Crime and Low Intensity Conflict,* Graham H Turbiville, ed. University of Illinois at Chicago, 1995

Military Cooperation with Civilian Law Enforcement Statute (10 USC 371-380) Dec. 1981

National Security Decision Directive On Narcotics (NSDD 221) April 8, 1986

New Republic "Nazi Retreat" Apr. 2, 1989, Bruce Reed

New York Times "Informer Says Siege Figure Offered to Sell Him Illegal Guns" Sep. 9, 1995

Rice, Paul Jackson. "New Laws and Insight's Encircle The Posse Commitatus Act" Individual

Study Project, U.S. Army War College, May 26, 1983

Ridgeway, James. *Blood in the Face: The Ku Klux Klan, Aryan Nations, Nazi Skinheads, and the Rise of a New White Culture.* 2nd ed. Basic Books. 1996

Rocky Mountain News "Who Painted The Phony Trail Of Guilt? Racist Militia Leader Denies Link to the Oklahoma Bombing, Stays Ready For a Shootout" Nov. 2, 1997, Kevin Flynn

Salt Lake City Weekly "Johnny's Rotten" Apr. 10, 2013

Seattle Times "Military Plays Role in Law Enforcement – Missions Involve Communications, Medical Aid and Weapons Training" Jul. 16, 1995, Kirk Spitzer

Time "Skinhead Against Skinhead" Aug. 9, 1993, David S. Jackson

U.S. Department of State, Bureau of International Narcotics Matters "International Narcotics Control Strategy Report" March 1987

U.S. House Of Representatives, House Hearing, "Law Enforcement: Are Federal, State, And Local Agencies Working Together Effectively?" Joint Hearing Before The Subcommittee On Criminal Justice, Drug Policy And Human Resources and the Subcommittees On Government Efficiency, Financial Management and Intergovernmental Relations and the Subcommittee On National Security, Veterans Affairs And International Relations of the Committee On Government Reform, Testimony of Joseph R. Greene, Acting Deputy Executive Associate Commissioner For Field Operations Immigration And Naturalization Service, Nov. 12, 2001, Serial No. 107-116, U.S. Government Printing Office, 2002

U.S. Senate, "The Federal Raid On Ruby Ridge, Idaho" Hearings Before The Subcommittee On Terrorism, Technology and Government Information, Sep. 6-Oct. 19, 1995, Serial NO. J-104-41

Washington Times "Military Training of Civilian Police Steadily Expands: Congress Has Paved the Way With Legislation" Sept. 9, 1999, Rowan Scarborough

Zeskind, Leonard. *Blood and Politics: The History of the White Nationalist Movement from the Margins to the Mainstream.* Farrar Straus Giroux. 2009

CHAPTER THREE:

PART THREE, AN INCOMMUNICABLE THING

For sources used but not directly quoted in the Chapter Three, Part Three, see:

Li, B., Mahan; et. al., "Longitudinal Health Study of US 1991 Gulf War Veterans: Changes in Health Status at 10-year Follow-up" *American Journal of Epidemiology*, 174 (7) 2011: 761-768

Arkansas Democrat-Gazette "Ailing Vets Last Victims of Desert Storm Correction 062794" Jun. 26, 1994

Army Times "Gulf War Syndrome Called Very Real: Research Still Needed, Senators Told" Oct. 8, 2007

Austin American Statesman "Strange Maladies Hit Gulf War Returnees" Aug. 15, 1992

Booth-Kewley, Stephanie; et. al., "Psychosocial Predictors of Military Misconduct" *The Journal of Nervous and Mental Disease*, 198 (2) 2010

Boston Globe "US Plans Registry to Track Gulf War-related Illnesses" Aug. 4, 1992

Buffalo News "She Carried The Aids Message: Wendi Modeste Talks to African American Community" May 24, 1992, Carl Allen

Buffalo News "Hot Line Calls Abate Since Doctor Revealed He Has HIV Infection Few Reported Seeking Aids Tests" June 6, 1992, Henry L. Davis

Buffalo News "VA Setting Up Machinery To Probe Gulf Vets Mysterious Ailments" Aug. 15, 1992, Randolph E. Schmid

Buffalo News "Public Clinics Advised to Test Almost All Patients For HIV" Aug. 28, 1992

Buffalo News "Exams of Local Gulf War Veterans Suffering Mystery Maladies Start" Sep. 19, 1992

Buffalo News "The VA Wants To Hear From Gulf War Veterans" January 31, 1994

Buffalo News "Gulf Vets Puzzled By Illness, Chemical Report" May 27, 1994, Jerry Zremski

Buffalo News "Gulf War Spawned No Mystery Disease, Pentagon Study Reaffirms" Aug. 2, 1995

Buffalo News "Debunking The Gulf War Syndrome" Dec. 24, 1996, Charles Krauthammer

Buffalo News "Local Gulf War Veterans To Testify About Illness" July 18, 1997, Jerry Zremski

Buffalo News "Mother Battles Air Force on Care for Son With Reaction to Anthrax Vaccine" Oct. 10, 2000, Terry Frank

Buffalo News "Treat Gulf War Condition; Study Concludes Symptoms Are Real and Government Help Should Follow" (editorial) Dec. 1, 2008

Dallas Morning News "Dallas Researcher's Team Finds Gulf War Illness Stems From Nerve Damage" Nov. 26, 2012, Scott Parks

Denver Post "VA: Burn Pit Registry Sought by Veterans Not Needed" Jun. 14, 2012, Rick Maze

Denver Post "Exposed to Burn Pits, Iraq Veteran from Idaho Pursues Environmental Career"

Dec. 28, 2012, Scott Maben

Europe Intelligence Wire "Genes May Determine Who Developed Gulf War Syndrome,

University of Buffalo Researchers Find; Variant in ACE Gene Appears to Cause Susceptibility to Environmental Triggers" July 28, 2004

Nicholson, Garth; Nancy Nicholson. "Diagnosis and Treatment of Mycoplasma Infections in

Persian Gulf War Illness – CFIDS Patients" *International Journal of Occupational Medicine, Immunology, and Toxicology* 5 (1996): 69-78

Gazette "A Toxic Legacy of War: For Victors and Vanquished Alike, Radioactive Fallout from Munitions Made of Depleted Uranium is Suspected of Wreaking Long Term Havoc with Health" Nov. 16, 2002

Giardino, Anthony E. "Combat Veterans, Mental Health Issues, and the Death Penalty: Addressing the Impact of Post- Traumatic Stress Disorder and Traumatic Brain Injury" *Fordham Law Review* 77 (2009): 2955-2995

Guardian "The New Gulf War Syndrome" Nov. 11, 2008, Nora Eisenberg

Greensboro News & Record "Scientist Ties Polio Vaccine to Diseases" Nov. 11, 1996

Johnson, Alison; James J. Tuite. *Gulf War Syndrome: Legacy of a Perfect War*. MCS Information Exchange, 2001.

Lockport Union Sun & Journal. Letter to the Editor, Feb. 11, 1992, Timothy McVeigh.

Lockport Union Sun & Journal. Letter to the Editor, March 10, 1992, Timothy McVeigh

Matsumoto, Gary. *Vaccine A: The Covert Government Experiment That's Killing Our Soldiers and Why GI's Are Only the First Victims*, Basic Books, 2009

Navy Times "Report Links Gulf War Illness to Pesticides, Nerve Agent Blocker" Dec. 12, 2008

New Scientist "Book Review: 'The Invisible Enemy' by Dorothy Crawford, Oxford University Press" Oct. 28, 2000

New Scientist "Gulf War Syndrome is Real, says US Report" Nov. 22, 2008

New York Times "Recruiting Problems in New York Slowing U.S. Trials of AIDS Drug" Dec. 18, 1988, Gina Kolata

New York Times "Personal Health" Oct. 10, 1996, James E. Brody

New York Times "Coming Together to Fight for a Troubled Veteran" July 17, 2011, Erica Goode

New York Times "Researchers Find Biological Evidence of Gulf War Illness" June 24, 2013

Nicolson, Garth L., et al. "Diagnosis and treatment of chronic mycoplasmal infections in Fibromyalgia and Chronic Fatigue Syndromes: relationship to Gulf War Illness." *Biomedical Therapy* 16 (1998): 266-271

O'Connor, Michael J. "Bearing True Faith and Allegiance-Allowing Recovery for Soldiers under Fire in Military Experiments that Violate the Nuremberg Code." *Suffolk Transnational Law Review* 25 (2001)

Ottawa Citizen "Conspiracy Theories Spin Out of Control on the Web" Nov. 16, 1996, Chris Cobb

Pittsburgh Post- Gazette "Hearings on Gulf Illness Promised; Veterans of '91 Desert Conflict Tell Specter that 150,000 Still Suffer From War Syndrome" Nov. 15, 1996, Steve Twedt

Rambo: First Blood (film) Ted Kotcheff, dir. Orion Pictures, 1982

Seattle Post-Intelligencer. "First Gulf War Still Claims Lives" Jan. 16, 2006

Spectrum "Tech Researchers to Study Insecticide Exposure" Nov. 19, 1998, Stewart MacInnis

Star Tribune "The Army Became His Enemy; Injured Veteran is Embittered by Extended Fight for Treatment, Benefits He Says He's Been Denied" Jun. 1, 1993, Neal Gendler

Tampa Bay Times "VA Reopens Gulf War Files: The Agency Will Reexamine Rejected Claims of Veterans Who Got Sick After Serving in the 1991 Conflict" Feb. 27, 2010, Stephanie Haynes

Telegraph Herald (Dubuque, IA) "Some Killers Utilize Military Training; McVeigh, Whitman: Experts Say Veterans Are Not More Likely to Be Murderers but Are More Proficient" Oct. 26, 2002

The Nation "The Pentagon's Radioactive Bullet: An Investigative Report by Bill Mesler" Oct. 21, 1996,Bill Messler

The Times "Gulf Shell Link to Illness Admitted" Jun. 10, 1993, Wolfgang Munchau

Toronto Star "Could Dust Be the Cause of War Vets' Ailments?" May 12, 2011

Toronto Star "Anti-Oxidants Found to Ease Gulf War Ills" Jun. 27, 2011

Toronto Star "Study Provides More Clues to Gulf War Illness and Hope" Nov. 26, 2012

USA Today "Coming Home: Trauma of War Hits Troops and Families" March 13, 1991

Virginian-Pilot "Editorial: Gulf War Syndrome Haunts Vets, Nation" Dec. 1, 2008

Virginia Tech News "Study Of Insecticide Neurotoxicity Yields Clues To Onset Of Parkinson's Disease" March 24, 2003

Virginia Tech Science Blog "Gulf War Troop Exposure to Pesticides To Be Studied By Virginia Tech Researchers" Nov. 10, 1998

Washington Post "Gulf Veterans Still Paying the Price; Some Troops Count Jobs, Marriages, Health Among War's Casualties" Jan. 17, 1992, Sandra Evans

Washington Post "Antibiotic Touted as Treatment for Gulf War Disease; Organism Found to Cause Infection" Oct. 31, 1999, Joyce Howard Price

Washington Post "A Judge in Fairfax Wants to Help Virginia's Veterans" June 6, 2014

Wheelwright, Jeff. *The Irritable Heart: The Medical Mystery of the Gulf War.* W.W. Norton & Co., 2001

CHAPTER THREE
PART FOUR:
HOWLING AT THE MOON

For sources used but not directly quoted in the Chapter Three, Part Four, see:

BBC News "Project Paperclip: Dark side of the Moon" Nov. 21, 2011, Andrew Walker

Buffalo News "UFO Reports Linked to Earthquakes" April 15, 1992

Buffalo News "Extraterrestrials Have Returned To Invade The National Psyche" June 7, 1992

Buffalo News "Calspan Wins Air Force Contract" Nov. 29, 1995

Buffalo News "Calspan Corp. Name Returns As Locals Buy The New Engineering Icon" Feb. 18, 2005

Buffalo News "UFO researcher discusses alien visits" Sep.28, 2005, Pam Kowalik

Buffalo News "Calspan honored for its contributions to aviation: Cheektowaga company's history includes testing of military planes and space shuttles" Dec. 2, 2010, Michelle Kearns

Business First of Buffalo "Calspan hoping sky isn't limit for aerospace merger" Aug.9, 1993

Business First of Buffalo "Calspan President leaves behind a space odyssey" Aug. 22, 1994

Business Wire "Local Ownership Group Purchases Former Calspan Corporation from General Dynamics; Buyout Saves Jobs and Preserves an Important Piece of Buffalo's Technology History" Feb.18, 2005

Campell, Mark R.; et. al., . "Hubertus Strughold: The 'Father of Space Medicine'" *Aviation, Space, and Environmental Medicine* 78:7 (2007) pg. 716-719

Cornell Bulletin "Curtis-Wright Corp. Gives Lab to Cornell; To Aid Air Research" Dec. 21, 1945

Cornell Bulletin "Aircraft Companies Donate Gift to Cornell Aeronautical Laboratory" Feb. 15, 1946

Cornell Bulletin "Scientists Form New Association of Atomic Study" Feb. 15, 1946

Daily Mail (London) "Are UFOs Just A CIA Con-Trick?" July 23, 2010

Eiband, David; Lynn R. Kern. "Generic drone control system" United States Patent 5,240,207, Filed Aug. 3, 1992, Assignee: U.S. Secretary of the Navy, Date of Patent Aug. 31, 1993

Flight International "Airborne Trials for see and avoid technologies" Aug.18, 2009

Funplacestofly.com "Mojave Airport/Spaceport, Mojave, CA" (Web), Cathy Hansen Good, Timothy. *Above Top Secret: The Worldwide UFO Coverup,* William Morrow & Company. 1988

Guardian "Mark Pilkington's top 10 books about UFOs" Sep. 1, 2010

Guardian "Snowden files: The real 'Men In Black,' Hollywood and the great UFO False Flag'" Aug. 15, 2014

Hanson, Lars. (Affidavit) "UFOs, Aliens, and 'Ex'-intelligence Agents: Who's Fooling Whom, The Inside Story of John Lear, Bill Cooper, and the Greatest Coverup in Human History" July 18, 1991

India Investment News "Random Media Announces Acquisitions of 'Escape From Tomorrow' and 'Mirage Men'" Dec. 12, 2013

International Herald Tribune "Fuel Costs Inspire Era Of Dirigible Dreamers" July 5, 2008

Lewis, Tyson; Richard Kahn."The Reptoid Hypothesis: Utopian and Dystopian Representational Motif's in David Icke's Alien Conspiracy Theory' *Utopian Studies* 16 (1) 2005: 45-74

Logansport Pharos-Tribune (Logansport, Indiana) "Arvin Forms Space Industry Venture" Sep. 3, 1992

Los Angeles Times "Arizona Militia Figure Is Shot To Death" Nov. 7, 2001

BBC News "SA Government steps into Aids row" Sep. 14, 2000

Makrinos, Stephen T. "High Altitude Airships for Homeland Security Operations: Providing Persistent Surveillance for Warfighters and First Responders" *Sea Technology,* 46 (8) Aug. 2005: 29-32

Moyer, S. A.; M. D. Talbot."Wind –Tunnell Test Techniques for Unmanned Aerial Vehicle Separation Investigations" *Journal Of Aircraft* 30 (8) May/ June 1994: 585-590

Newsweek "Fugitive Captured in Arizona Spectators cheer Arrest After Scuffle" May 13, 1995

New York Times "Company Briefs" Jan. 20, 1990

New York Times 'Terror In Oklahoma: The Overview: Bomb Inquiry Leads To Arrest of Biochemist' May 13, 1995

Pantagraph (Bloomington, IL) "Maryland Company Flying High As Makers of Unmanned Drones" Oct. 6, 1993

Philadelphia Inquirer "Biochemist is arrested, may be tied to McVeigh Steven Garrett Colbern was arrested in Arizona. The charge is not related to the Oklahoma blast." May 13, 1995

Plus Media Solutions "Washington: Almost 2,500 Now Killed by Covert US Drone Strikes Since Obama Inauguration Six Years Ago" Feb. 3, 2015

PR Newswire "Arvin's Calspan and Space Industries Form New Space Company" Sep.1, 1992

Robotics Business Review "Drones In Commercial Airspace To Drive A New Industrial Revolution" Aug. 3, 2012

Redfern, Nick. *On the Trail of the Saucer Spies: UFOs and Government Surveillance*, Anomalist Books, 2006

Santa Cruz Sentinel "Probe fails to tie drifter to bombing: Colbern says he knew McVeigh" May 14, 1995

Speakupwny.com "Buffalo needs a home to tell aviation story" Oct.25, 2005, Lee Chowaniec

Standard Speaker (Hazelton, PA) "Private Spacecraft Launch Delayed" May 20, 1993

Star.com "U.S. Military Drone Crashes Into Lake Ontario" Nov. 12, 2013

St. Louis Dispatch "Another arrest in bombing inquiry" May 13, 1995

Syracuse.com "Military Drones Grounded in Central New York Following Crash in Lake Ontario" Nov. 13, 2013

Syracuse.com "U.S. Navy Divers Suspend Search For Reaper Drone Lost in Lake Ontario" Dec. 18, 2013

Ukiah Daily Journal "Man linked to bombing fascinated by explosives" May 14, 1995

USA Today "Pilotless aircraft can detect Serb troops" April 6, 1999

Wall Street Journal "In Depth: A Scientists Nazi-Era Past Haunts Famed Space Prize- What Stughold Allegedly Did During War Has Fueled Controversy Over Award Names in His Honor" Dec.3, 2012, Lucette Lagnado

Washington Post "Biochemist arrested in bomb case; possible companion of suspect McVeigh held for questioning" May 13, 1995

Washington Post "3 books on UFOs" Oct. 13, 2010

Windsor Star (Ontario) "Unmanned blimp crashes in woods" July 28, 2011

Wired "Here Come: The Drones!" 20 (7) July 2012, Chris Anderson

CHAPTER FOUR
PART ONE:
DASTARDLY DOPPELGANGER

For sources used but not directly quoted in the Chapter Four, Part One, see:

Anti-Defamation League "Calendar Of Conspiracy: A Chronology Of Anti-Government Extremist Criminal Activity, October to December 1997" A Militia Watchdog Special Report 1(4) Feb. 18, 1998

Anti-Defamation League "Explosion Of Hate: The Growing Dangers Of The National Alliance" (report), 2000

Associated Press "CNN Witness says he saw McVeigh in Ryder truck" May 8, 1997

Associated Press "McVeigh was driving Ryder truck days before blast, witness says" May 8, 1997 Michael Fleeman

Berger, J.M. *"PATCON Revealed: An Exclusive Look Inside The FBI's Secret War With the Militia Movement"* Oct. 8, 2007, *Intelwire*

Buffalo News "Lee Harvey Oswald's Momentous Coincidences" Book Review, May 7, 1995, Neil Schmit.

Buffalo News "McVeigh Predicted Conspiracy Claims" Feb. 26, 2004, Dan Herbeck, Lou Michel.

Campbell, J.B. "Manchurian Shooters" *J.B. Campbell Extremism Online* (blog), Nov. 12, 2011

Carmichael, Thomas. "Lee Harvey Oswald as the Postmodern Subject: History and Intertextuality in Don DeLillo's Libra, The Names, and Mao II" *Contemporary Literature* 34 no. 2 (1993): 204-218.

Denver Post "Did McVeigh Botch a Larger Plot?" March 29, 1997, Howard Pankratz

Desert News "Court Marshal Proceedings Against 2 At HAFB Resolved" Nov. 30, 1989

Desert News "Arrest In Punchout" Dec. 19, 1989

Desert News "Did McVeigh Go To St. George Gun Show" May 21, 1995

Desert News "Nichols says bombing was FBI op" Feb. 21, 2007, George Fattah

Galveston Daily News (Galveston, Texas) "This Conspiracy Group's Out There" July 30, 1994

Hall, John R., "Public Narratives and the Apocalyptic Sect: From Jonestown to Mt.

Carmel" pg. 205-235 *Armageddon In Waco: Critical Perspectives on the Branch Davidian Conflict*, Stuart Wright (ed.) University of Chicago Press. 1995

Independent (London) "One-armed bandits and the two bit soldiers" Sep. 20, 1992, Phil Reeves

Joplin Globe "Protestor held in Joplin:: Ex-informant, in psychiatric ward, claims conspiracy in McVeigh case" May 11, 2001

Las Vegas Sun "Man Claims Entrapment After Arrest" Aug. 22, 1996, Rachael Levy

Los Angeles Times "Soldiers Of Fortune Meet To Share Arms, Tactics" Oct. 27, 1985

Mail on Sunday (London, England) "The American Way" Feb. 15, 1998

Mother Jones "In Search of John Doe No. 2: The Story the Feds Never Told About the Oklahoma City Bombing" July/Aug. 2007, James Ridgeway

Mother Jones "Did the FBI Bury Oklahoma City Bombing Evidence?" July 21, 2011

Newsweek "My Life as a White Supremacist: An FBI mole speaks for the first time about life in the seedy world of right-wing terror." Nov. 21, 2011, R.M. Schneiderman.

New York Times "Two Airmen Admit a Plot to Sell Jet Engines" Oct. 20, 1989

New York Times "Books of The Times; Revisiting Vietnam on Fantasy's Odd Battlefields" Feb. 11, 1994, Michiko Kakutani

New York Times "Terror in Oklahoma: The Overview; FBI Issues Alert For 2 More Sought In Bombing Inquiry" May 2, 1995, David Johnston

Nichols, James, D., *Freedom's End: Conspiracy In Oklahoma, As Told To Robert S. Papovich*. Freedom's End, 1997

Observer "Kill For God, America And Fun" Sep. 18, 1994, Ed Vulliamy

Oregonian (Portland, Oregon) "If He'd Been At Work" April 20, 1995, Dave Hogan

Panola Watchman (Carthage, Texas) "Bombing Leaves Family Worried For Older Sister" April 23, 1995

People Magazine "Soldiers Of Fortune Invade Charlotte, N.C. To Find Adventure, Love And Death" Nov. 8, 1982, Richard Woodley

Reason "FBI Fakers" Aug/Sep 2012, Ed Krayewski.

Rolling Stone Magazine "Armed and Dangerous (The NRA, Militias and White Supremacists are fostering a network of right wing warriors)" Nov. 2, 1995, Leonard Zeskind

Salt Lake Tribune "According to Oklahoma bombing conspirator, ranking officials were involved in the attack" Feb. 21, 2007, Pamela Manson

Salt Lake Tribune "Legal setback for Utah man whose brother died in Oklahoma prison" Aug. 7, 2007

Washington Post "AP: FBI Suspected McVeigh Link to Robbers" Feb. 25, 2004, John Solomon

Star Ledger (Newark, New Jersey) "Lawmen Get Warning of Plot on U.S. Targets" March 22, 1995, Robert Rudolf

Time Magazine "McVeigh Trial: The Third Man, Is another conspirator still at large? Who is Robert Jacques?" March 17, 1997, Mes Polk and Susan Candiotti

The Times "Oklahoma blast 'part of plot to murder judges'" March 31, 1997

Titusville Herald (Titusville, PA) "Hoosiers Protest Waco Action" Feb. 19, 1993

U.S. District Court For The District Of Utah, Central Division. *Jesse C. Trentadue V. United States Central Intelligence Agency, et. al.*, Plaintiff's Reply Memorandum, RE: Motion To Strike August 25, 2015 Hearing" Aug. 25, 2014, Case No. 2:08-cv-0788

Washington Post "Playing With Guns" March 13, 1994, David Morrell

Washington Times "ATF chief vows to keep an eye on religious cults", Nov. 2, 1993, Scott Shepard

Wright, Stuart A., "Construction and Escalation of a Cult Threat: Dissecting Moral Panic and Official Reaction to the Branch Davidians" pg. 75-94 in *Armageddon In Waco: Critical Perspectives on the Branch Davidian Conflict*, Stuart Wright (ed.) University of Chicago Press. 1995

CHAPTER FOUR
PART TWO
THE EXPERTS: INTRODUCTION

For sources used but not directly quoted in the Chapter Four, Part Two, see:

American Psychiatric Association, American Psychiatric Association. "Diagnostic and statistical manual of mental disorders (DSM)." Washington, DC: American Psychiatric Association. 1994

A Noble Lie: Oklahoma City 1995 (film) Free Mind Films, 2011, Director: James Lane. Writers: Holland Vendennieuwenhof, Wendy Painting

Associated Press "Prison Security Chief Loses Job For Tightening Safety" July 14, 1995

Bertini, Joseph. "Stings, stoolies, and agents provocateurs: Evaluating FBI undercover counterterrorism operations" PhD dissertation., Georgetown University, 2011

Bowart, W. H. *Operation Mind Control* Dell Publishing Co. Inc. 1978

Buffalo News "Lee Harvey Oswald's Momentous Coincidences" Book Review, May 7, 1995, Neil Schmit

Carena, Etzel., Weiner, Lupita A., "Evaluation Of Dissociation Throughout The Lifespan" *Psychotherapy: Theory, Research, Practice, Training.* 41 (4) 2004: 496 -508

Carmichael, Thomas. "Lee Harvey Oswald as the Postmodern Subject: History and Intertextuality in Don DeLillo's Libra, The Names, and Mao II" *Contemporary Literature* 34 (2) 1993: 204-21.

CNN. "The Road to Oklahoma" Nov. 19, 1995

Daily Oklahoman "El Reno Prison Guards Unite Behind Suspended Chief" Aug. 28, 1995, Nolan Clay

Daily Oklahoman "El Reno Prison Chief Will Fight Suspension" Aug. 29, 1995, Nolan Clay

Denver Post "Did McVeigh botch a larger plot?" March 29, 1997, Howard Pankratz

Denver Post "Racist claims wrong building hit Blast termed part of large slaying plot" March 29, 1997

Eisenman, Russell; F.A. Coyle, Jr. "Commonality In Sociopathy And Paranoia?" *Psychological Reports,* 17 (3) 1965

Gallimore, Josef Parnas., et. al., "The Concept of Psychosis: A Clinical and Theoretical Analysis" *Clinical Neuropsychiatry* 7 (2) 2010

Gallimore, Timothy. "Unresolved Trauma: Fuel for the Cycle of Violence and Terrorism" in *The Psychology of Terrorism: Clinical Aspects and Responses.* V. 2, Chris E. Stout Ed., Praeger, 2002

Hay, Bruce. "Sting Operations, Undercover Agents, and Entrapment" *Harvard Law Review* 70 (387) 2005

Hoffman, David "'I Have Seen The Dragon': Family Seeks Answers In Death Of McVeigh Prison Guard" *primenet.com* April 14, 1997

Kansas City Star "Extra Leg, Other Riddles Still Surround Bombing" June 15, 1997

Kleinman, Steven M. M.S., "KUBRK Counterintelligence Interrogation Review: Observations of an Interrogator, Lessons Learned and Avenues for Further Research" pg. 95-140 in *Educing Information: Interrogation: Science and Art, Foundations for the Future.* Intelligence Science Board, Center for Strategic Intelligence Research, National Defense Intelligence College, Intelligence Science Board, NDIC Press, Washington, D.C. , Feb. 2006

Kuo, Susan, S., "Official Indiscretions: Considering Sex Bargains with Government Informants" *University of California. Davis Law Review* 38 (1643) June 2005

Los Angeles Times "Leg From Bomb Rubble Said To Be Buried Victim's" Feb. 24, 1996

McKenzie, Stephanie A. "Coverpersons and Operators in Undercover Work: The Reappearance of False Identities" *The Canadian Journal Of Police & Security Services.* 3 (4) 2005

New York Times "More Federal Agencies Are Using Undercover Operations" Nov. 15, 2014, Eric Lichtblau and William M. Arkinnov

Prison Legal News "Two Former Oklahoma Prison Guards Get Deferred Sentences in Prisoner's Death" June 3, 2015, Matthew Clarke

Rock Creek Free Press "Unanswered Questions Haunt Family of Oklahoma City Bombing First Responder" 3(11) Nov. 2009, Wendy S. Painting

Rodrigues, Adriono., et. al., "Construct Representation and Definitions in Psychopathology: The Case of Delusion" *Philosophy, Ethics and Humanities in Medicine* 5 (5) 2010

Schafer, Ingo., Fisher, Helen L., et. al., "Dissociative symptoms in patients with schizophrenia: relationships with childhood trauma and psychotic symptoms." *Comprehensive Psychiatry.* 53 (4)) 2012: 364-371

Soldz, Stephen. "The 'Ethical Interrogation': The Myth of Michael Gelles and the al-Qahtani Interrogation" *dissientvoice.org,* Dec. 7, 2009

Spiegel, David, et al. "Dissociative disorders in DSM-5" *Depression And Anxiety* 28 (12) 2011: E17-E45

The Times "Oklahoma blast 'part of plot to murder judges'" May 31, 1997

Time "Defending McVeigh: The Extra Leg" May 22, 1997, Jennifer Mattos

Upstart Business Journal "Spy vs. Spy" Dec. 17, 2007, Douglas Frantz

CHAPTER FOUR
PART THREE
GUILTY AGENT OR ALL AMERICAN MIND CONTROL

For sources used but not directly quoted in the Chapter Four, Part Three, see:

Advisory Committee on Human Radiation Experiments, *Final Report of the Advisory Committee on Human Radiation Experiments,* Oxford University Press, 1996

Biderman, Albert D. *Cultural models of captivity relationships.* Bureau of Social Science Research Report. Washington, D.C. 339 (4) Feb. 1961

Berle, Adolf A.;Robert J. Lifton; Albert D. Biderman; Harold G. Wolff; Lawrence E. Hinkle. Symposium on Communist Brainwashing, Nov. 7, 1957

Business Recorder "Making of Suicide Bombers" June 20, 2010, Dr. Ghayur Ahub

Butler, Lisa D. ; Oxana Palesh. "Spellbound: Dissociation in the Movies" *Journal of Trauma & Dissociation* 5(2) 2008: 61-87

Cockburn, Alexander. *Whiteout: The CIA, Drugs, and the Press.* Verso. 1998

Cotter, Lloyd H. (M.D) "Operant Conditioning in a Vietnamese Mental Hospital," *American Journal of Psychiatry* 124 (1) July 1967

Daily Mail "Elephants on LSD and Other Bizarre Experiments: Where the quest for knowledge has led our nutty professor" Nov. 1, 2007

Doob, Leonard W. "The Strategies Of Psychological Warfare." *Public Opinion Quarterly* 13 (4) 1949: 635-644

Estabrooks. George H., *Hypnotism.* E.P. Dutton & Co. Inc., 1943

Estabrooks, George H. (PhD), "Hypnosis Comes Of Age" *Science Digest,* April 1971: 44-50

Farber, I. E; Harry F. Harlow; Louis Jolyon West. "Brainwashing, Conditioning, and DDD (Debility, Dependency, and Dread" *Sociometry.* 20(4) Dec. 1957

Harriman, P.L., "Critical Review of Recent Books: *Hypnotism* by G.H. Estabrooks, 1943"

Journal of Social Psychology, 20(2) 1944: 321-325

Heath, R. G., "Electrical self-stimulation of the brain in man" *American Journal Of Psychiatry,* 120 (6) 1963: 571-577

Heath, R. G., "Pleasure and brain activity in man. Deep and surface electrocenphalograms during orgasm." *Journal of Nervous and Mental Disease.* 165 (1) 1972: 3-18

Hinkle, Lawrence E., Wolff, Harold G. "Communist Interrogation and Indoctrination of 'Enemies of the States: Analysis of Methods Used by the Communist State Police (A Special Report) *AMA Archives of Neurology and Psychiatry* 76(2) 1956: 115–74

Kaye, Jeff. "Military Interrogations: Torture, Hypocrisy Predate 9/11" (blog) *firedoglake.com.* July 25, 2009

Lee, Martin A., Shlain, Bruce. *Acid dreams: the CIA, LSD, and the sixties rebellion.* Grove Press. 1985

Los Angeles Times, "Did the CIA hypnotize Sirhan Sirhan?: Conspiracy theory. Robert Kennedy assassin was really Manchurian Candidate, book says" editorial, Feb.28, 2005

Melley, Timothy. "Brainwashed! Conspiracy Theory and Ideology in the Postwar United States" New German Critique, 35 (1) Spring 2008

Melley, Timothy. Empire of Conspiracy: The Culture of Paranoia in Postwar America. Cornell University Press, 2000.

Melley, Timothy. The Covert Sphere: secrecy, fiction, and the national security state. Cornell University Press, 2001.

Melley, Timothy. "Brainwashed! Conspiracy Theory and Ideology in the Postwar United States"

New German Critique, 35 (1) Spring 2008

Melley, Timothy The Covert Sphere: Secrecy, Fiction, and the National Security State, Cornell University Press. 2012

Meltzer, H., "Book Review: Hypnotism by G.H. Estabrooks, 1943" Journal of Educational Psychology, 36 (1) Jan. 1945: 61,62

Moreno, Jonathan D., Mind Wars: Brian Science and the Military in the 21st Century. 2nd ed., Bellvue Literary Press. 2012

Nathan, Debbie. "A Nightmare World of Torture and Prison Guard Suicides" Counterpunch. Feb. 26, 2008

Pepper, William F. An Act of State: The Execution of Martin Luther King. Verso. 2003

Piasecki, Eugene G., "The History Of Special Warfare" Special Warfare 28(2) April 1, 2015

RAND Corporation "Are the Cominform Countries Using Hypnosis Techniques To Elicit Confession In Public Trials?" (Report) April 25, 1949

Ross, Colin A. (MD), "Ethics of CIA and Military Contracting by Psychiatrists and Psychologists" Ethical Human Psychology and Psychiatry, 9(1) 2007

San Francisco Weekly "Operation Midnight Climax: How the CIA Dosed S.F. Citizens with LSD" March 14 2012

Spiegel, Herbert (M.D)., "The Grade 5 Syndrome: The Highly Hypnotizable Person" International Journal of Clinical and Experimental Hypnosis, 22(4) 1974: 303-319

Suppes, Patrick; Bing Han; Zhong-Ling Lu. "Brain Wave Recognition of Words" Proceedings of the National Academy of Sciences of the United States of America, 94 (2) Dec. 1997

Suppes, Patrick; Bing Han; Zhong-Ling Lu. " Brain Wave Recognition of Sentences" Proceedings of the National Academy of Sciences of the United States of America, 95 (26) Dec. 1998: 15861-15866

The Guardian "A dose of madness" Aug. 8, 2002

The Public Record "Former Top Navy Psychologist Involved in Pre 9/11 Prisoner Abuse Case" July 24, 2009, Jeffery Kaye

The Public Record "Broken Faith: How a Navy Psychologist Drove A U.S. Prisoner to Attempt Suicide" Aug. 31, 2009, Jeffery Kaye

The Telegraph "Kennedy assassin dubbed Manchurian Candidate" March 2, 2011, Jon Swaine

The Times 'Robert Kennedy killed in CIA plot' June 2, 1993

Thomas, Gordon. Journey Into Madness: The True Story Of Secret CIA Mind Control and Medical Abuse. Bantam, 1989

USA Today "FBI Goes On Offensive vs. Tech Spies; China Linked to About One Third of All Economic Espionage Cases" July 24, 2007

Valentine, Douglas. "Sex, Drugs, and the CIA" Counterpunch. June 19, 2002

Wright, Evangeline. "Mind Control Experimentation: A Travesty of Human Rights in the United States" The Journal of Gender, Race & Justice. 9 (no issue listed) 2005

Young, Charles, S. "Missing in action: POW films, brainwashing and the Korean War 1954-1968"

Historical Journal of Film, Radio & Television 18 (1) 1998: 49-74

CHAPTER FOUR
PART FOUR
CALSPAN: RISE OF THE ROBOTS
AND THE DATABASE THAT COULD'

For sources used but not directly quoted in the Chapter Four, Part Four, see:

Advisory Committee on Human Radiation Experiments, *Final Report of the Advisory Committee on Human Radiation Experiments*, New York, Oxford University Press, 1996.

Alivistatos, Paul A., et. al., "A National Network Of Neurotechnology Centers For The BRAIN Initiative" *Neuron*, 88 (3) Nov. 2015: 445-448

Aviation Week & Space Technology "Defense Dept. Using EW Simulators To Gather Rapid, Affordable Data" Nov. 5, 1990, Bruce D. Nordwall

Buffalo News "Approve DNA Database, An Effective Anti-Crime Tool But Assure Reliability and Confidentiality" May 26, 1992

Buffalo News "Calspan honored for its contributions to aviation: Cheektowaga company's history includes testing of military planes and space shuttles" Dec. 2, 2010, Michelle Kearns

Buffalo News "Assembly Democrats oppose Cuomo DNA data expansion plan" March 7, 2012

BUG (film), William Friedkin, dir, L.I.F.T. Production, Bug LLC, DMK Medienfonds, Lionsgate 2006

Business Wire "Local Ownership Group Purchases Former Calspan Corporation from General Dynamics; Buyout Saves Jobs and Preserves an Important Piece of Buffalo's Technology History" Feb.18, 2005

Cell Press "US Neuroscientists Call For Creation Of 'Brain Observatories'" Oct. 15, 2014

Conspiracy Theory (film) Richard Donner, dir. Warner Brothers, 1997.

Cornell Daily Sun "Asian Déjà vu" Feb. 11, 1969

Daily News (New York) "SMART OUTFIT Superbriany-agent chips in with grid-dy 'Intelligence'" Jan. 7, 2014

Edmonton Journal (Alberta) "Man and Machine" Jan. 7, 2014

Herr, Andrew. "Will Humans Matter In The Wars Of 2030?" *Joint Force Quarterly*. April 1, 2015

International Herald Tribune "Future Of Technology Is Something To Think About" April 29, 2013, Nick Bilton

Investor's Business Daily "Defense Agency Pushed Its Tech Out Door" Dec. 17, 2012

Ishihata, H.; K. Tomoe; T. Takei; et. al,, "A Radio Frequency Identification Implanted in a Tooth can Communicate With the Outside World" *Biomedicine* 11(6) Nov. 2007: 683-685

Kidd, Devvy "McVeigh's Second Trial" (website) *NewsWithViews.com* Aug. 1, 2005

McCoy, Alfred W., *A Question of Torture: CIA Interrogation, From the Cold War to the War on Terror.* Henry Holt and Co., LLC, 2006

Medical Device Daily "New Ventures: Allied Minds Creates New Medical Device Subsidiary" Nov. 10, 2011

Nanaszko, Michael ., Little, Andrew., "Two Years Since The BRAIN Initiative: Update on Current Scientific and Technological Neuroscience Advancements" *World Neurosurgery*, 84 (5) Nov. 2015: 1182-1190

New York Post "The Future's So Bleak We Gotta Wear Blades" Aug. 4, 2013

New York Times "Gunman in Classroom Standoff Is Convicted" Jan. 13, 1996

New York Times "Man Sentenced in Albany Hostage Drama" Feb. 17, 1996

Ottawa Citizen "Military expands data collection capacity; Canadian Forces to share biometricinfo, methods with civilian departments" Dec. 1, 2012, David Pugliese

Pitts, John A. *The Human Factor: Biomedicine in the Manned Space Program to 1980.*

NASASP-4213, Washington, D. C: National Aeronautics and Space Administration, Scientific and Technical Information Branch, 1985

Pittsford Post-Gazette "CBS Stands By 'Intelligence'" Jan. 16, 2014

Rajagopalan, H.; Y. Rahmat-Samii. "On-body RFID tag design for human monitoring applications" *IEEE Antennas and Propagation Society International Symposium,* 2010

Rosenblatt, Peter L. III., et. al., "Systems And Methods For Providing Guidance Procedure With A Device" United States Patent 20140204190, Filed: July 19, 2013, Assignee: Allied Mind Devices, LLC, Date of Patent July 24, 2014

Rowan, Ford. *Technospies: The Secret Network That Spies on You –And You* G.P. Putnam and Sons, 1978

Salt Lake City Tribune "DNA Registries Present Hard Ethical Questions" Jan. 25, 1992

Scientific American "Does Sprouting New Brain Cells Cure Depression?" Sep. 25, 2006, JR Minkel

Scientific And Technical Information Branch of the National Aeronautics and Space Administration, "Aerospace Medicine and Biology, 1978 Cumulative Index, NASA SP-011 (189)" Washington, DC. Jan. 1979

The IPCRESS File (film) Sidney J. Furie, dir. J. Arthur Rank, 1965

The Manchurian Candidate (film) John Frankenheimer, United Artists, 1962

The Manchurian Candidate (film) Jonathan Demme, Paramount Pictures, 2004

The Terminal Man (film) Mike Hodges, dir., Warner Brothers, 1974

Thomas, Timothy L. "The Mind Has No Firewall" *Parameters,* Spring 1998: 84-92

Toronto Star "Crime and punishment of a delusional" Oct. 17, 2002, Vinay Menon

Young, Charles S. "Missing action: POW films, brainwashing and the Korean War, 1954–1968."

Historical Journal of Film, Radio and Television 18.1 (1998): 49-74

CHAPTER FOUR
PART FIVE
THE BOURNE SCENARIO

For sources used but not directly quoted in the Chapter Four, Part Four, see:

Buffalo News "McVeigh Predicted Conspiracy Claims" Feb. 26, 2004, Dan Herbeck, Lou Michel

Butler, Lisa D., Palesh, Oxana. "Spellbound: Dissociation in the Movies" *Journal of Trauma & Dissociation* 5(2) 2008: 61-87

Culver, Dick. "Introduction to The Saga of 'Lee Harvey' McVeigh" on *'Culvers Shooting Page'* (website) *Jouster.com.* March 23, 1997, updated 2004.

Maderia, Jody Lynee. *Killing McVeigh: The Death Penalty and the Myth of Closure.* University Press. 2012.

Rixon, Stewart "Was McVeigh Really Executed?" (website) *rumormillnews.com.* June 17, 2001

Skolnick, Sherman, H., "The Secrets of Timothy McVeigh" (website) *Skolnickreport.com.* June 15, 2001

St. Louis Post-Dispatch "Behind the mask of the execution doctor Revelations about Dr. Alan Doerhoff follow judge's halt of lethal injections" July 30, 2006

St. Louis Post-Dispatch "Execution doctor defends his work 'I'm more than willing to help' state, Doerhoff says; downplays 20 suits against him as part of 'malpractice crisis'" Aug. 1, 2006

St. Louis Post-Dispatch "Judge ousts state execution doctor" Sep. 14, 2006

St. Louis Post-Dispatch "The secret of Dr. X" May 29, 2007

St. Louis Post-Dispatch "Judge upholds execution procedure Ruling may clear way for Missouri to put killer to death on July 30." July 16, 2008

The Bourne Identity (film) Doug Liman, dir., Universal Pictures, 2002

The Bourne Legacy (film) Tony Gilroy, dir., Universal Pictures, 2012

The Bourne Supremacy (film) Paul Greengrass, dir., Universal Pictures, 2004

The Bourne Ultimatum (film) Paul Greengrass, dir., Universal Pictures, 2007

The Independent "FBI Admits it has more 'missing' McVeigh files" May 16, 2001

Washington Post "Mo. Execution Doctor Had History of Errors" July 30, 2006; *New York Times* "After Flawed Executions, States Resort to Secrecy" July 30, 2007

CHAPTER FIVE
WEARING THE WOLF'S HEAD

For sources used but not directly quoted in the Chapter Five, see:

Associated Press "Document: Oklahoma City Bombing Was Taped" April 20, 2004

Berger, J.M., "PATCON Revealed: An Exclusive Look Inside The FBI's Secret War With the Militia Movement" *Intelwire.* Oct. 8, 2007

Bertini, Joseph. "Stings, stoolies, and agents provocateurs: Evaluating FBI undercover counterterrorism operations" PhD dissertation., #1491298, Georgetown University, 2011

CNN. The Lone Wolf—the unknowable face of terror" Feb. 18, 2012, Paul Cruickshank., Tim Lister

Desert Morning News "Trial begins for S.L. man seeking answers" July 29, 2014

Foreign Policy. "Patriot Games: How the FBI spent a decade hunting white supremacists and missed Timothy McVeigh" April 18, 2012, J.M. Berger

Hay, Bruce "Sting Operations, Undercover Agents, and Entrapment" *Harvard Law Review,* 70 (2005)

Huffington Post "Oklahoma City Bombing Tapes Appear Edited" Sep. 27, 2009

Kansas City Star "Oklahoma City bombing: New evidence renews conspiracy debate" Jan. 17, 2006

Kuo, Susan, S., "Official Indiscretions: Considering Sex Bargains with Government Informants" *The Regents of the University of California U.C. Davis Law Review* 38 (1643) June 2005

Mother Jones "The informants: the FBI has built a massive network of spies to prevent another domestic attack. But are they busting terrorist plots--or leading them?" 36 (5) Sep. to Oct. 2011, Trever Aaaronson

New York Times "New Face of Terror Crimes: 'Lone Wolf' Weaned on Hate" Aug. 16, 1999, Jo Thomas

New York Times "More Federal Agencies Are Using Undercover Operations" Nov. 15, 2014, Eric Lichtblau and William M. Arkinnov

Newsweek "My Life as a White Supremacist: An FBI mole speaks for the first time about life in the seedy world of right-wing terror." Nov. 21, 2011, R.M. Schneiderman

National Public Radio "Terror Probes Have FBI's Informant Numbers Soaring" Aug. 21, 2011 (Show) All Things Considered

The Independent "FBI Admits it has more 'missing' McVeigh files" May 16, 2001

The Independent "Does one man on death row hold the secret of Oklahoma?" Jan. 29, 2004

The Oklahoman "Lawyer says bombing tapes edited" Sep. 28, 2009

Rolling Stone "The Plot Against Occupy" September 13, 2012, Sabrina Rubin.

Said, Wadie, E., "The terrorist informant" *Washington Law Review* 85 (4) 2010

Salt Lake Tribune "According to Oklahoma bombing conspirator, ranking officials were involved in the attack" Feb. 21, 2007, Pamela Manson

Salt Lake Tribune "Legal setback for Utah man whose brother died in Oklahoma prison" Aug. 7, 2007

Salt Lake Tribune "Utah Judge orders probe into why witness won't testify at trial" July 29, 2014

Salt Lake Tribune "Witnesses: Cameras were monitoring Oklahoma City federal building" July 20, 2014, Pamela Manson

Salt Lake City Tribune "FBI could be found in contempt in case of Utahn investigation brother's death" Nov. 10, 2014

Salt Lake City Tribune "Magistrate to investigate witness tampering claims in Utah man's Oklahoma City bombing records case" May 1, 2015

Sentinel & Enterprise (Fitchburg, MA) "Man: Video Shows 2nd Person Involved in

Okla. City bombing" July 28, 2014

U.S. District Court For The District Of Utah, Central Division, Jesse Trentadue V. United States Central Intelligence Agency, et. al. "Plaintiff's Reply Memorandum, RE: Motion To Strike August 25, 2015 Hearing" Aug. 25, 2014. Case No. 2:08-cv-0788

Washington Post "AP: FBI Suspected McVeigh Link to Robbers" Feb. 25, 2004, John Solomon

Stephen Jones Oklahoma City Bombing Archive

A listing of the Jones Collection documents can be found in the Finding Aid for The Stephen Jones Oklahoma City Bombing Archive, 1798 – 2003 (Bulk 1995 – 1997), Dolph Briscoe Center for American History, University of Texas at Austin. To my knowledge, as of 2012, I am the only person to have gone through the entire publicly available Stephen Jones Collection held at the University of Texas, Austin, a task that took me approximately four and a half years. I requested copies of many, but by no means, all of the documents purveyed and was allowed to take pictures of some of them. I have approximately 3000 pages of documents in my possession, first accessed through the Jones Collection. In some cases, notably FBI reports and McVeigh's military records, although I first accessed them through the Jones Collection, I later accessed the same documents through other sources and means and they are listed in this bibliography under 'Other Sources' rather than in the list of documents unique to the Jones Collection. All documents used in this book are on file with me, including all Jones Collection documents that informed or were directly referred to or quoted in this book.

While *all* of the Jones Collection documents in my possession informed this book, only a small portion were referred to or mentioned in it, and a much smaller portion, quoted directly. Documents unique to the Jones Collection, quoted directly or referred to in this book include, but are not limited to:

- Over 100 internal defense team memoranda and reports detailing Jones Team members' visits with Timothy McVeigh from June 1995 until December 1996. Jones Team members whose visits with McVeigh are directly quoted include Bob Wyatt, Lee Norton, Randy Coyne, Rob Nigh, Richard Reyna, Seymour Halleck, Anthony Semone, Amber McLaughlin, and Jaralyn Merritt.

- Over 50 internal defense team memoranda, reports, and transcripts detailing Jones Team members' conversations with witnesses or other parties of interest from May 1995 until August 1997. These individuals include (but are not limited to): Andrea

Augustine, Johnny Bangerter, Richard Coffman, Jeff Davis, Bobby Joe Farrington, Robert Millar, James Nichols, Gwen Strider, Mark Thomas, Linda Thompson, the Hodge family, Carl Lebron, Jennifer McVeigh, Bill McVeigh, Mickey Frazer, as well as other extended members of the McVeigh family, McVeigh family friends and neighbors and McVeigh's fellow soldiers and co-workers at various places of employment.

- Other internal Jones Team memorandum and reports (see 'Select List Of Internal Jones Team Memorandum And Reports').

- Numerous letters to or from members of the defense team including those written by and to Timothy McVeigh (see 'Select List Of Jones Team Letters').

- Other documents including court filings and exhibits used in trial (see 'Select List Of Additional Jones Team Documents'), many of which can be accessed elsewhere but some of which are unique to the Jones Collection.

- Hundreds of 'FBI 302 database forms' in which the Jones Team summarized FBI documents in their possession, most turned over by the government to the Jones Team during discovery (see 'Select List of FBI 302 Database Forms').

- McVeigh's partial military records, first accessed in the Jones Collection and then duplicated and expanded upon through my own FOIA requests (see 'Other Sources, Select List Of McVeigh Military/ Medical Records').

- Hundreds of FBI reports, many of which I have accessed both in the Jones Collection but also through other sources (see 'Other Sources, Select List Of FBI 302s).

SELECT LIST OF INTERNAL JONES TEAM MEMORANDUM AND REPORTS

June 9, 1995. To: Rob Nigh. From: Bob Wyatt. Sub: Tim McVeigh Witness File.

July 2, 1995. To: Stephen Jones & Dick Burr. From: Rob Nigh. Sub: Dr. Smith

July 3, 1995. To: Dick Burr, Rob Nigh, Stephen Jones. From: Lee Norton. Re: Mitigation Investigation.

July 3, 1995. To: Stephen, Rob, Bob, Julia. From: Dick. Re: Update on Lee Norton's work.

July 19, 1995. To: Stephen Jones, et. al., Rob Nigh, Dick Burr, Bob Wyatt, Julia Simms, Amber McLaughlin, Jim Hankins, Mike Roberts, Randy Coyne, Ann Bradley, Marty Reed, Wilma Sparks, Richard Reyna, Neil Hartley, Lee Norton, Scott Anderson, Kathryn Irons. From: Bob Wyatt. SUB: Tim McVeigh –Assignments/ Things To Do (Master List) (revised 8-1-95; 8-14-95; 11-14-95; 11-16-95).

Aug 23, 1995. To: All Attorneys. From: Rob Nigh. Sub: Military Records.

Aug. 31, 1995. To: Richard Burr, Esq. From: H. Anthony Semone, PhD. Re: Timothy McVeigh.

Sep. 8, 1995. To: Stephen Jones, (Nigh, Wyatt, et. al,) From: Dick Burr. Sub: Dr. Halleck's impressions after his initial interview with Tim.

Sep. 12, 1995. To: Kathryn. From: Dick. No Subject. Memo starts "We need to get some materials copied for Dr. Halleck."

Sep. 18, 1996. To: McVeigh In House Legal Team. From: Amber McLaughlin. Sub: Handwritten Directions To Emrick's Storage.

Sep. 24, 1995. Prepared by Col. James D. Weiskoph, U.S. Army, Retired. Sub: Pertaining To The Military, Finance, And Medical Records; Timothy James McVeigh.

Oct. 5, 1995. To: Stephen, et. al., From: Dick Burr. Sub: Meeting with Dr. Halleck, October 4, 1995.

Oct. 11, 1995. To: Tim McVeigh – File And Scott Anderson And McVeigh Defense Team. From: Jim Hankins. Sub: Document Review Of Documents Filed Under Seal With Magistrate Howland And Bill French.

Oct. 18, 1995. To: Stephen, Rob, Bob, et. al., From: Dick. Re: Some ideas about a theory of Defense—inspired by the Oct 12 meeting with Dr. Halleck, Dr. Semone, Lee Norton and Neil Hartley.

Oct. 27, 1995. To: Rob Nigh. From: Kate Rubin. Sub: Mental Health Data.

Oct. 27, 1995. To: Stephen, Rob. From: Dick RE: Thoughts engendered by ABC/NBC, our life history/ mental health evaluation process, and evolving thinking about defense themes.

Oct. 30, 1995. To: Stephen, Rob. From: Dick. No Subject. Memo begins "I wanted to bring you up to date on a variety of fronts from my end."

Nov. 1, 1995. To: Stephen Jones, (Burr, Nigh, Coyne, et. al.,) & Bob Miller A/K/A Roger Moore File. Sub: McVeigh: Inconsistencies By Roger Moore.

Nov. 6, 1995. To: Dick Burr. From: Stephen Jones. Sub: Tim McVeigh Re: Your conference with Tim Nov. 1, 1995.

Nov. 15, 1995. To: Stephen, From: Dick. RE: Your November 6 memo to me., our telephone conference today and the evolution of a potential defense strategy.

Nov. 29, 1995. From: Rob Nigh. Sub: Myers/ James Nichols, 10/20/95 (with attached transcript).

Dec. 5, 1995. To: Stephen Jones and Defense Team. From: Jim Hankins. Sub: McVeigh— Conference With Dr. Stephen Sloan Of 12/1/95.

Dec. 6, 1995. To: Bob Wyatt. From: Stephen Jones. SUB: Problems in Military Records.

Dec. 8, 1995. To: Stephen Jones/ Rob Nigh/ Dick Burr. From: Richard Reyna. Re: Research on Andreas Karl Strassmeir.

Dec. 10, 1995. To: Jim Hankins. From: Sam G. Sub: Transcript of Lebron/ McVeigh, Sep. 15, 1992 (with attached transcript).

Dec. 27, 1995. To: Military Records File. Official Records. Gen Memo File. From: Scott Anderson. Sub: PKG to Lawrence Myer.

Jan. 11, 1996. To: McVeigh Legal Team, General Memo File, Evidence File and Witness: Steve Hodge File. From: Robert Warren. Sub: McVeigh: Summary Of Letters To Steve Hodge.

Jan. 12, 1996. To: Stephen Jones. From: Wilma Sparks/ Marty Reed. Re: Info re Strass-meir/Mahon.

Jan. 13, 1996. To: Stephen Jones/ Rob Nigh. From: Richard Reyna. Ref: Response to the January 2, 1996 memorandum from Stephen Jones regarding Roger Moore.

Jan. 19, 1996. To: Stephen Jones. From: Amber McLaughlin. Sub: Storage Shed Chart.

Jan. 30, 1996. To: Bob Wyatt. From: Andrew Murphy. Sub: Witnesses, Discovery Items, And Chronology.

Feb. 7, 1996. To: Stephen Jones. From: Andrew Murphy. Sub: Steven G. Colburn's State-ment Summary.

Feb. 13, 1996. To: McVeigh Legal Team and Jennifer McVeigh File. From: Robert War-ren. Re: Summary of Tim McVeigh's letters to Jennifer McVeigh.

Feb. 15, 1996. To: Stephen Jones, (Nigh, Burr, et. al.,) From: Amber McLaughlin. Sub: Aliases used by Tim McVeigh & Terry Nichols.

Feb. 19, 1996. To: Stephen Jones/ Bob Wyatt. From: Wilma Sparks/ Marty Reed. Re: Johnny Bangerter's pirate phone records.

March 6, 1996. To: Stephen Jones. From: Richard Reyna. Sub: Telephone records/ John Bangerter.

March 11, 1996. To: McVeigh In House Legal Team. From: Amber McLaughlin. Sub: Phone Conversation Between Lawrence Myers and James Nichols, October 20, 1995.

March 13, 1996. To: Dick Burr. From: Stephen Jones. Sub: McVeigh.

March 14, 1996. To: Stephen Jones and McVeigh Defense Team. From: A.W. Reed. Sub: Files Search at Fort Riley, Kansas.

March 14, 1996. To: Stephen Jones. From: Jim Hankins. Sub: Art Reed/ McVeigh Mil-itary Records.

March 14, 1996. To: McVeigh File. From: Andrew Murphy. Sub: Phone Conversation between Andy and Dr. Jolly West (310) 825-0085 of UCLA.

March 15, 1996. To: McVeigh File. From: Stephen Jones. Sub: Phone conversation between John R. Smith, M.D. and Stephen Jones on March 12, 1996. Transcribed on March 15, 1996.

April 19, 1996. To: Stephen, Rob, Mental Health Mitigation File. From: Dick. Re: Meet-ing in Raleigh, NC, 4-18-96.

April 23, 1996. To: McVeigh In-House Legal Team. From: Amber McLaughlin. Sub: Sightings Of Tim McVeigh On April 18, 1995.

April 24, 1996. To: Dick Burr, (Norton, et., al). From: Stephen Jones. Sub: Mitigation Phase.

April 22, 1996. To: McVeigh Defense Team. From: Rob Nigh. Sub: Redacted Exculpato-ry Statements (with attached heavily redacted FBI reports about eye witnesses).

May 30, 1996. To: McVeigh Defense Team. From: Dick. Re: Review of Tim's letters with him, Part I-April 22, 1996.

June 12, 1996. To: Dick Burr and Stephen Jones. From: Amber McLaughlin. Sub: Mitigation Evidence.

July 22, 1996. To: Missing 302's File. From: Stephen Jones. Sub: FBI Interviews Mentioned In Newspaper.

July 23, 1996. To: Rob Nigh. From: Stephen Jones. Sub: Richard Lee Guthrie.

Aug 27, 1996. To: Stephen Jones /Robb Nigh. From: Richard Reyna. Ref: Michael Joseph Fortier- Association with the Aryan Movement.

Aug. 29, 1996. To: Stephen Jones, (Nigh, Merritt). From: Amber McLaughlin. Sub: Tim's Reply To Defense Request For Pay Phone Records.

Sep. 2-4, 1996. To: Stephen Jones/ Rob Nigh. Re: Michael Joseph Fortier's involvement in the bombing of the Alfred P. Murrah Federal Building, Oklahoma City, Oklahoma .

Sep. 24, 1996. To: Dick Burr, Mandy Welch. From: Stephen Jones. Sub: McVeigh – Your memo of Sep.19, 1996, Meeting with Dr. Halleck and Dr. Semone- Psychological Evaluation of Tim.

Sep. 26, 1996. To: Stephen Jones & Bob Wyatt. From: Amber McLaughlin. Sub: Prosecution Rule 17(C) Subpoenas

Oct. 14, 1996. To: Stephen Jones, (Nigh, Wyatt). From: Robert Warren. Sub: Appearance Of Conflicting Information From Tim.

Oct. 21, 1996. To: Bob Wyatt. From: Dick Burr. Re: Military Records. Oct. 21, 1996.

Oct. 28, 1996. To: David Fechheimer. From: Stephen Jones. Sub: National Alliance & Greg Pfaff.

Nov. 5, 1996. To: Mary Reed and Wilma Sparks. From: Stephen Jones. Sub: McVeigh: Subsequent Investigation Of Oklahoma City.

Nov. 18, 1996. To: McVeigh Legal Team. From: Robert Warren. Sub: Phone Conversation With Former Elohim City Resident.

Nov. 25, 1996. To: Dick Burr, (Nigh, Wyatt, Coyne). From: Stephen Jones. Sub: McVeigh: Letter To Tim.

Jan. 14, 1997. To: Stephen Jones and File. From: Ann Bradley. Sub: McVeigh-Grand Jury Summary Of Jennifer McVeigh Given August 2, 1995.

Jan. 16, 1997. To: File. From: Stephen Jones. Sub: Government Attempts To Leak And Influence The Press.

Feb. 24, 1997. To: Rob Nigh. From: Stephen Jones. Sub: Blank. Memo starts "We have never gotten a complete set of Tim McVeigh's military records although I have asked for them repeatedly."

March 27, 1997. To: Rob. From: Chris (Abacus Research & Investigation). No Subject. Memo starts "Per your request we have been trying to track Mike/Tim/Terry whereabouts on military leave but we have found we have incomplete military records."

April 2, 1997. To: Stephen Jones, Rob Nigh & Cheryl Ramsey. From: Amber McLaughlin. Sub: Defense Witnesses: Elliot's Body Shop; Dreamland; Geary Lake; Junction City and Kansas To Oklahoma City.

Undated. To: Stephen Jones. From: Ann Bradley. RE: Is he lying or isn't he?

Undated. No Heading. "Statements Of Timothy McVeigh."

Undated. No Heading. "Evidence that Mr. McVeigh was racist" entered as "Exhibit 6."

Undated. No Heading. "Summary of telephone activity on Daryl bridges phone card Dec.7, 1993 through April 17, 1995."

Undated. "Index-Hodge Letters."

SELECT LIST OF JONES TEAM LETTERS

July 13, 1995. To: Stephen (Jones). From: Tim McVeigh. No Subject. Letter begins, "I want to warn you of something."

Aug. 31, 1995. No recipient listed (to Jones Team). From: Timothy McVeigh. Re: Polygraph results of Thursday, August 31, 1995.

Aug. 31, 1995. To: Dick Burr, Esquire. From: H. Anthony Semone, PhD., Clinical Psychologist/Neuropsychologist. RE: Re: Timothy McVeigh.

Oct. 6, 1995. To: Ken Reding, Federal Correctional Institution, El Reno, OK. From: Richard Burr, Co-Council For Timothy McVeigh. Re: Tim McVeigh's cell and conditions of detention.

Oct. 10, 1995. To: Tim McVeigh. From: Stephen Jones. No Subject. Letter begins, "This letter is an exception to our general rule not to send you anything in writing."

Oct. 11, 1995. To: Stephen Jones. From: Timothy McVeigh. No Subject. Letter begins "I received your letter today. Thank you for the followup; that in itself shows me a lot."

Oct. 24, 1995. To: Stephen Jones. From: Michael Drosnin. No Subject. Letter begins "According to my source, there is at least one other conspirator in the bombing, a man your client met with in the month before the explosion."

March, 11, 1996. To: Stephen Jones, Attorney. From: John R. Smith, M.D., Inc. No subject. Letter begins "On Saturday, March 9, 1996, I spent three and one-half hours in an interview with Timothy McVeigh at his request."

May 13, 1996. To: Stephen (Jones). From: Timothy McVeigh. No Subject. Letter begins, "Please find enclosed items related to our phone conversation this evening – re: DNL."

May 24, 1996. To: Joseph Hartzler, Esquire., Assistant U.S. District Attorney, Dept. of Justice. Re: Video Film.

Nov. 6, 1996. To: Joseph Hartzler, Esq., DOJ. From: Stephen Jones. No Subject. Letter begins, "Please consider this letter Defendant McVeigh's first written request for Brady information."

Nov. 20, 1996. To: Beth Wilkinson, DOJ. From: Ronald G. Woods, Attorney At Law (Terry Nichols' defense attorney). No Subject. Letter begins, "On November 13m 1996, Judge Matsch ordered you to disclose whether Roger Moore, AKA Robert or Bob Miller, is or was a confidential informant for any government agency."

Nov. 22, 1996. To: Stephen Jones, Esq. From: Joseph H. Hartzler and Beth A. Wilkinson, Special Attorneys to the U.S. Attorney General (with attached partial list of gun shows and dates attended by Timothy McVeigh.)

Nov. 24, 1996. To: "All attorneys assigned to U.S. vs. McVeigh." From: Timothy McVeigh. Re: General Notice To Defense Team, Defense Strategy.

Dec. 3, 1996. To: Timothy McVeigh. From: Stephen Jones. Re: United States v. Timothy McVeigh.

Dec. 11, 1996. To: Timothy McVeigh. From: Stephen Jones. Re: United States v. Timothy McVeigh.

Jan. 24, 1997. To: Rob Nigh, Esq. From: Craig Bryant, Assistant Federal Public Defender. No Subject. Letter begins, "On January 15, 1997, I briefly spoke with Carol Howe at the federal courthouse in Tulsa."

March 9, 1997. To: Stephen Jones. From: Richard Reyna. No Subject. Letter begins, "I have spoken with Conroe, Texas attorney Don Brown who informed me of his conversations with you prior to your February 28, 1997 press conference.

March 20, 1997. To: Richard Reyna. From: Stephen Jones. Re: United States v. Timothy McVeigh.

May 2, 1997. To: Stephen Jones, Esquire. From: James L. Hankins. No Subject. Letter begins, "Based upon our conversation of Friday, April 25, 1997, I am taking this opportunity now to present my resignation effective Friday, May 9, 1997."

May 28, 1997. To: Tim McVeigh. From: Stephen Jones. Re: United States v. Timothy McVeigh. June 30, 1997. To: Mildred "Mickie" Frazer. From: Stephen Jones. No Subject. Letter begins, "I just wanted to tell you have sad I am for you and your family and for Tim that we did not have a better result."

Undated. To: "Everyone on my Legal Team." From: Tim McVeigh. No Subject. Letter begins, "I am having difficulty "coping" with a few recent events, and need some time to 'regroup.'"

Undated. To: Stephen (Jones). From: Me, Tim (McVeigh). No Subject. Letter begins, "I would not have enclosed correspondence from that Phoenix guy if I was considering "going alone."

Undated. No recipient noted (Jones Team). From: Timothy McVeigh. Re: Polygraph results.

SELECT LIST OF ADDITIONAL JONES TEAM DOCUMENTS

April 29, 1995. "Audiotape Summary" Bates No: A099, Description: WDNY #281 Tape 2, Location: Residence Inn, Room 828, Time Stamped: 0000-4015, Date Summarized: Oct. 10, 1996, Date Recorded: April 29, 1995 (Conversation between Jennifer McVeigh and Mickey Frazer) July 5, 1995. U.S. District Court, Western District Of Oklahoma. U.S. v. Timothy James

McVeigh. Case No. M-95-98-H. Motion To Prohibit Investigative Obstruction, To Remedy Violations Of Grand Jury Secrecy And Request For Evidentiary Hearing.

July 7, 1995. Affidavit of J.R. Smith. #12076-064. State of Oklahoma. County of Garfield.

Aug. 1995. Louis Jolyon West, M.D. Curriculum Vitae. University Of California, Los Angeles.

Sep. 5, 1995. Confidential Statement Of Timothy James McVeigh. El Reno, Oklahoma.

Dec. 29, 1995. United States Government Memorandum. Federal Correctional Institution. El Reno, Oklahoma. To: All Concerned. Reply To: Sam Calbone, Associate Warden. Sub: Attorneys Of Record, 22nd Revision, Timothy McVeigh (approved legal visitor list).

Jan. 22, 1996. Affidavit of Stephen Jones. State Of Oklahoma, County Of Garfield.

Aug. 28, 1996. United States Government Memorandum. Dept. Of Justice, Federal Bureau Of Prisons, FCI Englewood, Colorado. To: All Concerned. Reply To: Jonathan B. May, Paralegal Specialist. Sub: Legal Visitor List for Timothy McVeigh -2nd Revision.

Oct. 10, 1996. Alliance Services Investigative Memorandum. To: Michael E. Tigar, Ronald G. Woods, From: Roland Leeds. Re: Roger Moore. Case: Nichols.

Oct. 18, 1996. U.S. District Court, Colorado, Chief Judge Richard P. Matsch, U.S. v. Timothy James McVeigh and Terry Lynn Nichols. Criminal Action No. 96-CR-68-M. Response Of The United States To McVeigh's Amended Motion To Compel Production Of Classified Information. Sealed.

Dec. 18, 1996. Alliance Services Investigative Memorandum, To: Michael A. Tigar, Ronald G. Woods. From: John W. Hough. Sub: The Enigma of Roger Moore.

June 9, 1997. U.S. District Court, Colorado, Chief Judge Richard P. Matsch, U.S. v. Timothy James McVeigh and Terry Lynn Nichols, Criminal Action No. 96-CR-68-M. Order Granting Defendant McVeigh's Motion to Seal Proffer For Testimony Of Carol E. Howe.

SELECT LIST OF FBI 302 DATABASE FORMS

FBI 302 Database Form citations are sorted by the categories the Jones Team assigned to them and may contain the following information: (1) Date of FBI 302. (2) "Sub" Subject of Report as listed by Jones Team and various names mentioned. *Disclaimer: Names of individuals may reflect person interviewed by FBI or the names of people mentioned in report* (3) "Ed" Event Date, if listed (4) "LC" Location (5) "ATH" Author of FBI report (5) Report numbers, if listed.

CATEGORY: ELOHIM CITY:

May 10, 1995. Sub: Vernon Phillips, OHP, provided information on Andreas Strassmeir and Elohim City; Bruce Millar, Robert Grant Millar, McVeigh, Richard William Snell, Pricilla Ward, Suzie Ward, Sonny Ward, Kirk Lyons, V.A. Letruskie. #E-1866.

May 16, 1996. Sub: Confidential informant gave his opinion that Strassmeier, Millar and others residing in Elohim City would be involved in actual violence against the government including the bombing of the Alfred P. Murrah building; Robert Millar, Andrew Strassmeier, Protect I.D., John Strassmeier, McVeigh, Pete LNU. ED: April 19, 1995. LC: Elohim City, Oklahoma City. ATH: REDACTED. #D-15301.

CATEGORY: EYE WITNESS IDENTIFICATION:

June 8, 1995. Sub: Ann Mitchell was maid at Dixie Palms Motel when McVeigh stayed at motel and she tentatively ID'ed his Pontiac. ED: Feb. 25, 1995. LC: Dixie Palms Motel, St. George, Utah. ATH: Sa Robert Allan Spiva. #D-16386.

CATEGORY: FORENSIC AND LAB EVIDENCE:

April 24, 1995. Sub: Video recording of Ryder Truck and possible four wheel drive vehicle at bomb site. LC: Murrah Building. ED: April 19, 1995. ATH: SA Zelda A. Morris.

June 19, 1995. Sub: McVeigh on videotape taken on March 16, 1993 at the Mt. Carmel Compound; Bob Pecot. ED: March 1, 3, 1996. ATH: SA Pamela A. Matson. #D-15196.

July 26, 1995 to Sep. 8, 1995. Sub: Video tape surveillance. LC: Southewestern Bell, Regency Towen, Anthony's, Journal Record Building, Oklahoma City Public Library, other Oklahoma City sites. ATH: Pamela A. Matson. #E (insert).

CATEGORY: JOHN DOE 2:

April 27, 1995. Sub: Possible John Doe 2 In Kingman, Associated With Separatists. LC: Compound In Kingman. ATH: Steven F. Fillerup, Susan Stamper. #D-949.

CATEGORY: KINGMAN, AZ:

April 29, 1995. Sub: Sighting of McVeigh and another male and a pregnant female at the Golden Valley Landowners Association bingo game in 1994. LC: Kingman, AZ. ATH: SAs Bradford C. Petri; SA Phillip E. McClanahan. #D-1583.

May 10, 1995. Sub: McVeigh temporary employment, McVeigh's associations. LC: Kingman, AZ. ATH: Gilbert A. Hirschy, Melvin O. Cervantes. #D-1305.

CATEGORY: LIFE HISTORY, POST MILITARY:

May 1, 1995. Sub: Interview of dentist who filled one of McVeigh's teeth in Kingman, AZ on April 4, 1995; Jerry Sullivan, DDS. ATH: SA Robert E. Bumpers. #D-4955.

May 3, 1995. Sub: McVeigh's stay at the Belle Art Lodge in Kingman, AZ Jan. 31, 1995 to Feb. 8, 1995. ATH: SAs Donald E. Robinson, Ann C. Schultz. #D-1858.

May 11, 1995. Sub: Application For Employment With Loomis Armored, Inc., Las Vegas, NV; Nancy Kaufman; ATH: William A. Scrob. #D.

May 11, 1995. Sub: McVeigh's application for employment at Loomis Armored, Inc., Las Vegas, NV. McVeigh was not hired; Nancy Kaufman, Dr. D.E. Casey, M.D. ED: May 18, 1994. ATH:SA Brian P. Tone. #D-2239.

May 24, 1995. Sub: Kristen Foster describes her knowledge of McVeigh. LC: Kingman, AZ. ATH: Robert J. Demo, Kieth D. Tolhur.

June 20, 1995. Sub: McVeigh's employment at State Security Service; Richard A. Miller. ED:

Sep. 1, 1993. LC: Kingman, AZ. ATH: Tracey L. Thom(name cut off). #D-6367.

Aug. 31, 1995. Sub: McVeigh's stay at the Belle Art Lodge in Kingman, Az. ATH: SA Jerry D. Delap. #D-9924.

CATEGORY: MFORTIER:

Aug. 8, 1995. Sub: MFortier sell gun @ Crossroads Of The West Gunshow. ED: Feb. 25, 1995. LC: St. George, Utah. ATH: SA Schubert.

CATEGORY: OKLAHOMA CITY EYE WITNESSES:

April 22, 1995. Sub: US1 and US2 seen in OKC Albertsons on April 18, 1995 approx 9:30 –10pm; Robert Pettigrew, Becky Rupert, McVeigh, US1, US2. ED: April 18, 1995. ATH: SA Gregory M. Kuntz, FBI. #D-164.

April 24, 1995. Sub: Video tape taken from Regency Tower and its chain of custody; Rich Willis, SA Lou Ann Sandstorm, Karen Willis. ED: April 19, 1995. LC: Regency Tower Apartments, OKC. ATH: SA Lou Ann Sandstorm. #D-1818.

April 24, 1995. Sub: Man resembling McVeigh after bombing seen outside Leadership Square and made comment ["Shit Happens"]; Charles Henry Young. ED: April 19, 1995. LC: Oklahoma City, OK. ATH: SA Robert M. Fanning. #D-102.

Jan. 8, 1996 to Oct. 7, 1996. Sub: Review of three surveillance tapes of Total Service Station in Oklahoma City, OK. ATH: Kraig Graham. #D.

CATEGORY: ROGER MOORE AKA BOB MILLER:

May 15, 1995. Sub: Billy Joe Pierce, nee: Stanley, a former girlfriend of SColburn describes her relationship with him and what she knew about him. LC: Bullhead City, AZ; Laughlin, NV; Oatman, AZ. ED: Nov. 1994. ATH: SAs Robert E. Bumpers, Kimerly K. Mertz. #D-4551.

No dates listed. Sub: SColburn describes life as a fugitive and his relationship with McVeigh and RMoore; Tim Tuttle. LC: Phoenix, AZ; Oatman, AZ; Kingman, AZ. ATH: SAs H. Michael Warren, William R. Keefe. #D-5344.

CATEGORY: STATEMENT OF MOTIVES:

May 20, 1995. Sub: Steve Colbern's knowledge of and attempts to contact Tim Tuttle; Bob Anderson, Karen Anderson. ED: Nov. 1, 1994. LC: Ozarks; Kingman, AZ; Oatman, AZ; Little Rock, AK. ATH: Michael Warren, William R. Keefe.

CATEGORY: SUBPOENAS ISSUED AND EXECUTED:

May 18, 1995. Sub: On May 18, 1995, Phillips found register for McVeigh who stayed @ Dixie Palms on Feb. 25 and 26, 1995. LC: Dixie Palms Motel, St. George, UT; Dexter, NM. ATH: SA Raymond A. Hult. #D-3251.

CATEGORY: SUSPECT INDIVIDUALS OR GROUPS, MOTIVE

April 22, 1995. Sub: Foster's possible information of man in Kingman making bombs. ATH: Kenneth Williams. #D-16467.

June 1, 1995. Sub: Clark Vollmer stated he knows of Fortier, McVeigh, Rosencrans and Others; Steve Colbern. LC: Kingman Regional Medical Center, Kingman, Arizona. ATH: SAs Bradford C. Petrie, Kenneth J. Williams. #D-5880.

Aug. 11, 1995. Sub: Wedin's personal relationship with McVeigh; Janet Rose Wedin. ED: June 11, 1993. LC: Tyler, Texas. ATH: Michael S. Poche, James R. Wilkins. #D.

May 16 and 19, 1996. Sub: Activities of Steven Colbern In Mid and Late 1994, According To Associate Tom Ward. PL: Ventura, CA; Bullhead City, AZ; Oatman, AZ; Adelanto, CA; Old Woman Mountains, Eagle Rock, CA. ATH: SA Kevin D. Kelly. #E-3221 (insert).

CATEGORY: TELEPHONE RECORDS:

April 27, 1995. Sub: The government prepared a summary of 18 Bridges' calls which contains 32 variances from the Bridges' summary which we have been provided, including differences in the time of call, duration of call, date of call and additional calls not included on the Bridges' summary. ED: Various. ATH: SA Joe Navarro. #D-2527.

Aug. 15, 1995. Sub: Citizens Utility provided exact information of Bridges' calls placed from Kingman, AZ from Feb. 18, 1994 until April 11, 1995. LC: Kingman, AZ, Imperial Motel. ATH: Joseph Gray. #D-9234.

Oct. 2, 1995. Sub: In reference to Bridges' calls placed from the Imperial Motel from April 5, 1995 thru April 11, 1995. LC: Imperial Motel, Kingman AZ. ATH: SAs Timothy Kirham, Kevin Mooney. #D-10760.

Oct. 2, 1995. Sub: In reference to 3 Bridges' calls placed on Dec. 14 -15, 1994 from the Mohave Inn. LC: Mohave Inn, Kingman, AZ. ATH: SA Timothy Kirkham. #D-10766.

American Terrorist Collection

The American Terrorist Collection is a small, private collection held at the Friedsam Memorial Library, St. Bonaventure University containing letters from Timothy McVeigh to his authorized biographers, Dan Herbeck and Lou Michel (sometimes with news clippings) as well as transcripts of their conversations with them. In 2012, I was generously granted permission to access this archive and while researchers are not allowed to make copies of documents, I transcribed the great majority of material found in the collection.

Letters from Tim McVeigh to Dan Herbeck and Lou Michel, written from 1999 until 2001, are listed here by date of letter and folder number. Letters referred to or directly quoted in this book include:

1999: April 18, F8; April 21, F9; May 11, F11; May 12, F12; May 16 (Folder Unknown); May 19, F14; June 1, F17; June 12, F19; June 16, F20; June 18, F21; Aug. 30, F27.

2000: Jan. 22, F37; Feb. 12 and 13; Feb. 24, F45; Feb. 26, F46; April 25, F50; July 24, F53; Aug. 21, F56; Sep. 27, F60; Oct. (no day listed), F61; Oct. 11, F62; Nov. 5, F65; Nov. 23, F67; Nov. 24, F67; Dec. 30, F72.

2001: Jan. 6, F75; Jan. 8, F76; Jan. 9, F77; Feb. 14, F86; Feb. 14, F86; March 7, F92; April 19, F100; May 12, F109; May 23, F111.

Transcripts of Herbeck and Michel interviews with Timothy McVeigh in the Federal Correctional Facility in Florence, Colorado from May 6 to 9, 1999, are listed here by transcript tape (TT) and page number, referred to or quoted in this book include:

TT1, pg. 4; TT2, pg. 8-10; TT3, pg. 11, 12, 14; TT4, pg. 19; TT7, pg. 31; TT8, pg. 32, 33; TT9, pg. 36; TT9, pg. 36; TT 11, pg. 45, 52, 59; TT 12, pg. 55; TT13, pg. unknown; TT14, pg. 45; TT16, pg. 116.

Other Sources
Select List of FBI 302 Investigatory Reports

Several sources including Jones Archive, Trentadue, Peter Langan, Other Structure: (1)Name of Person Interviewed (2) Date of report (3) Subject of report (4) Location. Special Agents conducting interview/ investigation (5) report numbers, if listed; (6) dates of subsequent reports and agents listed on them.

Anderson, Karen Garland. April 29, 1995. Hot Springs, Arkansas. SAs Mark A. Jessie,

Steven Crutchfield. # D-811; May 3, 1995. SA Steven Crutchfield. # D-1525; May 19, 1995. SA Mark A. Jesse. # D-4401 and # D-5247; May 26, 1995. SAs Jonathan R. Hersley, Mark A. Jesse, James E. Judd, John R. Hippard. # D-5235; Oct. 25, 1995. SA Floyd J. Hays Jr., # D-10880 and # D-10660; Jan. 12, 1996. Oklahoma City, Oklahoma. SA John R. Hippard. # D-12897; Jan. 12, 1996. J. Hays Jr., #D-10880 and # D-10660 Anderson, Karen Garland and Roger Moore. May 19, 1995. Hot Springs, Arkansas. SA Mark A. Jesse #D-5559.

Boyd, Roy L. May 17, 1995 (re : Aryan Nations/ Other bomb targets). Florence, Arizona. SA Jerry L. Wagner. #-E-1298 Burke, Dianna Sanders (Officer, Wagoner Police Department). Dec. 11, 1995 (re: Roger Moore). Wagoner County, Oklahoma. SA James F. Charlie. # D-11941. Lead Control # 13754; March 21, 1996 (re:Roger Moore) SA James F. Charlie. # D-14318. Lead Control # 13754.

Coffman, Richard L. June 15, 1995. Richard L. Coffman. Laughlin, Nevada. SA Keith D. Tolhurst. #D-15876.

Confidential Source #OC-5357-D. June 22, 1995. (re: Roger Moore). Muskogee, Oklahoma. SA Rayburn Dee Collins. #E-2407.

Cox, Stephen M. (American Red Cross Station Manager) and Douglas F. Gibson. April 28, 1995. Manhattan Kansas. SA Charles G. Pritchett.

Drosnin, Michael. July 7, 1995. (re: 'Hector', paramilitary camps on outskirts of Kingman, Arizona). Kingman, Arizona. A Kevin J. Mooney. #D-7067.

Farrington, Bobby Joe. April 30, 1995 (re: Aryan Nations/ McVeigh). Tennessee Colony, Texas.

SAs Jeff Block, J. Dennis Murphy. # D-13458; May 2, 1995. (re: Aryan Nations/ McVeigh).

Fortier, Michael Joseph. April 24, 1995. Kingman, Arizona. SAs Blaine D. McIlwaine, Kenneth J. Williams. # D-2276.

Frazer, Mildred Noreen. April 24, 1995. Fort Pierce, Florida. SAs Jay T. Miller, Constantine Golovaty, Jeffery Serna. #A-1793.

Gelles, Michael G. (Dr., Psy, D., Naval Criminal Investigative Service. Dec. 11, 1995 (re: Hypnosis Services, Dec. 6, 1995. Re: Nora Young). Casville, MO. SAs Lou Ann Sandstrom, William E. Teater. #D-12742.

Grochowski, Dolores. Dec. 26, 1995 (re: Roger Moore). Las Vegas, Nevada. SA Richard E. McArthur. # E-6784. Lead Control #13792.

Lubeck, Bruce (Assistant U.S. Attorney, Salt Lake City). March 5, 1996 (re: "Operation Punchout" and Roger Moore. Feb. 27, 1996). Salt Lake City Utah. SA Ronald J. Van Vranken. # D-1367. (With attached Docket Sheet, Aug. 21, 1991).

McGown, Eric. May 4, 1995. (re : Dreamland Motel). SA Mark M. Button. Junction City, Kansas.

McLaughlin, Richard. Dec. 28, 1995 (re: Roger Moore, Dec. 18, 1995). Wagoner, Oklahoma. SA Peter Butler, James F. Charlie. # D-12655.

McVeigh, Jennifer Lynn. April 29, 1995 (Re: Letters from Timothy McVeigh, collected by SA Eric E. Kruss). Buffalo, New York. SA Regina Canale-Miles. #D-2911; May 7, 1995 (Signed Statement, May 1, 1995).SAs Caryl L. Cid, Dean G. Naum. #D-2075 ; (Signed statement May 2, 1995). #D-1969 ; May 10, 1995. SAs Caryl L. Cid, Dean G. Naum, J. Gary Dilaura. #D-2298 ; May 18, 1995 (Signed statement May 5, 1995). SA

Dean G. Naum, Caryl Cid. #D-1953.

Millikan, Roger. May 2, 1995. (Re: Tim McNey). SA Thomas K. Vest. # E-1006. Lead Control #9991.

Moore, Roger. May 19, 1995. Hot Springs, Arkansas. SAs Mark A. Jessie, Floyd J. Hays, Jr. # D-5206; May 19, 1995 SA Mark A. Jesse Sub. #4400; May 19, 1995 #D-4504 (with attached letter from Timothy McVeigh); May 27, 1995. Roger E. Moore. SAs Jonathan R. Hersley, Mark A. Jesse, James E. Judd, John R. Hippard. # D-9256.

Nehman, Wade Alan. Sep. 19, 1995. Tennessee Colony, Texas. SA Redacted. #E-7042. Lead Control # 13121.

Nicholas, Kevin. April 28, 1995. Owendale, Michigan. SAs Steve J. Dunphy, Norval P. Labadie, Hugh D. Ruegesggor. #- D-1234.

No Name Listed. May 17, 1995 (re: rented P.O. boxes in Kingman area/Jacks/Land/ Colbern). Kingman, Arizona. SAs Donald W. Jarrett, Robert E. Bumpers, Richard K. Gonzalez.

No Name Listed. Aug. 15, 1996. (re: Operation Punchout/ Roger Moore/ Roy, Utah). Denver, Colorado. SA Kraig R. Graham. #16800. Lead Control #15075.

Powell, Lance. May 2, 1996. (re: Roger Moore robbery). Royal, Arkansas. SA Floyd J. Hays. #D-14885. Lead Control #14681.

Powell, Verta. May 2, 1996. (re: Roger Moore robbery). Royal, Arkansas. SA Floyd J. Hays Jr. #D-1485 (last number missing). Lead Control #14681.

Powell, Walt. May 2, 1996 (re: Roger Moore robbery). Royal, Arkansas. SA Floyd J. Hays Jr. # D-14853. Lead Control #14681.

Rayas, Aleva (Bank Of America). May 1, 1995 (re: Gary A. Land). Kingman, Arizona; Independence, MO, and Rolla, MO. SA Callen D. Dalrymple.

Redacted Name. Aug. 17, 1995 (re: paramilitary camps on outskirts of Kingman, Arizona). SAs.

Redacted. #E-8034.

Rogers, Richard Latimer. May 11, 1995 (re : McVeigh). Kingman, Arizona. SAs Daniel Sturgill (FBI) and Ruben Chaves, Manuel Olmos (ATF). #D-1251.

Rosencrans, James W. July 1, 1995. Kingman, Arizona. SA Kenneth J. Williams and SA Bradford C. Petrie.

Tempelton, Bob. Dec. 13, 1995 (re: Crossroads Of The West Gun Show, Phoenix, AZ, Sep. 11-12, 1993 and April 23-24, 1994/ Tim Tuttle/ Investigation, In Response To Lead Control # 13257). Kaysville, Utah. FBI SA Ronald J. Vanranken, ATF SA Sherry Quindley. #7075.

Thompson, Linda. April 23, 1995. SA W. Timothy Pitchford. #E-3632. Lead Control # 12999. (Attached article: *The Indianapolis Star* "Government Behind Oklahoma Blast, Claims Militia Advocate" April 25, 1995).

Trezza, Anthony. July 5, 1995. (Re: McVeigh, Moore). Delta, Utah. SA James K. Colceri. #D-56120.

Trochman, John (Militia Of Montana). Jan. 30, 1996 (re: Roger "Bob" Moore and Karen Anderson). #E-7412.

Select Military Records

The following contains a partial chronological index of Timothy McVeigh's military and medical records, first accessed through the Jones Collection and then duplicated and expanded upon through Freedom Of Information Act Requests, received May 22, 2014. All documents on file with the author.

Record Index Form: McVeigh, Timothy J. Original Vault #V2988, New Vault # V500 654.

Folder #1: Service Documents (May 1988 to July 1993), 89 pages.

Folder #2: Awards, Decorations and Commendations (June 1989 to April 1993), 27 pages.

Folder #3: Medical Records (May 1988 to January 1992), 119 pages.

Folder #4: Microform (No Dates Listed) Redacted Materials, 3 pages.

Folder #5: Reference Correspondence (April 1995 to July 2002) Redacted Materials, 8 pages.

Folder #6: Original Containers (No Dates Listed) Redacted Materials, 14 pages.

Index

K

L